Lecture Notes in Computer Science 6602

Commenced Publication in 1973
Founding and Former Series Editors:
Gerhard Goos, Juris Hartmanis, and Jan van Leeuwen

W0051325

Editorial Board

David Hutchison, UK
Takeo Kanade, USA
Josef Kittler, UK
Jon M. Kleinberg, USA
Alfred Kobsa, USA
Friedemann Mattern, Switzerland
John C. Mitchell, USA
Moni Naor, Israel
Oscar Nierstrasz, Switzerland
C. Pandu Rangan, India
Bernhard Steffen, Germany
Madhu Sudan, USA
Demetri Terzopoulos, USA
Doug Tygar, USA
Gerhard Weikum, Germany

Advanced Research in Computing and Software Science

Subline of Lectures Notes in Computer Science

Subline Series Editors

Giorgio Ausiello, *University of Rome 'La Sapienza', Italy*
Vladimiro Sassone, *University of Southampton, UK*

Subline Advisory Board

Susanne Albers, *University of Freiburg, Germany*
Benjamin C. Pierce, *University of Pennsylvania, USA*
Bernhard Steffen, *University of Dortmund, Germany*
Madhu Sudan, *Microsoft Research, Cambridge, MA, USA*
Deng Xiaotie, *City University of Hong Kong*
Jeannette M. Wing, *Carnegie Mellon University, Pittsburgh, PA, USA*

Gilles Barthe (Ed.)

Programming Languages and Systems

20th European Symposium on Programming, ESOP 2011
Held as Part of the Joint European Conferences
on Theory and Practice of Software, ETAPS 2011
Saarbrücken, Germany, March 26–April 3, 2011
Proceedings

Springer

Volume Editor

Gilles Barthe
IMDEA Software
Facultad de Informatica (UPM)
Campus Montegancedo, 28660 Boadilla del Monte, Madrid, Spain
E-mail: gilles.barthe@imdea.org

ISSN 0302-9743 e-ISSN 1611-3349
ISBN 978-3-642-19717-8 e-ISBN 978-3-642-19718-5
DOI 10.1007/978-3-642-19718-5
Springer Heidelberg Dordrecht London New York

Library of Congress Control Number: 2011922331

CR Subject Classification (1998): D.2, F.3, C.2, D.3, H.4, D.1

LNCS Sublibrary: SL 1 – Theoretical Computer Science and General Issues

© Springer-Verlag Berlin Heidelberg 2011
This work is subject to copyright. All rights are reserved, whether the whole or part of the material is concerned, specifically the rights of translation, reprinting, re-use of illustrations, recitation, broadcasting, reproduction on microfilms or in any other way, and storage in data banks. Duplication of this publication or parts thereof is permitted only under the provisions of the German Copyright Law of September 9, 1965, in its current version, and permission for use must always be obtained from Springer. Violations are liable to prosecution under the German Copyright Law.
The use of general descriptive names, registered names, trademarks, etc. in this publication does not imply, even in the absence of a specific statement, that such names are exempt from the relevant protective laws and regulations and therefore free for general use.

Typesetting: Camera-ready by author, data conversion by Scientific Publishing Services, Chennai, India

Printed on acid-free paper

Springer is part of Springer Science+Business Media (www.springer.com)

Foreword

ETAPS 2011 was the 14th instance of the European Joint Conferences on Theory and Practice of Software. ETAPS is an annual federated conference that was established in 1998 by combining a number of existing and new conferences. This year it comprised the usual five sister conferences (CC, ESOP, FASE, FOSSACS, TACAS), 16 satellite workshops (ACCAT, BYTECODE, COCV, DICE, FESCA, GaLoP, GT-VMT, HAS, IWIGP, LDTA, PLACES, QAPL, ROCKS, SVARM, TERMGRAPH, and WGT), one associated event (TOSCA), and seven invited lectures (excluding those specific to the satellite events).

The five main conferences received 463 submissions this year (including 26 tool demonstration papers), 130 of which were accepted (2 tool demos), giving an overall acceptance rate of 28%. Congratulations therefore to all the authors who made it to the final programme! I hope that most of the other authors will still have found a way of participating in this exciting event, and that you will all continue submitting to ETAPS and contributing to make of it the best conference on software science and engineering.

The events that comprise ETAPS address various aspects of the system development process, including specification, design, implementation, analysis and improvement. The languages, methodologies and tools which support these activities are all well within its scope. Different blends of theory and practice are represented, with an inclination towards theory with a practical motivation on the one hand and soundly based practice on the other. Many of the issues involved in software design apply to systems in general, including hardware systems, and the emphasis on software is not intended to be exclusive.

ETAPS is a confederation in which each event retains its own identity, with a separate Programme Committee and proceedings. Its format is open-ended, allowing it to grow and evolve as time goes by. Contributed talks and system demonstrations are in synchronised parallel sessions, with invited lectures in plenary sessions. Two of the invited lectures are reserved for 'unifying' talks on topics of interest to the whole range of ETAPS attendees. The aim of cramming all this activity into a single one-week meeting is to create a strong magnet for academic and industrial researchers working on topics within its scope, giving them the opportunity to learn about research in related areas, and thereby to foster new and existing links between work in areas that were formerly addressed in separate meetings.

ETAPS 2011 was organised by the *Universität des Saarlandes* in cooperation with:

▷ European Association for Theoretical Computer Science (EATCS)
▷ European Association for Programming Languages and Systems (EAPLS)
▷ European Association of Software Science and Technology (EASST)

It also had support from the following sponsors, which we gratefully thank: DFG Deutsche Forschungsgemeinschaft; AbsInt Angewandte Informatik GmbH; Microsoft Research; Robert Bosch GmbH; IDS Scheer AG / Software AG; T-Systems Enterprise Services GmbH; IBM Research; gwSaar Gesellschaft für Wirtschaftsförderung Saar mbH; Springer-Verlag GmbH; and Elsevier B.V.

The organising team comprised:

General Chair:	*Reinhard Wilhelm*
Organising Committee:	*Bernd Finkbeiner, Holger Hermanns* (chair), *Reinhard Wilhelm, Stefanie Haupert-Betz, Christa Schäfer*
Satellite Events:	*Bernd Finkbeiner*
Website:	*Hernán Baró Graf*

Overall planning for ETAPS conferences is the responsibility of its Steering Committee, whose current membership is:

Vladimiro Sassone (Southampton, Chair), Parosh Abdulla (Uppsala), Gilles Barthe (IMDEA-Software), Lars Birkedal (Copenhagen), Michael O'Boyle (Edinburgh), Giuseppe Castagna (CNRS Paris), Marsha Chechik (Toronto), Sophia Drossopoulou (Imperial College London), Bernd Finkbeiner (Saarbrücken) Cormac Flanagan (Santa Cruz), Dimitra Giannakopoulou (CMU/NASA Ames), Andrew D. Gordon (MSR Cambridge), Rajiv Gupta (UC Riverside), Chris Hankin (Imperial College London), Holger Hermanns (Saarbrücken), Mike Hinchey (Lero, the Irish Software Engineering Research Centre), Martin Hofmann (LMU Munich), Joost-Pieter Katoen (Aachen), Paul Klint (Amsterdam), Jens Knoop (Vienna), Barbara König (Duisburg), Shriram Krishnamurthi (Brown), Juan de Lara (Madrid), Kim Larsen (Aalborg), Rustan Leino (MSR Redmond), Gerald Luettgen (Bamberg), Rupak Majumdar (Los Angeles), Tiziana Margaria (Potsdam), Ugo Montanari (Pisa), Luke Ong (Oxford), Fernando Orejas (Barcelona), Catuscia Palamidessi (INRIA Paris), George Papadopoulos (Cyprus), David Rosenblum (UCL), Don Sannella (Edinburgh), João Saraiva (Minho), Helmut Seidl (TU Munich), Tarmo Uustalu (Tallinn), and Andrea Zisman (London).

I would like to express my sincere gratitude to all of these people and organisations, the Programme Committee Chairs and members of the ETAPS conferences, the organisers of the satellite events, the speakers themselves, the many reviewers, all the participants, and Springer for agreeing to publish the ETAPS proceedings in the ARCoSS subline.

Finally, I would like to thank the Organising Chair of ETAPS 2011, Holger Hermanns and his Organising Committee, for arranging for us to have ETAPS in the most beautiful surroundings of Saarbrücken.

January 2011

Vladimiro Sassone
ETAPS SC Chair

Preface

This volume contains the papers presented at ESOP 2011, the 20th European Symposium on Programming held March 30-April 1, 2011, in Saarbrücken, Germany.

ESOP is an annual conference devoted to fundamental issues in the specification, design, analysis, and implementation of programming languages and systems. ESOP 2011 was the 20th edition in the series. The Programme Committee (PC) invited papers on all aspects of programming language research including: programming paradigms and styles, methods and tools to write and specify programs and languages, methods and tools for reasoning about programs, methods and tools for implementation, and concurrency and distribution.

Following previous editions, we maintained the page limit to 20 pages, and a rebuttal process of 72 hours during which the authors could respond to the reviews of their submission. This year, PC submissions were not allowed. We received 117 abstracts and in the end got 93 full submissions; one submission was withdrawn. The remaining 92 submissions received from 3 to 6, and on average 4, reviews; eventually the PC selected 24 papers for publication. These proceedings consist of Andrew Appel's invited paper, and of the 24 selected papers.

I would like to thank the PC and the subreviewers for their dedicated work in the paper selection process, and all authors who submitted their work to the conference. I would also like to thank the 2011 Organizing Committee, chaired by Holger Hermanns, and the Steering Committee, chaired by Vladimiro Sassone, for coordinating the organization of ETAPS 2011. Finally, I would like to thank Andrei Voronkov, whose EasyChair system proved (once more) invaluable throughout the whole process.

January 2011 Gilles Barthe

Preface

Conference Organization

Programme Chair

Gilles Barthe

Programme Committee

Nick Benton
Cristiano Calcagno
Radhia Cousot
Sophia Drossopoulou
Jean Goubault-Larrecq
Nicolas Halbwachs
Radha Jagadeesan
Gerwin Klein
Viktor Kuncak
Julia Lawall
Sorin Lerner
Frank Piessens
Arnd Poetzsch-Heffter
Francois Pottier
Shaz Qadeer
Andrey Rybalchenko
Andrei Sabelfeld
Peter Sewell
Tachio Terauchi
Vasco T. Vasconcelos
Jan Vitek
David Walker
Stephanie Weirich
Kwangkeun Yi

External Reviewers

Ahmed, Amal
Alglave, Jade
Amtoft, Torben
Ancona, Davide
Andronick, June
Askarov, Aslan
Balakrishnan, Gogul
Balland, Emilie
Banerjee, Anindya
Barnett, Michael
Berdine, Josh
Beringer, Lennart
Bertrane, Julien
Besson, Frédéric
Bierman, Gavin
Birgisson, Arnar
Bouajjani, Ahmed
Boulmé, Sylvain
Boyton, Andrew
Carbone, Marco
Casinghino, Chris
Castagna, Giuseppe
Chadha, Rohit
Chakravarty, Manuel
Chatzikokolakis, Konstantinos
Chen, Juan
Chen, Liqian
Chlipala, Adam
Choi, Wontai
Chong, Stephen
Chugh, Ravi
Cirstea, Horatiu
Comon-Lundh, Hubert
Compagnoni, Adriana
Corin, Ricardo
Cortier, Véronique
Cotton, Scott
Cremers, Cas
Crespo, Juan Manuel
D'Silva, Vijay

Daubignard, Marion
Desmet, Lieven
Devriese, Dominique
Dietl, Werner
Distefano, Dino
Dodds, Mike
Dumas, Marlon
Fahndrich, Manuel
Feller, Christoph
Feret, Jerome
Ferrara, Pietro
Filliatre, Jean-Christophe
Fournet, Cédric
Francalanza, Adrian
Gaillourdet, Jean-Marie
Gammie, Peter
Ganty, Pierre
Gay, Simon
Geilmann, Kathrin
Ghica, Dan
Gordon, Andy
Gotsman, Alexey
Goubault, Eric
Gray, Kathryn E.
Greenaway, David
Greenberg, Michael
Gupta, Ashutosh
Gurov, Dilian
Gvero, Tihomir
Hammer, Christian
Rydhof Hansen, Rene
Hedin, Daniel
Heeren, Bastiaan
Hobor, Aquinas
Honda, Kohei
Hu, Zhenjiang
Hurlin, Clément
Jacobs, Bart
Jacobs, Swen
Jaskelioff, Mauro
Jeffrey, Alan
Jensen, Simon
Jung, Yungbum
Kennedy, Andrew
Kim, Hanjun
Kim, Ik-Soon
Kim, Youil
Kinder, Johannes
Kolanski, Rafal
Kopp, Oliver
Koutavas, Vasileios
Kremer, Steve
Kunz, César
Kurnia, Ilham
König, Barbara
Laud, Peeter
Laviron, Vincent
Lee, Oukseh
Lee, Wonchan
Leroy, Xavier
Lopes, Nuno P.
Lozes, Etienne
Maffei, Matteo
Malkis, Alexander
Marinescu, Maria-Cristina
Marron, Mark
Martel, Matthieu
Martins, Francisco
Mass, Damien
Matsuda, Kazutaka
Mauborgne, Laurent
McCusker, Guy
McKinna, James
Meyer, Roland
Michaelson, Greg
Michel, Patrick
Might, Matthew
Miné, Antoine
Monniaux, David
Mostrous, Dimitris
Motika, Christian
Nguyen, Kim
Nilsson, Henrik
Noble, James
Nogueira, Pablo
Nordio, Martin
Oh, Hakjoo
Oliveira, Bruno
Owens, Scott
Pandya, Paritosh
Park, Sungwoo
Parkinson, Matthew

Petri, Gustavo
Pichardie, David
Pitcher, Corin
Plump, Detlef
Pratikakis, Polyvios
Rajan, Hridesh
Remy, Didier
Reus, Bernhard
Ringeissen, Christophe
Russo, Alejandro
Ryu, Sukyoung
Samborski-Forlese, Julian
Sands, David
Santos, André L.
Schmitt, Alan
Sevcik, Jaroslav
Shin, Jaeho
Silva, Josep
Skalka, Christian
Sozeau, Matthieu
Steffen, Martin
Strickland, Stephen T.
Summers, Alexander
Svenningsson, Josef
Thielecke, Hayo
Tsukada, Takeshi
Uustalu, Tarmo
Van Horn, David
Vanoverberghe, Dries
Venet, Arnaud
von Hanxleden, Reinhard
Wadler, Philip
Welsch, Yannick
Winwood, Simon
Yorgey, Brent
Zanella Béguelin, Santiago
Phillips, Andrew
Piskac, Ruzica
Plsek, Ales
Popeea, Corneliu
Rafnsson, Willard
Regis-Gianas, Yann
Rensink, Arend
Riba, Colin
Rompf, Tiark
Russo, Luis
S, Ramesh
Sanchez, Cesar
Sankaranarayanan, Sriram
Schaefer, Jan
Seidl, Helmut
Sewell, Thomas
Siek, Jeremy
Sjöberg, Vilhelm
Smans, Jan
Staton, Sam
Strackx, Raoul
Sumii, Eijiro
Suter, Philippe
Swierstra, Doaitse
Thiemann, Peter
Urzyczyn, Pawel
van der Meyden, Ron
van Staden, Stephan
Vaughan, Jeff
Vogels, Frederic
Vouillon, Jérôme
Wells, Joe
Westbrook, Edwin
Wrigstad, Tobias
Yu, Minlan
Zappa Nardelli, Francesco

Table of Contents

Verified Software Toolchain
(Invited Talk)

Andrew W. Appel

Princeton University

Abstract. The software toolchain includes static analyzers to check assertions about programs; optimizing compilers to translate programs to machine language; operating systems and libraries to supply context for programs. Our *Verified Software Toolchain* verifies with machine-checked proofs that the assertions claimed at the top of the toolchain really hold in the machine-language program, running in the operating-system context, on a weakly-consistent-shared-memory machine.

Our verification approach is modular, in that proofs about operating systems or concurrency libraries are oblivious of the programming language or machine language, proofs about compilers are oblivious of the program logic used to verify static analyzers, and so on. The approach is scalable, in that each component is verified in the semantic idiom most natural for that component.

Finally, the verification is *foundational:* the trusted base for proofs of observable properties of the machine-language program includes only the operational semantics of the machine language, not the source language, the compiler, the program logic, or any other part of the toolchain—even when these proofs are carried out by source-level static analyzers.

In this paper I explain some semantic techniques for building a verified toolchain.

Consider a software toolchain comprising,

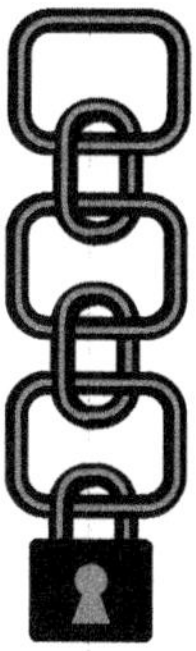

A *Static analyzer* or *program verifier* that uses program invariants to check assertions about the behavior of the source program.

A *compiler* that translates the source-language program to a machine-language (or other object-language) program.

A *runtime system* (or operating system, or concurrency library) that serves as the runtime context for external function calls of the machine-language program.

We want to construct a machine-checked proof, from the foundations of logic, that *Any claims by the static analyzer about observations of the source-language program will also characterize the observations of the compiled program.*

We may want to attach several different static analyzers to the same compiler, or choose among several compilers beneath the same analyzer, or substitute one operating system for another. The construction and verification of just one component, such as a compiler or a static analyzer, may be as large as one project team or research group can reasonably accomplish. For both of these reasons, the interfaces between

G. Barthe (Ed.): ESOP 2011, LNCS 6602, pp. 1–17, 2011.
© Springer-Verlag Berlin Heidelberg 2011

components—their specifications—deserve as much attention and effort as the components themselves.

We specify the observable behavior of a concurrent program (or of a single thread of that program) as its *input-output* behavior, so that the statement *Program p matches specification S* can be expressed independently of the semantics of the programming language in which *p* is written, or of the machine language. Of course, those semantics will show up in the proof of the claim! Sections 10 and 11 explain this in more detail.

But observable "input-output" behaviors of individual shared-memory threads are not just the input and output of atomic tokens: a lock-release makes visible (all at once) a whole batch of newly observable memory, a lock-aquire absorbs a similar batch, and a operating-system call (read into memory buffer, write from memory buffer, alloc memory buffer) is also an operation on a set of memory locations. Section 1 explains.

The main technical idea of this approach is to define a thread-local semantics for a well-synchronized concurrent program and use this semantics to trick the correctness proof of the *sequential* compiler to prove its correctness on a concurrent program. That is, take a sequential program; characterize its observable behavior in a way that ignores intensional properties such as individual loads and stores, and focus instead on (externally visible) system calls or lock-aquire/releases that transfer a whole batch of memory locations; split into thread-local semantics of individual threads; carry them through the modified sequential proof of compiler correctness; gather the resulting statements about observable interactions of individual threads into a statement about the observable behavior of the whole binary.

Because our very expressive program logic is most naturally proved sound with respect to an operational semantics with fancy features (permissions, predicates-in-the-heap) that don't exist in a standard operational semantics (or real computer), we need to erase them at some appropriate point. But when to erase? We do some erasure (what we call the transition from *decorated* op. sem. to *angelic* op. sem.) *before* the compiler-correctness proof; other erasure (from *angelic* to *erased*) should be done much later.

We organize our proof, in Coq, as follows. (Items marked • are either completed or nearly so; items marked ∘ are in the early stages; my principal coauthors on this research (in rough chronological order) are Sandrine Blazy, Aquinas Hobor, Robert Dockins, Lennart Beringer, and Gordon Stewart. Items marked – are plausible but not even begun.)

- • We specify an expressive *program logic* for source-language programs;
- ∘ we instrument the static analyzer to emit witnesses in the form of invariants;
- ∘ we reimplement just the *core* of the static analyzer (invariant checker, not invariant inference engine) and prove it correct w.r.t the program logic;
- • we specify a *decorated operational semantics* for source-language programs;
- • we prove the soundness of the program logic w.r.t. the decorated semantics;
- • we specify an *angelic operational semantics*;
- • we prove a correspondence between executions of the decorated and the angelic semantics;
- ⋆ we prove the correctness of the optimizing compiler w.r.t. the angelic operational semantics of the source and machine languages;

  - we prove the equivalence of executions in the angelic operational semantics in a *weakly consistent* memory model and in a *sequentially consistent* memory model;
- we specify an *erased* (i.e., quite conventional) *operational semantics* of the machine language;
- we prove a correspondence between executions of the angelic and erased semantics.

The composition of all these steps gives the desired theorem. Q.E.D.

The $\star$ verified optimizing compiler is not by our research group, it is the CompCert compiler by Leroy *et al.* [24] with whom we have been collaborating since 2006 on adjusting the CompCert interfaces and specifications to make this connection possible. Since Leroy *et al.*'s correctness proof of CompCert in Coq constitutes one of the components of our modular verification, it seemed reasonable to do the rest of our verification in Coq. In addition, some of the logical techniques we use require a logic with dependent types, and cannot be expressed (for example) in HOL (higher-order logic, a.k.a. Church's simple theory of types). We wanted to use a logic whose kernel theory (in this case, CiC) is trustworthy, machine-checkable, and well understood. Finally, we wanted a system with well-maintained software tools, mature libraries of tactics and theories, and a large user community. For all these reasons we use Coq for our Verified Software Toolchain (VST), and we have been happy with this choice.

1 Observables

Specifications of program behavior must be robust with respect to translation from source language to machine language. Although the states of source- and target-language programs may be expressed differently, we characterize the *observable behaviors* (or *observations*) of source- and target-language programs in the same language [15].

Our source language is a dialect of C with shared-memory concurrency using semaphores (locks). The C programs interact with the outside world by doing system calls—with communication via parameters as well as in memory shared with the operating system—and via lock synchronization (through shared memory). One thread of a shared-memory concurrent program interacts with other threads in much the same way that a client program interacts with an operating system. That is, the thread reads and writes memory to which the other threads (or operating system) have access; the thread synchronizes with the other threads (or OS) via special instructions (trap, compare-and-swap) or external function calls (read-from-file, semaphore-unlock). We want the notion of *observable behavior* to be sufficiently robust to characterize either kind of interaction.

For each system call, and at each lock acquire/release, some portion of the memory is observable. But on the other hand, some parts of memory should not be observable.[1] In private regions of memory, compilers should have the freedom to optimize loads and stores of sequential programs: to hoist loads/stores past each other, and past control operations, to eliminate redundant loads and stores, etc.—subject only to dataflow constraints.

[1] Of course, the operating system can observe any part of memory that it wants to. But the O.S. should not "care" about the thread's local data, while it does "care" about the contents of memory pointed to by the argument of a `write` system call.

Of course, with a naive or ill-synchronized approach to shared memory, it is possible for one thread to see another's loads and stores, and therefore the compiler might alter the output of a program by "optimizing" it. At least for the time being, we restrict our attention to well-synchronized programs—in which any thread's write (read) access to data is done while holding a semaphore granting exclusive (shared) permission to that data. In such a regime, we can achieve that *loads and stores are not observable events*. This is an important design principle.

"Volatile" variables with observable loads/stores can be treated in our framework, with each load or store transformed—by the front end—into a special synchronization operation. Leroy has recently instrumented the front end of CompCert to perform this transformation.

Extensional properties. This approach to program specification deliberately avoids intensional properties, i.e. those that characterize *how* the computation proceeds. This design decision frees the compiler to make very general program transformations. However, that means that we cannot specify properties such as execution time.

Permissions and synchronization. When a thread does a system call or a lock synchronization, there is implicitly a set of addresses that may be "observed." Our specification of observations makes this explicit as *permissions*. A thread that (at a given time) has write permission to a memory address can be sure that no other thread (or operating system) can observe it. Lock synchronizations and system calls can change a thread's permission in controlled and predictable ways. From the compiler's point of view, synchronizations and system calls are instances of *external function calls*, which can change memory permissions in almost arbitrary ways.

The permissions have no concrete runtime manifestation—since, of course, we are compiling to raw machine code on real machines. Instead, they are a "fictional" artifact of static program invariants: a static permission-based proof about a program says something about its non-stuck execution in a permission-carrying operational semantics. Then, the permissions present in our decorated and angelic operational semantics disappear in the erased operational semantics.

In fact, the difference between the decorated and angelic operational semantics is in how the permissions change at external function calls. The decorated operational semantics is annotated with sufficient program invariants to calculate the change in permissions; the angelic semantics is equipped with an "angel" that serves as an oracle for the change in permissions; see Section 7.

2 The Programming Language and Compiler

Our VST project was inspired in part by Leroy's CompCert verified optimizing C compiler [24]. CompCert is a remarkable achievement, on the whole and in many particulars. For example, the CompCert memory model by Leroy and Blazy [25] supports storing of bytes, integers, floats, and relocatable pointers in a byte-addressable memory; is sufficiently abstract to support relocation and the kinds of block-layout adjustments that occur during compilation; and is sufficiently general that the same memory model can be used for the source-level semantics, the target-machine semantics, and at every level in between. The tasteful design of the memory model is one reason for CompCert's success.

CompCert "merely" proves that, whenever it compiles a C program to assembly language, any safe execution in C corresponds to a safe execution in assembly with the same observable behavior. But where do safe C programs come from, and how can one characterize the observable behavior of those C programs? If those questions cannot be answered, then it might seem that CompCert is like a highly overengineered hammer without any nails.

Our Verified Software Toolchain uses *C minor* [24] as a source language. C minor is the high-level intermediate representation used in CompCert for the C programming language. CompCert compiles the C programming language (or rather, a very substantial subset called *C light* [9]) through 7 intermediate languages into assembly language for the PowerPC processor; the third language in this chain of 9 is C minor. For each language in the chain, Leroy has specified the syntax and operational semantics in the Coq theorem prover. Each of the 8 compiler phases between these intermediate languages is proved (in Coq) to preserve observational equivalence between its input (a program in one intermediate language) and its output (a program in the next language).

We chose to use C minor (instead of C light) as the target for VST, for two reasons: C minor is more friendly to Hoare-style reasoning as there are no side effects inside expressions;[2] and C minor can be used as a target language from source languages such as ML or Java.

3 Oracle Semantics

Remarkable as CompCert is, its original specification was too weak to express the interaction of a thread with its context—whether that context is the operating system or other concurrent threads. We want to remedy that weakness without making fundamental changes to the CompCert correctness proof.

We factor the operational semantics to separate *core programming-language* execution from execution steps in the *operating-system/runtime-system/concurrency context*, which we call the *oracle* for short. We do this because the same oracle will be applied to both the source- and machine-language programs; and because (conversely) different kinds of oracles will be applied to the same source- or machine-language program.

The CompCert C compiler [24] is proved correct with respect to a source-level operational semantics and a machine-level operational semantics. In early versions of CompCert, the source-level semantics was big-step and the machine-level was small-step. Each semantics generated a *trace*, a finite or infinite sequence of observable events, that is, system calls with atomic arguments and return values.

This specification posed obstacles for integration into our verified toolchain: the big-step semantics was inconvenient for reasoning about concurrent threads; the system calls did not permit shared memory between client and operating system (e.g. did not permit the conventional model of system calls); the lack of shared memory meant that

[2] More precisely, because C minor is not a subset of C, we had some flexibility to negotiate with Leroy a few modifications to the specification of C minor: e.g., unlike C minor 2006, C minor 2010 has no side-effects inside expressions.

a shared-memory concurrency model was difficult; the coarseness of memory-access permissions meant that concurrent separation logic was difficult; and so on.

Therefore we worked with Xavier Leroy to adjust the specification of CompCert's source-level operational semantics. Now it is a small-step semantics, with a lattice of permissions on each memory address. Instead of a trace model–in which the behavior of a program is characterized by a sequence of atomic values read or written, we characterize the behavior by the thread's history of (shared-memory) interactions with the oracle. Each state of the small-step semantics contains three components: oracle state Ω, memory m, and core state q. A *core step* is a small-step of computation that is *not* an external function call; an *oracle step* is taken whenever the computation is at an external function call. Each core step affects only m and q, leaving Ω unchanged; each oracle-step affects only Ω and m.

What is the oracle? If we are modeling the interaction of a sequential C program with its operating system, then the oracle is the operating system, and the external function calls are system calls. If we are modeling the interaction of a sequential C thread with all the other threads in a shared-memory concurrent computation, then the external function calls are lock-acquire and -release, and the oracle is *all the other threads.* An early version of this oracle model of concurrency is described by Hobor *et al.* [20,21].

The advantage of the oracle model is that, from the point of view of the C compiler and its correctness proof, issues of concurrency hardly intrude at all. Still, Hobor's oracle model was only partly modular: it successfully hid the internal details of the oracle from the compiler-correctness proof, but it did not hide all the details of the programming language from the oracle. This was a problem, because it was difficult to characterize the result of compiling a concurrent C program down to a concurrent machine-language program. Dockins [15] has a substantially more modular oracle model, which is the basis for the verified toolchain described here.

4 The Program Logic

Proofs of static analyses and program verifiers are (often) most convenient with respect to an *axiomatic semantics* (such as a Hoare Logic) of the programming language; we call this the *program logic*. Proofs of compilers and optimizations are (often) most convenient using an *operational semantics*.[3] Therefore for the source language we will need both an axiomatic and an operational semantics, as well as a machine-checked soundness proof that relates the two.

We intend to use the program logic as an intermediate step between a static analysis algorithm and an operational semantics. We would like to do this in a modular way—that is, prove several different static analyses correct w.r.t. the same program logic, then prove the program logic sound w.r.t. the operational semantics. Therefore we want the program logic to be as general and expressive as possible.

We start with a Hoare Logic for C minor: the judgement $\Gamma \vdash \{P\}c\{Q\}$ means that command c has precondition P and postcondition Q. Somewhat more precisely, if c starts in a state satisfying P, then either it safely infinite-loops or it reaches a state

[3] At the very least, the particular proof that we want to connect our system to—CompCert—is w.r.t. an operational semantics.

satisfying Q. However, C minor has two control-flow commands that can avoid a fall-through exit: exit n breaks out of n nested blocks (within a function), and return e evaluates e and returns its value from the current function-call. Thus, Q is really a triple of three postconditions; an ordinary assertion for fall-through, an assertion parameterized by n (equivalently, a list of assertions) for exit and an assertion parameterized by return-value for return.

To take a simple example, the judgement

$$\Gamma \vdash \{\exists x.\ (v \Downarrow x) * (x \overset{4,\pi}{\mapsto} 6) * (x{+}4 \overset{4,\top}{\mapsto} x)\}\ [v{+}4] :=_4 0\ \{\exists x.\ (v \Downarrow x) * (x \overset{4,\pi}{\mapsto} 6) * (x{+}4 \overset{4,\top}{\mapsto} 0)\}$$

can be read as follows: Before execution of the *store* statement, local variable v points to some address x; the current thread has partial permission π to read (but not necessarily write) a 4-byte integer (or pointer) at x; the current 4-byte contents of memory at x is 6; the thread has full permission $\top$ to read or write a 4-byte integer (or pointer) at $x + 4$; the current contentents at $x + 4$ is x. Furthermore, by the rules of $*$ in separation logic, x is not aliased to $x + 4$, though in this case we didn't need separation logic to tell us this obvious fact!

After the assignment, the situation is much the same except that the contents of $x + 4$ is now a null pointer. The exit and return postconditions (not shown) are both **false** since the store command neither exits nor returns.

The global context Γ maps addresses to their function specifications. The assertion $f : \{P\}\{Q\}$ means f has precondition P and postcondition Q.

Since C (and C minor) permits passing functions as pointers, in the program logic one can write $\exists v.\ (f \Downarrow v) * (v : \{P\}\{Q\})$, meaning that the name f evaluates to some pointer-value v, and v has precondition P, etc. Since the function can take a sequence of parameters and return an optional result, in fact P and Q are functions from value-list to assertion.

The operators $\exists, *, \mapsto$, and : are all constructed as definitions in Coq from the underlying logic. We use a "shallow embedding," but because of the almost-self-referential nature of some assertions ("$f(x)$ is a function whose precondition claims that x is a function whose precondition..."), the construction can be rather intricate; see Section 6.

In a Hoare logic one often needs to relate certain dynamic values appearing in a precondition to the same values in a postcondition. For example, consider the function int f(int x){return x + 1; }. One wants to specify that this function returns a value strictly greater than its argument. We write a specification such as,

$$\exists v.\ f \Downarrow v \wedge v : (\forall x : \mathsf{int}.\{\lambda a.a = x\}\{\lambda r.r > x\})$$

or, using a HOAS style for the : operator, $\exists v.\ f \Downarrow v \wedge v : [\mathsf{int}]\{P\}\{Q\}$ where $P = \lambda x \lambda a.(a = x)$ and $Q = \lambda x \lambda r.(r > x)$. This notation permits the shared information x to be of any Coq type τ, where in this example $\tau = \mathsf{int}$.

The use of HOAS (higher-order abstract syntax) hints that we shallowly embed the assertions in the surrounding logical framework, in this case Coq, to take advantage of all the binding structure there.

To reason about polymorphic functions or data abstraction, our Hoare logic permits universal and existential quantification: $\forall x : \tau.P \qquad \exists x : \tau.P$

where τ can be any Coq type, and P can contain free occurrences of x. Of course this is just Coq "notation" for the HOAS version: $\forall[\tau]P' \quad \exists[\tau]P'$
where P' is a function from τ to assertion.

It is particularly important that τ can be any Coq type *including* quantified assertions. That is, the quantification is *impredicative*. Impredicativity is necessary for reasoning about data abstraction, where the abstract types in the interface of one module can be themselves implemented by abstract types from the interface of another module.

To specify inductive datatypes, our program logic has an operator μ for recursively defined assertions: $\mu x.P(x)$ satisfies the fixpoint equation $\mu x.P(x) = P(\mu x.P(x))$, (or in HOAS $\mu P = P(\mu P)$), provided that P is a contractive function [6].

Ordinary Hoare logics have difficulty with pointers and arrays, especially with updates of fields and array slots. Therefore we use a *separation logic*, which is a Hoare logic based on the theory of bunched implications. In an ordinary Hoare logic, the assertion $P \wedge Q$ means that P holds on the current state and so does Q. In separation logic, $P * Q$ means that the current state can be expressed as the disjoint union of two parts, and P holds on the first part while Q holds on the second part. The assert emp holds on exactly the empty state, and **true** holds on any state. Thus the assertion $(P * Q) \wedge (R * \text{true})$ holds on any state s that can be broken into two pieces $s_1 \oplus s_2$, where P holds on one and Q on the other; *and* such that R holds on some substate of the state.

Our separation logic has a notion of partial ownership, or "permissions." The assertion $x \overset{\pi}{\mapsto} y$ means that the current state has exactly one address x in it; the contents of this address is the value y; and the current state has nonempty permission π to read (or perhaps also to write) the value. Permissions form a lattice; some permissions give read access, stronger permissions give write access, and the "top" permission gives the capability to deallocate the address. In contrast to previous permission models [11,29] ours is finite, constructive, general, and modeled in Coq [16].

Partial ownerships and overlapping visibility mean that "disjoint union" is an oversimplification to describe the $\oplus$ operator; we use a *separation algebra,* following Calcagno *et al.;* but we have a more general treatment of units and identities [16].

To reason about concurrent programs, we use a *concurrent separation logic* (CSL). O'Hearn [28] demonstrated that separation logic naturally extends to concurrency, as it limits each thread to the objects for which it has (virtual) permission to access. Portions of the heap can have their virtual ownership transferred from one thread to another by synchronization on semaphores. We have generalized O'Hearn's original CSL to account for dynamic creation of locks and threads [21]; Gotsman *et al.* made a similar generalization [18]. The assertion $\ell \overset{\pi}{\leadsto} R$ means that address ℓ is a lock (i.e., semaphore) with visibility (permission) π and resource invariant R. Permission $\pi < \top$ means that, most likely, some other thread(s) can see this lock as well; if only one thread could see ℓ then it would be difficult to use for synchronization! Any nonempty π gives permission to (attempt to) acquire the lock. Resource invariant R means that whenever a thread releases ℓ, it gives up a portion of memory satisfying the assertion R; whenever a thread acquires ℓ, it acquires a new portion of memory satisfying R. While ℓ is held, the thread can violate R until it is ready to release the lock.

The basic CSL triples for acquire/release are

$$\{\ell \overset{\pi}{\leadsto} R\}\ \mathsf{acquire}\,\ell\ \{R * \ell \overset{\pi}{\leadsto} R\} \qquad \{R * \ell \overset{\pi}{\leadsto} R\}\ \mathsf{release}\,\ell\ \{\ell \overset{\pi}{\leadsto} R\}.$$

In summary, programs have pointers, we want to reason about aliasing, hence Separation Logic rather than just Hoare Logic. Programs have higher-order functions, polymorphism, and data abstraction; hence we want impredicative quantification in the logic. Programs have concurrency, hence we want resource invariants. Finally, different front-end static analyses will make different demands on the program logic, so we want the program logic to be as expressive and general as we can possibly make it. We end up with *impredicative higher-order concurrent separation logic.*

5 Instrumenting Static Analyses

Hoare-style judgements can be proved in an interactive theorem prover by applying the inference rules of the program logic. But there are many kinds of program properties that, with much less user effort, a static analyzer can "prove" automatically. We are interested in removing the quotation marks from the previous sentence.

One way to connect a static analyzer to a program logic is to have the analyzer produce derivation trees in the logic. But this may require a large change to an existing analyzer, or significantly affect the software design of an analyzer; and the derivation trees will be huge. Another way would be to prove the analyzer correct, but analyzers are typically large programs implemented in languages with difficult proof theories; sometimes they have major components such as SAT solvers or ILP solvers.

We propose to instrument the analyzer in a different way. A typical analyzer infers program *invariants* from *assertions* provided by the user. In a sense, the invariants are the induction hypotheses needed to verify the assertions. We propose that the analyzer should output the program liberally sprinkled with invariants. A much simpler program than the analyzer, the *core* of the analyzer, can check that the invariants before and after each program statement (or perhaps, program block) match up.

We will implement the core of each analyzer in the Gallina functional programing language embedded in the Coq theorem prover. We will use Coq to prove the soundness of the core w.r.t. our program logic. Then we use Coq's program-extraction to obtain a Caml program that implements the core. The toolchain then starts with the full (untrusted, unverified) static analyzer, whose results are rechecked with the (verified) core analyzer.

My undergraduate student William Mansky conducted one successful experiment in this vein [26]: he reimplemented in Gallina the concurrent-separation-logic-based shape analysis by Gotsman *et al.* [19], and proved it correct[4] with respect to our program logic. He found that this shape analysis was simple enough that he could implement the entire analysis including invariant inference in Gallina, without needing an unverified front end.

[4] Well, almost proved. The problem is that Gotsman *et al.* assume a Concurrent Separation Logic with imprecise resource invariants, whereas our CSL (as is more standard [28]) requires precise resource invariants. The joy of discovering mismatches such as this is one of the rewards in doing end-to-end, top-to-bottom, machine-checked proofs such as the VST.

6 Semantic Modeling of Assertions

We want to interpret an assertion P as a predicate on the state of the computation: more or less, $s \models P$ is interpreted as $P(s)$. Some of our assertion forms characterize information about permissions, types, and predicates that are nowhere to be found in a "Curry-style" bare-bones operational semantics of a conventional target machine. Therefore we use more than one kind of operational semantics: a *decorated* semantics with extra information, an *angelic* semantics with partial information, and an *erased* semantics with even less information.

We have erasure theorems—that any nonstuck execution in the decorated semantics corresponds to a nonstuck execution in angelic semantics with similar observables, and ditto for the angelic to the erased semantics. Assertions require the decorated semantics.

A judgement $s \models 10 \overset{\pi_1}{\mapsto} 8 * 11 \overset{\pi_2}{\mapsto} 0$ means that s (in the decorated and angelic semantics) must contain not only 8 at address 10 and 0 at address 11, but must also keep track of the fact that there is exactly π_1 permission at 10, and π_2 at 11.

The assertions $\ell \overset{\pi}{\leadsto} R$ (meaning that ℓ is a lock with resource invariant R and visibility π) and $v : [\tau]\{P\}\{Q\}$ (v is a function with precondition P and postcondition Q) are interesting in that one assertion is characterizing the binding of an address (ℓ or v) to another assertion (R, P, Q).

Somehow the decorated state s must contain predicates; which in turn predicate over states. Achieving this—in connection with impredicative quantification and recursive assertions—is quite difficult; the semantic methods of the late 20th century were not up to the task. If we interpret assertions naively in set theory, we violate Cantor's paradox.

We solve this problem using the methods of Ahmed [4] as reformulated into the "Very Modal Model" [6] and "Indirection Theory" [22]. The recent formulation of Birkedal *et al.* [8] could also be used. The basic trick is that each state s indicates a degree of approximation (a natural number k_s). When $s \models \ell \overset{\pi}{\leadsto} R$, then the assertion R can be applied to states s' only strictly more approximately than k_s. When the computation takes a step $s \rightarrow s'$, it must "age" the state by making sure that s' is strictly more approximate than s, that is, $k_{s'} < k_s$.

In a decorated state an address can map to any of:

$\mathsf{val}_\pi\ v$	Memory data byte v with permission π
$\mathsf{lock}_\pi\ R$	Lock with resource-invariant R
$\mathsf{fun}_\pi\ [\tau]PQ$	Function entry point with precondition P, post Q

In the angelic semantics the predicates are removed—leaving only $\mathsf{val}_\pi\ v$, lock_π, fun_π—and in the erased semantics the permissions are removed.

7 Partial Erasure before Bisimulation

Our toolchain has, near the front end, a higher-order program logic; and near the back end, an optimizing compiler composed of successive phases. Each phase translates one language to another (or to itself with rewrites), and each phase comes equipped with a bisimulation proof that the observable behavior is unchanged.

The fact that program-states s contain "hair" such as approximation indices and predicates, poses some problems for the modularity of the top-to-bottom verification of the toolchain. To verify the soundness of the program logic w.r.t. the operational semantics, we need states s containing predicates. As explained in Section 6, Indirection Theory requires that predicates embedded in states must be at specific levels of approximation, and these need to be "aged" (made more approximate) at each step of the computation. On the other hand, to verify the correctness of the optimizing compiler the predicates are unneeded, and the aging hampers the bisimulation proofs. For example, a compiler phase might change the number of steps executed (and thus the amount of aging).

Thus we erase the predicates in moving from the decorated to the angelic semantics. But there are a few places where the predicates have an operational effect, and we replace these with an *angelic oracle* that supplies the missing information. All of our ageable predicates are within the Ω (oracle) component of the state; and thus this erasure has no effect on the m and q components.

Let address $\ell \overset{\pi}{\rightsquigarrow} R$ be a lock (semaphore) in Concurrent Separation Logic, with resource invariant R. R must be a precise separation-logic predicate, meaning that R is satisfied by a unique subheap (if any subset) of a given memory. When a thread releases this lock, the (unique) subheap satisfying R, of the current heap, is moved from thread-ownership to lock-pool ownership.

The operational effect on fully-erased memory is only that the semaphore goes from state 0 to state 1. The operational effect on decorated or angelic memory is that the permissions π of the thread (and of the lock pool) change. The way the permission-change $\Delta\pi$ is calculated, in the decorated semantics, is that R is fetched from the state and (classically, not constructively) evaluated.[5] That is, in a decorated state, at each lock address, is stored the resource invariant R.

Unlike decorated states, angelic states contain no predicates. Instead of calculating $\Delta\pi$ from R, the *angel* is an oracle that contains a list of all $\Delta\pi$ effects that would have (nonconstructively) satisfied from deleted predicates. At each semaphore-release operation, the next $\Delta\pi$ is consumed from the angel.

Dockins [15] shows the proof that *For each safe execution in the decorated semantics, there exists an angel that gives a safe execution in the angelic semantics with the same observable behavior.*

8 Bisimulation

After the static analyzer or a program verifier has proved something about the observable behavior of a source program in the decorated semantics, we partially erase to the angelic semantics. The compiler-correctness proof, showing that source-language and machine-language programs have identical observables, is done in the angelic semantics of the several intermediate languages.

[5] Our own proofs (and those of CompCert) do not use classical axioms such as choice and excluded middle; we use only some axioms of extensionality. But classical axioms are consistent with CiC+extensionality, so the user of our program logic may choose to use them. Therefore we do not assume that the satisfaction of R must be constructive.

The original CompCert proofs were done by bisimulation, with respect to a simple notion of finite or infinite traces of atomic events, with no shared memory. Because the CompCert languages are deterministic, the bisimulations reduce to simpler simulation proofs. These proofs rely on a set of general lemmas about simulations and bisimulations in small-step semantics equipped with observable traces.

We are able reuse the existing CompCert proofs with very little modification, by ensuring that our oracle/observable interface is as compatible as possible with the original trace-based specification. From oracles and observables, Dockins [15] proves a set of simulation lemmas very similar to the original versions in CompCert. From these, Leroy can easily adapt the CompCert proofs.[6] The fact that the operational semantics is angelic is almost invisible in the CompCert bisimulations, because the angel is consulted only at certain of the external function calls, and never during ordinary computation steps corresponding to instructions emitted by the compiler.

If there had been predicates in the heap (i.e. the decorated semantics), the bisimulations would have been harder to prove (and require more changes to the CompCert proofs), because the aging of predicates required by Indirection Theory would age the state by different amounts depending how many instructions a compiler optimization deletes.

Even so, there have been a few changes to the CompCert specification to accommodate our verified toolchain. In addition to the new notion of observables, CompCert now has an address-by-address permission map. Leroy has already modified CompCert (and its proof) to accommodate these permissions (CompCert 1.7, released 03/2010).

The need for permissions in the (angelic) operational semantics is in response to a problem explained by Boehm: "Threads cannot be implemented as a library." [10] He points out that hoisting loads and stores past aquire/release synchronizations can be unsafe optimizations, in shared-memory concurrent programs. He writes, "Here we point out the important issues, and argue that they lie almost exclusively with the compiler and the language specification itself, not with the thread library or its specification." Indeed, the permissions in our decorated or angelic semantics form such a specification, and CompCert is proved correct with respect to this specification.

9 Weak Memory Models

The angelic semantics (and its management of permissions) must be preserved down to the back end of the compiler, so that each optimization stage can correctly hoist loads/stores past other instructions. Only then can full erasure of permissions be done, into the erased semantics.

At this time, the program is still race-free, and the permissions in the angelic semantics allow a proof of this fact. This suggests that executions in a weakly consistent memory model should have the same observable behavior as sequentially consistent executions. It should be possible to prove this, for a given memory model, and to add this proof to the bottom of the verified software toolchain. Recent results in the formal specification of weak memory models [31,12] should be helpful in this regard.

---

[6] As of mid-2010, CompCert is not yet fully ported to the new model of observations.

10 Foundational Verification

Foundational verification is a machine-checked formal verification where we pay particular attention to the size and comprehensibility of the *trusted base*, which includes the specification of the theorem to be proved, the axiomatization of the logic, and the implementation of the proof checker.

It is instructive to use Proof-Carrying Code as a testbed for gedanken experiments about what constitutes the trusted base of a formal method for software. Then in the next section we can apply this methodology to the Verified Software Toolchain, and compare both the size of the trusted base and the strength of what can be proved.

Consider the claim that *Program P in the ML (or Java) language does not load or store addresses outside its heap*. What is the trusted base for a proof of this claim of memory safety? Implicit in this claim is that P is compiled by an ML (or Java) compiler to machine language. A full statement of this theorem in mathematical logic would include: (1) the specification of the operational semantics and instruction encodings of the machine language, (2) the specification of memory safety as a property of executions in the machine language, and (3) the entire ML (or Java) compiler. A verification is a proof of this theorem for P, and naively it might seem that part of this proof is a proof of correctness of the ML (or Java) compiler.

ML and Java are type-safe languages: a source-language program that type-checks cannot load or store outside the heap when executing in the source-language operational semantics. Consequently, the machine-language program should also be memory-safe, if the compiler is correct. Proof-carrying code (PCC) [27] was introduced as a way to remove the compiler from the trusted base, without having to prove the compiler correct—machine-checked compiler-correctness proofs seemed impractical in 1997. Instead of relying on a correct compiler, PCC instruments the (untrusted, possibly incorrect) compiler to translate the source-language types of program variables (in the source-language type system) to machine-language types of program registers (in some machine-language type system). Then one implements a program to type-check machine-language programs. Let P' be the compilation of P to machine-language; now the theorem is that *P' is memory-safe*. The trusted base includes the machine-language type-checker, but not the compiler: that is, one trusts that, or proves that, if P' type-checks then it is memory safe.

Proof-carrying code originally had three important limitations:

1. There is no guarantee that P' has the same observable (input/output) behavior as P, because the compiler is free to produce *any* program as output so long as it type-checks in the machine-language type system;
2. For each kind of source-level safety property that one wishes to proof-carry, one must instrument the compiler to translate source-level annotations to checkable machine-level annotations;
3. The claim that *Any program that type-checks in the machine-language type system has the desired safety property when it executes* is still proved only informally; that is, there was a LaTeXproof about an abstraction of a subset of the type-checker.

Foundational proof-carrying code [5] addresses this third point. We construct a formal specification of the machine-language syntax and semantics in a machine-checkable logic, and a specification of memory-safety in that same logic. Then the theorem is, *Program P' is memory-safe*, and neither the compiler nor the machine-language type annotations need be trusted; the type annotations are part of the *proof* of the theorem, and the proof need not be trusted because it is checked by machine.

The Princeton foundational proof-carrying code (FPCC) project, 1999-2005, demonstrated this approach for core Standard ML. We demonstrated that the trusted base could be reduced to less than 3000 lines of source code: about 800 for a proof checker, written in C and capable of checking proofs for any object logic representable in LF; a few lines for the representation of higher-order logic (HOL) in LF; and about 1500 lines to represent instruction encodings and instruction semantics of the Sparc processor [32]. We instrumented Standard ML of New Jersey to produce type annotations at each basic block [13] and we built a semantic soundness proof for the machine-level type system [1]. Other research groups also demonstrated FPCC for other compilers [17,14].

The late-20th-century limitation that inspired PCC and FPCC—that it is impractical to prove the correctness of an optimizing compiler—no longer applies. Several machine-checked compiler-correctness proofs have been demonstrated [23,24,30]. Proof-carrying code is no longer the state of the art.

11 What Is the Trusted Base?

Our main theorem is, *Claims by the static analyzer about the source-language program will characterize the observations of the compiled program.*

How is this statement to be represented in a machine-checkable logic? We may choose to use complex and sophisticated mathematical techniques to prove such a statement. The compiler may use sophisticated optimization algorithms, with correspondingly complex correctness proofs. We can tolerate such complexity in *proofs,* because proofs are machine-checked. But complexity in the statement of the theorem is undesirable, because some human—the eventual consumer of our proof—must be able to check whether we have proved the right thing.

A "claim" by a static analyzer relates a program p to the specification S of its observable behavior. That is, let A be the static analyzer, so that $A(p, S)$ means that the analyzer claims that every observation o of source-language program p is in the set S. Let C be the compiler, so that $C(p, p')$ means that source program p translates to machine-language program p'. Let M be the operational semantics of machine language, so that $M(p', o)$ means that program p' can run with observation o.

Then the main theorem is, $\forall p, p', S, o.\ A(p, S) \wedge C(p, p') \rightarrow M(p', o) \rightarrow o \in S$. That is, "if the analyzer claims that program p matches specification S, and the compiler compiles p to p', and p' executes on M with observation o, then o is permitted by S."

The *statement* of this theorem is independent of the semantics of the source language! If we expand all the definitions in this theorem, the "big" things are A, C, S, and M. The consumer of this theorem doesn't need to understand A or C, he just needs to make sure that A and C are installed, bit-for-bit, in his computer. The definition S is just the specification of the desired behavior of the program, and this will be as large or as concise as the user needs. The semantics M is only moderately large, depending on the machine architecture; in the FPCC project the Sparc architecture was specified in about 1500 lines of higher-order logic. [32]

What is *not* in the statement of this theorem is the operational or axiomatic semantics of the source language, or the semantic techniques used in defining the program logic! All of these are contained within the *proof* of the theorem, but they do not form part of the trusted based needed in interpreting what the theorem claims.

It seems paradoxical that a claim about the behavior of a program can be independent of the semantics of the programming language. But it works because of the end-to-end connection between the program logic and the compiler. The theorem can be read as, "When you apply the compiler to the syntax of this program, the result is a machine-language program with a certain behavior." That sentence can be uttered without reference to the particular source-language semantics.

What else do you need to trust? The analyzer A and compiler C are written in Gallina, the pure functional programming language embedded in the Coq theorem prover. Coq contains software s_1 to check proofs about Gallina programs, and software s_2 to translate Gallina to ML. The OCaml compiler s_3 translates ML to machine-language; the machine language runs with OCaml runtime-system s_4. All of these are in the trusted base, in the sense that bugs in the s_i can render the proved theorem useless.

FPCC had a much smaller trusted base, avoiding s_1–s_4.[7] But at least these components s_1–s_4 are fixed for all proofs and projects, and well tested by the community; and perhaps some of the techniques used in the FPCC project, such as a tiny independent proof checker, could be applied here as well to remove the s_i from the trusted base.

12 Conclusion

Highly expressive program logics require different semantic methods than compiler-correctness proofs. Proofs about a sequential thread require different kinds of reasoning than proofs about operating systems and concurrency. A top-to-bottom verified toolchain requires all these kinds of reasoning, and thus we choose the right formalism for each component, and prove the relationships between the formalisms. In this way we achieve a system that is sufficiently modular that its major components can be built and proved by entirely separate research groups.

In the process, more work goes into thinking about specifications and interfaces than into the individual components. This is not a bad thing, in the end.

A formal proof may be "wrong" for either of two reasons: There may be a mistake in one or more steps of the proof, so that the "proof" fails to prove the stated theorem; or the statement of the theorem may be not what was intended. Using a proof assistant to mechanically check the proof prevents the first kind of problem, but not the second. This is why I find it so important to do a big top-to-bottom system and connect all the components together in the same metalogic. For example, our paper in LICS'02 [2] was a correct proof of a nice-looking theorem (semantic model of a type system with mutable references, polymorphism, and recursive types) but only in the application to the big Foundational Proof-Carrying Code project did we discover that it was the wrong theorem: the type system had predicative quantification, but we needed impredicative. We had to go back to the drawing board and figure out how to do impredicativity as well

[7] For the explanation of why no compilers are in FPCC's trusted base, see [7, §8.2]. Unfortunately that argument does not apply to the VST.

[3,4]. Footnote 4 describes one such incident in the VST project, and there have been many more along the way. Big "systems" projects have an important place in research on the formal semantics of software.

Acknowledgments. Gilles Barthe, Lennart Beringer, Alexey Gotsman, Julia Lawall, Aleks Nanevski, Gordon Stewart, and Shaz Qadeer all gave me very helpful suggestions on how to organize and present this material. This research was supported in part by the Air Force Office of Scientific Research (grant FA9550-09-1-0138) and the National Science Foundation (grant CNS-0910448).

References

1. Ahmed, A., Appel, A.W., Richards, C.D., Swadi, K.N., Tan, G., Wang, D.C.: Semantic foundations for typed assembly languages. ACM Trans. Program. Lang. Syst. 32(3), 1–67 (2010)
2. Ahmed, A., Appel, A.W., Virga, R.: A stratified semantics of general references embeddable in higher-order logic. In: 17th Annual IEEE Symp. on Logic in Computer Science, pp. 75–86 (June 2002)
3. Ahmed, A., Appel, A.W., Virga, R.: An indexed model of impredicative polymorphism and mutable references (January 2003), `http://www.cs.princeton.edu/~appel/papers/impred.pdf`
4. Ahmed, A.J.: Semantics of Types for Mutable State. PhD thesis, Princeton University, Princeton, NJ, Tech Report TR-713-04 (November 2004)
5. Appel, A.W.: Foundational proof-carrying code. In: Symp. on Logic in Computer Science (LICS 2001), pp. 247–258. IEEE, Los Alamitos (2001)
6. Appel, A.W., Melliès, P.-A., Richards, C.D., Vouillon, J.: A very modal model of a modern, major, general type system. In: Proc. 34th Annual ACM SIGPLAN-SIGACT Symposium on Principles of Programming Languages (POPL 2007), pp. 109–122 (January 2007)
7. Appel, A.W., Michael, N.G., Stump, A., Virga, R.: A trustworthy proof checker. J. Automated Reasoning 31, 231–260 (2003)
8. Birkedal, L., Reus, B., Schwinghammer, J., Stovring, K., Thamsborg, J., Yang, H.: Step-indexed Kripke models over recursive worlds (2010) (submitted for publication)
9. Blazy, S., Dargaye, Z., Leroy, X.: Formal verification of a C compiler front-end. In: Symp. on Formal Methods, pp. 460–475 (2006)
10. Boehm, H.-J.: Threads cannot be implemented as a library. In: PLDI 2005: 2005 ACM SIGPLAN Conference on Programming Language Design and Implementation, New York, pp. 261–268 (2005)
11. Bornat, R., Calcagno, C., O'Hearn, P., Parkinson, M.: Permission accounting in separation logic. In: POPL 2005, pp. 259–270 (2005)
12. Boudol, G., Petri, G.: Relaxed memory models: an operational approach. In: POPL 2009, pp. 392–403 (2009)
13. Chen, J., Wu, D., Appel, A.W., Fang, H.: A provably sound TAL for back-end optimization. In: PLDI 2003: Proc. 2003 ACM SIGPLAN Conference on Programming Language Design and Implementation, pp. 208–219 (June 2003)
14. Crary, K., Sarkar, S.: Foundational certified code in the twelf metalogical framework. ACM Trans. Comput. Logic 9(3), 1–26 (2008)
15. Dockins, R., Appel, A.W.: Observational oracular semantics for compiler correctness and language metatheory (2011) (in preparation)

16. Dockins, R., Hobor, A., Appel, A.W.: A fresh look at separation algebras and share accounting. In: Hu, Z. (ed.) APLAS 2009. LNCS, vol. 5904, pp. 161–177. Springer, Heidelberg (2009)
17. Feng, X., Ni, Z., Shao, Z., Guo, Y.: An open framework for foundational proof-carrying code. In: Proc. 2007 ACM SIGPLAN International Workshop on Types in Language Design and Implementation (TLDI 2007), January 2007, pp. 67–78. ACM Press, New York (2007)
18. Gotsman, A., Berdine, J., Cook, B., Rinetzky, N., Sagiv, M.: Local reasoning for storable locks and threads. In: Shao, Z. (ed.) APLAS 2007. LNCS, vol. 4807, pp. 19–37. Springer, Heidelberg (2007)
19. Gotsman, A., Berdine, J., Cook, B., Sagiv, M.: Thread-modular shape analysis. In: PLDI 2007: 2007 ACM SIGPLAN Conference on Programming Language Design and Implementation (2007)
20. Hobor, A.: Oracle Semantics. PhD thesis, Princeton University (2008)
21. Hobor, A., Appel, A.W., Nardelli, F.Z.: Oracle semantics for concurrent separation logic. In: Gairing, M. (ed.) ESOP 2008. LNCS, vol. 4960, pp. 353–367. Springer, Heidelberg (2008)
22. Hobor, A., Dockings, R., Appel, A.W.: A theory of indirection via approximation. In: POPL 2010: Proc. 37th Annual ACM SIGPLAN-SIGACT Symposium on Principles of Programming Languages, pp. 171–184 (January 2010)
23. Klein, G., Nipkow, T.: A machine-checked model for a Java-like language, virtual machine and compiler. ACM Trans. on Programming Languages and Systems 28, 619–695 (2006)
24. Leroy, X.: Formal certification of a compiler back-end, or: programming a compiler with a proof assistant. In: POPL 2006, pp. 42–54 (2006)
25. Leroy, X., Blazy, S.: Formal verification of a C-like memory model and its uses for verifying program transformations. Journal of Automated Reasoning 41(1), 1–31 (2008)
26. Mansky, W.: Automating separation logic for Concurrent C minor. Undergraduate thesis (May 2008)
27. Necula, G.: Proof-carrying code. In: 24th ACM SIGPLAN-SIGACT Symp. on Principles of Programming Languages, pp. 106–119. ACM Press, New York (1997)
28. O'Hearn, P.W.: Resources, concurrency and local reasoning. Theoretical Computer Science 375(1), 271–307 (2007)
29. Parkinson, M.J.: Local Reasoning for Java. PhD thesis, University of Cambridge (2005)
30. Schirmer, N.: Verification of Sequential Imperative Programs in Isabelle/HOL. PhD thesis, Technische Universität München (2006)
31. Sewell, P., Sarkar, S., Owens, S., Nardelli, F.Z., Myreen, M.O.: x86-tso: a rigorous and usable programmer's model for x86 multiprocessors. Commun. ACM 53(7), 89–97 (2010)
32. Wu, D., Appel, A.W., Stump, A.: Foundational proof checkers with small witnesses. In: 5th ACM SIGPLAN International Conference on Principles and Practice of Declarative Programming (August 2003)

Polymorphic Contracts

João Filipe Belo[1], Michael Greenberg[1],
Atsushi Igarashi[2], and Benjamin C. Pierce[1]

[1] University of Pennsylvania
[2] Kyoto University

Abstract. *Manifest contracts* track precise properties by refining types with predicates—e.g., $\{x{:}\mathsf{Int} \mid x > 0\}$ denotes the positive integers. Contracts and polymorphism make a natural combination: programmers can give strong contracts to abstract types, precisely stating pre- and post-conditions while hiding implementation details—for example, an abstract type of stacks might specify that the pop operation has input type $\{x{:}\alpha\ \mathsf{Stack} \mid \mathsf{not}\,(\mathsf{empty}\,x)\}$. We formalize this combination by defining $\mathrm{F_H}$, a polymorphic calculus with manifest contracts, and establishing fundamental properties including type soundness and relational parametricity. Our development relies on a significant technical improvement over earlier presentations of contracts: instead of introducing a denotational model to break a problematic circularity between typing, subtyping, and evaluation, we develop the metatheory of contracts in a completely syntactic fashion, omitting subtyping from the core system and recovering it *post facto* as a derived property.

Keywords: contracts, refinement types, preconditions, postconditions, dynamic checking, parametric polymorphism, abstract datatypes, syntactic proof, logical relations, subtyping.

1 Introduction

Software contracts allow programmers to state precise properties—e.g., that a function takes a non-empty list to a positive integer—as concrete predicates written in the same language as the rest of the program; these predicates can be checked dynamically as the program executes or, more ambitiously, verified statically with the assistance of a theorem prover. Findler and Felleisen [5] introduced "higher-order contracts" for functional languages; these can take one of two forms: predicate contracts like $\{x{:}\mathsf{Int} \mid x > 0\}$, which denotes the positive numbers, and function contracts like $x{:}\mathsf{Int} \to \{y{:}\mathsf{Int} \mid y \geq x\}$, which denotes functions over the integers that return numbers larger than their inputs.

Greenberg, Pierce, and Weirich [7] contrast two different approaches to contracts: in the *manifest* approach, contracts are types—the type system itself makes contracts 'manifest'; in the *latent* approach, contracts and types live in different worlds (indeed, there may be no types at all, as in PLT Racket's contract system [1]). These two presentations lead to different ways of checking contracts. Latent systems run contracts with checks: for example, $\langle\{x{:}\mathsf{Int} \mid x > 0\}\rangle^{l}\ n$

G. Barthe (Ed.): ESOP 2011, LNCS 6602, pp. 18–37, 2011.
© Springer-Verlag Berlin Heidelberg 2011

checks that $n > 0$. If the check succeeds, then the entire expression will just return n. If it fails, then the entire program will "blame" the label l, raising an uncatchable exception $\Uparrow l$, pronounced "blame l". Manifest systems use casts, $\langle \mathsf{Int} \Rightarrow \{x{:}\mathsf{Int} \mid x > 0\} \rangle^l$ to convert values from one type to another (the left-hand side is the *source* type and the right-hand side is the *target* type). For predicate contracts, a cast will behave just like a check on the target type: applied to n, the cast either returns n or raises $\Uparrow l$. Checks and casts differ when it comes to function contracts. A function check $(\langle T_1 \rightarrow T_2 \rangle^l\ v)\ v'$ will reduce to $\langle T_2 \rangle^l\ (v\ (\langle T_1 \rangle^l\ v'))$, giving v the argument checked at the domain contract and checking that the result satisfies the codomain contract. A function cast $(\langle T_{11} \rightarrow T_{12} \Rightarrow T_{21} \rightarrow T_{22} \rangle^l\, v)\, v'$ will reduce to $\langle T_{12} \Rightarrow T_{22} \rangle^l\, (v\, (\langle T_{21} \Rightarrow T_{11} \rangle^l\, v'))$, wrapping the argument v' in a (contravariant) cast between the domain types and wrapping the result of the application in a (covariant) cast between the codomain types. The differences between checks and casts are discussed at length in [7]. Both presentations have their pros and cons: latent contracts are simpler to design and extend, while manifest contracts make a clearer connection between the static constraints captured by types and the dynamic checks performed by casts. In this work, we consider the manifest approach and endeavor to tame its principal drawback: the complexity of its metatheory. We summarize the issues here, comparing our work to previous approaches more thoroughly in Section 6.

Subtyping is the main source of complexity in the most expressive manifest calculi—those which have dependent functions and allow arbitrary terms in refinements [7,10]. These calculi have subtyping for two reasons. First, subtyping helps preserve types when evaluating casts with predicate contracts: if $\langle \mathsf{Int} \Rightarrow \{x{:}\mathsf{Int} \mid x > 0\} \rangle^l\, n \longrightarrow^* n$, then we need to type n at $\{x{:}\mathsf{Int} \mid x > 0\}$. Subtyping gives it to us, allowing n to be typed at any predicate contract it satisfies. Second, subtyping can show the equivalence of types with different but related term substitutions. Consider the standard dependent-function application rule:

$$\frac{\Gamma \vdash e_1 : (x{:}T_1 \rightarrow T_2) \qquad \Gamma \vdash e_2 : T_1}{\Gamma \vdash e_1\ e_2 : T_2[e_2/x]}$$

If $e_2 \longrightarrow e_2'$, how do $T_2[e_2/x]$ and $T_2[e_2'/x]$ relate? (An important question when proving preservation!) Subtyping shows that these types are really the same: the first type parallel reduces to the second, and it can be shown that parallel reduction between types implies mutual subtyping—that is, equivalence.

Subtyping brings its own challenges, though. A naïve treatment of subtyping introduces a circularity in the definition of the type system. Existing systems break this circularity by defining judgements in a careful order: first the evaluation relation and the corresponding parallel reduction relation; then a denotational semantics based on the evaluation relation and subtyping based on the denotational semantics; and finally the syntactic type system. Making this carefully sequenced series of definitions hold together requires a long series of tedious lemmas relating evaluation and parallel reduction. The upshot is that existing manifest calculi have taken considerable effort to construct.

We propose here a simpler approach to manifest calculi that greatly simplifies their definition and metatheory. Rather than using subtyping, we define a type conversion relation based on parallel reduction. This avoids the original circularity without resorting to denotational semantics. Indeed, we can use this type conversion to give a completely syntactic account of type soundness—with just a few easy lemmas relating evaluation and parallel reduction. Moreover, eliminating subtyping doesn't fundamentally weaken our approach, since we can define a subtyping relation and prove its soundness *post facto*.

We bring this new technique to bear on F_H, a manifest calculus with parametric polymorphism. Researchers have already studied the *dynamic* enforcement of parametric polymorphism in languages that mix (conventional, un-refined) static and dynamic typing (see Section 6); here we study the *static* enforcement of parametric polymorphism in languages that go beyond conventional static types by adding refinement types and dependent function contracts. Concretely, we offer four main contributions:

1. We devise a simpler approach to manifest contract calculi and apply it to F_H, proving type soundness using straightforward syntactic methods [19].
2. We offer the first operational semantics for *general* refinements, where refinements can apply to any type—not just base types.
3. We prove that F_H is relationally parametric—establishing that contract checking does not interfere with this desirable property.
4. We define a *post facto* subtyping relation and prove that "upcasts" from subtypes to supertypes always succeed in F_H, i.e., that subtyping is sound.

We begin with some examples in Section 2. We then describe F_H and prove type soundness in Section 3. We prove parametricity in Section 4 and the upcast lemma in Section 5. We discuss related work in Section 6 and conclude with ideas for future work in Section 7.

2 Examples

Like other manifest calculi, F_H checks contracts with casts: the cast $\langle T_1 \Rightarrow T_2\rangle^l$ takes a value of type T_1 (the source type) and ensures that it behaves (and is treated) like a T_2 (the target type). The l superscript is a *blame label*, used to differentiate between different casts and identify the source of failures. How we check $\langle T_1 \Rightarrow T_2\rangle^l\, v$ depends on the structure of T_1 and T_2. Checking predicate contracts with casts is easy: if v satisfies the predicate of the target type, the entire application goes to v; if not, then the program aborts, "raising" blame, written $\Uparrow l$. For example, $\langle \mathsf{Int} \Rightarrow \{x{:}\mathsf{Int} \mid x > 0\}\rangle^l\, 5 \longrightarrow^* 5$, since $5 > 0$. But $\langle \mathsf{Int} \Rightarrow \{x{:}\mathsf{Int} \mid x > 0\}\rangle^l\, 0 \longrightarrow^* \Uparrow l$, since $0 \not> 0$. When checking predicate contracts, only the target type matters—the type system guarantees that whatever value we have is well typed at the source type. Checking function contracts is a little trickier: what should $\langle \mathsf{Int} \to \mathsf{Int} \Rightarrow \{x{:}\mathsf{Int} \mid x > 0\} \to \{y{:}\mathsf{Int} \mid y > 5\}\rangle^l\, v$ do? We can't just open up v and check whether it always returns positives. The solution is to decompose the cast into its parts:

$$\begin{array}{l}\langle \mathsf{Int} \to \mathsf{Int} \Rightarrow \{x{:}\mathsf{Int} \mid x > 0\} \to \{y{:}\mathsf{Int} \mid y > 5\}\rangle^l\, v \quad \longrightarrow \\ \lambda x{:}\{x{:}\mathsf{Int} \mid x > 0\}.\ (\langle \mathsf{Int} \Rightarrow \{y{:}\mathsf{Int} \mid y > 5\}\rangle^l\, (v\, (\langle \{x{:}\mathsf{Int} \mid x > 0\} \Rightarrow \mathsf{Int}\rangle^l\, x)))\end{array}$$

Note that the domain cast is contravariant, while the codomain is covariant: the context will be forced by the type system to provide a positive number, so we need to cast the input to an appropriate type for v. (In this example, the contravariant cast $\langle \{x{:}\mathsf{Int} \mid x > 0\} \Rightarrow \mathsf{Int}\rangle^l$ will always succeed.) After v returns, we run the covariant codomain cast to ensure that v didn't misbehave. So:

$$\begin{aligned}\langle \mathsf{Int} \rightarrow \mathsf{Int} \Rightarrow \{x{:}\mathsf{Int} \mid x > 0\} \rightarrow \{y{:}\mathsf{Int} \mid y > 5\}\rangle^l\ (\lambda x{:}\mathsf{Int}.\ x)\, 6 &\longrightarrow^* 6 \\ \langle \cdots \rangle^l\ (\lambda x{:}\mathsf{Int}.\ 0)\, 6 &\longrightarrow^* \Uparrow l \\ \langle \cdots \rangle^l\ (\lambda x{:}\mathsf{Int}.\ 0)\, (\langle \mathsf{Int} \Rightarrow \{x{:}\mathsf{Int} \mid x > 0\}\rangle^{l'}\, 0) &\longrightarrow^* \Uparrow l'\end{aligned}$$

Note that we omitted the case where a cast function is applied to 0. It is an important property of our system that 0 doesn't have type $\{x{:}\mathsf{Int} \mid x > 0\}$!

With these preliminaries out of the way, we can approach our work: a manifest calculus with polymorphism. The standard polymorphic encodings of existential and product types transfer over to $\mathrm{F_H}$ without a problem. Indeed, our dependent functions allow us to go one step further and encode even dependent products such as $(x : \mathsf{Int}) \times \{y{:}\alpha\ \mathsf{List} \mid \mathsf{length}\ y = x\}$, which represents lists paired with their lengths. Let's look at an example combining contracts and polymorphism—an abstract datatype of natural numbers.

$$\begin{aligned}\mathsf{NAT} : \exists \alpha.\ &(\mathsf{zero} : \alpha) \times (\mathsf{succ} : (\alpha \rightarrow \alpha)) \times (\mathsf{iszero} : (\alpha \rightarrow \mathsf{Bool})) \times \\ &(\mathsf{pred} : \{x{:}\alpha \mid \mathsf{not}\,(\mathsf{iszero}\, x)\} \rightarrow \alpha)\end{aligned}$$

(We omit the implementation, a standard Church encoding.) The NAT interface hides our encoding of the naturals behind an existential type, but it also requires that pred is only ever applied to terms of type $\{x{:}\alpha \mid \mathsf{not}\,(\mathsf{iszero}\, x)\}$. Assuming that $\mathsf{iszero}\, v \longrightarrow^* \mathsf{true}$ iff $v = \mathsf{zero}$, we can infer that pred is never given zero as an argument. Consider the following expression, where I is the interface we specified for NAT and we omit the term binding for brevity:

$$\mathsf{unpack}\ \mathsf{NAT} : \exists \alpha.\ I\ \mathsf{as}\ \alpha, \_\ \ \mathsf{in}\ \mathsf{pred}\,(\langle \alpha \Rightarrow \{x{:}\alpha \mid \mathsf{not}\,(\mathsf{iszero}\, x)\}\rangle^l\, \mathsf{zero}) : \alpha$$

The application of pred directly to zero would not be well typed, since $\mathsf{zero} : \alpha$. On the other hand, the cast term is well typed, since we cast zero to the type we need. Naturally, this cast will ultimately raise $\Uparrow l$, because $\mathsf{not}\,(\mathsf{iszero}\,\mathsf{zero}) \longrightarrow^* \mathsf{false}$.

The example so far imposes constraints only on the *use* of the abstract datatype, in particular on the use of pred. To have constraints imposed also on the *implementation* of the abstract data type, consider the extension of the interface with a subtraction operation, sub, and a "less than or equal" predicate, leq. We now have the interface:

$$I' = I \times (\mathsf{leq} : \alpha \rightarrow \alpha \rightarrow \mathsf{Bool}) \times (\mathsf{sub} : (x{:}\alpha \rightarrow \{y{:}\alpha \mid \mathsf{leq}\, y\, x\} \rightarrow \{z{:}\alpha \mid \mathsf{leq}\, z\, x\}))$$

The sub function requires that its second argument isn't greater than the first, and it promises to return a result that isn't greater than the first argument.

We get contracts in interfaces by putting casts in the implementations. For example, the contracts on pred and sub are imposed when we "pack up" NAT; we write nat for the implementation type:

$$\mathsf{pack}\ \langle \mathsf{nat}, (\mathsf{zero}, \mathsf{succ}, \mathsf{iszero}, \mathsf{pred}, \mathsf{leq}, \mathsf{sub})\rangle\ \mathsf{as}\ \exists \alpha.\ I'$$

Types and contexts

$T ::= B \mid \alpha \mid x{:}T_1 \to T_2 \mid \forall\alpha.T \mid \{x{:}T \mid e\}$

$\Gamma ::= \emptyset \mid \Gamma, x{:}T \mid \Gamma, \alpha$

Terms

$e ::= x \mid k \mid \mathsf{op}\,(e_1, \ldots, e_n) \mid \lambda x{:}T.\ e \mid \Lambda\alpha.e \mid e_1\ e_2 \mid e\ T \mid$
$\quad \langle T_1 \Rightarrow T_2\rangle^l \mid \Uparrow l \mid \langle\{x{:}T \mid e_1\}, e_2, v\rangle^l$

$v ::= k \mid \lambda x{:}T.\ e \mid \Lambda\alpha.e \mid \langle T_1 \Rightarrow T_2\rangle^l$

$r ::= v \mid \Uparrow l$

$E ::= [\,]\ e_2 \mid v_1\ [\,] \mid [\,]\ T \mid \langle\{x{:}T \mid e\}, [\,], v\rangle^l \mid \mathsf{op}(v_1, \ldots, v_{i-1}, [\,], e_{i+1}, \ldots, e_n)$

Fig. 1. Syntax for $\mathrm{F_H}$

where:

$$\mathsf{pred} = \langle \mathsf{nat} \to \mathsf{nat} \Rightarrow \{x{:}\mathsf{nat} \mid \mathsf{not}\,(\mathsf{iszero}\,x)\} \to \mathsf{nat}\rangle^l\ \mathsf{pred}'$$
$$\mathsf{sub} = \langle \mathsf{nat} \to \mathsf{nat} \to \mathsf{nat} \Rightarrow x{:}\mathsf{nat} \to \{y{:}\mathsf{nat} \mid \mathsf{leq}\,y\,x\} \to \{z{:}\mathsf{nat} \mid \mathsf{leq}\,z\,x\}\rangle^l\ \mathsf{sub}'$$

That is, the existential type dictates that we must pack up *cast* versions of our implementations, pred' and sub'. Note, however, that the cast on pred' will never actually check anything at runtime: if we unfold the domain contract contravariantly, we see that $\langle\{x{:}\mathsf{nat} \mid \mathsf{not}\,(\mathsf{iszero}\,x)\} \Rightarrow \mathsf{nat}\rangle^l$ is a no-op. Instead, clients of NAT can only call pred with terms that are typed at $\{x{:}\mathsf{nat} \mid \mathsf{not}\,(\mathsf{iszero}\,x)\}$, i.e., by checking that values are nonzero with a cast into pred's input type. The story is the same for the contract on sub's second argument—the contravariant cast won't actually check anything. The codomain contract on sub, however, could fail if sub' mis-implemented subtraction.

We can sum up the situation for contracts in interfaces as follows: the positive parts of the interface type are checked and can raise blame—these parts are the responsibility of the implementation; the negative parts of the interface type are not checked by the implementation—clients must check these themselves before calling functions from the ADT. Distributing obligations in this way recalls Findler and Felleisen's seminal idea of client and server blame [5].

3 Defining $\mathrm{F_H}$

The syntax of $\mathrm{F_H}$ is given in Figure 1. For unrefined types we have: base types B, which must include Bool; type variables α; dependent function types $x{:}T_1 \to T_2$ where x is bound in T_2; and universal types $\forall\alpha.T$, where α is bound in T. Aside from dependency in function types, these are just the types of the standard polymorphic lambda calculus. As usual, we write $T_1 \to T_2$ for $x{:}T_1 \to T_2$ when x does not appear free in T_2. We also have predicate contracts, or *refinement types*, written $\{x{:}T \mid e\}$. Conceptually, $\{x{:}T \mid e\}$ denotes values v of type T for which $e[v/x]$ reduces to true. For each B, we fix a set $\mathcal{K}_B$ of the constants in that type; we require our typing rules for constants and our typing and evaluation rules for operations to respect this set. We also require that $\mathcal{K}_{\mathsf{Bool}} = \{\mathsf{true}, \mathsf{false}\}$.

In the syntax of terms, the first line is standard for a call-by-value polymorphic language: variables, constants, several monomorphic first-order operations op (i.e., destructors of one or more base-type arguments), term and type abstractions, and term and type applications. The second line offers the standard constructs of a manifest contract calculus [6,7,10], with a few alterations, discussed below.

Casts are the distinguishing feature of manifest contract calculi. When applied to a value of type T_1, the cast $\langle T_1 \Rightarrow T_2 \rangle^l$ ensures that its argument behaves—and is treated—like a value of type T_2. When a cast detects a problem, it raises blame, a label-indexed uncatchable exception written $\Uparrow l$. The label l allows us to trace blame back to a specific cast. (While our labels here are drawn from an arbitrary set, in practice l will refer to a source-code location.) Finally, we use active checks $\langle \{x{:}T \mid e_1\}, e_2, v \rangle^l$ to support a small-step semantics for checking casts into refinement types. In an active check, $\{x{:}T \mid e_1\}$ is the refinement being checked, e_2 is the current state of checking, and v is the value being checked. The type in the first position of an active check isn't necessary for the operational semantics, but we keep it around as a technical aid to type soundness. If checking succeeds, the check will return v; if checking fails, the check will blame its label, raising $\Uparrow l$. Active checks and blame are not intended to occur in source programs—they are runtime devices. (In a real programming language based on this calculus, casts will probably not appear explicitly either, but will be inserted by an elaboration phase. The details of this process are beyond the scope of the present work.)

The values in F_H are constants, term and type abstractions, and casts. We also define *results*, which are either values or blame. (Type soundness—a consequence of Theorems 2 and 3 below—will show that evaluation produces a result, but not necessarily a value.) In some earlier work [7,8], casts between function types applied to values were themselves considered values. We make the other choice here: excluding applications from the possible syntactic forms of values simplifies our inversion lemmas.

There are two notable features relative to existing manifest calculi: first, *any* type (even a refinement type) can be refined, not just base types (as in [6,7,8,10,12]); second, the third part of the active check form $\langle \{x{:}T \mid e_1\}, e_2, v \rangle^l$ can be any value, not just a constant. Both of these changes are motivated by the introduction of polymorphism. In particular, to support refinement of type variables we must allow refinements of *all* types, since any type can be substituted in for a variable.

Operational Semantics

The call-by-value operational semantics in Figure 2 are given as a small-step relation, split into two sub-relations: one for reductions ($\rightsquigarrow$) and one for congruence and blame lifting ($\longrightarrow$).

The latter relation is standard. The E_Reduce rule lifts $\rightsquigarrow$ reductions into $\longrightarrow$; the E_Compat rule turns $\longrightarrow$ into a congruence over our evaluation contexts; and the E_Blame rule lifts blame, treating it as an uncatchable exception. The reduction relation $\rightsquigarrow$ is more interesting. There are four different kinds of

Reduction rules $\boxed{e_1 \rightsquigarrow e_2}$

$$\mathsf{op}\,(v_1, \ldots, v_n) \rightsquigarrow [\![\mathsf{op}]\!]\,(v_1, \ldots, v_n) \qquad \text{E\_OP}$$
$$(\lambda x{:}T_1.\; e_{12})\; v_2 \rightsquigarrow e_{12}[v_2/x] \qquad \text{E\_BETA}$$
$$(\Lambda\alpha.e)\; T \rightsquigarrow e[T/\alpha] \qquad \text{E\_TBETA}$$

$$\langle T \Rightarrow T\rangle^l\, v \rightsquigarrow v \qquad \text{E\_REFL}$$
$$\langle x{:}T_{11} \to T_{12} \Rightarrow x{:}T_{21} \to T_{22}\rangle^l\, v \rightsquigarrow \qquad \text{E\_FUN}$$
$$\lambda x{:}T_{21}.\; (\langle T_{12}[\langle T_{21} \Rightarrow T_{11}\rangle^l\, x/x] \Rightarrow T_{22}\rangle^l\, (v\, (\langle T_{21} \Rightarrow T_{11}\rangle^l\, x)))$$
$$\text{when } x{:}T_{11} \to T_{12} \neq x{:}T_{21} \to T_{22}$$
$$\langle \forall\alpha.T_1 \Rightarrow \forall\alpha.T_2\rangle^l\, v \rightsquigarrow \Lambda\alpha.(\langle T_1 \Rightarrow T_2\rangle^l\, (v\,\alpha)) \qquad \text{E\_FORALL}$$
$$\text{when } \forall\alpha.T_1 \neq \forall\alpha.T_2$$

$$\langle \{x{:}T_1 \mid e\} \Rightarrow T_2\rangle^l\, v \rightsquigarrow \langle T_1 \Rightarrow T_2\rangle^l\, v \qquad \text{E\_FORGET}$$
$$\text{when } T_2 \neq \{x{:}T_1 \mid e\} \text{ and } T_2 \neq \{y{:}\{x{:}T_1 \mid e\} \mid e_2\}$$
$$\langle T_1 \Rightarrow \{x{:}T_2 \mid e\}\rangle^l\, v \rightsquigarrow \langle T_2 \Rightarrow \{x{:}T_2 \mid e\}\rangle^l\, (\langle T_1 \Rightarrow T_2\rangle^l\, v) \qquad \text{E\_PRECHECK}$$
$$\text{when } T_1 \neq T_2 \text{ and } T_1 \neq \{x{:}T' \mid e'\}$$
$$\langle T \Rightarrow \{x{:}T \mid e\}\rangle^l\, v \rightsquigarrow \langle \{x{:}T \mid e\}, e[v/x], v\rangle^l \qquad \text{E\_CHECK}$$

$$\langle \{x{:}T \mid e\}, \mathsf{true}, v\rangle^l \rightsquigarrow v \qquad \text{E\_OK}$$
$$\langle \{x{:}T \mid e\}, \mathsf{false}, v\rangle^l \rightsquigarrow \Uparrow l \qquad \text{E\_FAIL}$$

Evaluation rules $\boxed{e_1 \longrightarrow e_2}$

$$\frac{e_1 \rightsquigarrow e_2}{e_1 \longrightarrow e_2}\ \text{E\_REDUCE} \qquad \frac{e_1 \longrightarrow e_2}{E\,[e_1] \longrightarrow E\,[e_2]}\ \text{E\_COMPAT} \qquad \frac{}{E\,[\Uparrow l] \longrightarrow \Uparrow l}\ \text{E\_BLAME}$$

Fig. 2. Operational semantics

reductions: the standard lambda calculus reductions, structural cast reductions, cast staging reductions, and checking reductions.

The E_BETA, and E_TBETA rules should need no explanation—these are the standard call-by-value polymorphic lambda calculus reductions. The E_OP rule uses a denotation function $[\![-]\!]$ to give meaning to our first-order operations.

The E_REFL, E_FUN, and E_FORALL rules are structural cast reductions. E_REFL eliminates a cast from a type to itself; intuitively, such a cast should always succeed anyway. (We discuss this rule more in Section 4.) When a cast between function types is applied to a value v, the E_FUN rule produces a new lambda, wrapping v with a contravariant cast on the domain and covariant cast on the codomain. The extra substitution in the left-hand side of the codomain cast may seem suspicious, but in fact the rule must be this way in order for type preservation to hold (see [7] for an explanation). The E_FORALL rule is similar to E_FUN, generating a type abstraction with the necessary covariant cast. Side conditions on E_FORALL and E_FUN ensure that these rules apply only when E_REFL doesn't.

The E_FORGET, E_PRECHECK, and E_CHECK rules are cast-staging reductions, breaking a complex cast down to a series of simpler casts and checks. All of these rules require that the left- and right-hand sides of the cast be different—if they are the same, then E_REFL applies. The E_FORGET rule strips a layer of refinement off the left-hand side; in addition to requiring that the left- and right-hand sides are different, the preconditions require that the right-hand side isn't a refinement of the left-hand side. The E_PRECHECK rule breaks a cast into two parts: one that checks exactly one level of refinement and another that checks the remaining parts. We only apply this rule when the two sides of the cast are different and when the left-hand side isn't a refinement. The E_CHECK rule applies when the right-hand side refines the left-hand side; it takes the cast value and checks that it satisfies the right-hand side. (We don't have to check the left-hand side, since that's the type we're casting *from*.)

Before explaining how these rules interact in general, we offer a few examples. First, here is a reduction using E_CHECK, E_COMPAT, E_OP, and E_OK:

$$\begin{aligned}\langle \mathsf{Int} \Rightarrow \{x{:}\mathsf{Int} \mid x \geq 0\}\rangle^l\, 5 &\longrightarrow \langle \{x{:}\mathsf{Int} \mid x \geq 0\}, 5 \geq 0, 5\rangle^l \\ &\longrightarrow \langle \{x{:}\mathsf{Int} \mid x \geq 0\}, \mathsf{true}, 5\rangle^l \longrightarrow 5\end{aligned}$$

A failed check will work the same way until the last reduction, which will use E_FAIL rather than E_OK:

$$\begin{aligned}\langle \mathsf{Int} \Rightarrow \{x{:}\mathsf{Int} \mid x \geq 0\}\rangle^l\, (-1) &\longrightarrow \langle \{x{:}\mathsf{Int} \mid x \geq 0\}, -1 \geq 0, -1\rangle^l \\ &\longrightarrow \langle \{x{:}\mathsf{Int} \mid x \geq 0\}, \mathsf{false}, -1\rangle^l \longrightarrow \Uparrow l\end{aligned}$$

Notice that the blame label comes from the cast that failed. Here is a similar reduction that needs some staging, using E_FORGET followed by the first reduction we gave:

$$\begin{aligned}\langle \{x{:}\mathsf{Int} \mid x = 5\} \Rightarrow \{x{:}\mathsf{Int} \mid x \geq 0\}\rangle^l\, 5 &\longrightarrow \langle \mathsf{Int} \Rightarrow \{x{:}\mathsf{Int} \mid x \geq 0\}\rangle^l\, 5 \\ &\longrightarrow \langle \{x{:}\mathsf{Int} \mid x \geq 0\}, 5 \geq 0, 5\rangle^l \longrightarrow^* 5\end{aligned}$$

There are two cases where we need to use E_PRECHECK. First, when multiple refinements are involved:

$$\begin{aligned}\langle \mathsf{Int} \Rightarrow \{x{:}\{y{:}\mathsf{Int} \mid y \geq 0\} \mid x = 5\}\rangle^l\, 5 &\longrightarrow \\ \langle \{y{:}\mathsf{Int} \mid y \geq 0\} \Rightarrow \{x{:}\{y{:}\mathsf{Int} \mid y \geq 0\} \mid x = 5\}\rangle^l\, (\langle \mathsf{Int} \Rightarrow \{y{:}\mathsf{Int} \mid y \geq 0\}\rangle^l\, 5) &\longrightarrow^* \\ \langle \{y{:}\mathsf{Int} \mid y \geq 0\} \Rightarrow \{x{:}\{y{:}\mathsf{Int} \mid y \geq 0\} \mid x = 5\}\rangle^l\, 5 &\longrightarrow \\ \langle \{x{:}\{y{:}\mathsf{Int} \mid y \geq 0\} \mid x = 5\}, 5 = 5, 5\rangle^l &\longrightarrow^* \\ 5&\end{aligned}$$

Second, when casting a function or universal type into a refinement of a *different* function or universal type.

$$\begin{aligned}&\langle \mathsf{Bool} \rightarrow \{x{:}\mathsf{Bool} \mid x\} \Rightarrow \{f{:}\mathsf{Bool} \rightarrow \mathsf{Bool} \mid f\,\mathsf{true} = f\,\mathsf{false}\}\rangle^l\, v \longrightarrow \\ &\quad \langle \mathsf{Bool} \rightarrow \mathsf{Bool} \Rightarrow \{f{:}\mathsf{Bool} \rightarrow \mathsf{Bool} \mid f\,\mathsf{true} = f\,\mathsf{false}\}\rangle^l \\ &\quad\quad (\langle \mathsf{Bool} \rightarrow \{x{:}\mathsf{Bool} \mid x\} \Rightarrow \mathsf{Bool} \rightarrow \mathsf{Bool}\rangle^l\, v)\end{aligned}$$

E_REFL is necessary for simple cases, like $\langle \mathsf{Int} \Rightarrow \mathsf{Int}\rangle^l\, 5 \longrightarrow 5$. Hopefully, such a silly cast would never be written, but it could arise as a result of E_FUN or E_FORALL. (We also need E_REFL in our proof of parametricity; see Section 4.)

Cast evaluation follows a regular schema:

$$\text{REFL} \mid (\text{FORGET}^* \; (\text{REFL} \mid (\text{PRECHECK}^* \; (\text{REFL} \mid \text{FUN} \mid \text{FORALL})? \; \text{CHECK}^*)))$$

Let's consider the cast $\langle T_1 \Rightarrow T_2 \rangle^l\, v$. To simplify the following discussion, we define unref(T) as T without any outer refinements (though refinements on, e.g., the domain of a function would be unaffected); we write unref$_n(T)$ when we remove only the n outermost refinements:

$$\text{unref}(T) = \begin{cases} \text{unref}(T') & \text{if } T = \{x{:}T' \mid e\} \\ T & \text{otherwise} \end{cases}$$

First, if $T_1 = T_2$, we can apply E_REFL and be done with it. If that doesn't work, we'll reduce by E_FORGET until the left-hand side doesn't have any refinements. (N.B. we may not have to make any of these reductions.) Either all of the refinements will be stripped away from the source type, or E_REFL eventually applies and the entire cast disappears. Assuming E_REFL doesn't apply, we now have $\langle \text{unref}(T_1) \Rightarrow T_2 \rangle^l\, v$. Next, we apply E_PRECHECK until the cast is completely decomposed into one-step casts, once for each refinement in T_2:

$$\langle \text{unref}_1(T_2) \Rightarrow T_2 \rangle^l (\langle \text{unref}_2(T_2) \Rightarrow \text{unref}_1(T_2) \rangle^l \\ (\ldots\; (\langle \text{unref}(T_1) \Rightarrow \text{unref}(T_2) \rangle^l\, v) \;\ldots))$$

As our next step, we apply whichever structural cast rule applies to $\langle \text{unref}(T_1) \Rightarrow \text{unref}(T_2) \rangle^l\, v$, one of E_REFL, E_FUN, or E_FORALL. Now all that remains are some number of refinement checks, which can be dispatched by the E_CHECK rule (and other rules, of course, during the predicate checks themselves).

Static Typing

The type system comprises three mutually recursive judgments: context well formedness, type well formedness, and term well typing. The rules for contexts and types are unsurprising. The rules for terms are mostly standard. First, the T_APP rule is dependent, to account for dependent function types. The T_CAST rule is standard for manifest calculi, allowing casts between compatibly structured well formed types. Compatibility of type structures is defined in Figure 4; in short, compatible types erase to identical simple type skeletons. Note that we assign casts a non-dependent function type. The T_OP rule uses the ty function to assign (possibly dependent) monomorphic first-order types to our operations; we require that ty(op) and $[\![\text{op}]\!]$ agree.

Some of the typing rules—T_CHECK, T_BLAME, T_EXACT, T_FORGET, and T_CONV—are "runtime only". We don't expect to use these rules to type check source programs, but we need them to guarantee preservation. Note that the conclusions of these rules use a context Γ, but their premises don't use Γ at all. Even though runtime terms and their typing rules should only ever occur in an empty context, the T_APP rule substitutes terms into types—so a runtime term could end up under a binder. We therefore allow the runtime typing rules

Context well formedness $\boxed{\vdash \Gamma}$

$$\frac{}{\vdash \emptyset}\ \text{WF\_EMPTY} \qquad \frac{\vdash \Gamma \quad \Gamma \vdash T}{\vdash \Gamma, x{:}T}\ \text{WF\_EXTENDVAR} \qquad \frac{\vdash \Gamma}{\vdash \Gamma, \alpha}\ \text{WF\_EXTENDTVAR}$$

Type well formedness $\boxed{\Gamma \vdash T}$

$$\frac{\vdash \Gamma}{\Gamma \vdash B}\ \text{WF\_BASE} \qquad \frac{\vdash \Gamma \quad \alpha \in \Gamma}{\Gamma \vdash \alpha}\ \text{WF\_TVAR} \qquad \frac{\Gamma, \alpha \vdash T}{\Gamma \vdash \forall \alpha. T}\ \text{WF\_FORALL}$$

$$\frac{\Gamma \vdash T_1 \quad \Gamma, x{:}T_1 \vdash T_2}{\Gamma \vdash x{:}T_1 \to T_2}\ \text{WF\_FUN} \qquad \frac{\Gamma \vdash T \quad \Gamma, x{:}T \vdash e : \mathsf{Bool}}{\Gamma \vdash \{x{:}T \mid e\}}\ \text{WF\_REFINE}$$

Term typing $\boxed{\Gamma \vdash e : T}$

$$\frac{\vdash \Gamma \quad x{:}T \in \Gamma}{\Gamma \vdash x : T}\ \text{T\_VAR} \qquad \frac{\vdash \Gamma}{\Gamma \vdash k : \mathsf{ty}(k)}\ \text{T\_CONST} \qquad \frac{\emptyset \vdash T \quad \vdash \Gamma}{\Gamma \vdash \Uparrow l : T}\ \text{T\_BLAME}$$

$$\frac{\Gamma, x{:}T_1 \vdash e_{12} : T_2}{\Gamma \vdash \lambda x{:}T_1.\ e_{12} : x{:}T_1 \to T_2}\ \text{T\_ABS} \qquad \frac{\Gamma \vdash e_1 : (x{:}T_1 \to T_2) \quad \Gamma \vdash e_2 : T_1}{\Gamma \vdash e_1\ e_2 : T_2[e_2/x]}\ \text{T\_APP}$$

$$\frac{\begin{array}{c}\vdash \Gamma \qquad \mathsf{ty}(\mathsf{op}) = x_1 : T_1 \to \ldots \to x_n : T_n \to T \\ \Gamma \vdash e_i[e_1/x_1, \ldots, e_{i-1}/x_{i-1}] : T_i[e_1/x_1, \ldots, e_{i-1}/x_{i-1}]\end{array}}{\Gamma \vdash \mathsf{op}\,(e_1, \ldots, e_n) : T[e_1/x_1, \ldots, e_n/x_n]}\ \text{T\_OP}$$

$$\frac{\Gamma, \alpha \vdash e : T}{\Gamma \vdash \Lambda \alpha. e : \forall \alpha. T}\ \text{T\_TABS} \qquad \frac{\Gamma \vdash e_1 : \forall \alpha. T \quad \Gamma \vdash T_2}{\Gamma \vdash e_1\ T_2 : T[T_2/\alpha]}\ \text{T\_TAPP}$$

$$\frac{\Gamma \vdash T_1 \quad \Gamma \vdash T_2 \quad T_1 \parallel T_2}{\Gamma \vdash \langle T_1 \Rightarrow T_2 \rangle^l : T_1 \to T_2}\ \text{T\_CAST}$$

$$\frac{\vdash \Gamma \quad \emptyset \vdash \{x{:}T \mid e_1\} \quad \emptyset \vdash v : T \quad \emptyset \vdash e_2 : \mathsf{Bool} \quad e_1[v/x] \longrightarrow^* e_2}{\Gamma \vdash \langle \{x{:}T \mid e_1\}, e_2, v \rangle^l : \{x{:}T \mid e_1\}}\ \text{T\_CHECK}$$

$$\frac{\vdash \Gamma \quad \emptyset \vdash e : T \quad \emptyset \vdash T' \quad T \equiv T'}{\Gamma \vdash e : T'}\ \text{T\_CONV} \qquad \frac{\emptyset \vdash v : \{x{:}T \mid e\} \quad \vdash \Gamma}{\Gamma \vdash v : T}\ \text{T\_FORGET}$$

$$\frac{\vdash \Gamma \quad \emptyset \vdash v : T \quad \emptyset \vdash \{x{:}T \mid e\} \quad e[v/x] \longrightarrow^* \mathsf{true}}{\Gamma \vdash v : \{x{:}T \mid e\}}\ \text{T\_EXACT}$$

Fig. 3. Typing rules

Type compatibility $\boxed{T_1 \parallel T_2}$

$$\frac{}{T \parallel T}\ \text{C\_REFL} \qquad \frac{T_1 \parallel T_2}{\{x{:}T_1 \mid e\} \parallel T_2}\ \text{C\_REFINEL} \qquad \frac{T_1 \parallel T_2}{T_1 \parallel \{x{:}T_2 \mid e\}}\ \text{C\_REFINER}$$

$$\frac{T_{11} \parallel T_{21} \quad T_{12} \parallel T_{22}}{x{:}T_{11} \to T_{12} \parallel x{:}T_{21} \to T_{22}}\ \text{C\_FUN} \qquad \frac{T_1 \parallel T_2}{\forall\alpha.T_1 \parallel \forall\alpha.T_2}\ \text{C\_FORALL}$$

Fig. 4. Type compatibility

to apply in any well formed context, so long as the terms they type check are closed. The T_BLAME rule allows us to give any type to blame—this is necessary for preservation. The T_CHECK rule types an active check, $\langle\{x{:}T \mid e_1\}, e_2, v\rangle^l$. Such a term arises when a term like $\langle T \Rightarrow \{x{:}T \mid e_1\}\rangle^l\ v$ reduces by E_CHECK. The premises of the rule are all intuitive except for $e_1[v/x] \longrightarrow^* e_2$, which is necessary to avoid nonsensical terms like $\langle\{x{:}T \mid x \geq 0\}, \mathsf{true}, -1\rangle^l$, where the wrong predicate gets checked. The T_EXACT rule allows us to retype a closed value of type T at $\{x{:}T \mid e\}$ if $e[v/x] \longrightarrow^* \mathsf{true}$. This typing rule guarantees type preservation for E_OK: $\langle\{x{:}T \mid e_1\}, \mathsf{true}, v\rangle^l \longrightarrow v$. If the active check was well typed, then we know that $e_1[v/x] \longrightarrow^* \mathsf{true}$, so T_EXACT applies. Finally, the T_CONV rule allows us to retype expressions at convertible types: if $\emptyset \vdash e : T$ and $T \equiv T'$, then $\emptyset \vdash e : T'$ (or in any well formed context Γ). We define $\equiv$ as the symmetric, transitive closure of call-by-value respecting parallel reduction, which we write $\Rrightarrow$. The T_CONV rule is necessary to prove preservation in the case where $e_1\ e_2 \longrightarrow e_1\ e_2'$. Why? The first term is typed at $T_2[e_2/x]$ (by T_APP), but reapplying T_APP types the second term at $T_2[e_2'/x]$. Conveniently, $T_2[e_2/x] \Rrightarrow T_2[e_2'/x]$, so the two are convertible if we take parallel reduction as our type conversion. Naturally, we have to take the transitive closure so we can string together conversion derivations. We take the symmetric closure, since it is easier for us to work with an equivalence. In previous work, subtyping is used instead of the $\equiv$ relation; one of our contributions is the insight that subtyping—with its accompanying metatheoretical complications—is not an essential component of manifest calculi.

We define type compatibility and a few metatheoretically useful operators in Figure 4.

Lemma 1 (Canonical forms). *If $\emptyset \vdash v : T$, then:*

1. *If* $\mathrm{unref}(T) = B$ *then* $v = k \in \mathcal{K}_B$ *for some* v
2. *If* $\mathrm{unref}(T) = x{:}T_1 \to T_2$ *then* v *is*
   (a) $\lambda x{:}T_1'.\ e_{12}$ *and* $T_1' \equiv T_1$ *for some* x, T_1' *and* e_{12}, *or*
   (b) $\langle T_1' \Rightarrow T_2'\rangle^l$ *and* $T_1' \equiv T_1$ *and* $T_2' \equiv T_2$ *for some* T_1', T_2', *and* l
3. *If* $\mathrm{unref}(T) = \forall\alpha.T'$ *then* v *is* $\Lambda\alpha.v'$ *for some* v'.

Theorem 2 (Progress). *If $\emptyset \vdash e : T$, then either $e \longrightarrow e'$ or e is a result.*

Theorem 3 (Preservation). *If $\emptyset \vdash e : T$ and $e \longrightarrow e'$, then $\emptyset \vdash e' : T$.*

Closed terms $\boxed{r_1 \sim r_2 : T; \theta; \delta \text{ and } e_1 \simeq e_2 : T; \theta; \delta}$

$$
\begin{array}{rcl}
k \sim k : B; \theta; \delta & \iff & k \in \mathcal{K}_B \\
v_1 \sim v_2 : \alpha; \theta; \delta & \iff & \exists R T_1 T_2,\ \alpha \mapsto R, T_1, T_2 \in \theta \wedge v_1\ R\ v_2 \\
v_1 \sim v_2 : (x{:}T_1 \to T_2); \theta; \delta & \iff & \forall v_1' \sim v_2' : T_1; \theta; \delta,\ v_1\, v_1' \simeq v_2\, v_2' : T_2; \theta; \delta[v_1', v_2'/x] \\
v_1 \sim v_2 : \forall \alpha. T; \theta; \delta & \iff & \forall R T_1 T_2,\ v_1\, T_1 \simeq v_2\, T_2 : T; \theta[\alpha \mapsto R, T_1, T_2]; \delta \\
v_1 \sim v_2 : \{x{:}T \mid e\}; \theta; \delta & \iff & v_1 \sim v_2 : T; \theta; \delta \wedge \\
& & \theta_1(\delta_1(e))[v_1/x] \longrightarrow^* \mathsf{true} \wedge \theta_2(\delta_2(e))[v_2/x] \longrightarrow^* \mathsf{true} \\
\Uparrow l \sim \Uparrow l : T; \theta; \delta & & \\
& & \\
e_1 \simeq e_2 : T; \theta; \delta & \iff & \exists r_1 r_2, e_1 \longrightarrow^* r_1 \wedge e_2 \longrightarrow^* r_2 \wedge r_1 \sim r_2 : T; \theta; \delta
\end{array}
$$

Types $\boxed{T_1 \simeq T_2 : *; \theta; \delta}$

$$
\begin{array}{rcl}
B \simeq B : *; \theta; \delta & & \\
\alpha \simeq \alpha : *; \theta; \delta & & \\
x{:}T_{11} \to T_{12} \simeq x{:}T_{21} \to T_{22} : *; \theta; \delta & \iff & T_{11} \simeq T_{21} : *; \theta; \delta \wedge \\
& & \forall v_1 \sim v_2 : T_{11}; \theta; \delta, \\
& & \quad T_{12} \simeq T_{22} : *; \theta; \delta[v_1, v_2/x] \\
\forall \alpha. T_1 \simeq \forall \alpha. T_2 : *; \theta; \delta & \iff & \forall R T_1' T_2',\ T_1 \simeq T_2 : *; \theta[\alpha \mapsto R, T_1', T_2']; \delta \\
\{x{:}T_1 \mid e_1\} \simeq \{x{:}T_2 \mid e_2\} : *; \theta; \delta & \iff & T_1 \simeq T_2 : *; \theta; \delta \wedge \\
\multicolumn{3}{r}{\forall v_1 \sim v_2 : T_1; \theta; \delta,\ \theta_1(\delta_1(e_1))[v_1/x] \simeq \theta_2(\delta_2(e_2))[v_2/x] : \mathsf{Bool}; \theta; \delta}
\end{array}
$$

Open terms and types $\boxed{\Gamma \vdash \theta; \delta \text{ and } \Gamma \vdash e_1 \simeq e_2 : T \text{ and } \Gamma \vdash T_1 \simeq T_2 : *}$

$$
\begin{array}{rcl}
\Gamma \vdash \theta; \delta & \iff & \forall x{:}T \in \Gamma,\ \theta_1(\delta_1(x)) \simeq \theta_2(\delta_2(x)) : T; \theta; \delta \wedge \\
& & \forall \alpha \in \Gamma, \exists R T_1 T_2,\ \alpha \mapsto R, T_1, T_2 \in \theta \\
\Gamma \vdash e_1 \simeq e_2 : T & \iff & \forall \Gamma \vdash \theta; \delta,\ \theta_1(\delta_1(e_1)) \simeq \theta_2(\delta_2(e_2)) : T; \theta; \delta \\
\Gamma \vdash T_1 \simeq T_2 : * & \iff & \forall \Gamma \vdash \theta; \delta,\ T_1 \simeq T_2 : *; \theta; \delta
\end{array}
$$

Fig. 5. The logical relation for parametricity

Requiring standard weakening, substitution, and inversion lemmas, the syntactic proof of type soundness is straightforward. It is easy to restrict F_H to a simply typed calculus with a similar type soundness proof.

4 Parametricity

We prove relational parametricity for two reasons: (1) it gives us powerful reasoning techniques such as free theorems [17], and (2) it indicates that contracts don't interfere with type abstraction. Our proof is standard: we define a (syntactic) logical relation where each type is interpreted as a relation on terms and the relation at type variables is given as a parameter. In the next section, we will define a subtype relation and show that an upcast—a cast whose source type is a subtype of the target type—is logically related to the identity function. Since our logical relation is an adequate congruence, it is contained in contextual equivalence. Therefore, upcasts are *contextually equivalent* to the identity and can be eliminated without changing the meaning of a program.

We begin by defining two relations: $r_1 \sim r_2 : T; \theta; \delta$ relates closed results, defined by induction on types; $e_1 \simeq e_2 : T; \theta; \delta$ relates closed expressions which evaluate results in the first relation. The definitions are shown in Figure 5.[1] Both relations have three indices: a type T, a substitution θ for type variables, and a substitution δ for term variables. A type substitution θ, which gives the interpretation of free type variables in T, maps a type variable to a triple (R, T_1, T_2) comprising a binary relation R on terms and two closed types T_1 and T_2. We require that R be closed under parallel reduction (the $\Rrightarrow$ relation). A term substitution δ maps from variables to pairs of closed values. We write θ_i $(i = 1, 2)$ for a substitution that maps a type variable α to T_i where $\theta(\alpha) = (R, T_1, T_2)$. We denote projections δ_i similarly.

With these definitions out of the way, the term relation is mostly straightforward. First, $\Uparrow l$ is related to itself at every type. A base type B gives the identity relation on $\mathcal{K}_B$, the set of constants of type B. A type variable α simply uses the relation assumed in the substitution θ. Related functions map related arguments to related results. Type abstractions are related when their bodies are parametric in the interpretation of the type variable. Finally, two values are related at a refinement type when they are related at the underlying type and both satisfy the predicate; here, the predicate e gets closed by applying the substitutions. The $\sim$ relation on results is extended to the relation $\simeq$ on closed terms in a straightforward manner: terms are related if and only if they both terminate at related results. We extend the relation to open terms, written $\Gamma \vdash e_1 \simeq e_2 : T$, relating open terms that are related when closed by any "Γ-respecting" pair of substitutions θ and δ (written $\Gamma \vdash \theta; \delta$, also defined in Figure 5).

To show that a (well-typed) cast is logically related to itself, we also need a relation on types $T_1 \simeq T_2 : *; \theta; \delta$; we define this relation in Figure 5. We use the logical relation on terms to handle the arguments of function types and refinement types. Note that T_1 and T_2 are not necessarily closed; terms in refinement types, which should be related at Bool, are closed by applying substitutions. In the function/refinement type cases, the relation on a smaller type is universally quantified over logically related values. There are two choices of the type at which they should be related (for example, the second line of the function type case could change T_{11} to T_{21}), but it does not really matter which to choose since they are related types. Here, we have chosen the type from the left-hand side; in our proof, we justify this choice by proving a "type exchange" lemma that lets us replace a type index T_1 in the term relation by T_2 when $T_1 \simeq T_2 : *$. Finally, we lift our type relation to open terms: we write $\Gamma \vdash T_1 \simeq T_2 : *$ when two types are equivalent for any Γ-respecting substitutions.

It is worth discussing a few points peculiar to our formulation. First, we allow any relation on terms closed under parallel reduction to be used in θ; terms related at T need not be well typed at T. The standard formulation of a logical relation is well typed throughout, requiring that the relation R in every triple be well typed, only relating values of type T_1 to values of type T_2 (e.g., [14]). We have two motivations for leaving our relations untyped. First, functions of type

[1] To save space, we write $\Uparrow l \sim \Uparrow l : T; \theta; \delta$ separately instead of manually adding such a clause for each type.

$x{:}T_1 \rightarrow T_2$ must map related values ($v_1 \sim v_2 : T_1$) to related results...but at what type? While $T_2[v_1/x]$ and $T_2[v_2/x]$ are related in our type logical relation, terms that are well typed at one type won't necessarily be well typed at the other. Second, we prove in Section 5 that upcasts have no effect: if $T_1 <: T_2$, then $\langle T_1 \Rightarrow T_2\rangle^l \sim \lambda x{:}T_1.\ x : T_1 \rightarrow T_2$. That is, we want a cast $\langle T_1 \Rightarrow T_2\rangle^l$, of type $T_1 \rightarrow T_2$, to be related to the identity $\lambda x{:}T_1.\ x$, of type $T_1 \rightarrow T_1$: the cast and the identity won't (in general) have the same type. We therefore don't demand that two expressions related at T be well typed at T, and we allow *any* relation to be chosen as R, so long as it is closed under parallel reduction. Another peculiarity is in our treatment of substitutions and type indices. Just as the interpretation of free type variables in the logical relation's type index are kept in a substitution θ, we keep δ as a substitution for the free term variables that can appear in type indices. Keeping this substitution separate avoids a problem in defining the logical relation at function types. Consider a function type $x{:}T_1 \rightarrow T_2$: our *logical* relation says that values v_1 and v_2 are related at this type when they take related values to related results, i.e. if $v_1' \sim v_2' : T_1; \theta; \delta$, then we should be able to find $v_1\, v_1' \simeq v_2\, v_2'$. The question here is which type index we should use. If we keep our type indices closed (with respect to term variables), we cannot use T_2 on its own—we have to choose a binding for x! Knowles and Flanagan [10] deal with this problem by introducing the "wedge product" operator, which merges two types—one with v_1' substituted for x and the other with v_2' for x—into one. Instead of substituting eagerly, we put both bindings in δ and apply them when needed—the refinement type case. We think our formulation is more uniform with regard to free term/type variables, since eager substitution is a non-starter for type variables, anyway.

As we developed our proof, we found that the E_Refl rule

$$\langle T \Rightarrow T\rangle^l\, v \rightsquigarrow v$$

is not just a convenient way to skip decomposition of a trivial cast into smaller trivial casts (when T is a polymorphic or dependent function type); E_Refl is, in fact, crucial to obtaining parametricity in our syntactic setting. For example, by parametricity, we expect every value of type $\forall\alpha.\alpha \rightarrow \alpha$ to behave the same as the polymorphic identity function. One of the values of this type is $\Lambda\alpha.\langle\alpha \Rightarrow \alpha\rangle^l$. Without E_Refl, however, applying this type abstraction to a compound type, say $\mathsf{Bool} \rightarrow \mathsf{Bool}$, and a function f of type $\mathsf{Bool} \rightarrow \mathsf{Bool}$ would return, by E_Fun, a value that is syntactically different from f, breaking parametricity![2] With E_Refl, $\langle T \Rightarrow T\rangle^l$ returns the input immediately, regardless of T, just as the identity function. So, this rule is a technical necessity, ensuring that casts containing type variables behave parametrically. (Naturally, the evaluation of well-typed programs never encounters casts with uninstantiated type variables.)

We have relational parametricity—every well-typed term (under Γ) is related to itself for any Γ-respecting substitutions.

[2] Intuitively, we expect the returned value should behave the same as the input, though. Moreover, the subtyping we define is reflexive, so the upcast lemma we prove applies, as well—though, of course, we used E_Refl to prove it!

$\boxed{\Gamma \vdash T_1 <: T_2}$

$$\frac{}{\Gamma \vdash B <: B}\ \text{S\_BASE} \qquad \frac{}{\Gamma \vdash \alpha <: \alpha}\ \text{S\_TVAR} \qquad \frac{\Gamma, \alpha \vdash T_1 <: T_2}{\Gamma \vdash \forall \alpha. T_1 <: \forall \alpha. T_2}\ \text{S\_FORALL}$$

$$\frac{\Gamma \vdash T_{21} <: T_{11} \quad \Gamma, x{:}T_{21} \vdash T_{12}[\langle T_{21} \Rightarrow T_{11} \rangle^l\, x/x] <: T_{22}}{\Gamma \vdash x{:}T_{11} \to T_{12} <: x{:}T_{21} \to T_{22}}\ \text{S\_FUN}$$

$$\text{casts}(T) = \begin{cases} \langle T' \Rightarrow \{x{:}T' \mid e\} \rangle^l \circ \text{casts}(T') & \text{if } T = \{x{:}T' \mid e\} \\ \lambda x{:}T.\ x & \text{otherwise} \end{cases}$$

$$\frac{\begin{array}{l}\Gamma \vdash \text{unref}(T_1) <: \text{unref}(T_2) \\ \Gamma, x{:}\,\text{unref}(T_1) \vdash \text{casts}(T_1)\, x \supset \text{casts}(T_2)\, (\langle \text{unref}(T_1) \Rightarrow \text{unref}(T_2) \rangle^l\, x)\end{array}}{\Gamma \vdash T_1 <: T_2}\ \text{S\_REFINE}$$

$\boxed{\Gamma \vdash e_1 \supset e_2}$

$$\frac{\forall \Gamma \vdash \theta; \delta.\ (\exists v.\ \theta_1(\delta_1(e_1)) \longrightarrow^* v) \text{ implies } (\exists v.\ \theta_1(\delta_1(e_2)) \longrightarrow^* v)}{\Gamma \vdash e_1 \supset e_2}\ \text{IMP}$$

Fig. 6. Subtyping, implication, and closing substitutions

Theorem 4 (Parametricity)

1. *If* $\Gamma \vdash e : T$ *then* $\Gamma \vdash e \simeq e : T$, *and*
2. *If* $\Gamma \vdash T$ *then* $\Gamma \vdash T \simeq T : *$.

The proof is mostly standard, although—like the proof of semantic type soundness in Greenberg, Pierce, and Weirich [7]—it requires a separate reflexivity lemma for casts, as mentioned above. We make one small disclaimer: we have not completed the standard but tedious proof showing that parallel reduction implies cotermination at similar values, i.e., if $e_1 \Rrightarrow e_2$ and $e_1 \longrightarrow^* r_1$, then $e_2 \longrightarrow^* r_2$ such that $r_1 \Rrightarrow r_2$, and vice versa. We expect that our existing Coq proof of this fact for a similar operational semantics (from [7]) will adapt readily. Note that our proof of type soundness in Section 3 relies on much simpler properties of parallel reduction, which we *have* proved.

5 Subtyping and Upcast Elimination

Knowles and Flanagan [10] define a subtyping relation for their manifest calculus, λ_{H}, as a primitive notion of the system. Furthermore, they prove that upcast elimination is sound: if $T_1 <: T_2$, then $\langle T_1 \Rightarrow T_2 \rangle^l$ is equivalent to the identity function. Upcast elimination is, at heart, an optimization: since the cast can never fail, there is no point in running it. We define a subtyping relation for $\mathrm{F_H}$

and prove that upcast elimination is sound. To be clear, the type system of F_H doesn't have subtyping or a subsumption rule at all; we simply show that upcasts are logically related—and therefore contextually equivalent—to the identity.

We define subtyping in Figure 6. Our subtyping rules are similar to those in λ_H. The first three rules are standard. The rule for dependent function types is mostly usual: contravariant on argument types and covariant on return types. Here, we need to be careful about the type of x. Return types T_{12} and T_{22} should be compared under the assumption that x has T_{21}, which is a subtype of the other argument type T_{11} [4]. However, x in T_{12} has a different type, i.e., T_{11}, so we need to insert a cast to keep the subtyping relation well typed—F_H doesn't have subsumption!

Our rule for subtyping of refinements differs substantially from λ_H's, mostly because F_H allows refinements of arbitrary types, while λ_H only refines base types. The S_REFINE rule essentially says T_1 is a subtype of T_2 if (1) T_1 without the (outermost) refinements is a subtype of T_2 without the (outermost) refinements, and (2) for any v of type $\text{unref}(T_1)$, if $\text{casts}(T_1)\, v$ reduces to a value, so does $\text{casts}(T_2)\, \langle \text{unref}(T_1) \Rightarrow \text{unref}(T_2)\rangle^l\, v$, for any l. The intuition behind the second condition is that, for T_1 to be a subtype of T_2, the predicates in T_1 (combined by conjunction) should be stronger than those in T_2. Recall that $\text{casts}(T)$ is defined in Figure 6 as the composition of casts necessary to cast from $\text{unref}(T)$ to T. So, if application of $\text{casts}(T)$ to a value of $\text{unref}(T)$ does not raise blame, then the value can be typed at T by repeated use of T_EXACT.

If the implication in S_REFINE holds for a value v of type $\text{unref}(T_1)$, then either: (1) v did not pass the checks in $\text{casts}(T_1)$, so this value is not in T_1; or (2) v passed the checks in $\text{casts}(T_1)$ and $\langle \text{unref}(T_1) \Rightarrow \text{unref}(T_2)\rangle^l\, v$ passed all of the checks in $\text{casts}(T_2)$. So, if (1) or (2) hold for all values of type $\text{unref}(T_1)$, then it means that all values of type T_1 can be safely treated as if they had type T_2, i.e., T_1 a subtype of T_2.

Finally, we need a source of closing substitutions to compare the evaluation of the two casts. We use the closing substitutions from the logical relation at T as the source of "values of type T". (Arbitrarily, we take the values and types from the left.) There is a similar situation in the manifest calculi of Knowles and Flanagan [10] and Greenberg, Pierce, and Weirich [7]. They both define a denotational semantics for use in their refinement subtyping rule—but they *need* to do so, in order to avoid a circularity. We have no such issues, and make the decision because it is expedient.

We formulate our implication judgment in terms of cotermination at values rather than cotermination at true (as in [7,10]) because we have to contend with multiple layers of refinement in types—using cotermination at values reduces the amount of predicate bookkeeping we have to do.

Having defined subtyping, we are able to show that upcast elimination is sound.

Lemma 5 (Upcast lemma). *If* $\Gamma \vdash T_1 <: T_2$ *and* $\Gamma \vdash T_1$ *and* $\Gamma \vdash T_2$*, then* $\Gamma \vdash \langle T_1 \Rightarrow T_2\rangle^l \simeq \lambda x{:}T_1.\ x : T_1 \to T_2$.

6 Related Work

We discuss the related work in two parts. We first distinguish our work from the untyped contract systems that enforce parametric polymorphism *dynamically*, rather than statically as F_H does; we then discuss how F_H differs from existing manifest contract calculi in greater detail.

Dynamically Checked Polymorphism

The F_H type system enforces parametricity with type abstractions and type variables, while refinements are dynamically checked. Another line of work omits refinements, seeking instead to dynamically enforce parametricity—typically with some form of sealing (à la Pierce and Sumii [13]).

Guha et al. [9] define contracts with polymorphic signatures, maintaining abstraction with sealed "coffers"; they do not prove parametricity. Matthews and Ahmed [11] prove parametricity for a polymorphic multi-language system with a similar policy. Ahmed et al. [2] prove parametricity for a gradual typing [15] calculus which enforces polymorphism with a set of global runtime seals. Strickland et al. add support for dynamically checked variable-arity polymorphism to Typed Racket [16]. Ahmed et al. [3] define a polymorphic calculus for gradual typing, using local syntactic "barriers" instead of global seals. We believe that it is possible to combine F_H with the barrier calculus of Ahmed et al., yielding a polymorphic blame calculus [18]. We leave this to future work.

Manifest Systems

Wadler and Findler [18] gave a simple syntactic account of a calculus combining refinement types and gradual types [15]; they, like us, define subtyping *post facto*, proving theorems similar to the upcast lemma. They do not, however, support dependent function types. Gronski and Flanagan [8] compares non-dependent latent and manifest contract calculi.

Four existing manifest calculi have dependent function types (such as [6,7,10,12]) use subtyping and theorem provers as part of the definition of the type system. All four of these calculi have complicated metatheory. Ou et al. [12] restrict refinements and arguments of dependent functions to a conservative approximation of pure terms; they also place strong requirements on their prover. Knowles and Flanagan [10] as well as Greenberg, Pierce, and Weirich [7] use denotational semantics to give a firm foundation to Flanagan's earlier work [6]. We consider three systems in more detail: Knowles and Flanagan's λ_H (KF) [10]; Greenberg, Pierce, and Weirich's λ_H (GPW) [7]; and F_H. The rest of this subsection addresses the differences between KF, GPW, and F_H.

In Section 1, we discussed in general terms some of the complexity that KF and GPW encountered. What made KF and GPW so complicated? Both systems share the same two impediments in the preservation proof: preservation after active checks and after congruence steps in the argument position of applications. KF and GPW resolve both of these with subtyping, using a rule like the following for refinements:[3]

$$\frac{\forall \Gamma, x{:}\{x{:}B \mid \mathsf{true}\} \vdash \sigma.\ \sigma(e_1) \longrightarrow^* \mathsf{true\,implies}\,\sigma(e_2) \longrightarrow^* \mathsf{true}}{\Gamma \vdash \{x{:}B \mid e_1\} <: \{x{:}B \mid e_2\}}$$

Subtyping and the requirement that constants be assigned most specific types, —i.e., if $e[k/x] \longrightarrow^* \mathsf{true}$ for $k \in \mathcal{K}_B$ then $\emptyset \vdash \mathsf{ty}(k) <: \{x{:}B \mid e\}$—are used to show preservation of active checks. The two systems use subtyping to relate substituted types in different ways. KF use full beta reduction, showing that subtyping is closed under reduction. GPW use call-by-value reduction, showing that subtyping is closed under parallel reduction. Once these two difficulties are resolved, both preservation proofs are standard, given appropriate subtyping inversion lemmas.

So much for subtyping. Why do KF and GPW need denotational semantics? Spelled out pedantically, the subtyping rule above has the following premise:

$$\forall \sigma.\ \Gamma, x{:}\{x{:}B \mid \mathsf{true}\} \vdash \sigma\,\text{implies}\,(\sigma(e_1) \longrightarrow^* \mathsf{true\,implies}\,\sigma(e_2) \longrightarrow^* \mathsf{true})$$

That is, the well formedness of the closing substitution σ is in a negative position. Where do closing substitutions come from? We cannot use the typing judgment itself, as this would be ill-defined: term typing requires subtyping via subsumption; subtyping requires closing substitutions in a negative position via the refinement case; but closing substitutions require typing. We need another source of values: hence, denotational semantics. Both KF and GPW define syntactic term models of types to use as a source of values for closing substitutions, though the specifics differ.

After adding subtyping and denotational semantics, both KF and GPW are well defined and have syntactic proofs of type soundness. But in the process of proving syntactic type soundness, both languages proved semantic soundness theorems:

$$\Gamma \vdash e : T \text{ implies } \forall \Gamma \vdash \sigma,\ \sigma(e) \in [\![\sigma(T)]\!]$$

This theorem suffices for soundness of the language... so why bother with a syntactic proof? In light of this, GPW only proves semantic soundness. The situation in KF and GPW is unsatisfying: the syntactic proof of type soundness motivated subtyping, which motivated denotational semantics, which obviated the need for syntactic proof. Beyond this, the proofs are hard to scale: adding in polymorphism or state is a non-trivial task, since we must—before defining the type system!—construct an appropriate denotational semantics, which itself depends on our evaluation relation.

F_H solves the problem by avoiding subtyping—which is what forced the presence of closing substitutions and denotational semantics in the first place. The

[3] Readers familiar with the systems will recognize that we've folded the implication judgment into the relevant subtyping rule.

first issue in preservation—that of preserving refinement types after checks have finished—was resolved in KF and GPW with subtyping. We instead resolve it with a runtime rule that allows us to type values with any refinement they satisfy:

$$\frac{\vdash \Gamma \qquad \emptyset \vdash v : T \qquad \emptyset \vdash \{x{:}T \mid e\} \qquad e[v/x] \longrightarrow^{*} \mathsf{true}}{\Gamma \vdash v : \{x{:}T \mid e\}} \ \text{T\_EXACT}$$

Adding this rule eliminates one use of subtyping as well as the "most-specific type" restriction. If we "bit the bullet" and allowed non-empty contexts in T_EXACT, then we would need to apply a closing substitution to $e[v/x]$ before checking if it reduces to true. But the circularity in subtyping alluded to in Section 1 was caused by closing substitutions; we must avoid them! The second issue in preservation—that of conversion between $T_2[e_2/x]$ and $T_2[e_2'/x]$—can be resolved in a similar fashion. We define another runtime rule that allows us to convert types:

$$\frac{\vdash \Gamma \qquad \emptyset \vdash e : T \qquad \emptyset \vdash T' \qquad T \equiv T'}{\Gamma \vdash e : T'} \ \text{T\_CONV}$$

The conversion we use, $\equiv$, is defined as the symmetric, transitive closure of CBV-respecting parallel reduction. This is only as much equivalence as we need: if $e_2 \longrightarrow e_2'$, then $T_2[e_2/x] \equiv T_2[e_2'/x]$. These two rules suffice to keep subtyping out of F_H, which in turn avoids denotational semantics.

7 Future Work

We presented a simpler approach to manifest contract calculi, which we applied to construct F_H, a parametrically polymorphic manifest contract calculus. We hope to extend F_H with barriers for dynamically checked polymorphism [3], and with general recursion and state. (Though we acknowledge that state is a difficult open problem.) We also hope that F_H's operational semantics and (relatively) simple type system will help developers implement contracts.

Acknowledgments

Stephanie Weirich provided many insights throughout. Jianzhou Zhao's help with parametricity was invaluable; and a conversation about parametricity with Amal Ahmed and Stephanie Weirich was particularly illuminating. This work was supported in part by the National Science Foundation under grant 0915671, *Contracts for Precise Types*, in part by the JSPS Grant-in-Aid for Young Scientists (A) No. 21680002, and in part by the Portuguese Foundation for Science and Technology, POPH - QREN, under grant SFRH / BPD / 46065 / 2008.

References

1. PLT Racket Contracts, `http://pre.plt-scheme.org/docs/html/guide/contracts.html`
2. Ahmed, A., Findler, R.B., Matthews, J., Wadler, P.: Blame for all. In: Workshop on Script-to-Program Evolution, STOP (2009)
3. Ahmed, A., Findler, R.B., Siek, J., Wadler, P.: Blame for all. In: Principles of Programming Languages, POPL (2011)
4. Aspinall, D., Compagnoni, A.: Subtyping dependent types. Theor. Comput. Sci. 266(1-2), 273–309 (2001)
5. Findler, R.B., Felleisen, M.: Contracts for higher-order functions. In: International Conference on Functional Programming (ICFP), pp. 48–59 (2002)
6. Flanagan, C.: Hybrid type checking. In: POPL, pp. 245–256 (2006)
7. Greenberg, M., Pierce, B.C., Weirich, S.: Contracts made manifest. In: Principles of Programming Languages, POPL 2010 (2010)
8. Gronski, J., Flanagan, C.: Unifying hybrid types and contracts. In: Trends in Functional Programming, TFP (2007)
9. Guha, A., Matthews, J., Findler, R.B., Krishnamurthi, S.: Relationally-parametric polymorphic contracts. In: DLS, pp. 29–40 (2007)
10. Knowles, K., Flanagan, C.: Hybrid type checking (2010) (to appear in TOPLAS)
11. Matthews, J., Ahmed, A.: Parametric polymorphism through run-time sealing or, theorems for low, low prices! In: Gairing, M. (ed.) ESOP 2008. LNCS, vol. 4960, pp. 16–31. Springer, Heidelberg (2008)
12. Ou, X., Tan, G., Mandelbaum, Y., Walker, D.: Dynamic typing with dependent types. In: IFIP TCS, pp. 437–450 (2004)
13. Pierce, B., Sumii, E.: Relating cryptography and polymorphism (July 2000)
14. Pitts, A.M.: Typed operational reasoning. In: Pierce, B.C. (ed.) Advanced Topics in Types and Programming Languages, ch. 7, pp. 245–289. MIT Press, Cambridge (2005)
15. Siek, J.G., Taha, W.: Gradual typing for functional languages. In: Scheme and Functional Programming Workshop (September 2006)
16. Strickland, T.S., Tobin-Hochstadt, S., Felleisen, M.: Practical variable-arity polymorphism. In: Castagna, G. (ed.) ESOP 2009. LNCS, vol. 5502, pp. 32–46. Springer, Heidelberg (2009)
17. Wadler, P.: Theorems for free! In: Proceedings of ACM Conference on Functional Programming and Computer Architecture (FPCA 1989), pp. 347–359, London, UK (September 1989)
18. Wadler, P., Findler, R.B.: Well-typed programs can't be blamed. In: Castagna, G. (ed.) ESOP 2009. LNCS, vol. 5502, pp. 1–16. Springer, Heidelberg (2009)
19. Wright, A.K., Felleisen, M.: A syntactic approach to type soundness. Information and Computation 115, 38–94 (1992)

Proving Isolation Properties for Software Transactional Memory*

Annette Bieniusa and Peter Thiemann

University of Freiburg, Germany

Abstract. An algorithm for Software Transactional Memory (STM) is correct if it guarantees a proclaimed degree of isolation between concurrently executing transactions. A correctness proof requires explicit modeling of the effects of transaction bodies and the non-deterministic scheduling of their operations.

We provide a formalization of an STM algorithm that is explicit about all aspects required for a correctness proof: effects of operations, non-determinism, and modeling rollback. We prove that this algorithm is correct by showing that it implements opacity.

1 Introduction

Concurrent programming is notoriously difficult. Programs that rely on shared memory may exhibit race conditions or other strange effects caused by the subtleties of the underlying memory model. Traditionally, these defects are kept at bay through synchronization primitives like monitors, locks, and semaphores. However, these constructs complicate reasoning about programs considerably, not the least because they might give rise to deadlocks.

While an application aiming for ultimate performance has to tackle these obstacles and must rely on explicit reasoning with the synchronization primitives to construct a correctness proof, Software Transactional Memory (STM) is an alternative approach that gives high-level guarantees about the interaction of concurrent threads. In STM, read or write accesses to shared memory are only permitted inside a transaction, where a thread is guaranteed an isolation property which roughly states that it never sees an inconsistent memory snapshot.

The problems resulting from computations that observe inconsistencies in their memory snapshot are well-known. For example, in an interleaved execution of transactions `Tx1` and `Tx2`,

```
Tx1: read X;                   read X
Tx2:          write X; commit
```

the second read should return the same value as the first one (repeatable read) and, furthermore, transaction `Tx1` must not be allowed to commit because its outcome may be based on an obsolete value of X.

* This work was partially funded as part of the *JCell* project by the Federal Government of Germany under grant number 01IH08011.

G. Barthe (Ed.): ESOP 2011, LNCS 6602, pp. 38–56, 2011.
© Springer-Verlag Berlin Heidelberg 2011

For another example, consider the interleaved execution

```
Tx1:            read X;          commit
Tx2: write X;           abort;
```

where the read operation in Tx1 must not return the value written by Tx2 because it aborts instead of committing (phantom read). The first transaction Tx1 may commit unless there are inconsistencies involving other variables.

By avoiding observable inconsistencies, the semantics of transactional memory provides a comparatively simple model for concurrent programming. Instead of having the programmer associate several memory locations with a lock and requiring that the lock needs to be obtained before accessing any of these memory locations and released thereafter, accesses are grouped together in a transaction that runs at a proclaimed level of isolation. To prevent conflicting accesses, each STM algorithm has a built-in contention strategy that detects and resolves conflicts like the ones exhibited in the examples. The main question is thus what kind of isolation does an STM algorithm provide.

Prior work on the semantics of transactions [1,12] focused primarily on weak atomicity, which is important for hybrid applications (for example, an application that includes legacy code using locking as well as new transactional code) because it helps to study the interaction of transactional and non-transactional memory accesses. However, these formalizations do not account for the phenomena due to the interleaved execution of transactions. For example, in state-of-the-art algorithms like TL2 [4], threads may get stuck even when a fair scheduling of threads is provided because they are repeatedly forced to abort by other transactions' successful commits.

To illustrate the mechanism underlying the aborts, this paper pursues an approach that abstracts program execution by traces of memory accesses and transaction control operations. To this end, we define a monadic lambda calculus with threads and transactions, Λ_{STM}. Similar to approaches in research on isolation levels of database transactions, each memory access is modeled by an effect on the global store. By modeling an TM algorithm similar to TL2, the system is shown to implement the isolation level of opacity.

We claim the following contributions:

1. A formalization of a semantics of transactional memory that is suitable for proving properties of a TM implementation.
   A high-level semantics abstracts so many details that properties of the implementation become trivially evident [8]. A low-level semantics provides so many details that formal proof of its properties is no longer tractable. An example is pseudocode for an implementation. Our semantics keeps in the middle ground. It explicitly models the non-deterministic interleaving of the operations in each thread including operations in aborting transactions. However, it does not model implementation details like the construction of memory snapshots or the implementation of locks.
2. We prove that our semantics implements opacity [7], that is, all execution traces in our semantics are equivalent to serial execution traces, where the execution of critical regions (i.e., transaction bodies) is non-interleaved.

Overview. Section 2 starts with examples that illustrate the basic ideas. Then, section 3 presents the formalization of the system. Based on the operational semantics, section 4 continues with the characteristics of the model and shows the serializability of traces. The paper concludes with related work in section 5 and concludes in section 6.

2   Execution Traces

2.1   Successful Commits

If all transactions in a program run commit successfully at the highest isolation level, then the execution trace can be turned into a serializable one by adapting the scheduler's decisions. For an example, consider a trace where the scheduling interleaves two transactions t_1 and t_2 that read and write disjoint variables $x \neq y$ (*at* marks the start of a transaction and *co(x)* its commit which writes variable x):

$$t_1 \quad \overset{at_1 \quad r_1(x) \qquad\qquad\qquad co_1(x)}{\rule{5cm}{0.4pt}}$$

$$t_2 \quad \overset{at_2 \quad r_2(y) \qquad co_2(y)}{\rule{4cm}{0.4pt}}$$

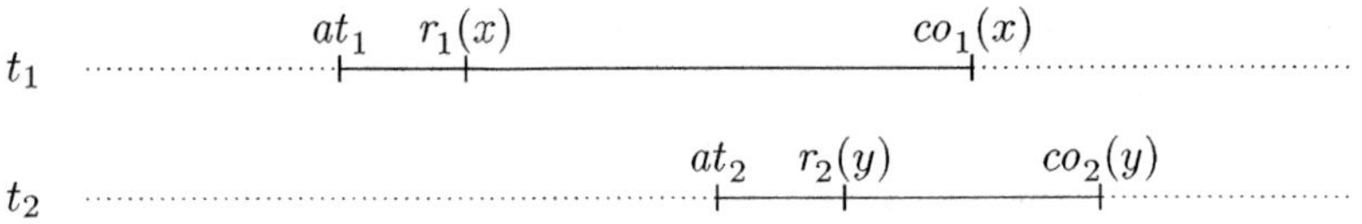

For this trace, there are two equivalent serial traces:

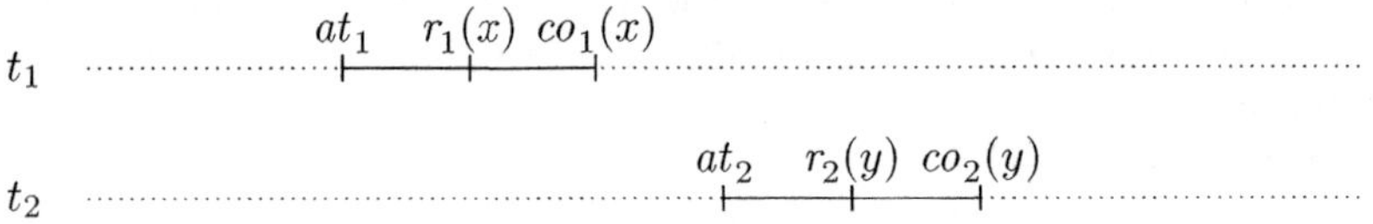

$$t_1 \quad \overset{at_1 \quad r_1(x) \; co_1(x)}{\rule{3cm}{0.4pt}}$$

$$t_2 \quad \overset{at_2 \quad r_2(y) \; co_2(y)}{\rule{3cm}{0.4pt}}$$

and

$$t_1 \quad \overset{at_1 \quad r_1(x) \; co_1(x)}{\rule{3cm}{0.4pt}}$$

$$t_2 \quad \overset{at_2 \quad r_2(y) \; co_2(y)}{\rule{3cm}{0.4pt}}$$

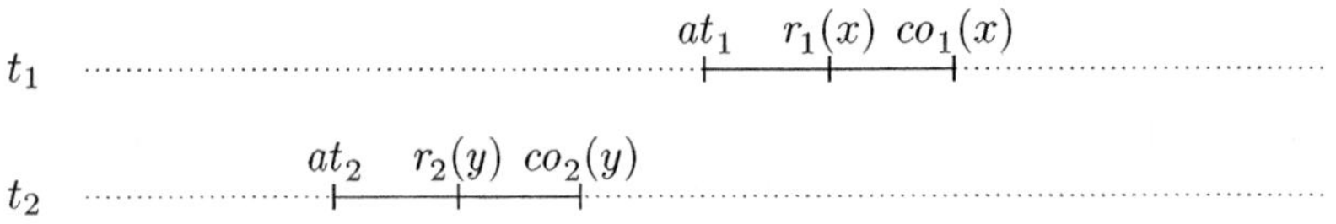

Both traces correspond to evaluations of the program to the same final store. During the evaluation, each transaction conceptually operates on its own memory snapshot, taken at the beginning of the transaction. As both transactions were able to finish successfully, their read and write sets cannot have elements in common, and all their operations are independent. Hence both serial traces are equivalent to the original one.

2.2   Read Conflicts

A read conflict occurs if one transaction commits a write operation to a variable that another transaction is just about to read. In that case, the reading transaction must not proceed because its snapshot is no longer consistent with the current store. Thus, the semantics forces the second transaction to abort.

As an example, consider the following trace:

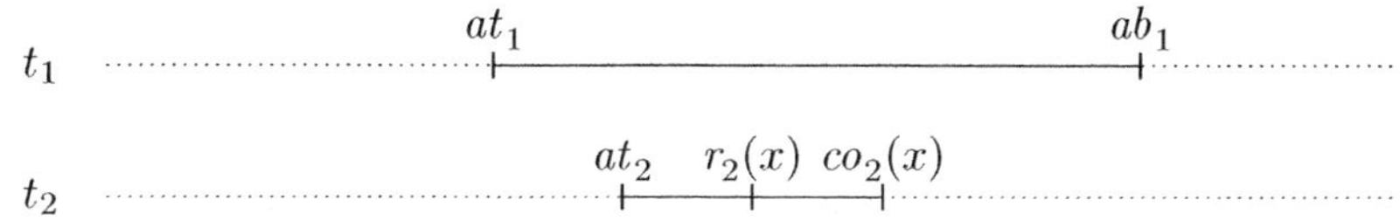

The trace illustrates a transaction t_1 which has to abort (indicated by ab) because of a read conflict on variable x (it does not produce a read effect because the read operation is never permitted, as explained above). Nevertheless, there is an equivalent serial trace:

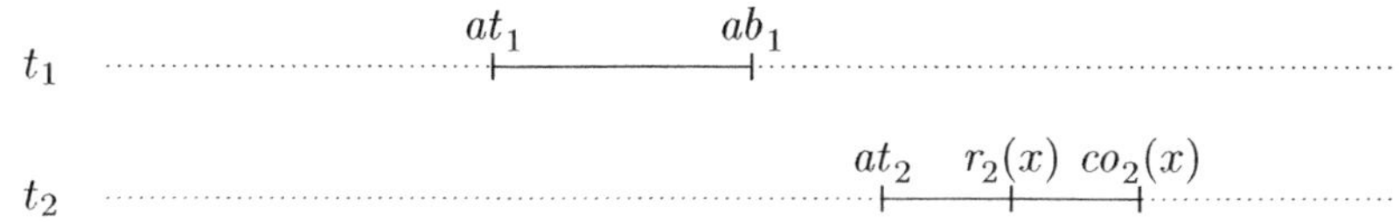

2.3 Snapshot Isolation

The next trace gives an example of a non-serializable execution:

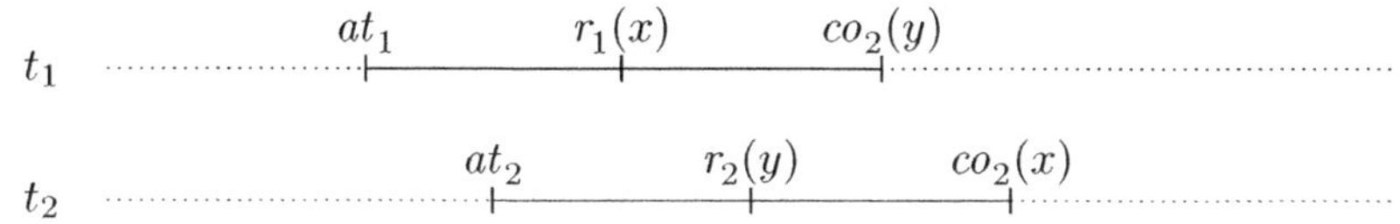

The transactions in this example do not have write or read conflicts as they update different memory locations. Yet, the memory locations that one transaction read are updated by the other. This effect is a *write skew anomaly* [2]. The trace is not serializable because a read operation is supposed to return the last value written to a variable. Hence, in a serial trace the latter operation would yield the value written by the first one.

Algorithms that allow traces with write skew anomalies implement a weaker isolation level called snapshot isolation. It requires that all transactions operate on reads that belong to one consistent memory snapshot. Updates that are committed between the begin of a transaction and its commit lead to conflicts only if the current transaction is about to update the same locations.

2.4 Semantics of Haskell's `orElse`

The STM library for Haskell [8], which is shipped with GHC, provides a construct m_1 `‘orElse‘` m_2. Its semantics specifies that if there is a failure during the execution of the `or` branch m_1 (because of a failed read due to a conflict with a concurrently running transaction or because of a `retry` instruction issued by the programmer), the write operations of the `or` branch are discarded, and `else` branch m_2 is executed instead.

Although the semantics of Haskell's STM does not permit write skew anomalies, it provides the programmer with information about conflicting memory accesses at run time. If the programmer exploits this information, the semantics

$$\begin{aligned}
&x \in \text{Var} \qquad l \in \text{Ref} \\
&v \in \text{Val} ::= l \mid \texttt{tt} \mid \texttt{ff} \mid () \mid \lambda x.e \\
&e \in \text{Exp} ::= v \mid x \mid e\ e \mid \texttt{if}\ e\ e\ e \mid \texttt{return}\ e \mid e \gg\!= e \\
&\qquad \mid \texttt{spawn}\ e \mid \texttt{atomic}\ e \mid (e, W_i, R_i, i, e, \mathcal{H}) \\
&\qquad \mid \texttt{newref}\ e \mid \texttt{readref}\ e \mid \texttt{writeref}\ e\ e
\end{aligned}$$

Fig. 1. Syntax of Λ_{STM}. Gray expressions arise only during evaluation.

of a program depends crucially on the scheduling of the threads. As the `else` branch is never entered in a serial execution (unless there is an explicition invocation of `retry`), Haskell STM actually implements an isolation level which is less restrictive than opacity but more restrictive than snapshot isolation.

This paper concentrates on serializability and opacity. It does not consider weaker isolation modes like snapshot isolation or Haskell's `orElse` construct.

3 Formalization of Transactions

This section formalizes an STM with lazy update, where all write operations are delayed till the commit operation. The formalization is based on a monadic call-by-value lambda calculus with references, threads, and transactions.

3.1 Syntax

Figure 1 contains the syntax of Λ_{STM}. A value is either a reference, a boolean, the unit constant, or a function. Expressions comprise these values, variables, function application, conditional, monadic return and bind, spawning of threads, transactions, transactions in progress (an intermediate expression not arising in source programs), and the usual operations on references. The expression $e_1; e_2$ abbreviates $(\lambda x.e_2)\ e_1$ where x does not appear free in e_2 and $e[v/x]$ denotes the capture-avoiding substitution of x by v in e.

Figure 2 defines the type system for Λ_{STM}. The type language consists of the types of the simply typed lambda calculus with base types boolean and unit, a reference type $\texttt{R}\,\tau$ for references pointing to values of type τ, function types, and a monadic type $\mu\,\tau$ for a monad returning values of type τ. There is a choice of two monads, `IO` for general monadic operations and `STM` for operations inside a transaction.

The typing judgment contains two environments: Σ tracks the type of memory locations, and Γ tracks the type of variables. There is a second, heap typing judgment that relates the type of each memory location to the (closed) value stored in it. The typing rules are syntax-directed and mostly standard.

3.2 Operational Semantics

Figure 3 introduces some further definitions for the operational semantics. A program state $\mathcal{H}, \mathcal{P}$ is a pair consisting of a heap and a thread pool. A thread

$$\text{Types} \quad \tau ::= \texttt{bool} \mid () \mid \texttt{R}\,\tau \mid \tau \rightarrow \tau \mid \mu\,\tau$$
$$\mu ::= \texttt{IO} \mid \texttt{STM}$$

$$\frac{}{\Sigma|\Gamma \vdash \texttt{ff} : \texttt{bool}}\ \textsc{T-False} \qquad \frac{}{\Sigma|\Gamma \vdash \texttt{tt} : \texttt{bool}}\ \textsc{T-True} \qquad \frac{}{\Sigma|\Gamma \vdash () : ()}\ \textsc{T-Unit}$$

$$\frac{\Gamma(x) = \tau}{\Sigma|\Gamma \vdash x : \tau}\ \textsc{T-Var} \qquad \frac{\Sigma(l) = \tau}{\Sigma|\Gamma \vdash l : \texttt{R}\,\tau}\ \textsc{T-Ref}$$

$$\frac{\Sigma|\Gamma, x : \tau_1 \vdash e : \tau_2}{\Sigma|\Gamma \vdash \lambda x.e : \tau_1 \rightarrow \tau_2}\ \textsc{T-Func} \qquad \frac{\Sigma|\Gamma \vdash e_2 : \tau_1 \rightarrow \tau_2 \qquad \Sigma|\Gamma \vdash e_1 : \tau_1}{\Sigma|\Gamma \vdash e_2\, e_1 : \tau_2}\ \textsc{T-App}$$

$$\frac{\Sigma|\Gamma \vdash e_1 : \texttt{bool} \qquad \Sigma|\Gamma \vdash e_2 : \tau \qquad \Sigma|\Gamma \vdash e_3 : \tau}{\Sigma|\Gamma \vdash \texttt{if}\ e_1\, e_2\, e_3 : \tau}\ \textsc{T-If}$$

$$\frac{\Sigma|\Gamma \vdash e : \tau}{\Sigma|\Gamma \vdash \texttt{return}\ e : \mu\,\tau}\ \textsc{T-Return}$$

$$\frac{\Sigma|\Gamma \vdash e_1 : \mu\,\tau \qquad \Sigma|\Gamma \vdash e_2 : \tau \rightarrow \mu\,\tau'}{\Sigma|\Gamma \vdash e_1 \gg\!= e_2 : \mu\,\tau'}\ \textsc{T-Bind}$$

$$\frac{\Sigma|\Gamma \vdash e : \texttt{IO}\,\tau}{\Sigma|\Gamma \vdash \texttt{spawn}\ e : \texttt{IO}\,()}\ \textsc{T-Spawn} \qquad \frac{\Sigma|\Gamma \vdash e : \texttt{STM}\,\tau}{\Sigma|\Gamma \vdash \texttt{atomic}\ e : \texttt{IO}\,\tau}\ \textsc{T-Atomic}$$

$$\frac{\Sigma|\Gamma \vdash e : \texttt{STM}\,\tau \qquad \Sigma|\Gamma \vdash e' : \texttt{STM}\,\tau \qquad \Sigma \vdash W_i \qquad \Sigma \vdash R_i \qquad \Sigma \vdash \mathcal{H}}{\Sigma|\Gamma \vdash (e, W_i, R_i, i, e', \mathcal{H}) : \texttt{IO}\,\tau}\ \textsc{T-Txn}$$

$$\frac{\Sigma|\Gamma \vdash e : \tau}{\Sigma|\Gamma \vdash \texttt{newref}\ e : \texttt{STM}\,(\texttt{R}\,\tau)}\ \textsc{T-Alloc} \qquad \frac{\Sigma|\Gamma \vdash e : \texttt{R}\,\tau}{\Sigma|\Gamma \vdash \texttt{readref}\ e : \texttt{STM}\,\tau}\ \textsc{T-Deref}$$

$$\frac{\Sigma|\Gamma \vdash e_1 : \texttt{R}\,\tau \qquad \Sigma|\Gamma \vdash e_2 : \tau}{\Sigma|\Gamma \vdash \texttt{writeref}\ e_1\, e_2 : \texttt{STM}\,()}\ \textsc{T-Assign}$$

$$\frac{\mathcal{H}(l) = (v, i) \Rightarrow \Sigma|[] \vdash v : \Sigma(l)}{\Sigma \vdash \mathcal{H}}$$

Fig. 2. Typing rules of Λ_{STM}

l	$\in$ Ref	
$\mathcal{P}$	$\in$ Program	$=$ ThreadId $\rightharpoonup$ Exp
T_i	$\in$ Transaction	$=$ Exp $\times$ Store $\times$ Store $\times$ Id $\times$ Exp $\times$ Store
$\mathcal{H}, R_i, W_i$	$\in$ Store	$=$ Ref $\rightharpoonup$ Val $\times$ Id
α	$\in$ Effect	$= \{\epsilon^t, sp^t, at_i^t, ab_i^t, co_i^t(\bar{l}), r_i^t(l), \epsilon_i^t\}$

Fig. 3. State related definitions

Evaluation contexts

$$\begin{aligned}\mathcal{E} &::= [] \; e \mid v \; [] \mid \texttt{if} \; [] \; e \; e' \\ \mathcal{M} &::= \texttt{newref} \; [] \mid \texttt{readref} \; [] \mid \texttt{writeref} \; [] \; e \mid \texttt{writeref} \; v \; [] \\ &\quad \mid \texttt{return} \; [] \mid [] \gg\!= e\end{aligned}$$

Expression evaluation $\rightarrow$

$$(\lambda x.e) \; v \rightarrow e[v/x]$$

$$\texttt{if tt} \; e \; e' \rightarrow e$$

$$\texttt{if ff} \; e \; e' \rightarrow e'$$

$$\frac{e \rightarrow e'}{\mathcal{E}[e] \rightarrow \mathcal{E}[e']}$$

Monadic evaluation $\curvearrowright$

$$\texttt{return} \; v \gg\!= e \curvearrowright e \; v$$

$$\frac{e \rightarrow e'}{e \curvearrowright e'} \qquad \frac{m \curvearrowright m'}{\mathcal{M}[m] \curvearrowright \mathcal{M}[m']}$$

Fig. 4. Operational semantics: Local evaluation steps

pool maps thread identifiers to expressions to be evaluated concurrently. The execution of a program is represented by a labeled transition relation between program states.

A transaction in progress is represented by a tuple $(e, W_i, R_i, i, e', \mathcal{H}')$. It consists of the expression e that is currently evaluated, the write set W_i and the read set R_i of the transaction, a (unique) transaction identifier i, a copy of the original transaction body e', and a copy $\mathcal{H}'$ of the heap taken at the beginning of the transaction. The latter two store the relevant state at the beginning of a transaction to facilitate the consistency check and the abort operation.

A reference corresponds to a heap location. All stores (the heap, the read set, and the write set of a transaction) map a reference to a pair of a value and a transaction identifier. The transaction identifier specifies the transaction which committed or, in case of the write set, attempts to commit the value to the global store. $S(l)$ denotes the lookup operation of a reference l in a heap S. It implies $l \in \mathrm{dom}(S)$. The store update operation $S[l \mapsto y]$ returns a store that is identical to S, except that it maps l to y. For two stores S_1 and S_2, we write $S_1[S_2]$ for the updated version of S_1 with all entries of S_2.

Operations can have different effects α on the global state: the begin transaction (at_i^t), abort transaction (ab_i^t), read reference l ($r_i^t(l)$), and commit writing references $\bar{l}$ ($co_i^t(\bar{l})$) indicating operations on the global shared heap, or empty effects (ϵ_i^t or ϵ^t), with t a thread identifier, and i a transaction id. The empty effects represent monadic reductions that occur outside a transaction (see top of Fig. 5).

The evaluation of a program with body e starts in an initial state $\langle\rangle, \{t_0 \mapsto e\}$ with an empty heap and a main thread t_0. A final state has the form $\mathcal{H}, \{t_0 \mapsto$

$$\frac{\mathcal{P}(t) = m \qquad m \curvearrowright m'}{\mathcal{H}, \mathcal{P} \stackrel{\epsilon^t}{\Longrightarrow} \mathcal{H}, \mathcal{P}[t \mapsto m']} \text{ IO-MONAD}$$

$$\frac{\mathcal{P}(t) = \mathcal{M}[\texttt{spawn}\ m] \qquad t' \text{ fresh}}{\mathcal{H}, \mathcal{P} \stackrel{sp^t}{\Longrightarrow} \mathcal{H}, \mathcal{P}[t \mapsto \mathcal{M}[\texttt{return}\ ()], t' \mapsto m]} \text{ SPAWN}$$

$$\frac{\mathcal{P}(t) = \mathcal{M}[\texttt{atomic}\ m] \qquad T_i = (m, \langle\rangle, \langle\rangle, i, m, \mathcal{H}) \qquad i \text{ fresh}}{\mathcal{H}, \mathcal{P} \stackrel{at_i^t}{\Longrightarrow} \mathcal{H}, \mathcal{P}[t \mapsto \mathcal{M}[T_i]]} \text{ ATOMIC}$$

$$\frac{\mathcal{P}(t) = \mathcal{M}[(m, W_i, R_i, i, m', \mathcal{H}')] \qquad m \curvearrowright m''}{\mathcal{H}, \mathcal{P} \stackrel{\epsilon_i^t}{\Longrightarrow} \mathcal{H}, \mathcal{P}[t \mapsto \mathcal{M}[(m'', W_i, R_i, i, m', \mathcal{H}')]]} \text{ STM-MONAD}$$

$$\frac{\mathcal{P}(t) = \mathcal{M}[(\mathcal{M}'[\texttt{newref}\ v], W_i, R_i, i, m', \mathcal{H}')] \qquad l \notin \mathcal{H}, \mathcal{P}}{\mathcal{H}, \mathcal{P} \stackrel{\epsilon_i^t}{\Longrightarrow} \mathcal{H}, \mathcal{P}[t \mapsto \mathcal{M}[(\mathcal{M}'[\texttt{return}\ l], W_i[l \mapsto (v, i)], R_i, i, m', \mathcal{H}')]]} \text{ ALLOC}$$

$$\frac{\mathcal{P}(t) = \mathcal{M}[(\mathcal{M}'[\texttt{writeref}\ l\ v], W_i, R_i, i, m', \mathcal{H}')]}{\mathcal{H}, \mathcal{P} \stackrel{\epsilon_i^t}{\Longrightarrow} \mathcal{H}, \mathcal{P}[t \mapsto \mathcal{M}[(\mathcal{M}'[\texttt{return}\ ()], W_i[l \mapsto (v, i)], R_i, i, m', \mathcal{H}')]]} \text{ WRITE}$$

$$\frac{\begin{array}{c}\mathcal{P}(t) = \mathcal{M}[(\mathcal{M}'[\texttt{readref}\ l], W_i, R_i, i, m', \mathcal{H}')] \\ l \notin \text{dom}(W_i) \cup \text{dom}(R_i) \qquad \mathcal{H}(l) = \mathcal{H}'(l) = (v, j)\end{array}}{\mathcal{H}, \mathcal{P} \stackrel{r_i^t(l)}{\Longrightarrow} \mathcal{H}, \mathcal{P}[t \mapsto \mathcal{M}[(\mathcal{M}'[\texttt{return}\ v], W_i, R_i[l \mapsto (v, j)], i, m', \mathcal{H}')]]} \text{ READGLOBAL}$$

$$\frac{\begin{array}{c}\mathcal{P}(t) = \mathcal{M}[(\mathcal{M}'[\texttt{readref}\ l], W_i, R_i, i, m', \mathcal{H}')] \\ l \notin \text{dom}(W_i) \qquad R_i(l) = (v, i)\end{array}}{\mathcal{H}, \mathcal{P} \stackrel{\epsilon_i^t}{\Longrightarrow} \mathcal{H}, \mathcal{P}[t \mapsto \mathcal{M}[(\mathcal{M}'[\texttt{return}\ v], W_i, R_i, i, m', \mathcal{H}')]]} \text{ READRSET}$$

$$\frac{\mathcal{P}(t) = \mathcal{M}[(\mathcal{M}'[\texttt{readref}\ l], W_i, R_i, i, m', \mathcal{H}')] \qquad W_i(l) = (v, i)}{\mathcal{H}, \mathcal{P} \stackrel{\epsilon_i^t}{\Longrightarrow} \mathcal{H}, \mathcal{P}[t \mapsto \mathcal{M}[(\mathcal{M}'[\texttt{return}\ v], W_i, R_i, i, m', \mathcal{H}')]]} \text{ READWSET}$$

$$\frac{\mathcal{P}(t) = \mathcal{M}[(m, W_i, R_i, i, m', \mathcal{H}')]}{\mathcal{H}, \mathcal{P} \stackrel{ab_i^t}{\Longrightarrow} \mathcal{H}, \mathcal{P}[t \mapsto \mathcal{M}[\texttt{atomic}\ m']]} \text{ ROLLBACK}$$

$$\frac{\begin{array}{c}\mathcal{P}(t) = \mathcal{M}[(\texttt{return}\ v, W_i, R_i, i, m', \mathcal{H}')] \\ \mathit{check}(R_i, \mathcal{H}) = \mathit{ok} \qquad \mathcal{H}' = \mathcal{H}[W_i] \qquad \bar{l} = \text{dom}(W_i)\end{array}}{\mathcal{H}, \mathcal{P} \stackrel{co_i^t(\bar{l})}{\Longrightarrow} \mathcal{H}, \mathcal{P}[t \mapsto \mathcal{M}[v]]} \text{ COMMIT}$$

Fig. 5. Operational semantics: Global evaluation steps

$$\frac{\forall l \in \text{dom}(R_i) : R_i(l) = \mathcal{H}(l)}{check(R_i, \mathcal{H}) = ok} \text{ Check-Ok}$$

$$\frac{\exists l \in \text{dom}(R_i) : R_i(l) \neq \mathcal{H}(l)}{check(R_i, \mathcal{H}) = bad} \text{ Check-Bad}$$

Fig. 6. Operational semantics: Helper relations

$v_0, \ldots, t_n \mapsto v_n\}$. The rules in Figures 4 and 5 define the semantics of the language constructs. In Fig. 4, $\mathcal{E}[\bullet]$ denotes an evaluation context for an expression and $\mathcal{M}[\bullet]$ an evaluation context for monadic expressions. We write m to indicate that an expression has monadic type.

The `IO` monad is the top-level evaluation mode. Each reduction step $\stackrel{\alpha}{\Longrightarrow}$ chooses an expression from the thread pool $\mathcal{P}$. The non-determinism in this choice models an arbitrary scheduling of threads.

Spawning a thread (Spawn) creates a new entry in the thread pool and returns unit in the parent thread.

An atomic expression at the top-level (Atomic) creates a new transaction in progress with the expression to be evaluated, an empty read and write set, and a fresh transaction identifier (that has never been used before in a particular evaluation). Further, a copy of the expression m is needed for possible rollbacks, and a copy of the current heap to mark the beginning of the transaction.

Any evaluation step that can take place outside a transaction, can also take place inside (STM-Monad).

Allocation of a new reference (Alloc) must check that the reference is not yet allocated in the heap. But it must also check that the reference is not yet allocated in any concurrently running transaction to avoid accidental overwrites when both transactions commit. This condition is indicated by $l \notin \mathcal{H}, \mathcal{P}$, eschewing a formal definition.

Write operations (Write) are straightforward. They just affect the local write set and store the value along with the current transaction identifier.

The read operation on references (ReadGlobal) needs to consult the global state. If a reference cannot be read from the local read or write set, it is accessed in the current global heap. To maintain the transaction's consistency, the read operation is successful only if the value has not been updated since the transaction's beginning. The value and transaction identifier as registered in the heap for this reference are then added to the read set and the value is returned to the transactional computation.

If a reference is present in the read set, but not in the write set, then its value is taken from the read set (ReadRSet).

If the reference is present in the write set, then its value is taken from the write set, without checking the read set (ReadWSet).

If none of the preceding three cases holds at a read, then the transaction aborts and rolls back via Rollback by abandoning the transaction in progress and reinstalling the saved transaction body m' as an atomic block. In fact, this rule has no precondition so that a rollback may happen non-deterministically at any time during a transaction. This way, it is easy to extend our model with an explicit user abort or retry operation. Furthermore, this rule covers the abort both when reading fails as well as when the commit operation fails.

When committing (Commit), the heap is checked for updates to the references which are found in the transaction's read set since the start of the transaction. There are two cases:

The check is successful: None of the variables read by the transaction have been committed by another transaction in the meantime. Therefore, the transaction may publish its writes atomically to the shared heap and return to the IO monad.

The check fails: The only applicable rule is Rollback. The transaction aborts and restarts.

Each of these reductions generates the appropriate effect label on the transition relation. Thus, each sequence of labeled reductions uniquely determines a sequence of labels, which we call the trace of the reduction sequence. Unlike other formalizations, the interleaving of transactions as well as the abort operations are visible in the trace.

Theorem 1 (Type soundness). *The type system in Figure 2 is sound with respect to the operational semantics of Λ_{STM}.*

Proof. The proof is by establishing type preservation and progress in the usual way [15]. The proof of progress relies crucially on the use of the Rollback rule if the comparison of heap entries in ReadGlobal or Commit fails. □

4 Opacity

Many TM systems implemented opacity before it was even defined. Examples systems are DSTM [9], McRT-STM [13], and TL2 [4]. Thus, opacity may be called a standard isolation property of STM. It states that any permitted interleaving of transactions must have an equivalent serialized execution. Furthermore, even aborting transactions are required to view memory locations only in a consistent way.

We can prove formally that the semantics for Λ_{STM} satisfies opacity. To this end, we give a definition for well-formedness of execution traces in terms of the effects they exhibit.

We then show that reordering certain evaluation steps leads to equivalent reductions sequences. Reductions are considered equivalent if each read operation returns the same value, each commit operation commits the same values, and each transaction's outcome (abort or commit) is the same. To see which reordering yields equivalent reductions, we define a notion of dependency on effects.

Finally, we show that all reduction sequences produced by the operational semantics are equivalent to some reduction sequence with a serial trace, up to the assignment of unique labels to the transactions. Without loss of generality, we only consider finite traces: for infinite traces, we would be able to establish our results for all finite prefixes.

4.1 Well-Formedness

The well-formedness of a trace depends largely on temporal relations between effects. We denote by α any effect from a trace $\bar{\alpha}$, α_j denotes the effect at index j in the trace, α^t an effect from thread t, and α_i^t an effect from transaction T_i in thread t.

Further, $\bar{\alpha}|_t$ is the subset of all effects from thread t, and $\bar{\alpha}|_{t,i}$ the subsets of all effects from transaction i in thread t.

Definition 1 (Effect traces). *For a trace $\bar{\alpha}$, a total order on the effects $\alpha \in \bar{\alpha}$ is defined by their position in the effect trace. For $i, j \in \{1, \ldots, |\bar{\alpha}|\}$ and $i \leq j$, we use the abbreviation*

$$\bar{\alpha} \vdash \alpha_i < \alpha_j$$

to denote that an effect α_i is happening before α_j in an trace $\bar{\alpha}$. Similarly,

$$\bar{\alpha} \vdash \bar{\beta} < \bar{\gamma}$$

extends the relation to sets of effects if it holds pairwise for all elements.

Definition 2 (Well-formed traces). *A* trace *$\bar{\alpha}$ is the sequence $\bar{\alpha} = \alpha_1 \ldots \alpha_n$ of effects $\alpha_i \in$ **Effect**$, i \in 1, \ldots, n$. A trace $\bar{\alpha}$ is* well-formed *iff the following conditions hold:*

- *There is no effect for a thread before its spawn effect.*

$$\alpha^t \in \bar{\alpha} \Rightarrow sp^t \in \bar{\alpha} \wedge \bar{\alpha} \vdash sp^t < \alpha^t$$

- *There is no effect for a transaction T_i before its atomic effect.*

$$r_i^t(l) \in \bar{\alpha} \Rightarrow at_i^t \in \bar{\alpha} \wedge \bar{\alpha} \vdash at_i^t < r_i^t(l)$$

$$co_i^t(\bar{l}) \in \bar{\alpha} \Rightarrow at_i^t \in \bar{\alpha} \wedge \bar{\alpha} \vdash at_i^t < co_i^t(\bar{l})$$
$$ab_i^t \in \bar{\alpha} \Rightarrow at_i^t \in \bar{\alpha} \wedge \bar{\alpha} \vdash at_i^t < ab_i^t$$

- *There is no read effect for a transaction T_i after its commit or abort effect.*

$$co_i^t(\bar{l}) \in \bar{\alpha} \Rightarrow \forall r_i^t(l) \in \bar{\alpha} : \bar{\alpha} \vdash r_i^t(l) < co_i^t(\bar{l})$$

$$ab_i^t \in \bar{\alpha} \Rightarrow \forall r_i^t(l) \in \bar{\alpha} : \bar{\alpha} \vdash r_i^t(l) < ab_t^i$$

- *A transaction may have either a commit or an abort effect, but not both.*

$$co_i^t(\bar{l}) \in \bar{\alpha} \Rightarrow ab_i^t \notin \bar{\alpha}$$

$$ab_i^t \in \bar{\alpha} \Rightarrow co_i^t(\bar{l}) \notin \bar{\alpha}$$

– *There are no non-transactional effects within a transaction.*

$$\epsilon^t \in \bar{\alpha} \Rightarrow \nexists i : \bar{\alpha} \vdash at_i^t < \epsilon^t < co_i^t(\bar{l}) \text{ or } \bar{\alpha} \vdash at_i^t < \epsilon^t < ab_i^t$$

– *Transactional effects from the same thread do not interleave.*

$$\forall t \, \forall i \neq j : \bar{\alpha} \vdash \bar{\alpha}|_{t,i} < \bar{\alpha}|_{t,j} \text{ or } \bar{\alpha} \vdash \bar{\alpha}|_{t,j} < \bar{\alpha}|_{t,i}$$

Definition 3 (Pending transactions). *A transaction T_i is pending in a trace $\bar{\alpha}$ if it has neither a commit or an abort effect:*

$$ab_i^t \notin \bar{\alpha} \text{ and } co_i^t(\bar{l}) \notin \bar{\alpha}$$

In contrast to other definitions of well-formed execution traces (e.g. [14]), we do not include the condition that the order of all reads and writes in the transaction is preserved in the effect traces. The operational semantics guarantees that each transaction is working on a consistent view of the shared memory as indexed by its time stamp. A read operation returns the last value written, either by another transaction which updated the global heap, or by the transaction itself in a local write step. Further, all write operations are published (i.e., made visible to other transactions) only after the successful commit. Therefore, the trace reflects the order of the globally visible effects of the read and write operations. The local reads and writes have no globally visible effect.

Lemma 1. *All traces produced by type-correct programs are well-formed.*

Proof. Type-correct programs allow only certain compositions of transactional phases. Effects are only produced when evaluating expressions in the `STM` monad. An at_i^t effect is only produced when entering the `STM` monad. All read effects are produced within the `STM` part, and the evaluation of a transactional expression finishes with either an ab_i^t or $co_i^t(\bar{l})$ effect. □

Well-formedness of a trace relates the effects of one transaction to each other. Complementary, an isolation level defines a relation between the effects of all transactions that participate in a trace [2]. Serializability, for example, is one of these isolation levels.

Definition 4 (Serial traces). *A well-formed trace $\bar{\alpha}$ is serial if for any two transactions T_i and T_j ($i \neq j$), all effects from T_i occur before all effects from T_j, or vice versa:*

$$\forall i \neq j : \bar{\alpha} \vdash \bar{\alpha}|_{t_i,i} < \bar{\alpha}|_{t_j,j} \text{ or } \bar{\alpha} \vdash \bar{\alpha}|_{t_j,j} < \bar{\alpha}|_{t_i,i}$$

In contrast to other approaches, we do not exclude aborting or pending transactions in the definition for serial traces. Therefore, we actually model opaque traces.

Definition 5 (Control dependency). *An effect α_i has a* control dependency *on an effect α_j, $\alpha_i \rhd_c \alpha_j$, iff they must occur in that order in any well-formed trace. A control dependency exists in the following cases:*

- $at_i^t \triangleright_c r_i^t(l)$
- $at_i^t \triangleright_c co_i^t(\bar{l})$
- $at_i^t \triangleright_c ab_i^t$
- $r_i^t(l) \triangleright_c ab_i^t$
- $r_i^t(l) \triangleright_c co_i^t(\bar{l})$

Definition 6 (Data dependency). *An effect α_i has a* data dependency *on an effect α_j, $\alpha_i \triangleright_d \alpha_j$, if they exhibit a write-read, read-write or write-write conflict. A data dependency exists in the following cases where $i \neq j$:*

- $r_i^t(l) \triangleright_d co_j^{t'}(\bar{l})$ *if* $l \in \bar{l}$
- $co_i^t(\bar{l}) \triangleright_d r_j^{t'}(l)$ *if* $l \in \bar{l}$
- $co_i^t(\bar{l}) \triangleright_d co_j^{t'}(\bar{l}')$ *if* $\bar{l} \cap \bar{l}' \neq \emptyset$

Definition 7 (Dependency). *An effect α_i is* dependent *on an effect α_j, $\alpha_i \triangleright \alpha_j$, iff α_i is either control or data dependent on α_j and $\bar{\alpha} \vdash \alpha_i < \alpha_j$ in a trace $\bar{\alpha}$. Effects that are not dependent are called* independent. *A trace of effects $\overline{\alpha}$ is independent from another trace of effects $\overline{\alpha}'$ iff all effects $\alpha_m \in \overline{\alpha}$ are independent from all effects $\alpha_k \in \overline{\alpha}'$.*

Definition 8 (Dependent transactions). *A transaction T_i is dependent on a transaction T_j if $\alpha_i \triangleright \alpha_j$ for an effect α_i from T_i and an effect α_j from T_j.*

Definition 9 (Trace dependencies). *Let $\bar{\alpha}$ be a well-formed trace. The trace dependencies $\Delta(\bar{\alpha})$ are defined as the set of all tuples of dependent effects in this trace:*

$$\Delta(\bar{\alpha}) = \{(\alpha_i, \alpha_j) \mid \alpha_i \triangleright \alpha_j\}$$

The trace dependencies impose a partial order on a trace. We are interested in equivalent traces that satisfy the same order and are permutations of each other. However, the order of trace items inside of every individual thread must not be changed. We call permutations that leave the relative ordering inside every thread unchanged *admissible permutations.* We prove that we can admissibly permute a trace such that it is serial, and that execution of this trace ends in the same program state.

In the scope of this paper, the term *serializability* actually refers to conflict serializability [14]. In contrast to view seriazability, which defines traces to be equivalent if the same data items are read and written, conflict serializability requires that equivalent traces preserve all dependencies.

Definition 10 (Equivalence of traces). *A trace $\bar{\alpha}$ is* equivalent *to a trace $\bar{\beta}$ iff $\bar{\beta}$ is an admissibly permutation of $\bar{\alpha}$ and $\Delta(\bar{\alpha}) = \Delta(\bar{\beta})$.*

Definition 11 (Equivalence of program states). *A program state $\mathcal{P}$ is equivalent to a program state $\mathcal{P}'$, $\mathcal{P} \sim \mathcal{P}'$ iff for all threads i either $\mathcal{P}(i) = \mathcal{P}'(i)$ or $\mathcal{P}(i) = \mathcal{M}[(m_1, W_i, R_i, i, m_2, \mathcal{H})], \mathcal{P}'(i) = \mathcal{M}[(m_1, W_i, R_i, i, m_2, \mathcal{H}')]$ and $\mathcal{H}|_{R_i} = \mathcal{H}'|_{R_i}$.*

Definition 12 (Equivalence of evaluation states). *An evaluation state $\mathcal{H}, \mathcal{P}$ is equivalent to an evaluation state $\mathcal{H}', \mathcal{P}'$ iff $\mathcal{H} = \mathcal{H}'$ and $\mathcal{P} \sim \mathcal{P}'$.*

Lemma 2 (Permutation of reduction steps). *Let R be the two-step reduction*

$$\mathcal{H}, \mathcal{P} \stackrel{\alpha_i}{\Longrightarrow} \mathcal{H}_0, \mathcal{P}_0 \stackrel{\alpha_j}{\Longrightarrow} \mathcal{H}', \mathcal{P}_0'.$$

If α_i is independent from α_j, then there exists an equivalent reduction sequence R' of the form

$$\mathcal{H}, \mathcal{P} \stackrel{\alpha_j}{\Longrightarrow} \mathcal{H}_1, \mathcal{P}_1 \stackrel{\alpha_i}{\Longrightarrow} \mathcal{H}', \mathcal{P}_1'$$

and $\mathcal{P}_0' \sim \mathcal{P}_1'$.

Proof. Case distinction on all independent effects.

Effect-free operations ($\alpha_i = \epsilon^t$ or $\alpha_j = \epsilon_i^t$) are either pure or work on local (transactional) state. Therefore, these steps can get swapped with any operation while resulting in the same heap and thread pool. Reduction steps which result in an abort only modify the transactions' local state. The same holds for read operations. For commit effects, it holds that subsequent independent commit operations change disjoint parts of the global heap. The rules for inconsistency checks require that read and write sets of concurrently running transactions are disjoint in case of successful commit. Therefore reordering independent commit operations has no influence on the heap's final state, and produces equivalent program states. □

In our semantics the begin of a transaction defines its relative order to other transactions. Yet, this order is only partial for transactions that perform their operations interleaved. In this case, they all only commit successfully if their operations do not conflict with each other. The following lemma shows that for these transactions, any relative order is permissive.

Lemma 3 (Permutation of committing transactions). *Let $\bar{\alpha}$ be a well-formed trace with $\bar{\alpha} = \bar{\alpha}' co_i^t(\bar{l})$ and $\bar{\alpha}'$ serial. Further, let T_j be a transaction with $at_j^{t_j} \in \bar{\alpha}$ and $\bar{\alpha} \vdash at_i^{t_i} < at_j^{t_j} < co_i^{t_i}(\bar{l})$ and there does not exist a k with $\bar{\alpha} \vdash at_i^{t_i} < at_k^{t_k} < at_j^{t_j}$. Then $\bar{\alpha}$ is equivalent to a trace $\bar{\beta}$ with $\bar{\beta} \vdash \alpha_j < at_i^{t_i}$ for all effects α_j of transaction T_j.*

Proof. According to the restrictions, the trace must have the following structure:

$$\bar{\alpha} = \alpha_{pre}, at_i^{t_i}, \overline{r_i^{t_i}(l)}, at_j^{t_j}, \overline{r_j^{t_j}(l)}, (ab_i^{t_i} | co_i^{t_i}(\bar{l})), \alpha_{post}$$

There are no dependencies between $at_j^{t_j}$ and any $r_i^{t_i}(l)$, or $at_j^{t_j}$ and $at_i^{t_i}$, or any $r_i^{t_i}(l)$ and any $r_j^{t_j}(l)$. By Lemma 3 this is therefore equivalent to trace

$$\alpha_{pre}, at_j^{t_j}, \overline{r_j^{t_j}(l)}, at_i^{t_i}, \overline{r_i^{t_i}(l)}, (ab_i^{t_i} | co_i^{t_i}(\bar{l})), \alpha_{post}$$

Case distinction on the status of T_j.

- *Case* $ab_j^{t_j} \in \bar{\alpha}$: There is no dependency between $ab_j^{t_j}$ and any effect of T_i, so by Lemma 2, the trace is equivalent to

$$\alpha_{pre}, at_j^{t_j}, \overline{r_j^{t_j}(l)}, ab_j^{t_j}, at_i^{t_i}, \overline{r_i^{t_i}(l)}, \alpha_{post}$$

- *Case* $co_j^{t_j}(\bar{l}) \in \bar{\alpha}$: Assume that $r_i^{t_i}(l) \triangleright co_j^{t_j}(\bar{l})$. Then, the validation of the transaction T_i in rule Commit would fail and $co_i^{t_i}(\bar{l}) \notin \bar{\alpha}$ in contradiction to the assumption. Hence, $co_j^{t_j}(\bar{l})$ is not dependent on any effect of T_i, and by Lemma 2, the trace is equivalent to

$$\alpha_{pre}, at_j^{t_j}, \overline{r_j^{t_j}(l)}, co_j^{t_j}(\bar{l}), at_i^{t_i}, \overline{r_i^{t_i}(l)}, \alpha_{post}$$

- *Case* T_j is pending: Then the trace $\bar{\alpha}$ is equivalent to

$$\alpha_{pre}, at_j^{t_j}, \overline{r_j^{t_j}(l)}, at_i^{t_i}, \overline{r_i^{t_i}(l)}, \alpha_{post}$$

End case distinction on the status of T_j. □

In the remainder of this section, we identify which subsequences of a trace are not serial, and specify an algorithm that moves the effects to the appropriate place.

Lemma 4 (Conflicts). *Let* $\bar{\alpha}$ *be a well-formed trace. Then* $\bar{\alpha}$ *is either serial, or there exists an* α_k *such that the prefix* $\alpha_1 \ldots \alpha_k$ *is serial and*

1. α_k *and* α_{k+1} *are independent, or*
2. $\alpha_k = r_i^{t_i}(l)$ *and* $\alpha_{k+1} = co_j^{t_j}(\bar{l})$ *with* $l \in \bar{l}$.

Proof. We consider all possible combinations of effects which might occur in a well-formed trace. Cases that are left out lead violate well-formedness.
Case distinction on α_i and α_{k+1} where $i \neq j$.

- *Case* $\alpha_k = \epsilon^{t_i}$ or $\alpha_{k+1} = \epsilon^{t_j}$: serial or independent.
- *Case* $\alpha_k = \epsilon_j^{t_i}$ or $\alpha_{k+1} = \epsilon_j^{t_j}$: serial or independent.
- *Case* $\alpha_k = at_i^{t_i}$ and $\alpha_{k+1} = at_j^{t_j}$: serial.
- *Case* $\alpha_k = at_i^{t_i}$ and $\alpha_{k+1} = r_i^{t_i}(l)$: serial.
- *Case* $\alpha_k = at_i^{t_i}$ and $\alpha_{k+1} = r_j^{t_j}(l)$: independent.
- *Case* $\alpha_k = at_i^{t_i}$ and $\alpha_{k+1} = co_i^{t_i}(\bar{l})$: serial.
- *Case* $\alpha_k = at_i^{t_i}$ and $\alpha_{k+1} = co_j^{t_j}(\bar{l})$: independent.
- *Case* $\alpha_k = at_i^{t_i}$ and $\alpha_{k+1} = ab_i^{t_i}$: serial.
- *Case* $\alpha_k = at_i^{t_i}$ and $\alpha_{k+1} = ab_j^{t_j}$: independent.
- *Case* $\alpha_k = r_i^{t_i}(l)$ and $\alpha_{k+1} = r_j^{t_j}(l')$: independent.
- *Case* $\alpha_k = r_i^{t_i}(l)$ and $\alpha_{k+1} = r_i^{t_i}(l')$: serial.
- *Case* $\alpha_k = r_i^{t_i}(l)$ and $\alpha_{k+1} = co_i^{t_i}(\bar{l})$: serial.
- *Case* $\alpha_k = r_i^{t_i}(l)$ and $\alpha_{k+1} = co_j^{t_j}(\bar{l})$: If $l \in \bar{l}$, then this is the second case in the lemma. Otherwise independent.

- *Case* $\alpha_k = r_i^{t_i}(l)$ and $\alpha_{k+1} = ab_i^{t_i}$: serial.
- *Case* $\alpha_k = r_i^{t_i}(l)$ and $\alpha_{k+1} = ab_j^{t_j}$: independent.
- *Case* $\alpha_k = co_i^{t_i}(\bar{l})$ and $\alpha_{k+1} = co_j^{t_j}(\bar{l'})$: According to the operational semantics, it must hold that $\bar{l} \cap \bar{l'} = \emptyset$. Therefore, the effects are independent.
- *Case* $\alpha_k = co_i^{t_i}(\bar{l})$ and $\alpha_{k+1} = ab_j^{t_j}$: independent.

End case distinction on α_i and α_{k+1} where $i \neq j$. □

For the proof of opacity, we define an algorithm which produces for a serializable trace an equivalent serial trace.

---

while $\bar{\alpha}$ is not serial **do**
  choose α_k and α_{k+1} such that $\alpha_1 \dots \alpha_k$ is serial and $\alpha_1 \dots \alpha_{k+1}$ is not serial
  if α_k and α_{k+1} are independent **then** swap α_k with α_{k+1}
  else if $\alpha_k = r_i^{t_i}(l)$ and $\alpha_{k+1} = co_j^{t_j}(\bar{l})$ with $l \in \bar{l}$ **then**
    permute transactions in prefix such that prefix ends with transaction j
  end if
end while

Fig. 7. Reordering transactions for opacity

The algorithm in Figure 7 has the following properties:

1. It terminates on all traces produced by a type-correct programs in Λ_{STM}.
2. For any trace input of a type-correct program in Λ_{STM}, it gives an equivalent serial trace.

We prove these properties in several steps.

Lemma 5 (Termination). *The algorithm terminates on all traces of type-correct programs in* Λ_{STM}.

Proof. We show that the algorithm only performs a finite number of swaps for each pair of effects. Further, for each iteration of the while loop, either a permutation or a swap is performed. The transaction permutations are performed at most $n!$ times, where n is the number of all transactions that participates in a trace. Let m_t denote the number of effects that a transaction produces, and $m = \max m_t$. For every permutation, each pair of effects is swapped at most once ($(m-1)!$). As each trace consists only of a finite number of effects, the algorithm performs at most $n!(m-1)!$ many swap operations. □

Lemma 6 (Permutation). *The output of the algorithm is a permutation of the input trace.*

Proof. All operations on the trace are permutations of effects. Therefore, effects are neither removed from nor added to the input trace. □

Lemma 7 (Dependencies). *The algorithm does not change any dependencies in the trace.*

Proof. Effects are only swapped when they are independent or when permuting transactions. In the latter case, the dependencies in the trace are respected as is shown in Lemma 3. □

Lemma 8 (Correctness of the algorithm). *The output of the algorithm is an equivalent serial trace.*

Proof. By Lemmas 6 and 7, the output is equivalent to the input trace. By Lemma 5, the algorithm terminates on all traces from type-correct programs. In this case, the condition for entering the while loop is falsified, and therefore the trace is serial. □

Theorem 2 (Opacity). *Let $\mathcal{P}_0$ be a type-correct program. Further, let R be a sequence of reductions*

$$\mathcal{H}_0, \mathcal{P}_0 \stackrel{\alpha_1}{\Longrightarrow} \dots \stackrel{\alpha_n}{\Longrightarrow} \mathcal{H}_n, \mathcal{P}_n.$$

Then there exists an equivalent sequence R' of the form

$$\mathcal{H}_0, \mathcal{P}_0 \stackrel{\alpha'_1}{\Longrightarrow} \dots \stackrel{\alpha'_n}{\Longrightarrow} \mathcal{H}_n, \mathcal{P}'_n$$

such that $\bar{\alpha}(R')$ is serial.

Proof. We apply the algorithm for serialization of traces to the traces of R. Because the algorithm only requires the permutation of independent effects, by Lemma 2 the result is an equivalent reduction sequence with serial trace. □

5 Related Work

Weikum and Vossen [14] include a comprehensive overview on theory and practice of transactional systems. Although their work is based on databases, the presented results relate to all transaction-based execution environments. They differentiate in detail between several notions of serializability, and give soundness proofs for all major commit protocols.

Jagannathan and coworkers [10] specify a formal system for transactions with nesting implemented by a versioning and a locking algorithm. They do not model aborts, but stuck executions are implicitly rolled back. They show that the presented algorithms implement serializability.

Abadi and coworkers [1] formalize the semantics of the Automatic Mutual Exclusion (AME) programming model. Similarly, Moore and Grossman [12] provide a formal model with small-step operational semantics for an impure functional language. Both works focus on the treatment of memory locations inside and outside of transactions, and in which cases the notion of weak and strong atomicity coincide.

Doherty and coworkers [5] give a formalization for transactional memory in terms of an I/O automaton. Their specifications are of different granularities and aim to for machine-checked correctness proofs of implementations.

Opacity was introduced by Guerraoui and Kapalka [7] as a correctness criterion for transactional memory. They also show how opacity can be efficiently implemented for different relaxed memory models [6].

Our work is partially inspired by Lipton's work [11] on a reduction theory for proving properties of concurrent programs. His main idea was to identify certain statements that may be moved to the left or to the right in the trace of an interleaved execution. In particular, he establishes that lock acquisition can always be moved to the right over a statements executing in another thread, whereas lock release is a left mover. The commonality is that we are also reordering traces to prove isolation properties, but the difference is that we consider a transactional framework which also includes explicit transaction aborts.

6 Conclusion and Outlook

Transactional memory has evolved as a serious subdomain in concurrent programming. Yet, to this day only few formal models exists that give insight into properties of TM algorithms and its concrete semantics.

This paper presents the formalization of a TM algorithm with lazy update in terms of a monadic lambda calculus. The formal model incorporates all standard TM operations and introduces their abstractions as effects on the global state. The type system enforces strong atomicity semantics by restricting access to shared memory to the STM monad. Based on the traces, the semantics is shown to implement the isolation level of opacity.

We are currently extending the calculus with additional features like I/O actions and repair facilities for conflicts [3]. So far, the small core calculus and its effect system facilitated the development of the enriched interface.

It is also possible to adapt the operational semantics such that it implements other isolation levels like snapshot isolation. The technique of reordering can be used in a similar fashion to transform execution traces to a canonical form of traces produced by snapshot isolation.

References

1. Abadi, M., Birrell, A., Harris, T., Isard, M.: Semantics of transactional memory and automatic mutual exclusion. In: POPL 2008: Proceedings of the 35th annual ACM SIGPLAN-SIGACT symposium on Principles of programming languages, pp. 63–74. ACM, New York (2008)
2. Berenson, H., Bernstein, P., Gray, J., Melton, J., O'Neil, E., O'Neil, P.: A critique of ansi sql isolation levels. In: SIGMOD 1995: Proceedings of the 1995 ACM SIGMOD International Conference on Management of Data, pp. 1–10. ACM, New York (1995)
3. Bieniusa, A., Middelkoop, A., Thiemann, P.: Brief announcement: Actions in the twilight - concurrent irrevocable transactions and inconsistency repair. In: Richa, A.W., Guerraoui, R. (eds.) PODC, pp. 71–72. ACM, New York (2010)

4. Dice, D., Shalev, O., Shavit, N.: Transactional locking II. In: Dolev, S. (ed.) DISC 2006. LNCS, vol. 4167, pp. 194–208. Springer, Heidelberg (2006)
5. Doherty, S., Groves, L., Luchangco, V., Moir, M.: Towards formally specifying and verifying transactional memory. In: Proceedings of the RefineNet Workshop 2009 (REFINE 2009). Electronic Notes in Theoretical Computer Science (2009)
6. Guerraoui, R., Henzinger, T.A., Kapalka, M., Singh, V.: Transactions in the jungle. In: auf der Heide, F.M., Phillips, C.A. (eds.) SPAA, pp. 263–272. ACM, New York (2010)
7. Guerraoui, R., Kapalka, M.: On the correctness of transactional memory. In: Chatterjee, S., Scott, M.L. (eds.) PPOPP, pp. 175–184. ACM, New York (2008)
8. Harris, T., Marlow, S., Jones, S.P., Herlihy, M.: Composable memory transactions. In: Sixteenth ACM SIGPLAN Symposium on Principles and Practice of Parallel Programming, Chicago, IL, USA, pp. 48–60. ACM Press, New York (2005)
9. Herlihy, M., Luchangco, V., Moir, M., Scherer III, W.N.: Software transactional memory for dynamic-sized data structures. In: PODC 2003: Proceedings of the Twentysecond Annual Symposium on Principles of Distributed Computing, Boston, Massachusetts, pp. 92–101. ACM Press, New York (2003)
10. Jagannathan, S., Vitek, J., Welc, A., Hosking, A.: A transactional object calculus. Sci. Comput. Program 57(2), 164–186 (2005)
11. Lipton, R.J.: Reduction: A method of proving properties of parallel programs. Commun. ACM 18(12), 717–721 (1975)
12. Moore, K.F., Grossman, D.: High-level small-step operational semantics for transactions. In: POPL 2008: Proceedings of the 35th annual ACM SIGPLAN-SIGACT symposium on Principles of programming languages, pp. 51–62. ACM, New York (2008)
13. Saha, B., Adl-Tabatabai, A.-R., Hudson, R.L., Minh, C.C., Hertzberg, B.: McRT-STM: a high performance software transactional memory system for a multi-core runtime. In: PPoPP 2006: Proceedings of the 11th ACM SIGPLAN symposium on Principles and practice of parallel programming, New York, NY, USA, pp. 187–197 (2006)
14. Weikum, G., Vossen, G.: Transactional information systems: theory, algorithms, and the practice of concurrency control and recovery. Morgan Kaufmann Publishers Inc., San Francisco (2001)
15. Wright, A., Felleisen, M.: A syntactic approach to type soundness. Information and Computation 115(1), 38–94 (1994)

Typing Copyless Message Passing

Viviana Bono, Chiara Messa, and Luca Padovani

Dipartimento di Informatica, Università di Torino, Italy

Abstract. We present a calculus that models a form of process interaction based on copyless message passing, in the style of Singularity OS. The calculus is equipped with a type system ensuring that well-typed processes are free from faults, leaks, and communication errors. The type system is essentially linear, but we show that linearity alone is inadequate. On the one hand, it is too strict when dealing with heap-allocated objects; on the other hand, it leaves room for scenarios where well-typed processes leak significant amounts of memory. We address these problems using dedicated types for keeping track of dereferenced pointers and by basing the type system upon an original variant of session types.

1 Introduction

Singularity OS is the prototype of a dependable operating system where software-isolated processes (SIPs) run in the same address space. Process interaction occurs solely through the exchange of messages over asynchronous, FIFO channels consisting of a pair of related endpoints (the channel *peers*), such that any message sent over one of the endpoints is received on the other endpoint. The communication overhead is tamed by copyless message passing: only *pointers* to messages are physically transferred from one process to another. Static analysis guarantees *process isolation*, namely that every process can only access memory it owns exclusively.

In this paper, we present CoreSing#, a calculus that captures the essential features of Singularity. We equip the calculus with a type system ensuring that well-typed processes are free from communication errors, memory faults, and memory leaks. We avoid communication errors by associating each endpoint with an endpoint type specifying the sequence of input/output actions allowed on that endpoint. Endpoint types are a variant of session types [7,8,13] tailored to the Singularity communication model. For example, the recursive endpoint type

$$T = \mathbf{rec}\, X.!\{\mathtt{arg}.?\{\mathtt{ack}.X\},\mathtt{quit}.\mathbf{end}\}$$

indicates that a process can send an arbitrary number of arg-tagged messages and can close the endpoint only after it has sent a quit-tagged message. After every arg-tagged message, the process must be ready to receive an ack-tagged message coming from the process using the peer endpoint. Communication errors are avoided by imposing that peer endpoints are typed by *dual* session types. For example, the dual of T is $\overline{T} = \mathbf{rec}\, X.?\{\mathtt{arg}.!\{\mathtt{ack}.X\},\mathtt{quit}.\mathbf{end}\}$, which specifies complementary actions with respect to those occurring in T.

To avoid memory faults and memory leaks, our type system relies essentially on the *linear usage* of pointers, although linearity alone proves to be inadequate. As a matter of fact, linearity is not enough to guarantee the absence of leaks. For instance the function

G. Barthe (Ed.): ESOP 2011, LNCS 6602, pp. 57–76, 2011.
© Springer-Verlag Berlin Heidelberg 2011

```
void foo() { (e, f) = open(); send(arg, f, e); close(f); }
```

creates the two endpoints e and f of a channel, sends e as the argument of an arg-tagged message on f, and closes f. This function uses e and f linearly and it is typable by associating e and f with suitable endpoint types. Yet, foo leaks some memory: after the **close** instruction, no reference to e is left to the process, therefore the arg-tagged message will never be deallocated. This memory leak can be avoided by imposing a simple restriction on the endpoint types. The idea is to define a notion of *weight* for endpoint types which roughly gives the "size" of the message queues in the endpoints having those types and to restrict endpoint types to those having finite weight. Then, one can show that foo is typable only if endpoint types with infinite weight are allowed.

From another point of view, linearity is too restrictive and must be relaxed, since *using* a pointer does not necessarily mean *consuming* the resource it points to. For example, the same endpoint can be used multiple times, as specified by its endpoint type. We must also deal with cases where a process owns a cell (that is, a one-field structure) but not its content. This happens after executing the instruction

```
send(arg, e, *a);
```

which sends the content of a in an arg-tagged message on endpoint e. The process performing the **send** no longer owns (the memory located at) *a after this instruction, but it still owns (the memory located at) a. We address this issue by distinguishing *cell types* $*t$ from *exposed cell types* $*\bullet$. The former ones denote memory cells that a process owns together with their content (of type t); the latter ones denote memory cells that a process owns, but whose content is owned by a different process. In the code fragment above, a has type $*t$ for some t *before* the **send**, and type $*\bullet$ *after* the **send**. This prevents a from being dereferenced multiple times, until the process regains ownership of its content, typically by assigning some value it owns into *a.

CoreSing# can be seen as a formalization of the language Sing#, which is an extension of C# specifically tailored to the implementation of Singularity processes. In particular, we provide a purely type-based framework to explain *channel contracts* and the **expose** construct in Sing# programs.

In Sing#, a channel contract describes an interaction pattern between the users of the two endpoints. For instance, the Sing# contract

```
contract C {
  initial state Transfer { !arg → WaitAck; !quit → End }
  state WaitAck { ?ack → Transfer }
  final state End { } }
```

describes a pattern where the process using the so-called *exporting endpoint* behaves as specified by the endpoint type T defined above, while the process using the *importing endpoint* behaves as specified by $\overline{T}$. There are clear analogies between contracts and endpoint types: the contract describes an interaction between two processes in terms of states and transitions, with a bias towards one of the two processes; the endpoint type describes the behavior of a single process involved in the interaction.

Regarding the **expose** construct, it is used by the Sing# compiler to keep track of memory ownership. In particular, Sing# allows pointer dereferentiation only within **expose** blocks. To illustrate the point, consider the following code fragments:

```
expose (a)                    expose (a)
{ send(arg, *a, b); }         { send(arg, b, *a); *a = new T(); }
```

The effect of **expose**(a) is to transfer the ownership of *a from a to the process exposing the pointer. If the process still owns *a at the end of the **expose** block, the construct is well typed. In the fragment on the left hand side, *a is owned by the process before and after the **send**, even though the type associated with a might have changed since the **send** can possibly change the state of *a's contract. In the fragment on the right hand side, the process loses ownership of *a after the **send**, but it assigns the pointer to a newly allocated object into *a. The same assignment in the left fragment would cause a memory leak, while omitting the assignment in the right fragment would prevent the **expose** block from being well typed. Distinguishing between cells with type $*t$ and cells with type $*\bullet$ is all we need to capture the static semantics of **expose**(a) blocks in Sing#. At the beginning of the block, a is accessed and its type turns from $*t$ to $*\bullet$; within the block it is possible to (linearly) use *a; at the end of the block, *a is assigned with a (possibly different) pointer that the process owns, thus turning a's type from $*\bullet$ back to some $*s$.

Related work. Session types have been introduced as a structuring mechanism in distributed systems, where processes engage into a conversation by first establishing a *private session* and then carrying on the conversation within the protected scope of the session. The session type prescribes, for each process involved in the session, the sequence and type of messages the process is allowed to send or expected to receive at each given time. Endpoint types are dyadic, "finite-weight" session types describing the exchange of heap pointers. There exist session type theories guaranteeing not only the absence of communication errors, but also the *global progress* of systems. While definitely interesting, we do not care about global progress in this work, since it can be achieved by means of orthogonal mechanisms, as shown for example in [3,1].

Aspects of the Singularity OS and of Sing# have already been formalized and studied elsewhere. In particular, [14] and [16] introduce general frameworks for reasoning on (pseudo-)linear access to shared memory. Regarding channel contracts, [12] shows that they are implementable without deadlocks if they are *deterministic* and *autonomous*. The first condition requires that there cannot be two transitions that differ only for the target state. The autonomous condition requires that every two transitions departing from the same state are either two sends or two receives. These conditions make it possible to split contracts into pairs of dual session types, and to fit existing session type theories in our setting in such a natural way. To keep session types simple, however, we do not model Singularity contracts where a final state has outgoing transitions. More expressive session types [2] could be adopted, but then we should presumably impose also the *synchronizing* restriction on channel contracts, as investigated in [14]. In [4] it was already observed that, to prevent inconsistencies related to the ownership of messages, special care is required when sending endpoints. There, the authors show that sending endpoints in a *send-state* condition is safe. Our investigation provides further motivations to restrict the endpoints that can be sent as messages. Also, our "finite-weight" condition generalizes the *send-state* condition in [4]. Other works [4,6] introduce apparently similar, "finite-weight" restrictions on session types to make sure that message queues of the corresponding channels are bounded. In our case, the weight concerns a different measure and the restriction prevents the creation of cycles involving channel queues in the heap (see Section 3 for details).

Our work shares many aspects with [14,15], where the authors develop a proof system for a significant fragment of Sing#. The proof system is based on a variant of *separation logic* [9,11] and permits the derivation of Hoare triples of the form $\{A\}\ p\ \{B\}$ where p is a program and A and B are logical formulas describing the state of the heap before and after the execution of p. A judgment $\{\mathsf{emp}\}\ p\ \{\mathsf{emp}\}$ indicates that if p is executed in the empty heap (the pre-condition emp), then it leaks no memory (the post-condition emp). However, leaks in [14] manifest themselves only when both endpoints of any channel used in p have been closed. In particular, it is possible to derive the judgment $\{\mathsf{emp}\}$ `foo()` $\{\mathsf{emp}\}$ for the function `foo` we have shown above, although it is intuitively clear that `foo` does indeed leak some memory. We tighten the definition of "leak" and we are able to declare `foo` ill typed. Endpoint types allow us to easily detect communication errors, while this aspect is still to be investigated in the setting of [14].

Structure of the paper. In Section 2 we present the syntax and semantics of CoreSing# and we formalize faults, leaks, and communication errors. Section 3 presents the type system for CoreSing# and the soundness results. In Section 4 we briefly sketch some extensions of the type system which are supported by Sing#. We conclude in Section 5.

2 Syntax and Semantics of CoreSing#

Let us fix some notation: we use P, Q, ... to range over processes and a, b, ... to range over *heap pointers* (or simply *pointers*) taken from some infinite set `Pointers`; we use x, y, ... to range over *variables* taken from some infinite set `Variables` disjoint from `Pointers` and we let u, v, ... range over *names*, which are elements of `Pointers` $\cup$ `Variables`; finally, we let X, ... range over *process variables*. In the following, we will write $\tilde{a}$, $\tilde{x}$, $\tilde{u}$, ... for denoting sequences of pointers, variables, and names, respectively. We will sometimes treat $\tilde{u}$ as the set of names occurring in the sequence $\tilde{u}$.

The language of processes, defined by the grammar in Table 1, essentially is a pi-calculus equipped with tag-based message dispatching and primitives for handling heap-allocated objects (cells and endpoints). To keep the model manageable and the presentation within the page limits we only consider cells, but multi-field structures can be accommodated with reasonable effort. The process $\mathbf{0}$ is idle and performs no action. Terms $\mathbf{rec}\ X.P$ and X are used for building recursive processes, as usual. The process $u!\mathtt{m}\langle\tilde{u}\rangle.P$ sends a message $\mathtt{m}\langle\tilde{u}\rangle$ on the endpoint u and continues as P. A *message* is made of a *tag* $\mathtt{m}$ along with its *parameters* $\tilde{u}$. The process $\sum_{i\in I} u?\mathtt{m}_i(\tilde{x}_i).P_i$ waits for a message from the endpoint u. The tag $\mathtt{m}_i$ of the received message determines the continuation P_i where the variables x_i are instantiated with the parameters of the message. The process $\mathbf{cell}(a,u).P$ creates a new cell located at a, initializes it with u, and continues as P. Similarly, $\mathbf{open}(a,b).P$ creates a *channel*, represented as a pair of endpoints a and b. We will say that b is the peer endpoint of a and vice-versa. The process $\mathbf{free}(u)$ declares that the object located at u is no longer in use. The process $\mathbf{expose}(u,x).P$ reads the content of the cell located at u and binds it to x in the continuation P, while $\mathbf{unexpose}(u,v).P$

assigns v to the cell located at u. These primitives are named **expose** and **unexpose** because they are strictly related with the **expose** construct in Singularity. In Section 3 we will see that they also represent complementary scoping primitives. The processes $P \oplus Q$ and $P \mid Q$ are standard and respectively denote the non-deterministic choice and the parallel composition of P and Q.

Table 1. Syntax of CoreSing# processes and of heap objects

$P ::=$		**Process**	$\mu ::=$		**Heap**
	$\mathbf{0}$	(idle)		$\emptyset$	(empty)
	$\mid X$	(variable)		$\mid a \mapsto a$	(cell)
	$\mid \mathbf{free}(u)$	(garbage)		$\mid a \mapsto [a,q]$	(endpoint)
	$\mid \mathbf{open}(a,a).P$	(open channel)		$\mid \mu,\mu$	(composition)
	$\mid \mathbf{cell}(a,u).P$	(create cell)			
	$\mid \mathbf{expose}(u,x).P$	(expose cell)	$q ::=$		**Queue**
	$\mid \mathbf{unexpose}(u,u).P$	(unexpose cell)		ε	(empty)
	$\mid u!\mathtt{m}\langle\tilde{u}\rangle.P$	(send)		$\mid \mathtt{m}\langle\tilde{a}\rangle$	(message)
	$\mid \sum_{i\in I} u?\mathtt{m}_i(\tilde{x}_i).P_i$	(receive)		$\mid q :: q$	(composition)
	$\mid P \oplus P$	(choice)			
	$\mid P \mid P$	(composition)			
	$\mid \mathbf{rec}\ X.P$	(recursion)			

The sets of free and bound names of every process P, respectively denoted by $\mathrm{fn}(P)$ and $\mathrm{bn}(P)$, are almost standard. Beware that the process $\mathbf{cell}(a,u).P$ binds a but not u, which is thus free. The construct **rec** X is the only binder for process variables. We restrict recursive processes so that in every term **rec** $X.P$ we have $\mathrm{fn}(P) \cap \mathrm{bn}(P) = \emptyset$. This makes sure that in the unfolding $P\{\mathbf{rec}\ X.P/X\}$ of a recursive process no name occurring free in P is accidentally captured.

Heaps, ranged over by μ, ..., are finite maps from pointers to heap objects represented as terms defined according to the syntax in Table 1: the heap $\emptyset$ is empty; the heap $a \mapsto b$ is made of a cell located at a that contains b; the heap $a \mapsto [b,q]$ is made of an endpoint located at a which is a structure referring to the peer endpoint b and containing a *queue* q of messages waiting to be read from a. Heap compositions μ, μ' are defined only when the domains of the heaps being composed, which we denote by $\mathrm{dom}(\mu)$ and $\mathrm{dom}(\mu')$, are disjoint. We assume that heaps are equal up to commutativity and associativity of composition and that $\emptyset$ is neutral for composition. *Queues*, ranged over by q, ..., are finite ordered sequences of messages $\mathtt{m}_1\langle\tilde{c}_1\rangle :: \cdots :: \mathtt{m}_n\langle\tilde{c}_n\rangle$. We build queues from the empty queue ε and concatenation of messages by means of ::. We assume that queues are equal up to associativity of :: and that ε is neutral for ::.

We define the operational semantics of processes as the combination of a structural congruence relation, which equates processes we never want to distinguish, and a reduction relation. Structural congruence, denoted by $\equiv$, is the least congruence relation that includes alpha conversion on bound names, commutativity and associativity of $\mid$, and the law $P \mid \mathbf{0} \equiv P$.

CoreSing# processes never interact directly with each other: every action performed by a process has some effect (or depends) on the heap, and processes communicate with

Table 2. Reduction of systems

(R-CELL)
$$(\mu;\mathbf{cell}(a,b).P) \rightarrow (\mu, a \mapsto b; P)$$

(R-OPEN)
$$(\mu;\mathbf{open}(a,b).P) \rightarrow (\mu, a \mapsto [b,\varepsilon], b \mapsto [a,\varepsilon]; P)$$

(R-CHOICE)
$$(\mu;P \oplus Q) \rightarrow (\mu;P)$$

(R-EXPOSE)
$$(\mu, a \mapsto b; \mathbf{expose}(a,x).P) \rightarrow (\mu, a \mapsto b; P\{b/x\})$$

(R-REC)
$$(\mu;\mathbf{rec}\, X.P) \rightarrow (\mu;P\{\mathbf{rec}\, X.P/X\})$$

(R-UNEXPOSE)
$$(\mu, a \mapsto b; \mathbf{unexpose}(a,c).P) \rightarrow (\mu, a \mapsto c; P)$$

(R-SEND)
$$(\mu, a \mapsto [b,q], b \mapsto [a,q']; a!\mathtt{m}\langle\tilde{c}\rangle.P) \rightarrow (\mu, a \mapsto [b,q], b \mapsto [a, q' :: \mathtt{m}\langle\tilde{c}\rangle]; P)$$

(R-RECEIVE)
$$\frac{k \in I}{(\mu, a \mapsto [b, \mathtt{m}_k\langle\tilde{c}\rangle :: q]; \sum_{i\in I} a?\mathtt{m}_i(\tilde{x}_i).P_i) \rightarrow (\mu, a \mapsto [b,q]; P_k\{\tilde{c}/\tilde{x}_k\})}$$

(R-STRUCT)
$$\frac{P \equiv P' \qquad (\mu;P') \rightarrow (\mu';Q') \qquad Q' \equiv Q}{(\mu;P) \rightarrow (\mu';Q)}$$

(R-PAR)
$$\frac{(\mu;P) \rightarrow (\mu';P')}{(\mu;P \mid Q) \rightarrow (\mu';P' \mid Q)}$$

each other by means of the heap. Therefore, the reduction relation defines the transitions of *systems* instead of processes, where a system is a pair $(\mu;P)$ of a heap μ and a process P. The reduction relation $\rightarrow$, inductively defined in Table 2, is described in the following paragraph. (R-CELL) and (R-OPEN) respectively create a new cell and a new channel. The channel consists of two fresh endpoints which refer to each other and have an empty queue. The cell is properly initialized with the pointer specified in the process. Both reductions are possible provided that the newly introduced pointers do not already occur in $\mathrm{dom}(\mu)$, for otherwise the heap in the resulting system would be undefined. (R-CHOICE) (and its symmetric, omitted) is a standard choice rule, saying that a process $P \oplus Q$ may autonomously reduce to either P or Q leaving the heap unchanged. For the sake of simplicity, we do not specify the test performed by the process, since it is irrelevant for the investigation we are pursuing. (R-EXPOSE) reads the content of a cell and binds it to a variable in the continuation process. As usual, $P\{b/x\}$ denotes the capture-avoiding substitution of every free occurrence of x in P with b. (R-UNEXPOSE) describes the assignment of a pointer c to the content of a cell pointed to by a whose previous content was b. The pointers b and c may be equal, in which case the reduction is a no-op. (R-SEND) describes the sending of a message $\mathtt{m}\langle\tilde{c}\rangle$ on the endpoint a. The message is enqueued at the end of a's peer endpoint queue. (R-RECEIVE) describes a process waiting for a message from the endpoint a. The message at the front of a's queue is removed from the queue, its tag is used for selecting some branch $k \in I$, and its parameters instantiate the variables $\tilde{x}_k$. If the queue is not empty and the first message in the queue does not match any of the tags $\{\mathtt{m}_i \mid i \in I\}$, then no reduction occurs and the process is stuck. The rule implicitly assumes that the sequence $\tilde{c}$ of parameters in the message and the sequence $\tilde{x}_k$ of variables in the process have equal length. This will be enforced by the type system in Section 3. (R-STRUCT) describes reductions modulo structural congruence. It plays an essential role in ensuring that **cell**$(a,b).P$ and **open**$(a,b).P$ are never stuck, because a and b can always be alpha converted to some pointers not occurring in $\mathrm{dom}(\mu)$. Finally, (R-PAR) expresses reductions under parallel composition. Observe that the heap is treated globally, even when it is only a sub-process to reduce. There is no reduction for **free**(a) processes: it is technically convenient to treat them as persistent processes so that we can easily track which pointers have been properly deallocated. A process willing to deallocate a pointer a and to continue as P afterwards can be modelled as **free**$(a) \mid P$. In the following we write $\Rightarrow$ for the reflexive, transitive closure of $\rightarrow$, and we write $(\mu;P) \not\rightarrow$ if there exist no μ' and P' such that $(\mu;P) \rightarrow (\mu';P')$.

In this work we focus on three properties of systems: we wish every system to be fault free, where a fault is an attempt to use a pointer not corresponding to an allocated object or to use a pointer in some way which is not allowed by the object it refers to; we wish every system to be leak free, where a leak is a region of the heap that some process allocates and that becomes unreachable because no reference to it is directly or indirectly available to the processes in the system; finally, we wish every system to enjoy (a limited form of) progress, meaning that no process in the system should get stuck while reading messages from a non-empty queue. We conclude this section by making these properties precise, using CoreSing# as the reference calculus.

Before we move on, we need to formalize the reachability of a heap object with respect to a set of *root* pointers. Intuitively, a process P may directly reach any object located at some pointer in the set $\mathrm{fn}(P)$ (we can think of the pointers in $\mathrm{fn}(P)$ as of the local variables of the process stored in its stack); from these pointers, the process may reach other heap objects by exposing cells and by reading messages from the queue of the endpoints it can reach.

Definition 2.1 (Reachable pointers). *Let $A \subseteq$ `Pointers`. We write $\mathrm{reach}(A,\mu)$ for the least set A' that includes A and such that:*

- *$a \in A'$ and $a \mapsto b \in \mu$ implies $b \in A'$;*
- *$a \in A'$ and $a \mapsto [b, q :: \mathtt{m}\langle\tilde{c}\rangle :: q'] \in \mu$ implies $\tilde{c} \subseteq A'$.*

Observe that the peer of an endpoint located at a may not be reachable, because the calculus has no primitive operator to access the b component in the heap $a \mapsto [b,q]$. We now define well-behaved systems formally.

Definition 2.2 (Well-behaved process). *We say that the process P is* well behaved *if $(\emptyset;P) \Rightarrow (\mu;Q)$ implies: (1) $\mathrm{fn}(Q) \subseteq \mathrm{dom}(\mu)$; (2) $\mathrm{dom}(\mu) \subseteq \mathrm{reach}(\mathrm{fn}(Q),\mu)$; (3) $Q \equiv P_1 \mid P_2$ implies $\mathrm{fn}(P_1) \cap \mathrm{fn}(P_2) = \emptyset$; (4) $Q \equiv P_1 \mid P_2$ and $(\mu;P_1) \not\rightarrow$ where P_1 does not have unguarded parallel compositions imply either $P_1 = \mathbf{0}$ or $P_1 =$* **free**(a) *or $P_1 = \sum_{i \in I} a?\mathtt{m}_i(x_i).P_i$ where the queue in the endpoint located at a is empty.*

Let us comment on the conditions (1–4) in Definition 2.2 and see how they capture the desirable properties discussed earlier. *Absence of faults* is formalized as the combination of conditions (1), (3), and (4). Indeed, (1) ensures that any pointer that is directly reachable refers to an allocated object. Since Definition 2.2 quantifies over *every* possible reduction of P, condition (1) must hold for every pointer that is indirectly reachable. Condition (3) implies that no well-behaving process can access a deallocated object or can deallocate the same object twice, because in CoreSing# we keep track of deallocated objects by means of persistent $\textsf{free}(u)$ processes. For example, the process $\textsf{expose}(a,x).\textsf{expose}(a,y).(\textsf{free}(a) \mid \textsf{free}(x) \mid \textsf{free}(y))$ violates condition (3) because it deallocates the content of the cell located at a twice. Finally, condition (4) ensures that a stable, atomic process cannot be an attempt to **(un)expose** an endpoint or to send or receive a message using a pointer that refers to a cell. *Absence of leaks* is formalized as condition (2), requiring that the set of pointers reachable from Q must include the whole domain of the heap. The processes $\textsf{open}(a,b).\mathbf{0}$ and $\textsf{expose}(a,x).\textsf{free}(x)$ are simple examples of violation of condition (2). *Progress* is formalized as condition (4), implying that if $(\mu;Q)$ is a stuck configuration, then every non-terminated process in Q is waiting for a message on an endpoint having an empty queue. This configuration corresponds to a genuine deadlock where every process in some set is waiting for a message that is to be sent by another process in the same set. The same condition requires that a deallocated endpoint must have an empty queue.

3 Type System

Types. Types describe the nature of objects allocated in the heap. According to Table 1, the heap contains *cells* and *endpoints*, therefore we want to discriminate these entities using different types. Since endpoints can be used for complex interactions involving messages with different tags, the type of endpoints will be a structured term describing a protocol, in the same spirit of *session types*. Also, we will discriminate between cells that have been exposed from those that have not. For the sake of minimality we only focus on types for linear entities. Non-linear entities, which are essential in practice, can be added by means of orthogonal extensions of the type system, as shown e.g. in [13].

Table 3. Syntax of types

$t ::=$		**Type**	$T ::=$		**Endpoint Type**
	$*t$	(cell type)		$\textsf{end}$	(termination)
$\mid$	$*\bullet$	(exposed cell type)	$\mid$	X	(variable)
$\mid$	T	(endpoint type)	$\mid$	$!\{\mathtt{m}_i.T_i\}_{i\in I}$	(internal choice)
			$\mid$	$?\{\mathtt{m}_i.T_i\}_{i\in I}$	(external choice)
			$\mid$	$\textsf{rec}\, X.T$	(recursive type)

Types, ranged over by t, s, ..., and endpoint types, ranged over by T, S, ..., are defined in Table 3. The *cell type* $*t$ describes a cell whose content has type t; the *exposed cell type* $*\bullet$ also describes a cell, but it says nothing about the content of the cell and therefore makes the cell visible but inaccessible. Endpoint types describe the sequence of actions that processes can perform on a given endpoint. The endpoint type $\textsf{end}$ describes an endpoint on which no further action, save for deallocation, is possible. The internal choice $!\{\mathtt{m}_i.T_i\}_{i\in I}$ describes an endpoint on which a process can send any message with tag $\mathtt{m}_i$ for $i \in I$. Depending on the tag $\mathtt{m}_i$ of the message, the process must then use the endpoint according to the endpoint type T_i. The external choice $?\{\mathtt{m}_i.T_i\}_{i\in I}$ describes an endpoint from which a process is supposed to receive a message which is guaranteed to have a tag $\mathtt{m}_i$ for some $i \in I$. After the message is received, the process must use the endpoint according to the endpoint type T_i. In both choices we assume that $I \neq \emptyset$ and that $i, j \in I$ with $i \neq j$ implies $\mathtt{m}_i \neq \mathtt{m}_j$ (this corresponds to the deterministic condition for Sing# contracts). When I is a singleton, we will usually write $!\mathtt{m}.T$ instead of $!\{\mathtt{m}.T\}$, and similarly for external choices. We use endpoint variables and terms of the form $\mathbf{rec}\ X.T$ for describing recursive protocols, as usual. For instance, $\mathbf{rec}\ X.!\mathtt{m}.X$ describes an endpoint on which a process must send an infinite number of m-tagged messages. We forbid non-contractive endpoint types such as $\mathbf{rec}\ X.X$ requiring that every recursion variable is guarded by an internal or external choice. We assume that a recursive endpoint type $\mathbf{rec}\ X.T$ and its unfolding $T\{\mathbf{rec}\ X.T/X\}$ are equal.

We assume a global environment Σ associating message tags with sequences of types. A judgment of the form $\Sigma \vdash \mathtt{m} : \langle t_1, \dots, t_n \rangle$ indicates that messages tagged by m have n parameters with type $t_1, \dots, t_n$, in this order. This obliges a sender of a m-tagged message to provide n parameters with these types and guarantees a receiver of a m-tagged message that the n parameters have these types.

A crucial notion regarding endpoint types is that of *duality*. Intuitively, two peer endpoints should be typed by dual endpoint types to guarantee that the communications on them occur without errors. For example, the endpoint types $!\{\mathtt{m}_i.\mathbf{end}\}_{i \in I}$ and $?\{\mathtt{m}_i.\mathbf{end}\}_{i \in I}$ are dual: every message sent by the sender process is accepted by the receiver. More generally, the dual of an endpoint type T, denoted by $\overline{T}$, is obtained by swapping internal and external choices, while **end** is invariant. Formally:

$$\overline{\mathbf{end}} = \mathbf{end} \qquad \overline{X} = X \qquad \overline{\mathbf{rec}\ X.T} = \mathbf{rec}\ X.\overline{T}$$
$$\overline{!\{\mathtt{m}_i.T_i\}_{i \in I}} = ?\{\mathtt{m}_i.\overline{T}_i\}_{i \in I} \qquad \overline{?\{\mathtt{m}_i.T_i\}_{i \in I}} = !\{\mathtt{m}_i.\overline{T}_i\}_{i \in I}$$

Typing the Heap. The heap plays a primary role, not just because it enables the interaction between processes, but also because most properties of well-behaved processes are direct consequences of related properties of the heap. Therefore, just as we will check well typedness of a process P with respect to some context that associates the pointers occurring in P with the corresponding types, we will also need to check that the heap is consistent with respect to the same context. This leads to a notion of well-typed heap that we develop in this section. The mere fact that we have this notion does not mean that we need to type-check the heap at runtime. Well typedness of the heap will be a consequence of well typedness of processes, and the empty heap will be trivially well typed.

The context Δ we use for typing heaps (and processes) does not specify an association for every location of the heap, as this would be redundant. For example, the association $a : *t$ tells us not only that a is a pointer to a cell, but also that the content of the cell, which is another pointer, has itself type t. Therefore, the association $b : t$ is redundant, assuming that b is the content of the cell located at a, insofar the context contains the association $a : *t$. The context we use for typing a heap μ is defined on a proper subset of $\mathrm{dom}(\mu)$ which happens to be the set of pointers that the processes of the system have direct access to. The reader can think of $\mathrm{dom}(\Delta)$ as playing a similar role as the *roots* of a garbage collector. The composition of two contexts Δ_1 and Δ_2, denoted by Δ_1, Δ_2, is defined only when $\mathrm{dom}(\Delta_1) \cap \mathrm{dom}(\Delta_2) = \emptyset$.

Informally, well-typedness of a heap with respect to some context Δ entails the following properties:

(Consistency) Every allocated object is consistent with the corresponding type in the context. Hence, associations $a : *t$ and $a : *\bullet$ in the context correspond to cells $a \mapsto b$ in the heap; analogously, associations $a : T$ in the context correspond to endpoints $a \mapsto [b, q]$ in the heap such that each message in q has parameters that are consistent with the their type, as determined by the tag of the message; also, the tag is among the ones occurring in T (we will make this more precise shortly).

(Reachability) Every allocated object is reachable from exactly one of the pointers in $\mathrm{dom}(\Delta)$. This has two implications: first, there is no leak in a well-typed heap provided that every pointer in $\mathrm{dom}(\Delta)$ occurs in some process; second, a well-typed heap has no overlapping of the objects that can be reached from different roots, therefore each allocated object is "owned" by exactly one root. Since the roots will be distributed linearly among the processes in the system (different processes cannot share the same root) this immediately guarantees that different processes have access to disjoint regions of the heap.

(Duality) Peer endpoints have dual endpoint types. This invariant is needed for ensuring that communications occurring on peer endpoints are error free.

We split heap type checking in two parts: first we define a well-formedness relation $\Delta \Vdash \mu$, meaning that μ satisfies the consistency and reachability conditions we have informally described above. Then, we say that μ is well typed with respect to Δ when $\Delta \Vdash \mu$ holds and the duality condition is also satisfied. We proceed this way because consistency and reachability are more conveniently defined in terms of a deduction system, while duality is a global property that involves pairs of peer endpoints, which may be (and usually are) located in disjoint regions of the heap.

Table 4. Well-formedness rules for the heap

(T-MEM EMPTY)
$$\emptyset \Vdash \emptyset$$

(T-MEM OPEN)
$$a : *\bullet \Vdash a \mapsto b$$

(T-MEM CELL)
$$\frac{b : t \Vdash \mu}{a : *t \Vdash \mu, a \mapsto b}$$

(T-MEM SPLIT)
$$\frac{\Delta_1 \Vdash \mu_1 \qquad \Delta_2 \Vdash \mu_2}{\Delta_1, \Delta_2 \Vdash \mu_1, \mu_2}$$

(T-MEM ENDPOINT)
$$\frac{\Sigma \vdash \mathtt{m}_i : \langle \tilde{t}_i \rangle \ ^{(i=1..n)} \qquad \{\tilde{c}_i : \tilde{t}_i\}_{i=1..n} \Vdash \mu \qquad \mathrm{tail}(T, \mathtt{m}_1 \cdots \mathtt{m}_n) \text{ is defined}}{a : T \Vdash \mu, a \mapsto [b, \mathtt{m}_1\langle \tilde{c}_1 \rangle :: \cdots :: \mathtt{m}_n \langle \tilde{c}_n \rangle]}$$

The relation $\Vdash$ is defined in Table 4. In the derivation of a judgment $\Delta \Vdash \mu$ both the context Δ and the heap μ are treated linearly, implying that μ should contain all and only the objects that are reachable from the roots in Δ. Axiom (T-MEM EMPTY) states that the empty heap is well formed only with respect to the empty context. Axiom (T-MEM OPEN) states that the heap $a \mapsto b$ is well formed with respect to the context $a : *\bullet$ regardless of what b is associated with. Since the type system for processes will prevent access to b, the heap region rooted at b is not accessible if a is typed by $*\bullet$. Rule (T-MEM CELL) states that the heap containing $a \mapsto b$ is well formed with respect to the context $a : *t$ if it is well formed with respect to the context $b : t$.

Rule (T-MEM SPLIT) allows to check well formedness of a compound heap μ_1, μ_2 by means of a compound context Δ_1, Δ_2. Rule (T-MEM ENDPOINT) states that the heap $a \mapsto [b, q]$ is well formed with respect to the context $a : T$, provided that the heap rooted at the parameters of the messages in q is well formed with respect to the context determined by the tags of the messages, and that T does indeed specify that the messages in q are expected to be received *in the order in which they occur in* q. The last check is enforced by means of a partial function $\mathsf{tail}(T, \mathtt{m}_1 \cdots \mathtt{m}_n)$, which is defined by induction on n as follows:

$$\mathsf{tail}(T, \varepsilon) = T \qquad \frac{k \in I \qquad \mathsf{tail}(T_k, \tilde{\mathtt{m}}) = S}{\mathsf{tail}(?\{\mathtt{m}_i.T_i\}_{i \in I}, \mathtt{m}_k \tilde{\mathtt{m}}) = S}$$

We will use tail again to enforce an even stronger relation between the endpoint types of peer endpoints. For the time being, observe that if q is not empty, then T must begin with as many external choices as the number of messages in the queue. Therefore, in a well-formed heap every endpoint associated with an endpoint type **end** or $!\{\mathtt{m}_i.T_i\}_{i \in I}$ must have an empty queue.

Although the context Δ in a judgment $\Delta \Vdash \mu$ only specifies type associations for the roots of μ it will occasionally be useful to access the type associations for all of the pointers in $\mathsf{dom}(\mu)$. To this purpose, we define a closure operator over contexts.

Definition 3.1 (Context closure). *Let $\Delta \Vdash \mu$. The* closure *of Δ with respect μ, denoted by $[\Delta; \mu]$, is the set of all the judgments $a : t$ that occur in the derivation of $\Delta \Vdash \mu$.*

The following result provides us with a sanity check on the closure of a context: when $\Delta \Vdash \mu$ the closure of Δ with respect to μ contains the associations for all the objects allocated in μ and every allocated object is reachable from $\mathsf{dom}(\Delta)$.

Proposition 3.1. *If $\Delta \Vdash \mu$, then* $\mathsf{dom}(\mu) = \mathsf{dom}([\Delta; \mu]) \subseteq \mathsf{reach}(\mathsf{dom}(\Delta), \mu)$.

We are now ready to complete the definition of well-typed heap, by imposing additional constraints on peer endpoints.

Definition 3.2 (Well-typed heap). *We say that μ is* well typed *under Δ, notation $\Delta \vdash \mu$, if $\Delta \Vdash \mu$ and for every $a \mapsto [b, \mathtt{m}_1\langle \tilde{c}_1 \rangle :: \cdots :: \mathtt{m}_n\langle \tilde{c}_n \rangle] \in \mu$ we have:*

1. $b \mapsto [a, \mathtt{m}'_1\langle \tilde{c}'_1 \rangle :: \cdots :: \mathtt{m}'_m\langle \tilde{c}'_m \rangle] \in \mu$;
2. $\min\{n, m\} = 0$;
3. $\mathsf{tail}(T, \mathtt{m}_1 \cdots \mathtt{m}_n) = \overline{\mathsf{tail}(S, \mathtt{m}'_1 \cdots \mathtt{m}'_m)}$ *where $a : T \in [\Delta; \mu]$ and $b : S \in [\Delta; \mu]$.*

Item (1) requires that, for every endpoint $a \in \mathsf{dom}(\mu)$, its peer is also in $\mathsf{dom}(\mu)$. Item (2) states that at most one of the queues of peer endpoints can contain messages. Item (3) states that the residual endpoint types associated with peer endpoints after removing the prefixes determined by the tags of the messages in the corresponding queues must be dual. Observe that, by rule (T-MEM ENDPOINT), both $\mathsf{tail}(T, \mathtt{m}_1 \cdots \mathtt{m}_n)$ and $\mathsf{tail}(S, \mathtt{m}'_1 \cdots \mathtt{m}'_m)$ are defined and that duality is an involution ($\overline{\overline{T}} = T$), therefore the items hold for both peers of a channel.

Table 5. Typing rules for processes

(T-IDLE)
$$\Gamma;\emptyset \vdash \mathbf{0}$$

(T-VAR)
$$\Gamma,\{X \mapsto \Delta\};\Delta \vdash X$$

(T-FREE CELL)
$$\Gamma; u : *\bullet \vdash \mathbf{free}(u)$$

(T-FREE ENDPOINT)
$$\Gamma; u : \mathbf{end} \vdash \mathbf{free}(u)$$

(T-OPEN)
$$\frac{\Gamma;\Delta, a : T, b : \overline{T} \vdash P}{\Gamma;\Delta \vdash \mathbf{open}(a,b).P}$$

(T-CELL)
$$\frac{\Gamma;\Delta, a : *t \vdash P}{\Gamma;\Delta, u : t \vdash \mathbf{cell}(a,u).P}$$

(T-EXPOSE)
$$\frac{\Gamma;\Delta, u : *\bullet, x : t \vdash P}{\Gamma;\Delta, u : *t \vdash \mathbf{expose}(u,x).P}$$

(T-REC)
$$\frac{\Gamma,\{X \mapsto \Delta\};\Delta \vdash P \qquad \mathrm{dom}(\Delta) = \mathrm{fn}(P)}{\Gamma;\Delta \vdash \mathbf{rec}\, X.P}$$

(T-UNEXPOSE)
$$\frac{\Gamma;\Delta, u : *t \vdash P}{\Gamma;\Delta, u : *\bullet, v : t \vdash \mathbf{unexpose}(u,v).P}$$

(T-CHOICE)
$$\frac{\Gamma;\Delta \vdash P \qquad \Gamma;\Delta \vdash Q}{\Gamma;\Delta \vdash P \oplus Q}$$

(T-SEND)
$$\frac{k \in I \qquad \Sigma \vdash \mathtt{m}_k : \langle \tilde{t} \rangle \qquad \Gamma;\Delta, u : T_k \vdash P}{\Gamma;\Delta, u : !\{\mathtt{m}_i.T_i\}_{i\in I}, \tilde{v} : \tilde{t} \vdash u!\mathtt{m}_k\langle \tilde{v} \rangle.P}$$

(T-PAR)
$$\frac{\Gamma;\Delta_1 \vdash P \qquad \Gamma;\Delta_2 \vdash Q}{\Gamma;\Delta_1,\Delta_2 \vdash P \mid Q}$$

(T-RECEIVE)
$$\frac{\Sigma \vdash \mathtt{m}_i : \langle \tilde{t}_i \rangle \ ^{(i\in I)} \qquad \Gamma;\Delta, u : T_i, \tilde{x}_i : \tilde{t}_i \vdash P_i \ ^{(i\in I)}}{\Gamma;\Delta, u : ?\{\mathtt{m}_i.T_i\}_{i\in I} \vdash \sum_{i\in I} u?\mathtt{m}_i(\tilde{x}_i).P_i}$$

Typing Processes. We now turn our attention to the typing rules for processes, which are inductively defined in Table 5. Judgments have the form $\Gamma;\Delta \vdash P$ where Δ is the same context we use for typing heaps. The additional context Γ is used for typing recursive processes and therefore plays a role in two rules only, (T-VAR) and (T-REC). The unusual premise $\mathrm{dom}(\Delta) = \mathrm{dom}(P)$ in rule (T-REC) enforces a weak form of contractivity on recursive processes. It states that **rec** $X.P$ is well typed under Δ only if P actually uses the names in $\mathrm{dom}(\Delta)$. Normally, divergent processes such as **rec** $X.X$ can be typed in every context. If this were the case, the process **open**(a,b).**rec** $X.X$, which leaks a and b, would be well typed. The idle process is well typed in the empty context only. As we have seen in the typing rules for the heap, the empty context can only be used for typing the empty heap, therefore rule (T-IDLE) says that the terminated process has no leaks. Rules (T-FREE CELL) and (T-FREE ENDPOINT) state that a process **free**(u) is well typed provided that u is the only name owned by the process and that it corresponds to either an exposed cell (with type $*\bullet$) or to an endpoint on which no further interaction is possible (with type **end**). Rules (T-OPEN) and (T-CELL) are used for respectively typing the creation of a new channel and of a new cell. In both cases the newly created pointers are visible in the continuation; in (T-OPEN) the rule guesses two dual endpoint types that, associated with the two endpoints, permits to type check the continuation; in (T-CELL), the name used for the cell initialization is discharged from the context and becomes unavailable in the continuation, unless the cell is exposed. Rules (T-CHOICE) and (T-PAR) are standard. Rule (T-SEND) states that a process $u!\mathtt{m}\langle \tilde{v} \rangle.P$ is well typed if u is associated with an endpoint type that permits the output of $\mathtt{m}$-tagged messages and the parameters of the message have the expected type as specified in the global context Σ. Also, the continuation P must be well typed in a context where the parameters have been discharged and the endpoint u is typed according to the endpoint type determined by the tag of the message. Rule (T-RECEIVE) deals with inputs: a process waiting for a message from an endpoint $a : ?\{\mathtt{m}_i.T_i\}_{i\in I}$ is well typed if it can deal with any $\mathtt{m}_i$-tagged message. The continuation process may use the endpoint according to the endpoint type T_i and can access the message's parameters. Rule (T-EXPOSE) states that the exposure of a cell is well typed only if the cell has not already been exposed (its type is $*t$ for some t and not $*\bullet$) and if the continuation correctly uses its content and the exposed cell itself. Rule (T-UNEXPOSE) shows that an exposed cell can be assigned any pointer that the process owns. Observe that the resulting type of the cell may differ from the one the cell had before exposure. This may happen for two reasons: either because the cell is assigned a different content having a different type, or because the type of the cell's content has changed, even if the content itself has not (endpoint types change over time, even though the pointer to them stays the same).

It turns out that the function `foo` in the introduction (properly encoded in CoreSing#) would be well typed in the empty context, as shown by the derivation below:

$$\dfrac{\dfrac{\Sigma \vdash \mathtt{m} : \langle ?\mathtt{m}.\mathbf{end}\rangle \qquad \dfrac{}{a : \mathbf{end} \vdash \mathbf{free}(a)}\ (\text{T-FREE ENDPOINT})}{a : !\mathtt{m}.\mathbf{end}, b : ?\mathtt{m}.\mathbf{end} \vdash a!\mathtt{m}\langle b\rangle.\mathbf{free}(a)}\ (\text{T-SEND})}{\vdash \mathbf{open}(a,b).a!\mathtt{m}\langle b\rangle.\mathbf{free}(a)}\ (\text{T-OPEN})$$

As we have anticipated, this apparently harmless process produces a leak:

$$(\emptyset; \mathbf{open}(a,b).a!\mathtt{m}\langle b\rangle.\mathbf{free}(a)) \Rightarrow (a \mapsto [b,\varepsilon], b \mapsto [a,\mathtt{m}\langle b\rangle]; \mathbf{free}(a))$$

The endpoint b is no longer accessible by the process nor has it been properly deallocated. Furthermore, even if there were a mechanism for accessing b (for example, by peeking into the endpoint located at a) and for reading the message from b's queue, this would be catastrophic from the point of view of types: the actual type of b is $?\mathtt{m}.\mathbf{end}$, but as we remove the message from its queue it turns to **end**. The b in the message, however, would maintain the "old" type $?\mathtt{m}.\mathbf{end}$, thus the actual and the inferred types for b would no longer coincide, with potentially catastrophic consequences. A closer look at the heap in the reduction above reveals that the problem lies in the cycle involving b: it is as if the $b \mapsto [a,\mathtt{m}\langle b\rangle]$ region of the heap needs not be owned by any process because it "owns" itself. In summary, we should tighten our type system and make sure that no cycle involving endpoint queues is created in the heap. In the process above this problem would not be too hard to detect, as the fact that a and b are peer endpoints is apparent from the syntax of the process. In general, however, detecting whether an endpoint is sent over its peer requires a runtime check, which is not a viable solution as we aim at static verification of processes.

An alternative approach for attacking the problem which does not require any change to the typing rules in Table 5 stems from the observation that infinite values (the endpoint located at b above fits well in this category) usually inhabit recursive types. The type of b is in fact recursive, although only implicitly: we have $b : T$ where $T : ?\mathtt{m}.\mathbf{end}$ and $\Sigma \vdash \mathtt{m} : \langle T\rangle$. Forbidding this implicit recursion would prevent the creation of cycles in the heap, but it would also unnecessarily restrict our language. For example, the endpoint type $S = !\mathtt{m}'.\mathbf{end}$ where $\Sigma \vdash \mathtt{m}' : \langle S\rangle$ would never cause the creation of cycles in the heap, even though it is implicitly recursive. The reason is that, if we are sending an endpoint $b : S$ over $a : S$, then its peer endpoint must have the dual type $?\mathtt{m}'.\textbf{end}$ and therefore must be different from a. In general, cycles in the heap originate from non-empty queues, and non-empty queues are always associated with endpoints whose type begins with an external choice. The idea then is to give each endpoint type a *weight* that estimates the length of any chain of pointers originating from the queue. Endpoint types **end** and internal choices will always have a null weight, since the well formedness conditions for the heap already guarantee emptiness of the queues of the endpoints with these types.

The weight of a type is formally defined thus:

Definition 3.3 (Weight). *Let $\Downarrow$ be the largest relation such that $t \Downarrow n$ implies either:*

- $t = *\bullet$ *or* $t = \textbf{end}$ *or* $t = !\{\mathtt{m}_i.T_i\}_{i\in I}$, *or*
- $t = *s$ *and* $s \Downarrow n$, *or*
- $t = \textbf{rec}\, X.T$ *and* $T\{t/X\} \Downarrow n$, *or*
- $t = ?\{\mathtt{m}_i.T_i\}_{i\in I}$ *and* $n > 0$ *and* $\Sigma \vdash \mathtt{m}_i : \langle s_1, \dots, s_n\rangle$ *implies* $s_j \Downarrow n-1$, *and* $T_i \Downarrow n$ *for every* $i \in I$.

We define the weight *of a type t as* $\|t\| = \min\{n \in \mathbb{N} \cup \{\infty\} \mid t \Downarrow n\}$.

Intuitively, $t \Downarrow n$ means that the weight of t is bounded by n, hence $\|t\|$ is the least of t's bounds. In the examples we have discussed above, we have $\|T\| = \infty$ and $\|S\| = 0$. In the following we let $\|\tilde{t}\| = \max_{s\in\tilde{t}} \|s\|$. Observe that the weight of an endpoint type may change over time, as the endpoint type changes. For example $\|!\mathtt{m}.?\mathtt{m}.\textbf{end}\| = 0$ and $\|?\mathtt{m}.\textbf{end}\| = 1$ assuming $\Sigma \vdash \mathtt{m} : \langle\rangle$. For our purposes, the following property is particularly important:

Proposition 3.2. *Let* $\Sigma \vdash \mathtt{m}_i : \langle \tilde{t}_i \rangle$. *Then* $\max_{i\in I} \|\tilde{t}_i\| < \|?\{\mathtt{m}_i.T_i\}_{i\in I}\|$.

The reason why the restriction to types with finite weight is sufficient for proving the soundness of the type system lies in the following proposition relating the reachability of pointers and the weights of the corresponding types.

Proposition 3.3. *Let* $a : t \Vdash \mu$ *and* $b : s \in [a : t; \mu]$. *Then* $\|s\| \leq \|t\|$.

Proposition 3.3 is useful for deducing that some pointer b is not reachable from a. If $a : t \Vdash \mu$ and we know that b must be associated with some type s such that $\|t\| < \|s\|$, then we can conclude $b \notin \mathrm{dom}([a : t; \mu])$. In the specific case of endpoints, suppose we are type checking a process $c!\mathtt{m}\langle a\rangle.\mathbf{0}$ where $a : t$. Clearly c must be associated with some endpoint type of the form $!\{\mathtt{m}_i.T_i\}_{i\in I}$ and its peer, say b, with the corresponding dual endpoint type $s = ?\{\mathtt{m}_i.\overline{T}_i\}_{i\in I}$. From Proposition 3.2 we deduce that $\|t\| < \|s\|$, therefore we can conclude $a \neq b$ by Proposition 3.3. In particular, we are not enqueueing b into its own queue.

We should remark that restricting endpoint types so that they have finite weight does not necessarily guarantee that the heap is free of cycles. For instance, both the following partially specified processes create cycles in the heap:

$$P_1 \stackrel{\text{def}}{=} \textbf{open}(a,b).\textbf{cell}(c,b).\textbf{expose}(c,x).a!\mathtt{m}\langle c\rangle.Q_1$$
$$P_2 \stackrel{\text{def}}{=} \textbf{open}(a,b).\textbf{cell}(c,a).\textbf{cell}(d,c).\textbf{expose}(d,x).\textbf{expose}(x,y).\textbf{unexpose}(x,d).Q_2$$

and the reader may easily verify that it is possible to find appropriate Q_1 and Q_2 such that P_1 and P_2 are closed and well typed. The cycles created in these examples are harmless because the exposed cell type $*\bullet$ is a boundary which processes cannot trespass.

We can now present the subject reduction theorem followed by the soundness of the type system. Subject reduction is slightly non-standard, in the sense that types in the context may change as the process reduces. This is common in session type theories, since session types are behavioral types. In our case, also cell types can change (from $*t$ to $*\bullet$ and vice-versa). In addition, we need to type heaps as well as processes, and we write $\Delta \vdash (\mu;P)$ when $\Delta \vdash \mu$ and $\Delta \vdash P$.

Theorem 3.1 (Subject reduction). *Let* $\Delta \vdash (\mu;P)$ *and* $(\mu;P) \to (\mu';P')$. *Then* $\Delta' \vdash (\mu';P')$ *for some* Δ'.

In the statement of Theorem 3.1 we content ourselves of finding an appropriate context Δ' for typing the reduced process correctly as this is all one needs for proving the soundness of the type system. However, the proof of Theorem 3.1 necessarily relies on a stronger statement showing how Δ' is derived from Δ. Technically the most difficult part of the proof deals with regions of the heap that change owner: when a process $P_1 \mid P_2$ reduces because P_1 sends a message, the parameters of the message may transfer to the region of the heap owned by P_2. Thus, even though the context used for typing P_2 does not change (it is P_1 that reduces), the proof that the heap owned by P_2 is still well formed may change significantly. The finite-weight restriction on session types plays a crucial role to ensure that the new heap is well formed.

Theorem 3.2 (Soundness). *If* $\vdash P$, *then* P *is well behaved.*

We conclude this section with two remarks. The first one is that item (4) in Definition 2.2 is weaker than deadlock freedom. For example, the process

$$\mathbf{open}(a,b).a?\mathtt{m}().b!\mathtt{m}\langle\rangle.(\mathbf{free}(a) \mid \mathbf{free}(b))$$

is well typed assuming $a : ?\mathtt{m}.\mathbf{end}$ and $b : !\mathtt{m}.\mathbf{end}$ where $\Sigma \vdash \mathtt{m} : \langle\rangle$. This process deadlocks after the creation of the two endpoints, because it attempts at reading from endpoint a before any message is sent on its peer b. Incidentally, the example above shows that it is possible to have a deadlock also when only one channel is created.

The second remark regards the expressiveness of our framework, and in particular the possible limitations due to the finite-weight restriction we impose on types. The following example shows how to work around this restriction in a scenario where the use of types with infinite weight would be natural (a similar workaround was suggested in [6]).

Example 3.1 (Linear lists). We can represent a linear list as an endpoint from which one of two kinds of messages can be received: a `nil`-tagged message indicates that the list is empty; a `cons`-tagged message indicates that the list has at least one element, and the parameters of the message are the head of the list and its tail, which is itself a list. Reading a message from the endpoint corresponds to deconstructing the list and the tag-based dispatching of messages implements pattern matching. According to this intuition, the type of lists with elements of type t would be encoded as

$\mathtt{List}(t) = ?\{\mathtt{nil}.\mathbf{end}, \mathtt{cons}_t.\mathbf{end}\}$ where $\Sigma \vdash \mathtt{nil} : \langle\rangle$ and $\Sigma \vdash \mathtt{cons}_t : \langle t, \mathtt{List}(t)\rangle$, except that in this case we have $\|\mathtt{List}(t)\| = \infty$. To fix this, we require users of the list to signal the imminent deconstruction by sending a dummy, use-tagged message on the endpoint. This corresponds to defining $\mathtt{List}(t) = !\mathtt{use}.?\{\mathtt{nil}.\mathbf{end}, \mathtt{cons}_t.\mathbf{end}\}$ where $\Sigma \vdash \mathtt{use} : \langle\rangle$. One can now define syntactic sugar for creating and deconstructing linear lists, thus:

$$
\begin{array}{rcl}
\mathtt{let}\ a = \mathtt{nil}\ \mathtt{in}\ P & \stackrel{\text{def}}{=} & \mathbf{open}(a,b).(P \mid b?\mathtt{use}().b!\mathtt{nil}\langle\rangle.\mathbf{free}(b)) \\
\mathtt{let}\ a = \mathtt{cons}_t\langle u,v\rangle\ \mathtt{in}\ P & \stackrel{\text{def}}{=} & \mathbf{open}(a,b).(P \mid b?\mathtt{use}().b!\mathtt{cons}_t\langle u,v\rangle.\mathbf{free}(b)) \\
\mathtt{match}\ u\ \mathtt{with} & \stackrel{\text{def}}{=} & u!\mathtt{use}\langle\rangle. \\
\mathtt{nil} \to P & & \quad (\ u?\mathtt{nil}().(\mathbf{free}(u) \mid P) \\
\mathtt{cons}_t(x,y) \to Q & & \quad\ + u?\mathtt{cons}_t(x,y).(\mathbf{free}(u) \mid Q)\ )
\end{array}
$$

The interested reader can verify that these processes are well typed . ■

4 Extensions

Non-linear usage of endpoints in output actions. An interesting feature of [14] is the possibility of sending an endpoint over itself. In our setting, this would be modeled as a process $P = u!\mathtt{m}\langle u\rangle.Q$ for some tag $\mathtt{m}$ with a parameter of the appropriate type. In [14] this feature actually plays a fundamental role: there the two endpoints of a channel must be closed simultaneously, hence it is natural to have a mechanism that reunites two peer endpoints by receiving one from the other. The process P above fails to type check according to the rules described in Section 3 because the endpoint u is used non-linearly both as the endpoint on which the communication occurs and as the message parameter. It is possible to relax the type system by adding the following rule:

$$
\text{(T-SELF SEND)}\quad
\frac{k \in I \qquad \Sigma \vdash \mathtt{m}_k : \langle \tilde{t}_1, T_k, \tilde{t}_2\rangle \qquad \Gamma;\Delta \vdash P}{\Gamma;\Delta, u : !\{\mathtt{m}_i.T_i\}_{i\in I}, \tilde{v}_1 : \tilde{t}_1, \tilde{v}_2 : \tilde{t}_2 \vdash u!\mathtt{m}_k\langle \tilde{v}_1, u, \tilde{v}_2\rangle.P}
$$

There are two differences with respect to (T-SEND), all of which regard the endpoint u: first of all, u occurs twice, as the endpoint on which the message is sent as well as in the parameters of the message itself, possibly preceded and followed by more parameters. The two occurrences of u are treated differently with respect to types: the parameter u is preventively given type T_k, which corresponds to the correct type of u *after* the sending action has occurred. This is safe because, by the time the message is received, the send action has already completed. The second difference is that the endpoint u is no longer available in the continuation P, since it has been sent away.

Rule (T-SELF SEND) cannot compromise well formedness of the heap, in the sense that no cycles can be created even though the rule appears to embed some circularity. The reason is that, by sending an endpoint over itself, we can rest assured that the endpoint will be enqueued in the queue of a *different* endpoint, namely its peer.

Subtyping. The most common way to increase flexibility of a type system is to introduce a *subtyping* relation $\leqslant$ that establishes an (asymmetric) compatibility between different types: any value of type t can be safely used where a value of type s is expected when $t \leqslant s$. In the flourishing literature on session types several notions of subtyping relations have been investigated [5,2,13,10]. Here we show how to extend our model with a subtyping relation which is a straightforward adaptation of the subtyping defined in [5].

Definition 4.1 (Subtyping relation). *The* subtyping relation $\leqslant$ *is the largest relation such that* $t \leqslant s$ *implies:*

1. $t = *\bullet$ *implies* $s = *\bullet$;
2. $t = *t'$ *implies* $s = *s'$ *and* $t' \leqslant s'$;
3. $t = \mathbf{end}$ *implies* $s = \mathbf{end}$;
4. $t = !\{\mathtt{m}_i.T_i\}_{i\in I}$ *implies* $s = !\{\mathtt{m}_j.S_j\}_{j\in J}$ *with* $J \subseteq I$ *and* $T_j \leqslant S_j$ *for every* $j \in J$;
5. $t = ?\{\mathtt{m}_i.T_i\}_{i\in I}$ *implies* $s = ?\{\mathtt{m}_j.S_j\}_{j\in J}$ *with* $I \subseteq J$ *and* $T_i \leqslant S_i$ *for every* $i \in I$.

The key point for understanding $\leqslant$ is to focus on the concept of endpoint use: using an endpoint with type **end** means closing it; using an endpoint with type $!\{\mathtt{m}_i.T_i\}_{i\in I}$ means sending a message with tag $\mathtt{m}_k$ for some $k \in I$ and using the endpoint according to T_k thereafter; using an endpoint with type $?\{\mathtt{m}_i.T_i\}_{i\in I}$ means being ready to receive any message with tag $\mathtt{m}_i$ for every $i \in I$ and using the endpoint according to T_k thereafter. This leads to the invariance of **end**, contravariance of internal choice, and covariance of external choice in Definition 4.1. For instance, it is safe to use an endpoint $u : !\{\mathtt{m}_i.T_i\}_{i\in I\cup J}$ where $v : !\{\mathtt{m}_i.T_i\}_{i\in I}$ is expected because the process using v will send a message with tag $\mathtt{m}_k$ for some $k \in I$. Then $k \in I \cup J$, hence the process is using u correctly according with its type. It may look surprising that $\leqslant$ is covariant with respect to cell types, namely that $t \leqslant s$ implies $*t \leqslant *s$. This relation is sound in our setting because access to the content of a cell is disciplined by means of open cell types: the type $*t$ only states the type of the values that can be *read* from the cell, not the type of the values that can be *written* in the cell.

Using this subtyping relation, we can relax the type system with a weaker rule for output actions, along with a subsumption rule:

$$\text{(T-SEND')}\ \frac{\Sigma \vdash \mathtt{m} : \langle \tilde{s} \rangle \qquad \tilde{t} \leqslant \tilde{s} \qquad \Gamma; \Delta, u : T \vdash P}{\Gamma; \Delta, u : !\mathtt{m}.T, \tilde{v} : \tilde{t} \vdash u!\mathtt{m}\langle \tilde{v} \rangle.P} \qquad \text{(T-SUB)}\ \frac{\Gamma; \Delta, u : S \vdash P \qquad T \leqslant S}{\Gamma; \Delta, u : T \vdash P}$$

In rule (T-SEND') the endpoint type associated with u precisely states the type of message that is sent and the actual parameters of the message are allowed to have a subtype of the expected type ($\tilde{t} \leqslant \tilde{s}$ is the point-wise extension of $\leqslant$ to tuples of types). Rule (T-SUB) is a bit unusual, since it allows to have a smaller type in the conclusion. This can be explained as the fact that the typing rules do not assign types to processes, and the subtyping relation changes the type of a name in the context.

We have seen in Section 3 that type weights play a crucial role in ensuring that the type theory is sound. In principle, since it is the (expected) type of the parameters of a message that determines the weight of the endpoint type where the message tag occurs, one might fear that subtyping could be exploited for circumventing the finiteness restriction we impose on the weight of types. This is not the case, and the rationale is remarkably simple. As the following proposition states, the weight of types changes in accordance with the subtyping relation, therefore any application of subtyping can only *decrease* the actual weight of types.

Proposition 4.1. $t \leqslant s$ *implies* $\|t\| \leq \|s\|$.

According to Definition 4.1, being a subtype does not necessarily mean being a "simpler" type. For example, we have $!\{\mathtt{m}_1.T_1, \mathtt{m}_2.T_2\} \leqslant !\mathtt{m}_1.T_1$. Yet, the weight of internal choices is zero, regardless of the number of (and the tags occurring in) branches. Had we assigned weights to endpoint types merely looking at the message tags occurring in them, as we initially suggested in Section 3, Proposition 4.1 would not hold.

Unrestricted closing of endpoints. A difference between Sing# and CoreSing# is that in the former language endpoints can be closed at any time while in CoreSing# this can only happen when their endpoint type is **end**. The restricted viewpoint we have adopted is consistent with the philosophy of session types, where the type of an endpoint describes not only the capabilities of a channel, but also the obligations that a process owning that channel is bound to. Sing# is more permissive about the closing of endpoints because, in a controlled environment such as Singularity, it might be desirable to abruptly terminate communications under exceptional circumstances.

If we relax the obligation to send messages on an endpoint when its type says so, we might introduce new deadlocks. Therefore we need to devise appropriate mechanisms for notifying processes that are blocked on input operations on closed endpoints and for spawning dedicated handlers when these situations occur. Closed endpoints are easily detectable in CoreSing# because of persistent **free**(a) processes. Therefore, we only need to annotate input processes thus

$$P \ ::= \ \cdots \ \mid \ \Sigma_{i \in I}\, u?\mathtt{m}_i(\tilde{x}_i).P_i \ \mathtt{or}\ P \ \mid \ \cdots$$

by adding a *handler* branch '$\cdots$ or P' which is selected if the queue associated with u is empty and the peer endpoint of u has been closed. This behavior is formalized by rule (R-RECEIVE CLOSE) in Table 6. In the reduced process a **free**(a) term appears, meaning that the endpoint used for input cannot be used by the handler.

This is not enough to avoid deadlocks caused by prematurely closed endpoints, because the queue of a closed endpoint may contain messages that that have other endpoints as parameters. Since no process can access these messages anymore, we must properly close every endpoint occurring in the queue of a closed endpoint. To this aim we enrich the reduction relation with rule (R-COLLECT), which formalizes a basic step of the garbage collector we have just described: any message $\mathtt{m}\langle\tilde{c}\rangle$ in the queue of a closed endpoint is dequeued and deallocated by a process **collect**$(\tilde{c} : \tilde{t})$ which is inductively defined at the bottom of Table 6. The process uses information provided by the type system to navigate through the structure of the objects to be deallocated. This will possibly fire rules (R-RECEIVE CLOSE) and (R-COLLECT) recursively.

Table 7 presents the revised typing rules for handling the unrestricted closing of endpoints. It is now possible to prove that well-typed processes are well behaved and that, in addition, if a process is blocked waiting for a message on some endpoint a it is because the peer endpoint of a has not been closed.

Table 6. Garbage collector and additional reduction rules

Reduction rules

(R-RECEIVE CLOSE)
$(\mu, a \mapsto [b, \varepsilon]; \sum_{i \in I} a?\mathtt{m}_i(\tilde{x}_i).P_i \texttt{ or } Q \mid \mathsf{free}(b)) \rightarrow (\mu, a \mapsto [b, \varepsilon]; Q \mid \mathsf{free}(a) \mid \mathsf{free}(b))$

(R-COLLECT)
$$\frac{\Sigma \vdash \mathtt{m} : \langle \tilde{t} \rangle}{(\mu, a \mapsto [b, \mathtt{m}\langle \tilde{c} \rangle :: q]; \mathsf{free}(a)) \rightarrow (\mu, a \mapsto [b, q]; \mathsf{free}(a) \mid \mathsf{collect}(\tilde{c} : \tilde{t}))}$$

Garbage collector process

$$\begin{aligned} \mathsf{collect}(u : *\bullet) = \mathsf{collect}(u : T) &= \mathsf{free}(u) \\ \mathsf{collect}(u : *t) &= \mathsf{expose}(u, x).(\mathsf{free}(u) \mid \mathsf{collect}(x : t)) \\ \mathsf{collect}(u_1 : t_1, \dots, u_n : t_n) &= \mathsf{collect}(u_1 : t_1) \mid \cdots \mid \mathsf{collect}(u_n : t_n) \end{aligned}$$

Table 7. Updated typing rules for unrestricted endpoint closing

(T-FREE ENDPOINT')
$\Gamma; u : T \vdash \mathsf{free}(u)$

(T-RECEIVE')
$$\frac{\Sigma \vdash \mathtt{m}_i : \langle \tilde{t}_i \rangle \ ^{(i \in I)} \qquad \Gamma; \Delta, u : T_i, \tilde{x}_i : \tilde{t}_i \vdash P_i \ ^{(i \in I)} \qquad \Gamma; \Delta \vdash Q}{\Gamma; \Delta, u : ?\{\mathtt{m}_i.T_i\}_{i \in I} \vdash \sum_{i \in I} u?\mathtt{m}_i(\tilde{x}_i).P_i \texttt{ or } Q}$$

5 Conclusions

We have defined the static analysis for a calculus where processes communicate through the exchange of *pointers*. Verified processes are guaranteed to be free from memory faults, they do not leak memory, and do not fail on input actions. In this respect our work shares many objectives with [14], although our approach is *type-based*, whereas the one in [14] is *proof-based*. The proof-based approach relies on an expressive variant of separation logic and is therefore more general, in terms of properties of the heap that can be stated and verified. The type-based approach we have presented is tailored for guaranteeing the three properties above only, but it is simple to understand and efficient in practice (type checking and subtyping can be implemented in linear time).

Our type system has been inspired by session type theories, in a broad sense. The basic idea of session types, and of behavioral types in general, is that operating on a (linearly used) value may change its type, and thus the capabilities of that value thereafter. Endpoint types express the capabilities of endpoints, in terms of the type of messages that can be sent or received and in which order. Cell types and open cell types are, in a sense, behavioral types for (linear) heap cells: accessing the content of a cell changes its type from $*t$ to $*\bullet$; assigning the content of a cell does the inverse. In fact, it would be possible to encode cells and cell types in terms of endpoints and endpoint types, if only endpoint types were polymorphic.

The finite-weight restriction we impose on endpoint types is original to the best of our knowledge. Singularity restricts communications so that only endpoints in a *send-state*, those whose type begins with an internal choice, can be safely sent as messages.

The restriction is motivated by the implementation of ownership transfer in Singularity, where it is the sender's responsibility to explicitly tag sent messages with their new owner; therefore, a race can arise if the endpoint that the message is sent to changes owner (a detailed description can be found in [4]). We have shown that uncontrolled sending of endpoints may also produce memory leaks. Our finite-weight relaxes the send-state restriction, because endpoints in a send-state always have a null weight.

Acknowledgments. We are grateful to Lorenzo Bettini for discussions on the notion of memory leak, to Nobuko Yoshida for comments on an early version of this paper, and to the anonymous referees for the detailed and useful reviews.

References

1. Bettini, L., Coppo, M., D'Antoni, L., De Luca, M., Dezani-Ciancaglini, M., Yoshida, N.: Global Progress in Dynamically Interleaved Multiparty Sessions. In: van Breugel, F., Chechik, M. (eds.) CONCUR 2008. LNCS, vol. 5201, pp. 418–433. Springer, Heidelberg (2008)
2. Castagna, G., Dezani-Ciancaglini, M., Giachino, E., Padovani, L.: Foundations of session types. In: PPDP 2009, pp. 219–230. ACM, New York (2009)
3. Dezani-Ciancaglini, M., de Liguoro, U., Yoshida, N.: On Progress for Structured Communications. In: Barthe, G., Fournet, C. (eds.) TGC 2007 and FODO 2008. LNCS, vol. 4912, pp. 257–275. Springer, Heidelberg (2008)
4. Fähndrich, M., Aiken, M., Hawblitzel, C., Hodson, O., Hunt, G., Larus, J.R., Levi, S.: Language support for fast and reliable message-based communication in singularity os. In: EuroSys 2006, pp. 177–190. ACM, New York (2006)
5. Gay, S., Hole, M.: Subtyping for session types in the π-calculus. Acta Informatica 42(2-3), 191–225 (2005)
6. Gay, S., Vasconcelos, V.T.: Linear type theory for asynchronous session types. Journal of Functional Programming 20(01), 19–50 (2010)
7. Honda, K.: Types for dyadic interaction. In: Best, E. (ed.) CONCUR 1993. LNCS, vol. 715, pp. 509–523. Springer, Heidelberg (1993)
8. Honda, K., Vasconcelos, V.T., Kubo, M.: Language primitives and type disciplines for structured communication-based programming. In: Hankin, C. (ed.) ESOP 1998. LNCS, vol. 1381, pp. 122–138. Springer, Heidelberg (1998)
9. O'Hearn, P.W., Reynolds, J.C., Yang, H.: Local reasoning about programs that alter data structures. In: Fribourg, L. (ed.) CSL 2001 and EACSL 2001. LNCS, vol. 2142, pp. 1–19. Springer, Heidelberg (2001)
10. Padovani, L.: Session types at the mirror. EPTCS 12, 71–86 (2009)
11. Reynolds, J.C.: Separation logic: A logic for shared mutable data structures. In: LICS 2002, pp. 55–74. IEEE, Los Alamitos (2002)
12. Stengel, Z., Bultan, T.: Analyzing singularity channel contracts. In: ISSTA 2009, pp. 13–24. ACM, New York (2009)
13. Vasconcelos, V.T.: Fundamentals of session types. In: Bernardo, M., Padovani, L., Zavattaro, G. (eds.) SFM 2009. LNCS, vol. 5569, pp. 158–186. Springer, Heidelberg (2009)
14. Villard, J., Lozes, É., Calcagno, C.: Proving copyless message passing. In: Hu, Z. (ed.) APLAS 2009. LNCS, vol. 5904, pp. 194–209. Springer, Heidelberg (2009)
15. Villard, J., Lozes, É., Calcagno, C.: Tracking heaps that hop with heap-hop. In: Esparza, J., Majumdar, R. (eds.) TACAS 2010. LNCS, vol. 6015, pp. 275–279. Springer, Heidelberg (2010)
16. Walker, D., Gregory Morrisett, J.: Alias types for recursive data structures. In: Harper, R. (ed.) TIC 2000. LNCS, vol. 2071, pp. 177–206. Springer, Heidelberg (2001)

Measure Transformer Semantics for Bayesian Machine Learning

Johannes Borgström[1], Andrew D. Gordon[1], Michael Greenberg[2], James Margetson[1], and Jurgen Van Gael[1]

[1] Microsoft Research
[2] University of Pennsylvania

Abstract. The Bayesian approach to machine learning amounts to inferring posterior distributions of random variables from a probabilistic model of how the variables are related (that is, a prior distribution) and a set of observations of variables. There is a trend in machine learning towards expressing Bayesian models as probabilistic programs. As a foundation for this kind of programming, we propose a core functional calculus with primitives for sampling prior distributions and observing variables. We define combinators for measure transformers, based on theorems in measure theory, and use these to give a rigorous semantics to our core calculus. The original features of our semantics include its support for discrete, continuous, and hybrid measures, and, in particular, for observations of zero-probability events. We compile our core language to a small imperative language that has a straightforward semantics via factor graphs, data structures that enable many efficient inference algorithms. We use an existing inference engine for efficient approximate inference of posterior marginal distributions, treating thousands of observations per second for large instances of realistic models.

1 Introduction

In the past 15 years, statistical machine learning has unified many seemingly unrelated methods through the Bayesian paradigm. With a solid understanding of the theoretical foundations, advances in algorithms for inference, and numerous applications, the Bayesian paradigm is now the state of the art for learning from data. The theme of this paper is the idea of writing Bayesian models as probabilistic programs, which was pioneered by Koller et al. [16] and is recently gaining in popularity [31,30,9,4,14]. In particular, we draw inspiration from Csoft [37], an imperative language with an informal probabilistic semantics. Csoft is the native language of Infer.NET [25], a software library for Bayesian reasoning. A compiler turns Csoft programs into factor graphs [18], data structures that support efficient inference algorithms [15]. This paper borrows ideas from Csoft and extends them, placing the semantics on a firm footing.

Bayesian Models as Probabilistic Expressions. Consider a simplified form of TrueSkill [11], a large-scale online system for ranking computer gamers. There is a population of players, each assumed to have a skill, which is a real number that cannot be directly observed. We observe skills only indirectly via a series of matches. The problem is to infer the skills of players given the outcomes of the matches. In a Bayesian setting, we

G. Barthe (Ed.): ESOP 2011, LNCS 6602, pp. 77–96, 2011.
© Springer-Verlag Berlin Heidelberg 2011

represent our uncertain knowledge of the skills as continuous probability distributions. The following probabilistic expression models the situation by generating probability distributions for the players' skills, given three played games (observations).

```
// prior distributions, the hypothesis
let skill() = random (Gaussian(10.0,20.0))
let Alice,Bob,Cyd = skill(),skill(),skill()
// observe the evidence
let performance player = random (Gaussian(player,1.0))
observe (performance Alice > performance Bob) //Alice beats Bob
observe (performance Bob > performance Cyd) //Bob beats Cyd
observe (performance Alice > performance Cyd) //Alice beats Cyd
// return the skills
Alice,Bob,Cyd
```

A run of this expression goes as follows. We sample the skills of the three players from the *prior distribution* **Gaussian**(10.0, 20.0). Such a distribution can be pictured as a bell curve centred on 10.0, and gradually tailing off at a rate given by the *variance*, here 20.0. Sampling from such a distribution is a randomized operation that returns a real number, most likely close to the mean. For each match, the run continues by sampling an individual performance for each of the two players. Each performance is centred on the skill of a player, with low variance, making the performance closely correlated with but not identical to the skill. We then observe that the winner's performance is greater than the loser's. An *observation* **observe** M always returns (), but represents a constraint that M must hold. A whole run is valid if all encountered observations are true. The run terminates by returning the three skills.

A classic computational method to learn the posterior distribution of each of the skills is by Monte Carlo sampling [21]. We run the expression many times, but keep just the valid runs—the ones where the sampled skills correspond to the observed outcomes. We then compute the means of the resulting skills by applying standard statistical formulas. In the example above, the *posterior distribution* of the returned skills has moved so that the mean of Alice's skill is greater than Bob's, which is greater than Cyd's.

Deterministic algorithms based on factor graphs [18,15] are an efficient alternative to Monte Carlo sampling. To the best of our knowledge, all prior inference techniques for probabilistic languages, apart from Csoft and recent versions of IBAL [32], are based on nondeterministic inference using some form of Monte Carlo sampling. The benefit of using factor graphs in Csoft is to support deterministic but approximative inference algorithms, which are known to be significantly more efficient than sampling methods, where applicable.

Observations with zero probability arise commonly in Bayesian models. For example, in the model above, a drawn game would be modelled as the performance of two players being observed to be equal. Since the performances are randomly drawn from a continuous distribution, the probability of them actually being equal is zero, so we would not expect to see *any* valid runs in a Monte Carlo simulation. (To use Monte Carlo methods, one must instead write that the absolute difference between two drawn performances is less than some small ε.) However, our semantics based on measure theory makes sense of such observations, and corresponds to inference as achieved by algorithms on factor graphs.

Plan of the Paper. We propose Fun:

- Fun is a functional language for Bayesian models with primitives for probabilistic sampling and observations (Section 2).
- Fun has a rigorous probabilistic semantics as measure transformers (Section 3).
- Fun has an efficient implementation: our system compiles Fun to Imp (Section 4), a subset of Csoft, and then relies on Infer.NET (Section 5).

Our main contribution is a framework for finite measure transformer semantics, which supports discrete measures, continuous measures, and mixtures of the two, and also supports observations of zero probability events.

As a substantial application, we supply measure transformer semantics for Fun, Imp, and factor graphs, and use the semantics to verify the translations in our compiler. Theorem 2 establishes the correctness of the translation from Fun to Imp and the factor graph semantics of Imp.

We designed Fun to be a subset of the F# dialect of ML [36], for implementation convenience: F# reflection allows easy access to the abstract syntax of a program. All the examples in the paper have been executed with our system, described in Section 5.

We end the paper with a description of related work (Section 6) and some concluding remarks (Section 7). A companion technical report [5] includes: detailed proofs; extensions of Fun, Imp, and our factor graph notations with array types suitable for inference on large datasets; listings of examples including versions of large-scale algorithms; and a description, including performance numbers, of our practical implementation of a compiler from Fun to Imp, and a backend based on Infer.NET.

2 Bayesian Models as Probabilistic Expressions

We present a core calculus, Fun, for Bayesian reasoning via probabilistic functional programming with observations.

2.1 Syntax, Informal Semantics, and Bayesian Reading

Expressions are strongly typed, with types t built up from base scalar types b and pair types. We let c range over constant data of scalar type, n over integers and r over real numbers. We write $\mathrm{ty}(c) = t$ to mean that constant c has type t. For each base type b, we define a *zero element* 0_b. We have arithmetic and Boolean operations on base types.

Types, Constant Data, and Zero Elements:

$a,b ::= \mathbf{bool} \mid \mathbf{int} \mid \mathbf{real}$	Base types
$t ::= \mathbf{unit} \mid b \mid (t_1 * t_2)$	Compound types

$\mathrm{ty}(()) = \mathbf{unit} \quad \mathrm{ty}(\mathbf{true}) = \mathrm{ty}(\mathbf{false}) = \mathbf{bool} \quad \mathrm{ty}(n) = \mathbf{int} \quad \mathrm{ty}(r) = \mathbf{real}$

$0_{\mathbf{bool}} = \mathbf{true} \qquad 0_{\mathbf{int}} = 0 \qquad 0_{\mathbf{real}} = 0.0$

Signatures of Arithmetic and Logical Operators: $\otimes : b_1, b_2 \rightarrow b_3$

$\&\&, ||, =$: **bool**, **bool** $\rightarrow$ **bool** $\quad >, =$: **int**, **int** $\rightarrow$ **bool**
$+, -, *$: **int**, **int** $\rightarrow$ **int** $\quad >$: **real**, **real** $\rightarrow$ **bool** $\quad +, -, *$: **real**, **real** $\rightarrow$ **real**

We have several standard probability distributions as primitive: $D : t \rightarrow u$ takes parameters in t and yields a random value in u.

Signatures of Distributions: $D : (x_1 : b_1 * \cdots * x_n : b_n) \rightarrow b$

Bernoulli : (success : **real**) $\rightarrow$ **bool**
Binomial : (trials : **int** $*$ success : **real**) $\rightarrow$ **int**
Poisson : (rate : **real**) $\rightarrow$ **int**
DiscreteUniform : (max : **int**) $\rightarrow$ **int**
Gaussian : (mean : **real** $*$ variance : **real**) $\rightarrow$ **real**
Beta : (a : **real** $*$ b : **real**) $\rightarrow$ **real**
Gamma : (shape : **real** $*$ scale : **real**) $\rightarrow$ **real**

The expressions and values of Fun are below. Expressions are in a limited syntax akin to A-normal form, with let-expressions for sequential composition.

Fun: Values and Expressions

$V ::= x \mid c \mid (V,V)$	Value
$M,N ::=$	Expression
V	value
$V_1 \otimes V_2$	arithmetic or logical operator
$V.1$	left projection from pair
$V.2$	right projection from pair
if V **then** M_1 **else** M_2	conditional
let $x = M$ **in** N	let (scope of x is N)
random $(D(V))$	primitive distribution
observe V	observation

In the discrete case, Fun has a standard *sampling semantics*; the formal semantics for the general case comes later. A run of a closed expression M is the process of evaluating M to a value. The evaluation of most expressions is standard, apart from sampling and observation.

To run **random** $(D(V))$, where $V = (c_1, \ldots, c_n)$, choose a value c at random, with probability given by the distribution $D(c_1, \ldots, c_n)$, and return c.

To run **observe** V, always return (). We say the observation is *valid* if and only if the value V is some zero element 0_b.

Due to the presence of sampling, different runs of the same expression may yield more than one value, with differing probabilities. Let a run be *valid* so long as every encountered observation is valid. The sampling semantics of an expression is the conditional probability of returning a particular value, given a valid run.

(Boolean observations are akin to assume statements in assertion-based program specifications, where runs of a program are ignored if an assumed formula is false.)

Example: Two Coins, Not Both Tails

```
let heads1 = random (Bernoulli(0.5)) in
let heads2 = random (Bernoulli(0.5)) in
let u = observe (heads1 || heads2) in
(heads1,heads2)
```

The subexpression **random** (**Bernoulli**(0.5)) generates **true** or **false** with equal likelihood. The whole expression has four distinct runs, each with probability $1/4$, corresponding to the possible combinations of Booleans heads1 and heads2. All these runs are valid, apart from the one for heads1 = **false** and heads2 = **false** (representing two tails), since the observation **observe**(**false**||**false**) is not valid. The sampling semantics of this expression is a probability distribution assigning probability $1/3$ to the values (**true**, **false**), (**false**, **true**), and (**true**, **true**), but probability 0 to the value (**false**, **false**).

The sampling semantics allows us to interpret an expression as a Bayesian model. We interpret the distribution of possible return values as the *prior probability* of the model. The constraints on valid runs induced by observations represent new evidence or training data. The conditional probability of a value given a valid run is the *posterior probability*: an adjustment of the prior probability given the evidence or training data.

Thus, the expression above can be read as a Bayesian model of the problem: *I toss two coins. I observe that not both are tails. What is the probability of each outcome?*

2.2 Syntactic Conventions and Monomorphic Typing Rules

We identify phrases of syntax up to consistent renaming of bound variables. Let $\mathrm{fv}(\phi)$ be the set of variables occurring free in phrase ϕ. Let $\phi\{^{\psi}/_{x}\}$ be the outcome of substituting phrase ψ for each free occurrence of variable x in phrase ϕ. We treat function definitions as macros with call-by-value semantics. In particular, in examples, we write first-order non-recursive function definitions in the form **let** $f\ x_1\ \dots\ x_n = M$, and we allow function applications $f\ M_1\ \dots\ M_n$ as expressions. We consider such a function application as being a shorthand for the expression **let** $x_1 = M_1$ **in** ... **let** $x_n = M_n$ **in** M, where the bound variables $x_1, \dots, x_n$ do not occur free in $M_1, \dots, M_n$. We allow expressions to be used in place of values, via insertion of suitable let-expressions. For example, (M_1,M_2) stands for **let** $x_1 = M_1$ **in let** $x_2 = M_2$ **in** (x_1,x_2), and $M_1 \otimes M_2$ stands for **let** $x_1 = M_1$ **in let** $x_2 = M_2$ **in** $x_1 \otimes x_2$, when either M_1 or M_2 or both is not a value. Let $M_1;M_2$ stand for **let** $x = M_1$ **in** M_2 where $x \notin \mathrm{fv}(M_2)$. The notation $t = t_1 * \dots * t_n$ for tuple types means the following: when $n = 0$, $t =$ **unit**; when $n = 1$, $t = t_1$; and when $n > 1, t = t_1 * (t_2 * \dots * t_n)$. In listings, we rely on syntactic abbreviations available in F#, such as layout conventions (to suppress **in** keywords) and writing tuples as $M_1, \dots, M_n$ without enclosing parentheses.

Let a *typing environment*, Γ, be a list of the form $\varepsilon, x_1 : t_1, \dots, x_n : t_n$; we say Γ is *well-formed* and write $\Gamma \vdash \diamond$ to mean that the variables x_i are pairwise distinct. Let $\mathrm{dom}(\Gamma) = \{x_1, \dots, x_n\}$ if $\Gamma = \varepsilon, x_1 : t_1, \dots, x_n : t_n$. We sometimes use the notation $\overline{x:t}$ for $\Gamma = \varepsilon, x_1 : t_1, \dots, x_n : t_n$ where $\overline{x} = x_1, \dots, x_n$ and $\overline{t} = t_1, \dots, t_n$.

The typing rules for this monomorphic first-order language are standard.

Representative Typing Rules for Fun Expressions: $\Gamma \vdash M : t$

(FUN OPERATOR)
$$\frac{\otimes : b_1, b_2 \to b_3 \quad \Gamma \vdash V_1 : b_1 \quad \Gamma \vdash V_2 : b_2}{\Gamma \vdash V_1 \otimes V_2 : b_3}$$

(FUN RANDOM)
$$\frac{D : (x_1 : b_1 * \cdots * x_n : b_n) \to b \quad \Gamma \vdash V : (b_1 * \cdots * b_n)}{\Gamma \vdash \textbf{random}\ (D(V)) : b}$$

(FUN OBSERVE)
$$\frac{\Gamma \vdash V : b}{\Gamma \vdash \textbf{observe}\ V : \textbf{unit}}$$

3 Semantics as Measure Transformers

If we can only sample from discrete distributions, the semantics of Fun is straightforward. In our technical report, we formalize the sampling semantics of the previous section as a small-step operational semantics for the fragment of Fun where every **random** expression takes the form **random** (**Bernoulli**(c)) for some real $c \in (0,1)$. A reduction $M \to^p M'$ means that M reduces to M' with non-zero probability p.

We cannot give such a semantics to expressions that sample from continuous distributions, such as **random** (**Gaussian**$(1,1)$), since the probability of any particular sample is zero. A further difficulty is the need to observe events with probability zero, a common situation in machine learning. For example, consider the naive Bayesian classifier, a common, simple probabilistic model. In the training phase, it is given objects together with their classes and the values of their pertinent features. Below, we show the training for a single feature: the weight of the object. The zero probability events are weight measurements, assumed to be normally distributed around the class mean. The outcome of the training is the posterior weight distributions for the different classes.

Naive Bayesian Classifier, Single Feature Training:

```
let wPrior() = sample (Gaussian(0.5,1.0))
let Glass,Watch,Plate = wPrior(),wPrior(),wPrior()
let weight objClass objWeight =
    observe (objWeight−(sample (Gaussian(objClass,1.0))))
weight Glass .18; weight Glass .21
weight Watch .11; weight Watch .073
weight Plate .23; weight Plate .45
Watch,Glass,Plate
```

Above, the call to weight Glass .18 modifies the distribution of the variable Glass. The example uses **observe** (x−y) to denote that the difference between the weights x and y is 0. The reason for not instead writing x=y is that conditioning on events of zero probability without specifying the random variable they are drawn from is not in general well-defined, cf. Borel's paradox [12]. To avoid this issue, we instead observe the random variable x−y of type **real**, at the value 0.

To give a formal semantics to such observations, as well as to mixtures of continuous and discrete distributions, we turn to measure theory, following standard sources [3]. Two basic concepts are measurable spaces and measures. A measurable space is a set of values equipped with a collection of *measurable* subsets; these measurable sets generalize the events of discrete probability. A finite *measure* is a function that assigns a numeric size to each measurable set; measures generalize probability distributions.

3.1 Types as Measurable Spaces

We let Ω range over sets of possible outcomes; in our semantics Ω will range over $\mathbb{B} = \{\mathbf{true}, \mathbf{false}\}$, $\mathbb{Z}$, $\mathbb{R}$, and finite Cartesian products of these sets. A *σ-algebra* over Ω is a set $\mathcal{M} \subseteq \mathcal{P}(\Omega)$ which (1) contains $\varnothing$ and Ω, and (2) is closed under complement and countable union and intersection. A *measurable space* is a pair $(\Omega, \mathcal{M})$ where $\mathcal{M}$ is a σ-algebra over Ω; the elements of $\mathcal{M}$ are called *measurable sets*. We use the notation $\sigma_\Omega(S)$, when $S \subseteq \mathcal{P}(\Omega)$, for the smallest σ-algebra over Ω that is a superset of S; we may omit Ω when it is clear from context. If $(\Omega, \mathcal{M})$ and $(\Omega', \mathcal{M}')$ are measurable spaces, then the function $f : \Omega \to \Omega'$ is *measurable* if and only if for all $A \in \mathcal{M}'$, $f^{-1}(A) \in \mathcal{M}$, where the *inverse image* $f^{-1} : \mathcal{P}(\Omega') \to \mathcal{P}(\Omega)$ is given by $f^{-1}(A) \triangleq \{\omega \in \Omega \mid f(\omega) \in A\}$. We write $f^{-1}(x)$ for $f^{-1}(\{x\})$ when $x \in \Omega'$.

We give each first-order type t an interpretation as a measurable space $\mathcal{T}[\![t]\!] \triangleq (\mathbf{V}_t, \mathcal{M}_t)$ below. We write $()$ for $\varnothing$, the unit value.

Semantics of Types as Measurable Spaces:

$\mathcal{T}[\![\mathbf{unit}]\!] = (\{()\}, \{\{()\}, \varnothing\})$ $\qquad$ $\mathcal{T}[\![\mathbf{bool}]\!] = (\mathbb{B}, \mathcal{P}(\mathbb{B}))$
$\mathcal{T}[\![\mathbf{int}]\!] = (\mathbb{Z}, \mathcal{P}(\mathbb{Z}))$ $\qquad$ $\mathcal{T}[\![\mathbf{real}]\!] = (\mathbb{R}, \sigma_{\mathbb{R}}(\{[a,b] \mid a, b \in \mathbb{R}\}))$
$\mathcal{T}[\![t * u]\!] = (\mathbf{V}_t \times \mathbf{V}_u, \sigma_{\mathbf{V}_t \times \mathbf{V}_u}(\{m \times n \mid m \in \mathcal{M}_t,\ n \in \mathcal{M}_u\}))$

The set $\sigma_{\mathbb{R}}(\{[a,b] \mid a, b \in \mathbb{R}\})$ in the definition of $\mathcal{T}[\![\mathbf{real}]\!]$ is the Borel σ-algebra on the real line, which is the smallest σ-algebra containing all closed (and open) intervals. Below, we write $f : t \to u$ to denote that $f : \mathbf{V}_t \to \mathbf{V}_u$ is measurable, that is, that $f^{-1}(B) \in \mathcal{M}_t$ for all $B \in \mathcal{M}_u$.

3.2 Finite Measures

A *finite measure* μ on a measurable space $(\Omega, \mathcal{M})$ is a function $\mathcal{M} \to \mathbb{R}^+$ that is countably additive, that is, if the sets $A_0, A_1, \ldots \in \mathcal{M}$ are pairwise disjoint, then $\mu(\cup_i A_i) = \sum_i \mu(A_i)$. We write $|\mu| \triangleq \mu(\Omega)$. Let $\mathtt{M}\,t$ be the set of finite measures on the measurable space $\mathcal{T}[\![t]\!]$. We make use of the following constructions on measures.

- Given a function $f : t \to u$ and a measure $\mu \in \mathtt{M}\,t$, there is a measure $\mu f^{-1} \in \mathtt{M}\,u$ given by $(\mu f^{-1})(B) \triangleq \mu(f^{-1}(B))$.
- Given a finite measure μ and a measurable set B, we let $\mu|_B(A) \triangleq \mu(A \cap B)$ be the restriction of μ to B.
- We can add two measures on the same set as $(\mu_1 + \mu_2)(A) \triangleq \mu_1(A) + \mu_2(A)$.
- The (independent) product $(\mu_1 \times \mu_2)$ of two measures is also definable, and satisfies $(\mu_1 \times \mu_2)(A \times B) = \mu_1(A) \cdot \mu_2(B)$. (Existence and uniqueness follows from the Hahn-Kolmogorov theorem.)
- Given a measure μ on the measurable space $\mathcal{T}[\![t]\!]$, a measurable set $A \in \mathcal{M}_t$ and a function $f : t \to \mathbf{real}$, we write $\int_A f\, d\mu$ or equivalently $\int_A f(x)\, d\mu(x)$ for standard (Lebesgue) integration. This integration is always well-defined if μ is finite and f is non-negative and bounded from above.

- Given a measure μ on a measurable space $\mathcal{T}[\![t]\!]$ let a function $\dot{\mu} : t \to \textbf{real}$ be a *density* for μ iff $\mu(A) = \int_A \dot{\mu}\, d\lambda$ for all $A \in \mathcal{M}$, where λ is the standard Lebesgue measure on $\mathcal{T}[\![t]\!]$. (We also use λ-notation for functions, but we trust any ambiguity is easily resolved.)

Standard Distributions. Given a closed well-typed Fun expression **random** $(D(V))$ of base type b, we define a corresponding finite measure $\mu_{D(V)}$ on measurable space $\mathcal{T}[\![b]\!]$.

In the discrete case, we first define probability masses $D(V)\ c$ of single elements, and hence of singleton sets, and then define the measure $\mu_{D(V)}$ as a countable sum.

Masses $D(V)\ c$ and Measures $\mu_{D(V)}$ for Discrete Probability Distributions:

$\textbf{Bernoulli}(p)\ \textbf{true} \triangleq p$	if $0 \le p \le 1$, 0 otherwise
$\textbf{Bernoulli}(p)\ \textbf{false} \triangleq 1-p$	if $0 \le p \le 1$, 0 otherwise
$\textbf{Binomial}(n,p)\ i \triangleq \binom{i}{n} p^i/n!$	if $0 \le p \le 1$, 0 otherwise
$\textbf{DiscreteUniform}(m)\ i \triangleq 1/m$	if $0 \le i < m$, 0 otherwise
$\textbf{Poisson}(l)\ n \triangleq e^{-l} l^n/n!$	if $l,n \ge 0$, 0 otherwise
$\mu_{D(V)}(A) \triangleq \sum_i D(V)\ c_i$	if $A = \bigcup_i \{c_i\}$ for pairwise distinct c_i

In the continuous case, we first define probability densities $D(V)\ r$ at individual elements r. and then define the measure $\mu_{D(V)}$ as an integral. Below, we write $\mathbf{G}$ for the standard Gamma function, which on naturals n satisfies $\mathbf{G}(n) = (n-1)!$.

Densities $D(V)\ r$ and Measures $\mu_{D(V)}$ for Continuous Probability Distributions:

$\textbf{Gaussian}(m,v)\ r \triangleq e^{-(r-m)^2/2v}/\sqrt{2\pi v}$	if $v > 0$, 0 otherwise
$\textbf{Gamma}(s,p)\ r \triangleq r^{s-1}e^{-pr}p^s/\mathbf{G}(s)$	if $r,s,p > 0$, 0 otherwise
$\textbf{Beta}(a,b)\ r \triangleq r^{a-1}(1-r)^{b-1}\mathbf{G}(a+b)/(\mathbf{G}(a)\mathbf{G}(b))$	if $a,b \ge 0$ and $0 \le r \le 1$, 0 otherwise
$\mu_{D(V)}(A) \triangleq \int_A D(V)\, d\lambda$	where λ is the Lebesgue measure

The Dirac δ measure is defined on the measurable space $\mathcal{T}[\![b]\!]$ for each base type b, and is given by $\delta_c(A) \triangleq 1$ if $c \in A$, 0 otherwise. We write δ for $\delta_{0.0}$.

The notion of density can be generalized as follows, yielding an unnormalized counterpart to conditional probability. Given a measure μ on $\mathcal{T}[\![t]\!]$ and a measurable function $p : t \to b$, we consider the family of events $p(x) = c$ where c ranges over $\mathbf{V}_b$. We define $\dot{\mu}[A||p=c] \in \mathbb{R}$ (the μ-density at $p = c$ of A) following [8], by:

Conditional Density: $\dot{\mu}[A||p=c]$

$\dot{\mu}[A||p=c] \triangleq \lim_{i\to\infty} \mu(A \cap p^{-1}(B_i))/\int_{B_i} 1\, d\lambda$ if the limit exists and is the same for all sequences $\{B_i\}$ of closed sets converging regularly to c.

Where defined, letting $A \in \mathcal{M}_a, B \in \mathcal{M}_b$, conditional density satisfies the equation

$$\int_B \dot{\mu}[A||p=x]\ d(\mu p^{-1})(x) = \mu(A \cap p^{-1}(B)).$$

In particular, we have $\dot{\mu}[A||p=c]=0$ if b is discrete and $\mu(p^{-1}(c))=0$. To show that our definition of conditional density generalizes the notion of density given above, we have that if μ has a continuous density $\dot{\mu}$ on some neighbourhood of $p^{-1}(c)$ then

$$\dot{\mu}[A||p=c] = \int_A \delta_c(p(x))\dot{\mu}(x)\,d\lambda(x).$$

3.3 Measure Transformers

We will now recast some standard theorems of measure theory as a library of combinators, that we will later use to give semantics to probabilistic languages. A *measure transformer* is a function from finite measures to finite measures. We let $t \leadsto u$ be the set of functions $\mathtt{M}\,t \to \mathtt{M}\,u$. We use the following combinators on measure transformers in the formal semantics of our languages.

Measure Transformer Combinators:

$\mathtt{pure} \in (t \to u) \to (t \leadsto u)$
$\ggg \in (t_1 \leadsto t_2) \to (t_2 \leadsto t_3) \to (t_1 \leadsto t_3)$
$\mathtt{choose} \in (\mathbf{V}_t \to (t \leadsto u)) \to (t \leadsto u)$
$\mathtt{extend} \in (\mathbf{V}_t \to \mathtt{M}\,u) \to (t \leadsto (t * u))$
$\mathtt{observe} \in (t \to b) \to (t \leadsto t)$

The definitions of these combinators occupy the remainder of this section. We recall that μ denotes a measure and A a measurable set, of appropriate types.

To lift a pure measurable function to a measure transformer, we use the combinator $\mathtt{pure} \in (t \to u) \to (t \leadsto u)$. Given $f : t \to u$, we let $\mathtt{pure}\,f\;\mu\;A \triangleq \mu f^{-1}(A)$, where μ is a measure on $\mathcal{T}[\![t]\!]$ and A is a measurable set from $\mathcal{T}[\![u]\!]$.

To sequentially compose two measure transformers we use standard function composition, defining $\ggg \in (t_1 \leadsto t_2) \to (t_2 \leadsto t_3) \to (t_1 \leadsto t_3)$ as $T \ggg U \triangleq U \circ T$.

The combinator $\mathtt{choose} \in (\mathbf{V}_t \to (t \leadsto u)) \to (t \leadsto u)$ makes a conditional choice between measure transformers, if its first argument is measurable and has finite range. Intuitively, $\mathtt{choose}\,K\;\mu$ first splits $\mathbf{V}_t$ into the equivalence classes modulo K. For each equivalence class, we then run the corresponding measure transformer on μ restricted to the class. Finally, the resulting finite measures are added together, yielding a finite measure. We let $\mathtt{choose}\,K\;\mu\;A \triangleq \sum_{T\in\mathrm{range}(K)} T(\mu|_{K^{-1}(T)})(A)$. In particular, if K is a binary choice mapping all elements of B to T_B and all elements of $C=\overline{B}$ to T_C, we have $\mathtt{choose}\,K\;\mu\;A = T_B(\mu|_B)(A)+T_C(\mu|_C)(A)$. (In fact, our only uses of choose in this paper are in the semantics of conditional expressions in Fun and conditional statements in Imp, and in each case the argument K to choose is a binary choice.)

The combinator $\mathtt{extend} \in (\mathbf{V}_t \to \mathtt{M}\,u) \to (t \leadsto (t * u))$ extends the domain of a measure using a function yielding measures. It is reminiscent of creating a dependent pair, since the distribution of the second component depends on the value of the first. For $\mathtt{extend}\,m$ to be defined, we require that for every $A \in \mathcal{M}_u$, the function $f_A \triangleq \lambda x.m(x)(A)$ is measurable, non-negative and bounded from above. This will always be the case in our semantics for Fun, since we only use the standard distributions for m above. We let $\mathtt{extend}\,m\;\mu\;AB \triangleq \int_{\mathbf{V}_t} m(x)(\{y \mid (x,y)\in AB\})\,d\mu(x)$, where we integrate over the first component (call it x) with respect to the measure μ, and the integrand is the measure $m(x)$ of the set $\{y \mid (x,y) \in A\}$ for each x.

The combinator observe $\in (t \to b) \to (t \rightsquigarrow t)$ conditions a measure over $\mathcal{T}[\![t]\!]$ on the event that an indicator function of type $t \to b$ is zero. Here observation is *unnormalized* conditioning of a measure on an event. We define:

$$\texttt{observe}\ p\ \mu\ A \triangleq \begin{cases} \dot{\mu}[A||p = 0_b] & \text{if } \mu(p^{-1}(0_b)) = 0 \\ \mu(A \cap p^{-1}(0_b)) & \text{otherwise} \end{cases}$$

As an example, if $p : t \to \textbf{bool}$ is a predicate on values of type t, we have

$$\texttt{observe}\ p\ \mu\ A = \mu(A \cap \{x \mid p(x) = \textbf{true}\}).$$

In the continuous case, if $\mathbf{V}_t = \mathbb{R} \times \mathbb{R}^k$, $p = \lambda(y,x).(y - c)$ and μ has density $\dot{\mu}$ then

$$\texttt{observe}\ p\ \mu\ A = \int_A \dot{\mu}(y,x)\, d(\delta_c \times \lambda)(y,x) = \int_{\{x \mid (c,x) \in A\}} \dot{\mu}(c,x)\, d\lambda(x).$$

Notice that observe p μ A can be greater than $\mu(A)$, for which reason we cannot restrict ourselves to transformation of (sub-)probability measures.

3.4 Measure Transformer Semantics of Fun

In order to give a compositional denotational semantics of Fun programs, we give a semantics to open programs, later to be placed in some closing context. Since observations change the distributions of program variables, we may draw a parallel to while programs. In this setting, we can give a denotation to a program as a function from variable valuations to a return value and a variable valuation. Similarly, we give semantics to an open Fun term by mapping a measure over assignments to the term's free variables to a joint measure of the term's return value and assignments to its free variables. This choice is a generalization of the (discrete) semantics of pWHILE [2].

First, we define a data structure for an evaluation environment assigning values to variable names, and corresponding operations. Given an environment $\Gamma = x_1{:}t_1, \ldots, x_n{:}t_n$, we let $\mathtt{S}\langle\Gamma\rangle$ be the set of states, or finite maps $s = \{x_1 \mapsto V_1, \ldots, x_n \mapsto V_n\}$ such that for all $i = 1, \ldots, n$, $\varepsilon \vdash V_i : t_i$. We let $\mathcal{T}[\![\mathtt{S}\langle\Gamma\rangle]\!] \triangleq \mathcal{T}[\![t_1 * \cdots * t_n]\!]$ be the measurable space of states in $\mathtt{S}\langle\Gamma\rangle$. We define $\mathrm{dom}(s) \triangleq \{x_1, \ldots, x_n\}$. We define the following operators.

Auxiliary Operations on States and Pairs:

$\texttt{add}\,x\ (s,V) \triangleq s \cup \{x \mapsto V\}$	if $\varepsilon \vdash V : t$ and $x \notin \mathrm{dom}(s)$, s otherwise.
$\texttt{lookup}\,x\ s \triangleq s(x)$	if $x \in \mathrm{dom}(s)$, $()$ otherwise.
$\texttt{drop}\,X\ s \triangleq \{(x \mapsto V) \in s \mid x \notin X\}$	$\texttt{fst}((x,y)) \triangleq x$ $\quad$ $\texttt{snd}((x,y)) \triangleq y$

We apply these combinators to give a semantics to Fun programs as measure transformers. We assume that all bound variables in a program are different from the free variables and each other. Below, $\mathcal{V}[\![V]\!]\ s$ gives the valuation of V in state s, and $\mathcal{A}[\![M]\!]$ gives the measure transformer denoted by M.

Measure Transformer Semantics of Fun:

$$\mathcal{V}[\![x]\!]\ s \triangleq \texttt{lookup}\, x\, s$$
$$\mathcal{V}[\![c]\!]\ s \triangleq c$$
$$\mathcal{V}[\![(V_1,V_2)]\!]\ s \triangleq (\mathcal{V}[\![V_1]\!]\ s, \mathcal{V}[\![V_2]\!]\ s)$$

$$\mathcal{A}[\![V]\!] \triangleq \texttt{pure}\ \lambda s.(s, \mathcal{V}[\![V]\!]\ s)$$
$$\mathcal{A}[\![V_1 \otimes V_2]\!] \triangleq \texttt{pure}\ \lambda s.(s, ((\mathcal{V}[\![V_1]\!]\ s) \otimes (\mathcal{V}[\![V_2]\!]\ s)))$$
$$\mathcal{A}[\![V.1]\!] \triangleq \texttt{pure}\ \lambda s.(s, \texttt{fst}(\mathcal{V}[\![V]\!]\ s))$$
$$\mathcal{A}[\![V.2]\!] \triangleq \texttt{pure}\ \lambda s.(s, \texttt{snd}(\mathcal{V}[\![V]\!]\ s))$$

$$\mathcal{A}[\![\mathbf{if}\ V\ \mathbf{then}\ M\ \mathbf{else}\ N]\!] \triangleq \texttt{choose}\ \lambda s.\texttt{if}\ \mathcal{V}[\![V]\!]\ s\ \texttt{then}\ \mathcal{A}[\![M]\!]\ \texttt{else}\ \mathcal{A}[\![N]\!]$$
$$\mathcal{A}[\![\mathbf{random}\ (D(V))]\!] \triangleq \texttt{extend}\ \lambda s.\mu_{D(\mathcal{V}[\![V]\!]\ s)}$$
$$\mathcal{A}[\![\mathbf{observe}\ V]\!] \triangleq (\texttt{observe}\ \lambda s.\mathcal{V}[\![V]\!]\ s) \ggg \texttt{pure}\ \lambda s.(s, ())$$
$$\mathcal{A}[\![\mathbf{let}\ x = M\ \mathbf{in}\ N]\!] \triangleq \mathcal{A}[\![M]\!] \ggg \texttt{pure}\ (\texttt{add}\ x) \ggg \mathcal{A}[\![N]\!] \ggg \texttt{pure}\ \lambda(s,y).((\texttt{drop}\ \{x\}\ s), y)$$

A value expression V returns the valuation of V in the current state, which is left unchanged. Similarly, binary operations and projections have a deterministic meaning given the current state. An **if** V expression runs the measure transformer given by the **then** branch on the states where V evaluates true, and the transformer given by the **else** branch on all other states, using the combinator `choose`. A primitive distribution **random** $(D(V))$ extends the state measure with a value drawn from the distribution D, with parameters V depending on the current state. An observation **observe** V modifies the current measure by restricting it to states where V is zero. It is implemented with the `observe` combinator, and it always returns the unit value. The expression **let** $x = M$ **in** N intuitively first runs M and binds its return value to x using `add`. After running N, the binding is discarded using `drop`.

Lemma 1. *If* $s : \mathtt{S}\langle\Gamma\rangle$ *and* $\Gamma \vdash V : t$ *then* $\mathcal{V}[\![V]\!]\ s \in \mathbf{V}_t$.

Lemma 2. *If* $\Gamma \vdash M : t$ *then* $\mathcal{A}[\![M]\!] \in \mathtt{S}\langle\Gamma\rangle \rightsquigarrow (\mathtt{S}\langle\Gamma\rangle * t)$.

The measure transformer semantics of Fun is hard to use directly, except in the case of discrete measures where they can be directly implemented: a naive implementation of $\mathtt{M}\langle\mathtt{S}\langle\Gamma\rangle\rangle$ is as a map assigning a probability to each possible variable valuation. If there are N variables, each sampled from a Bernoulli distribution, in the worst case there are 2^N paths to be explored in the computation, each of which corresponds to a variable valuation. In this simple case, the measure transformer semantics of closed programs also coincides with the sampling semantics. We write $\mathrm{P}_M[\mathsf{value} = V \mid \mathsf{valid}]$ for the probability that a run of M returns V given that all observations in the run succeed.

Theorem 1. *Suppose* $\varepsilon \vdash M : t$ *for some* M *only using* **Bernoulli** *distributions. If* $\mu = \mathcal{A}[\![M]\!]\ \delta_{()}$ *and* $\varepsilon \vdash V : t$ *then* $\mathrm{P}_M[\mathsf{value} = V \mid \mathsf{valid}] = \mu(\{V\})/|\mu|$.

A consequence of the theorem is that our measure transformer semantics is a generalization of the sampling semantics for discrete probabilities. For this theorem to hold, it is critical that `observe` denotes unnormalized conditioning (filtering). Otherwise programs that perform observations inside the branches of conditional expressions would have undesired semantics. As the following example shows, the two program fragments **observe** (x=y) and **if** x **then observe** (y=**true**) **else observe** (y=**false**) would have different measure transformer semantics although they have the same sampling semantics.

Simple Conditional Expression: M_{if}

```
let x = sample (Bernoulli(0.5))
let y = sample (Bernoulli(0.1))
if x then observe (y=true) else observe (y=false)
y
```

In the sampling semantics, the two valid runs are when x and y are both **true** (with probability 0.05), and both **false** (with probability 0.45), so we have $\mathrm{P}[\textbf{true} \mid \mathsf{valid}] = 0.1$ and $\mathrm{P}[\textbf{false} \mid \mathsf{valid}] = 0.9$.

If, instead of the unnormalized definition $\texttt{observe}\ p\ \mu\ A = \mu(A \cap \{x \mid p(x)\})$, we had either of the flawed definitions

$$\texttt{observe}\ p\ \mu\ A = \frac{\mu(A \cap \{x \mid p(x)\})}{\mu(\{x \mid p(x)\})} \quad \text{or} \quad |\mu| \frac{\mu(A \cap \{x \mid p(x)\})}{\mu(\{x \mid p(x)\})}$$

then $\mathcal{A}[\![M_{\text{if}}]\!]\ \delta_{()}\ \{\textbf{true}\} = \mathcal{A}[\![M_{\text{if}}]\!]\ \delta_{()}\ \{\textbf{false}\}$, which would invalidate the theorem.

Let $M' = M_{\text{if}}$ with **observe** $(x = y)$ substituted for the conditional expression. With the actual or either of the flawed definitions of `observe` we have $\mathcal{A}[\![M']\!]\ \delta_{()}\ \{\textbf{true}\} = (\mathcal{A}[\![M']\!]\ \delta_{()}\ \{\textbf{false}\})/9$.

4 Semantics as Factor Graphs

A naive implementation of the measure transformer semantics of the previous section would work directly with measures of states, whose size could be exponential in the number of variables in scope. For large models, this becomes intractable. In this section, we instead give a semantics to Fun programs as *factor graphs* [18], whose size will be linear in the size of the program. We define this semantics in two steps. We first compile the Fun program into a program in the simple imperative language Imp, and then the Imp program itself has a straightforward semantics as a factor graph. Our semantics formalizes the way in which our implementation maps F# programs to Csoft programs, which are evaluated by Infer.NET by constructing suitable factor graphs. The implementation advantage of translating F# to Csoft, over simply generating factor graphs directly [22], is that the translation preserves the structure of the input model (including array processing in our full language), which can be exploited by the various inference algorithms supported by Infer.NET.

4.1 Imp: An Imperative Core Calculus

Imp is an imperative language, based on the static single assignment (SSA) intermediate form. It is a sublanguage of Csoft, the input language of Infer.NET [25], and is intended to have a simple semantics as a factor graph. A composite statement C is a sequence of statements, each of which either stores the result of a primitive operation in a location, observes the contents of a location to be zero, or branches on the value of a location. Imp shares the base types b with Fun, but has no tuples.

Syntax of Imp:

$l, l', \dots$	Locations (variables) in global store
$E, F ::= c \mid l \mid (l \otimes l)$	Expression
$I ::=$	Statement
$\quad l \leftarrow E$	assignment
$\quad l \overset{s}{\leftarrow} D(l_1, \dots, l_n)$	random assignment
$\quad \textbf{observe}_b\ l$	observation
$\quad \textbf{if}\ l\ \textbf{then}_{\Sigma_1}\ C_1\ \textbf{else}_{\Sigma_2}\ C_2$	conditional
$C ::= \textbf{nil} \mid I \mid (C; C)$	Composite Statement

When making an observation $\textbf{observe}_b$, we make explicit the type b of the observed location. In the form $\textbf{if}\ l\ \textbf{then}_{\Sigma_1}\ C_1\ \textbf{else}_{\Sigma_2}\ C_2$, the environments Σ_1 and Σ_2 declare the local variables assigned by the **then** branch and the **else** branch, respectively. These annotations simplify type checking and denotational semantics.

The typing rules for Imp are standard. We consider Imp typing environments Σ to be a special case of Fun environments Γ, where variables (locations) always map to base types. The judgment $\Sigma \vdash C : \Sigma'$ means that the composite statement C is well-typed in the initial environment Σ, yielding additional bindings Σ'.

Part of the Type System for Imp: $\Sigma \vdash C : \Sigma'$

(IMP SEQ)
$$\frac{\Sigma \vdash C_1 : \Sigma' \qquad \Sigma, \Sigma' \vdash C_2 : \Sigma''}{\Sigma \vdash C_1; C_2 : (\Sigma', \Sigma'')}$$

(IMP NIL)
$$\frac{\Sigma \vdash \diamond}{\Sigma \vdash \textbf{nil} : \varepsilon}$$

(IMP ASSIGN)
$$\frac{\Sigma \vdash E : b \qquad l \notin \mathrm{dom}(\Sigma)}{\Sigma \vdash l \leftarrow E : \varepsilon, l{:}b}$$

(IMP OBSERVE)
$$\frac{\Sigma \vdash l : b}{\Sigma \vdash \textbf{observe}_b\ l : \varepsilon}$$

(IMP IF)
$$\frac{\Sigma \vdash l : \textbf{bool} \quad \Sigma \vdash C_1 : \Sigma'_1 \quad \Sigma \vdash C_2 : \Sigma'_2 \quad \{\Sigma'_i\} = \{\Sigma_i, \Sigma'\}}{\Sigma \vdash \textbf{if}\ l\ \textbf{then}_{\Sigma_1}\ C_1\ \textbf{else}_{\Sigma_2}\ C_2 : \Sigma'}$$

4.2 Translating from Fun to Imp

The translation from Fun to Imp is a mostly routine compilation of functional code to imperative code. The main point of interest is that Imp locations only hold values of base type, while Fun variables may hold tuples. We rely on *patterns* p and *layouts* ρ to track the Imp locations corresponding to Fun environments. The technical report has the detailed definition of the following notations.

Notations for the Translation from Fun to Imp:

$p ::= l \mid () \mid (p, p)$	pattern: group of Imp locations to represent Fun value
$\rho ::= (x_i \mapsto p_i)^{i \in 1..n}$	layout: finite map from Fun variables to patterns
$\Sigma \vdash p : t$	in environment Σ, pattern p represents Fun value of type t
$\Sigma \vdash \rho : \Gamma$	in environment Σ, layout ρ represents environment Γ
$\rho \vdash M \Rightarrow C, p$	given ρ, expression M translates to C and pattern p

4.3 Factor Graphs

A factor graph [18] represents a joint probability distribution of a set of random variables as a collection of multiplicative factors. Factor graphs are an effective means of stating conditional independence properties between variables, and enable efficient algebraic inference techniques [27,38] as well as sampling techniques [15, Chapter 12]. We use factor graphs with *gates* [26] for modelling if-then-else clauses; gates introduce second-order edges in the graph.

Factor Graphs:

$G ::= \mathsf{new}\ \overline{x:b}\ \mathsf{in}\ \{e_1,\dots,e_m\}$	Graph
$x, y, z, \dots$	Nodes (random variables)
$e ::=$	Edge
$\mathsf{Equal}(x,y)$	equality $(x = y)$
$\mathsf{Constant}_c(x)$	constant $(x = c)$
$\mathsf{Binop}_\otimes(x,y,z)$	binary operator $(x = y \otimes z)$
$\mathsf{Sample}_D(x,y_1,\dots,y_n)$	sampling $(x \sim D(y_1,\dots,y_n))$
$\mathsf{Gate}(x,G_1,G_2)$	gate (if x then G_1 else G_2)

In a graph $\mathsf{new}\ \overline{x:b}\ \mathsf{in}\ \{e_1,\dots,e_m\}$, the variables x_i are bound; graphs are identified up to consistent renaming of bound variables. We write $\{e_1,\dots,e_m\}$ for $\mathsf{new}\ \varepsilon\ \mathsf{in}\ \{e_1,\dots,e_m\}$. We write $\mathrm{fv}(G)$ for the variables occurring free in G. Here is an example factor graph G_E. (The corresponding Fun source code is listed in the technical report.)

Factor Graph for Epidemiology Example:

$$
\begin{aligned}
G_\mathrm{E} = \{&\mathsf{Constant}_{0.01}(p_d), \mathsf{Sample}_B(\mathsf{has\_disease}, p_d),\\
&\mathsf{Gate}(\mathsf{has\_disease},\\
&\quad \mathsf{new}\ p_p : \mathbf{real}\ \mathsf{in}\ \{\mathsf{Constant}_{0.8}(p_p), \mathsf{Sample}_B(\mathsf{positive\_result}, p_p)\},\\
&\quad \mathsf{new}\ p_n : \mathbf{real}\ \mathsf{in}\ \{\mathsf{Constant}_{0.096}(p_n), \mathsf{Sample}_B(\mathsf{positive\_result}, p_n)\}),\\
&\mathsf{Constant}_{\mathbf{true}}(\mathsf{positive\_result})\}
\end{aligned}
$$

A factor graph typically denotes a probability distribution. The probability (density) of an assignment of values to variables is equal to the product of all the factors, averaged over all assignments to local variables. Here, we give a slightly more general semantics of factor graphs as measure transformers; the input measure corresponds to a prior factor over all variables that it mentions. Below, we use the Iverson brackets, where $[p]$ is 1 when p is true and 0 otherwise. We let $\delta(x = y) \triangleq \delta_0(x - y)$ when x, y denote real numbers, and $[x = y]$ otherwise.

Semantics of Factor Graphs: $\mathcal{J}[\![G]\!]_\Sigma^{\Sigma'} \in \mathrm{S}\langle\Sigma\rangle \rightsquigarrow \mathrm{S}\langle\Sigma,\Sigma'\rangle$

$$
\begin{aligned}
&\mathcal{J}[\![G]\!]_\Sigma^{\Sigma'}\ \mu\ A \triangleq \textstyle\int_A (\mathcal{J}[\![G]\!]\ s)\ d(\mu \times \lambda)(s)\\
&\mathcal{J}[\![\mathsf{new}\ \overline{x:b}\ \mathsf{in}\ \{\overline{e}\}]\!]\ s \triangleq \textstyle\int_{\mathbf{V}_{*_i b_i}} \prod_j (\mathcal{J}[\![e_j]\!]\ (s,\overline{x}))\, d\lambda(\overline{x})\\
&\mathcal{J}[\![\mathsf{Equal}(l,l')]\!]\ s \triangleq \delta(\mathtt{lookup}\ l\ s = \mathtt{lookup}\ l'\ s)\\
&\mathcal{J}[\![\mathsf{Constant}_c(l)]\!]\ s \triangleq \delta(\mathtt{lookup}\ l\ s = c)\\
&\mathcal{J}[\![\mathsf{Binop}_\otimes(l,w_1,w_2)]\!]\ s \triangleq \delta(\mathtt{lookup}\ l\ s = \mathtt{lookup}\ w_1\ s \otimes \mathtt{lookup}\ w_2\ s)
\end{aligned}
$$

$\mathcal{J}[\![\mathsf{Sample}_D(l, v_1, \ldots, v_n)]\!]\ s \triangleq \mu_{D(\texttt{lookup}\ v_1\ s, \ldots, \texttt{lookup}\ v_n\ s)}(\texttt{lookup}\ l\ s)$
$\mathcal{J}[\![\mathsf{Gate}(v, G_1, G_2)]\!]\ s \triangleq (\mathcal{J}[\![G_1]\!]\ s)^{[\texttt{lookup}\ v\ s]}(\mathcal{J}[\![G_2]\!]\ s)^{[\neg\texttt{lookup}\ v\ s]}$

4.4 Factor Graph Semantics for Imp

An Imp statement has a straightforward semantics as a factor graph. Here, observation is defined by the value of the variable being the constant 0_b.

Factor Graph Semantics of Imp: $G = \mathcal{G}[\![C]\!]$

$\mathcal{G}[\![\mathbf{nil}]\!] \triangleq \varnothing$
$\mathcal{G}[\![C_1; C_2]\!] \triangleq \mathcal{G}[\![C_1]\!] \cup \mathcal{G}[\![C_2]\!]$

$\mathcal{G}[\![l \leftarrow c]\!] \triangleq \{\mathsf{Constant}_c(l)\}$
$\mathcal{G}[\![l \leftarrow l']\!] \triangleq \{\mathsf{Equal}(l, l')\}$
$\mathcal{G}[\![l \leftarrow l_1 \otimes l_2]\!] \triangleq \{\mathsf{Binop}_\otimes(l, l_1, l_2)\}$
$\mathcal{G}[\![l \xleftarrow{s} D(l_1, \ldots, l_n)]\!] \triangleq \{\mathsf{Sample}_D(l, l_1, \ldots, l_n)\}$
$\mathcal{G}[\![\mathbf{observe}_b\ l]\!] \triangleq \{\mathsf{Constant}_{0_b}(l)\}$
$\mathcal{G}[\![\mathbf{if}\ l\ \mathbf{then}_{\Sigma_1}\ C_1\ \mathbf{else}_{\Sigma_2}\ C_2]\!] \triangleq \{\mathsf{Gate}(l, \mathsf{new}\ \Sigma_1\ \mathsf{in}\ \mathcal{G}[\![C_1]\!], \mathsf{new}\ \Sigma_2\ \mathsf{in}\ \mathcal{G}[\![C_2]\!])\}$

The following theorem asserts that the semantics of Fun coincides with the semantics of Imp for compatible measures, which are defined as follows. If $T : t \rightsquigarrow u$ is a measure transformer composed from the combinators of Section 3 and $\mu \in \mathtt{M}\,t$, we say that T is *compatible* with μ if every application of $\texttt{observe}\ f$ to some μ' in the evaluation of $T(\mu)$ satisfies either that f is discrete or that μ has a continuous density on some ε-neighbourhood of $f^{-1}(0.0)$.

The statement of the theorem needs some additional notation. If $\Sigma \vdash p : t$ and $s \in \mathtt{S}\langle\Sigma\rangle$, we write $p\ s$ for the reconstruction of an element of $\mathcal{T}[\![t]\!]$ by looking up the locations of p in the state s. We define as follows operations $\texttt{lift}$ and $\texttt{restrict}$ to translate between states consisting of Fun variables ($\mathtt{S}\langle\Gamma\rangle$) and states consisting of Imp locations ($\mathtt{S}\langle\Sigma\rangle$), where flatten takes a mapping from patterns to values to a mapping from locations to base values.

$$\texttt{lift}\ \rho \triangleq \lambda s.\,\mathrm{flatten}\,\{\rho(x) \mapsto \mathcal{V}[\![x]\!]\ s \mid x \in \mathrm{dom}(\rho)\}$$
$$\texttt{restrict}\ \rho \triangleq \lambda s.\,\{x \mapsto \mathcal{V}[\![\rho(x)]\!]\ s \mid x \in \mathrm{dom}(\rho)\}$$

Theorem 2. *If $\Gamma \vdash M : t$ and $\Sigma \vdash \rho : \Gamma$ and $\rho \vdash M \Rightarrow C, p$ and measure $\mu \in \mathtt{M}\langle\mathtt{S}\langle\Gamma\rangle\rangle$ is compatible with $\mathcal{A}[\![M]\!]$ then there exists Σ' such that $\Sigma \vdash C : \Sigma'$ and:*
$\mathcal{A}[\![M]\!]\ \mu = (\texttt{pure}\ (\texttt{lift}\ \rho) \ggg \mathcal{J}[\![\mathcal{G}[\![C]\!]]\!]_{\Sigma}^{\Sigma'} \ggg \texttt{pure}\ (\lambda s.\ (\texttt{restrict}\ \rho\ s, p\ s)))\ \mu.$

Proof. Via a direct measure transformer semantics for Imp. The proof is by induction on the typing judgments $\Gamma \vdash M : t$ and $\Sigma \vdash C : \Sigma'$. □

5 Implementation Experience

We implemented a compiler from Fun to Imp in F#. We wrote two backends for Imp: an exact inference algorithm based on a direct implementation of measure transformers for discrete measures, and an approximating inference algorithm for continuous measures, using Infer.NET [25]. Translating Imp to Infer.NET is relatively straightforward, and amounts to a syntax-directed series of calls to Infer.NET's object-oriented API.

We have statistics on a few of the examples we have implemented. The lines of code number includes F# code that loads and processes data from disk before loading it into Infer.NET. The times are based on an average of three runs. All of the runs are on a four-core machine with 4GB of RAM. The Naive Bayes program is the naive Bayesian classifier of the earlier examples. The Mixture model is another clustering/-classification model. TrueSkill is a tournament ranking model, and adPredictor is a simplified version of a model to predict the likelihood that a display advertisment will be clicked. In the two long-running examples, time is spent mostly loading and processing data from disk and running inference in Infer.NET. TrueSkill spends the majority of its time (64%) in Infer.NET, performing inference. AdPredictor spends most of the time in pre-processing (58%), and only 40% in inference. The time spent in our compiler is negligible, never more than a few hundred milliseconds.

Summary of our Basic Test Suite:

	LOC	Observations	Variables	Time
Naive Bayes	28	9	3	<1s
Mixture	33	3	3	<1s
TrueSkill	68	15,664	84	6s
adPredictor	78	300,752	299,594	3m30s

In summary, our implementation strategy allowed us to build an effective prototype quickly and easily: the entire compiler is only 2079 lines of F#; the Infer.NET backend is 600 lines; the discrete backend is 252 lines. Our implementation, however, is only a prototype, and has limitations. On the one hand, Infer.NET supports a limited set of operations on specific combinations of probabilistic and deterministic arguments. Our discrete backend, on the other hand, is limited to small models using only finite measures.

6 Related Work

To the best of our knowledge, this paper introduces the first rigorous measure-theoretic semantics shown to be in agreement with a factor graph semantics for a probabilistic language with observation and sampling from continuous distributions. Hence, we lay a firm foundation for inference on probabilistic programs via modern message-passing algorithms on factor graphs.

Formal Semantics of Probabilistic Languages. There is a long history of formal semantics for probabilistic languages with sampling primitives, often combined with recursive computation. One of the first semantics is for Probabilistic LCF [35], which augments the core functional language LCF with weighted binary choice, for discrete distributions. Kozen [17] develops a probabilistic semantics for while-programs augmented with random assignment. He develops two provably equivalent semantics; one more operational, and the other a denotational semantics using partially ordered Banach spaces.

Imp is simpler than Kozen's language, as Imp has no unbounded while-statements, so the semantics of Imp need not deal with non-termination. On the other hand, observations are not present in Kozen's language.

Jones and Plotkin [13] investigate the probability monad, and apply it to languages with discrete probabilistic choice. Ramsey and Pfeffer [33] give a stochastic λ-calculus with a measure-theoretic semantics in the probability monad, and provide an embedding within Haskell; they do not consider observations. We can generalize the semantics of **observe** to this setting as filtering in the probability monad (yielding what we may call a sub-probability monad), as long as the events that are being observed are discrete or have non-zero probability. However, zero-probability observations of real variables do not translate easily to the probability monad, as the following example shows. Let N be an expression returning a continuous distribution, for example, **sample** (**Gaussian**(0.0,1.0)), and let f x = **observe** x. The probability monad semantics of the program **let** x = N **in** f x of the stochastic λ-calculus is $[\![N]\!] \gg= \lambda y.[\![\mathsf{f}\ \mathsf{x}]\!]\{\mathsf{x} \mapsto y\}$, which yields the measure $\mu(A) = \int_{\mathbb{R}} (\mathbf{M}[\![[\![\mathsf{f}\ \mathsf{x}]\!]\{\mathsf{x} \mapsto y\}]\!])(A)\ d\mathbf{M}[N](y)$. Here the probability $(\mathbf{M}[\![[\![\mathsf{f}\ \mathsf{x}]\!]\{x \mapsto y\}]\!])(A)$ is zero except when $y = 0$, where it is some real number. Since the N-measure of $y = 0$ is zero, the whole integral is zero for all A (in particular $\mu(\mathbb{R}) = 0$), whereas the intended semantics is that x is constrained to be zero with probability 1 (so in particular $\mu(\mathbb{R}) = 1$).

The probabilistic concurrent constraint programming language pcc of Gupta, Jagadeesan, and Panangaden [10] is also intended for describing probability distributions using independent sampling and constraints. Our use of observations corresponds to constraints on random variables in pcc. In the finite case, pcc also relies on a sampling semantics with observation (constraints) denoting filtering. To admit continuous distributions, pcc adds general fixpoints and defines the semantics of a program as the limit of finite unrollings of its fixpoints, if defined. This can lead to surprising results, for example, that the distribution resulting from observing that two uniform distributions are equal may not itself be uniform. In contrast, our goal is an efficient implementation via factor graphs, which led us to work directly with standard distributions and to have a semantics of observation that is independent of the program text.

McIver and Morgan [23] develop a theory of abstraction and refinement for probabilistic while programs, based on weakest preconditions. They reject a subdistribution transformer semantics in order to admit demonic nondeterminism in the language.

We conjecture that Fun and Imp could in principle be conferred semantics within a probabilistic language supporting general recursion, by encoding observations by placing the whole program within a conditional sampling loop, and by encoding Gaussian and other continuous distributions as repeated sampling using recursive functions. Still, our choices in formulating the semantics of Fun and Imp were to include some distributions as primitive, and to exclude recursion; compared to encodings within probabilistic languages with recursion, these choices have these advantages: (1) our measure transformer semantics relies on relatively elementary measure theory, with no need to express non-termination or to compute limits when defining the model; (2) our semantics is compositional rather than relying on a global sampling loop; and (3) our semantics has a direct implementation via message-passing algorithms on factor graphs, with efficient implementations of primitive distributions.

Probabilistic Languages for Machine Learning. Koller et al. [16] pioneered the idea of representing a probability distribution using first-order functional programs with discrete random choice, and proposed an inference algorithm for Bayesian networks and stochastic context-free grammars. Observations happen outside their language, by returning the distributions $P[A \wedge B], P[A \wedge \neg B], P[\neg A]$ which can be used to compute $P[B \mid A]$.

Park et al. [30] propose $\lambda_\circ$, the first probabilistic language with formal semantics applied to actual machine learning problems involving continuous distributions. The formal basis is sampling functions, which uniformly supports both discrete and continuous probability distributions, and inference is by Monte Carlo methods. The calculus $\lambda_\circ$ does not include observations, but enables conditional sampling via fixpoints and rejection.

Infer.NET [25] is a software library that implements the approximate deterministic algorithms expectation propagation [27] and variational message passing [38], as well as Gibbs sampling, a nondeterministic algorithm. Infer.NET models are written in a probabilistic subset of C#, known as Csoft [37]. Csoft allows **observe** on zero probability events, but its semantics has not previously been formalized and it is currently only implemented as an internal language of Infer.NET. IBAL [32] has observations and uses a factor graph semantics, but only works with discrete datatypes and thus does not need advanced probability theory. Moreover, there seems to be no proof that the factor graph denotation of an IBAL program yields the same distribution as the direct semantics, an important goal of the present work. HANSEI [14] is a programming library for OCaml, based on explicit manipulation of discrete probability distributions as lists, and sampling algorithms based on coroutines. HANSEI uses an explicit `fail` statement, which is equivalent to **observe false** and so cannot be used for conditioning on zero probability events.

FACTORIE [22] is a Scala library for explicitly constructing factor graphs. Although there are many Bayesian modelling languages, Csoft and IBAL are the only previous languages implemented by a compilation to factor graphs. Church [9] is a probabilistic form of the untyped functional language Scheme, equipped with conditional sampling and a mechanism of stochastic memoization. Queries are implemented using Monte Carlo methods. Blaise [4] supports the compositional construction of sophisticated probabilistic models, and decouples the choice of inference algorithm from the specification of the distribution. WinBUGS [28] is a popular language for explicitly describing distributions suitable for Monte Carlo analysis.

Other Uses of Probabilistic Languages. Probabilistic languages with formal semantics find application in many areas apart from machine learning, including databases [6], model checking [19], differential privacy [24,34], information flow [20], and cryptography [1]. A recent monograph on semantics for labelled Markov processes [29] focuses on bisimulation-based equational reasoning. The syntax and semantics of Imp is modelled on an existing probabilistic language [2] without observations.

Erwig and Kollmansberger [7] describe a library for probabilistic functional programming in Haskell. The library is based on the probability monad, and uses a finite representation suitable for small discrete distributions; the library would not suffice to provide a semantics for Fun or Imp with their continuous and hybrid distributions.

7 Conclusion

Our direct contribution is a rigorous semantics for a probabilistic programming language that also has an equivalent factor graph semantics. We have shown that probabilistic functional programs with iteration over arrays, but without the complexities of general recursion, are a concise representation for complex probability distributions arising in machine learning. An implication of our work for the machine learning community is that probabilistic programs can be written directly within an existing declarative language (Fun—a subset of F#), linked by comprehensions to large datasets, and compiled down to lower level Bayesian inference engines.

For the programming language community, our new semantics suggests some novel directions for research. What other primitives are possible—non-generative models, inspection of distributions, on-line inference on data streams? Can we verify the transformations performed by machine learning compilers such as Infer.NET compiler for Csoft? Are there type systems for avoiding zero probability exceptions, or to ensure that we only generate factor graphs that can be handled by our back-end?

Acknowledgements. We gratefully acknowledge discussions with Ralf Herbrich, Tom Minka, and John Winn. Comments from Nikhil Swamy, Dimitrios Vytiniotis, and the anonymous reviewers were helpful.

References

1. Abadi, M., Rogaway, P.: Reconciling two views of cryptography (the computational soundness of formal encryption). J. Cryptology 15(2), 103–127 (2002)
2. Barthe, G., Grégoire, B., Béguelin, S.Z.: Formal certification of code-based cryptographic proofs. In: POPL, pp. 90–101. ACM, New York (2009)
3. Billingsley, P.: Probability and Measure, 3rd edn. Wiley, Chichester (1995)
4. Bonawitz, K.A.: Composable Probabilistic Inference with Blaise. PhD thesis, MIT, Available as Technical Report MIT-CSAIL-TR-2008-044 (2008)
5. Borgström, J., Gordon, A.D., Greenberg, M., Margetson, J., Van Gael, J.: Measure transformer semantics for Bayesian machine learning. Technical report, Microsoft Research (2011)
6. Dalvi, N.N., Ré, C., Suciu, D.: Probabilistic databases: diamonds in the dirt. Commun. ACM 52(7), 86–94 (2009)
7. Erwig, M., Kollmansberger, S.: Functional pearls: Probabilistic functional programming in Haskell. J. Funct. Program. 16(1), 21–34 (2006)
8. Fraser, D.A.S., McDunnough, P., Naderi, A., Plante, A.: On the definition of probability densities and sufficiency of the likelihood map. J. Probability and Mathematical Statistics 15, 301–310 (1995)
9. Goodman, N., Mansinghka, V.K., Roy, D.M., Bonawitz, K., Tenenbaum, J.B.: Church: a language for generative models. In: UAI, pp. 220–229. AUAI Press (2008)
10. Gupta, V., Jagadeesan, R., Panangaden, P.: Stochastic processes as concurrent constraint programs. In: POPL 1999, pp. 189–202 (1999)
11. Herbrich, R., Minka, T., Graepel, T.: TrueSkill(TM): A Bayesian skill rating system. In: Advances in Neural Information Processing Systems 20 (2007)
12. Jaynes, E.T.: 15.7 The Borel-Kolmogorov paradox. In: Probability Theory: The Logic of Science, pp. 467–470. CUP (2003)

13. Jones, C., Plotkin, G.D.: A probabilistic powerdomain of evaluations. In: LICS, pp. 186–195. IEEE Computer Society, Los Alamitos (1989)
14. Kiselyov, O., Shan, C.: Monolingual probabilistic programming using generalized coroutines. In: UAI (2009)
15. Koller, D., Friedman, N.: Probabilistic Graphical Models. The MIT Press, Cambridge (2009)
16. Koller, D., McAllester, D.A., Pfeffer, A.: Effective Bayesian inference for stochastic programs. In: AAAI/IAAI, pp. 740–747 (1997)
17. Kozen, D.: Semantics of probabilistic programs. J. Comput. Syst. Sci. 22(3), 328–350 (1981)
18. Kschischang, F.R., Frey, B.J., Loeliger, H.-A.: Factor graphs and the sum-product algorithm. IEEE Transactions on Information Theory 47(2), 498–519 (2001)
19. Kwiatkowska, M.Z., Norman, G., Parker, D.: Quantitative analysis with the probabilistic model checker PRISM. ENTCS 153(2), 5–31 (2006)
20. Lowe, G.: Quantifying information flow. In: CSFW, pp. 18–31. IEEE Computer Society, Los Alamitos (2002)
21. MacKay, D.J.C.: Information Theory, Inference, and Learning Algorithms. CUP (2003)
22. McCallum, A., Schultz, K., Singh, S.: FACTORIE: Probabilistic programming via imperatively defined factor graphs. In: Poster at 23rd Annual Conference on Neural Information Processing Systems, NIPS (2009)
23. McIver, A., Morgan, C.: Abstraction, refinement and proof for probabilistic systems. Monographs in computer science. Springer, Heidelberg (2005)
24. McSherry, F.: Privacy integrated queries: an extensible platform for privacy-preserving data analysis. In: SIGMOD Conference, pp. 19–30. ACM, New York (2009)
25. Minka, T., Winn, J., Guiver, J., Kannan, A.: Infer.NET 2.3 (November 2009), Software available from `http://research.microsoft.com/infernet`
26. Minka, T., Winn, J.M.: Gates. In: NIPS, pp. 1073–1080. MIT Press, Cambridge (2008)
27. Minka, T.P.: Expectation Propagation for approximate Bayesian inference. In: UAI, pp. 362–369. Morgan Kaufmann, San Francisco (2001)
28. Ntzoufras, I.: Bayesian Modeling Using WinBUGS. Wiley, Chichester (2009)
29. Panangaden, P.: Labelled Markov processes. Imperial College Press, London (2009)
30. Park, S., Pfenning, F., Thrun, S.: A probabilistic language based upon sampling functions. In: POPL, pp. 171–182. ACM, New York (2005)
31. Pfeffer, A.: IBAL: A probabilistic rational programming language. In: Nebel, B. (ed.) IJCAI, pp. 733–740. Morgan Kaufmann, San Francisco (2001)
32. Pfeffer, A.: The design and implementation of IBAL: A General-Purpose Probabilistic Language. In: Statistical Relational Learning. MIT Press, Cambridge (2007)
33. Ramsey, N., Pfeffer, A.: Stochastic lambda calculus and monads of probability distributions. In: POPL, pp. 154–165 (2002)
34. Reed, J., Pierce, B.C.: Distance makes the types grow stronger: A calculus for differential privacy. In: ICFP, pp. 157–168 (2010)
35. Saheb-Djahromi, N.: Probabilistic LCF. In: Winkowski, J. (ed.) MFCS 1978. LNCS, vol. 64, pp. 442–451. Springer, Heidelberg (1978)
36. Syme, D., Granicz, A., Cisternino, A.: Expert F#. Apress (2007)
37. Winn, J., Minka, T.: Probabilistic programming with Infer.NET. Machine Learning Summer School lecture notes (2009), `http://research.microsoft.com/~minka/papers/mlss2009/`
38. Winn, J.M., Bishop, C.M.: Variational message passing. Journal of Machine Learning Research 6, 661–694 (2005)

Transfer Function Synthesis without Quantifier Elimination

Jörg Brauer[1] and Andy King[2]

[1] Embedded Software Laboratory, RWTH Aachen University, Germany
[2] Portcullis Computer Security Limited, Pinner, UK

Abstract. Recently it has been shown how transfer functions for linear template constraints can be derived for bit-vector programs by operating over propositional Boolean formulae. The drawback of this method is that it relies on existential quantifier elimination, which induces a computational bottleneck. The contribution of this paper is a novel method for synthesising transfer functions that does not rely on quantifier elimination. We demonstrate the practicality of the method for generating transfer functions for both intervals and octagons.

1 Introduction

In model checking [3] the behaviour of a system is formally specified with a model. All paths through the program are then exhaustively checked against its requirements. The detailed nature of the requirements entails that the program is simulated in a fine-grained way, sometimes down to the level of individual bits. Because of the complexity of this reasoning there has been much interest in representing states of a program symbolically, as Boolean functions, which enables states that share commonality to be represented without duplicating their commonality.

The key idea in abstract interpretation [10] is to abstract away from the detailed nature of states. Then the program checker operates over classes of related states — collections of states that are equivalent in some sense — rather than individual states. If the number of classes is small, then all the paths through the program can be examined without incurring the problems of state-space explosion. When carefully constructed, the classes of states can preserve sufficient information to prove correctness. However, sometimes so much detail is lost when working with classes that the technique cannot infer useful information. This is because it critically depends on the expressiveness of the classes and the class transformers chosen to model the instructions that arise in the program. Class transformers are traditionally known as transfer functions [16]; they express how input states are mapped to output states by an instruction. If an input state is described by a class, then the transfer function is required to simulate the execution of the instruction by computing a class which faithfully describes the output state. Constructing transfer functions is difficult, especially when the instructions are low-level and operate over finite machine arithmetic.

G. Barthe (Ed.): ESOP 2011, LNCS 6602, pp. 97–115, 2011.
© Springer-Verlag Berlin Heidelberg 2011

This is because classes are themselves expressed as high-level geometric concepts such as affine and polyhedral spaces, presenting a semantic gap that has to be bridged.

The seminal work of Reps and his colleagues [29] advocated the automatic synthesis of transfer functions, though recently the topic has attracted increasing attention [6,19,23] because of the desire to generate transfer functions for blocks rather than single instructions. This can improve precision when there is a close coupling between the operations that constitute a block [19], which is often the case when recovering high-level semantics from assembly code, for instance, recovering a 16-bit addition from two consecutive 8-bit additions with carry.

1.1 Deriving Transfer Functions by Quantifier Elimination

Boolean formulae are germane to the problem of transfer function synthesis since the semantics of blocks are naturally represented as input-output relations — a technique that is colloquially referred to as bit-blasting [7]. This formulation of the semantics of a block dovetails with the quantifier-based approach [23] to transfer function synthesis since, when a formula is presented in CNF, existential and universal quantifier elimination can be realised straightforwardly [20].

To illustrate the role of quantification, suppose a formula models a block that mutates a single register whose values on entry and exit are represented by bit-vectors $\boldsymbol{x}$ and $\boldsymbol{x}'$, respectively. To derive a transfer function for interval analysis, it is necessary to ascertain how the maximal value of $\boldsymbol{x}'$, denoted $\boldsymbol{x}'_u$, relates to the minimal and maximal values of $\boldsymbol{x}$, denoted $\boldsymbol{x}_\ell$ and $\boldsymbol{x}_u$. The value of $\boldsymbol{x}'_u$ can be specified in logic [6,23] by asserting that: (i) for every value of $\boldsymbol{x}$ that falls in the interval $[\boldsymbol{x}_\ell, \boldsymbol{x}_u]$, the value of $\boldsymbol{x}'_u$ is greater or equal to $\boldsymbol{x}'$, and (ii) for some value of $\boldsymbol{x}$ in $[\boldsymbol{x}_\ell, \boldsymbol{x}_u]$, the output $\boldsymbol{x}'$ takes the value of $\boldsymbol{x}'_u$. The "for some" can be expressed with existential quantification, but the "for every" can only be expressed with universal quantification. By applying quantifier elimination, a direct relationship between $\boldsymbol{x}_\ell$, $\boldsymbol{x}_u$, and $\boldsymbol{x}'_u$ can be found, yielding a mechanism for computing $\boldsymbol{x}'_u$ in terms of $\boldsymbol{x}_l$ and $\boldsymbol{x}_u$.

1.2 The Drawbacks of Quantifier Elimination

Transfer function synthesis thus involves eliminating quantified variables from $\forall \boldsymbol{y} : \varphi$ where φ is a system of propositional constraints and $\boldsymbol{y}$ is a tuple of variables. When φ is propositional, a CNF formula ψ that is equisatisfiable, denoted $\equiv$, to φ can be straightforwardly found [27] by introducing fresh variables, denoted $\boldsymbol{z}$, to give $\varphi \equiv \exists \boldsymbol{z} : \psi$. The transfer function synthesis problem then amounts to solving $\forall \boldsymbol{y} : \exists \boldsymbol{z} : \psi$ where ψ is in CNF. Alternating quantifiers also arise when transfer functions are synthesised from piece-wise linear constraints [23].

To eliminate existentially quantified variables, resolution [20, Chap. 9.2.3] is applied, which may be prohibitively expensive: the quadratic nature of each resolution step compromises tractability as the size of $\boldsymbol{z}$ increases. The size of $\boldsymbol{z}$ is proportional to the number of logical connectives in φ which, in turn, depends on the size of the bit-vectors and the complexity of the block under consideration. It is therefore no surprise that this approach has only been demonstrated for blocks of microcontroller code where the word-size is just 8 bits [6]. Thus far, the complexity of resolution has thwarted the wider applicability of this technique, even when applied carefully, which motivates the search for alternative methods.

1.3 Avoiding Quantifier Elimination

Our contribution is to eliminate the need for existential quantifier elimination altogether and replace resolution with successive calls to a SAT solver, where the number of calls grows linearly with the word-size. To illustrate, consider an octagon [22] which consists of a system of inequalities of the form $\pm x \pm y \leq d$. For each of these inequalities, our approach derives the least $d \in \mathbb{Z}$ (which is uniquely determined) such that the inequality holds for all feasible values of x and y as defined by some predicate.

As an example, consider the inequality $x + y \leq d$. The constant d is characterised as $d = \min\{c \in \mathbb{Z} \mid \forall \boldsymbol{x} : \forall \boldsymbol{y} : P(\boldsymbol{x}, \boldsymbol{y}) \wedge (\boldsymbol{x} + \boldsymbol{y} \leq c)\}$ where $P(\boldsymbol{x}, \boldsymbol{y})$ is a predicate constraining the values of bit-vectors $\boldsymbol{x}$ and $\boldsymbol{y}$. Further, given a machine with word-length w, the maximal value in an unsigned representation is given as $2^w - 1$, and thus we can derive an initial constraint $0 \leq d \wedge d \leq 2 \cdot (2^w - 1)$ for d, which can be expressed disjunctively as $\mu_\ell \vee \mu_u$ where:

$$\mu_\ell = (0 \leq d \wedge d \leq 2^w - 1) \qquad \mu_u = (2^w \leq d \wedge d \leq 2 \cdot (2^w - 1))$$

To determine which disjunct characterises d, it is sufficient to test the formula $\exists \boldsymbol{x} : \exists \boldsymbol{y} : P(\boldsymbol{x}, \boldsymbol{y}) \wedge (\boldsymbol{x} + \boldsymbol{y} \geq 2^w)$ for *satisfiability*. If satisfiable, then μ_u is entailed by d, and μ_ℓ otherwise. We proceed by decomposing the new characterisation into a disjunction and repeating this step w times to give d exactly. When a transfer function is formulated as a system of guarded affine updates [6, Sect. 2] then this range refinement technique can be applied to synthesise guards on the input values of variables.

The second contribution is to finesse the need for quantifier elimination in the generation of the input-output transformers that constitute the updates of the transfer functions. We demonstrate this construction not only for intervals, but for transfer functions over octagons. The method is based on computing an affine abstraction of a Boolean formula. Operationally, an update is applied to those inputs that satisfy the respective guard; the update details how the bounds of an input interval are mapped to new bounds of an output interval. In the case of octagons, the update maps the constants on the input octagonal inequalities to new constants on the output inequalities. Deriving updates for octagons requires range refinement to be interleaved with affine abstraction, which represents a third contribution. As a fourth contribution, we suggest a simple way of evaluating these transfer functions.

1.4 Outline of the Approach

Overall, the paper proposes a systematic technique for inferring transfer functions that are defined as systems of guarded updates. Transfer functions are inferred for a block by modeling each instruction as one of (at most) three Boolean functions, according to whether it overflows, underflows or does neither (is exact). A mode combination is then chosen for each instruction, and a single Boolean formula is constructed for the block by composing a formula for each instruction in the prescribed mode. If the composed formula is unsatisfiable, then the mode combination is inconsistent. Otherwise the mode combination is feasible and describes one type of wrapping (or non-wrapping) behaviour that can be realised within the block. The formula is then used to distill a guard paired with an update; one pair is computed for each feasible mode combination.

The guard, which is the optimal octagonal abstraction of the formula, is constructed one octagonal constraint at a time, by applying a form of dichotomy search, which amounts to a series of calls a SAT solver, as is explained in Sect. 2. The update component of the pair specifies how, when the guard is satisfied, the constraints in an input octagon are mapped to constraints in the output octagon (or in the degenerative case how to adjust bounds on intervals). Computing the update amounts to inferring a relationship between the bound on an output constraint and the bounds on the input constraints. Such a relationship can again be derived by repeated SAT solving, as detailed in Sect. 3. Replicating this construction for each of the output constraints gives the update operation for the feasible mode combination.

All these techniques are illustrated for blocks of 32-bit AVR UC3 assembly code [1], though the techniques are completely generic. We present experimental evidence in Sect. 5 which shows that the techniques presented in the paper are able to synthesise transfer functions for blocks where previous approaches based on quantifier elimination were prohibitively expensive. Sect. 6 surveys the related work and Sect. 7 concludes.

2 Deriving Guards

We express the concrete semantics of a block with Boolean formulae. Whereas universal quantifier elimination is attractive computationally, this is not so for the elimination of existentially quantified variables. We overcome this problem by reformulating the construction given in [6] for the synthesis of guards.

2.1 Deriving Interval Guards by Range Refinement

Consider deriving a transfer function for the operation `INC R0`, which increments the value of `R0` by one and stores the result in `R0`. For this example, we assume that the operands are unsigned. We represent the value of `R0` by a bit-vector $\boldsymbol{r0}$ and let $\langle \boldsymbol{r0} \rangle = \sum_{i=0}^{31} 2^i \cdot \boldsymbol{r0}[i]$ where $\boldsymbol{r0}[i]$ denotes the ith element of $\boldsymbol{r0}$. The instruction itself can operate in one of two modes: (1) it overflows (iff $\langle \boldsymbol{r0} \rangle = 2^{32} - 1$) or (2) it is exact (otherwise). The semantics of these two modes can be expressed as two formulae:

$$\begin{array}{ll} (1) & \varphi_O(\boldsymbol{X}) = \varphi(\boldsymbol{X}) \wedge (\bigwedge_{i=0}^{31} \boldsymbol{r0}[i]) \\ (2) & \varphi_E(\boldsymbol{X}) = \varphi(\boldsymbol{X}) \wedge (\bigvee_{i=0}^{31} \neg \boldsymbol{r0}[i]) \end{array}$$

where $\varphi(\boldsymbol{X})$ encodes the increment over bit-vectors $\boldsymbol{X} = \{\boldsymbol{r0}, \boldsymbol{r0}'\}$ as follows:

$$\varphi(\boldsymbol{X}) = \bigwedge_{i=0}^{31} \left(\boldsymbol{r0}'[i] \leftrightarrow \boldsymbol{r0}[i] \oplus \bigwedge_{j=0}^{i-1} \boldsymbol{r0}[j]\right)$$

Both formulae can be converted into CNF by introducing fresh variables $\boldsymbol{z}$. We therefore denote the resulting formulae by $\varphi_E(\boldsymbol{X}, \boldsymbol{z})$ and $\varphi_O(\boldsymbol{X}, \boldsymbol{z})$. Following our initial approach [6], the transfer function for a multi-modal block (where the internal instructions can wrap) is described as a system of guarded updates. In the one-dimensional case, octagonal guards coincide with intervals. Each guard constitutes an upper-approximation of those inputs that are compatible with the specific mode. In case of the increment, we derive guards g_O and g_E defined as:

$$\begin{array}{lll} (1) & g_O = 2^{32} - 1 & \leq \langle \boldsymbol{r0} \rangle \leq 2^{32} - 1 \\ (2) & g_E = 0 & \leq \langle \boldsymbol{r0} \rangle \leq 2^{32} - 2 \end{array}$$

To obtain these guards, we solve a series of SAT instances, rather than following a monolithic all-in-one approach based on quantifier elimination [6]. To illustrate, consider the computation of a least upper bound d for $\langle \boldsymbol{r0} \rangle$ for the formula $\varphi_E(\boldsymbol{X}, \boldsymbol{z})$. We start by putting:

$$\psi_E^1(\boldsymbol{X}, \boldsymbol{z}) = \varphi_E(\boldsymbol{X}, \boldsymbol{z}) \wedge \langle \boldsymbol{r0} \rangle \geq 2^{31}$$

As 2^{31} is a power of two, we can finesse the need for a complicated Boolean encoding of the predicate $\geq$ by using the equivalent formula:

$$\psi_E^{\mathsf{simp},1}(\boldsymbol{X}, \boldsymbol{z}) = \varphi_E(\boldsymbol{X}, \boldsymbol{z}) \wedge \boldsymbol{r0}[31]$$

which is simpler both to formulate and to solve. Then, the satisfiability of $\psi_E^{\mathsf{simp},1}(\boldsymbol{X}, \boldsymbol{z})$ shows that $\boldsymbol{r0}$ takes a value in the range $2^{31} \leq \langle \boldsymbol{r0} \rangle \leq 2^{32} - 1$. Consequently, d occurs in the same range. We can thus further refine this range by testing:

$$\psi_E^2(\boldsymbol{X}, \boldsymbol{z}) = \varphi_E(\boldsymbol{z}) \wedge \langle \boldsymbol{r0} \rangle \geq (2^{31} + 2^{30})$$

for satisfiability, or equivalently $\varphi_E^{\mathsf{simp},2}(\boldsymbol{X}, \boldsymbol{z}) = \varphi_E(\boldsymbol{z}) \wedge \boldsymbol{r0}[31] \wedge \boldsymbol{r0}[30]$. As $\psi_E^{\mathsf{simp},2}(\boldsymbol{X}, \boldsymbol{z})$ is satisfiable, we infer that d satisfies $2^{30} + 2^{31} \leq d \leq 2^{32} - 1$. The method continues to refine the constraint on d into two equally sized halves. Only in the last iteration is the satisfiability check found to fail from which we conclude that $d = \sum_{i=1}^{31} 2^i = 2^{32} - 2$. Overall, this deduction requires 32 SAT instances, but the similarity of the instances suggests that the overhead can be mitigated somewhat by incremental SAT.

2.2 Deriving Octagonal Guards by Range Refinement

In a second example, we show how to extend the refinement technique from intervals to octagons. To illustrate the method, consider the following fragment:

```
1 : ADD R0, R1;     2 : MOV R2, R0;     3 : EOR R2, R1;     4 : LSL R2;
5 : SBC R2, R2;     6 : ADD R0, R2;     7 : EOR R0, R2;
```

This program corresponds to an assignment `R0' := isign(R0+R1,R1)` for signed values. The function `isign` assigns `abs(R0+R1)` to `R0` if `R1` is positive, and `-abs(R0+R1)` otherwise. `R2` is used as a temporary register. The sum of `R0` and `R1` is computed by instruction (1), and instructions (2) – (7) implement `isign`. The semantics of even this simple block is not obvious due to the bounded nature of machine arithmetic. For instance, if `abs` is applied to the smallest representable integer -2^{31} then the result is 2^{31} subject to overflow, which gives -2^{31}. To derive octagons that describe such corner cases, we have to consider all combinations of over- and underflow modes of the instructions. In the above program, the instructions `ADD` (sum) and `LSL` (left-shift) can wrap in different ways, and thus are multi-modal. Neither `EOR` nor `MOV` can wrap; they are both uni-modal. Note that in general, the instruction `SBC` (subtract-with-carry) is multi-modal. However, in the case of two equal operands, the instruction can only result in 0 or -1, depending on the carry-flag. We thus ignore the wrapping of `SBC R2, R2` and consider it to be uni-modal for simplicity. Note that only overflows occurred in the previous example since the single operand was unsigned.

Finding the feasible mode-combinations. In what follows, let $\mu(\boldsymbol{X})$ denote the Boolean encoding of the instruction `ADD R0, R1` over bit-vectors $\boldsymbol{X} = \{\boldsymbol{r0}, \boldsymbol{r1}, \ldots\}$ obtained through static single assignment conversion. The semantics of `ADD R0, R1` is to compute the sum of `R0` and `R1` and store the result in `R0`. Since we are now working with signed objects, let $\langle\langle \boldsymbol{x} \rangle\rangle = (\sum_{i=0}^{w-2} 2^i \cdot \boldsymbol{x}[i]) - 2^{w-1} \cdot \boldsymbol{x}[w-1]$ denote the value of $\boldsymbol{x}$ where $\boldsymbol{x}[31]$ is interpreted as the sign-bit. Then, `ADD R0, R1` has three modes of operation: overflow, underflow and exact operation. Underflow occurs, for example, if the arithmetic sum of $\langle\langle \boldsymbol{r0} \rangle\rangle$ and $\langle\langle \boldsymbol{r1} \rangle\rangle$ is less than -2^{31}. The semantics of these modes can be expressed as three Boolean formulae:

$$\mu_O(\boldsymbol{X}) = \mu(\boldsymbol{X}) \wedge \neg\boldsymbol{r0}[31] \wedge \neg\boldsymbol{r1}[31] \wedge \boldsymbol{r0}'[31]$$
$$\mu_U(\boldsymbol{X}) = \mu(\boldsymbol{X}) \wedge \boldsymbol{r0}[31] \wedge \boldsymbol{r1}[31] \wedge \neg\boldsymbol{r0}'[31]$$
$$\mu_E(\boldsymbol{X}) = \mu(\boldsymbol{X}) \wedge (\boldsymbol{r0}[31] \vee \boldsymbol{r1}[31] \vee \neg\boldsymbol{r0}'[31]) \wedge (\neg\boldsymbol{r0}[31] \vee \neg\boldsymbol{r1}[31] \vee \boldsymbol{r0}'[31])$$

The instruction `LSL R2` shifts `R2` to the left by one bit-position, and the most-significant bit is moved into the carry-flag. If the carry-flag is set, an overflow occurs. Let $\nu_O(\boldsymbol{X})$ and $\nu_E(\boldsymbol{X})$ thus express the overflow and exact modes of `LSL R2`. In an analogous way to the first `ADD`, let $\eta_O(\boldsymbol{X})$, $\eta_U(\boldsymbol{X})$ and $\eta_E(\boldsymbol{X})$ express the semantics of the instruction `ADD R0, R2`. Using these encodings that satisfy a single mode, we can compose a Boolean formula for a fixed mode-combination that expresses the possibility of one mode of one operation being consistent with another mode of another operation; the unsatisfiability of this formula indicates that the chosen modes are inconsistent. For example, the combination of $\mu_U(\boldsymbol{X})$, $\nu_E(\boldsymbol{X})$ and $\eta_E(\boldsymbol{X})$ is infeasible. The above block constitutes $3 \cdot 2 \cdot 3$ combinations of modes, but only 6 of which are satisfiable. We thus have to derive guards only for the feasible combinations.

Deriving guards for the feasible mode-combinations. Consider the case where (1) underflows, (4) overflows and (6) is exact, with the corresponding formula denoted $\xi(\boldsymbol{X})$. To derive an octagonal abstraction of the inputs that satisfy $\xi(\boldsymbol{X})$, first consider the problem of computing the least upper bound d for the octagonal expression $-\langle\!\langle \boldsymbol{r0} \rangle\!\rangle - \langle\!\langle \boldsymbol{r1} \rangle\!\rangle$. To do so, let κ be a formula encoding $\langle\!\langle \boldsymbol{d} \rangle\!\rangle = -\langle\!\langle \boldsymbol{r0} \rangle\!\rangle - \langle\!\langle \boldsymbol{r1} \rangle\!\rangle$ where $\boldsymbol{d}$ is signed and κ is extended to 34 bits to prevent wraps in the octagonal expression (cp. [9, Sect. 3.3]). Then check:

$$\psi^1(\boldsymbol{X}) = \xi(\boldsymbol{X}) \wedge \kappa \wedge \neg \boldsymbol{d}[33]$$

for satisfiability to derive a coarse approximation of d. The satisfiability of $\psi^1(\boldsymbol{X})$ shows that $d \geq 0$. We thus proceed with testing:

$$\psi^2(\boldsymbol{X}) = \xi(\boldsymbol{X}) \wedge \kappa \wedge \neg \boldsymbol{d}[33] \wedge \boldsymbol{d}[32]$$

for satisfiability. Satisfiability of $\psi^2(\boldsymbol{X})$ shows that $d \geq 2^{32}$. Following this strategy, the remaining instantiated formulae are unsatisfiable, and we thus infer the exact bound $\langle\!\langle \boldsymbol{d} \rangle\!\rangle = 2^{32}$. Rearranging $-\langle\!\langle \boldsymbol{r0} \rangle\!\rangle - \langle\!\langle \boldsymbol{r1} \rangle\!\rangle \leq 2^{32}$ we obtain $-2^{32} \leq \langle\!\langle \boldsymbol{r0} \rangle\!\rangle + \langle\!\langle \boldsymbol{r1} \rangle\!\rangle$. Using the same tactic, we derive $\langle\!\langle \boldsymbol{r0} \rangle\!\rangle + \langle\!\langle \boldsymbol{r1} \rangle\!\rangle \leq -2^{31} - 1$. Repeating this tactic for all five feasible mode-combinations, we obtain the following optimal octagonal guards:

$$\begin{array}{lclcl}
g_{O^{(1)},O^{(4)},U^{(6)}} & = & 2^{31} \leq \langle\!\langle \boldsymbol{r0} \rangle\!\rangle + \langle\!\langle \boldsymbol{r1} \rangle\!\rangle \leq 2^{31} & \wedge & 0 \leq \langle\!\langle \boldsymbol{r1} \rangle\!\rangle \leq 2^{31} - 1 \\
g_{E^{(1)},E^{(4)},E^{(6)}} & = & -2^{31} \leq \langle\!\langle \boldsymbol{r0} \rangle\!\rangle + \langle\!\langle \boldsymbol{r1} \rangle\!\rangle \leq 2^{31} - 1 & & \\
g_{U^{(1)},O^{(4)},E^{(6)}} & = & -2^{32} \leq \langle\!\langle \boldsymbol{r0} \rangle\!\rangle + \langle\!\langle \boldsymbol{r1} \rangle\!\rangle \leq -2^{31} - 1 & & \\
g_{E^{(1)},O^{(4)},E^{(6)}} & = & 0 \leq \langle\!\langle \boldsymbol{r0} \rangle\!\rangle + \langle\!\langle \boldsymbol{r1} \rangle\!\rangle \leq 2^{31} - 1 & \wedge & -2^{31} \leq \langle\!\langle \boldsymbol{r1} \rangle\!\rangle \leq 1 \\
g_{O^{(1)},O^{(4)},E^{(6)}} & = & 2^{31} + 1 \leq \langle\!\langle \boldsymbol{r0} \rangle\!\rangle + \langle\!\langle \boldsymbol{r1} \rangle\!\rangle \leq 2^{32} & &
\end{array}$$

Redundant inequalities, which are themselves entailed by the given guards, are omitted for clarity of presentation.

Complexity. A total of $4 \cdot 34 + 4 \cdot 33$ SAT instances is solved for each guard. This is due to the bit-extended representation for constraints $\pm v_1 \pm v_2 \leq d$, whereas 33 bits are used for constraints $\pm v_1 \leq d$. While this may appear large, it is important to appreciate that the number of SAT instances grows linearly with the bit-width. By way of comparison with [6], adding a single propositional variable to a formula can increase the complexity of resolution quadratically.

3 Deriving Updates

Transformers over template constraints have been previously formulated using quantification [6,23]. To avoid this, we derive affine relationships between output variables and input variables. These relations are then lifted to symbolic constraints that detail how the bounds of an input interval are mapped to the bounds of an output interval. The technique is then refined to support octagons. Note that Sect. 3.2 and Sect. 3.3 are just given for pedagogical purposes; only Sect. 3.4 provides a linear symbolic update operation that is optimal.

3.1 Inferring Affine Equalities

Our algorithm computes an affine abstraction of the models for a given mode-combination. To solve for affine input-output relations, let $\boldsymbol{X}$ denote the set of bit-vectors as before. Consider the Boolean formula $\xi(\boldsymbol{X})$ for the case where (1) underflows, (4) overflows and (6) is exact. The process of deriving an affine abstraction follows the scheme given in [6, Sect. 3.2]. It starts with solving the formula $\xi(\boldsymbol{X})$, which produces a model $\mathbf{m}_1$ where:

$$\mathbf{m}_1 = \{\, \langle\!\langle \boldsymbol{r0'} \rangle\!\rangle = -2^{31} \,, \quad \langle\!\langle \boldsymbol{r1'} \rangle\!\rangle = -1 \,, \quad \langle\!\langle \boldsymbol{r0} \rangle\!\rangle = -2^{31}+1 \,, \quad \langle\!\langle \boldsymbol{r1} \rangle\!\rangle = -1 \,\}$$

We can equivalently write $\mathbf{m}_1$ as a matrix, denoted $\mathbf{M}_1$. With variable ordering $\langle \boldsymbol{r0'}, \boldsymbol{r1'}, \boldsymbol{r0}, \boldsymbol{r1} \rangle$ on columns, this gives:

$$\mathbf{M}_1 = \left[\begin{array}{cccc|l} 1&0&0&0 & -2^{31} \\ 0&1&0&0 & -1 \\ 0&0&1&0 & -2^{31}+1 \\ 0&0&0&1 & -1 \end{array}\right]$$

We then add a disequality constraint $\langle\!\langle \boldsymbol{r1} \rangle\!\rangle \neq -1$ to $\xi(\boldsymbol{X})$ in order to obtain a new solution that is not covered by $\mathbf{M}_1$. Denote this formula by $\xi'(\boldsymbol{X})$. Then, solving for $\xi'(\boldsymbol{X})$ produces a different model $\mathbf{m}_2$, say:

$$\mathbf{m}_2 = \{\, \langle\!\langle \boldsymbol{r0'} \rangle\!\rangle = -2^{31}+2 \,, \quad \langle\!\langle \boldsymbol{r1'} \rangle\!\rangle = -3 \,, \quad \langle\!\langle \boldsymbol{r0} \rangle\!\rangle = -2^{31}+1 \,, \quad \langle\!\langle \boldsymbol{r1} \rangle\!\rangle = -3 \,\}$$

Joining $\mathbf{M}_1$ with $\mathbf{M_2}$, which is likewise obtained from $\mathbf{m}_2$, yields a matrix that describes that affine relations common to both models:

$$\mathbf{M}_1 \sqcup \mathbf{M}_2 = \left[\begin{array}{cccc|l} 1&0&0&0 & -2^{31} \\ 0&1&0&0 & -1 \\ 0&0&1&0 & -2^{31}+1 \\ 0&0&0&1 & -1 \end{array}\right] \sqcup \left[\begin{array}{cccc|l} 1&0&0&0 & -2^{31}+2 \\ 0&1&0&0 & -3 \\ 0&0&1&0 & -2^{31}+1 \\ 0&0&0&1 & -3 \end{array}\right] = \left[\begin{array}{cccc|l} 1&1&0&0 & -2^{31}-1 \\ 0&1&0&-1 & 0 \\ 0&0&1&0 & -2^{31}+1 \end{array}\right]$$

Our algorithm now attempts to find a model that violates the constraint given through the last row, that is, $\langle\!\langle \boldsymbol{r0} \rangle\!\rangle = -2^{31}+1$. Adding a disequality constraint to $\xi'(\boldsymbol{X})$ yields a new formula $\xi''(\boldsymbol{X})$, for which a SAT solver finds a model:

$$\mathbf{m}_3 = \{\, \langle\!\langle \boldsymbol{r0'} \rangle\!\rangle = -2^{31} \,, \quad \langle\!\langle \boldsymbol{r1'} \rangle\!\rangle = -4 \,, \quad \langle\!\langle \boldsymbol{r0} \rangle\!\rangle = -2^{31}+4 \,, \quad \langle\!\langle \boldsymbol{r1} \rangle\!\rangle = -4 \,\}$$

Then, we join $\mathbf{M}_1 \sqcup \mathbf{M}_2$ with $\mathbf{M}_3$ to give:

$$\left[\begin{array}{cccc|l} 1&1&0&0 & -2^{31}-1 \\ 0&1&0&-1 & 0 \\ 0&0&1&0 & -2^{31}+1 \end{array}\right] \sqcup \left[\begin{array}{cccc|l} 1&0&0&0 & -2^{31} \\ 0&1&0&0 & -4 \\ 0&0&1&0 & -2^{31}+4 \\ 0&0&0&1 & -4 \end{array}\right] = \left[\begin{array}{cccc|l} 1&0&1&1 & -2^{32} \\ 0&1&0&-1 & 0 \end{array}\right]$$

Adding a disequality constraint to suppress $\langle\!\langle \boldsymbol{r1'} \rangle\!\rangle - \langle\!\langle \boldsymbol{r1} \rangle\!\rangle = 0$ yields an unsatisfiable formula, likewise for $\langle\!\langle \boldsymbol{r0'} \rangle\!\rangle + \langle\!\langle \boldsymbol{r1} \rangle\!\rangle + \langle\!\langle \boldsymbol{r0} \rangle\!\rangle = -2^{32}$. Indeed, we have

$$(\mathbf{M}_1 \sqcup \mathbf{M}_2) \sqcup \mathbf{M}_3 = \textstyle\bigsqcup_{i \in \mathbb{N}} \mathbf{M}_i$$

where $\mathbf{M}_i$ are matrices describing different models m_i of $\xi(\boldsymbol{X})$. Indeed, an affine summary of a mode-combination is in some sense universally quantified, since its relation is satisfied by every model. Moreover $(\mathbf{M}_1 \sqcup \mathbf{M}_2) \sqcup \mathbf{M}_3$ represents the best affine abstraction of $\xi(\boldsymbol{X})$ [6,19]. The resulting equations, however, express relationships between variables but not between symbolic intervals. As it turns out, we can lift $(\mathbf{M}_1 \sqcup \mathbf{M}_2) \sqcup \mathbf{M}_3$ to an equation system over intervals by applying a set of straightforward transformations.

Complexity. Note that the chain-length in the affine domain is linear in the number of variables in the system [18]. Thus, the number of iterations required to compute a fixed point is bounded by the number of variables and does not depend on the bit-width.

3.2 Lifting Affine Equalities to Interval Updates

We explain how to transform $(\mathbf{M}_1 \sqcup \mathbf{M}_2) \sqcup \mathbf{M}_3$ over variables in $\boldsymbol{X}$ into an equation system over range boundaries. To do so, let $\boldsymbol{V} \subseteq \boldsymbol{X}$ denote the bit-vectors on entry of the block, and let $\boldsymbol{V}' \subseteq \boldsymbol{X}$ denote the bit-vectors on exit. Further, introduce fresh variables

$$\boldsymbol{V}_\ell = \{\boldsymbol{r0}_\ell, \boldsymbol{r1}_\ell\} \quad \boldsymbol{V}_u = \{\boldsymbol{r0}_u, \boldsymbol{r1}_u\} \quad \boldsymbol{V}'_\ell = \{\boldsymbol{r0}'_\ell, \boldsymbol{r1}'_\ell\} \quad \boldsymbol{V}'_u = \{\boldsymbol{r0}'_u, \boldsymbol{r1}'_u\}$$

and if necessary transform the equations such that the left-hand side consists of only one variable in $\boldsymbol{V}'$. For the above equations, this gives:

$$\begin{aligned} \langle\!\langle \boldsymbol{r1}' \rangle\!\rangle &= \langle\!\langle \boldsymbol{r1} \rangle\!\rangle \\ \langle\!\langle \boldsymbol{r0}' \rangle\!\rangle &= -\langle\!\langle \boldsymbol{r0} \rangle\!\rangle - \langle\!\langle \boldsymbol{r1} \rangle\!\rangle - 2^{32} \end{aligned}$$

These equations imply the following affine relations on interval boundaries:

$$\begin{aligned} \langle\!\langle \boldsymbol{r1}' \rangle\!\rangle_u &= \langle\!\langle \boldsymbol{r1}' \rangle\!\rangle_u & \qquad \langle\!\langle \boldsymbol{r0}' \rangle\!\rangle_u &= -\langle\!\langle \boldsymbol{r1} \rangle\!\rangle_\ell - \langle\!\langle \boldsymbol{r0} \rangle\!\rangle_\ell - 2^{32} \\ \langle\!\langle \boldsymbol{r1}' \rangle\!\rangle_\ell &= \langle\!\langle \boldsymbol{r1}' \rangle\!\rangle_\ell & \qquad \langle\!\langle \boldsymbol{r0}' \rangle\!\rangle_\ell &= -\langle\!\langle \boldsymbol{r1} \rangle\!\rangle_u - \langle\!\langle \boldsymbol{r0} \rangle\!\rangle_u - 2^{32} \end{aligned}$$

To derive such as system, transform each of the original equations into the form $\lambda_{\boldsymbol{v}'} \cdot \boldsymbol{v}' = \sum_{\boldsymbol{v} \in \boldsymbol{V}} \lambda_{\boldsymbol{v}} \cdot \boldsymbol{v} + d$ where $\boldsymbol{v}' \in \boldsymbol{V}'$, $\lambda_{\boldsymbol{v}'} > 0$ and $\lambda_{\boldsymbol{v}} \in \mathbb{Z}$ for all $\boldsymbol{v} \in \boldsymbol{V}$. This can always be achieved due to the variable ordering. For example, the system below on the left can be transformed into the system on the right by applying elementary row operations:

$$\left[\begin{array}{cccc|c} 1 & -1 & 0 & 0 & 1 \\ 0 & 1 & 0 & -1 & 2 \end{array}\right] \quad \rightsquigarrow \quad \left[\begin{array}{cccc|c} 1 & 0 & 0 & -1 & 3 \\ 0 & 1 & 0 & -1 & 2 \end{array}\right]$$

Note that the leading coefficients are positive. We then replace each original equation by a pair of equations as follows:

$$\begin{aligned} \lambda_{\boldsymbol{v}'} \cdot \boldsymbol{v}'_u &= \textstyle\sum_{\boldsymbol{v} \in \boldsymbol{X}} \lambda_{\boldsymbol{v}} \cdot \beta(\lambda_{\boldsymbol{v}}, \boldsymbol{v}) + d \\ \lambda_{\boldsymbol{v}'} \cdot \boldsymbol{v}'_\ell &= \textstyle\sum_{\boldsymbol{v} \in \boldsymbol{X}} \lambda_{\boldsymbol{v}} \cdot \beta(-\lambda_{\boldsymbol{v}}, \boldsymbol{v}) + d \end{aligned}$$

The map $\beta : \mathbb{Z} \times \boldsymbol{V} \to (\boldsymbol{V}_\ell \cup \boldsymbol{V}_u)$ is defined as $\beta(\lambda, \boldsymbol{v}) = \boldsymbol{v}_\ell$ if $\lambda < 0$ and $\beta(\lambda, \boldsymbol{v}) = \boldsymbol{v}_u$ otherwise. The key idea when constructing the upper bound is to replace each occurrence of a variable in the original system with its upper bound in case its coefficient is positive, and with its lower bound otherwise. This task is performed by β. An analogous technique is applied when defining the lower bound. Applying this technique to all affine systems, we obtain the following five transfer functions (with the identity constraints on $\boldsymbol{r1}'_\ell$ and $\boldsymbol{r1}'_u$ omitted):

$$f_{O^{(1)},O^{(4)},U^{(6)}} = \begin{cases} (\langle\!\langle \boldsymbol{r0}' \rangle\!\rangle_\ell = -2^{31}) \wedge \\ (\langle\!\langle \boldsymbol{r0}' \rangle\!\rangle_u = -2^{31}) \end{cases}$$

$$f_{E^{(1)},E^{(4)},E^{(6)}} = \begin{cases} (\langle\!\langle \boldsymbol{r0}' \rangle\!\rangle_\ell = \langle\!\langle \boldsymbol{r0}_\ell \rangle\!\rangle + \langle\!\langle \boldsymbol{r1}_\ell \rangle\!\rangle) \wedge \\ (\langle\!\langle \boldsymbol{r0}' \rangle\!\rangle_u = \langle\!\langle \boldsymbol{r0}_u \rangle\!\rangle + \langle\!\langle \boldsymbol{r1}_u \rangle\!\rangle) \end{cases}$$

$$f_{U^{(1)},O^{(4)},E^{(6)}} = \begin{cases} (\langle\!\langle \boldsymbol{r0}' \rangle\!\rangle_\ell = -2^{32} - \langle\!\langle \boldsymbol{r0}_u \rangle\!\rangle - \langle\!\langle \boldsymbol{r1}_u \rangle\!\rangle) \wedge \\ (\langle\!\langle \boldsymbol{r0}' \rangle\!\rangle_u = -2^{32} - \langle\!\langle \boldsymbol{r0}_\ell \rangle\!\rangle - \langle\!\langle \boldsymbol{r1}_\ell \rangle\!\rangle) \end{cases}$$

$$f_{E^{(1)},O^{(4)},E^{(6)}} = \begin{cases} (\langle\!\langle \boldsymbol{r0}' \rangle\!\rangle_\ell = -\langle\!\langle \boldsymbol{r0}_u \rangle\!\rangle - \langle\!\langle \boldsymbol{r1}_u \rangle\!\rangle) \wedge \\ (\langle\!\langle \boldsymbol{r0}' \rangle\!\rangle_u = -\langle\!\langle \boldsymbol{r0}_\ell \rangle\!\rangle - \langle\!\langle \boldsymbol{r1}_\ell \rangle\!\rangle) \end{cases}$$

$$f_{O^{(1)},O^{(4)},E^{(6)}} = \begin{cases} (\langle\!\langle \boldsymbol{r0}' \rangle\!\rangle_\ell = 2^{32} - \langle\!\langle \boldsymbol{r0}_u \rangle\!\rangle - \langle\!\langle \boldsymbol{r1}_u \rangle\!\rangle) \wedge \\ (\langle\!\langle \boldsymbol{r0}' \rangle\!\rangle_u = 2^{32} - \langle\!\langle \boldsymbol{r0}_\ell \rangle\!\rangle - \langle\!\langle \boldsymbol{r1}_\ell \rangle\!\rangle) \end{cases}$$

To illustrate the accuracy of this result, consider the application of the transfer function $f_{U^{(1)},O^{(4)},E^{(6)}}$ to the input intervals defined by:

$$\langle\!\langle \boldsymbol{r0}_\ell \rangle\!\rangle = -2^{31} \qquad \langle\!\langle \boldsymbol{r0}_u \rangle\!\rangle = -2^{31} + 4 \qquad \langle\!\langle \boldsymbol{r1}_\ell \rangle\!\rangle = -20 \qquad \langle\!\langle \boldsymbol{r1}_u \rangle\!\rangle = -10$$

Then, the above transfer function defines the output intervals by modelling the wrap that occurs in the first instruction `ADD R0 R1` to give $\langle\!\langle \boldsymbol{r0}'_\ell \rangle\!\rangle = -2^{31} + 6$ and $\langle\!\langle \boldsymbol{r0}'_u \rangle\!\rangle = -2^{31} + 20$.

3.3 Lifting Affine Equalities to Octagonal Updates

Consider deriving a transfer function for octagons for `ADD R0 R1; LSL R0` where `ADD` and `LSL` operate in exact modes. Computing the affine relation for this mode-combination gives $(\langle\!\langle \boldsymbol{r0}' \rangle\!\rangle = 2 \cdot \langle\!\langle \boldsymbol{r0} \rangle\!\rangle + 2 \cdot \langle\!\langle \boldsymbol{r1} \rangle\!\rangle) \wedge (\langle\!\langle \boldsymbol{r1}' \rangle\!\rangle = \langle\!\langle \boldsymbol{r1} \rangle\!\rangle)$. We aim to construct an update that maps octagonal input constraints with symbolic constants to octagonal outputs likewise with symbolic constants of the form:

$$\left\{ \begin{array}{r} \langle\!\langle \boldsymbol{r0} \rangle\!\rangle \le d_1 \\ \langle\!\langle \boldsymbol{r1} \rangle\!\rangle \le d_2 \\ -\langle\!\langle \boldsymbol{r0} \rangle\!\rangle \le d_3 \\ -\langle\!\langle \boldsymbol{r1} \rangle\!\rangle \le d_4 \\ \hline \langle\!\langle \boldsymbol{r0} \rangle\!\rangle + \langle\!\langle \boldsymbol{r1} \rangle\!\rangle \le d_5 \\ -\langle\!\langle \boldsymbol{r0} \rangle\!\rangle - \langle\!\langle \boldsymbol{r1} \rangle\!\rangle \le d_6 \\ -\langle\!\langle \boldsymbol{r0} \rangle\!\rangle + \langle\!\langle \boldsymbol{r1} \rangle\!\rangle \le d_7 \\ \langle\!\langle \boldsymbol{r0} \rangle\!\rangle - \langle\!\langle \boldsymbol{r1} \rangle\!\rangle \le d_8 \end{array} \right\} \rightsquigarrow \left\{ \begin{array}{r} \langle\!\langle \boldsymbol{r0}' \rangle\!\rangle \le 2 \cdot (d_1 + d_2) \\ \langle\!\langle \boldsymbol{r1}' \rangle\!\rangle \le d_2 \\ -\langle\!\langle \boldsymbol{r0}' \rangle\!\rangle \le 2 \cdot (d_3 + d_4) \\ -\langle\!\langle \boldsymbol{r1}' \rangle\!\rangle \le d_4 \\ \langle\!\langle \boldsymbol{r0}' \rangle\!\rangle + \langle\!\langle \boldsymbol{r1}' \rangle\!\rangle \le 2 \cdot d_1 + 3 \cdot d_2 \\ -\langle\!\langle \boldsymbol{r0}' \rangle\!\rangle - \langle\!\langle \boldsymbol{r1}' \rangle\!\rangle \le 2 \cdot d_3 + 3 \cdot d_4 \\ -\langle\!\langle \boldsymbol{r0}' \rangle\!\rangle + \langle\!\langle \boldsymbol{r1}' \rangle\!\rangle \le 2 \cdot (d_3 + d_4) + d_2 \\ \langle\!\langle \boldsymbol{r0}' \rangle\!\rangle - \langle\!\langle \boldsymbol{r1}' \rangle\!\rangle \le 2 \cdot (d_1 + d_2) + d_4 \end{array} \right\}$$

We start by constructing an update operation that uses the unary input constraints only, as indicated by the bar separator. We modify the method presented in Sect. 2.4 so as to express output constraints in terms of symbolic

Table 1. Intermediate results for inferring exact affine transformers for octagons

	$\langle\langle d'_1\rangle\rangle$	$\langle\langle d_1\rangle\rangle$	$\langle\langle d_2\rangle\rangle$	$\langle\langle d_3\rangle\rangle$	$\langle\langle d_4\rangle\rangle$	$\langle\langle d_5\rangle\rangle$	$\langle\langle d_6\rangle\rangle$	$\langle\langle d_7\rangle\rangle$	$\langle\langle d_8\rangle\rangle$	$\max(\langle\langle d'\rangle\rangle)$
m_1	1	1	1	0	0	1	0	1	1	2
m_2	8	3	3	−1	−1	5	−2	2	0	10
m_3	22	8	7	0	1	13	3	4	0	26
m_4	4	0	3	2	0	3	1	6	3	6

variables $d_1, \ldots, d_4$ from the input constraints. We obtain the four output unary constraints by an analogous technique as before by substituting the symbolic minima and maxima for the symbolic output constants. The binary output constraints are derived by linear combinations of the unary output constraints.

Since the output constraints do not use relational information from the inputs, such as $\langle\langle \boldsymbol{r0}\rangle\rangle + \langle\langle \boldsymbol{r1}\rangle\rangle \leq d_5$, we obtain a sub-optimal update. To illustrate, suppose $0 \leq \langle\langle \boldsymbol{r0}\rangle\rangle \leq 4$, $0 \leq \langle\langle \boldsymbol{r1}\rangle\rangle \leq 1$ and $\langle\langle \boldsymbol{r0}\rangle\rangle + \langle\langle \boldsymbol{r1}\rangle\rangle \leq 4$. Then we derive:

$$0 \leq \langle\langle \boldsymbol{r0'}\rangle\rangle \leq 10 \qquad 0 \leq \langle\langle \boldsymbol{r1'}\rangle\rangle \leq 1 \qquad 0 \leq \langle\langle \boldsymbol{r0'}\rangle\rangle + \langle\langle \boldsymbol{r1'}\rangle\rangle \leq 11$$

The optimal octagonal abstraction, however, confers the constraints $\langle\langle \boldsymbol{r0'}\rangle\rangle \leq 8$ and $\langle\langle \boldsymbol{r0'}\rangle\rangle + \langle\langle \boldsymbol{r1'}\rangle\rangle \leq 8$. Although the above method fails to propagate the effect of some inputs into the outputs, it retains the property that the update can be constructed straightforwardly in linear time by lifting the affine relations. In what follows, we will describe how to derive more precise affine relations for the outputs.

3.4 Inferring Affine Inequalities for Octagonal Updates

To derive more precise affine updates for octagons, let $\xi(\boldsymbol{X})$ denote the propositional encoding for `ADD R0 R1; LSL R0` where again `ADD` and `LSL` operate in exact modes. Consider inequality $\langle\langle \boldsymbol{r0'}\rangle\rangle \leq d'_1$ in the output octagon and in particular the problem of discovering a relationship between d'_1 and the symbolic constants $d_1, \ldots, d_8$ of the input octagon, as detailed previously.

We proceed by introducing signed 34-bit vectors $\boldsymbol{d_1}, \ldots, \boldsymbol{d_8}$ to represent the symbolic constants $d_1, \ldots, d_8$. Further, let κ denote a Boolean formula that holds iff the eight inequalities $\langle\langle \boldsymbol{r0}\rangle\rangle \leq \langle\langle \boldsymbol{d_1}\rangle\rangle, \ldots, \langle\langle \boldsymbol{r0}\rangle\rangle - \langle\langle \boldsymbol{r1}\rangle\rangle \leq \langle\langle \boldsymbol{d_8}\rangle\rangle$ simultaneously hold. Furthermore, let η denote a formula that encodes the equality $\langle\langle \boldsymbol{r0'}\rangle\rangle = \langle\langle \boldsymbol{d'_1}\rangle\rangle$ where $\boldsymbol{d'_1}$ is a signed bit-vector representing d'_1. Presenting the compound formula $\kappa \wedge \xi(\boldsymbol{X}) \wedge \eta$ to a SAT solver produces a model:

$$\boldsymbol{m}_1 = \{\, \langle\langle \boldsymbol{d'_1}\rangle\rangle = 1, \langle\langle \boldsymbol{d_1}\rangle\rangle = 1, \langle\langle \boldsymbol{d_2}\rangle\rangle = 1, \ldots, \langle\langle \boldsymbol{d_7}\rangle\rangle = 1, \langle\langle \boldsymbol{d_8}\rangle\rangle = 1 \,\}$$

which is fully detailed in Tab. 1. The assignment $\langle\langle \boldsymbol{d'_1}\rangle\rangle = 1$ does not necessarily represent the maximum value of $\langle\langle \boldsymbol{d'_1}\rangle\rangle$ for the partial assignment $\langle\langle \boldsymbol{d_1}\rangle\rangle = 1, \ldots, \langle\langle \boldsymbol{d_8}\rangle\rangle = 1$. Thus let ζ_1 denote a formula that holds iff $\langle\langle \boldsymbol{d_1}\rangle\rangle = 1, \ldots, \langle\langle \boldsymbol{d_8}\rangle\rangle = 1$ all hold. Then range refinement can be applied to find the maximal value of $\langle\langle \boldsymbol{d'_1}\rangle\rangle$ subject to $\kappa \wedge \xi(\boldsymbol{X}) \wedge \eta \wedge \zeta$. This gives $\langle\langle \boldsymbol{d'_1}\rangle\rangle = 2$ and a model:

$$\boldsymbol{m}'_1 = \{\langle\langle \boldsymbol{d'_1}\rangle\rangle = 2, \langle\langle \boldsymbol{d_1}\rangle\rangle = 1, \ldots, \langle\langle \boldsymbol{d_8}\rangle\rangle = 1\}$$

An affine summary of all such maximal models can be found by interleaving range refinement with affine join. Thus suppose the matrix $\mathbf{M}_1$ is constructed from $\boldsymbol{m}'_1$ by using the variable ordering $\langle d'_1, d_1, \ldots, d_8 \rangle$ on columns:

$$\mathbf{M}_1 = \left[\begin{array}{ccccccccc|c} 1&0&0&0&0&0&0&0&0&2 \\ 0&1&0&0&0&0&0&0&0&1 \\ 0&0&1&0&0&0&0&0&0&1 \\ 0&0&0&1&0&0&0&0&0&0 \\ 0&0&0&0&1&0&0&0&0&0 \\ 0&0&0&0&0&1&0&0&0&1 \\ 0&0&0&0&0&0&1&0&0&0 \\ 0&0&0&0&0&0&0&1&0&1 \\ 0&0&0&0&0&0&0&0&1&1 \end{array}\right]$$

The method proceeds in an analogous fashion to before by constructing a formula μ that holds iff $\langle\!\langle \boldsymbol{d_8} \rangle\!\rangle \neq 1$ holds. Solving the formula $\kappa \wedge \xi(\boldsymbol{X}) \wedge \eta \wedge \mu$ gives the model $\boldsymbol{m}_2$ detailed in Tab. 1. The model $\boldsymbol{m}_2$, itself, defines a formula ζ_2 that is equi-satisfiable with the conjunction of $\langle\!\langle \boldsymbol{d_1} \rangle\!\rangle = 3, \ldots, \langle\!\langle \boldsymbol{d_8} \rangle\!\rangle = 0$. Maximising $\langle\!\langle \boldsymbol{d'_1} \rangle\!\rangle$ subject to $\kappa \wedge \xi(\boldsymbol{X}) \wedge \eta \wedge \zeta_2$ gives $\langle\!\langle \boldsymbol{d'_1} \rangle\!\rangle = 10$ which defines the model

$$\boldsymbol{m}'_2 = \{\langle\!\langle \boldsymbol{d'_1} \rangle\!\rangle = 10, \langle\!\langle \boldsymbol{d_1} \rangle\!\rangle = 3, \ldots, \langle\!\langle \boldsymbol{d_8} \rangle\!\rangle = 0\}$$

and $\mathbf{M}_2$, which in turn yields the join $\mathbf{M}_1 \sqcup \mathbf{M}_2$ as follows:

$$\mathbf{M}_1 \sqcup \mathbf{M}_2 = \left[\begin{array}{ccccccccc|c} 1&0&0&0&0&-2&0&0&0&0 \\ 0&1&-1&0&0&0&0&0&0&0 \\ 0&0&0&1&-2&0&0&0&0&0 \\ 0&0&0&0&0&0&1&2&0&2 \\ 0&0&0&0&0&0&0&1&1&1 \end{array}\right]$$

Repeating this process two more times then gives:

$$\boldsymbol{m}'_3 = \{\langle\!\langle \boldsymbol{d'_1} \rangle\!\rangle = 26, \langle\!\langle \boldsymbol{d_1} \rangle\!\rangle = 8, \ldots, \langle\!\langle \boldsymbol{d_8} \rangle\!\rangle = 0\}$$
$$\boldsymbol{m}'_4 = \{\langle\!\langle \boldsymbol{d'_1} \rangle\!\rangle = 6, \langle\!\langle \boldsymbol{d_1} \rangle\!\rangle = 0, \ldots, \langle\!\langle \boldsymbol{d_8} \rangle\!\rangle = 3\}$$

$$\mathbf{M}_1 \sqcup \mathbf{M}_2 \sqcup \mathbf{M}_3 = \left[\begin{array}{ccccccccc|c} 1&0&0&0&0&-2&0&0&0&0 \\ 0&1&-1&1&-1&0&0&0&0&0 \end{array}\right]$$

$$\mathbf{M}_1 \sqcup \mathbf{M}_2 \sqcup \mathbf{M}_3 \sqcup \mathbf{M}_4 = \left[\begin{array}{ccccccccc|c} 1&0&0&0&0&-2&0&0&0&0 \end{array}\right]$$

The system $\mathbf{M}_1 \sqcup \mathbf{M}_2 \sqcup \mathbf{M}_3 \sqcup \mathbf{M}_4$ then expresses the relationship $\langle\!\langle \boldsymbol{d'_1} \rangle\!\rangle = 2 \cdot \langle\!\langle \boldsymbol{d_5} \rangle\!\rangle$.

To verify that $\langle\!\langle \boldsymbol{d'_1} \rangle\!\rangle = 2 \cdot \langle\!\langle \boldsymbol{d_5} \rangle\!\rangle$ is a fixed point, unlike before, it not sufficient to impose the disequality $\langle\!\langle \boldsymbol{d'_1} \rangle\!\rangle \neq 2 \cdot \langle\!\langle \boldsymbol{d_5} \rangle\!\rangle$ and check for unsatisfiability. This is because $\langle\!\langle \boldsymbol{d'_1} \rangle\!\rangle$ is defined through maximisation. Instead the check amounts to testing whether $\kappa \wedge \xi(\boldsymbol{X}) \wedge \eta$ is unsatisfiable when combined with a formula encoding the strict inequality $\langle\!\langle \boldsymbol{d'_1} \rangle\!\rangle > 2 \cdot \langle\!\langle \boldsymbol{d_5} \rangle\!\rangle$. Since the combined system is unsatisfiable, we conclude that the update for this mode-combination includes $d'_1 = 2 \cdot d_5$. The complete affine update consists of:

$$\begin{array}{llll} d'_1 = 2 \cdot d_5 & d'_2 = d_2 & d'_3 = 2 \cdot d_6 & d'_4 = d_4 \\ d'_5 = 2 \cdot d_5 + d_2 & d'_6 = 2 \cdot d_6 + d_4 & d'_7 = 2 \cdot d_6 + d_2 & d'_8 = 2 \cdot d_5 + d_4 \end{array}$$

Observe that these linear symbolic update operations are optimal.

Reflections on octagonal transfer functions. Interestingly, Miné [22, Fig. 27] also discusses the relative precision of transfer functions, though where the base semantics is polyhedral rather than Boolean. Using his classification, the transfer functions derived using the synthesis techniques presented in Sect. 3.3 and 3.4 might be described as medium and exact.

3.5 Inferring Bounds for Octagons

For a final example, consider the following code block:

1 : `AND R0, 15;` 2 : `AND R1, 15;` 3 : `XOR R0, R1;` 4 : `ADD R0, R1;`

The operations `AND` and `XOR` are uni-modal; `ADD` is multi-modal but it only operates in exact mode for this block. For this single mode no affine relationship exists between the symbolic constants d_i that characterise the input octagon and those d'_i that characterise the output octagon.

However, even in such cases, it can be still possible to find a d'_1 such that $\langle\langle \boldsymbol{r0}' \rangle\rangle \leq d'_1$ by applying range refinement. This gives $d'_1 = 30$. Repeating this tactic for remaining the symbolic output constants yields:

$$\begin{array}{llll} d'_1 = 30 & d'_2 = 15 & d'_3 = 0 & d'_4 = 0 \\ d'_5 = 45 & d'_6 = 0 & d'_7 = 0 & d'_8 = 15 \end{array}$$

4 Evaluating Transfer Functions

Thus far, we have described how to derive transfer functions for intervals and octagons where the functions are systems of guards paired with affine updates, without reference to how they are evaluated. In our previous work [6], the application of a transfer function amounted to solving a series of integer linear programs (ILPs). To illustrate, suppose a transfer function consists of a single guard g and update u pair and let c denote a system of octagonal constraints on the input variables. A single output inequality in the output system, c', such as $r0' + r1' \leq d'_5$, can be derived by maximising $r0' + r1'$ subject to the linear system $c \wedge g \wedge u$. To construct c' in its entirety requires the solution of $O(n^2)$ ILPs where n is the number of registers (or variables) in the block. Although steady progress has been made on deriving safe bounds for integer programs [26], a more attractive solution computationally would avoid ILPs altogether.

4.1 A Single Guard and Update Pair

Affine updates, as derived in Sect. 3.4, relate symbolic constants on the inequalities in the input octagon to those of the output octagon. These updates confer a different, simpler, evaluation model. To compute $r0' + r1' \leq d'_5$ in c' it is sufficient to compute $c \sqcap g$ [22] which is the octagon that describes the conjoined system $c \wedge g$. This can be computed in quadratic-time when g is a single inequality and in cubic-time otherwise [22]. The meet $c \sqcap g$ then defines values for the symbolic constants d_i, though these values may include $-\infty$ and ∞. The value of d'_5 is defined by its affine update, that is, as a weighted sum of the d_i values. If there is no affine update for d'_5, then its value defaults to ∞. If bounds have been inferred for output octagons (Sect 3.5), then the d'_i can possibly be refined with a tighter bound. This evaluation mechanism thus replaces ILP with arithmetic that is both conceptually simple and computationally efficient. This is significant since transfer functions are themselves computed many times during fixpoint evaluation.

4.2 A System of Guard and Update Pairs

The above evaluation procedure needs to be applied for each guard g and update u pair for which $c \sqcap g$ is satisfiable. Thus several output octagons may be derived for a single block. We do not prescribe how these octagons should be combined, for example, a disjunctive representation is one possibility [13]. However, the simplest tactic is undoubtedly to apply the merge operation for octagons [22] (though this entails closing the output octagons).

5 Experiments

We have implemented the techniques described in this paper in JAVA using the SAT4J solver [21], so as to integrate with our analysis framework for machine code [30], called [MC]SQUARE, which is also coded in JAVA. All experiments were performed on a MACBOOK PRO equipped with a 2.6 GHz dual-core processor and 4 GB of RAM, but only a single core was used in our experiments.

To evaluate transfer function synthesis without quantifier elimination, Tab. 2 compares the results for intervals for different blocks of assembly code to those obtained using the technique described in [6]. Column *#instr* contains the number of instructions, whereas column *#bits* gives the bit-width. (The 8-bit and 32-bit versions of the AVR instruction sets are analogous.) Then, *#affine* presents the number of affine relations for each block. The columns *runtime* contain the runtime and the number of SAT instances. The overall runtime of the elimination-based algorithm [6] is given in column *old* (∞ is used for timeout, which is set to 30s). Transfer function synthesis for blocks of up to 10 instruction is evaluated, which is a typical size for microcontroller code. For these size blocks, we have never observed more than 10 feasible mode combinations.

Comparison. Using quantifier elimination, all instances could be solved in a reasonable amount of time for 8-bit instructions. However, only the small instances could be solved for 32 bits (and only then because the Boolean encodings for the instructions were minimised prior to the synthesis of the transfer functions). It is also important to appreciate that none of the timeouts was caused by the SAT solver; it was resolution that failed to produce results in reasonable time. By way of comparison, synthesising guards for different overflow modes requires most runtime in our new approach, caused by the fact that the number of SAT

Table 2. Experimental results for synthesis of transfer functions

block	#instr	#affine	#bits	runtime			
				guards / #SAT	affine / #SAT	overall	old
`inc`	1	2	8	0.2s / 40	0.1s / 5	0.3s	0.2s
			32	0.5s / 136	0.2s / 5	1.0s	23.0s
`inc+shift`	2	3	8	0.3s / 60	0.1s / 8	0.4s	0.3s
			32	0.8s / 216	0.2s / 8	1.0s	∞
`swap`	3	1	8	—	0.1s / 3	0.1s	0.1s
			32	—	0.1s / 3	0.1s	0.2s
`inc+flip`	4	2	8	0.2s / 40	0.2s / 5	0.4s	0.5s
			32	0.9s / 216	0.3s / 5	1.2s	∞
`abs`	5	3	8	2.5s / 216	0.3s / 8	2.8s	0.8s
			32	6.5s / 792	0.3s / 8	6.8s	∞
`inc+abs`	6	3	8	2.6s / 216	0.3s / 8	2.9s	1.4s
			32	6.7s / 792	0.3s / 8	7.0s	∞
`sum+isign`	7	5	8	4.1s / 360	0.2s / 18	4.3s	4.5s
			32	10.7s / 1320	0.4s / 18	11.1s	∞
`exchange+abs`	10	3	8	2.8s / 216	0.3s / 8	3.1s	9.5s
			32	7.2s / 792	0.3s / 8	7.5s	∞

instances to be solved grows linearly with the number of bits and quadratically with the number of variables (the number of octagonal inequalities is quadratic in the number of variables). Computing the affine updates consumes only a fraction of the overall time. In terms of precision, the results coincide with those previously generated [6].

The block for `swap` is interesting since it consists of three consecutive exclusive-or instructions, for which there is no coupling between different bits of the same register. The block is also unusual in that it is uni-modal with vacuous guards. These properties make it ideal for resolution. Even in this situation, the new technique scales better. In fact, the Boolean formulae that we present to the solver are almost trivial by modern standards, the main overhead coming from repeated SAT solving rather than solving a single large instance. SAT4J does reuse clauses learnt in an earlier SAT instances, though it does not permit clauses to be incrementally added and rescinded which is useful when solving maximisation problems [6]. Thus the timings given above are very conservative; indeed SAT4J was chosen to maintain the portability of [MC]SQUARE rather than for raw performance. Nevertheless, these timings very favourably compare with those required to compute transfer functions for intervals using BDDs [28], where in excess of 24 hours is required for single 8-bit instructions.

Deriving octagonal transfer functions. The process of deriving octagonal transfer functions by lifting (Sect. 3.3) requires an imperceivable overhead compared to computing affine relations themselves, indeed it is merely syntactic rewriting. The runtimes required for inferring affine inequalities by alternating range refinement and affine join (Sect. 3.4), however, is typically 3 or 4 times slower than those of computing the guards; the number of symbolic constants on the output inequalities corresponds exactly to the number of input guards. (We refrain from giving exact times since this component has not been tuned.)

Further optimisations. Since transfer functions are program dependent, one could first use a simple form of range analysis [5] to over-approximate the ranges a register can assume. These ranges can be encoded in the formulae, thereby pruning out some mode-combinations. For example, it is rarely the case that the absolute value function is actually applied to the smallest representable integer.

6 Related Work

Although the problem of constructing transfer functions has been recognised for over twenty years, for example, by Cousot and Halbwachs [12] for the polyhedral domain and by Granger [14] for linear congruences, automatic synthesis has only recently become a practical proposition due to emergence of robust decision procedures [19,29] and quantifier elimination techniques [20,23,24].

Transfer functions [29] can always be found for domains that satisfy the finite ascending chain condition, provided one is prepared to pay the cost of calling a decision procedure repeatedly on each application of a transformer. This motivates applying a decision procedure in order to compute optimal transfer functions offline, prior to the actual analysis [6,19].

Our previous work [6] shows how bit-blasting and quantifier elimination can be applied to synthesise transformers for bit-vector programs. This work was inspired by that of Monniaux [23,24] on synthesising transfer functions for piecewise linear programs. Although his approach extends beyond octagons [32], it is unclear how to express some instructions (such as exclusive-or) in terms of linear constraints. Universal quantification, as used in both approaches, also appears in work on inferring linear template constraints by Gulwani et al. [15]. There, the authors apply Farkas' lemma in order to transform universal quantification into existential quantification, albeit at the cost of completeness since Farkas' lemma prevents integral reasoning. However, crucially, neither Monniaux nor Gulwani et al. provide a way to model integer overflow. By way of contrast, our approach explains how to systematically handle wrap-around arithmetic in the transfer function itself whilst sidestepping quantifier elimination.

Transfer functions have been automatically synthesised for intervals using BDDs by applying interval subdivision [28]. If $g : [0, 2^8 - 1] \to [0, 2^8 - 1]$ is a unary operation on an unsigned byte, then its transformer $f : D \to D$ on $D = \{\emptyset\} \cup \{[\ell, u] \mid 0 \leq \ell \leq u < 2^8\}$ can be defined recursively. If $\ell = u$ then $f([\ell, u]) = g(\ell)$ whereas if $\ell < u$ then $f([\ell, u]) = f([\ell, m-1]) \sqcup f([m, u])$ where $m = \lfloor u/2^n \rfloor 2^n$ and $n = \lfloor \log_2(u - \ell + 1) \rfloor$. Binary operations can likewise be decomposed. The 8-bit inputs, ℓ and u, can be represented as 8-bit vectors, as can the 8-bit outputs, so as to represent f with a BDD. This permits caching to be applied when f is computed, which reduces the time needed to compute a best transformer to approximately one day for each 8-bit operation.

The classical approach to handling overflow is to verify that they do not occur using unbounded domains as implemented in the ASTRÉE tool [11]. However, for the domain of polyhedra, it is also possible to revise the concretisation map to reflect the effect of truncation [31]. Another choice is to deploy congruence relations [14] where the modulus is a power of two [19,25]. Finally, bit-blasting has been combined with range inference elsewhere [5,8], though neither of these papers address relational abstraction nor transfer function synthesis.

7 Concluding Discussion

Synopsis. This paper revisits the problem of synthesising transfer functions for programs whose semantics is defined over finite bit-vectors. The irony is that although Boolean formula initially appear attractive for synthesis because of the simplicity of universal projection [6], their real strength is the fact that they are discrete. This permits octagonal inequalities to be inferred by repeated satisfiability testing, avoiding the need for quantifier elimination, and in particular the complexity of resolution. The force of this observation is that it extends transfer function synthesis to architectures whose word size exceeds 8 bits, strengthening the case for low-level code verification [4,30].

Future work. The problem of synthesising transfer functions is not dissimilar to that of inferring ranking functions for bit-vector programs [9]. The existence of a ranking function on a path π with a transition relation $r_\pi(\boldsymbol{x}, \boldsymbol{x}')$ amounts to solving the formula $\exists \boldsymbol{c} : \forall \boldsymbol{x} : \forall \boldsymbol{x}' : r_\pi(\boldsymbol{x}, \boldsymbol{x}') \rightarrow (p(\boldsymbol{c}, \boldsymbol{x}) < p(\boldsymbol{c}, \boldsymbol{x}'))$ where $p(\boldsymbol{c}, \boldsymbol{x})$ is a polynomial over the bit-vector $\boldsymbol{x}$ and $\boldsymbol{c}$ is a bit-vector of coefficients. However, if intermediate variables $\boldsymbol{y}$ are needed to express $r_\pi(\boldsymbol{x}, \boldsymbol{x}')$, $p(\boldsymbol{c}, \boldsymbol{x})$, $p(\boldsymbol{c}, \boldsymbol{x}')$ or $<$, then the formula actually takes the form $\exists \boldsymbol{c} : \forall \boldsymbol{x} : \forall \boldsymbol{x}' : \exists \boldsymbol{y} : \nu$ where $\exists \boldsymbol{y} : \nu \equiv r_\pi(\boldsymbol{x}, \boldsymbol{x}') \rightarrow (p(\boldsymbol{c}, \boldsymbol{x}) < p(\boldsymbol{c}, \boldsymbol{x}'))$. This formula is similar to those solved in [6] by elimination which begs the question of whether this problem, like that of transfer function synthesis, can be recast to avoid elimination altogether.

We will also investigate whether transfer functions can be found, not only for sequences of instructions, but also for entire loops [17,23]. Existing approaches for the specification of (least inductive) loop invariants rely on existential quantification, and the natural question is whether the techniques proposed in this paper can annul this complexity. It is also interesting to note that octagons derived using our approach are tightly closed [22]. Intuitively, this means that all hyperplanes defined through inequalities actually touch the enclosed volume. However, the octagons may contain redundant inequalities, and therefore it will be interesting to see if simplification is worthwhile [2] and, if so, whether non-redundant octagons can be directly derived using SAT.

Acknowledgements. The first author was supported, in part, by the DFG research training group 1298 *Algorithmic Synthesis of Reactive and Discrete-Continuous Systems* and the by the DFG Cluster of Excellence on Ultra-high Speed Information and Communication, German Research Foundation grant DFG EXC 89.

The second author was funded, in part, by a Royal Society travel grant, reference TG092357, and a Royal Society Industrial Fellowship, reference IF081178. We thank David Monniaux and Stefan Kowalewski for interesting technical discussions, as well as moral support, in this line of scientific enquiry.

References

1. Atmel Products. AVR32 Architecture Manual (2007), http://www.atmel.com/
2. Bagnara, R., Hill, P.M., Zaffanella, E.: Weakly-relational shapes for numeric abstractions: improved algorithms and proofs of correctness. Formal Methods in System Design 35(3), 279–323 (2009)
3. Baier, C., Katoen, J.-P.: Principles of Model Checking. The MIT Press, Cambridge (2008)
4. Balakrishnan, G., Reps, T.: WYSINWYX: What You See Is Not What You eXecute. ACM Trans. Program. Lang. Syst. 32(6) (2010)
5. Barrett, E., King, A.: Range and Set Abstraction Using SAT. Electronic Notes in Theoretical Computer Science 267(1), 17–27 (2010)
6. Brauer, J., King, A.: Automatic Abstraction for Intervals using Boolean Formulae. In: Cousot, R., Martel, M. (eds.) SAS 2010. LNCS, vol. 6337, pp. 167–183. Springer, Heidelberg (2010)
7. Clarke, E., Kroening, D., Lerda, F.: A tool for checking ANSI-C programs. In: Jensen, K., Podelski, A. (eds.) TACAS 2004. LNCS, vol. 2988, pp. 168–176. Springer, Heidelberg (2004)
8. Codish, M., Lagoon, V., Stuckey, P.J.: Logic programming with satisfiability. Theory and Practice of Logic Programming 8(1), 121–128 (2008)
9. Cook, B., Kroening, D., Rümmer, P., Wintersteiger, C.: Ranking Function Synthesis for Bit-Vector Relations. In: Esparza, J., Majumdar, R. (eds.) TACAS 2010. LNCS, vol. 6015, pp. 236–250. Springer, Heidelberg (2010)
10. Cousot, P., Cousot, R.: Abstract Interpretation: A Unified Lattice model for Static Analysis of Programs by Construction or Approximation of Fixpoints. In: POPL, pp. 238–252. ACM Press, New York (1977)
11. Cousot, P., Cousot, R., Feret, J., Mauborgne, L., Mine, A., Monniaux, D., Rival, X.: The Astrée analyser. In: Sagiv, M. (ed.) ESOP 2005. LNCS, vol. 3444, pp. 21–30. Springer, Heidelberg (2005)
12. Cousot, P., Halbwachs, N.: Automatic Discovery of Linear Restraints Among Variables of a Program. In: POPL, pp. 84–97. ACM Press, New York (1978)
13. Giacobazzi, R., Ranzato, F.: Optimal domains for disjunctive abstract interpretation. Sci. Comput. Program. 32(1-3), 177–210 (1998)
14. Granger, P.: Static Analysis of Arithmetical Congruences. International Journal of Computer Mathematics 30(13), 165–190 (1989)
15. Gulwani, S., Srivastava, S., Venkatesan, R.: Program Analysis as Constraint Solving. In: PLDI, pp. 281–292. ACM Press, New York (2008)
16. Kam, J.B., Ullman, J.D.: Monotone Data Flow Analysis Frameworks. Acta Informatica 7, 305–317 (1997)
17. Kapur, D.: Automatically Generating Loop Invariants Using Quantifier Elimination. In: Deduction and Applications, vol. 05431, IBFI (2005)
18. Karr, M.: Affine Relationships among Variables of a Program. Acta Informatica 6, 133–151 (1976)

19. King, A., Søndergaard, H.: Automatic Abstraction for Congruences. In: Barthe, G., Hermenegildo, M. (eds.) VMCAI 2010. LNCS, vol. 5944, pp. 197–213. Springer, Heidelberg (2010)
20. Kroening, D., Strichman, O.: Decision Procedures. Springer, Heidelberg (2008)
21. Le Berre, D.: SAT4J: Bringing the power of SAT technology to the Java platform (2010), http://www.sat4j.org/
22. Miné, A.: The Octagon Abstract Domain. Higher-Order and Symbolic Computation 19(1), 31–100 (2006)
23. Monniaux, D.: Automatic Modular Abstractions for Linear Constraints. In: POPL, pp. 140–151. ACM Press, New York (2009)
24. Monniaux, D.: Quantifier Elimination by Lazy Model Enumeration. In: Touili, T., Cook, B., Jackson, P. (eds.) CAV 2010. LNCS, vol. 6174, pp. 585–599. Springer, Heidelberg (2010)
25. Müller-Olm, M., Seidl, H.: Analysis of Modular Arithmetic. ACM Trans. Program. Lang. Syst. 29(5) (August 2007)
26. Neumaier, A., Shcherbina, O.: Safe Bounds in Linear and Mixed-Integer Linear Programming. Math. Program. 99(2), 283–296 (2004)
27. Plaisted, D.A., Greenbaum, S.: A Structure-Preserving Clause Form Translation. Journal of Symbolic Computation 2(3), 293–304 (1986)
28. Regehr, J., Reid, A.: HOIST: A System for Automatically Deriving Static Analyzers for Embedded Systems. ACM SIGOPS Operating Systems Review 38(5), 133–143 (2004)
29. Reps, T., Sagiv, M., Yorsh, G.: Symbolic Implementation of the Best Transformer. In: Steffen, B., Levi, G. (eds.) VMCAI 2004. LNCS, vol. 2937, pp. 252–266. Springer, Heidelberg (2004)
30. Schlich, B.: Model Checking of Software for Microcontrollers. ACM Trans. Embed. Comput. Syst. 9(4), 1–27 (2010)
31. Simon, A., King, A.: Taming the Wrapping of Integer Arithmetic. In: Riis Nielson, H., Filé, G. (eds.) SAS 2007. LNCS, vol. 4634, pp. 121–136. Springer, Heidelberg (2007)
32. Simon, A., King, A., Howe, J.M.: The Two Variable Per Inequality Abstract Domain. Higher-Order and Symbolic Computation (to appear)

Semantics of Concurrent Revisions

Sebastian Burckhardt and Daan Leijen

Microsoft Research

Abstract. Enabling applications to execute various tasks in parallel is difficult if those tasks exhibit read and write conflicts. We recently developed a programming model based on *concurrent revisions* that addresses this challenge in a novel way: each forked task gets a conceptual copy of all the shared state, and state changes are integrated only when tasks are joined, at which time write-write conflicts are deterministically resolved.

In this paper, we study the precise semantics of this model, in particular its guarantees for determinacy and consistency. First, we introduce a revision calculus that concisely captures the programming model. Despite allowing concurrent execution and locally nondeterministic scheduling, we prove that the calculus is confluent and guarantees determinacy. We show that the consistency guarantees of our calculus are a logical extension of snapshot isolation with support for conflict resolution and nesting. Moreover, we discuss how custom merge functions can provide stronger guarantees for particular data types that are tailored to the needs of the application.

Finally, we show we can visualize the nonlinear history of state in our computations using *revision diagrams* that clarify the synchronization between tasks and allow local reasoning about state updates.

1 Introduction

With the recent broad availability of shared-memory multiprocessors, many more application developers now have a strong motivation to tap into the potential performance benefits of parallel execution. Exploiting parallel hardware can be relatively easy if the application performs computations for which parallel algorithms are well known or straightforward to develop (such as for scientific problems or multimedia applications). However, traditional parallelization strategies often do not satisfactorily address how to execute different application tasks that access shared data in parallel.

For example, consider an office application that needs to perform five different tasks: (1) save a snapshot of the document to disk, (2) react to keyboard input by the user who is editing the document, (3) perform a spellcheck of the document, (4) render the document on the screen, and (5) exchange document updates with collaborating remote users.

Executing such tasks in parallel is not simple, because all of them potentially access the same data (such as the document) at the same time. For instance, in a case study on parallelizing a game application [3] we discovered that the parallel execution of the physics task and the render task is essential to achieve decent speedup on multiple cores. But these tasks naturally exhibit read-write conflicts: The physics task modifies

G. Barthe (Ed.): ESOP 2011, LNCS 6602, pp. 116–135, 2011.
© Springer-Verlag Berlin Heidelberg 2011

all coordinates of game objects (to simulate elapsed time) while the render task reads all coordinates (to render a snapshot of the scene).

Avoiding, negotiating, or resolving such conflicts between parallel tasks can be quite challenging with traditional synchronization models. In fact, many programmers are deterred by the engineering complexity of performing explicit, manual synchronization (such as by using locks and critical sections) or replication (such as by creating temporary copies or using double buffering).

Our proposed programming model, *concurrent revisions* [8], simplifies parallelization of conflicting tasks by (conceptually) copying shared state automatically on a fork. Tasks execute in complete isolation because each has its own copy of the shared data (e.g. the document or the coordinates, in the above examples), somewhat analogous to source control systems that allow multiple programmers to work on the same code at the same time by creating local copies of files, and checking changed files back into the repository.

```
x = 0;
y = 0;

r = rfork { x = 1; }
y = x;
rjoin r;

print x, y;
```

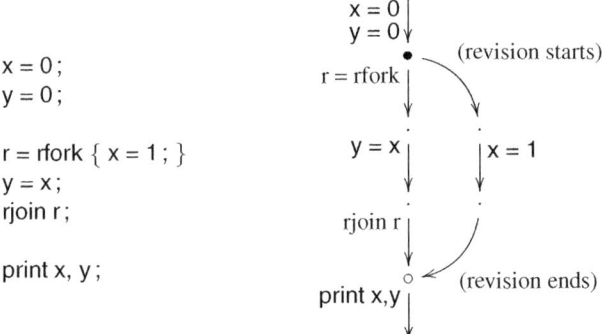

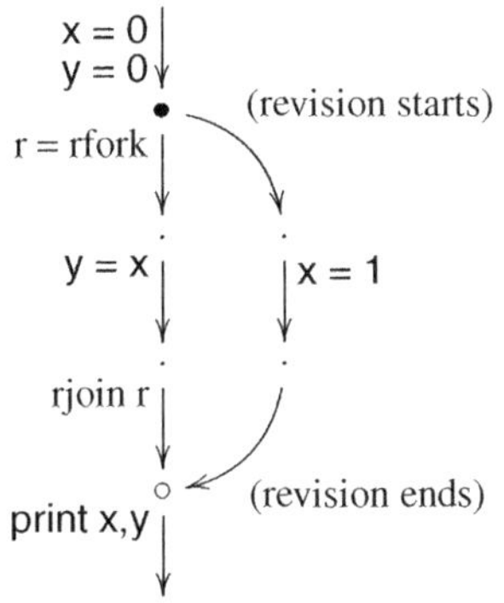

Fig. 1. An example of a revision diagram (on the right) representing the execution of a program (on the left). The effect of the write $x = 1$ is confined to its revision until that revision is joined. Thus the print statement prints (1,0).

For example, consider the code in Fig. 1 which illustrates the basic concept of *forking and joining revisions* and how to visualize executions using *revision diagrams*. The program on the left forks a concurrent revision, obtaining a handle r which it later joins. The forked revision executes the assignment $x = 1$, but the effect of this assignment is confined to that revision until it is joined, at which point all of its changes are applied to the joining revision. The diagram shows how the state is forked and joined (each vertex represents a state, and curved arrows represent fork and join), as well as how the state is locally updated by revisions (vertical arrows represent steps by revisions). Note that because revisions are isolated, data can flow only along edges in the diagram. Moreover, because the program specifies where to join revisions and does not depend on scheduling and timing, the execution is determinate.

Our previous work [8] has already provided some evidence that this concurrent revision model can be implemented efficiently enough to achieve satisfactory parallelization speedups, and that it is easier to use than locks or transactions [3]. However, our previous work left many important questions about the semantics unaddressed, in particular relating to determinacy and consistency guarantees. The purpose of our work presented in this paper is to address these questions rigorously and provide precise answers. We make the following contributions:

1. We give a minimal calculus describing the concurrent revision model. Because the calculus is small, it is well suited as a semantic reference and as an experimental tool to study various extensions or implementations. In fact, it was inspired (and is very similar to) the AME calculus [24] which served a similar purpose in the context of transactional memory. Note that we published a preliminary version of this calculus (without discussion or proofs) in the previous paper [8].
2. Even though the calculus is intrinsically concurrent, we prove that it guarantees determinacy.
3. We give a comprehensive discussion of consistency guarantees and state merging. We show that in the absence of write-conflicts and nesting, revisions are analogous to transactions with snapshot isolation. We also show how the introduction of custom *merge* functions into the calculus can allow the programmer to achieve stronger consistency guarantees tailored to the needs of the application.
4. We formalize the notion of a *revision diagram* (informally introduced in [8]). These diagrams capture the revision history of an execution, by showing the order and nesting of forks and joins. Moreover, they illustrate data flow, since information can propagate only along edges. We contrast revision diagrams with other commonly used task graphs (such as DAGs or SP-graphs) and prove that they are semilattices.

Overall, our work shows that the revision model preserves some of the best properties of sequential programs (deterministic execution, local reasoning about state updates) without forcing programmers to manually isolate parallel tasks, and without restricting parallel executions to be fully equivalent to a sequential execution. Rather, parallelism is expressed directly and explicitly, and always exploitable even if the tasks exhibit conflicts.

2 Discussion

We start with a high-level informal discussion of various aspects of the revision model, such as determinacy, nesting of revisions, handling of write-write conflicts, and revision diagrams. Moreover, we compare revisions to related work on transactional memory and determinacy.

2.1 Revisions vs. Interleaved Tasks

In our model, revisions are the basic unit of concurrency. They function much like asynchronous tasks that are forked and joined, and they may themselves fork and join other tasks. We chose the term 'revision' to emphasize the semantic similarity to branches in source control systems where programmers work with a local snapshot of the shared source code.

In particular, on every revisional fork (rfork), the system conceptually copies the entire state and each branch works on its own local copy. Every revision is completely

(sequential consistency)	(transactional memory)	(concurrent revisions)
x = 0 ; y = 0 ;	x = 0 ; y = 0 ;	x = 0 ; y = 0 ;
t = fork {	t = fork { atomic {	r = rfork {
if (x = 0) y++ ;	if (x = 0) y++ ;	if (x = 0) y++ ;
}	}}	}
if (y = 0) x++ ;	atomic { if (y = 0) x++ ; }	if (y = 0) x++ ;
join t ;	join t ;	rjoin r ;
assert((x = 0 ∧ y = 1) ∨	assert((x = 0 ∧ y = 1) ∨	assert(x = 1 ∧ y = 1);
(x = 1 ∧ y = 0) ∨	(x = 1 ∧ y = 0));	;
(x = 1 ∧ y = 1));	;	;

Fig. 2. Outcomes under different programming models

isolated from the others and there is no possibility of communication through shared state. Any updates in a revision only become re-integrated once the revision is joined. Since there is no possibility of stateful interleavings with other threads, intra-revision reasoning (that is, reasoning about code executing within a revision) is sequential.

The revision model is a significant departure from memory models that interleave tasks at the level of individual instructions, such as sequential consistency [21]. Moreover, this difference is not simply a matter of the interleaving granularity. Transactional memory, for example, interleaves tasks at the granularity of atomic blocks [22, 15]. However, coarser interleaving does not in itself guarantee determinacy of executions, as the relative order of the atomic blocks is unspecified. Thus, whether we use sequential consistency or transactional memory, the interleaving chosen during an execution depends on nondeterministic arbitration which can vary between executions. In contrast, with our concurrent revision model, the precise structure of forks and joins is completely determined by the program and independent of runtime scheduling.

We illustrate this difference in Figure 2 where we compare the results of a program for these three models. The program forks a concurrent branch where each branch increments a variable x or y respectively depending on the value of the other variable (y and x respectively). Under sequential consistency, there are many interleavings possible and there are three distinct possibilities for the values of x and y. In the second program, we use transactional memory to limit the possible interleavings by executing each branch atomically. This effectively serializes the execution and we see either $x = 0 \wedge y = 1$ or $x = 1 \wedge y = 0$ depending on how the branches are scheduled. Using revisions, the outcome is always determinate: both branches get their own local (conceptual) copy of the state, and both branches will increment the variables ending in $x = 1 \wedge y = 1$.

2.2 Local Reasoning vs. Serializability

As Figure 2 shows, we can truly reason about each branch locally without considering any interleavings. However, note also that there is no equivalent sequential execution for this example. The lack of equivalence to some sequential execution is no accident: requiring such equivalence fundamentally limits the concurrency that can be practically exploited if tasks exhibit conflicts. For the kind of applications we have in mind, conflicts may be quite frequent.

With revisions, conflicts never destroy the available parallelism and never cause rollbacks. These choices provide substantial practical benefits over the use of rollbacks in optimistic transactional memory, which does not fare well in the presence of frequent conflicts, and cannot be easily combined with I/O [33].

Comfortably reasoning about application behavior in the absence of serializability requires understanding and conceptualizing a nonlinear history of state. We achieve this by introducing revision diagrams that directly visualize how the global state can be forked, updated, and joined (Fig. 1, Fig. 3). Revisions correspond to vertical chains in the diagram, and are connected by curved arrows that represent the forks and joins. We sometimes label the revisions with the actions they perform. Such diagrams visualize clearly how information may flow (it follows the edges) and how effects become visible upon the join. In Section 5 we show that the diagrams have a formal and well-defined meaning with relation to the calculus.

2.3 State Merging

When joining a revision, two copies of the state need to be merged together, which naturally raises two questions:

1. Can we always find a common ancestor state to help us determine if either side has made changes, and what those changes are?
2. If both sides have made changes, how do we resolve such write-write conflicts? (Note that there are no read-write or write-read conflicts between revisions.)

We answer the first question by showing how our calculus keeps track of the ancestor state (Section 3), and by showing that revision diagrams are semilattices and the ancestor state is in fact the greatest common ancestor (Section 5).

We address the second question by discussing several sensible merge policies. A key insight that makes state merging practical and convenient is that we need not define merge functions or policies globally, but can do so separately for each variable. In fact, we used this insight in previous work to parallelize a game application [8] by declaring the policy for each variable using special *isolation types*. Such isolation types allow the user to convey deep semantic knowledge that helps to exploit the available parallelism even if there are numerous conflicts.

In this paper, we consider a number of different merge policies. Note that these happen at the granularity of individual memory locations, not on the global state.

- (Join overwrites). This policy is the default in our basic calculus (Section 3). On a write-write conflict, the value of the joined revision overwrites the value of the joining revision.
- (Custom merge function). We can use a user-defined merge function to resolve conflicts deterministically (Section 4.1).
- (Give up and report). We can refuse to merge write-write conflicts and report the failure to the user, who can take some appropriate action. (Section 4.3).

What we found a bit surprising is that the (Join overwrites)-policy is very useful in practice even though it appears to 'lose state'. This is because it lets us precisely control which revisions should take precedence over others by ordering the joins accordingly. For instance, if writes by revision B should take priority over writes by revision A, we can simply join B after joining A. The (Custom merge function)-policy was useful very specifically for implementing collections, which are often updated in a commutative way by concurrent revisions. We did not have any use for the (Give Up and Report)-policy in the game.

Isolation types are also sensible from a software engineering perspective: in a large application an architect can annotate the shared data structures with their merge policy, while the code that uses such data types stays the same: in particular, programmers have no need to use atomic regions or locks when accessing such data types and can reason about it without considering interleaved executions.

2.4 Nesting of Revisions

Nesting of revisions is a natural consequence of the fact that revisions can themselves fork and join other revisions. We show a progression of nesting in the four left most examples of Fig. 3. The (regular) and (overlap) diagrams do not nest revisions beyond a depth of 1 (that is, only the main revision is forking and joining revisions). The (nested) diagram shows simple nesting, where a revision forks a child of depth 2 and then joins it (before being joined itself). The (bridge) diagram shows that child revisions can "survive" their parents (i.e. be joined later), and that revisions can be joined by a different revision than where they were forked.

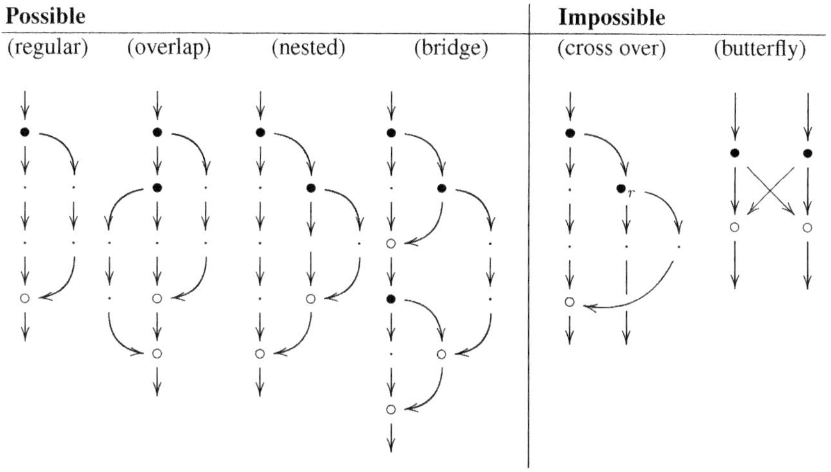

Fig. 3. Some examples of revision diagrams. The four on the left are all valid revision diagrams. On the right are two examples of impossible revision diagrams: the first one is not possible since the main branch cannot join on the outer revision as the (fresh) outer revision handle r cannot be part of its state. The right-most diagram cannot be constructed for similar reasons, in particular, all revision diagrams are semi-lattices (Theorem 3).

However, not all diagrams are possible, because revision handles must flow along edges. The two right-most examples in Fig. 3 show impossible revision diagrams. We prove some structural properties of revision diagrams in Section 5, in particular that revision diagrams are semi-lattices (Theorem 3).

Note that the structure of revision diagrams is entirely dynamic, not lexical. In particular, once a revision is forked, its handle can be stored in arbitrary data structures and be joined at an arbitrary later point of time. In some sense, revisions behave like futures whose side effects are delayed, and take effect atomically at the moment when the future is forced.

Although we present a fully dynamic model, it is of course possible to design a language that statically restricts the use of joins, to make stronger scheduling guarantees (as done in Cilk++ [14, 29]) or to simplify the most common usage patterns and to eliminate common user mistakes (as done in X10 [23]). In fact, many models (including an earlier version of our calculus) use a restricted "fork-join" parallelism [7,5]. Whether such restrictions are necessary or beneficial is beyond the scope of this paper. For now, we are content with stating that it is relatively easy to add them if desired, while it would be difficult to remove them from a calculus that depends on restrictive assumptions.

2.5 Related Work

Just as we do with revisions, proponents of transactions have long recognized that providing strong guarantees such as serializability [27] or linearizability [17] can be overly conservative for some applications, and have proposed alternate guarantees such as multi-version concurrency control [26] or snapshot isolation (SI) [4, 11, 30]. In fact, revisions can be understood as a natural generalization of snapshot isolation, extended to handle resolution of write-write conflicts following some policy (as discussed in Section 2.3), and to support nesting (as discussed in Section 2.4). We examine the relationship to snapshot isolation more formally in Section 4.3.

There has been much prior work on programming models for concurrency [25, 12, 1, 31, 2, 6]. Recently, many researchers have proposed programming models for deterministic concurrency [7, 5, 32, 28], creating renewed interest in an old problem previously known as determinacy [10]. All of these models differ semantically from revisions, and are quite a bit more restrictive. As they guarantee that the execution is equivalent to some sequential execution, they cannot easily resolve all conflicts on commit (like revisions do). Thus, they must restrict tasks from producing such conflicts either statically (by type system) or dynamically (pessimistic with blocking, or optimistic with abort and retry).

To the best of our knowledge, our combination of snapshot isolation and deterministic conflict resolution, as first presented in [8], is a novel way to simplify the parallelization of tasks that exhibit conflicts.

Isolation types are similar to Cilk++ hyperobjects [13]: both use type declarations by the programmer to change the semantics of shared variables. Cilk++ hyperobjects may split, hold, and reduce values. Although these primitives can (if properly used) achieve an effect similar to revisions, they do not provide a similarly seamless semantics. In particular, the determinacy guarantees are fragile, i.e. do not hold for all programs. For instance, the following program may finish with either $x == 2$ or $x == 1$:

```
reducer_opadd⟨int⟩ x = 0;
cilk_spawn { x++ }
if (x= 0) x++;
cilk_sync
```

Isolation types are also similar to the idea of transactional boosting, coarse-grained transactions, and semantic commutativity [16, 19, 20], which eliminate false conflicts by raising the abstraction level. Isolation types go farther though: for example, the type versioned⟨T⟩ does not just avoid false conflicts, but resolves true conflicts deterministically (in a not necessarily serializable way).

3 Revision Calculus

For reference and to remove potential ambiguities, we now present a formal calculus for revisions. It is based on a similar calculus introduced by prior work on AME (automatic mutual exclusion) [24].

Notations. To present the formal syntax and semantics succinctly, we use some standard and nonstandard notations for partial functions. For sets A, B, we write $A \rightharpoonup B$ for the set of partial functions from A to B. For $f, g \in A \rightharpoonup B$, $a \in A$, $b \in B$, and $A' \subset A$, we adopt the following notations: $f(a) = \bot$ means $a \notin \mathsf{dom}(f)$, ϵ is the empty partial function with $\mathsf{dom}(\epsilon) = \varnothing$, $f[a \mapsto b]$ is the partial function that is equivalent to f except that $f(a) = b$, and $f{::}g$ is the partial function that is equivalent to g on $\mathsf{dom}(g)$ and equivalent to f on $A \setminus \mathsf{dom}(g)$. In our transition rules, we use patterns of the form $f(a_1 \mapsto b_1) \ldots (a_n \mapsto b_n)$ (where $n \geq 1$)) to match partial functions f that satisfy $f(a_i) = b_i$ for all $1 \leq i \leq n$.

3.1 Syntax and Semantics

We show the syntax and semantics of our calculus concisely in Fig. 4. The syntax (top left) represents a standard functional calculus, augmented with references. References can be created (ref e), read ($!e$) and assigned ($e := e$). The result of a fork expression rfork e is a revision identifier from the set *Rid*, and can be used in a rjoin e expression (note that e is an expression, not a constant, thus the revision being joined can vary dynamically).

To define evaluation order within an expression, we syntactically define execution contexts (Fig. 4 right column, in the middle). An execution context $\mathcal{E}$ is an expression "with a hole $\square$", and as usual we let $\mathcal{E}[e]$ be the expression obtained from $\mathcal{E}$ by replacing the hole $\square$ with e.

The operational semantics (Fig. 4, bottom) describes transitions of the form $s \rightarrow_r s'$ which represent a step by revision r from global state s to global state s'. Consider first the definition of global states (Fig. 4, top right). A global state is a partial function from revision identifiers to local states: there is no shared global state. The local state has three parts (σ, τ, e): the snapshot σ is a partial function that represents the initial state that this revision started in, the local store τ is a partial function that represents all the locations this revision has written to, and e is the current expression.

Syntactic Symbols

$$
\begin{array}{lcl}
v \in \mathit{Val} & ::= & c \mid x \mid l \mid r \mid \lambda x.e \\
c \in \mathit{Const} & ::= & \mathsf{unit} \mid \mathsf{false} \mid \mathsf{true} \\
l \in \mathit{Loc} & & \\
r \in \mathit{Rid} & & \\
x \in \mathit{Var} & & \\
e \in \mathit{Expr} & ::= & v \\
 & \mid & e\ e \mid (e\,?\,e : e) \\
 & \mid & \mathsf{ref}\ e \mid !e \mid e := e \\
 & \mid & \mathsf{rfork}\ e \mid \mathsf{rjoin}\ e
\end{array}
$$

State

$$
\begin{array}{lcl}
s \in \mathit{GlobalState} & = & \mathit{Rid} \rightharpoonup \mathit{LocalState} \\
\mathit{LocalState} & = & \mathit{Snapshot} \times \mathit{LocalStore} \times \mathit{Expr} \\
\sigma \in \mathit{Snapshot} & = & \mathit{Loc} \rightharpoonup \mathit{Val} \\
\tau \in \mathit{LocalStore} & = & \mathit{Loc} \rightharpoonup \mathit{Val}
\end{array}
$$

Execution Contexts

$$
\begin{array}{lcl}
\mathcal{E} & = & \square \\
 & \mid & \mathcal{E}\ e \mid v\ \mathcal{E} \mid (\mathcal{E}\,?\,e : e) \\
 & \mid & \mathsf{ref}\ \mathcal{E} \mid !\mathcal{E} \mid \mathcal{E} := e \mid l := \mathcal{E} \\
 & \mid & \mathsf{rjoin}\ \mathcal{E}
\end{array}
$$

Operational Semantics

$$
\begin{array}{lll}
(\mathit{apply}) & s(r \mapsto \langle \sigma, \tau, \mathcal{E}[(\lambda x.e)\ v] \rangle) & \rightarrow_r s[r \mapsto \langle \sigma, \tau, \mathcal{E}[[v/x]e] \rangle] \\
(\mathit{if\text{-}true}) & s(r \mapsto \langle \sigma, \tau, \mathcal{E}[(\mathsf{true}\,?\,e_1 : e_2)] \rangle) & \rightarrow_r s[r \mapsto \langle \sigma, \tau, \mathcal{E}[e_1] \rangle] \\
(\mathit{if\text{-}false}) & s(r \mapsto \langle \sigma, \tau, \mathcal{E}[(\mathsf{false}\,?\,e_1 : e_2)] \rangle) & \rightarrow_r s[r \mapsto \langle \sigma, \tau, \mathcal{E}[e_2] \rangle]
\end{array}
$$

$$
\begin{array}{llll}
(\mathit{new}) & s(r \mapsto \langle \sigma, \tau, \mathcal{E}[\mathsf{ref}\ v] \rangle) & \rightarrow_r s[r \mapsto \langle \sigma, \tau[l \mapsto v], \mathcal{E}[l] \rangle] & \text{if } l \notin s \\
(\mathit{get}) & s(r \mapsto \langle \sigma, \tau, \mathcal{E}[!l] \rangle) & \rightarrow_r s[r \mapsto \langle \sigma, \tau, \mathcal{E}[(\sigma{::}\tau)(l)] \rangle] & \text{if } l \in \mathrm{dom}(\sigma{::}\tau) \\
(\mathit{set}) & s(r \mapsto \langle \sigma, \tau, \mathcal{E}[l := v] \rangle) & \rightarrow_r s[r \mapsto \langle \sigma, \tau[l \mapsto v], \mathcal{E}[\mathsf{unit}] \rangle] & \text{if } l \in \mathrm{dom}(\sigma{::}\tau)
\end{array}
$$

$$
\begin{array}{llll}
(\mathit{fork}) & s(r \mapsto \langle \sigma, \tau, \mathcal{E}[\mathsf{rfork}\ e] \rangle) & \rightarrow_r s[r \mapsto \langle \sigma, \tau, \mathcal{E}[r'] \rangle][r' \mapsto \langle \sigma{::}\tau, \epsilon, e \rangle] & \text{if } r' \notin s
\end{array}
$$

$$
\begin{array}{lll}
(\mathit{join}) & s(r \mapsto \langle \sigma, \tau, \mathcal{E}[\mathsf{rjoin}\ r'] \rangle)(r' \mapsto \langle \sigma', \tau', v \rangle) & \rightarrow_r s[r \mapsto \langle \sigma, \tau{::}\tau', \mathcal{E}[\mathsf{unit}] \rangle][r' \mapsto \bot] \\
(\mathit{join}_\epsilon) & s(r \mapsto \langle \sigma, \tau, \mathcal{E}[\mathsf{rjoin}\ r'] \rangle)(r' \mapsto \bot) & \rightarrow_r \epsilon
\end{array}
$$

Fig. 4. Syntax and Semantics of the revision calculus

The rules for the operational semantics (Fig. 4, bottom) all follow the same general structure: a transition $s \rightarrow_r s'$ matches the local state for r on the left, and describes how the next step of revision r changes the state.

The first three rules (*apply*), (*if-true*), and (*if-false*)) reflect standard semantics of application and conditional. They affect only the local expression. The next three rules (*new*), (*get*), and (*set*) reflect operations on the store. Thus, they affect both the local store and the local expression. The (*new*) rule chooses a fresh location (we simply write $l \notin s$ to express that l does not appear in any snapshot or local store of s). The last two rules reflect synchronization operations. The rule (*fork*) starts a new revision, whose local state consists of (1) a snapshot that is initialized to the current state $\sigma{::}\tau$, (2) a local store that is the empty partial function, and (3) an expression that is the expression supplied with the fork. Note that (*fork*) chooses a fresh revision identifier (we simply write $r \notin s$ to express that r is not mapped by s, and does not appear in any snapshot or local store of s). The rule (*join*) updates the local store of the revision that performs the join by merging the snapshot, master, and revision states (in accordance with the declared isolation types), and removes the joined revision. We call r the joining revision (or joiner), and r' the joined revision (or joinee). A join can only proceed if the joinee has executed all the way to a value (which is ignored). The final rule (join_ϵ) is added to prevent joining a revision handle more than once. If a revision handle is joined a second time, the joinee is no longer in the domain of s, and the entire state transitions to a special error state represented by the empty partial function ϵ (this state can not be reached in any other way, and has no outgoing transitions).

3.2 Executions

As usual, we let $\rightarrow$ be the union of all $\rightarrow_r$ where $r \in \mathit{Rid}$. Furthermore, we use the following notations for repeated steps: we say $s \rightarrow^n s'$ if s' can be reached from s in exactly n $\rightarrow$-steps, we say $s \rightarrow^* s'$ (transitive reflexive closure) if it can be reached in zero or more steps, $s \rightarrow^+ s'$ (transitive closure) if it can be reached in one or more steps, and $s \rightarrow^? s'$ (reflexive closure) if it can be reached in zero or one steps.

We define global executions of expressions as follows. First, an expression e is a *program expression* if it does not contain any revision identifiers (expressions may contain revision identifiers during execution, but not initially). We say a sequence of transitions $s_0 \rightarrow s_1 \rightarrow \cdots \rightarrow s_n$ is an *execution* of a program expression e if $s_0 = \{(r, (\epsilon, \epsilon, e)\}$ for some $r \in \mathit{Rid}$. We call such an execution *maximal* if there exists no s' such that $s_n \rightarrow s'$. Finally, given a program expression e we write $e \downarrow s$ if there exists a maximal execution for e with final state s.

3.3 Determinacy

A surprising property of our calculus is that executions are determinate and not dependent on a specific 'schedule'. Before we can state this precisely, we need a notion of equivalence of states modulo renaming of revisions and locations.

For a permutation α of *Rid* and a global state s let $\alpha(s)$ be the global state obtained by replacing all revision identifiers r that occur in s with $\alpha(r)$. Similarly, define $\beta(s)$ for a permutation β of *Loc*. We say two states s, s' are equivalent upto $\alpha\beta$-renaming, written as $s \approx s'$, if there exist permutations α of *Rid* and β of *Loc* such that $s = \alpha(\beta(s'))$.

We now state the main result of this section: executions are determinate modulo renaming of locations and revisions.

Theorem 1 (Determinacy). *Let e be a program expression, and let $e \downarrow s$ and $e \downarrow s'$. Then $s \approx s'$.*

Before proving this theorem, we make a few observations, and establish a few lemmas and an important confluence theorem.

Note that some executions may terminate in the special error state ϵ if they attempt to join the same revision more than once. Our use of a special error state is important to guarantee determinacy. Suppose two revisions try to join a third revision simultaneously (i.e. there is a race between two joins). Without the rule ($join_\epsilon$) the different schedules may lead to different final states. However, with ($join_\epsilon$), all executions are forced to eventually end up at ϵ, maintaining determinacy.

To prepare for the proof, we now state and prove a local determinism lemma and a confluence theorem.

Lemma 1 (Local Determinism). *If $s_1 \approx s_1'$ and $s_1 \rightarrow_r s_2$ and $s_1' \rightarrow_r s_2'$, then $s_2 \approx s_2'$.*

Proof. First we observe that by construction, each evaluation context $\mathcal{E}$ contains at most one hole and that there is no choice in which redex to evaluate next. We can now do a case analysis on $\mathcal{E}[e]$ where e is a redex. For a fixed revision r, such expression context is matched uniquely by at most one operational rule. Moreover, each rule is deterministic modulo $\alpha\beta$-equivalence. This is trivial for all operations except (*new*) and (*fork*) that create new locations and revisions respectively. Given a state $s(r \mapsto \langle \sigma, \tau, \mathcal{E}[\mathsf{ref}\ v] \rangle)$, rule (*new*) can create different names for the new location, i.e. $s = s(r \mapsto \langle \sigma, \tau[l \mapsto v], \mathcal{E}[l] \rangle)$ or $s' = s(r \mapsto \langle \sigma, \tau[l' \mapsto v], \mathcal{E}[l'] \rangle)$. If $l = l'$ this is equivalent directly. If $l \neq l'$ we can apply α-renaming with $\alpha = [l/l']$ where $s = \alpha(s')$ which holds since $l' \notin s'$ and $l \notin s$ due to the side condition on (*new*) (and by definition $s \approx s'$). We prove equivalence similarly for (*fork*).

Lemma 2 (Strong Local Confluence). *Let s_1 and s_1' be reachable states that satisfy $s_1 \approx s_1'$. Then, if $s_1 \to_r s_2$ and $s_1' \to_{r'} s_2'$, then there exist equivalent states $s_3 \approx s_3'$ such that both $s_2 \to_{r'}^{?} s_3$ and $s_2' \to_r^{?} s_3'$.*

Proof. First we observe that when $r = r'$, the lemma follows directly from the local-determinism lemma. We continue the proof for the case $r \neq r'$, and do a case distinction on the kind of the two operational steps appearing in the assumption of the theorem. We use the term *local step* to denote a step that is not (*fork*), (*join*), and (*join*$_\epsilon$).

- (*local*) / (*local*). The rules affect independent parts of the state s and thus commute. As before, we may need to use α-renaming for the (*new*) case.
- (*local*) / (*fork*),(*join*). Same argument; note that the forked/joined revision can not be the same as the local one because of the side condition $r' \notin s$ (for fork) or because the joinee can not take a step (for join).
- (*join*$_\epsilon$) / any. The claim follows because if we could apply (*join*$_\epsilon$) in some state but perform a different rule, then (*join*$_\epsilon$) still applies.
- (*fork*) / (*fork*). In this case the side condition $r' \notin s$ ensures that both forks will fork a unique revision. As shown in the proof of the previous lemma, we can safely apply β-renaming to show both end states are equivalent.
- (*fork*) / (*join*). Observe that the (*join*) cannot join on the revision that forks (since its expression is not a value). Also, the side condition $r' \notin s$ ensures that a unique revision is forked that is different from r and r' in the (*join*) rules.
- (*join*) / (*join*). The matched states are $s(r \mapsto \langle \sigma, \tau, \mathcal{E}[\mathsf{rjoin}\ r_1] \rangle)(r_1 \mapsto \langle \sigma_1, \tau_1, v_1 \rangle)$ and $s(r' \mapsto \langle \sigma', \tau', \mathcal{E}'[\mathsf{rjoin}\ r_2] \rangle)(r_2 \mapsto \langle \sigma_2, \tau_2, v_2 \rangle)$. We have two possibilities. First, if $r_1 \neq r_2$, both joins commute directly. Otherwise, $r_1 = r_2$. In this case the joinee is shared . Thus, taking step $\to_r$ leads to a state where $s(r_1 \mapsto \bot)$ and step $\to_{r'}$ must use (*join*$_\epsilon$) ending in state ϵ, which is also the outcome for the opposite order.

Theorem 2 (Confluence). *For any reachable states $s_1 \approx s_1'$, it holds that if $s_1 \to^* s_2$ and $s_1' \to^* s_2'$, then there exist equivalent states $s_3 \approx s_3'$ such that both $s_2 \to^* s_3$ and $s_2' \to^* s_3'$.*

Proving confluence from strong local confluence is well-known and often illustrated using tiling of diagrams. It is useful for several applications (e.g. the lambda calculus or general term rewriting) but can also be understood more abstractly as a property of binary relations [18]. We include a quick proof sketch for reference.

Proof. First, lift the step relation $\rightarrow$ to equivalence classes of states modulo $\approx$. Let x, y, z, u range over equivalence classes, and consider the following three properties:

1. $\forall xyz : x \rightarrow y \wedge x \rightarrow z \Rightarrow \exists u : y \rightarrow^{?} u \wedge z \rightarrow^{?} u$
2. $\forall n : \forall xyz : x \rightarrow^{?} y \wedge x \rightarrow^{n} z \Rightarrow \exists u : y \rightarrow^{*} u \wedge z \rightarrow^{?} u$
3. $\forall n : \forall xyz : x \rightarrow^{n} y \wedge x \rightarrow^{*} z \Rightarrow \exists u : y \rightarrow^{*} u \wedge z \rightarrow^{*} u$

We can then show that (1) the first claim follows from strong local confluence, (2) the second claim follows from the first by induction over n, (3) the third claim follows from the second by induction over n, and (4) the theorem follows from the third claim.

We now conclude with the proof of theorem 1. Given a program expression e and two maximal executions $s_0 \rightarrow^{*} s$ and $s'_0 \rightarrow^{*} s'$ for e, we know $s_0 \approx s'_0$ (by the way we defined initial states for e), so by the confluence theorem there exist $s_1 \approx s'_1$ such that $s \rightarrow^{*} s_1$ and $s' \rightarrow^{*} s'_1$. But since s and s' are maximal it must be the case that $s = s_1$ and $s' = s'_1$ and thus $s \approx s'$ as claimed.

4 State Merging

The basic calculus introduced in the previous section provides little flexibility as to how write-write conflicts should be resolved. We now show how to modify the calculus so that it can support custom merge functions (Section 4.1), how it can be understood as an extension of snapshot isolation (Section 4.3), and how we can provide stronger consistency guarantees for abstract data types using sequential merge functions (Section 4.4).

$$(\textit{join-merge})\ s(r \mapsto \langle \sigma, \tau, \mathcal{E}[\mathsf{rjoin}\ r'] \rangle)(r' \mapsto \langle \sigma', \tau', v \rangle) \quad \rightarrow_r$$
$$s[r \mapsto \langle \sigma, \mathsf{merge}(\tau, \tau', \sigma'), \mathcal{E}[\mathsf{unit}] \rangle][r' \mapsto \bot]$$

where
$$\mathsf{merge}(\tau, \tau', \sigma')(l) = \begin{cases} \tau(l) & \text{if } \tau'(l) = \bot \\ \tau'(l) & \text{if } \sigma'(l) = \tau(l) \\ \mathsf{merge}_l(\tau(l), \tau'(l), \sigma'(l)) & \text{otherwise} \end{cases}$$

Fig. 5. Extending the revision calculus with merge functions

4.1 Merge Functions

Figure 5 extends the basic calculus with flexible merge functions. There is just one change to the basic calculus where we replace the (*join*) rule with the (*join-merge*) rule. Instead of composing the new state as $\tau{::}\tau'$ we call a custom $\mathsf{merge}(\tau, \tau', \sigma')$ function that merges the states. If there is no (write-write) conflict at a particular location, this function behaves just like our earlier composition. In case of conflict, the value at a location l after a join is determined by a location specific function $\mathsf{merge}_l : \mathit{Val} \times \mathit{Val} \times \mathit{Val} \rightarrow \mathit{Val}$ which is defined separately for each location l.

Note that the choice of merge function does not influence determinacy. The determinacy proof remains intact regardless of what merge function is chosen (as long as it is a function of its three inputs). In particular, we need not restrict our attention to commutative or associative functions only.

The merge_l function subsumes the semantics of the previous calculus where a joinee takes precedence since we can define the default merge function as:

$$\mathsf{merge}_l(v, v', v_0) = v' \quad \text{(joinee wins)}$$

Similarly, we can implement the dual strategy where updates to a specific location are ignored if there is a write-write conflict:

$$\mathsf{merge}_l(v, v', v_0) = v \quad \text{(joiner wins)}$$

Note that sometimes, we may wish to define merge functions involving more than a single variable. In our calculus we can do so by using composite types to group several variables into a single location and merge them collectively.

4.2 Commutative Merges

We call a merge function *commutative* if $\mathsf{merge}_l(v, v', v_0) = \mathsf{merge}_l(v', v, v_0)$. Clearly, the default merge function is not commutative, but many others are. For example, a reasonable merge function for sets could be:

$$\mathsf{merge}_l(s, s', s_0) = s \cup s'$$

which is commutative. This is not the only reasonable merge function though. Consider the following venn diagram that shows how the sets s, s', and s_0 may interact:

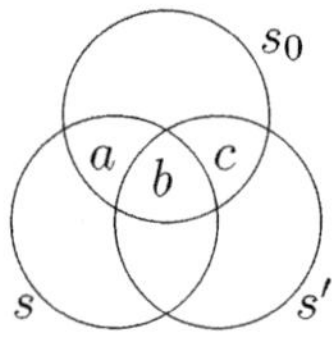

When taking the union of s and s', we always include the regions a, b, and c. One can argue however that to end up with s' from s_0, the elements in a were explicitly removed (and similarly for s with region c). Another reasonable merge function may respect such removals and remove region a and c from the final result. We can specify this as:

$$\mathsf{merge}_l(s, s', s_0) = (s - s_0) \cup (s' - s_0) \cup (s \cap s')$$

which is also commutative. Note that when all operations on the set are additive, both of these merge functions produce the same result since $s_0 \subseteq (s \cap s')$ in that case.

Ultimately, this discussion simply illustrates that the choice of a merge function should be informed by what operations are performed (additions only, removals only, both, etc.). We discuss this idea more formally in Section 4.4, where we show that by restricting the operations on an abstract data type, we can find merge functions can provide particularly strong guarantees.

$$\begin{array}{lll}
(\textit{join-ok}) & s(r \mapsto \langle \sigma, \tau, \mathcal{E}[\mathsf{rjoin}\ r'] \rangle)(r' \mapsto \langle \sigma', \tau', v \rangle) & \rightarrow_r \\
& s[r \mapsto \langle \sigma, \mathsf{merge}(\tau, \tau', \sigma'), \mathcal{E}[\mathsf{true}] \rangle][r' \mapsto \bot] & \text{if } \neg\mathsf{fail}(\tau, \tau', \sigma') \\
(\textit{join-fail}) & s(r \mapsto \langle \sigma, \tau, \mathcal{E}[\mathsf{rjoin}\ r'] \rangle)(r' \mapsto \langle \sigma', \tau', v \rangle) & \rightarrow_r \\
& s[r \mapsto \langle \sigma, \tau, \mathcal{E}[\mathsf{false}] \rangle][r' \mapsto \bot] & \text{if } \mathsf{fail}(\tau, \tau', \sigma')
\end{array}$$

$$\text{where} \quad \mathsf{fail}(\tau, \tau', \sigma') = \mathsf{undef} \in \mathsf{rng}(\mathsf{merge}(\tau, \tau', \sigma'))$$

Fig. 6. Extending the merge calculus with failing joins

4.3 Snapshot Isolation

We now explain how to view our system as a generalization of *snapshot isolation* [4], a concurrency control algorithm that is widely used in the database community, and has for example been implemented by Oracle and Microsoft SQL Server (with minor variations). We use the definition given by Fekete *et al.* [11].

We claim that our revision calculus is a generalization of snapshot isolation, augmented by (1) the ability to gracefully resolve write-write conflict when a suitable merge function exists for a particular location, and (2) support nontrivial nesting (Fig. 3) while maintaining a simple and precise semantics. To see why this is the case, we perform the reverse process: we (1) introduce the ability to fail on write-write conflicts, and (2) remove nesting from revisions.

Removing nesting is straightforward (for example, we can disallow forks by all revisions but the main revision). As for failing on conflicts, we proceed as follows. To mirror how transactions fail (and discard state), we introduce the notion of a failing join as follows.

- We change the merge calculus slightly, by redefining the local merge functions so that they can return a special value indicating that there is an unresolvable conflict:

$$\mathsf{merge}_l : \mathit{Val} \times \mathit{Val} \times \mathit{Val} \rightarrow (\mathit{Val} \cup \{\mathsf{undef}\})$$

- We extend the merge calculus by replacing (*join-merge*) with two new rules. The (*join-ok*) rule is equivalent to the previous (*join-merge*) rule but can only be applied now if all of the location specific merge functions are defined. The rule (*join-fail*) applies if at least one of the merges failed and simply ignores all updates in the joinee. Both rules now return a boolean to the joiner, where true indicates that the join was successful, and false indicates that it was not.

Consider now the definition of snapshot isolation: A transaction A executing under snapshot isolation operates on a snapshot of the database taken at the start of the transaction. When the transaction concludes, it will successfully commit only if the values updated by the transaction A were not updated by any other transaction B that committed after transaction A started.

We can succinctly describe this behaviour in our calculus by letting every merge_l function fail:

$$\mathsf{merge}_l(v, v', v_0) = \mathsf{undef} \qquad \text{(snapshot isolation)}$$

When discussing snapshot isolation there is sometimes confusion whether a transaction should abort if there was a concurrent *silent write* in the main branch where the original value has been left unchanged. In our formal calculus there is no such confusion: due to the second case of the merge function (Fig. 5), concurrent silent writes on the main branch will not cause a transaction to fail. Note that we can still model the behaviour where silent writes cause a transaction to fail by assigning sequence numbers to each value (ensuring that $\sigma'(l) \neq \tau(l)$ on silent writes). Dually, we can *ignore* silent writes on the child branch by modifying the merge function:

$$\mathsf{merge}_l(v, v', v_0) = ((v' = v_0)\,?\,v' : \mathsf{undef}) \quad \text{(ignore silent wr)}$$

4.4 Abstract Data Types and Sequential Merges

As Theorem 1 shows, our calculus is always determinate, but we have seen in the introduction that it is not always serializable (Fig. 2). However, we can sometimes guarantee equivalence to a sequential execution by raising the abstraction level of operations on data, and constructing merge functions that are tailored to the operations that are performed.

For example, consider a program location x that is initially zero and for which we define the merge function $\mathsf{merge}_x(v, v', v_0) = v + v' - v_0$. Furthermore, assume that a program performs only one type of operation on x, namely *add*(i), which adds an integer i to it. Then the final value of x is always consistent with a serial execution of all the *add* operations that occurred in the program. We now explain this idea more formally.

Abstract Data Types. We define an *abstract data type* to be a tuple (V, o, Op, op) where V is a set of values, $o \in V$ is an initial value, Op is a set of operations, and $op : Op \times V \rightharpoonup V$ is a partial function. In our formalization, the set Op includes argument and return values of operations, and op is partial because not all operations apply in all states.

Example 1. We can define an integer register (i.e. a memory location holding an integer that can be read and written) as $IntReg = (\mathbb{Z}, 0, Op, op)$ where

$$Op = \{get(v) \mid v \in \mathbb{Z}\} \cup \{set(v) \mid v \in \mathbb{Z}\}$$

$$op(v, o) = \begin{cases} w \text{ if } o = set(w) \\ v \text{ if } o = get(v) \\ \perp \text{ if } o = get(v') \text{ and } v \neq v' \end{cases}$$

Sequential Merge Functions. Sometimes we can find merge functions that can simulate a deterministic, linear interleaving of the operations. We call such merge functions *sequential*. This concept is quite useful in practice since the programmer can design the application specifically to enable sequential merge functions, by restricting what type of operations may happen in concurrent revisions. For example, if an application performs aggregation of results, sequential merges usually exist.

To study the effect of entire sequences of operations, we introduce the following concise notations. We consider operation sequences as words in Op^*, and write $u(v)$ (where $u \in Op^*$ and $v \in Val$) for the combined effect of all the operations in the sequence u (left to right) applied to the value v, which may be undefined. For example, this means that for operation sequences $u, w \in Op^*$ and a value v, we have $uw(v) = w(u(v))$ if $u(v) \neq \bot$ and $w(u(v)) \neq \bot$. We now define sequential merge functions as:

Definition 1. *Let $\mathcal{A} = (V, o, Op, op)$ be an abstract data type. We say a merge function $\mathsf{m} : V \times V \times V \to V$ is* sequential *for $\mathcal{A}$ if for all operation sequences $u, w_1, w_2 \in Op^*$ such that $u(o) \neq \bot$, $uw_1(o) \neq \bot$ and $uw_2(o) \neq \bot$, both of the following are true:*

1. $uw_1w_2(o) \neq \bot$
2. $\mathsf{m}(uw_1(o), uw_2(o), u(o)) = uw_1w_2(o)$

The advantage of a sequential merge function is that it guarantees the appearance that all operations were executed sequentially, with the operations of the joined revision happening at the time of the join.

Note that condition 1 of Def. 1 does not depend on the actual merge function, but is a property of the abstract data type. This property may not be satisfiable, thus sequential merge functions do not exist for all abstract data types. For example, the abstract data type *IntReg* defined in Example 1 does not permit sequential merging because it can be the case that $w_1 = set(1)$, $w_2 = get(0)$ in which case always $uw_1w_2(0) = \bot$.

Abelian Data Types. Particularly simple to merge are certain abstract data types with commutative operations that we call *abelian*. More formally, call an abstract data type (V, o, Op, op) *abelian* if there exists a binary operation $+$ on V, and a function $\delta : Op \to V$ such that (1) $(V, +)$ is an abelian group with neutral element o, and (2) for all $a \in Op$ we have $a(v) = v + \delta(a)$.

We conclude this section with a lemma that shows how to construct sequential merge functions for abelian data types.

Lemma 3. *For an abelian data type (V, o, Op, op) with operation $+$, the merge function : $\mathsf{m}(v_1, v_2, v) = v_1 + v_2 - v$ is sequential.*

Proof. Let $w_1 = \sum_{i=1}^{n} a_i$ and $w_2 = \sum_{i=1}^{m} b_i$ and $v = u(o)$. Then claim 2 is satisfied: $\mathsf{m}(uw_1(o), uw_2(o), u(o)) = \mathsf{m}(w_1(u(o)), w_2(u(o)), u(o)) = \mathsf{m}(v + \sum_{i=1}^{n} a_i, v + \sum_{i=1}^{m} b_i, v) = v + \sum_{i=1}^{n} a_i + v + \sum_{i=1}^{m} b_i - v = v + \sum_{i=1}^{n} a_i + \sum_{i=1}^{m} b_i = w_1w_2(u(o)) = uw_1w_2(o)$. This implies also that claim 1 is satisfied.

5 Revision Diagrams

In this section we describe and formally define *revision diagrams*, a special kind of graph that visually represent the dataflow of computations of our calculus. Revision diagrams are an essential tool to understand how to program with revisions, somewhat analogous to the role of stream diagrams for stream programming. Revision diagrams are not equivalent to other graph classes commonly used for representing concurrent

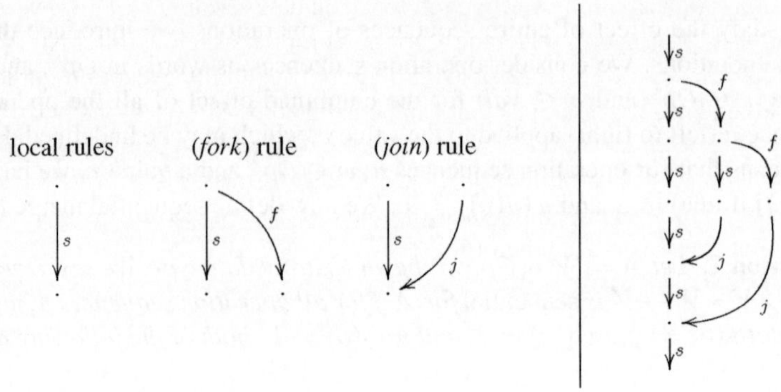

Fig. 7. **(a)** Left: the diagrams illustrate how revision diagrams are constructed incrementally by transition rules adding vertices. **(b)** Right: a typical example of a revision diagram.

or parallel qcomputations, such as directed acyclic graphs (DAGs), or series-parallel graphs (SP-graphs). The goal of this section is to formally define revision diagrams and to shed more light on their general structure.

Intuitively, revision diagrams represent executions, with vertices being states and edges being transitions. Technically, revision diagrams are labeled graphs:

Definition 2. *A* fsj-graph G *is a tuple* $G = (V, E)$ *where* V *is a set of vertices and* $E \subset V \times \{f, s, j\} \times V$ *is a set of labeled edges.*

Graph Notations. We use the usual terminology for graphs, but emphasize a relational view of edges. For a fixed graph $G = (V, E)$, we define a binary relation $\xrightarrow{f}$ on vertices such that $(u \xrightarrow{f} v) \overset{\text{def}}{\Leftrightarrow} ((u, f, v) \in E)$, and similarly for $\xrightarrow{j}$ and $\xrightarrow{s}$. We also define the relation $\rightarrow \overset{\text{def}}{=} (\xrightarrow{f} \cup \xrightarrow{j} \cup \xrightarrow{s})$.

To define the revision diagram for a given execution, we extend the original operational semantics so that a fsj-graph is constructed alongside the executing program. More formally, we extend the original transition relation $\rightarrow$ to an extended transition relation $\rightarrow_d$ (where d is just a label for easier distinction) on states $(s, (V, E), \rho, \gamma)$ where: $s \in \mathit{GlobalState}$ is a global state as defined previously, (V, E) is a fsj-graph, $\rho : V \rightarrow \mathit{Rid}$ maps vertices to revision they belong to, and $\gamma : \mathit{Rid} \rightharpoonup V$ is a partial function that maps a revision to the last (current) vertex of that revision.

The graph is constructed incrementally by adding new vertices, and edges from the existing graph to the new vertices, as illustrated in Fig. 7 (a). The precise transition rules for $\rightarrow_d$ are defined in Fig. 8. Intutively, the constructed graphs represents excecutions in the following sense (for an example, see Fig. 7 (b)):

- Each vertex $v \in V$ belongs to a particular revision $\rho(v)$ and represents the local state of that revision at a certain point of time.
- The set of all vertices belonging to the same revisions is totally ordered by $\xrightarrow{s}$, the successor relation, which describes how the local state of that revision evolves over time.
- Each edge in $\xrightarrow{f}$ represents the forking of a new revision. Its destination vertex is the first vertex of the new revision.

- Each edge in $\xrightarrow{j}$ represents the joining of a revision. Its source vertex is that last vertex of the revision being joined.

We define the initial states to be $(s_0, G_0, \rho_0, \gamma_0)$ where $s_0 = (r, (\epsilon, \epsilon, e))$ is an initial global state (that is, r is a revision identifier and e is an expression not containing any revision identifiers), $G_0 = (\{v\}, \emptyset)$ is a singleton graph, and $\rho_0 = \{v \mapsto r\}$, $\gamma_0 = \{r \mapsto v\}$. We say a state (s, G, ρ, γ) is *reachable* if there exists an initial state from which it can be reached by zero or more $\rightarrow_d$-transitions.

Definition 3. *A* revision diagram *is an fsj-graph G that is part of some reachable state* (s, G, ρ, γ).

It is easy to see (comparing the definitions of $\rightarrow$ and $\rightarrow_d$) that for any execution $s_0 \rightarrow^* s_n$ such that $s_n \neq \epsilon$, we can find a corresponding extended execution, and vice versa. Note that this may entail the renaming of revision identifiers in the $\rightarrow$-execution, because the latter does allow the reuse of revision identifiers after the revision has been joined while $\rightarrow_d$ does not. Our main theorem can now be stated as:

$$
\begin{array}{lll}
(\mathit{apply}) & (s(r \mapsto \langle \sigma, \tau, \mathcal{E}[(\lambda x.e)\ v]\rangle),\ (V,E), \rho, \gamma\ ) \quad \rightarrow_d \quad (\text{if } v \notin V) \\
& (s[r \mapsto \langle \sigma, \tau, \mathcal{E}[[v/x]e]\rangle],\ (V \cup v, E \cup \gamma(r) \xrightarrow{s} v), \rho[v \mapsto r], \gamma[r \mapsto v]\ ) \\
(\mathit{if\text{-}true}) & (s(r \mapsto \langle \sigma, \tau, \mathcal{E}[(\mathsf{true}\,?\,e_1 : e_2)]\rangle),\ (V,E), \rho, \gamma\ ) \quad \rightarrow_d \quad (\text{if } v \notin V) \\
& (s[r \mapsto \langle \sigma, \tau, \mathcal{E}[e_1]\rangle],\ (V \cup v, E \cup \gamma(r) \xrightarrow{s} v), \rho[v \mapsto r], \gamma[r \mapsto v]\ ) \\
(\mathit{if\text{-}false}) & (s(r \mapsto \langle \sigma, \tau, \mathcal{E}[(\mathsf{false}\,?\,e_1 : e_2)]\rangle),\ (V,E), \rho, \gamma\ ) \quad \rightarrow_d \quad (\text{if } v \notin V) \\
& (s[r \mapsto \langle \sigma, \tau, \mathcal{E}[e_2]\rangle],\ (V \cup v, E \cup \gamma(r) \xrightarrow{s} v), \rho[v \mapsto r], \gamma[r \mapsto v]\ ) \\
(\mathit{new}) & (s(r \mapsto \langle \sigma, \tau, \mathcal{E}[\mathsf{ref}\ v]\rangle),\ (V,E), \rho, \gamma\ ) \quad \rightarrow_d \quad (\text{if } l \notin s \text{ and } v \notin V) \\
& (s[r \mapsto \langle \sigma, \tau[l \mapsto v], \mathcal{E}[l]\rangle],\ (V \cup v, E \cup \gamma(r) \xrightarrow{s} v), \rho[v \mapsto r], \gamma[r \mapsto v]\ ) \\
(\mathit{get}) & (s(r \mapsto \langle \sigma, \tau, \mathcal{E}[!l]\rangle),\ (V,E), \rho, \gamma\ ) \quad \rightarrow_d \quad (\text{if } l \in \mathsf{dom}(\sigma{::}\tau) \text{ and } v \notin V) \\
& (s[r \mapsto \langle \sigma, \tau, \mathcal{E}[(\sigma{::}\tau)(l)]\rangle]\ (V \cup v, E \cup \gamma(r) \xrightarrow{s} v), \rho[v \mapsto r], \gamma[r \mapsto v]\ ) \\
(\mathit{set}) & (s(r \mapsto \langle \sigma, \tau, \mathcal{E}[l := v]\rangle),\ (V,E), \rho, \gamma\ ) \quad \rightarrow_d \quad (\text{if } l \in \mathsf{dom}(\sigma{::}\tau) \text{ and } v \notin V) \\
& (s[r \mapsto \langle \sigma, \tau[l \mapsto v], \mathcal{E}[\mathsf{unit}]\rangle],\ (V \cup v, E \cup \gamma(r) \xrightarrow{s} v), \rho[v \mapsto r], \gamma[r \mapsto v]) \\
(\mathit{fork}) & (s(r \mapsto \langle \sigma, \tau, \mathcal{E}[\mathsf{rfork}\ e]\rangle)\ (V,E), \rho, \gamma\ ) \rightarrow_d \ (\text{if } r' \notin s,\ v,w \notin V \text{ and } r' \notin \mathsf{rng}(\rho)) \\
& (s[r \mapsto \langle \sigma, \tau, \mathcal{E}[r']\rangle][r' \mapsto \langle \sigma{::}\tau, \epsilon, e\rangle], \\
& (V \cup \{v,w\}, E \cup \{\gamma(r) \xrightarrow{s} v, \gamma(r) \xrightarrow{f} w\}), \rho[v \mapsto r][w \mapsto r'], \gamma[r \mapsto v][r' \mapsto w]\ ) \\
(\mathit{join}) & (s(r \mapsto \langle \sigma, \tau, \mathcal{E}[\mathsf{rjoin}\ r']\rangle)(r' \mapsto \langle \sigma', \tau', v\rangle)\ (V,E), \rho, \gamma\ ) \quad \rightarrow_d \quad (\text{if } v \notin V) \\
& (s[r \mapsto \langle \sigma, \tau{::}\tau', \mathcal{E}[\mathsf{unit}]\rangle][r' \mapsto \bot], \\
& (V \cup v, E \cup \{\gamma(r) \xrightarrow{s} v, \gamma(r') \xrightarrow{j} v\}), \rho[v \mapsto r], \gamma[r \mapsto v][r' \mapsto \bot]\ )
\end{array}
$$

Fig. 8. Operational rules for $\rightarrow_d$. The rules match the ones in Fig. 4, except for the highlighted parts, and for the omission of (*join*$_\epsilon$).

Theorem 3. *Let* $G = (V, E)$ *be a revision diagram. Then G is a semilattice, i.e. for any two vertices* $x, y \in V$, *there exists a greatest common ancestor.*

While plausible, this result is not obvious, as it hinges on where exactly revisions can be joined from: If we could join revisions from anywhere (e.g. if we used sequential consistency without isolating revisions), the graphs would be general DAGs which are not always semilattices (e.g. see Fig. 3, on the right). On the other hand, if our revisions were simply nested like trees (as enforced in Cilk, for example), the resulting graphs would be SP-graphs which can be easily proved to always be semilattices. For revision diagrams, however, the proof of the semilattice property is somewhat subtle as it depends on the fact that revisions can be joined only from locations that are downstream from the fork (since revision handles must flow along lines). For a detailed proof of this theorem as well as other useful or interesting properties of revision diagrams see the companion Tech Report [9].

6 Conclusion and Future Work

We have presented a novel programming model based on concurrent revisions. First, we presented a concise calculus that shows how revisions can maintain determinacy despite nondeterministic scheduling. Then we provided a discussion of how state merging can be tailored to the needs of the application. Finally, we formalized revision diagrams, the fundamental tool to visualize nonlinear histories of state, and showed how they differ from other task graphs. In future work, we may further investigate state merging and serialization guarantees. We are also interested in enhancing the calculus with reactive inputs and outputs and extending the determinacy guarantee to such applications.

Acknowledgments. We thank Tim Harris, Tom Ball and Manuel Fähndrich for their helpful feedback.

References

1. Aditya, S., Arvind, Augustsson, L., Maessen, J.-W., Nikhil, R.: Semantics of pH: A Parallel Dialect of Haskell. In: Hudak, P. (ed.) Proc. Haskell Workshop, La Jolla, CA, USA, pp. 35–49 (June 1995)
2. Allen, E., Chase, D., Flood, C., Luchangco, V., Maessen, J.-W., Ryu, S., Steele Jr., G.: Project fortress: A multicore language for multicore processors. In: Linux Mag. (September 2007)
3. Baldassin, A., Burckhardt, S.: Lightweight software transactions for games. In: Workshop on Hot Topics in Parallelism, HotPar (2009)
4. Berenson, H., Bernstein, P., Gray, J., Melton, J., O'Neil, E., O'Neil, P.: A critique of ANSI SQL isolation levels. In: Proceedings of SIGMOD, pp. 1–10 (1995)
5. Berger, E., Yang, T., Liu, T., Novark, G.: Grace: Safe multithreaded programming for C/C++. In: OOPSLA (2009)
6. Blelloch, G., Chatterjee, S., Hardwick, J., Sipelstein, J., Zagha, M.: Impl. of a portable nested data-parallel language. Journal of Par. and Dist. Comp. 21(1), 4–14 (1994)
7. Bocchino, R., Adve, V., Dig, D., Adve, S., et al.: A type and effect system for deterministic parallel java. In: OOPSLA (2009)
8. Burckhardt, S., Baldassin, A., Leijen, D.: Concurrent programming with revisions and isolation types. In: OOPSLA (October 2010)
9. Burckhardt, S., Leijen, D.: Semantics of concurrent revisions. Technical Report MSR-TR-2010-94, Microsoft Research (2010)

10. Denning, P., Dennis, J.: The resurgence of parallelism. Commun. ACM 53(6) (2010)
11. Fekete, A., Liarokapis, D., O'Neil, E., O'Neil, P., Shasha, D.: Making snapshot isolation serializable. ACM Trans. Database Syst. 30(2), 492–528 (2005)
12. Flanagan, C., Felleisen, M.: The semantics of future and its use in program optimization, Rice University, pp. 209–220 (1995)
13. Frigo, M., Halpern, P., Leiserson, C.E., Lewin-Berlin, S.: Reducers and other cilk++ hyperobjects. In: Sym. on Par. Algorithms and Architectures, SPAA, pp. 79–90 (2009)
14. Frigo, M., Leiserson, C., Randall, K.: The implementation of the Cilk-5 multithreaded language. In: Programming Language Design and Impl., PLDI, pp. 212–223 (1998)
15. Harris, T., Cristal, A., Unsal, O., Ayguadé, E., Gagliardi, F., Smith, B., Valero, M.: Transactional memory: An overview. IEEE Micro 27(3), 8–29 (2007)
16. Herlihy, M., Koskinen, E.: Transactional boosting: a methodology for highly-concurrent transactional objects. In: Principles and Practice of Parallel Programming, PPoPP, pp. 207–216 (2008)
17. Herlihy, M., Wing, J.: Linearizability: a correctness condition for concurrent objects. ACM Trans. Program. Lang. Syst. 12(3), 463–492 (1990)
18. Huet, G.: Confluent reductions: Abstract properties and applications in term rewriting systems. J. ACM 27(4) (October 1980)
19. Koskinen, E., Parkinson, M., Herlihy, M.: Coarse-grained transactions. In: Principles of Programming Languages, POPL, pp. 19–30 (2010)
20. Kulkarni, M., Pingali, K., Walter, B., Ramanarayanan, G., Bala, K., Chew, L.: Optimistic parallelism requires abstractions. In: PLDI (2007)
21. Lamport, L.: How to make a multiprocessor computer that correctly executes multiprocess programs. IEEE Trans. Comp. C-28(9), 690–691 (1979)
22. Larus, J., Rajwar, R.: Transactional Memory. Morgan & Claypool (2007)
23. Lee, J., Palsberg, J.: Featherweight x10: a core calculus for async-finish parallelism. In: Principles and Practice of Parallel Programming, PPoPP 2010 (2010)
24. Martin, A., Birrell, A., Harris, T., Isard, M.: Semantics of transactional memory and automatic mutual exclusion. In: Principles of Prog. Lang. POPL, pp. 63–74 (2008)
25. Moreau, L.: The semantics of scheme with future. In: ACM SIGPLAN International Conference on Functional Programming, ICFP 1996, pp. 146–156 (1996)
26. Bernstein, P.A., Goodman, N.: Multiversion concurrency control—theory and algorithms. ACM Trans. Database Syst. 8(4), 465–483 (1983)
27. Bernstein, P.A., Hadzilacos, V., Goodman, N.: Concurrency Control and Recovery in Database Systems. Addison-Wesley, Reading (1987)
28. Pratikakis, P., Spacco, J., Hicks, M.: Transparent proxies for java futures. SIGPLAN Not. 39(10), 206–223 (2004)
29. Randall, K.: Cilk: Efficient Multithreaded Computing. PhD thesis, Dept. of Electrical Engineering and Computer Science. MIT, Cambridge (1998)
30. Riegel, T., Fetzer, C., Felber, P.: Snapshot isolation for software transactional memory. In: Workshop on Transactional Computing, TRANSACT (2006)
31. Steele, G.: Parallel programming and parallel abstractions in fortress. In: Hagiya, M. (ed.) FLOPS 2006. LNCS, vol. 3945, pp. 1–1. Springer, Heidelberg (2006)
32. Welc, A., Jagannathan, S., Hosking, A.: Safe futures for java. In: OOPSLA, pp. 439–453 (2005)
33. Welc, A., Saha, B., Adl-Tabatabai, A.-R.: Irrevocable transactions and their applications. In: Symposium on Parallel Algorithms and Architectures, SPAA, pp. 285–296 (2008)

Type-Based Access Control in Data-Centric Systems

Luís Caires[1], Jorge A. Pérez[1], João Costa Seco[1],
Hugo Torres Vieira[1], and Lúcio Ferrão[2]

[1] CITI and Departamento de Informática, Faculdade de Ciências e Tecnologia,
Universidade Nova de Lisboa
[2] OutSystems SA

Abstract. Data-centric multi-user systems, such as web applications, require flexible yet fine-grained data security mechanisms. Such mechanisms are usually enforced by a specially crafted security layer, which adds extra complexity and often leads to error prone coding, easily causing severe security breaches. In this paper, we introduce a programming language approach for enforcing access control policies to data in data-centric programs by static typing. Our development is based on the general concept of refinement type, but extended so as to address realistic and challenging scenarios of permission-based data security, in which policies dynamically depend on the database state, and flexible combinations of column- and row-level protection of data are necessary. We state and prove soundness and safety of our type system, stating that well-typed programs never break the declared data access control policies.

1 Introduction

Data-centric multi-user software systems are a pervasive class of software applications, where transactions manipulate information stored in a shared database on behalf of several different users, playing several different roles. In the case of web-based systems, of which common examples are collaborative applications or social networks, the number of users may be extremely large, and the security requirements critical. Indeed, such systems require very flexible yet fine-grained data security mechanisms, including dynamic, role-based access control. Moreover, web applications are usually developed and executed in heterogeneous multiple-tier environments. Access control to data in such environments is typically performed at runtime by specially crafted security code, which mediates between the application code and the relational database management system. Such a security layer is hard to construct, error prone, and may easily cause severe security breaches. To make things a bit harder, access control policies are usually dependent on stored data and meta-data, and highly dynamic. Addressing such security requirements is frequently hindered by the expressiveness gap that exists between the required access control policies at the application side, and the actual security mechanisms provided by database engines.

Properly mapping the access control policies defined at the application side into associated database mechanisms is often difficult, if not impossible, also because multiple application profiles should be related to only a few database profiles. As an unfortunate side result, the enforcement of access control policies at the database level is kept to a minimum, promoting security breaches, as a consequence of the lack of protection

G. Barthe (Ed.): ESOP 2011, LNCS 6602, pp. 136–155, 2011.
© Springer-Verlag Berlin Heidelberg 2011

between layers. It is therefore important to identify new verification methods to prevent programmers from inadvertently violating access control constraints in such common scenarios of permission-based data-centric security.

In this work we develop a programming language approach for expressing and verifying access control policies to data in (relational) data-centric programs by means of static type checking. More precisely, we introduce a core language λ_{DB} which includes typeful programming constructs to manipulate (query and update) data stored in data "entities", to be physically represented by database tables (cf. the relational model). The associated type system allows access control policies to be associated to data entities, allowing queries and updates to the database to be validated against the declared constraints, taking into account also the particular information stored, and the current static state of the current principal. In λ_{DB}, access control policies are explicitly represented at the level of types: we endow λ_{DB} with dependent refinement types, which ensure that well-typed programs do not violate prescribed access control policies.

Access control mechanisms available in database systems are supported by fixed relations between users, operations, and tables. This basic approach induces a so called "column-level" protection in database tables, based on the *static structure* of the data model. Such a static form of access control, however, is far from enough, because in common situations the authorization to access a particular piece of information depends on information also stored in the database. For example, in web applications, it is very common to find data with security requirements such as, e.g., "only the manager of a proposal is able to modify it" or "only intranet users can see the submitted applications". Similarly, dynamic properties such as "only the current friends of a user can see his/her photos" are familiar. Notice that, the predicate "friend" as used here is dynamic and state dependent: a user can be granted a permission (by being selected as "friend"), that may be later revoked by other transaction. Any access control mechanism for data-centric systems should therefore be flexible and expressive enough to capture state dependencies of these kinds, which covers the notion of "row-level" protection to database entities. Our type system fully addresses such a challenging combination of column-level, row-level, and authorization permissions to enable the static verification of policies such as the one above, enabling the type-checker to issue an error whenever the programmer inadvertently tries to compile insecure code.

Our approach is based on associating expressive conditions as guards to basic operations on data entities (read, update, insert, etc.), and verify such conditions at the appropriate points in the code by static checking. In this way, it is possible to encode usual database permissions (but also more general conditions), and verify the program's conformance to the access control policies. To this end we build on the notion of *refinement types* [13,15], extended to a setting where properties depend both on the static state and on the dynamic state when manipulating entity tables. Intuitively, a refinement type $\{x : \beta \mid C\}$ classifies values of type β for which the logical expression C holds; for instance, $\{x : \mathsf{int} \mid x > 0\}$ is the type of the positive integers. This also allows a type environment to be seen as a refined property of the declared objects, so that for instance, we may say that a typing environment $\Delta = \Delta', a : \{x : \beta \mid C\}$ entails $C\{a/x\}$, written $\Delta \vdash C\{a/x\}$, where C is some condition about the program state. We also consider the combination of refinement types with functional dependent types, something

```
entity Person [ userid: string; public: string;
              photo: picture; secret: string; ]
  read public where true;
  read userid where Auth(uid);
  read secret where Auth(uid) and uid = userid;
  read photo where Auth(uid) and Friends(userid,uid);
  write where Auth(userid);

entity Friend [ user: string; friend: string; ]
  invariant Friends(user,friend)
  write where Auth(user)
```

Fig. 1. Some Sample Database Entities

particularly useful to express general pre- and post- conditions [15]. In the context of access control to database entities, refinement types are useful to express what conditions are valid for each program fragment and, ultimately, to implement flexible mechanisms for access control. Notice however, that our requirements for dynamic row-level protection, as captured in the typing rules for database reading and updating constructs, are not naturally expressible in existing refinement type systems, due to the dependence of refinements on the actual data stored in database entities.

We illustrate our approach with a sequence of simple examples, in the scenario of a social network application. The data model contains, among other elements, entities *Person* and *Friend*, defined in Fig. 1. Entities are defined by enumerating their field names and types, together with a set of access control policies associated to them. Here we focus on the "friendship" relation, implemented by entity `Friend`, and on using it to control the access users have to each others' data. Each permission clause is composed by (i) the kind of access granted (either read or write); (ii) the list of entity fields it protects; and (iii) a condition, expressed as a logical formula. Field names occur in the logical conditions, to allow them to refer to data in the entity row. The intended semantics is that the disjunction of the set of all access control policies for a given kind of access and field name must be valid for the corresponding operations to be applied. Intuitively, the capabilities associated to a list of database columns will only be granted if the associated conditions hold in the context of evaluation. In general, the evaluation context entails primitive properties (e.g., expressing authorizations), which may be explicitly asserted, or hold as a consequence of logical deduction from the primitive ones (conceptually stored in a *log* [15]). The elementary propositions of such formulas are predicates parameterized by language identifiers and constants.

In our case, entity `Person` declares four read permissions and one write permission. The first read permission stipulates that field `public` is always readable, as its associated condition (true) always holds. The contents of field `userid` of a row is only readable if `Auth(uid)` holds for some `uid` (identifiers not field names are existentially quantified variables). The third read permission states that field `secret` should be accessible only if predicate `Auth(userid)` holds in the current state. When a condition in a permission clause refers to field names, its validity depends on the actual data stored on each entity row. Free names in the conditions (for example `uid`) are existential parameters in each permission, and will be instantiated by concrete values at verification time. In the example, we assume that `Auth(`$user_1$`)` asserts that user named $user_1$ is authenticated in the system. The consequence of this condition is that an authenticated user can only select the field `secret` from those rows in which field `userid` corresponds to its own userid (for brevity, we omit the (trusted) code that establishes predicate `Auth(_)` in the login process). The fourth read permission states that an authenticated user (with name $user_2$) can access the field `photo` of another user (with name $user_1$) only in the case that predicate `Friends(`$user_1$`,`$user_2$`)` is valid. The write permission applies to every field in `Person` and is self-explanatory.

The specification of entity *Friend* features a write permission and an invariant clause. The invariant clause says that for each one of the rows $[user = user_1, friend = user_2]$ actually stored in entity `Friend`, the proposition `Friends(`$user_1$`,`$user_2$`)` always holds. Intuitively, the invariant must hold of a tuple in order for it to be added to the table, so that it is known to hold for every tuple read from the table; invariants in entity declarations express refinements over the actually stored data. As specified by the write permission, a row such as $[user = user_1, friend = user_2]$, asserting $user_2$ to be a friend of $user_1$ can only be created, updated, or deleted in a context where the condition (authorization) `Auth(`$user_1$`)` holds. The permissions thus enforce that friends can only be added (or removed) by the authenticated user $user_1$ to a data record having her as key, and only if the condition `Friends(`$user_1$`,`$user_2$`)` holds in the current state. This last condition may hold either because it may be obtained as effect of a query, or by calling a trusted library (which may establish it by an explicit assume statement).

Permission clauses as introduced in this example, also support reasoning about row- and column-level protection when accessing data. For instance, the following query, expressed in a LINQ [16] like syntax,

```
from p in Person where true select public
```

is well-typed and safe since the condition in the permission associated to field `public` always holds (true). Other fields are protected by stronger conditions. For instance, reading the contents of the `secret` field of a row is only possible for the rows where `userid=`*name* and `Auth(`*name*`)`. For example, the query

```
from p in Person where p.userid=loggeduser select secret
```

will only type-check in a context where `Auth(loggeduser)` holds, for some given `loggeduser` while the query

```
from p in Person where true select secret
```

will not type-check. We now consider the definitions of some functions on entities. Consider a function that fetches the field `secret` of a given user, with type

```
getSecret: {n:string | Auth(n)} → string
```

The refined parameter type acts as a pre-condition, since function `getSecret` can only be called if the argument is a string `s` such that predicate `Auth(s)` holds. We define `getSecret` using a query on entity `Person`, as follows:

```
def getSecret(name:{n:string | Auth(n)}):string = {
  let l = (from p in Person
           where p.userid = name
           select p.secret) in
  if isEmpty(l) then NULL else head(l) }
```

According to the declarations in Fig. 1, the context of the query expression selecting field `secret` is required to satisfy predicate `Auth(p.userid)` for the selected rows. This is obtained directly from the typing `name:{n:string | Auth(n)}` and from the query's where clause `p.userid = name`, which holds for all rows in the result of the query. Notice that we assumed given two predefined operations `isEmpty` and `head` to handle the results of queries.

As a last example, we define a function for fetching the photo of a given user. We will need two parameters, the logged-on user name and the user name whose photo is sought. The function `getPhoto` would then have the following type:

```
getPhoto: {n:string | Auth(n)} × string → picture
```

Reading the field photo requires the owner of the photo to be known as a friend of the authenticated user, expressed by the predicate `Friends(−,−)`.

Recall that `Friends(`$user_i$`,`$user_j$`)` relation is managed dynamically by the application, by inserting and deleting rows from entity `Friend`. Now, given users $user_1$ and $user_2$ where we know that `Auth(`$user_1$`)` is valid (from the function type parameters), we may statically establish that predicate `Friends(`$user_2$`,`$user_1$`)` is valid. This is done by querying such a row in entity `Friend`. We thus have

```
def getPhoto(name:{n:string | Auth(n)},
             othername:string):picture = {
  if isFriendOf(othername,name) then
    let l = (from p in Person
             where p.userid = othername
             select p.photo) in
    if isEmpty(l) then NULL else head(l)
  else NULL }
```

The conditions for reading field `photo` can be deduced from the context, which entails `Auth(name)` (from the parameter type) and `Friends(othername,name)` (from the result of the `isFriendOf` call). Notice how our type system actually forces the programmer to perform a runtime test, by consulting the `Friend` entity before retrieving the photo. To that end, we may use an auxiliary function `isFriendOf`, with type

```
isFriendOf: u:string×v:string → {b:bool | b ⇒ Friends(u,v)}
```

and which encapsulates the table access, and whose return (refined) type entails the friendship of the given parameters, defined as follows:

```
def isFriendOf(user:string, friend:string):
      {b:bool | b ⇒ Friends(user,friend)} = {
  let l = (from f in Friends
           where f.user = user
                 and f.friend = friend
           select f) in
  if isEmpty(l) then false
  else {head(l); true} }
```

We assume that read permissions for `user` and `friend` are true by default. Notice that the type of `head(l)` entails `Friends(user,friend)`, resulting from the entity invariant.

The rest of the paper is structured as follows. Sections 2 and 3 introduce the syntax and operational semantics of the λ_{DB} language, where a key notion of access control compliance is also defined (Definition 3.7). In Section 4, a type system for ensuring safety is proposed and its main results are stated, namely type preservation under reduction (Theorem 4.6), progress (Theorem 4.7), and typeful access control compliance (Corollary 4.8). Section 5 discusses related work.

2 Syntax

In this section we present the syntax of λ_{DB} and describe its main constructs. λ_{DB} contains a *functional core*, several constructs for *storage and manipulation* of data entities, and *logical operators* for expressing the knowledge about properties of data in programs. The syntax of λ_{DB} expressions (e), logical propositions (C), values (v), terms (V) and permissions (ρ) is given in Fig. 2, where we assume given infinite sets of names Λ (ranged over by $m, n, o, \ldots$) and of variables $\mathcal{V}$ (ranged over by $t, x, y, z, \ldots$). The distinguished variable *this* is used in table permissions to refer to a table row.

Expressions include values v, application $e(v)$, records $[m_1 = e_1, \ldots, m_k = e_k]$, where each m_i is a field, and field access $e.m$. λ_{DB} values include the unit value $()$, true and false, variables, and abstractions $\lambda x{:}\tau.e$, where τ is the type of x. A value may also be a record or a collection $v_1, \ldots, v_k$. We often use the overbar to abbreviate

$e ::=$	*(Expressions)*
v	(Value)
$\mid\ e\ (v)$	(Application)
$\mid\ [\overline{m = e}]$	(Record)
$\mid\ e.m$	(Field Selection)
$\mid\ e\ op\ e$	(Operation)
$\mid\ e\,?\,e : e$	(Conditional)
$\mid$ let $x = e$ in e	(Let)
$\mid\ e_1, \ldots, e_k$	(Collection)
$\mid$ create $t : \beta_{\overline{\rho}}$ in e	(Create)
$\mid$ from x in t where e select e	(Select)
$\mid$ update x in t where e with e	(Update)
$\mid$ append e to t	(Append)
$\mid$ delete x in t where e	(Delete)
$\mid$ assume C	(Assume)
$\mid$ assert C	(Assert)

$C, R, W ::=$	*(Propositions)*
$p(\overline{V})$	(Predicate)
$\mid\ V = V$	(Equality)
$\mid\ C \wedge C$	(Conjunction)
$\mid\ C \implies C$	(Implication)

$u, v ::=$	*(Values)*
$()$	(Unit value)
$\mid$ true	(True)
$\mid$ false	(False)
$\mid\ x$	(Variable)
$\mid\ \lambda x : \tau.e$	(Abstraction)
$\mid\ [\overline{m = v}]$	(Record)
$\mid\ v_1, \ldots, v_k$	(Collection)
$\mid\ \star(v)$	(Classified Value)

$V ::=$	*(Terms)*
$()$	(Unit value)
$\mid$ true	(True)
$\mid$ false	(False)
$\mid\ x$	(Variable)
$\mid\ \lambda x : \tau.e$	(Abstraction)
$\mid\ [\overline{m = V}]$	(Record)
$\mid\ V_1, \ldots, V_k$	(Collection)
$\mid\ \star(V)$	(Classified Term)
$\mid\ V.m$	(Field Selection)

$\rho ::=$	*(Permissions)*
$\mathtt{rd}(m, R)$	(Read)
$\mid\ \mathtt{wr}(m, W)$	(Write)

Fig. 2. Syntax of λ_{DB}: Expressions, Logical Propositions, Values, Terms, Permissions

indexed sets; this way, e.g., $[\overline{m = v}]$ stands for $[m_1 = v_1, \ldots, m_k = v_k]$ and $\overline{v}$ stands for $v_1, \ldots, v_k$. If $r' = [\ldots, m_i = v_i', \ldots]$, then we denote v_i' by r'_{m_i}. Database tables are modeled by references to collections of records. To represent high security data (data not accessible according to the permissions and the current knowledge) we introduce *classified* values $\star(v)$, meaning that value v is not accessible to the current program. Classified values $\star(v)$ cannot appear in source programs, but are useful for expressing the language semantics and its properties, namely the notion of access control compliance (Definition 3.7). Notice that the language of values is included in the language of terms, and that the language of terms is included in the language of expressions.

A field access expression $e.m$, provided e evaluates to a record with a field named m, evaluates to the contents of the m field of such record. We assume some unspecified set of operations over basic values (ranged over by *op*) and write e_1 *op* e_2 to represent the application of the operation to the result of evaluating expressions e_1 and e_2. Expressions also include a conditional statement $e_1 \mathbin{?} e_2 : e_3$, with the expected meaning: if e_1 then evaluate e_2 otherwise evaluate e_3. The let expression let $x = e_1$ in e_2 assigns the value obtained by evaluating e_1 to variable x, and binds x with scope e_2 (notice that let is not representable through function application since we require the argument of application to be a value, for typing purposes). The collection of expressions $e_1, \ldots, e_k$ allows to build collections of values by evaluating $e_1, \ldots, e_k$. Also, we assume the extension of the language with other basic values, and with basic language constructs encoded in a standard way. For instance, we use $e_1; e_2$ to denote the sequential composition of expressions. We use the notation $fn()$ to refer to the set of free names of expressions, defined as expected. Logical conditions, for example database access permissions, are expressed in λ_{DB} with propositions C. Logical propositions are a predicate on a sequence of terms $p(\overline{V})$, a term equality test $V_1 = V_2$, a conjunction $C_1 \wedge C_2$, or an implication $C_1 \Rightarrow C_2$. Note that we separately define values v (which appear in programs) from terms V (which appear in propositions). Terms add to values the field selection construct, in such way allowing propositions to talk about properties of record fields, but the intuition is that terms denote values.

Database constructs are SQL-like. Expression create $t : \beta_{\overline{p}}$ in e creates a new database table and binds it to variable t in scope e. The create expression uses the *table type* $\beta_{\overline{p}}$, which specifies access control policies for t. A full account of types is given in Section 4; for now it suffices to say that a type $\beta_{\overline{p}}$, associates t with a (record) type β for its rows and a set of *permissions* $\overline{p}$. As discussed earlier, permissions define access control policies at the level of database entities, based on logical conditions. There are two kinds of permissions: a permission $\mathtt{rd}(m, R)$ specifies that field m can be read only if condition R is deducible from the current knowledge. Similarly, permission $\mathtt{wr}(m, W)$ specifies that field m can be modified only if condition W is deducible from the current knowledge. In a permission $\mathtt{rd}(m, R)$ or $\mathtt{wr}(m, W)$, the (current) database row to which they apply to is denoted by the reserved variable *this*, and any other free variables are considered to be existentially quantified with scope R or W, respectively. For example, $\mathtt{rd}(\mathtt{address}, auth(x) \wedge x = this.id)$ specifies that field address can only be read if there is a value s for which $auth(s)$ holds and $this.id = s$.

Expression from x in t where e_1 select e_2 specifies a read access to the table t: it returns the collection of all values obtained by applying the select expression e_2 to all

$e^r ::= e$ (Expression) | $\text{from}_t^r\ x$ in e where e select e (Runtime Select)
| $\text{update}_t^r\ e$ with e (Runtime Update) | $\text{delete}_t^r\ e$ where e (Runtime Delete)

Fig. 3. Syntax of λ_{DB} Runtime Expressions

the rows in t for which the where boolean expression e_1 evaluates to true. Variable x is bound with scope e_1 and e_2.

Expression update x in t where e_1 with e_2 updates the fields in the rows of t that satisfy the where condition e_1 according to the record obtained by evaluating e_2 for every such row. Variable x is bound with scope e_1 and e_2. Expression append e to t adds to t the collection of values obtained by evaluating e. Expression delete x in t where e deletes from t the rows that satisfy the condition e. Variable x is bound with scope e. In examples we specify the database permissions together with entity *invariants* (see, e.g., Fig. 1). Such invariant specifications are syntactic sugar for table type refinements, as the following example illustrates. Consider entity `Friend` in Fig. 1. The corresponding λ_{DB} declaration, letting $\overline{p} = \mathtt{rd}(user, Auth(user)), \mathtt{wr}(friend, Auth(user))$, is:
create $Friend\colon \{x\colon [user\colon string;\ friend\colon string] \mid Friends(x.user, x.friend)\}_{\overline{p}}\ \ldots$

As other languages with refinement types, λ_{DB} expressions include statements for adding and checking assertions at runtime: assume C specifies that proposition C should be assumed true from the current state on, while assert C checks whether proposition C is true in the current state. For our model to make sense, the use of assume C commands is forbidden to regular users and only allowed in trusted code, accessible to user code through trusted APIs (following the approach of [6]).

3 Operational Semantics

We now present the operational semantics of λ_{DB} and introduce a notion of *access control compliance* for λ_{DB} programs. The semantics is defined using a reduction relation and evaluation contexts [19]. Reduction is defined between *configurations* of the form $(S; C; e)$, where S is a *state*, e is an *expression*, and C is a proposition defining the current *knowledge*. A *reduction step* of the form $(S; C; e) \rightarrow (S'; C'; e')$ means that expression e in state S with knowledge C evolves in one computation step to expression e' in state S' with knowledge C'. State S is a mapping from table names (variables) to collections of basic values, each one annotated with a set of permissions $\overline{p}$: $S \triangleq \{t_1 \mapsto \langle v_1 \rangle_{\overline{p}_1}, \ldots, t_k \mapsto \langle v_k \rangle_{\overline{p}_k}\}$. We use $S(t)$ to refer to the element $\langle v \rangle_{\overline{p}}$ such that $t \mapsto \langle v \rangle_{\overline{p}} \in S$. We note $dom(S)$ the set of table names defined in state S. *Runtime expressions* (e^r), representing intermediate states in the computation of database operations, are given in Fig. 3. In the following, we use e to denote e^r, where appropriate. *Evaluation contexts* specify the structure of language expressions whose inner expressions are active and may reduce. We write $\mathcal{C}[e]$ to represent the expression obtained by replacing the hole $\cdot$ by e in the evaluation context $\mathcal{C}[\cdot]$. The syntax of evaluation contexts is given in Fig. 4. Reduction relies on an auxiliary notion of knowledge entailment:

Definition 3.1 (Entailment). *Let C and C' be logical propositions. We define $C \vdash C'$ (C entails C') if the proposition $C \Rightarrow C'$ is derivable in classical propositional logic extended with equality over terms in V and the axiom scheme $[\overline{m = v}].m_i = v_i$.*

$$
\begin{array}{lllll}
\mathcal{C}[\cdot] ::= \cdot & \text{(Hole)} & \mid \overline{v}, \mathcal{C}[\cdot], \overline{e} & \text{(Collection)} \\
\mid \mathsf{from}^{\tau}_{t}\ x \ \mathsf{in}\ v\ \mathsf{where}\ \mathcal{C}[\cdot]\ \mathsf{select}\ e & \text{(From)} & \mid \mathsf{let}\ x = \mathcal{C}[\cdot]\ \mathsf{in}\ e & \text{(Let)} \\
\mid \mathsf{update}^{\tau}_{t}\ v\ \mathsf{with}\ \overline{v\,?\,e : e}, \mathcal{C}[\cdot]\,?\,e : e, \overline{e} & \text{(Update-If)} & \mid \mathcal{C}[\cdot]\ (v) & \text{(Application)} \\
\mid \mathsf{update}^{\tau}_{t}\ v\ \mathsf{with}\ \overline{v}, \mathcal{C}[\cdot], \overline{e} & \text{(Update)} & \mid \mathcal{C}[\cdot]\,?\,e : e & \text{(If)} \\
\mid \mathsf{append}\ \mathcal{C}[\cdot]\ \mathsf{to}\ t & \text{(Append)} & \mid \mathcal{C}[\cdot]\ op\ e & \text{(Op Left)} \\
\mid \mathsf{delete}^{\tau}_{t}\ v\ \mathsf{where}\ \mathcal{C}[\cdot] & \text{(Delete)} & \mid v\ op\ \mathcal{C}[\cdot] & \text{(Op Right)} \\
\mid [\overline{n = v}, o = \mathcal{C}[\cdot], \overline{m = e}] & \text{(Record)} & \mid \mathcal{C}[\cdot].n & \text{(Field)}
\end{array}
$$

Fig. 4. Syntax of Evaluation Contexts

$$(S; C; \mathsf{true}?e_1{:}e_2) \rightarrow (S; C; e_1)\ (\textit{r-if-true}) \quad (S; C; \mathsf{false}?e_1{:}e_2) \rightarrow (S; C; e_2)\ (\textit{r-if-false})$$

$$(S; C; \mathsf{let}\ x{=}v\ \mathsf{in}\ e) \rightarrow (S; C; e\{{}^{v}\!/\!_{x}\})(\textit{r-let}) \quad (S; C; (\lambda x{:}\tau.e)(v)) \rightarrow (S; C; e\{{}^{v}\!/\!_{x}\})(\textit{r-app})$$

$$\frac{v \neq \star(v')}{(S;\ C;\ [\ldots, n = v, \ldots].n) \rightarrow (S;\ C;\ v)}(\textit{r-field}) \quad \frac{(S;\ C;\ e_1) \rightarrow (S';\ C';\ e_1')}{(S;\ C;\ \mathcal{C}[e_1]) \rightarrow (S';\ C';\ \mathcal{C}[e_1'])}(\textit{r-cont})$$

$$(S;\ C;\ \mathsf{assume}\ C') \rightarrow (S;\ C \wedge C';\ ())(\textit{r-assume}) \quad \frac{C \vdash C'}{(S;\ C;\ \mathsf{assert}\ C') \rightarrow (S;\ C;\ ())}(\textit{r-assert})$$

Fig. 5. Reduction Rules for Basic Operations

For example, we have $(x.m = \mathsf{true} \Rightarrow q(x.m)) \wedge x = [m = \mathsf{true}] \vdash q(\mathsf{true})$.
We may now precisely define the reduction relation on configurations.

Definition 3.2 (Reduction). *Reduction, noted $(S;\ C;\ e) \rightarrow (S';\ C';\ e')$, is inductively defined by the rules in Fig. 5, 6, and 7.*

In order to express the notion of compliance with access control policies, we instrument our semantics so that access to values in the state is guarded by the permissions associated to the corresponding tables. We use the notion of classified value to mark the data for which permissions are not entailed by the current knowledge. The rules in Fig. 5 capture the reductions for the conditional expression (*r-if-true*) and (*r-if-false*), let (*r-let*), and application (*r-app*) in a standard way. Rule (*r-field*) states that a record value indexed by a field name reduces to the corresponding field value, provided it is not a classified value. Rule (*r-cont*) allows for reduction to take place internally to a given evaluation context. Rule (*r-assume*) applies to expressions of the form assume C' which reduce to the unit value and add proposition C' to the knowledge in the resulting configuration. By rule (*r-assert*), an expression of the form assert C' reduces, to the unit value, provided that proposition C' is entailed by the current knowledge.

Fig. 6 and 7 present the reduction rules for the operations on database tables. Rule (*r-create*) specifies the creation of a new entry in the state, by associating a fresh table name with an empty collection. Rule (*r-from*) specifies the first step of the evaluation of a from expression by reducing to an intermediate expression. Crucially, the resulting runtime expression from$^{\tau}$ takes a *filtered* copy of the values associated with table t in the state, according to the *filter*() operation defined as follows:

$$\frac{t' \notin dom(S) \cup fn(e)}{(S; C;\ \text{create } t : \beta_{\overline{\rho}} \text{ in } e) \longrightarrow (S, t' \mapsto \langle\emptyset\rangle_{\overline{\rho}}; C;\ e\{^{t'}/_{t}\})}\ (r\text{-}create)$$

$$\frac{S(t) = \langle\overline{v}\rangle_{\overline{\rho}} \qquad \overline{v}' = filter(\overline{v})^{\overline{\rho}}_{C}}{(S; C;\ \text{from } x \text{ in } t \text{ where } e_1 \text{ select } e_2) \longrightarrow (S; C;\ \text{from}^r_t\ x \text{ in } \overline{v}' \text{ where } \overline{e_1\{^{v'}/_{x}\}} \text{ select } e_2)}\ (r\text{-}from)$$

$$\frac{S(t) = \langle\overline{v}\rangle_{\overline{\rho}} \qquad \overline{v}' = filter(\overline{v})^{\overline{\rho}}_{C}}{(S; C;\ \text{update } x \text{ in } t \text{ where } e_1 \text{ with } e_2) \longrightarrow (S; C;\ \text{update}^r_t\ \overline{v} \text{ with } \overline{(e_1\ ?\ e_2 : [\,])\{^{v'}/_{x}\}})}\ (r\text{-}update)$$

$$\frac{S(t) = \langle\overline{v}\rangle_{\overline{\rho}} \qquad \overline{v}' = filter(\overline{v})^{\overline{\rho}}_{C}}{(S; C;\ \text{delete } x \text{ in } t \text{ where } e) \longrightarrow (S; C;\ \text{delete}^r_t\ \overline{v} \text{ where } \overline{e\{^{v'}/_{x}\}})}\ (r\text{-}delete)$$

$$\frac{ok2write(\overline{v})^{\overline{\rho}}_{C}}{(S, t \mapsto \langle\overline{u}\rangle_{\overline{\rho}}; C;\ \text{append } \overline{v} \text{ to } t) \longrightarrow (S, t \mapsto \langle\overline{u}, \overline{v}\rangle_{\overline{\rho}}; C;\ ())}\ (r\text{-}append)$$

Fig. 6. Reduction Rules for Table Operations

$$\frac{\overline{u} = \{v'_k \mid v_k = \text{true}\}}{(S; C;\ \text{from}^r_t\ x \text{ in } \overline{v}' \text{ where } \overline{v} \text{ select } e_2) \longrightarrow (S; C;\ \overline{e_2\{^{u}/_{x}\}})}\ (r\text{-}from^r)$$

$$\frac{\forall_i\ (e^3_i = e^1_i \land u_i = \text{true}) \lor (e^3_i = e^2_i \land u_i = \text{false})}{(S; C;\ \text{update}^r_t\ \overline{v} \text{ with } \overline{u\ ?\ e^1 : e^2}) \longrightarrow (S; C;\ \text{update}^r_t\ \overline{v} \text{ with } \overline{e^3})}\ (r\text{-}update\text{-}if^r)$$

$$\frac{\overline{u} = \overline{v} \bullet \overline{v}' \qquad ok2update(\overline{v}, \overline{v}')^{\overline{\rho}}_{C}}{(S, t \mapsto \langle u'\rangle_{\overline{\rho}}; C;\ \text{update}^r_t\ \overline{v} \text{ with } \overline{v}') \longrightarrow (S, t \mapsto \langle\overline{u}\rangle_{\overline{\rho}}; C;\ ())}\ (r\text{-}update^r)$$

$$\frac{\overline{u} = \{v_k \mid v'_k = \text{false}\} \qquad ok2write(\{v_k \mid v'_k = \text{true}\})^{\overline{\rho}}_{C}}{(S, t \mapsto \langle u'\rangle_{\overline{\rho}}; C;\ \text{delete}^r_t\ \overline{v} \text{ where } \overline{v}') \longrightarrow (S, t \mapsto \langle\overline{u}\rangle_{\overline{\rho}}; C;\ ())}\ (r\text{-}delete^r)$$

Fig. 7. Reduction Rules for Runtime Expressions

Definition 3.3 (Filtering). *Given a set of permissions $\overline{\rho}$, a proposition C, and a record $r = [\overline{m = v}]$, we define filtering of r under $C, \overline{\rho}$, by $filter(r)^{\overline{\rho}}_{C} \triangleq [\overline{m = v'}]$ where:*

$$v'_i = \begin{cases} v_i & \text{if exists } \mathtt{rd}(m_i, R) \in \overline{\rho} \text{ and } \theta \text{ such that } C \vdash \theta(R\{^{r}/_{this}\}) \\ \star(v_i) & otherwise \end{cases}$$

We set $filter(v_1, \ldots, v_n)^{\overline{\rho}}_{C} = filter(v_1)^{\overline{\rho}}_{C}, \ldots, filter(v_n)^{\overline{\rho}}_{C}$.

The filtering operation marks a value v_i in a record field as *classified* if no instance of its read permissions is derivable from the current knowledge C, replacing v_i by $\star(v_i)$ in the resulting record. A substitution θ (a finite function from variables to terms) is used to instantiate all free variables in a permission condition by closed values (except for the reserved variable *this*). From now on, we use $\theta(C)$ assuming that the domain of θ is the set of free variables in C, except *this*. Filtering causes a program to get stuck if it attempts to select a classified value from a record read from a table later on in the computation.

In the runtime counterpart of expression from x in t where e_1 select e_2, expression e_1 is expanded to a collection of expressions, where each element $(e_1\{v'_i/x\})$ instantiates the cursor variable x with one of the filtered rows (v'_i) of table t. Notice that the from^r expression freezes the current (filtered) state of table t, so as to use it when producing the final result. Rule (*r-from^r*) applies to a from^r expression where all conditional expressions are values, and reduces to a collection of expressions, obtained by replacing the cursor variable x by each one of the selected rows in the select expression e_2.

By rule (*r-update*), an update expression reduces to a runtime expression update^r, that expresses the modifications to the selected rows of t, via a collection of conditional constructs $(e_1?e_2:[])$, where the cursor variable x is replaced by the filtered values of table t. If the condition e_1 yields true, the modified field values are computed by expression e_2, otherwise the result is an empty record denoting that no modification is to be performed in that particular row. Rule (*r-update-if^r*), is applied after the evaluation of all conditions, and performs the corresponding selections. This three-step evaluation ensures the expected semantics where conditions are all evaluated first. Finally, rule (*r-update^r*) actually updates the table in the resulting state. The record update operation below is used to update the collection associated to table name t in the state. It takes two records r,r' and produces a record based on the first argument, replacing its field values with the values of the second record whenever they exist.

Definition 3.4 (Record Update). *Let* $r = [\overline{m = v}]$ *and* $r' = [\overline{m' = v'}]$ *be two records with* $\overline{m'} \subseteq \overline{m}$. *The update of record* r *by* r', *noted* $r \bullet r'$, *is defined by*

$$r \bullet r' \triangleq [\overline{m = u}] \text{ where } u_i = (\text{if } m_i \in \overline{m'} \text{ then } r'_{m_i} \text{ else } r_{m_i})$$

We set $\overline{r} \bullet \overline{r'} = r_1 \bullet r'_1, \ldots, r_n \bullet r'_n$.

For example $[pwd = foo, uid = 9] \bullet [uid = 0] = [pwd = foo, uid = 0]$.

Rule (*r-delete*) specifies that a delete expression reduces to the runtime expression delete^r, in which the where expression is expanded into a collection of boolean tests, again instantiating the cursor variable x with the filtered records $\overline{v'}$. Rule (*r-delete^r*) updates the values in table t in the resulting state, by keeping only the ones whose corresponding test yields false. Rule (*r-append*) reduces to a configuration where the collection associated with table name t is imperatively augmented with values $\overline{v}$. The operations update, delete, and append depend on the runtime verification that the current knowledge entails the necessary write permissions. Rule update^r expression depends on test $ok2update()$ that checks only the modified fields in a record when compared with the original row, while rules (*r-delete^r*) and (*r-append^r*) depend on the test $ok2write()$ which checks permissions for all fields in the table rows.

Definition 3.5 (Write and Update Permission Checks). *Given* $r = [\overline{m = u}]$ *and* $r' = [\overline{m' = v}]$ *(with* $\overline{m'} \subseteq \overline{m}$*), a set of permissions* $\overline{p}$ *for* r, *and a proposition* C, *we define the write and update permission checks,* $ok2write(r)^{\overline{p}}_C$, *and* $ok2update(r, r')^{\overline{p}}_C$ *by:*

$$ok2write(r)^{\overline{p}}_C \triangleq \forall_{m_i \in \overline{m}}\ \exists W_i, \theta_i(\mathtt{wr}(m_i, W_i) \in \overline{p} \text{ and } C \vdash \theta_i(W_i\{r/this\}))$$

$$ok2update(r, r')^{\overline{p}}_C \triangleq$$

$$\forall_{m_i \in \overline{m'}}\ (r_{m_i} = r'_{m_i}) \vee \exists W_i, \theta_i(\mathtt{wr}(m_i, W_i) \in \overline{p} \text{ and } C \vdash \theta_i(W_i\{r'/this\}))$$

We set $ok2write(\overline{v})^{\overline{p}}_C = ok2write(v_1)^{\overline{p}}_C \wedge \ldots \wedge ok2write(v_n)^{\overline{p}}_C$,
and $ok2update(\overline{v}, \overline{u})^{\overline{p}}_C = ok2update(v_1, u_1)^{\overline{p}}_C \wedge \ldots \wedge ok2update(v_n, u_n)^{\overline{p}}_C$.

$\beta, \phi ::=$	$\texttt{unit}$	(Unit Type)	$\tau, \sigma ::=$	β	(Basic Type)
$\mid$	$\texttt{bool}$	(Boolean Type)	$\mid$	β^*	(Collection Type)
$\mid$	$[\overline{m : \beta}]$	(Record Type)	$\mid$	$\Pi x : \tau.\, \tau$	(Dependent Function Type)
$\mid$	$\{x : \beta \mid C\}$	(Refinement Type)			

Fig. 8. Syntax for Types

We may now define the notion of error for λ_{DB} configurations.

Definition 3.6 (Error). *A configuration* $(S; C; e)$ *is an* error *if* e *is not a value and there are no* S', C', e' *such that* $(S; C; e) \to (S'; C'; e')$.

Notice that a configuration $(S; C; e)$ immediately attempting to select a field of a record containing a hidden (classified) value is an error, since by the premise of *(r-field)*, it has no reduction. Given that classified values are only introduced in data access primitives by filtering out data in fields for which no read permission is available, we define:

Definition 3.7 (Data Access Control Compliance). *A configuration is* data access control compliant *if no computation from it gets stuck in a field selection (r-field), update, delete, or append operation, due to a* $ok2write()$ *or* $ok2update()$ *test failure.*

It is then clear that programs that do not get into errors are in particular access control compliant. In the next section, we introduce a type system that statically ensures that well-typed programs do not get into errors, and are therefore access control compliant.

4 Type System

In this section we present our type system, which ensures that well-typed programs are data access control compliant. The syntax of types is defined in Fig. 8. We have basic types (β): $\texttt{unit}$, $\texttt{bool}$, the record type $[m_1 : \beta_1, \ldots, m_k : \beta_k]$, and refinement types $\{x : \beta \mid C\}$, which capture values of type β for which the proposition C holds (x is bound with scope C). Types also include collection types β^* which type collections of values of type β, and dependent function types $\Pi x : \tau.\sigma$, the type of functions that given a value x of type τ return a value of type σ, where x may occur on σ. As usual, the standard function type $\tau \to \sigma$ is represented by $\Pi x : \tau.\sigma$, where x does not occur in σ. Notice that we forbid collections of functions, collections of collections, etc, for simplicity. We also introduce table types, denoted $\beta_{\overline{\rho}}$ to classify table names. Recall that table names are imperatively bound to collection of values of type β, and have their contents are guarded by a set of permissions $\overline{\rho}$.

We now present our typing relation. A typing judgment of the form $\Delta \vdash e : \tau$ says that expression e has type τ under environment Δ. Also, we use $\Delta \vdash C$ to say that knowledge C is logically entailed from the knowledge in environment Δ (see below). We introduce an auxiliary type constructor, not expected to appear on source programs, but needed to type records where some fields may contain secured data. Such types, called projected types, have the form $\beta\lfloor_{\overline{m}}$, where β is a record type or an (hereditary) refinement of a record type, and are only used to type the query "cursor" in the scope of database table operations. Intuitively, $\beta\lfloor_{\overline{m}}$ means the same as β, but selection on a "classified" field (a field not in $\overline{m}$) is not allowed in well-typed programs. Crucially, types containing projected types as subexpressions are not allowed, so that the projection construction in only allowed to occur at the top level of any type. This condition is important to block illegal information flows out of trusted where and select clauses. In the sequel, we range both types τ and projected types $\beta\lfloor_{\overline{m}}$ using μ.

Type declarations, ranged over by γ, are assignments of types to variables, defined as either $x : \tau$ (normal type) or as $x : \tau\lfloor_{\overline{m}}$ (projected type) or as $t : \beta_{\overline{\rho}}$ (table type). For example, $x : [\mathtt{name} : \beta_1, \mathtt{email} : \beta_2, \mathtt{address} : \beta_3]\lfloor_{\mathtt{name},\mathtt{email}}$ is a type declaration that specifies that the only fields accessible in variable x are `name` and `email`, while field `address` is not accessible. A typing environment, ranged over by Δ, is a sequence of typing declarations $\gamma_1, \ldots, \gamma_k$. A well-formed typing environment satisfies a domain closure property on type declarations (from left to right). We say typing environment Δ is well-formed if for all γ such that $\Delta = \Delta', \gamma, \Delta''$ and $\gamma = x : \tau$ or $\gamma = x : \tau\lfloor_{\overline{m}}$ or $\gamma = x : \beta_{\overline{\rho}}$ then $x \notin fn(\Delta')$, where there is a notion of *free names* of environments, declarations, and types (we use $fn()$, taking into account names in the domain and in the types). From this point on, we assume typing environments are always well-formed. Also, we use Δ_π to denote the environment obtained by deleting from Δ all identifiers which are assigned non-basic types. To define the knowledge of a type environment, we introduce the auxiliary notion of term environment. This is the same as the notion of environment, but where *term declarations* may assign types to *terms* V (see Fig. 2), not just to variables. So a type environment is also a term environment. Given a term environment Δ, we may consider the knowledge it expresses about the terms it specifies, as a set (taken as the conjunction) of propositions.

Definition 4.1 (Knowledge). *The knowledge of a term declaration γ, noted $kn(\gamma)$, is inductively defined on types by:*

$$kn(V{:}\{x{:}\beta \mid C\}) \triangleq \{C\{^V/_x\}\} \cup kn(V{:}\beta) \qquad kn(V{:}[\overline{m{:}\beta}]) \triangleq \bigcup_{m_i \in \overline{m}} kn(V.m_i{:}\beta_i)$$
$$kn(V{:}\{x{:}\beta \mid C\}\lfloor_{\overline{m}}) \triangleq \{C\{^V/_x\}\} \cup kn(V{:}\beta\lfloor_{\overline{m}}) \qquad kn(V{:}[\overline{m{:}\beta}]\lfloor_{\overline{n}}) \triangleq \bigcup_{m_i \in \overline{n}} kn(V.m_i{:}\beta_i)$$

and as $kn(\gamma) \triangleq \emptyset$ for other types. Then $kn(\Delta)$ is given by $kn(\Delta, \gamma) = kn(\Delta) \cup kn(\gamma)$, and $kn(\emptyset) = \emptyset$. We often identify the set $kn(\Delta)$ with the conjunction of its elements.

Definition 4.2 (Derivable Knowledge). *Given a term environment Δ, formula C is derivable knowledge from Δ, noted by $\Delta \vdash C$, if $kn(\Delta) \vdash C$.*

Logical entailment has been defined in Definition 3.1. We can verify that knowledge is preserved by term substitution, that is, $kn(\Delta)\{^V/_x\} = kn(\Delta\{^V/_x\})$, and we also have that $\Delta \vdash V{:}\mu$ implies $\Delta \vdash kn(V{:}\mu)$. We can now define:

Definition 4.3 (Typing). *Typing is expressed by judgment $\Delta \vdash e : \mu$, stating expression e is well-typed by μ in environment Δ. Typing rules are given in Figs. 9, 10, and 11.*

We first discuss the typing rules that do not concern database operations, depicted in Fig. 9. Rules (*t-assert*), (*t-assume*), (*t-refine*), (*t-term-refine*), and (*t-unrefine*) express standard principles in refinement type theories (see, e.g., [15]), with some simplifications, due to the absence of subtyping in our presentation. Rule (*t-assert*) checks if the environment knowledge supports the specified proposition. Rule (*t-assume*) (remember

$$\frac{\Delta \vdash C}{\Delta \vdash \mathsf{assert}\ C : \mathtt{unit}}\,(\textit{t-assert}) \qquad \Delta \vdash \mathsf{assume}\ C : \{\_ : \mathtt{unit} \mid C\}\ (\textit{t-assume})$$

$$\Delta \vdash () : \mathtt{unit}\ (\textit{t-unit}) \qquad \frac{\Delta \vdash V : \beta \qquad \Delta \vdash C(V)}{\Delta \vdash V : \{x : \beta \mid C(x)\}}\,(\textit{t-term-refine})$$

$$\frac{\Delta \vdash e : \beta \qquad \Delta, x : \beta \vdash C(x)}{\Delta \vdash e : \{x : \beta \mid C(x)\}}\,(\textit{t-refine}) \qquad \frac{\Delta \vdash e : \{x : \beta \mid C(x)\}}{\Delta \vdash e : \beta}\,(\textit{t-unrefine})$$

$$\frac{\Delta \vdash e : \Pi x : \tau.\ \sigma \qquad \Delta \vdash v : \tau}{\Delta \vdash e(v) : \sigma\{^{v}/x\}}\,(\textit{t-app}) \qquad \frac{\Delta \vdash e_1 : \sigma \qquad \Delta, x : \sigma \vdash e_2 : \tau}{\Delta \vdash \mathsf{let}\ x = e_1\ \mathsf{in}\ e_2 : \tau}\,(\textit{t-let})$$

$$\frac{\Delta, x : \tau \vdash e : \sigma}{\Delta \vdash \lambda x : \tau.e : (\Pi x : \tau.\ \sigma)}\,(\textit{t-fun}) \qquad \frac{op : \tau_1 \to \tau_2 \to \sigma \qquad \forall_{i \in 1,2}\ \Delta \vdash e_i : \tau_i}{\Delta \vdash e_1\ op\ e_2 : \sigma}\,(\textit{t-op})$$

$$\frac{\Delta \vdash e_1 : \{b : \mathtt{bool} \mid C(b)\} \qquad \Delta, \_ : \{\_ : \mathtt{unit} \mid C(\mathsf{true})\} \vdash e_2 : \tau \qquad \Delta, \_ : \{\_ : \mathtt{unit} \mid C(\mathsf{false})\} \vdash e_3 : \tau}{\Delta \vdash e_1\,?\,e_2 : e_3 : \tau}\,(\textit{t-if})$$

$$\Delta, x : \tau, \Delta' \vdash x : \tau\ (\textit{t-id}) \qquad \frac{\forall_i\ \Delta \vdash e_i : \beta_i}{\Delta \vdash [\overline{m = e}] : [\overline{m : \beta}]}\,(\textit{t-record}) \qquad \frac{\forall_i\ \Delta \vdash e_i : \beta}{\Delta \vdash \overline{e} : \beta*}\,(\textit{t-collection})$$

$$\frac{\Delta \vdash e : [\ldots, n : \beta, \ldots]}{\Delta \vdash e.n : \beta}\ (\textit{t-field}) \qquad \frac{\Delta \vdash v : [\ldots, n : \beta, \ldots]\lfloor_{\overline{m}} \qquad n \in \overline{m}}{\Delta \vdash v.n : \beta}\ (\textit{t-fieldProj})$$

$$\frac{\forall_i\ ((v_i = \star(u_i) \wedge m_i \notin \overline{n}) \vee \Delta \vdash v_i : \beta_i)}{\Delta \vdash [\overline{m = v}] : [\overline{m : \beta}]\lfloor_{\overline{n}}}\,(\textit{t-recProj}) \qquad \Delta, x : \tau\lfloor_{\overline{m}}, \Delta' \vdash x : \tau\lfloor_{\overline{m}}\ (\textit{t-idProj})$$

$$\frac{\Delta \vdash x : \tau\lfloor_{\overline{m}} \qquad \textit{fields}(\tau) = \overline{m}}{\Delta \vdash x : \tau}\ (\textit{t-allFields})$$

Fig. 9. Typing Rules (I)

that assume is only to be used in trusted code, not user code) types the assume witness (with unit type) with its logical refinement, which may then be added to the current knowledge (namely, via a let x = assume C in ...).

We now consider the basic typing rules for database operations (see Fig. 10). Typing rules for related runtime expressions follow similar lines and are shown in Fig. 11. Rule (*t-from*) specifies that a from expression is well-typed if the environment knowledge entails the permissions needed to access the data in the table (I, J, K, L are sets of record field labels). The where expression e_1 returns a boolean b such that $C(x, b)$ for the given record x. Thus if x is selected by the test e_1, we know $C(x, \mathsf{true})$ holds. Notice that e_1 itself is only allowed to use table fields m_j ($m_j \in J$) for which the appropriate read permissions R_{m_j} are entailed by the current knowledge Δ. Using this additional piece of knowledge ($C(x, \mathsf{true})$), taking into account that the result of the where test is true for the selected rows, the set of permissions R_{m_k}, for fields $m_k \in K$, is derived. Notice that the refinement predicate obtained for the where expression (i.e., $C(x, b)$) carries information about the actual data being selected. This allows us to capture the intended row-level access control conditions, as all necessary read permissions are valid for each

$$\frac{\begin{array}{c}\Delta(t) = \beta_{\{\mathtt{rd}(m_i,R_{m_i})\,|\,m_i\in I\}\cup\overline{\rho}} \qquad J,K \subseteq I \\ \Delta \vdash \bigwedge_{m_j\in J}\theta_j(R_{m_j}) \qquad \Delta_\pi, x : \beta\lfloor_J \vdash e_1 : \{b : \mathtt{bool} \mid C(x,b)\} \\ \Delta \vdash C(\mathit{this}, \mathsf{true}) \implies \bigwedge_{m_k\in K}\theta_k(R_{m_k}) \\ \Delta, x : \beta\lfloor_K, \_ : \{\_ : \mathtt{unit} \mid C(x,\mathsf{true})\} \vdash e_2 : \phi\end{array}}{\Delta \vdash \mathsf{from}\ x\ \mathsf{in}\ t\ \mathsf{where}\ e_1\ \mathsf{select}\ e_2 : \phi^*}\ (\textit{t-from})$$

$$\frac{\begin{array}{c}\Delta(t) = \beta_{\{\mathtt{rd}(m_i,R_{m_i})\,|\,m_i\in I\}\cup\{\mathtt{wr}(m_l,W_{m_l})\,|\,m_l\in L\}\cup\overline{\rho}} \qquad J,K \subseteq I \qquad L \subseteq K \\ \Delta \vdash \bigwedge_{m_j\in J}\theta_j(R_{m_j}) \qquad \Delta_\pi, x : \beta\lfloor_J \vdash e_1 : \{b : \mathtt{bool} \mid C(x,b)\} \\ \Delta \vdash C(\mathit{this}, \mathsf{true}) \implies \bigwedge_{k\in K}\theta_{m_k}(R_{m_k}) \\ \beta = \{r : \tau \mid I(r)\} \quad I(r) \vdash H(r) \quad H(r) \wedge U(r) \vdash I(r) \quad \phi = \{r : |\tau|_K \mid U(r)\} \\ D(y) = (\bigwedge_{m_l\in K-L} y.m_l = x.m_l) \wedge \bigwedge_{m_l\in L}\theta_{m_l}(W_{m_l}\{y/\mathit{this}\}) \\ \Delta, x : \beta\lfloor_K, \_ : \{\_ : \mathtt{unit} \mid C(x,\mathsf{true})\} \vdash e_2 : \{y : \phi \mid D(y)\}\end{array}}{\Delta \vdash \mathsf{update}\ x\ \mathsf{in}\ t\ \mathsf{where}\ e_1\ \mathsf{with}\ e_2 : \mathtt{unit}}\ (\textit{t-update})$$

$$\frac{\begin{array}{c}\Delta(t) = \beta_{\{\mathtt{rd}(m_j,R_{m_j})\,|\,m_j\in J\}\cup\{\mathtt{wr}(m_l,W_{m_l})\,|\,m_l\in L\}\cup\overline{\rho}} \qquad \mathit{fields}(\beta) = L \\ \Delta \vdash \bigwedge_{m_j\in J}\theta_j(R_{m_j}) \qquad \Delta_\pi, x : \beta\lfloor_J \vdash e : \{b : \mathtt{bool} \mid C(x,b)\} \\ \Delta \vdash C(\mathit{this}, \mathsf{true}) \implies \bigwedge_{m_l\in L}\theta_l(W_{m_l})\end{array}}{\Delta \vdash \mathsf{delete}\ x\ \mathsf{in}\ t\ \mathsf{where}\ e : \mathtt{unit}}\ (\textit{t-delete})$$

$$\frac{\begin{array}{c}\Delta(t) = \beta_{\{\mathtt{wr}(m_l,W_{m_l})\,|\,m_l\in L\}\cup\overline{\rho}} \qquad \mathit{fields}(\beta) = L \\ \Delta \vdash e : \{x : \beta \mid \bigwedge_{m_l\in L}\theta_l(W_{m_l}\{x/\mathit{this}\})\}^*\end{array}}{\Delta \vdash \mathsf{append}\ e\ \mathsf{to}\ t : \mathtt{unit}}\ (\textit{t-append})$$

$$\frac{\Delta, t : \beta_{\overline{\rho}} \vdash e : \tau \qquad \beta = \{r : \beta_r \mid I(r)\} \quad \beta_r \text{ is a record type}}{\Delta \vdash \mathsf{create}\ t : \beta_{\overline{\rho}}\ \mathsf{in}\ e : \tau}\ (\textit{t-create})$$

Fig. 10. Typing Rules (II)

selected row. For soundness, we type the test in the pure part of the environment Δ_π. This ensures that computation of where clauses will never generate new knowledge, even if they may generate side effects.

Notice that the type of the cursor x is projected to the set of accessible fields when typing the where and select expressions, so that only the fields for which permissions are entailed may be selected (see Rule (*t-fieldProj*)). Also, to derive the permissions, we type the cursor identifier x with the (row) element type for the table (β), projected to the accessible fields (either m_j or m_k). The typing of the select expression ensures that ϕ is the type of the values returned; in general, ϕ may implicitly include information on the invariants of entity t as a refinement.

Rule (*t-fieldProj*) types the field access to an identifier which type declaration is projected in a set of field names and where this set contains the accessed field. In rule (*t-allFields*), an environment that specifies a projected type declaration for identifier n types it with the (unrestricted) type τ, provided the projection is over all fields of type τ — we use *fields*(τ) to denote the set of fields of the record type τ, possibly occurring under a refinement type. The combined use of rules (*t-allFields*) and (*t-fieldProj*) ensures that a record value typed by a projected type can only be used as a non protected record when the projection is over the whole set of fields. Otherwise, the only admissible behavior on such a value will be to select a field in the projection set. This ensures a tight control on the information flow of secured data. In particular, classified (high) values $\star(v)$ will never be leaked outside the context of a database operation, such as a where or a select computation, since protected types are not used elsewhere, due to our typing and syntactic constraints.

Rule (*t-update*) implements a reasoning similar to (*t-from*), as far as the where test is concerned, with fields in J selected for safe reading, based on available read permissions R_{m_j}. However, to type the with clause e_2, we must check: (1) that e_2 copies without modification ($y.m_l = x.m_l$) the fields in $K - L$ for which write permissions are not deduced, and (2) that write permissions W_{m_k} are currently entailed for all potentially modified fields m_k. In general, write permissions W_{m_k} may refer to readable fields (allowed by R_{m_l}), where $L \subseteq K$ (only readable fields may be updated), but not to other (classified) fields. So, we require in the rule that the permissions $W_{m_l}(r)$ may only refer to fields of r in K. All these conditions explain the refinement $D(y)$ of ϕ. To ensure that the updated row would satisfy the table type $\beta = \{r : \tau \mid I(r)\}$ (expressing invariant $I(r)$) we verify, through a frame reasoning, that the conjunction of the properties of the update records produced by e_2 together with the properties of the classified part imply the table invariant $I(r)$ for the updated record r. So, we require that $H(r)$ only refers to fields of τ not in K and $U(r)$ only refers to fields of τ in K. Notice that the base record type of ϕ is the same of β, but with fields out of K removed (noted $|\tau|_K$). All these conditions ensure that the update $v_3 = v_1 \bullet v_2$ in rule (*r-update-if*) is well defined, and that neither invariants nor write permissions are violated at runtime.

The remaining rules follow similar ideas: (*t-delete*) verifies that write permissions are available for all fields of all records selected by the where test, and (*t-append*) requires write access to all table fields. We now introduce well-typed configurations.

Definition 4.4 (Well-typed Configuration and State). *A configuration $(S; C; e)$ is well-typed in environment Δ (noted $\Delta \vdash (S; C; e)$ if (a) $\Delta \vdash e : \tau$; (b) $\Delta \vdash S$; and (c) for all $C_i \in kn(\Delta)$, $C \vdash C_i$. We also define $\Delta \vdash S$ by for all $(t \mapsto \langle\overline{v}\rangle_{\overline{\rho}}) \in S$ we have $\Delta(t) = \beta_{\overline{\rho}}$ and for all $v_i \in \overline{v}$, $\Delta \vdash v_i : \beta$.*

Notice that (c) states that the runtime condition C (the log) is stronger that the static knowledge entailed by Δ. This fact is used in our proofs to express that any statically verified condition (assertions, permissions) also holds at runtime.

We now present our main results, which ensure that programs that go through our typing rules are access control compliant (in addition to being of course error (stuck) free in the usual sense). The main statements are Theorem 4.6 (Type Preservation) — well-typing is invariant under reduction — Theorem 4.7 (Progress) — well-typed expressions are either values or have a reduction — and Corollary 4.8 — well-typed expressions comply with access control policies. Detailed proofs may be found in [9]. We first present our type preservation result, which relies on two substitution lemmas.

Lemma 4.5 (Substitution)

1. *(Entailment) Let $\Delta, x : \mu, \Delta' \vdash C$. If $\Delta \vdash V : \mu$ then $\Delta, (\Delta'\{^V/_x\}) \vdash C\{^V/_x\}$.*
2. *(Typing) Let e be an expression where $\Delta, x : \mu, \Delta' \vdash e : \sigma$. If $\Delta \vdash v : \mu$ then $\Delta, (\Delta'\{^v/_x\}) \vdash e\{^v/_x\} : \sigma\{^v/_x\}$.*

Theorem 4.6 (Type Preservation). *Let* $\Delta \vdash (S; C; e)$. *If* $(S; C; e) \rightarrow (S'; C'; e')$ *then there is* Δ' *such that* $\Delta, \Delta' \vdash (S', C', e')$.

Theorem 4.6 says that any reduction step in well-typed configuration leads to a well-typed configuration, where the typing of the final configuration is possibly extended so as to capture added knowledge (e.g., in case of an assume) or new locations of tables (via create) in the state. Our second result states that a closed well-typed configuration $(S; C; e)$ either has a value as its distinguished expression e, or has a reduction (it is not stuck). In particular, it is not an error.

Theorem 4.7 (Progress). *Let* $\Delta \vdash (S; C; e)$ *and* $fn(e) \subseteq dom(S)$. *Then either* e *is a value or* $(S; C; e) \rightarrow (S'; C'; e')$.

Theorem 4.7 states closed well-typed programs never get stuck on a expression which is not a value, and thus, in particular, well-typed configurations never get stuck on an assert C statement. Also notice that access to a classified record value is never attempted performed by well-typed programs, and safety of database updates, deletes, and appends, is also ensured by the validity of runtime control assertions such as $ok2write()$, which ultimately depend on assertion checking. By Theorems 4.6 and 4.7 we conclude:

Corollary 4.8 (Data Access Control Compliance). *Let* $\Delta \vdash (S; C; e)$ *and* $fn(e) \subseteq dom(S)$. *Then* $(S; C; e)$ *is data access control compliant.*

Corollary 4.8 tells us, in a technically precise way, that well-typed configurations never attempt to read data from tables which is forbidden by the prescribed policies, neither store in tables data that violates the prescribed policies or table invariants.

5 Discussion and Related Work

Refinement types were introduced in [13] in the context of ML type theory. Recently, Gordon and co-authors have developed a general theory of refinement types for a concurrent λ-calculus [15]. Their approach is applied in [6], where refinement types are interpreted as logic assertions which are used to verify authentication/authorization properties in security protocols. Our model builds on the general framework of refinement types, but does not seem naturally expressible within it; in fact, a key ingredient of our approach is the integration of refinements with coarse-grained typing principles for database operations, allowing access policies to selectively depend on the stored data, on a row-level basis, as required in realistic scenarios. We have no perspective on how to model our typed language in other related languages, including Fine [17], mainly because of the need to tightly integrate the constraints needed to statically type-check the trusted from and update constructs, parametric on general filtering where tests.

Several (proposals of) programming and/or modeling languages integrating data operations into programs — often in the form of SQL-like operations — have been put forward recently; examples include LINQ [16], Cω [8], Links [11], Ur/Web [10], Dminor [7], and M; some of these works have tackled security issues. Our work shares the same general goals with [10]. However, the underlying approaches are very different. In [10] access policies are defined as queries and programs are checked (using symbolic evaluation techniques) so as to guarantee any data exchanged with the database is contained in the result set of some policy, while access control policies may depend on the actual data and on the knowledge held by the user performing the query — captured by *known*, a distinguished predicate. In our approach access control policies also depend on the actual data; they are expressed in terms of arbitrary logical expressions which can capture, for instance, the knowledge held by the user or some data relationship, thus introducing extra flexibility. Another fundamental difference between our work and [10] lies on the conception of access control itself. The approach in [10] enforces a strong distinction between the access control capabilities of the (trusted) server and those of its (untrusted) clients. In our work, thanks to refinement types, access control can be treated in a more uniform way: the actual access control permissions of a participant (server or clients) depends on the knowledge currently available to it. This is reflected in the handling of where clauses: in [10] the data by a where clause is not subject to access control checks, which allows for queries that implicitly leak non-accessible information while in our approach the where test code is subject to access control checks in a uniform way, which excludes queries that access classified information, in the precise sense of Corollary 4.8.

Dminor [7] combines refinement types and expressions enforcing dynamic type tests. Although a basic form of select expressions is expressible in Dminor (by means of an accumulator construct), it does not support other database-like expressions nor offers a simple way of enforcing fine-grained access control permissions over data entities, two of the distinguishing features of λ_{DB}. The approach of [7] is related to the work in RFC in [6], which we reviewed above. Links [11] is a typed functional programming language for web applications. In [5] a secure compilation strategy for Links is formalized by a concurrent λ-calculus, endowed with a refinement type system, but not addressing data management operations. SELinks [12] extends Links with label-based security policies. In SELinks security labels are associated to objects which contain sensible data; a labeled object is not accessible. Policy enforcement functions are used to safely "unlabel" objects, thus implementing the semantics associated to the security labels. A type system [18] ensures the correct mediation between application code and the policy enforcement functions. Our focus is on data access control, based on logical conditions on the data itself, where permissions are directly taken in account while typing database primitives, by means of refinement types, allowing for fine-grained policies to be directly verified in application level SQL-like database manipulation code.

6 Concluding Remarks

We have presented a type-based approach to statically enforce access control to persistent data in data-centric software systems such as web applications. We believe that our proposal provides a useful mechanism to enforce the preservation of protection (in the general sense of [1]) between application-level security and database-level security management. Our technical development is based on a core language λ_{DB}, which includes comprehensive SQL-like operations, and is equipped with a refinement type system. Refinement types are combined with access permissions, allowing the system to control unsecure information flows across database operations. Although simple to use, at least in principle, our approach is expressive enough to enforce access control policies at a very fine-grained level, in particular allowing security constraints to dynamically depend on the stored data, as is often the case in real applications. Our main results certify that our type system excludes error configurations, namely systems that violate access control policies, in a technically precise sense. In future work, we intend to extend our model with more sophisticated permission and access control concerns. For simplicity and usability, our refinements logic is a simple classical logic, where deduced facts are monotonically accumulated, while database contents keeps changing overtime. Nevertheless, this approach is already very useful and consistent with the scenario of web-based applications, where all the state resides in the database, and operations are implemented by independent short-running requests. Our type system ensures that no data access violations may occur in a transaction, given the currently visible database stored data and related policies. Nevertheless, it would be interesting to study the adoption in our framework of more expressive logics (e.g., [3,14,4]), and to research the interplay between refinement types and types for information flow [2].

Acknowledgements. We thank Carnegie Mellon—PT INTERFACES 44-2009-12, CITI, and OutSystems SA. Thanks to Frank Pfenning for insightful discussions. The anonymous referees are also thanked for their extremely useful comments and criticisms.

References

1. Abadi, M.: Protection in Programming-Language Translations. In: Larsen, K.G., Skyum, S., Winskel, G. (eds.) ICALP 1998. LNCS, vol. 1443, pp. 868–883. Springer, Heidelberg (1998)
2. Abadi, M.: Access Control in a Core Calculus of Dependency. In: Reppy, J.H., Lawall, J.L. (eds.) Proc. of ICFP 2006, pp. 263–273. ACM, New York (2006)
3. Abadi, M.: Logic in Access Control (Tutorial Notes). In: Proc. of FOSAD. LNCS, vol. 5705, pp. 145–165. Springer, Heidelberg (2009)
4. Abadi, M., Burrows, M., Lampson, B.W., Plotkin, G.D.: A Calculus for Access Control in Distributed Systems. ACM Trans. Program. Lang. Syst. 15(4), 706–734 (1993)
5. Baltopoulos, I.G., Gordon, A.D.: Secure Compilation of a Multi-Tier Web Language. In: Proc. of TLDI 2009, pp. 27–38. ACM, New York (2009)
6. Bengtson, J., Bhargavan, K., Fournet, C., Gordon, A.D., Maffeis, S.: Refinement Types for Secure Implementations. In: Proc. of CSF 2008, pp. 17–32. IEEE Computer Society, Los Alamitos (2008)
7. Bierman, G.M., Gordon, A.D., Hritcu, C., Langworthy, D.: Semantic Subtyping with an SMT Solver. In: Proc. of ICFP 2010, pp. 105–116. ACM, New York (2010)
8. Bierman, G., Meijer, E., Schulte, W.: The Essence of Data Access in Cω. In: Gao, X.-X. (ed.) ECOOP 2005. LNCS, vol. 3586, pp. 287–311. Springer, Heidelberg (2005)
9. Caires, L., Pérez, J.A., Seco, J.C., Vieira, H.T., Ferrão, L.: Type-based Access Control in Data-Centric Systems. Technical Report DIFCTUNL 3/10, U. Nova de Lisboa (2010)
10. Chlipala, A.: Static Checking of Dynamically-Varying Security Policies in Database-Backed Applications. In: Proc. of OSDI 2010, USENIX Association (2010)
11. Cooper, E., Lindley, S., Wadler, P., Yallop, J.: Links: Web Programming Without Tiers. In: de Boer, F.S., Bonsangue, M.M., Graf, S., de Roever, W.-P. (eds.) FMCO 2006. LNCS, vol. 4709, pp. 266–296. Springer, Heidelberg (2007)
12. Corcoran, B.J., Swamy, N., Hicks, M.W.: Cross-Tier, Label-Based Security Enforcement for Web Applications. In: SIGMOD Conference 2009, pp. 269–282. ACM, New York (2009)
13. Freeman, T., Pfenning, F.: Refinement Types for ML. In: Proc. of PLDI 1991, pp. 268–277. ACM, New York (1991)

14. Garg, D., Bauer, L., Bowers, K.D., Pfenning, F., Reiter, M.K.: A Linear Logic of Authorization and Knowledge. In: Gollmann, D., Meier, J., Sabelfeld, A. (eds.) ESORICS 2006. LNCS, vol. 4189, pp. 297–312. Springer, Heidelberg (2006)
15. Gordon, A.D., Fournet, C.: Principles and Applications of Refinement Types. Technical Report MSR-TR-2009-147, Microsoft Research (2009)
16. Meijer, E., Beckman, B., Bierman, G.: LINQ: Reconciling Object, Relations and XML in the .NET Framework. In: SIGMOD Conference 2006, pp. 706–706. ACM, New York (2006)
17. Swamy, N., Chen, J., Chugh, R.: Enforcing Stateful Authorization and Information Flow Policies in Fine. In: Gordon, A.D. (ed.) ESOP 2010. LNCS, vol. 6012, pp. 529–549. Springer, Heidelberg (2010)
18. Swamy, N., Corcoran, B.J., Hicks, M.: Fable: A Language for Enforcing User-defined Security Policies. In: Proc. of IEEE S&P 2008, pp. 369–383. IEEE Computer Society, Los Alamitos (2008)
19. Wright, A.K., Felleisen, M.: A Syntactic Approach to Type Soundness. Information and Computation 115, 38–94 (1994)

Appendix: Typing Rules for Runtime Expressions

$$\frac{\begin{array}{c}\Delta(t) = \beta_{\{\mathtt{rd}(m_i, R_{m_i}) \,|\, m_i \in I\} \cup \overline{\rho}} \qquad J, K \subseteq I \\ \Delta \vdash \bigwedge_{m_j \in J} \theta_{m_j}(R_{m_j}) \qquad \forall_{v_i \in \overline{v}}\ \Delta \vdash v_i : \beta\lfloor_J \\ \forall_{e_i \in \overline{e}}\ \Delta_\pi \vdash e_i : \{b : \mathtt{bool} \mid C(v_i, b)\} \qquad \Delta \vdash C(\mathit{this}, \mathsf{true}) \implies \bigwedge_{m_k \in K} \theta_{m_k}(R_{m_k}) \\ \Delta, x : \beta\lfloor_K, \_ : \{\_ : \mathtt{unit} \mid C(x, \mathsf{true})\} \vdash e_2 : \phi\end{array}}{\Delta \vdash \mathsf{from}^r_t\ x\ \mathsf{in}\ \overline{v}\ \mathsf{where}\ \overline{e}\ \mathsf{select}\ e_2 : \phi^\star}$$

$$\frac{\begin{array}{c}\Delta(t) = \beta_{\{\mathtt{rd}(m_i, R_{m_i}) \,|\, m_i \in I\} \cup \{\mathtt{wr}(m_l, W_{m_l}) \,|\, m_l \in L\} \cup \overline{\rho}} \qquad J, K \subseteq I \quad L \subseteq K \\ \Delta \vdash \bigwedge_{m_j \in J} \theta_{m_j}(R_{m_j}) \qquad \forall_{v_i \in \overline{v}}\ \Delta \vdash v_i : \beta \qquad \forall_{v'_i \in \overline{v}'}\ \Delta \vdash v'_i : \beta\lfloor_J \\ \forall_{e'_i \in \overline{e}'}\ \Delta_\pi \vdash e'_i : \{b : \mathtt{bool} \mid C(v'_i, b)\} \qquad \Delta \vdash C(\mathit{this}, \mathsf{true}) \implies \bigwedge_{m_k \in K} \theta_{m_k}(R_{m_k}) \\ \beta = \{r : \tau \mid I(r)\} \quad I(r) \vdash H(r) \quad H(r) \wedge U(r) \vdash I(r) \quad \phi = \{r : |\tau|_K \mid U(r)\} \\ e''_i = e_2\{{}^{v'_i}\!/x\} \quad D(y) = (\bigwedge_{m_l \in K-L} y.m_l = x.m_l) \wedge \bigwedge_{m_l \in L} \theta_{m_l}(W_{m_l}\{{}^{y}\!/\mathit{this}\}) \\ \Delta, x : \beta\lfloor_K, \_ : \{\_ : \mathtt{unit} \mid C(x, \mathsf{true})\} \vdash e_2 : \{y : \phi \mid D(y)\}\end{array}}{\Delta \vdash \mathsf{update}^r_t\ \overline{v}\ \mathsf{with}\ \overline{e'\,?\,e'' : []} : \mathtt{unit}}$$

$$\frac{\begin{array}{c}\Delta(t) = \beta_{\{\mathtt{rd}(m_k, R_{m_k}) \,|\, m_k \in K\} \cup \{\mathtt{wr}(m_l, W_{m_l}) \,|\, m_l \in L\} \cup \overline{\rho}} \qquad L \subseteq K \\ \forall_{v_i \in \overline{v}}\ \Delta \vdash v_i : \beta \qquad \Delta \vdash C(\mathit{this}, \mathsf{true}) \implies \bigwedge_{m_k \in K} \theta_{m_k}(R_{m_k}) \\ \beta = \{r : \tau \mid I(r)\} \quad I(r) \vdash H(r) \quad H(r) \wedge U(r) \vdash I(r) \quad \phi = \{r : |\tau|_K \mid U(r)\} \\ D(y)(\bigwedge_{m_l \in K-L} y.m_l = x.m_l) \wedge \bigwedge_{m_l \in L} \theta_{m_l}(W_{m_l}\{{}^{y}\!/\mathit{this}\}) \\ \forall_{e_i \in \overline{e}}\ (e_i = []) \vee \\ (\Delta \vdash v'_i : \beta\lfloor_K \wedge \Delta, \_ : \{\_ : \mathtt{unit} \mid C(v'_i, \mathsf{true})\} \vdash e_i : \{y : \phi \mid D(y)\{{}^{v'_i}\!/x\}\})\end{array}}{\Delta \vdash \mathsf{update}^r_t\ \overline{v}\ \mathsf{with}\ \overline{e} : \mathtt{unit}}$$

$$\frac{\begin{array}{c}\Delta(t) = \beta_{\{\mathtt{rd}(m_j, R_{m_j}) \,|\, m_j \in J\} \cup \{\mathtt{wr}(m_l, W_{m_l}) \,|\, l \in L\} \cup \overline{\rho}} \qquad \mathit{fields}(\beta) = L \\ \Delta \vdash \bigwedge_{m_j \in J} \theta_{m_j}(R_{m_j}) \qquad \forall_{v_i \in \overline{v}}\ \Delta \vdash v_i : \beta \qquad \forall_{v'_i \in \overline{v}'}\ \Delta \vdash v'_i : \beta\lfloor_J \\ \forall_{e_i \in \overline{e}}\ \Delta_\pi \vdash e_i : \{b : \mathtt{bool} \mid C(x, b)\} \qquad \Delta \vdash C(\mathit{this}, \mathsf{true}) \implies \bigwedge_{m_l \in L} \theta_{m_l}(W_{m_l})\end{array}}{\Delta \vdash \mathsf{delete}^r_t\ \overline{v}\ \mathsf{where}\ \overline{e} : \mathtt{unit}}$$

Fig. 11. Typing Rules (III)

Linear Absolute Value Relation Analysis*

Liqian Chen[1], Antoine Miné[2,3], Ji Wang[1], and Patrick Cousot[2,4]

[1] National Laboratory for Parallel and Distributed Processing, Changsha, P.R. China
{lqchen,wj}@nudt.edu.cn
[2] École Normale Supérieure, Paris, France
{mine,cousot}@di.ens.fr
[3] CNRS, France
[4] CIMS, New York University, New York, NY, USA

Abstract. Linear relation analysis (polyhedral analysis), devoted to discovering linear invariant relations among variables of a program, remains one of the most powerful abstract interpretations but is subject to convexity limitations. *Absolute value* enjoys piecewise linear expressiveness and thus natively fits to encode certain *non-convex* properties. Based on this insight, we propose to use *linear absolute value relation analysis* to discover linear relations among values and absolute values of program variables. Under the framework of abstract interpretation, the analysis yields a new numerical abstract domain, namely the abstract domain of *linear absolute value inequalities* ($\Sigma_k a_k x_k + \Sigma_k b_k|x_k| \leq c$), which can be used to analyze programs involving piecewise linear behaviors (e.g., due to conditional branches or absolute value function calls). Experimental results of our prototype are encouraging; The new abstract domain can find non-convex invariants of interest in practice.

1 Introduction

Abstract interpretation [7] provides a general framework for static analysis. One predominant application is numerical static analysis, i.e., to discover numerical properties of a program statically and automatically. *Linear relation analysis* [9], devoted to discovering linear invariant relations among variables of a program, is one of the earliest but still most powerful abstract interpretations. It yields the known *convex polyhedra* abstract domain ($\Sigma_k a_k x_k \leq c$) [9], since the set of the reachable states at each program point is abstracted as a convex polyhedron. Over the last 30 years, linear relation analysis has a wide range of applications, especially in the field of analysis and verification of programs and hybrid systems [14]. Moreover, a variety of weakly (linear) relational abstract domains have been proposed in recent years, for discovering restricted forms of linear relations, such as the Octagon domain ($\pm x \pm y \leq c$) [21], the Two Variables Per Inequality (TVPI) domain ($ax + by \leq c$) [28], and the Template Polyhedra domain ($\Sigma_k a_k x_k \leq c$ where variable coefficients a_k are fixed beforehand) [25].

The concrete semantics of a program often involves *non-convex* behaviors. E.g., conditional branch statements often introduce disjunctive behaviors, since different

* This work is supported by the INRIA project "Abstraction" common to CNRS and ENS in France, and by the National Natural Science Foundation of China under Grant No.60725206.

G. Barthe (Ed.): ESOP 2011, LNCS 6602, pp. 156–175, 2011.
© Springer-Verlag Berlin Heidelberg 2011

computations are performed depending on whether the condition evaluates to true or false. Besides, many program properties that users may be interested in are non-convex, e.g., the division-by-zero error. However, the polyhedra abstract domain together with weakly (linear) relational abstract domains can express only convex sets (without resorting to powerset extensions). The convexity limitations may lead to imprecision in the analysis and thus can cause many false alarms.

Absolute value (AV) is a fundamental concept in mathematics and of high relevance in practice. AV function is essentially a kind of *piecewise linear* functions, and thus fits to express piecewise linear behaviors in a program that account for a large class of non-convex behaviors in practice. Moreover, complex non-linear program behaviors can be abstracted into piecewise linear behaviors, as in the field of hybrid systems. On the other hand, AV functions are provided by many modern programming languages, e.g., the *abs* (absolute value of an integer), *fabs* (absolute value of a floating-point number) functions in the C language. And several commonly used mathematical functions such as *fmin* (minimum value), *fmax* (maximum value), *fdim* (positive difference) in the C99 standard can be also expressed by AV functions, e.g., $\max(x, y) = \frac{1}{2}(|x-y| + x + y)$. Besides, rounding errors in floating-point arithmetic can be also abstracted by AV functions: $|round(x) - x| \leq \varepsilon_{\text{rel}} \cdot |x| + \varepsilon_{\text{abs}}$ where ε_{rel} denotes a relative error and ε_{abs} denotes an absolute error [20]. In addition, in Sect. 2.4, we will show that linear constraints with interval coefficients which may appear in numerical static analysis [4] can be also rewritten via AV functions. However, due to non-linearity, AV functions are rarely considered during program analysis and verification.

In this paper, we propose an analysis to discover *linear absolute value relations* among variables of a program, i.e., linear relations among the values and the absolute values of variables. The analysis yields a new abstract domain, namely the abstract domain of *linear absolute value inequalities* (AVI), to infer relationships of the form $\Sigma_k a_k x_k + b_k |x_k| \leq c$ over program variables x_k $(k = 1, \ldots, n)$ where constants $a_k, b_k, c \in \mathbb{R}$ are automatically inferred by the analysis. The new domain is more expressive than the classic convex polyhedra domain and allows expressing certain non-convex (even unconnected) sets due to the utilization of absolute value. Its domain operations are constructed based a double description method. The preliminary experimental results of the prototype implementation are promising on benchmark programs; AVI can find non-convex invariants of interest in practice.

To sum up, this paper aims at exploiting the piecewise-linear expressiveness of absolute value to design non-convex abstract domains which can be used to capture disjunctive information in a program and which for example will apply to programs involving AV(-like) function calls. In other words, this paper is dedicated to coping with disjunctive behaviors of a program at the level of abstract domains, with no need to resort to other techniques to deal with disjunctions [3,8,24].

The rest of the paper is organized as follows. Section 2 shows the equivalence among linear absolute value inequality systems, extended linear complementary problem (XLCP) systems and interval linear inequality systems. Section 3 presents a double description method for XLCP on top of that for polyhedra. Section 4 proposes an abstract domain of linear AV inequalities based on the double description method for XLCP.

Section 5 presents our prototype implementation together with preliminary experimental results. Section 6 discusses some related work before Section 7 concludes.

2 Linear Absolute Value Inequality Systems and Their Equivalents

2.1 Linear Absolute Value Inequality Systems (AVIs)

Let $|\cdot|$ denote absolute value (AV). We consider the following system of linear absolute value inequalities (AVI)

$$Ax + B|x| \leq c \tag{1}$$

where $A, B \in \mathbb{R}^{m\times n}$ and $c \in \mathbb{R}^m$.

Theorem 1. *Any AV inequality*

$$\textstyle\sum_i a_i x_i + \sum_{i\neq p} b_i|x_i| + b_p|x_p| \leq c$$

where $b_p > 0$, can be reformulated as a conjunction of two AV inequalities

$$\begin{cases} \sum_i a_i x_i + \sum_{i\neq p} b_i|x_i| + b_p x_p \leq c \\ \sum_i a_i x_i + \sum_{i\neq p} b_i|x_i| - b_p x_p \leq c \end{cases}$$

Theorem 1 implies that any AVI system $Ax + B|x| \leq c$ can be reformulated as an AVI system $A'x + B'|x| \leq c$ where $B' \leq 0$.

2.2 Extended Linear Complementarity Problems (XLCPs)

Given a matrix $M \in \mathbb{R}^{n\times n}$ and a vector $q \in \mathbb{R}^n$, the (standard) linear complementarity problem (LCP) is defined as the problem of finding vectors x^+ and x^- such that

$$x^+ = Mx^- + q \tag{2}$$
$$x^+, x^- \geq 0 \tag{3}$$
$$(x^+)^T x^- = 0. \tag{4}$$

Note that if x^+ and x^- are solutions of the above LCP, then it follows from (3-4) that

$$x_i^+ x_i^- = 0 \qquad \text{for } i = 1, \ldots, n$$

i.e., for each i the following holds: If $x_i^+ > 0$ then $x_i^- = 0$ holds, and if $x_i^- > 0$ then $x_i^+ = 0$ holds. In other words, the zero patterns of x_i^+ and x_i^- are complementary. Thus, condition (4) is called the *complementarity condition* of the above LCP. The LCP problem is one of the fundamental problems in mathematical optimization theory, which subsumes many mathematical programming problems such as linear programs, quadratic programs [6]. Here, we present one extension of the LCP that is of interest to us.

Given $M, N \in \mathbb{R}^{m\times n}$ and a vector $q \in \mathbb{R}^m$, find $x^+, x^- \in \mathbb{R}^n$ such that

$$Mx^+ + Nx^- \leq q \tag{5}$$
$$x^+, x^- \geq 0 \tag{6}$$
$$(x^+)^T x^- = 0. \tag{7}$$

We call the above problem eXtended Linear Complementarity Problem (XLCP), since it can be proved equivalent to eXtended LCP of Mangasarian and Pang [19].

2.3 Interval Linear Inequality Systems (ILIs)

Let $\mathbf{x} = [\underline{x}, \overline{x}]$ be an interval with its bounds (endpoints) $\underline{x} \leq \overline{x}$. Let $\mathbb{IR}$ be the set of all real intervals $[\underline{a}, \overline{a}]$ where $\underline{a}, \overline{a} \in \mathbb{R}$. Let $\underline{A}, \overline{A} \in \mathbb{R}^{m \times n}$ be two matrices with $\underline{A} \leq \overline{A}$ where the order is defined element-wise, then the set of matrices $\mathbf{A} = [\underline{A}, \overline{A}] = \{A \in \mathbb{R}^{m \times n} : \underline{A} \leq A \leq \overline{A}\}$ is called an *interval matrix* and the matrices $\underline{A}, \overline{A}$ are called its bounds. Let us define the *center matrix* of $\mathbf{A}$ as $A_c = \frac{1}{2}(\underline{A} + \overline{A})$ and the *radius matrix* as $\triangle_A = \frac{1}{2}(\overline{A} - \underline{A})$. Then, $\mathbf{A} = [\underline{A}, \overline{A}] = [A_c - \triangle_A, A_c + \triangle_A]$. Note that $\triangle_A \geq 0$ always holds.

Let b be a regular vector in $\mathbb{R}^m$. The following system of interval linear inequalities

$$\mathbf{A}x \leq b$$

denotes an *interval linear inequality system* (ILI), that is, the *family* of all systems of linear inequalities $Ax \leq b$ such that $A \in \mathbf{A}$. A vector $x \in \mathbb{R}^n$ is called a *weak solution* of the interval linear inequality system $\mathbf{A}x \leq b$, if it satisfies $Ax \leq b$ for some $A \in \mathbf{A}$.

2.4 Equivalence among AVIs, XLCPs and ILIs

Equivalence between AVIs and XLCPs. Let $x = (x_i)_{i=1}^n$ be a vector. Let vectors x^+ and x^- be defined by $x^+ = (\max(x_i, 0))_{i=1}^n$ and $x^- = (\max(-x_i, 0))_{i=1}^n$, so that

$$x^+ \geq 0, x^- \geq 0, (x^+)^T x^- = 0$$

and

$$x = x^+ - x^-, \qquad |x| = x^+ + x^- \tag{8}$$

$$x^+ = \frac{1}{2}(x + |x|), \qquad x^- = \frac{1}{2}(|x| - x) \tag{9}$$

wherein $|x| = (|x_i|)_{i=1}^n$.

According to (8), AVI (1) can be reformulated as the following XLCP:

$$\begin{aligned} (A + B)x^+ + (B - A)x^- &\leq c \\ x^+, x^- &\geq 0 \\ (x^+)^T x^- &= 0 \end{aligned}$$

Similarly, according to (9), XLCP (5-7) can be reformulated as the following AVI:

$$\frac{1}{2}(M - N)x + \frac{1}{2}(M + N)|x| \leq q$$

Equivalence between AVIs and ILIs. From Theorem 2.19 in [23] (which states that a vector $x \in \mathbb{R}^n$ is a weak solution of $\mathbf{A}x \leq b$ iff it satisfies $A_c x - \triangle_A |x| \leq b$) together with Theorem 1 in this paper, we can prove that any system of absolute value inequalities $Ax + B|x| \leq b$ can be reformulated as a system of interval linear inequalities $\mathbf{A}'x \leq b'$ where $A, B \in \mathbb{R}^{m \times n}, b \in \mathbb{R}^m, \mathbf{A}' \in \mathbb{IR}^{k \times n}, b' \in \mathbb{R}^k$. The converse also holds.

Example 1. Consider the following AVI: $\{|x| \leq 1, -|x| \leq -1\}$. Its corresponding XLCP will be $\{x^+ + x^- \leq 1, -x^+ - x^- \leq -1, x^+ \geq 0, x^- \geq 0, (x^+)^T x^- = 0\}$, and its corresponding ILI will be $\{x \leq 1, -x \leq 1, [-1, 1]x \leq -1\}$.

Until now, we have shown the equivalence among AVIs, XLCPs and ILIs, which indicates that we can reuse the method that can solve one of them to solve the others. In this paper, we reduce AVIs (as well as ILIs) to XLCPs and propose a double description method to characterize all solutions of an XLCP. On the other hand, the equivalence implies that the AVI domain proposed in this paper can be reused to infer other kinds of equivalent relations, e.g., to deal with linear constraints with interval coefficients that may appear in numerical static analysis [4]. In Sect. 4.1, we will see that the AVI domain is as expressive as the existing interval polyhedra domain [4] (that employs ILIs for domain representation) but enjoys better (optimal) domain operations.

3 Double Description Method for XLCP

By Minkowski-Weyl theorem [26], the set $P \subseteq \mathbb{R}^n$ is a polyhedron, iff it is finitely generated, i.e., there exist finite sets $V, R \in \mathbb{R}^n$ such that P can be generated by (V, R):

$$P = \left\{ \sum_{i=1}^{|V|} \lambda_i V_i + \sum_{j=1}^{|R|} \mu_j R_j \;\middle|\; \forall i, \lambda_i \geq 0, \forall j, \mu_j \geq 0, \sum_{i=1}^{|V|} \lambda_i = 1 \right\}$$

where $|V|$, $|R|$ denote the cardinality of sets V, R respectively. Elements in V are called *extreme points*, while elements in R are called *extreme rays*. Using the double description method, a convex polyhedron can be represented by either its constraint representation $\{Ax \leq b\}$ or its generator representation (V, R). The two representations are duals: Each can be computed from the other by Chernikova's algorithm [18]. And the classic convex polyhedra abstract domain [9] is designed based on the dual representations.

In this section, we will construct a double description method for XLCP, on top of that for convex polyhedra. The main idea is the following. Intuitively, (5-6) of an XLCP describes a convex polyhedron $P = \{x^+ \in \mathbb{R}^n, x^- \in \mathbb{R}^n \mid Mx^+ + Nx^- \leq q, x^+ \geq 0, x^- \geq 0\}$, while the complementary condition (7) specifies that $x_i^+ = 0 \vee x_i^- = 0$ holds for all $i = 1, \ldots, n$, which indicates 2^n complementary patterns. Overall, XLCP (5-7) can be considered as a union of a set of polyhedra, the number of which is in the worst case 2^n (one for each complementary pattern). E.g., when $n = 1$, XLCP (5-7) is equivalent to the union of 2^1 polyhedra: $\{x^+ \in \mathbb{R}^n, x^- \in \mathbb{R}^n \mid Mx^+ + Nx^- \leq q, x^+ = 0, x^- \geq 0\} \cup \{x^+ \in \mathbb{R}^n, x^- \in \mathbb{R}^n \mid Mx^+ + Nx^- \leq q, x^+ \geq 0, x^- = 0\}$. It is worth noting that first not all generators g of P will be the generators of XLCP (5-7), since g may not satisfy the complementary condition. Second, even for those generators of P that satisfy the complementary condition, not all combinations of them will result in solutions of XLCP (5-7). Essentially, we need to group generators according to the complementary patterns such that each group corresponds to a convex polyhedron and any combination of generators in one group will always result in a solution of XLCP (5-7).

Example 2. Consider the following XLCP: $\{-x^+ - x^- \leq -1, x^+ \leq 2, x^- \leq 2, x^+ \geq 0, x^- \geq 0, x^+ x^- = 0\}$. As shown in Fig. 1, the polyhedral generators of $\{-x^+ - x^- \leq -1, x^+ \leq 2, x^- \leq 2, x^+ \geq 0, x^- \geq 0\}$ will be

$$(V, R) = \left(\begin{pmatrix} x^+ \\ x^- \end{pmatrix} : \left\{ \begin{pmatrix} 1 \\ 0 \end{pmatrix}, \begin{pmatrix} 2 \\ 0 \end{pmatrix}, \begin{pmatrix} 0 \\ 1 \end{pmatrix}, \begin{pmatrix} 0 \\ 2 \end{pmatrix}, \begin{pmatrix} 2 \\ 2 \end{pmatrix} \right\}, \ \emptyset \right)$$

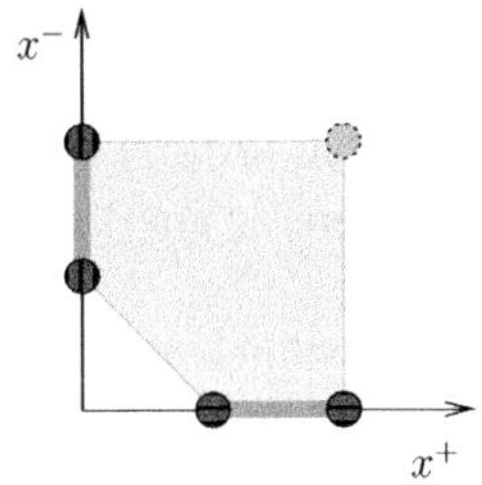

Fig. 1. Generators and their grouping for XLCP

Firstly, the extreme point $(2\ 2)^T$ does not satisfy the complementary condition $x^+x^- = 0$, and thus should be removed, since no combination involving $(2\ 2)^T$ will satisfy $x^+x^- = 0$ either. Secondly, for other extreme points that satisfy the complementary condition, not all convex combinations of them will satisfy $x^+x^- = 0$, e.g., convex combinations of $(1\ 0)^T$ and $(0\ 1)^T$. To precisely characterize the solution set of the original XLCP, two groups need to be constructed such that any convex combination of extreme points from either group (without mixing) forms a XLCP solution:

$$\left\{ \left(\begin{pmatrix} x^+ \\ x^- \end{pmatrix} : \left\{ \begin{pmatrix} 1 \\ 0 \end{pmatrix}, \begin{pmatrix} 2 \\ 0 \end{pmatrix} \right\}, \emptyset \right), \left(\begin{pmatrix} x^+ \\ x^- \end{pmatrix} : \left\{ \begin{pmatrix} 0 \\ 1 \end{pmatrix}, \begin{pmatrix} 0 \\ 2 \end{pmatrix} \right\}, \emptyset \right) \right\}$$

Taking the first group as an example, the convex combinations between extreme points $(1\ 0)^T$ and $(2\ 0)^T$ from the first group define points lying on the line segment connecting $(1\ 0)^T$ and $(2\ 0)^T$. Indeed, all those points are solutions of the original XLCP.

3.1 Conversion from the Constraint to the Generator Representation

3.1.1 Homogeneous Case

Finding non-negative solutions of a polyhedral cone satisfying the complementary condition. Let us denote $x = (x^+, x^-)^T$, where $x \in \mathbb{R}^{2n}, x^+, x^- \in \mathbb{R}^n$. Now we consider a set of the form

$$C_\pm = \{x \in \mathbb{R}^{2n} \mid Ax \geq 0, x \geq 0, (x^+)^T x^- = 0\}$$

A vector $y \in \mathbb{R}^{2n}$ is said to be a *complementary generator* of $C_\pm$, iff y is a polyhedral generator of $\{x \mid Ax \geq 0, x \geq 0\}$ and satisfies $(y^+)^T y^- = 0$. One simple way to find all the complementary generators for $C_\pm$ is to first calculate all the polyhedral generators of $\{x \mid Ax \geq 0, x \geq 0\}$ using Chernikova's algorithm [18] and then remove those generators that do not satisfy $(x^+)^T x^- = 0$ at the very end of the whole process. However, this may cause a lot of unnecessary computation, and even combinatorial explosion.

We aim to design a method that can generate directly only complementary generators, by taking into account the complementary condition during the intermediate computation. First, let $C = \{x \mid Ax \geq 0, x \geq 0\}$ be a polyhedral cone and let y be a vector in C. Let D be the matrix associated with the constraint system of C, i.e., $D = \begin{bmatrix} A \\ I \end{bmatrix}$ where $I \in \mathbb{R}^{n \times n}$ denotes the identity matrix. We use $S(y, D) = \{a \mid a \text{ is a row of } D \text{ such that } ay = 0\}$ to denote the set of rows saturated by y. Let Q be the non-redundant set of polyhedral generators of C. Note that generators of pointed polyhedral cone are all extreme rays except the extreme point 0. We apply the following rule to check adjacency: Two rays y_1 and y_2 are *adjacent* in Q, denoted as $adjacent(y_1, y_2) = true$, if $|S(y_1, D) \cap S(y_2, D)| \geq 1$ and there is no y' distinct from y_1, y_2 in Q such that $S(y_1, D) \cap S(y_2, D) \subseteq S(y', D)$.

Let $Q_{\pm} = \{y_1, \ldots, y_r\}$ be the non-redundant set of complementary extreme rays of $C_{\pm}$. Let $H = \{x \mid cx \geq 0\}$. Three sets can be defined with respect to the product cy_i:

$$Q_{\pm}^{=} = \{y \mid y \in Q_{\pm}, cy = 0\}$$
$$Q_{\pm}^{>} = \{y \mid y \in Q_{\pm}, cy > 0\}$$
$$Q_{\pm}^{<} = \{y \mid y \in Q_{\pm}, cy < 0\}.$$

The non-redundant set of complementary extreme rays of the new cone $C_{\pm} \cap H$, denoted as $Q'_{\pm}$, can be then constructed as:

$$Q'_{\pm} = Q_{\pm}^{=} \cup Q_{\pm}^{>} \cup \overline{Q}_{\pm}$$

where $\overline{Q}_{\pm}$ is defined by:

$$\{y \mid cy = 0, y = \lambda y_1 + \mu y_2, (y_1, y_2) \in Q_{\pm}^{>} \times Q_{\pm}^{<}, adjacent^c(y_1, y_2), \lambda > 0, (y^+)^T y^- = 0\}$$

where $adjacent^c(y_1, y_2) = true$, if $|S(y_1, D) \cap S(y_2, D)| >= 1$ and there is no y' distinct from y_1, y_2 in $Q_{\pm}$ such that $S(y_1, D) \cap S(y_2, D) \subseteq S(y', D)$.

Note that to state $adjacent^c(y_1, y_2) = true$, we check over only the set $Q_{\pm}$ that is a subset of Q since some of the elements in Q may not satisfy the complementary condition. Thus, it may happen that $adjacent^c(y_1, y_2) = true$ (defined via $Q_{\pm}$) but $adjacent(y_1, y_2) = false$ (defined via Q). However, in fact, in this case it can be proved that no positive combination of such y_1 and y_2 will satisfy the complementary condition. Let R be the set of extreme rays for $C = \{x \mid Ax \geq 0, x \geq 0\}$. Let R^c be the resulting set of complementary extreme rays for $C_{\pm} = \{x \mid Ax \geq 0, x \geq 0, (x^+)^T x^- = 0\}$ computed by the above method via $Q_{\pm}$. The following theorem guarantees the correctness of the above incremental process of computing complementary extreme rays for $C_{\pm}$.

Theorem 2. *R^c contains all and only complementary extreme rays, that is, $R^c = R \cap \{y \mid y^+ y^- = 0\}$.*

Theorem 2 implies that R^c is equivalent to the result given by first computing all extreme rays (i.e., R) for C and then removing at the very end those extreme rays that do not satisfy the complementary condition.

Grouping complementary extreme rays. Note that not all non-negative combinations of rays in R^c satisfy the complementary condition $(x^+)^T x^- = 0$ and thus are necessary in $C_{\pm}$. To precisely describe $C_{\pm}$, we need to classify R^c into several groups such that the grouping result $R^{cc} = \langle R^c_{s_1}, \ldots, R^c_{s_i}, \ldots, R^c_{s_m} \rangle$ satisfies

1. $\cup_{i=1}^m R^c_{s_i} = R^c$, and
2. Within each group $R^c_{s_i}$, any nonnegative combination y of rays in $R^c_{s_i}$ satisfies the complementary condition $(y^+)^T y^- = 0$.

Note that R^{cc} is a cover of R^c. To construct such groups, we use the following method. First, we construct an undirected graph Θ, where each $r_i^c \in R^c$ corresponds to one node in Θ. And there is an edge between two nodes r_i^c and r_j^c, if the resulting vector $s = \max\{r_i^c, r_j^c\}$ satisfies $(s^+)^T s^- = 0$. The goal then is to find all the maximal complete subgraphs in Θ, each of which corresponds to one group $R_{s_i}^c$ in R^c. After that, we can characterize $C_\pm$.

Theorem 3. *Let* $C_\pm = \{x \mid Ax \geq 0, x \geq 0, (x^+)^T x^- = 0\}$ *and let* $R^{cc} = \langle R_{s_1}^c, \ldots, R_{s_i}^c, \ldots, R_{s_m}^c \rangle$ *be the grouping result of its complementary extreme rays. Then* $x \in C_\pm$, *iff there exists some* i $(i \in \mathbb{N}, 1 \leq i \leq m)$ *such that*

$$x = \sum_{r_k^c \in R_{s_i}^c} \mu_k r_k^c$$

where $\mu_k \geq 0$.

Intuitively, Theorem 3 states that $C_\pm$ is a union of a set of polyhedral cones and each group $R_{s_i}^c$ corresponds to one polyhedral cone. While the sufficient condition is obvious, the necessary condition can be proved as follows: Suppose $y \in C_\pm = \{x \mid Ax \geq 0, x \geq 0, (x^+)^T x^- = 0\}$. First, we know that y can be and can only be generated through a positive combination of a subset of rays in $R^c = R \cap \{x \mid (x^+)^T x^- = 0\}$, since the result z of any positive combination involving $r \in R \setminus R^c$ will not satisfy $(z^+)^T z^- = 0$. Assume that y can be generated through a positive combination of a set of rays R_y^c where $R_y^c \subseteq R^c$, which implies that any nonnegative combination of rays in R_y^c will satisfy the complementary condition. Hence, any $R_{s_i}^c$ satisfying $R_y^c \subseteq R_{s_i}^c$ can generate y. Therefore, there exists some i $(1 \leq i \leq m)$ such that $y = \sum_{r_k^c \in R_{s_i}^c} \mu_k r_k^c$ where $\mu_k \geq 0$.

3.1.2 Inhomogeneous Case

Finding non-negative solutions of a convex polyhedron. By introducing a fresh variable $h \in \mathbb{R}$, the inhomogeneous linear system $\{Ax \geq b, x \geq 0\}$ (where $x \in \mathbb{R}^{2n}$) can be transformed into an equivalent homogeneous one: $\{[A \;\; -b]y \geq 0, y \geq 0\}$ where $y = (x\ h)^T$ is a column $(2n+1)$-vector with $h \geq 0$.

Each extreme ray r of the above homogeneous system has the form of $r = (x\ h)^T$ with $h \geq 0$. We use r_h to denote the h component of the vector r. For each extreme ray r, there are two possibilities: $r_h = 0$ or $r_h > 0$. The set of extreme rays of the homogeneous system, denoted as R^h, can be divided into two groups: $R^0 = \{r \mid r \in R^h, r_h = 0\}$ and $R^1 = \{r/r_h \mid r \in R^h, r_h > 0\}$. Then, we extract the x part out of the vectors from R^0 and R^1. Assume that we get $R = \{x \mid (x\ 0)^T \in R^0\}$ and $V = \{x \mid (x\ 1)^T \in R^1\}$. The generators in V are called *extreme points* while the generators in R are called *extreme rays* of the inhomogeneous system. In other words, we get the generator representation $G = (V, R)$ for the inhomogeneous system $\{Ax \geq b, x \geq 0\}$.

Finding non-negative solutions of a convex polyhedron satisfying the complementary condition. Similarly as above, from the set of complementary extreme rays of $\{y \mid Ay \geq 0, y \geq 0, (x^+)^T x^- = 0, y = (x^+\ x^-\ h)^T\}$ which can be obtained via the method in Sect. 3.1.1, we can derive the set of complementary generators $G^c = (V^c, R^c)$ for

$$P_\pm = \{x \mid Ax \geq b, x \geq 0, (x^+)^T x^- = 0\}.$$

Again, to precisely describe $P_\pm$, we need to classify G^c into several groups such that the grouping result $G^{cc} = \langle G^c_{s_1}, \ldots, G^c_{s_i}, \ldots, G^c_{s_m} \rangle$ where $G^c_{s_i} = (V^c_{s_i}, R^c_{s_i})$, satisfies

1. $\cup_{i=1}^m V^c_{s_i} = V^c$, $\cup_{i=1}^m R^c_{s_i} = R^c$, and
2. Within each group $G^c_{s_i}$, any sum z of an arbitrary convex combination of extreme points from $V^c_{s_i}$ and an arbitrary nonnegative combination of extreme rays from $R^c_{s_i}$, satisfies the complementary condition $(z^+)^T z^- = 0$.

Similarly, to construct such groups, we can use algorithms that find all the maximal complete subgraphs of an undirected graph. Now we can characterize $P_\pm$.

Theorem 4. *Let $P_\pm = \{x \in \mathbb{R}^{2n} \mid Ax \geq b, x \geq 0, (x^+)^T x^- = 0\}$, and let $G^{cc} = \langle G^c_{s_1}, \ldots, G^c_{s_i}, \ldots, G^c_{s_m} \rangle$ be the grouping result of its complementary generators where $G^c_{s_i} = (V^c_{s_i}, R^c_{s_i})$. Then $x \in P_\pm$, iff there exists some i ($i \in \mathbb{N}, 1 \leq i \leq m$) such that*

$$x = \sum_{v_j^c \in V^c_{s_i}} \lambda_j v_j^c + \sum_{r_k^c \in R^c_{s_i}} \mu_k r_k^c$$

where $\lambda_j, \mu_k \geq 0, \Sigma_j \lambda_j = 1$.

Theorem 4 states that $P_\pm$ is a union of a set of convex polyhedra, the number of which is s_m. Each group $G^c_{s_i}$ describes a polyhedron. Note that s_m is not necessarily equal to the number of complementary patterns (i.e., 2^n), since a certain complementary pattern may define an empty polyhedron and the union of some polyhedra stemming from distinct complementary patterns may be exactly representable by a single polyhedron.

It is worth noting that generating all the maximal complete subgraphs of an undirected graph is an NP-complete problem [10]. Fortunately, as we will see in Sect. 4, to design the AVI abstract domain, we do not need to group the complementary generators, since no domain operation requires G^{cc} and all domain operations can be implemented based on only a non-redundant set of complementary generators G^c. In this paper, the notion of G^{cc} is only useful to get Theorem 4 which is interesting as it precisely characterizes the topological properties of $P_\pm$ and shows that $P_\pm$ is essentially a (possibly) non-convex union of a set of convex polyhedra.

3.2 Conversion from the Generator to the Constraint Representation

Let $G^c = (V^c, R^c)$ be the set of complementary generators of a convex polyhedron $P_\pm$ satisfying $\{x \geq 0, (x^+)^T x^- = 0\}$. We now consider the problem of constructing the constraint representation for $P_\pm$ from G^c. It can be achieved by the following steps:

1. Consider $G^c = (V^c, R^c)$ as the regular generator representation of some convex polyhedron. Then we use the standard Chernikova's algorithm to compute the corresponding polyhedral constraint representation, i.e., a linear system such as
$$M'x^+ + N'x^- \leq b'$$
2. Add $x^+, x^- \geq 0$ to the above system and remove those constraints from $M'x^+ + N'x^- \leq b'$ that become redundant after adding $x^+, x^- \geq 0$. Suppose we get
$$\begin{aligned} Mx^+ + Nx^- &\leq b \\ x^+, x^- &\geq 0 \end{aligned}$$

3. Add $(x^+)^T x^- = 0$ to the above system, and we get

$$\begin{aligned} Mx^+ + Nx^- &\leq b \\ x^+, x^- &\geq 0 \\ (x^+)^T x^- &= 0 \end{aligned}$$

which will be the XLCP constraint representation for $P_\pm$.

Observe that the resulting XLCP constraint representation for $P_\pm$ is not necessarily non-redundant. However, this does not matter much for designing abstract domains, since a non-redundant generator representation for $P_\pm$ can be ensured.

4 An Abstract Domain of Linear Absolute Value Inequalities

In this section, we propose a new abstract domain, namely the abstract domain of linear absolute value inequalities (AVI). The key point is to use a system of linear absolute value inequalities as the domain representation. AVI can be used to infer relationships of the form $\Sigma_k a_k x_k + \Sigma_k b_k |x_k| \leq c$ over program variables x_k $(k = 1, \ldots, n)$, where constants $a_k, b_k, c \in \mathbb{R}$ are automatically inferred by the analysis.

4.1 Representation

An AVI domain element $\mathbf{P}$ is described as an AVI system $Ax + B|x| \leq c$, where $A, B \in \mathbb{R}^{m \times n}, c \in \mathbb{R}^m$, and m is the number of constraints in the system. It represents the set $\gamma(\mathbf{P}) = \{x \in \mathbb{R}^n \mid Ax + B|x| \leq c\}$, in which each point $x \in \gamma(\mathbf{P})$ represents a possible program environment (or state), i.e., an assignment of numerical/real values to program variables.

From Sect. 2, we know that a linear AV inequality system is equivalent to an interval linear inequality system. Thus the AVI domain is as expressive as the interval polyhedra abstract domain [4]. In other words, each AVI domain element is geometrically an interval polyhedron. Hence, the set of AVI domain elements has the same topological properties as the set of interval polyhedra:

- An AVI domain element is non-convex (even unconnected) in general.
- The intersection of an AVI domain element with each orthant in $\mathbb{R}^n$ gives a (possibly empty) convex polyhedron.

Specifically, from Theorem 6 in Sect. 4.2, we will see that the set union of bounded convex polyhedra with one per each (closed) orthant can be exactly represented by one AVI domain element.

Expressiveness lifting. Note that in the AVI domain representation, absolute value $|\cdot|$ applies to only (single) variables rather than expressions. E.g., consider the relation $y = x - |x+1| + |x-1|$ which encodes the following piecewise linear function

$$y = \begin{cases} x+2 & \text{if } x \leq -1 \\ -x & \text{if } -1 \leq x \leq 1 \\ x-2 & \text{if } x \geq 1 \end{cases}$$

whose plot is shown in Fig. 2. The AVI domain can not express directly this piecewise linear function (in the space of x, y), since $|\cdot|$ applies to two expressions: $x+1$ and $x-1$. Indeed, in Fig. 2 the region in each orthant is not a convex polyhedron.

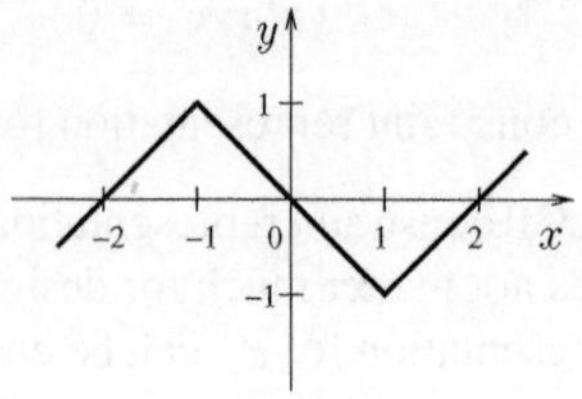

Fig. 2. A piecewise linear function

In order to express such piecewise linear relations, we lift the expressiveness of the AVI domain by introducing new auxiliary variables to denote those expressions that appear inside the AV function. E.g., we could introduce two auxiliary variables v_1, v_2 to denote the values of the expressions $x + 1$ and $x - 1$ respectively. Then using AVI domain elements in the space with higher dimension (involving 4 variables: x, y, v_1, v_2), such as $\{y = x - |v_1| + |v_2|, v_1 = x + 1, v_2 = x - 1\}$, we could express complex piecewise linear relations in the space over lower dimension (involving 2 variables: x, y), such as $y = x - |x + 1| + |x - 1|$. Note that $\{y = x - |v_1| + |v_2|, v_1 = x + 1, v_2 = x - 1\}$ is indeed an AVI domain element. Following the same strategy, we can also express piecewise linear relations with nestings of absolute value functions. E.g., to express $y = ||x| - 1| + ||z| - 2|$, by introducing auxiliary variables v_1, v_2, we could use $\{y = |v_1| + |v_2|, v_1 = |x| - 1, v_2 = |z| - 2\}$.

In fact, a large subclass of piecewise linear functions of practical interest can be represented via AV functions through a so-called canonical (piecewise linear) representation [5], as known in the field of circuits and systems. Thus, most piecewise linear relations of interest in the program could be also expressed by the AVI domain, provided that necessary auxiliary variables are introduced.

4.2 Domain Operations

In the convex polyhedra domain, domain operations can be implemented based on the double description method for convex polyhedra [9]. Similarly, we will construct domain operations for the AVI domain based on the double description method for AVI systems (which are equivalent to XLCPs). During the implementation, we maintain the map between abstract environments over x and abstract environments over x^+, x^- as:

$$x = x^+ - x^-, \qquad |x| = x^+ + x^-$$
$$x^+ = \frac{1}{2}(x + |x|), \qquad x^- = \frac{1}{2}(|x| - x)$$

where x^+, x^- satisfy

$$x^+ \geq 0, x^- \geq 0, (x^+)^T x^- = 0$$

More precisely, we will construct domain operations for the AVI domain over x, based on the double description method for XLCP over x^+, x^-. Note that for the implementation of the AVI domain, we need only the set of complementary generators $G^c = (V^c, R^c)$, without resorting to the grouping information G^{cc} of the complementary generators. And the cost of the AVI domain is dominated by the dual conversions between XLCP constraints and complementary generators.

For the sake of simplicity, from now on, we assume that the AVI element **P** corresponds to the following XLCP system:

$$\begin{array}{c} Mx^+ + Nx^- \leq b \\ x^+ \geq 0, x^- \geq 0, (x^+)^T x^- = 0 \end{array}$$

and we denote its set of complementary generators as

$$G^c = (V^c, R^c).$$

Now, we describe the implementation of most common domain operations required for static analysis over the AVI domain, some of which require only constraints or generators while some of which require both.

(1) Lattice operations

- Emptiness test: **P** is empty, iff $V^c = \emptyset$.
  From now on, let $\mathbf{P}, \mathbf{P}'$ be two non-empty AVI domain elements.
- Inclusion test: $\mathbf{P} \sqsubseteq \mathbf{P}'$ that is $\gamma(\mathbf{P}) \subseteq \gamma(\mathbf{P}')$, iff

$$\forall v \in V^c, M' v^+ + N' v^- \leq b' \quad \wedge \quad \forall r \in R^c, M' r^+ + N' r^- \leq 0$$

- Meet: $\mathbf{P} \sqcap \mathbf{P}'$ is an AVI domain element whose XLCP system is

$$\begin{array}{c} Mx^+ + Nx^- \leq b \\ M'x^+ + N'x^- \leq b' \\ x^+ \geq 0, x^- \geq 0, (x^+)^T x^- = 0 \end{array}$$

- Join: $\mathbf{P} \sqcup \mathbf{P}'$ is the least AVI domain element containing **P** and $\mathbf{P}'$, whose set of complementary generators is the union of those of **P** and $\mathbf{P}'$: $(V^c \cup V'^c, R^c \cup R'^c)$. We show by the following theorem that this join operation is optimal, i.e., its output gives the smallest AVI domain element containing the two input elements.

Theorem 5. *Given two* AVI *domain elements* **P** *and* $\mathbf{P}'$*, for any* AVI *domain element* **Q** *satisfying* $\gamma(\mathbf{P}) \subseteq \gamma(\mathbf{Q})$ *and* $\gamma(\mathbf{P}') \subseteq \gamma(\mathbf{Q})$*, we have* $\gamma(\mathbf{P} \sqcup \mathbf{P}') \subseteq \gamma(\mathbf{Q})$.

From this theorem together with Theorem 4, we have the following theorem that explores further the expressiveness of the AVI domain.

Theorem 6. *Given a set of bounded convex polyhedra with one per each closed orthant, their set union can be exactly represented by one* AVI *domain element (through the same set of variables).*

Note that, however, Theorem 6 may not hold when one of the input AVI domain elements is not bounded. Theorem 6 implies that given two AVI systems that are bounded, the result of the AVI join is equivalent to the result given by the set union of convex polyhedral hulls in each orthant.

(2) Transfer functions

- Test transfer function: $\tau[\![cx + d|x| \leq e]\!]^{\#}(\mathbf{P})$, whose XLCP system is defined as

$$\begin{aligned} Mx^+ + Nx^- &\leq b \\ (c+d)x^+ + (d-c)x^- &\leq e \\ x^+ \geq 0, x^- \geq 0, (x^+)^T x^- &= 0 \end{aligned}$$

- Projection: $\tau[\![x_j := random()]\!]^{\#}(\mathbf{P})$, whose set of complementary generators is defined as $(V^c, R^c \cup \{e_j^+, e_j^-, -e_j^+, -e_j^-\})$, where e_j^+ denotes a canonical basis vector wherein all the components are 0 except $x_j^+ = 1$, and e_j^- denotes a canonical basis vector wherein all the components are 0 except $x_j^- = 1$. Observe that $\tau[\![x_j := random()]\!]^{\#}(\mathbf{P})$ is optimal in the AVI domain, although its result may be less precise than $\exists x_j.\mathbf{P} \stackrel{\text{def}}{=} \{x[x_j/y] \mid x \in \gamma(\mathbf{P}), y \in \mathbb{R}\}$ which may be not an AVI domain element, where $x[x_j/y]$ denotes the vector x in which the j-th element is replaced with y.
- Assignment transfer function: $\tau[\![x_j := \Sigma_i a_i x_i + \Sigma_i b_i |x_i| + c]\!]^{\#}(\mathbf{P})$, can be modeled using test transfer function, projection and variable renaming as follows:

$$\left(\tau[\![x_j := random()]\!]^{\#} \circ \tau[\![\Sigma_i a_i x_i + \Sigma_i b_i |x_i| + c - x'_j = 0]\!]^{\#}(\mathbf{P})\right)[x'_j/x_j]$$

Note that the assignment transfer function is optimal but not exact. E.g., assignments may cause a polyhedron in one orthant to cross orthant boundaries. In such case, the result in each orthant is then updated to a possible overapproximation of the polyhedral convex hull of the regions which belong to that orthant after the transfer operation.

(3) Widening

- Widening: Given two AVI domain elements $\mathbf{P} \sqsubseteq \mathbf{P}'$, we define

$$\mathbf{P} \triangledown \mathbf{P}' \stackrel{\text{def}}{=} \mathcal{S}_1 \cup \mathcal{S}_2 \cup \{x^+, x^- \geq 0, (x^+)^T x^- = 0\}$$

where

$$\begin{aligned} \mathcal{S}_1 &= \{\varphi_1 \in (Mx^+ + Nx^- \leq b) \mid \mathbf{P}' \models \varphi_1\}, \\ \mathcal{S}_2 &= \left\{ \varphi_2 \in (M'x^+ + N'x^- \leq b') \,\middle|\, \begin{array}{l} \exists \varphi_1 \in (Mx^+ + Nx^- \leq b), \\ \gamma(\mathbf{P}) = \gamma((\mathbf{P} \setminus \{\varphi_1\}) \cup \{\varphi_2\}) \end{array} \right\} \end{aligned}$$

The above widening for the AVI domain is designed following the same principle as the standard widening of the convex polyhedra domain. The first set $\mathcal{S}_1$ contains all inequalities from the $Mx^+ + Nx^- \leq b$ part of $\mathbf{P}$ that are not violated by the larger $\mathbf{P}'$, while $\mathcal{S}_2$ consists of inequalities from the $M'x^+ + N'x^- \leq b'$ part of $\mathbf{P}'$ that can be exchanged with an inequality from the $Mx^+ + Nx^- \leq b$ part of $\mathbf{P}$ without changing the represented state. $\mathcal{S}_2$ ensures that the result is independent of the (syntactic) representation of $\mathbf{P}$ and $\mathbf{P}'$. Here, we use $\varphi_1 \in (Mx^+ + Nx^- \leq b)$ to denote that φ_1 is one constraint from the system $Mx^+ + Nx^- \leq b$. Let φ_1 be $(cx^+ + dx^- \leq e)$. The entailment $\mathbf{P}' \models \varphi_1$ can be implemented by checking

$$\forall v' \in V'^c, c\,v'^+ + d\,v'^- \le e \quad \wedge \quad \forall r' \in R'^c, c\,r'^+ + d\,r'^- \le 0$$

Next, we use the following example to show in detail how AVI domain operations can be constructed based on the double description method. We choose to show the join operation, since the join is rather interesting (especially when comparing it with polyhedral convex hull of the convex polyhedra domain [9] as well as weak join of the interval polyhedra domain [4]).

Example 3. Consider two AVI domain elements $\mathbf{P}' = \{(x\ y)^T \mid 1 \le x \le 2, -1 \le y \le 1\} = \{(x^+\ x^-\ y^+\ y^-)^T \mid 1 \le x^+ - x^- \le 2, -1 \le y^+ - y^- \le 1, x^+ \ge 0, x^- \ge 0, y^+ \ge 0, y^- \ge 0, x^+x^- = 0, y^+y^- = 0\}$ and $\mathbf{P}'' = \{(x\ y)^T \mid -2 \le x \le -1\} = \{(x^+\ x^-\ y^+\ y^-)^T \mid -2 \le x^+ - x^- \le -1, x^+ \ge 0, x^- \ge 0, y^+ \ge 0, y^- \ge 0, x^+x^- = 0, y^+y^- = 0\}$, shown in Figure 3(1). Note that $\mathbf{P}'$ is a bounded convex polyhedron while $\mathbf{P}''$ is an unbounded convex polyhedron. And the polyhedral convex hull of $\mathbf{P}'$ and $\mathbf{P}''$ results in $\{(x\ y)^T \mid -2 \le x \le 2\}$ that is a convex polyhedron. Since $\mathbf{P}''$ is unbounded, we can not apply Theorem 6 to the set union of $\mathbf{P}'$ and $\mathbf{P}''$ which indeed cannot be exactly described by any AVI domain element (through the same set of variables).

First, if we omit the condition $x^+x^- = 0 \wedge y^+y^- = 0$, the set of regular (polyhedral) generators for $\mathbf{P}'$ and $\mathbf{P}''$ over $(x^+, x^-, y^+, y^-)^T$ will be respectively

$$(V_{\mathbf{P}'}, R_{\mathbf{P}'}) = \left(\begin{pmatrix} x^+ \\ x^- \\ y^+ \\ y^- \end{pmatrix} : \left\{\begin{pmatrix}1\\0\\0\\0\end{pmatrix}, \begin{pmatrix}2\\0\\0\\0\end{pmatrix}, \begin{pmatrix}1\\0\\0\\1\end{pmatrix}, \begin{pmatrix}2\\0\\0\\1\end{pmatrix}, \begin{pmatrix}1\\0\\1\\0\end{pmatrix}, \begin{pmatrix}2\\0\\1\\0\end{pmatrix}\right\}, \left\{\begin{pmatrix}1\\1\\0\\0\end{pmatrix}, \begin{pmatrix}0\\0\\1\\1\end{pmatrix}\right\}\right)$$

$$(V_{\mathbf{P}''}, R_{\mathbf{P}''}) = \left(\begin{pmatrix} x^+ \\ x^- \\ y^+ \\ y^- \end{pmatrix} : \left\{\begin{pmatrix}0\\1\\0\\0\end{pmatrix}, \begin{pmatrix}0\\2\\0\\0\end{pmatrix}\right\}, \left\{\begin{pmatrix}0\\0\\0\\1\end{pmatrix}, \begin{pmatrix}0\\0\\1\\0\end{pmatrix}, \begin{pmatrix}1\\1\\0\\0\end{pmatrix}\right\}\right)$$

If we take into account $x^+x^- = 0 \wedge y^+y^- = 0$, we get the sets of complementary generators for $\mathbf{P}'$and $\mathbf{P}''$ over $(x^+, x^-, y^+, y^-)^T$:

$$(V^c_{\mathbf{P}'}, R^c_{\mathbf{P}'}) = \left(\begin{pmatrix} x^+ \\ x^- \\ y^+ \\ y^- \end{pmatrix} : \left\{\begin{pmatrix}1\\0\\0\\0\end{pmatrix}, \begin{pmatrix}2\\0\\0\\0\end{pmatrix}, \begin{pmatrix}1\\0\\0\\1\end{pmatrix}, \begin{pmatrix}2\\0\\0\\1\end{pmatrix}, \begin{pmatrix}1\\0\\1\\0\end{pmatrix}, \begin{pmatrix}2\\0\\1\\0\end{pmatrix}\right\}, \emptyset\right)$$

$$(V^c_{\mathbf{P}''}, R^c_{\mathbf{P}''}) = \left(\begin{pmatrix} x^+ \\ x^- \\ y^+ \\ y^- \end{pmatrix} : \left\{\begin{pmatrix}0\\1\\0\\0\end{pmatrix}, \begin{pmatrix}0\\2\\0\\0\end{pmatrix}\right\}, \left\{\begin{pmatrix}0\\0\\0\\1\end{pmatrix}, \begin{pmatrix}0\\0\\1\\0\end{pmatrix}\right\}\right)$$

And $(V^c_{\mathbf{P}'} \cup V^c_{\mathbf{P}''}, R^c_{\mathbf{P}'} \cup R^c_{\mathbf{P}''})$ will be the set of complementary generators for $\mathbf{P}' \sqcup \mathbf{P}''$, i.e.,

$$\left(\begin{pmatrix} x^+ \\ x^- \\ y^+ \\ y^- \end{pmatrix} : \left\{\begin{pmatrix}1\\0\\0\\0\end{pmatrix}, \begin{pmatrix}2\\0\\0\\0\end{pmatrix}, \begin{pmatrix}1\\0\\0\\1\end{pmatrix}, \begin{pmatrix}2\\0\\0\\1\end{pmatrix}, \begin{pmatrix}1\\0\\1\\0\end{pmatrix}, \begin{pmatrix}2\\0\\1\\0\end{pmatrix}, \begin{pmatrix}0\\1\\0\\0\end{pmatrix}, \begin{pmatrix}0\\2\\0\\0\end{pmatrix}\right\}, \left\{\begin{pmatrix}0\\0\\0\\1\end{pmatrix}, \begin{pmatrix}0\\0\\1\\0\end{pmatrix}\right\}\right)$$

Then, by converting it into the constraint representation, we will get the following XLCP system for $\mathbf{P}' \sqcup \mathbf{P}''$:

$$\{1 \le x^+ + x^- \le 2, x^+ \ge 0, x^- \ge 0, x^+x^- = 0, y^+ \ge 0, y^- \ge 0, y^+y^- = 0\}$$

Finally, we can get the following AVI representation for $\mathbf{P}' \sqcup \mathbf{P}''$:

$$\mathbf{P}' \sqcup \mathbf{P}'' = \{(x\ y)^T \mid 1 \le |x| \le 2\}$$

And the regions of the inputs $\mathbf{P}'$ and $\mathbf{P}''$ together with the output $\mathbf{Q}$ of the AVI join operation are shown in Figure 3.

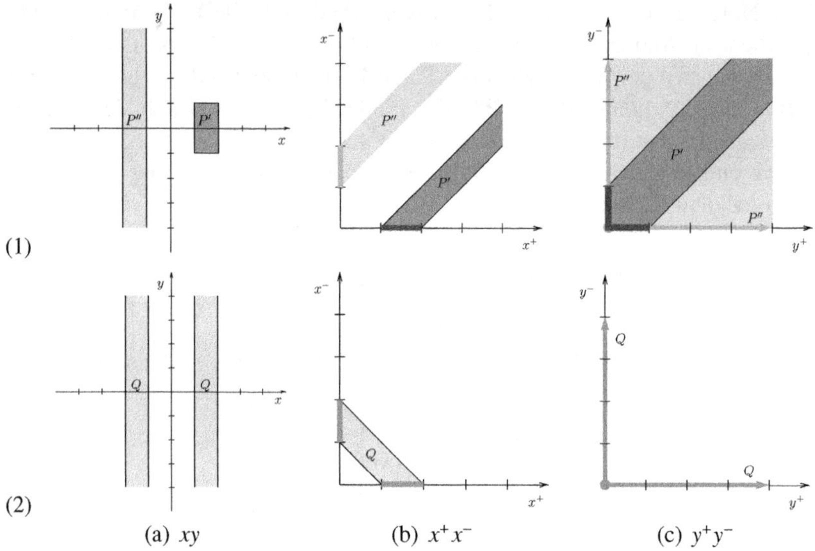

Fig. 3. Subfigure (1) shows the two input AVI domain elements of the join: $\mathbf{P}' = \{1 \le x \le 2, -1 \le y \le 1\}$ and $\mathbf{P}'' = \{-2 \le x \le -1\}$, while subfigure (2) shows the join over the AVI domain: $\mathbf{Q} = \mathbf{P}' \sqcup \mathbf{P}'' = \{1 \le |x| \le 2\}$. The columns (a), (b), (c) depict the regions over the xy, x^+x^-, y^+y^- planes respectively.

5 Implementation and Experimental Results

Our prototype domain, rAVI, is developed based on Sect. 4 using multi-precision rational numbers. It makes use of GMP (the GNU Multiple Precision arithmetic library) [1] and NewPolka [15] that is a rational implementation of the convex polyhedra domain. rAVI is interfaced to the APRON numerical abstract domain library [15]. Our experiments were conducted using the INTERPROC [16] static analyzer. In order to assess the precision and efficiency of rAVI, we compare the obtained invariants and the performance of rAVI with NewPolka as well as our previous work *itvPol* which is a sound floating-point implementation of the interval polyhedra domain [4].

To demonstrate the expressiveness of rAVI, two simple programs are shown in Figs. 4-5, together with the invariants generated by the analyzer. In Fig. 4, for *AVtest1*, the initial state consists of four points that are respectively from 4 different orthants over the x-y plane: $(1, 1), (-1, 1), (-1, -1), (1, -1)$. The loop increases the values of x and y in each orthant simultaneously, along the direction $y = x$ and $y = -x$ respectively. At program point ①, rAVI can prove that $|y| = |x| \wedge |x| \geq 1$ while NewPolka obtains no information. *itvPol* can only prove that $[-1, 1]x \leq -1 \wedge [-1, 1]y \leq -1$ (i.e., $|x| \geq 1 \wedge |y| \geq 1$) and thus can not find any relations among x and y due to the weak join used in *itvPol* [4].

```
real x, y;
assume x = 1 or x = −1;
assume y = 1 or y = −1;
while (true) {
① if (x ≥ 0) { x := x + 1; }
   else      { x := x − 1; }
   if (y ≥ 0) { y := y + 1; }
   else      { y := y − 1; }
}
```

Loc	NewPolka	*itvPol*	rAVI
①	$\top$ (no information)	$[-1, 1]x \leq -1$ $\wedge[-1, 1]y \leq -1$	$\lvert x\rvert = \lvert y\rvert \wedge \lvert x\rvert \geq 1$

Fig. 4. Program AVtest1 (left) and the generated invariants (right)

The program CmplxTest1 shown in Fig. 5 comes from [13] where it is used as an example for analyzing time complexity of the program. Here, we modify a bit the program by introducing a fresh variable t to denote the value of $n - x0$. The main goal is to find an upper bound for the loop counter i. However, NewPolka and *itvPol* can not find any upper bound for i, while rAVI can prove that $i \leq \frac{1}{2}(|t| + t)$, i.e., $i \leq \max(0, n - x0)$, which shows that the time complexity of CmplxTest1 is $\max(0, n - x0)$ in terms of the input parameters $x0, n$.

```
CmplxTest1(int x0, n)
   x := x0; i := 0;
   t := n − x0;
   while (x < n) {
      i := i + 1;
      x := x + 1;
   } ①
```

Loc	NewPolka	*itvPol*	rAVI
①	$i \geq 0$ $\wedge i = x - x0$	$i \geq 0$	$i \geq 0$ $\wedge i = x - x0$ $\wedge i \leq \frac{1}{2}(\lvert t\rvert + t)$ $\wedge \ldots$

Fig. 5. Program CmplxTest1 (left) and the generated invariants related to i (right)

Table 1 shows the comparison of performance and result invariants for a selection of benchmark examples. Programs AVtest1, CmplxTest1 correspond to those programs shown in Figs. 4-5. CmplxTest1-3 come from [13] wherein they are used for analyzing time complexity of programs. program4 and program5 come from our previous work [4]. "#vars" indicates the total number of program variables in each program. And for each program, the value of the widening delay parameter for INTERPROC is set to 1. "#iter." gives the number of increasing iterations during the analysis.

Table 1. Experimental results for benchmark examples

Program		NewPolka		itvPol		rAVI		Res.	
name	#vars	#iter.	*t(ms)*	#iter.	*t(ms)*	#iter.	*t(ms)*	Inv.	
AVtest1	2	4	11	4	45	4	48	⊐	⊐
AVtest2	2	4	8	3	14	4	31	⊐	⊐
AVtest3	2	4	9	4	16	5	73	⊐	⊐
CmplxTest1	5	4	7	4	26	4	57	⊐	⊐
CmplxTest2	5	6	10	6	34	6	150	⊐	⊐
CmplxTest3	8	4	17	4	242	4	310	⊐	⊐
program4	1	5	2	4	4	4	10	⊐	=
program5	2	6	9	5	20	8	45	⊐	⊐

Invariants. The column "Res. Inv." compares the invariants obtained. The left sub-column compares rAVI with NewPolka while the right sub-column compares rAVI with itvPol. A "⊐" indicates that rAVI outputs stronger invariants than NewPolka or *itvPol*, while a "=" indicates that rAVI outputs equivalent invariants as NewPolka or *itvPol*. The results in Table 1 show that rAVI outputs stronger invariants than NewPolka for all these examples. Note that traditional convex domains (such as the convex polyhedra domain) are not fit for the benchmark examples shown in Table 1, since these programs involve non-convex properties that are out of the expressiveness of convex domains.

And in most cases, rAVI outputs stronger invariants than *itvPol*, although the two domains have the same expressiveness. This is because domain operations in rAVI are optimal while most domain operations in *itvPol* are weak (e.g., the join operation). For *program4*, the two domains generate equivalent invariants, because this program involves only one variable and most domain operations in *itvPol* become optimal in this case. During the experiments, we observed that most linear absolute value invariants generated by rAVI are essentially due to piecewise linear behaviors in the program, e.g., branches inside loops. In the examples CmplxTest1-3 that are used to show time complexity, the piecewise linear behaviors mainly come from case by case discussions over the difference between the loop counter and the input parameter (or the initial value), e.g., whether the difference is greater than 0 or not.

Performance. The column "t(ms)" presents the analysis times in milliseconds when the analyzer runs on a 2.4GHz PC with 2GB of RAM running Fedora Linux. From Table 1, we can see that rAVI is much less efficient than NewPolka, because for these examples the polyhedra generated by NewPolka during the analysis are rather simple (with very few or even no non-trivial constraints). Similarly, we can see that rAVI is less efficient than *itvPol*, because *itvPol* is implemented based on floating-point arithmetic and also because domain operations in *itvPol* are weak operations with low computational cost.

6 Related Work

In numerical static analysis, linear relations are considered as the most important kind of numerical relations among variables of a program. The convex polyhedra abstract domain [9], devoted to linear relation analysis, is one of the earliest but still remains one of the most powerful and commonly used numerical abstract domains. For the sake of efficiency, a variety of weakly relational abstract domains are designed as subdomains of the convex polyhedra domain, such as the Octagon domain [21], the Two Variables Per Inequality (TVPI) domain [28], the Template Polyhedra domain [25], and the SubPolyhedra domain [17]. However, this paper goes the other direction. Rather than aiming at discovering restricted forms of linear relations, we generalize the linear relation analysis to linear absolute value relation analysis that allows discovering a kind of piecewise linear relations.

Numerical abstract domains often use conjunctions of convex constraints as the domain representation, and thus most domains can only represent convex sets. The convexity limitations may lead to imprecision during analysis. To deal with disjunctions, a known solution in abstract interpretation is to use disjunctive completion [8,11], such as powerset extension. However, it can be very costly and widening operators for such domains are difficult to design [3].

There also exists much work on elaborating the control flow information of the program to improve the precision. Rival and Mauborgne [22] proposed the trace partitioning abstract domain, which is based on the partitioning of program traces. Sankaranarayanan et al. [24] showed that a fixed point computed over a powerset extension corresponds to a fixed point over the base domain computed on an elaboration of the control flow graph of the program. Simon [27] used a boolean flag to encode the union of two polyhedra and to perform control flow splitting when necessary.

This paper aims at designing abstract domains that can natively encode non-convex information. Until now, few existing abstract domains natively allow representing non-convex sets, e.g., congruences [12], max-plus polyhedra [2], domain lifting by max expressions [13], interval polyhedra [4].

The AVI domain that we introduce in this paper is closest to our previous work on the interval polyhedra domain [4]. The AVI domain is as expressive as the interval polyhedra domain, but differs from it in the following respects: First, the AVI domain enjoys optimal domain operations while operations in the interval polyhedra domain are not optimal; Second, for representation, the AVI domain uses the double description method while the interval polyhedra domain uses solely constraints; Third, to implement domain operations, the AVI domain employs Chernikova's algorithm while the interval polyhedra domain employs linear programming and Fourier-Motzkin elimination algorithms; Finally, prototype rAVI for the AVI domain is implemented via rational numbers while prototype *itvPol* for the interval polyhedra domain in [4] is implemented via floating point numbers.

7 Conclusion

In this paper, we present an analysis to discover linear absolute value relations among variables of a program ($\Sigma_k a_k x_k + \Sigma_k b_k |x_k| \leq c$), which generalizes the classic linear relation analysis ($\Sigma_k a_k x_k \leq c$) [9]. The analysis explores absolute value (AV) to describe piecewise linear relations in the program, as a mean to deal with non-convex or non-linear behaviors in the program. First, we show the equivalence among linear AV inequality systems, extended linear complementarity problem (XLCP) systems and interval linear inequality systems. The equivalence implies that linear AV relation analysis can be reused to infer other kinds of equivalent relations in a program, such as interval linear relations which is of high relevance in numeric static analysis [4]. Then, we construct a double description method for XLCP on top of that for convex polyhedra. On this basis, we propose an abstract domain of linear AV inequalities that natively allows expressing non-convex properties and enjoys optimal transfer functions. The AVI domain is implemented using rational numbers based on the double description method for XLCP. Experimental results are encouraging: The AVI domain can discover interesting non-convex properties, especially for programs involving piecewise linear behaviors.

It remains for future work to consider automatic methods to introduce auxiliary variables on the fly that can be used inside the AV function to improve the precision of AVI analysis. Another direction of work is to consider weakly relational abstract domains over absolute value, with less expressiveness but higher efficiency.

References

1. Gnu multiple precision arithmetic library, `http://gmplib.org/`.
2. Allamigeon, X., Gaubert, S., Goubault, E.: Inferring min and max invariants using max-plus polyhedra. In: Alpuente, M., Vidal, G. (eds.) SAS 2008. LNCS, vol. 5079, pp. 189–204. Springer, Heidelberg (2008)
3. Bagnara, R., Hill, P.M., Zaffanella, E.: Widening operators for powerset domains. In: Steffen, B., Levi, G. (eds.) VMCAI 2004. LNCS, vol. 2937, pp. 135–148. Springer, Heidelberg (2004)
4. Chen, L., Miné, A., Wang, J., Cousot, P.: Interval polyhedra: An abstract domain to infer interval linear relationships. In: Palsberg, J., Su, Z. (eds.) SAS 2009. LNCS, vol. 5673, pp. 309–325. Springer, Heidelberg (2009)
5. Chua, L.O., Deng, A.-C.: Canonical piecewise-linear representation. IEEE Trans. on Circuits and Systems 35(1), 101–111 (1988)
6. Cottle, R.W., Pang, J.-S., Stone, R.E.: The Linear Complementarity Problem. Academic Press, New York (1992)
7. Cousot, P., Cousot, R.: Abstract interpretation: a unified lattice model for static analysis of programs by construction or approximation of fixpoints. In: ACM POPL 1977, pp. 238–252. ACM Press, New York (1977)
8. Cousot, P., Cousot, R.: Systematic design of program analysis frameworks. In: ACM POPL 1979, pp. 269–282. ACM Press, New York (1979)
9. Cousot, P., Halbwachs, N.: Automatic discovery of linear restraints among variables of a program. In: ACM POPL 1978, pp. 84–96. ACM Press, New York (1978)
10. Garey, M.R., Johnson, D.S.: Computers and Intractability: A Guide to the Theory of NP-Completeness. W. H. Freeman & Co, New York (1979)
11. Giacobazzi, R., Ranzato, F.: Optimal domains for disjunctive abstract interpretation. Sci. Comput. Program 32(1-3), 177–210 (1998)
12. Granger, P.: Static analysis of arithmetical congruences. International Journal of Computer Mathematics, 165–199 (1989)
13. Gulavani, B.S., Gulwani, S.: A numerical abstract domain based on expression abstraction and max operator with application in timing analysis. In: Gupta, A., Malik, S. (eds.) CAV 2008. LNCS, vol. 5123, pp. 370–384. Springer, Heidelberg (2008)
14. Halbwachs, N., Proy, Y.E., Roumanoff, P.: Verification of real-time systems using linear relation analysis. Formal Methods in System Design 11(2), 157–185 (1997)

15. Jeannet, B., Miné, A.: Apron: A library of numerical abstract domains for static analysis. In: Bouajjani, A., Maler, O. (eds.) CAV 2009. LNCS, vol. 5643, pp. 661–667. Springer, Heidelberg (2009)
16. Lalire, G., Argoud, M., Jeannet, B.: Interproc., http://pop-art.inrialpes.fr/people/bjeannet/bjeannet-forge/interproc/
17. Laviron, V., Logozzo, F.: Subpolyhedra: A (more) scalable approach to infer linear inequalities. In: Jones, N.D., Müller-Olm, M. (eds.) VMCAI 2009. LNCS, vol. 5403, pp. 229–244. Springer, Heidelberg (2009)
18. LeVerge, H.: A note on Chernikova's algorithm. Technical Report 635, IRISA, France (1992)
19. Mangasarian, O.L., Pang, J.S.: The extended linear complementarity problem. SIAM J. Matrix Anal. Appl. 16(2), 359–368 (1995)
20. Miné, A.: Relational abstract domains for the detection of floating-point run-time errors. In: Schmidt, D. (ed.) ESOP 2004. LNCS, vol. 2986, pp. 3–17. Springer, Heidelberg (2004)
21. Miné, A.: The octagon abstract domain. Higher-Order and Symbolic Computation 19(1), 31–100 (2006)
22. Rival, X., Mauborgne, L.: The trace partitioning abstract domain. ACM Transactions on Programming Languages and Systems (TOPLAS) 29(5) (2007)
23. Rohn, J.: Solvability of systems of interval linear equations and inequalities. In: Linear Optimization Problems with Inexact Data, pp. 35–77. Springer, Heidelberg (2006)
24. Sankaranarayanan, S., Ivancic, F., Shlyakhter, I., Gupta, A.: Static analysis in disjunctive numerical domains. In: Yi, K. (ed.) SAS 2006. LNCS, vol. 4134, pp. 3–17. Springer, Heidelberg (2006)
25. Sankaranarayanan, S., Sipma, H., Manna, Z.: Scalable analysis of linear systems using mathematical programming. In: Cousot, R. (ed.) VMCAI 2005. LNCS, vol. 3385, pp. 25–41. Springer, Heidelberg (2005)
26. Schrijver, A.: Theory of linear and integer programming. John Wiley & Sons, Inc., Chichester (1986)
27. Simon, A.: Splitting the Control Flow with Boolean Flags. In: Alpuente, M., Vidal, G. (eds.) SAS 2008. LNCS, vol. 5079, pp. 315–331. Springer, Heidelberg (2008)
28. Simon, A., King, A., Howe, J.M.: Two Variables per Linear Inequality as an Abstract Domain. In: Leuschel, M. (ed.) LOPSTR 2002. LNCS, vol. 2664, pp. 71–89. Springer, Heidelberg (2003)

Generalizing the Template Polyhedral Domain*

Michael A. Colón[1] and Sriram Sankaranarayanan[2]

[1] U.S. Naval Research Laboratory, Washington, DC
colon@itd.nrl.navy.mil
[2] University of Colorado, Boulder, CO
srirams@colorado.edu

Abstract. Template polyhedra generalize weakly relational domains by specifying arbitrary fixed linear expressions on the left-hand sides of inequalities and undetermined constants on the right. The domain operations required for analysis over template polyhedra can be computed in polynomial time using linear programming. In this paper, we introduce the generalized template polyhedral domain that extends template polyhedra using fixed left-hand side expressions with bilinear forms involving program variables and unknown parameters to the right. We prove that the domain operations over generalized templates can be defined as the "best possible abstractions" of the corresponding polyhedral domain operations. The resulting analysis can straddle the entire space of linear relation analysis starting from the template domain to the full polyhedral domain.

We show that analysis in the generalized template domain can be performed by dualizing the join, post-condition and widening operations. We also investigate the special case of template polyhedra wherein each bilinear form has at most two parameters. For this domain, we use the special properties of two dimensional polyhedra and techniques from fractional linear programming to derive domain operations that can be implemented in polynomial time over the number of variables in the program and the size of the polyhedra. We present applications of generalized template polyhedra to strengthen previously obtained invariants by converting them into templates. We describe an experimental evaluation of an implementation over several benchmark systems.

1 Introduction

In this paper, we present some generalizations of the template polyhedral domain. Template polyhedral domains [34,32] were introduced in our earlier work as a generalization of domains such as *intervals* [10], *octagons* [28], *octahedra* [7], *pentagons* [26] and *logahedra* [20]. The characteristic feature of these domains is

* This material is based upon work supported by the National Science Foundation (NSF) under Grant No. 0953941 and the Office of Naval Research (ONR). Any opinions, findings, and conclusions or recommendations expressed in this material are those of the author(s) and do not necessarily reflect the views of NSF or ONR.

G. Barthe (Ed.): ESOP 2011, LNCS 6602, pp. 176–195, 2011.
© Springer-Verlag Berlin Heidelberg 2011

that assertions are restricted to a form that makes the analysis tractable. For instance, the assertions involved in the octagon domain are of the form $\pm x \pm y \leq c$ for each pair of program variables x and y, along with some unspecified constant $c \in \mathbb{R}$. The goal of the program analysis is to discover a suitable set of constants so that the resulting assertions are inductive, or equivalently, form a (post-) fixed point under the program's semantics [11].

In this paper, we generalize template polyhedral domains to consider templates with a linear expression on the left-hand side and a bilinear form on the right-hand side that specifies a parameterized linear expression. For instance, our analysis can handle template inequalities of the form $x - y \leq c_1 z + c_2 w + d$, wherein x, y, z, w are program variables and c_1, c_2, d are unknown parameters for which values will be computed by the analysis so that the entire expression forms a program invariant. This generalization can straddle the space of numerical domains from weakly relational domains (bilinear form is an unknown constant) to the full polyhedral domain (bilinear form has all the program variables) [12,8]. The main contributions of this paper are as follows:

- We generalize template polyhedra to consider the case where each template can be of the form $e \leq f$, wherein e is a linear expression over the program variables and f is a bilinear form over the program variables involving unknown parameters that are to be instantiated by the analysis.
- We prove that the domain operations can be performed *output sensitively* in polynomial time for the special case of two unknown parameters in each template. Our technique uses *fractional linear programming* [5] to simulate Jarvis's march for two dimensional polyhedra [9,23].
- We describe potential applications of our ideas to improve fixed points computed by other numerical domain analyses. These applications partially address the question of how to select generalized templates and use them in a numerical domain analysis framework.

We evaluate our approach against polyhedral analysis by using generalized templates to improve the fixed points computed by polyhedral analysis on several benchmark programs taken from the literature [3,34]. We find that the ideas presented in this paper help to improve the fixed point in many of these benchmarks by discovering new relations not implied by the previously computed fixed points.

2 Preliminaries

Throughout the paper, let $\mathbb{R}$ represent the set of real numbers. We fix a set of *variables* $X = \{x_1, \ldots, x_n\}$, which often correspond to the variables of the program under study.

Polyhedra. We recall some standard results on polyhedra. A *linear expression* e is of the form $a_1x_1 + \cdots + a_nx_n + b$, wherein each $a_i \in \mathbb{R}$ and $b \in \mathbb{R}$. The expression is said to be *homogeneous* if $b = 0$. For a linear expression $e = a_1x_1 + \cdots + a_nx_n + b$, let $\textsc{vars}(e) = \{x_i | a_i \neq 0\}$.

Definition 1 (Linear Assertions). *A* linear inequality *is of the form* $a_1x_1 + \cdots + a_nx_n + b \leq 0$. *A* linear assertion *is a finite conjunction of linear inequalities.*

Note that the linear inequality $0 \leq 0$ represents the assertion *true*, whereas the inequality $1 \leq 0$ represents *false*. An assertion can be written in matrix form as $A\boldsymbol{x} \leq \boldsymbol{b}$, where A is an $m \times n$ matrix, while $\boldsymbol{x} = (x_1, \ldots, x_n)$ and $\boldsymbol{b} = (b_1, \ldots, b_m)$ are n- and m-dimensional vectors, respectively. The ith row of the matrix form is an inequality that will be written as $A_i\boldsymbol{x} \leq \boldsymbol{b}_i$. Note that each equality is represented by a pair of inequalities. The set of points in $\mathbb{R}^n$ satisfying a linear assertion $\varphi : A\boldsymbol{x} \leq \boldsymbol{b}$ is denoted $[\![\varphi]\!] : \{\boldsymbol{x} \in \mathbb{R}^n \mid A\boldsymbol{x} \leq \boldsymbol{b}\}$. Such a set is called a *polyhedron*. Given two linear assertions φ_1 and φ_2, we define the entailment relation $\varphi_1 \models \varphi_2$ iff $[\![\varphi_1]\!] \subseteq [\![\varphi_2]\!]$.

The representation of a polyhedron by a linear assertion is known as its *constraint representation*. Alternatively, a polyhedron can be represented explicitly by a finite set of vertices and rays, known as its *generator representation*. There are several well-known algorithms for converting from one representation to the other. Highly engineered implementations of these algorithms such as the Apron [24] and Parma Polyhedral (PPL) [2] libraries implement the conversion between constraint and genrator representations, which is a key primitive for implementing the domain operations required to carry out abstract interpretation over polyhedra [12]. Nevertheless, conversion between the constraint and the generator representations still remains intractable for polyhedra involving a large number of variables and constraints.

Linear Programming. We briefly describe the theory of linear programming. Details may be found in standard textbooks, such as Schrijver [35].

Definition 2 (Linear Programming). *A canonical instance of the* linear programming (LP) problem *is of the form* $\mathsf{min.}\ \ e\ \mathsf{s.t.}\ \ \varphi$, *for a linear assertion* φ *and a linear expression* e, *called the* objective function.

The goal is to determine a solution of φ for which e is minimal. An LP problem can have one of three results: (1) an optimal solution; (2) $-\infty$, i.e, e is unbounded from below in φ; and (3) $+\infty$, i.e, φ has no solutions.

It is well-known that an optimal solution, if it exists, is realized at a vertex of the polyhedron. Therefore, the optimal solution can be found by evaluating e at each of the vertices. Enumerating all the vertices is very inefficient because the number of generators can be exponential in the number of constraints in the worst-case. The popular SIMPLEX algorithm (due to Danzig [35]) employs a sophisticated hill-climbing strategy that converges on an optimal vertex without necessarily enumerating all vertices. In theory, SIMPLEX is worst-case exponential. However, in practice, SIMPLEX is efficient for most problems. Interior point methods and ellipsoidal techniques are guaranteed to solve linear programs in polynomial time [5].

Fractional Linear Programs. Fractional Linear Programs (FLPs) will form an important primitive for computing abstractions and transfer functions of generalized template polyhedra. We describe the basic facts about these in this section. More details about FLPs are available elsewhere [5].

Definition 3. *A fractional linear program is an optimization problem of the following form:*

$$\text{min.}\ \frac{\boldsymbol{a}^T\boldsymbol{x} + a_0}{\boldsymbol{c}^T\boldsymbol{x} + c_0}\ \text{s.t.}\ A\boldsymbol{x} \leq \boldsymbol{b},\ \boldsymbol{c}^T\boldsymbol{x} + c_0 > 0\,. \tag{1}$$

A fractional linear program can be solved by *homogenizing* it to an "equivalent" LP [5]:

$$\text{min.}\ \boldsymbol{a}^T\boldsymbol{x} + a_0 z\ \text{s.t.}\ A\boldsymbol{x} \leq \boldsymbol{b}z\ \wedge \boldsymbol{c}^T\boldsymbol{x} + c_0 z = 1\ \wedge\ z \geq 0\,. \tag{2}$$

If the LP (2) has an optimal solution $(\boldsymbol{x}^*, z^*)$ such that $z^* > 0$ then $\frac{1}{z^*}\boldsymbol{x}^*$ is an optimal solution to the FLP (1). Furthermore, $\frac{1}{z^*}\boldsymbol{x}^*$ is also a vertex of the polyhedron $A\boldsymbol{x} \leq \boldsymbol{b}$. If, on the other hand, $z^* = 0$, the optimal solution to (1) is an extreme ray of the polyhedron $A\boldsymbol{x} \leq \boldsymbol{b}$. Finally if LP (2) is infeasible then the FLP (1) is infeasible.

Transition Systems. We will briefly define transition systems over real-valued variables as the model of computation used throughout this paper. It is possible to abstract a given program written in a language such as C or Java with arrays, pointers and dynamic memory calls into abstract numerical models. Details of this translation, known as *memory modeling*, are available elsewhere [22,6,4]. To ensure simplicity, our presentation here does not include techniques for handling function calls. Nevertheless, function calls can be handled using standard extensions of this approach.

Definition 4 (Transition System). *A* transition system Π *is represented by a tuple* $\langle X, L, \mathcal{T}, \ell_0, \Theta\rangle$*, where*

- $X = \{x_1, \ldots, x_n\}$ *is a set of* variables. *For each variable* $x_i \in X$*, there is an associated* primed variable x_i'*, and the set of primed variables is denoted by* X'*. The variables of* X *are collectively denoted as a vector* $\boldsymbol{x}$*;*
- L *is a finite set of* locations*;*
- $\mathcal{T}$ *is a finite set of* transitions. *Each transition* $\tau \in \mathcal{T}$ *consists of a tuple* $\tau : \langle \ell, m, \rho_\tau\rangle$ *wherein* $\ell, m \in L$ *are the* pre- *and the* post-locations *of the transition,* $\rho_\tau[X, X']$ *is the* transition relation *that relates the current state variables* X *and the next-state variables* X'*;*
- $\ell_0 \in L$ *represents the* initial location*; and*
- Θ *is the* initial condition, *specified as an assertion over* X*. It represents the set of initial values of the program variables.*

A transition system is *linear* iff the variables X range over the domain of real numbers, each transition $\tau \in \mathcal{T}$ has a *linear transition relation* ρ_τ that is represented as a linear assertion over $X \cup X'$, and finally, the initial condition Θ is a linear assertion over X. Further details on transition systems, including their operational semantics and the definition of invariants, are available from standard references [27].

3 Generalized Templates

In this section, we introduce the *generalized template domain.* To begin with, we recall expression templates. A template T is a set of homogeneous linear expressions $\{e_1, \ldots, e_m\}$ over program variables X. The approach of template expressions was formalized in our previous work [34,32]. Let $X = \{x_1, \ldots, x_n\}$ be the set of program variables and $C = \{c_1, c_2, \ldots, d_1, d_2, \ldots\}$ denote a set of unknown *parameters.*

Definition 5 (Bilinear Form). *A* bilinear form *over X and C is given by an expression of the form*

$$f: \left(\sum_{i\in I} c_i x_i\right) + d, \text{ wherein } I \subseteq \{1, \ldots, n\}$$

Given the bilinear form f above, let $\text{VARS}(f) : \{x_i \mid i \in I\}$ *and let* $\text{PARS}(f) : \{c_i \mid i \in I\} \cup \{d\}$ *denote the parameters involved in f.*

Given a mapping $\mu : C \to \mathbb{R}$, a bilinear form $f : d + \sum_{i\in I} c_i x_i$ can be mapped to the linear expression $f[\mu] : \mu(d) + \sum_{i\in I} \mu(c_i)x_i$

Definition 6 (Generalized Templates). *A* generalized template *G consists of a set of entries: $G = \{(e_1, f_1), \ldots, (e_m, f_m)\}$, where for each $i \in \{1, \ldots, m\}$, e_i is a homogeneous linear expression over X, and f_i is a bilinear form over C and X. The entry (e_j, f_j) represents the linear inequality $e_j \leq f_j$, where the left-hand side is a fixed linear expression and the right-hand side is a parameterized linear expression represented as a bilinear form.*

We assume that two bilinear forms f_i and f_j, for $i \neq j$, cannot share common parameters, i.e., $\text{PARS}(f_i) \cap \text{PARS}(f_j) = \emptyset$. *Finally, we assume that for each entry (e_i, f_i) in a generalized template G,* $\text{VARS}(e_i) \cap \text{VARS}(f_i) = \emptyset$, *i.e, the left- and right-hand sides share no variables.*

Example 1. Consider program variables $X = \{x_1, x_2, x_3\}$ and parameters $C = \{c_1, c_2, c_3, c_4, d_1, d_2, d_3\}$. An example of a generalized template follows:

$$G: \left\{ \begin{array}{ll} (e_1 : x_1 & , \ f_1 : c_1x_2 + c_2x_3 + d_1), \\ (e_2 : x_2 & , \ f_2 : c_3x_3 + d_2), \\ (e_3 : x_3 - 2x_1 & , \ f_3 : c_4x_2 + d_3) \end{array} \right\}.$$

Notation. For a bilinear form f_j, will use the variable d_j to denote the constant coefficient and $c_{j,k}$ to denote the parameter for the coefficient of the variable x_k.

Generalized templates define an infinite family of convex polyhedra called *generalized template polyhedra.*

Definition 7 (Generalized Template Polyhedron). *Given a template G, a polyhedron $\varphi : \bigwedge_i \ A_i\boldsymbol{x} \leq \boldsymbol{b}_i$ is a* generalized template polyhedron *(GTP) iff φ is the empty polyhedron, or each inequality $\varphi_i : \ A_i\boldsymbol{x} \leq \boldsymbol{b}_i$ in φ can be cast as the instantiation of some entry $(e_j, f_j) \in G$ in one of the following ways:*

Vertex Instantiation: $\varphi_i : \; e_j \leq f_j[\mu_{ij}]$ *for some map* $\mu_{ij} : \textsc{pars}(f_j) \to \mathbb{R}$ *that instantiates the parameters in* $\textsc{pars}(f_j)$ *to some real values.*
Ray Instantiation: $\varphi_i : \; \mathbf{0} \leq f_j[\mu_{ij}]$ *for some map* $\mu_{ij} : \textsc{pars}(f_j) \to \mathbb{R}$.

The rationale behind ray instantiation will be made clear presently. A *conformance map* γ between a GTP $\varphi : A\boldsymbol{x} \leq \boldsymbol{b}$ and its generalized template G, maps every inequality $\varphi_i : A_i\boldsymbol{x} \leq \boldsymbol{b}_i$ to some entry $\gamma(i) \in G$ so that φ_i may be viewed as a vertex or a ray instantiation of the template entry $\gamma(i)$. If a conformance map exists, then φ is said to *conform* to G.

If φ is a GTP that conforms to the template G, it is possible that (1) a single inequality in φ can be expressed as instantiations of multiple entries in G, and (2) a single entry (e_j, f_j) can be instantiated as multiple inequalities (or no inequalities) in φ. In other words, conformance maps between φ and G, can be many-to-one and non-surjective.

Example 2. Recalling the template G from Example 1, the polyhedron $\varphi_1 \wedge \cdots \wedge \varphi_4$, below, conforms to G:

$$\begin{array}{l|l} \varphi_1 & x_1 \leq 1 \\ \varphi_2 & x_1 \leq x_3 - 10 \end{array} \qquad \begin{array}{l|l} \varphi_3 & x_2 \qquad\quad \leq 2x_3 - 10 \\ \varphi_4 & x_3 - 2x_1 \leq 3x_2 + 1 \end{array}$$

The conformance map is given by

$$\gamma : 1 \mapsto (e_1, f_1), 2 \mapsto (e_1, f_1), 3 \mapsto (e_2, f_2), 4 \mapsto (e_3, f_3)\,.$$

On the other hand, the polyhedron $x_1 \leq 1 \;\wedge\; x_1 \geq 5$, does not conform to G, whose definition in this example does not permit lower bounds for the variable x_1. ■

We now describe the abstract domain of generalized templates, consisting of all the generalized template polyhedra (GTP) that conform to the template G. We will denote the set of all GTPs given a template G as Ψ_G and use the standard entailment amongst linear assertions as the ordering amongst GTPs. Theorem 2 shows that the structure $\langle \Psi_G, \models \rangle$, induced by the generalized template G, is a lattice.

Note 1. Using ray instantiations, the empty polyhedron *false* can be viewed as a GTP for any template G. We define the two polyhedra *true* and *false* to belong to Ψ_G for any G, including $G = \emptyset$.

Abstraction. We now define the abstraction map α_G that transforms a given convex polyhedron $\varphi : A\boldsymbol{x} \leq \boldsymbol{b}$ into a GTP $\psi_G : \; \alpha_G(\varphi)$. If φ is empty, then the abstraction $\alpha_G(\varphi)$ is defined to be *false*. For the ensuing discussion, we assume that φ is a non-empty polyhedron. Our abstraction map is the *best possible*, yielding the "smallest" GTP in Ψ_G through a process of dualization using Farkas' lemma [8]:

(1) For each $(e_j, f_j) \in G$, we wish to compute the set of all values of the unknown parameters in $\textsc{pars}(f_j)$ so that the entailment $\varphi : A\boldsymbol{x} \leq \boldsymbol{b} \models e_j \leq f_j$ holds. For convenience, we express $e_j \leq f_j$ as $\boldsymbol{c}^T\boldsymbol{x} \leq d$ wherein $\boldsymbol{c}, d$ consist of linear expressions over the unknowns in $\textsc{pars}(f_i)$.

(2) Applying Farkas' lemma to the entailment above yields a dual polyhedron φ_j^D, whose variables include the unknowns in $\text{PARS}(f_j)$ and some vector of *multipliers* $\boldsymbol{\lambda}$. This dual polyhedron is written as:

$$A\boldsymbol{x} \le \boldsymbol{b} \models \boldsymbol{c}^T\boldsymbol{x} \le d\,, \text{ holds}$$
$$\text{iff}$$
$$\varphi_j^D : (\exists\, \boldsymbol{\lambda} \ge 0)\ A^T\boldsymbol{\lambda} = \boldsymbol{c},\ \boldsymbol{b}^T\boldsymbol{\lambda} \le d.$$

(3) We eliminate the multipliers $\boldsymbol{\lambda}$ from φ_j^D to obtain ψ_j over variables $\text{PARS}(f_j)$.
(4) If ψ_j is empty, then the abstraction is defined as the universal polyhedron. Otherwise, each vertex $\boldsymbol{v}_i$ of ψ_j is instantiated to an inequality by *vertex instantiation*: $e_j \le f_j[\text{PARS}(f_j) \mapsto \boldsymbol{v}_i]$ Similarly, each ray $\boldsymbol{r}_k$ of ψ_j is instantiated to an inequality by *ray instantiation*: $\boldsymbol{0} \le f_j[\text{PARS}(f_j) \mapsto \boldsymbol{r}_k]$.

The overall result is the conjunction of all inequalities obtained by vertex and ray instantiation for all the entries of G. In practice, this result has many redundant constraints. These redundancies can be eliminated using LP solvers [32].

In the general case, the elimination of $\boldsymbol{\lambda}$ in step (3) may be computed exactly using the double description method [31] or Fourier-Motzkin elimination [35]. However, in Section 4 we show techniques where the elimination can be performed in output-sensitive polynomial time when $|\text{PARS}(f_j)| \le 2$ (even when $|\boldsymbol{\lambda}|$ is arbitrary) using fractional linear programming. In Section 5, we show how the result of the elimination can be *approximated* soundly using LP solvers.

Theorem 1. *For any polyhedron φ and template G, let $\psi : \alpha_G(\varphi)$ be the abstraction computed using the procedure above. (A) ψ is a GTP conforming to G, i.e, $\psi \in \Psi_G$, (B) $\varphi \models \psi$ and (C) ψ is the best abstraction of φ in the lattice: $(\forall \psi' \in \Psi_G)\ \varphi \models \psi'$ iff $\psi \models \psi'$.*

Proofs of all the theorems will be provided in an extended version of this paper. As a consequence, the existence of a best abstraction allows us to prove that $\langle \Psi_G, \models \rangle$ is itself a lattice.

Theorem 2. *The structure $\langle \Psi_G, \models \rangle$ forms a lattice, and furthermore, the maps $(\alpha_G, \mathsf{identity})$ form a Galois connection between this lattice and the lattice of polyhedra.*

Example 3 (Abstraction). We illustrate the process of abstraction through an example. Consider the polyhedron φ over two variables x, y:

$$\varphi : x \le 2\ \wedge\ x \ge 1\ \wedge\ y \le 2\ \wedge\ y \ge 1\,.$$

We wish to compute $\alpha_G(\varphi)$ for the following template $\left\{ \begin{array}{l} (e_1 :\ x, f_1 :\ c_1 y + d_1) \\ (e_2 :\ y, f_2 :\ c_2 x + d_2) \end{array} \right\}$.
We will now illustrate computing the polyhedron $\psi_1[c_1, d_1]$ corresponding to the entry $(e_1 :\ x, f_1 :\ c_1 y + d_1)$. To do so, we wish to find values of c_1, d_1 that

satisfy the entailment $\varphi : (x \in [1,2] \ \wedge \ y \in [1,2]) \models x \leq c_1 y + d_1$. Dualizing, using Farkas' lemma, we obtain the following constraints

$$(\exists \lambda_1, \lambda_2, \lambda_3, \lambda_4 \geq 0) \begin{bmatrix} \lambda_1 - \lambda_2 = 1 \\ \lambda_3 - \lambda_4 = -c_1 \\ 2\lambda_1 - \lambda_2 + 2\lambda_3 - \lambda_4 \leq d_1 \end{bmatrix}.$$

Eliminating $\lambda_{1,2,3,4}$ yields the polyhedron: $\psi_1 : \ c_1 + d_1 \geq 2 \ \wedge \ 2c_1 + d_1 \geq 2$. The polyhedron ψ_1 has a vertex $\boldsymbol{v}_1 : (0, 2)$ and rays $\boldsymbol{r}_1 : (1, -1)$ and $\boldsymbol{r}_2 : (-\frac{1}{2}, 1)$.

We obtain the inequality $e_1 \leq f_1[\boldsymbol{v}_1] : x \leq 0y + 2$ by instantiating the vertex. Similarly, instantiating using *ray instantiation* yields: $0 \leq f_1[\boldsymbol{r}_1] : 0 \leq y - 1$ and $0 \leq f_1[\boldsymbol{r}_2] : 0 \leq \frac{-1}{2} y + 1$. Considering the second entry (e_2, f_2) yields the inequality $y \leq 2$ through a vertex instantiation and the inequalities $x \geq 1$ and $x \leq 2$ using ray instantiation. Conjoining the results from both entries, we obtain $\alpha_G(\varphi)$, which is equivalent to φ. ■

Why Ray Instantiation? We can now explain the rationale behind ray instantiation in our domain. If ray instantiation is not included then the best abstraction clause in Theorem 1 will no longer hold (see proof in extended version). Example 4, below, serves as a counter-example. Further, $\langle \Psi_G, \models \rangle$ is no longer a lattice since the least upper bound Ψ_G may no longer exist. This can complicate the construction of the abstract domain. Ray instantiations are necessary to capture the rays of the dual polytope obtained in step (3) of the abstraction process. Let us assume that $\boldsymbol{r}$ is a ray of a dual polytope $\psi[\boldsymbol{c}]$ that contains all values of $\boldsymbol{c}$ so that the primal entailment $\varphi \models e_i \leq f_i[\boldsymbol{c}]$ holds. In other words, for any $\boldsymbol{c}_0 \in [\![\psi]\!]$, the inequality $I : e_i \leq f_i[\boldsymbol{c}_0]$ is entailed by φ. If ψ contains a ray $\boldsymbol{r}$ then $\boldsymbol{c}_0 + \gamma \boldsymbol{r} \in [\![\psi]\!]$ for any $\gamma \geq 0$. This models infinitely many inequalities, all of which are consequences of φ:

$$\overline{I}(\gamma) : \ e_i \leq f_i[\boldsymbol{c}_0 + \gamma \boldsymbol{r}] = e_i \leq f_i[\boldsymbol{c}_0] + \gamma f_i[\boldsymbol{r}],$$

for $\gamma \geq 0$. Note that, in general, the inequality $\overline{I}(\gamma_1)$ need not be a consequence of $\overline{I}(\gamma_2)$ for $\gamma_1 \neq \gamma_2$. Including the ray instantiation $\hat{I} : \ \mathbf{0} \leq f_i[\boldsymbol{r}]$ allows us to write each inequality $\overline{I}(\gamma)$ as a proper consequence of just two inequalities $I, \hat{I}$, i.e, $\overline{I}(\gamma) : I + \gamma \hat{I}$.

Example 4. If ray instantiation is disallowed, then the abstraction $\alpha_G(\varphi)$ obtained for Example 3 will be $x \leq 2 \wedge y \leq 2$. However, this is no longer the best abstraction possible. For example, each polyhedron $x \leq 2 \wedge y \leq 2 \wedge x \leq \alpha y + 2 - \alpha$, for $\alpha \geq 0$, belongs to Ψ_G and is a better abstraction. However, larger values of α yield strictly stronger abstractions without necessarily having a strongest abstraction. Allowing ray instantiation lets us capture the inequality $0 \leq y - 1$ so that there is once again a best abstraction. ■

Post-Conditions. We now discuss the computation of post-conditions (transfer functions) across a transition $\tau : \langle \ell, m, \rho_\tau[\boldsymbol{x}, \boldsymbol{x}'] \rangle$.

Let φ be a GTP conforming to a template G. Our goal is to compute $post_G(\varphi, \tau)$, given a transition τ. Since $\rho_\tau[\boldsymbol{x}, \boldsymbol{x}']$ is a linear assertion, the best post-condition that we may hope for is given by the abstraction of the post-condition over the polyhedral domain: $\alpha_G(post_{poly}(\varphi, \tau))$. We show that the post-condition $post_G(\varphi, \tau)$ can be computed effectively, without computing $post_{poly}$, by modifying the algorithm for computing α_G.

1. Compute a convex polyhedron $P[\boldsymbol{x}, \boldsymbol{x}'] :\ \varphi \wedge\ \rho_\tau[\boldsymbol{x}, \boldsymbol{x}']$ whose variables range over both the current and the next state variables: $\boldsymbol{x}, \boldsymbol{x}'$. If P is empty, then the result of post-condition is empty.
2. For each entry $(e_j, f_j) \in G$, we consider the entailment $P[\boldsymbol{x}, \boldsymbol{x}'] \models e_j[\boldsymbol{x} \mapsto \boldsymbol{x}'] \leq f_j[\boldsymbol{x} \mapsto \boldsymbol{x}']$.
3. Dualizing, using Farkas' lemma, we compute a polyhedron ψ_j over the parameters in $\text{PARS}(f_j)$.
4. If ψ_j is non-empty, instantiate the inequalities of the result using the vertices and rays of ψ_j. The result is the conjunction of all the vertex-instantiated and ray-instantiated inequalities.

Theorem 3. $post_G(\varphi, \tau) = \alpha_G(post_{poly}(\varphi, \tau))$.

For the case of transition relations that arise from assignments in basic blocks of programs, the post-condition computation can be optimized by substituting the next state variables $\boldsymbol{x}'$ with expressions in terms of $\boldsymbol{x}$ before computing the dualization.

Example 5 (Post-Condition Computation). Recall the template G from Example 3. Let $\varphi :\ x \in [1, 2],\ y \in [1, 2]$. Consider the transition τ with transition relation ρ_τ:

$$\rho_\tau[x, y, x', y'] :\ x' = x + 1\ \wedge\ y' = y + 1\,.$$

Our goal is to compute $post_G(\varphi, \tau)$. To do so, we first compute $P :\ \varphi\ \wedge\ \rho_\tau$:

$$P[\boldsymbol{x}, \boldsymbol{x}'] :\ 1 \leq x \leq 2\ \wedge\ 1 \leq y \leq 2\ \wedge\ x' = x + 1\ \wedge\ y' = y + 1\,.$$

We consider the entailment $P \models x' \leq c_1 y' + d_1$ arising from the first entry of the template. We may substitute $x + 1$ for x' and $y + 1$ for y' in the entailment yielding:

$$x \in [1, 2]\ \wedge\ y \in [1, 2]\ \models\ x + 1 \leq c_1(y + 1) + d_1\ \ =\ \ x \leq c_1 y + (d_1 + c_1 - 1)\,.$$

After dualizing and eliminating the multipliers, we obtain $\psi_1[c_1, d_1] : 2c_1 + d_1 \geq 3 \wedge 3c_1 + d_1 \geq 3$. This is generated by the vertex $\boldsymbol{v}_1 : (3, 0)$ and rays $\boldsymbol{r}_1 :\ (\frac{1}{2}, -1)$ and $\boldsymbol{r}_2 :\ (\frac{-1}{3}, 1)$, yielding inequalities $x \leq 3,\ y \leq 3,$ and $y \geq 2$ through vertex and ray instantiation. The overall post-condition is $x \in [2, 3], y \in [2, 3]$. ■

For common program assignments of the form $x := x + c$, where c is a constant, the post-condition computation can be optimized so that dualization can be avoided. Similar optimizations are possible for assignments of the form $x := c$. The post-condition for non-linear transitions can be obtained by abstracting them as (interval) linear assignments or using non-linear programming techniques. We refer the reader to work by Miné for more details [29].

Join. Join over the polyhedral domain is computed by the convex hull operation. For the case of GTPs, join is obtained by first computing the convex hull and then abstracting it using α_G. However, this can be more expensive than computing the polyhedral convex hull. We provide an alternate and less expensive scheme that is once again based on Farkas' lemma. This join will be effectively computable in output-sensitive polynomial time when $|\text{PARS}(f_j)| \le 2$ for each template entry.

Let φ_1 and φ_2 be two GTPs conforming to a template G. We wish to compute the join $\varphi_1 \sqcup_G \varphi_2$ that is the least upper bound of φ_1 and φ_2 in Ψ_G.

1. For each entry $(e_j, f_j) \in G$, we encode the entailments
$$\varphi_1 \models e_j \le f_j \text{ and } \varphi_2 \models e_j \le f_j .$$
2. Let $\psi_1[\text{PARS}(f_j)]$ and $\psi_2[\text{PARS}(f_j)]$ be the polyhedra that result from encoding the entailments using Farkas' lemma and eliminating the multipliers for φ_1 and φ_2, respectively.
3. Let $\psi : \psi_1 \wedge \psi_2$ be the intersection. ψ captures all the linear inequalities that (a) fit the template $e_j \le f_j$ and (b) are entailed by φ_1 as well as φ_2.
4. If ψ is non-empty, compute the generators of ψ and instantiate by vertex and ray instantiation.

The conjunction of all the inequalities so obtained for all the entries in G forms the resulting join.

Theorem 4. *For GTPs φ_1, φ_2 corresponding to template G, $\varphi : \varphi_1 \sqcup_G \varphi_2$ is the least upper bound in Ψ_G of φ_1 and φ_2.*

Widening. Given φ_1 and φ_2, the standard widening $\varphi_1 \nabla \varphi_2$ drops those inequalities of φ_1 that are not entailed by φ_2. The result is naturally guaranteed to be in Ψ_G provided φ_1 and φ_2 are. Furthermore, the entailment for each inequality can be checked using linear programming [32]. Termination of this scheme is immediate since we drop constraints. *Mutually redundant* constraints used in the standard polyhedral widening can also be considered for the widening [18].

Note 2. Care must be taken not to apply the abstraction operator on the result φ of the widening. It is possible to construct examples wherein widening may drop a redundant constraint in φ_1 that can be restored by the application of the α_G operator [28].

Inclusion Checking. Since our lattice uses the same ordering as polyhedra, inclusion checking can be performed in polynomial time using LP solvers.

Complexity. Thus far, we have presented the GTP domain. The complexity of various operations may vary depending on the representation chosen for GTPs. We assume that each GTP is represented as a set of constraints.

The abstraction of convex polyhedra, computation of join and computation of post-condition require the elimination of multipliers $\boldsymbol{\lambda}$ from the assertion obtained after dualization using Farkas' lemma. The number of multipliers $\boldsymbol{\lambda}$ equals the number of constraints in the polyhedron being abstracted. This number is of the same order as the number of variables in the program plus the number of constraints in the polyhedron. It still remains open if the elimination of the $\boldsymbol{\lambda}$ multipliers can be performed efficiently by avoiding the exponential blow-up that is common for general polyhedra. We present two techniques to avoid this problem:

1. We present algorithms for the special case when each template entry has no more than two parameters. In this case, our algorithms run in time that is polynomial in the sizes of the inputs and the outputs.
2. The problem of sound approximations of the results of the elimination that can be computed in polynomial time will be tackled in Section 5.

4 Two Parameters per Template Entry

In this section, we present efficient algorithms when each template entry has at most two parameters. Following the discussion on complexity in the previous section, we directly enumerate the generators of the projection of a dual form $P[c, d, \boldsymbol{\lambda}]$ onto c and d using repeated LP and FLP instances. The efficiency of the remaining operations over GTPs follow from the fact that they can all be reduced to computing α_G.

Abstraction. Our goal is to present an efficient algorithm for α_G when each entry of G has at most two unknown parameters. Specifically, let G be a template with entries of the form (e_i, f_i), wherein e_i is an arbitrary linear expression over the program variables and f_i is of the form $c_i x_j + d_i$, for some variable x_j and unknown parameters c_i, d_i.

Let $\varphi[x_1, \ldots, x_n]$ be a polyhedron over the program variables. If φ is empty, then the abstraction is empty. We assume for the remainder of this section that φ is a non-empty polyhedron. We compute $\alpha_G(\varphi)$ by dualizing the entailment below, for each entry (e_i, f_i):

$$\varphi[x_1, \ldots, x_n] \;\models\; e_i \leq c_i x_j + d_i \,. \tag{3}$$

Using Farkas' lemma, we obtain the dual form

$$\psi_i[c_i, d_i] : \; (\exists\, \boldsymbol{\lambda} \geq 0)\; P[c_i, d_i, \boldsymbol{\lambda}] \tag{4}$$

We present a technique that computes the vertices and rays of ψ_i using a series of fractional linear programs without explicitly eliminating $\boldsymbol{\lambda}$. We first note the following useful fact:

Lemma 1. *The vector $(0, 1)$ is a ray of ψ_i. Furthermore, since φ is non-empty, the vector $(0, -1)$ cannot be a ray of ψ_i.*

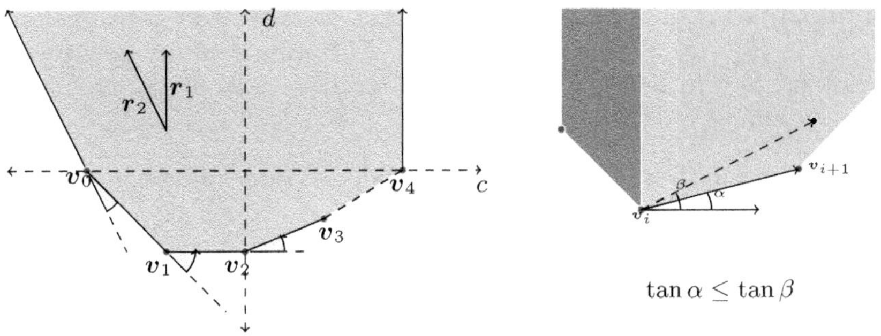

Fig. 1. Finding vertices and extreme rays of a 2D polygon by adapting Jarvis's march. The solid line connects vertices discovered so far. Each edge is discovered by means of an angle sweep starting from the previously discovered vertex.

4.1 Projecting to Two Dimensions Efficiently

In this section, we consider a polyhedron $P[c, d, \boldsymbol{\lambda}]$ as in (4). Our goal is to compute the vertices and rays of $\psi : (\exists \boldsymbol{\lambda})\ P$ efficiently. If P is empty, then the resulting projection is also the empty polyhedron. For the remainder of this section, P is assumed to be non-empty.

The overall technique for computing the vertices of ψ simulates Jarvis's march for computing the convex hull of a set of points in two dimensions [23,9]. In this case, however, the polyhedron P is specified implicitly as the projection of a higher dimensional polyhedron. Figure 1 illustrates the idea behind this algorithm. The algorithm starts with some initial point guaranteed to be on the boundary of the polyhedron. Given a vertex $\boldsymbol{v}_i$ (or the initial point), the next vertex or extreme ray is computed in two steps:

1. Sweep a ray in a clockwise or counterclockwise direction from the current vertex until it touches the polyhedron. This ray defines an edge of the projection. Our algorithm performs the ray sweep by solving a suitably formulated FLP.
2. Find the farthest point in the polyhedron along this edge. If a farthest point can be found, then it is a vertex of the projection. Otherwise, the edge is an extreme ray. This step is formulated as a linear program in our algorithm.

We now discuss Steps 1 and 2 in detail.

Finding an Edge Using FLP. Let $\boldsymbol{v} :\ (a, b)$ be some vertex of ψ. Consider the following optimization problem:

$$\text{min.}\ \frac{d-b}{c-a}\ \text{s.t.}\ \ c > a\ \wedge\ P[c, d, \boldsymbol{\lambda}] \tag{5}$$

In effect, the optimization yields a *direction of least slope* joining $(c, d) \in [\![\psi]\!]$ and (a, b), where $c > a$. The optimization problem above is a *fractional linear program* [5] (also Cf. Section 2).

Lemma 2. *(a) If the FLP* (5) *is infeasible, then there is no point to the right of* (a, b) *in* $[\![\psi]\!]$. *(b) For non-empty* φ*, the FLP cannot be unbounded. (c) An optimal solution to the FLP yields the direction of least slope, as required by Jarvis's march.*

Finding the Farthest Point Along an Edge. Once a direction with slope θ is found starting from a vertex (a, b), we wish to find a vertex along this direction. This vertex can be found by solving the following LP:

$$\text{max. } c - a \text{ s.t. } c - a \geq 0 \wedge d = b + \theta(c - a) \wedge P[c, d, \boldsymbol{\lambda}] \tag{6}$$

In effect, we seek the maximum offset along the direction θ starting from (a, b) such that the end point (c, d) remains in ψ. The LP above cannot be infeasible (since $(c, d) = (a, b)$ is a feasible point). If the LP above is unbounded then we obtain an extreme ray of ψ. Otherwise, we obtain an end-point that is a vertex of ψ. The overall algorithm is similar to Jarvis's march as presented in standard textbooks (Cf. Cormen, Leiserson and Rivest, Ch. 35.3 [9] or R.A. Jarvis's original paper [23]). Rather than perform a "clockwise" and a "counterclockwise" march, we make use of the fact that $(0, 1)$ is a ray of ψ and perform an equivalent "leftward" and a "rightward" march.

1. We start by finding some point on the boundary of ψ. Let $(a, b, \boldsymbol{\lambda})$ be some feasible point in P. We solve the problem $\text{min. } d \text{ s.t. } c = a \wedge P[c, d, \boldsymbol{\lambda}]$. The point $\boldsymbol{v}_0$ can be treated as a starting point that is guaranteed to lie on the boundary of ψ. Note, however, that $\boldsymbol{v}_0$ is not necessarilty a vertex of ψ. Since φ is assumed non-empty, the LP above cannot be unbounded.
2. We describe the rightward march. Each vertex $\boldsymbol{v}_{i+1}$ is discovered after computing $\boldsymbol{v}_1, \ldots, \boldsymbol{v}_i$. Let $\boldsymbol{v}_i : (a_i, b_i)$ be the last vertex discovered.
   (a) Obtain least slope by solving the FLP problem in (5).
   (b) If the FLP is infeasible, then stop. $\boldsymbol{v}_i$ is the right-most vertex and the vector $(0, 1)$ an extreme ray.
   (c) Solve the LP in (6). An optimal solution yields a vertex $\boldsymbol{v}_{i+1}$. Otherwise, if the LP is unbounded, we obtain an extreme ray of ψ and $\boldsymbol{v}_i$ is the right-most vertex.
3. The leftward march can be performed using the reflection $T : c' \mapsto -c, d' \mapsto d$, carried out as a substitution in the polyhedron P. The resulting generators are reflected back.

Each generator discovered by our algorithm requires solving FLP and LP instances. Furthermore, the initial point can itself be found by solving at most two LP instances. Since LPs and FLPs can be solved efficiently, we have presented an efficient, *output-sensitive* algorithm for performing the abstraction. This algorithm, in turn, can be used as a primitive to compute the join and the post-condition efficiently, as well.

Note 3. It must be mentioned that an efficient (output-sensitive) algorithm for each abstract domain operation does not necessarily imply that the overall analysis itself can also be performed efficiently in terms of program size and template size. For instance, it is conceivable that the intermediate polyhedra and their coefficients can grow arbitrarily large during the course of the analysis by repeated applications of joins and post-conditions. This is a possibility for most strongly-relational domains, including the two variables per inequality domain proposed by Simon et al. [37]. Nevertheless, in practice, we find that a careful implementation can control this blow-up effectively by means of widening.

5 Efficient Approximations

In Section 4, we discussed the special case in which each bilinear form in a template has at most two parameters. We presented an efficient algorithm for computing the abstraction operation. However, if $|\textsc{pars}(f_j)| > 2$, we are forced to resort to expensive elimination techniques using Fourier-Motzkin elimination [35] or the double description method [31]. An alternative is to perform the elimination approximately to obtain $\psi[\boldsymbol{c}, d]$ such that

$$\psi[\boldsymbol{c}, d] \models (\exists\, \boldsymbol{\lambda})\ P[\boldsymbol{c}, d, \boldsymbol{\lambda}]\,.$$

Note that, since we are working with the dual representation, we seek to *under-approximate* the result of the elimination.

We consider two methods for deriving an under-approximation of ψ_j by computing some of its generators. The under-approximations presented here are similar to those used in earlier work by Kanade *et al.* involving one of the authors of this paper [25].

Finding Vertices by Linear Programming. We simply solve k linear programs, each yielding a vertex, by choosing some fixed or random objective $f_i[\boldsymbol{c}, d]$ and solving $\mathsf{min.}\ f_i\ \mathsf{s.t.}\ P[\boldsymbol{c}, d, \boldsymbol{\lambda}],\ \boldsymbol{\lambda} \geq 0$. The solution yields a vertex (or a ray) of the feasible region $(\boldsymbol{c}, d, \boldsymbol{\lambda})$. By projecting $\boldsymbol{\lambda}$ out, we obtain a point inside ψ_j or a ray of ψ_j, alternatively.

Finding Vertices by Ray-Shooting. Choose a point $(\boldsymbol{c}_0, d_0)$ known to be inside ψ_j (using a linear programming). Let $\boldsymbol{r}$ be some direction. We seek a point of the form $(\boldsymbol{c}_0, d_0) + \gamma r$ for some $\gamma \in \mathbb{R}$ by solving the following LP:

$$\mathsf{max.}\ \ \gamma\ \mathsf{s.t.}\ \ ((\boldsymbol{c}_0, d_0) + \gamma \boldsymbol{r}) \in [\![P[\boldsymbol{c}, d, \boldsymbol{\lambda}]\ \wedge\ \boldsymbol{\lambda} \geq 0]\!]\,.$$

Any solution yields a point inside ψ_j by projection. If the LP is unbounded, we conclude that $\boldsymbol{r}$ is a ray of ψ_j.

We refer the reader to Kanade et al. [25] for more details on how under-approximation techniques described above can be used to control the size of the polyhedral representation.

6 Applications

In this section, we present two applications of the ideas presented thus far. In doing so, we seek to answer the following question: *how do we derive interesting templates without having the user of the analysis tool specify them*? Note that our previous work provides heuristics for guessing an initial set of templates in a property directed manner and enriching this set based on pre-condition computations [34].

Improving Fixed-Points. Template polyhedra can be used to improve post-fixed points that are computed using other known techniques for numerical domains. For instance, suppose we perform a polyhedral analysis for some program and compute invariants $\varphi : e_1 \leq 0, \ldots, e_m \leq 0$ for linear expressions $e_1, \ldots, e_m$. A local fixed point improvement template could specify entries of the form (e_i, f_i), wherein $e_i \leq 0$ is an inequality involved in the polyhedral invariant and f_i is a bilinear form involving the program variables that do not appear in e_i. Improvement of fixed points can be attempted under more restrictive settings where the inequalities $e_i \leq 0$ are obtained from a less expensive analysis.

Variable Packing. Packing of variables is a commonly used tactic to tackle the high complexity of domain operations in numerical domains [4,22]. An alternative to packing would involve using generalized templates by specifying expressions of the form $0 \leq c_1x_1 + \cdots + c_kx_k$ as the template at a particular location where a variable pack of $\{x_1, \ldots, x_k\}$ is to be employed. This allows us to seamlessly reason about multiple packs at different program locations and integrate the reasoning about packs during the course of the analysis.

7 Implementation and Experiments

In this section, we describe our experimental evaluation of several of the ideas presented in this paper on some benchmarks.

Implementation. The generalized template polyhedral domain presented in this paper has been implemented using the Parma Polyhedral Library (PPL) for manipulating polyhedra [2]. Our implementation supports general templates with arbitrarily many RHS parameters using generator enumeration capabilities of PPL. The special case of templates with at most two parameters has been implemented using the LP solver available in PPL. The analysis engine uses a naive iteration with delayed widening followed by the narrowing of post-fixed points, for a bounded number of iterations.

Note 4. In this paper, we have described an algorithm for performing abstraction using polyhedral projection (elimination of multiplier variables for dualization). Our implementation uses a different technique based directly on generator enumeration: to compute $\alpha(\varphi)$ we simply compute the generators of φ and derive the dual constraints for each template entry from the generators of φ. This has been done since PPL has an efficiently engineered generator enumeration algorithm. Therefore, our implementation performs a single vertex enumeration up-front and re-uses the result for each template entry, as opposed to eliminating multipliers for each template entry.

Template Construction. The overall template construction is based on a pre-computed fixed point. For our experiments, we use the polyhedral domain to generate these fixed points. Next, using each inequality $e \leq 0$ in the result

Table 1. Experimental evaluation of the GTP domain on some benchmark examples using various methods for forming templates. All timings are in seconds. #tpl: # of templates, #entries: average/min/max number of entries per template, # FP Impr: # of templates that improve the fixed point, T_{poly}: polyhedral analysis time, T_{flp}: average time per template with FLP, T_{ve}: average time per template with vertex enum.

Name	#var	#trs	M1 #tpl	M1 #entries avg	M1 #entries (min,max)	M1 #fp imp	M1 T_{poly}	M1 T_{flp} avg	M1 T_{ve} avg
lifo	8	10	42	1.0	1 , 1	6	0.02	0.02	0.00
tick3i	8	9	78	1.0	1 , 1	0	0.03	0.02	0.01
pool	9	6	64	1.1	1 , 2	8	0.01	0.03	0.01
ttp	9	20	968	1.4	1 , 2	64	0.06	0.02	0.01
cars2	10	7	149	1.1	1 , 2	4	13.5	0.06	0.01
req-gr	11	8	81	1.3	1 , 2	25	0.01	0.06	0.02
cprot	12	8	100	1.3	1 , 2	27	0.02	0.07	0.02
CSM	13	8	131	1.4	1 , 2	27	0.02	0.06	0.02
cprod	18	14	233	1.2	1 , 2	38	0.06	0.13	0.05
incdec	32	28	854	1.1	1 , 2	103	1	0.41	0.23
mesh2x2	32	32	940	1.1	1 , 2	212	1	0.51	0.29
bigjava	45	37	1856	1.4	1 , 2	129	239	0.85	0.48

Name	#tpl	M2 #entries avg	M2 #entries (min,max)	M2 T_{flp} avg	M2 T_{ve} avg	M2 #fp impr	M3 #entries avg	M3 #entries (min,max)	M3 T avg	M3 #fp impr
lifo	7	6.0	6 , 6	0.6	0.0	6	1.0	1 , 1	0.0	0
tick3i	14	5.6	3 , 7	0.1	0.0	0	1.0	1 , 1	0.0	0
pool	10	7.1	4 , 8	0.5	0.0	8	1.2	1 , 2	0.0	3
ttp	140	9.5	5 , 16	0.4	0.0	32	1.4	1 , 2	0.0	2
cars2	18	9.3	7 , 18	1.4	0.2	3	1.1	1 , 2	0.1	1
req-gr	9	11.3	10 , 16	1.5	0.2	9	1.3	1 , 2	0.0	8
cprot	10	13.4	11 , 20	2.0	0.3	10	1.4	1 , 2	0.0	9
CSM	12	15.3	7 , 22	2.5	0.5	12	1.4	1 , 2	0.0	7
cprod	16	18.1	12 , 32	7.4	1.5	15	1.3	1 , 2	0.1	13
incdec	29	32.7	16 , 60	43.6	87.8	29	1.1	1 , 2	1.1	7
bigjava	44	60.4	34 , 86	67.1	50.4	42	1.4	1 , 2	1.7	8

computed by the polyhedral domain, we compare three methods for forming templates: (**M1**) Create *multiple templates* per invariant inequality, each template consisting of a single entry of the form $e \leq c_j x_j + d_j$, for each $x_j \not\in \textsc{vars}(e)$, (**M2**) Create *one template* per inequality, each template consisting of multiple entries of the form $e \leq c_j x_j + d_j$, for each $x_j \not\in \textsc{vars}(e)$, and finally, (**M3**) Create *one template* per inequality, consisting of a single entry of the form $e \leq \sum_j c_j x_j + d$ for all variables $x_j \not\in \textsc{vars}(e)$. For equalities $e = 0$, we consider entries of the form $e \leq c_j x_j + d_j$ and $e \geq c'_j x_j + d'_j$, modifying the methods above appropriately.

Furthermore, for methods **M1** and **M2**, we compare the implementation using vertex enumeration against the fractional LP implementation for the key primitive of abstraction, which also underlies the implementation of the join and post-condition operations. Since the fractional LP algorithm produces the same result as the vertex enumeration, we did not observe any difference in the generated invariants. We compare the running times for these techniques.

Results. Table 1 reports on the time taken for the initial polyhedral analysis run, the number of templates, avg/min/max of the number of entries per template and the number of analysis runs that discovered a stronger invariant. The benchmarks have been employed in our previous work [34] as well as other tools [3]. They range in size from small (≤ 10 program variables) to large (≥ 30 program variables). The initial widening delay was set to 4 for each run of the polyhedral analysis.

We note that our domain can be used to infer invariants that are not consequences of the polyhedral domain invariants. This validates the usefulness of generalized templates for improving fixed points. The results using method **M2** show that analysis using generalized templates can be expensive when the number of entries in each template is large. However, method **M2** also provides a fixed point improvement for almost all the templates that were run, whereas in method **M1**, roughly 10% of the runs resulted in a fixed point improvement. Even though method **M3** does not allow us to use fractional linear programming, it presents a good tradeoff between running time and the possibility of fixed point improvement.

The comparison between running times for the fractional LP approach and the basic approach using vertex enumeration yields a surprising result: on most larger benchmarks, the fractional LP approach (which is polynomial time, in theory) is *slower* than the vertex enumeration. A closer investigation reveals that each vertex enumeration pass yields very few (~ 10) vertices and extreme rays. Therefore, the well-engineered generator enumeration implementation in PPL invoked once, though exponential in worst-case, can outperform our technique which requires repeated calls to LP solvers. On the other hand, the constraints in the dual form $P[c, d, \boldsymbol{\lambda}]$ obtained by Farkas' Lemma are common to all the LP and FLP solver invocations during a run of our algorithm. Incremental solvers used in SMT solvers such as Z3 [13], could potentially be adapted to speed our algorithm up.

Finally, the comparison here has been carried out against invariants obtained by polyhedral analysis. In the future, we wish to evaluate our domain against other types of invariant generation tools such as VS3 [38] and InvGen [17].

8 Related Work

Polyhedral analysis was first introduced by Cousot & Halbwachs [12] using the abstract interpretation framework [11]. Further work has realized the usefulness of domains based on convex polyhedra to the analysis of hybrid systems [19], control software [4], and systems software [36,21,22,14]. However, these advances have avoided the direct use of the original polyhedral domain due to the high cost of domain operations such as convex hulls and post-conditions [35]. In spite of impressive advances made by polyhedra libraries such as PPL, the combinatorial explosion in the number of generators cannot be overcome, in general [2].

However, it is also well-known that these operations can be performed at a lower polynomial cost (in terms of the problem size and the output size) for two dimensional polyhedra [9,35]. This fact has been used to design fast program analysis techniques to compute invariants that involve at most two program variables [37]. Further restricting the coefficients to units (± 1), yields the weakly-relational octagon domain wherein the process of reasoning about the constraints can be reduced to graph operations [28].

The restriction to at most two variables for each invariant and unit coefficients has been observed to be quite useful for proving absence of runtime errors [21]. On the other hand, current evidence suggests that invariants involving three or more variables are often crucial for proving safety of string operations and user-defined assertions [33].

Template polyhedral domains attempt to avoid the exponential complexity of polyhedral domain operations by fixing templates that represent the form of the desired invariants [34]. Recently, there have been many advances in our understanding of template polyhedral domains. Techniques such as policy iteration and strategy iteration have exploited ideas from max-plus algebra to show that the least fixed point in weakly-relational domains is computable [15,16]. These techniques have been extended to handle templates with non-linear inequalities using ideas from convex programming [1,16]. The possibility that some of these results may generalize to the domain presented in this paper remains open.

The problem of modular template polyhedral analysis has been studied by Monniaux [30], wherein summaries for templates are derived by dualization using Farkas' lemma followed by quantifier elimination in the theory of linear arithmetic. This work has also extended the template domain to handle floating point semantics for control software. Srivastava and Gulwani [38] present a verification technique using templates that can specify a richer class of templates involving quantifiers and various Boolean combinations of predicates. However, their approach for computing transformers works by restricting the coefficients to a finite set and "*bit blasting*" using SAT solvers. The logahedron domain uses a similar restriction [20]. Invariants with unit coefficients are quite useful for reasoning about runtime properties of low-level code. However, it is as yet unclear if verifying functional properties in domains such as control systems will necessitate invariants with arbitrary coefficients.

9 Conclusion

We have presented a generalization of the template domain with arbitrary bilinear forms, along with efficient algorithms for computing the domain operations when the template has at most two parameters per entry. Our experimental results demonstrate that our techniques can be applied to strengthen the invariants computed by other numerical domains. In the future, we plan to investigate techniques such as policy and strategy iteration for analysis over generalized templates. Extensions to non-linear templates and the handling of floating point semantics are also of great interest.

References

1. Adjé, A., Gaubert, S., Goubault, E.: Coupling policy iteration with semi-definite relaxation to compute accurate numerical invariants in static analysis. In: Gordon, A.D. (ed.) ESOP 2010. LNCS, vol. 6012, pp. 23–42. Springer, Heidelberg (2010)
2. Bagnara, R., Ricci, E., Zaffanella, E., Hill, P.M.: Possibly not closed convex polyhedra and the Parma Polyhedra Library. In: Hermenegildo, M.V., Puebla, G. (eds.) SAS 2002. LNCS, vol. 2477, pp. 213–229. Springer, Heidelberg (2002)
3. Bardin, S., Finkel, A., Leroux, J., Petrucci, L.: FAST: fast accelereation of symbolic transition systems. In: Hunt Jr., W.A., Somenzi, F. (eds.) CAV 2003. LNCS, vol. 2725, pp. 118–121. Springer, Heidelberg (2003)
4. Blanchet, B., Cousot, P., Cousot, R., Feret, J., Mauborgne, L., Miné, A., Monniaux, D., Rival, X.: Design and implementation of a special-purpose static program analyzer for safety-critical real-time embedded software (invited chapter). In: Mogensen, T.Æ., Schmidt, D.A., Sudborough, I.H. (eds.) The Essence of Computation. LNCS, vol. 2566, pp. 85–108. Springer, Heidelberg (2002)
5. Boyd, S., Vandenberghe, S.: Convex Optimization. Cambridge University Press, Cambridge (2004), `http://www.stanford.edu/~boyd/cvxbook.html`
6. Chatterjee, S., Lahiri, S.K., Qadeer, S., Rakamaric, Z.: A reachability predicate for analyzing low-level software. In: Grumberg, O., Huth, M. (eds.) TACAS 2007. LNCS, vol. 4424, pp. 19–33. Springer, Heidelberg (2007)
7. Clarisó, R., Cortadella, J.: The octahedron abstract domain. Science of Computer Programming 64(1), 115–139 (2007)
8. Colón, M.A.: Deductive Techniques for Program Analysis. PhD thesis, Stanford University (2003)
9. Corman, T., Leiserson, C.F., Rivest, R.: Introduction to Algorithms. McGraw Hill, New York (1990)
10. Cousot, P., Cousot, R.: Static determination of dynamic properties of programs. In: Proc. ISOP 1976, Dunod, Paris, France, pp. 106–130 (1976)
11. Cousot, P., Cousot, R.: Abstract Interpretation: A unified lattice model for static analysis of programs by construction or approximation of fixpoints. In: POPL, pp. 238–252 (1977)
12. Cousot, P., Halbwachs, N.: Automatic discovery of linear restraints among the variables of a program. In: POPL 1978, pp. 84–97 (January 1978)
13. de Moura, L.M., Bjørner, N.: Z3: An efficient SMT solver. In: Ramakrishnan, C.R., Rehof, J. (eds.) TACAS 2008. LNCS, vol. 4963, pp. 337–340. Springer, Heidelberg (2008)
14. Ferrara, P., Logozzo, F., Fähndrich, M.: Safer unsafe code for .NET. In: OOPSLA, pp. 329–346. ACM, New York (2008)
15. Gaubert, S., Goubault, E., Taly, A., Zennou, S.: Static analysis by policy iteration on relational domains. In: De Nicola, R. (ed.) ESOP 2007. LNCS, vol. 4421, pp. 237–252. Springer, Heidelberg (2007)
16. Gawlitza, T., Seidl, H.: Precise fixpoint computation through strategy iteration. In: De Nicola, R. (ed.) ESOP 2007. LNCS, vol. 4421, pp. 300–315. Springer, Heidelberg (2007)
17. Gupta, A., Rybalchenko, A.: InvGen: An efficient invariant generator. In: Bouajjani, A., Maler, O. (eds.) CAV 2009. LNCS, vol. 5643, pp. 634–640. Springer, Heidelberg (2009)
18. Halbwachs, N., Proy, Y.-E., Roumanoff, P.: Verification of real-time systems using linear relation analysis. Formal Methods in System Design 11(2), 157–185 (1997)

19. Henzinger, T.A., Ho, P.: HyTech: The Cornell hybrid technology tool. In: Antsaklis, P.J., Kohn, W., Nerode, A., Sastry, S.S. (eds.) HS 1994. LNCS, vol. 999, pp. 265–293. Springer, Heidelberg (1995)
20. Howe, J., King, A.: Logahedra: A new weakly relational domain. In: Liu, Z., Ravn, A.P. (eds.) ATVA 2009. LNCS, vol. 5799, pp. 306–320. Springer, Heidelberg (2009)
21. Ivančić, F., Sankaranarayanan, S., Shlyakhter, I., Gupta, A.: Buffer overflow analysis using environment refinement 2009. Draft (2009)
22. Ivančić, F., Shlyakhter, I., Gupta, A., Ganai, M.K.: Model checking C programs using F-SOFT. In: ICCD, pp. 297–308. IEEE Computer Society, Los Alamitos (2005)
23. Jarvis, R.A.: On the identification of the convex hull of a finite set of points in the plane. Information Processing Letters 2(1), 18–21 (1973)
24. Jeannet, B., Miné, A.: Apron: A library of numerical abstract domains for static analysis. In: Bouajjani, A., Maler, O. (eds.) CAV 2009. LNCS, vol. 5643, pp. 661–667. Springer, Heidelberg (2009)
25. Kanade, A., Alur, R., Ivančić, F., Ramesh, S., Sankaranarayanan, S., Sashidhar, K.: Generating and analyzing symbolic traces of Simulink/Stateflow models. In: Bouajjani, A., Maler, O. (eds.) CAV 2009. LNCS, vol. 5643, pp. 430–445. Springer, Heidelberg (2009)
26. Logozzo, F., Fähndrich, M.: Pentagons: A weakly relational abstract domain for the efficient validation of array accesses. Sci. Comp. Prog. 75(9), 796–807 (2010)
27. Manna, Z., Pnueli, A.: Temporal Verification of Reactive Systems: Safety. Springer, New York (1995)
28. Miné, A.: A new numerical abstract domain based on difference-bound matrices. In: Danvy, O., Filinski, A. (eds.) PADO 2001. LNCS, vol. 2053, pp. 155–172. Springer, Heidelberg (2001)
29. Miné, A.: Symbolic methods to enhance the precision of numerical abstract domains. In: Emerson, E.A., Namjoshi, K.S. (eds.) VMCAI 2006. LNCS, vol. 3855, pp. 348–363. Springer, Heidelberg (2005)
30. Monniaux, D.: Automatic modular abstractions for template numerical constraints. Logical Methods in Computer Science 6(3) (2010)
31. Motzkin, T.S., Raiffa, H., Thompson, G.L., Thrall, R.M.: The double description method. In: Contributions to the theory of games. Annals of Mathematics Studies, vol. 2, pp. 51–73. Princeton University Press, Princeton (1953)
32. Sankaranarayanan, S., Colón, M.A., Sipma, H., Manna, Z.: Efficient strongly relational polyhedral analysis. In: Emerson, E.A., Namjoshi, K.S. (eds.) VMCAI 2006. LNCS, vol. 3855, pp. 111–125. Springer, Heidelberg (2006)
33. Sankaranarayanan, S., Ivančić, F., Gupta, A.: Program analysis using symbolic ranges. In: Riis Nielson, H., Filé, G. (eds.) SAS 2007. LNCS, vol. 4634, pp. 366–383. Springer, Heidelberg (2007)
34. Sankaranarayanan, S., Sipma, H.B., Manna, Z.: Scalable analysis of linear systems using mathematical programming. In: Cousot, R. (ed.) VMCAI 2005. LNCS, vol. 3385, pp. 25–41. Springer, Heidelberg (2005)
35. Schrijver, A.: Theory of Linear and Integer Programming. Wiley, Chichester (1986)
36. Simon, A.: Value-Range Analysis of C Programs: Towards Proving the Absence of Buffer Overflow Vulnerabilities. Springer, Heidelberg (2008)
37. Simon, A., King, A., Howe, J.M.: Two variables per linear inequality as an abstract domain. In: Leuschel, M. (ed.) LOPSTR 2002. LNCS, vol. 2664, pp. 71–89. Springer, Heidelberg (2003)
38. Srivastava, S., Gulwani, S.: Program verification using templates over predicate abstraction. In: PLDI 2009, pp. 223–234. ACM, New York (2009)

Dataflow Analysis for Datarace-Free Programs

Arnab De, Deepak D'Souza, and Rupesh Nasre

Department of Computer Science and Automation,
Indian Institute of Science, Bangalore, India
{arnabde,deepakd,nasre}@csa.iisc.ernet.in

Abstract. Memory models for shared-memory concurrent programming languages typically guarantee sequential consistency (SC) semantics for datarace-free (DRF) programs, while providing very weak or no guarantees for non-DRF programs. In effect programmers are expected to write only DRF programs, which are then executed with SC semantics. With this in mind, we propose a novel scalable solution for dataflow analysis of concurrent programs, which is proved to be sound for DRF programs with SC semantics. We use the synchronization structure of the program to propagate dataflow information among threads without requiring to consider all interleavings explicitly. Given a dataflow analysis that is sound for sequential programs and meets certain criteria, our technique automatically converts it to an analysis for concurrent programs.

Keywords: dataflow analysis, datarace-free program, concurrency.

1 Introduction

In recent years several new semantics based on relaxed memory models have been proposed for concurrent programs, most notably the Java Memory Model [20], and the C++ Memory Model [2]. While the aim of the relaxed semantics is to facilitate aggressive compiler optimizations and efficient execution on hardware, the guarantees they provide can be quite different from the standard "Sequentially Consistent" (SC) semantics. A common guarantee that they typically provide however is that programs *without* dataraces will run with SC semantics. For programs *with* dataraces there are very weak guarantees: the Java Memory Model [20] essentially ensures that there will be no "out-of-thin-air" values read, while the C++ memory model [2] specifies no semantics for such programs.

The prevalence of this so-called "SC-for-DRF" semantics makes the class of datarace-free programs with sequentially consistent semantics an important one from a static analysis point of view. An analysis technique that is sound for this class of programs can in principle be used by a compiler-writer for the *general* class of programs, as long as the ensuing transformation preserves the weak guarantees described above. From a verification point of view as well, most programs should be first checked for datarace-freedom and then a sound analysis for datarace-free programs can be used to prove other properties.

With this in mind, in this paper we propose a novel and scalable dataflow analysis technique for concurrent programs that is sound for datarace-free programs

G. Barthe (Ed.): ESOP 2011, LNCS 6602, pp. 196–215, 2011.
© Springer-Verlag Berlin Heidelberg 2011

under the SC semantics. Given a sequential dataflow analysis that meets certain criteria, our technique automatically produces an efficient and fairly precise analysis for concurrent programs. The criteria that the underlying analysis must meet is that each dataflow fact should be dependent on the contents of some associated lvalue (an *lvalue* is an expression that refers to memory locations at runtime). Several sequential dataflow analyses such as null-pointer analysis, interval analysis and constant propagation satisfy this criteria. Our technique gives useful information (in terms of precision of the inferred data-flow facts) at points where the corresponding lvalue is *read*. For example, in the case of null-pointer analysis, the dataflow fact "*NonNull*(`p`)" is dependent on the contents of the lvalue "`p`" and is relevant before a statement that dereferences (and therefore, reads) "`p`". Similarly, the fact that an lvalue has a constant value at a program point is dependent on the contents of the lvalue and is relevant at statements that read that lvalue.

The main challenge in lifting an analysis for sequential programs to concurrent programs is that multiple threads can simultaneously modify a shared memory location. Traditionally the analysis techniques for concurrent programs address this problem in one of the following ways: they either invalidate the analyzed fact if there is any possible interference from any other thread [3,15], making the analysis very imprecise, or they exhaustively explore all possible interleavings [27], leading to poor scalability. In contrast, our analysis technique uses the synchronization structure of the program to propagate dataflow facts between threads. The main insight we use is that it is sufficient to propagate dataflow facts between threads only at corresponding synchronization points (like from an "`unlock(l)`" statement to a "`lock(l)` statement"). We also show how our framework can be integrated with a context-sensitive analysis.

We implemented our technique in a framework for automatically converting dataflow analyses for sequential Java programs to sound analyses for concurrent programs and instantiated it for a null-dereference analysis. Our initial experience with the tool shows that the analysis runs in a few seconds on real benchmark programs and is able to prove a high percentage of dereferences to be safe. We also developed a prototype implementation for concurrent C programs. This allows us to compare our technique empirically with the state-of-the-art Radar tool [3], and show that our tool is more precise on a few medium-sized benchmarks.

2 Overview of Our Approach

In this section we informally illustrate our technique with the help of a few examples. We consider the null-pointer analysis where the goal is to compute a set of dataflow facts for each edge of the program which tell us which lvalues are non-null along all executions reaching that edge. Examples of such dataflow facts can be *NonNull*(`p->data`) for the program in Figure 1.

Note that value of the dataflow fact *NonNull*(`p->data`) at runtime depends on the contents of the memory location corresponding to the lvalue `p->data`.

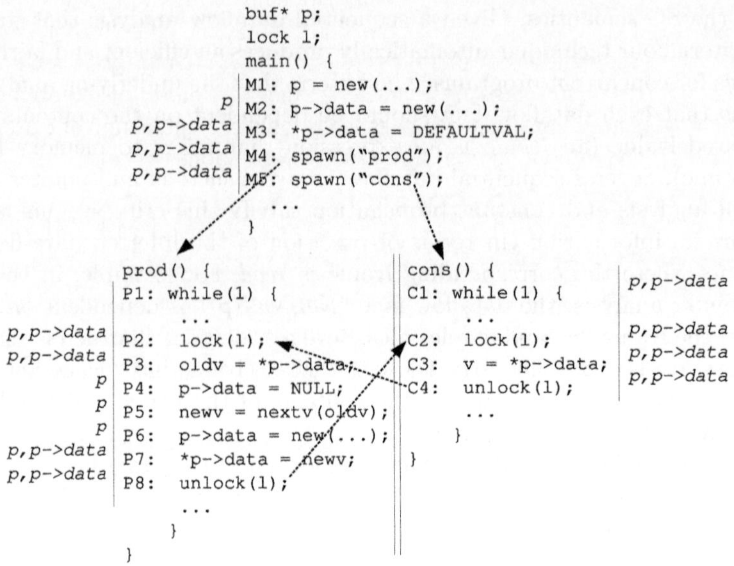

Fig. 1. Program 1

Hence, at runtime, the value of this fact can only be modified by writing to the memory locations corresponding to `p->data` or `p`, possibly through some alias. Moreover, the value of the fact *NonNull*(`p->data`) is relevant only before the statements where `p->data` is dereferenced or `p->data` is assigned to some other pointer or `p->data` is compared to `NULL`. For example, in Figure 1, this fact is relevant before the statements `M3`, `P3`, `P7` and `C3`, but not before `P6` or `M2`. Note that at all edges where this fact is relevant, the successor statements read `p->data`. Our analysis guarantees that for a given datarace-free program, if a fact is computed to be true at a program edge where the fact is relevant, then it is indeed true at that program edge in all executions of the program.

Figure 1 shows a simple concurrent producer-consumer program, where data is shared through a shared location, pointed to by `p`. The call to `new` returns newly allocated memory. Note that the `main` thread sets the pointers `p` and `p->data` to non-null values. The `prod` thread sets `p->data` to null after locking `l`, but restores its non-nullity before unlocking `l`. As a result, the `cons` thread can dereference `p` and `p->data` without checking for non-nullity after locking `l`. This code has no null-pointer dereferences in any of its executions. Clearly, the threads in this code depend on each other to make the pointers non-null before any other thread can access them. We also note the the program has no dataraces.

Let us again consider the dataflow fact *NonNull*(`p->data`) in the program of Figure 1. As the program is datarace-free, if a thread writes to `p->data` or `p` and some other thread reads `p->data` later in the execution, then these accesses must be synchronized, i.e. there must be a release action (e.g. `unlock` or `spawn`) by the first thread, followed by an acquire action (e.g. `lock` or first action of a thread) by the second thread, between the write and the read. In other words, in any execution of the program, the action that modifies the dataflow fact and the action before which it is relevant either belong to the same thread or are synchronized.

As the first step of our analysis, we introduce new edges between nodes of the control-flow graphs (CFGs) representing different threads. These edges correspond to possible "release-acquire" pairs at runtime. We refer to this unified set of CFGs with added edges as the *sync-CFG*. Figure 1 shows the edges we add for this program as dashed arrows - from `spawn` to the first instruction of the child thread and from the `unlock` to `lock` statements if they access the same lock variable and if they can possibly run in parallel.

In the next step of our analysis, we perform a sequential dataflow analysis on this *sync-CFG* to compute a set of dataflow facts at each program edge that conservatively approximates the *join-over-all-paths* (JOP) solution over the *sync-CFG*.

In Figure 1, we show the lvalues discovered to be non-null by our analysis at different program points in *italics*. As `p->data` is non-null at point `M5` in the `main` thread before spawning the `cons` thread, this fact gets propagated to the first instruction `C1` of the `cons` thread though one of the added edges, and from there to the `lock` instruction at `C2`. Similarly, although `p->data` is set to null in the `prod` thread at `P4`, it is set back to non-null at `P6` before the `unlock`. This facts also gets propagated to the `lock` statement of the `cons` thread through the edge `P8` to `C2`. As `p->data` is non-null in both the paths joining at the `C2` of the `cons` thread, we can determine `p->data` to be non-null before the `lock` statement in all executions. This makes the fact *NonNull*(`p->data`) to be true before the deference of `p->data` at `C3`.

The reason why our analysis works is that if, in an execution, an action modifies the dataflow fact *NonNull*(`p->data`) and it is relevant at some later action, then there exists a static path from the statement of the first action to the statement of the second action in the *sync-CFG* and the static dataflow function corresponding to this path will conservatively approximate the effect of the execution path segment from the first action to the second action on the dataflow fact. As an example, consider the interleaved execution path fragment [`P6`,`C1`,`P7`,`P8`,`C2`,`C3`] where `P6` modifies *NonNull*(`p->data`) and it is relevant at `C3`. There is a static path in the *sync-CFG* [`P6`,`P7`,`P8`,`C2`,`C3`] which has the same effect on this dataflow fact as the execution path segment.

We note that at points where a fact is *not* relevant our analysis may compute incorrect values. For example our analysis computes *NonNull*(`p->data`) to be true at `C1` although the interleaved execution path segment [`P4`,`C1`] can make it false. However, the fact *NonNull*(`p->data`) is not relevant at `C1`.

Let us now consider a buggy version of the program, presented in Figure 2. The `main` thread is the same as Figure 1. This program is also DRF, but the `prod` thread releases the lock after setting `p->data` to null at `P4`, and acquires the lock again before setting it to non-null. If the `cons` thread dereferences `p->data`

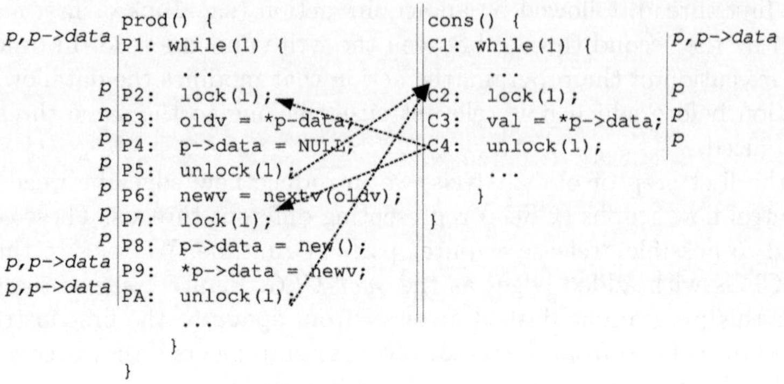
prod() {
P1: while(1) {
...
P2: lock(1);
P3: oldv = *p->data;
P4: p->data = NULL;
P5: unlock(1);
P6: newv = nextv(oldv);
P7: lock(1);
P8: p->data = new();
P9: *p->data = newv;
PA: unlock(1);
...
}
}
p,p->data
p
p
p
p
p
p
p
p,p->data
p,p->data
cons() {
C1: while(1) {
...
C2: lock(1);
C3: val = *p->data;
C4: unlock(1);
...
}
}
p,p->data
p
p
p

Fig. 2. Program 2

in between these two actions, it will dereference a null-pointer. For example, the execution path segment [P4,P5,C2,C3] will result in null-pointer dereference. Note that there is a static path [P4,P5,C2,C3] in the *sync-CFG* that also sets the fact *NonNull*(`p->data`) to false before `C3`. Hence our analysis will detect that `p->data` can be null before the dereference at `C3`. Note that here also we incorrectly compute *NonNull*(`p->data`) to be true at `C1` as the modification of this fact at `P4` is not propagated to `C1`. Nevertheless, as the program is datarace-free, before the `cons` thread reads `p->data`, it must synchronize with the `prod` thread and the modified value for the fact *NonNull*(`p->data`) is propagated to the `cons` thread through the corresponding static edge ([`P5`,`C2`] in this case).

3 Related Work

There are quite a few works on dataflow analysis of concurrent programs in the literature and they differ considerably in terms of technique, precision and applicability. Some works [16,11,6] create parallel flow graphs similar to our technique and perform a modified version of sequential analysis on them, but unlike us, their techniques are applicable to very specific analyses, such as bit-vector analysis or gen-kill analysis. In particular, they do not handle the analyses where the value of a dataflow fact can depend on some other dataflow fact. For example, in null-pointer analysis, `p` is non-null after a statement `p = q` only if `q` is non-null before the statement. Unlike our technique, they also do not consider many features of modern concurrent programs such as unbounded threads, synchronization using locks/volatiles etc. For example, the pointer-analysis algorithm presented in [23] considers only structured par-begin/par-end like synchronization constructs.

On the other hand, there are a few works such as [15] that kill the dataflow facts whenever there is a possible interference. Similarly, Radar [3] uses a datarace detection engine to conservatively kill a dataflow fact whenever there is a possible race on the lvalues corresponding to the fact. Our technique is more precise than theirs as we propagate the dataflow facts precisely. For example, in Figure 1, Radar cannot detect the dereference of `p->data` in the `cons` thread to be safe. Recently Farzan et al. [7] presented a compositional technique for dataflow analysis, but it is applicable to only bit-vector analyses.

Model checkers such as [27] provide an alternative technique to find if a property holds at a particular program point. They typically exhaustively enumerate all interleavings of a program, resulting in poor scalability. CHESS [21] prunes the number of interleavings by context switching only at the synchronization points, assuming the program is datarace-free, but scalability still remains an issue. In contrast ours is a static analysis which does not explore interleavings explicitly. Moreover, due to infinite state-spaces, model checking of real programming languages cannot cover all program behaviors. Thread modular analyses [8,9,10] can analyze each thread separately, but either require user-defined annotations denoting some invariants or try to infer them automatically, limiting their scalability and precision. Recently, Malkis et al. [19] proposed a thread-modular abstraction refinement technique where the set of reachable "global states" is computed as the cartesian abstraction of sets of reachable "local" states. If a global state is infeasible, an abstraction refinement step excludes it from the cartesian abstraction. This technique assumes the number of dynamic threads to be statically bound. It is not implemented for real programs and the analysis-refinement cycle limits its scalability.

4 Preliminaries

4.1 Program Structure

In this section we formalize the structure of the subject programs for our analysis. For ease of presentation, we use a simple core language that has the representative features of real programming languages with shared-memory concurrency.

The program is composed of a finite number of named thread codes[1], one of which is designated as the *main thread*. The program is denoted as $P = (T_0, \ldots, T_k)$, where each T_i is name of a static thread. Each thread T_i is represented as a control flow graph (CFG) C_i where each node represents a statement in the program. We do not consider procedures at this point (context-sensitive interprocedural analysis is described in Section 8). In the rest of the paper, we use the terms *nodes* and *statements* interchangeably to refer to the static statements in the program.

Figure 3 defines the syntax of the language partially. Variables are declared globally. The non-terminal *Decl* in Figure 3 describes a variable declaration. A regular (non-synchronization) variable can be of some basic type or structure type or pointer type. A *synchronization variable* is either a lock or a thread identifier.

[1] We refer the code of a thread as a *static thread* and the runtime instance of a thread as a *dynamic thread*.

```
Decl      ::= VarType <var> | Lock <lockvar> | ThreadId <tid>
VarType   ::= BasicType | VarType*

Stmt      ::= AsgnStmt | BranchStmt | SyncStmt | skip
AsgnStmt  ::= Lval := Expr
Lval      ::= <var> | *Lval
SyncStmt  ::= lock <lockvar> | unlock <lockvar>
            | <tid> := spawn <T> | join <tid> | start | end
```

Fig. 3. Partial syntax of the language

Statements (*Stmt* in Figure 3) are of following types: *assignment*, *branch*, *synchronization* and *skip*. Assignment statements (*AsgnStmt* in Figure 3) assigns the value of an expression to an lvalue, which is either a declared variable or dereference of an lvalue. Expressions are arithmetic or logical expressions over constants and lvalues or "address of" expressions. Branch conditions can be any Boolean expression.

For an lvalue l, we define $deref(l)$ to be the set of lvalues that are dereferenced in the expression of l. Formally,

$$deref(l) = \begin{cases} \{l'\} \cup deref(l') & \text{if } l \text{ is of the form } *l' \\ \emptyset & \text{otherwise.} \end{cases}$$

For example, if `p` is a variable and `**p` is an lvalue, then $deref(**\mathtt{p}) = \{\mathtt{p}, *\mathtt{p}\}$.

We call an lvalue l *relevant* at a program edge E and its successor node N if l is syntactically part of the expression read at the node N. Note that, if l is relevant at a program edge/node, all lvalues in $deref(l)$ are also relevant at that program edge. In the program of Figure 1, at `C3`, the relevant lvalues are `p`, `p->data` and `*p->data`. We consider only well-typed programs without pointer arithmetic.

Synchronization statements (*SyncStmt* in Figure 3) are of special interest to us. Each thread has a *start* node and an *end* node, containing special `start` and `end` statements, respectively. Threads are spawned by `spawn` statements that take static thread names as parameters and return thread ids of the child threads. A parent thread waits for a child thread to finish using a `join` statement. The `lock` and `unlock` statements have the standard semantics for reentrant locks. Only synchronization statements can access synchronization variables. Although we consider only these synchronization statements in this paper, our technique can be applied to programming languages with other synchronization statements that have acquire/release semantics (described in Section 4.2), such as read/write of volatiles in the Java programming language [12].

For a CFG $C = (Nodes, Edges, E_0, E_\sharp)$, $Nodes$ denotes the set of nodes, $Edges \subseteq Nodes \times Nodes$ denotes the set of edges, $E_0 \notin Edges$ denotes a special *start edge* with no predecessor node and $E_\sharp \notin Edges$ denotes a special *end edge* with no successor node in C. For a node N, $epred(N) = \{E \in Edges \mid \exists N' \in Nodes : E = \langle N', N\rangle\}$ denotes the set of predecessor edges of N and

$npred(N) = \{N' \in Nodes \mid \langle N', N\rangle \in Edges\}$ denotes the set of predecessor nodes of N. For an edge $E = \langle N, N'\rangle$, $\{N\}$ is the singleton set of predecessor node of E, denoted by $npred(E)$ and the set $epred(npred(E))$ is the set of predecessor edges of E, denoted by $epred(E)$. Similarly, *esucc* and *nsucc* denote the sets of successor edges and successor nodes for an edge or a node, respectively. Although we overload these notations, the meaning should be clear from the context. Each CFG has a *start node* N_0 which is the successor node of E_0 and an *end node* $N_\sharp$ which is the predecessor node of $E_\sharp$. Let N_0^M and E_0^M denote the start node and the start edge of the main thread and $N_\sharp^M$ and $E_\sharp^M$ denote the end node and the end edge of the main thread, respectively.

A *path* Π in a CFG C is defined as a sequence of nodes $\langle N_0', \ldots, N_n'\rangle$ of C, such that there is an edge in C between N_i' and N_{i+1}' for every i, $0 \leq i < n$. A path Π is called an *initial path* in C if the first node of the path is the node N_0, the start node in C.

4.2 Execution

Let P be a program written in the language described in Section 4.1. An *action* is a dynamic instance of a statement in an execution. For an action a, $stmt(a)$ denotes the corresponding static statement or node and $thread\_id(a)$ denotes the dynamic thread id of the thread performing the action.

An *interleaving* of P is a sequence of actions $\langle a_0, \ldots, a_n\rangle$, $stmt(a_0) = N_0^M$, possibly from different dynamic threads, such that the projection of the sequence to any thread id is consistent with the sequential semantics of that thread, given the values of reads of shared variables. If I is an interleaving of P, $I[i]$ denotes the ith action in the interleaving. Let a be an action in an interleaving I. By $eprev(a)$ and $enext(a)$ we denote the program point (CFG edge) reached in the thread executing a just before and after executing a, respectively. Similarly, by $next(a)$ we mean the next action in I that belongs to the same dynamic thread as a. Thus, $next(a) = I[j]$ if $a = I[i]$ and $thread\_id(a_i) = thread\_id(a_j)$, $i < j$ and there is no k, $i < k < j$ such that $thread\_id(a_i) = thread\_id(a_k)$. If $a' = next(a)$, then we say $a = prev(a')$.

Synchronization actions are of two types: `spawn`, `end` and `unlock` actions are the *release* actions, where as `join`, `start` and `lock` actions are the *acquire* actions.

An interleaving I of program P is *synchronization-valid* if

- each `unlock` action is preceded by a *matching* `lock` action. For every prefix of I, number of unlock actions on a lock variable by a dynamic thread must be less than or equal to the number of lock actions performed by the same dynamic thread on the same lock,
- locks maintain mutual exclusion property. If a is a `lock` action performed by a dynamic thread t on a lock `l`, then for any thread $t' \neq t$, the number of `unlock` actions performed on `l` by t' before a in I must be exactly equal to the number of `lock` actions on `l` by t' before a in I.

- The `start` action of any thread (except the `main` thread) is preceded by a corresponding `spawn` action that returns a thread id which is the same as the started thread,
- each `join` action is preceded by the end action of the thread it waits for.

An interleaving is *sequentially consistent* (SC) if every read of a memory location reads the value written by the last preceding write to the same memory location in the interleaving. We assume that there is an initial write to every memory location whenever the memory is allocated in an execution. An *sc-execution* is simply a synchronization-valid and sequentially consistent interleaving.

4.3 Datarace-Free Programs

Two non-synchronization actions in an sc-execution are *conflicting* if they both access a common memory location and at least one of them writes to that memory location.

Given an sc-execution $\mathcal{E}$ of a program P, we say a release action *synchronizes-with* subsequent acquire actions corresponding to it. More specifically, an `unlock` action synchronizes with any subsequent `lock` action on the same lock variable, a `spawn` action synchronizes with the `start` action of the thread it spawns and an end action synchronizes with the `join` action that waits for the thread to finish. If in $\mathcal{E}$, an action a synchronizes with an action b, it is denoted by $a <_{sw}^{\mathcal{E}} b$.

Similarly, if in an sc-execution $\mathcal{E}$, $a = \mathcal{E}[i]$ and $b = \mathcal{E}[j]$ are two actions such that $thread\_id(a) = thread\_id(b)$, $i < j$ and there is no k, $i < k < j$, such that $thread\_id(\mathcal{E}[k]) = thread\_id(\mathcal{E}[i])$, then there is a *program-order* relation between a and b, denoted by $a <_{po}^{\mathcal{E}} b$. Note that if $a <_{po}^{\mathcal{E}} b$, then there is an edge from $stmt(a)$ to $stmt(b)$ in the CFG of the corresponding static thread.

The *happens-before* order induced by an sc-execution $\mathcal{E}$, is a partial-order on the actions of $\mathcal{E}$, denoted by $\leq_{hb}^{\mathcal{E}}$, and is defined as the reflexive transitive closure of $<_{sw}^{\mathcal{E}}$ and $<_{po}^{\mathcal{E}}$ relations.

An sc-execution $\mathcal{E}$ is *datarace-free* if every pair of conflicting actions are related by the happens-before order. A program is datarace-free if all sc-executions of the program are datarace-free. This definition of datarace-freedom is equivalent to the more intuitive definition [24] - in any sc-execution of a datarace-free program, two conflicting actions from different dynamic threads cannot happen immediately after one another.

Many programming languages such as Java [20] and C++ [2] guarantee that any execution of a datarace-free program in these languages is equivalent to some sc-execution. We assume that the memory model of our language guarantees sequentially consistent semantics for datarace-free programs and we are only interested in datarace-free programs in this paper. Henceforth we refer to an sc-execution simply as an *execution*.

5 Analysis for Sequential Programs

In this section, we characterize the class of the analyses for sequential programs that can be converted to analyses for concurrent programs using our technique.

This class essentially consists of the "value set analysis" (Section 5.1) and any consistent abstraction (Section 5.2) of it.

We assume the sequential program to consist of a single `main` thread. It may not have any synchronization statement except for the `start` and `end` statements of the main thread. Let us denote the sequential program by P and its CFG by $C = (Nodes, Edges, E_0, E_\sharp)$.

5.1 Value Set Analysis

Intuitively, the value set semantics of a program is an abstract semantics where the state at each program edge is a map from the each lvalue read or written in the program to a set of values. The analysis characterizes a conservative approximation of such a state for each program edge E, i.e. the set of values corresponding to an lvalue l in the solution should include every value contained in the memory location corresponding to l at E in any execution of the program P reaching E.

Formally, the *value set analysis* $\mathcal{VS}$ for a program P is a tuple $(\mathcal{L}_{\mathcal{VS}}, \mathcal{F}_{\mathcal{VS}})$ where $\mathcal{L}_{\mathcal{VS}}$ is the lattice of abstract states and $\mathcal{F}_{\mathcal{VS}}$ is the set of static flow functions. An abstract state in this semantics is a map $LVals \rightarrow 2^{Values}$, where $LVals$ is the set of lvalues read/written in program P and $Values$ is the set of values that can be contained in any memory location. The domain of such states is denoted as $ValueSets$. Hence the lattice $\mathcal{L}_{\mathcal{VS}}$ is a join-lattice $(ValueSets, \preceq, \top, \bot, \sqcup)$, where for $vs, vs' \in ValueSets$ and $S \subseteq ValueSets$

- $vs \preceq vs'$ iff $\forall l \in LVals : vs(l) \subseteq vs'(l)$
- $\top = \lambda\, l.\, Values$
- $\bot = \lambda\, l. \emptyset$
- $\bigsqcup S = \lambda\, l. \bigcup_{vs \in S} vs(l)$.

We allow the analysis to be flow-sensitive and (partially) path-sensitive. Hence, the static flow function for any node N is of the form $F_N : ValueSets \times Edges \rightarrow ValueSets$, allowing it to propagate different abstract states along different successor edges. The flow functions for different types of statements are defined below. Given an expression e, the denotation $[\![e]\!] : ValueSets \rightarrow 2^{Values}$ is a function that returns a set of values obtained from evaluating e on all possible *concrete states* corresponding to a given value set. For an lvalue l, $AliasSet(l)$ denotes the set of lvalues that may represent the same memory location as l. Note that for sequential programs, the $AliasSet$ can be computed from the value sets itself or from some sound pointer analysis such as [1].

If $N \in AsgnStmt$ and is of the form `l := e`, $F_N(vs, \_) = vs'$, where

$$vs'(l') = \begin{cases} [\![\mathtt{e}]\!](vs) & \text{if } l' = \mathtt{l} \\ [\![\mathtt{e}]\!](vs) \cup vs(l') & \text{if } l' \in AliasSet(\mathtt{l}) \\ Values & \text{if } \mathtt{l} \in AliasSet(deref(l')) \\ vs(l') & \text{otherwise.} \end{cases}$$

Intuitively, we destructively update the value set of the lvalue at the LHS, but conservatively update the value set of an lvalue that may be alias of the LHS.

If an lvalue is dependent on some alias of the LHS, the memory location corresponding to that lvalue might change. Hence its value set is set to $\top$.

If $N \in \mathit{BranchStmt}$ and the branch condition is e, then $F_N(vs, \mathit{true\_branch}) = vs'$ and $F_N(vs, \mathit{false\_branch}) = vs''$, where

$$\forall l, v : v \in vs'(l) \text{ iff } v \in vs(l) \wedge \exists \hat{vs} : \hat{vs}(l) = \{v\} \wedge \mathit{true} \in [\![\mathrm{e}]\!](\hat{vs})$$
$$\forall l, v : v \in vs''(l) \text{ iff } v \in vs(l) \wedge \exists \hat{vs} : \hat{vs}(l) = \{v\} \wedge \mathit{false} \in [\![\mathrm{e}]\!](\hat{vs}).$$

Intuitively, a value v is included in the value set of an lvalue l along the true branch if e can evaluate to *true* with v contained in l. The false branch is similar. Branch statements do not generate any value that was not there in the input value set. Flow functions for other statements are identity functions.

A concrete state of a program P is a map $cs : \mathit{LVals} \rightarrow \mathit{Values}$. Given an action a from an execution $\mathcal{E}$ of the program P, $\mathit{pre}(a)$ and $\mathit{post}(a)$ denote the concrete states immediately before and after a is executed, respectively. If $a_\sharp$ is the last action of $\mathcal{E}$, $\mathit{post}(\mathcal{E}) = \mathit{post}(a_\sharp)$. Given a program edge E, let $\Xi(E)$ denote the set of executions of the program *up to* E, i.e., $\Xi(E) = \{\mathcal{E} \mid \mathcal{E} = \langle a'_0, \ldots, a'_\sharp\rangle \text{ and } E = \mathit{enext}(a'_\sharp)\}$. Then for any edge E, the collecting value set CVS at E is defined to be

$$\mathit{CVS}[E] = \lambda l. \bigcup_{\mathcal{E} \in \Xi(E)} \mathit{post}(\mathcal{E})(l). \tag{1}$$

Let $\mathcal{E} = \langle a'_0, \ldots, a'_n\rangle$ be an execution of the sequential program P. $\Pi_\mathcal{E} = \langle N'_0, \ldots, N'_n\rangle$ is the path corresponding to $\mathcal{E}$ where for all i, $0 \leq i \leq n$, $N'_i = \mathit{stmt}(a'_i)$. Note that for a sequential program, there is an edge in the CFG between N'_i and N'_{i+1} for all i, $0 \leq i < n$. For any analysis $\mathcal{A} = (\mathcal{L}, \mathcal{F})$, the flow function for the path $\Pi_\mathcal{E}$ with the initial state $d \in \mathcal{L}$ along the edge E is defined by $F_{\Pi_\mathcal{E}}(vs, E) = F_{N'_n}(F_{N'_{n-1}}(\ldots(F_{N'_0}(vs, E'_0)\ldots), E'_{n-1}), E)$, where each $E'_i = \langle N'_i, N'_{i+1}\rangle$, $E \in \mathit{esucc}(N'_n)$ and each $F_{N'_i} \in \mathcal{F}$. Let $\Sigma(E)$ be the set of initial paths up to E. Then the ideal *join-over-all-paths* (JOP) solution of the analysis $\mathcal{A}$ on P, denoted by $J_\mathcal{A}$, at any edge E, is given by

$$J_\mathcal{A}[E] = \bigsqcup_{\Pi \in \Sigma(E)} F_\Pi(\top, E). \tag{2}$$

For value set analysis, the static flow functions over-approximate the runtime behavior, i.e. $\forall l \in \mathit{LVals}\colon v = \mathit{post}(a_n)(l) \Rightarrow v \in F_{\Pi_\mathcal{E}}(\top, \mathit{enext}(a_n))$. We assume the flow function of an empty path to be identity. Hence for a sequential program, $\mathit{CVS} \preceq J_{\mathcal{VS}}$.

Any dataflow analysis (say $\mathcal{A}$) characterizes a further conservative approximation of the JOP by the least solution $S_\mathcal{A}$ for the following set of equations:

$$\begin{aligned} X[E_0] &= \top \\ \forall E \in (\mathit{Edges} - \{E_0\}) : X[E] &= \bigsqcup_{E' \in \mathit{epred}(E)} F_{\mathit{npred}(E)}(X[E'], E). \end{aligned} \tag{3}$$

As described in standard literature e.g. [13], if flow functions are monotonic, $J_\mathcal{A} \preceq S_\mathcal{A}$. In particular, $\mathit{CVS} \preceq J_{\mathcal{VS}} \preceq S_{\mathcal{VS}}$. Note that the least solution always exists, but may not be computable for value set analysis. If the underlying lattice has bounded height, the least solution for $\mathcal{A}$ can be computed using an algorithm like Kildall's [14].

5.2 Abstractions of Value Set Semantics

In this section, we define *consistent abstractions* [4] of the value set semantics. An analysis $\mathcal{A} = (\mathcal{L}, \mathcal{F})$, where $\mathcal{L} = (\mathcal{D}, \preceq)$, is a consistent abstraction of $\mathcal{VS}$ if there are a monotonic abstraction function $\alpha\colon \mathit{ValueSets} \to \mathcal{D}$ and a monotonic concretization function $\gamma\colon \mathcal{D} \to \mathit{ValueSets}$, such that

- $\forall x \in \mathcal{D} : x = \alpha(\gamma(x))$.
- $\forall vs \in \mathit{ValueSets} : vs \preceq \gamma(\alpha(vs))$.
- $\forall E \in \mathit{Edges} : S_{\mathcal{VS}}[E] \preceq \gamma(S_{\mathcal{A}}[E])$ and $\alpha(S_{\mathcal{VS}}[E]) \preceq S_{\mathcal{A}}[E]$.

Cousot and Cousot [4] provide sufficient "local" conditions to check that one abstraction is a consistent abstraction of another.

5.3 Null-Pointer Analysis

In this section, we describe a simple *null-pointer analysis NPA* as an example of a consistent abstraction of the value set analysis. This analysis can be used to prove a pointer to be non-null when it is dereferenced. Given a program P, an abstract state is a map of the form $\mathit{LVals} \to \{\mathit{NonNull}, \mathit{MayNull}\}$, where LVals is the set of lvalues in P. The domain of the analysis $\mathcal{D}_{NPA}$ is a set of all such maps. The concretization function $\gamma : \mathcal{D}_{NPA} \to \mathit{ValueSets}$ is defined below for $d \in \mathcal{D}_{NPA}$:

$$\gamma(d)(l) = \begin{cases} \mathit{Values} & \text{if } d(l) = \mathit{MayNull} \\ \mathit{Values} - \{\texttt{NULL}\} & \text{if } d(l) = \mathit{NonNull}. \end{cases}$$

Similarly, if a value set contains NULL, the abstraction function maps it to *MayNull*, otherwise to *NonNull*.

For $d_1, d_2 \in \mathcal{D}_{NPA}$ and $l \in \mathit{LVals}$, the join operation is defined below:

$$d_1 \sqcup d_2(l) = \begin{cases} \mathit{NonNull} & \text{if } d_1(l) = d_2(l) = \mathit{NonNull} \\ \mathit{MayNull} & \text{otherwise.} \end{cases}$$

The flow functions for a node N, edge E and state d are given below. By $d[l \leftarrow a]$ we denote a map same as d except that $d(l) = a$.

If N is of the form `if (l != NULL)`:

$$F_N(d, E) = \begin{cases} d[l \leftarrow \mathit{NonNull}] & \text{if } E \text{ is the true edge} \\ d & \text{otherwise.} \end{cases}$$

If N is of the form `l := e`:

$$F_N(d, E)(l') = \begin{cases} \mathit{NonNull} \text{ if } l' = \texttt{l},\ e \text{ is an lvalue, and } d(e) = \mathit{NonNull} \\ d(l') \qquad \text{if } l' \notin \mathit{AliasSet}(\texttt{l}) \text{ and } \texttt{l} \notin \mathit{AliasSet}(\mathit{deref}(l')) \\ d(l') \qquad \text{if } l' \in \mathit{AliasSet}(\texttt{l}),\ e \text{ is an lvalue,} \\ \qquad\qquad \text{and } d(e) = \mathit{NonNull} \\ \mathit{MayNull} \text{ otherwise.} \end{cases}$$

The flow functions for all other statements are identity functions. It is easy to see that this is an abstraction of the value set analysis.

6 Analysis for Concurrent Programs

Given a concurrent program P and a dataflow analysis $\mathcal{A}$ for sequential programs, our technique converts $\mathcal{A}$ to an analysis for P that is sound if P is datarace-free and $\mathcal{A}$ falls into the class of analyses described in Section 5. We assume availability of a sound may-alias analysis. For example, flow-insensitive may-alias analyses such as [1] are sound for concurrent programs.

1. **Construction of the sync-CFG:** We first construct an extended CFG C for P, called *sync-CFG*, as follows. We begin by taking the disjoint union of the CFGs of threads of P. We then add the *may-synchronize-with* (msw) edges between nodes of these CFGs as described below. These edges are added between nodes that might participate in a *synchronizes-with* relation at runtime. More specifically, we add the the following types of edges:
   1. From a `spawn` node to the `start` node of the child thread.
   2. From an `end` node to the corresponding `join` node of the parent thread.
   3. From an `unlock` node to a `lock` node, if they access the same lock and if the corresponding threads may run in parallel.

   In case the exact set of edges are difficult be compute, we can use any over-approximation of it. For example, if locks can be aliased (not possible in the language described in Section 4.1), we use the may-alias analysis to find out whether a `lock`/`unlock` pair may access the same lock variable at run-time. Similarly, simple control flow based techniques can be used to conservatively detect whether two threads can run in parallel. Figure 1 shows the msw edges added for the shown program fragment.
2. **Constructing Flow functions:** Flow functions of the synchronization statements are simply identity functions. Flow functions of other nodes are same as that of $\mathcal{A}$.
3. **Constructing and Solving Flow Equations:** The sync-CFG C corresponds to a (non-deterministic) sequential program. We construct the flow equations for our analysis $\mathcal{A}$ over C as given in Equation 3. Finally, we compute the least solution of these set of equations over the sync-CFG C.

Interpreting the Result. As we show in Section 7, the solution given by our technique conservatively approximates the value sets of relevant lvalues at a program edge, while it may not be sound for non-relevant lvalues. Hence the client of the analysis must use the result to reason about only relevant lvalues. For example, in the program of Figure 1, our analysis wrongly concludes that `p->data` must be non-null at `C1`, but `p->data` is not relevant at `C1`. On the other hand, it finds `p->data` to be non-null at `C3` where it is relevant and this fact is sound.

Alternatively, to present a solution that is sound for all lvalues, we define a program dependent operation *havoc* on value set states as follows. For $vs \in \mathit{ValueSets}$, $E \in \mathit{Edges}$ and $l \in \mathit{LVals}$,

$$\mathit{havoc}(vs, E)(l) = \begin{cases} \mathit{Values} & \text{if } l \text{ is not relevant at } E \\ vs(l) & \text{otherwise.} \end{cases}$$

Then for an abstract analysis $\mathcal{A}$, $\alpha(\mathit{havoc}(\gamma(S_{\mathcal{A}})[E], E))$ (or any conservative approximation of it) is the final solution at edge E. This step essentially sets the abstract values of non-relevant lvalues at every program point to the most conservative value. Hence, this method produces useful results only for relevant lvalues at each program edge, but is sound for all lvalues.

As each component analysis can be computed in time polynomial in size of the original program, the entire algorithm takes time polynomial in size of the original program.

7 Proof of Soundness

7.1 For Value Set Analysis

In this section we prove that given a datarace-free concurrent program P, the solution characterized by the technique described in Section 6 is a conservative approximation of the collecting semantics defined by Equation 1 for value set analysis with respect to the relevant lvalues at each program edge. Note that the least solution to the equation system 3 is a conservative approximation of the JOP solution over the sync-CFG C of P. Thus it is sufficient for our purpose to argue that if there is an execution of P in which an lvalue l has a value v at a program edge E where l is relevant, then there is an initial path in the *sync-CFG* to E along which the value v is included in the value set of l at E. This is shown in Lemma 2 below. We begin with a lemma that will be useful in proving Lemma 2.

Lemma 1. *Let* $\mathcal{E} = \langle a_0, \ldots, a_j \rangle$ *be an execution of the program* P. *Let* l *be a relevant lvalue at* $\mathit{stmt}(a_j)$ *and* $v = \mathit{pre}(a_j)(l)$. *Let* M *be the set of memory locations corresponding to the lvalues* $\{l\} \cup \mathit{deref}(l)$ *at* a_j. *Let* a_i, $i < j$ *be the last action before* a_j *that writes to a memory location in* M. *Then there exists a static path* Π *in the sync-CFG* C *from* $\mathit{stmt}(\mathit{next}(a_i))$ *to* $\mathit{stmt}(\mathit{prev}(a_j))$ *such that* $\forall vs \in \mathit{ValueSets}\colon v \in vs(l) \Rightarrow v \in F_{\Pi}(vs, E)(l)$, *where* $E = \mathit{eprev}(a_j)$.

Proof. As l is relevant at $\mathit{stmt}(a_j)$, a_j reads all the memory locations of M. As a_i is the last action before a_j that writes to one of these memory locations, a_i and a_j are conflicting. As the program is datarace-free, we must have $a_i \leq_{hb}^{\mathcal{E}} a_j$. Recall that the happens-before relation is the reflexive transitive closure of program-order and synchronizes-with relations. It is easy to see that if for two actions b and b' from $\mathcal{E}$, $b <_{po}^{\mathcal{E}} b'$ or $b <_{sw}^{\mathcal{E}} b'$, then there is an edge in C from $\mathit{stmt}(b)$ to $\mathit{stmt}(b')$. Hence, a path Π' from $\mathit{stmt}(a_i)$ to $\mathit{stmt}(a_j)$ in C can be constructed by joining the edges of C corresponding to these *po* and *sw* relations. As neither a_i nor a_j can be synchronization actions (they read/write to lvalues), hence, in Π', $stmt(a_i)$ is succeeded by $stmt(next(a_i))$ and $stmt(a_j)$ is preceded by $stmt(prev(a_j))$. Clearly, this path is a subsequence of the list of nodes corresponding to $a_i, \ldots, a_j$. We further obtain Π from Π' by excluding $stmt(a_i)$ and $stmt(a_j)$ from Π'.

By contradiction, let vs be a value set state such that $v \in vs(l)$ and $v \notin F_\Pi(vs, E)$. Then there must be a node N and an edge E in Π such that $E \in esucc(N)$ and there is a value set state vs' such that $v \in vs'(l)$ and $v \notin F_N(vs', E)(l)$. From the definition of flow functions from Section 5.1, this can be possible only in the following two cases:

- N is an assignment to l. As a_i was the last assignment to any memory location in M, the memory location corresponding to l does not change after a_i till a_j. If LHS of N was l, then the corresponding action in $a_{i+1}, \ldots, a_{j-1}$ must have written to a memory location in M, which is not possible because of the choice of a_i.
- N is a branch statement and E is the true successor edge and the condition e is such that it does not evaluate to true when l has a value v. This is not possible as the execution took the true branch E with the value v in l. The argument is similar for the false branch.

Hence, there can be no such vs and the lemma is proved. □

Lemma 2. *Let $\mathcal{E} = \langle a_0, \ldots, a_j \rangle$ be an execution of P. Let l be an lvalue relevant at $stmt(a_j)$ and $v = pre(a_j)(l)$. Let $N = stmt(a_j)$ and $E \in epred(N)$ in C. Then there exists an initial static path Θ in C from N_0^M up to E, such that $v \in F_\Theta(\top, E)(l)$.*

Proof. We prove the lemma by induction on the length $k = j + 1$ of the execution $\mathcal{E}$.

Base case: If $k = 0$, $\Theta = \epsilon$ (empty path) and $F_\Theta(\top, E) = \top$. Clearly, $v \in \top(l)$.

Induction step: Let us assume the result for $k < n$ and consider the case for $k = n$.

Let a_i be the last action in $\mathcal{E}$ before a_j which writes to a memory location corresponding to the lvalues in $\{l\} \cup deref(l)$ at a_j. Then we have $v = post(a_i)(l)$ as the value contained in l cannot change after a_i in $\mathcal{E}$. As $\hat{N} = stmt(a_i)$ is an assignment statement, let us denote the singleton edge in $esucc(\hat{N})$ by $\hat{E}$. Then either of the following is true:

1. $\hat{N}$ writes to a memory location corresponding to an lvalue in $deref(l)$ at a_j. In this case, any path $\hat{\Theta}$ from N_0^M to $\hat{N}$ (both inclusive) in C will have $v \in F_{\hat{\Theta}}(\top, \hat{E})(l)$, as the flow function of $\hat{N}$ sets the value set of l to *Values*. It is easy to see that if a node gets executed, then there is a path from N_0^M to that node in C.
2. $\hat{N}$ writes to the memory location corresponding to l. Let the RHS be the expression e. As the length of $\langle a_0, \ldots, a_i \rangle$ is less than k, by the induction hypothesis, there is a path Θ'' from N_0^M up to but not including $\hat{N}$, such

that for all lvalue l' read in e, $v' = pre(a_i)(l') \Rightarrow v' \in F_{\Theta''}(\top, epred(a_i))(l')$. Let $\hat{\Theta} = \Theta''.\hat{N}$. From the definition of static flow function, this implies $v \in F_{\hat{\Theta}}(\top, \hat{E})(l)$.

Now let Π be the path from $stmt(next(a_i))$ to $stmt(prev(a_j))$, excluding both, as given by Lemma 1. Clearly, $E = eprev(a_j)$. Let $\Theta = \hat{\Theta} \cdot \Pi$. As $v \in F_{\hat{\Theta}}(\top, \hat{E})(l)$ and $v = post(a_i)(l)$, using Lemma 1, we have $v \in F_{\Theta}(\top, E)(l)$. □

We finally prove the following soundness theorem:

Theorem 1. *Let P be a datarace-free concurrent program. Let $S_{\mathcal{VS}}$ be the solution returned by our technique and let CVS be the collecting value set of P. If l is an lvalue relevant at an edge E, then $CVS[E](l) \subseteq S_{\mathcal{VS}}[E](l)$.*

Proof. As already observed in the beginning of this section, since our analysis finds a conservative approximation of the *join-over-all-paths* solution over the paths of *sync-CFG* C of P, it is sufficient to show that if there is an execution of P which has a value v in an lvalue l at a program edge E where l is relevant, then there is an initial path in C to E along which the value v is included in the value set of l at E. This is a direct consequence of Lemma 2. Hence the theorem is proved. □

The following corollary is immediate from Theorem 1 and definition of *havoc*.

Corollary 1. *For a datarace-free program P and for all edges E, $CVS[E] \preceq havoc(S_{\mathcal{VS}}[E], E)$.*

7.2 For Abstractions of Value Set Semantics

We now show that the havoced solution characterized by our technique for any consistent abstraction of value set semantics conservatively approximates the collecting semantics for value set analysis for a datarace-free program.

Theorem 2. *Let $\mathcal{A}$ be a consistent abstraction of the value set semantics and $S_{\mathcal{A}}$ be the solution returned by our analysis for a datarace-free concurrent program P. Then for all edges E, $CVS[E] \preceq havoc(\gamma(S_{\mathcal{A}})[E], E)$.*

Proof. From definition of consistent abstraction, $S_{\mathcal{VS}} \preceq \gamma(S_{\mathcal{A}})$. As *havoc* is monotonic, $havoc(S_{\mathcal{VS}}[E], E) \preceq havoc(\gamma(S_{\mathcal{A}})[E], E)$. From Corollary 1, we have $CVS[E] \preceq havoc(S_{\mathcal{VS}}[E], E)$. Thus, $CVS[E] \preceq havoc(\gamma(S_{\mathcal{A}})[E], E)$. □

8 Context-Sensitive Analysis

In this section, we describe how a context-sensitive technique, namely the *call-string approach* [25], can be integrated into our framework. Due to lack of space, we only give an informal description here - for details see [5].

A thread now consists of a number of procedures, each with their own rooted CFGs. Each thread has an *entry procedure*. Execution of a thread starts with the execution of the `start` node of the entry procedure. We define two new types of statements: *CallStmt* of the form `<procname>()`, where `<procname>` is the name of some procedure, and *ReturnStmt* of the form `return`. The control flow structure of a thread is represented by an *Interprocedural Control Flow Graph* (ICFG), which is obtained by taking disjoint union of all the CFGs of all the procedures of the thread and adding *call edges* (from call statements to the root nodes of the called procedures' CFGs) and *return edges* (from return statements to the statements immediately following the corresponding call statements calling the procedures containing the return statements). Note that in any CFG, there are no direct edges from call statements to the next statements.

A call-string is a (possibly empty) sequence of call statements. The domain of the call-string analysis consists of sets of abstract dataflow states tagged with call-strings. Intuitively, these tags represent the call stack when an execution reaches a program point with that abstract value. Clearly, same abstract value can reach a program point with different tags. For sequential programs, the join operation joins only those abstract values whose tags match. Flow functions of nodes other than call and return do not modify the tags, but modify the abstract values like their context-insensitive counterparts. Flow functions for call statements do not modify the abstract value, but modify the call-string tags by pushing the call statement. Flow functions of return statements propagate only those abstract values along a return edge whose tags have the corresponding call statement as the last element of the string. They also pop the last element from such call-string tags. For details of call-string approach for sequential programs, see [25].

In case of datarace-free concurrent programs, any abstract state reachable at a release node tagged with any call-string should be joined with all abstract states reachable at the corresponding acquire node, as the release and the acquire nodes may belong to different dynamic threads at runtime and there is no relation among the call-strings of different threads. If the abstract state corresponding to some call-string is $\perp$ at the acquire node, it implies that the call-string is not reachable at that program node. Hence we join the propagated value only with the call-strings that are mapped to non-bottom values. In practice, we use an approximate but sound call-string approach where a call-string is represented by a finite length suffix, as described in [25]. Details of our context-sensitive technique can be found in [5].

9 Implementation

We implemented our technique into a framework named STAND (for STatic ANanlysis for Datarace-free programs) that automatically converts dataflow analyses for sequential Java programs to analyses for concurrent program. We use Soot [26] as the frontend and SPARK [17] for the alias analysis. We instantiated STAND for null-dereference analysis and ran it on three large Java programs, `jdbm` (a transactional persistence engine), `jdbf` (an object-relational mapping system) and `jtds` (a JDBC driver). Developers of these programs fixed the dataraces detected by Chord [22] and hence, they are likely to be datarace-free. We used a 2.27 GHz Intel Xeon machine with 2 GB RAM for experiments.

We report the percentage of dereferences proven to be safe for our benchmark programs in column *% safe* of Table 1. We observe that on an average, STAND is able to prove over 80% of the dereferences safe. We compare our precision with an unsound sequential analysis that is obtained by removing the msw edges (except for edges from `spawn` to `start`) from a sync-CFG and running the same underlying sequential analysis on the modified graph. Note that this analysis is unsound as it does not account for the interference from other threads. The column *% seq-safe* denotes the percentage of dereferences shown to be safe by this unsound, sequential analysis. We observe that the difference between *% safe* and *% seq-safe* is small. Hence it can be concluded that the loss of precision in STAND can largely be attributed to the underlying sequential analysis. Finally, we report the total analysis time in two parts: *SPARK time* denotes the time taken by the SPARK alias analysis and *STAND time* denotes the time taken by our analysis excluding alias analysis. Note that the analysis time of STAND after alias analysis is fairly small for these benchmark programs.

Table 1. Results using STAND

Benchmark	LOC (w/o lib)	% safe	% seq-safe	STAND time(s)	SPARK time(s)
jdbm	19077	79.5	81.0	2.518	35
jdbf	15923	81.9	82.8	2.883	120
jtds	66318	80.3	84.3	1.709	51

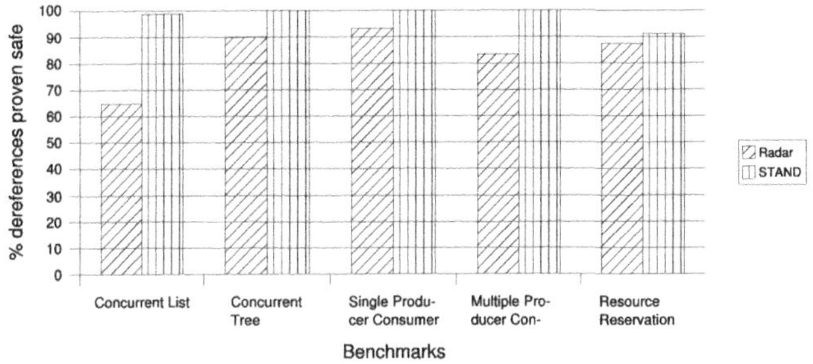

Fig. 4. Precision comparison between Radar and Stand

We also compare STAND with Radar [3] by implementing null-pointer analysis for concurrent C programs using LLVM [18] frontend. We executed Radar and STAND on five concurrent programs (average size $>$ 1 KLOC) implementing some classic concurrent algorithms and data-structures. The precision results given in Figure 4 shows that STAND is consistently more precise than Radar. We manually confirmed the reason behind this precision difference is that Radar kills a dataflow fact whenever some other thread possibly affects that fact whereas STAND propagates the exact facts from one thread to another. The analysis time of STAND for these programs is only 0.8 seconds on average.

Acknowledgments. We thank Ankur Sinha for helping with the experiments.

References

1. Andersen, L.O.: Program Analysis and Specialization for the C Programming Language. Ph.D. thesis, DIKU, University of Copenhagen (1994)
2. Boehm, H.J., Adve, S.V.: Foundations of the C++ Concurrency Memory Model. In: Proceedings of the 2008 ACM SIGPLAN Conference on Programming Language Design and Implementation, pp. 68–78. ACM, New York (2008)
3. Chugh, R., Voung, J.W., Jhala, R., Lerner, S.: Dataflow Analysis for Concurrent Programs Using Datarace Detection. In: Proceedings of the 2008 ACM SIGPLAN Conference on Programming Language Design and Implementation, pp. 316–326. ACM, New York (2008)
4. Cousot, P., Cousot, R.: Abstract Interpretation: A Unified Lattice Model for Static Analysis of Programs by Construction or Approximation of Fixpoints. In: Proceedings of the 4th ACM SIGACT-SIGPLAN Symposium on Principles of programming languages, pp. 238–252. ACM, New York (1977)
5. De, A., D'Souza, D., Nasre, R.: Dataflow Analysis for Datarace-Free Programs. Tech. Rep. IISc-CSA-TR-2010-8, Computer Science and Automation, Indian Institute of Science, India (December 2010), `http://aditya.csa.iisc.ernet.in/TR/2010/8/`
6. Dwyer, M.B., Clarke, L.A.: Data Flow Analysis for Verifying Properties of Concurrent Programs. In: Proceedings of the 2nd ACM SIGSOFT Symposium on Foundations of Software Engineering, pp. 62–75. ACM, New York (1994)
7. Farzan, A., Kincaid, Z.: Compositional Bitvector Analysis for Concurrent Programs with Nested Locks. In: Cousot, R., Martel, M. (eds.) SAS 2011. LNCS, vol. 6337, pp. 253–270. Springer, Heidelberg (2011)
8. Flanagan, C., Freund, S., Qadeer, S.: Thread-Modular Verification for Shared-Memory Programs. In: Le Métayer, D. (ed.) ESOP 2002. LNCS, vol. 2305, pp. 262–277. Springer, Heidelberg (2002)
9. Flanagan, C., Qadeer, S.: Thread-Modular Model Checking. In: Ball, T., Rajamani, S.K. (eds.) SPIN 2003. LNCS, vol. 2648, p. 624. Springer, Heidelberg (2003)
10. Gotsman, A., Berdine, J., Cook, B., Sagiv, M.: Thread-Modular Shape Analysis. In: Proceedings of the 2007 ACM SIGPLAN Conference on Programming Language Design and Implementation, pp. 266–277. ACM, New York (2007)
11. Grunwald, D., Srinivasan, H.: Data Flow Equations for Explicitly Parallel Programs. In: Proceedings of the 4th ACM SIGPLAN Symposium on Principles and Practice of Parallel Programming, pp. 159–168. ACM, New York (1993)
12. JSR-133 Expert Group: JSR-133: Java Memory Model and Thread Specification (August 2004), `http://www.cs.umd.edu/~pugh/java/memoryModel/jsr133.pdf`
13. Kam, J.B., Ullman, J.D.: Monotone Data Flow Analysis Frameworks. Acta Inf. 7, 305–317 (1977)
14. Kildall, G.A.: A Unified Approach to Global Program Optimization. In: Proceedings of the 1st ACM SIGACT-SIGPLAN Symposium on Principles of Programming Languages, pp. 194–206. ACM, New York (1973)
15. Knoop, J., Steffen, B., Vollmer, J.: Parallelism for Free: Efficient and Optimal Bitvector Analyses for Parallel Programs. ACM Trans. Program. Lang. Syst. 18(3), 268–299 (1996)

16. Lee, J., Padua, D.A., Midkiff, S.P.: Basic Compiler Algorithms for Parallel Programs. In: Proceedings of the 7th ACM SIGPLAN Symposium on Principles and Practice of Parallel Programming, pp. 1–12. ACM, New York (1999)
17. Lhoták, O.: Spark: A Flexible Points-to Analysis Framework for Java. Master's thesis, McGill University (December 2002)
18. LLVM Project. The LLVM Compiler Infrastructure, `http://llvm.org/`
19. Malkis, A., Podelski, A., Rybalchenko, A.: Thread-Modular Counterexample-Guided Abstraction Refinement. In: Cousot, R., Martel, M. (eds.) SAS 2010. LNCS, vol. 6337, pp. 356–372. Springer, Heidelberg (2010)
20. Manson, J., Pugh, W., Adve, S.V.: The Java Memory Model. In: Proceedings of the 32nd ACM SIGPLAN-SIGACT Symposium on Principles of Programming Languages, pp. 378–391. ACM, New York (2005)
21. Musuvathi, M., Qadeer, S.: Iterative Context Bounding for Systematic Testing of Multithreaded Programs. In: Proceedings of the 2007 ACM SIGPLAN Conference on Programming Language Design and Implementation, pp. 446–455. ACM, New York (2007)
22. Naik, M., Aiken, A., Whaley, J.: Effective Static Race Detection for Java. In: Proceedings of the 2006 ACM SIGPLAN conference on Programming Language Design and Implementation, pp. 308–319. ACM, New York (2006)
23. Rugina, R., Rinard, M.: Pointer Analysis for Multithreaded Programs. In: Proceedings of the ACM SIGPLAN 1999 Conference on Programming Language Design and Implementation, pp. 77–90. ACM, New York (1999)
24. Sevcik, J.: Program Transformations in Weak Memory Models. Ph.D. thesis, University of Edinburgh (2008)
25. Sharir, M., Pnueli, A.: Two Approaches to Interprocedural Data Flow Analysis, ch. 7, pp. 189–234. Prentice-Hall, Englewood Cliffs (1981)
26. Valle-Rai, R.: Soot: A Java Bytecode Optimization Framework. Master's thesis, McGill University (July 2000)
27. Visser, W., Havelund, K., Brat, G., Park, S.: Model Checking Programs. In: Proceedings of the 15th IEEE International Conference on Automated Software Engineering, p. 3. IEEE Computer Society, Washington, DC (2000)

Compiling Information-Flow Security to Minimal Trusted Computing Bases

Cédric Fournet[1,2] and Jérémy Planul[1]

[1] MSR-INRIA
[2] Microsoft Research

Abstract. Information-flow policies can express strong security requirements for programs run by distributed parties with different levels of trust. However, this security is hard to preserve as programs get compiled to distributed systems with (potentially) compromised machines. For instance, many programs involve computations too sensitive to be trusted to any of those machines. Also, many programs are not perfectly secure (non-interferent); as they selectively endorse and declassify information, their relative security becomes harder to preserve.

We develop a secure compiler for distributed information flows. To minimize trust assumptions, we rely on cryptographic protection, and we exploit hardware and software mechanisms available on modern architectures, such as secure boots, trusted platform modules, and remote attestation.

We present a security model for these mechanisms in an imperative language with dynamic code loading. We define program transformations to generate trusted virtual hosts and to run them on untrusted machines. We obtain confidentiality and integrity theorems under realistic assumptions, showing that the compiled distributed system is at least as secure as the source program.

1 Programming with TPMs

When designing or reviewing the security of a system, a first step is to identify its trusted computing base (TCB), that is, the set of components that need to be trusted to achieve a given level of security. For general-purpose networked machines, this set is large and complex; it includes the hardware, an operating system, a runtime environment and their libraries (maybe 10^8 LOCs overall) plus drivers, applications, and dynamically loaded code. This leads to a best-effort approach to security, at odds with formal verification, which provides strong guarantees only for smaller, simpler systems.

Minimal TCBs. Modern computer architectures provide hardware support for reducing TCBs and protecting privileged operations. Thus, most computers come bundled with some form of secure coprocessor with a dedicated secure instruction set—for example, most laptops now embed a Trusted Platform Module (TPM) (TCG, 2005) and many high-end processors feature a special *late launch* functionality (AMD's Secure Virtual Machine Architecture, 2005, and Intel's Trusted Execution Technology, 2009). These instructions can run a given piece of code in isolation, with strong code-based identity and privileged cryptographic operations, for instance to seal persistent state or to perform remote attestation. Such hardware mechanisms can greatly reduce the TCB of security applications, by removing the need to trust the host operating system

G. Barthe (Ed.): ESOP 2011, LNCS 6602, pp. 216–235, 2011.
© Springer-Verlag Berlin Heidelberg 2011

and other applications, and thus help protect critical data and computations from malicious software. TPMs are routinely used for secure booting, e.g. BitLocker (Microsoft, 2006) guards access to the master keys for disk encryption, so that the disk content may be read only after authenticating the user and the operating system. Research papers also describe e.g. how to build secure online payment systems (Balfe and Paterson, 2008) and how to use late launches to run small pieces of application code in isolation (McCune et al., 2008, 2009). Still, the secure instructions are remarkably seldom used in practice. We believe that the complexity of their low-level interface and the lack of programming tools are major obstacles to their mainstream adoption for writing security applications.

Information-flow security. At a more abstract level, language-based security often relies on information flow policies (Denning, 1976; Myers and Liskov, 2000). Each variable is assigned a level in a security lattice; this level indicates the intended integrity and confidentiality of any information stored in this variable. Thus, a program is deemed completely secure (non-interferent) if an adversary that can access only low-level information cannot gain (or influence) any higher-level information by executing the program. Static analyses and type systems have been developed to verify that a program is secure with regards to a given policy. Further, it is sometimes possible to compile such programs to a given system while preserving their security properties. Hence, Jif (Myers et al., 2001) and FlowCaml (Pottier and Simonet, 2003) provide security type-checking for Java and Caml, respectively. Further, Jif/Split (Zdancewic et al., 2002; Zheng et al., 2003) and Swift (Chong et al., 2009) automatically partition distributed programs into local code, each running at a given security level, representing the level of trust granted to each host in a distributed system. As can be expected, program partitioning fails when no host is sufficiently trusted to run some parts of the computation, such as code that operates on secrets provided by mutually-suspicious parties. Cryptographically-blinded evaluation techniques (Diffie and Hellman, 1976) can sometimes solve this problem, but with a high performance overhead. Instead, in this paper, we systematically rely on secure hardware to virtually 'boot' short-lived, trusted environments for executing privileged code.

Example: applying for a loan. Consider a program involving two parties, a bank that offers loans, and a client that wishes to apply for a loan without disclosing private information (at least until the loan is granted). Suppose also that the bank does not want to disclose the parameters used for evaluating loan applications. Although the client and the bank do not trust one another, they may agree to securely run the loan-evaluation code on a TPM-enabled client machine. This simple computation is depicted below.

The bank sends its (encrypted, signed) secret input (x_b) to the client; the client forwards it to the code running the loan evaluation, together with its own input (y_c), using shared local memory; after securely booting, the TPM-protected code decrypts its input, evaluates the loan, and returns its results; finally, the client gets its result (y'_c) and may forward the (encrypted, signed) output (x'_b) to the bank if the loan is granted.

The messages passed between the bank and TPM-protected code must be cryptographically protected, so that for instance the bank input may be read and processed only by that code—not by the client or the network. The code protected by the TPM is short but complex as regards information flows: the inputs are endorsed (letting the

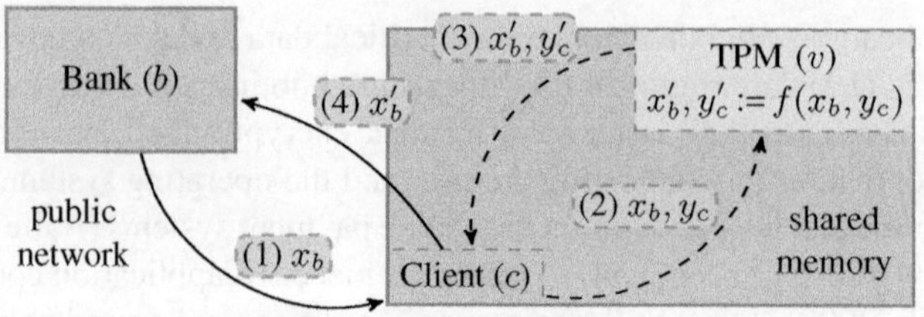

client accept the bank input and vice versa) then the outputs are declassified (releasing partial information from the client input to the bank and vice versa). Also, this code must refuse to run multiple loan evaluations for different client inputs without the bank's consent, as this may enable the extraction of the bank input.

Compiling with minimal TCBs. We compile imperative programs with security and locality annotations to distributed programs using cryptography and TPMs, and we show that our compilation scheme preserves information-flow security under standard cryptographic assumptions.

To this end, we specify a subset of the TPM instructions within a core imperative programming language. Our model aims at formal simplicity while still reflecting the main security features of hardware and cryptographic specifications, at a level of detail sufficient for reasoning about information flows. We model secure instructions to manage monotonic counters; measure code; run code in isolation; cryptographically sign data using the private attestation key of the TPM; and cryptographically seal and unseal data associated with some code.

We use this imperative language as the target of a new security-preserving compiler, built by adapting and extending recent work on cryptographic support for enforcing information-flow policies (Fournet and Rezk, 2008; Fournet et al., 2009). In their work, imperative commands are annotated with a host location, indicating where to run the command. Each location is also given a security level, used to type the source program. Their compiler, CFLOW, generates a protocol for securing the transfer of control between locations, as specified by the control flow of the source program, and selective encryption and authentication for securing the exchange of data.

We add support for dynamic code linking and a more permissive type system, enabling us to compile source programs that perform almost arbitrary declassifications and endorsements. We also provide runtime support for implementing highly-trusted locations by relying on secure instructions on relatively less trusted machines. Hence, we obtain distributed systems composed of ordinary application code and privileged code, with custom cryptographic support to coordinate their execution, such that all information-flow properties of the source program are preserved.

In summary, our main contributions are:

1. An operational semantics for modelling TPM-based security, focusing on TCB reduction by higher-order programming, with sample code and security properties.
2. A robust, flexible extension of CFLOW, enabling endorsement and declassification in typed source programs, with improved security definitions and theorems.
3. A compilation scheme for booting trusted hosts on demand, taking advantage of TPM attestation, with correctness and security theorems.

Contents. Section 2 defines an imperative, probabilistic, higher-order programming language. Section 3 defines information-flow policies, active adversaries, and target security properties. Section 4 describes and formalizes secure hardware instructions. Section 5 presents the CFLOW compiler and its theorems. Section 6 shows how to use TPM capabilities to implement secure virtual hosts, such as those produced by CFLOW.

An extended paper, the CFLOW compiler, and various code samples are available at **`http://msr-inria.inria.fr/projects/sec/cflow`**. The extended paper presents additional materials, including proofs; experimental results obtained by adapting CFLOW to generate statically-linked C code and running it on several small virtual machines; discussions on our shared memory model and scheduling; and additional results on attested boot sequences when the adversary can schedule, reboot, and corrupt host machines (but not their TPMs).

2 An Imperative Higher-Order Language

We define a probabilistic while-language with a command to turn data into executable code, used later to model dynamic code loading and TPM capabilities. The grammar for expressions and commands is

$$\begin{aligned} e &::= x \mid op(e_1, \ldots, e_n) \\ P &::= x := e \mid x := f(x_1, \ldots, x_n) \mid \mathit{skip} \mid P; P \\ &\quad\mid \text{if } e \text{ then } P \text{ else } P \mid \text{while } e \text{ do } P \mid \text{link}\, e\, [\widetilde{P}]\, \ell \mid X \end{aligned}$$

where op and f range over deterministic and probabilistic n-ary functions, respectively, with arity $n \geq 0$. Expressions e consist of variables and operations. We write op for nullary constructors $op()$. We assume given (polynomial-time) functions for standard boolean and arithmetic constants $(0, 1, \ldots)$ and operators $(||, +, \ldots)$. Commands P consist of variable assignments, using deterministic expressions and probabilistic functions, composed into sequences, conditionals, and loops, plus a link command for dynamically loading, linking, and running code. We write $\widetilde{P}$ for a tuple of commands $P_1, \ldots, P_n$ for some $n \geq 0$. Command variables X are placeholders for commands, bound in command contexts and when running link commands. As usual, we often use anonymous command variables in command contexts, writing $P[\widetilde{Q}]$ instead of $P[\widetilde{Q}/\widetilde{X}]$. For instance, $(X_1;X_2;X_1)[P_1,P_2]$ stands for $P_1;P_2;P_1$.

Commands as Data. We use data constructors to represent commands (and their expressions) as expressions, such as $op\_if(e_1,e_2,e_3)$ for conditionals and op_x for variable x. For instance, the command $c := c + 5$ is represented by $op\_assign(op_c, (op\_plus\ (op_c,5)))$. To ease the writing of expressions representing commands, we let $\langle P \rangle$ be the expression that represents command P. Command expressions can also contain variables; these variables are quoted within $\langle P \rangle$. For instance, the expression $op\_assign(op_c, (op\_plus(op_c,t)))$ is written $\langle c := c + `t \rangle$.

The command $\text{link}\, e\, [\widetilde{P}]\, \ell$ dynamically checks that the result of expression e represents a valid command at level ℓ (the role of ℓ is explained below) parameterized by subcommand variables $\widetilde{P}$, and then runs that command after replacing each X_i with the command P_i. We write link $e\ \ell$ instead of link $e\ []\ \ell$ when $\widetilde{P}$ is empty. These checks occur at link-time, before running the command, as would be the case with a high-level virtual machine. In contrast, low-level protection for executable and data memory is usually enforced later, at runtime (e.g. by triggering memory page faults). Thus, for instance, information flows due to low-level memory error handling are outside the scope of our model. See also Askarov and Sabelfeld (2009) for a information-flow model of dynamic loading with run-time monitoring.

Probabilistic Semantics. The full paper details our operational semantics; in this presentation we only present our main notations. We use a probabilistic semantics mainly to model cryptographic algorithms as commands.

Program configurations are of the form $\langle P, \mu\rangle$ where P is a program and μ is a *memory*, that is, a function from variables to values. Our operational semantics is defined by a probabilistic reduction step relation $\rightsquigarrow_p$ between configurations, with $0 < p \leq 1$. We give below our rule for link commands (with $p = 1$).

$$\text{(LINK)}\quad \frac{[\![e]\!](\mu) = \langle P\rangle \qquad \vdash P : \ell}{\langle \text{link}\, e\, [\widetilde{P}]\, \ell, \mu\rangle \rightsquigarrow_1 \langle P[\widetilde{P}/\widetilde{X}], \mu\rangle}$$

We write $\Pr[\langle P, \mu\rangle; \varphi]$ for the probability that P terminates with a final memory that meets condition φ. When P always terminates, that is, $\Pr[\langle P, \mu\rangle; \mathit{true}] = 1$, we write $\rho_\infty(\langle P, \mu\rangle)$ for the final distribution of memories obtained by running P with initial memory μ. For a given domain X, we write $\mu_{|X}$ for μ restricted to X and $\rho_{|X}$ for the projection of ρ on X, that is, $\rho_{|X}(\mu_{|X}) = \sum_{\mu' | \mu_{|X} = \mu'_{|X}} \rho(\mu')$.

Cryptographic assumptions. We consider only polynomial-time commands, and rely on standard computational definitions and assumptions for cryptography primitives; see the full paper for the details.

We use functions $\mathcal{G}_e$, $\mathcal{E}$, $\mathcal{D}$ and $\mathcal{G}_{\mathcal{SE}}$, $\mathcal{SE}$, $\mathcal{SD}$ for public-key and symmetric-key generation, encryption, and decryption; functions $\mathcal{G}_s()$, $\mathcal{S}$, and $\mathcal{V}$ for public-key generation, signing, and verification; functions $\mathcal{G}_\mathcal{M}$, $\mathcal{M}$, and $\mathcal{V}_\mathcal{M}$ for MAC key generation, computation, and verification; and functions $\mathcal{G}$ and $\mathcal{H}$ for pseudo-random hash function initialization and application.

3 Information Flow Security

Next, we define information-flow policies, we describe their enforcement by typing, and we discuss support for potentially-unsafe information flows. We then model active adversaries as command contexts, and give the general form of our target security properties.

Security Labels. We annotate each variable with a security label. These labels specify the programmer's security intent. Except for dynamic links, they do not affect the operational semantics of programs. The security labels form a lattice $(\mathcal{L}, \leq)$ obtained as the product of two lattices, for confidentiality levels $(\mathcal{L}_C, \leq_C)$ and for integrity levels $(\mathcal{L}_I, \leq_I)$. We write $\bot_\mathcal{L}$ and $\top_\mathcal{L}$ for the smallest and largest elements of $\mathcal{L}$, and $\sqcup$ and $\sqcap$

$$\text{(TSUBC)}\ \frac{\vdash P:\ell \quad \ell' \leq \ell}{\vdash P:\ell'} \qquad \text{(TFUN)}\ \frac{\vdash \widetilde{y}:\Gamma(x)}{\vdash x := f(\widetilde{y}) : \Gamma(x)} \qquad \text{(TSEQ)}\ \frac{\vdash P:\ell \quad \vdash P':\ell}{\vdash P;P' : \ell} \qquad \text{(TSKIP)}\ \frac{}{\vdash \mathit{skip} : \top}$$

$$\text{(TCOND)}\ \frac{\vdash e:\ell \quad \vdash P:\ell \quad \vdash P':\ell}{\vdash \text{if } e \text{ then } P \text{ else } P' : \ell} \qquad \text{(TWHILE)}\ \frac{\vdash e:\ell \quad \vdash P : \ell}{\vdash \text{while } e \text{ do } P : \ell} \qquad \text{(TVAR)}\ \frac{}{\vdash X : (\bot_C, \top_I)}$$

Strict rules:

$$\text{(TASSIGN STRICT)}\ \frac{\vdash e:\Gamma(x)}{\vdash x := e : \Gamma(x)} \qquad \text{(TLINK STRICT)}\ \frac{\vdash e:\ell \quad \vdash \widetilde{P}:(\bot_C,\top_I)}{\vdash \text{link}\, e\, [\widetilde{P}]\, \ell : \ell}$$

Lax rules:

$$\text{(TASSIGN ENDORSE)}\ \frac{\vdash e:(c,\_) \quad c \leq C(x)}{\vdash x := e : \Gamma(x)} \qquad \text{(TASSIGN ROBUST)}\ \frac{\vdash e:(c,\_) \quad c \not\leq C(x)}{\vdash x := e : \Gamma(x) \sqcap (\top_C, R(c))} \qquad \text{(TLINK PRIVILEGED)}\ \frac{\vdash e:\ell \quad \vdash \widetilde{P}:\ell \quad \ell \leq \ell'}{\vdash \text{link}\, e\, [\widetilde{P}]\, \ell' : \ell}$$

Fig. 1. Security type system (for a fixed policy Γ)

for the least upper bound and greatest lower bound of two elements of $\mathcal{L}$, respectively. We write $\bot_C$, $\bot_I$, $\top_C$, and $\top_I$ for the smallest and largest elements of $\mathcal{L}_C$ and $\mathcal{L}_I$, respectively. In examples, we often use a four-point lattice defined by $LH < HH < HL$ and $LH < LL < HL$, where LH for instance is low-confidentiality high-integrity.

For a given label $\ell = (\ell_C, \ell_I)$ of $\mathcal{L}$, the confidentiality label ℓ_C specifies a read level for variables, while the integrity label ℓ_I specifies a write level; the meaning of $\ell \leq \ell'$ is that ℓ' is at least as confidential (can be read by fewer entities) and at most as trusted (can be written by more entities) than ℓ (Myers et al., 2006). We let $C(\ell) = \ell_C$ and $I(\ell) = \ell_I$ be the projections that yield the confidentiality and integrity parts of a label. Hence, the partial order on $\mathcal{L}$ is defined as $\ell \leq \ell'$ iff $C(\ell) \leq_C C(\ell')$ and $I(\ell) \leq_I I(\ell')$. We overload $\leq_C$ and $\leq_I$, letting $\ell \leq_C \ell'$ be $C(\ell) \leq_C C(\ell')$ and $\ell \leq_I \ell'$ be $I(\ell) \leq_I I(\ell')$. We let $\ell^I \doteq (\bot_C, I(\ell))$ be the label with low confidentiality and the integrity of ℓ.

Policies. Memory policies are functions Γ from variables to security labels. We define *low equality* between memories, memory distributions, and distributions, relative to a label $\ell \in \mathcal{L}$: letting $S = \{x \mid \Gamma(x) \leq \ell\}$, we define $\mu =_\ell \mu'$ as $\mu_{|S} = \mu'_{|S}$, $\rho =_\ell \rho'$ as $\rho_{|S} = \rho'_{|S}$, and $d =_\ell d'$ as $d_{|S} = d'_{|S}$.

A Strict Type System for Non-interference. As a starting point, we equip our language with a type system that enforces (termination-insensitive) non-interference. Typing judgments for commands are of the form $\Gamma \vdash P : \ell$. We often omit the policy Γ when it is clear from the context.

The typing rules for commands appear in Figure 1 (excluding the 'lax' rules). We omit the standard typing rules for expressions, such that $\vdash e : \ell$ when $\Gamma(x) \leq \ell$ for each variable x read in e. This type system is similar to those typically used for non-interference (see e.g. Sabelfeld and Myers, 2003). The only new rule is TLINK STRICT: the command $\text{link}\, e\, [\widetilde{P}]\, \ell$, when executed, will check that the expression e represents a valid command at level ℓ before running it. Accordingly, we type the command also at level ℓ, after checking that its actual auxiliary commands have level $(\bot_C, \top_I)$, as anticipated by rule TVAR. (We considered typing auxiliary commands and command variables at other levels, but this is not needed for our present purpose.) We also check that the expression e has level ℓ, to keep track of the implicit flow from command values to their runtime effects. To illustrate this rule, consider two variables $secret$ and x at levels $\ell_s = \Gamma(secret)$ and $\ell_x = \Gamma(x)$ such that $\ell_s \not\leq \ell_x$. We have:

1. $x := secret$ is not typable.
2. $\vdash$ link $\langle x := secret \rangle$ $\ell : \ell$ but runtime type checking will fail.
3. link $\langle x :=$ '$secret \rangle$ ℓ_x is not typable (preventing a flow from the command expression).
4. $\vdash$ link $\langle x :=$ '$secret \rangle$ $\ell_s : \ell_s$ but runtime type checking will fail.
5. link $\langle$if $secret$ then $X\rangle[\, x := 0 \,]$ ℓ_s is not typable unless $\ell_x = (\bot_C, \top_I)$.
6. $\vdash$ link $\langle$if $secret$ then $X\rangle[\, x := 0 \,]$ $\ell_s : \ell_s$ if $\ell_x = (\bot_C, \top_I)$ but runtime type checking will also fail (preventing an implicit flow from running the auxiliary command).

With the strict typing rules, typing guarantees non-interference:

Theorem 1 (Non-interference). *Let Γ be a security policy, P a (strictly) well-typed command, $\ell \in \mathcal{L}$, and μ_0 and μ_1 two initial memories such that P always terminates.*
If $\mu_0 =_\ell \mu_1$, then $\rho_\infty(\langle P, \mu_0 \rangle) =_\ell \rho_\infty(\langle P, \mu_1 \rangle)$.

Declassifications and Endorsements. Our strict type system thus excludes many useful programs that (by design) selectively declassify secrets or endorse untrusted values.

Example 1 (Password protection). Consider a program that releases a secret after verifying a password entered in variable *guess*:

if $guess = pwd$ then $r := secret$

with $\Gamma(guess) = LL$, $\Gamma(pwd) = HH$, $\Gamma(r) = LH$, and $\Gamma(secret) = HH$. Although this program is arguably secure, it endorses *guess* (which is a priori untrusted), declassifies the outcome of the test (which is secret, since *pwd* is), then possibly declassifies $secret$.

Consider now a system that provides a subcommand that conditionally releases a secret after verifying a password, and tolerates up to three failed attempts (to protect against brute-force attacks on the password):

$c := 0;$
link a[if $c < 3$ && $guess = pwd$ then $r := secret$ else c++] LL

using a counter variable c with $\Gamma(c) = LH$ and a variable a with $\Gamma(a) = LL$ for dynamically loading code that may call this subcommand. Intuitively, a contains arbitrary low-level code, representing an active adversary, that cannot leak *pwd* or *secret* and cannot write *pwd*, *secret*, or *c*. If linking succeeds, this code can only access the secret by calling its privileged subcommand, and only the first three calls may succeed. For instance, running the command above with an initial memory where a is set to the command *guess* := 0; while *guess* < 10 && *r* = 0 do { *X*; *guess*++ }

leaks *secret* to *r* only if *pwd* is 0, 1, or 2. More generally, if we also assume that *pwd* is sampled at random, the probability that any adversary command learns anything about *secret* is bounded by the sum of the probabilities of the three most probable passwords ($3/N$ if there are N uniformly distributed passwords).

We intend to compile such programs, letting the programmer take responsibility for the source properties of her program, but still ensuring that the compilation process does not introduce any further potentially-unsafe information flows.

Robustness. In the example above, the programmer deliberately declassifies information. Moreover, the declassification depends on the low-integrity variable *guess*, thereby letting the adversary influence what is declassified. This is generally dangerous; for instance, our example would be entirely broken with $\Gamma(pwd) = HL$. Conversely, a declassification is *robust* when it does not depend on low-integrity data, and thus cannot be influenced by active adversaries (Zdancewic and Myers, 2001; Sabelfeld and Myers, 2004; Chong and Myers, 2006; Askarov and Myers, 2010). We support non-robust declassifications, treating them as a high-integrity endorsement followed by a robust declassification, and we rely on a *robustness function*, $R : \mathcal{L}_C \to \mathcal{L}_I$, that indicates the minimum integrity level required to declassify each confidentiality level. Although we allow endorsement and non-robust declassification, in the following, we still usually demand that our security policies be robust:

Definition 1 (Robust policies). *For a given robustness function R, $\ell \in \mathcal{L}$ is robust when $I(\ell) \le R(C(\ell))$; Γ is robust for R when $\Gamma(x)$ is robust for all $x \in \mathrm{dom}(\Gamma)$.*

A More Permissive Type System. For typing source programs, we define a new type system, whose typing rules allow declassifications and endorsements but take them into account to compute the level of the command (sometimes called its 'program counter' level). The typing rules appear in Figure 1, using three new 'lax' typing rules instead of the 'strict' ones. The rules TASSIGN ENDORSE and TASSIGN ROBUST are two generalization of rule TASSIGN STRICT. TASSIGN ENDORSE is TASSIGN STRICT only when e has at least the integrity of x; otherwise, the assignment endorses e. Irrespective of e, the command is typed at the level of x. TASSIGN ROBUST enables the declassification of e into x ($c \not\leq C(x)$) but it records this privileged operation by raising the command type up to the associated robust integrity level $R(c)$. The rule TLINK PRIVILEGED generalizes TLINK STRICT by allowing the caller to link e with auxiliary commands at arbitrary levels of integrity, but it records those levels in the type of the command. This endorses at link-time any calls to the auxiliary commands, since dynamic typing of the callee ignores the integrity of auxiliary command variables (rule TVAR).

The lax type system enforces two fundamental properties. First, if a command has level ℓ, then it does not write variables below ℓ. Second, a command at level ℓ may declassify values of confidentiality c only if $I(\ell) \le R(c)$.

Theorem 2 (Containment). *Let Γ be a policy, $\ell \in \mathcal{L}$, P a command, and μ a memory such that P terminates. If $\vdash P : \ell'$ and $\ell' \not\leq \ell$, then $\rho_\infty(\langle P, \mu\rangle) =_\ell \mu$.*

Theorem 3 (Robust non-interference). *Let Γ be a policy, $\ell \in \mathcal{L}$, $c \in \mathcal{L}_C$ such that $I(\ell) \not\leq R(c)$, and $L = \{x \mid c \not\leq C(x)\}$. Let P be a command and μ_0, μ_1 memories such that P terminates. If $\vdash P : \ell$ and $\mu_{0|L} = \mu_{1|L}$, then $\rho_\infty(\langle P, \mu_0 \rangle)_{|L} = \rho_\infty(\langle P, \mu_1 \rangle)_{|L}$.*

Active Adversaries. In the following, our security properties are parameterized by the power of the adversary, defined by a security level $\alpha \in \mathcal{L}$. We say that a command A is an adversary command (respectively an adversary command context) if it reads only variables of lower confidentiality than $C(\alpha)$, write only variables of higher integrity than $I(\alpha)$, and use links only with a level above α. We are interested in robustness functions that ensure adversaries can read any variable they can write, at least when the policy Γ is robust.

Definition 2. *R is robust against an adversary level α when, for all confidentiality levels $c \in \mathcal{L}_C$, if $I(\alpha) \leq R(c)$, then $c \leq C(\alpha)$.*

Our next theorem guarantees that, with R robust against α and with a robust security policy, an adversary command does not gain additional expressiveness by using link. This justifies our condition on link in the definition of adversary commands.

Theorem 4. *Let α be an adversary level, R be a robustness function robust against α, Γ be a security policy robust for R, and A an adversary command. There exists an adversary command A' with no link commands such that, for all memory μ, if A terminates on μ, then A' terminates on μ and $\rho_\infty(\langle A, \mu \rangle) = \rho_\infty(\langle A', \mu \rangle)$.*

Properties of Program Transformations. We finally present the main properties we establish for our compiler, as regards both security and functional correctness. The properties are stated below for an abstract program transformation between source and target programs; they are instantiated before each of our main theorems in Sections 5 and 6.

We are interested in transformations that operate on programs that are (possibly) not perfectly secure, so we cannot define security as the preservation of non-interference. Instead, for each of our transformations, we demand that there is an inverse map from target adversaries to source adversaries, essentially showing how to 'decompile' each attack into an attack already present before the transformation is applied.

We consider system configurations obtained by composing an imperative program $P \in \mathcal{P}$, an adversary (e.g. a command context) $A \in \mathcal{A}$, and an initial state (e.g. a memory) $\mu \in \mathcal{M}$. Their semantics is given by an evaluation function, written $\langle\!\langle \cdot \rangle\!\rangle : \mathcal{P} \to \mathcal{A} \to \mathcal{M} \to \mathcal{M}$, and an observational equivalence on states, written $\approx \subseteq \mathcal{M}^2$. For a given program and an arbitrary adversary, we are interested in the properties of final states up to $\approx$. For instance, if we consider commands for a client and a bank scheduled by an adversary that controls the network, we may let programs range over pairs of commands Q_c, Q_b, let adversaries range over binary command contexts, let $\approx$ be low-equality on memory distributions, and use the evaluation function

$$\langle\!\langle (Q_c, Q_b), A, \mu \rangle\!\rangle \doteq \rho_\infty(\langle A[Q_c, Q_b], \mu \rangle)$$

Given definitions for source $(\mathcal{P}, \mathcal{A}, \mathcal{M}, \approx, \langle\!\langle\rangle\!\rangle)$ and target $(\mathcal{P}', \mathcal{A}', \mathcal{M}', \approx', \langle\!\langle\rangle\!\rangle')$ configurations, we consider *program transformations*, written $[\![\cdot]\!] : \mathcal{P} \to \mathcal{P}'$, together with *state projections* (that is, surjective functions), written $\pi : \mathcal{M}' \rightarrow \mathcal{M}$. (The role of π is to erase any auxiliary variable introduced by the transformation.) We arrive at the following definitions:

Definition 3 (Security). $(\llbracket\cdot\rrbracket, \pi)$ *is secure when, for every source program* $P \in \mathcal{P}$ *and target adversary* $A' \in \mathcal{A}'$, *there is a source adversary* $A \in \mathcal{A}$ *such that, for every target initial memory* $\mu' \in \mathcal{M}'$, *we have* $\langle\!\langle P, A, \pi(\mu')\rangle\!\rangle \approx \pi\langle\!\langle \llbracket P \rrbracket, A', \mu'\rangle\!\rangle'$.

Definition 4 (Correctness). $(\llbracket\cdot\rrbracket, \pi)$ *is correct when, for every source program* $P \in \mathcal{P}$ *and source adversary* $A \in \mathcal{A}$, *there is a target adversary* $A' \in \mathcal{A}'$ *such that, for every target initial memory* $\mu' \in \mathcal{M}'$, *we have* $\langle\!\langle P, A, \pi(\mu')\rangle\!\rangle \approx \pi\langle\!\langle \llbracket P \rrbracket, A', \mu'\rangle\!\rangle'$.

The two definitions differ in their quantification on adversaries. Informally, all attacks must be reflected, but not all of them need to be preserved, so we expect functional correctness only for a well-behaved subset of adversaries, acting for instance as reliable networks and fair schedulers, and we will use a smaller set $\mathcal{A}$ for Definition 4 than for Definition 3.

4 Command Semantics for Secure Instructions

We model a core subset of the security features available on modern processors with a TPM. Aiming at formal simplicity, we do not account for all the details of their hardware specification, but still intend to reflect their gist. We set an (intuitively high) robust security level ℓ_{TPM} for the hardware, and assign that level to fixed variables that model parts of the hardware-protected memory, together with fixed commands that model secure instructions and have privileged access to these variables. (Their initialization is described at the end of the section.) We then model software as commands linked to these privileged subcommands, thereby gaining indirect access to protected variables.

Related Work. We briefly discuss prior models and analyses for TPMs. Abadi and Wobber (2004) give an authorization logic for a precursor of the TPM. Gürgens et al. (2008) analyze several TCG protocols. Millen et al. (2007) study remote attestation using a model-checker. Datta et al. (2009) develop a logic for reasoning about attestation and secure boots. Our model of the TPM differs from theirs in its use of information flows, memory policies, and cryptographic assumptions. It also covers confidentiality properties and deals with sealing and unsealing.

Monotonic Counters. The TPM features a collection of monotonic counters, that is, persistent protected memory whose contents can only be read and incremented, but not reset (TCG, 2006, p 681). Such counters are essential for protection against replays.

We model just one of these counters, using a public variable c at the integrity level of the TPM. Thus, our counter can be read by any command but it is exclusively assigned by the fixed command INC below. In particular, c cannot be reset or decremented.

$$\text{INC} \doteq \quad c := c{+}1 \qquad\qquad \Gamma(c) = \ell^I_{TPM}$$

(Concretely, TPMs manage a few independent counters with finer access control, and the operating system is in charge of restricting increments to prevent denial of service.)

Example 2. Continuing with our password example, we may use the monotonic counter to reliably keep track of guessing attempts:

link a[if $c < 3$ && $guess = pwd$ then $r := secret$ else INC] LL

Platform Configuration Registers. The TPM also features a collection of Platform Configuration Registers (PCR), which are cleared when the machine reboots, then selectively written by TPM commands. As detailed in the full paper, these registers usually contain measurements of the code running on the machine. PCRs are specialized: the first PCRs are used for static root of trust measurements as the machine boots (SRTM) (Grawrock, 2007), while PCRs 17–19 are used for dynamic root of trust measurements (DRTM) and may be selectively reset without rebooting (TCG, 2006; AMD, 2005). PCRs are read as high-integrity implicit parameters for many other TPM commands, such as attestation and seals. We model PCRs as variables h_i at level ℓ^I_{TPM}. For simplicity, we use just two registers, h_1 for SRTM, modified only by EXTEND$_1$, and h_{17} for DRTM, initialized by SKINIT and modified by EXTEND$_{17}$, as explained below.

EXTEND$_i$ appends some code identity to h_i and can be used to record a delegation chain starting from a secure kernel (TCG, 2006, p 284). To keep the size of h_i constant, the chain is implemented as a nested hash, using a cryptographic hash functions $\mathcal{H}$. We model it as

$$\text{EXTEND}_i \doteq \quad h_i := \mathcal{H}(h_i|\mathit{identity}) \qquad \Gamma(h_i) = \ell^I_{TPM} \qquad \Gamma(\mathit{identity}) = (\bot_C, \top_I)$$

where '|' is bitstring concatenation and *identity* is a public-untrusted variable .

SKINIT sets the code identity in h_{17} to (the hash of) a new command passed as input, usually called a 'secure kernel', then runs that command, and finally clears h_{17} (AMD, 2005, p 53). We model it as an assignment to h_{17} from the content of a public-untrusted variable *kernel*, followed by a link of *kernel* with subcommands parameters that pass to the new kernel the rest of the TPM interface (written $\widetilde{TPM}$), then a reset of h_{17}. We let $\widetilde{TPM} \doteq \{\text{INC}, \text{EXTEND}_{17}, \text{ATTEST}_{17}, \text{SEAL}_{17}, \text{UNSEAL}_{17}\}$.

$$\text{SKINIT} \doteq \quad h_{17} := \mathcal{H}(kernel);\ \text{link}\ kernel[\widetilde{TPM}]\ \ell^I_{system};\ h_{17} := 0$$

Thus, h_{17} either is at its default value 0 or it holds the identity of the kernel that is currently running, possibly extended by a chain of hashes that records further identity information. Concretely, the command SKINIT loads code at a privileged (kernel) level. This is reflected in our model by the link label ℓ^I_{system}. It is the responsibility of the operating system to validate the kernels passed by user commands before calling SKINIT e.g. to prevent privilege escalation. In the following, we assume that the hash function used for all assignment to PCRs is collision-resistant and yields fixed-sized hash values (so that concatenation of a hash with another value is injective).

Remote Attestation. Each TPM uses a fixed public-key-signature keypair, set during manufacturing, and used to uniquely identify and authenticate this particular TPM.

ATTEST signs an input value and a subset of the PCRs with the private signing key (TCG, 2006). The resulting signature guarantees that this value has been 'attested' by a command running on a machine with this TPM and these PCR values. This signature can be verified by any command that knows the verification key for the TPM, typically running on a remote machine; the verifier can then interpret the authenticated value and PCRs. We model attestation with two variables for the TPM keypair, k^{+}_{TPM} of level ℓ^{I}_{TPM} and k^{-}_{TPM} of level ℓ_{TPM}, and two commands

$$\mathrm{ATTEST}_i \doteq \quad \mathit{tag} := \mathcal{S}(i|h_i|\mathit{plain},\, k^{-}_{TPM})$$

$$\mathrm{VERIFY}_i \doteq \quad \text{if } \mathcal{V}(i|\mathit{source}|\mathit{plain},\, \mathit{tag},\, k^{+}_{TPM}) \text{ then } X$$

with public-untrusted inputs *source* and *plain* for the presumed value of h_i and the attested value, and output *tag* for the signature. These commands rely on public-key signing ($\mathcal{S}$) and signature-verification ($\mathcal{V}$) functions. Since the verification key is public, VERIFY need not be a privileged command; its variable X stands for the command guarded by the cryptographic verification.

Sealing. SEAL encrypts and signs the content of a variable together with the current identity of the sender and the intended identity of the receiver (TCG, 2006, p 298). Conversely UNSEAL decrypts a variable and verifies its signature, then verifies the identity of the sender and the current identity of the receiver (TCG, 2006, p 364). The TPM can handle several nonmigratable keys, but we only model sealing and unsealing keyed with fixed hardware secrets $s.ke$ and $s.ka$, both at level ℓ_{TPM}.

$$\begin{aligned}\mathrm{SEAL}_i \doteq \quad & \mathit{enc} := \mathcal{SE}(\mathit{plain},s.ke);\ \mathit{mac} := \mathcal{M}(i|h_i|\mathit{target}|\mathit{enc},s.ka);\\ & \mathit{cipher} := \mathit{enc}|\mathit{mac};\ \mathit{enc} := 0;\ \mathit{mac} := 0\end{aligned}$$

$$\begin{aligned}\mathrm{UNSEAL}_i \doteq \quad & \mathit{enc}|\mathit{mac} := \mathit{cipher};\\ & \text{if } \mathcal{V}_{\mathcal{M}}(i|\mathit{source}|h_i|\mathit{enc},\, \mathit{mac},\, s.ka)\\ & \text{then } \mathit{plain} := \mathcal{SD}(\mathit{enc},s.ke) \text{ else } \mathit{plain} := 0;\\ & \mathit{enc} := 0;\ \mathit{mac} := 0\end{aligned}$$

where $\mathit{enc}|\mathit{mac} := \mathit{cipher}$ is syntactic sugar for assigning to *enc* and *mac* substrings of *cipher* at fixed indexes (since the size of *mac* is fixed). As illustrated in the rest of the paper, SEAL and UNSEAL can be used to emulate a persistent, secure memory, and to communicate securely between TPM commands.

Security and Functionality Properties for Seals. We specify the cryptographic properties of SEAL and UNSEAL by relating them to an ideal implementation that maintains a global table for all values sealed so far and encrypts 0s instead of the actual plaintexts. (The full paper define similar security and functionality properties for attestation.)

$$\begin{aligned}\mathrm{SEAL}^0_i \doteq \quad & \mathit{enc} := \mathcal{SE}(0,s.ke);\ \mathit{mac} := \mathcal{M}(i|h_i|\mathit{target}|\mathit{enc},s.ka);\\ & \mathit{cipher} := \mathit{enc}|\mathit{mac};\ \mathit{log}_i := \mathit{log}_i + ((h_i|\mathit{target}|\mathit{enc}),\mathit{plain})\\ & \mathit{enc} := 0;\ \mathit{mac} := 0\end{aligned}$$

$$\begin{aligned}\mathrm{UNSEAL}^0_i \doteq \quad & \text{if } \mathcal{V}_{\mathcal{M}}(i|\mathit{source}|h_i|\mathit{enc},\, \mathit{mac},\, s.ka)\\ & \text{then } \mathit{plain} := \mathit{assoc}(\mathit{log}_i,(\mathit{source}|h_i|\mathit{enc})) \text{ else } \mathit{plain} := 0;\\ & \mathit{enc} := 0;\ \mathit{mac} := 0\end{aligned}$$

Security means that, provided s is generated uniformly at random and no other part of the code accesses s or log, no probabilistic polynomial program can distinguish between (SEAL, UNSEAL) and (SEAL^0,UNSEAL^0). This property can be reduced to indistinguishability against chosen plaintext attacks for encryption and resistance against forgery attacks for signing.

Functionality means that UNSEAL is a partial inverse of SEAL: unsealing a value sealed with matching source and target hashes always yields the plain sealed value.

Auxiliary Notations. For convenience, we define simple macros for calling SEAL and UNSEAL. (The full paper defines similar macros for our other security commands.)

$$x := \text{SEAL}_i(e_v, e_t) \doteq \quad \mathit{target} := e_t;\ \mathit{plain} := e_v;\ \text{SEAL}_i;$$
$$x := \mathit{cipher};\ \mathit{target} := 0;\ \mathit{plain} := 0;\ \mathit{cipher} := 0$$

$$x := \text{UNSEAL}_i(e_c, e_s) \doteq \quad \mathit{source} := e_s;\ \mathit{cipher} := e_c;\ \text{UNSEAL}_i;$$
$$x := \mathit{plain};\ \mathit{source} := 0;\ \mathit{cipher} := 0;\ \mathit{plain} := 0$$

Example 3. Continuing with our password example, we define code that seals the secret and the password to itself (using the current value of h_{17}) within a public-untrusted variable. Thus, protected by the TPM key, the secret and the password can only be retrieved by re-running this code. When re-run, the code behaves as in the password example, retrieving the password and the secret then granting access to the secret if the password is guessed in less than three attempts.

```
kernel := ⟨
  if c = 0 then store := SEAL((pwd,secret),h17)
  else { pwd,secret := UNSEAL(store,h17);
         if c < 4 && guess = pwd then r := secret};
  INC; pwd := 0; secret := 0 ⟩;
SKINIT;A [SKINIT]
```

Assuming that, initially, $c = 0$ and *pwd* is sampled at random, the probability that a polynomial adversary learns anything about *secret* is bounded by the sum of the probabilities of the three most probable passwords plus the (negligible) probabilities that the adversary finds a collision in the hash function or breaks the cryptography used in SEAL and UNSEAL.

Initialization. The protected variables of the TPM must be initialized before use. We write TPM_0 for the initialization command. Informally, this command runs once as the TPM is manufactured. It generates cryptographic keys and sets h_1, h_{17}, and c to zero. For cryptographic reasons, we also need to randomly sample $\mathcal{H}$ in a family of universal one-way hash functions; this is modelled as an implicit parameter ν for $\mathcal{H}$. Concretely, the public key of the TPM may also be certified by some authority, so that its high integrity can be dynamically verified.

$$TPM_0 \doteq \quad k^-_{TPM}, k^+_{TPM} := \mathcal{G}_e();\ s.ke := \mathcal{G}_{\mathcal{SE}}();\ s.ka := \mathcal{G}_{\mathcal{M}}();\ \nu := \mathcal{G}();$$
$$h_1 := 0;\ h_{17} := 0;\ c := 0$$

5 CFLOW Revisited

We describe the CFLOW compiler, giving its specification and outlining its algorithms; we refer to Fournet et al. (2009) for a detailed presentation. The compiler takes a source program plus security and locality policies, and outputs a cryptographically-protected distributed program. We improve on earlier work by handling more source programs, with endorsements and declassification, and by providing more precise theorems.

Source language, with locations. We consider a finite set of hosts, or locations, $\{1, 2, \ldots, i, b, c, v, \ldots, n\}$ intended to represent units of trust (principals) and of locality (runtime environments). The source language is the language of Section 2 extended with host annotations:

$$P ::= \ldots \mid b : P$$

The locality command $b : P$ states that command P should run on host b. Locality commands can be nested, as in $c : \{P_c; v : P_v\}$. We assume that every source program has a locality command at top level, setting an initial host. Since variables are transparently shared between hosts, locality annotations do not affect our semantics for commands.

Typing locality commands rules. We extend our security policy to assign a level $\Gamma(b)$ to each host b; this level indicates which variables b can read and write. We only consider robust hosts, such that $I(b) \leq R(C(b))$. We use the typing rule

$$\text{(TLOCALITY)}\quad \frac{\vdash P : \ell \qquad I(b) \leq_I I(\ell)}{\vdash (b : P) : (\bot, I(\ell))}$$

The rule states that locality commands are public, thereby reflecting that the transfer of control between hosts can be observed by the adversary.

We illustrate CFLOW for the example in the introduction. The source code and its policy specify levels of protection, but leave the choice of cryptographic mechanisms to the compiler. The actual source and compiled programs are available online.

Example 4 (Applying for a loan: source code). The code is

$$b\text{: } \{x_b := e_b\};\ c\text{:}\{y_c := e_c\};\ v\text{: } \{x'_b, y'_c := f(x_b, y_c)\};\ b\text{: } \{\mathit{print}(x'_b)\};\ c\text{: } \{\mathit{print}(y'_c)\}$$

It involves three hosts: a client c with $\Gamma(c) = (C_c, I_c)$, a bank b with $\Gamma(b) = (C_b, I_b)$, and a 'virtual' host v with $\Gamma(v) = (C_c \sqcup C_b, I_c \sqcap I_b)$ for the TPM-attested code on the client machine. All variables indexed by b, c or v are private to b, c or v, respectively. For instance, $\Gamma(x_c) = (C_c, I_c)$. The bank and the client first write their secret values (in x_b and y_c); then v computes the two results (x'_b and y'_c); finally, the bank and the client print them (locally). With this source command, for instance, an adversary at the level of the bank cannot read the client secret, and vice versa.

Compiler transformation. The compiler inputs a command with localities P and a security policy Γ, and outputs an initialization command, Q_0, used to specify initial trust assumptions, plus a series of commands $\widetilde{Q}$ that include one command Q_i for each host i that occurs in the source program. We write Γ' for the security policy of these commands. Informally, Q_i is a single command that implements and schedules all code fragments of P located on i. After type checking, the compilation proceeds in 4 passes:

1. The source program is sliced into local threads, each running on a single host.
2. The distributed control flow between threads is protected, using dynamic checks on auxiliary program-counter variables, so that the adversary cannot run high-integrity threads out of schedule.
3. Relying on a single-static-assignment transformation, each variable shared between different hosts (including the program counters) is replaced by a series of local replicas, with explicit transfers between replicas.
4. Depending on their security levels, memory transfers between replicas are cryptographically protected, by inserting encryptions to transfer instead low-confidentiality encrypted values, and inserting authentication primitives to transfer instead low-integrity values. The compiler determines which symmetric keys to use for these operations, and generates an initial key-exchange protocol to distribute them. After this pass, the only variables shared between different hosts are (1) the signature verification keys used by the initial protocol, and (2) public-untrusted variables at level $(\bot, \top)$. (The compiler also generates untrusted code for scheduling these commands and transferring public-untrusted data.)

These 4 passes define a program transformation $Q_0, \widetilde{Q} \doteq [\![P]\!]$ such that each command Q_i has type ℓ_i^I. Next, we instantiate Definitions 3 and 4 for this transformation.

Source programs and their adversaries. We let source programs range over well-typed polynomial commands with locality annotations Informally, source programs enable their active adversaries to run whenever they pass control between hosts (since the adversary controls at least the network). To each source command P, we associate the command context $\widehat{P}$ obtained from P by replacing every subcommand of the form $b : P'$ by a command context with two command variables $X; P'; X'$. For a given adversary level α, we let $\widetilde{A}$ range over tuples of polynomial adversary commands, with one command for each command variable. Hence, $\widehat{P}[\widetilde{A}]$ ranges over commands that interleave the code of P with adversary commands. (This is analogous to models of non-interference for concurrency, where the adversary runs between any two program steps.) Thus, we define source evaluation by

$$\langle\!\langle P, A, \mu \rangle\!\rangle \doteq \rho_\infty \langle \widehat{P}[A], \mu \rangle$$

Implementations and their adversaries. Implementation programs range over our compiler outputs $Q_0, \widetilde{Q}$. Once Q_0 has run, we simulate concurrency by letting the adversary explicitly schedule commands ($\widetilde{Q}$) that represent parallel threads of computation (rather than having $\widehat{P}$ schedule $\widetilde{A}$). The resulting low-level model realistically accounts for all interleavings of these threads. Implementation adversaries range over adversaries command contexts A' with one hole for each host. Thus, we define target evaluation by

$$\langle\!\langle (Q_0, \widetilde{Q}), A', \mu' \rangle\!\rangle \doteq \rho_\infty \langle Q_0; A'[\widetilde{Q}], \mu' \rangle$$

We let π be the erasure of all variables added in Γ': $\pi(\mu') = \mu'_{|dom(\mu)}$ and we define equivalence on final memory distributions ($\rho_0 \approx \rho_1$) as computational indistinguishability: for all polynomial commands T, $|\Pr[\langle T, \rho_0 \rangle; g = 0] - \Pr[\langle T, \rho_1 \rangle, g = 0]|$ is negligible. (We use indistinguishability instead of distribution equality because our compiler relies on cryptographic security assumptions.)

With the definitions above, our new compilation theorem for CFLOW is

Theorem 5. *Let $\alpha \in \mathcal{L}$ be such that R is robust against α. Let Γ be a robust policy. $([\![\cdot]\!], \pi)$ is secure; and $([\![\cdot]\!], \pi)$ is correct when $\alpha = (\bot_C, \top_I)$.*

The theorem demands that the source policy Γ be robust (Definition 1), so that the adversary can read any shared variable that it can write. This hypothesis stems from our decision to support endorsements in source programs. In particular, the control flow integrity enforced by pass 2 may otherwise fail to protect programs that combine endorsements and declassifications, as illustrated below.

Example 5 (Non-robust shared variables). Consider a source program that writes a secret s with $\Gamma(s) = HH$ into a (non robust) variable x with $\Gamma(x) = HL$, then erases the content of x, and finally declassifies x by copying it to p with $\Gamma(p) = LL$:

$$P \doteq 1\!:\!\{x := s\}; 2\!:\!\{x := 0\}; 3\!:\!\{p := x\}$$

Let $\alpha = LL$. With our source semantics, the command context

$$\widehat{P} \doteq X_1; x := s; X_2; x := 0; X_3; p := x; X_4$$

ensures that p finally contains either 0 or a value written by the adversary, but not the value of s. In the implementation, however, the two local commands at hosts 1 and 2 have low integrity, so pass 2 does not guarantee their sequential execution, and an implementation adversary that schedules Q_2 before Q_1 lead Q_3 to declassify s into p.

Cryptographic protection (pass 4) is also problematic for programs that share non-robust variables, such as x in Example 5. Although their confidentiality is protected by encryption, an implementation adversary can swap their contents (by swapping their encrypted values) and similarly lead the program to declassify the wrong data.

Simulation vs non-interference. Instead of Theorem 5, Fournet et al. (2009) show that two classes of information-flow properties of the source program are preserved in the implementation. Our security result is more precise; it guarantees that, for any attack against our implementation, there is also an attack against the source program, with the same information leakage. The theorem below confirms that our new result generally subsumes theirs, and thus yields strong computational non-interference properties. (We refer to Fournet et al. (2009) and to the full paper for the definitions and discussion of their notion of computational non-interference for confidentiality and for integrity.)

Theorem 6 (Computational Non-Interference). *If a transformation $([\![\cdot]\!], \pi)$ is secure, then it preserves computational confidentiality and integrity.*

Example 6 (Simplified implementation). Continuing with our example, and in preparation for the next section, we give a simplified, hand-written implementation of Example 4 that illustrates the main mechanisms of CFLOW while avoiding those irrelevant here. For instance, the ordering of $x_b := e_b$ and $y_c := e_c$ is irrelevant; the ordering of $x_b := e_b$ and $x'_b, y'_c := f(x_b, y_c)$ is protected because $x'_b, y'_c := f(x_b, y_c)$ does not run unless x_b has been verified. So, instead of the globally shared and signed programs counter, we use one local anti-replay counter for each host. Communications between b and v are cryptographically protected, but we let v and c share local memory (since v will run on c's machine). Otherwise, all the new (communication) variables are public and untrusted; the only shared high-integrity variables are the public keys (k_b^+ and k_v^+). The commands are :

$$\begin{aligned}
Q_0 &\doteq k_b^-, k_b^+ := \mathcal{G}_e(); k_v^-, k_v^+ := \mathcal{G}_e() \\
Q_b &\doteq \text{if } c_b{=}1 \text{ then } \{\, c_b{+}{+};\ x_b{:=}\ e_b;\ x_e := \mathcal{E}(x_b, k_v^+);\ x_s := \mathcal{S}(x_e, k_b^-) \,\} \\
&\quad \text{else if } c_b = 2 \text{ then } \{\, c_b{+}{+};\ \text{if } \mathcal{V}(x'_e, x'_s, k_v^+) \text{ then } \mathit{print}(\mathcal{D}(x'_e, k_b^-)) \,\} \\
Q_c &\doteq \text{if } c_c{=}1 \text{ then } \{\, c_c{+}{+};\ y_c := e_c \,\} \text{ else if } c_c{=}2 \text{ then } \{\, c_c{+}{+};\ \mathit{print}(y'_c) \,\} \\
Q_v &\doteq \text{if } c_v{=}1 \text{ then} \\
&\quad \{\, c_v{+}{+};\ \text{if } \mathcal{V}(x_e, x_s, k_b^+) \text{ then } \{\, x_v := \mathcal{D}(x_e, k_v^-);\ x'_v, y'_c := f(x_v, y_c); \\
&\qquad\qquad x'_e := \mathcal{E}(x'_v, k_b^+);\ x'_s := \mathcal{S}(x_e, k_v^-) \,\}\,\}
\end{aligned}$$

6 Implementing Virtual Hosts on TPMs

Section 5 shows how to compile an imperative program with shared access-controlled memory into a distributed program protected by cryptography. The resulting program runs on a series of machines, and preserves the security properties of the source program, subject to the assumption that each local command Q_b of the distributed implementation runs on a machine with (at least) the security of its declared level ℓ_b. However, for many useful programs, it is difficult to find such machines for the most trusted parts of the computation.

This section introduces a transformation that relies on secure instructions to boot trusted virtual machines. This transformation applies to any distributed programs, including those produced by CFLOW in Section 5. Before giving general definitions and theorems, we illustrate the transformation on Example 6.

Example 7 (Securely booting Q_v). The command Q_v requires a machine trusted by both the client and the bank. Assume that the bank trusts the client TPM for running Q_v and knows its public key for attestation. We may use the code

$$\begin{aligned}
Q_0 &\doteq k_b^-, k_b^+ := \mathcal{G}_e(); k_{TPM}^-, k_{TPM}^+ := \mathcal{G}_e(); c := 0; \\
Q_b &\doteq \text{if } c_b{=}1 \text{ then } \{\, c_b{+}{+};\ x_b{:=}\ e_b; \\
&\qquad \text{if VERIFY}(\mathcal{H}(\langle K_v \rangle), k_v^+, \mathit{cert}_v) \\
&\qquad [\, b.k_v^+ := k_v^+;\ x_e := \mathcal{E}(x_b, k_v^+);\ x_s := \mathcal{S}(x_e, k_b^-) \,]\,\} \\
&\quad \text{else if } c_b{=}2 \text{ then } \{\, c_b{+}{+};\ \text{if } \mathcal{V}(x'_e, x'_s, k_v^+) \text{ then } \mathit{print}(\mathcal{D}(x'_e, k_b^-)) \,\} \\
Q_c &\doteq \text{if } c_c{=}1 \text{ then } \{\, c_c{+}{+};\ y_c := e_c \,\} \text{ else if } c_c{=}2 \text{ then } \{\, \mathit{print}(y'_c) \,\} \\
Q_v &\doteq \mathit{kernel} := \langle K_v \rangle;\ \text{SKINIT} \\
K_v &\doteq \text{if } c{=}0 \text{ then} \\
&\quad \{\, \text{INC};\ k_v^-, k_v^+ := \mathcal{G}_e();\ \mathit{cert}_v := \text{ATTEST}(k_v^+);\ \mathit{key} := \text{SEAL}(k_v^-, h) \,\} \\
&\quad \text{else if } c{=}1 \text{ then} \\
&\quad \{\, \text{INC};\ k_v^- := \text{UNSEAL}(\mathit{key}, h); \\
&\qquad \text{if } \mathcal{V}(x_e, x_s, k_b^+) \text{ then } \{\, x_v := \mathcal{D}(x_e, k_v^-);\ x'_v, y'_c := f(x_v, y_c); \\
&\qquad\qquad x'_e := \mathcal{E}(x'_v, \text{`}k_b^+);\ x'_s := \mathcal{S}(x'_e, k_v^-) \,\}\,\}
\end{aligned}$$

In contrast with the host commands of Section 5, TPM-attested host commands do not have a persistent, protected local memory to keep their trusted key pair. Instead, as we dynamically set up host v, we generate its key pair, we use remote attestation to convince the bank to encrypt its secret towards the implementation of Q_v, and we simulate the persistent local memory using seal/unseal and the TPM counter to protect against replays.

A General Transformation. Our transformation takes as input a policy Γ, a tuple of typed commands $\widetilde{Q}$ for hosts $\widetilde{b}$, including the command of a virtual host v, and a subset of the variables $\widetilde{x}$ of Q_v (informally, $\widetilde{x}$ represents the private, trusted local state of v). It assumes the existence of a TPM on host a, at least as trusted as v and not used in the source program. It generates an implementation policy Γ' and a series of implementation commands Q'_0, $\widetilde{Q}'$, defined below. We let $\widetilde{Q}$ range over commands such that

1. no command in $\widetilde{Q} \setminus Q_v$ accesses $\widetilde{x}$ (i.e. the variables of $\widetilde{x}$ are local to Q_v);
2. Q_v does not read $\widetilde{x}$ before initializing them;
3. $\vdash Q_b : \ell_b^I$ for $b \in \widetilde{b}$;
4. $\vdash Q_v : \ell_{TPM}^I$ (i.e. the TPM is as trusted as Q_v); and
5. $R(C(\ell_{TPM})) \not\leq I(\ell_b)$ for $b \in \widetilde{b}$ (i.e. no host can access the TPM private variables).

Initialization. Recall that the commands $\widetilde{Q}$ (including Q_v) rely on trusted variables formally initialized in Q_0. In contrast, our implementation of Q_v uses SKINIT, so its own initialization is deferred until runtime and must be explicitly coded. For simplicity, we assume that, for each host $b \in \widetilde{b}$, initialization is a command of the form $Q_{0,b} \doteq k_b^-, k_b^+ := \mathcal{G}_e();\ldots$ that writes private variables and generates a single keypair, with v initialized last. We also assume that the keys written in Q_0 are not overwritten in $\widetilde{Q}$. (These assumptions hold with the CFLOW compiler, up to a reordering of hosts.)

6. $Q_0 \doteq (Q_{0,b};)_{b \neq v}; Q_{0,v}$;
7. no command in $\widetilde{Q} \setminus Q_b$ accesses variables written in $Q_{0,b}$ except for k_b^+ for $b \in \widetilde{b}$ (i.e. the variables initialized in $Q_{0,b}$ are local to Q_b);
8. no command in $\widetilde{Q}$ writes k_b^+, k_b^- for $b \in \widetilde{b}$.

Implementation of Q_0. Initialization is obtained from Q_0 by adding initialization for the TPM and removing initialization for v: $Q'_0 \doteq \mathit{TPM}_0; (Q_{0,b}; b.k_v^+ := 0;)_{b \neq v}$.

Implementation of Q_v. The command Q'_v uses SKINIT to dynamically launch a secure kernel K_v that implements Q_v:

$$
\begin{array}{rcl}
Q'_v & \doteq & \mathit{kernel} := \langle K_v \rangle;\ a.\mathrm{SKINIT} \\
K_v & \doteq & a.\mathrm{INC}; \\
& & \quad \text{if } a.c = c_v^0{+}1 \text{ then } \{\ v.c := a.c;\ Q_{v,0};\ \mathit{cert}_v := a.\mathrm{ATTEST}_{17}(k_v^+)\} \\
& & \qquad\qquad\qquad\qquad \text{else } \{\ k_v^- | k_v^+ | v.c | v.\widetilde{x} := a.\mathrm{UNSEAL}_{17}(\mathit{store}_v, a.h_{17}); \\
& & \qquad\qquad\qquad\qquad\qquad\quad \text{if } v.c = a.c \text{ then } Q_v\ \{v.x/x, x \in \widetilde{x}\}\{\text{`}k_b^+/k_b^+, b \neq v\}\}; \\
& & \quad \mathit{store}_v := a.\mathrm{SEAL}_{17}((k_v^-, k_v^+ | v.c{+}1 | v.\widetilde{x}), a.h_{17}));\ k_v^-, v.c, v.\widetilde{x} := 0
\end{array}
$$

The variables $v.\widetilde{x}$ (and $v.c$) are volatile for each run of Q'_v; they can be public and untrusted, but must be cleared before returning. By eliminating trusted and confidential variables, the transformation lowers the level of Q_v hence the level required to run it.

The identity of K_v is verified by the other hosts, so the command Q'_v itself need not be trusted. The other new variables k_v^+, cert$_v$, store$_v$ are also (formally) public and untrusted. They need not be trusted for security, although an adversary that can overwrite them may cause the system to fail. The value c_v^0 is a constant of the program and corresponds to the initial value of the TPM monotonic counter.

Implementation of Q_b for $b \neq v$, $b \in \widetilde{b}$. As it runs for the first time, each host command Q'_b verifies the attested public key for v and stores it in a new local variable, $b.k_v^+$, a local trusted copy to be used instead of k_v^+ in Q_b. To this end, Q'_b recomputes the expected value of h, including the values for c_v^0 and any other keys $k_{b'}^+$ used in Q_v, and verifies its concatenation with the received public key k_v^+ using the trusted verification key of the supporting TPM.

$$Q'_{b,i} \doteq \text{if } b.k_v^+ = 0 \text{ then } \{ \text{ if } a.\text{VERIFY}(v.\mathcal{H}(\langle K_v \rangle), k_v^+, cert_v)[\, b.k_v^+ := k_v^+] \, \} \\ \text{else } \{ \, Q_{b,i}\{b.k_v^+/k_v^+\} \, \}$$

Implementation of Γ. The formal implementation of Γ is $\Gamma' = \Gamma\{v.\widetilde{x}, v.c, k_v^+, cert_v, store_v \mapsto (\bot, \top)\}\{b.k_v^+ \mapsto \ell_b, b \neq v\}$.

Security and functional correctness. We express the security and functional correctness of our transformation as instances of definitions 3 and 4. Source programs range over commands $\widetilde{Q}$ that meet conditions 1–8 above. Source adversaries are parameterized by α and range over adversary command contexts for Γ. The commands of the distributed programs are scheduled by the adversary after the execution of Q_0; formally:

$$\langle\!\langle \widetilde{Q}, A, \mu \rangle\!\rangle \doteq \rho_\infty \langle Q_0; A[\widetilde{Q}], \mu \rangle$$

Implementation programs $[\![\widetilde{Q}]\!]$ range over $\widetilde{Q}'$, as defined above. Implementation adversaries are parameterized by α and range over valid adversary command contexts for Γ'. The commands of the distributed program are scheduled by the adversary after the execution of Q'_0 but additionally, the adversary and Q_v have access to protected versions of the subroutine SKINIT$_a$: we let

$$S' \doteq Q'_0; A'[a.\text{SKINIT}_{\alpha'}, \widetilde{Q}', Q'_v[a.\text{SKINIT}_{\ell''_v}]]$$

$$\langle\!\langle \widetilde{Q}', A', \mu' \rangle\!\rangle' \doteq \rho_\infty(\langle S', \mu' \rangle)$$

where $a.\text{SKINIT}_\ell$ runs $a.$SKINIT after testing that *kernel* contains code typed at level ℓ.

We let π be the erasure of all variables added in Γ': $\pi(\mu') = \mu'_{|dom(\mu)}$ and we define equivalence on final memory distributions ($\rho_0 \approx \rho_1$) as computational indistinguishability: for all polynomial commands T such that T does not read $\{\widetilde{x}, k_v^-, k_v^+\}$, $|\Pr[\langle T, \rho_0 \rangle; g = 0] - \Pr[\langle T, \rho_1 \rangle; g = 0]|$ is negligible. Relying on these definitions, our main theorem for virtual hosts on TPMs is

Theorem 7. *Let $\alpha \in \mathcal{L}$ be such that R is robust against α. Let Γ be a robust policy. $([\![\cdot]\!], \pi)$ is secure; $([\![\cdot]\!], \pi)$ is correct when $\alpha = (\bot_C, \top_I)$.*

Since its input and output are in the same format, the transformation and its theorem can be applied several times to implement a series of virtual hosts using different TPMs.

Acknowledgments. We thank Karthik Bhargavan, Gurvan le Guernic, Jean-Jacques Lévy, Himanshu Raj, Tamara Rezk, and the anonymous reviewers for their help.

References

Abadi, M., Wobber, T.: A logical account of NGSCB. In: de Frutos-Escrig, D., Núñez, M. (eds.) FORTE 2004. LNCS, vol. 3235, pp. 1–12. Springer, Heidelberg (2004)

AMD. AMD64 virtualization: Secure virtual machine architecture reference manual

Askarov, A., Myers, A.: A semantic framework for declassification and endorsement. Prog. Languages and Systems, 64–84 (2010)

Askarov, A., Sabelfeld, A.: Tight enforcement of information-release policies for dynamic languages. In: CSF (2009)

Balfe, S., Paterson, K.G.: e-EMV: Emulating EMV for internet payments using trusted computing technology. In: STC 2008, pp. 81–92 (2008)

Chong, S., Myers, A.C.: Decentralized robustness. In: 19th IEEE CSFW 2006, p. 12 (2006)

Chong, S., Liu, J., Myers, A.C., Qi, X., Vikram, K., Zheng, L., Zheng, X.: Secure web applications via automatic partitioning. In: CACM (2009)

Datta, A., Franklin, J., Garg, D., Kaynar, D.: A logic of secure systems and its application to trusted computing. In: S&P 2009, pp. 221–236 (2009)

Denning, D.E.: A lattice model of secure information flow. In: CACM (1976)

Diffie, W., Hellman, M.E.: New directions in cryptography. IEEE TIT (1976)

Fournet, C., Rezk, T.: Cryptographically sound implementations for typed information-flow security. In: POPL 2008, pp. 323–335 (January 2008)

Fournet, C., Le Guernic, G., Rezk, T.: A security-preserving compiler for distributed programs: from information-flow policies to cryptographic mechanisms. In: CCS 2009, ACM, New York (2009)

Grawrock, D.: TCG Specification Architecture Overview, Rev. 1.4 (2007)

Gürgens, S., Rudolph, C., Scheuermann, D., Atts, M., Plaga, R.: Security evaluation of scenarios based on the TCGs TPM specification. In: Biskup, J., López, J. (eds.) ESORICS 2007. LNCS, vol. 4734, pp. 438–453. Springer, Heidelberg (2007)

Halderman, J., Schoen, S., Heninger, N., Clarkson, W., Paul, W., Calandrino, J., Feldman, A., Appelbaum, J., Felten, E.: Lest we remember: cold-boot attacks on encryption keys. In: CACM (2009)

Intel. Intel Trusted Execution Technology Software Development Guide (2009)

McCune, J., Parno, B., Perrig, A., Reiter, M., Isozaki, H.: Flicker: An execution infrastructure for TCB minimization. In: 3rd ACM SIGOPS/EuroSys, pp. 315–328. ACM, New York (2008)

McCune, J., Qu, N., Li, Y., Datta, A., Gligor, V., Perrig, A.: Efficient TCB Reduction and Attestation. CMU-CyLab-09-003 9 (2009)

Microsoft. Windows BitLocker drive encryption (2006)

Millen, J., Guttman, J., Ramsdell, J., Sheehy, J., Sniffen, B., Bedford, M.: Analysis of a measured launch. In: MITRE (2007)

Myers, A.C., Liskov, B.: Complete, safe information flow with decentralized labels. In: 19th IEEE Symposium on Research in Security and Privacy (RSP), Oakland, California (May 1998)

Myers, A.C., Liskov, B.: Protecting privacy using the decentralized label model. In: TOSEM (2000)

Myers, A.C., Zheng, L., Zdancewic, S., Chong, S., Nystrom, N.: Jif: Java information flow (2001)

Myers, A.C., Sabelfeld, A., Zdancewic, S.: Enforcing robust declassification and qualified robustness. JCS 14(2), 157–196 (2006)

Pottier, F., Simonet, V.: Information flow inference for ML. In: ACM TOPLAS (2003)

Sabelfeld, A., Myers, A.C.: Language-based information-flow security. In: IEEE J-SAC (2003)

Sabelfeld, A., Myers, A.C.: A model for delimited information release. Software Security-Theories and Systems, 174–191 (2004)

Trusted Computing Group. Client Specific TPM Interface Specification (TIS), Version 1.2 (2005)

Trusted Computing Group. TCG Software Stack (TSS 1.2). Trusted Computing Group (2006)

Zdancewic, S., Myers, A.C.: Robust declassification. In: CSFW 2001, pp. 15–23 (2001)

Zdancewic, S., Zheng, L., Nystrom, N., Myers, A.C.: Secure program partitioning. In: TOCS (2002)

Zheng, L., Chong, S., Myers, A.C., Zdancewic, S.: Using replication and partitioning to build secure distributed systems. In: 15th IEEE Symposium on Security and Privacy (2003)

Improving Strategies via SMT Solving*

Thomas Martin Gawlitza and David Monniaux
CNRS/VERIMAG
{Thomas.Gawlitza,David.Monniaux}@imag.fr**

Abstract. We consider the problem of computing numerical invariants of programs by abstract interpretation. Our method eschews two traditional sources of imprecision: (i) the use of widening operators for enforcing convergence within a finite number of iterations (ii) the use of merge operations (often, convex hulls) at the merge points of the control flow graph. It instead computes the least inductive invariant expressible in the domain at a restricted set of program points, and analyzes the rest of the code en bloc. We emphasize that we compute this inductive invariant precisely. For that we extend the strategy improvement algorithm of Gawlitza and Seidl [17]. If we applied their method directly, we would have to solve an exponentially sized system of abstract semantic equations, resulting in memory exhaustion. Instead, we keep the system implicit and discover strategy improvements using SAT modulo real linear arithmetic (SMT). For evaluating strategies we use linear programming. Our algorithm has low polynomial space complexity and performs for contrived examples in the worst case exponentially many strategy improvement steps; this is unsurprising, since we show that the associated abstract reachability problem is Π_2^p-complete.

1 Introduction

Motivation. Static program analysis attempts to derive properties about the run-time behavior of a program without running the program. Among interesting properties are the numerical ones: for instance, that a given variable x always has a value in the range $[12, 41]$ when reaching a given program point. An analysis solely based on such interval relations at all program points is known as *interval analysis* [11]. More refined numerical analyses include, for instance, finding for each program point an enclosing polyhedron for the vector of program variables [13]. In addition to obtaining facts about the values of numerical program variables, numerical analyses are used as building blocks for e.g. pointer and shape analyses.

However, by Rice's theorem, only trivial properties can be checked automatically [26]. In order to check non-trivial properties we are usually forced to use *abstractions*. A systematic way for inferring properties automatically w.r.t. a given abstraction is given through the *abstract interpretation* framework of Cousot and Cousot [12]. This framework *safely over-approximates* the run-time behavior of a program.

When using the abstract interpretation framework, we usually have two sources of imprecision. The first source of imprecision is the abstraction itself: for instance, if the

* This work was partially funded by the ANR project ASOPT.
** VERIMAG is a joint laboratory of CNRS, Université Joseph Fourier and Grenoble INP.

G. Barthe (Ed.): ESOP 2011, LNCS 6602, pp. 236–255, 2011.
© Springer-Verlag Berlin Heidelberg 2011

property to be proved needs a non-convex invariant to be established, and our abstraction can only represent convex sets, then we cannot prove the property. Take for instance the C-code y = 0; **if** (x <= −1 || x >= 1) { **if** (x == 0) y = 1; }. No matter what the values of the variables x and y are before the execution of the above C-code, after the execution the value of y is 0. The invariant $|x| \geq 1$ in the "then" branch is not convex, and its convex hull includes $x = 0$. Any static analysis method that computes a convex invariant in this branch will thus also include $y = 1$. In contrast, our method avoids enforcing convexity, except at the heads of loops.

The second source of imprecision are the safe but imprecise methods that are used for solving the *abstract semantic equations* that describe the abstract semantics: such methods safely over-approximate exact solutions, but do not return exact solutions in all cases. The reason is that we are concerned with abstract domains that contain infinite ascending chains, in particular if we are interested in numerical properties: the complete lattice of all n-dimensional closed real intervals, used for interval analysis, is an example. The traditional methods are based on Kleene fixpoint iteration which (purely applied) is not guaranteed to terminate in interesting cases. In order to enforce termination (for the price of imprecision) traditional methods make use of the widening/narrowing approach of Cousot and Cousot [12]. Grossly, widening extrapolates the first iterations of a sequence to a possible limit, but can easily overshoot the desired result. In order to avoid this, various tricks are used, including "widening up to" [27, Sec. 3.2], "delayed" or with "thresholds" [6]. However, these tricks, although they may help in many practical cases, are easily thwarted. Gopan and Reps [25] proposed "lookahead widening", which discovers new feasible paths and adapts widening accordingly; again this method is no panacea. Furthermore, analyses involving widening are *non-monotonic*: stronger preconditions can lead to weaker invariants being automatically inferred; a rather non-intuitive behaviour. Since our method does not use widening at all, it avoids these problems.

Our Contribution. We fight both sources of imprecision noted above:

- In order to improve the precision of the abstraction, we abstract sequences of if-then-else statements without loops en bloc. In the above example, we are then able to conclude that $y \neq 0$ holds. In other words: we abstract sets of states only at the heads of loops, or, more generally, at a cut-set of the control-flow graph (a cut-set is a set of program points such that removing them would cut all loops).
- Our main technical contribution consists of a practical method for precisely computing abstract semantics of affine programs w.r.t. the template linear constraint domains of Sankaranarayanan et al. [42], with sequences of if-then-else statements which do not contain loops abstracted en bloc. Our method is based on a strict generalization of the strategy improvement algorithm of Gawlitza and Seidl [17, 18, 22]. The latter algorithm could be directly applied to the problem we solve in this article, but the size of its input would be exponential in the size of the program, because we then need to explicitly enumerate all program paths between cut-nodes which do not cross other cut-nodes. In this article, we give an algorithm with low polynomial memory consumption that uses exponential time in the worst case. The basic idea consists in avoiding an explicit enumeration of all paths through sequences of if-then-else-statements which do not contain loops. Instead we use a

SAT modulo real linear arithmetic solver for improving the current strategy locally. For evaluating each strategy encountered during the strategy iteration, we use linear programming.
- As a byproduct of our considerations we show that the corresponding abstract reachability problem is Π_2^p-complete. In fact, we show that it is Π_2^p-hard even if the loop invariant being computed consists in a single $x \leq C$ inequality where x is a program variable and C is the parameter of the invariant. Hence, exponential worst-case running-time seems to be unavoidable.

Related Work. Recently, several alternative approaches for computing numerical invariants (for instance w.r.t. to template linear constraints) were developed:

Strategy Iteration. Strategy iteration (also called *policy iteration*) was introduced by Howard for solving stochastic control problems [29, 40] and is also applied to two-players zero-sum games [28, 39, 45] or min-max-plus systems [7]. Adjé et al. [2], Costan et al. [9], Gaubert et al. [16] developed a strategy iteration approach for solving the abstract semantic equations that occur in static program analysis by abstract interpretation. Their approach can be seen as an alternative to the traditional widening/narrowing approach. The goal of their algorithm is to compute least fixpoints of monotone self-maps f, where $f(x) = \min \{\pi(x) \mid \pi \in \Pi\}$ for all x and Π is a family of self-maps. The assumption is that one can efficiently compute the least fixpoint $\mu\pi$ of π for every $\pi \in \Pi$. The π's are the (min-)strategies. Starting with an arbitrary min-stratgy $\pi^{(0)}$, the min-strategy is successively improved. The sequence $(\pi^{(k)})_k$ of attained min-strategies results in a decreasing sequence $\mu\pi^{(0)} > \mu\pi^{(1)} > \cdots > \mu\pi^{(k)}$ that stabilizes, whenever $\mu\pi^{(k)}$ is a fixpoint of f — not necessarily the least one. However, there are indeed important cases, where minimality of the obtained fixpoint can be guaranteed [1]. Moreover, an important advantage of their algorithm is that it can be stopped at any time with a safe over-approximation. This is in particular interesting if there are infinitely many min-strategies [2]. Costan et al. [9] showed how to use their framework for performing interval analysis without widening. Gaubert et al. [16] extended this work to the following *relational* abstract domains: The *zone domain* [33], the *octagon domain* [34] and in particular the *template linear constraint domains* [42]. Gawlitza and Seidl [17] presented a practical (max-)strategy improvement algorithm for computing least solutions of *systems of rational equations*. Their algorithm enables them to perform a template linear constraint analysis *precisely* — even if the mappings are not non-expansive. This means: Their algorithm always computes *least* solutions of abstract semantic equations — not just some solutions.

Acceleration Techniques. Gonnord [23], Gonnord and Halbwachs [24] investigated an improvement of linear relation analysis that consists in computing, when possible, the exact (abstract) effect of a loop. The technique is fully compatible with the use of widening, and whenever it applies, it improves both the precision and the performance of the analysis. Gawlitza et al. [20], Leroux and Sutre [31] studied cases where interval analysis can be done in polynomial time w.r.t. a uniform cost measure, where memory accesses and arithmetic operations are counted for $\mathcal{O}(1)$.

Quantifier Elimination. Recent improvements in SAT/SMT solving techniques have made it possible to perform quantifier elimination on larger formulas [36]. Monniaux

[37] developed an analysis method based on quantifier elimination in the theory of rational linear arithmetic. This method targets the same domains as the present article; it however produces a richer result. It can not only compute the least invariant inside the abstract domain of a loop, but also express it as a function of the precondition of the loop; the method outputs the source code of the optimal abstract transformer mapping the precondition to the invariant. Its drawback is its high cost, which makes it practical only on small code fragments; thus, its intended application is *modular analysis*: analyze very precisely small portions of code (functions, modules, nodes of a reactive data-flow program, ...), and use the results for analyzing larger portions, perhaps with another method, including the method proposed in this article.

Mathematical Programming. Colón et al. [8], Cousot [10], Sankaranarayanan et al. [41] presented approaches for generating linear invariants that uses *non-linear constraint solving*. Leconte et al. [30] propose a mathematical programming formulation whose constraints define the space of all post-solutions of the abstract semantic equations. The objective function aims at minimizing the result. For programs that use affine assignments and affine guards, only, this yields a *mixed integer linear programming* formulation for interval analysis. The resulting mathematical programming problems can then be solved to guaranteed global optimality by means of general purpose branch-and-bound type algorithms.

2 Basics

Notations. $\mathbb{B} = \{0, 1\}$ denotes the set of Boolean values. The set of real numbers is denoted by $\mathbb{R}$. The complete linearly ordered set $\mathbb{R} \cup \{-\infty, \infty\}$ is denoted by $\overline{\mathbb{R}}$. We call two vectors $x, y \in \overline{\mathbb{R}}^n$ *comparable* iff $x \leq y$ or $y \leq x$ holds. For $f : X \to \overline{\mathbb{R}}^m$ with $X \subseteq \overline{\mathbb{R}}^n$, we set $\mathrm{dom}(f) := \{x \in X \mid f(x) \in \mathbb{R}^m\}$ and $\mathrm{fdom}(f) := \mathrm{dom}(f) \cap \mathbb{R}^n$. We denote the i-th row (resp. the j-th column) of a matrix A by $A_{i\cdot}$ (resp. $A_{\cdot j}$). Accordingly, $A_{i\cdot j}$ denotes the component in the i-th row and the j-th column. We also use this notation for vectors and mappings $f : X \to Y^k$.

Assume that a fixed set $\mathbf{X}$ of variables and a domain $\mathbb{D}$ is given. We consider equations of the form $\mathbf{x} = e$, where $\mathbf{x} \in \mathbf{X}$ is a variable and e is an expression over $\mathbb{D}$. A *system* $\mathcal{E}$ of (fixpoint) equations is a finite set $\{\mathbf{x}_1 = e_1, \ldots, \mathbf{x}_n = e_n\}$ of equations, where $\mathbf{x}_1, \ldots, \mathbf{x}_n$ are pairwise distinct variables. We denote the set $\{\mathbf{x}_1, \ldots, \mathbf{x}_n\}$ of variables occurring in $\mathcal{E}$ by $\mathbf{X}_{\mathcal{E}}$. We drop the subscript whenever it is clear from the context.

For a variable assignment $\rho : \mathbf{X} \to \mathbb{D}$, an expression e is mapped to a value $[\![e]\!]\rho$ by setting $[\![\mathbf{x}]\!]\rho := \rho(\mathbf{x})$ and $[\![f(e_1, \ldots, e_k)]\!]\rho := f([\![e_1]\!]\rho, \ldots, [\![e_k]\!]\rho)$, where $\mathbf{x} \in \mathbf{X}$, f is a k-ary operator, for instance $+$, and $e_1, \ldots, e_k$ are expressions. Let $\mathcal{E}$ be a system of equations. We define the unary operator $[\![\mathcal{E}]\!]$ on $\mathbf{X} \to \mathbb{D}$ by setting $([\![\mathcal{E}]\!]\rho)(\mathbf{x}) := [\![e]\!]\rho$ for all $\mathbf{x} = e \in \mathcal{E}$. A solution is a variable assignment ρ such that $\rho = [\![\mathcal{E}]\!]\rho$ holds. The set of solutions is denoted by $\mathbf{Sol}(\mathcal{E})$.

Let $\mathbb{D}$ be a complete lattice. We denote the *least upper bound* and the *greatest lower bound* of a set $X \subseteq \mathbb{D}$ by $\bigvee X$ and $\bigwedge X$, respectively. The least element $\bigvee \emptyset$ (resp. the greatest element $\bigwedge \emptyset$) is denoted by $\bot$ (resp. $\top$). We define the binary operators $\vee$ and $\wedge$ by $x \vee y := \bigvee\{x, y\}$ and $x \wedge y := \bigwedge\{x, y\}$ for all $x, y \in \mathbb{D}$, respectively.

For $\square \in \{\vee, \wedge\}$, we will also consider $x_1 \square \cdots \square x_k$ as the application of a k-ary operator. This will cause no problems, since the binary operators $\vee$ and $\wedge$ are associative and commutative. An expression e (resp. an equation $\mathbf{x} = e$) is called *monotone* iff all operators occurring in e are monotone.

The set $\mathbf{X} \to \mathbb{D}$ of all *variable assignments* is a complete lattice. For $\rho, \rho' : \mathbf{X} \to \mathbb{D}$, we write $\rho \lhd \rho'$ (resp. $\rho \rhd \rho'$) iff $\rho(\mathbf{x}) < \rho'(\mathbf{x})$ (resp. $\rho(\mathbf{x}) > \rho'(\mathbf{x})$) holds for all $\mathbf{x} \in \mathbf{X}$. For $d \in \mathbb{D}$, $\underline{d}$ denotes the variable assignment $\{\mathbf{x} \mapsto d \mid \mathbf{x} \in \mathbf{X}\}$. A variable assignment ρ with $\underline{\bot} \lhd \rho \lhd \underline{\top}$ is called *finite*. A pre-solution (resp. post-solution) is a variable assignment ρ such that $\rho \leq [\![\mathcal{E}]\!]\rho$ (resp. $\rho \geq [\![\mathcal{E}]\!]\rho$) holds. The set of all pre-solutions (resp. the set of all post-solutions) is denoted by $\mathbf{PreSol}(\mathcal{E})$ (resp. $\mathbf{PostSol}(\mathcal{E})$). The least fixpoint (resp. the greatest fixpoint) of an operator $f : \mathbb{D} \to \mathbb{D}$ is denoted by μf (resp. νf), provided that it exists. Thus, the least solution (resp. the greatest solution) of a system $\mathcal{E}$ of equations is denoted by $\mu[\![\mathcal{E}]\!]$ (resp. $\nu[\![\mathcal{E}]\!]$), provided that it exists. For a pre-solution ρ (resp. for a post-solution ρ), $\mu_{\geq\rho}[\![\mathcal{E}]\!]$ (resp. $\nu_{\leq\rho}[\![\mathcal{E}]\!]$) denotes the least solution that is greater than or equal to ρ (resp. the greatest solution that is less than or equal to ρ). From Knaster-Tarski's fixpoint theorem we get: Every system $\mathcal{E}$ of monotone equations over a complete lattice has a least solution $\mu[\![\mathcal{E}]\!]$ and a greatest solution $\nu[\![\mathcal{E}]\!]$. Furthermore, $\mu[\![\mathcal{E}]\!] = \bigwedge \mathbf{PostSol}(\mathcal{E})$ and $\nu[\![\mathcal{E}]\!] = \bigvee \mathbf{PreSol}(\mathcal{E})$.

Linear Programming. We consider linear programming problems (LP problems for short) of the form $\sup \{c^\top x \mid x \in \mathbb{R}^n, Ax \leq b\}$, where $A \in \mathbb{R}^{m \times n}$, $b \in \mathbb{R}^m$, and $c \in \mathbb{R}^n$ are the inputs. The convex closed polyhedron $\{x \in \mathbb{R}^n \mid Ax \leq b\}$ is called the *feasible space*. The LP problem is called *infeasible* iff the feasible space is empty. An element of the feasible space, is called *feasible solution*. A feasible solution x that maximizes $c^\top x$ is called *optimal solution*.

LP problems can be solved in polynomial time through interior point methods [32, 43]. Note, however, that the running-time then crucially depends on the sizes of occurring numbers. At the danger of an exponential running-time in contrived cases, we can also instead rely on the simplex algorithm: its running-time is *uniform*, i.e., independent of the sizes of occurring numbers (given that arithmetic operations, comparison, storage and retrieval for numbers are counted for $\mathcal{O}(1)$).

SAT Modulo Real Linear Arithmetic. The set of SAT modulo real linear arithmetic formulas Φ is defined through the grammar $e ::= c \mid x \mid e_1 + e_2 \mid c \cdot e'$, $\Phi ::= a \mid e_1 \leq e_2 \mid \Phi_1 \vee \Phi_2 \mid \Phi_1 \wedge \Phi_2 \mid \overline{\Phi'}$. Here, $c \in \mathbb{R}$ is a constant, x is a real valued variable, e, e', e_1, e_2 are real-valued linear expressions, a is a Boolean variable and $\Phi, \Phi', \Phi_1, \Phi_2$ are formulas. An *interpretation* I for a formula Φ is a mapping that assigns a real value to every real-valued variable and a Boolean value to every Boolean variable. We write $I \models \Phi$ for "I is a *model* of Φ", i.e., $[\![c]\!]I = c$, $[\![x]\!] = I(x)$, $[\![e_1 + e_2]\!]I = [\![e_1]\!]I + [\![e_2]\!]I$, $[\![c \cdot e']\!]I = c \cdot [\![e']\!]I$, and:

$$
\begin{array}{rlrl}
I \models a & \iff I(a) = 1 & I \models e_1 \leq e_2 & \iff [\![e_1]\!]I \leq [\![e_2]\!]I \\
I \models \Phi_1 \vee \Phi_2 & \iff I \models \Phi_1 \text{ or } I \models \Phi_2 & I \models \Phi_1 \wedge \Phi_2 & \iff I \models \Phi_1 \text{ and } I \models \Phi_2 \\
I \models \overline{\Phi'} & \iff I \not\models \Phi' & &
\end{array}
$$

A formula is called *satisfiable* iff it has a model. The problem of deciding, whether or not a given SAT modulo real linear arithmetic formula is satisfiable, is NP-complete. There nevertheless exist efficient solver implementations for this decision problem [15].

In order to simplify notations we also allow matrices, vectors, the operations $\geq$, $<, >, \neq, =$, and the Boolean constants 0 and 1 to occur.

Collecting and Abstract Semantics. The programs that we consider in this article use real-valued variables $x_1, \ldots, x_n$. Accordingly, we denote by $x = (x_1, \ldots, x_n)^\top$ the vector of all program variables. For simplicity, we only consider elementary statements of the form $x := Ax + b$, and $Ax \leq b$, where $A \in \mathbb{R}^{n \times n}$ (resp. $\mathbb{R}^{k \times n}$), $b \in \mathbb{R}^n$ (resp. $\mathbb{R}^k$), and $x \in \mathbb{R}^n$ denotes the vector of all program variables. Statements of the form $x := Ax + b$ are called *(affine) assignments*. Statements of the form $Ax \leq b$ are called *(affine) guards*. Additionally, we allow statements of the form $s_1; \cdots; s_k$ and $s_1 \mid \cdots \mid s_k$, where $s_1, \ldots, s_k$ are statements. The operator ; binds tighter than the operator $|$, and we consider ; and $|$ to be right-associative, i.e., $s_1 \mid s_2 \mid s_3$ stands for $s_1 \mid (s_2 \mid s_3)$, and $s_1; s_2; s_3$ stands for $s_1; (s_2; s_3)$. The set of statements is denoted by $\mathbf{Stmt}$. A statement of the form $s_1 \mid \cdots \mid s_k$, where s_i does not contain the operator $|$ for all $i = 1, \ldots, k$, is called *merge-simple*. A merge-simple statement s that does not use the $|$ operator at all is called *sequential*. A statement is called *elementary* iff it neither contains the operator $|$ nor the operator ;.

The *collecting semantics* $[\![s]\!] : 2^{\mathbb{R}^n} \to 2^{\mathbb{R}^n}$ of a statement $s \in \mathbf{Stmt}$ is defined by

$$[\![x := Ax + b]\!]X := \{Ax + b \mid x \in X\}, \qquad [\![Ax \leq b]\!]X := \{x \in X \mid Ax \leq b\},$$
$$[\![s_1; \cdots; s_k]\!] := [\![s_k]\!] \circ \cdots \circ [\![s_1]\!] \qquad [\![s_1 \mid \cdots \mid s_k]\!]X := [\![s_1]\!]X \cup \cdots \cup [\![s_k]\!]X$$

for $X \subseteq \mathbb{R}^n$. Note that the operators ; and $|$ are associative, i.e., $[\![(s_1; s_2); s_3]\!] = [\![s_1; (s_2; s_3)]\!]$ and $[\![(s_1 \mid s_2) \mid s_3]\!] = [\![s_1 \mid (s_2 \mid s_3)]\!]$ hold for all statements s_1, s_2, s_3.

An *(affine) program* G is a triple $(N, E, \mathbf{st})$, where N is a finite set of *program points*, $E \subseteq N \times \mathbf{Stmt} \times N$ is a finite set of control-flow edges, and $\mathbf{st} \in N$ is the *start program point*. As usual, the *collecting semantics* V of a program $G = (N, E, \mathbf{st})$ is the least solution of the following constraint system:

$$\mathbf{V}[\mathbf{st}] \supseteq \mathbb{R}^n \qquad \mathbf{V}[v] \supseteq [\![s]\!](\mathbf{V}[u]) \quad \text{for all } (u, s, v) \in E$$

Here, the variables $\mathbf{V}[v]$, $v \in N$ take values in $2^{\mathbb{R}^n}$. The components of the collecting semantics V are denoted by $V[v]$ for all $v \in N$.

Let $\mathbb{D}$ be a complete lattice (for instance the complete lattice of all n-dimensional closed real intervals). Let the partial order of $\mathbb{D}$ be denoted by $\leq$. Assume that $\alpha : 2^{\mathbb{R}^n} \to \mathbb{D}$ and $\gamma : \mathbb{D} \to 2^{\mathbb{R}^n}$ form a Galois connection, i.e., for all $X \subseteq \mathbb{R}^n$ and all $d \in \mathbb{D}$, $\alpha(X) \leq d$ iff $X \subseteq \gamma(d)$. The *abstract semantics* $[\![s]\!]^\sharp : \mathbb{D} \to \mathbb{D}$ of a statement s is defined by $[\![s]\!]^\sharp := \alpha \circ [\![s]\!] \circ \gamma$. The *abstract semantics* $V^\sharp$ of an affine program $G = (N, E, \mathbf{st})$ is the least solution of the following constraint system:

$$\mathbf{V}^\sharp[\mathbf{st}] \geq \alpha(\mathbb{R}^n) \qquad \mathbf{V}^\sharp[v] \geq [\![s]\!]^\sharp(\mathbf{V}^\sharp[u]) \quad \text{for all } (u, s, v) \in E$$

Here, the variables $\mathbf{V}^\sharp[v]$, $v \in N$ take values in $\mathbb{D}$. The components of the abstract semantics $V^\sharp$ are denoted by $V^\sharp[v]$ for all $v \in N$. The abstract semantics $V^\sharp$ safely over-approximates the collecting semantics V, i.e., $\gamma(V^\sharp[v]) \supseteq V[v]$ for all $v \in N$.

Using Cut-Sets to Improve Precision. Usually, only sequential statements (these statements correspond to *basic blocks*) are allowed in control flow graphs. However, given a cut-set C, one can systematically transform any control flow graph G into an equivalent control flow graph G' of our form (up to the fact that G' has fewer program points than G) with increased precision of the abstract semantics. However, for the sake of simplicity, we do not discuss these aspects in detail. Instead, we consider an example:

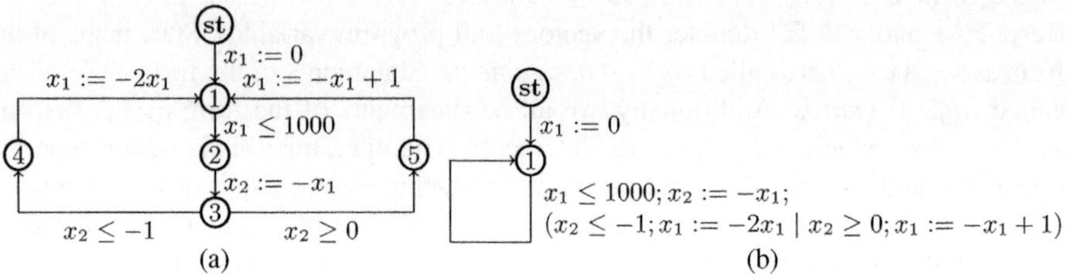

Fig. 1.

Example 1 (Using Cut-Sets to improve Precision). As a running example throughout the present article we use the following C-code:

```
int x_1, x_2; x_1 = 0; while (x_1 <= 1000) { x_2 = -x_1;
  if (x_2 < 0) x_1 = -2 * x_1; else x_1 = -x_1 + 1; }
```

This C-code is abstracted through the affine program $G_1 = (N_1, E_1, \mathbf{st})$ which is shown in Figure 1.(a). However, it is unnecessary to apply abstraction at every program point; it suffices to apply abstraction at a cut-set of G_1. Since all loops contain program point 1, a cut-set of G_1 is $\{1\}$. Equivalent to applying abstraction only at program point 1 is to rewrite the control-flow graph w.r.t. the cut-set $\{1\}$ into a control-flow graph G equivalent w.r.t. the collecting semantic. The result of this transformation is drawn in Figure 1.(b). This means: the affine program for the above C-code is $G = (N, E, \mathbf{st})$, where $N = \{\mathbf{st}, 1\}$, $E = \{(\mathbf{st}, x_1 := 0, 1), (1, s, 1)\}$, and

$$s' = x_1 \leq 1000; x_2 := -x_1 \qquad s_1 = x_2 \leq -1; x_1 := -2x_1$$

$$s_2 = -x_2 \leq 0; x_1 := -x_1 + 1 \qquad s = s'; (s_1 \mid s_2)$$

Let V_1 denote the collecting semantics of G_1 and V denote the collecting semantics of G. G_1 and G are equivalent in the following sense: $V[v] = V_1[v]$ holds for all program points $v \in N$. W.r.t. the abstract semantics, G is, is we will see, strictly more precise than G_1. In general we at least have $V^\sharp[v] \subseteq V_1^\sharp[v]$ for all program points $v \in N$. This is independent of the abstract domain.[1] □

Template Linear Constraints. In the present article we restrict our considerations to *template linear constraint domains* [42]. Assume that we are given a fixed *template constraint matrix* $T \in \mathbb{R}^{m \times n}$. The template linear constraint domain is $\overline{\mathbb{R}}^m$. As shown

[1] We assume that we have given a Galois-connection and thus in particular monotone best abstract transformers.

by Sankaranarayanan et al. [42], the concretization $\gamma : \overline{\mathbb{R}}^m \to 2^{\mathbb{R}^n}$ and the abstraction $\alpha : 2^{\mathbb{R}^n} \to \overline{\mathbb{R}}^m$, which are defined by

$$\gamma(d) := \{x \in \mathbb{R}^n \mid Tx \leq d\} \qquad \forall d \in \overline{\mathbb{R}}^m,$$
$$\alpha(X) := \bigwedge\{d \in \overline{\mathbb{R}}^m \mid \gamma(d) \supseteq X\} \qquad \forall X \subseteq \mathbb{R}^n,$$

form a Galois connection. The template linear constraint domains contain *intervals*, *zones*, and *octagons*, with appropriate choices of the template constraint matrix [42].

In a first stage we restrict our considerations to sequential and merge-simple statements. Even for these statements we avoid unnecessary imprecision, if we abstract such statements en bloc instead of abstracting each elementary statement separately:

Example 2. In this example we use the interval domain as abstract domain, i.e., our complete lattice consists of all n-dimensional closed real intervals. Our affine program will use 2 variables, i.e., $n = 2$. The complete lattice of all 2-dimensional closed real intervals can be specified through the template constraint matrix $T = \begin{pmatrix}-I & I\end{pmatrix}^\top \in \mathbb{R}^{4\times 2}$, where I denotes the identity matrix. Consider the statements $s_1 = x_2 := x_1$, $s_2 = x_1 := x_1 - x_2$, and $s = s_1; s_2$ and the abstract value $I = [0,1] \times \mathbb{R}$ (a 2-dimensional closed real interval). The interval I can w.r.t. T be identified with the abstract value $(0, \infty, 1, \infty)^\top$. More generally, w.r.t. T every 2-dimensional closed real interval $[l_1, u_1] \times [l_2, u_2]$ can be identified with the abstract value $(-l_1, -l_2, u_1, u_2)^\top$. If we abstract each elementary statement separately, then we in fact use $[\![s_2]\!]^\sharp \circ [\![s_1]\!]^\sharp$ instead of $[\![s]\!]^\sharp$ to abstract the collecting semantics $[\![s]\!]$ of the statement $s = s_1; s_2$. The following calculation shows that this can be important: $[\![s]\!]^\sharp I = [0,0] \times [0,1] \neq [-1,1] \times [0,1] = [\![s_2]\!]^\sharp([0,1] \times [0,1]) = ([\![s_2]\!]^\sharp \circ [\![s_1]\!]^\sharp)I$. The imprecision is caused by the additional abstraction. We lose the information that the values of the program variables x_1 and x_2 are equal after executing the first statement. □

Another possibility for avoiding unnecessary imprecision in the above example would consist in adding additional rows to the template constraint matrix. Although this works for the above example, it does not work in general, since still only convex sets can be described, but sometimes non-convex sets are required (cf. with the example in the introduction).

Provided that s is a merge-simple statement, $[\![s]\!]^\sharp d$ can be computed in polynomial time through linear programming:

Lemma 1 (Merge-Simple Statements). *Let s be a merge-simple statement and $d \in \overline{\mathbb{R}}^m$. Then $[\![s]\!]^\sharp d$ can be computed in polynomial time through linear programming.* □

However, the situation for arbitrary statements is significantly more difficult, since, by reducing SAT to the corresponding decision problem, we can show the following:

Lemma 2. *The problem of deciding, whether or not, for a given template constraint matrix T, and a given statement s, $[\![s]\!]^\sharp \underline{\infty} > \underline{-\infty}$ holds, is NP-complete.*

Before proving the above lemma, we introduce $\vee$-strategies for statements as follows:

Definition 1 **($\vee$-Strategies for Statements).** *A $\vee$-strategy σ for a statement s is a function that maps every position of a $|$-statement, (a statement of the form $s_0 \mid s_1$) within s to 0 or 1. The application $s\sigma$ of a $\vee$-strategy σ to a statement s is inductively defined by $s\sigma = s$, $(s_0 \mid s_1)\sigma = s_{\sigma(\mathrm{pos}(s_0|s_1))}\sigma$, and $(s_0; s_1)\sigma = (s_0\sigma; s_1\sigma)$, where s is an elementary statement, and s_0, s_1 are arbitrary statements. For all occurrences s', $\mathrm{pos}(s')$ denotes the position of s', i.e., $\mathrm{pos}(s')$ identifies the occurrence.* □

Proof. Firstly, we show containment in NP. Assume $[\![s]\!]^\sharp \underline{\infty} > \underline{-\infty}$. There exists some k such that the k-th component of $[\![s]\!]^\sharp \underline{\infty}$ is greater than $-\infty$. We choose k non-deterministically. There exists a $\vee$-strategy σ for s such that the k-th component of $[\![s\sigma]\!]^\sharp \underline{\infty}$ equals the k-th component of $[\![s]\!]^\sharp \underline{\infty}$. We choose such a $\vee$-strategy non-deterministically. By Lemma 1, we can check in polynomial time, whether the k-th component of $[\![s\sigma]\!]^\sharp \underline{\infty}$ is greater than $-\infty$. If this is fulfilled, we accept.

In order to show NP-hardness, we reduce the NP-hard problem SAT to our problem. Let Φ be a propositional formula with n variables. W.l.o.g. we assume that Φ is in normal form, i.e., there are no negated sub-formulas that contain $\wedge$ or $\vee$. We define the statement $s(\Phi)$ that uses the variables of Φ as program variables inductively by $s(z) := z = 1$, $s(\overline{z}) := z = 0$, $s(\Phi_1 \wedge \Phi_2) := s(\Phi_1); s(\Phi_2)$, and $s(\Phi_1 \vee \Phi_2) := s(\Phi_1) \mid s(\Phi_2)$, where z is a variable of Φ, and Φ_1, Φ_2 are formulas. Here, the statement $Ax = b$ is an abbreviation for the statement $Ax \leq b; -Ax \leq -b$. The formula Φ is satisfiable iff $[\![s(\Phi)]\!]\mathbb{R}^n \neq \emptyset$ holds. Moreover, even if we just use the interval domain, $[\![s(\Phi)]\!]\mathbb{R}^n \neq \emptyset$ holds iff $[\![s(\Phi)]\!]^\sharp \underline{\infty} > \underline{-\infty}$ holds. Thus, Φ is satisfiable iff $[\![s(\Phi)]\!]^\sharp \underline{\infty} > \underline{-\infty}$ holds. □

Obviously, $[\![(s_1 \mid s_2); s]\!] = [\![s_1; s \mid s_2; s]\!]$ and $[\![s; (s_1 \mid s_2)]\!] = [\![s; s_1 \mid s; s_2]\!]$ for all statements s, s_1, s_2. We can transform any statement s into an equivalent merge-simple statement s' using these rules. We denote the merge-simple statement s' that is obtained from an arbitrary statement s by applying the above rules in some canonical way by $[s]$. Intuitively, $[s]$ is an explicit enumeration of all paths through the statement s.

Lemma 3. *For every statement s, $[s]$ is merge-simple, and $[\![s]\!] = [\![[s]]\!]$. The size of $[s]$ is at most exponential in the size of s.* □

However, in the worst case, the size of $[s]$ is exponential in the size of s. For the statement $s = (s_1^{(1)} \mid s_1^{(2)}); \cdots; (s_k^{(1)} \mid s_k^{(2)})$, for instance, we get $[s] = |_{(a_1,\ldots,a_k)\in\{1,2\}^k}\, s_1^{(a_1)}; \cdots; s_k^{(a_k)}$. After replacing all statements s with $[s]$ it is in principle possible to use the methods of Gawlitza and Seidl [17] in order to compute the abstract semantics $V^\sharp$ precisely. Because of the exponential blowup, however, this method would be impractical in most cases. [2]

Our new method that we are going to present avoids this exponential blowup: instead of enumerating all program paths, we shall visit them only as needed. Guided by a SAT modulo real linear arithmetic solver, our method selects a path through s only when it is *locally profitable* in some sense. In the worst case, an exponential number of paths

[2] Note that we cannot expect a polynomial-time algorithm, because of Lemma 2: even without loops, abstract reachability is NP-hard. Even if all statements are merge-simple, we cannot expect a polynomial-time algorithm, since the problem of computing the winning regions of parity games is polynomial-time reducible to abstract reachability [19].

may be visited (Section 7); but one can hope that this does not happen in many practical cases, in the same way that SAT and SMT solving perform well on many practical cases even though they in principle may visit an exponential number of cases.

Abstract Semantic Equations. The first step of our method consists of rewriting our program analysis problem into a *system of abstract semantic equations* that is interpreted over the reals. For that, let $G = (N, E, \mathbf{st})$ be an affine program and $V^\sharp$ its abstract semantics. We define the system $\mathcal{C}(G)$ of *abstract semantic inequalities* to be the smallest set of inequalities that fulfills the following constraints:

- $\mathcal{C}$ contains the inequality $\mathbf{x}_{\mathbf{st},i} \geq \alpha_{i\cdot}(\mathbb{R}^n)$ for every $i \in \{1, \ldots, m\}$.
- $\mathcal{C}$ contains the inequality $\mathbf{x}_{v,i} \geq [\![s]\!]^\sharp_{i\cdot}(\mathbf{x}_{u,1}, \ldots, \mathbf{x}_{u,m})$ for every control-flow edge $(u, s, v) \in E$ and every $i \in \{1, \ldots, m\}$.

We define the system $\mathcal{E}(G)$ of *abstract semantic equations* by $\mathcal{E}(G) := \mathcal{E}(\mathcal{C}(G))$. Here, for a system $\mathcal{C}' = \{\mathbf{x}_1 \geq e_{1,1}, \ldots, \mathbf{x}_1 \geq e_{1,k_1}, \ldots, \mathbf{x}_n \geq e_{n,1}, \ldots, \mathbf{x}_n \geq e_{n,k_n}\}$ of inequalities, $\mathcal{E}(\mathcal{C}')$ is the system $\mathcal{E}(\mathcal{C}') = \{\mathbf{x}_1 = e_{1,1} \vee \cdots \vee e_{1,k_1}, \ldots, \mathbf{x}_n = e_{n,1} \vee \cdots \vee e_{n,k_n}\}$ of equations. The system $\mathcal{E}(G)$ of abstract semantic equations captures the abstract semantics $V^\sharp$ of G:

Lemma 4. $(V^\sharp[v])_{i\cdot} = \mu[\![\mathcal{E}(G)]\!](\mathbf{x}_{v,i})$ *for all program points* v, $i \in \{1, \ldots, m\}$. □

Example 3 (Abstract Semantic Equations). We again consider the program G of Example 1. Assume that the template constraint matrix $T \in \mathbb{R}^{2\times 2}$ is given by $T_{1\cdot} = (1, 0)$ and $T_{2\cdot} = (-1, 0)$. Let $V^\sharp$ denote the abstract semantics of G. Then $V^\sharp[1] = (2001, 2000)^\top$. $\mathcal{E}(G)$ consists of the following abstract semantic equations:

$$\mathbf{x}_{\mathbf{st},1} = \infty \qquad \mathbf{x}_{1,1} = [\![x_1 := 0]\!]^\sharp_{1\cdot}(\mathbf{x}_{\mathbf{st},1}, \mathbf{x}_{\mathbf{st},2}) \vee [\![s]\!]^\sharp_{1\cdot}(\mathbf{x}_{1,1}, \mathbf{x}_{1,2})$$
$$\mathbf{x}_{\mathbf{st},2} = \infty \qquad \mathbf{x}_{1,2} = [\![x_1 := 0]\!]^\sharp_{2\cdot}(\mathbf{x}_{\mathbf{st},1}, \mathbf{x}_{\mathbf{st},2}) \vee [\![s]\!]^\sharp_{2\cdot}(\mathbf{x}_{1,1}, \mathbf{x}_{1,2})$$

As stated by Lemma 4, we have $(V^\sharp[1])_{1\cdot} = \mu[\![\mathcal{E}(G)]\!](\mathbf{x}_{1,1}) = 2001$, and $(V^\sharp[1])_{2\cdot} = \mu[\![\mathcal{E}(G)]\!](\mathbf{x}_{1,2}) = 2000$. □

3 A Lower Bound on the Complexity

In this section we show that the problem of computing abstract semantics of affine programs w.r.t. the interval domain is Π^p_2-hard. Π^p_2-hard problems are conjectured to be harder than both NP-complete and co-NP-complete problems. For further information regarding the polynomial-time hierarchy see e.g. Stockmeyer [44].

Theorem 1. *The problem of deciding, whether, for a given program G, a given template constraint matrix T, and a given program point v,* $V^\sharp[v] > \underline{-\infty}$ *holds, is* Π^p_2*-hard.*

Proof. We reduce the Π^p_2-complete problem of deciding the truth of a $\forall\exists$ propositional formula [46] to our problem. Let $\Phi = \forall x_1, \ldots, x_n. \exists y_1, \ldots, y_m. \Phi'$ be a formula without free variables, where Φ' is a propositional formula. We consider the affine program $G = (N, E, \mathbf{st})$, with program variables $x, x', x_1, \ldots, x_n, y_1, \ldots, y_m$, where $N = \{\mathbf{st}, 1, 2\}$, and $E = \{(\mathbf{st}, x := 0, 1), (1, s, 1), (1, x \geq 2^n, 2)\}$ with

$$s = x' := x; (x' \geq 2^{n-1}; x' := x' - 2^{n-1}; x_n := 1 \mid x' \leq 2^{n-1} - 1; x_n := 0); \cdots$$
$$(x' \geq 2^{1-1}; x' := x' - 2^{1-1}; x_1 := 1 \mid x' \leq 2^{1-1} - 1; x_1 := 0);$$
$$s(\Phi');\ x := x + 1$$

The statement $s(\Phi')$ is defined as in the proof of Lemma 2.

In intuitive terms: this program initializes x to 0. Then, it enters a loop: it computes into $x_1, \ldots, x_n$ the binary decomposition of x, then it attempts to nondeterministically choose $y_1, \ldots, y_m$ so that ϕ' is true. If this is possible, it increments x by one and loops. Otherwise, it just loops. Thus, there is a terminating computations iff Φ holds.

Then Φ holds iff $V[2] \neq \emptyset$. For the abstraction, we consider the interval domain. By considering the Kleene-Iteration, it is easy to see that $V[2] \neq \emptyset$ holds iff $V^\sharp[2] > \underline{-\infty}$ holds. Thus Φ holds iff $V^\sharp[2] > \underline{-\infty}$ holds. □

4 Determining Improved Strategies

In this section we develop a method for computing local improvements of strategies through solving SAT modulo real linear arithmetic formulas.

In order to decide, whether or not, for a given statement s, a given $j \in \{1, \ldots, m\}$, a given c, and a given $d \in \overline{\mathbb{R}}^m$, $[\![s]\!]^\sharp_j.d > c$ holds, we construct the following SAT modulo real linear arithmetic formula (we use existential quantifiers to improve readability):

$$\Phi(s, d, j, c) :\equiv \exists v \in \mathbb{R} \,.\, \Phi(s, d, j) \wedge v > c$$
$$\Phi(s, d, j) :\equiv \exists x \in \mathbb{R}^n, x' \in \mathbb{R}^n \,.\, Tx \leq d \wedge \Phi(s) \wedge v = T_{j\cdot}x'$$

Here, $\Phi(s)$ is a formula that relates every $x \in \mathbb{R}^n$ with all elements from the set $[\![s]\!]\{x\}$. It is defined inductively over the structure of s as follows:

$$\Phi(x := Ax + b) :\equiv x' = Ax + b$$
$$\Phi(Ax \leq b) :\equiv Ax \leq b \wedge x' = x$$
$$\Phi(s_1; s_2) :\equiv \exists x'' \in \mathbb{R}^n \,.\, \Phi(s_1)[x''/x'] \wedge \Phi(s_2)[x''/x]$$
$$\Phi(s_1 \mid s_2) :\equiv (\overline{a_{\mathrm{pos}(s_1|s_2)}} \wedge \Phi(s_1)) \vee (a_{\mathrm{pos}(s_1|s_2)} \wedge \Phi(s_2))$$

Here, for every position p of a subexpression of s, a_p is a Boolean variable. Let $\mathrm{Pos}_{|}(s)$ denote the set of all positions of $|$-subexpressions of s. The set of free variables of the formula $\Phi(s)$ is $\{x, x'\} \cup \{a_p \mid p \in \mathrm{Pos}_{|}(s)\}$. A valuation for the variables from the set $\{a_p \mid p \in \mathrm{Pos}_{|}(s)\}$ describes a path through s. We have:

Lemma 5. *$[\![s]\!]^\sharp_j.d > c$ holds iff $\Phi(s, d, j, c)$ is satisfiable.* □

Our next goal is to compute a $\vee$-strategy σ for s such that $[\![s\sigma]\!]^\sharp_j.d > c$ holds, provided that $[\![s]\!]^\sharp_j.d > c$ holds. Let s be a statement, $d \in \overline{\mathbb{R}}^m$, $j \in \{1, \ldots, m\}$, and $c \in \mathbb{R}$. Assume that $[\![s]\!]^\sharp_j.d > c$ holds. By Lemma 5, there exists a model M of $\Phi(s, d, j, c)$. We define the $\vee$-strategy σ_M for s by $\sigma_M(p) := M(a_p)$ for all $p \in \mathrm{Pos}_{|}(s)$. By again applying Lemma 5, we get $[\![s\sigma]\!]^\sharp_j.d > c$. Summarizing we have:

Lemma 6. *By solving the SAT modulo real linear arithmetic formula $\Phi(s, d, j, c)$ that can be obtained from s in linear time, we can decide, whether or not $[\![s]\!]^\sharp_{j\cdot}.d > c$ holds. From a model M of this formula, we can obtain a $\vee$-strategy σ_M for s such that $[\![s\sigma_M]\!]^\sharp_{j\cdot}.d > c$ holds in linear time.* □

$$
\begin{aligned}
\Phi(s, (0,0)^\top, 1, 0) &\equiv \exists v \in \mathbb{R} \,.\, \Phi(s, (0,0)^\top, 1) \wedge v > 0 \\
\Phi(s, (0,0)^\top, 1) &\equiv \exists x \in \mathbb{R}^2, x' \in \mathbb{R}^2 \,.\, x_{1\cdot} \le 0 \wedge -x_{1\cdot} \le 0 \wedge \Phi(s) \wedge v = x'_{1\cdot} \\
\Phi(s') &\equiv \exists x'' \in \mathbb{R}^2 \,.\, x_{1\cdot} \le 1000 \wedge x''_{1\cdot} = x_{1\cdot} \wedge x''_{2\cdot} = x_{2\cdot} \wedge x'_{1\cdot} = x''_{1\cdot} \wedge x'_{2\cdot} = -x''_{1\cdot} \\
&\equiv x_{1\cdot} \le 1000 \wedge x'_{1\cdot} = x_{1\cdot} \wedge x'_{2\cdot} = -x_{1\cdot} \\
\Phi(s_1) &\equiv \exists x'' \in \mathbb{R}^2 \,.\, x_{2\cdot} \le -1 \wedge x''_{1\cdot} = x_{1\cdot} \wedge x''_{2\cdot} = x_{2\cdot} \wedge x'_{1\cdot} = -2x''_{1\cdot} \wedge x'_{2\cdot} = x''_{2\cdot} \\
&\equiv x_{2\cdot} \le -1 \wedge x'_{1\cdot} = -2x_{1\cdot} \wedge x'_{2\cdot} = x_{2\cdot} \\
\Phi(s_2) &\equiv \exists x'' \in \mathbb{R}^2 \,.\, -x_{2\cdot} \le 0 \wedge x''_{1\cdot} = x_{1\cdot} \wedge x''_{2\cdot} = x_{2\cdot} \wedge x'_{1\cdot} = -x''_{1\cdot} + 1 \wedge x'_{2\cdot} = x''_{2\cdot} \\
&\equiv x_{2\cdot} \le 0 \wedge x'_{1\cdot} = -x_{1\cdot} + 1 \wedge x'_{2\cdot} = x_{2\cdot} \\
\Phi(s_1 \mid s_2) &\equiv (\overline{a_1} \wedge \Phi(s_1)) \vee (a_1 \wedge \Phi(s_2)) \equiv (\overline{a_1} \wedge x_{2\cdot} \le -1 \wedge x'_{1\cdot} = -2x_{1\cdot} \wedge x'_{2\cdot} = x_{2\cdot}) \\
&\qquad \vee (a_1 \wedge x_{2\cdot} \le 0 \wedge x'_{1\cdot} = -x_{1\cdot} + 1 \wedge x'_{2\cdot} = x_{2\cdot}) \\
\Phi(s) &\equiv \exists x'' \in \mathbb{R}^2 \,.\, \Phi(s')[x''/x'] \wedge \Phi(s_1 \mid s_2)[x''/x] \\
&\equiv x_{1\cdot} \le 1000 \wedge ((\overline{a_1} \wedge -x_{1\cdot} \le -1 \wedge x'_{1\cdot} = -2x_{1\cdot} \wedge x'_{2\cdot} = -x_{1\cdot}) \\
&\qquad \vee (a_1 \wedge -x_{1\cdot} \le 0 \wedge x'_{1\cdot} = -x_{1\cdot} + 1 \wedge x'_{2\cdot} = -x_{1\cdot}))
\end{aligned}
$$

Fig. 2. Formula for Example 4

Example 4. We again continue Example 1 and 3. We want to know, whether $[\![s]\!]^\sharp_{1\cdot}.(0,0)^\top > 0$ holds. For that we compute a model of the formula $\Phi(s, (0,0)^\top, 1, 0)$ which is written down in Figure 2. $M = \{a_1 \mapsto 1\}$ is a model of the formula $\Phi(s, (0,0)^\top, 1, 0)$. Thus, we have $0 < [\![s\sigma_M]\!]^\sharp_{1\cdot}.(0,0)^\top = [\![s'; s_2]\!]^\sharp_{1\cdot}.(0,0)^\top$ by Lemma 6. □

It remains to compute a model of $\Phi(s, d, j, c)$. Most of the state-of-the-art SMT solvers, as for instance Yices [14, 15], support the computation of models directly; if unsupported, one can compute the model using standard self-reduction techniques.

The semantic equations we are concerned with in the present article have the form $\mathbf{x} = e_1 \vee \cdots \vee e_k$, where each expression e_i, $i = 1, \ldots, k$ is either a constant or an expression of the form $[\![s]\!]^\sharp_{j\cdot}(\mathbf{x}_1, \ldots, \mathbf{x}_m)$. We now extent our notion of $\vee$-strategies in order to deal with the occurring right-hand sides:

Definition 2 **($\vee$-Strategies).** *The $\vee$-strategy for all constants is the 0-tuple $()$. The application $c()$ of $()$ to a constant $c \in \overline{\mathbb{R}}$ is defined by $c() := c$ for all $c \in \overline{\mathbb{R}}$. A $\vee$-strategy σ for an expression $[\![s]\!]^\sharp_{j\cdot}(\mathbf{x}_1, \ldots, \mathbf{x}_m)$ is a $\vee$-strategy for s. The application $([\![s]\!]^\sharp_{j\cdot}(\mathbf{x}_1, \ldots, \mathbf{x}_m))\sigma$ of σ to $[\![s]\!]^\sharp_{j\cdot}(\mathbf{x}_1, \ldots, \mathbf{x}_m)$ is defined by $([\![s]\!]^\sharp_{j\cdot}(\mathbf{x}_1, \ldots, \mathbf{x}_m))\sigma := [\![s\sigma]\!]^\sharp_{j\cdot}(\mathbf{x}_1, \ldots, \mathbf{x}_m)$. A $\vee$-strategy for an expression $e = e_0 \vee e_1$, where, for each $i \in \{0, 1\}$, e_i is either a constant or an expression of the form $[\![s]\!]^\sharp_{j\cdot}(\mathbf{x}_1, \ldots, \mathbf{x}_m)$, is a pair (p, σ), where $p \in \{0, 1\}$ and σ is a $\vee$-strategy for e_p. The application $e(p, \sigma)$ of (p, σ) to $e = e_0 \vee e_1$ is defined by $e(p, \sigma) = e_p\sigma$. A $\vee$-strategy σ for a system $\mathcal{E} = \{\mathbf{x}_1 = e_1, \ldots, \mathbf{x}_n = e_n\}$ of abstract semantic equations is a mapping $\{\mathbf{x}_i \mapsto \sigma_i \mid i = 1, \ldots, n\}$, where σ_i is a $\vee$-strategy for e_i for all $i = 1, \ldots, n$. We set $\mathcal{E}(\sigma) := \{\mathbf{x}_1 = e_1(\sigma(\mathbf{x}_1)), \ldots, \mathbf{x}_n = e_n(\sigma(\mathbf{x}_n))\}$.* □

Using the same ideas as above, we can prove the following lemma which finally enables us to use a SAT modulo real linear arithmetic solver for improving $\vee$-strategies for systems of abstract semantic equations locally.

Lemma 7. *Let* $\mathbf{x} = e$ *be an abstract semantic equation,* ρ *a variable assignment, and* $c \in \overline{\mathbb{R}}$. *By solving a SAT modulo real linear arithmetic formula that can be obtained from* e, ρ *and* c *in linear time, we can decide, whether or not* $[\![e]\!]\rho > c$ *holds. From a model* M *of this formula, we can in linear time obtain a* $\vee$*-strategy* σ_M *for* e *such that* $[\![e\sigma_M]\!]\rho > c$ *holds.* □

5 Solving Systems of Concave Equations

In order to solve systems of abstract semantic equations (see the end of Section 2) we generalize the $\vee$-strategy improvement algorithm of Gawlitza and Seidl [22] as follows:

Concave Functions. A set $X \subseteq \mathbb{R}^n$ is called *convex* iff $\lambda x + (1 - \lambda)y \in X$ holds for all $x, y \in X$ and all $\lambda \in [0, 1]$. A mapping $f : X \to \mathbb{R}^m$ with $X \subseteq \mathbb{R}^n$ convex is called *convex* (resp. *concave*) iff $f(\lambda x + (1 - \lambda)y) \leq$ (resp. $\geq$) $\lambda f(x) + (1 - \lambda)f(y)$ holds for all $x, y \in X$ and all $\lambda \in [0, 1]$. Note that f is concave iff $-f$ is convex. Note also that f is convex (resp. concave) iff $f_{i\cdot}$ is convex (resp. concave) for all $i = 1, \ldots, m$.

We extend the notion of convexity/concavity from $\mathbb{R}^n \to \mathbb{R}^m$ to $\overline{\mathbb{R}}^n \to \overline{\mathbb{R}}^m$ as follows: Let $f : \overline{\mathbb{R}}^n \to \overline{\mathbb{R}}^m$, and $I : \{1, \ldots, n\} \to \{-\infty, \mathrm{id}, \infty\}$. Here, $-\infty$ denotes the function that assigns $-\infty$ to every argument, id denotes the identity function, and ∞ denotes the function that assigns ∞ to every argument. We define the mapping $f^{(I)} : \overline{\mathbb{R}}^n \to \overline{\mathbb{R}}^m$ by $f^{(I)}(x_1, \ldots, x_n) := f(I(1)(x_1), \ldots, I(n)(x_n))$ for all $x_1, \ldots, x_n \in \overline{\mathbb{R}}$. A mapping $f : \overline{\mathbb{R}}^n \to \overline{\mathbb{R}}^m$ is called *concave* iff $f_{i\cdot}$ is continuous on $\{x \in \overline{\mathbb{R}}^n \mid f_{i\cdot}(x) > -\infty\}$ for all $i \in \{1, \ldots, m\}$, and the following conditions are fulfilled for all $I : \{1, \ldots, n\} \to \{-\infty, \mathrm{id}, \infty\}$:

1. $\mathrm{fdom}(f^{(I)})$ is convex.
2. $f^{(I)}|_{\mathrm{fdom}(f^{(I)})}$ is concave.
3. For all $i \in \{1, \ldots, m\}$ the following holds: If there exists some $y \in \mathbb{R}^n$ such that $f_{i\cdot}^{(I)}(y) \in \mathbb{R}$, then $f_{i\cdot}^{(I)}(x) < \infty$ for all $x \in \mathbb{R}^n$.

A mapping $f : \overline{\mathbb{R}}^n \to \overline{\mathbb{R}}^m$ is called *convex* iff $-f$ is concave. In the following we are only concerned with mappings $f : \overline{\mathbb{R}}^n \to \overline{\mathbb{R}}^m$ that are monotone and concave.

We slightly extend the definition of concave equations of Gawlitza and Seidl [22]:

Definition 3 (Concave Equations). *An expression* e *(resp. equation* $\mathbf{x} = e$*) over* $\overline{\mathbb{R}}$ *is called* basic concave expression *(resp.* basic concave equation*) iff* $[\![e]\!]$ *is monotone and concave. An expression* e *(resp. equation* $\mathbf{x} = e$*) over* $\overline{\mathbb{R}}$ *is called* concave *iff* $e = \bigvee E$, *where* E *is a set of basic concave expressions.* □

The class of systems of concave equations strictly subsumes the class of *systems of rational equations* and even the class of *systems of rational LP-equations* as defined by Gawlitza and Seidl [17, 21] (cf. [22]).

For this paper it is important to observe that every system of abstract semantic equations (cf. Section 2) is a system of concave equations: For every statement s, the expression $[\![s]\!]^\sharp_{j\cdot}(\mathbf{x}_1, \ldots, \mathbf{x}_m)$ is a concave expression, since (1) the expression $([\![s]\!]^\sharp_{j\cdot}(\mathbf{x}_1, \ldots, \mathbf{x}_m))\sigma$ is a basic concave expression for all $\vee$-strategies σ, (i.e. $[\![s\sigma]\!]^\sharp_{j\cdot}$ is monotone and concave) and (2) the expression $[\![s]\!]^\sharp_{j\cdot}(\mathbf{x}_1, \ldots, \mathbf{x}_m)$ can be written as the expression $\bigvee_{\sigma \in \Sigma}([\![s]\!]^\sharp_{j\cdot}(\mathbf{x}_1, \ldots, \mathbf{x}_m))\sigma$. Here, Σ denotes the set of all $\vee$-strategies. Hence, we can generalize the concept of $\vee$-strategies as follows:

Strategies. A $\vee$-*strategy* σ for $\mathcal{E}$ is a function that maps every expression $\bigvee E$ occurring in $\mathcal{E}$ to one of the $e \in E$. We denote the set of all $\vee$-strategies for $\mathcal{E}$ by $\Sigma_{\mathcal{E}}$. We drop subscripts, whenever they are clear from the context. For $\sigma \in \Sigma$, the expression $e\sigma$ denotes the expression $\sigma(e)$. Finally, we set $\mathcal{E}(\sigma) := \{\mathbf{x} = e\sigma \mid \mathbf{x} = e \in \mathcal{E}\}$.

The Strategy Improvement Algorithm. We briefly explain the strategy improvement algorithm (cf. [21, 22]). It iterates over $\vee$-strategies. It maintains a current $\vee$-strategy and a current *approximate* to the least solution. A so-called *strategy improvement operator* is used for determining a next, improved $\vee$-strategy. In our application, the strategy improvement operator is realized by a SAT modulo real linear arithmetic solver (cf. Section 4). Whether or not a $\vee$-strategy represents an *improvement* may depend on the current approximate. It can indeed be the case that a switch from one $\vee$-strategy to another $\vee$-strategy is only then *profitable*, when it is known, that the least solution is of a certain size. Hence, we talk about an *improvement* of a $\vee$-strategy w.r.t. an approximate:

Definition 4 (Improvements). *Let $\mathcal{E}$ be a system of monotone equations over a complete linear ordered set. Let $\sigma, \sigma' \in \Sigma$ be $\vee$-strategies for $\mathcal{E}$ and ρ be a pre-solution of $\mathcal{E}(\sigma)$. The $\vee$-strategy σ' is called* improvement of σ w.r.t. ρ *iff the following conditions are fulfilled: (1) If $\rho \notin \mathbf{Sol}(\mathcal{E})$, then $[\![\mathcal{E}(\sigma')]\!]\rho > \rho$. (2) For all $\bigvee$-expressions e occurring in $\mathcal{E}$ the following holds: If $\sigma'(e) \neq \sigma(e)$, then $[\![e\sigma']\!]\rho > [\![e\sigma]\!]\rho$. A function $P_\vee$ which assigns an improvement of σ w.r.t. ρ to every pair (σ, ρ), where σ is a $\vee$-strategy and ρ is a pre-solution of $\mathcal{E}(\sigma)$, is called* $\vee$-strategy improvement operator. □

In many cases, there exist several, different improvements of a $\vee$-strategy σ w.r.t. a pre-solution ρ of $\mathcal{E}(\sigma)$. Accordingly, there exist several, different strategy improvement operators. One possibility for improving the current strategy is known as *all profitable switches* [4, 5]. Carried over to the case considered here, this means: For the improvement σ' of σ w.r.t. ρ we have: $[\![\mathcal{E}(\sigma')]\!]\rho = [\![\mathcal{E}]\!]\rho$, i.e., σ' represents the best local improvement of σ at ρ. We denote σ' by $P_\vee^{\text{eager}}(\sigma, \rho)$ [17–19, 21].

Now we can formulate the strategy improvement algorithm for computing least solutions of systems of monotone equations over complete linear ordered sets. This algorithm is parameterized with a $\vee$-strategy improvement operator $P_\vee$. The input is a system $\mathcal{E}$ of monotone equations over a complete linear ordered set, a $\vee$-strategy σ_{init} for $\mathcal{E}$, and a pre-solution ρ_{init} of $\mathcal{E}(\sigma_{\text{init}})$. In order to compute the *least* and not some *arbitrary* solution, we additionally assume that $\rho_{\text{init}} \leq \mu[\![\mathcal{E}]\!]$ holds:

Algorithm 1. The Strategy Improvement Algorithm

Input : - A system $\mathcal{E}$ of monotone equations over a complete linear ordered set
- A $\vee$-strategy σ_{init} for $\mathcal{E}$
- A pre-solution ρ_{init} of $\mathcal{E}(\sigma_{\text{init}})$ with $\rho_{\text{init}} \leq \mu[\![\mathcal{E}]\!]$

$\sigma \leftarrow \sigma_{\text{init}}$; $\rho \leftarrow \rho_{\text{init}}$; **while** $(\rho \notin \mathbf{Sol}(\mathcal{E}))$ $\{\sigma \leftarrow P_{\vee}(\sigma, \rho)$; $\rho \leftarrow \mu_{\geq \rho}[\![\mathcal{E}(\sigma)]\!]$; $\}$ **return** ρ;

Lemma 8. *Let $\mathcal{E}$ be a system of monotone equations over a complete linear ordered set. For $i \in \mathbb{N}$, let ρ_i be the value of the program variable ρ and σ_i be the value of the program variable σ in the strategy improvement algorithm after the i-th evaluation of the loop-body. The following statements hold for all $i \in \mathbb{N}$:*
1. $\rho_i \leq \mu[\![\mathcal{E}]\!]$.
2. $\rho_i \in \mathbf{PreSol}(\mathcal{E}(\sigma_{i+1}))$.
3. If $\rho_i < \mu[\![\mathcal{E}]\!]$, then $\rho_{i+1} > \rho_i$.
4. If $\rho_i = \mu[\![\mathcal{E}]\!]$, then $\rho_{i+1} = \rho_i$. □

An immediate consequence of Lemma 8 is the following: Whenever the strategy improvement algorithm terminates, it computes the least solution $\mu[\![\mathcal{E}]\!]$ of $\mathcal{E}$.

At first we are interested in solving systems of concave equations with *finitely* many strategies and *finite* least solutions. We show that our strategy improvement algorithm terminates and thus returns the least solution in this case at the latest after considering all strategies. Further, we give an important characterization for $\mu_{\geq \rho}[\![\mathcal{E}(\sigma)]\!]$.

Feasibility. In order to prove termination we define the following notion of feasibility:

Definition 5 (Feasibility ([22])). *Let $\mathcal{E}$ be a system of basic concave equations. A finite solution ρ of $\mathcal{E}$ is called ($\mathcal{E}$-)*feasible *iff there exists $\mathbf{X}_1, \mathbf{X}_2 \subseteq \mathbf{X}$ and some $k \in \mathbb{N}$ such that the following statements hold:*
1. $\mathbf{X}_1 \cup \mathbf{X}_2 = \mathbf{X}$, and $\mathbf{X}_1 \cap \mathbf{X}_2 = \emptyset$.
2. There exists some $\rho' \lhd \rho|_{\mathbf{X}_1}$ such that $\rho' \mathbin{\dot\cup} \rho|_{\mathbf{X}_2}$ is a pre-solution of $\mathcal{E}$, and $\rho = [\![\mathcal{E}]\!]^k(\rho' \mathbin{\dot\cup} \rho|_{\mathbf{X}_2})$.
3. There exists a $\rho' \lhd \rho|_{\mathbf{X}_2}$ such that $\rho' \lhd ([\![\mathcal{E}]\!]^k(\rho|_{\mathbf{X}_1} \mathbin{\dot\cup} \rho'))|_{\mathbf{X}_2}$.
*A finite pre-solution ρ of $\mathcal{E}$ is called ($\mathcal{E}$-)*feasible *iff $\mu_{\geq \rho}[\![\mathcal{E}]\!]$ is a feasible finite solution of $\mathcal{E}$. A pre-solution $\rho \lhd \underline{\infty}$ is called feasible iff $e = -\infty$ for all $\mathbf{x} = e \in \mathcal{E}$ with $[\![e]\!]\rho = -\infty$, and $\rho|_{\mathbf{X}'}$ is a feasible finite pre-solution of $\{\mathbf{x} = e \in \mathcal{E} \mid \mathbf{x} \in \mathbf{X}'\}$, where $\mathbf{X}' := \{\mathbf{x} \mid \mathbf{x} = e \in \mathcal{E}, [\![e]\!]\rho > -\infty\}$.*

A system $\mathcal{E}$ of basic concave equations is called feasible *iff there exists a feasible solution ρ of $\mathcal{E}$.* □

The following lemmas ensure that our strategy improvement algorithm stays in the feasible area, whenever it is started in the feasible area.

Lemma 9 ([22]). *Let $\mathcal{E}$ be a system of basic concave equations and ρ be a feasible pre-solution of $\mathcal{E}$. Every pre-solution ρ' of $\mathcal{E}$ with $\rho \leq \rho' \leq \mu_{\geq \rho}[\![\mathcal{E}]\!]$ is feasible.* □

Lemma 10 ([22]). *Let $\mathcal{E}$ be a system of concave equations, σ be a $\vee$-strategy for $\mathcal{E}$, ρ be a feasible solution of $\mathcal{E}(\sigma)$, and σ' be an improvement of σ w.r.t. ρ. Then ρ is a feasible pre-solution of $\mathcal{E}(\sigma')$.* □

In order to start in the feasible area, we simply start the strategy improvement algorithm with the system $\mathcal{E} \vee -\infty := \{\mathbf{x} = e \vee -\infty \mid \mathbf{x} = e \in \mathcal{E}\}$, a $\vee$-strategy σ_{init} for $\mathcal{E} \vee -\infty$ such that $(\mathcal{E} \vee -\infty)(\sigma_{\text{init}}) = \{\mathbf{x} = -\infty \mid \mathbf{x} = e \in \mathcal{E}\}$, and the feasible pre-solution $\underline{-\infty}$ of $(\mathcal{E} \vee -\infty)(\sigma_{\text{init}})$.

It remains to determine $\mu_{\geq\rho}[\![\mathcal{E}]\!]$. Because of Lemma 9 and Lemma 10, we are allowed to assume that ρ is a feasible pre-solution of the system $\mathcal{E}$ of basic concave equations. This is important in our strategy improvement algorithm. The following lemma in particular states that we have to compute the greatest finite pre-solution.

Lemma 11 ([22]). *Let $\mathcal{E}$ be a feasible system of basic concave equations with $e \neq -\infty$ for all $\mathbf{x} = e \in \mathcal{E}$. There exists a greatest finite pre-solution ρ^* of $\mathcal{E}$ and ρ^* is the only feasible solution of $\mathcal{E}$. If ρ is a finite pre-solution of $\mathcal{E}$, then $\rho^* = \mu_{\geq\rho}[\![\mathcal{E}]\!]$.* □

Termination. Lemma 11 implies that our strategy improvement algorithm has to consider each $\vee$-strategy at most once. Thus, we have shown the following theorem:

Theorem 2. *Let $\mathcal{E}$ be a system of concave equations with $\mu[\![\mathcal{E}]\!] \lhd \underline{\infty}$. Assume that we can compute the greatest finite pre-solution ρ_σ of each $\mathcal{E}(\sigma)$, if $\mathcal{E}(\sigma)$ is feasible. Our strategy improvement algorithm computes $\mu[\![\mathcal{E}]\!]$ and performs at most $|\Sigma|+|\mathbf{X}|$ strategy improvement steps. The algorithm in particular terminates, whenever Σ is finite.* □

6 Computing Greatest Finite Pre-solutions

For all systems $\mathcal{E}$ of abstract semantic equations (see Section 2) and all $\vee$-strategies σ, $\mathcal{E}(\sigma)$ is a system of abstract semantic equations, where each right-hand side is of the form $[\![s]\!]^\sharp_{j\cdot}(\mathbf{x}_1, \ldots, \mathbf{x}_m)$, where s is a sequential statement and $\mathbf{x}_1, \ldots, \mathbf{x}_m$ are variables. We call such a system of abstract semantic equations a system of *basic* abstract semantic equations. It remains to explain how we can compute the greatest finite solution of such a system — provided that it exists.

Let $\mathcal{E}$ be a system of basic abstract semantic equations with a greatest finite pre-solution ρ^*. We can compute ρ^* through linear programming as follows:

We assume w.l.o.g. that every sequential statement s that occurs in the right-hand sides of $\mathcal{E}$ is of the form $Ax \leq b; x := A'x + b'$, where $A \in \mathbb{R}^{k\times n}, b \in \mathbb{R}^k, A' \in \mathbb{R}^{n\times n}, b' \in \mathbb{R}^n$. This can be done w.l.o.g., since every sequential statement can be rewritten into this form in polynomial time. We define the system $\mathcal{C}$ of linear inequalities to be the smallest set that fulfills the following properties: For each equation

$$\mathbf{x} = [\![Ax \leq b; x := A'x + b']\!]^\sharp_{j\cdot}(\mathbf{x}_1, \ldots, \mathbf{x}_m),$$

the system $\mathcal{C}$ contains the following constraints:

$$\mathbf{x} \leq T_{j\cdot}A'(\mathbf{y}_1, \ldots, \mathbf{y}_n)^\top + T_{j\cdot}b' \qquad A_{i\cdot}(\mathbf{y}_1, \ldots, \mathbf{y}_n)^\top \leq b_i \text{ for all } i = 1, \ldots, k$$
$$T_{i\cdot}(\mathbf{y}_1, \ldots, \mathbf{y}_n)^\top \leq \mathbf{x}_i \text{ for all } i = 1, \ldots, m$$

Here, $\mathbf{y}_1, \ldots, \mathbf{y}_n$ are fresh variables. Then $\rho^*(\mathbf{x}) = \sup\,\{\rho(\mathbf{x}) \mid \rho \in \mathbf{Sol}(\mathcal{C})\}$. Thus ρ^* can be determined by solving $|\mathbf{X}_\mathcal{E}|$ linear programming problems each of which can be constructed in linear time. We can do even better by determining an optimal solution of the linear programming problem $\sup \left\{\sum_{\mathbf{x} \in \mathbf{X}_{\mathcal{E}}} \rho(\mathbf{x}) \mid \rho \in \mathbf{Sol}(\mathcal{C})\right\}$. Then the optimal values for the variables $\mathbf{x} \in \mathbf{X}_{\mathcal{E}}$ determine ρ^* (cf. Gawlitza and Seidl [17, 21]). Summarizing we have:

Lemma 12. *Let $\mathcal{E}$ be a system of basic abstract semantic equations with a greatest finite pre-solution ρ^*. Then ρ^* can be computed by solving a linear programming problem that can be constructed in linear time.* □

Example 5. We again use the definitions of Example 3. Consider the system $\mathcal{E}$ of basic abstract semantic equations that consists of the equations

$$\mathbf{x}_{1,1} = [\![s'; s_2]\!]^\sharp_{1\cdot}(\mathbf{x}_{1,1}, \mathbf{x}_{1,2}) \qquad \mathbf{x}_{1,2} = [\![s'; s_1]\!]^\sharp_{2\cdot}(\mathbf{x}_{1,1}, \mathbf{x}_{1,2}),$$

where $s' := x_1 \leq 1000; x_2 := -x_1$, $s_1 := x_2 \leq -1; x_1 := -2x_1$, and $s_2 := -x_2 \leq 0; x_1 := -x_1 + 1$. Our goal is to compute the greatest finite pre-solution ρ^* of $\mathcal{E}$. Firstly, we note that $[\![s'; s_2]\!] = [\![x_1 \leq 0; (x_1, x_2) := (-x_1 + 1, -x_1)]\!]$ and $[\![s'; s_1]\!] = [\![(x_1, -x_1) \leq (1000, -1); (x_1, x_2) := (-2x_1, -x_1)]\!]$ hold. Accordingly, we have to find an optimal solution for the following linear programming problem:

$$\begin{array}{lllll} \text{maximize } \mathbf{x}_{1,1} + \mathbf{x}_{1,2} & & & & \\ \quad \mathbf{x}_{1,1} \leq -\mathbf{y}_1 + 1 & \mathbf{x}_{1,2} \leq 2\mathbf{y}'_1 & \mathbf{y}_1 \leq 0 & \mathbf{y}'_1 \leq 1000 & \mathbf{y}_1 \leq \mathbf{x}_{1,1} \\ \quad -\mathbf{y}'_1 \leq -1 & -\mathbf{y}_1 \leq \mathbf{x}_{1,2} & \mathbf{y}'_1 \leq \mathbf{x}_{1,1} & -\mathbf{y}'_1 \leq \mathbf{x}_{1,2} & \end{array}$$

An optimal solution is $\mathbf{x}_{1,1} = 2001$, $\mathbf{x}_{1,2} = 2000$, $\mathbf{y}_1 = -2000$, and $\mathbf{y}'_1 = 1000$. Thus $\rho^* = \{\mathbf{x}_{1,1} \mapsto 2001,\ \mathbf{x}_{1,2} \mapsto 2000\}$ is the greatest finite pre-solution of $\mathcal{E}$. □

Summarizing, we have shown our main theorem:

Theorem 3. *Let $\mathcal{E}$ be a system of abstract semantic equations with $\mu[\![\mathcal{E}]\!] \lhd \underline{\infty}$. Our strategy improvement algorithm computes $\mu[\![\mathcal{E}]\!]$ and performs at most $|\Sigma| + |\mathbf{X}|$ strategy improvement steps. For each strategy improvement step, we have to do the following:*

1. *Find models for $|\mathbf{X}|$ SAT modulo real linear arithmetic formulas, each of which can be constructed in linear time.*
2. *Solve a linear programming problem which can be constructed in linear time.*

Proof. The statement follows from Lemmas 9, 10, 11, 12 and Theorem 2. □

Our techniques can be extended straightforwardly in order to get rid of the pre-condition $\mu[\![\mathcal{E}]\!] \lhd \underline{\infty}$. However, for simplicity we eschew these technicalities in the present article.

7 An Upper Bound on the Complexity

In Section 3, we have provided a lower bound on the complexity of computing abstract semantics of affine programs w.r.t. the template linear domains. In this section we show that the corresponding decision problem is not only Π_2^p-hard, but in fact Π_2^p-complete:

Theorem 4. *The problem of deciding, whether or not, for a given affine program G, a given template constraint matrix T, and a given program point v, $V^\sharp[v] > \underline{-\infty}$ holds, is in Π_2^p.*

Proof. (Sketch) We have to show that the problem of deciding, whether or not, for a given affine program G, a given template constraint matrix T, a given program point v, and a given $i \in \{1, \ldots, m\}$, $(V^\sharp[v])_{i\cdot} = -\infty$ holds, is in co$-\Pi_2^p = \Sigma_2^p = \mathrm{NP}^{\mathrm{NP}}$. In polynomial time we can guess a $\vee$-strategy σ for $\mathcal{E}' := \mathcal{E}(G)$ and compute the *least feasible solution* ρ of $\mathcal{E}'(\sigma)$ (see Gawlitza and Seidl [17]). Because of Lemma 2, we can use a NP oracle to determine whether or not there exists an improvement of the strategy σ w.r.t. ρ. If this is not the case, we know that $\rho \geq \mu[\![\mathcal{E}']\!]$ holds. Therefore, by Lemma 4, we have $\rho(\mathbf{x}_{v,i}) \geq (V^\sharp[v])_{i\cdot}$. Thus we can accept, whenever $\rho(\mathbf{x}_{v,i}) = -\infty$ holds. □

Finally, we give an example where our strategy improvement algorithm performs exponentially many strategy improvement steps. It is similar to the program in the proof of Theorem 1. For all $n \in \mathbb{N}$, we consider the program $G_n = (N, E, \mathbf{st})$, where $N = \{\mathbf{st}, 1\}$, $E = \{(\mathbf{st}, x_1 := 0; y_1 := 1; y_2 := 2y_1; \ldots; y_n := 2y_{n-1}, 1), (1, s, 1)\}$, and

$$\begin{aligned} s \ = \ & x_2 := x_1; (x_2 \geq y_n; x_2 := x_2 - y_n \mid x_2 \leq y_n - 1); \cdots \\ & (x_2 \geq y_1; x_2 := x_2 - y_1 \mid x_2 \leq y_1 - 1);\ x_1 := x_1 + 1. \end{aligned}$$

It is sufficient to use a template constraint matrix that corresponds to the interval domain. It is remarkable that the strategy iteration does not depend on the strategy improvement operator in use. At any time there is exactly one possible improvement until the least solution is reached. All strategies for the statement s will be encountered. Thus, the strategy improvement algorithm performs 2^n strategy improvement steps. Since the size of G_n is $\Theta(n)$, exponentially many strategy improvement steps are performed.

8 Conclusion

We presented an extension of the strategy improvement algorithm of Gawlitza and Seidl [17, 18, 22] which enables us to use a SAT modulo real linear arithmetic solver for determining improvements of strategies w.r.t. current approximates. Due to this extension, we are able to compute abstract semantics of affine programs w.r.t. the template linear constraint domains of Sankaranarayanan et al. [42], where we abstract sequences of if-then-else statements without loops en bloc. This gives us additional precision. Additionally, We provided one of the few "hard" complexity results regarding precise abstract interpretation.

It remains to practically evaluate the presented approach and to compare it systematically with other approaches. Besides this, starting from the present work, there are several directions to explore. One can for instance try to apply the same ideas for non-linear templates [22], or to use linearization techniques [35].

References

[1] Adjé, A., Gaubert, S., Goubault, E.: Computing the smallest fixed point of nonexpansive mappings arising in game theory and static analysis of programs. ArXiv e-prints (June 2008)

[2] Adjé, A., Gaubert, S., Goubault, E.: Coupling policy iteration with semi-definite relaxation to compute accurate numerical invariants in static analysis. In: Gordon, A.D. (ed.) ESOP 2010. LNCS, vol. 6012, pp. 23–42. Springer, Heidelberg (2010)
[3] Ball, T., Jones, R.B. (eds.): CAV 2006. LNCS, vol. 4144. Springer, Heidelberg (2006)
[4] Björklund, H., Sandberg, S., Vorobyov, S.: Optimization on completely unimodal hypercubes. Technichal report 2002-18, Uppsala University (2002)
[5] Bjorklund, H., Sandberg, S., Vorobyov, S.: Complexity of Model Checking by Iterative Improvement: the Pseudo-Boolean Framework. In: Broy, M., Zamulin, A.V. (eds.) PSI 2003. LNCS, vol. 2890, pp. 381–394. Springer, Heidelberg (2004)
[6] Blanchet, B., Cousot, P., Cousot, R., Feret, J., Mauborgne, L., Miné, A., Monniaux, D., Rival, X.: A static analyzer for large safety-critical software. In: Programming Language Design and Implementation (PLDI), ACM, New York (2003)
[7] Cochet-Terrasson, J., Gaubert, S., Gunawardena, J.: A Constructive Fixed Point Theorem for Min-Max Functions. Dynamics and Stability of Systems 14(4), 407–433 (1999)
[8] Colón, M.A., Sankaranarayanan, S., Sipma, H.: Linear invariant generation using nonlinear constraint solving. In: Hunt Jr., W.A., Somenzi, F. (eds.) CAV 2003. LNCS, vol. 2725, pp. 420–432. Springer, Heidelberg (2003)
[9] Costan, A., Gaubert, S., Goubault, E., Martel, M., Putot, S.: A Policy Iteration Algorithm for Computing Fixed Points in Static Analysis of Programs. In: Etessami, K., Rajamani, S.K. (eds.) CAV 2005. LNCS, vol. 3576, pp. 462–475. Springer, Heidelberg (2005)
[10] Cousot, P.: Proving program invariance and termination by parametric abstraction, Lagrangian relaxation and semidefinite programming. In: Cousot, R. (ed.) VMCAI 2005. LNCS, vol. 3385, pp. 1–24. Springer, Heidelberg (2005)
[11] Cousot, P., Cousot, R.: Static Determination of Dynamic Properties of Programs. In: Second Int. Symp. on Programming, Dunod, Paris, France (1976)
[12] Cousot, P., Cousot, R.: Abstract interpretation: A unified lattice model for static analysis of programs by construction or approximation of fixpoints. In: POPL (1977)
[13] Cousot, P., Halbwachs, N.: Automatic discovery of linear restraints among variables of a program. In: POPL (1978)
[14] Dutertre, B., de Moura, L.: The Yices SMT solver. Tool paper (August 2006), http://yices.csl.sri.com/tool-paper.pdf
[15] Dutertre, B., de Moura, L.M.: A fast linear-arithmetic solver for dpll(t). In: Ball, Jones [3]
[16] Gaubert, S., Goubault, E., Taly, A., Zennou, S.: Static analysis by policy iteration on relational domains. In: Nicola [38]
[17] Gawlitza, T., Seidl, H.: Precise relational invariants through strategy iteration. In: Duparc, J., Henzinger, T.A. (eds.) CSL 2007. LNCS, vol. 4646, pp. 23–40. Springer, Heidelberg (2007)
[18] Gawlitza, T., Seidl, H.: Precise fixpoint computation through strategy iteration. In: Nicola [38]
[19] Gawlitza, T., Seidl, H.: Precise interval analysis vs. parity games. In: Cuéllar, J., Maibaum, T.S.E., Sere, K. (eds.) FM 2008. LNCS, vol. 5014, pp. 342–357. Springer, Heidelberg (2008)
[20] Gawlitza, T., Leroux, J., Reineke, J., Seidl, H., Sutre, G., Wilhelm, R.: Polynomial precise interval analysis revisited. In: Albers, S., Alt, H., Näher, S. (eds.) Efficient Algorithms. LNCS, vol. 5760, pp. 422–437. Springer, Heidelberg (2009)
[21] Gawlitza, T.M., Seidl, H.: Solving systems of rational equations through strategy iteration. Technical report, TUM (2009)
[22] Gawlitza, T.M., Seidl, H.: Computing relaxed abstract semantics w.r.t. quadratic zones precisely. In: Cousot, R., Martel, M. (eds.) SAS 2010. LNCS, vol. 6337, pp. 271–286. Springer, Heidelberg (2010)

[23] Gonnord, L.: Accélération abstraite pour l'amélioration de la précision en analyse des relations linéaires. PhD thesis, Université Joseph Fourier (October 2007), http://tel.archives-ouvertes.fr/tel-00196899/en/
[24] Gonnord, L., Halbwachs, N.: Combining widening and acceleration in linear relation analysis. In: Yi, K. (ed.) SAS 2006. LNCS, vol. 4134, pp. 144–160. Springer, Heidelberg (2006)
[25] Gopan, D., Reps, T.W.: Lookahead widening. In: Ball, Jones [3]
[26] Rice, H.G.: Classes of recursively enumerable sets and their decision problems. In: Transactions of the American Mathematical Society, vol. 74. AMS, Providence (1953)
[27] Halbwachs, N.: Delay analysis in synchronous programs. In: Courcoubetis, C. (ed.) CAV 1993. LNCS, vol. 697, pp. 333–346. Springer, Heidelberg (1993)
[28] Hoffman, A., Karp, R.: On Nonterminating Stochastic Games. Management Sci. 12, 359–370 (1966)
[29] Howard, R.: Dynamic Programming and Markov Processes. Wiley, NY (1960)
[30] Leconte, J., Roux, S.L., Liberti, L., Marinelli, F.: Code verification by static analysis: a mathematical programming approach. Technical report, LIX, Ecole Polytechnique, Palaiseau (August 2009)
[31] Leroux, J., Sutre, G.: Accelerated data-flow analysis. In: Riis Nielson, H., Filé, G. (eds.) SAS 2007. LNCS, vol. 4634, pp. 184–199. Springer, Heidelberg (2007)
[32] Megiddo, N.: On the Complexity of Linear Programming. In: Bewley, T. (ed.) Advances in Economic Theory: 5th World Congress, Cambridge University Press, Cambridge (1987)
[33] Miné, A.: A new numerical abstract domain based on difference-bound matrices. In: Danvy, O., Filinski, A. (eds.) PADO 2001. LNCS, vol. 2053, pp. 155–172. Springer, Heidelberg (2001)
[34] Miné, A.: The octagon abstract domain. In: WCRE (2001)
[35] Miné, A.: Domaines numériques abstraits faiblement relationnels. PhD thesis, École polytechnique (2004)
[36] Monniaux, D.: A quantifier elimination algorithm for linear real arithmetic. In: Cervesato, I., Veith, H., Voronkov, A. (eds.) LPAR 2008. LNCS (LNAI), vol. 5330, pp. 243–257. Springer, Heidelberg (2008)
[37] Monniaux, D.: Automatic modular abstractions for linear constraints. In: Shao, Z., Pierce, B.C. (eds.) POPL, pp. 140–151. ACM, New York (2009)
[38] Nicola, R.D.: Programming Languages and Systems, ESOP 2007. LNCS, vol. 4421. Springer, Heidelberg (2007)
[39] Puri, A.: Theory of Hybrid and Discrete Systems. PhD thesis, University of California, Berkeley (1995)
[40] Puterman, M.L.: Markov Decision Processes: Discrete Stochastic Dynamic Programming. Wiley, New York (1994)
[41] Sankaranarayanan, S., Sipma, H., Manna, Z.: Constraint-based linear-relations analysis. In: Giacobazzi, R. (ed.) SAS 2004. LNCS, vol. 3148, pp. 53–68. Springer, Heidelberg (2004)
[42] Sankaranarayanan, S., Sipma, H.B., Manna, Z.: Scalable analysis of linear systems using mathematical programming. In: Cousot, R. (ed.) VMCAI 2005. LNCS, vol. 3385, pp. 25–41. Springer, Heidelberg (2005)
[43] Schrijver, A.: Theory of linear and integer programming. John Wiley & Sons, Inc., New York (1986)
[44] Stockmeyer, L.J.: The polynomial-time hierarchy. Theoretical Computer Science 3(1), 1–22 (1976)
[45] Vöge, J., Jurdziński, M.: A Discrete Strategy Improvement Algorithm for Solving Parity Games. In: Emerson, E.A., Sistla, A.P. (eds.) CAV 2000. LNCS, vol. 1855, pp. 202–215. Springer, Heidelberg (2000)
[46] Wrathall, C.: Complete sets and the polynomial-time hierarchy. Theor. Comput. Sci. 3(1), 23–33 (1976)

Typing Local Control and State Using Flow Analysis

Arjun Guha, Claudiu Saftoiu, and Shriram Krishnamurthi

Brown University

Abstract. Programs written in scripting languages employ idioms that confound conventional type systems. In this paper, we highlight one important set of related idioms: the use of local control and state to reason informally about types. To address these idioms, we formalize run-time tags and their relationship to types, and use these to present a novel strategy to integrate typing with flow analysis in a modular way. We demonstrate that in our separation of typing and flow analysis, each component remains conventional, their composition is simple, but the result can handle these idioms better than either one alone.

1 Introduction

"Scripting" languages are widely used in software development. Their lack of static types is touted as a positive feature that enables rapid prototyping. As programs grow large and complex, programmers need tools to reason about their code. A retrofitted type system, which would provide additional static guarantees, would help programmers manage evolution. However, care must be taken so that common idioms aren't deemed untypable; otherwise, either many programs or the languages themselves would have to change.

In section 2, we present examples from the aforementioned scripting languages that make heavy use of control and state to reason about "types". In section 3, we introduce a core calculus that can express the essence of these examples and a simple type system for this core calculus; but this type system alone cannot type-check our examples. In section 5, we present a program analysis that can reason about the idioms in our examples. One of our contributions is to clarify the relationship between static types and runtime tags (section 4), which scripting languages often confuse; we exploit this relationship to integrate type-checking with flow analysis in a tractable manner. In section 6, we present a simple proof of soundness for the combination of typing and flow analysis.

We have built an experimental type checker for JavaScript that uses these ideas. The implementation, discussion, and elided proofs, are available from `http://www.cs.brown.edu/research/plt/dl/flowtyping/v1/`.

2 Control and State in Scripting Languages

We consider examples from canonical scripting languages. Our first example is the JavaScript function in figure 1, which serializes arbitrary values to strings.

G. Barthe (Ed.): ESOP 2011, LNCS 6602, pp. 256–275, 2011.
© Springer-Verlag Berlin Heidelberg 2011

```
1 // adapted from the Prototype library, v. 1.6.1
2 function serialize(val) {
3   switch (typeof val) {
4     case "undefined":
5     case "function":
6       return false;
7     case "boolean":
8       return val ? "true" : "false";
9     case "number":
10      return "" + val;
11    case "string":
12      return val;
13  }
14
15  if (val === null) { return "null"; }
16
17  var fields = [ ];
18  for (var p in val) {
19    var v = serialize(val[p]);
20    if (typeof v === "string") {
21      fields.push(p + ": " + v);
22    }
23  }
24  return "{ " + fields.join(", ") + " }";
25 }
```

Fig. 1. Non-local control in JavaScript

Functions and the special value `undefined` cannot be serialized, so for these it returns `false`. Since `val` may be any value, in a typed dialect of JavaScript, `serialize` should have a type equivalent to $\top \rightarrow \mathsf{Str} \cup \mathsf{Bool}$.

Let us informally reason about the type-safety of `serialize`. On line 3, the function branches on the result of `typeof val`. In JavaScript, the `typeof` operator[1] returns a string representing the "runtime type" of its argument. Thereafter:

- For `case "undefined"`, control falls through to line 5.
- On line 5, for `case "function"`, the function returns `false`.
- On line 7, for `case "boolean"`, the function branches on `val` and returns either `"true"` or `"false"`. `val` is a boolean because none of the preceding cases fall through to line 7.
- On line 9, for `case "number"`, the function uses string concatenation to coerce the number `val` to a string. Thus, `val` is a number because none of the preceding cases fall through to line 9.
- On line 11, for `case "string"`, the function returns `val`. Thus, `val` is a string because none of the preceding cases fall through to here.

[1] To be precise, `typeof` does not return a (static) type but a (runtime) tag. This distinction becomes significant in section 4.

```
1 # From the Python 2.5.2 standard libraries
2 def insort_right(a, x, lo=0, hi=None):
3     if hi is None:
4         hi = len(a)
5     while lo < hi:
6         mid = (lo+hi)//2
7         if x < a[mid]: hi = mid
8         else: lo = mid+1
9     a.insert(lo, x)
```

Fig. 2. Heap-sensitive reasoning in Python

This `switch` is missing a case! If `typeof val === "object"`, none of the earlier cases match and control will fall through. However, since all the explicitly handled cases return, we know that `typeof val === "object"` holds on lines 15–24.

JavaScript has a value `null` and `typeof null === "object"`. Therefore, line 15 tests for `null` and if the test is `true`, the program returns `"null"`. However, if the test is `false`, because the conditional does not have a `false`-branch, control proceeds to line 17. Since the `true`-branch returns, `val !== null` holds on lines 17–24. We can safely use `val` as an object on these lines. Lines 20 and 21 also employ flow-directed reasoning, but are relatively trivial. Therefore, we can conclude that `serialize` is safe.

Heap-Sensitive Reasoning. Let us consider a Python example. The function `insort_right` (figure 2) inserts the argument `x` into the sorted array `a`, preserving sortedness. The additional optional arguments, `lo` and `hi`, are expected to be integers that specify the portion of array `a` to be returned.

The intended defaults are `lo=0` and `hi=len(a)`. However, the values of other arguments are not in scope when these expressions are evaluated. Therefore, `hi=len(a)` would signal an unbound identifier error. Instead, the program uses the default `hi=None` (which better guards against premature use than would a numeric default like `0`). The test on line 3 and the side-effect on line 4 ensure that `hi` is an integer in the continuation of the `if`-statement (lines 5–9). This function relies not only on control-flow, but on the interaction of control and state to reason about types.

Dynamic Dispatch and Type Tests. We reasoned about the use of `serialize` and `insort_right` by following their convoluted control-flow and side-effects, instead of merely following their syntactic structure. A reader may argue that these functions are "bad style", so a type system can legitimately reject them. For example, an easily typable alternative to `serialize` is to extend the builtin prototypes (`Object`, `String`, etc.) with a `serialize` method and rely on dynamic dispatch, instead of reflection. Unfortunately, extending builtin classes runs into the fragile base class problem [17] and is thus considered bad practice (e.g., [6]).

Irrespective of these options, the code above reflects what programmers do in practice. Figure 3 offers a conservative estimate of the prevalence of type

Checks For	JS Gadgets	Python stdlib	Ruby stdlib	Django	Rails
`undefined/null`[a]	3,298	1,686	538	868	712
`instanceof`[b]	17	613	1,730	647	764
`typeof`[c]	474	381		4	
field-presence[d]		504	171	348	719
Total Checks	3,789	3,184	2,439	1,867	2,195
LOC	617,766	313,938	190,002	91,999	294,807

[a] `None` in Python, and `nil` in Ruby.
[b] `isinstance` in Python, and `.is_a?` and `.instance_of?` in Ruby.
[c] `type` in Python.
[d] `hasattr` in Python, and `.respond_to?` in Ruby.

Fig. 3. Tag Checks and Related Checks

tests and related checks across a broad corpus of code, by counting occurrences of type testing operators. We believe these numbers undercount, since they do not account for heap-sensitive reasoning and other type testing patterns. For example, we do not try to estimate how often JavaScript programs test for the presence of a field, because this operation is syntactically indistinguishable from field lookup.

Perspective. The examples above make heavy use of local control and state to reason informally about "types". A static type system that admits these programs will need to support this style of reasoning and various other features (e.g., objects). The book-keeping needed to account for control and state can pervade the entire type system and occlude its typing of other features. Our novel *flow typing* system therefore separates typing from the account of flows and state. We present flow typing for an explicitly typed core calculus. We view type inference as a programmer convenience [9] that we leave for future work.

3 Semantics and Types

To present formal type and flow analysis systems, we have to settle on a run-time semantics. The languages under consideration have a kernel of higher-order functions and state that is essentially the same. This kernel is almost sufficient for our presentation, but we need to pick control operators and primitive operators, which do vary between languages. For now we will pick operators based on JavaScript, and return to this issue in section 5.

Figure 4 specifies the syntax and semantics of λ_S, which is a core calculus that is sufficient for our exposition of flow typing. λ_S includes higher-order functions, mutable references, conditionals, a control operator (**break**), and JavaScript-inspired primitives. Type annotations (discussed below) are ignored during evaluation. Although λ_S has first-class references, note that JavaScript, Python, and Ruby do not. However, first-class references allow us to model mutable variables and stateful objects [8, Section 2.1].

identifiers	x
locations	l
constants	$c = num \mid str \mid bool \mid \textbf{undefined}$
values	$v = x \mid c \mid \textbf{func}(x \cdots) : T \texttt{ \{ } e \texttt{ \} } \mid l$
expressions	$e = v \mid \textbf{let } x = e_1 \textbf{ in } e_2 \mid e_f(e_1 \cdots e_n) \mid op_n(e_1 \cdots e_n)$
	$\mid \textbf{if } (e_1) \texttt{ \{ } e_2 \texttt{ \} } \textbf{else} \texttt{ \{ } e_3 \texttt{ \} } \mid \textbf{break } label\ e \mid label : T \texttt{ \{ } e \texttt{ \} }$
	$\mid \textbf{ref } e \mid \textbf{deref } e \mid \textbf{setref } e_1\ e_2$
evaluation contexts	$E = \bullet \mid \textbf{let } x = E \textbf{ in } e \mid E(e_1 \cdots e_n) \mid v_f(v \cdots Ee \cdots)$
	$\mid op_n(v \cdots Ee \cdots) \mid \textbf{break } label\ E \mid \textbf{if } (E) \texttt{ \{ } e_2 \texttt{ \} } \textbf{else} \texttt{ \{ } e_3 \texttt{ \} }$
	$\mid label : T \texttt{ \{ } E \texttt{ \} } \mid \textbf{ref } E \mid \textbf{deref } E \mid \textbf{setref } E\ e \mid \textbf{setref } v\ E$
stores	$\sigma = \cdot \mid (l, v)\,\sigma$
types	$T = \mathsf{Str} \mid \mathsf{Bool} \mid \mathsf{Undef} \mid T_1 \cup T_2 \mid T_1 \cdots \to T \mid \mathsf{Ref}\ T \mid \bot \mid \top$

(E-Let) $\sigma E\langle \textbf{let } x = v \textbf{ in } e \rangle \to \sigma E\langle e[x/v] \rangle$

(E-Prim) $\sigma E\langle op_n(v \cdots) \rangle \to \sigma E\langle \delta_n(op_n, v \cdots) \rangle$

(β_v) $\sigma E\langle \textbf{func}(x \cdots) \texttt{ \{ } e \texttt{ \} } (v \cdots) \rangle \to \sigma E\langle e[x/v \cdots] \rangle$

(E-Break) $\sigma E_1\langle label : \texttt{\{ } E_2\langle \textbf{break } label\ v \rangle \texttt{ \}} \rangle \to \sigma E_1\langle v \rangle$, when $label \notin E_2$

(E-Label-Pop) $\sigma E\langle label : \texttt{\{ } v \texttt{ \}} \rangle \to \sigma E\langle v \rangle$

(E-Ref) $\sigma E\langle \textbf{ref } v \rangle \to (l, v), \sigma E\langle l \rangle$ l fresh

(E-Deref) $\sigma E\langle \textbf{deref } l \rangle \to \sigma E\langle \sigma(l) \rangle$

(E-SetRef) $\sigma E\langle \textbf{setref } l\ v \rangle \to \sigma[l/v] E\langle l \rangle$

$\delta_1(\textbf{tagof}, num) = \texttt{"number"}$
$\delta_1(\textbf{tagof}, \textbf{undefined}) = \texttt{"undefined"}$
$\delta_1(\textbf{tagof}, str) = \texttt{"string"}$
$\delta_1(\textbf{tagof}, bool) = \texttt{"boolean"}$
$\delta_1(\textbf{tagof}, l) = \texttt{"location"}$
$\delta_1(\textbf{tagof}, \textbf{func}(x \cdots) \texttt{ \{ } e \texttt{ \}}) = \texttt{"function"}$

$\delta_2(\texttt{===}, v, v) = \textbf{true}$
$\delta_2(\texttt{===}, v_1, v_2) = \textbf{false}$, when $v_1 \neq v_2$
$\delta_2(\texttt{-}, num_1, num_2) = num_1 - num_2$

Fig. 4. Syntax and Semantics of λ_S

In this paper, the static types of λ_S are much richer than its runtime tags. Therefore, we use a more technically precise name, **tagof**, to model the `typeof` operator of real scripting languages. The **break** operator can model both `break` and `return` statements of JavaScript. **break** aborts the current continuation up to a matching label, and returns a value. We specify the semantics of three primitives, of which physical equality (===) and **tagof** appear extensively in flow-directed

$$(\text{S-Refl})\ T <: T \qquad (\text{S-Trans})\frac{S <: U \qquad U <: T}{S <: T} \qquad (\text{S-Bot})\ \bot <: T$$

$$(\text{S-Top})\ T <: \top \qquad (\text{S-Arr})\frac{S' <: S \cdots \qquad T <: T'}{S \cdots \to T <: S' \cdots \to T'}$$

$$(\text{S-Ref})\frac{T <: S \qquad S <: T}{\mathsf{Ref}\ S <: \mathsf{Ref}\ T} \qquad (\text{S-UnionE})\frac{S_1 <: T \qquad S_2 <: T}{S_1 \cup S_2 <: T}$$

$$(\text{S-UnionL})\ S <: S \cup T \qquad (\text{S-UnionR})\ T <: S \cup T$$

Fig. 5. Subtyping in λ_S

$$ty_1(\textbf{tagof}) = \top \to \mathsf{Str} \qquad ty_2(\texttt{===}) = \top \times \top \to \mathsf{Bool} \qquad ty_2(\texttt{-}) = \mathsf{Num} \times \mathsf{Num} \to \mathsf{Num}$$

$$(\text{T-Loc})\frac{\Sigma(l) = T}{\Sigma; \Gamma \vdash l : T} \qquad (\text{T-Sub})\frac{\Sigma; \Gamma \vdash e : S \qquad S <: T}{\Sigma; \Gamma \vdash e : T}$$

$$(\text{T-Abs})\frac{\Sigma; \Gamma', x : S, \cdots \vdash e : T \qquad \Gamma' = \Gamma \text{ with labels removed}}{\Sigma; \Gamma \vdash \textbf{func}(x \cdots) : S \cdots \to T\{\ e\ \} : S \cdots \to T}$$

$$(\text{T-SetRef})\frac{\Sigma; \Gamma \vdash e_1 : \mathsf{Ref}\ S \qquad \Sigma; \Gamma \vdash e_2 : T \qquad T <: S}{\Sigma; \Gamma \vdash \textbf{setref}\ e_1\ e_2 : \mathsf{Ref}\ T}$$

$$(\text{T-If})\frac{\Sigma; \Gamma \vdash e_1 : \mathsf{Bool} \qquad \Sigma; \Gamma \vdash e_2 : T \qquad \Sigma; \Gamma \vdash e_3 : T}{\Sigma; \Gamma \vdash \textbf{if}\ (e_1)\ \{\ e_2\ \}\ \textbf{else}\ \{\ e_3\ \} : T}$$

$$(\text{T-Label})\frac{\Sigma; \Gamma, label : T \vdash e : T}{\Sigma; \Gamma \vdash label{:}T\ \{\ e\ \} : T} \qquad (\text{T-Break})\frac{\Gamma(label) = T \qquad \Sigma, \Gamma \vdash e : T}{\Sigma; \Gamma \vdash \textbf{break}\ label\ e : \bot}$$

Fig. 6. Typing λ_S (Essential Rules)

reasoning (figure 1). Other expressions, such as **tagof** x `!== "string"`, are a simple extension of our theory.

Figure 4 also specifies the syntax of types, T. Types include untagged unions and a top type $\top$, which were motivated in section 2. We also include the type of locations, Ref T, and a bottom type $\bot$ for control operators that do not return a value. Given these types, subtyping (figure 5) is conventional.

Our typing relation is also mostly conventional. We present select typing judgments in figure 6. Note that the typing environment binds identifiers and labels. By T-SetRef, we can write subtypes to locations.[2] Finally, like JavaScript, λ_S programs cannot **break** across function boundaries, so we statically disallow it by dropping labels when typing functions (T-Abs).

[2] This is a simple restriction of source and sink types [20, Chapter 15.5].

$r = \{\texttt{"string"}, \texttt{"boolean"}, \texttt{"number"}, \texttt{"undefined"}, \texttt{"function"}, \texttt{"location"}\}$
$R = \mathcal{P}(r)$

$$\begin{aligned}
&runtime : T \rightarrow R \\
&runtime(\mathsf{Str}) &&= \{\texttt{"string"}\} \\
&runtime(\mathsf{Bool}) &&= \{\texttt{"boolean"}\} \\
&runtime(\mathsf{Num}) &&= \{\texttt{"number"}\} \\
&runtime(\mathsf{Undef}) &&= \{\texttt{"undefined"}\} \\
&runtime(S \cup T) &&= runtime(S) \cup runtime(T) \\
&runtime(S \cdots \rightarrow T) &&= \{\texttt{"function"}\} \\
&runtime(\bot) &&= \emptyset \\
&runtime(\top) &&= r \\
&runtime(\mathsf{Ref}\ T) &&= \{\texttt{"location"}\}
\end{aligned}$$

$$\begin{aligned}
&static : R \times T \rightarrow T \\
&static(R, \mathsf{Str}) &&= \mathsf{Str}, \text{if } \texttt{"string"} \in R \\
&static(R, \mathsf{Bool}) &&= \mathsf{Bool}, \text{if } \texttt{"boolean"} \in R \\
&static(R, \mathsf{Num}) &&= \mathsf{Num}, \text{if } \texttt{"number"} \in R \\
&static(R, \mathsf{Undef}) &&= \mathsf{Undef}, \text{if } \texttt{"undefined"} \in R \\
&static(R, S \cdots \rightarrow T) &&= S \cdots \rightarrow T, \text{if } \texttt{"function"} \in R \\
&static(R, S \cup T) &&= static(R, S) \cup static(R, T) \\
&static(R, S \cup T) &&= static(R, S), \text{if } static(R, T) \text{ is undefined} \\
&static(R, S \cup T) &&= static(R, T), \text{if } static(R, S) \text{ is undefined} \\
&static(R, \top) &&= \top \\
&static(R, \mathsf{Ref}\ T) &&= \mathsf{Ref}\ \top
\end{aligned}$$

Fig. 7. Relationship Between Types and Tags

4 Relating Static Types and Runtime Tags

Consider the following JavaScript program:

```
function f(x) {
  if (typeof x === "string") { return 0; }
  else { return (x-1); } }
f(200)
```

We can model this in λ_S as follows, with x as a local variable and the **break**s representing `return` statements and the intended type annotation inserted:[3]

```
let f = ref func(y) : Num ∪ Str → Num {
  return:Num {
    let x = ref y in
    if (tagof (deref x) === "string") { break return 0 }
    else { break return ((deref x) - 1) } } }
in (deref f)(200)
```

Both the λ_S and original JavaScript programs run without error, returning 199.

[3] In earlier work, we desugared JavaScript to λ_{JS} in this form [8].

$$e = \cdots \mid \textbf{tagcheck}\ R\ e \mid \textbf{tagerr}$$
$$E = \cdots \mid \textbf{tagcheck}\ R\ E$$

$$(\text{E-TagCheck})\ \frac{\delta_1(\textbf{tagof}, v) \in R}{\sigma E\langle \textbf{tagcheck}\ R\ v\rangle \rightarrow \sigma E\langle v\rangle}$$

$$(\text{E-TagCheck-Err})\ \frac{\delta_1(\textbf{tagof}, v) \notin R}{\sigma E\langle \textbf{tagcheck}\ R\ v\rangle \rightarrow \sigma E\langle \textbf{tagerr}\rangle}$$

$$(\text{T-Check})\ \frac{\Sigma; \Gamma \vdash e : S \qquad static(R, S) = T}{\Sigma; \Gamma \vdash \textbf{tagcheck}\ R\ e : T} \qquad (\text{T-TagErr})\ \Sigma; \Gamma \vdash \textbf{tagerr} : \bot$$

Fig. 8. Typing and Evaluation of Checked Tags

This λ_S program fails to type in the type checker of the previous section because - expects its operands to be numbers, but **deref** x has type Num ∪ Str. However, the tag-test informs us, the reader, that x has the static type Str in the true branch; the type annotation on y bounds its range of values, and thus enables us to conclude that x has type Num in the false branch. Thus, the dynamic test and static type annotation collude to demonstrate that this program is statically safe. Our goal is to enable the static type checker to arrive at the same conclusion.

To support such reasoning, a retrofitted type system must relate static types and runtime tags. We show this in figure 7. *runtime* maps types to tag *sets* (due to the presence of unions), but since types are much richer than tags, we cannot distinguish all static types at runtime, e.g., all arrow types are mapped to the tag `"function"` (objects would be modeled similarly). *static* lets us narrow a type based on a known tag. For example, if a value has type Str ∪ Num and its tag set is {`"number"`}, then *static* produces the type Num. Note that *static* is partial: for example, *static*({`"number"`}, Str) is undefined.

Since *static* relates types and tags, our type system can use it to account for runtime tag-tests. We use *static* by extending λ_S with an auxiliary construct, **tagcheck** R e (figure 8), which narrows the type of e based on the tag set R. By judiciously inserting **tagcheck**s, we can make our example typable.[4] We thus offer **tagcheck** as an appropriate cast-like operator for scripting languages.

A **tagcheck** expression can fail in three ways. Two are static: when the tag set R is incompatible with the type of e, *static* is undefined; even if it is compatible, the resulting type may not be what the context expects. However, the third failure is dynamic: if e reduces to v and **tagof**(v) $\notin R$, then evaluation gets stuck with a **tagerr** (E-TagCheck-Err). This error condition manifests itself when we try to prove a type soundness theorem.

[4] Section 5 presents an efficient technique to insert **tagcheck**s automatically, so they are hidden from the programmer.

The preservation lemma is conventional:

Lemma 1 (Preservation) *If $\Sigma, \cdot \vdash e : T$, $\Sigma \vdash \sigma$, and $\sigma e \rightarrow \sigma' e'$, then there exists a Σ', such that:*

i. $\Sigma', \cdot \vdash \sigma' e' : T$, *and*
ii. $\Sigma \subseteq \Sigma'$.

However, programs can get stuck on **tagerr**s:

Lemma 2 (Progress) *If $\Sigma, \cdot \vdash e : T$ and $\Sigma \vdash \sigma$, then either:*

i. $e \in v$, *or*
ii. there exist σ' *and* e', *such that* $\sigma e \rightarrow \sigma' e'$, *or*
iii. $e = E\langle$**tagerr**$\rangle$, *for some* E.

Thus, the type soundness theorem is unsatisfying because of (iii.) of the lemma above. We could try to "repair" the type system; indeed, a sufficiently complicated type system might not need **tagcheck**s and **tagerr**s at all. Our key idea is to admit **tagerr**s to keep the type system simple, and then discharge them by other means.

5 Automatically Inserting Safe tagchecks

We need a way to automatically insert **tagcheck**s that fail neither statically nor at runtime. The **tagcheck**-insertion technique needs to be sound and handle uses of local control and state that we presented in section 2. Unlike conventional type systems, flow analyses are well-suited to such reasoning styles, so we consider flow analysis here. Unfortunately, whole-program analysis of functional and object-oriented languages is non-modular and expensive (section 7). Moreover, we need to relate abstract heaps produced by flow analysis to types produced by type-checking. We address these problems broadly, before formally presenting one particular analysis (section 6).

The goal of the flow analysis is to compute the tag-sets necessary for **tagcheck** expressions. Therefore, the domain of the analysis will be tag-sets augmented by some book-keeping information. Returning to the example from section 4, the comments illustrate the kind of information we need from flow analysis:

```
let f = ref func(y) : Num ∪ Str → Num {
  return:Num { /* tagof(y) ∈ {"number","string"} */
    let x = ref y in /* x = ref y, tagof(y) ∈ {"number","string"} */
    if (tagof (deref x) === "string") { /* same as line 3 */
      break return 0 /* x = ref y, tagof(y) ∈ {"string"} */
    }
    else {
      break return ((deref x) - 1) /* x = ref y, tagof(y) ∈ {"number"} */
   } } }
in (deref f)(200)
```

The flow analysis should compute that $x =$ **ref** y at all program points, and that on lines 4 and 8, **tagof**$(y) \in \{$"number", "string"$\}$ and **tagof**$(y) \in \{$"number"$\}$, respectively. This information is enough to mechanically transform the program, replacing the (**deref** x) expressions with **tagcheck** $\{$"number", "string"$\}$ (**deref** x) on line 4 and **tagcheck** $\{$"string"$\}$ (**deref** x) on line 8. Section 6 details a control-sensitive, heap-sensitive analysis that produces results such as this.

This analysis, like our type system, is mostly conventional. It is peculiar in populating the initial abstract heap with **tagof**$(y) \in \{$"number", "string"$\}$. A whole-program analysis might have used the application on line 10 to populate the heap with the argument value of 200. In contrast, our analysis remains local but exploits the type annotation on y, thus determining that **tagof**(y) is in *runtime*(Num ∪ Str) $= \{$"number", "string"$\}$.

We thus use types to modularize our flow analysis, so the analysis can remain strictly *intra*procedural. The time complexity of flow analysis is therefore a function of the size of individual functions in the program, which does not tend to grow as programs get larger. (Of course, the choice of function calls as modularity boundaries is not essential.) However, this does reduce precision, as we see below.

Assignment and Aliasing. Our analysis is locally heap-sensitive and can type-check the following imperative variant of the example function:

```
let f = ref func(y) : Num ∪ Str → Num {
  let x = ref y in
  let _ = if (tagof (deref x) == "string") { setref x 1 }
          else { false } in
  (deref x) - 1 /* x = ref y, tagof(y) ∈ {"number"} */ }
in (deref f)(200)
```

However, since we restart the analysis at function applications, we do not track non-local effects. In the following example, since foo(x) may assign either a number or a string to x, the analysis we present in section 6 simply restarts on all function applications. Thus we cannot insert a useful **tagcheck** around the subsequent **deref** x, so the example is untypable:

```
let g = ref func(y) : Num ∪ Str → Num {
  let x = ref y in
  let _ = setref x 10 in
  let _ = foo(x) in
  (deref x) /* x = ref y,tagof(y) ∈ {"number","string"} */}
in (deref g)("test")
```

More sophisticated analyses that tracked ownership or aliasing could make such examples typeable.

Soundness. Given that our flow analysis ignores actual arguments, is it sound? To show that a flow analysis is sound, we must define an acceptability relation and prove that statically computed abstract heaps remain acceptable under evaluation. However, here is a trivial variation of our example that violates acceptability:

	JavaScript	Python	Ruby
Loops	✓	✓	✓
Exceptions	✓	✓	✓
Generators		✓	✓
Labelled Statements	✓		
Switch fall-through	✓		
Continuations			✓

Fig. 9. Control Features of Scripting Languages

values	$V = x \mid c \mid l \mid \textbf{func}(x \cdots)\texttt{:}T \texttt{ \{ } M \texttt{ \}} \mid \textbf{func}(x \cdots) \texttt{ \{ } M \texttt{ \}}$
binding expressions	$B = V \mid \textbf{ref } V \mid \textbf{deref } V \mid \textbf{setref } V_1 \; V_2 \mid op_n\,(V_1 \cdots V_n)$
	$\mid \textbf{tagcheck } R \; V \mid \textbf{tagerr}$
unlabeled expressions	$N = \textbf{let } x = B \textbf{ in } M \mid V_f\,(V \cdots)$
	$\mid \textbf{if } (V) \texttt{ \{ } M_1 \texttt{ \} } \textbf{else} \texttt{ \{ } M_2 \texttt{ \}}$
labelled expressions	$M = N^{\hat{l}}$
stores	$S = \cdot \mid (l, V)\, S$

Fig. 10. Syntax of λ_S in CPS

```
let f = ref func(y) : Num ∪ Str → Num { /* ... as before ... */ }
in (deref f) (true)
```

The flow analysis ignores the actual argument **true** (tagged `"boolean"`) and instead assumes that the type annotation is correct. That is, it assumes that at runtime, y is tagged either `"number"` or `"string"`. Thus, we obtain only a weak soundness lemma (lemma 4).

Although flow analysis admits such mis-applied functions, the type system ensures that function applications are well-typed. Conversely, although the type system admits **tagerr**s at runtime, the flow analysis only inserts **tagcheck**s that provably do not produce **tagerr**s. Hence, each component resolves the other's weakness and in concert they combine to statically check programs that they cannot verify alone.

6 Flow Analysis via CPS

A glaring issue with λ_S is that it has a single control operator, while real scripting languages support a plethora of control operators (figure 9). To avoid presenting an overly **break**-specific program analysis, we convert λ_S to CPS. CPS has the added advantage of naming intermediate terms, thereby simplifying our analysis. CPS is, however, not a requirement; we only use it for convenience.

6.1 CPS Transformation

Figure 10 specifies the syntax of CPS-λ_S, which, with the exception of V, is a syntactic restriction of λ_S. V includes administrative functions (explained shortly).

$\widehat{S} : \hat{l} \to R$	abstract store
$\widehat{\Gamma} : x \to \widehat{V}$	abstract environments

$$\widehat{V} = R \mid \mathsf{Ref}\ \hat{l} \mid \mathsf{Deref}\ \hat{l}\ R \mid \mathsf{LocTagof}\ \hat{l} \mid \mathsf{LocType}\ \hat{l}\ R$$

$$\frac{R_1 \subseteq R_2}{R_1 \sqsubseteq R_2} \qquad \mathsf{LocTagof}\ \hat{l} \sqsubseteq \{\texttt{"string"}\} \qquad \mathsf{LocType}\ \hat{l}\ R \sqsubseteq \{\texttt{"boolean"}\}$$

$$\mathsf{Deref}\ \hat{l}\ R \sqsubseteq R \qquad \mathsf{Ref}\ \hat{l} \sqsubseteq \{\texttt{"location"}\}$$

Fig. 11. Analysis Domains

We specify the CPS transformation using a technique developed by Sabry and Felleisen [21]. The transformation is defined by four mutually-recursive functions that respectively map programs, expressions, values, and evaluation contexts from direct-style to CPS:

$$\mathcal{P}_k : \sigma e \to SM \qquad \Phi : v \to V \qquad \mathcal{C}_k : e \to M \qquad \mathcal{K}_k : E \to V$$

For illustration, consider representative cases of these functions:

$$\begin{aligned}
\mathcal{P}_k[\![(l,v)\cdots e]\!] &= (l,\Phi(v))\cdots\mathcal{C}_k[\![e]\!] \\
\Phi[\![\mathsf{func}(x\cdots):S\cdots\to T\ \{\ e\ \}]\!] &= \mathsf{func}(k,x\cdots):(T\to\bot)\times S\cdots\to\bot\ \{\ \mathcal{C}_k[\![e]\!]\ \} \\
\mathcal{C}_k[\![E\langle v_f\,(v_{arg}\cdots)\rangle]\!] &= \Phi[\![v_f]\!]\,(\mathcal{K}_k[\![E]\!],\Phi[\![v_{arg}]\!]\cdots) \\
\mathcal{K}_k[\![E\langle \mathsf{let}\ x\ =\ \bullet\ \mathsf{in}\ e\rangle]\!] &= \mathsf{func}(x)\ \{\ \mathcal{C}_k[\![E\langle e\rangle]\!]\ \}
\end{aligned}$$

In the last case above, the transformation introduces functions not found in the source program to receive the bound value. Since all evaluation contexts are transformed into such "administrative" functions, all control structures are thus transformed into applications of administrative functions.

For succinctness, we do not introduce continuation-passing operators, and instead let-bind operators' results. We elide the semantics of CPS-λ_S, since it is essentially the same as the semantics in figure 4. This style of definition makes it easy to prove that direct-evaluation corresponds to CPS-evaluation, which is necessary to relate typing and flow analysis.

Lemma 3 (Soundness of CPS Transformation) *If $\sigma e \to \sigma' e'$ using reduction rule R, then $\mathcal{P}_k[\![\sigma e]\!] \twoheadrightarrow \mathcal{P}_k[\![\sigma' e']\!]$ using reduction rules R, E-Let, and $\widehat{\beta_v}$.*

In the lemma above, $\widehat{\beta_v}$ denotes the reduction rule for administrative functions (defined exactly as β_v). The lemma roughly states that intermediate redexes in CPS are applications of administrative functions and let-expressions.

6.2 Modular Flow Analysis

Figure 11 specifies our abstract values and the lattice that relates them. Abstract stores ($\widehat{S}$) map abstract locations ($\hat{l}$) to tag sets (R). (Abstract locations

```
1 let f = func(k, y):(Num → ⊥) × Num ∪ Str → ⊥ {
2   // By V-Restart, k = {"function"}, y = {"number", "string"}
3   let x = ref y in // By F-Alloc, x = Ref l̂; l̂ = {"number", "string"}
4   let t1' = deref x in // By F-Deref, t' = Deref x Ŝ(l̂)
5   let t1 = tagcheck {"number","string"} t1' in // By F-TagCheck, t1 = t1'
6   let t2 = typeof t1' in // By F-Typeof, t2 = LocTypeof l̂
7   let t3 = (t2 === "string") in // By F-TypeIs-Str, t3 = LocType l̂ {"string"}
8     if (t3) { // By F-If-Split applied to l̂
9       k(0) } // By F-App, with l̂ = {"number"}
10    else {
11      let t4' = deref x in // By F-Deref, t4' = Deref x Ŝ(l̂); l̂ = {"number"}
12      let t4 = tagcheck {"number"} t4' in // By F-TagCheck, t4 = t4'
13      let t5 = t4' - 1 in
14        k(t5) } }
15 in let f' = deref f
16 in f'(k_init,200)
```

Fig. 12. tagcheck Insertion

are labels on expressions, introduced by CPS.) On the other hand, abstract environments ($\widehat{\Gamma}$) map identifiers to abstract values ($\widehat{V}$) that will account for tag-tests.

For example, figure 12 presents our example from the previous section in CPS. The comment on line 2 specifies the initial abstract environment, computed by applying *runtime* to the arguments. The remaining comments specify how the abstract heap and environment are transformed by each statement. These transformation are *acceptable*, as specified by our acceptability relation (figure 13).

Note that the user-written identifier x is bound to a heap-location. However, the CPS-introduced identifiers, which name the subexpressions that reason about x, are not heap-allocated. We exploit this stratification in our analysis domains to simplify the proof of soundness. The abstract heap and environment contain values that locally reason about the heap. For soundness, V-Restart therefore discards the abstract heap and uses *reset* and *del* to widen heap-dependent abstract values to simple tag sets.

Assignment and Aliasing. In figure 14, we account for the effects of assignments to tag sets. If a program sets an abstract location $\hat{l}$, then F-SetRef simply updates $\hat{l}$ in the abstract store of its continuation. However, the environment may bind identifiers to abstract values that reason about $\hat{l}$. Therefore, we use *del* to widen $\hat{l}$-dependent values to simple tag sets.

Local variables cannot reference each other. However, we use references to model mutable objects as well. A local variable bound to a mutable object is a reference to a reference, and these objects can be aliased. In these cases, we stop tracking the potentially-aliased abstract location, once again using *del*.

$$
\begin{array}{ll}
del : \hat{l}, \widehat{\Gamma} \rightarrow \widehat{\Gamma} & \\
del(\hat{l}, \cdot) & = \cdot \\
del(\hat{l}, x : \mathsf{Deref}\ \hat{l}\ R, \widehat{\Gamma}) & = x : R, del(\hat{l}, \widehat{\Gamma}) \\
del(\hat{l}, x : \mathsf{LocTagof}\ \hat{l}, \widehat{\Gamma}) & = x : \{\texttt{"string"}\}, del(\hat{l}, \widehat{\Gamma}) \\
del(\hat{l}, x : \mathsf{LocType}\ \hat{l}\ R, \widehat{\Gamma}) & = x : \{\texttt{"boolean"}\}, del(\hat{l}, \widehat{\Gamma}) \\
del(\hat{l}, x : \mathsf{Ref}\ \hat{l}, \widehat{\Gamma}) & = x : r, del(\hat{l}, \widehat{\Gamma}) \\
del(\hat{l}, x : \widehat{V}, \widehat{\Gamma}) & = x : \widehat{V}, del(\hat{l}, \widehat{\Gamma}) \\
reset(\widehat{\Gamma}) & = del(\hat{l}_1, del(\hat{l}_2, ..., del(\hat{l}_n, \widehat{\Gamma}))), \forall \hat{l}_i \in \widehat{\Gamma}
\end{array}
$$

$\boxed{\widehat{\Gamma} \triangleright V \rightsquigarrow \widehat{V}}$

$$
\text{(V-Restart)}\ \frac{\cdot; x : runtime(T) \cdots, reset(\widehat{\Gamma}) \vDash M}{\widehat{\Gamma} \triangleright \mathbf{func}(x \cdots) : T \cdots \rightarrow \bot\ \{\ M\ \} \rightsquigarrow \texttt{"function"}}
$$

$$
\text{(V-Const)}\ \widehat{\Gamma} \triangleright c \rightsquigarrow \delta_1(, c) \qquad \text{(V-Id)}\ \widehat{\Gamma} \triangleright x \rightsquigarrow \widehat{\Gamma}(x)
$$

$$
\text{(V-Sub)}\ \frac{\widehat{\Gamma} \triangleright V \rightsquigarrow \widehat{V} \qquad \widehat{V} \sqsubseteq \widehat{V'}}{\widehat{\Gamma} \triangleright V \rightsquigarrow \widehat{V'}}
$$

$\boxed{\widehat{S}; \widehat{\Gamma} \vDash M}$

$$
\text{(F-LetVal)}\ \frac{\begin{array}{c}\widehat{\Gamma} \triangleright V \rightsquigarrow \widehat{V} \\ \widehat{S}; x : \widehat{V}, \widehat{\Gamma} \vDash M\end{array}}{\widehat{S}; \widehat{\Gamma} \vDash \mathbf{let}\ x\ \texttt{=}\ V\ \mathbf{in}\ M} \qquad \text{(F-Alloc)}\ \frac{\begin{array}{c}\widehat{\Gamma} \triangleright V \rightsquigarrow R \\ \hat{l} : R, \widehat{S}; x : \mathsf{Ref}\ \hat{l}, \widehat{\Gamma} \vDash M\end{array}}{\widehat{S}; \widehat{\Gamma} \vDash \mathbf{let}^{\hat{l}} x\ \texttt{=}\ \mathbf{ref}\ V\ \mathbf{in}\ M}
$$

$$
\text{(F-Deref)}\ \frac{\widehat{\Gamma} \triangleright V \rightsquigarrow \mathsf{Ref}\ \hat{l} \qquad \widehat{S}(\hat{l}) = R \qquad \widehat{S}; x : \mathsf{Deref}\ \hat{l}\ R, \widehat{\Gamma} \vDash M}{\widehat{S}; \widehat{\Gamma} \vDash \mathbf{let}\ x\ \texttt{=}\ \mathbf{deref}\ V\ \mathbf{in}\ M}
$$

$$
\text{(F-Tagof)}\ \frac{\widehat{\Gamma} \triangleright V \rightsquigarrow \mathsf{Deref}\ \hat{l}\ R \qquad \widehat{S}; x : \mathsf{LocTagof}\ \hat{l}, \widehat{\Gamma} \vDash M}{\widehat{S}; \widehat{\Gamma} \vDash \mathbf{let}\ x\ \texttt{=}\ \mathbf{tagof}\ V\ \mathbf{in}\ M}
$$

$$
\text{(F-TypeIs-Str)}^{a}\ \frac{\widehat{\Gamma} \triangleright V \rightsquigarrow \mathsf{LocTagof}\ \hat{l} \qquad \widehat{S}; x : \mathsf{LocType}\ \hat{l}\ \{\texttt{"string"}\}, \widehat{\Gamma} \vDash M}{\widehat{S}; \widehat{\Gamma} \vDash \mathbf{let}\ x\ \texttt{=}\ V\ \texttt{===}\ \texttt{"string"}\mathbf{in}\ M}
$$

$$
\text{(F-TagCheck)}\ \frac{\widehat{\Gamma} \triangleright V \rightsquigarrow R \qquad \widehat{S}; x : R, \widehat{\Gamma} \vDash M}{\widehat{S}; \widehat{\Gamma} \vDash \mathbf{let}\ x\ \texttt{=}\ \mathbf{tagcheck}\ R\ V\ \mathbf{in}\ M}
$$

$$
\text{(F-If-Split)}\ \frac{\widehat{\Gamma} \triangleright V \rightsquigarrow \mathsf{LocType}\ \hat{l}\ R \qquad \widehat{S}[\hat{l} := R]; \widehat{\Gamma} \vDash M_1 \qquad \widehat{S}[\hat{l} := \widehat{S}(\hat{l}) \backslash R]; \widehat{\Gamma} \vDash M_2}{\widehat{S}; \widehat{\Gamma} \vDash \mathbf{if}\ \texttt{(}V\texttt{)}\ \texttt{\{}\ M_1\ \texttt{\}}\ \mathbf{else}\ \texttt{\{}\ M_2\ \texttt{\}}}
$$

$$
\text{(F-App)}\ \frac{\widehat{\Gamma} \triangleright V_f \rightsquigarrow \widehat{V_f} \qquad \widehat{\Gamma} \triangleright V \rightsquigarrow R \cdots}{\widehat{S}; \widehat{\Gamma} \vDash V_f\,(V \cdots)}
$$

[a] F-TypeIsStr is easily generalized to arbitrary tags; we specialize it to strings for presentation only.

Fig. 13. Acceptability of Flow Analysis (Essential Rules)

$$\text{(F-SetRef)}\ \frac{\widehat{\Gamma} \rhd V_1 \leadsto \mathsf{Ref}\ \hat{l} \qquad \widehat{\Gamma} \rhd V_2 \leadsto R \qquad \widehat{S}[\hat{l} := R]; x : \mathsf{Ref}\ \hat{l}, del(\hat{l}, \widehat{\Gamma}) \models M}{\widehat{S}; \widehat{\Gamma} \models \textbf{let}\ x\ =\ \textbf{setref}\ V_1\ V_2\ \textbf{in}\ M}$$

$$\text{(F-Ref-Alias)}\ \frac{\widehat{\Gamma} \rhd V \leadsto \mathsf{Ref}\ \hat{l} \qquad \widehat{S}; x : r, del(\hat{l}, \widehat{\Gamma}) \models M}{\widehat{S}; \widehat{\Gamma} \models \textbf{let}\ x\ =\ \textbf{ref}\ V\ \textbf{in}\ M}$$

Fig. 14. Assignment and Aliasing

F-Ref-Alias in figure 14 tackles aliasing in **ref** expressions. Similar rules apply to other syntactic forms.

Monotone Framework. Our algorithm for computing tagchecks is a simple monotone framework [15] directly derived from the rules in figure 13. The monotone framework computes the abstract store and environment at each labelled expression. We use this information to insert **tagcheck**s into our programs.

Consider each expression of the form:

$\textbf{let}^{\hat{l}}\ r\ =\ \textbf{deref}\ x\ \textbf{in}\ M$

Let $\widehat{\Gamma}$ and $\widehat{S}$ be the computed abstract environment and store at $\hat{l}$. If $\widehat{\Gamma}(\hat{l}) = \mathsf{Ref}\ \hat{l}'$, then we transform the expression to:

$\textbf{let}\ r'^{\hat{l}}\ =\ \textbf{deref}\ x\ \textbf{in}$
$\textbf{let}\ r\ =\ \textbf{tagcheck}\ \widehat{S}(\hat{l}')\ r'\ \textbf{in}$
M

For type-checking, this inserted **tagcheck** is mapped back to the original, direct-style program.

The administrative functions, if applied, can exponentially increase the size of programs. Therefore, we leave certain administrative redexes unapplied (e.g., continuations of **if**-expressions). The CPS transformation is therefore linear time and our flow analysis computes meets through administrative functions.

Complexity. Our flow analysis is a monotonic ascent of a lattice of finite height. For a program of N terms our analysis computes an abstract store and environment at each term. The domain of abstract stores and environments are both of size $O(N)$. The range of the abstract store is R, and $|R|$ is a constant. The range of the abstract environment is $\widehat{V}$, where $\widehat{V}$ contains the elements of R. The additional elements of $\widehat{V}$ are incomparable with each other and are all less than the elements of R. Hence, the height of $\widehat{V}$ is just 1 greater than the height of R. Thus, the analysis needs time quadratic in the program size. In practice, our prototype implementation type-checks real-world JavaScript programs in seconds on modest machines.

Soundness. In addition to figure 13 and figure 14, we require trivial rules for cases where our flow analysis cannot determine useful information. These additional rules admit all other expressions, except **tagerr**s and possibly-faulty **tagcheck**s. Soundness also requires auxiliary rules that reason about the concrete values in the store that are introduced by evaluation. We elided the concrete store from figures 13 and 14 for clarity; in the following lemmas, we introduce it.

Lemma 4 (Soundness) *If* $\hat{S}, \cdot \vDash SM$ *and* $SM \rightarrow S'M'$ *then either:*

i. $\hat{S}', \cdot \vDash S'M'$, *or*
ii. M *is a* β_v*-redex,* $\textbf{func}\,(x\cdots)\ :\ T\cdots \rightarrow \bot\ \{\ N\ \}(V\cdots)$, *where for some* V, $\delta_1(\textbf{tagof}, V) \notin runtime(T)$.

6.3 Combining Typing and Flow Analysis

We can now prove a stronger progress result that eliminates **tagerr**s.

Theorem 1 (Strengthened Progress) *If:*

i. $\Sigma; \cdot \vdash e : T$,
ii. $\Sigma \vdash \sigma$, *and*
iii. $\widehat{S}; \cdot \vDash \mathcal{P}_k[\![\sigma e]\!]$,

then either:

i. $e \in v$, *or*
ii. There exist σ' *and* e', *such that* $\sigma e \rightarrow \sigma' e'$.

Proof: This follows from lemma 2, with the possibility of **tagerr**s eliminated by inspection of figure 13—flow analysis does not admit expressions with **tagerr**s. ■

Theorem 1 requires a corresponding, combined preservation theorem.

Theorem 2 (Combined Preservation) *If:*

i. $\Sigma; \cdot \vdash e : T$,
ii. $\Sigma \vdash \sigma$,
iii. $\widehat{S}; \cdot \vDash \mathcal{P}_k[\![\sigma e]\!]$, *and*
iv. $\sigma e \rightarrow \sigma' e'$,

then there exist Σ' *and* $\widehat{S}'$, *such that:*

i. $\Sigma'; \cdot \vdash e' : T$,
ii. $\Sigma' \vdash \sigma'$,
iii. $\Sigma \subseteq \Sigma'$, *and*
iv. $\hat{S}'; \cdot \vDash \mathcal{P}_k[\![\sigma' e']\!]$.

Proof: Conclusions (i.), (ii.), and (iii.) follow immediately from lemma 1. For conclusion (iv.), apply lemma 3 to hypothesis (iv.) to get a reduction sequence, $\mathcal{P}_k[\![\sigma e]\!] \twoheadrightarrow \mathcal{P}_k[\![\sigma' e']\!]$. Apply lemma 4 at each step, eliminating case (ii.) of the lemma as follows. By lemma 3, intermediate expressions are not β_v-redexes, so case (ii.) does not apply. Suppose e itself has an active β_v-redex:

$$e = E\langle \textbf{func}(x\cdots)\ :\ U\cdots \rightarrow S\ \{\ e_f\ \}(v\cdots)\rangle$$

$$\frac{\Gamma \vdash e_1 : \tau_1; \phi_1 \qquad \Gamma + \phi_1 \vdash e_2 : \tau_2; \phi_2 \qquad \Gamma - \phi_1 \vdash e_3 : \tau_3; \phi_3 \\ \vdash \tau_2 <: \tau \qquad \vdash \tau_3 <: \tau \qquad \phi = combpred(\phi_1, \phi_2, \phi_3)}{\Gamma \vdash (\textbf{if}\, e_1\, e_2\, e_3) : \tau; \phi}$$

Fig. 15. If-splitting in Typed Scheme [23]

Once transformed to CPS, e has the form

$$\textsf{func}(k, x \cdots) \ : \ (S \to \perp) \times U \cdots \to \perp \ \{ \ M_p \ \}(V \cdots)$$

where $V \cdots$ are $v \cdots$ in CPS. Since e is typed, there exists a Γ such that:

$$\Sigma; \Gamma \vdash \textsf{func}(x \cdots) \ : \ U \cdots \to S \ \{ \ e_f \ \}(v \cdots) : S$$

For all v, $\Sigma; \Gamma \vdash v : U$ by inversion. Hence $\delta_1(\textsf{tagof}, v) \in \mathit{runtime}(U)$. Since conversion to CPS does not change tags, $\delta_1(\textsf{tagof}, v) = \delta_1(\textsf{tagof}, V)$, case (ii.) of lemma 4 does not apply. ■

7 Related Work

Typed Scheme. Typed Scheme [23,24] is a type system designed to admit Scheme idioms. Typed Scheme uses *occurrence typing* to account for type tests and type predicates. However, occurrence typing is unsound in the presence of imperative features; thus, it is "turned off" when imperative features are used. Unlike the Scheme programs that Typed Scheme types, programs in mainstream scripting languages make heavy use of imperative features, which we handle.

Technically, we develop a type system and flow analysis that are complementary by design (Lemmas 2 and 4), which combine soundly (Theorems 1 and 2), and which can be enriched independently within the framework of these two lemmas. We conjecture that a similar structure could be extracted from Typed Scheme, as the type system is augmented with meta-functions that update the environment (see Typed Scheme's use of $\Gamma+$ and $\Gamma-$ to affect the environment, and *combpred* to prop type tests to the context in **if** (figure 15)). We believe these are similar to transfer functions for dataflow analyses. However, Typed Scheme is not organized in this manner.

Intensional Polymorphism. Intensional polymorphism [2] provides a `typecase` construct that allows programs to inspect and dispatch on the type of values at runtime. This requires a term-level representation of types at runtime, which is only possible when the static and dynamic semantics of a programming language are co-designed. The present work, Typed Scheme, and other retrofitted type systems (discussed below) do not have access to their types at runtime. Type dispatch in a retrofitted type system happens indirectly. For example, Typed Scheme uses predicates [23], while our work relies on the relationship between static types and runtime tags (section 4).

Other Retrofitted Type Systems. Soft Scheme [25] performs type inference for Scheme programs. It handles the full language of the time, and has a limited form of if-splitting. It does not pay any additional attention to the interaction of types and control flow. This is reasonable because it, like Typed Scheme, is focused on Scheme programs that are mostly functional. However, this means that it too cannot handle the kinds of examples shown in this paper and found in many scripting languages.

Anderson et al. [1] tackle type inference for JavaScript. However, their language is extremely limited, and their type system cannot tackle the idioms discussed in this paper (section 2).

Heidegger and Thiemann's [10] *recency types* account for ad hoc object initialization patterns that are pervasive in JavaScript, but does not address the problems that this paper does. Our work does not account for objects. Our preliminary investigation suggests that the two approaches are complementary and can fruitfully be combined.

Henglein and Rehof [12] present a translation of Scheme to ML that uses type inference to minimize runtime projections. However, their "type system does not model control flow information" [12, Section 6.5], which is the goal of our work.

Diamondback Ruby [5] is a type system and type inference for Ruby. Although its type language includes union types, it does not account for type-tests to discriminate members of unions, which is the focus of our work. The authors state that "support for occurrence types would be useful future work".

Types and Flow Analysis. Shivers shows how control-flow can be extended to account for type-tests [22, Chapter 9]. However, whole-program analysis for functional and object-oriented languages is non-modular and expensive [4] or difficult to make effective [3]. Meunier et al. [16] develops a modular analysis for an untyped language by using contracts as sources and sinks for abstract values. We exploit type annotations in the same manner. However, unlike contracts, which are assumed to be correct, typing ensures that type annotations are correct. Since all functions have type annotations, our flow analysis problem is significantly more tractable than in an untyped language with optional contracts.

Jensen et al. [13,14] and MrSpidey [4] use flow analysis to recover precise type-like information for arbitrary JavaScript and Scheme programs, respectively. A significant advantage of flow analysis is that it does not require type annotations. Our work requires and exploits type annotations to achieve modularity, which leads to quadratic time complexity in theory that appears to translate into practice (section 6.2).

There are known equivalences between various type systems and control-flow analyses, e.g., Heintze [11], Nielson and Nielson [18], and Palsberg and O'Keefe [19]. The aforementioned works extend type systems to calculate information that is conventionally calculated by flow analyses. In contrast, our type system is oblivious to control flow information (figure 6). We use a separate flow analysis to account for control-sensitive and heap-sensitive reasoning (section 5). We independently prove typing and flow analysis sound, then show that they combine in a simple way (section 6.3).

Definite assignment analysis is a commonly used flow analysis that augments typing (e.g., see the Java Language Specification [7, Chapter 16]). Definite assignment analysis conservatively ensures that variables are assigned before they are used. Hence, the analysis rejects programs as untypable when all variables are not definitely assigned. In contrast, our analysis augments the type system to accept programs that would otherwise be untypable.

Acknowledgements

We thank Nicholas Cameron, Matthias Felleisen, and the anonymous reviewers for their careful comments on earlier drafts. We also thank Gilad Bracha, Cormac Flanagan, Jasvir Nagra, Steven Reiss, Ankur Taly, and Jan Vitek for enlightening discussions. This work is partially supported by the NSF and by Google.

References

1. Anderson, C., Giannini, P., Drossopoulou, S.: Towards type inference for javaScript. In: Gao, X.-X. (ed.) ECOOP 2005. LNCS, vol. 3586, pp. 428–452. Springer, Heidelberg (2005)
2. Crary, K., Weirich, S., Morrisett, G.: Intentional polymorphism in type-erasure semantics. In: ACM SIGPLAN International Conference on Functional Programming (1998)
3. Flanagan, C., Felleisen, M.: Componential set-based analysis. In: ACM SIGPLAN Conference on Programming Language Design and Implementation (1997)
4. Flanagan, C., Flatt, M., Krishnamurthi, S., Weirich, S., Felleisen, M.: Catching bugs in the web of program invariants. In: ACM SIGPLAN Conference on Programming Language Design and Implementation (1996)
5. Furr, M., An, J.D., Foster, J.S., Hicks, M.: Static type inference for Ruby. In: ACM Symposium on Applied Computing (2009)
6. Google JavaScript style guide, `http://google-styleguide.googlecode.com/svn/trunk/javascriptguide.xml`
7. Gosling, J., Joy, B., Steele, J.G.L., Bracha, G.: The Java Language Specification, 3rd edn. Addison Wesley, Reading (2005)
8. Guha, A., Saftoiu, C., Krishnamurthi, S.: The essence of javaScript. In: D'Hondt, T. (ed.) ECOOP 2010. LNCS, vol. 6183, pp. 126–150. Springer, Heidelberg (2010)
9. Harper, R., Mitchell, J.C.: On the type structure of Standard ML. ACM Transactions on Programming Languages and Systems 15(2) (1993)
10. Heidegger, P., Thiemann, P.: Recency types for dynamically-typed, object-based languages: Strong updates for JavaScript. In: ACM SIGPLAN International Workshop on Foundations of Object-Oriented Languages (2009)
11. Heintze, N.: Control-flow analysis and type systems. In: International Static Analysis Symposium (1995)
12. Henglein, F., Rehof, J.: Safe polymorphic type inference for a dynamically typed language: Translating Scheme to ML. In: ACM SIGPLAN International Conference on Functional Programming (1995)
13. Jensen, S.H., Møller, A., Thiemann, P.: Type analysis for JavaScript. In: International Static Analysis Symposium (2009)

14. Jensen, S.H., Møller, A., Thiemann, P.: Interprocedural analysis with lazy propagation. In: International Static Analysis Symposium (2010)
15. Kildall, G.A.: A unified approach to global program optimization. In: ACM SIGPLAN-SIGACT Symposium on Principles of Programming Languages (1973)
16. Meunier, P., Findler, R.B., Felleisen, M.: Modular set-based analysis from contracts. In: ACM SIGPLAN-SIGACT Symposium on Principles of Programming Languages (2006)
17. Mikhajlov, L., Sekerinski, E.: A study of the fragile base class problem. In: European Conference on Object-Oriented Programming (1998)
18. Nielson, F., Nielson, H.R.: Type and effect systems. In: Olderog, E.-R., Steffen, B. (eds.) Correct System Design. LNCS, vol. 1710, p. 114. Springer, Heidelberg (1999)
19. Palsberg, J., O'Keefe, P.: A type system equivalent to flow analysis. In: ACM SIGPLAN-SIGACT Symposium on Principles of Programming Languages (1995)
20. Pierce, B.C.: Types and Programming Languages. MIT Press, Cambridge (2002)
21. Sabry, A., Felleisen, M.: Reasoning about programs in continuation-passing style. LISP and Symbolic Computation 6(3) (1993)
22. Shivers, O.: Control-Flow Analysis of Higher-Order Languages. PhD thesis, Carnegie Mellon University (1991)
23. Tobin-Hochstadt, S., Felleisen, M.: The design and implementation of Typed Scheme. In: ACM SIGPLAN-SIGACT Symposium on Principles of Programming Languages (2008)
24. Tobin-Hochstadt, S., Felleisen, M.: Logical types for untyped languages. In: ACM SIGPLAN International Conference on Functional Programming (2010)
25. Wright, A.K., Cartwright, R.: A practical soft type system for Scheme. ACM Transactions on Programming Languages and Systems 19(1) (1997)

Barriers in Concurrent Separation Logic

Aquinas Hobor and Cristian Gherghina

National University of Singapore

Abstract. We develop and prove sound a concurrent separation logic for Pthreads-style barriers. Although Pthreads barriers are widely used in systems, and separation logic is widely used for verification, there has not been any effort to combine the two. Unlike locks and critical sections, Pthreads barriers enable simultaneous resource redistribution between multiple threads and are inherently stateful, leading to significant complications in the design of the logic and its soundness proof. We show how our logic can be applied to a specific example program in a modular way. Our proofs are machine-checked in Coq.

1 Introduction

In a shared-memory concurrent program, threads communicate via a common memory. Programmers use synchronization mechanisms, such as critical sections and locks, to avoid data races. In a data race, threads "step on each others' toes" by using the shared memory in an unsafe manner. Recently, concurrent separation logic has been used to formally reason about shared-memory programs that use critical sections and (first-class) locks [18,15,13,14]. Programs verified with concurrent separation logic are provably data-race free.

What about shared-memory programs that use other kinds of synchronization mechanisms, such as semaphores? The general assumption is that other mechanisms can be implemented with locks, and that reasonable Hoare rules can be derived by verifying their implementation. Indeed, the first published example of concurrent separation logic was implementing semaphores using critical sections [18]. Unfortunately, not all synchronization mechanisms can be easily reduced to locks in a way that allows for a reasonable Hoare rule to be derived. In this paper we introduce a Hoare rule that natively handles one such synchronization mechanism, the Pthreads-style barrier.

Pthreads (POSIX Threads) is a widely-used API for concurrent programming, and includes various procedures for thread creation/destruction and synchronization [7]. When a thread issues a barrier call it waits until a specified number (typically all) of other threads have also issued a barrier call; at that point, all of the threads continue. Although barriers do not get much attention in theory-oriented literature, they are very common in actual systems code. PARSEC is the standard benchmarking suite for multicore architectures, and has thirteen workloads selected to provide a realistic cross-section for how concurrency is used in practice today; a total of five (38%) of PARSEC's workloads use barriers, covering the application domains of financial analysis (blackscholes),

G. Barthe (Ed.): ESOP 2011, LNCS 6602, pp. 276–296, 2011.
© Springer-Verlag Berlin Heidelberg 2011

computer vision (bodytrack), engineering (canneal), animation (fluidanimate), and data mining (streamcluster) [4]. A common use for barriers is to manage large numbers of threads in a pipeline setting. For example, in a video-processing algorithm, each thread might read from some shared common area containing the most recently completed frame while writing to some private area that will contain some fraction of the next frame. (A thread might need to know what is happening in other areas of the previous frame to properly handle objects entering or exiting its part of the current frame.) In the next iteration, the old private areas become the new shared common area as the algorithm continues.

Our key insight is that a barrier is used to simultaneously redistribute ownership of resources (typically, permission to read/write memory cells) between multiple threads. In the video-processing example, each thread starts out with read-only access to the previous frame and write access to a portion of the current frame. At the barrier call, each thread gives up its write access to its portion of the (just-finished) frame, and receives back read-only access to the entire frame. Separation logic (when combined with fractional permissions [5,11]) can elegantly model this kind of resource redistribution. Let Pre_i be the preconditions held upon entering the barrier, and $Post_i$ be the postconditions that will hold after being released; then the following equation is *almost* true:

$$\mathop{\ast}_i Pre_i \quad = \quad \mathop{\ast}_i Post_i \tag{1}$$

Pipelined algorithms often operate in stages. Since barriers are used to ensure that one computation has finished before the next can start, the barriers need to have stages as well—a piece of ghost state associated with the barrier. We model this by building a finite automata into the barrier definition. We then need an assertion, written $\mathsf{barrier}(bn, \pi, cs)$, which says that barrier bn, owned with fractional permission π, is currently in state cs. The state of a barrier changes exactly as the threads are released from the barrier. We can correct equation (1) by noting that barrier bn is transitioning from state cs (current state) to state ns (next state), and that the other resources (frame F) are not modified:

$$\begin{array}{rcl} \mathop{\ast}_i Pre_i & = & F * \mathsf{barrier}(bn, \blacksquare, cs) \\ \mathop{\ast}_i Post_i & = & F * \mathsf{barrier}(bn, \blacksquare, ns) \end{array} \tag{2}$$

We use the symbol $\blacksquare$ to denote the full (~100%) permission, which we require so that no thread has a "stale" view of the barrier state. Although the on-chip (or *erased*) operational behavior of a barrier is conceptually simple[1], it may be already apparent that the verification can rapidly become quite complicated.

Contributions

1. We give a formal characterization for sound barrier definitions.
2. We design a natural Hoare rule in separation logic for verifying barrier calls.

[1] Suspend each thread as it arrives; keep a counter of the number of arrived threads; and when all of the threads have arrived, resume the suspended threads.

3. We give a formal resource-aware *unerased* concurrent operational semantics for barriers and prove our Hoare rules sound with respect to our semantics.
4. Our soundness results are machine-checked in Coq and are available at:

   `www.comp.nus.edu.sg/~hobor/barrier`

2 Syntax, Separation Algebras, Shares, and Assertions

Here we briefly introduce preliminaries: the syntax of our language, separation algebras, share accounting, and the assertions of our separation logic.

2.1 Programming Language Syntax

To let us focus on the barriers, most of our programming language is pure vanilla. We define four kinds of (tagged) values v: TRUE, FALSE, ADDR($\mathbb{N}$), and DATA($\mathbb{N}$). We have two (tagged) expressions e: C(v) and V(x), where x are local variable names (just $\mathbb{N}$ in Coq). To make the example more interesting we add the arithmetical operations to e. We write bn for a barrier number, with bn $\in \mathbb{N}$.

We have ten commands c: `skip` (do nothing), $x := e$ (local variable assignment), $x := [e]$ (load from memory), $[e_1] := e_2$ (store to memory), x:= `new` e (memory allocation), `free` e (memory deallocation), $c_1;\ \ c_2$ (instruction sequence), `if` e `then` c_1 `else` c_2 (if-then-else), `while` e $\{c\}$ (loops), and **barrier** bn (wait for barrier bn). To run commands $c_1 \ldots c_n$ in parallel (which, like O'Hearn, we only allow at the top level [18]), we write $c_1 || \ldots || c_n$. To avoid clogging the presentation, we elide a setup sequence before the parallel composition.

2.2 Disjoint Multi-unit Separation Algebras

Separation algebras are mathematical structures used to model separation logic. We use a variant described by Dockins *et al.* called a disjoint multi-unit separation algebra (hereafter just "DSA") [11]. Briefly, a DSA is a set S and an associated three-place partial *join relation* $\oplus$, written $x \oplus y = z$, such that:

A function:	$x \oplus y = z_1 \;\Rightarrow\; x \oplus y = z_2 \;\Rightarrow\; z_1 = z_2$
Commutative:	$x \oplus y \;=\; y \oplus x$
Associative:	$x \oplus (y \oplus z) \;=\; (x \oplus y) \oplus z$
Cancellative:	$x_1 \oplus y = z \;\Rightarrow\; x_2 \oplus y = z \;\Rightarrow\; x_1 = x_2$
Multiple units:	$\forall x.\ \exists u_x.\ x \oplus u_x = x$
Disjointness:	$x \oplus x = y \;\Rightarrow\; x = y$

A key concept is the idea of an *identity*: x is an identity if $x \oplus y = z$ implies $y = z$. One fundamental property of identities is that x is an identity if and only if $x \oplus x = x$. Dockins also develops a series of standard constructions (*e.g.*, product, functions, etc.) for building complicated DSAs from simpler DSAs. We make use of this idea to construct a variety of separation algebras as needed, usually with the concept of *share* as the "foundational" DSA.

2.3 Shares

Separation logic is a logic of *resource ownership*. Concurrent algorithms sometimes want to have threads share some common resources. Bornat *et al.* introduced the concept of *fractional share* to handle the necessary accounting [5]. Shares form a DSA; a *full share* (complete ownership of a resource) can be broken into various *partial shares*; these shares can then be rejoined into the full share. The *empty share* is the identity for shares. We often need non-empty (strictly *positive*) shares, denoted by π. A critical invariant is that the sum of each thread's share of a given object is no more or less than the full share.

The semantic meaning of partial shares varies; here we use them in two distinct ways. We require the full share to modify a memory location; in contrast, we only require a positive share to read from one. There is no danger of a data race even though we do not require the full share to read: if a thread has a positive share of some location, no other thread can have a full share for the same location. We use fractional permissions differently for barriers: each precondition includes some positive share of the barrier itself and we require that the preconditions combine to imply the full share of the barrier (plus a frame F).

In the Coq development we use a share model developed Dockins *et al.* that supports sophisticated fractional ownership schemes [11]. Here we simplify this model into four elements: the full share ■; two **distinct** nonempty partial shares, ◩ and ◪, and the empty share □. The key point is that ◩ $\oplus$ ◪ = ■.

2.4 Assertion Language

We model the assertions of separation logic following Dockins *et al.* [11]. Our states σ are triples of a stack, heap, and barrier map ($\sigma = (s, h, b)$). Local variables live in stacks s (functions from variable names to values). In contrast, a heap h contains the locations shared between threads; heaps are partial functions from addresses to pairs of positive shares and values. We also equip our heaps with a distinguished location, called the *break*, that tracks the boundary between allocated and unallocated locations. The break lets us provide semantics for the x:= `new` e instruction in a natural way by setting x equal to the current break and then incrementing the break. Since threads share a common break, there is a backdoor communication channel; however the existence of this channel is a small price to pay for avoiding the necessity of a concurrent garbage collector. We ensure that the threads see the same break by equipping our break with ownership shares just as we equip normal memory locations with shares.

We denote the empty heap (which lacks ownership for both all memory locations and the distinguished break location) by h_0. Of note, our expressions e are evaluated only in the context of the stack; we write $s \vdash e \Downarrow v$ to mean that e evaluates to v in the context of the stack s. Finally, the barrier map b is a partial function from barrier numbers to pairs of barrier states (represented as natural numbers) and positive shares; we denote the empty barrier map by b_0.

An *assertion* is a function from states to truth values (`Prop` in Coq). As is common, we define the usual logical connectives via a straightforward embedding into the metalogic; for example, the object-level conjunction $P \wedge Q$ is defined as

$\lambda\sigma.\ (P\sigma)\wedge(Q\sigma)$. We will adopt the convention of using the same symbol for both the object-level operators and the meta-level operators to avoid symbol bloat; it should be clear from the context which operator applies in a given situation. We provide all of the standard connectives ($\top, \bot, \wedge, \vee, \Rightarrow, \neg, \forall, \exists$).

We model the connectives of separation logic in the standard way[2]:

$$
\begin{array}{lcl}
\mathsf{emp} & = & \lambda(s,h,b).\ h = h_0 \ \wedge\ b = b_0 \\
P * Q & = & \lambda\sigma.\ \exists\sigma_1,\sigma_2.\ \sigma_1 \oplus \sigma_2 = \sigma \ \wedge\ P(\sigma_1) \ \wedge\ Q(\sigma_2) \\
e_1 \overset{\pi}{\mapsto} e_2 & = & \lambda(s,h,b).\ \exists a, v.\ (s \vdash e_1 \Downarrow \mathtt{ADDR}(a)) \ \wedge\ (s \vdash e_2 \Downarrow v) \ \wedge \\
 & & \quad b = b_0 \ \wedge\ h(a) = (v,\pi) \ \wedge\ \mathsf{dom}(h) = \{a\} \ \wedge\ \mathsf{break}(h) = \Box \\
\mathsf{barrier}(bn,\pi,s) & = & \lambda(s,h,b).\ h = h_0 \ \wedge\ b(bn) = (s,\pi) \ \wedge\ \mathsf{dom}(b) = \{bn\}
\end{array}
$$

The fractional maps-to assertion, $e_1 \overset{\pi}{\mapsto} e_2$, means that the expression e_1 is pointing to an address a in memory; a is owned with positive share π, and contains the evaluated value v of e_2. The fractional maps-to assertion does not include any ownership of the break. The barrier assertion, $\mathsf{barrier}(bn,\pi,s)$, means that the barrier bn, owned with positive share π, is in state s.

We also lift program expressions into the logic: $e \Downarrow v$, which evaluates e with σ's stack (*i.e.*, $\lambda(s,h,b).\ h = h_0 \wedge b = b_0 \wedge s \vdash e \Downarrow v$); $[e]$, equivalent to $e \Downarrow \mathtt{TRUE}$; and $x = v$, equivalent to $\mathtt{V}(x) \Downarrow v$. These assertions have a "built-in" emp.

3 Example

We present a detailed example inspired by a video decompression algorithm. The code and a detailed-but-informal description of the barrier definition is given in Figure 1.[3] Two threads cooperate to repeatedly compute the elements of two size-two arrays x and y. In each iteration, each thread writes to a single cell of the "current" array, and reads from both cells of the "previous" array.

In Figure 1 we give a pictorial representation of the state machine associated with the barrier used in the code using the following specialized notation:

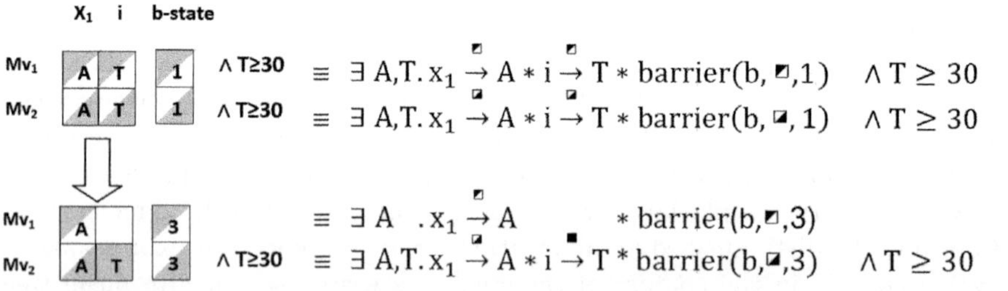

This notation is used to express the pre- and postconditions for a given barrier transition. Each row is a pictorial representation (values, barrier states, and shares) of a formula in separation logic as indicated above. The preconditions are

[2] Our Coq definition for emp is different but equivalent to the definition given here.
[3] In our Coq development we give the full formal description of the example barrier.

0: $\{x_1 \stackrel{\blacksquare}{\longmapsto} 0 * x_2 \stackrel{\blacksquare}{\longmapsto} 0 * y_1 \stackrel{\blacksquare}{\longmapsto} 0 * y_2 \stackrel{\blacksquare}{\longmapsto} 0 * i \stackrel{\blacksquare}{\longmapsto} 0 * \mathsf{barrier}(bn, \blacksquare, 0)\}$

0': $\{x_1 \stackrel{◩}{\longmapsto} 0 * x_2 \stackrel{◩}{\longmapsto} 0 * y_1 \stackrel{◩}{\longmapsto} 0 * y_2 \stackrel{◩}{\longmapsto} 0 * i \stackrel{◩}{\longmapsto} 0 * \mathsf{barrier}(bn, ◩, 0)\}$	$\{x_1 \stackrel{◪}{\longmapsto} 0 * x_2 \stackrel{◪}{\longmapsto} 0 * y_1 \stackrel{◪}{\longmapsto} 0 * y_2 \stackrel{◪}{\longmapsto} 0 * i \stackrel{◪}{\longmapsto} 0 * \mathsf{barrier}(bn, ◪, 0)\}$

```
...
barrier b;
n := 0;
while n < 30 {
    a1 := [x1];
    a2 := [x2];
    [y1] := (a1+2*a2);
    barrier b;
    a1 := [y1];
    a2 := [y2];
    [x1] := (a1+2*a2);
    n := (n+1);
    [i] := n;
    barrier b;

}
barrier b;
[i] := 0;
...
```

```
...
barrier b;          // b transitions 0→1
m := 0;
while m < 30 {
    a1 := [x1];
    a2 := [x2];
    [y2] := (a1+3*a2);
    barrier b;      // b transitions 1→2
    a1 := [y1];
    a2 := [y2];
    [x2] := (a1+3*a2);


    barrier b;      // b transitions 2→1
    m := [i];
}
barrier b;          // b transitions 1→3
...
```

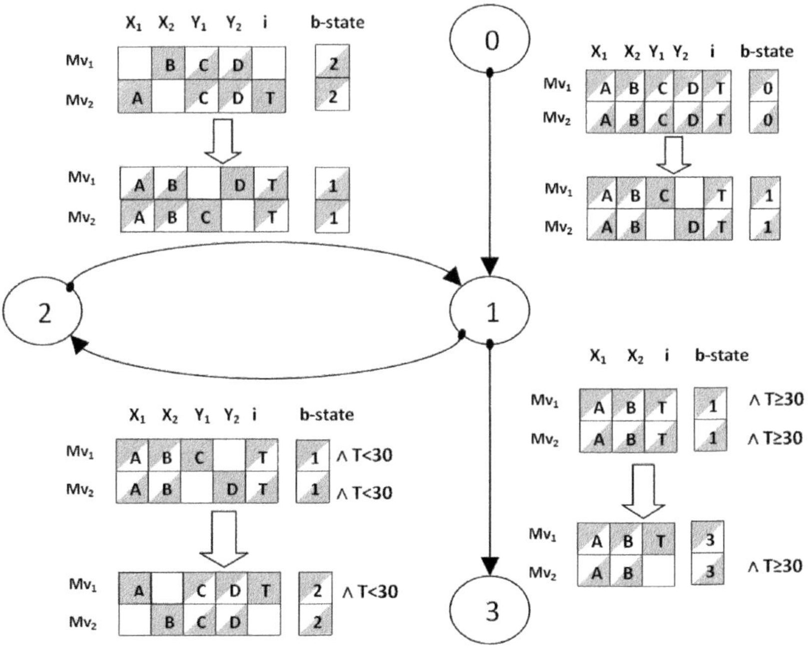

Fig. 1. Example: Code and Barrier Diagram

on top (one per row) and the postconditions below. Each row is associated with a *move*; move 1 is a pair of the first precondition row and the first postcondition row, etc. A barrier that is waiting for n threads will have n moves; n can be fewer than the total number of threads. We do not require that a given thread always takes the same move each time it reaches a given barrier transition.

Note that only the permissions on the memory cells change during a transition; the contents (values) do not.[4] The exception to this is the special column on the right side, which denotes the assertion associated with the barrier itself. As the barrier transitions, this value changes from the previous state to the next; we require that the sum of the preconditions includes the full share of the barrier assertion to guarantee that no thread has an out-of-date view of the barrier's state. Observe that all of the preconditions join together, and, except for the state of the barrier itself, are exactly equal to the join of the postconditions.

The initial state of the machine is given as an assertion in line 0. The machine starts with full ownership of the array cells x_1, x_2, y_1, and y_2, as well as an additional cell i, used as a condition variable. The barrier b is fully-owned and is in state 0. The initial state is then partitioned into two parts on line 0', with the left thread (A) and right thread (B) getting the shares ◩ and ◪, respectively.

Not shown (between lines 0' and 1) is thread-specific initialization code; perhaps both threads read both arrays and perform consistency checks. The real action starts with the barrier call on line 1, which ensures that this initialization code has completed. Thread A takes move 1 and thread B takes move 2. Afterwards, thread A has full ownership over y_1 and thread B has full ownership over y_2; the ownership of x_1, x_2, and i remains split between A and B. While the ownership of the barrier is unchanged, it is now in state 1.

We then enter the main loop on line 3. On lines 4–5, both threads read from the shared cells x_1 and x_2, and on line 6 both threads update their fully-owned cell. The barrier call on line 7 ensures that these updates have been completed before the threads continue. Since the value T at memory location i is less than 30, only the 1–2 transition is possible; the 1–3 transition requires T$\geq$ 30. Thread A takes move 1 and thread B takes move 2[5]; afterwards, both threads have partial shares of y_1 and y_2, thread A has the full share of x_1 and the condition cell i, and thread B has the full share of x_2; the barrier is in state 2.

Lines 8–10 are mirrors of lines 4–6. On lines 11–12, thread A updates the condition cell i. The barrier on line 13 ensures that the updates on lines 10 and 12 have completed before the threads continue; thread A takes move 2 while thread B takes move 1. Afterwards, the threads have the same permissions they had on entering the loop: A has full ownership of y_1, B has full ownership of y_2, and they share ownership of x_1, x_2, and i; the barrier is again in state 1.

---

[4] We use the same quantified variable names before and after the transition because an outside observer can tell that the values are the same. A local verification can use ghost state to prove the equality; alternatively we could add the ability to move the quantifier to other parts of the diagram, *e.g.*, over an entire pre-post pair.

[5] In this example a given thread always takes the same move for a given transition; however, this is not forced by the rules of our logic.

BarDef	≡	{ bd_bn : *Nat*	barrier id
(barrier definition)		bd_limit : *Nat*	# of threads
		bd_states : *list* BarStateDef}	state list
BarStateDef	≡	{bsd_bn : *Nat*	barrier id
(barrier state)		bsd_cs : *Nat*	state id
		bsd_directions : *list* BarMoveList	transition list
		bsd_limit : *Nat*}	# of threads
BarMoveList	≡	{bml_dest : *Nat*	next state
(transition)		bml_bn : *Nat*	barrier id
		bml_cs : *Nat*	current state
		bml_limit : *Nat*	# of threads
		bml_moves : *list* (assert × assert)}	pre/post pairs

Fig. 2. Barrier Definitions

On line 14, thread B reads from the condition variable i, and then the program loops back to line 3. After 30 iterations, the loop exits and control moves to the barrier on line 16. Observe that since the (shared) value T at memory location i is greater than or equal to 30, only the 1–3 transition is possible; the 1–2 transition requires T$<$ 30. Thread A takes move 1 while thread B takes move 2; afterwards, both threads are sharing ownership of x_1, x_2, y_1, and y_2 (since the transition from 1 to 3 does not mention y_1 and y_2 they are unchanged). Thread A has full permission over the condition variable i; the barrier is in state 3. Finally, on line 17, thread A updates i; the barrier on line 16 ensures that thread B's read of i on line 14 has already occurred.

4 Barrier Definitions and Consistency Requirements

We present the type of a barrier definition in Figure 2 in the form of a data structure. The definitions include numerous consistency requirements; in Coq these are maintained with dependent types. From the top down, a barrier definition (BarDef) consists of a barrier identifier (*i.e.*, barrier number), the number of threads the barrier is synchronizing, and a list of barrier state definitions. For programs that have more than one barrier, the individual barrier definitions will be collected into a list and barrier number j will be in list slot j.

A barrier state definition (BarStateDef) consists of a barrier number, the number of threads synchronized, a state id, and a transition list; such that:

1. the barrier number matches the barrier number in the containing BarDef
2. the limit matches the limit of the containing BarDef[6]
3. the state identifier j indicates that this BarStateDef is the j element of the containing BarDef's list of state definitions
4. the directions are *mutually exclusive*

[6] A command to dynamically alter the number of threads a barrier managed might allow different states/transitions to wait for different numbers of threads.

The first three are unexciting; we will discuss mutual exclusion shortly.

A transition (BarMoveList) contains a barrier number (bn), number of threads synchronized, current state identifier (cs), next state identifier (ns), and list of precondition/postcondition pairs (the *move list*). We require that:

1. bn matches the barrier number in the containing BarStateDef
2. the limit matches the limit in the containing BarStateDef
3. cs matches the state identifier in the containing BarStateDef
4. the length of list of moves (bml_moves) is equal to the limit (bml_limit)
5. all of the pre/postconditions in the movelist ignore the stack, focusing only on the memory and barrier map. Since stacks are private to each thread (on a processor these would be registers), it does not make sense for them to be mentioned in the "public" pre/post conditions.
6. all of the preconditions in the movelist are *precise*. Precision is a technical property involving the identifiability of states satisfying an assertion.[7]
7. each precondition P includes some positive share of the barrier assertion with bn and cs, *i.e.*, $\exists \pi.\ P \Rightarrow \top * \mathsf{barrier}(\mathsf{bn}, \pi, \mathsf{cs})$.
8. the sum of the preconditions must equal the sum of the postconditions, except for the state of the barrier; moreover, the sum of the preconditions must include the full share of the barrier (equation (2), repeated here):

$$\begin{array}{ccc} \mathop{\bigstar}_i Pre_i & = & F * \mathsf{barrier}(\mathsf{bn}, \blacksquare, \mathsf{cs}) \\ \mathop{\bigstar}_i Post_i & = & F * \mathsf{barrier}(\mathsf{bn}, \blacksquare, \mathsf{ns}) \end{array}$$

Items 1–4 are simple bookkeeping; items 5–7 are similar to technical requirements required in other variants of concurrent separation logic [18,14,13]. As previously mentioned, the fundamental insight of this approach is property (8).

The function lookup_move simplifies the lookup of a move in a BarDef:

$$\mathsf{lookup\_move}(bd, cs, dir, mv) = bd.\mathsf{bd\_states}[cs].\mathsf{bsd\_directions}[dir].\mathsf{bml\_moves}[mv]$$

Using this notation, we can express the important requirement that all directions in the barrier state cs of the barrier definition bd are mutually exclusive:

$$\begin{array}{c} \forall dir_1, dir_2, mv_1, mv_2, pre_1, pre_2.\ dir_1 \neq dir_2 \Rightarrow \\ \mathsf{lookup\_move}(bd, cs, dir_1, mv_1) = (pre_1, \_) \Rightarrow \\ \mathsf{lookup\_move}(bd, cs, dir_2, mv_2) = (pre_2, \_) \Rightarrow \\ (\top * pre_1) \wedge (\top * pre_2) \ \equiv\ \bot \end{array}$$

In other words, it is *impossible* for any of the preconditions of more than one transition (of a given state) to be true at a time. The simplest way to understand this is to consider the 1–2 and 1–3 transitions in the example program. The 1–2 transition requires that the value in memory cell i be strictly less than 30; in contrast, the 1–3 transition requires that *the same cell* contains a value greater

[7] Precision may not be required; another property (tentatively christened "token") that might serve would be if, for any precondition P, $P * P \equiv \bot$. Note that precision in conjunction with item (6) implies P is a token.

than or equal to 30. Plainly these are incompatible; but in fact the above property is stronger: *both* of the moves on the 1–2 transition, and *both* of the moves on the 1–3 transition include the incompatibility. Thus, if thread A takes transition 1–2, it knows for certain that thread B *cannot* take transition 1–3. This way we ensure that both threads always agree on the barrier's current state.

5 Hoare Logic

Our Hoare judgment has the form $\Gamma \vdash \{P\}\ c\ \{Q\}$, where Γ is a list of barrier definitions as given in §4, P and Q are assertions in separation logic, and c is a command. Our Hoare rules come in three groups: standard Hoare logic (Skip, If, Sequence, While, Assignment, Consequence); standard separation logic (Frame, Store, Load, New, Free); and the barrier rule. We give groups two and three in Figure 3; group one is standard and elided. We note four points for group two.

First, as explained in §2.4, the assertions $e \Downarrow v$, $[e]$ and $x = v$ are bundled with an assertion that the heap and barrier map are empty(*i.e.*, $e \Downarrow v \quad \Rightarrow \quad \mathsf{emp}$); thus, we use the separating conjunction when employing them. Second, the rules are in "side-condition-free form". Thus, instead of presenting the load rule as $\Gamma \vdash \{e_1 \overset{\pi}{\mapsto} e_2\}\ x := [e_1]\ \{x = e_2 * e_1 \overset{\pi}{\mapsto} e_2\}$, which is aesthetically attractive but untrue in the pesky case when e_2 depends on x (*e.g.*, $x := [x]$), we use a form that is less visually pleasing but does not require side conditions.[8] It is straightforward to restore rules with side conditions via the Consequence rule. Third, our Store and Free rules require the full share of location e_1; in contrast, our Load rule only requires some positive share; this is consistent with our use of fractional permissions as explained in §2.3. Fourth, memory allocation and deallocation are more complicated in concurrent settings than in sequential settings, and so the New and Free rules cause nontrivial complications in the semantic model.

The Hoare rule for barriers is so simple that at first glance it may be hard to understand. The variables for the current state cs, direction dir, and move

$$\frac{\Gamma \vdash \{P\}\ c\ \{Q\} \quad \mathsf{closed}(F, c)}{\Gamma \vdash \{F * P\}\ c\ \{F * Q\}}\ \text{Frame} \qquad \frac{}{\Gamma \vdash \{e_1 \overset{\blacksquare}{\mapsto} \_\}\ [e_1] := e_2\ \{e_1 \overset{\blacksquare}{\mapsto} e_2\}}\ \text{Store}$$

$$\frac{}{\Gamma \vdash \{e_1 \overset{\pi}{\mapsto} e_2 * e_1 \Downarrow v_1 * e_2 \Downarrow v_2\}\ x := [e_1]\ \{\mathtt{C}(v_1) \overset{\pi}{\mapsto} \mathtt{C}(v_2) * x = v_2\}}\ \text{Load}$$

$$\frac{}{\Gamma \vdash \{e \Downarrow v\}\ x := \mathtt{new}\ e\ \{\mathtt{V}(x) \overset{\blacksquare}{\mapsto} \mathtt{C}(v)\}}\ \text{New} \qquad \frac{}{\Gamma \vdash \{e_1 \overset{\blacksquare}{\mapsto} e_2\}\ \mathtt{free}\ e_1\ \{\mathsf{emp}\}}\ \text{Free}$$

$$\frac{\Gamma[bn] = bd \qquad \mathsf{lookup\_move}(bd, cs, dir, mv) = (P, Q)}{\Gamma \vdash \{P\}\ \textbf{barrier bn}\ \{Q\}}\ \text{Barrier}$$

Fig. 3. Hoare rules (not pictured: Skip, If, Sequence, While, Assign, and Consequence)

[8] Recall from §2: $\mathtt{V}(x)$ and $\mathtt{C}(v)$ are expression constructors for locals and constants. In addition, $\mathsf{closed}(F, c)$ means that F does not depend on locals modified by c.

mv appear to be free in the lookup_move! However, things are not quite as unconstrained as they initially appear. Recall from §4 that one of the consistency requirements for the precondition P is that P implies an assertion about the barrier itself: $P \Rightarrow Q * \mathsf{barrier}(bn, \pi, cs)$; thus at a given program point we can only use directions and moves from the current state. Similarly, recall from §4 that since the directions are mutually exclusive, dir is uniquely determined.

This leaves the question of the uniqueness of mv. If a thread only satisfies a single precondition, then the move mv is uniquely determined. Unfortunately, it is simple to construct programs in which a thread enters a barrier while satisfying the preconditions of multiple moves. What saves us is that we are developing a logic of partial correctness. Since preconditions to moves must be precise and nonempty (*i.e.*, token), only one thread is able to satisfy a given precondition at a time. The pigeonhole principle guarantees that if a thread holds multiple preconditions then some other thread will not be able to enter the barrier; in this case, the barrier call will never return and we can guarantee any postcondition.

We now apply the Barrier rule to the barrier calls in line 13 from our example program; the lookup_moves are direct from the barrier state diagram:

$$\text{Thread A} \begin{cases} \mathsf{lookup\_move}(b, 2, 1, 2) = (P, Q) \\ P = y_1 \overset{\text{◩}}{\longmapsto} v_{y1} * y_2 \overset{\text{◩}}{\longmapsto} v_{y2} * x_1 \overset{\text{■}}{\mapsto} v_{x1} * i \overset{\text{■}}{\mapsto} v_i * \mathsf{barrier}(bn, \text{◩}, \mathit{2}) \\ \underline{Q = y_1 \overset{\text{■}}{\mapsto} v_{y1} * x_1 \overset{\text{◩}}{\longmapsto} v_{x1} * x_2 \overset{\text{◩}}{\longmapsto} v_{x2} * i \overset{\text{◩}}{\longmapsto} v_i * \mathsf{barrier}(bn, \text{◩}, \mathit{1})} \\ \Gamma \vdash \{P\}\ \mathbf{barrier\ b}\ \{Q\} \end{cases}$$

$$\text{Thread B} \begin{cases} \mathsf{lookup\_move}(b, 2, 1, 1) = (P, Q) \\ P = y_1 \overset{\text{◪}}{\longmapsto} v_{y1} * y_2 \overset{\text{◪}}{\longmapsto} v_{y2} * x_2 \overset{\text{■}}{\mapsto} v_{x2} * \mathsf{barrier}(bn, \text{◪}, \mathit{2})\} \\ \underline{Q = y_2 \overset{\text{■}}{\mapsto} v_{y2} * x_1 \overset{\text{◪}}{\longmapsto} v_{x1} * x_2 \overset{\text{◪}}{\longmapsto} v_{x2} * i \overset{\text{◪}}{\longmapsto} v_i * \mathsf{barrier}(bn, \text{◪}, \mathit{1})\}} \\ \Gamma \vdash \{P\}\ \mathbf{barrier\ b}\ \{Q\} \end{cases}$$

Note that in this line of the example program, the frame is emp in both threads.

Not shown in Figure 3 is a parallel composition rule. As in [14], each thread is verified independently using the Hoare rules given; a top-level safety theorem proves that the entire concurrent machine behaves as expected.

6 Semantic Models

Our operational semantics is divided into three parts: purely sequential, which executes all of the instructions except for barrier in a thread-local manner; concurrent, which manages thread scheduling and handles the barrier instruction; and oracular, which provides a pseudosequential view of the concurrent machine to enable simple proofs of the sequential Hoare rules. Our setup follows Hobor *et al.* very closely and we refer readers there for more detail [15,14].

Purely sequential semantics. The purely sequential semantics executes the instructions `skip`, $x := e$, $x := [e]$, $[e_1] := e_2$, $x :=$ `new` e, `free` e, c_1; c_2, `if` e `then` c_1 `else` c_2, and `while` e $\{c\}$. The form of the sequential step judgment is $(\sigma, c) \mapsto (\sigma', c')$. Here σ is a state (triple of stack, heap, barrier map), just as in §2.4 and c is a command of our language. The semantics of the sequential instructions is standard; the only "tricky" part is that the machine gets stuck if one tries to write to a location for which one does not have full permission or read from a location for which one has no permission; *e.g.*, here is the store rule:

$$\frac{\begin{array}{ccc} & s \vdash e_1 \Downarrow \mathtt{C(ADDR}(n)\mathtt{)} & s \vdash e_2 \Downarrow v \\ n < \mathsf{break}(h) & h(n) = (\blacksquare, v') & h' = [n \mapsto (\blacksquare, v)]h \end{array}}{\big((s, h, b),\ [e_1] := e_2; c\big) \ \mapsto\ \big((s, h', b), c\big)} \ \mathsf{sstep-store}$$

The test that $n < \mathsf{break}(h)$ ensures that the address for the store is "in bounds"—that is, less than the current value of the break between allocated and unallocated memory; since we are updating the memory we require that the permission associated with the location n full ($\blacksquare$). We say that this step relation is *unerased* since these bounds and permission checks are virtual rather than on-chip.

We define the other cases of the step relation in a similar way. Observe that if we were in a sequential setting the proof of the Hoare store rule would be straightforward; this is likewise the case for the other cases of the sequential step relation and their associated Hoare rules. If the sequential step relation reaches a barrier call **barrier** bn then it simply gets stuck.

Concurrent semantics. We define the notion of a *concurrent state* in Figure 4. A concurrent state contains a scheduler Ω (modeled as a list of natural numbers), a distinguished heap called the *allocation pool*, a list of *threads*, and a *barrier pool*[9]. The allocation pool is the owner of all of the unallocated memory cells (plus the ownership of the break between allocated and unallocated cells); before we run a thread we transfer the allocation pool into the local heap owned by the thread so that `new` can transfer a cell from this pool into the local heap of a thread when required. When we suspend the thread we remove (what is left of) the allocation pool from its heap so that we can transfer it to the next thread.

A thread contains a (sequential) state (stack, heap, and barrier map) and a *concurrent control*, which is either $\mathsf{Running}(c)$, meaning the thread is available to run command c, or $\mathsf{Waiting}(bn, dir, mv, c)$, meaning that the thread is currently waiting on barrier bn to make move mv in direction dir; after the barrier call completes the thread will resume running with command c.

The barrier pool ($\mathsf{Barpool}$) contains a list of *dynamic barrier statuses* (DBSes) as well as a state which is the join of all of the states inside the DBSes. Each DBS consists of a barrier number (which must be its index into the array of its containing $\mathsf{Barpool}$), a barrier definition (from §4), and a *waitpool* (WP). A waitpool consists of a direction option (`None` before the first barrier call in a given

[9] There is also a series of consistency requirements such as the fact that all of the heaps in the threads and barrier pool join together with the allocation pool into one consistent heap; in the mechanization this is carried around via a dependent type as a fifth component of the concurrent state. We elide this proof from the presentation.

Cstate	$\equiv$	{ cs_sched : list $\mathbb{N}$	schedule
		cs_allocpool : heap	alloc pool
		cs_thds : list Thread	thread pool
		cs_barpool : Barpool}	barrier pool
Thread	$\equiv$	{ th_stk : stack	
		th_hp : heap	
		th_bs : BarrierMap	local view of barrier states
		th_ctl : conc_ctl}	running or waiting
conc_ctl	$\equiv$	| Running(c)	executing code c
		| Waiting(bn, dir, mv, c)	waiting on bn
Barpool	$\equiv$	{ bp_bars : list DyBarStatus	dynamic barrier status
		bp_st : stack $\times$ heap $\times$ BarrierMap}	current state
DyBarStatus	$\equiv$	{ dbs_bn : $\mathbb{N}$	barrier id
		dbs_wp : Waitpool	waiting thread pool
		dbs_bd : BarDef}	
Waitpool	$\equiv$	{ wp_dir : $\mathbb{N}$ *option*	direction id
		wp_slots : list slot *option*	taken slots
		wp_limit : $\mathbb{N}$	
		wp_st : stack $\times$ heap $\times$ BarrierMap}	current state
slot	$\equiv$	(thread_id $\times$ heap $\times$ BarrierMap)	waiting slot

Fig. 4. Concurrent state

state; thereafter the unique direction for the next state), a limit (the number of threads synchronized by the barrier, and comes from the barrier definition in the enclosing DBS), a *slot* list, and a state (which is the join of all of the states in the slot list). A slot is a heap and barrier map (the stack is unneeded since barrier pre/postconditions ignore it) as well as a thread id (whence the heap and barrier map came as a precondition, and to which the postcondition will return).

The concurrent step relation is $(\Omega, ap, thds, bp) \rightsquigarrow (\Omega', ap', thds', bp')$, where Ω, ap, $thds$, and bp are the scheduler, allocation pool, thread list, and barrier pool respectively. The concurrent step relation has only four cases; the following case CStep-Seq is used to run all of the sequential commands:

$$\frac{\begin{array}{ccc} thds[i] = (s, h, b, \mathsf{Running}(c)) & h \oplus ap = h' & ((s, h', b), c) \mapsto ((s', h'', b), c') \\ h''' \oplus ap' = h'' & \mathsf{isAllocPool}(ap') & thds' = [i \mapsto (s', h''', b, \mathsf{Running}(c'))]thds \end{array}}{(i :: \Omega, thds, ap, bp) \rightsquigarrow (i :: \Omega, thds', ap', bp)} \;\text{CStep-Seq}$$

That is, we look up the thread whose thread id is at the head of the scheduler, join in the allocation pool, and run the sequential step relation. If the command c is a barrier call then the sequential relation will not be able to run and so the CStep-Seq relation will not hold; otherwise the sequential step relation will be able to handle any command. After we have taken a sequential step, we subtract out the (possibly diminished) allocation pool, and reinsert the modified sequential state into the thread list. Since we quantify over all schedulers and our language does not have input/output, it is sufficient to utilize a non-preemptive scheduler; for further justification on the use of such schedulers see [14].

The second case of the concurrent step relation handles the case when a thread has reached the last instruction, which must be a `skip`:

$$\frac{thds[i] = \mathsf{Running}(\mathtt{skip})}{(i :: \Omega, thds, ap, bp) \leadsto (\Omega, thds, ap, bp)} \text{ CStep-Exit}$$

When we reach the end of a thread we simply context switch to the next thread.

The interesting cases occur when the instruction for the running thread is a barrier call; here the CStep-Seq rule does not apply. The concurrent semantics handles the barrier call directly via the last two cases of the step relation; before presenting these cases we will first give a technical definition called fill_barrier_slot:

$$\frac{\begin{array}{c} thds[i] = \mathsf{Thread}(stk,\ hp,\ bs,\ (\mathsf{Running}\ (barrier\ bn\ ;\ c))) \\ \mathsf{lookup\_move}(bp.bp\_bars[bn],\ dir,\ mv) = (pre, post) \\ hp' \oplus hp'' = hp \qquad bs' \oplus bs'' = bs \qquad pre(stk, hp', bs') \\ \mathsf{bp\_inc\_waitpool}\ (bp,\ bn,\ dir,\ mv,\ (i,\ (hp',\ bs'))) = bp' \\ thds' = [i \rightarrow (\mathsf{Thread}(\ stk,\ hp'',\ bs'',\ (\mathsf{Waiting}\ (bn,\ dir,\ mv,\ c))))]\ thds \end{array}}{\mathsf{fill\_barrier\_slot}\ \ (thds,\ bp,\ bn,\ i) = (thds',\ bp')}$$

The predicate fill_barrier_slot gives the details of removing the (sub)state satisfying the precondition of the barrier from the thread's state, inserting it into the barrier pool, and suspending the calling thread. The predicate bp_inc_waitpool does the insertion into the barrier pool; the details of manipulating the data structure are straightforward but lengthy to formalize[10].

We are now ready to give the first case for the barrier, used when a thread executes a barrier but is not the last thread to do so:

$$\frac{\begin{array}{c} \mathsf{fill\_barrier\_slot}\ \ (thds,\ bp,\ bn,\ i) = (thds',\ bp') \\ \neg\ \mathsf{bp\_ready}\ \ (bp',\ bn) \end{array}}{((i :: \Omega), ap, thds, bp) \leadsto (\Omega, ap, thds', bp')} \text{ CStep-Suspend}$$

After using fill_barrier_slot, CStep-Suspend checks to see if the barrier is full by counting the number of slots that have been filled in the appropriate wait pool by using the bp_ready predicate, and then context switches.

If the barrier is ready then instead of using the CStep-Suspend case of the concurrent step relation, we must use the CStep-Release case:

$$\frac{\begin{array}{c} \mathsf{fill\_barrier\_slot}\ \ (thds,\ bp,\ bn,\ i) = (thds',\ bp') \\ \mathsf{bp\_ready}\ \ (bp',\ bn) \\ \mathsf{bp\_transition}\ \ (bp',\ bn,\ out) = bp'' \\ \mathsf{transition\_threads}\ \ (out,\ thds') = thds'' \end{array}}{((i :: \Omega), ap, thds, bp) \leadsto (\Omega, ap, thds'', bp'')} \text{ CStep-Release}$$

The first requirement of CStep-Release is exactly the same as CStep-Suspend: we suspend the thread and transfer the appropriate resources to the barrier

[10] In Coq things are trickier since we track some technical side conditions via dependent types so this relation also ensures that these side conditions remain satisfied.

pool. However, now all of the threads have arrived at the barrier and so it is ready. We use the bp_transition predicate to go through the barrier's slots in the waitpool, combine the associated heaps and barrier maps, redivide these resources according to the barrier postconditions, and remove the associated resources from the barrier pool into a list of slots called out. Finally, the states in out are combined with the suspended threads, which are simultaneously resumed by the transition_threads predicate. The formal definitions of the bp_transition and transition_threads predicates are extremely complex and very tedious and we refer interested readers to the mechanization.

Oracle semantics. Following Hobor *et al.* [15,14], we define a third *oracular semantics*: $(\sigma, o, c) \mapsto (\sigma', o', c')$. Here the sequential state σ and command c are exactly the same as in the purely sequential step. The new parameter o is an oracle, a kind of box containing "the rest" of the concurrent machine—that is, o contains a scheduler, a list of other threads, and a barrier pool.

The oracle semantics behaves exactly the same way as the purely sequential semantics on all of the instructions except for the barrier call, with the oracle o being passed through unchanged. That is to say:

$$\frac{(\sigma, c) \;\mapsto\; (\sigma', c')}{(\sigma, o, c) \;\mapsto\; (\sigma', o, c')}\ \text{os-seq}$$

When the oracle semantics reaches a barrier instruction, it consults the oracle o to determine the state of the machine after the barrier:

$$\frac{\mathsf{consult}(h, b, o) = (h', b', o')}{((s, h, b), o, \textbf{barrier}\ \mathsf{bn};\ c) \;\mapsto\; ((s, h', b'), o', c)}\ \text{os-consult}$$

The formal definition of the consult relation is detailed in [15,14] but the idea is simple. To consult the oracle, one unpacks the concurrent machine and runs (classically) all of the other threads until control returns to the original thread; consult then returns the current h' and b' (that resulted from the barrier call) and repackages the concurrent machine into the new oracle o'. The final case of the oracle semantics occurs when the concurrent machine never returns control (because it got stuck or due to sheer perversion of the scheduler):

$$\frac{\nexists r.\ \mathsf{consult}(h, b, o) = r \qquad (i.e.,\ \mathsf{consult\ diverges})}{((s, h, b), o, \textbf{barrier}\ \mathsf{bn};\ c) \;\mapsto\; ((s, h, b), o, \textbf{barrier}\ \mathsf{bn};\ c)}\ \text{os-diverge}$$

When control will never return, it does not matter what this thread does as long as it does not get stuck; accordingly we enter an (infinite) loop.

Soundness proof outline. Our soundness argument falls into several parts. We define our Hoare tuple in terms of our oracle semantics using a definition by Appel and Blazy [2]; this definition was designed for a sequential language and we believe that other standard sequential definitions for Hoare tuples would work as well[11]. We then prove (in Coq) all of the Hoare rules for the sequential

[11] We change Appel and Blazy's definition so that our Hoare tuple guarantees that the allocation pool is available for verifying the Hoare rule for x:= `new` e.

instructions; since the os-seq case of the oracle semantics provides a straight lift into the purely sequential semantics this is straightforward[12].

Next, we prove (in Coq) the soundness for the barrier rule. This turns out to be much more complicated than a proof of the soundness of (non-first-class) locks and took the bulk of the effort. There are two points of particular difficulty: first, the excruciatingly painful accounting associated with tracking resources during the barrier call as they move from a source thread (as a precondition), into the barrier pool, and redistribution to the target thread(s) as postcondition(s). The second difficulty is proving that a thread that enters a barrier while holding more than one precondition will never wake up; the analogy is a door with n keys distributed among n owners; if an owner has a second key in his pocket when he enters then one of the remaining owners will not be able to get in.

After proving the Hoare rules from Figure 3 sound with respect to the oracle semantics, the remaining task is to connect the oracle semantics to the concurrent semantics—that is, *oracle soundness*. Oracle soundness says that if each of the threads on a machine are safe with respect to the oracle semantics, then the entire concurrent machine combining the threads together is safe. The (very rough) analogy to this result in Brookes' semantics is the parallel decomposition lemma. Here we use a progress/preservation style proof closely following that given in [14, *pp.*242–255]; the proof was straightforward and quite short to mechanize. A technical advance over previous work is that the progress/preservation proofs do not require that the concurrent semantics be deterministic. In fact, allowing the semantics to be nondeterministic simplified the proofs significantly.

A direct consequence of oracle soundness is that if each thread is verified with the Hoare rules, and is loaded onto a single concurrent machine, then if the machine does not get stuck and if it halts then all of the postconditions hold.

Erasure. One can justly observe that our concurrent semantics is not especially realistic; *e.g.*, we: explicitly track resource ownership permissions (*i.e.*, our semantics is *unerased*); have an unrealistic memory allocator/deallocator and scheduler; ignore issues of byte-addressable memory; do not store code in the heap; and so forth. We believe that we could connect our semantics to a more realistic semantics that could handle each of these issues, but most of them are orthogonal to barriers. For brevity we will comment only on erasing the resource accounting since it forms the heart of our soundness result.

We have defined, in Coq, an *erased* sequential and concurrent semantics. An erased memory is simply a pair of a break address and a total function from addresses to values. The run-time state of an erased barrier is simply a pair of naturals: the first tracking the number of threads currently waiting on the barrier, and the second giving the final number of threads the barrier is waiting for. We define a series of erase functions that take an unerased type (memory/barrier status/thread/etc.) to an erased one by "forgetting" all permission information.

[12] The Hoare rule for loops (While) is only proved on paper. The loop rule is known to be painful to mechanize and so the mechanization was skipped due to time constraints. It has been proved in Coq for similar (indeed, more complicated from a sequential control-flow perspective) settings in previous work [2,15].

File	LOC	Time	Description
SLB_Base	1,182	2s	Utility lemmas (largely list facts)
SLB_Lang	1,240	11s	States, program syntax, assertion model
SLB_BarDefs	265	2s	Barrier definitions
SLB_CLang	3,230	1m7s	Dynamic concurrent state
SLB_SSem	415	17s	Sequential semantics
SLB_Sem	784	33s	Concurrent semantics
SLB_ESSem	230	5s	Erased semantics
SLB_ESEquiv	650	30s	Erasure proofs
SLB_OSem	1,942	2m10s	Oracular semantics
SLB_HRules	170	2s	Definition of Hoare tuples
SLB_OSound	426	30s	Soundness of oracle semantics
SLB_HRulesSound	1,664	1m14s	Soundness proofs for Hoare rules
SLB_Ex	2,700	48s	Example of a barrier definition
Total	14,898	7m34s	

Fig. 5. Proof structure, size and compilation times (2.66GHz, 8GB)

The sequential erased semantics is quite similar to the unerased one, with the exception that we do not check if we have read/write permission before executing a load/store. The concurrent erased semantics is much simpler than the complicated accounting-enabled semantics explained above since all that is needed to handle the barrier is incrementing/resetting a counter, plus some modest management of the thread list to suspend/resume threads. Critically, our erased semantics is a computable function, enabling program evaluation. Finally, we have proved that our unerased semantics is a conservative approximation to our erased one: that is, if our unerased concurrent machine can take a step from some state Σ to Σ', then our erased machine takes a step from $\mathsf{erase}(\Sigma)$ to $\mathsf{erase}(\Sigma')$.

7 Coq Development

We detail our Coq development in Figure 5. We use the Mechanized Semantic Library [1] for the definitions of share models, separation algebras, and various utility lemmas/tactics. In addition to the standard Coq axioms, we use dependent and propositional extensionality and the law of excluded middle.

Over 7,000 lines of the development is devoted to proving the soundness of the Hoare rule for barriers, largely in the files SLB_BarDefs.v, SLB_CLang.v, SLB_Sem.v, SLB_OSem.v, SLB_HRules.v, and a small part of SLB_HRulesSound.v. The rest of the concurrent semantics, the oracle semantics, and the soundness of the oracle semantics (~the parallel decomposition lemma) require approximately 1,000 lines, largely in the files SLB_Sem.v, SLB_HRules.v, and SLB_OSound. The erased semantics requires 230 lines in the file SLB_ESSem.v, while the associated equivalence proofs require 650 lines in the file SLB_ESEquiv.v.

The sequential semantics and proofs for the associated Hoare rules require approximately 2,000 lines drawn from the files SLB_Lang.v, SLB_SSem.v,

SLB_HRules.v, and SLB_HRulesSound.v. We estimate that the proof of the loop rule would require a further 2,000-3,000 lines. The model of our assertions and the program syntax are both in SLB_Lang.v. Utility lemmas/tactics (SLB_Base.v) and the example barrier (SLB_Ex.v) complete the development.

8 Limitations and Future Work

We have two obvious directions for future work. First, we can extend the logic by making the barriers first-class (i.e., dynamic barrier creation/destruction). In the present work we thought we could simplify the proofs by having statically declared barriers in the style of O'Hearn [18]. This turned out to be somewhat of a mistake: since we were forced to track the barrier states (and partial shares) explicitly in the Hoare logic, we estimate that 90% of the work required to make the barriers first-class has already been done in the present work; moreover, a further 8% (the intrinsic contravariant circularity) would be easy to handle via indirection theory [16]. With perfect foresight (or if it were nontrivial to restart a large mechanized proof), we would have certainly made the barriers first-class.

Second, we do not address the tricky problem of program analysis. One place where we believe that automatic program verification could be easily applied is in verifying that barrier definitions meet the various soundness requirements. We would also like to investigate verifying program text containing barrier calls; one place to begin is constructing a verifier for programs that use OpenMP [10].

9 Related Work

Calcagno *et al.* proposed separation algebras as models of separation logic [9]; fractional permissions were discussed by Bornat *et al.* [5]. In our work we use the share model and separation algebra development of Dockins *et al.* [11,1].

O'Hearn's concurrent separation logic focused on programs that used critical regions [18,6]; subsequent work by Hobor *et al.* and Gotsman *et al.* added first-class locks and threads [15,13,14]. Our basic soundness techniques (unerased semantics tracks resource accounting; oracle semantics isolates sequential and concurrent reasoning from each other; etc.) follow Hobor *et al.* Recently both Villard *et al.* and Bell *et al.* extended concurrent separation logic to channels [3,19]. The work on channels is similar to ours in that both Bell and Villard track additional dynamic state in the logic and soundness proof. Bell tracks communication histories while Villard tracks the state of a finite state automata associated with each communication channel. Of all of the previous soundness results, only Hobor *et al.* had a machine-checked soundness proof; it was incomplete.

An interesting question is whether is it possible to reason about barriers in a setting with locks or channels. The question has both an operational and a logical flavor. Speaking operationally, in a practical sense the answer is no: for performance reasons barriers are not implemented with channels or locks. If we ignore performance, however, it **is** possible to implement barriers with channels or locks[13]. The logical part of the question then becomes, are the program logics

[13] Indeed, it is possible to implement channels and locks in terms of each other.

defined by O'Hearn, Hobor, Gotsman, Villard, or Bell (including their coauthors) strong enough to reason about the (implementation of) barriers in the style of the logic we have presented? As far as we can tell each previous solution is missing at least one required feature, so in a strict sense, the answer here is again no.

For illustration we examine what seems to be the closest solution to ours: the copyless message passing channels of Villard *et al.* Operationally speaking, the best way to implement barriers seems to be by adding a central authority that maintains a channel with each thread using a barrier. When a thread hits a barrier, it sends "waiting" to the central authority, and then waits until it receives "proceed". In turn, the central authority waits for a "waiting" message from each thread, and then sends each of them a "proceed" message. Fortunately Villard allows the central authority to wait on multiple channels simultaneously.

The question then becomes a logical one. Although it should not pose any fundamental difficulty, their logic would first need to enhanced with fractional permissions; in fact we believe that Villard's Heap-Hop tool already uses the same fractional permission model (by Dockins *et al.*) that we do[14]. Since Villard uses automata to track state, we think it probable, but not certain, that our barrier state machines can be encoded as a series of his channel state machines.

There are some problems to solve. Villard requires certain side conditions on his channels; we require other kinds of side conditions on our barriers; these conditions do not seem fully compatible[15]. Assuming that we can weaken/strengthen conditions appropriately, we reach a second problem with the side conditions: some of our side conditions (*e.g.*, mutual exclusion) are restrictions on the shape of the entire diagram; in Villard's setting the barrier state diagram has been partitioned into numerous separate channel state machines. Verifying our side conditions seems to require verification of the relationships that these channel state machines have to each other; the exact process is unclear.

Once the matter of side conditions is settled, there remains the issue of verifying the individual threads and the central authority. Villard's logic seems to have all that is required for the individual threads; the question is how difficult it would be to verify the central authority. Here we are less sure but suspect that with enough ghost state/instructions it can be done.

There remains a question as to whether it is a good idea to reason about barriers via channels (or locks). We suspect that it is not a good idea, even ignoring the fact that actual implementations of barriers do not use channels. The main problem seems to be a loss of intuition: by distributing the barrier state machine across numerous channel state machines and the inclusion of necessary ghost state, it becomes much harder to see what is going on. We believe that one of the major contributions of our work is that our barrier rule is extremely simple; with a quick reference to the barrier state diagram it is easy to determine what is going on. There is a secondary problem: we believe that our barrier rule

[14] To be precise, Heap-Hop uses the code extracted from the fractional permission Coq proof development by Dockins *et al.*

[15] For example, Villard requires determinacy whereas we do not; he would also require that the postconditions of barriers be precise whereas we do not; etc.

will look and behave essentially the same way in a setting with first-class barriers in which it is possible to define functions that are polymorphic over the barrier diagram; even assuming a channel logic enriched in a similar way, the verification of a polymorphic central authority seems potentially formidable.

Finally, work on concurrent program analysis is in the early stages; Gotsman *et al.*, Calcagno *et al.*, and Villard *et al.* give techniques that cover some use cases involving locks and channels but much remains to be done [12,8,20].

Connection to an upcoming result by Jacobs and Piessens. We recently learned that Jacobs and Piessens have an impressive upcoming result on modular fine-grained concurrency [17]. Jacobs was able to reason about our example program using his VeriFast tool by designing an implementation of barriers using locks and reducing our barrier diagram to a large disjunction for a resource invariant. However, there are some costs. First, VeriFast requires the user to add annotations, such as function pre- and postconditions, loop invariants, folds/unfolds, etc. In the case of our 30-line example program, more than 600 lines of annotation were required, not including the code/annotiations for the barrier implementation itself; in contrast, using our logic, verifying the example program is extremely simple. Second, it was harder to gain insight into the program from the disjunction-form of the invariant; in contrast we find our barrier diagrams straightforward. Finally, it is unclear to us whether the reduction is always possible or whether it was only enabled by the relative simplicity of our example program. That said, Jacobs and Piessens have the only logic proven to be able to reason about barriers as derived from a more general mechanism.

10 Conclusion

We have designed and proved sound a program logic for Pthreads-style barriers. Our development includes a formal design for barrier definitions and a series of soundness conditions to verify that a particular barrier can be used safely. Our Hoare rules can verify threads independently, enabling a thread-modular approach. Our soundness proof defines an operational semantics that explicitly tracks permission accounting during barrier calls and is machine-checked in Coq.

Acknowledgements. We thank Christian Bienia for showcasing numerous example programs containing barriers, Christopher Chak for help on an early version of this work, Jules Villard for useful comments in general and in particular on the relation of our logic to the logic of his Heap-Hop tool, and Bart Jacobs for discovering how to verify our example program in his VeriFast tool.

References

1. Appel, A., Dockins, R., Hobor, A.: Mechanized Semantic Library (2009-2010), `http://msl.cs.princeton.edu`
2. Appel, A.W., Blazy, S.: Separation logic for small-step C minor. In: Schneider, K., Brandt, J. (eds.) TPHOLs 2007. LNCS, vol. 4732, pp. 5–21. Springer, Heidelberg (2007)

3. Bell, C.J., Appel, A.W., Walker, D.: Concurrent separation logic for pipelined parallelization. In: Cousot, R., Martel, M. (eds.) SAS 2010. LNCS, vol. 6337, pp. 151–166. Springer, Heidelberg (2010)
4. Bienia, C.: Benchmarking Modern Multiprocessors. PhD thesis, Princeton University, Department of Computer Science, Princeton, NJ (December 2010)
5. Bornat, R., Calcagno, C., O'Hearn, P., Parkinson, M.: Permission accounting in separation logic. In: POPL, pp. 259–270 (2005)
6. Brookes, S.D.: A semantics for concurrent separation logic. In: Gardner, P., Yoshida, N. (eds.) CONCUR 2004. LNCS, vol. 3170, pp. 16–34. Springer, Heidelberg (2004)
7. Butenhof, D.R.: Programming with POSIX Threads. Addison-Wesley, Reading (1997)
8. Calcagno, C., Distefano, D., Vafeiadis, V.: Bi-abductive resource invariant synthesis. In: Hu, Z. (ed.) APLAS 2009. LNCS, vol. 5904, pp. 259–274. Springer, Heidelberg (2009)
9. Calcagno, C., O'Hearn, P.W., Yang, H.: Local action and abstract separation logic. In: Symposium on Logic in Computer Science (2007)
10. Chandra, R., Menon, R., Dagum, L., Kohr, D., Maydan, D., McDonald, J.: Parallel Programming in OpenMP. Morgan Kaufmann, San Francisco (2000)
11. Dockins, R., Hobor, A., Appel, A.W.: A fresh look at separation algebras and share accounting. In: Hu, Z. (ed.) APLAS 2009. LNCS, vol. 5904, pp. 161–177. Springer, Heidelberg (2009)
12. Gotsman, A., Berdine, J., Cook, B.: Interprocedural Shape Analysis with Separated Heap Abstractions. In: Yi, K. (ed.) SAS 2006. LNCS, vol. 4134, pp. 240–260. Springer, Heidelberg (2006)
13. Gotsman, A., Berdine, J., Cook, B., Rinetzky, N., Sagiv, M.: Local reasoning for storable locks and threads. In: Shao, Z. (ed.) APLAS 2007. LNCS, vol. 4807, pp. 19–37. Springer, Heidelberg (2007)
14. Hobor, A.: Oracle semantics. Technical Report TR-836-08, Princeton (2008)
15. Hobor, A., Appel, A.W., Nardelli, F.Z.: Oracle semantics for concurrent separation logic. In: Gairing, M. (ed.) ESOP 2008. LNCS, vol. 4960, pp. 353–367. Springer, Heidelberg (2008)
16. Hobor, A., Dockins, R., Appel, A.W.: A theory of indirection via approximation. In: POPL 2010, pp. 171–185 (2010)
17. Jacobs, B., Piessens, F.: Expressive modular fine-grained concurrency specification. In: POPL (to appear, 2011)
18. O'Hearn, P.W.: Resources, concurrency and local reasoning. Theoretical Computer Science 375(1), 271–307 (2007)
19. Villard, J., Lozes, É., Calcagno, C.: Proving copyless message passing. In: Hu, Z. (ed.) APLAS 2009. LNCS, vol. 5904, pp. 194–209. Springer, Heidelberg (2009)
20. Villard, J., Lozes, É., Calcagno, C.: Tracking heaps that hop with heap-hop. In: Esparza, J., Majumdar, R. (eds.) TACAS 2010. LNCS, vol. 6015, pp. 275–279. Springer, Heidelberg (2010)

From Exponential to Polynomial-Time Security Typing via Principal Types

Sebastian Hunt[1] and David Sands[2]

[1] City University London
[2] Chalmers University of Technology, Sweden

Abstract. Hunt and Sands (POPL'06) studied a flow sensitive type (FST) system for multi-level security, parametric in the choice of lattice of security levels. Choosing the powerset of program variables as the security lattice yields a system which was shown to be equivalent to Amtoft and Banerjee's Hoare-style independence logic (SAS'04). Moreover, using the powerset lattice, it was shown how to derive a principal type from which all other types (for all choices of lattice) can be simply derived. Both of these earlier works gave "algorithmic" formulations of the type system/program logic, but both algorithms are of exponential complexity due to the iterative typing of While loops. Later work by Hunt and Sands (ESOP'08) adapted the FST system to provide an erasure type system which determines whether some input is correctly erased at a designated time. This type system is inherently exponential, requiring a double typing of the erasure-labelled input command. In this paper we start by developing the FST work in two key ways: (1) We specialise the FST system to a form which only derives principal types; the resulting type system has a simple algorithmic reading, yielding principal security types in polynomial time. (2) We show how the FST system can be simply extended to check for various degrees of termination sensitivity (the original FST system is completely termination insensitive, while the erasure type system is fully termination sensitive). We go on to demonstrate the power of these techniques by combining them to develop a type system which is shown to correctly implement erasure typing in polynomial time. Principality is used in an essential way to reduce type derivation size from exponential to linear.

1 Introduction

The control of information flow is at the heart of many security goals. The classic multi-level security policy says that if a piece of data is considered secret from the perspective of a certain observer of a system, then during execution of the system there should be no information flow from the datum to that observer. Denning and Denning [DD77] pioneered the use of program analysis to statically determine if the information flow properties of a program satisfy a certain multi-level security policy.

A significant trend in the last 10 years has been the use of *security type systems* to formulate the analysis of secure information flow in programs, and to aid in a rigorous proof of its correctness.

The most well-cited works in this area [DD77, VSI96] are *flow-**in**sensitive*, meaning that a *fixed security level* is associated with each variable or data container. To understand the limitations of flow-insensitivity in this context consider the following code

G. Barthe (Ed.): ESOP 2011, LNCS 6602, pp. 297–316, 2011.
© Springer-Verlag Berlin Heidelberg 2011

fragment which swaps the values of two secrets and then swaps the values of two non secrets, via a temporary variable:

```
tmp := secret1; secret1 := secret2; secret2 := tmp;
tmp := public1; public1 := public2; public2 := tmp;
```

The program above is not typeable in a flow-insensitive system because the variable `tmp` cannot be correctly assigned a *single* security level. In a flow sensitive system this obviously secure program becomes typeable because the level of variable `tmp` can vary over time to more accurately reflect the security level of its contents.

Our earlier work [HS06] studies a flow-sensitive type (FST) system for multi-level security, parametric in the choice of lattice of security levels. It is shown that choosing the powerset of program variables as the security lattice yields a system which is equivalent to Amtoft and Banerjee's Hoare-style independence logic [AB04]. Moreover, using the powerset lattice, it is is shown how to derive a *principal typing* from which all other typings (for all choices of lattice) can be simply derived. The FST system is reviewed in Section 2. Later work by Hunt and Sands [HS08] adapts the FST system to provide an *erasure* type system which determines whether some input is correctly erased at a designated time. In this formulation, flow-sensitivity is essential to erasure typing.

The original FST system and the system of Amtoft and Banerjee (including [AB07]) provided "algorithmic" formulations of the type system/program logic, but both algorithms are of exponential complexity due to the iterative typing of While loops.

The erasure type system includes at its core a variant of the FST system. The core differs slightly from the earlier FST system in that it is termination-sensitive (meaning that it does not ignore those dependencies which arise purely from termination behaviour). The key to the erasure typing, however, is the typing of the erasure-labelled input command:

$$\text{input } x : L_1 \text{ erased to } L_2 \text{ after } C$$

This command inputs a value from the channel of security level L_1 and places it in variable x, and then executes command C. The erasure specification "erased to L_2" says that after execution of C the value that was input will only be observable to observers at level L_2 and above. So in particular if level L_2 is sufficiently high (so that there are no observers at all) then the information is completely erased.

To type this command we first establish that C is well typed in a context where x initially has type L_1. But then to deal with the erasure condition we perform a *second* typing in which we assume that x initially has type L_2, and where we ignore the effects of any output statements in C.

From an algorithmic perspective, the erasure type system is more inherently exponential than the underlying FST system, in the sense that the non-algorithmic typing derivations themselves can be exponential in the size of the original program. This is due to a subprogram C being typed twice within the erasure-labelled input rule.

Contributions. In this paper we start by developing the FST work in two key ways:

1. We specialise the FST system to a form which *only* derives principal typings (Section 2.2); the resulting type system is compact and simple – arguably simpler than all the previous descriptions of flow-sensitive security analyses – and at the same

time admits a direct algorithmic reading, yielding principal security typings in polynomial time (Section 2.4).

2. We show (Section 3) how the FST system can be simply generalised to be parametric in the degree of termination-sensitivity (the original FST system is completely termination-insensitive, while the erasure type system is fully termination-sensitive). From the principal typing of a program we can then deduce both termination-sensitive (i.e. sensitive to information flows transmitted by the termination status of a program) and termination-insensitive information flow properties.

We go on to demonstrate the power of these techniques by combining them to develop a type system which is shown to correctly implement erasure typing in polynomial time (Section 4). Principality is used in an essential way to reduce type derivation size from exponential to linear. Again, the key idea is to specialise the system so that it only derives principal typings. The notion of principality is sufficiently general that the two different typings of the erasure command can be derived cheaply by instantiating a single principal typing.

Finally (Section 5) we sketch how the FST system can be extended to handle recursive procedures in polynomial time. The analysis is polymorphic (and hence context-sensitive) in the procedures, but strikingly the extension to this case does not need to introduce type variables, and the algorithm does not require the introduction of type constraints and constraint solving.

Related work is discussed in Section 6.

2 Flow-Sensitive Security Types

We begin by recalling from [HS06] the algorithmic version of the FST system[1]. See Fig. 1. We refer to this system as *Flow Core* (FC). In the While rule, **fix** denotes the least fixed-point operator. Well definedness depends on the fact that the typing rules define a monotone function (see below).

$$\text{Skip}\frac{}{p \vdash \Gamma\ \{\mathbf{skip}\}\ \Gamma} \qquad \text{Assign}\frac{a = \Gamma(E)}{p \vdash \Gamma\ \{x := E\}\ \Gamma[x \mapsto p \sqcup a]}$$

$$\text{Seq}\frac{p \vdash \Gamma\ \{C_1\}\ \Gamma_1 \quad p \vdash \Gamma_1\ \{C_2\}\ \Gamma_2}{p \vdash \Gamma\ \{C_1\ ;\ C_2\}\ \Gamma_2}$$

$$\text{If}\frac{a = \Gamma(E) \quad p \sqcup a \vdash \Gamma\ \{C_i\}\ \Gamma_i \quad i = 1, 2}{p \vdash \Gamma\ \{\mathbf{if}\ E\ C_1\ C_2\}\ (\Gamma_1 \sqcup \Gamma_2)}$$

$$\text{While}\frac{\Gamma_f = \mathbf{fix}(\lambda\Gamma.\ \mathbf{let}\ p \sqcup \Gamma(E) \vdash \Gamma\ \{C\}\ \Gamma'\ \mathbf{in}\ \Gamma' \sqcup \Gamma_0)}{p \vdash \Gamma_0\ \{\mathbf{while}\ E\ C\}\ \Gamma_f}$$

Fig. 1. Flow Core (FC)

[1] There are some notational differences from the original presentation.

Notation: we will be defining a number of alternative type systems; in most cases we use an undecorated turnstile ($\vdash$) in judgements, relying on context to clarify which particular type system we mean; where we need to make our intention more explicit (typically, when comparing different systems) we decorate the turnstile with a subscript (for example, writing $\vdash_{\text{FC}}$ for the Flow Core system).

All the type systems we consider are concerned with tracking information flows with respect to various hierarchies of security levels; each such hierarchy consists of a join-semilattice with a least element (that is, a partial order in which all finite sets have a least upper bound). Wherever we say join-semilattice in the sequel we mean one with a least element; we overload $\bot$ to mean the least element of whatever join-semilattice is under discussion. Each security level models a class of users, grouped according to how much they are permitted to observe; if $a \sqsubseteq b$ then b-users can see everything a-users can see, and maybe more. Let $\mathcal{L}$ be a join-semilattice. Typing judgements in Flow Core have the form

$$p \vdash \Gamma\ \{C\}\ \Gamma'$$

where C is a command, $p \in \mathcal{L}$ represents the security level of the "program counter", and $\Gamma, \Gamma' : PVar \to \mathcal{L}$ are environments mapping program variables to security levels. ($PVar$ is the finite set of variables used in whatever top-level program is being analysed. Formally this should be an explicit parameter of the typing judgement, but glossing over this detail saves us from notational clutter without causing any significant problems.) Throughout the paper we treat function spaces such as $PVar \to \mathcal{L}$ as join-semilattices, inheriting their lattice structure pointwise from $\mathcal{L}$ (so $\Gamma \sqcup \Gamma' = \lambda x.\Gamma(x) \sqcup \Gamma'(x)$, etc). In these rules, $\Gamma(E)$ means the join of the levels assigned to the free variables in the expression E:

$$\Gamma(E) = \bigsqcup_{x \in \mathsf{fv}(E)} \Gamma(x)$$

When E has *no* free variables (it only involves constants) then $\Gamma(E) = \bigsqcup\{\} = \bot$. We leave the syntax of expressions unspecified; semantic soundness assumes that expressions are free of side-effects and are interpreted as total functions of the values of their free variables.

Note that $\mathcal{L}$ is an implicit parameter in the definition of Flow Core, so Flow Core actually defines a *family* of type systems, indexed by the choice of $\mathcal{L}$.

Although the current paper is not primarily concerned with semantic soundness, it is helpful to have some intuitions. By assigning levels to variables, an environment determines a policy, for each level $a \in \mathcal{L}$, stating which parts of a memory state a-users should be allowed to see. Say that two memory states are *a-equivalent under policy Γ* iff they agree on all variables x such that $\Gamma(x) \sqsubseteq a$. Then the intended semantics of a judgement $p \vdash \Gamma\ \{C\}\ \Gamma'$ is that it should satisfy

1. C only changes variables x for which $\Gamma'(x) \sqsupseteq p$; and
2. for all a, if two initial memory states are a-equivalent under Γ, the corresponding final stores after execution of C will be a-equivalent under Γ'.

Semantic soundness of Flow Core with respect to this specification is proved in [HS06].

The use of two type environments (pre- and post-) in Flow Core deserves some explanation. For a top-level program executed in batch mode, it is perhaps more natural for a security policy to specify a single assignment of levels to variables, applying both before and after the program executes. But it is the use of two distinct environments which allows Flow Core to be flow-sensitive. Consider again the swap program from the introduction:

```
tmp := secret1; secret1 := secret2; secret2 := tmp;
tmp := public1; public1 := public2; public2 := tmp;
```

It is a simple exercise to verify that this can be typed in Flow Core with $low \vdash \Gamma\ \{P\}\ \Gamma$ for Γ mapping `tmp` and the public variables to *low*, and mapping the secret variables to *high*. The first assignment raises the level of `tmp` from *low* to *high*; this is modelled by fact that the post-environment for the corresponding sub-derivation is not Γ but $\Gamma' = \Gamma[\texttt{tmp} \mapsto high]$. The assignment `tmp := public1` later reduces the level back down to *low*; this is modelled by the fact that the post-environment for the corresponding sub-derivation is $\Gamma'[\texttt{tmp} \mapsto low] = \Gamma$. In general, to enforce a policy specified by a single Γ, we would compute the typing $\bot \vdash \Gamma\ \{P\}\ \Gamma'$ and then check that $\Gamma' \sqsubseteq \Gamma$ (it is safe for a program to make variables *less* informative than the policy allows). In a language with IO channels, we are more likely to require a fixed policy for channels and assume that program variables are not directly observable at all. This scenario can also be modelled using essentially the same approach (see Section 4).

Flow Core is described in [HS06] as "algorithmic", by which we mean that the rules are syntax directed and that, for a given choice of p, Γ, they determine exactly one derivation for each C. A consequence is that Flow Core is *functional*: for each command C, for all p, Γ, there exists a unique Γ' such that $p \vdash \Gamma\ \{C\}\ \Gamma'$ (it is also monotonic in p and Γ). In [HS06] finite convergence of the While rule's fixed-point construction was trivially guaranteed by the requirement that $\mathcal{L}$ should be finite; here we have relaxed that constraint by requiring only that $\mathcal{L}$ should have finite joins. Nonetheless, finite convergence is guaranteed because environments are finite and the typing rules only ever construct elements of $\mathcal{L}$ which are finite joins of lattice elements actually used in the initial environment. Note that the use of **fix** makes the typing of nested while loops exponential, since the body of a loop will be typed repeatedly, once for each iteration towards the fixed-point.

2.1 FST with a pc-Variable

The principal typings result presented in [HS06] is slightly less general than we would like (and than we need in what follows) because it is restricted to "top-level" typings, by which we mean typings where p is $\bot$. To generalise the result we make a small change to Flow Core: we adjoin a new variable $\mathbf{pc}$ to model the program counter and we track $\mathbf{pc}$ in the type environments, along with the program variables, rather than reserving a special place for it in the syntax of judgements. The slight disadvantage is that the If and While rules must now explicitly "reset" $\mathbf{pc}$ in their post-environments. The advantage is that we can easily state a fully general principal typings result, paving the way to the key contributions of the current paper. Let $Var = PVar \cup \{\mathbf{pc}\}$. Type environments are extended to this new domain, thus $\Gamma : Var \rightarrow \mathcal{L}$. Except for the "resets" mentioned previously, when $\mathbf{pc}$ is updated in the new type rules it is always *increased*. It is convenient to introduce some notation for such increasing updates: we write $\Gamma[x \mathrel{+}= a]$ to mean $\Gamma[x \mapsto \Gamma(x) \sqcup a]$. We refer to the modified system as *Flow Core-pc* (FPC). The rules are presented in Fig. 2.

$$\text{Skip}\frac{}{\vdash \Gamma\ \{\mathbf{skip}\}\ \Gamma} \qquad \text{Assign}\frac{p = \Gamma(\mathbf{pc}) \quad a = \Gamma(E)}{\vdash \Gamma\ \{x := E\}\ \Gamma[x \mapsto p \sqcup a]}$$

$$\text{Seq}\frac{\vdash \Gamma\ \{C_1\}\ \Gamma_1 \quad \vdash \Gamma_1\ \{C_2\}\ \Gamma_2}{\vdash \Gamma\ \{C_1\ ;\ C_2\}\ \Gamma_2}$$

$$\text{If}\frac{p = \Gamma(\mathbf{pc}) \quad a = \Gamma(E) \quad \vdash \Gamma[\mathbf{pc} \mathrel{+}= a]\ \{C_i\}\ \Gamma_i \quad i = 1,2}{\vdash \Gamma\ \{\mathbf{if}\ E\ C_1\ C_2\}\ (\Gamma_1 \sqcup \Gamma_2)[\mathbf{pc} \mapsto p]}$$

$$\text{While}\frac{p = \Gamma(\mathbf{pc}) \quad \Gamma_f = \mathbf{fix}(\lambda\Gamma.\,\mathbf{let}\ \vdash \Gamma[\mathbf{pc} \mathrel{+}= \Gamma(E)]\ \{C\}\ \Gamma'\ \mathbf{in}\ \Gamma' \sqcup \Gamma_0)}{\vdash \Gamma_0\ \{\mathbf{while}\ E\ C\}\ \Gamma_f[\mathbf{pc} \mapsto p]}$$

Fig. 2. Flow Core-pc (FPC)

It is easily checked that derivations in Flow Core-pc preserve the type assignment for **pc**:

Lemma 1. *If* $\vdash \Gamma\ \{C\}\ \Gamma'$ *then* $\Gamma'(\mathbf{pc}) = \Gamma(\mathbf{pc})$.

A straightforward induction on C then establishes that Flow Core-pc is essentially equivalent to Flow Core:

Theorem 1. $p \vdash_{\mathrm{FC}} \Gamma\ \{C\}\ \Gamma'$ *iff* $\vdash_{\mathrm{FPC}} \Gamma[\mathbf{pc} \mapsto p]\ \{C\}\ \Gamma'[\mathbf{pc} \mapsto p]$

Note that while the theorem appears to leave open the possibility that there may be Flow Core-pc derivations $\vdash \Gamma\ \{C\}\ \Gamma'$ without any counterpart in Flow Core, this is ruled out by Lemma 1.

2.2 Principal Typings

Intuitively, a *principal typing* for a term is a typing from which all its other typings may be simply recovered. In this section we show that every command does indeed have a principal Flow Core-pc typing in this sense. More formally, the most general definition of principal typing is due to Wells [Wel02]. We do not use Wells' definition in the current paper but it is a simple corollary of Theorem 2 (see below) that our principal typings are indeed principal according to that definition.

The following lemma establishes a property of Flow Core-pc which is fundamental to the rest of the technical development. Say that a map α is *join-preserving* if it preserves all finite joins or, equivalently, if $\alpha(\bot) = \bot$ and $\alpha(a \sqcup b) = \alpha(a) \sqcup \alpha(b)$. It turns out that join-preserving maps allow us freely to translate one valid typing into another.

Lemma 2. *Let* $\mathcal{L}, \mathcal{J}$ *be join-semilattices, let* $\Gamma, \Gamma' : \mathit{Var} \to \mathcal{L}$ *and let* $\alpha : \mathcal{L} \to \mathcal{J}$ *be join-preserving. If* $\vdash \Gamma\ \{C\}\ \Gamma'$ *then* $\vdash \alpha \circ \Gamma\ \{C\}\ \alpha \circ \Gamma'$.

The proof of this lemma essentially relies only on the fact that environment update and $\sqcup$ are the key operations used in the type rules. This also holds for all the other algorithmic type systems presented in the current paper and so the lemma easily extends to them. We rely on this fact without further comment in the sequel.

Principal typings are constructed by choosing $\mathcal{P}(\mathit{Var})$ as the security lattice. In what follows we let Δ range over type environments just in this case (thus $\Delta : \mathit{Var} \rightarrow \mathcal{P}(\mathit{Var})$). The semantic content of such a Δ can be understood simply as a set of dependencies: $y \in \Delta(x)$ means "y depends on x". On this reading, it would be very natural to represent environments directly as binary relations rather than functions, so that we could write, for example, $x \ \Delta \ y$ in place of $y \in \Delta(x)$. However, using a different representation just when $\mathcal{L} = \mathcal{P}(\mathit{Var})$ would make it awkward to relate $\mathcal{P}(\mathit{Var})$ typings to typings for other choices of $\mathcal{L}$, which is necessary to establish our principal typings result. To square this circle we introduce a notion of *monadic composition*.

For any finite set B, join-semilattice $\mathcal{L}$ and $g : B \rightarrow \mathcal{L}$, define $g^\dagger : \mathcal{P}(B) \rightarrow \mathcal{L}$ by $g^\dagger(X) = \bigsqcup_{x \in X} g(x)$. In much of what follows, $\mathcal{L}$ will itself be a powerset, in which case it is implicit that $\sqcup$ is $\cup$. Note that, for any $g : B \rightarrow \mathcal{L}$, $g^\dagger$ is join-preserving: $g^\dagger(X \cup Y) = g^\dagger(X) \sqcup g^\dagger(Y)$ and $g^\dagger(\{\}) = \bot$. Now, given $f : A \rightarrow \mathcal{P}(B)$ and $g : B \rightarrow \mathcal{L}$, define the monadic composition $f \,;\, g : A \rightarrow \mathcal{L}$ by $f \,;\, g = g^\dagger \circ f$. Note that given two type environments $\Delta, \Delta' : \mathit{Var} \rightarrow \mathcal{P}(\mathit{Var})$, the relational reading of $\Delta \,;\, \Delta'$ is simply relational composition (abusing notation, $x \ \Delta \,;\, \Delta' \ y$ iff $\exists z. x \ \Delta \ z \wedge z \ \Delta' \ y$).

Lemma 3 (Kleisli Axioms). *For each finite set A, let $\eta_A : A \rightarrow \mathcal{P}(A)$ be the map $x \mapsto \{x\}$. Then:*

1. $\eta_A{}^\dagger = \mathrm{id}_{\mathcal{P}(A)}$
2. $\eta_A \,;\, f = f$ *for* $f : A \rightarrow \mathcal{L}$
3. $f^\dagger \,;\, g = (f \,;\, g)^\dagger$ *for* $f : A \rightarrow \mathcal{P}(B)$ *and* $g : B \rightarrow \mathcal{L}$

If we restrict attention to the cases where $\mathcal{L}$ is a powerset, these are exactly the Kleisli axioms for the canonical powerset monad (see, for example, [Mog89]).

Note that η_{Var} (as defined in Lemma 3) is the environment $\lambda x \in \mathit{Var}. \{x\}$. Henceforth we just write η for η_{Var}. The relational reading of η is just the identity relation.

Let $\vdash \eta \ \{C\} \ \Delta$ (since Flow Core-pc is functional, such a typing exists and is uniquely determined by C). It is this typing which we claim as the principal typing for C. The following theorem justifies the claim by showing how every other typing for C can be recovered from this one:

Theorem 2 (Principal Typings). *Let $\vdash \eta \ \{C\} \ \Delta$. Then $\vdash \Gamma \ \{C\} \ \Gamma'$ iff $\Gamma' = \Delta \,;\, \Gamma$.*

Proof. Since the type system is functional, it suffices to show that $\vdash \Gamma \ \{C\} \ \Delta \,;\, \Gamma$. By definition of monadic composition, $\Delta \,;\, \Gamma = \Gamma^\dagger \circ \Delta$. Since $\Gamma^\dagger$ preserves unions, Lemma 2 says that $\vdash \Gamma^\dagger \circ \eta \ \{C\} \ \Gamma^\dagger \circ \Delta$ or, equivalently, $\vdash \eta \,;\, \Gamma \ \{C\} \ \Delta \,;\, \Gamma$. By the second Kleisli axiom, $\eta \,;\, \Gamma = \Gamma$, thus $\vdash \Gamma \ \{C\} \ \Delta \,;\, \Gamma$. □

From now on we refer to Δ simply as the principal *type* for C (this is the only part of the principal typing which is specific to C, since the other component is always η).

2.3 The Principal Type System

We formulate a type system which *only* constructs principal types and in which every sub-derivation also derives a principal type. This system is arrived at by specialising

Flow Core-pc to the case that $\mathcal{L} = \mathcal{P}(Var)$ and $\Gamma = \eta$ and using the Principal Typings Theorem to replace each sub-derivation by a principal type derivation. Crucially, this allows us to replace the multiple sub-derivations required in the While rule by a single derivation, thus removing the exponential cost which they incur. There is just one eureka step in the specialisation of the While rule; we implement the fixed-point construction as a transitive closure. We write Δ^* for the *reflexive-transitive closure* of Δ, defined in the standard way but transposed into functional form:

$$\Delta^* = \bigsqcup_{n \geq 0} \Delta^n$$

where $\Delta^0 = \eta$ and $\Delta^{n+1} = \Delta \; ; \; \Delta^n$. (Note that the "infinite join" in this definition will actually be finite, since *Var* is finite, though even without this constraint it would be well-defined, since $Var \rightarrow \mathcal{P}(Var)$ would still be a complete lattice.)

$$\text{Skip}\,\frac{}{\vdash \mathbf{skip} : \eta} \qquad \text{Assign}\,\frac{}{\vdash x := E : \eta[x \mapsto \{\mathbf{pc}\} \cup \text{fv}(E)]}$$

$$\text{Seq}\,\frac{\vdash C_i : \Delta_i \quad i = 1,2}{\vdash C_1 \; ; \; C_2 : \Delta_2 \; ; \; \Delta_1}$$

$$\text{If}\,\frac{\vdash C_i : \Delta_i \quad \Delta_i' = \Delta_i \; ; \; \eta[\mathbf{pc} \mathrel{+}= \text{fv}(E)] \quad i = 1,2}{\vdash \mathbf{if}\ E\ C_1\ C_2 : (\Delta_1' \sqcup \Delta_2')[\mathbf{pc} \mapsto \{\mathbf{pc}\}]}$$

$$\text{While}\,\frac{\vdash C : \Delta \quad \Delta_f = (\Delta \; ; \; \eta[\mathbf{pc} \mathrel{+}= \text{fv}(E)])^*}{\vdash \mathbf{while}\ E\ C : \Delta_f[\mathbf{pc} \mapsto \{\mathbf{pc}\}]}$$

Fig. 3. Flow Principal (FP)

Theorem 3. *Flow Principal derives principal types:* $\vdash_{\text{FPC}} \eta \; \{C\} \; \Delta$ *iff* $\vdash_{\text{FP}} C : \Delta$.

Proof sketch: Proof is by a simple induction on the structure of C showing that each Flow Principal rule is the specialisation of its Flow Core-pc counterpart, using the Principal Typings Theorem to replace sub-derivations with principal type derivations. For example, consider the Seq rule. The Flow Core-pc derivation is:

$$\text{Seq}\,\frac{\vdash \eta \; \{C_1\} \; \Delta_1 \qquad \vdash \Delta_1 \; \{C_2\} \; \Delta_2'}{\vdash \eta \; \{C_1 \; ; \; C_2\} \; \Delta_2'}$$

The derivation for C_2 is not principal, so we replace it by $\vdash \eta \; \{C_2\} \; \Delta_2$ and then apply the Principal Typings Theorem to derive $\Delta_2' = \Delta_2 \; ; \; \Delta_1$.

The proof for the While rule is slightly more involved, because we have to show that the reflexive-transitive closure in the Flow Principal rule correctly implements the fixed-point specified in the Flow Core-pc rule, but in essence we are able to equate each term in an ascending chain for the transitive closure with the corresponding term in the fixed-point chain.

2.4 Complexity

Flow Principal (Fig. 3) has a direct algorithmic reading. Here we sketch the complexity based on a direct implementation of a relational reading of the rules.

The key operations that must be implemented to construct a type are composition (;), update ($[\cdot \mapsto \cdot]$), union, and reflexive-transitive closure ($*$). Representing binary relations as boolean matrices has a long tradition in program analysis (see e.g. [Pro59]). In this representation we have one row for each element of the domain and one column for each element of the range. Thus in the case of our relations between variables, Δ is represented by a matrix for which there is a 1 in the row for x and column for y if and only if $x \; \Delta \; y$. Composition is then realised by boolean matrix multiplication, union is just boolean matrix addition (pointwise conjunction), and the single-value update operation is just row replacement. Using this representation we can easily construct a polynomial time complexity for type inference:

Theorem 4. *Flow Principal can be used to construct principal types in $O(nv^3)$ where n is the size of the program and v is the number of variables.*

Proof. Since the size of a type derivation is $O(n)$ there are thus $O(n)$ operations required to construct the type. Considering the cost of the operations, the potentially expensive operations are composition and reflexive-transitive closure. Adopting the boolean matrix representation, the matrices have size v^2, and thus the cost of composition (matrix multiplication) is v^3. Using Warshall's algorithm the cost of transitive (and reflexive) closure is also v^3. Hence the total cost of constructing the principal type is $O(nv^3)$.

3 Termination Typing

The FC system, like Denning and Denning's original flow-insensitive analysis of secure information, enforces an imperfect notion of information flow which has become known as *termination-insensitive noninterference*. Under this version of noninterference, information leaks are permitted if they are transmitted purely by the program's termination behaviour (i.e., whether it terminates or not). This imperfection is the price to pay for having a security condition which is relatively liberal (e.g. allowing while-loops whose termination may depend on the value of a secret) and easy to check.

But in some circumstances (for example in the presence of IO [AHSS08]) it may be desirable to enforce a stronger condition such as termination-sensitive security in which a secret is not permitted to transmit information even through termination. For example, suppose that h is high and l is low, then the following programs are not termination-sensitive secure:

```
if h then (while true skip) else skip; l := 1
```

```
(while h skip) ; l := 1
```

(An example of a system enforcing this stronger condition is [AB04].) In what follows we generalise the FST system to track the *degree* of termination-sensitivity. This provides a variant of the system from which a principal type provides both termination-sensitive and termination-insensitive typings, and even typings which lie between the two [DS09], for example where we can abide some termination leakage from a large piece of data (on the basis that the rate of leakage is low) but not for small data.

The idea is to add a termination variable $\mathbf{t}$ to the state to record the levels upon which termination of the command may depend. This corresponds to the *termination effect* from [Bou05] (a similar component can be found in earlier type systems [Smi01, BC01]).[2] The only rule which needs to consider the value of the termination variable is the While-rule. Consider the While rule in Fig. 2. The fixed-point constructs an environment Γ_f in which $\mathbf{pc}$ records the maximum level of data which can influence the value of the loop condition. We therefore need to modify the rule to ensure that it raises $\mathbf{t}$ to this level. Modifying the While rule in this way gives us a new type system which we refer to as *Flow Termination* (FT). See Fig. 4. It is clear by comparing the

$$\text{While}\,\frac{p = \Gamma(\mathbf{pc}) \quad \Gamma_f = \mathbf{fix}(\lambda\Gamma.\,\mathbf{let}\ \vdash \Gamma[\mathbf{pc} \mathrel{+}= \Gamma(E)]\ \{C\}\ \Gamma'\ \mathbf{in}\ \Gamma' \sqcup \Gamma_0)}{\vdash \Gamma_0\ \{\mathbf{while}\ E\ C\}\ \Gamma_f[\mathbf{pc} \mapsto p, \mathbf{t} \mathrel{+}= \Gamma_f(\mathbf{pc})]}$$

Fig. 4. Flow Termination (FT) (*extends Flow Core-pc*)

two versions of the While rule that Flow Termination is functional and is a conservative extension of Flow Core-pc.

After typing a program, the type of the termination variable can be used to determine whether a certain degree of termination-sensitivity has been achieved. To have termination-sensitivity we must demand that the type of $\mathbf{t}$ is $\bot$ - i.e. termination depends only on public inputs. For termination-insensitivity one can simply ignore $\mathbf{t}$. This generalisation to include termination-sensitivity is required for the erasure types considered in the next section.

Although we do not focus on the semantic soundness of the systems in this paper, it is useful to understand the semantic content of the termination variable. We can state it informally as follows: suppose $\vdash_{\text{FT}} \Gamma\ \{C\}\ \Gamma'$ and $a = \Gamma'(\mathbf{t})$. Now suppose that M and N are two memory states (mappings from variables to values) which are a-equivalent under policy Γ. Then C terminates starting with memory state M iff it terminates starting with memory state N.

The Principal Typings Theorem also holds for the Flow Termination system:

Theorem 5. *Let* $\vdash_{\text{FT}} \eta\ \{C\}\ \Delta$. *Then* $\vdash_{\text{FT}} \Gamma\ \{C\}\ \Gamma'$ *iff* $\Gamma' = \Delta\ ;\ \Gamma$.

Specialising the new While rule in the obvious way, we obtain a modified version of Flow Principal which computes principal types for Flow Termination. We refer to this system as *Termination Principal* (TP). See Fig. 5.

Theorem 6. TP *derives principal types:* $\vdash_{\text{FT}} \eta\ \{C\}\ \Delta$ *iff* $\vdash_{\text{TP}} C : \Delta$.

[2] We do not attempt to make the system more liberal in the manner of [Bou05, Smi01, BC01]; this is possible but would require a more pervasive change whereby the type of a variable is a pair of levels.

$$\text{While}\frac{\vdash C : \Delta \quad \Delta_f = (\Delta \,;\, \eta[\mathbf{pc} \mathrel{+}= \text{fv}(E)])^*}{\vdash \mathbf{while}\; E\; C : \Delta_f[\mathbf{pc} \mapsto \{\mathbf{pc}\}, \mathbf{t} \mathrel{+}= \Delta_f(\mathbf{pc})]}$$

Fig. 5. Termination Principal (TP) (*extends Flow Principal*)

4 Erasure Types

In this section we derive a polynomial time implementation of the erasure type system from [HS08]. This system uses flow-sensitivity in an essential way to enforce a certain kind of data erasure policy. As explained in the introduction, the system appears to be inherently exponential because it makes essential use of a double typing of the body of the erasure-labelled input command (the Erase rule in Fig.6). Even so, because the core of the erasure type system is an FST system of essentially the same kind as the one from [HS06], we are able to apply the techniques from Sections 2 and 3 above. This enables us to implement erasure typing by transforming the original system into a polynomial-time system for deriving principal types.

4.1 Non-algorithmic Erasure Type System

Figure 6 presents the type system from [HS08]. Here the syntax $\mathbf{input}\; x : a \nearrow b\; \mathbf{in}\; C$ abbreviates the construction "input x : a erased to b after C" discussed in the Introduction. We refer to this system as *Erasure Basic* (EB). In rule Erase, deleteOutput(C) operates on the syntax of C, producing a copy of C in which each **output** command has been replaced by **skip**. Thus to type an erasing input command we have to type its body, C, *twice*, under two different type environments. The first typing enforces non-interference with respect to the security level of the input-channel, while the second typing enforces non-interference with respect to the erasure level; **output** commands in C are ignored during the second typing because the erasure level only applies *after* C has executed.

$$\text{Skip}\frac{}{p \vdash \Gamma\; \{\mathbf{skip}\}\; \Gamma} \qquad \text{Assign}\frac{a = \Gamma(E)}{p \vdash \Gamma\; \{x := E\}\; \Gamma[x \mapsto p \sqcup a]}$$

$$\text{Erase}\frac{p \vdash \Gamma[x \mapsto a]\; \{C\}\; \Gamma' \quad p \vdash \Gamma[x \mapsto b]\; \{C'\}\; \Gamma' \quad p \sqsubseteq a \quad C' = \text{deleteOutput}(C)}{p \vdash \Gamma\; \{\mathbf{input}\; x : a \nearrow b\; \mathbf{in}\; C\}\; \Gamma'}$$

$$\text{Output}\frac{b = \Gamma(E) \qquad p \sqcup b \sqsubseteq a}{p \vdash \Gamma\; \{\mathbf{output}\; E\; \mathbf{on}\; a\}\; \Gamma}$$

$$\text{Seq}\frac{p \vdash \Gamma\; \{C_1\}\; \Gamma' \quad p \vdash \Gamma'\; \{C_2\}\; \Gamma''}{p \vdash \Gamma\; \{C_1 \,;\, C_2\}\; \Gamma''} \qquad \text{If}\frac{a = \Gamma(E) \quad p \sqcup a \vdash \Gamma\; \{C_i\}\; \Gamma' \quad i = 1, 2}{p \vdash \Gamma\; \{\mathbf{if}\; E\; C_1\; C_2\}\; \Gamma'}$$

$$\text{While}\frac{\Gamma(E) = \bot \quad \bot \vdash \Gamma\; \{C\}\; \Gamma}{\bot \vdash \Gamma\; \{\mathbf{while}\; E\; C\}\; \Gamma} \qquad \text{Sub}\frac{p_1 \vdash \Gamma_1\; \{C\}\; \Gamma_1'}{p_2 \vdash \Gamma_2\; \{C\}\; \Gamma_2'} \quad p_2 \sqsubseteq p_1, \Gamma_2 \sqsubseteq \Gamma_1, \Gamma_1' \sqsubseteq \Gamma_2'$$

Fig. 6. Erasure Basic (EB)

Note that this type system is non-algorithmic. Additionally, in contrast to the FST systems above, it is *not* parametric in the choice of security lattice; input and output commands refer (independently of the type system) to elements from some lattice, which means that programs can only be typed with respect to that particular lattice. Both these issues are addressed in Section 4.2 below.

In this system we are primarily concerned with information flows on the I/O channels. The (flow-sensitive) typing of program variables is thus only a means to the end of checking that the I/O flows comply with the required security policy. Since the type system is monotone in Γ, if a program can be typed at all, it can be typed for the smallest Γ. We say that a command C is *typeable* iff there exists a Γ such that $\bot \vdash \bot \, \{C\} \, \Gamma$.

In the following sections we proceed as follows:

1. We develop an algorithmic version of Erasure Basic. At the same time, we generalise the system by introducing auxiliary variables to model the program counter, the termination channel and the IO channels. This allows all constraints to be removed from the type system (rules Erase, Output and While) and makes it parametric in the choice of security type lattice. We establish correctness of the new system with respect to Erasure Basic.
2. We formulate and prove a principal typings result for the generalised system.
3. We specialise the generalised system to one which produces just principal types. This principal types system has the same complexity as the earlier one (Section 2.4).

4.2 Generalised Erasure Type System

We introduce the following additional variables (assumed disjoint from the program variables $PVar$):

- The variables $\mathbf{pc}$ and $\mathbf{t}$, playing the same roles as in Flow Core-pc and Flow Termination above (Sections 2.1 and 3).
- Disjoint sets $IVar$ and $OVar$ of *channel variables*.

We modify the language syntax to use channel variables in place of fixed channel names. Input commands now have the form $\mathbf{input}\ x : i_1 \nearrow i_2\ \mathbf{in}\ C$, with $i_1, i_2 \in IVar$. Output commands have the form $\mathbf{output}\ E\ \mathbf{on}\ o$, with $o \in OVar$. These are the only places in the syntax where channel variables appear. Commands written in the original syntax are encoded in the new syntax by application of injective maps $a \mapsto i_a : \mathcal{L} \to IVar$ and $a \mapsto o_a : \mathcal{L} \to OVar$. For a command C in the old syntax, we denote its encoding in the new syntax by $\widehat{C}$. Thus $\mathbf{input}\ x : a \nearrow b\ \mathbf{in}\ C$ becomes $\mathbf{input}\ x : i_a \nearrow i_b\ \mathbf{in}\ \widehat{C}$ and $\mathbf{output}\ E\ \mathbf{on}\ a$ becomes $\mathbf{output}\ E\ \mathbf{on}\ o_a$. In the rest of the paper C denotes a command in the new syntax unless explicitly stated otherwise.

Environments become maps $\Gamma : Var \to \mathcal{L}$, where $Var = PVar \cup \{\mathbf{pc}, \mathbf{t}\} \cup IVar \cup OVar$. The rules for the generalised system are presented in Fig. 7. We refer to this system as *Erasure General* (EG).

Some intuitions for the Erasure General rules:

- Once information has flowed to a channel, it has "escaped" the system. This is reflected in the rules by ensuring that, as for $\mathbf{t}$, the post-assignment for a channel variable is always at least as great as its pre-assignment.

$$\text{Skip}\frac{}{\vdash \Gamma\ \{\mathbf{skip}\}\ \Gamma} \qquad \text{Assign}\frac{p = \Gamma(\mathbf{pc}) \quad a = \Gamma(E)}{\vdash \Gamma\ \{x := E\}\ \Gamma[x \mapsto p \sqcup a]}$$

$$\text{Erase}\frac{\begin{array}{c} p = \Gamma(\mathbf{pc}) \quad a_j = \Gamma(i_j) \quad \vdash \Gamma[x \mapsto p \sqcup a_j]\ \{C\}\ \Gamma_j \quad j = 1,2 \\ \forall y \in \mathit{Var}.\Gamma'(y) = \begin{cases} \Gamma_1(y) & \text{if } y \in \mathit{OVar} \\ \Gamma_1(y) \sqcup \Gamma_2(y) & \text{otherwise} \end{cases} \end{array}}{\vdash \Gamma\ \{\mathbf{input}\ x : i_1 \nearrow i_2\ \mathbf{in}\ C\}\ \Gamma'[i_1 \mathrel{+}= p]}$$

$$\text{Output}\frac{p = \Gamma(\mathbf{pc}) \quad b = \Gamma(E)}{\vdash \Gamma\ \{\mathbf{output}\ E\ \mathbf{on}\ o\}\ \Gamma[o \mathrel{+}= p \sqcup b]}$$

$$\text{Seq}\frac{\vdash \Gamma\ \{C_1\}\ \Gamma_1 \quad \vdash \Gamma_1\ \{C_2\}\ \Gamma_2}{\vdash \Gamma\ \{C_1\ ;\ C_2\}\ \Gamma_2}$$

$$\text{If}\frac{p = \Gamma(\mathbf{pc}) \quad a = \Gamma(E) \quad \vdash \Gamma[\mathbf{pc} \mathrel{+}= a]\ \{C_i\}\ \Gamma_i \quad i = 1,2}{\vdash \Gamma\ \{\mathbf{if}\ E\ C_1\ C_2\}\ (\Gamma_1 \sqcup \Gamma_2)[\mathbf{pc} \mapsto p]}$$

$$\text{While}\frac{p = \Gamma(\mathbf{pc}) \quad \Gamma_f = \mathbf{fix}(\lambda\Gamma.\,\mathbf{let}\ \vdash \Gamma[\mathbf{pc} \mathrel{+}= \Gamma(E)]\ \{C\}\ \Gamma'\ \mathbf{in}\ \Gamma' \sqcup \Gamma_0)}{\vdash \Gamma_0\ \{\mathbf{while}\ E\ C\}\ \Gamma_f[\mathbf{pc} \mapsto p, \mathbf{t} \mathrel{+}= \Gamma_f(\mathbf{pc})]}$$

Fig. 7. Erasure General (EG)

- In Erasure Basic the Erase rule imposes the constraint that $p \sqsubseteq a$, where a is the (fixed) input channel type. In Erasure General this constraint has been removed but the post-environment is updated ($\Gamma'[i_1 \mathrel{+}= p]$) in a way which effectively allows the constraint to be checked by examining the final result of the type derivation. The $p \sqcup b \sqsubseteq a$ constraint in the Output rule is handled similarly.
- In Erasure Basic the While rule imposes the constraint that $\Gamma(E) = \bot$. Erasure General uses $\mathbf{t}$ to track whatever termination flows there may be, without building in any constraint on what is allowed. Again, flows not permitted by Erasure Basic can be caught by examining the final result.
- The generalised Erase rule still requires a double typing of the command body. But rather than deleting output commands in the second typing, we are able simply to discard those parts of the derived environment relating to output channels. This is achieved by the definition of Γ', which discriminates between output channel variables and others.

Lemma 4. *Erasure General (Fig. 7) is functional and if* $\vdash \Gamma\ \{C\}\ \Gamma'$ *then:*

1. $\Gamma'(\mathbf{pc}) = \Gamma(\mathbf{pc})$
2. *For all* $x \in \{\mathbf{t}\} \cup \mathit{IVar} \cup \mathit{OVar}$, $\Gamma'(x) \sqsupseteq \Gamma(x)$.

The following theorem shows how each Erasure Basic typing can be recovered from a specified Erasure General typing. They key observation is that the Erasure Basic constraints are satisfied iff the termination and channel variable type assignments are invariant in the specified Erasure General typing. Given $\Gamma : \mathit{PVar} \to \mathcal{L}$ and $p \in \mathcal{L}$, let $\widehat{\Gamma}^p : \mathit{Var} \to \mathcal{L}$ be defined by $\widehat{\Gamma}^p = \Gamma[\mathbf{pc} \mapsto p, \mathbf{t} \mapsto \bot][i_a \mapsto a, o_a \mapsto a]_{a \in \mathcal{L}}$.

Theorem 7. *Let C be a command in the original syntax and let $\vdash_{\mathrm{EG}} \widehat{\Gamma}^p \; \{\widehat{C}\} \; \Gamma'$. Then $p \vdash_{\mathrm{EB}} \Gamma \; \{C\} \; \Gamma_1$ iff there exists $\Gamma_2 \sqsubseteq \Gamma_1$ such that $\Gamma' = \widehat{\Gamma_2}^p$.*

Corollary 1. *Let C be a command in the original syntax and let $\vdash_{\mathrm{EG}} \bot \; \{\widehat{C}\} \; \Gamma$. Then C is typeable in Erasure Basic iff $\Gamma(\mathbf{t}) = \bot$ and $\Gamma(i_a) = a$ and $\Gamma(o_a) = a$ for each $a \in \mathcal{L}$.*

Thus the problem of Erasure Basic typing is reduced to the problem of constructing a specific Erasure General typing and then checking that the levels of the termination and channel variables remain fixed.

4.3 Principal Types for Erasure Typing

The Erasure General system is sufficiently similar to the earlier FST systems that the principal typings result carries over with no significant extra work:

Theorem 8 (Principal Erasure Typings). *Let $\vdash_{\mathrm{EG}} \eta \; \{C\} \; \Delta$ (see Fig. 7). Then $\vdash_{\mathrm{EG}} \Gamma \; \{C\} \; \Gamma'$ iff $\Gamma' = \Delta \,;\, \Gamma$.*

Proof. As for Theorem 2.

Using the Principal Erasure Typings Theorem we can specialise Erasure General to derive a system which produces only principal erasure types, just as we did in Section 2.2 for the FST system. The derived rules are shown in Fig. 8. We refer to this system as *Erasure Principal* (EP).

$$\text{Erase}\;\frac{\vdash C : \Delta \quad \Delta_j = \Delta \,;\, \eta[x \mapsto \{\mathbf{pc}, i_j\}] \quad j = 1,2 \qquad \Delta'(x) = \begin{cases} \Delta_1(x) & \text{if } x \in OVar \\ \Delta_1(x) \sqcup \Delta_2(x) & \text{otherwise} \end{cases}}{\vdash \mathbf{input}\; x : i_1 \nearrow i_2 \;\mathbf{in}\; C : \Delta'[i_1 \mathrel{+}= \{\mathbf{pc}\}]}$$

$$\text{Output}\;\frac{}{\vdash \mathbf{output}\; E \;\mathbf{on}\; o : \eta[o \mathrel{+}= \{\mathbf{pc}\} \cup \mathrm{fv}(E)]}$$

Fig. 8. Erasure Principal (EP) (*extends Termination Principal*)

Theorem 9. *Erasure Principal derives principal types: $\vdash_{\mathrm{EG}} \eta \; \{C\} \; \Delta$ iff $\vdash_{\mathrm{EP}} C : \Delta$.*

Note that Erasure Principal contains no multiple typings. Indeed, the complexity analysis of Theorem 4 carries over unchanged to Erasure Principal, showing that it is $O(nv^3)$.

5 Procedures

In this section we outline the extension of the FST system to a procedural language to obtain a context-sensitive procedural analysis. In a type-based setting a standard approach is to use type variables to represent any possible calling context in a parametric way. This in turn requires the generation of constraints on the values of such type variables. The key observation here is that the underlying FST system is already sufficiently "polymorphic" to enable a smooth extension of the system to procedures without the need for type variables and type constraints. Because of recursion, the algorithm requires a fixed-point iteration over the analysis of procedure bodies, but this remains polynomial-time.

First let us divide the set of program variables into two disjoint sets $\{x_1, x_2, \ldots\}$ and $\{y_1, y_2 \ldots\}$ which will be used for a procedure's formal in-parameters and formal out-parameters, respectively. We assume that procedure names form a finite indexed set $\mathit{ProcName} = \{p_i\}_{i \in A}$. A program Prog is a set

$$\mathit{Prog} = \{p_i(\mathbf{in}\ x_1, \ldots, x_{n_i}; \mathbf{out}\ y_1, \ldots, y_{m_i})\ C_i\}_{i \in A}$$

where $n_i, m_i \geq 0$ and $\mathrm{fv}(C_i) \cap \mathit{PVar} \subseteq \{x_1, \ldots, x_{n_i}, y_1, \ldots, y_{m_i}\}$ (no global variables). The grammar of commands from Section 4 is extended with procedure calls:

$$C ::= \cdots \mid\ p_i(E_1, \ldots E_{n_i}; z_1, \ldots, z_{m_i})$$

where the actual out-parameters $z_1, \ldots, z_{m_i}$ are required to be distinct. For the operational semantics we can assume that there is a distinguished procedure $\mathit{main} \in \mathit{ProcName}$ defined with zero parameters. The intended semantics of a procedure call is call-by-value, return-by-value. Formal out-parameters are initialised to constant values, formal in-parameters are initialised with the values of the actual in-parameters and the actual out-parameters are assigned from the formal out-parameters at the end of the procedure call.

When extending the FST system to handle procedures it is desirable to make the type system *context-sensitive*, so that the analysis of a given call takes into account the context in which it is called. One natural way to achieve this in a compositional type-based setting is to make the analysis of procedures *polymorphic* in the security levels of their parameters. To do this, in turn, would require the introduction of type variables. However, we can bypass this step altogether. Since our principal type system is already "polymorphic" we can directly extend it to handle procedures in a context-sensitive way without making any major changes to the system (such as the introduction of type variables and an algorithm based on the solution of type constraints).

Each procedure will be typed by a function $\mathit{Var} \to \mathcal{P}(\mathit{Var})$. A program typing Ψ will be a function which gives a type to each procedure, i.e., $\Psi : \mathit{ProcName} \to \mathit{Var} \to \mathcal{P}(\mathit{Var})$. Given such a program typing we can type a command. The previous typing rules are unchanged.

The basic form of the new rule to handle procedure calls is:

$$\frac{\Delta = \Psi(p_i)}{\Psi \vdash p_i(\vec{E}; \vec{z}) : (\Delta_{\mathbf{out}_i}\ ;\ \Delta\ ;\ \Delta_{\mathbf{in}_i})[v \mapsto \{v\}]_{v \in \mathit{PVar} - \vec{z}}}$$

where:

$\Delta_{\mathbf{in}_i}$ describes the initial dependencies of the formal parameters; the formal in-parameters are initially dependent on the actual in-parameters, while the formal out-parameters are initialised to constants and so start with no dependencies, thus:

$$\Delta_{\mathbf{in}_i} = \eta[x_j \mapsto \mathrm{fv}(E_j), y_k \mapsto \{\}]_{j \in \{1 \ldots n_i\}, k \in \{1 \ldots m_i\}}$$

$\Delta_{\mathbf{out}_i}$ describes the assignment of the actual out-parameters from the formal out-parameters, thus:

$$\Delta_{\mathbf{out}_i} = \eta[z_k \mapsto \{y_k, \mathbf{pc}\}]_{k\in\{1...m_i\}}$$

If we wish to think of this in terms of instantiation of the polymorphic procedure type Δ, then $\Delta_{\mathbf{in}_i}$ is the instantiation of the in-parameter types and $\Delta_{\mathbf{out}_i}$ is the instantiation of the out-parameter types. The update in the conclusion of the rule implements the local scoping of the procedure's formal parameters; since we disallow global variables, the only effect of a procedure call on program variables in the calling context is to update the actual out-parameters, thus it acts as the identity (dependency $v \mapsto \{v\}$) on all other program variables.

As it stands, this rule does not correctly track termination flows arising from the potential for non-terminating recursions. A conservative solution would be simply to apply the update $[\mathbf{t} \mathrel{+}= \{\mathbf{pc}\}]$ to the type. A more precise typing would be obtained by using an auxiliary analysis to distinguish between those procedures which are guaranteed not to recurse infinitely (in which case the $\mathbf{t}$ update is not required) and those which may; a cheap approach would simply use the structure of the program's call graph.

In order to type the commands we need a procedure typing which is consistent with the whole program. Such a typing is described by the following rule:

$$\text{Prog}\;\frac{\forall i \in A.\, \Psi \vdash C_i : \Delta_i \quad \Psi(p_i) = \Delta_i}{\vdash \mathit{Prog} : \Psi}$$

The recursive calls from a procedure are handled no differently to any other calls, so in conventional terms the type system could be said to use polymorphic recursion.

Example. Consider the swap operation in the introduction represented as a procedure:

```
swap(in x1, x2; out y1, y2) y1 := x2 ; y2 := x1
```

Using the obvious syntactic sugar for in-out parameters, the code sequence in the introduction could then be written:

```
swap(in out secret1, secret2);
swap(in out public1, public2);
```

The type for swap would be $\Delta = \eta[\mathtt{y1} \mapsto \{\mathtt{x2}, \mathbf{pc}\}, \mathtt{y2} \mapsto \{\mathtt{x1}, \mathbf{pc}\}]$. Abbreviating `secret1` as `s1` and `secret2` as `s2`, and defining $\Delta_{\mathbf{in}} = \eta[\mathtt{x1} \mapsto \{\mathtt{s1}\}, \mathtt{x2} \mapsto \{\mathtt{s2}\}]$ and $\Delta_{\mathbf{out}} = \eta[\mathtt{s1} \mapsto \{\mathtt{y1}, \mathbf{pc}\}, \mathtt{s2} \mapsto \{\mathtt{y2}, \mathbf{pc}\}]$, the typing for the first call above would thus be:

$$(\Delta_{\mathbf{out}}; \Delta; \Delta_{\mathbf{in}})[v \mapsto \{v\}]_{v\in\{\mathtt{x1},\mathtt{x2},\mathtt{y1},\mathtt{y2}\}} = \eta[\mathtt{s1} \mapsto \{\mathtt{s2}, \mathbf{pc}\}, \mathtt{s2} \mapsto \{\mathtt{s1}, \mathbf{pc}\}]$$

and the typing for the second call would be analogous.

5.1 Procedure Typing, Algorithmically

Although the Prog rule describes a valid typing it is not algorithmic. To obtain the minimal valid typing we construct an ascending chain of approximations:

$$\Psi_0 = \lambda p_i.\lambda x.\,\{\}$$
$$\Psi_{n+1} = \lambda p_i.\Delta \quad \text{where } \Psi_n \vdash C_i : \Delta$$

The complexity of typing commands is unchanged (since typing procedure call is cheap), so the cost of each iteration is $O(nv^3)$ as before. The number of iterations to reach a fixed-point is constant if the call-graph is not recursive (it is bounded by the depth of the call graph). In the presence of recursion we can bound the number of iterations at $O(v^2)$ (the height of the powerset of variables multiplied by the number of variables). In Theorem 4, v denoted the number of global variables and channels in the program. Since we no longer have global variables, v now denotes the number of channel variables plus the maximum number of parameters of any procedure.

6 Related Work

To our knowledge, this is the first published work which shows how flow-sensitive multi-level security typing can be achieved in polynomial time. Our own previous work [HS06] includes an "algorithmic" type system which has exponential complexity. We also showed that the system of Amtoft and Banerjee [AB04] is equivalent to a particular instance of ours, but the published algorithmic versions of their system [AB04, AB07] are also exponential.

We are not claiming, however, that the core algorithm presented in the current paper is optimal. The specialised principal type systems we have described effectively reduce the general security typing problem to a pure dependency analysis and there are a number of previously published polynomial algorithms for implementing essentially similar dependency analyses:

- The work of Banâtre et al [BB93a, BBL94, BB93b] presents dependency analyses which are similar to the Amtoft and Banerjee system. [BBL94] in particular is for a similar language and takes an algorithmic approach. The algorithm involves constructing and then traversing a graph whose nodes correspond to program points. [BB93b] is one of the only papers which attempts formally to relate a dependency analysis to multi-level security analysis. The account is not entirely satisfactory, since the details of the multi-level analysis are not made explicit, but the conclusion is that the dependency analysis subsumes multi-level security analysis. This is also implicit in Andrews and Reitman's information flow logic [AR80], whereby a logical flow deduction is made independently of a particular policy assigning security levels to variables. The principal typings result of [HS06] confirms that conclusion but also shows that (a) dependency analysis is itself a *special case* of flow-sensitive multi-level security analysis and (b) if multi-level security in a given lattice is the property of interest, dependency analysis doesn't provide any additional precision.
- Algorithms for program slicing also incorporate dependency analysis and it is intuitively clear that they could be adapted to implement the principal type systems of the current paper. Weiser [Wei84] describes an $O(n^2)$ algorithm for building an individual slice, which would yield an $O(n^2v)$ algorithm for calculating the full matrix of dependencies (applying it once per variable).

  Later work by Horwitz et al [HRB90] casts the slicing problem as a graph traversal problem and extends the basic algorithm to the inter-procedural case, using a powerful grammar-based technique to analyse procedure calls in a context-sensitive manner. Hammer and Snelting [HS09, Ham10] explicitly apply this graph-based

approach to the problem of information flow analysis. The algorithm presented by Horwitz et al is polynomial but the accompanying algorithmic analysis is stated for measures which are specific to their grammar constructions, preventing any straightforward comparison with the algorithm sketched for procedures in the current paper. More fundamentally, it is not clear how to relate the relative precision of the two approaches.
- The dependency analysis of Bergeretti and Carré [BC85] shares the same motivations as the slicing work (aiding with program comprehension, testing and debugging). Although the analysis is described in a more informal and arguably less straightforward way, their algorithm seems to be essentially equivalent to the basic principal types system described in the current paper and indeed their analysis of its complexity is $O(nv^3)$, in agreement with ours. The paper does not deal with the extension to recursive procedures. This work forms the basis of the information flow analysis of the commercial *Spark Examiner tool* [CH04], suggesting that it is algorithmically adequate.

A number of papers deal with the implementation of security type systems for similar languages e.g. [VS97, DS06] and for more complex ones [PS03], but these all have flow-insensitive treatments of imperative variables. Other algorithmic but non type-based treatments of flow-sensitive information flow include Clark et al's flow logic approach [CHH02].

Regarding erasure there is rather little prior work; the type system of the authors [HS08] and the concurrently developed system described by Chong and Myers [CM08] are perhaps the only examples. Chong and Myers do not describe an algorithm, although there approach is implemented in a restricted form as part of the Jif compiler. Their approach is incomparable because it concerns a different kind of erasure specification: it is assumed that there is an additional runtime mechanism which will overwrite all data with a certain label at a designated erasure time. The purpose of the types system is to ensure that there will be no sensitive data "left behind" when this is done. This makes less work for the static analysis and one can get away with a flow-insensitive system.

7 Conclusions and Future Work

We have presented a new approach to type-based security analysis which hinges on specialisation to principal types. The approach leads to a novel high-level structural description of a principal typing which has a direct algorithmic reading. By taking advantage of principality we provide polynomial complexity for systems which were previously presented in an implicitly exponential manner.

One direction for future work would be to see if this development can be carried over to richer language features (e.g. [ABB06]). Do dynamic allocation, structured data and aliasing fundamentally change the algorithmic approach?

Another direction would be to consider the theoretical question of expressiveness. Among analyses which extract no information about expressions beyond the free variables that they contain, is the analysis optimal? In the context of slicing, Weiser gives an example which can be used to show that our analysis is not optimal ([Wei84], Fig 3).

However if we consider the class of analyses which are also invariant under loop and recursion unrolling (as we believe ours is) then we suspect that an optimality result may be within reach.

Acknowledgements. This work was partly funded by the European Commission under the WebSand project and the Swedish research agencies SSF and VR. The first author carried out part of this work while on sabbatical, very kindly hosted by Mark Harman's CREST group at UCL. Discussions with Tobias Gedell and Daniel Hedin in the early stages of this work provided valuable insights. Jens Krinke helped us navigate the related work on program slicing. Niklas Broberg and Josef Svenningsson provided helpful comments on an earlier draft. Thanks to the anonymous referees for their very helpful comments and suggestions for improvement.

References

[AB04] Amtoft, T., Banerjee, A.: Information flow analysis in logical form. In: Giacobazzi, R. (ed.) SAS 2004. LNCS, vol. 3148, pp. 100–115. Springer, Heidelberg (2004)

[AB07] Amtoft, T., Banerjee, A.: A logic for information flow analysis with an application to forward slicing of simple imperative programs. Science of Computer Programming 64(1), 3–28 (2007)

[ABB06] Amtoft, T., Bandhakavi, S., Banerjee, A.: A logic for information flow in object-oriented programs. In: POPL 2006: Conference record of the 33rd ACM SIGPLAN-SIGACT symposium on Principles of programming languages, pp. 91–102. ACM, New York (2006)

[AHSS08] Askarov, A., Hunt, S., Sabelfeld, A., Sands, D.: Termination insensitive noninterference leaks more than just a bit. In: Jajodia, S., Lopez, J. (eds.) ESORICS 2008. LNCS, vol. 5283, pp. 333–348. Springer, Heidelberg (2008)

[AR80] Andrews, G.R., Reitman, R.P.: An axiomatic approach to information flow in programs. TOPLAS 2(1), 56–75 (1980)

[BB93a] Banâtre, J.-P., Bryce, C.: Information flow control in a parallel language framework. In: Proc. IEEE Computer Security Foundations Workshop, pp. 39–52 (June 1993)

[BB93b] Banâtre, J.-P., Bryce, C.: A security proof system for networks of communicating processes. Research Report RR-2042, INRIA (1993)

[BBL94] Banâtre, J.-P., Bryce, C., Le Métayer, D.: Compile-time detection of information flow in sequential programs. In: Gollmann, D. (ed.) ESORICS 1994. LNCS, vol. 875, pp. 55–73. Springer, Heidelberg (1994)

[BC85] Bergeretti, J.-F., Carré, B.: Information-flow and data-flow analysis of while-programs. ACM TOPLAS 7(1), 37–61 (1985)

[BC01] Boudol, G., Castellani, I.: Noninterference for concurrent programs. In: Yu, Y., Spirakis, P.G., van Leeuwen, J. (eds.) ICALP 2001. LNCS, vol. 2076, pp. 382–395. Springer, Heidelberg (2001)

[Bou05] Boudol, G.: On typing information flow. In: Van Hung, D., Wirsing, M. (eds.) ICTAC 2005. LNCS, vol. 3722, pp. 366–380. Springer, Heidelberg (2005)

[CH04] Chapman, R., Hilton, A.: Enforcing security and safety models with an information flow analysis tool. Ada Lett. XXIV(4), 39–46 (2004)

[CHH02] Clark, D., Hankin, C., Hunt, S.: Information flow for Algol-like languages. Journal of Computer Languages 28(1), 3–28 (2002)

[CM08] Chong, S., Myers, A.C.: End-to-end enforcement of erasure and declassification. In: CSF, pp. 98–111. IEEE Computer Society, Los Alamitos (2008)

[DD77] Denning, D.E., Denning, P.J.: Certification of programs for secure information flow. Comm. of the ACM 20(7), 504–513 (1977)

[DS06] Deng, Z., Smith, G.: Type inference and informative error reporting for secure information flow. In: ACM-SE 44: Proceedings of the 44th annual Southeast regional conference, pp. 543–548. ACM, New York (2006)

[DS09] Demange, D., Sands, D.: All Secrets Great and Small. In: Castagna, G. (ed.) ESOP 2009. LNCS, vol. 5502, pp. 207–221. Springer, Heidelberg (2009)

[Ham10] Hammer, C.: Experiences with pdg-based ifc. In: Second International Symposium Engineering Secure Software and Systems, pp. 44–60 (2010)

[HRB90] Horwitz, S., Reps, T.W., Binkley, D.: Interprocedural slicing using dependence graphs. ACM TOPLAS 12(1), 26–60 (1990)

[HS06] Hunt, S., Sands, D.: On flow-sensitive security types. In: POPL 2006, Proceedings of the 33rd Annual. ACM SIGPLAN - SIGACT. Symposium. on Principles of Programming Languages (January 2006)

[HS08] Hunt, S., Sands, D.: Just forget it - the semantics and enforcement of information erasure. In: Gairing, M. (ed.) ESOP 2008. LNCS, vol. 4960, pp. 239–253. Springer, Heidelberg (2008)

[HS09] Hammer, C., Snelting, G.: Flow-sensitive, context-sensitive, and object-sensitive information flow control based on program dependence graphs. International Journal of Information Security 8(6), 399–422 (2009)

[Mog89] Moggi, E.: Computational lambda-calculus and monads. In: Proc. IEEE Symp. on Logic in Computer Science, pp. 14–23 (1989)

[Pro59] Prosser, R.T.: Applications of boolean matrices to the analysis of flow diagrams. In: IRE-AIEE-ACM 1959 (Eastern): Papers presented at the December 1-3, 1959, eastern joint IRE-AIEE-ACM computer conference, pp. 133–138. ACM, New York (1959)

[PS03] Pottier, F., Simonet, V.: Information flow inference for ML. ACM TOPLAS 25(1), 117–158 (2003)

[Smi01] Smith, G.: A new type system for secure information flow. In: Proc. IEEE Computer Security Foundations Workshop, June 2001, pp. 115–125 (2001)

[VS97] Volpano, D., Smith, G.: A type-based approach to program security. In: Bidoit, M., Dauchet, M. (eds.) CAAP 1997, FASE 1997, and TAPSOFT 1997. LNCS, vol. 1214, pp. 607–621. Springer, Heidelberg (1997)

[VSI96] Volpano, D., Smith, G., Irvine, C.: A sound type system for secure flow analysis. J. Computer Security 4(3), 167–187 (1996)

[Wei84] Weiser, M.: Program slicing. IEEE Transactions on Software Engineering 10(4), 352–357 (1984)

[Wel02] Wells, J.B.: The essence of principal typings. In: Widmayer, P., Triguero, F., Morales, R., Hennessy, M., Eidenbenz, S., Conejo, R. (eds.) ICALP 2002. LNCS, vol. 2380, pp. 913–925. Springer, Heidelberg (2002)

Secure the Clones*

Static Enforcement of Policies for Secure Object Copying

Thomas Jensen, Florent Kirchner, and David Pichardie

INRIA Rennes – Bretagne Atlantique, France
`firstname.lastname@inria.fr`

Abstract. Exchanging mutable data objects with untrusted code is a delicate matter because of the risk of creating a data space that is accessible by an attacker. Consequently, secure programming guidelines for Java stress the importance of using defensive copying before accepting or handing out references to an internal mutable object. However, implementation of a copy method (like clone()) is entirely left to the programmer. It may not provide a sufficiently deep copy of an object and is subject to overriding by a malicious sub-class. Currently no language-based mechanism supports secure object cloning. This paper proposes a type-based annotation system for defining modular copy policies for class-based object-oriented programs. A copy policy specifies the maximally allowed sharing between an object and its clone. We present a static enforcement mechanism that will guarantee that all classes fulfill their copy policy, even in the presence of overriding of copy methods, and establish the semantic correctness of the overall approach in Coq. The mechanism has been implemented and experimentally evaluated on clone methods from several Java libraries.

1 Introduction

Exchanging data objects with untrusted code is a delicate matter because of the risk of creating a data space that is accessible by an attacker. Consequently, secure programming guidelines for Java such as those proposed by Sun [13] and CERT [5] stress the importance of using defensive *copying* or *cloning* before accepting or handing out references to an internal mutable object. There are two aspects of the problem:

1. If the result of a method is a reference to an internal mutable object, then the receiving code may modify the internal state. Therefore, it is recommended to make copies of mutable objects that are returned as results, unless the intention is to share state.
2. If an argument to a method is a reference to an object coming from hostile code, a local copy of the object should be created. Otherwise, the hostile code may be able to modify the internal state of the object.

A common way for a class to provide facilities for copying objects is to implement a `clone()` method that overrides the cloning method provided by `java.lang.Object`.

* This work was supported by the ANSSI, the ANR, and the *Région Bretagne*, respectively under the Javasec, Parsec, and Certlogs projects.

G. Barthe (Ed.): ESOP 2011, LNCS 6602, pp. 317–337, 2011.
© Springer-Verlag Berlin Heidelberg 2011

The following code snippet, taken from Sun's Secure Coding Guidelines for Java, demonstrates how a `date` object is cloned before being returned to a caller:

```
public class CopyOutput {
    private final java.util.Date date;
    ...
    public java.util.Date getDate() {
        return (java.util.Date)date.clone(); }
}
```

However, relying on calling a polymorphic `clone` method to ensure secure copying of objects may prove insufficient, for two reasons. First, the implementation of the `clone()` method is entirely left to the programmer and there is no way to enforce that an untrusted implementation provides a sufficiently *deep* copy of the object. It is free to leave references to parts of the original object being copied in the new object. Second, even if the current `clone()` method works properly, sub-classes may override the `clone()` method and replace it with a method that does not create a sufficiently deep clone. For the above example to behave correctly, an additional class invariant is required, ensuring that the `date` field always contains an object that is of class `Date` and not one of its sub-classes. To quote from the CERT guidelines for secure Java programming: *"Do not carry out defensive copying using the clone() method in constructors, when the (non-system) class can be subclassed by untrusted code. This will limit the malicious code from returning a crafted object when the object's clone() method is invoked."* Clearly, we are faced with a situation where basic object-oriented software engineering principles (sub-classing and overriding) are at odds with security concerns. To reconcile these two aspects in a manner that provides semantically well-founded guarantees of the resulting code, this paper proposes a formalism for defining *cloning policies* by annotating classes and specific copy methods, and a static enforcement mechanism that will guarantee that all classes of an application adhere to the copy policy. We do not enforce that a copy method will always return a target object that is functionally equivalent to its source. Rather, we ensure non-sharing constraints between source and targets, expressed through a copy policy, as this is the security-critical part of a copy method in a defensive copying scenario.

1.1 Cloning of Objects

For objects in Java to be cloneable, their class must implement the empty interface `Cloneable`. A default `clone` method is provided by the class `Object`: when invoked on an object of a class, `Object.clone` will create a new object of that class and copy the content of each field of the original object into the new object. The object and its clone share all sub-structures of the object; such a copy is called *shallow*.

It is common for cloneable classes to override the default clone method and provide their own implementation. For a generic `List` class, this could be done as follows:

```
public class List<V> implements Cloneable
{
    public V value;
    public List<V> next;
```

```
    public List(V val, List<V> next) {
    this.value = val;
    this.next = next; }

    public List<V> clone() {
        return new List(value,(next==null)?null:next.clone()); }
}
```

Notice that this cloning method performs a shallow copy of the list, duplicating the spine but sharing all the elements between the list and its clone. Because this amount of sharing may not be desirable (for the reasons mentioned above), the programmer is free to implement other versions of `clone()`. For example, another way of cloning a list is by copying both the list spine and its elements[1], creating what is known as a *deep* copy.

```
public List<V> deepClone() {
  return new List((V) value.clone(),
                  (next==null ? null : next.deepClone())); }
```

A general programming pattern for methods that clone objects works by first creating a shallow copy of the object by calling the `super.clone()` method, and then modifying certain fields to reference new copies of the original content. This is illustrated in the following snippet, taken from the class `LinkedList` in Fig. 8:

```
public Object clone() {  ...
  clone = super.clone();  ...
  clone.header = new Entry<E>(null, null, null); ...
  return clone;}
```

There are two observations to be made about the analysis of such methods. First, an analysis that tracks the depth of the clone being returned will have to be flow-sensitive, as the method starts out with a shallow copy that is gradually being made deeper. This makes the analysis more costly. Second, there is no need to track precisely modifications made to parts of the memory that are not local to the clone method, as clone methods are primarily concerned with manipulating memory that they allocate themselves. This will have a strong impact on the design choices of our analysis.

1.2 Copy Policies

The first contribution of the paper is a proposal for a set of semantically well-defined program annotations, whose purpose is to enable the expression of policies for secure copying of objects. Introducing a copy policy language enables class developers to state explicitly the intended behavior of copy methods. In the basic form of the copy policy formalism, fields of classes are annotated with `@Shallow` and `@Deep`. Intuitively, the annotation `@Shallow` indicates that the field is referencing an object, parts of which may be referenced from elsewhere. The annotation `@Deep(X)` on a field `f` means that *a*) the object referenced by this field `f` cannot itself be referenced from elsewhere, and

[1] To be type-checked by the Java compiler it is necessary to add a cast before calling `clone()` on `value`. A cast to a sub interface of `Cloneable` that declares a `clone()` method is necessary.

b) the field `f` is copied according to the copy policy identified by `X`. Here, `X` is either the name of a specific policy or if omitted, it designates the default policy of the class of the field. For example, the following annotations:

```
class List  { @Shallow V value;   @Deep List next;   ...}
```

specifies a default policy for the class `List` where the `next` field points to a list object that also respects the default copy policy for lists. Any method in the `List` class, labelled with the @Copy annotation, is meant to respect this default policy.

In addition it is possible to define other copy policies and annotate specific *copy methods* (identified by the annotation @Copy(...)) with the name of these policies. For example, the annotation[2]

```
DL: { @Deep V value; @Deep(DL) List next;};
@Copy(DL) List<V> deepClone() {
  return new List((V) value.clone(),
                  (next==null ? null  : next.deepClone())); }
```

can be used to specify a list-copying method that also ensures that the `value` fields of a list of objects are copied according to the copy policy of their class (which is a stronger policy than that imposed by the annotations of the class `List`). We give a formal definition of the policy annotation language in Section 2.

The annotations are meant to ensure a certain degree of non-sharing between the original object being copied and its clone. We want to state explicitly that the parts of the clone that can be accessed via fields marked @`Deep` are unaccessible from any part of the heap that was accessible before the call to `clone`(). To make this intention precise, we provide a formal semantics of a simple programming language extended with policy annotations and define what it means for a program to respect a policy (Section 2.2).

1.3 Enforcement

The second major contribution of this work is to make the developer's intent, expressed by copy policies, statically enforceable using a type system. We formalize this enforcement mechanism by giving an interpretation of the policy language in which annotations are translated into graph-shaped type structures. For example, the annotations of the `List` class defined above will be translated into the graph that is depicted to the right in Fig. 1 (`res` is the name given to the result of the copy method). The left part shows the concrete heap structure.

Unlike general purpose shape analysis, we take into account the programming methodologies and practice for copy methods, and design a type system specifically tailored to the enforcement of copy policies. This means that the underlying analysis must be able to track precisely all modifications to objects that the copy method allocates itself (directly or indirectly) in a flow-sensitive manner. Conversely, as copy methods should not modify non-local objects, the analysis will be designed to be more approximate when tracking objects external to the method under analysis, and the type system will accordingly refuse methods that attempt such non-local modifications. As

[2] Our implementation uses a sightly different policy declaration syntax because of the limitations imposed by the Java annotation language.

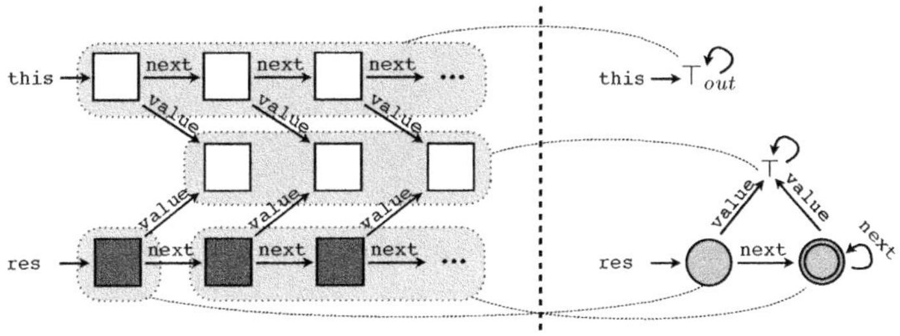

Fig. 1. A linked structure (left part) and its abstraction (right part)

a further design choice, the annotations are required to be verifiable modularly on a class-by-class basis without having to perform an analysis of the entire code base, and at a reasonable cost.

As depicted in Fig. 1, concrete memory cells are either abstracted as *a*) $\top_{out}$ when they are not allocated in the copy method itself (or its callee); *b*) $\top$ when they are just marked as *maybe-shared*; and *c*) circle nodes of a deterministic graph when they are locally allocated. A single circle furthermore expresses a singleton concretization. In this example, the abstract heap representation matches the graph interpretation of annotations, which means that the instruction set that produced this heap state satisfies the specified copy policy.

Technically, the intra-procedural component of our analysis corresponds to heap shape analysis with the particular type of graphs that we have defined. Operations involving non-local parts of the heap are rapidly discarded. Inter-procedural analysis uses the signatures of copy methods provided by the programmer. Inheritance is dealt with by stipulating that inherited fields retain their "shallow/deep" annotations. Redefinition of a method must respect the same copy policy and other copy methods can be added to a sub-class. The detailed definition of the analysis, presented as a set of type inference rules, is given in Section 3.

2 Language and Copy Policies

The formalism is developed for a small, imperative language extended with basic, class-based object-oriented features for object allocation, field access and assignment, and method invocation. A program is a collection of classes, organized into a tree-structured class hierarchy via the $extends$ relation. A class consists of a series of copy method declarations with each its own policy X, its name m, its formal parameter x and commands c to execute. A sub-class inherits the copy methods of its super-class and can re-define a copy method defined in one of its super-classes. We only consider copy methods. Private methods (or static methods of the current class) are inlined by the type checker. Other method calls (to virtual methods) are modeled by a special instruction $x{:=}?(y)$ that assigns an arbitrary value to x and possibly modifies all heap cells reachable from y (except itself). The other commands are standard. The copy method call $x{:=}m_{cn:X}(y)$ is a virtual call. The method to be called is the copy method of name m defined or inherited by the (dynamic) class of the object stored in variable y. The subscript annotation $cn{:}X$ is used as a static constraint. It is supposed that the type of y is guaranteed to be

$$x, y \in Var \qquad f \in Field \qquad m \in Meth \qquad cn \in Class_{\mathrm{id}} \qquad X \in Policy_{\mathrm{id}}$$

$$\begin{array}{rrl}
p \in & Prog ::= & \overline{cl} \\
cl \in & Class ::= & class\ cn\ [extends\ cn]\ \{\overline{pd}\ \overline{md}\} \\
pd \in & PolicyDecl ::= & X : \{\tau\} \\
\tau \in & Policy ::= & \overline{(X, f)} \\
md \in & MethDecl ::= & \mathsf{Copy}(X)\ m(x){:=}c \\
c \in & Comm ::= & x{:=}y \mid x{:=}y.f \mid x.f{:=}y \mid x{:=}null \\
& & \mid x := new\ cn \mid x{:=}m_{cn:X}(y) \mid x{:=}?(y) \mid return\ x \\
& & \mid c; c \mid if\ (*)\ then\ c\ else\ c\ fi \mid while\ (*)\ do\ c\ done
\end{array}$$

Notations: We write $\preceq$ for the reflexive transitive closure of the subclass relation induced by a (well-formed) program that is fixed in the rest of the paper. We write $\overline{x}$ a sequence of syntactic elements of form x.

Fig. 2. Language Syntax

a sub-class of class cn and that cn defines a method m with a copy policy X. This is ensured by standard bytecode verification and method resolution.

We suppose given a set of policy identifiers $Policy_{\mathrm{id}}$, ranged over by X. A copy policy declaration has the form $X : \{\tau\}$ where X is the identifier of the policy signature and τ is a policy. The policy τ consists of a set of field annotations (X, f) ; ... where f is a *deep* field that should reference an object which can only be accessed via the returned pointer of the copy method and which respects the copy policy identified by X. The use of policy identifiers makes it possible to write recursive definitions of copy policies, necessary for describing copy properties of recursive structures. Any other field is implicitly *shallow*, meaning that no copy properties are guaranteed for the object referenced by the field. No further copy properties are given for the sub-structure starting at *shallow* fields. For instance, the default copy policy of the class `List` presented in Sec. 1.2 writes: $\{(\mathtt{List.default}, \mathtt{next})\}$.

We assume that for a given program, all copy policies have been grouped together in a finite map $\Pi_p : Policy_{\mathrm{id}} \to Policy$. In the rest of the paper, we assume this map is complete, *i.e.* each policy name X that appears in an annotation is bound to a unique policy in the program p.

The semantic model of the language defined here is store-based:

$$\begin{array}{rl}
l \in Loc & \\
v \in Val & = Loc \cup \{\diamond\} \\
\rho \in Env & = Var \to Val \\
o \in Object & = Field \to Val \\
h \in Heap & = Loc \rightharpoonup_{\mathrm{fin}} (Class_{\mathrm{id}} \times Object) \\
\langle \rho, h, A \rangle \in State & = Env \times Heap \times \mathcal{P}(Loc)
\end{array}$$

A program state consists of an environment ρ of local variables, a store h of locations mapping[3] to objects in a heap and a set A of locally allocated locations in the current method or one of its callees. This last component does not influence the semantic transitions: it is necessary to express the type system interpretation exposed in Sec. 3, but is not used in the final soundness theorem. Each object is modeled in turn as a finite

[3] We note $\rightharpoonup_{\mathrm{fin}}$ for partial functions on finite domains.

$$\frac{}{(x{:=}y, \langle \rho, h, A\rangle) \rightsquigarrow \langle \rho[x \mapsto \rho(y)], h, A\rangle} \quad \frac{}{(x{:=}null, \langle \rho, h, A\rangle) \rightsquigarrow \langle \rho[x \mapsto \diamond], h, A\rangle}$$

$$\frac{\rho(y) \in \mathrm{dom}(h)}{(x{:=}y.f, \langle \rho, h, A\rangle) \rightsquigarrow \langle \rho[x \mapsto h(\rho(y), f)], h, A\rangle} \quad \frac{\rho(x) \in \mathrm{dom}(h)}{(x.f{:=}y, \langle \rho, h, A\rangle) \rightsquigarrow \langle \rho, h[(\rho(x), f) \mapsto \rho(y)], A\rangle}$$

$$\frac{l \notin \mathrm{dom}(h)}{(x := new\ cn, \langle \rho, h, A\rangle) \rightsquigarrow \langle \rho[x \mapsto l], h[l \mapsto (cn, o_\diamond)], A \cup \{l\}\rangle}$$

$$\frac{}{(return\ x, \langle \rho, h, A\rangle) \rightsquigarrow \langle \rho[ret \mapsto \rho(x)], h, A\rangle}$$

$$\frac{h(\rho(y)) = (cn_y, \_) \quad lookup(cn_y, m) = (\mathsf{Copy}(X')\ m(a){:=}c) \quad cn_y \preceq cn \qquad (c, \langle \rho_\diamond[a \mapsto \rho(y)], h, \emptyset\rangle) \rightsquigarrow \langle \rho', h', A'\rangle}{(x{:=}m_{cn:X}(y), \langle \rho, h, A\rangle) \rightsquigarrow \langle \rho[x \mapsto \rho'(ret)], h', A \cup A'\rangle}$$

$$\frac{\begin{array}{c}\mathrm{dom}(h) \subseteq \mathrm{dom}(h') \quad \forall l \in \mathrm{dom}(h) \setminus \mathrm{Reach}_h(\rho(y)),\ h(l) = h'(l) \\ \forall l \in \mathrm{dom}(h) \setminus \mathrm{Reach}_h(\rho(y)),\ \forall l', l \in \mathrm{Reach}_{h'}(l') \Rightarrow l' \in \mathrm{dom}(h) \setminus \mathrm{Reach}_h(\rho(y)) \\ v \in \{\diamond\} + \mathrm{Reach}_h(\rho(y)) \cup (\mathrm{dom}(h') \setminus \mathrm{dom}(h))\end{array}}{(x{:=}?(y), \langle \rho, h, A\rangle) \rightsquigarrow \langle \rho[x \mapsto v], h', A \setminus \mathrm{Reach}^+_h(\rho(y))\rangle}$$

$$\frac{(c_1, \langle \rho, h, A\rangle) \rightsquigarrow \langle \rho_1, h_1, A_1\rangle \quad (c_2, \langle \rho_1, h_1, A_1\rangle) \rightsquigarrow \langle \rho_2, h_2, A_2\rangle}{(c_1; c_2, \langle \rho, h, A\rangle) \rightsquigarrow \langle \rho_2, h_2, A_2\rangle}$$

$$\frac{(c_1, \langle \rho, h, A\rangle) \rightsquigarrow \langle \rho_1, h_1, A_1\rangle}{(if\ (*)\ then\ c_1\ else\ c_2\ fi, \langle \rho, h, A\rangle) \rightsquigarrow \langle \rho_1, h_1, A_1\rangle} \quad \frac{(c_2, \langle \rho, h, A\rangle) \rightsquigarrow \langle \rho_2, h_2, A_2\rangle}{(if\ (*)\ then\ c_1\ else\ c_2\ fi, \langle \rho, h, A\rangle) \rightsquigarrow \langle \rho_2, h_2, A_2\rangle}$$

$$\frac{}{(while\ (*)\ do\ c\ done, \langle \rho, h, A\rangle) \rightsquigarrow \langle \rho, h, A\rangle} \quad \frac{(c; while\ (*)\ do\ c\ done, \langle \rho, h, A\rangle) \rightsquigarrow \langle \rho', h', A'\rangle}{(while\ (*)\ do\ c\ done, \langle \rho, h, A\rangle) \rightsquigarrow \langle \rho', h', A'\rangle}$$

Notations: We write $h(l, f)$ for the value $o(f)$ such that $l \in \mathrm{dom}(h)$ and $h(l) = o$. We write $h[(l, f) \mapsto v]$ for the heap h' that is equal to h except that the f field of the object at location l now has value v. Similarly, $\rho[x \mapsto v]$ is the environment ρ modified so that x now maps to v. The object $o_\diamond$ is the object satisfying $o_\diamond(f) = \diamond$ for all field f, and $\rho_\diamond$ is the environment such that $\rho_\diamond(x) = \diamond$ for all variables x. We consider methods with only one parameter and name it p. *lookup* designates the dynamic lookup procedure that, given a class name cn and a method name m, find the first implementation of m in the class hierarchy starting from the class of name cn and scanning the hierarchy bottom-up. It returns the corresponding method declaration. ret is a specific local variable name that is used to store the result of each method. $\mathrm{Reach}_h(l)$ (resp. $\mathrm{Reach}^+_h(l)$) denotes the set of values that are reachable from any sequence (resp. any non-empty sequence) of fields in h.

Fig. 3. Semantic Rules

function from field names to values (references or the specific $\diamond$ reference for null values). We do not deal with base values such as integers because their immutable values are irrelevant here.

The operational semantics of the language is defined (Fig. 3) by the evaluation relation $\rightsquigarrow$ between configurations $Comm \times State$ and resulting states $State$. The set of locally allocated locations is updated by both the $x := new\ cn$ and the $x{:=}m_{cn:X}(y)$ statements. The execution of an unknown method call $x{:=}?(y)$ results in a new heap h' that keeps all the previous objects that were not reachable from $\rho(l)$. It assigns the variable x a reference that was either reachable from $\rho(l)$ in h or that has been allocated during this call and hence not present in h.

2.1 Policies and Inheritance

We impose restrictions on the way that inheritance can interact with copy policies. A method being re-defined in a sub-class can impose further constraints on how fields of the objects returned as result should be copied. A field already annotated *deep* with policy X must have the same annotation in the policy governing the re-defined method but a field annotated as *shallow* can be annotated *deep* for a re-defined method.

Definition 1 (Overriding Copy Policies). *A program p is well-formed with respect to overriding copy policies if and only if for any method declaration* $\mathsf{Copy}(X')\ m(x){:=}\dots$ *that overrides* (i.e. *is declared with this signature in a subclass of a class cl) another method declaration* $\mathsf{Copy}(X)\ m(x){:=}\dots$ *declared in cl, we have*

$$\Pi_p(X) \subseteq \Pi_p(X').$$

Example 1. The `java.lang.Object` class provides a `clone()` method of policy $\{\}$ (because its native `clone()` method is *shallow* on all fields). A class `A` declaring two fields `f` and `g` can hence override the `clone()` method and give it a policy $\{(X, \mathtt{g})\}$. If a class `B` extends `A` and overrides `clone()`, it must assign it a policy of the form $\{(X, \mathtt{g});\ \dots\}$ and could declare the field `f` as *deep*. In our implementation, we let the programmer leave the policy part that concerns fields declared in superclasses implicit, as it is systematically inherited.

2.2 Semantics of Copy Policies

The informal semantics of the copy policy annotation of a method is:

> A copy method satisfies a copy policy X if and only if no memory cell that is reachable from the result of this method following only fields with *deep* annotations in X, is reachable from another local variable of the caller.

We formalize this by giving, in Fig. 4, a semantics to copy policies based on access paths. An access path consists of a variable x followed by a sequence of field names f_i separated by a dot. An access path π can be evaluated to a value v in a context $\langle \rho, h \rangle$ with a judgment $\langle \rho, h \rangle \vdash \pi \Downarrow v$. Each path π has a root variable $\downarrow\!\pi \in \mathit{Var}$. A judgment $\vdash \pi : \tau$ holds when a path π follows only deep fields in the policy τ.

Definition 2 (Secure Copy Method). *A method m is said* secure *wrt. a copy signature* $\mathsf{Copy}(X)\{\tau\}$ *if and only if for all heaps* $h_1, h_2 \in \mathit{Heap}$*, local environments* $\rho_1, \rho_2 \in \mathit{Env}$*, locally allocated locations* $A_1, A_2 \in \mathcal{P}(\mathit{Loc})$*, and variables* $x, y \in \mathit{Var}$*,*

$$(x{:=}m_{cn:X}(y), \langle \rho_1, h_1, A_1 \rangle) \leadsto \langle \rho_2, h_2, A_2 \rangle \ \textit{implies}\ \ \rho_2, h_2, x \models \tau$$

Note that because of virtual dispatch, the method executed by such a call may not be the method found in cn but an overridden version of it. The security policy requires that all overriding implementations still satisfy the policy τ.

Lemma 1 (Monotonicity of Copy Policies wrt. Overriding)

$$\tau_1 \subseteq \tau_2 \ \textit{implies}\ \forall h, \rho, x,\ \ \rho, h, x \models \tau_2 \Rightarrow \rho, h, x \models \tau_1$$

Access path syntax

$$\pi \in \mathbb{P} ::= x \mid \pi.f$$

Access path evaluation

$$\langle \rho, h \rangle \vdash x \Downarrow \rho(x) \qquad \frac{\langle \rho, h \rangle \vdash \pi \Downarrow l \quad h(l) = o}{\langle \rho, h \rangle \vdash \pi.f \Downarrow o(f)}$$

Access path root

$$\downarrow x = x \quad \downarrow \pi.f = \downarrow \pi$$

Access path satisfying a policy

We suppose given $\Pi_p : Policy_{\text{id}} \rightarrow Policy$ the set of copy policies of the considered program p.

$$\frac{}{\vdash x : \tau} \qquad \frac{(X_1\ f_1) \in \tau, (X_2\ f_2) \in \Pi_p(X_1), \cdots, (X_n\ f_n) \in \Pi_p(X_{n-1})}{\vdash x.f_1.\ldots.f_n : \tau}$$

Policy semantics

$$\frac{\left.\begin{array}{l}\forall \pi, \pi' \in \mathbb{P}, \forall l, l' \in Loc,\ x = \downarrow\pi, \quad \downarrow\pi' \neq x, \\ \qquad \langle \rho, h \rangle \vdash \pi \Downarrow l\,, \quad \langle \rho, h \rangle \vdash \pi' \Downarrow l'\,, \\ \qquad \vdash \pi : \tau \end{array}\right\} \text{implies } l \neq l'}{\rho, h, x \models \tau}$$

Fig. 4. Copy Policy Semantics

Proof. Under these hypotheses, for all access paths π, $\vdash \pi : \tau_1$ implies $\vdash \pi : \tau_2$. Thus the result holds by definition of $\models$.

Thanks to this lemma, it is sufficient to prove that each method is secure wrt. its own copy signature to ensure that all potential overridings will be also secure.

3 Type and Effect System

The annotations defined in the previous section are convenient for expressing a copy policy but are not sufficiently expressive for reasoning about the data structures being copied. The static enforcement of a copy policy hence relies on a translation of policies into a graph-based structure (that we shall call types) describing parts of the environment of local variables and the heap manipulated by a program. In particular, the types can express useful alias information between variables and heap cells. In this section, we define the set of types, an approximation (sub-typing) relation $\sqsubseteq$ on types, and an inference system for assigning types to each statement and to the final result of a method.

The set of types is defined using the following symbols:

$$\begin{array}{ll} n \in \boldsymbol{N} & t \in \boldsymbol{t} = \boldsymbol{N} + \{\bot, \top_{out}, \top\} \\ \Gamma \in Var \rightarrow \boldsymbol{t} & \Delta \in \boldsymbol{\Delta} = \boldsymbol{N} \rightharpoonup_{\text{fin}} Field \rightarrow \boldsymbol{t} \\ \Theta \in \mathcal{P}(\boldsymbol{N}) & T \in \boldsymbol{T} = (Var \rightarrow \boldsymbol{t}) \times \boldsymbol{\Delta} \times \mathcal{P}(\boldsymbol{N}) \end{array}$$

We assume given a set $\boldsymbol{N}$ of nodes. A value can be given a *base type* t in $\boldsymbol{N} + \{\bot, \top_{out}, \top\}$. A node n means the value has been locally allocated. The symbol $\bot$ means that the value is equal to the null reference $\diamond$. The symbol $\top_{out}$ means that the value contains a location that cannot reach a locally allocated object. The symbol $\top$ is the specific "no-information" base type. A type is a triplet $T = (\Gamma, \Delta, \Theta) \in \boldsymbol{T}$ where

- Γ is a typing environment that maps (local) variables to base types.
- Δ is a graph whose nodes are elements of $\boldsymbol{N}$. The edges of the graphs are labeled with field names. The successors of a node is a base type. Edges over-approximate the concrete points-to relation.

Θ is a set of nodes that represents necessarily only one concrete cell each. Nodes in Θ are eligible to strong-update while others (weaks nodes) can only be weakly updated.

In order to link types to the heap structures they represent, we will need to state reachability predicates in the abstract domain. Therefore, the path evaluation relation is extended to types using the following inference rules:

$$\frac{}{[\Gamma,\Delta]\vdash x \Downarrow \Gamma(x)} \quad \frac{[\Gamma,\Delta]\vdash \pi \Downarrow n}{[\Gamma,\Delta]\vdash \pi.f \Downarrow \Delta[n,f]} \quad \frac{[\Gamma,\Delta]\vdash \pi \Downarrow \top}{[\Gamma,\Delta]\vdash \pi.f \Downarrow \top} \quad \frac{[\Gamma,\Delta]\vdash \pi \Downarrow \top_{out}}{[\Gamma,\Delta]\vdash \pi.f \Downarrow \top_{out}}$$

Notice both $\top_{out}$ and $\top$ are considered as sink nodes for path evaluation purposes[4].

3.1 From Annotation to Type

The set of all copy policies $\Pi_p \subseteq \mathit{PolicyDecl}$ can be translated into a graph Δ_p as described hereafter. We assume a naming process that associates to each policy name $X \in \mathit{Policy}_{\mathrm{id}}$ of a program a unique node $n'_X \in \boldsymbol{N}$.

$$\Delta_p = \bigcup_{X:\{(X_1,f_1);\ldots;(X_k,f_k)\}\in\Pi_p} \left[(n'_X, f_1) \mapsto n'_{X_1}, \cdots, (n'_X, f_k) \mapsto n'_{X_k}\right]$$

Given this graph, a policy $\tau = \{(X_1, f_1); \ldots; (X_k, f_k)\}$ that is declared in a class cl is translated into a triplet:

$$\Phi(\tau) = \left(n_\tau, \Delta_p \cup \left[(n_\tau, f_1) \mapsto n'_{X_1}, \cdots, (n_\tau, f_k) \mapsto n'_{X_k}\right], \{n_\tau\}\right)$$

Note that we *unfold* the possibly cyclic graph Δ_p with an extra node n_τ in order to be able to catch an alias information between this node and the result of a method, and hence declare n_τ as strong. Take for instance the type in Fig. 1: were it not for this unfolding step, the type would have consisted only in a weak node and a $\top$ node, with the variable `res` mapping directly to the former. Note also that it is not necessary to keep (and even to build) the full graph Δ_p in $\Phi(\tau)$ but only the part that is reachable from n_τ.

3.2 Type Interpretation

The semantic interpretation of types is given in Fig. 5, in the form of a relation

$$\langle \rho, h, A\rangle \sim [\Gamma, \Delta, \Theta]$$

that states when a local allocation history A, a heap h and an environment ρ are coherent with a type (Γ, Δ, Θ). The interpretation judgment amounts to checking that (i) for every path π that leads to a value l in the concrete memory and to a type t in the graph, the auxiliary type interpretation $\langle \rho, h, A\rangle, [\Gamma, \Delta] \Vdash v \sim t$ holds; (ii) every strong node

[4] The sink nodes status of $\top$ (resp. $\top_{out}$) can be understood as a way to state the following invariant enforced by our type system: when a cell points to an unspecified (resp. foreign) part of the heap, all successors of this cell are also unspecified (resp. foreign).

Auxiliary type interpretation

$$\frac{}{\langle\rho,h,A\rangle,[\Gamma,\Delta]\Vdash\diamond\sim t}\qquad\frac{}{\langle\rho,h,A\rangle,[\Gamma,\Delta]\Vdash r\sim\top}\qquad\frac{\mathrm{Reach}_h(l)\cap A=\emptyset}{\langle\rho,h,A\rangle,[\Gamma,\Delta]\Vdash l\sim\top_{out}}$$

$$\frac{l\in A\qquad n\in\mathrm{dom}(\Sigma)\qquad\forall\pi,\ \langle\rho,h\rangle\vdash\pi\Downarrow l\Rightarrow\langle\Gamma,\Sigma\rangle\vdash\pi\Downarrow n}{\langle\rho,h,A\rangle,[\Gamma,\Delta]\Vdash l\sim n}$$

Main type interpretation

$$\frac{\begin{array}{l}\forall\pi,\forall t,\forall l,\\ \quad\left.\begin{array}{l}[\Gamma,\Sigma]\vdash\pi\Downarrow t\\ \langle\rho,h\rangle\vdash\pi\Downarrow r\end{array}\right\}\Rightarrow\langle\rho,h,A\rangle,[\Gamma,\Delta]\Vdash r\sim t\end{array}\qquad\begin{array}{l}\forall n\in\Theta,\ \forall\pi,\forall\pi',\forall l,\forall l',\\ \quad\left.\begin{array}{l}[\Gamma,\Sigma]\vdash\pi\Downarrow n\ \wedge\ [\Gamma,\Sigma]\vdash\pi'\Downarrow n\\ \langle\rho,h\rangle\vdash\pi\Downarrow l\ \wedge\ \langle\rho,h\rangle\vdash\pi'\Downarrow l'\end{array}\right\}\Rightarrow l=l'\end{array}}{\langle\rho,h,A\rangle\sim[\Gamma,\Delta,\Theta]}$$

Fig. 5. Type Interpretation

in Θ represents a uniquely reachable value in the concrete memory. The auxiliary judgment $\langle\rho,h,A\rangle,[\Gamma,\Delta]\Vdash v\sim t$ is defined by case on t. The null value is represented by any type. The symbol $\top$ represents any value and $\top_{out}$ those values that do not allow to reach a locally allocated location. A node n represents a locally allocated memory location l such that every concrete path π that leads to l in $\langle\rho,h\rangle$ leads to node n in $\langle\Gamma,\Delta\rangle$.

We now establish a semantic link between policy semantics and type interpretation. We show that if the final state of a copy method can be given a type of the form $\Phi(\tau)$ then this is a secure method wrt. the policy τ.

Theorem 1. *Let $\Phi(\tau)=(n_\tau,\Delta_\tau,\Theta_\tau)$, $\rho\in Env$, $A\in\mathcal{P}(Loc)$, and $x\in Var$. Assume that, for all $y\in Var$ such that y is distinct from x, A is not reachable from $\rho(y)$ in a given heap h,* i.e. *$Reach_h(\rho(y))\cap A=\emptyset$. If there exists a state of the form $\langle\rho',h,A\rangle$, a return variable* res *and a local variable type Γ' such that $\rho'(\mathsf{res})=\rho(x)$, $\Gamma'(\mathsf{res})=n_\tau$ and $\langle\rho',h,A\rangle\sim[\Gamma',\Delta_\tau,\Theta_\tau]$, then $\rho,h,x\models\tau$ holds.*

Proof. We consider two paths π' and π such that $x=\downarrow\pi$, $\downarrow\pi'\neq x$, $\langle\rho,h\rangle\vdash\pi'\Downarrow l$, $\vdash\pi:\tau$, $\langle\rho,h\rangle\vdash\pi\Downarrow l$ and look for a contradiction. Since $\vdash\pi:\tau$, there exists a node $n\in\Delta_\tau$ such that $[\Gamma',\Delta_\tau]\vdash\pi\Downarrow n$. Furthermore $\langle\rho',h\rangle\vdash\pi\Downarrow l$ so we can deduce that $l\in A$. Thus we obtain a contradiction with $\langle\rho,h\rangle\vdash\pi'\Downarrow l$ because any path that starts from a variable other than x cannot reach the elements in A.

3.3 Sub-typing

To manage control flow merge points we rely on a sub-typing relation $\sqsubseteq$ described in Fig. 6. A sub-type relation $(\Gamma_1,\Delta_1,\Theta_1)\sqsubseteq(\Gamma_2,\Delta_2,\Theta_2)$ holds if and only if (ST_1) there exists a fusion function σ from $\mathrm{dom}(\Delta_1)$ to $\mathrm{dom}(\Delta_2)+\{\top\}$. σ is a mapping that merges nodes and edges in Δ_1 such that (ST_2) every element t_1 of Δ_1 accessible from a path π is mapped to an element t_2 of Δ_2 accessible from the same path, such that $t_1\leq_\sigma t_2$. In particular, this means that all successors of t_1 are mapped to successors of t_2. Incidentally, because $\top$ acts as a sink on paths, if t_1 is mapped to $\top$, then all its successors are mapped to $\top$ too. Finally, when a strong node in Δ_1 maps to a strong node in Δ_2, this image node cannot be the image of any other node in Δ_1—in other terms, σ is injective on strong nodes (ST_3).

Value sub-typing judgment

$$\frac{t \in \boldsymbol{t}}{\bot \leq_\sigma t} \quad \frac{t \in \boldsymbol{t} \backslash \boldsymbol{N}}{t \leq_\sigma \top} \quad \frac{}{\top_{out} \leq_\sigma \top_{out}} \quad \frac{n \in \boldsymbol{N}}{n \leq_\sigma \sigma(n)}$$

Main sub-typing judgment

$$\frac{\begin{array}{ll} (\mathrm{ST}_1) & \sigma \in \boldsymbol{N}(\Delta_1) \rightarrow \boldsymbol{N}(\Delta_2) + \{\top\} \\ (\mathrm{ST}_2) & \forall t_1 \in \boldsymbol{t}, \forall \pi \in \mathbb{P}, [\Gamma_1, \Delta_1] \vdash \pi \Downarrow t_1 \Rightarrow \exists t_2 \in \boldsymbol{t}, t_1 \leq_\sigma t_2 \wedge [\Gamma_2, \Delta_2] \vdash \pi \Downarrow t_2 \\ (\mathrm{ST}_3) & \forall n_2 \in \Theta_2,\ \exists n_1 \in \Theta_1,\ \sigma^{-1}(n_2) = \{n_1\} \end{array}}{(\Gamma_1, \Delta_1, \Theta_1) \sqsubseteq (\Gamma_2, \Delta_2, \Theta_2)}$$

Fig. 6. Sub-typing

Intuitively, it is possible to go up in the type partial order either by merging, or by forgetting nodes in the initial graph. The following example shows three ordered types and their corresponding fusion functions. On the left, we forget the node pointed to by y and hence forget all of its successors (see (ST_2)). On the right we fusion two strong nodes to obtain a weak node.

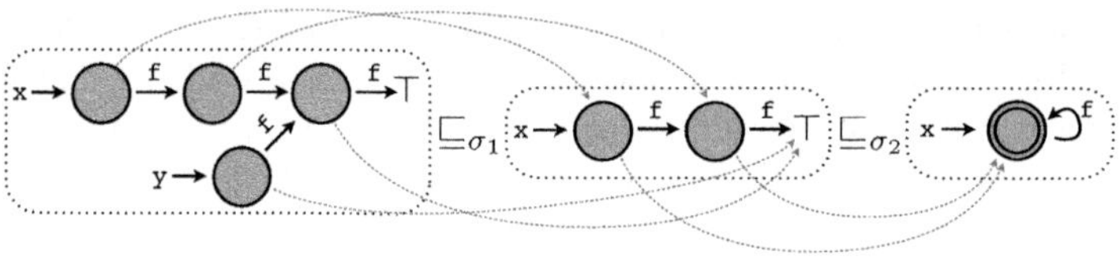

The logical soundness of this sub-typing relation is formally proved with the following theorem.

Theorem 2. *For any type* $T_1, T_2 \in \boldsymbol{T}$ *and state* $\langle \rho, h, A \rangle$, $T_1 \sqsubseteq T_2$ *and* $\langle \rho, h, A \rangle \sim [T_1]$ *imply* $\langle \rho, h, A \rangle \sim [T_2]$.

Proof. See [10] and the companion Coq development.

3.4 Type and Effect System

The type system verifies, statically and class by class, that a program respects the copy policy annotations relative to a declared copy policy. The core of the type system concerns the typability of commands, which is defined through the following judgment:

$$\Gamma, \Delta, \Theta \vdash c : \Gamma', \Delta', \Theta'.$$

The judgment is valid if the execution of command c in a state satisfying type (Γ, Δ, Θ) will result in a state satisfying $(\Gamma', \Delta', \Theta')$ or will diverge.

Typing rules are given in Fig. 7. We explain a selection of rules in the following. The rules for *if* $(*)$ *then else fi*, *while* $(*)$ *do done*, sequential composition and most of the assignment rules are standard for flow-sensitive type systems. The rule for $x :=$ *new* "allocates" a fresh node n with no edges in the graph Δ and let $\Gamma(x)$ reference this node.

There are two rules concerning the instruction $x.f{:=}y$ for assigning values to fields. If the variable x is represented by node n, then either the node is strong and we update

Command typing rules

$$\frac{}{\Gamma, \Delta, \Theta \vdash x{:=}y : \Gamma[x \mapsto \Gamma(y)], \Delta, \Theta} \qquad \frac{n \text{ fresh in } \Delta}{\Gamma, \Delta, \Theta \vdash x := new\ cn : \Gamma[x \mapsto n], \Delta[(n, \_) \mapsto \bot], \Theta \cup \{n\}}$$

$$\frac{\Gamma(y) = t \qquad t \in \{\top_{out}, \top\}}{[\Gamma, \Delta, \Theta] \vdash x{:=}y.f : \Gamma[x \mapsto t], \Delta, \Theta} \qquad \frac{\Gamma(y) = n}{\Gamma, \Delta, \Theta \vdash x{:=}y.f : \Gamma[x \mapsto \Delta[n, f]], \Delta, \Theta}$$

$$\frac{\Gamma(x) = n \quad n \in \Theta}{\Gamma, \Delta, \Theta \vdash x.f{:=}y : \Gamma, \Delta[n, f \mapsto \Gamma[y]], \Theta}$$

$$\frac{\Gamma(x) = n \quad n \notin \Theta \quad (\Gamma, \Delta[n, f \mapsto \Gamma[y]], \Theta) \sqsubseteq (\Gamma', \Delta', \Theta') \quad (\Gamma, \Delta, \Theta) \sqsubseteq (\Gamma', \Delta', \Theta')}{\Gamma, \Delta, \Theta \vdash x.f{:=}y : \Gamma', \Delta', \Theta'}$$

$$\frac{\begin{array}{ll}\Gamma, \Delta, \Theta \vdash c_1 : \Gamma_1, \Delta_1, \Theta_1 & (\Gamma_1, \Delta_1, \Theta_1) \sqsubseteq (\Gamma', \Delta', \Theta') \\ \Gamma, \Delta, \Theta \vdash c_2 : \Gamma_2, \Delta_2, \Theta_2 & (\Gamma_2, \Delta_2, \Theta_2) \sqsubseteq (\Gamma', \Delta', \Theta')\end{array}}{\Gamma, \Delta, \Theta \vdash if\ (*)\ then\ c_1\ else\ c_2\ fi : \Gamma', \Delta', \Theta'}$$

$$\frac{\Gamma', \Delta', \Theta' \vdash c : \Gamma_0, \Delta_0, \Theta_0 \quad (\Gamma, \Delta, \Theta) \sqsubseteq (\Gamma', \Delta', \Theta') \quad (\Gamma_0, \Delta_0, \Theta_0) \sqsubseteq (\Gamma', \Delta', \Theta')}{\Gamma, \Delta, \Theta \vdash while\ (*)\ do\ c\ done : \Gamma', \Delta', \Theta'}$$

$$\frac{\Gamma, \Delta, \Theta \vdash c_1 : \Gamma_1, \Delta_1, \Theta_1 \quad \Gamma_1, \Delta_1, \Theta_1 \vdash c_2 : \Gamma_2, \Delta_2, \Theta_2}{\Gamma, \Delta, \Theta \vdash c_1; c_2 : \Gamma_2, \Delta_2, \Theta_2}$$

$$\frac{\Pi_p(X) = \tau \quad \Phi(\tau) = (n_\tau, \Delta_\tau) \quad nodes(\Delta) \cap nodes(\Delta_\tau) = \emptyset \quad (\Gamma[y] = \bot) \vee (\Gamma[y] = \top_{out})}{\Gamma, \Delta, \Theta \vdash x{:=}m_{cn:X}(y) : \Gamma[x \mapsto n_\tau], \Delta \cup \Delta_\tau, \Theta \cup \{n_\tau\}}$$

$$\frac{\begin{array}{c}\Pi_p(X) = \tau \quad \Phi(\tau) = (n_\tau, \Delta_\tau) \quad nodes(\Delta) \cap nodes(\Delta_\tau) = \emptyset \\ KillSucc_n(\Gamma, \Delta, \Theta) = (\Gamma', \Delta', \Theta') \quad \Gamma[y] = n\end{array}}{\Gamma, \Delta, \Theta \vdash x{:=}m_{cn:X}(y) : \Gamma'[x \mapsto n_\tau], \Delta' \cup \Delta_\tau, \Theta' \cup \{n_\tau\}}$$

$$\frac{(\Gamma[y] = \bot) \vee (\Gamma[y] = \top_{out})}{\Gamma, \Delta, \Theta \vdash x{:=}?(y) : \Gamma[x \mapsto \top_{out}], \Delta, \Theta} \qquad \frac{KillSucc_n(\Gamma, \Delta, \Theta) = (\Gamma', \Delta', \Theta') \quad \Gamma[y] = n}{\Gamma, \Delta, \Theta \vdash x{:=}?(y) : \Gamma'[x \mapsto \top_{out}], \Delta', \Theta'}$$

$$\Gamma, \Delta, \Theta \vdash return\ x : \Gamma[ret \mapsto \Gamma[x]], \Delta, \Theta$$

Method typing rule

$$\frac{\begin{array}{c}[\cdot \mapsto \bot][x \mapsto \top_{out}], \emptyset, \emptyset \vdash c : \Gamma, \Delta, \Theta \\ \Pi_p(X) = \tau \quad \Phi(\tau) = (n_\tau, \Delta_\tau) \quad (\Gamma, \Delta, \Theta) \sqsubseteq (\Gamma[ret \mapsto n_\tau], \Delta_\tau, \{n_\tau\})\end{array}}{\vdash \mathsf{Copy}(X)\ m(x){:=}c}$$

Program typing rule

$$\frac{\forall cl \in p,\ \forall md \in cl, \quad \vdash md}{\vdash p}$$

Notations: We write $\Delta[(n, \_) \mapsto \bot]$ for the update of Δ with a new node n for which all successors are equal to $\bot$. We write $KillSucc_n$ for the function that removes all nodes reachable from n (with at least one step) and sets all its successors equal to $\top$.

Fig. 7. Type System

(or add) the edge in the graph Δ from node n labeled f to point to the value of $\Gamma(y)$, or it is only weak and we must merge the previous shape with its updated version.

As for method calls, two cases arise depending on whether the method is copy-annotated or not. In each case we must also discuss the type of the argument y. On the one hand, if a method is associated with a copy policy τ, we compute the corresponding type (n_τ, Δ_τ) and type the result of $x{:=}m_{cn:X}(y)$ starting in (Γ, Δ, Θ) with the result type consisting of the environment Γ where x now points to n_τ, the heap described by the disjoint union of Δ and Δ_τ, and the set of strong nodes augmented with n_τ. If y is a locally allocated memory location of type n, we must remove all nodes reachable from n, and set all its successors to $\top$. On the other hand, the method is not associated with a copy policy. If the parameter y is null or not locally allocated we know that x points to a non-locally allocated object. Else y is a locally allocated memory location of type n, and we must kill all its successors in the abstract heap.

Finally, the rule for method definition verifies the coherence of the result of analysing the body of a method m with its copy annotation $\Phi(\tau)$. Type checking extends trivially to all methods of the program.

Note the absence of a rule for typing an instruction $x.f{:=}y$ when $\Gamma(x) = \top$ or $\top_{out}$. In a first attempt, a sound rule would have been

$$\frac{\Gamma(x) = \top}{\Gamma, \Delta \vdash x.f{:=}y : \Gamma, \Delta[\,\cdot, f \mapsto \top]}$$

Because x may point to any part of the local shape we must conservatively forget all knowledge about the field f. Moreover we should also warn the caller of the current method that a field f of his own local shape may have been updated. We choose to simply reject copy methods with such patterns. Such a strong policy has at least the merit to be easily understandable to the programmer: a copy method should only modify locally allocated objects to be typable in our type system. For similar reasons, we reject methods that attempt to make a method call on a reference of type $\top$ because we can not track side effect modifications of such methods without loosing the modularity of the verification mechanism.

We first establish a standard subject reduction theorem and then prove type soundness. We assume that all methods of the considered program are well-typed.

Theorem 3 (Subject Reduction). *Assume* $T_1 \vdash c : T_2$ *and* $\langle \rho_1, h_1, A_1 \rangle \sim [T_1]$. *If* $(c, \langle \rho_1, h_1, A_1 \rangle) \rightsquigarrow \langle \rho_2, h_2, A_2 \rangle$ *then* $\langle \rho_2, h_2, A_2 \rangle \sim [T_2]$.

Theorem 4. *If* $\vdash p$ *then all methods* m *declared in the program* p *are secure.*

For the proofs see [10] and the companion Coq development.

Example 2 (Case Study: `java.util.LinkedList`*).* In this example, we demonstrate the use of the type system on a challenging example taken from the standard Java library. The class `java.util.LinkedList` provides an implementation of doubly-linked lists. A list is composed of a first cell that points through a field `header` to a collection of doubly-linked cells. Each cell has a link to the previous and the next cell and also to an element of (parameterized) type E. The clone method provided in `java.lang` library implements a shallow copy where only cells of type E may be shared between the source and the result of the copy. In Fig. 8 we present a modified version of the original source code: we have inlined all method calls, except those to copy methods and removed exception handling that leads to an abnormal return from methods[5]. Note that one method call in the original code was virtual and hence prevented inlining. Is has been necessary to make a private version of this method. This makes sense because such a virtual call actually constitutes a potentially dangerous hook in a cloning method, as a re-defined implementation could be called when cloning a subclass of `Linkedlist`.

In Fig. 8 we provide several intermediate types that are necessary for typing this method (T_i is the type before executing the instruction at line i). The call to

[5] Inlining is automatically performed by our tool and exception control flow graph is managed as standard control flow but omitted here for simplicity.

```
1 class LinkedList<E> implements Cloneable {
2   private @Deep Entry<E> header;
3
4   private static class Entry<E> {
5     @Shallow E element;
6     @Deep Entry<E> next;
7     @Deep Entry<E> previous;
8   }
9
10  @Copy public Object clone() {
11    LinkedList<E> clone = null;
12    clone = (LinkedList<E>) super.clone();
13    clone.header = new Entry<E>;
14    clone.header.next = clone.header;
15    clone.header.previous = clone.header;
16    Entry<E> e = this.header.next;
17    while (e != this.header) {
18      Entry<E> n = new Entry<E>;
19      n.element = e.element;
20      n.next = clone.header;
21      n.previous = clone.header.previous;
22      n.previous.next = n;
23      n.next.previous = n;
24      e = e.next;
25    }
26    return clone;
27  }
28 }
```

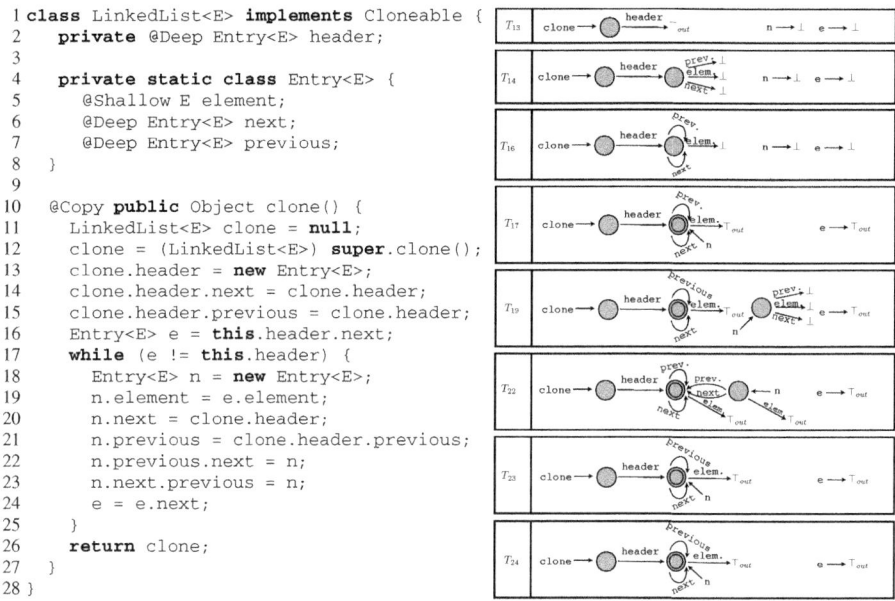

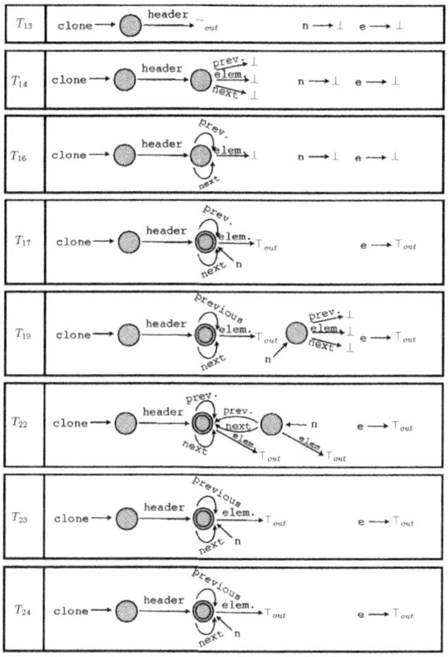

Fig. 8. Intermediate Types for `java.util.LinkedList.clone()`

`super.clone` at line 12 creates a shallow copy of the header cell of the list, which contains a reference to the original list. The original list is thus shared, a fact which is represented by an edge to $\top_{out}$ in type T_{13}.

The copy method then progressively constructs a deep copy of the list, by allocating a new node (see type T_{14}) and setting all paths `clone.header`, `clone.header.next` and `clone.header.previous` to point to this node. This is reflected in the analysis by a *strong update* to the node representing path `clone.header` to obtain the type T_{16} that precisely models the alias between paths `clone.header`, `clone.header.next` and `clone.header.previous` (the Java syntax used here hides the temporary variable that is introduced to be assigned the value of `clone.header` and then be updated).

This type T_{17} is the loop invariant necessary for type checking the whole loop. It is a super-type of T_{16} (updated with $e \mapsto \top_{out}$) and of T_{24} which represents the memory at the end of the loop body. The body of the loop allocates a new list cell (pointed to by variable `n`) (see type T_{19}) and inserts it into the doubly-linked list. The assignment in line 22 updates the weak node pointed to by path `n.previous` and hence merges the strong node pointed to by `n` with the weak node pointed to by `clone.header`, representing the spine of the list. The assignment at line 23 does not modify the type T_{23}.

Notice that the types used in this example show that a flow-insensitive version of the analysis could not have found this information. A flow-insensitive analysis would force the merge of the types at all program points, and the call to `super.clone` return a type that is less precise than the types needed for the analysis of the rest of the method.

4 Inference

In order to type-check a method with the previous type system, it is necessary to infer intermediate types at each loop header and conditional junction points. A standard approach consists in turning the previous typing problem into a fixpoint problem in a suitable sup-semi-lattice structure. This section presents the lattice that we put on $(\boldsymbol{T}, \sqsubseteq)$. Proofs are generally omitted by lack of space but can be found in the companion report. Typability is then checked by computing a suitable least-fixpoint in this lattice. We end this section by proposing a widening operator that is necessary to prevent infinite iterations.

We write $\equiv$ for the equivalence relation defined by $T_1 \equiv T_2$ if and only if $T_1 \sqsubseteq T_2$ and $T_2 \sqsubseteq T_1$. Although this entails that $\sqsubseteq$ is a partial order structure on top of $(\boldsymbol{T}, \equiv)$, equality and order testing remains difficult using only this definition. Instead of considering the quotient of $\boldsymbol{T}$ with $\equiv$, we define a notion of *well-formed* types on which $\sqsubseteq$ is antisymmetric. To do this, we assume that the set of nodes, variable names and field names are countable sets and we note n_i (resp. x_i and f_i) the ith node (resp. variable and field). A type (Γ, Δ, Θ) is *well-formed* if every node in Δ is reachable from a node in Γ and the nodes in Δ follow a canonical numbering based on a breadth-first traversal of the graph. Any type can be *garbage-collected* into a canonical well-formed type by removing all unreachable nodes from variables and renaming all remaining nodes using a fixed strategy based on a total ordering on variable names and field names and a breadth-first traversal. We note GC this transformation. The following example shows the effect of GC using a canonical numbering.

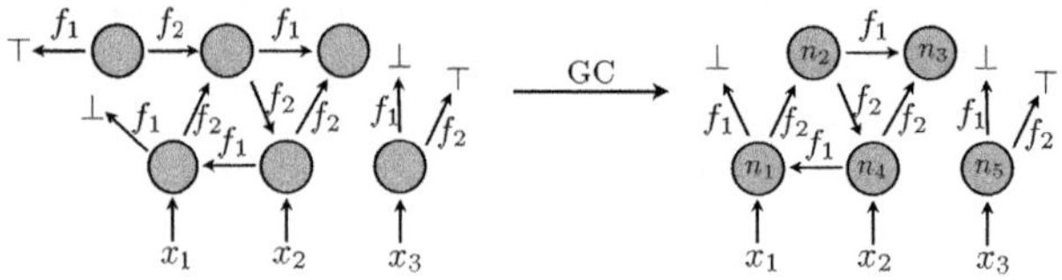

Since by definition, $\sqsubseteq$ only deals with reachable nodes, the GC function is a $\equiv$-morphism and respects type interpretation. This means than inference engine can at any time replace a type by a garbage-collected version. This is useful to perform an equivalence test in order to check fixpoint iteration ending.

Lemma 2. *For all well-formed types* $T_1, T_2 \in \boldsymbol{T}, T_1 \equiv T_2$ *iff* $T_1 = T_2$.

Definition 3. *Let* $\sqcup$ *be an operator that merges two types according to the algorithm in Fig. 9.*

The procedure has $T_1 = (\Gamma_1, \Delta_1, \Theta_1)$ and $T_2 = (\Gamma_2, \Delta_2, \Theta_2)$ as input, then takes the following steps.

1. It first makes the disjunct union of Δ_1 and Δ_2 into a non-deterministic graph (NDG) α, where nodes are labelled by sets of elements in $\boldsymbol{t}$. This operation is performed by the `lift` function, that maps nodes to singleton nodes, and fields to transitions.

```
// Initialization.
// α−nodes are sets in t.
// α−transitions can be
//     non−deterministic.
α = lift(Γ1,Γ2,Δ1 ∪ Δ2)

// Start with environments.
for {(x,t);(x,t′)} ⊆ (Γ1 × Γ2) {
  fusion({t,t′})
}

// Propagate in α.
while ∃f ∈ Field, ∃u ∈ α, |succ(u,f)| > 1 {
  fusion(succ(u,f))
}

// Return to types.
(Γ,Δ,Θ) = ground(Γ1,Γ2,α)
```

```
// N is a set of t ∈ t.
// (|N|) denotes the node in α
//     labelled by the set N.
void fusion (N) {
  α ← α + (|N|)
  for t ∈ N {
    for f ∈ Field {
      if ∃u, α(t,f) = u {
        // Re−route outbound edges.
        α ← α[((|N|),f) ↦ u]
      }
      if ∃n′, α(n′,f) = t {
        // Re−route inbound edges.
        α ← α[(n′,f) ↦ (|N|)]
  }}
  α ← α − u
}}
```

Fig. 9. Join Algorithm

2. It joins together the nodes in α referenced by Γ_i using the `fusion` algorithm[6].
3. Then it scans the NDG and merges all nondeterministic successors of nodes.
4. Finally it uses the `ground` function to recreate a graph Δ from the now-*deterministic* graph α. This function operates by pushing a node set to a node labelled by the $\leq_\sigma$-sup of the set. The result environment Γ is derived from Γ_i and α before the Δ-reconstruction.

All state fusions are recorded in a map σ which binds nodes in $\Delta_1 \cup \Delta_2$ to nodes in Δ.

Theorem 5. *The operator $\sqcup$ defines a sup-semi-lattice on types.*

Proof. See [10].

The poset structure does not enjoy the ascending chain condition. The following chain is an example infinite ascending chain.

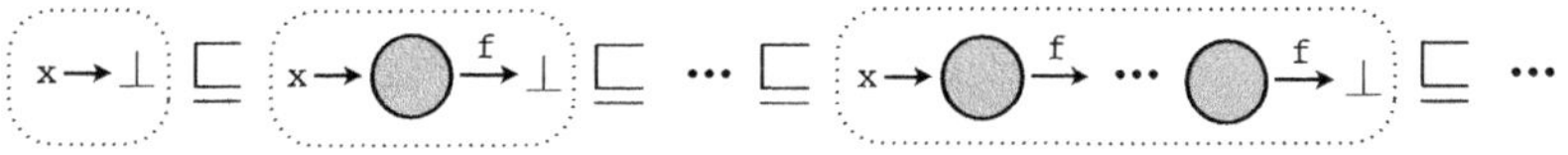

We have then to rely on a widening [7] operator to enforce termination of fixpoint computation. Here we follow a very pragmatic approach and define a widening operator $\nabla \in \boldsymbol{T} \times \boldsymbol{T} \rightarrow \boldsymbol{T}$ that takes the result of $\sqcup$ and that collapses together (with the operator `fusion` defined above) any node n and its predecessors such that the minimal path reaching n and starting from a local variable is of length at least 2.

5 Experiments

The policy language and its enforcement mechanism has been implemented in the form of a security tool for Java byte code. Standard Java `@interface` declarations are used

[6] Remark that Γ_i-bindings are not represented in α, but that node set fusions are trivially traceable. This allows us to safely ignore Γ_i during the following step and still perform a correct graph reconstruction.

to specify native annotations, which enable development environments such as Eclipse or Netbeans to parse, identify and auto-complete @`Shallow`, @`Deep`, and @`Copy` tags. Source code annotations are being made accessible to bytecode analysis frameworks. Both the policy extraction and enforcement components are implemented using the Javalib/Sawja static analysis libraries[7] to derive annotations and intermediate code representations.

In its standard mode, the tool performs a modular verification of annotated classes. We have run experiments on several classes of the standard library (specially in the package `java.util`) and have successfully checked realistic copy signatures for them (see the companion web page for examples). These experiments have also confirmed that the policy enforcement mechanism facilitates re-engineering into more compact implementations of cloning methods in classes with complex dependencies, such as those forming the `gnu.xml.transform` package. For example, in the `Stylesheet` class an inlined implementation of multiple deep copy methods for half a dozen fields can be rewritten to dispatch these functionalities to the relevant classes, while retaining the expected copy policy. This is made possible by the modularity of our enforcement mechanism, which validates calls to external cloning methods as long as their respective policies have been verified. However, some cloning methods will necessarily be beyond the reach of the analysis. We have identified one such method in GNU Classpath's `TreeMap` class, where the merging of information at control flow merge points destroys too much of the inferred type graph. A disjunctive form of abstraction seems necessary to verify a deep copy annotation on such programs and we leave this as a challenging extension.

The analysis is also capable of processing un-annotated methods, albeit with less precision than when copy policies are available—this is because it cannot rely on annotations to infer external copy method types. Nevertheless, this capability allows us to test our tool on two large code bases. The 17000 classes in Sun's `rt.jar` and the 7000 in the GNU Classpath have passed our scanner un-annotated. Among the 459 `clone()` methods we found in these classes, only 15 have been rejected because of an illegal assignment or method call and we were unable to infer the minimal signatures $\{\}$ (the same signature as `java.lang.Object.clone()`) in 78 methods. Our prototype confirms the efficiency of the enforcement technique because all these verifications took only 25s on a laptop computer.

Our prototype, the Coq formalization and proofs, as well as examples of annotated classes can be found at `http://www.irisa.fr/celtique/ext/clones`.

6 Related Work

Several proposals for programmer-oriented annotations of Java programs have been published following Bloch's initial proposal of an annotation framework for the Java language [4]. These proposals define the syntax of the annotations but often leave their exact semantics unspecified. A notable exception is the set of annotations concerning non-null annotations [8] for which a precise semantic characterization has emerged [9]. Concerning security, the GlassFish environment in Java offers program annotations of

[7] `http://sawja.inria.fr`

members of a class (such as `@DenyAll` or `@RolesAllowed`) for implementing role-based access control to methods.

To the best of our knowledge, the current paper is the first to propose a formal, semantically founded framework for secure cloning through program annotation and static enforcement. The closest work in this area is that of Anderson *et al.* [2] who have designed an annotation system for C data structures in order to control sharing between threads. Annotation policies are enforced by a mix of static and run-time verification. On the run-time verification side, their approach requires an operator that can dynamically "cast" a cell to an unshared structure. In contrast, our approach offers a completely static mechanism with statically guaranteed alias properties.

Aiken *et al.* proposes an analysis for checking and inferring local non-aliasing of data [1]. They propose to annotate C function parameters with the keyword `restrict` to ensure that no other aliases to the data referenced by the parameter are used during the execution of the method. A type and effect system is defined for enforcing this discipline statically. This analysis differs from ours in that it allows aliases to exist as long as they are not used whereas we aim at providing guarantees that certain parts of memory are without aliases. The properties tracked by our type system are close to escape analysis [3,6] but the analyses differ in their purpose. While escape analysis tracks locally allocated objects and tries to detect those that do not escape after the end of a method execution, we are specifically interested in tracking locally allocated objects that escape from the result of a method, as well as analyse their dependencies with respect to parameters.

Our static enforcement technique falls within the large area of static verification of heap properties. A substantial amount of research has been conducted here, the most prominent being region calculus [14], separation logic [11] and shape analysis [12]. Of these three approaches, shape analysis comes closest in its use of shape graphs. Shape analysis is a large framework that allows to infer complex properties on heap allocated data-structures like absence of dangling pointers in C or non-cyclicity invariants. In this approach, heap cells are abstracted by shape graphs with flexible object abstractions. Graph nodes can either represent a single cell, hence allowing strong updates, or several cells (summary nodes). *Materialization* allows to split a summary node during cell access in order to obtain a node pointing to a single cell. The shape graphs that we use are not intended to do full shape analysis but are rather specialized for tracking sharing in locally allocated objects. We use a different naming strategy for graph nodes and discard all information concerning non-locally allocated references. This leads to an analysis which is more scalable than full shape analysis, yet still powerful enough for verifying complex copy policies as demonstrated in the concrete case study `java.util.LinkedList`.

7 Conclusions and Perspectives

Cloning of objects is an important aspect of exchanging data with untrusted code. Current language technology for cloning does not provide adequate means for defining and enforcing a secure copy policy statically; a task which is made more difficult by important object-oriented features such as inheritance and re-definition of cloning methods.

We have presented a flow-sensitive type system for statically enforcing copy policies defined by the software developer through simple program annotations. The annotation formalism is compatible with the inheritance-based object oriented programing language and deals with dynamic method dispatch. The verification technique is designed to enable modular verification of individual classes, in order to provide a framework that can form part of an extended, security-enhancing Java byte code verifier. By specifically targeting the verification of copy methods, we consider a problem for which it is possible to deploy a localized version of shape analysis that avoids the complexity of a full shape analysis framework.

The present paper constitutes the formal foundations for a secure cloning framework. All theorems except those of Section 4 have been mechanized in the Coq proof assistant. Mechanization has been of great help to get right the soundness arguments but has been made particularly challenging because of the storeless nature of our type interpretation.

Several issues merit further investigations in order to develop a full-fledged software security verification tool. In the current approach, virtual methods without copy policy annotations are considered as black boxes that may modify any object reachable from its arguments. An extension of our copy annotations to virtual calls should be worked out if we want to enhance our enforcement technique and accept more secure copying methods. More advanced verifications will be possible if we develop a richer form of type signatures for methods where the formal parameters may occur in copy policies, in order to express a relation between copy properties of returning objects and parameter fields. The challenge here is to provide sufficiently expressive signatures which at the same time remain humanly readable software contracts. The current formalisation has been developed for a sequential model of Java. We believe that the extension to interleaving multi-threading semantics would be feasible without major changes to the type system because we only manipulate thread-local pointers. Spelling out the formal details of this argument is left for further work.

References

1. Aiken, A., Foster, J.S., Kodumal, J., Terauchi, T.: Checking and inferring local non-aliasing. In: Proc. of PLDI 2003, pp. 129–140. ACM Press, New York (2003)
2. Anderson, Z., Gay, D., Naik, M.: Lightweight annotations for controlling sharing in concurrent data structures. In: Proc. of PLDI 2009, pp. 98–109. ACM Press, New York (2009)
3. Blanchet, B.: Escape analysis for object-oriented languages: Application to Java. In: Proc. of OOPSLA, pp. 20–34. ACM Press, New York (1999)
4. Bloch, J.: JSR 175: A metadata facility for the Java programming language, September 30 (2004), `http://jcp.org/en/jsr/detail?id=175`
5. CERT. The CERT Sun Microsystems Secure Coding Standard for Java (2010), `https://www.securecoding.cert.org`
6. Choi, J.D., Gupta, M., Serrano, M.J., Sreedhar, V.C., Midkiff, S.P.: Escape analysis for java. In: Proc. of OOPSLA, pp. 1–19. ACM Press, New York (1999)
7. Cousot, P., Cousot, R.: Abstract interpretation: a unified lattice model for static analysis of programs by construction or approximation of fixpoints. In: Proc. of POPL 1977, pp. 238–252. ACM Press, New York (1977)
8. Fähndrich, M., Leino, K.R.M.: Declaring and checking non-null types in an object-oriented language. In: Proc. of OOPSLA 2003, pp. 302–312. ACM Press, New York (2003)

9. Hubert, L., Jensen, T., Pichardie, D.: Semantic foundations and inference of non-null annotations. In: Barthe, G., de Boer, F.S. (eds.) FMOODS 2008. LNCS, vol. 5051, pp. 132–149. Springer, Heidelberg (2008)
10. Jensen, T., Kirchner, F., Pichardie, D.: Secure the clones, Extended version (2010), http://www.irisa.fr/celtique/ext/clones
11. O'Hearn, P.W., Yang, H., Reynolds, J.C.: Separation and information hiding. In: Proc. of POPL 2004, pp. 268–280. ACM Press, New York (2004)
12. Sagiv, S., Reps, T.W., Wilhelm, R.: Parametric shape analysis via 3-valued logic. ACM Trans. Program. Lang. Syst. 24(3), 217–298 (2002)
13. Sun Develper Network. Secure Coding Guidelines for the Java Programming Language, version 3.0 (2010), http://java.sun.com/security/seccodeguide.html
14. Tofte, M., Talpin, J.-P.: Region-based memory management. Information and Computation 132(2), 109–176 (1997)

Biochemical Reaction Rules with Constraints

Mathias John[1,2], Cédric Lhoussaine[1,2],
Joachim Niehren[1,3], and Cristian Versari[4]

[1] BioComputing, LIFL (CNRS UMR8022) & IRI (CNRS USR3078)
[2] University of Lille 1
[3] INRIA, Lille
[4] University of Bologna

Abstract. We propose *React*(C), an expressive programming language for stochastic modeling and simulation in systems biology that is based on biochemical reactions with constraints. We prove that *React*(C) can express the stochastic π-calculus, in contrast to previous rule-based programming languages, and further illustrate the high expressiveness of *React*(C). We present a stochastic simulator for *React*(C) independently of the choice of the constraint language C. Our simulator decides for a given reaction rule whether it can be applied to the current biochemical solution. We show that this decision problem is NP-complete for arbitrary constraint systems C and that it can be solved in polynomial time for rules of bounded arity. In practice, we propose to solve this problem by constraint programming.

1 Introduction

The paradigm of chemical reactions is predominant in programming languages used for modeling and simulation in systems biology [6,9,3,19,1]. Chemical reactions are advantageous in that they can be given both, a continuous semantics in terms of ordinary differential equations (ODEs) as well as a stochastic semantics in terms of continuous time Markov chains (CTMCs). While ODEs describe deterministically the average dynamics of molecule populations, CTMCs describe the probabilities and speed of molecular interactions in an individual-based manner. The continuous semantics of a system of chemical reactions is an abstraction of its more precise stochastic semantics.

Biochemical reactions in the κ-calculus are widely accepted as a useful modeling language for systems biology [4,12,5,6]. The underlying idea is to model biochemical reactions as graph rewrite rules. The following rewrite rule, for instance, states that a C-molecule with a free binding site 1 can be linked to an A-B complex by using the free binding site 1 of A (while the complex uses binding sites 2 of A and 1 of B).

$$A(1+2^y), B(1^y), C(1) \xrightarrow{4.5} (\nu x)A(1^x+2^y), B(1^y), C(1^x)$$

The stochastic rate 4.5 determines the distribution of the speed of this interactions according to the law of mass-action.

G. Barthe (Ed.): ESOP 2011, LNCS 6602, pp. 338–357, 2011.
© Springer-Verlag Berlin Heidelberg 2011

The alternative paradigm of agent-based modeling languages attracted also much interest for modeling and simulation in systems biology. It underlies the stochastic π-calculus and its many extensions, [18,21,14,17,23,11], BioAmbients [20], BlenX or beta-binders [22], etc. The close relationship between modeling languages of both paradigms was first pointed out by Cardelli [2]. He identified the fragment of the stochastic π-calculus without ν-binders with systems of chemical reactions with the same CTMCs in order to obtain a continuous semantics of π-calculus processes in terms of ODEs. So far, however, there exists no positive result showing the expressiveness of the stochastic π-calculus for any language of chemical reactions. There exists a result for the π-calculus without stochastic semantics, which was shown equally expressive to the join calculus, a programming language based on chemical reaction rules, by Fournet et. al. [7]. Unfortunately, the encoding presented cannot be adapted to a stochastic setting in any obvious manner. Conversely, Danos and Laneve [6] showed that binary reaction rules of the κ-calculus without ν-binders on the left-hand side can be encoded in the π-calculus. The stochastic semantics is preserved as shown in [15]. A main limitation of the κ-calculus compared to the π-calculus is the restriction to graph rather than hypergraph rewriting.

In this paper we present *React*(C), a language of biochemical reaction rules with constraints. *React*(C) extends on the κ-calculus by hyperedge rewriting in particular. The graph rewrite rule from the κ-calculus above, for instance, can be written as follows, where `free` is a constant standing for a free binding site:

$$A(\texttt{free}; y), B(y), C(\texttt{free}) \xrightarrow{4.5} (\nu x)\ A(x; y), B(y), C(x)$$

Note that names of binding sites are identified by positions in *React*(C). The usefulness of hypergraph rewriting can be illustrated at modeling compartments, where the natural idea is to attribute each molecule by its compartment's name, i.e., to introduce a hyperedge per compartment that links all its molecules. One can then constrain reactions to happen only within a same compartment. For instance, consider a dimerization reaction between two A-molecules in the same compartment x:

$$A(x, \texttt{free}), A(x, \texttt{free}) \xrightarrow{3.1} (\nu z) A(x; z), A(x; z)$$

Variables with numeric values and arithmetic constraints are supported by *React*(C) too. These are useful for modeling dynamic volumes of compartments and to cope with alternative kinetics as those of the π-calculus. Simpler finite domain constraints were proposed for biological modeling in [13] and in BioCham. The following reaction rule for instance states that a polymerase bound at the *DNA* nucleotide with position x can advance to the next nucleotide at position $y = x + 1$ if x belongs to the finite domain $\{1, \ldots 47\} \setminus \{37\}$. The speed is given by the law of Mass action with a stochastic rate of 4.5.

$$\forall x \in \{1, \ldots 47\} \setminus \{37\}.\ Pol(x), \textsc{Dna}(y) \xrightarrow{\texttt{if } y=x+1 \texttt{ then } 4.5 \texttt{ else } 0} \textsc{Dna}(x), Pol(y)$$

Finally, *React*(C) enables general kinetics beside Mass action and Michaelis-Menten. Note that BioCham [3] and SBML [9] support both these kinetics but neither variables nor ν-binders.

Our main technical contribution is a proof that *React*(C) can indeed express the stochastic π-calculus, even if restricted to binary reaction rules with equality constraints and arithmetics on real numbers. This result is relevant since the π-calculus is the usual yardstick for the expressiveness of concurrent languages. Our result also illustrates that *React*(C) can express extensions of the stochastic π-calculus with constraints such as π@ [23] (without priorities) and the attributed π-calculus [11]. This means that all previous models in these languages carry over to *React*(C) in a systematic manner. Hyperedges and constraints thus provide the missing link between rule-based and agent-based modeling languages.

We present a stochastic simulation algorithm for *React*(C) that is independent of the choice of the constraint language C. Our simulator must decide for a given reaction rule whether it can be applied to the current biochemical solution. We show that this decision problem is NP-complete for arbitrary constraint systems C and that it can be solved in polynomial time for rules of bounded arity. In practice, we propose to solve this problem by constraint programming.

Our hardness proof relies on hypergraphs, so it does not apply to the κ-calculus. Indeed, the so called rigidity property of the κ-calculus (Lemma 3 of [5]) fails for *React*(C). Rigidity states that a matching of a connected pattern is entirely determined by matching only a single one of its molecules. It implies that the matching problem for the κ-calculus restricted to rules with connected patterns can be solved in P-time. The general case with multiple connected components remains open. We leave it also open whether the scalable simulation algorithm for the κ-calculus from [5] can be lifted to *React*(C) in any sense.

Outline. We start with a small language *React*$^=$ of biochemical reaction rules with equality constraints in Section 2 and show that it can express the stochastic π-calculus in Section 3 and 4. The main remaining problem not discussed so far, is to link stochastic mass-actions semantics with redex based stochastic semantics as in the stochastic π-calculus. The full language *React*(C) is presented in Section 5 and our simulation algorithm based on constraint programming in Section 6.

2 Reaction Rules with Equality Constraints

We present a small language of biochemical reaction rules with equality constraints *React*$^=$ that can express the stochastic π-calculus. We equip *React*$^=$ with a stochastic semantics that follows the usual law of Mass action.

We assume a signature $\mathcal{A}$ of molecule names $A \in \mathcal{A}$, each of which has a fixed arity in $ar(A) \in \mathbb{N}_0$. We also assume an infinite set $\mathcal{N}$ of (link) names ranged over by x, y and write $\tilde{x}$ for a possibly empty sequence of names $x_1; \ldots; x_n$. A molecule a is a term $A(\tilde{x})$ with $n = ar(A)$.

We define the biochemical solutions of *React*$^=$ in Fig. 1 as terms s that are constructed from molecules $A(\tilde{x})$, the composition operator s, s', and the empty solution $\mathbf{0}$. We often think of a biochemical solution as a (hyper-) graph of molecules that are linked by (hyper-) edges. For instance $A(x), B(x)$ describes the graph with two nodes $A(x)$ and $B(x)$ linked by a single edge named x. Such

Solutions	$s ::= A(\tilde{x}) \mid s, s' \mid \mathbf{0}$	where $A \in \mathcal{A}$, $\tilde{x} \in \mathcal{N}$
Rate expressions	$e ::= \texttt{if } x_1{=}x_2 \texttt{ then } e_1 \texttt{ else } e_2$	where $x_1, x_2 \in \mathcal{N}$
	$\mid e_1 + e_2 \mid e_1 * e_2 \mid d$	and $d \in \mathbb{R}_0^+$
Reaction rules	$r ::= s \xrightarrow{e} (\nu\tilde{x})s'$	where $fn(r) = fn(s)$
Reactions	$\rho ::= s \xrightarrow{d} s'$	

Fig. 1. Syntax of reaction rules of language $React^{=}$

Precongruence	$(s_1, s_2), s_3 \approx s_1, (s_2, s_3)$	$s_1, s_2 \approx s_2, s_1$	$s, \mathbf{0} \approx s$
Congruence	$\dfrac{s \approx s' \quad \sigma : \mathcal{N} \to \mathcal{N} \text{ injective}}{s \equiv s'\sigma}$		

Fig. 2. Precongruence and congruence on solutions

graphs do neither depend on the order of molecules nor on the concrete choice of link names. For instance, the same graph is obtained by solutions $B(y), A(y)$ and $A(x), B(x)$.

In Fig. 2, we define two congruence relations on solutions. The precongruence $\approx$ captures order independence. It is the least equivalence relation on solutions that renders the composition operator "," associative and commutative with the neutral element $\mathbf{0}$. We write $[s]_{\approx}$ for the equivalence class of a solution s. Clearly, we can identify precongruence classes with multisets of molecules. The weaker congruence relation $\equiv$ accounts for the irrelevance of concrete names in addition. It is defined such that $s \equiv s'$ if and only if there exists a solution $s'' \approx s$ and an injective function $\sigma : \mathcal{N} \to \mathcal{N}$ such that $s' = s''\sigma$, i.e., the term obtained by renaming all names x in s'' to $\sigma(x)$.

We write $fn(s)$ for the set of names occurring in s. As usual, we define iterated compositions $\prod_{i=1}^{0} s_i = \mathbf{0}$, $\prod_{i=1}^{n} s_i = (\prod_{i=1}^{n-1} s_i), s_n$, and $s^m = \prod_{i=1}^{m} s$. If $a_1, \ldots, a_n$ are pairwise distinct molecules then we define $\dot{\prod}_{i=1}^{n} a_i^{m_i} = \prod_{i=1}^{n} a_i^{m_i}$. Modulo precongruence, this term stands for the multiset with m_i occurrences of molecule a_i.

Reactions ρ are terms of the form $s_1 \xrightarrow{d} s_2$. They can be applied to rewrite solutions congruent to s, s_1 to some solution congruent to s, s_2:

$$(\text{REACT})\ \frac{s_1' \equiv s, s_1 \quad s, s_2 \equiv s_2'}{s_1 \xrightarrow{d} s_2 \vdash s_1' \to s_2'}$$

Judgements $\rho \vdash s_1' \to s_2'$ capture the non-deterministic semantics of reactions. Note that the rate constant d is irrelevant here; it matters in the stochastic semantics only, see below.

Reaction rules r are terms of the form $s \xrightarrow{e} (\nu\tilde{x})s'$. They are to be understood as schemas that define sets of reactions, one reaction per substitution

$$(\text{COND}_1)\ \frac{e_1 \Downarrow d_1}{\texttt{if } x{=}x \texttt{ then } e_1 \texttt{ else } e_2 \Downarrow d_1} \qquad (\text{COND}_2)\ \frac{x_1 \neq x_2 \quad e_2 \Downarrow d_2}{\texttt{if } x_1{=}x_2 \texttt{ then } e_1 \texttt{ else } e_2 \Downarrow d_2}$$

$$(\text{REALS})\ \frac{d \in \mathbb{R}_0^+}{d \Downarrow d} \qquad (+)\ \frac{e_1 \Downarrow d_1 \quad e_2 \Downarrow d_2}{e_1 + e_2 \Downarrow d_1 +^{\mathbb{R}} d_2} \qquad (*)\ \frac{e_1 \Downarrow d_1 \quad e_2 \Downarrow d_2}{e_1 * e_2 \Downarrow d_1 *^{\mathbb{R}} d_2}$$

Fig. 3. Big-step evaluator of rate expressions

$$(\text{INST})\ \frac{\sigma : fn(s) \to N \quad \sigma' : \{\tilde{x}\} \to \mathcal{N} \backslash (N \cup fn(s)) \text{ injective} \quad e\sigma \Downarrow d}{s \xrightarrow{e} (\nu\tilde{x})s' \Downarrow_{\sigma,N} s\sigma \xrightarrow{d} s'\sigma'\sigma}$$

Fig. 4. Instantiation and evaluation of reactions rules to reactions

$\sigma : \mathcal{N} \to \mathcal{N}$. Reaction rules contain a rate expressions e. Substitutions σ instantiating the rule are applied to e before evaluation, yielding another rate expression that we denote by $e\sigma$. Before formalizing the semantics of reaction rules, we need to define the values of rate expressions.

A rate expression e is a term built from constants $d \in \mathbb{R}_0^+$, addition $e+e$, multiplication $e * e$, and rate-valued equality constraints $\texttt{if } x_1{=}x_2 \texttt{ then } e_1 \texttt{ else } e_2$. We write $fn(e)$ for the set of names occurring in e and *Exprs* for the set of all rate expressions. Usual Boolean-valued constraints are subsumed, as for instance the conjunctive equality and inequality constraints $x{=}y \wedge y{\neq}z$ by rate expression $\texttt{if } x{=}y \texttt{ then } (\texttt{if } y{=}z \texttt{ then } 0 \texttt{ else } 1) \texttt{ else } 0$. In Fig. 3, we define an evaluator for rate expressions $\Downarrow$: $\mathit{Exprs} \to \mathbb{R}_0^+$ as usual. Note that this evaluator always terminates: neither there exist program errors nor non-termination.

A reaction rule $r = s \xrightarrow{e} (\nu\tilde{x})s'$ uses the new operator $(\nu\tilde{x})$ that binds the names in $\tilde{x}$ with scope s' similarly to the new operator of the π-calculus. It requires the creation of new names $\tilde{x}$ with scope s'. Being new means to not occur in the current solution to which the rule is applied. The free names of $(\nu\tilde{x})s'$ are thus defined by $fn((\nu\tilde{x})s') = fn(s') \setminus \{\tilde{x}\}$, and the free names of the reaction rule by $fn(r) = fn(s) \cup fn(e) \cup fn((\nu\tilde{x})s')$.

The instantiation (INST) of a reaction rule $r = s \xrightarrow{e} (\nu\tilde{x})s'$ to some reaction is defined in Fig. 4. There, we assume that $N \subseteq \mathcal{N}$ is a finite set of names – this will be the set of names of the current chemical reaction – and that $\sigma : fn(s) \to N$ is a substitution. Even though the domain of σ is restricted to $fn(s)$ we can still apply σ to r, since $fn(r) = fn(s)$ is assumed in the syntax of $\mathit{React}^{=}$. As a consequence, there exist only finitely many such substitutions and thus only finitely many rule instances to be considered (for some fixed new-name generator). The application of σ to r is defined as follows. First, some new-name generator $\sigma' : \{\tilde{x}\} \to \mathcal{N} \setminus (N \cup fn(s))$ introduces new names fresh for N and $fn(s)$ on r.h.s. of r, second, substitution σ is applied to the resulting rule, third, the expression $e\sigma$ is evaluated to some real number d. In this case, we say that r can be instantiated ρ by σ and N, where $\rho = s\sigma \xrightarrow{d} s'\sigma'\sigma$, and write $r \Downarrow_{\sigma,N} \rho$.

$$(\text{COUNT})\ \frac{s \approx \prod_{i=1}^{n} a_i^{m_i} \quad s' \approx \prod_{i=1}^{n+m} a_i^{m'_i}}{count(s;s') = \prod_{i=1}^{n} \binom{m'_i}{m_i}} \qquad (\text{REACT}_{\text{MA}})\ \frac{s'_1 \approx s, s_1 \quad s, s_2 \equiv s'_2}{s_1 \xrightarrow{d} s_2 \vdash s'_1 \xrightarrow{d * count(s_1;s'_1)} s'_2}$$

$$(\text{RULES}_{\text{MA}})\ \frac{s_1 \equiv s'_1 \quad d = \sum_{r \in R} \sum_{\{(d',\sigma) \ \mid \ r \Downarrow_{\sigma, fn(s'_1)} \rho,\ \rho \vdash s'_1 \xrightarrow{d'} s_2\}} d'}{R \vdash s_1 \xrightarrow[\text{MA}]{d} s_2}$$

Fig. 5. Stochastic mass-action semantics of $React^{=}$

The non-deterministic semantics of a reaction rule can now be defined by reduction to the non-deterministic semantics of reactions:

$$(\text{RULE})\ \frac{r \Downarrow_{\sigma, fn(s)} \rho \quad \rho \vdash s \rightarrow s'}{r \vdash s \rightarrow s'}$$

The set of free names of the current solution s is passed over to the instantiator $r \Downarrow_{\sigma, fn(s)} \rho$, in order to ensure that new-bound names are instantiated by fresh names for the current solution. Recall that only finitely many substitutions $\sigma : fn(r) \rightarrow fn(s)$ are to be considered. These are the possible matchings of the left hand side of the rule with the current solution.

The stochastic semantics of $React(C)$ in Fig. 5 refines the non-deterministic semantics. The rate of a reaction rule now determines the probability and speed of its application according to the law of mass action. Inference rule (COUNT) defines $count(s; s')$ which is the number of occurrences of multiset $[s]_{\approx}$ in multiset $[s']_{\approx}$. Note that it has a unique value independently of the choice of s and s' in their congruence class, i.e. the ordering on the multiset elements imposed by s and s' does not affect the result. Furthermore, recall that $\binom{m}{m'} = 0$ if $m' > m$, so that $count(s; s') = 0$ if multiset $[s]_{\approx}$ is not contained in $[s']_{\approx}$. Inference rule (REACT_{MA}) states how to apply a reaction rule $s_1 \xrightarrow{d} s_2$ to a solution s'_1. This works as in the non-deterministic case (REACT) except that an application rate $d * count(s_1; s'_1)$ is computed. Inference rule (RULES_{MA}) describes applications of systems of chemical reactions R to a given solution s while producing s'. The situation is analoguous to the non-deterministic semantics in (RULE) except that we now have to sum up the application rates d' of all instantiations σ of reaction rules in R to reactions that can reduce s to s'.

The stochastic semantics of $React(C)$ defines a CTMC for each set of chemical reactions. The states of this Markov chain are equivalence classes $[s]_{\equiv}$ of solutions s modulo full congruence. Its state transitions are obtained by applying reactions rules according to rule (RULES_{MA}). That is, reaction rates of all instantiations of rules in R that lead to the same state $[s]_{\equiv}$ are summed up providing the rate of a single transition. Note that the precongruence must be used while counting (since different renamings should not be counted). Consider, e.g., solution $s = A(x), A(y)$ and rule $r = A(x_1), A(x_2) \xrightarrow{2.1} A(x_1)$. For r we obtain two possible instantiations $\sigma = \{(x_1, x), (x_2, y)\}$ and $\sigma' = \{(x_1, y), (x_2, x)\}$ both leading to the same state $[s']_{\equiv} = [s'']_{\equiv}$ where $s' = A(x)$ and $s'' = A(y)$. Thus, we obtain one transition $[s]_{\equiv} \xrightarrow{4.2} [s']_{\equiv}$.

$$(\text{RED})\quad \frac{s_1 = \prod_{i=1}^{n} a_i \quad s_2 = \prod_{i=1}^{n'} a'_i}{\mathit{redex}(s_1; s_2) = \{\ell : \{1,\dots,n\} \to \{1,\dots,n'\} \text{ injective} \mid a'_{\ell(i)} = a_i \text{ for all } i \in \{1,\dots,n\}\}}$$

$$(\text{REACT}_{\text{RED}})\quad \frac{s'_1 \approx s, s_1 \quad s, s_2 \equiv s'_2 \quad d \in \mathbb{R}^+ \quad \ell \in \mathit{redex}(s_1; s'_1)}{s_1 \xrightarrow{d} s_2 \vdash s'_1 \xrightarrow[\ell]{d} s'_2}$$

$$(\text{RULES}_{\text{RED}})\quad \frac{s'_1 \equiv s_1 \quad d = \sum_{r \in R} \sum_{\{(d',\ell) \mid r \Downarrow_{\sigma,\mathit{fn}(s'_1)} \rho,\ \rho \vdash s'_1 \xrightarrow[\ell]{d'} s_2\}} d'}{R \vdash s_1 \xrightarrow[\text{RED}]{d} s_2}$$

Fig. 6. Stochastic redex semantics of language $\mathit{React}^{=}_{\text{RED}}$

3 An Alternative Stochastic Semantics

We provide an alternative stochastic semantics for systems of reaction rules in the small language that is based on redexes in analogy to the usual semantics of the stochastic π-calculus. We call the small language with the redex semantics $\mathit{React}^{=}_{\text{RED}}$ and show that $\mathit{React}^{=}_{\text{RED}}$ can be encoded into $\mathit{React}^{=}$ while preserving CTMCs. This encoding will provide the first part of our encoding of the stochastic π-calculus into $\mathit{React}^{=}$.

The particularity of a redex semantics is that it treats solutions as lists in some fixed order. It then enumerates all redexes by which a smaller list can be mapped into a larger list. A redex of a solution $s_1 = \prod_{i=1}^{n} a_i$ in a solution $s_2 = \prod_{i=1}^{n'} a'_i$ is an injective function $\ell : \{1,\dots,n\} \to \{1,\dots,n'\}$, such that $a'_{\ell(i)} = a_i$ for all $i \in \{1,\dots,n\}$. Note that ℓ depends on the order of molecules in s_1 and s_2. For instance, solution A, A has two redexes in itself, $\ell_1 = \{(1,1),(2,2)\}$ and $\ell_2 = \{(1,2),(2,1)\}$, even though $\mathit{count}(A,A;A,A) = \binom{2}{2} = 1$. The reason is that the notion of redexes is order sensitive in contrast to the notion of multiset inclusion on which function *count* used in the Mass action semantics is based.

The stochastic redex semantics rules are given in Fig. 6. The language of reaction rules with this semantics is called $\mathit{React}^{=}_{\text{RED}}$. Definition (RED) introduces the set $\mathit{redex}(s_1; s_2)$ of all redexes by which s_1 matches s_2. Inference rule ($\text{REACT}_{\text{RED}}$) applies a reaction at a redex to a solution. Rule ($\text{RULES}_{\text{RED}}$) treats the application of all instances of reaction rules to a solution. Notice that in contrast to rule (RULES_{MA}) of $\mathit{React}^{=}$, rule ($\text{RULES}_{\text{RED}}$) does not consider substitutions to identify rule instances, since redexes can be used for this purpose equally well.

Lemma 1. *For all r, ℓ, and s there exists at most one σ, such that $r \Downarrow_{\sigma,\mathit{fn}(s)} \rho$ and $\rho \vdash s \xrightarrow[\ell]{d} s'$.*

Proof. Let r be the rule $s_1 \xrightarrow{e} (\nu\tilde{x})s_2$. Since $r \Downarrow_{\sigma,\mathit{fn}(s)} \rho$, rule (INST) provides that $\sigma : \mathit{fn}(s_1) \to \mathit{fn}(s)$. By the definition of rule ($\text{REACT}_{\text{RED}}$), for all names $x \in \mathit{fn}(s_1)$ it holds that the values $\sigma(x)$ are uniquely determined by ℓ and S. $\square$

$$\llbracket s \xrightarrow{e} (\nu\tilde{x})s' \rrbracket =_{\text{def}} s \xrightarrow{\llbracket e \rrbracket_s} (\nu\tilde{x})s'$$

$$\llbracket e \rrbracket_{\prod_{i=1}^{n} A_i(\tilde{x}_i)} =_{\text{def}} e * \prod_{i=1}^{n} \sum_{j=i}^{n} \mathsf{eq}(A_i(\tilde{x}_i); A_j(\tilde{x}_j)), \text{ with}$$

$$\mathsf{eq}(A_1(\tilde{x}_1); A_2(\tilde{x}_2)) =_{\text{def}} \begin{cases} 0 & \text{if } A_1 \neq A_2 \\ \mathsf{eq}'(\tilde{x}_1; \tilde{x}_2) & \text{if } A_1 = A_2 \end{cases}$$

$$\mathsf{eq}'((x_1; \tilde{x}_1); (x_2; \tilde{x}_2)) =_{\text{def}} \texttt{if } x_1 = x_1' \texttt{ then } \mathsf{eq}'(\tilde{x}_1; \tilde{x}_2) \texttt{ else } 0$$

$$\mathsf{eq}'((); ()) =_{\text{def}} 1$$

Fig. 7. Encoding from $React^{=}_{\text{RED}}$ to $React^{=}$

In order to find an encoding from $React^{=}_{\text{RED}}$ to $React^{=}$, we need to quantify the discrepancy between $count(s_1; s_2)$ and the cardinality $\#redex(s_1, s_2)$. Since redexes are order sensitive, this is given by the difference between a combination without repetition (Mass action) and a variation without repetition (redexes). That is for each molecule a_i in a solution $\prod_{i=1}^{n} a_i$ the number of positions $i' > i$ need to be counted, where $a_i = a_{i'}$. In a solution $s \approx \prod_{i=1}^{n} a_i^{m_i}$ this number is given by $m_i!$ for molecule a_i.

Lemma 2. *For all solutions $s \approx \prod_{i=1}^{n} a_i^{m_i}$, $s' \approx \prod_{i=1}^{n+m} a_i^{m'_i}$ such that $m_i \leq m'_i$ for all $i \in \{1, \ldots, n\}$:*

$$\#redex(s; s') = \prod_{i=1}^{n} \binom{m'_i}{m_i} * m_i! = count(s; s') * \prod_{i=1}^{n} m_i!$$

Based on a claim that the number of redexes does not depend on the concrete order fixed by a solution, the proof is straightforward by induction on n.

We present the encoding $\llbracket\cdot\rrbracket : React^{=}_{\text{RED}} \to React^{=}$ in Fig. 7. The basic idea is to balance the difference between Mass action and redex quantification by counting the number of permutations of molecule places in solution lists according to the ideas above. Our encoding from $React^{=}_{\text{RED}}$ to $React^{=}$ is correct, in that it preserves CTMCs.

Proposition 1. *The encoding $\llbracket\cdot\rrbracket : React^{=}_{\text{RED}} \to React^{=}$ preserves the* CTMC, *in that for all rule sets $R \in React^{=}_{\text{RED}}$ and solutions s it holds $R \vdash s \xrightarrow[\text{RED}]{d} s'$ if and only if $\llbracket R \rrbracket \vdash s \xrightarrow[\text{MA}]{d} s'$.*

The proof basically proceeds by structural induction on the rules of the stochastic semantics of $React^{=}_{\text{RED}}$ and $React^{=}$. It is based on Lemma 1 and on another lemma that states that for all reaction rules $s_1 \xrightarrow{e} s_2$ of $React^{=}_{\text{RED}}$ and substitutions σ, it holds that if $s_1\sigma \approx \prod_{i=1}^{m} a_i^{m_i}$ and $e\sigma \Downarrow d \in \mathbb{R}^+$ then $\llbracket e \rrbracket_{s_1} \Downarrow d * \prod_{i=1}^{m} m_i!$, so that Lemma 2 can be applied.

4 Expressing the Stochastic π-Calculus

In this section, we propose an encoding of the stochastic π-calculus into $React^{=}_{\text{RED}}$ preserving the underlying CTMC, according to $React^{=}_{\text{RED}}$ alternative semantics of

Prefixes	$\pi ::= x?\tilde{y}$	receiver	where $x, \tilde{y}, \tilde{z} \in \mathcal{N}$
	$\mid x{:}d!\tilde{z}$	sender	and $d \in \mathbb{R}_0^+$
Sums	$M ::= \pi.P$	prefixed process	
	$\mid M_1 + M_2$	choice	
Processes	$P, Q, O ::= A(\tilde{x})$	defined process	where $A \in \mathcal{A}$
	$\mid P_1 \mid P_2$	parallel composition	
	$\mid (\nu x)P$	channel creation	
	$\mid \mathbf{0}$	idle process	
Definitions	$D ::= A(\tilde{x}) \triangleq M$	process definition	where $fn(M) \subseteq \{x\}$

Fig. 8. Syntax of the π-calculus

Sect. 3. The definition of the π-calculus we propose here corresponds to its "biochemical" variant: the bodies of parametric process definitions are sums of prefixed processes, possibly restricted. In order to simplify the presentation of the encoding, but not at the expense of the expressiveness, the syntax given in Fig. 8 excludes ν-operators over sums. Free names and structural congruence are defined as usual for π-calculus reduction semantics.

The stochastic semantics of the π-calculus as given in Fig. 9 refines the usual non-deterministic semantics. It is based on standard indexing of processes and prefixes, which allows the enumeration of all the pairs of prefixes that give rise to some reduction, as well as on the presence of *normal forms*, that allow the very compact expression of a process as a parallel composition of defined processes possibly preceded by restrictions.

In order to formalize the encoding from the π-calculus to reaction rules, we define a standard correspondence between (sets of) π-calculus process definitions and (sets of) rules. For the sake of readability, our encoding relies on the following assumptions:

- The set of names $\mathcal{N}$ of the π-calculus is that of $React^{=}_{\mathrm{RED}}$ and all free names on the right hand side of a definition $A(\tilde{x}) \triangleq P$ are bound on the left, i.e. $fn(P) \subseteq \{\tilde{x}\}$.
- The set of molecule names $\mathcal{A}$ of the π-calculus is that of $React^{=}_{\mathrm{RED}}$ and the number of names $|\tilde{x}|$ in definitions $A(\tilde{x}) \triangleq P$ must be equal to the *arity* of A fixed by $\mathcal{A}$. Furthermore all formal parameters in $\tilde{x}$ must be pairwise distinct and there exists no multiple definitions, that is for any pair of definitions $A_i(\tilde{x}_i) \triangleq P_i, i \in 1, 2$, it holds that $A_1 \neq A_2$.

Definition 1 (Normal form). *Processes $P = (\nu\tilde{x})\Pi_i A_i(\tilde{y}_i)$ are said to be in normal form. The subset of $\mathcal{P}$ of processes in normal form is denoted as $\widehat{\mathcal{P}}$. Thus, in the following, $\hat{P}$ denotes a process in normal form.*

Modulo the usual structural congruence rules any process can be put into normal form:

$$(\text{COMS}_\pi)\ \frac{P_1 = \sum_h \pi^1_h.P^1_h \quad P_2 = \sum_h \pi^2_h.P^2_h \quad \pi^1_l = x{:}d!\tilde{z} \quad \pi^2_m = x?\tilde{y} \quad |\tilde{y}| = |\tilde{z}|}{P_1 \mid P_2 \xrightarrow[(l,m)]{d} P^1_i \mid P^2_j[\tilde{z}/\tilde{y}]}$$

$$(\text{DEFS}_\pi)\ \frac{A_1(\tilde{x}_1) \triangleq M_1 \quad A_2(\tilde{x}_2) \triangleq M_2 \quad M_1[\tilde{y}_1/\tilde{x}_1] \mid M_2[\tilde{y}_2/\tilde{x}_2] \xrightarrow[(l,m)]{d} Q}{A_1(\tilde{y}_1) \mid A_2(\tilde{y}_2) \xrightarrow[(l,m)]{d} Q}$$

$$(\text{REDUCTS}_\pi)\ \frac{\begin{array}{l} P = (\nu\tilde{y}) \prod_{h=1}^n A_h(\tilde{x}_h) \\ A_j(\tilde{x}_j) \mid A_k(\tilde{x}_k) \xrightarrow[(l,m)]{d} Q \end{array} \quad O \equiv (\nu\tilde{y})(Q \mid \prod_{h\in\{1,\ldots,n\}\setminus\{j,k\}} A_h(\tilde{x}_h))}{P \xrightarrow[(j,l,k,m)]{d} O}$$

$$(\text{SUMS}_\pi)\ \frac{P \equiv P' \quad d = \sum_{\{(d',(j,l,k,m)) \mid P' \xrightarrow[(j,l,k,m)]{d'} O\}} d'}{P \xrightarrow{r} O}$$

Fig. 9. Stochastic semantics for the π-calculus

Lemma 3 (Congruent normal form). *For every π-calculus process P, there exists $\widehat{P} \equiv P$ such that $\widehat{P}$ is in normal form.*

Each process may be put in several different normal forms. In order to define the encoding from processes to solutions, we need to choose a unique normal form $\phi(P)$ for each P. Of course, the associative and commutative properties of structural congruence, as well as α-renaming, allow several distinct normalization functions $\phi(\cdot)$ to be defined. For our purpose, the specific choice is not relevant, as long as the same $\phi(\cdot)$ is always selected hereinafter.

Lemma 4 (Normalization function). *There exists (at least) one surjective and total function $\phi : \mathcal{P} \to \widehat{\mathcal{P}}$ such that $\forall P \in \mathcal{P} : \phi(P) \equiv P$ and $\forall P \in \widehat{\mathcal{P}}$: $\phi(P) = P$.*

Normal forms are useful to define the stochastic semantics of the π-calculus, given in Fig. 9. This semantics relies on redexes which are here tuples that locate a pair of complementary prefixes. In the reduction

$$(\nu\tilde{x})(A_1(\tilde{x}_1), \ldots, A_n(\tilde{x}_n)) \xrightarrow[(j,l,k,m)]{d} Q$$

an interaction with rate d involves the lth (output) prefix of process A_j and the mth (input) prefix of process A_k. From those located interactions, rule (SUMS_π) sums up the rates of the reductions leading to a common state, so that the specific pairs of complementary prefixes are forgotten.

Similarly to the stochastic semantics of the π-calculus, the encoding of the π-calculus in $React^{=}_{\text{RED}}$ relies on the correspondence between the redexes of these two languages. Such encoding consists in two parts: the first one allows the translation of parametric process definitions to reaction rules, the second one defines a tight correspondence between π-calculus processes and $React^{=}_{\text{RED}}$ solutions.

The translation of parametric process definitions occurs in two steps: first, a rule is generated for each redex that locates a pair of complementary prefixes, which do not necessarily share the same subject name; then, the rates of identical rules are summed up. In order to illustrate these informal ideas, let us consider the following process definitions:

$$A(x,\dot{x}) \triangleq x{:}d!\dot{x}.\mathbf{0} + x{:}d!\dot{x}.\mathbf{0} + \dot{x}?z.B(x,\dot{x},z)$$
$$B(y,\dot{y},\ddot{y}) \triangleq y{:}d'!\ddot{y}.(\nu z)A(y,z) + \dot{y}{:}d''!\ddot{y}.B(y,\dot{y},\ddot{y})$$

Depending on how those definitions are instantiated, at most 4 interactions can occur. Those are given by redexes (j,l,k,m) identifying the lth output prefix of the jth definition and the mth input prefix of the kth definition[1]. For the above definition, those redexes are $(1,1,1,3)$, $(1,2,1,3)$, $(2,1,1,3)$ and $(2,2,1,3)$. A rule, constrained by the equality of the subject of the prefixes, corresponds to each redex:

$$(1,1,1,3) : A(x,\dot{x}), A(y,\dot{y}) \xrightarrow{\texttt{if } x=\dot{y} \texttt{ then } d \texttt{ else } 0} B(y,\dot{y},\dot{x})$$
$$(1,2,1,3) : A(x,\dot{x}), A(y,\dot{y}) \xrightarrow{\texttt{if } x=\dot{y} \texttt{ then } d \texttt{ else } 0} B(y,\dot{y},\dot{x})$$
$$(2,1,1,3) : B(y,\dot{y},\ddot{y}), A(x,\dot{x}) \xrightarrow{\texttt{if } y=\dot{x} \texttt{ then } d' \texttt{ else } 0} (\nu z)A(y,z), B(x,\dot{x},\ddot{y})$$
$$(2,2,1,3) : B(y,\dot{y},\ddot{y}), A(x,\dot{x}) \xrightarrow{\texttt{if } \dot{y}=\dot{x} \texttt{ then } d'' \texttt{ else } 0} B(y,\dot{y},\ddot{y}), B(x,\dot{x},\ddot{y})$$

We get rid of the redex indexing of rules by summing up the rates of identical rules, and thus we obtain the following rule-based model that corresponds to the above π-calculus definitions:

$$\left\{\begin{array}{l} A(x,\dot{x}), A(y,\dot{y}) \xrightarrow{2*\texttt{if } x=\dot{y} \texttt{ then } d \texttt{ else } 0} B(y,\dot{y},\dot{x}), \\ B(y,\dot{y},\ddot{y}), A(x,\dot{x}) \xrightarrow{\texttt{if } y=\dot{x} \texttt{ then } d' \texttt{ else } 0} (\nu z)A(y,z), B(x,\dot{x},\ddot{y}), \\ B(y,\dot{y},\ddot{y}), A(x,\dot{x}) \xrightarrow{\texttt{if } \dot{y}=\dot{x} \texttt{ then } d'' \texttt{ else } 0} B(y,\dot{y},\ddot{y}), B(x,\dot{x},\ddot{y}) \end{array}\right\}$$

We can now formalize the encoding. First we define the translation of π-calculus process definitions in reaction rules, then we formalize how to translate a process to a solution (and back to a process again).

Definition 2 (From process definitions to reaction rules). *Let $\mathcal{D}$ be a finite set of process definitions of π-calculus, $\mathcal{D} = \{\delta_s | \delta_s = A_s(\tilde{x}_s) \triangleq \sum_{t=1}^{n_s} \pi_s^t.P_s^t\}$ with cardinality $|\mathcal{D}|$. The tuple $R'_{\mathcal{D}}$ of reaction rules corresponding to $\mathcal{D}$ is defined as $R'_{\mathcal{D}} = \{(i, r_i) | r_i = s_i \xrightarrow{e_i} (\nu\tilde{x}_i)s'_i\}$, where i is a composite index $i = (j,l,k,m)$ for all j,l,k,m such that:*

- *the jth and k^{th} definitions in $\mathcal{D}$ are $\delta_j = A_j(\tilde{x}_j) \triangleq \sum_{t=1}^{n_j} \pi_j^t.P_j^t$ and $\delta_k = A_k(\tilde{x}_k) \triangleq \sum_{t=1}^{n_k} \pi_k^t.P_k^t$ if $k \neq j$ and $\delta_k = A_j(\tilde{x}'_j) \triangleq \sum_{t=1}^{n_j} \pi_j^t.P_j^t[\tilde{x}'_j/\tilde{x}_j]$ otherwise, for some fresh names $\tilde{x}'_j$;*
- *$1 \leq l \leq n_j$ and $1 \leq m \leq n_k$*

[1] Note that here we refer to j^{th} and k^{th} definitions while in the stochastic semantics the same redex refers to the jth and k^{th} processes of the current state.

– $\pi_j^l = y_1{:}d!\tilde{z}_o$ *and* $\pi_k^m = y_2?\tilde{z}_i$ *with* $|\tilde{z}_o| = |\tilde{z}_i|$;
– $s_i = A_j(\tilde{x}_j), A_k(\tilde{x}_k)$ *and* $s_i' = \phi(\ P_j^l \ \mid \ P_k^m[\tilde{z}_o/\tilde{z}_i]\ )$
– $e_i = \texttt{if}\ y_1{=}y_2\ \texttt{then}\ d\ \texttt{else}\ 0.$

Given a rule r*, the multiplicity* $\mathrm{M}(r)$ *of* r *in* $R'_{\mathcal{D}}$ *is defined as* $\mathrm{M}(r) = |\ \{i \mid (i,r) \in R'_{\mathcal{D}}\}\ |$. *The set* $R_{\mathcal{D}}$ *of reaction rules corresponding to* $\mathcal{D}$ *is defined as*

$$R_{\mathcal{D}} = \{s \xrightarrow{\mathrm{M}(r)*e} (\nu\tilde{x})s' \mid (i,r) \in R'_{\mathcal{D}} \text{ for some } i \text{ and } r = s \xrightarrow{e} (\nu\tilde{x})s'\}$$

In practice, the translation of a process in a solution removes the restrictions in front of the process and preserves the names of defined processes and of channels.

Definition 3 (From processes to solutions). *Let* P *be a* π*-calculus process, with* $\widehat{P} = (\nu\tilde{z})(A_1(\tilde{x}_1) \mid \cdots \mid A_n(\tilde{x}_n))$. *The solution* s_P *corresponding to* P *is defined as* $s_P = A_1(\tilde{x}_1), \ldots, A_n(\tilde{x}_n)$.

The reverse translation adds again restrictions in front of the process, by preserving all the names.

Definition 4 (From solutions to processes). *Let* s *be a solution, with* $s = A_1(\tilde{x}_1) \mid \cdots \mid A_n(\tilde{x}_n)$. *The process* P_s *corresponding to* s *is defined as* $P_s = (\nu\tilde{x}_1)\ldots(\nu\tilde{x}_n)P_s^{-(\nu)}$, *with* $P_s^{-(\nu)} = A_1(\tilde{x}_1), \ldots, A_n(\tilde{x}_n)$.

The remarkable expressiveness of $React^{=}_{\mathrm{RED}}$ allows it to provide a tight correspondence with the π-calculus: in fact, the state space generated by a π-calculus process P without free names is isomorphic to the one generated by its corresponding solution s_P. Moreover, the transition rate between any pair of states is preserved by the encoding, so that the CTMC associated with any π-calculus process P without free names is isomorphic to the one associated with its corresponding solution s_P. This important property is captured by the following theorem.

Theorem 1. *Let* $\mathcal{D}$ *be a finite set of process definitions of* π*-calculus,* $R_{\mathcal{D}}$ *be the set of reaction rules corresponding to* $\mathcal{D}$ *according to Def. 2. Let* P *be a* π*-calculus process with* $\mathrm{fn}(P) = \emptyset$. *Then:*

1. $P \xrightarrow{d} P' \quad \Rightarrow \quad R_{\mathcal{D}} \vdash s_P \xrightarrow[\mathrm{RED}]{d} s_{P'}$;
2. $R_{\mathcal{D}} \vdash s_P \xrightarrow[\mathrm{RED}]{d} s' \quad \Rightarrow \quad P \xrightarrow{d} P_{s'}$.

Surely, it is possible to relax the requirement of absence of free names for π-calculus processes at the price of losing isomorphism, since some process transitions are lost. Still it would be easy to identify again the isomorphic subchain of CTMC of the corresponding solution of $React^{=}_{\mathrm{RED}}$.

5 Biochemical Reaction Rules with General Constraints

In this section, we define a powerful language of biochemical reaction rules, *React*(C), which besides others permits constraints in an arbitrary constraint system C, ν-binders on the left hand side, reflexivity, and general kinetics.

We define constraint languages like in higher-order logic in the simply typed call-by-value λ-calculus, extended by pairs, letrec expressions, case statements for matching molecules or solutions, and constants. We parametrize our λ-calculus by choice of base types, molecule constructors, and constants with a fixed semantics. Therefore, parameter C of *React*(C) is assumed to be a tuple $C = (\mathcal{B}, \mathcal{A}, \mathcal{C}, [[.]])$ with the following properties:

- $\mathcal{B} = \{\iota, \ldots\}$ is a set of type constants such as $\texttt{nat}_0$ (non zero natural numbers) and `real` for real numbers. Simple types build $\mathcal{B}$ and 3 further constants are defined in Fig. 10. They are ranged over by τ.
- $\mathcal{A} = \{A : \tilde{\tau}, \ldots\}$ is a set of typed molecule names, $\tilde{\tau}$ is a tuple of types.
- $\mathcal{C} = \{c : \tau, \ldots\}$ is a set of typed constants. If $\tau = \tau_1 \to \ldots \to \tau_n \to \tau'$ for some nonfunctional type τ' then we say that the arity of c is $ar(c) = n$. This set may contain constants for arithmetic functions such as $+ : \texttt{nat}_0 \to \texttt{nat}_0 \to \texttt{nat}_0$.
- for every constant $c : \tau_1 \to \ldots \to \tau_n \to \tau''$ of arity n, there is a function $[[c : \tau]]_s : \mathit{Vals}(\tau_1) \times \ldots \times \mathit{Vals}(\tau_n) \to \mathit{Vals}(\tau'')$. Here, $\mathit{Vals}(\tau)$ is the set of values of type τ which are closed in that the only remaining variables are to type `link`, which is defined as usual for the simply typed λ-calculus (see Figs. 10 and 11).

Note that simple types τ include, beside type constants in $\mathcal{B}$ and function types, two forms of molecule types, $A(\tilde{\tau})$ for molecules of species A with parameters of type $\tilde{\tau}$ and a constant `mol` which is the type of molecules. Furthermore, there is a type constant `sol` for solutions and a type `link` for link names.

Expressions as defined in Fig. 10 consist of λ-calculus terms extended with constants, molecule and solution data terms, and their respective matching constructs. Rules for their evaluation are provided in Fig. 12. A solution expression is a list of expressions $e_1, \ldots, e_n$ that the type system forces to evaluate to molecules. The special term `current_sol` evaluates to the current solution (that is the current state). In the matching `case_mol` e `of` $A(\tilde{x})$ `then` e_1 `else` e_2 variables $\tilde{x}$ scope over e_1. If e evaluates to a molecule $A(\tilde{v})$ then e_1 is evaluated with variables $\tilde{x}$ binding values $\tilde{v}$. Otherwise, e_2 is evaluated. Similarly, in the matching `case_sol` e `of` x^y, z `then` e_1 `else` e_2, variables x, y and z scope over e_1. If e evaluates to $A(\tilde{v}), s$ then e_1 is evaluated where x binds to $A(\tilde{v})$, y binds to the multiplicity of $A(\tilde{v})$ in solution $A(\tilde{v}), s$, and z binds to s with all occurrences of $A(\tilde{v})$ removed from s.Otherwise, that is when e evaluates to the empty solution, e_2 is evaluated. Values of this constraint language are standard.

Language *React*(C) has full support for reflexivity, meaning that the current solution can always be reflected into a value of the language. This is a powerful feature, since it permits to express global constraints on the current solution,

Types	$\tau ::= \iota \mid \tau \to \tau \mid A(\tilde{\tau}) \mid \texttt{sol} \mid \texttt{mol} \mid \texttt{link}$	where $\iota \in \mathcal{B},\ A \in \mathcal{A}$
Expres- sions	$e \in \mathit{Exprs} ::= c \mid x \mid \lambda x.e \mid ee$	where $c \in \mathcal{C},\ x, y, z \in \mathcal{N}$
	$\mid \texttt{letrec}\ x = e\ \texttt{in}\ e \mid A(\tilde{e})$	
	$\mid \texttt{case\_mol}\ e\ \texttt{of}\ A(\tilde{x})\ \texttt{then}\ e\ \texttt{else}\ e \mid \mathbf{0} \mid e, e$	
	$\mid \texttt{current\_sol} \mid \texttt{case\_sol}\ e\ \texttt{of}\ x^y, z\ \texttt{then}\ e\ \texttt{else}\ e$	
Solution patterns	$p \in \mathit{Pats} ::= A(\tilde{x}) \mid p, p \mid \mathbf{0}$	
Solutions	$s \in \mathit{Sols} ::= A(\tilde{v}) \mid s, s \mid \mathbf{0}$	
Values	$v \in \mathit{Vals} ::= x \mid \mathbf{0} \mid s \mid \lambda x.e \mid c\ v_1 \ldots v_k$	where $0 \le k < ar(c)$ or $k = 0$
Reaction rules	$r ::= (\nu\tilde{x})p \xrightarrow{e} (\nu\tilde{y})s$	where $fn(r) \subseteq fn((\nu\tilde{x})p)$ and $\{\tilde{y}\} \cap (fn(r) \cup fn(e) \cup \{\tilde{x}\}) = \emptyset$

Fig. 10. Expressions and values of *React*(*C*)

which do not only depend on the subsolution matching the left-hand-side of a rule.

In particular, we can rely on reflexivity in order to support arbitrary kinetics, as we illustrate by the following sequence of examples. There, we assume that C supports a constant $=: \texttt{mol} \to \texttt{mol} \to \texttt{nat}_0$ for the equality function on molecules and $+ : \texttt{nat}_0 \to \texttt{nat}_0 \to \texttt{nat}_0$ for the addition over natural numbers. We start with a function that counts all molecules of a solution.

$$\mathit{count\_mols} \triangleq \lambda s.\ \texttt{letrec}\ f = (\texttt{case\_sol}\ s\ \texttt{of}\ x^y, z\ \texttt{then}\ y + (fz)\ \texttt{else}\ 0)\ \texttt{in}\ fs$$

Similarly, we can count the number of A named molecules in a solution:

$$\mathit{count}_A \triangleq \lambda s.\ \texttt{letrec}\ f = \texttt{case\_sol}\ s\ \texttt{of}\ x^y, z\ \texttt{then}\ \texttt{case\_mol}\ x\ \texttt{of}\ A(x_1, \ldots, x_k)\ \texttt{then}\ 1 + (fz)\ \texttt{else}\ (fz)\ \texttt{else}\ 0\ \texttt{in}\ fs$$

It is also possible to have a function that receives a molecule and a solution and counts the number of this molecule in a solution. For instance, *count_mol* $A()\ A(), B(), A()$ is supposed to evaluate to 2.

$$\mathit{count\_mol} \triangleq \lambda m \lambda s.\ \texttt{letrec}\ f = \texttt{case\_sol}\ s\ \texttt{of}\ x^y, z\ \texttt{then}\ (\texttt{if}\ x = m\ \texttt{then}\ 1 + (fz)\ \texttt{else}\ (fz))\ \texttt{else}\ 0\ \texttt{in}\ fs$$

Our next objective is to define function *count* as needed to define the Mass action kinetics. Here we use the additional function constant *binom* : $\texttt{nat}_0 \to \texttt{nat}_0 \to \texttt{nat}_0$ that computes binomial coefficients. This means that we assume that the

$$(\text{T-VAR})\ \frac{x:\tau\in\Gamma}{\Gamma\vdash x:\tau_1}\quad (\text{T-FUN})\ \frac{\Gamma,x:\tau_1\vdash e:\tau_2}{\Gamma\vdash \lambda x.e:\tau_1\to\tau_2}\quad (\text{T-SPEC})\ \frac{A:\tilde{\tau}\in\mathcal{A}\quad \Gamma\vdash\tilde{e}:\tilde{\tau}}{\Gamma\vdash A(\tilde{e}):A(\tilde{\tau})}$$

$$(\text{T-APP})\ \frac{\Gamma\vdash e_1:\tau_1\to\tau_2\quad \Gamma\vdash e_2:\tau_1}{\Gamma\vdash e_1e_2:\tau_2}\quad (\text{T-REC})\ \frac{\Gamma,x:\tau'\vdash e_1:\tau'\quad \Gamma,x:\tau'\vdash e_2:\tau}{\Gamma\vdash \mathtt{letrec}\ x=e_1\ \mathtt{in}\ e_2:\tau}$$

$$(\text{T-CONST})\ \frac{c:\tau\in\mathcal{C}}{\Gamma\vdash c:\tau}\quad (\text{T-MATCH})\ \frac{\Gamma\vdash e_1:\mathtt{mol}A:\tilde{\tau'}\in\mathcal{A}\quad \Gamma,\tilde{x}:\tilde{\tau'}\vdash e_2:\tau\Gamma\vdash e_3:\tau}{\Gamma\vdash \mathtt{case\_mol}\ e_1\ \mathtt{of}\ A(\tilde{x})\ \mathtt{then}\ e_2\ \mathtt{else}\ e_3:\tau}$$

$$(\text{T-MOL})\ \frac{\Gamma\vdash e:A(\tilde{\tau})}{\Gamma\vdash e:\mathtt{mol}}\quad (\text{T-SELF})\ \frac{}{\Gamma\vdash \mathtt{current\_sol}:\mathtt{sol}}\quad (\text{T-SOL-ELEM})\ \frac{\Gamma\vdash e:\mathtt{mol}}{\Gamma\vdash e:\mathtt{sol}}$$

$$(\text{T-SOL-APPEND})\ \frac{\Gamma\vdash e:\mathtt{sol}\quad \Gamma\vdash e':\mathtt{sol}}{\Gamma\vdash e,e':\mathtt{sol}}\quad (\text{T-RULE-SET})\ \frac{\forall r\in R\quad \vdash r}{\vdash R}$$

$$(\text{T-MULT})\ \frac{\Gamma\vdash e_1:\mathtt{sol}\quad \Gamma,x:\mathtt{mol},y:\mathtt{nat},z:\mathtt{sol}\vdash e_2:\tau\quad \Gamma\vdash e_3:\tau}{\Gamma\vdash \mathtt{case\_sol}\ e_1\ \mathtt{of}\ x^y,z\ \mathtt{then}\ e_2\ \mathtt{else}\ e_3:\tau}$$

$$(\text{T-RULE})\ \frac{dom(\Gamma)=(fn(P)\cup fn(e))\backslash\{\tilde{x}\}\qquad \Gamma,\tilde{x}:\mathtt{link}\vdash p:\mathtt{sol}\quad \Gamma,\tilde{x}:\mathtt{link}\vdash e:\mathtt{real}\quad \Gamma,\tilde{x},\tilde{y}:\mathtt{link}\vdash s:\mathtt{sol}}{\vdash(\nu\tilde{x})p\xrightarrow{e}(\nu\tilde{y})s}$$

Fig. 11. Type system for expressions and rules

constraint language C provides this constant, such that for all natural numbers n and m and solutions s it holds that $[[binom]]_s(n,m)=\binom{n}{m}$.

$$\begin{aligned}count \triangleq \lambda s_1\lambda s_2.\ \mathtt{letrec}\ f = \mathtt{case\_sol}\ s_1\ \mathtt{of}\ x^y,z\ \mathtt{then}\\ (binom\ (count\_mol\ x\ s_2)\\ (count\_mol\ x\ s_1))*(f z)\\ \mathtt{else}\ 0\ \mathtt{in}\ f s\end{aligned}$$

Reaction rules are enriched with ν-binders on the left-hand side, similarly to the κ-calculus. They have thus the form $(\nu\tilde{x})p\xrightarrow{e}(\nu\tilde{y})s$. ν-bound variables on the right hand side should not occur elsewhere in the rule. ν-bound variables on the left hand side must match link names that are entirely removed from the solution by rule application, see Fig. 13. Typing rule (T-RULE) for rules ensures that ν-bound variables have `link` type, that reactant and product patterns are of `sol` type and that e has `real` type, see Fig. 11. For a well-typed rule set R and a solution s, typing is preserved by reduction.

Proposition 2 (Subject reduction). *Let R be a rule set and s be a solution, if $\Gamma\vdash s$ for some typing context Γ, and $\vdash R$, and $R\vdash s\xrightarrow{d}s'$ then $\Gamma\vdash s'$.*

6 Stochastic Simulator

We propose a stochastic simulator that applies to both $React^=$ and $React(C)$ and is independent of the choice of constraint system C. We also discuss the

$$\frac{}{v \Downarrow_s v} \qquad \frac{e_1 \Downarrow_s \lambda x.e \quad e_2 \Downarrow_s v' \quad e[v'/x] \Downarrow_s v}{e_1 e_2 \Downarrow_s v} \qquad \frac{e_1 \Downarrow_s v_1 \neq \lambda x.e \quad e_2 \Downarrow_s v_2 \quad v_1 v_2 \Downarrow_s v}{e_1 e_2 \Downarrow_s v}$$

$$\frac{c : \tau \in \mathcal{C} \quad ar(x) = n \quad e_1 \Downarrow_s v_1 \quad \dots \quad e_n \Downarrow_s v_n}{c\ e_1 \dots e_n \Downarrow_s [[c]]_s(v_1, \dots, v_n)} \qquad \frac{e_2[e_1/x] \Downarrow_s v}{\texttt{letrec}\ x = e_1\ \texttt{in}\ e_2 \Downarrow_s v}$$

$$\frac{\tilde{e} \Downarrow_s \tilde{v}}{A(\tilde{e}) \Downarrow_s A(\tilde{v})} \qquad \frac{e_1 \Downarrow_s A(\tilde{v}') \quad e_2[\tilde{v'}/\tilde{x}] \Downarrow_s v}{\texttt{case\_mol}\ e_1\ \texttt{of}\ A(\tilde{x})\ \texttt{then}\ e_2\ \texttt{else}\ e_3 \Downarrow_s v}$$

$$\frac{e_1 \Downarrow_s B(\tilde{v}') \quad A \neq B \quad e_3 \Downarrow_s v}{\texttt{case\_mol}\ e_1\ \texttt{of}\ A(\tilde{x})\ \texttt{then}\ e_2\ \texttt{else}\ e_3 \Downarrow_s v}$$

$$\frac{e_1 \Downarrow_s s_1 \quad s_1 \equiv \prod_{i=1}^n a_i^{m_i} \quad s_1 = a_1, s_1' \quad s_2 \equiv \prod_{i=2}^n a_i^{m_i} \quad e_2[a/x, m_1/y, s_2/z] \Downarrow_s v}{\texttt{case\_sol}\ e_1\ \texttt{of}\ x^y, z\ \texttt{then}\ e_2\ \texttt{else}\ e_3 \Downarrow_s v}$$

$$\frac{e_1 \Downarrow_s \mathbf{0} \quad e_3 \Downarrow_s v}{\texttt{case\_sol}\ e_1\ \texttt{of}\ x^y, z\ \texttt{then}\ e_2\ \texttt{else}\ e_3 \Downarrow_s v} \qquad \frac{e \Downarrow_s s \quad e' \Downarrow_s s'}{e, e' \Downarrow_s s, s'} \qquad \frac{}{\texttt{current\_sol} \Downarrow_s s}$$

Fig. 12. Big-step evaluation of expressions

$$(\textsc{inst})\ \frac{\sigma : fn((\nu\tilde{x})p) \cup fn(e) \to Vals \text{ type preserving} \quad e\sigma'\sigma \Downarrow d \qquad \sigma' : \{\tilde{x}\} \to N \backslash N' \text{ injective} \quad \sigma'' : \{\tilde{x}'\} \to \mathcal{N} \backslash (N \cup fn((\nu\tilde{x})p) \cup fn(e)) \text{ injective}}{(\nu\tilde{x})p \xrightarrow{e} (\nu\tilde{x}')s \Downarrow_{\sigma,\sigma',N,N'} p\sigma'\sigma \xrightarrow{d} s\sigma''\sigma}$$

$$(\textsc{react})\ \frac{s_1' \approx s, s_1 \quad s, s_2 \equiv s_2' \quad d \in \mathbb{R}^+}{s_1 \xrightarrow{d} s_2 \vdash s_1' \xrightarrow{d} s_2'}$$

$$(\textsc{sum})\ \frac{s_1' \equiv s_1 \quad d = \sum_{r \in R} \sum_{\{(d',\sigma,\sigma') \mid r \Downarrow_{\sigma,\sigma',fn(s_1'),fn(s_2)} \rho,\ \rho \vdash s_1' \xrightarrow{d'} s_2\}} d'}{R \vdash s_1 \xrightarrow[\text{MA}]{d} s_2}$$

Fig. 13. Stochastic mass-action semantics of *React*(C)

algorithmic complexity of a single simulation step. It should be noted that the efficient simulation algorithm for the κ-calculus [5], which updates matches of rules dynamically, cannot be generalized in any obvious manner, since hyperedges spoil the principle of rigidity (unique matches for connected patterns).

A stochastic simulator allows to execute a system of chemical reaction rules R on a biochemical solution s. It then computes traces by repeatedly applying the reaction rules in R to the current solution, with s as the initial solution. Note that these traces also contain the time delays Δ for every step. Our simulator is given in Fig. 14. It may compute infinite traces but the overall simulation time could easily be limited. Given the current solution s, the rule set R, and the current time point t, our simulator computes the set of applicable reactions (l, r, s') of R on s with their rates r and selects one of them non-deterministically by Gillespie's SSA algorithm [8] and also returns its time delay Δ. Note that label l is some pair $(\sigma, fn(s'))$ for $React^=$ and some pair $(\sigma, \sigma', fn(s), fn(s'))$ for

```
simulate(s,t) // with system of reaction rules R
  let Reacts = {(d,(l,r,s')) | r ∈ R, r ⇓_l ρ, ρ ⊢ s -d-> s'} // compute all potential
      reaction steps
  let (d,(l,r,s'),Δ) = SSA(Reacts) // choose transition and time delay by SSA
  output(d,(l,r,s'),Δ) // trace the chosen reaction
  simulate(s',t+Δ)
```

Fig. 14. Stochastic Simulator for *React*$^=$ and *React*(C)

React(C) where σ' takes care of the ν-binders on the left-hand side of r. The algorithm then outputs the selected step, its rate, and its delay and continues with s' at time point $t + \Delta$.

Algorithmically, the main problem to be solved by the simulator is to compute the set of applicable reactions for a given system R of rules and a solution s. The following proposition states that every step of the simulator can be done in polynomial time under the assumption that the maximal arity n of reaction rules is bounded. This result is relevant, since the encoding of definitions of the stochastic π-calculus produces only reactions rules of arity 2. We define the size $|r|$ of a rule as the number of its symbols, and similarly the size $|s|$ of a solution.

Proposition 3. *Let r be a reaction rule $(\nu\tilde{x})\prod_{i=1}^{n} A_i(\tilde{x}_i) \xrightarrow{e} (\nu\tilde{x}')p'$ and s a solution $\prod_{j=1}^{m} A'_j(\tilde{v}'_j)$ then the set of possible instantiations $\{l \mid r \Downarrow_l \rho,\ \rho \vdash\ s \xrightarrow{d} s'\}$ can be computed in time $O(|r| + |s| + m^n)$.*

Proof. We enumerate all injective functions $\ell : \{1,\ldots,n\} \to \{1,\ldots,m\}$ and tests whether they define a redex. There are m^n many of such functions and testing whether ℓ is a redex costs time $O(|s| + |r|)$. Again this is enough, since all free variables of r occur freely on the left hand side. □

Note that a naive approach that enumerates all possible assignments of pattern variables to values in s leads to an algorithm in $O(|r|^{|s|})$ which is exponential in the solution size and thus unfeasible.

The next proposition shows that we cannot obtain a simulator with steps in polynomial time, neither for *React*(C) nor for *React*$^=$, without imposing additional restrictions such as a bound on the maximal arity of reaction rules. The input is a reaction rule r and a solution s and the output is "yes" if and only if r is applicable to s, i.e., if there exists a substitution σ such that $r \Downarrow_{\sigma,fn(s)} \rho$ and $\rho \vdash\ s \xrightarrow{d} s'$.

Proposition 4. *The reaction-applicability problem is* NP*-complete for both* *React*$^=$ *and* *React*(C).

Proof. The generate and test algorithm in the Proof of Proposition 3 can be run in non-deterministic polynomial time, so reaction applicability is in NP.

In order to prove NP-hardness, we show that 3SAT can be reduced to reaction-applicability in polynomial time. We illustrate the ideas of our encoding at the following two 3SAT clauses as an example.

$$(b_1 \vee \overline{b_2}) \wedge (b_1 \vee b_2 \vee \overline{b_3})$$

We now express theses clauses by a reaction rule $p \xrightarrow{d} s'$ that is supposed to match a solution s. For each of the two clauses C_i where $1 \leq i \leq 2$, we fix a variable x_i which will match either of the three Boolean variable b_1, b_2, b_3 and that z_i matches the value of this Boolean variable in variable assignments satisfying the clauses. We use molecule names in $\mathcal{A} = \{C_i, E_{ij} \mid 1 \leq i, j \leq 2\}$.

1. The first clause is expressed by adding a reactant $C_1(x_1, z_1)$ to pattern p and molecules $C_1(b_1, 1), C_1(b_2, 0)$ to the solution s.
2. The second clause is expressed by adding a reactant $C_2(x_2, z_2)$ to pattern p and molecules $C_2(b_1, 1), C_2(b_2, 1), C_2(b_3, 0)$ to the solution s.
3. In order to express that z_i must match the Boolean that is assigned to the Boolean variable matching x_i, we encode condition $x_i = x_j \Rightarrow z_i = z_j$ for all $1 \leq i < j \leq 2$. This can be done by adding the reactants $E_{ij}(x_i, x_j, z_i, z_j)$ to pattern p and the following molecules to solution s:
$$\prod_{\beta,\beta' \in \mathbb{B}} \prod_{1 \leq k \neq l \leq 3} E_{ij}(b_k, b_k, \beta, \beta), E_{ij}(b_k, b_l, \beta, \beta')$$
So if x_i and x_j match the same b_k then z_i and z_j must match the same Boolean β. Otherwise, there is no restriction.

Pattern p grows linearly in the size of the clauses, while solution s grows both, quadratically with the number of clauses and quadratically with the number of Boolean variables, and thus polynomially in the size of the clauses. □

Computing matching redexes by constraint programming. We propose to use constraint programming in order to find an algorithm that computes the set of applicable reactions for a given system R of reaction rules and a biochemical solution s with a complexity less than the worst complexity $O(|r| + |s| + m^n)$. This is relevant, since this algorithm will always need quadratic time for each step of binary rules, while one would hope for linear time in many cases.

Rather than generating all redex candidates ℓ and then testing whether ℓ is indeed a redex of r and s, we define a constraint that states whether a redex candidate for a solution is indeed a redex and then solve this constraint by constraint programming, i.e. by propagating and splitting rather than generating and testing. For a given solution $s = \prod_{i=1}^{n} a_i^{m_i}$ and a reaction $\prod_{i=1}^{m} p_i \xrightarrow{e} s'$, the constraint $\psi(r, s)$ is defined as follows:

$$\begin{aligned}\psi(\textstyle\prod_{i=1}^{m} p_i \xrightarrow{e} s',\ \prod_{i=1}^{n} a_i^{m_i}) \;=\; & e \Downarrow d \in \mathbb{R}^+ \;\wedge_{i=1}^{m} I_i \in \{1, \ldots, n\} \wedge p_i = a_{I_i} \wedge \\ & \wedge_{i=1}^{m} \#\{j \mid I_i = I_j\} \leq m_i\end{aligned}$$

We use finite domain variables I_i and so called element constraints for expressing $\wedge_{i=1}^{m} I_i \in \{1, \ldots, n\} \wedge p_i = a_{I_i}$ which states that all p_i match a_{I_i} (line 2). Strong propagators for element constraints are provided by all current constraint programming libraries. Additional requirements are that the number of patterns matched to the same molecule must not exceed the number of that molecule in the solution (line 3) and that e evaluates to a successful value (line 1).

7 Conclusion

We introduced a new language of biochemical reaction rules with constraints *React*(C) that is highly expressive. We sowed that with equality constraints and hyperedges the missing features for subsuming the expressiveness of the stochastic π-calculus are provided. Besides constraints *React*(C) supports reflexivity, which enables modelers to define arbitrary kinetics.

We presented a simulator for *React*(C) that computes steps in polynomial time, under the assumption that the arity of reaction rules is bounded. We showed that efficient simulation is impossible without this assumption. A constraint programming solution that may often avoid the higher polynomials in the worst case was presented. An implementation is under way.

In future work, we would like to show that the attributed π-calculus $\pi(C)$ can be encoded in *React*(C) restricted to binary rules. Furthermore, we conjecture that the imperative π-calculus can be encoded into *React*(C) restricted to ternary rules. This would prove that *React*(C) subsumes BioAmbients as well. The relationship of *React*(C) to Bigraphs is also to be elaborated.

References

1. Blinov, M.L., Faeder, J.R., Goldstein, B., Hlavacek, W.S.: Bionetgen: software for rule-based modeling of signal transduction based on the interactions of molecular domains. Bioinformatics 20(17), 3289–3291 (2004)
2. Cardelli, L.: From processes to odes by chemistry. In: IFIP TCS. IFIP, vol. 273, pp. 261–281. Springer, Heidelberg (2008)
3. Chabrier-Rivier, N., Fages, F., Soliman, S.: The biochemical abstract machine biocham. In: Danos, V., Schachter, V. (eds.) CMSB 2004. LNCS (LNBI), vol. 3082, pp. 172–191. Springer, Heidelberg (2005)
4. Danos, V., Feret, J., Fontana, W., Harmer, R., Krivine, J.: Abstracting the differential semantics of rule-based models: Exact and automated model reduction. In: 25th LICS, pp. 362–381. IEEE Press, Los Alamitos (2010)
5. Danos, V., Feret, J., Fontana, W., Krivine, J.: Scalable simulation of cellular signaling networks. In: Shao, Z. (ed.) APLAS 2007. LNCS, vol. 4807, pp. 139–157. Springer, Heidelberg (2007)
6. Danos, V., Laneve, C.: Formal molecular biology. TCS 325(1), 69–110 (2004)
7. Fournet, C., Gonthier, G.: The reflexive cham and the join-calculus. In: POPL, pp. 372–385. ACM Press, New York (1996)
8. Gillespie, D.T.: A general method for numerically simulating the stochastic time evolution of coupled chemical reactions. Journal of Computational Physics 22(4), 403–434 (1976)
9. Gilroy, S.W., Harrison, M.D.: SBML: a user interface mark-up language based on interaction style. Int. J. Web Eng. Technol. 4(2), 207–234 (2008)
10. John, M., Lhoussaine, C., Niehren, J.: Dynamic compartments in the imperative pi calculus. In: Degano, P., Gorrieri, R. (eds.) CMSB 2009. LNCS, vol. 5688, pp. 235–250. Springer, Heidelberg (2009)
11. John, M., Lhoussaine, C., Niehren, J., Uhrmacher, A.: The attributed pi calculus with priorities. In: Priami, C., Breitling, R., Gilbert, D., Heiner, M., Uhrmacher, A.M. (eds.) Transactions on Computational Systems Biology XII. LNCS, vol. 5945, pp. 13–76. Springer, Heidelberg (2010)

12. Krivine, J., Danos, V., Benecke, A.: Modelling epigenetic information maintenance: A kappa tutorial. In: Bouajjani, A., Maler, O. (eds.) CAV 2009. LNCS, vol. 5643, pp. 17–32. Springer, Heidelberg (2009)
13. Kuttler, C., Lhoussaine, C., Nebut, M.: Rule-based modeling of transcriptional attenuation at the tryptophan operon. In: Priami, C., Breitling, R., Gilbert, D., Heiner, M., Uhrmacher, A.M. (eds.) Transactions on Computational Systems Biology XII. LNCS, vol. 5945, pp. 199–228. Springer, Heidelberg (2010)
14. Kuttler, C., Lhoussaine, C., Niehren, J.: A stochastic pi calculus for concurrent objects. In: Anai, H., Horimoto, K., Kutsia, T. (eds.) Ab 2007. LNCS, vol. 4545, pp. 232–246. Springer, Heidelberg (2007)
15. Laneve, C., Pradalier, S., Zavattaro, G.: From biochemistry to stochastic processes. ENTCS 253(3), 167–185 (2009)
16. Papanikolaou, N.: The space and motion of communicating agents author: Robin Milner. SIGACT News 41(3), 51–55 (2010)
17. Phillips, A., Cardelli, L.: Efficient, correct simulation of biological processes in the stochastic pi-calculus. In: Calder, M., Gilmore, S. (eds.) CMSB 2007. LNCS (LNBI), vol. 4695, pp. 184–199. Springer, Heidelberg (2007)
18. Priami, C.: Stochastic pi-calculus. Comput. J. 38(7), 578–589 (1995)
19. Ramsey, S., Orrell, D., Bolouri, H.: Dizzy: Stochastic simulation of large-scale genetic regulatory networks. J. Bioinformatics and Computational Biology 3(2), 415–436 (2005)
20. Regev, A., Panina, E.M., Silverman, W., Cardelli, L., Shapiro, E.Y.: Bioambients: an abstraction for biological compartments. TCS 325(1), 141–167 (2004)
21. Regev, A., Shapiro, E.: Cells as Computation. Nature 419, 343 (2002)
22. Romanel, A., Priami, C.: On the computational power of BlenX. TCS 411(2), 542–565 (2010)
23. Versari, C.: A core calculus for a comparative analysis of bio-inspired calculi. In: De Nicola, R. (ed.) ESOP 2007. LNCS, vol. 4421, pp. 411–425. Springer, Heidelberg (2007)

A Testing Theory for a Higher-Order Cryptographic Language*
(Extended Abstract)

Vasileios Koutavas and Matthew Hennessy

Trinity College Dublin
{Vasileios.Koutavas, Matthew.Hennessy}@scss.tcd.ie

Abstract. We study a higher-order concurrent language with cryptographic primitives, for which we develop a sound and complete, first-order testing theory for the preservation of safety properties. Our theory is based on co-inductive set simulations over transitions in a first-order Labelled Transition System. This keeps track of the knowledge of the observer, and treats transmitted higher-order values in a symbolic manner, thus obviating the quantification over functional contexts. Our characterisation provides an attractive proof technique, and we illustrate its usefulness in proofs of equivalence, including cases where bisimulation theory does not apply.

1 Introduction

The verification of higher-order distributed systems that employ security protocols is now more than ever relevant to software development. Extensions of the π-calculus [18] with cryptographic primitives, such as the spi-calculus [3] and the applied π-calculus [1], have provided an effective framework for modelling security and authentication protocols of first-order systems [3,1,4,8,2,5,9,6,11,10]. It is only natural that similar extensions to the *higher-order π-calculus* (HOπ) [19] would be equally effective for modelling and verifying security and authentication protocols of higher-order systems, such as distributed systems in which code is communicated between principals over public channels [17,25].

This paper is inspired by the work of Maffeis et al. [17], where the focus is in the safety of higher-order authentication protocols. The authors use a higher-order version of the spi-calculus, augmented with a combination of static and dynamic typing that enables the use of untrusted code in the dynamic verification of authentication policies. They call this "Code-Carrying Authorisation".

Our goal is to develop behavioural theories for such a language, and in this paper we make the first step by studying safety in the language HOspi, a version of HOπ augmented with the symmetric cryptographic primitives of the spi-calculus and an extremely simple type system. To the extent of our knowledge, this is the first theory of safety for such a language.

* This research was supported by SFI project SFI 06 IN.1 1898.

G. Barthe (Ed.): ESOP 2011, LNCS 6602, pp. 358–377, 2011.
© Springer-Verlag Berlin Heidelberg 2011

Even in HOspi there are examples of systems that use Code-Carrying Authorisation similar to those in [17]. Consider a rather simple part of a conference server that expects the submission of a review for a particular paper by a particular reviewer Rev_1 or any legitimate delegate reviewer:

$$\begin{aligned}\mathsf{Conf} = \mathtt{inp}\, \mathit{subm}(x_{subm}).\, \mathtt{dec}\, x_{subm}\, \mathtt{as}\, \{\!|\, (x_r, f_{prf})\,|\!\}_{s_p} \\ \mathtt{in}\, \nu a.\, \mathtt{fork}\, f_{prf}(\{\!|\, a\,|\!\}_{s_{rev_1}}).\, \mathtt{inp}\, a().\, \mathtt{outp}\, \mathit{ok}(x_r).\, \mathbf{0}\end{aligned}$$

The paper has been associated by the server to key s_p and the reviewer to key s_{rev_1}. After receiving a possible submission on *subm*, the server verifies that the sender had access to the paper by successfully decrypting the input message with s_p. The message contains the review (bound to x_r) and a function (bound to f_{prf}) which can be used to prove that the review came from Rev_1 or by a delegate reviewer. To do this, the server generates a fresh channel a, encrypts it with the key s_{rev_1}, and gives it as an argument to the function. The legitimacy of the review is verified by an input on a, which can only be matched by an output in the function bound to f_{prf}, after it successfully decrypts its argument.

Reviewer Rev_1 can submit a review by the following code:

$$\begin{aligned}\mathsf{Rev}_1 &= \mathtt{outp}\, \mathit{subm}(\{\!|\, r, \mathsf{F}_{prf_1}\,|\!\}_{s_p}).\, \mathbf{0} \\ \text{where } \mathsf{F}_{prf_1} &= \lambda x.\, \mathtt{dec}\, x\, \mathtt{as}\, \{\!|\, z\,|\!\}_{s_{rev_1}}\, \mathtt{in}\, \mathtt{outp}\, z().\, \mathbf{0}\end{aligned}$$

Alternatively, Rev_1 can delegate the review of the paper to Rev_2 by giving to the latter access to the paper (i.e. the key s_p) and a function that can be used to prove the delegation:

$$\begin{aligned}\mathsf{Rev}_1' &= \mathtt{outp}\, \mathit{deleg}(\{\!|\, s_p, \mathsf{F}_{del_{12}}\,|\!\}_{s_{rev_2}}).\, \mathbf{0} \\ \mathsf{F}_{del_{12}} &= \lambda(x, y).\, \mathtt{dec}\, x\, \mathtt{as}\, \{\!|\, z\,|\!\}_{s_{rev_1}}\, \mathtt{in}\, \mathtt{outp}\, y(\{\!|\, z\,|\!\}_{s_{rev_2}}).\, \mathbf{0}\end{aligned}$$

When this function is applied to a challenge $\{\!|\, a\,|\!\}_{s_{rev_1}}$ bound to x and a continuation channel bound to y, it sends the challenge $\{\!|\, a\,|\!\}_{s_{rev_2}}$ on y. Hence, Rev_2 can submit a review using the following code:

$$\begin{aligned}\mathsf{Rev}_2 &= \mathtt{inp}\, \mathit{deleg}(x_{deleg}).\, \mathtt{dec}\, x_{deleg}\, \mathtt{as}\, \{\!|\, x_p, f_{del_{12}}\,|\!\}_{s_{rev_2}} \\ &\qquad \mathtt{in}\, \mathtt{outp}\, \mathit{subm}(\{\!|\, r, \mathsf{F}_{prf_2}\,|\!\}_{x_p}).\, \mathbf{0} \\ \mathsf{F}_{prf_2} &= \lambda x.\, \nu b.\, \mathtt{fork}\, f_{del_{12}}(x, b).\, \mathtt{inp}\, b(y).\, \mathtt{dec}\, y\, \mathtt{as}\, \{\!|\, z\,|\!\}_{s_{rev_2}}\, \mathtt{in}\, \mathtt{outp}\, z().\, \mathbf{0}\end{aligned}$$

One would want to prove that the system where Rev_1 submits a review is equivalent to the system where the review is delegated to Rev_2. This can be done by proving that the system

$$\mathsf{Sys}_1 = \nu s_p, s_{rev_1}, s_{rev_2}.\, (\mathsf{Conf} \mid \mathsf{Rev}_1 \mid \mathsf{D})$$

is observationally equivalent to

$$\mathsf{Sys}_2 = \nu s_p, s_{rev_1}, s_{rev_2}.\, (\mathsf{Conf} \mid \mathsf{Rev}_1' \mid \mathsf{Rev}_2)$$

where D generates dummy traffic on channel *deleg*.

It is important therefore to develop techniques for proving the equivalence of higher-order concurrent systems with cryptographic primitives. These techniques depend on the particular choice of semantic equivalence, ranging from branching-time equivalences, such as *reduction barbed congruence* [25,1,4,13] and *bisimulation equivalence* [2], to linear-time equivalences, such as *may-testing equivalence* [3,4,12] and must-testing equivalence [12]. We aim at developing proof techniques that are adaptable to many semantic equivalences;[1] here we focus on *safe equivalence*, which is closely related to may-testing equivalence [7].

There are two main previous approaches that could potentially be used for proving safe equivalence for HOspi. The first would be to adapt Sangiorgi's well-known translation from the HOπ with finite types into the standard π-calculus [20], based on *triggers*, thereby in principle allowing first-order proof principles to be applied to HOspi. However it is unclear how the translation could be adapted to HOspi in a way that will be fully abstract and useful in proofs of equivalence. The second approach would be to make use of *environmental bisimulations* [23], which has been shown to provide a sound, complete and useful proof technique for reduction barbed congruence in Applied HOπ, a higher-order concurrent language with cryptographic primitives [25]. However, environmental bisimulations do not provide a complete proof principle for linear-time semantic equivalences, such as safe equivalence.

Here we pursue an alternative strategy similar to that of Jeffrey and Rathke [14], developing a proof technique which works at the level of a Labelled Transition System (LTS) for HOspi. The success of LTS-based reasoning for first-order calculi makes us confident that this approach is adaptable to semantic equivalences other than safe equivalence, and to higher-order concurrent languages with richer type-systems, as that by Maffeis et al. [17].

Configurations in our LTS record the interaction of the observer with the process, as well as the knowledge of the observer at every step of this interaction. This is similar in spirit to the environments used in environmental bisimulations [23,25] and in proof techniques for first-order cryptographic calculi [2,4]. Our LTS is first-order because it employs a *symbolic treatment* of higher-order values generated by the context, which obviates the need for quantification over functional contexts. Our approach is informed by the translation to triggers but avoids the complexities and incompleteness issues of a potential translation to a first-order language. We believe this to be the first first-order semantics for a higher-order language with cryptographic primitives.

We develop a sound and complete first-order co-inductive proof principle for safe equivalence for HOspi processes in terms of novel *set simulations*. These are essentially simulations over our first-order LTS between configurations and sets of configurations.

The symbolic treatment of functions in the LTS is a sound approach for HOspi because the language allows attackers to only apply functions or test them for equality. A variation of the language and theory that can express more

[1] For example semantic equivalences that can be used to prove security properties such as safety and non-interference.

Syntax

$$x, y, f \in \mathsf{Var} \qquad a, b, c, n, k, r \in \mathsf{Name} \qquad u, v \in \mathsf{Var} \cup \mathsf{Name}$$

$$T ::= \mathsf{Nm} \mid \mathsf{Pr} \mid T \times T \mid \mathsf{Enc}(T) \qquad \text{Type}$$

$$\begin{aligned} P, Q ::= {} & \mathbb{0} \mid \mathtt{outp}\, u(V{:}T).\, P \mid \mathtt{inp}\, u(x{:}T).\, P \mid (P \mid P) \mid \nu n.\, P \mid \mathtt{fork}\, V(u).\, P \qquad \text{Proc} \\ \mid {} & \mathtt{if}\, V = V\, \mathtt{then}\, P\, \mathtt{else}\, P \mid \mathtt{let}\, f = \lambda x.\, P\, \mathtt{in}\, P \\ \mid {} & \mathtt{match}\, V\, \mathtt{as}\, (x, y)\, \mathtt{in}\, P \mid \mathtt{decr}\, V\, \mathtt{as}\, \{\!|\, x \,|\!\}_u\, \mathtt{in}\, P\, \mathtt{else}\, P \end{aligned}$$

$$U, V, W ::= x \mid n \mid (V, V) \mid \lambda_r x.\, P \mid \{\!|\, V \,|\!\}_k \qquad \text{Val}$$

Reduction Semantics

$\mathtt{outp}\, c(V{:}T).\, P \mid \mathtt{inp}\, c(x{:}T).\, Q$	$\to P \mid Q\{V/x\}$		(RCOMM)
$\mathtt{decr}\, \{\!\|\, V \,\|\!\}_k\, \mathtt{as}\, \{\!\|\, x \,\|\!\}_k\, \mathtt{in}\, P\, \mathtt{else}\, Q$	$\to P\{V/x\}$		(RDEC-S)
$\mathtt{decr}\, \{\!\|\, V \,\|\!\}_l\, \mathtt{as}\, \{\!\|\, x \,\|\!\}_k\, \mathtt{in}\, P\, \mathtt{else}\, Q$	$\to Q$	if $k \neq l$	(RDEC-F)
$\mathtt{match}\, (V, U)\, \mathtt{as}\, (x, y)\, \mathtt{in}\, P$	$\to P\{V/x, U/y\}$		(RMTCH)
$\mathtt{let}\, f = \lambda x.\, P\, \mathtt{in}\, Q$	$\to \nu r.\, Q\{\lambda_r x.\, P/f\}$	if $r \notin fn(P, Q)$	(RLET)
$\mathtt{fork}\, (\lambda_r x.\, P)(n).\, Q$	$\to P\{n/x\} \mid Q$		(RAPP)
$\mathtt{if}\, U = V\, \mathtt{then}\, P\, \mathtt{else}\, Q$	$\to P$	if $\vdash equal(U, V)$	(RIF-T)
$\mathtt{if}\, U = V\, \mathtt{then}\, P\, \mathtt{else}\, Q$	$\to Q$	if $\nvdash equal(U, V)$	(RIF-F)
$P_1 \mid Q$	$\to P_2 \mid Q$	if $P_1 \to P_2$	(RPAR)
$\nu a.\, P_1$	$\to \nu a.\, P_2$	if $P_1 \to P_2$	(RNU)
P_1	$\to P_2$	if $P_1 \equiv P_1' \to P_2' \equiv P_2$	(RCNG)

Fig. 1. Syntax and reduction semantics of HOspi

sophisticated attackers, for example attackers that can learn the complete source-level text of transmitted code, as in Applied HOπ [25], would also be possible, but not first-order, and it would be closer to the theory of Sato and Sumii [25].

The language and reduction semantics are given in Section 2 while the LTS of configurations is in Section 3. In Section 5 we explain set simulations and state their soundness and completeness. We illustrate the usefulness of set simulations in Section 6, by giving coinductive proofs relating higher-order systems, such as those discussed above. The paper concludes with discussion of related and future work in Section 7.

2 Semantics of HOspi

We study the language HOspi, a higher-order concurrent calculus with primitives for symmetric-key cryptography, similar to those of the spi-calculus [3]. Public-key cryptography can be added to the language without any significant change to the semantics and the theory of the following sections. The syntax and reduction semantics of HOspi are shown in Figure 1. We employ the standard π-calculus abbreviations; $(\equiv)$ is the standard π-calculus structural equivalence.

We use a lightweight dynamic type system for HOspi which helps streamline the presentation of our theory. *Closed values* in HOspi, ranged over by V and U, are either names of type Nm, process abstractions $(\lambda_r x.\, P)$ of type Pr, pairs of type $T \times T'$, and messages encrypted with a name $(\{\!|\, V \,|\!\}_k)$ of type

$\mathsf{Enc}(T)$. Abstractions, for simplicity, can be applied to names with the construct $\mathtt{fork}\,(\lambda_r x.\, P)(n).\, Q$ and fork the body P as a new process in parallel with the continuation Q (RAPP). We write $\mathtt{fork}\,(\lambda_r x.\, P)(n)$ when the continuation is $\mathbf{0}$.

Communication happens by synchronisation of an output ($\mathtt{outp}\, c(V{:}T).\, P$) and an input ($\mathtt{inp}\, c(x{:}T).\, Q$) over a common channel c (RCOMM). The dynamic type system guarantees that communication happens only when the transmitted and the expected value have the same type. Restriction ($\nu n.\, P$) encodes privacy of information, such as keys, which can be extruded by communication.

In a cryptographic calculus it is important for processes or attackers to be able to detect the retransmission of messages. This creates the requirement for an equality semantics defined at any type, including function type (RIF-T, RIF-F). We use an equality semantics, denoted by *equal* and present in languages like Scheme, which identifies only functional values representing the same object, identical names, and pairs and encrypted packages with equal components. Object identity for functional values is possible by requiring each such value to be generated by the construct $\mathtt{let}\, f = \lambda x.\, P\, \mathtt{in}\, Q$, which annotates the value with a fresh name r (RLET). Equality at function type is thus reduced to equality of names. Such an equality construct is convenient for a symbolic treatment of functions in the following sections. We call a closed process with no functional values *source-level*; the reduction semantics of Figure 1 are defined only for processes derivable by a source-level process, which guarantees that functional values annotated with the same name were generated by a single `let` statement.

The remaining reduction rules are rather standard and deal with decryption of messages (RDEC-S, RDEC-F), the deconstruction of pairs (RMTCH), and π-calculus processes (RPAR, RNU, RCNG). We omit the `else` branch of decryption if it is $\mathbf{0}$.

A safety property can be formulated as a safety test T^ω; a process which reports bad behaviour on a special channel ω. Let us write $R\!\downarrow_\omega$ whenever $R \equiv \nu\tilde{n}.\, \mathtt{outp}\, \omega(V{:}T).\, R_1 \mid R_2$, and $\omega \notin \{\tilde{n}\}$.

Definition 2.1 (Passing Safety Tests). *A process P passes a safety test T^ω, written P cannot T^ω, when $P \mid T^\omega \rightarrow^* R$ implies $R\not\downarrow_\omega$.*

Definition 2.2 (Safety Preservation). *Two source-level processes P and Q are related by $P \sqsubseteq_{\mathsf{safe}} Q$ when for all source-level tests T^ω, P cannot T^ω implies Q cannot T^ω. We use $P \simeq_{\mathsf{safe}} Q$ to denote the associated equivalence.*

The reader familiar with [7] will recognise this safe-preorder as the inverse of the well-known *may-testing* preorder. An important property of ($\sqsubseteq_{\mathsf{safe}}$), as with other contextual equivalences, is that it enables compositional reasoning.

Proposition 2.3 (Compositional Reasoning). *If $P \sqsubseteq_{\mathsf{safe}} Q$ then $P \mid R \sqsubseteq_{\mathsf{safe}} Q \mid R$ and $\nu n.\, P \sqsubseteq_{\mathsf{safe}} \nu n.\, Q$.*

3 First-Order Semantics

We describe the interaction between a process and an observer by transitions in an LTS. The LTS uses *configurations* that record the values transmitted from the process to the observer and vice versa, the knowledge of the observer, and the private knowledge of the process. The LTS is *first-order*: only the names that annotate abstractions are exchanged between the process and the observer, not the abstractions themselves. Below we explain the details of configurations and transitions in this LTS.

3.1 Configurations

An LTS configuration describes the state of a process interrogated by an observer and takes the form $\langle H \parallel K \parallel I \rangle \triangleright \mathcal{P}$ where

- K is the current knowledge of the observer, a finite set of names
- I is the current private knowledge of the process, the set of names known to the process $\mathcal{P}$ but not the observer
- H is the history of the interaction between the observer and the process, in which the messages exchanged are accessible via indices
- $\mathcal{P}$ is an extended process, which may contain pointers to values in the history.

The interrogation of the process by the observer proceeds by the exchange of messages between them, each message being recorded in H, and available for use in future interactions. We first explain how these interactions take place, and how they are recorded.

Example 3.1. First we consider the configuration

$$\langle H_0 \parallel K \parallel s, r \rangle \triangleright \mathtt{outp}\, c(\{\!|\, \lambda_r x.\, P_0 \,|\!\}_s).\, P_1$$

where the key s (and the annotation r) are private to the configuration. Suppose the channel name c is known to the observer; that is $c \in K$. Then the process can output the encrypted message on c, resulting in the configuration

$$\langle H_1 \parallel K \parallel s, r \rangle \triangleright P_1$$

where $H_1 = H_0, \kappa {\mapsto} \{\!|\, \lambda_r x.\, P_0 \,|\!\}_s$. The history is extended with a new entry, indexed by the fresh κ, which records the message received, $\{\!|\, \lambda_r x.\, P_0 \,|\!\}_s$; these indices κ of messages received from the process are taken from a distinct set of *output abstract names* (OAName) The observer now has access to this message via the index κ, but not to the contents since the key s is private to the process.

If $P_1 = \mathtt{outp}\, c(s).\, P_2$, it can send the key s to the observer and end up in the configuration

$$\langle H_1 \parallel K, s \parallel r \rangle \triangleright P_2$$

Here the history has not changed since it is only necessary to record the non-base values used in the interactions. But the knowledge of the observer has been extended with the key s. Now using this key the observer has access to the abstraction and may apply it to a name or use it in a message sent back to the process. However in the latter case, in order to maintain a clear interface between the observer and process, the abstraction itself is not used. For example if $P_2 = \mathbf{inp}\, c(x).\, P_3$, the above configuration can transition to

$$\langle H_2 \,\|\, K, s \,\|\, r\rangle \rhd P_3\{\iota/x\}$$

where H_2 is the history $H_1, (\iota \mapsto \{\!|\, \kappa.\mathsf{decr}_s \,|\!\}_l)$, ι is a fresh index taken from a separate set of *input abstract names* (IAName) used for recording the messages sent from the observer to the process, and l is any key in the observers knowledge (K, s). But note that the process actually only receives the input index ι, and in the history the *observer pattern* $\kappa.\mathsf{decr}_s$ represents the actual abstraction $\lambda_r x.\, P_0$ previously received from the process. □

Thus, in a configuration the history H records the non-base messages exchanged, using $\kappa \in$ OAName for those sent by the process, and $\iota \in$ IAName for those received by the process. We use the following metavariables to range over these sets.

$$\iota \in \mathsf{IAName} \qquad \alpha \in \mathsf{AName} = \mathsf{IAName} \cup \mathsf{OAName}$$
$$\kappa \in \mathsf{OAName} \qquad \zeta \in \mathsf{AName} \cup \mathsf{Name}$$

Moreover, as we have seen in the previous example, observers can access data bound to output names in the history using *observer patterns* in order to further interrogate the process. As we will see, the process can dually access data bound to input names in the history using *process patterns*. The structure of these patterns is:

$$\phi ::= \iota \mid \phi.\mathsf{op} \quad \mathsf{ProcPattern} \qquad \mathsf{op} ::= 1 \mid 2 \mid \mathsf{decr}_s \quad \mathsf{Op}$$
$$\psi ::= \kappa \mid \psi.\mathsf{op} \quad \mathsf{ObsPattern} \qquad \pi \in \mathsf{Pattern} = \mathsf{ProcPattern} \cup \mathsf{ObsPattern}$$

The process (observer) pattern ι (resp. κ) refers to the value in the history that is bound to that name; $\pi.i$ refers to the ith projection of the value referred to by π, and $\pi.\mathsf{decr}_s$ refers to the contents of a message encrypted with s and referred to by π.[2] Therefore we extend the syntax for values (AVal) and processes (AProc) to contain such patterns ($\mathcal{U}, \mathcal{V} ::= \ldots \mid \pi \quad \mathsf{AVal}$).

The meta-function $fan(\mathcal{P})$ gives the abstract names in $\mathcal{P}$, and $T(\alpha)$ gives the type of the abstract name α. Patterns are typed by the following rules.

$$\frac{}{\vdash \alpha : T(\alpha)} \qquad \frac{\vdash \pi : T_1 \times T_2}{\vdash \pi.i : T_i} \qquad \frac{\vdash \pi : \mathsf{Enc}(T)}{\vdash \pi.\mathsf{decr}_s : T}$$

The observer may use its accumulating knowledge K, together with the abstract values received from the process, occurring in the history H, to further the interrogation of the process. However, unlike [21,23,25], in order to keep the LTS first-order we severely restrict the ability of the observer to construct higher-order values. The soundness of our technique in Section 5 shows that this restriction does not compromise the possible observations made in the LTS.

[2] The use of s in the pattern $\pi.\mathsf{decr}_s$ is only for quantifying over possible patterns, given a set of known keys.

Example 3.2. Consider the following configuration

$$\langle H_0 \parallel K \parallel \cdot \rangle \rhd \mathtt{inp}\, c(x).\, \mathtt{inp}\, c(y).\, \mathtt{dec}\, x\, \mathtt{as}\, \{\!|\, z \,|\!\}_y\, \mathtt{in}\, \mathtt{fork}\, z(n)$$

where $c \in K$. The process is expecting an encrypted function on the channel c. In our LTS the observer can only supply a *symbolic* representation of an abstraction, denoted $\Diamond_r$, informally representing an arbitrary but unknown function annotated with the name r. So after the first input we get the configuration

$$\langle H_1 \parallel K, s, r \parallel \cdot \rangle \rhd \mathtt{inp}\, c(y).\, \mathtt{dec}\, \iota_1\, \mathtt{as}\, \{\!|\, z \,|\!\}_y\, \mathtt{in}\, \mathtt{fork}\, z(n)$$

where $H_1 = H_0, (\iota_1 \mapsto \{\!|\, \Diamond_r \,|\!\}_s)$. The key s and annotation r are freshly generated by the observer and are added to the knowledge.

After the key s is passed to the process by the next input we get

$$\langle H_1 \parallel K, s, r \parallel \cdot \rangle \rhd \mathtt{dec}\, \iota_1\, \mathtt{as}\, \{\!|\, z \,|\!\}_s\, \mathtt{in}\, \mathtt{fork}\, z(n)$$

The process can now use the key s to decrypt the message indexed by ι_1. However, in order to keep the process independent of the actual observer interrogating it (i.e. avoid the propagation of observer-generated non-base values in the process), our operational semantics will ensure that the successful decryption of pattern ι_1 will actually generate the process pattern $\iota_1.\mathsf{decr}_s$, and we obtain the configuration

$$\langle H_1 \parallel K, s, r \parallel \cdot \rangle \rhd \mathtt{fork}\, (\iota_1.\mathsf{decr}_s)(n)$$

The pattern $\iota_1.\mathsf{decr}_s$ gives to the process access to the "function" $\Diamond_r$ in the history H_1. However, since this is purely symbolic its application to n cannot lead to any real computation; as we will see, this symbolic application is recorded by the LTS. □

Well-formed histories map abstract names to values of the same type. Moreover, indexed input values contain only observer patterns and indexed output values contain only process patterns, and all references to abstract names are to the left of each binding.

$$\begin{array}{l} \text{if } (\iota \mapsto \mathcal{V}) \in H \text{ then } \mathit{fan}(\mathcal{V}) \subset \mathsf{OAName} \\ \text{if } (\kappa \mapsto \mathcal{V}) \in H \text{ then } \mathit{fan}(\mathcal{V}) \subset \mathsf{IAName} \\ \text{if } H, \alpha \mapsto \mathcal{V}, H' \text{ then } \mathit{fan}(\mathcal{V}) \subseteq \mathit{dom}(H) \end{array}$$

Given a well-formed history H and a pattern π we define the partial dereferencing operation $H_K(\mathcal{V})$, relative to the knowledge K:

$$\begin{array}{lll} H_K(\mathcal{V}) = \mathcal{V} & \text{if } \mathcal{V} \notin \mathsf{Pattern} \\ H_K(\alpha) = \mathcal{V} & \text{if } (\alpha \mapsto \mathcal{V}') \in H \text{ and } H_K(\mathcal{V}') = \mathcal{V} \\ H_K(\pi.\mathsf{decr}_s) = \mathcal{V} & \text{if } H_K(\pi) = \{\!|\, \mathcal{V}' \,|\!\}_s,\ H_K(\mathcal{V}') = \mathcal{V}, \text{ and } s \in K \\ H_K(\pi.i) = H_K(\mathcal{V}_i) & \text{if } H_K(\pi) = (\mathcal{V}'_1, \mathcal{V}'_2) \text{ and } H_K(\mathcal{V}'_i) = \mathcal{V}_i \end{array}$$

We write $H(\mathcal{V})$ when only the first two rules are used and $H_*(\mathcal{V})$ when the knowledge contains all names.

The closure of the observers knowledge K under decryption of messages in the history H is given by the construction $K^\star_H$.

$$\frac{(\zeta, H', K') \in inp_{H,K,I}(T) \qquad c \in K}{\langle H \parallel K \parallel I\rangle \rhd \mathtt{inp}\,\mathsf{c}(x{:}T).\mathcal{P} \xrightarrow{c?\zeta} \langle H, H' \parallel K, K' \parallel I\rangle \rhd \mathcal{P}\{\zeta/x\}}\ \textsc{TIn}$$

$$\frac{(\zeta, H', K') \in outp(\mathcal{V}{:}T) \qquad I' = I\backslash(K, K')^\star_{H,H'} \qquad c \in K}{\langle H \parallel K \parallel I\rangle \rhd \mathtt{outp}\,\mathsf{c}(\mathcal{V}{:}T).\mathcal{P} \xrightarrow{c!\zeta} \langle H, H' \parallel (K, K')^\star_{H,H'} \parallel I'\rangle \rhd \mathcal{P}}\ \textsc{TOut}$$

$$\frac{\begin{array}{l}\langle H \parallel K, I \parallel \cdot\rangle \rhd \mathcal{P} \xrightarrow{c!\zeta} \langle H, H' \parallel K' \parallel \cdot\rangle \rhd \mathcal{P}' \\ \langle H \parallel K, I \parallel \cdot\rangle \rhd \mathcal{Q} \xrightarrow{c?\zeta_{fr}} \langle H'' \parallel K'' \parallel \cdot\rangle \rhd \mathcal{Q}' \qquad \zeta_{fr} \notin fan(\mathcal{Q})\end{array}}{\langle H \parallel K \parallel I\rangle \rhd \mathcal{P} \mid \mathcal{Q} \xrightarrow{\tau} \langle H \parallel K \parallel I\rangle \rhd \mathcal{P}' \mid \mathcal{Q}'\{H'(\zeta)/\zeta_{fr}\}}\ \textsc{TComm}$$

$$\frac{H_K(\psi) = \lambda_r x.\,\mathcal{Q}}{\langle H \parallel K \parallel I\rangle \rhd \mathcal{P} \xrightarrow{\mathsf{app}(\psi,r,n)} \langle H \parallel K \parallel I\rangle \rhd \mathcal{P} \mid \mathcal{Q}\{n/x\}}\ \textsc{TApp-Obs}$$

$$\frac{H_{K\cup I}(\phi) = \Diamond_r \qquad I' = I\backslash(K, n)^\star_H}{\langle H \parallel K \parallel I\rangle \rhd \mathtt{fork}\,\phi(n).\mathcal{P} \xrightarrow{\mathtt{sig}(r,n)} \langle H \parallel (K, n)^\star_H \parallel I'\rangle \rhd \mathcal{P}}\ \textsc{TApp-}\Diamond$$

$$\frac{H_{K\cup I}(\mathcal{V}) = \lambda_r x.\,\mathcal{P}}{\langle H \parallel K \parallel I\rangle \rhd \mathtt{fork}\,\mathcal{V}(n).\,Q \xrightarrow{\tau} \langle H \parallel K \parallel I\rangle \rhd \mathcal{P}\{n/x\} \mid \mathcal{Q}}\ \textsc{TApp-}\lambda$$

Fig. 2. Main LTS rules (omitting symmetric rules)

Definition 3.3 (Knowledge closure). *$n \in K^\star_H$ if $n \in K$ or $\exists\psi.H_{(K^\star_H)}(\psi) = n$.*

In the rest of this paper will only consider *well-formed* configurations, and we will use C to range over them.

Definition 3.4. *$\langle H \parallel K \parallel I\rangle \rhd \mathcal{P}$ is well-formed when:*

- *H is well-formed, and K is closed ($K^\star_H \subseteq K$)*
- Observer values use only K: $\forall(\iota \mapsto \mathcal{V}) \in H.\ fn(\mathcal{V}) \subseteq K$.
- Private and global names are distinct: $K \cap I = \emptyset$.
- Closed: $fv(codom(H), \mathcal{P}) = \emptyset$, $fn(codom(H), \mathcal{P}) \subseteq K \cup I$, and $fan(codom(H), P) \subseteq dom(H)$.
- Well-annotated: *if $\lambda_r x.\mathcal{P}$ is in the configuration then $r \in I$; if $\lambda_r x.\mathcal{P}'$ is also in the configuration then $\mathcal{P} = \mathcal{P}'$; if $\Diamond_r$ in the codomain of H then $r \in K$.*

3.2 Transitions

Our LTS defines labelled transitions between the configurations, briefly discussed informally in the examples of the previous section. The main transitions of the LTS are shown in Figure 2, subject to the well-formedness conditions for configurations.

Rule TOUT describes an output on channel c, labelled by $c!\zeta$. The channel name c must be in the knowledge of the observer and the effect of the action on the configuration is calculated using the auxiliary relation $outp(\mathcal{V} : T)$:

$$(n, \cdot, \{n\}) \in outp(n : \mathsf{Nm}) \qquad (\kappa, (\kappa \mapsto \mathcal{V}), \emptyset) \in outp(\mathcal{V} : T) \text{ if } T \neq \mathsf{Nm}$$

Thus, if the output value $\mathcal{V}$ is a name it is added directly to the observers knowledge; otherwise it is added to the history H via a new index. In both cases the output transition may allow the observer to discover previously private names known only to the process, by decrypting the current and previous messages. This knowledge extension of the observer is taken into account by the closure of the environment's knowledge $(\ )^\star_H$.

Rule TIN describes an input transition, labelled by $c?\zeta$; as for the output rule, the channel name c must be in the knowledge of the observer. The input value of type T is provided by the set $inp_{H,K,I}(T)$ as a tuple of an abstract or actual name ζ, a history extension H', and a knowledge extension K':

$$\begin{array}{lll}
(n, \cdot, \{n\}) & \in inp_{H,K,I}(\mathsf{Nm}) & \text{if } n \notin I \\
(\iota, (\iota \mapsto \Diamond_r), \{r\}) & \in inp_{H,K,I}(\mathsf{Pr}) & \\
(\iota, (\iota \mapsto (H_1(\zeta_1), H_2(\zeta_2))), (K_1, K_2)) & & \\
 & \in inp_{H,K,I}(T_1 \times T_2) & \text{if } (\zeta_i, H_i, K_i) \in inp_{H,K,I}(T_i) \\
(\iota, (\iota \mapsto \{\!| H_1(\zeta) |\!\}_s), (K_1, K_2)) & \in inp_{H,K,I}(\mathsf{Enc}(T)) & \text{if } (\zeta, H_1, K_1) \in inp_{H,K,I}(T) \\
 & & \text{and } (s, \cdot, K_2) \in inp_{H,K,I}(\mathsf{Nm}) \\
(\iota, (\iota \mapsto \psi), \emptyset) & \in inp_{H,K,I}(T) & \text{if } \vdash H_K(\psi) : T \neq \mathsf{Nm}
\end{array}$$

At type Nm, the input value is a name disjoint from the private names of the process I that can be either in K or fresh. At type Pr, the input can be the symbol $\Diamond_r$ and r is added in the knowledge K. The cases for $T_1 \times T_2$ and $\mathsf{Enc}(T)$ proceed by induction on the type, returning a singleton history extension and the union of the knowledge extension. At any non-base type, an output pattern can be used to reference a value that was previously sent to the observer.

Communication is achieved by rule TCOMM. Here, one of the processes inputs a fresh (actual or abstract) name, which is replaced by the value output by the other and may be indexed in the history. This is a τ-transition in which the observer does not participate; therefore the history H and knowledge K remain unchanged.

At any point in time the observer may choose to apply to a name n one of the abstractions reachable by an observer pattern ψ using keys from the knowledge K (TAPP-OBS). Intuitively this means that the abstraction in question $\lambda_r x.\, \mathcal{Q}$ was previously sent by the process to the observer, perhaps as the contents of an encrypted message, but which can be now decrypted with the current knowledge K. The resulting transition, labelled $\mathsf{app}(\psi, r, n)$, causes the application to run in parallel with the observed process.

TAPP-$\Diamond$ encodes the situation where the process applies an unknown abstraction that was created by the observer; such abstractions are only reachable by the process via a process pattern ϕ that uses keys from $K \cup I$. The effect of this rule is merely a signal $\mathtt{sig}(r, n)$ to the observer containing the annotation of the

TDECR-S

$$\frac{H \vdash \mathcal{V}.\mathsf{decr}_s \rightsquigarrow \mathcal{V}'}{\langle H \parallel K \parallel I\rangle \rhd \mathtt{decr}\,\mathcal{V}\,\mathtt{as}\,\{\!|\,x\,|\!\}_s\,\mathtt{in}\,\mathcal{P}\,\mathtt{else}\,\mathcal{Q} \xrightarrow{\tau} \langle H \parallel K \parallel I\rangle \rhd \mathcal{P}\{\mathcal{V}'/x\}}$$

TDECR-F

$$\frac{H_{K\cup I}(\mathcal{V}) = \{\!|\,\mathcal{V}'\,|\!\}_l \qquad s \neq l}{\langle H \parallel K \parallel I\rangle \rhd \mathtt{decr}\,\mathcal{V}\,\mathtt{as}\,\{\!|\,x\,|\!\}_s\,\mathtt{in}\,\mathcal{P}\,\mathtt{else}\,\mathcal{Q} \xrightarrow{\tau} \langle H \parallel K \parallel I\rangle \rhd \mathcal{Q}}$$

TCOND-T

$$\frac{H \vdash \mathit{equal}(\mathcal{V}_1, \mathcal{V}_2)}{\langle H \parallel K \parallel I\rangle \rhd \mathtt{if}\,\mathcal{V}_1 = \mathcal{V}_2\,\mathtt{then}\,\mathcal{P}\,\mathtt{else}\,\mathcal{Q} \xrightarrow{\tau} \langle H \parallel K \parallel I\rangle \rhd \mathcal{P}}$$

TCOND-F

$$\frac{H \vdash \neg\mathit{equal}(\mathcal{V}_1, \mathcal{V}_2)}{\langle H \parallel K \parallel I\rangle \rhd \mathtt{if}\,\mathcal{V}_1 = \mathcal{V}_2\,\mathtt{then}\,\mathcal{P}\,\mathtt{else}\,\mathcal{Q} \xrightarrow{\tau} \langle H \parallel K \parallel I\rangle \rhd \mathcal{Q}}$$

TMATCH

$$\frac{H \vdash \mathcal{V}.1 \rightsquigarrow \mathcal{V}_1 \qquad H \vdash \mathcal{V}.2 \rightsquigarrow \mathcal{V}_2}{\langle H \parallel K \parallel I\rangle \rhd \mathtt{match}\,\mathcal{V}\,\mathtt{as}\,(x_1, x_2)\,\mathtt{in}\,\mathcal{P} \xrightarrow{\tau} \langle H \parallel K \parallel I\rangle \rhd \mathcal{P}\{\mathcal{V}_1/x_1, \mathcal{V}_2/x_2\}}$$

TDEF-λ

$$\frac{r \notin I \cup K}{\langle H \parallel K \parallel I\rangle \rhd \mathtt{let}\,x = \lambda y.\mathcal{P}\,\mathtt{in}\,\mathcal{Q} \xrightarrow{\tau} \langle H \parallel K \parallel I, r\rangle \rhd \mathcal{Q}\{\lambda_r y.\mathcal{P}/x\}}$$

TPAR-L

$$\frac{\langle H \parallel K \parallel I\rangle \rhd \mathcal{P} \xrightarrow{\mu} \langle H' \parallel K' \parallel I'\rangle \rhd \mathcal{P}'}{\langle H \parallel K \parallel I\rangle \rhd \mathcal{P} \mid \mathcal{Q} \xrightarrow{\mu} \langle H' \parallel K' \parallel I'\rangle \rhd \mathcal{P}' \mid \mathcal{Q}}$$

TNU

$$\frac{a \notin I \cup K}{\langle H \parallel K \parallel I\rangle \rhd \nu a.\mathcal{P} \xrightarrow{\tau} \langle H \parallel K \parallel I, a\rangle \rhd \mathcal{P}}$$

Fig. 3. More LTS rules (omitting symmetric rules)

abstraction that was applied and the argument given. The resulting process is just the continuation of the application. As we will see, this transition is sufficient to reason about applications of input values and can be seen as a form of trigger semantics [19,20,14]. The process can also apply a process-generated abstraction, which is a τ-step in the LTS (TAPP-λ) since the application is unobservable.

The rest of the LTS rules are shown in Figure 3 and encode silent transitions and a congruence rule for parallel composition (TPAR-L). Rules TDECR-S and TDECR-F reduce a successful and an unsuccessful decryption using the following evaluation predicate:

$$
\begin{array}{ll}
H, K \vdash \{\!|\,\mathcal{V}\,|\!\}_S.\mathsf{decr}_s \rightsquigarrow \mathcal{V} & \\
H, K \vdash (\mathcal{V}_1, \mathcal{V}_2).i \rightsquigarrow \mathcal{V}_i & \\
H, K \vdash \phi.\mathsf{op} \rightsquigarrow \phi.\mathsf{op} & \text{if } H_K(\phi.\mathsf{op}) = \mathcal{V} \neq n \\
H, K \vdash \phi.\mathsf{op} \rightsquigarrow n & \text{if } H_K(\phi.\mathsf{op}) = n
\end{array}
$$

The important point in the rule TDECR-S is that if the encrypted message $\mathcal{V}$ is a process pattern, that refers to some data in the history H, then the successful decryption returns not the actual contents of the message but rather another process pattern with which the contents can be extracted from the history.

Rule TMATCH reduces the decomposition of a pair using the same evaluation predicate, while rules TCOND-T and TCOND-F reduce conditionals using a standard equality predicate that dereferences all patterns:

$$
\begin{array}{ll}
H \vdash equal(n, n) & \\
H \vdash equal(\Diamond_r, \Diamond_r) & \\
H \vdash equal(\lambda_r x.\, \mathcal{P}, \lambda_r x.\, \mathcal{Q}) & \\
H \vdash equal(\{\!|\mathcal{V}|\!\}_S, \{\!|\mathcal{V}'|\!\}_S) & \text{if } H \vdash equal(\mathcal{V}, \mathcal{V}') \\
H \vdash equal((\mathcal{V}_1, \mathcal{V}_2), (\mathcal{V}_1', \mathcal{V}_2')) & \text{if } H \vdash equal(\mathcal{V}_1, \mathcal{V}_1') \text{ and } H \vdash equal(\mathcal{V}_2, \mathcal{V}_2') \\
H \vdash equal(\pi, \mathcal{V}') & \text{if } H \vdash equal(H_*(\pi), \mathcal{V}') \\
H \vdash equal(\mathcal{V}, \pi) & \text{if } H \vdash equal(\mathcal{V}, H_*(\pi))
\end{array}
$$

Bound names in the process are promoted to actual names at the level of the configuration by a τ-move (TNU) that simplifies the handling of extrusion.

We write $\stackrel{\mu}{\Rightarrow}$ to mean the reflexive, transitive closure of $\stackrel{\tau}{\rightarrow}$, if $\mu = \tau$, and $\stackrel{\tau}{\Rightarrow}\stackrel{\mu}{\rightarrow}\stackrel{\tau}{\Rightarrow}$ otherwise. We call $\stackrel{t}{\Rightarrow}$ a *weak trace* of $\mathcal{C}$ if it is a sequence of non-τ actions $t = \mu_1 \dots \mu_n$ and for some $\mathcal{C}'$, $\mathcal{C} \stackrel{\tau}{\Rightarrow}\stackrel{\mu_1}{\longrightarrow}\stackrel{\tau}{\Rightarrow} \dots \stackrel{\tau}{\Rightarrow}\stackrel{\mu_n}{\longrightarrow}\stackrel{\tau}{\Rightarrow} \mathcal{C}'$.

The following propositions show that silent transitions do not change the history and knowledge of a configuration, weakly correspond to reduction steps of HOspi, and are invariant to transfer of knowledge between the process and the environment.

Proposition 3.5. *If* $\langle H_1 \parallel K_1 \parallel I_1 \rangle \rhd P \stackrel{\tau}{\rightarrow} \langle H_2 \parallel K_2 \parallel I_2 \rangle \rhd Q'$ *then* $H_1 = H_2$ *and* $K_1 = K_2$.

Proposition 3.6. *If* $P \rightarrow Q$ *then there exist* $\widetilde{a}$, $\widetilde{c}$, Q', *such that* $fn(P) \subseteq \widetilde{c}$, $Q \equiv \nu\widetilde{a}.\, Q'$ *and* $\langle \cdot \parallel \widetilde{c} \parallel \cdot \rangle \rhd P \stackrel{\tau}{\longrightarrow}^* \langle \cdot \parallel \widetilde{c} \parallel \widetilde{a} \rangle \rhd Q'$.

Proposition 3.7. *If* $\langle \cdot \parallel \widetilde{c} \parallel \widetilde{a} \rangle \rhd P \stackrel{\tau}{\rightarrow} \langle \cdot \parallel \widetilde{c} \parallel \widetilde{b} \rangle \rhd Q$ *then* $\nu\widetilde{a}.\, P \rightarrow^* \nu\widetilde{b}.\, Q$.

Proposition 3.8 (Knowledge Transfer)

$$
\begin{array}{l}
\langle H_1 \parallel K_1 \parallel I_1, b \rangle \rhd P \stackrel{\tau}{\rightarrow} \langle H_2 \parallel K_2 \parallel I_2, b \rangle \rhd Q \quad \textit{iff} \\
\langle H_1 \parallel K_1, b \parallel I_1 \rangle \rhd P \stackrel{\tau}{\rightarrow} \langle H_2 \parallel K_2, b \parallel I_2 \rangle \rhd Q
\end{array}
$$

Finally, private names can be renamed to fresh names without affecting the transitions of the configuration.

Lemma 3.9. *If* $\langle H \parallel K \parallel I, a \rangle \rhd \mathcal{P} \stackrel{\mu}{\rightarrow} \langle H' \parallel K' \parallel I', a \rangle \rhd Q$ *and* $b \notin I' \cup K'$ *then* $\langle H\{b/a\} \parallel K \parallel I, b \rangle \rhd \mathcal{P}\{b/a\} \xrightarrow{\mu\{b/a\}} \langle H'\{b/a\} \parallel K' \parallel I', b \rangle \rhd Q\{b/a\}$.

4 History Equivalence

Given a history H of a configuration $\mathcal{C}$, an observer with knowledge K can make a number of tests on the values previously output by $\mathcal{C}$ and bound to output abstract names in H: it can attempt to decode encrypted values with keys from K, and compare values reachable with keys from K with other constructed values. The following equivalence states when two histories are indistinguishable by these tests for a given knowledge K.

Definition 4.1 (History Equivalence ($\simeq$)). *Two histories H, H' are equivalent under the knowledge K, and we write $K \vdash H \simeq H'$, if*

$$dom(H) = dom(H') \qquad (\iota \mapsto \mathcal{V}) \in H \text{ iff } (\iota \mapsto \mathcal{V}) \in H'$$
$$\forall \psi, \mathcal{V}.\quad fn(\psi, \mathcal{V}) \subseteq K \;\wedge\; fan(\psi, \mathcal{V}) \subseteq dom(H) \cap \mathsf{OAName}$$
$$\implies (H \vdash equal(\psi, \mathcal{V}) \text{ iff } H' \vdash equal(\psi, \mathcal{V}))$$

Intuitively the first two conditions of the above definition require that equivalent histories describe the same sequence of inputs and outputs, and the observer-generated inputs are equal. The final condition compares values in the history, reachable by an observer pattern ψ using keys from K, with any other value that the observer can construct. These tests subsume the decryption tests of the observer.

Example 4.2. Consider an observer with knowledge K, where $k_1, k_2 \notin K$, and the histories $H = (\kappa_1 \mapsto \{\!|\, a \,|\!\}_{k_1})$ and $H' = (\kappa_1 \mapsto \{\!|\, a \,|\!\}_{k_2})$. The observer can test whether the message in each of the histories is encrypted with a known key $k \in K$ by attempting to decrypt it using k. This test, which fails in both histories, is encoded in the definition of ($\simeq$) by the equality: $equal(\kappa_1, \{\!|\, \kappa_1.\mathsf{decr}_k \,|\!\}_k)$.

In fact, under the given knowledge K, the two histories are indistinguishable by an observer and $K \vdash H \simeq H'$. If, after an output of the configuration, the knowledge K is extended with the key k_1 then the observer can distinguish the two histories by successfully decrypting the message in H and failing to do so in H'. The equality that distinguishes the histories in this case is $equal(\kappa_1, \{\!|\, \kappa_1.\mathsf{decr}_{k_1} \,|\!\}_{k_1})$, which is true under H and false under H'. □

Example 4.3. Consider $a, k_2 \in K$, $k_1 \notin K$, and the histories $H = (\kappa_1 \mapsto \{\!|\, a \,|\!\}_{k_1})$ and $H' = (\kappa_1 \mapsto \{\!|\, b \,|\!\}_{k_1})$. The observer cannot distinguish the two histories as any decryption test will fail for both. If after a transition the histories become

$$H = (\kappa_1 \mapsto \{\!|\, a \,|\!\}_{k_1},\; \kappa_2 \mapsto \{\!|\, k_1 \,|\!\}_{k_2}) \qquad H' = (\kappa_1 \mapsto \{\!|\, b \,|\!\}_{k_1},\; \kappa_2 \mapsto \{\!|\, k_1 \,|\!\}_{k_2})$$

the observer can decrypt the second message and increase the knowledge K with the key k_1. With the new knowledge, the decryption of the first message reveals that its content is different in H and H'. This is captured in the definition of ($\simeq$) by the following equality that holds only under H: $equal(\kappa_1.\mathsf{decr}_{k_1}, a)$. □

Example 4.4. The observer can also test two outputs of the configuration for equality. Thus, even with an empty knowledge, the histories

$$H = (\kappa_1 \mapsto \{\!|\, a \,|\!\}_k, \kappa_2 \mapsto \{\!|\, a \,|\!\}_k) \qquad H' = (\kappa_1 \mapsto \{\!|\, a \,|\!\}_k,\; \kappa_2 \mapsto \{\!|\, b \,|\!\}_k)$$

are distinguished. This is captured by the equality $equal(\kappa_1, \kappa_2)$. □

The necessary equality tests to decide $K \vdash H \simeq H'$ are *finite*. If we ignore function types, we can easily verify this statement by considering that the length of a history, the type of each position in the history, and the values of each type using a finite knowledge K are finite. For function types, we observe that the histories of well-formed configurations (Definition 3.4) contain functions $\lambda_r x.\mathcal{P}$ with r in the private names of the configuration, and therefore $r \notin K$. This means that in a well-formed configuration any equality $H \vdash \mathit{equal}(\psi, \lambda_r x.\mathcal{P})$ with $r \in K$ is false—these tests are unnecessary.

However, $(\simeq)$ tests functions for equality via the use of patterns and $\Diamond$-values.

Example 4.5. Consider the knowledge $K = \{r\}$ and the histories $H = (\iota \mapsto \Diamond_r, \kappa \mapsto \iota)$ and $H' = (\iota \mapsto \Diamond_r, \kappa \mapsto \lambda_{r'} x.\,\mathtt{fork}\,\iota(x))$. The first history describes a process that outputs the same function that it received as an input, while the second its eta-expansion. These histories are distinguishable by an observer using the test $\mathit{equal}(\kappa, \Diamond_r)$, which is true under H but not under H'. □

The finite-test equivalence $(\simeq)$ is not too permissive as it implies that the equivalence theory of values under related histories is the same. Moreover, we extend history equivalence to configurations.

Proposition 4.6. *If $K \vdash H \simeq H'$ then for all values $\mathcal{V}_1, \mathcal{V}_2$ with $\mathit{fn}(\mathcal{V}_1, \mathcal{V}_2) \subseteq K$ and $\mathit{fan}(\mathcal{V}_1, \mathcal{V}_2) \subseteq \mathit{dom}(H)$: $H \vdash \mathit{equal}(\mathcal{V}_1, \mathcal{V}_2)$ iff $H' \vdash \mathit{equal}(\mathcal{V}_1, \mathcal{V}_2)$.*

Definition 4.7. $\langle H \parallel K \parallel I \rangle \triangleright \mathcal{P} \simeq \langle H' \parallel K' \parallel I' \rangle \triangleright \mathcal{Q}$ *if* $K = K' \wedge K \vdash H \simeq H'$.

5 Set Simulations

Here we give a coinductive characterisation of safety preservation for HOspi based on *set simulations*. This gives a convenient, and complete, proof methodology which, moreover, is amenable to the usual up-to techniques [22]. Indeed our formulation is already up-to τ-moves. In this extended abstract we give a sketch of the characterisation. A *set simulation* is a relation between configurations and sets of configurations, ranged over by $\mathcal{S}$. For the definition we need to extend LTS transitions to sets.

Definition 5.1 (Set Transition). *If $\mathcal{S}$ is a set of configurations: $\mathcal{S} \xrightarrow{\mu} \mathcal{S}'$ when $\mathcal{S}'$ is non-empty and $\mathcal{S}' \subseteq \{\mathcal{C}' \mid \exists \mathcal{C} \in \mathcal{S}.\ \mathcal{C} \xrightarrow{\mu} \mathcal{C}'\}$; $\mathcal{S} \stackrel{\mu}{\Rightarrow} \mathcal{S}'$ when $\mathcal{S}'$ is non-empty and $\mathcal{S}' \subseteq \{\mathcal{C}' \mid \exists \mathcal{C} \in \mathcal{S}.\ \mathcal{C} \stackrel{\mu}{\Rightarrow} \mathcal{C}'\}$.*

Definition 5.2 (Set Simulation up-to τ). *A relation $\mathcal{X}$ between configurations and sets of configurations is a set simulation up-to τ if for all $\mathcal{C}\ \mathcal{X}\ \mathcal{S}$:*

1. *there exists $\mathcal{C}' \in \mathcal{S}$ such that $\mathcal{C} \simeq \mathcal{C}'$*
2. *if $\mathcal{C} \stackrel{\mu}{\Rightarrow} \mathcal{C}'$ and $\mu \neq \tau$ then there exists $\mathcal{S}'$ such that $\mathcal{S} \stackrel{\mu}{\Rightarrow} \mathcal{S}'$ and $\mathcal{C}' \stackrel{\tau}{\Rightarrow}\mathcal{X}\ \mathcal{S}'$.*

The definition for a set simulation up-to τ is monotone; therefore the largest set simulation up-to τ exists and we write it as $(\preceq)$. Set similarity up-to τ is sound and complete with respect to the safety preorder.

Theorem 5.3 (Soundness and Completeness of $(\preceq)$). *$P \sqsubseteq_{\mathsf{safe}} Q$ iff $\langle \cdot \parallel K \parallel \cdot \rangle \triangleright Q \preceq \{\langle \cdot \parallel K \parallel \cdot \rangle \triangleright P\}$.*

The main intuition of set simulations is that they are insensitive to the branching behaviour of processes.

Example 5.4. Consider the following example:

$$P = \mathtt{outp}\, a().\, (\mathtt{outp}\, b().\, \mathbb{0} + \mathtt{outp}\, c().\, \mathbb{0})$$
$$Q = \mathtt{outp}\, a().\, \mathtt{outp}\, b().\, \mathbb{0} + \mathtt{outp}\, a().\, \mathtt{outp}\, c().\, \mathbb{0}$$

These two terms are not bisimilar because when P takes an a-move, Q would need to match it, committing to one of the two branches. From a safety perspective, however, the two terms are equivalent since there is no safety test that distinguishes them. We can construct a set simulation that relates the two possible states of Q with a single state of P, which effectively delays the choice of a particular branch of Q; here we let $\mathcal{C}(R) = \langle \cdot \parallel \{a, b, c\} \parallel \cdot \rangle \rhd R$:

$$\{(\mathcal{C}(P), \{\mathcal{C}(Q)\}),\ (\mathcal{C}(\mathtt{outp}\, b().\, \mathbb{0} + \mathtt{outp}\, c().\, \mathbb{0}), \{\mathcal{C}(\mathtt{outp}\, b().\, \mathbb{0}), \mathcal{C}(\mathtt{outp}\, c().\, \mathbb{0})\})\}$$

□

6 Examples

6.1 Messaging Servers

As our first example we consider a specification of a messaging service with load balancing, which allows its clients to send a message once (using the state channel st), and distributes clients to a number of transmission servers, each listening to a separate channel in the set S. For simplicity the load balancing algorithm is abstracted away by an internal choice operator, denoted by Σ:

$$\begin{aligned}&\mathsf{MServer}_{req,res,p,S}\\ &\quad = \nu sk, st.\, \mathtt{inp}\, req(x).\, \mathtt{dec}\, x\, \mathtt{as}\, \{\!|\, y_{ck} \,|\!\}_p\, \mathtt{in}\\ &\qquad\qquad \sum_{s\in S}(\mathtt{outp}\, res(\{\!|\lambda_r x.\, \mathtt{inp}\, st().\, \mathtt{outp}\, s(\{\!|\, x \,|\!\}_{sk}).\, \mathbb{0} \,|\!\}_{y_{ck}}).\, \mathtt{outp}\, st().\, \mathbb{0})\end{aligned}$$

Here the choice of server is decided before the client receives a response from the server. However, an implementation of this service may delegate this decision to the code sent to the client:

$$\begin{aligned}&\mathsf{MServer}'_{req,res,p,S}\\ &\quad = \nu sk, st.\, \mathtt{inp}\, req(x).\, \mathtt{dec}\, x\, \mathtt{as}\, \{\!|\, y_{ck} \,|\!\}_p\, \mathtt{in}\\ &\qquad\qquad \mathtt{outp}\, res(\{\!|\, \lambda_r x.\, \mathtt{inp}\, st().\, \sum_{s\in S}\mathtt{outp}\, s(\{\!|\, x \,|\!\}_{sk}).\, \mathbb{0} \,|\!\}_{y_{ck}}).\, \mathtt{outp}\, st().\, \mathbb{0}\end{aligned}$$

It is not possible to show that the safety properties of the specification $\mathsf{MSys} = \nu p.\,(\mathsf{Client} \mid \mathsf{MServer})$ are preserved by the implementation $\mathsf{MSys}' = \nu p.\,(\mathsf{Client} \mid \mathsf{MServer}')$ in a behavioural theory based on bisimulations. This is because the two systems are not bisimilar: the choice of the messaging channel from S happens before the message on *res* in MSys, and after that message in MSys'. However, using our linear theory of safety we can prove this equivalence. The interesting direction is proving $\mathsf{MSys}' \precapprox_{\mathsf{safe}} \mathsf{MSys}$.

We do this proof by reasoning *compositionally*. By Proposition 2.3, it suffices to show that $\mathsf{MServer}' \lessapprox_{\mathsf{safe}} \mathsf{MServer}$. We consider the following continuations of $\mathsf{MServer}$ and $\mathsf{MServer}'$.

$\mathsf{Srv}_1 = \mathtt{inp}\ req(x)\ldots$	$\mathsf{Srv}'_1 = \mathtt{inp}\ req(x)\ldots$
$\mathsf{Srv}_2(ck,s) = \mathtt{outp}\ res(\{\!\mid \mathsf{F}(s) \mid\!\}_{ck})\ldots$	$\mathsf{Srv}'_2(ck) = \mathtt{outp}\ res(\{\!\mid \mathsf{F}' \mid\!\}_{ck})\ldots$
$\mathsf{Srv}_3 = \mathtt{outp}\ st().\mathbf{0}$	$\mathsf{Srv}'_3 = \mathtt{outp}\ st().\mathbf{0}$
$\mathsf{Srv}_4(s) = \mathtt{outp}\ s(\{\!\mid x \mid\!\}_{sk}).\mathbf{0}$	$\mathsf{Srv}'_4(s) = \mathtt{outp}\ s(\{\!\mid x \mid\!\}_{sk}).\mathbf{0}$
$\mathsf{F}(s) = \lambda_r x.\ \mathtt{inp}\ st().\ \mathtt{outp}\ s(\{\!\mid x \mid\!\}_{sk}).\mathbf{0}$	$\mathsf{F}' = \lambda_r x.\ \mathtt{inp}\ st().\ \sum_{s\in S} \mathtt{outp}\ s(\{\!\mid x \mid\!\}_{sk}).\mathbf{0}$

We let $K_0 = \{req, res, p\} \cup S$ and $I_0 = \{sk, st\}$ and the configurations of $\mathsf{MServer}$:

$$\begin{aligned}
\mathcal{C}_1 &= \langle \cdot \parallel K_0 \parallel I_0 \rangle \rhd \mathsf{Srv}_1 \\
\mathcal{C}_2(H,K,ck,s) &= \langle H \parallel K_0 \uplus K, ck \parallel I_0, r \rangle \rhd \mathsf{Srv}_2(ck,s) \\
\mathcal{C}_3(H,K) &= \langle H \parallel K_0 \uplus K \parallel I_0, r \rangle \rhd \mathsf{Srv}_3 \\
\mathcal{C}_4(H,K,R,s) &= \langle H \parallel K_0 \uplus K \parallel I_0, r \rangle \rhd \mathsf{Srv}_4(\mathsf{s}) \mid R \\
\mathcal{C}_5(H,K,I,R) &= \langle H \parallel K_0 \uplus K \parallel I \rangle \rhd R
\end{aligned}$$

and the corresponding configurations of $\mathsf{MServer}'$ obtained by replacing Srv_1 to Srv_4 by Srv'_1 to Srv'_4, respectively.

As shown in Figure 4, the choice of the messaging channel in $\mathsf{MServer}$ happens before the response of the server, and after that in $\mathsf{MServer}'$. Hence, in our set simulation we relate each configuration $\mathcal{C}'_2(H', K, ck)$ and $\mathcal{C}'_3(H', K)$, where the value $\{\!\mid \mathsf{F}' \mid\!\}_{ck}$ has been indexed by some κ in H', with the set $S_2(H', K, ck)$ and $S_3(H', K, \kappa, ck)$, respectively:

$$\begin{aligned}
S_2(H,K,ck) &= \{\mathcal{C}_2(H,K,ck,s) \mid s \in S\} \\
S_3(H',K,\kappa,ck) &= \{\mathcal{C}_3(H,K,ck,s) \mid\ s \in S,\ H(\kappa) = \{\!\mid \mathsf{F}(s) \mid\!\}_{ck}, \\
&\qquad (\forall \alpha \neq \kappa.\, H(\alpha) = H'(\alpha))\}
\end{aligned}$$

We construct the relation of well-formed configurations:

$$\begin{aligned}
\mathcal{X} = \{&(\langle \cdot \parallel K_0 \parallel \cdot \rangle \rhd \mathsf{MServer}, \{\langle \cdot \parallel K_0 \parallel \cdot \rangle \rhd \mathsf{MServer}'\}),\ \ (\mathcal{C}'_1, \{\mathcal{C}_1\})\} \\
\cup\ \{&(\mathcal{C}'_2(H,K,ck), \mathcal{S}_2(H,K,ck)) \mid \exists \iota_1.\ \ H(\iota_1) = \{\!\mid ck \mid\!\}_p\} \\
\cup\ \{&(\mathcal{C}'_3(H',K), \mathcal{S}_3(H',K,\kappa,ck)\}) \mid\ H'(\kappa) = \{\!\mid \mathsf{F}' \mid\!\}_{ck},\ ck \in K\} \\
\cup\ \{&(\mathcal{C}'_4(H',K,R), \{\mathcal{C}_4(H,K,R)\}) \mid R \text{ deadlocked and } \Phi(H,H')\} \\
\cup\ \{&(\mathcal{C}'_5(H',K,I',R), \{\mathcal{C}_5(H,K,I,R)\}) \mid R \text{ deadlocked and} \\
&\qquad r \in I, r \in I' \text{ and } \Phi(H,H')\}
\end{aligned}$$

$$\text{where } \Phi(H,H') \stackrel{\text{def}}{=} \exists \kappa.\ H(\kappa) = \{\!\mid \mathsf{F}(s) \mid\!\}_{ck} \text{ and } H'(\kappa) = \{\!\mid \mathsf{F}' \mid\!\}_{ck} \text{ and } (\forall \alpha \neq \kappa.\, H(\alpha) = H'(\alpha))$$

We prove that $\mathcal{X}$ is a set simulation up-to τ by considering the possible weak transitions from these configurations, the main of which are shown in Figure 4, and by showing that configurations related in $\mathcal{X}$ are also related in $(\simeq)$. The latter is easy since related histories contain either identical values, or abstractions with the same annotations ($\mathsf{F}(s)$ and F').

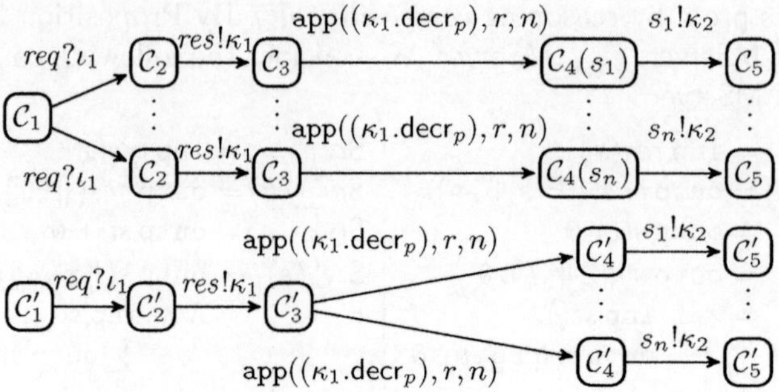

Fig. 4. Main transitions of MServer and MServer′

6.2 Example 2: Conference Servers

We now prove that the conference system Sys_2, shown in the introduction, preserves the safety properties of Sys_1. Here the function annotations are not important and we omit them. We also assume that functions can be applied to non-base values, which can be encoded by:

$$\mathtt{fork}\,(\lambda x.\, P)(V) \stackrel{\text{def}}{=} \nu c.\,\mathtt{fork}\,(\lambda y.\,\mathtt{inp}\,y(x).\,P)(c).\,\mathtt{outp}\,c(V).\,\mathbf{0}$$

We prove that $\mathsf{Sys}_1 \sqsubseteq_{\mathsf{safe}} \mathsf{Sys}_2$ by using Theorem 5.3 and giving a set simulation $\mathcal{X}$ such that $\mathsf{Sys}_2\ \mathcal{X}\ \{\mathsf{Sys}_1\}$. First we consider the dummy process D and the continuations of Conf and Rev_2:

$$\mathsf{D}_1 = \mu X.\,\mathtt{inp}\,del_{12}(x).\,X \qquad \mathsf{D}_2 = \mu X.\,\mathtt{outp}\,del_{12}(\{\!|\, s, \lambda.\,\mathbf{0}\,|\!\}_s).\,X$$

$$\mathsf{D} = \mathsf{D}_1 \mid \nu s.\,\mathsf{D}_2 \qquad \mathsf{Conf}_1 = \mathtt{outp}\,ok(r).\,\mathbf{0}$$

$$\mathsf{Rev}_{21} = \mathtt{outp}\,subm(\{\!|\, r, \mathsf{F}_{prf_2}\{\mathsf{F}_{del_{12}}/f_{del_{12}}\}\,|\!\}_{s_p}).\,\mathbf{0}$$

$$\mathsf{Rev}_{22}(\iota) = \mathtt{outp}\,subm(\{\!|\, r, \mathsf{F}_{prf_2}\{(\iota.\mathsf{decr}_{s_{rev_1}}.2)/f_{del_{12}}\}\,|\!\}_{s_p}).\,\mathbf{0}$$

We let $K_0 = \{subm, del_{12}, r\}$ and $I_0 = \{s_p, s_{rev_1}, s\}$, and consider the families of configurations for Sys_1:

$$\begin{aligned}
\mathcal{C}_1 &= \langle \cdot \parallel K_0 \parallel I_0 \rangle \rhd \mathsf{Conf} \mid \mathsf{Rev}_1 \mid \mathsf{D}_1 \mid \mathsf{D}_2\\
\mathcal{C}_2(H,K) &= \langle H \parallel K_0 \uplus K \parallel I_0 \rangle \rhd \mathsf{Conf} \mid \mathsf{D}_1 \mid \mathsf{D}_2\\
\mathcal{C}_3(H,K) &= \langle H \parallel K_0 \uplus K \parallel I_0 \rangle \rhd \mathsf{Conf}_1 \mid \mathsf{D}_1 \mid \mathsf{D}_2\\
\mathcal{C}_4(H,K) &= \langle H \parallel K_0 \uplus K \parallel I_0 \rangle \rhd \mathsf{D}_1 \mid \mathsf{D}_2\\
\mathcal{C}_5(H,K) &= \langle H \parallel K_0 \uplus K \parallel I_0 \rangle \rhd \mathsf{Rev}_1 \mid \mathsf{D}_1 \mid \mathsf{D}_2
\end{aligned}$$

We also let $I'_0 = \{s_p, s_{rev_1}, s_{rev_2}\}$, and consider for Sys_2:

$$\begin{aligned}
\mathcal{C}'_1 &= \langle \cdot \parallel K_0 \parallel I'_0 \rangle \rhd \mathsf{Conf} \mid \mathsf{Rev}'_1 \mid \mathsf{Rev}_2\\
\mathcal{C}'_2(H,K) &= \langle H \parallel K_0 \uplus K \parallel I'_0 \rangle \rhd \mathsf{Conf} \mid \mathsf{Rev}_2\\
\mathcal{C}'_{31}(H,K) &= \langle H \parallel K_0 \uplus K \parallel I'_0 \rangle \rhd \mathsf{Conf} \mid \mathsf{Rev}_{21}\\
\mathcal{C}'_{32}(H,K,\iota) &= \langle H \parallel K_0 \uplus K \parallel I'_0 \rangle \rhd \mathsf{Conf} \mid \mathsf{Rev}_{22}(\iota)\\
\mathcal{C}'_4(H,K) &= \langle H \parallel K_0 \uplus K \parallel I'_0 \rangle \rhd \mathsf{Conf}\\
\mathcal{C}'_5(H,K) &= \langle H \parallel K_0 \uplus K \parallel I'_0 \rangle \rhd \mathsf{Conf}_1\\
\mathcal{C}'_6(H,K,R) &= \langle H \parallel K_0 \uplus K \parallel I'_0 \rangle \rhd R
\end{aligned}$$

Here R will represent the process in states that do not lead to an output on ok. The proof is completed by showing that the following relation is a set simulation up-to τ. The proof is similar to the one in the previous example, but due to space constrains here we give only the relation.

$$\begin{aligned}
\mathcal{X} = \{ & ((\cdot \parallel K_0 \parallel \cdot) \triangleright \mathsf{Sys}_2, \{(\cdot \parallel K_0 \parallel \cdot) \triangleright \mathsf{Sys}_1\}), \quad (\mathcal{C}'_1, \{\mathcal{C}_1\}), \\
& \cup \{(\mathcal{C}'_2(H', K), \{\mathcal{C}_1(H, K)\}) \mid \exists \kappa.\ \Phi_1(H, H', \kappa)\} \\
& \cup \{(\mathcal{C}'_{31}(H, K), \{\mathcal{C}_1(H, K)\})\} \\
& \cup \{(\mathcal{C}'_{32}(H', K, \iota), \{\mathcal{C}_1(H, K)\}) \mid \exists \iota \in dom(H).\ \Phi_1(H, H', \kappa) \wedge H'(\iota) = \kappa\} \\
& \cup \{(\mathcal{C}'_4(H', K), \{\mathcal{C}_2(H, K)\}) \mid \Phi_2(H, H')\} \\
& \cup \{(\mathcal{C}'_5(H', K), \{\mathcal{C}_3(H, K)\}) \mid H = H' \vee \Phi_1(H, H') \vee \Phi_2(H, H')\} \\
& \cup \{(\mathcal{C}'_6(H', K, \mathbf{0}), \{\mathcal{C}_4(H, K)\}) \mid H_0 = H'_0 \vee \Phi_1(H_0, H'_0) \vee \Phi_2(H_0, H'_0)\} \\
& \cup \mathcal{Y}
\end{aligned}$$

where

$$\begin{aligned}
\Phi_1(H, H', \kappa) &\stackrel{\text{def}}{=} \exists H_0.\ H = H_0, (\kappa \mapsto \{\!|\, s, \lambda.\mathbf{0} \,|\!\}_s) \wedge H' = H_0, (\kappa \mapsto \{\!|\, s_p, \mathsf{F}_{del_{12}} \,|\!\}_{s_{rev_2}}) \\
\Phi_2(H, H') &\stackrel{\text{def}}{=} \exists H_0, H'_0, F.\ H = H_0, (\kappa \mapsto \{\!|\, r, \mathsf{F}_{prf_1} \,|\!\}_{s_p}) \wedge H' = H'_0, (\kappa \mapsto \{\!|\, r, F \,|\!\}_{s_p}) \\
& \qquad \wedge \big(\ (H_0 = H'_0 \wedge F = \mathsf{F}_{prf_2}\{\mathsf{F}_{del_{12}}/f_{del_{12}}\}) \vee \\
& \qquad\qquad (\exists \iota, \kappa, .\ \Phi_1(H_0, H'_0, \kappa) \wedge H'_0(\iota) = \kappa \wedge \\
& \qquad\qquad\qquad F = \mathsf{F}_{prf_2}\{(\iota.\mathsf{decr}_{s_{rev_2}}.2)/f_{del_{12}}\})\ \big)
\end{aligned}$$

and $\mathcal{Y}$ relates the configurations that do not lead to a signal on *ok*:

$$\begin{aligned}
\mathcal{Y} = \{ & (\mathcal{C}'_6(H, K, (\mathsf{Conf} \mid \mathsf{Rev}'_1)), \{\mathcal{C}_2(H, K)\})\} \\
& \cup \{(\mathcal{C}'_6(H', K, \mathsf{Conf}), \{\mathcal{C}_2(H, K)\}) \mid \exists \kappa.\ \Phi_1(H, H', \kappa)\} \\
& \cup \{(\mathcal{C}'_6(H, K, R), \{\mathcal{C}_4(H, K)\}) \mid R \in \{\mathsf{Rev}'_1, (\mathsf{Rev}'_1 \mid \mathsf{Rev}_2), \mathsf{Rev}_{21}\}\} \\
& \cup \{(\mathcal{C}'_6(H', K, \mathsf{Rev}_2), \{\mathcal{C}_4(H, K)\}) \mid \exists \kappa.\ \Phi_1(H, H', \kappa)\} \\
& \cup \{(\mathcal{C}'_6(H', K, \mathsf{Rev}_{22}(\iota)), \{\mathcal{C}_4(H, K)\}) \mid \exists \kappa.\ \Phi_1(H, H', \kappa) \wedge H'(\iota) = \kappa\}
\end{aligned}$$

7 Related and Future Work

We have proposed a behavioural testing theory for safe equivalence for a higher-order version of the spi-calculus. We have given a characterisation of safety preservation in terms of novel *set simulations*, which provides a sound and complete proof methodology for process equivalence; the usefulness of the methodology has been demonstrated via simple illustrative examples. The LTS in our proof methodology makes extensive use of the *current knowledge* of observers, or adversaries, a generalisation of similar ideas for the first-order spi-calculus [2,4], and environmental bisimulations [23,25].

Sato and Sumii [25] defined a higher-order version of the applied π-calculus called the *Applied HOπ* calculus, developed a bisimulation method which is sound and complete with respect to reduction barbed congruence, and gave bisimulation proofs for secrecy properties of example higher-order systems. This work uses a strong assumption about the power of attackers: higher-order terms are sent over channels as decomposable syntax objects. The resulting proof methodology is significantly different from ours, employing *environmental bisimulations* and sophisticated *up-to-context* techniques [23]. However, bisimulations do not provide a complete proof technique for linear-time equivalences, such as safe equivalence. We believe that an LTS-based theory can be developed for safe equivalence for Applied HOπ, but that would not be first-order as for HOspi, where a weak assumption about attackers is used. We leave this to future work.

Sangiorgi has given a translation of HOπ with finite types to the π-calculus [20,19] based on *triggers*, and a full-abstraction proof. This translation, generating a fresh trigger at every output, would be unsound for HOspi where transmitted functions can be tested for equality. An adaptation of the translation where a trigger is generated at every function definition [24, Sec. 13.2] would be sound but incomplete, at least without the use of a complex type system in the target language [24, pg. 402]. To the extent of our knowledge the details of such a translation have not been published. However, our LTS directly encodes the intuitions of the translation, avoiding the issues with full-abstraction.

Jeffrey and Rathke [14] used *symbolic triggers*, an encoding of triggers as extended processes in an LTS, to prove that bisimilarity in their LTS characterises reduction barbed congruence in the presence of recursive types, where Sangiorgi's fully-abstract translation does not apply. Our LTS takes this idea a step further by encoding a notion of triggers within the interaction history recorded in the configurations. This allows us to define a first-order theory for HOspi, a more intricate language that HOπ. Also we study a linear-time semantic equivalence, via set simulations, rather than reduction barbed congruence and bisimulation.

We believe that the approach to higher-order semantics we follow here, using an augmented LTS of configurations, is robust. In addition to safety for HOspi, we have followed this approach to characterise reduction barbed congruence for HOπ [15], and we believe that other equivalences, such as must-equivalence [12], can be similarly treated. Different cryptographic primitives, such as those used in the applied π-calculus, can also be easily accommodated. We believe that this approach can be applied to higher-order cryptographic languages with more complex type-systems such as the language in [17].

Symbolic techniques that reduce the quantification over first-order messages have been developed for the spi- and applied π-calculus [8,5,9]. Our symbolic treatment addresses the quantification over higher-order, rather than first-order, values. The use of simple types keeps the quantification over first-order messages finite up to fresh names.

Finally, we intend to investigate possible connections between our operational notion of histories and game semantics models for HOπ [16].

Acknowledgements. We are thankful to Eijiro Sumii and the anonymous referees for useful comments on this work.

References

1. Abadi, M., Fournet, C.: Mobile values, new names, and secure communication. SIGPLAN Not. 36(3), 104–115 (2001)
2. Abadi, M., Gordon, A.D.: A bisimulation method for cryptographic protocols. Nordic Journal of Computing 5, 267–303 (1998)

3. Abadi, M., Gordon, A.D.: A calculus for cryptographic protocols: The spi calculus. Inf. Comput. 148(1), 1–70 (1999)
4. Boreale, M., De Nicola, R., Pugliese, R.: Proof techniques for cryptographic processes. SIAM J. Comput. 31(3), 947–986 (2001)
5. Borgström, J., Briais, S., Nestmann, U.: Symbolic bisimulation in the spi calculus. In: Gardner, P., Yoshida, N. (eds.) CONCUR 2004. LNCS, vol. 3170, pp. 161–176. Springer, Heidelberg (2004)
6. Borgström, J., Nestmann, U.: On bisimulations for the spi calculus. Math. Structures in Comp. Sc. 15(3), 487–552 (2005)
7. De Nicola, R., Hennessy, M.C.B.: Testing equivalences for processes. Theoretical Computer Science 34(1-2), 83–133 (1984)
8. Delaune, S., Kremer, S., Ryan, M.D.: Symbolic bisimulation for the applied pi calculus. J. of Comp. Security 18(2), 317–377 (2010)
9. Durante, L., Sisto, R., Valenzano, A.: Automatic testing equivalence verification of spi calculus specifications. ACM Trans. Softw. Eng. Methodol. 12(2), 222–284 (2003)
10. Fournet, C., Gordon, A.D., Maffeis, S.: A type discipline for authorization in distributed systems. In: CSF 2007, pp. 31–48. IEEE Computer Society, Los Alamitos (2007)
11. Fournet, C., Gordon, A.D., Maffeis, S.: A type discipline for authorization policies. ACM Trans. Program. Lang. Syst. 29(5) (2007)
12. Hennessy, M.: The security pi-calculus and non-interference. J. Log. Algebr. Program 63(1), 3–34 (2005)
13. Honda, K., Yoshida, N.: A uniform type structure for secure information flow. ACM Trans. Program. Lang. Syst. 29(6) (2007)
14. Jeffrey, A., Rathke, J.: Contextual equivalence for higher-order pi-calculus revisited. LMCS 1(1:4) (2005)
15. Koutavas, V., Hennessy, M.: First-order reasoning for higher-order concurrency (February 2010) (manuscript)
16. Laird, J.: Game semantics for higher-order concurrency. In: Arun-Kumar, S., Garg, N. (eds.) FSTTCS 2006. LNCS, vol. 4337, pp. 417–428. Springer, Heidelberg (2006)
17. Maffeis, S., Abadi, M., Fournet, C., Gordon, A.D.: Code-carrying authorization. In: Jajodia, S., Lopez, J. (eds.) ESORICS 2008. LNCS, vol. 5283, pp. 563–579. Springer, Heidelberg (2008)
18. Milner, R.: Comunicating and Mobile Systems: the π-Calculus. Cambridge University Press, Cambridge (1999)
19. Sangiorgi, D.: Expressing Mobility in Process Algebras: First-Order and Higher-Order Paradigms. PhD thesis, Univ. of Edinburgh (1992)
20. Sangiorgi, D.: From pi-calculus to higher-order pi-calculus–and back. In: Gaudel, M.-C., Jouannaud, J.-P. (eds.) CAAP 1993, FASE 1993, and TAPSOFT 1993. LNCS, vol. 668, pp. 151–166. Springer, Heidelberg (1993)
21. Sangiorgi, D.: Bisimulation for higher-order process calculi. Information and Computation 131(2), 141–178 (1996)
22. Sangiorgi, D.: On the bisimulation proof method. Mathematical Structures in Comp. Sci. 8(5), 447–479 (1998)
23. Sangiorgi, D., Kobayashi, N., Sumii, E.: Environmental bisimulations for higher-order languages. In: LICS (2007)
24. Sangiorgi, D., Walker, D.: The π-calculus: a Theory of Mobile Processes. Cambridge University Press, Cambridge (2001)
25. Sato, N., Sumii, E.: The higher-order, call-by-value applied pi-calculus. In: Hu, Z. (ed.) APLAS 2009. LNCS, vol. 5904, pp. 311–326. Springer, Heidelberg (2009)

A New Method for Dependent Parsing

Trevor Jim and Yitzhak Mandelbaum

AT&T Labs–Research

Abstract. *Dependent grammars* extend context-free grammars by allowing semantic values to be bound to variables and used to constrain parsing. Dependent grammars can cleanly specify common features that cannot be handled by context-free grammars, such as length fields in data formats and significant indentation in programming languages. Few parser generators support dependent parsing, however. To address this shortcoming, we have developed a new method for implementing dependent parsers by extending existing parsing algorithms. Our method proposes a point-free language of dependent grammars, which we believe closely corresponds to existing context-free parsing algorithms, and gives a novel transformation from conventional dependent grammars to point-free ones.

To validate our technique, we have specified the semantics of both source and target dependent grammar languages, and proven our transformation sound and complete with respect to those semantics. Furthermore, we have empirically validated the suitability of our point-free language by adapting four parsing engines to support it: an Earley parsing engine; a GLR parsing engine; memoizing, arrow-style parser combinators; and PEG parser combinators.

1 Introduction

Context-free grammars are widely used in data format and programming language specifications and are the foundation of many parsing tools. Unfortunately, they are not powerful enough to *fully* specify the syntax of most data formats and programming languages—these require context-sensitive features. For example, XML has balanced tags; many data formats have unbounded length fields; C and C++ have typedef names; Python, Haskell, and many markup languages have significant indentation; Javascript has optional line-ending semicolons; Standard ML has user-defined infix operators; and Ruby and command-line shells have "here documents."

Specifications that use grammars, therefore, augment them with prose describing the context-sensitive features of the syntax. This half-formal approach is not ideal. Often, it results in an ambiguous or incomplete specification, which leads to incompatible implementations. This problem is so severe that some communities have abandoned grammars altogether, e.g., the syntax of HTML5 is specified by a state machine given in pseudo-code [7].

Moreover, a specification given as a grammar plus prose cannot serve as the input to a parser generator or automated analysis. In the best case, the implementor will be able to figure out a "lexer hack" that hides context-sensitive

G. Barthe (Ed.): ESOP 2011, LNCS 6602, pp. 378–397, 2011.
© Springer-Verlag Berlin Heidelberg 2011

features away from the grammar, which can then be processed separately by a parser generator. However, such tricks are hard to discover, and the result is not easy to understand, analyze, or replicate—witness the fact that there are many parser generators producing *parsers written in* Haskell or Python, but very few of them generate *parsers of* Haskell or Python.

In previous work, we used *dependent grammars* to cleanly specify context-sensitive syntax [10]. Dependent grammars extend context-free grammars by allowing semantic values to be bound to variables and used to guide subsequent parsing. For example, the value of a length field can be used to constrain the length of a following sequence, or the indentation of a line can be used to control the block structure of a Python program or Cisco IOS configuration section. We found dependent grammars to be an excellent formalism for specifying the kinds of context-sensitivity required in practical examples.

We also implemented dependent parsing, by extending Earley's algorithm for context-free parsing with semantic values, environments, and parsing constraints. This was more difficult. In particular, the machinery of environments had to be propagated throughout every part of the algorithm and correctness proof. This was delicate work, considering that there is a history of erroneous algorithms in the area (for example, Earley's algorithm for parse forest reconstruction did not account for all parse trees [17], and Tomita's original GLR algorithm fails to terminate on grammars with ϵ-rules and hidden left recursion [18]).

Dozens of other context-free parsing algorithms have been developed over many years, and we would like to adapt them for dependent parsing. Moreover, we would like to take advantage of existing *implementations* of these algorithms, because some of them have been finely tuned and represent many man-years of work. It is worth mentioning that, often, these sophisticated parsing engines do not even operate directly on grammars—instead, grammars are compiled into lower-level representations (for example, automatons), which are then "executed" by the parsing engine. Adding dependency to these engines by our previous method would involve complex changes to both the front-end and back-end, a prohibitive amount of work.

Therefore, we have developed a much simpler method of extending existing parsing algorithms to perform dependent parsing. Its key characteristics are:

- We introduce a new grammar *intermediate language* that supports dependent parsing without requiring environment machinery in the parsing engine.
- We compile a user-level dependent grammar into the intermediate language by a series of *source-to-source transformations* which move all environment manipulations into semantic actions of the intermediate language.

While there is a wealth of prior work on compiling away environment manipulations, from combinatory algebras to more recent work like Paterson's arrow notation [14], our work is distinguished by being compatible with a wide variety of existing parsing algorithms and engines (see Section 8 for further discussion). To demonstrate this compatibility, we have built four back ends for our dependent parser generator, each based on a different context-free parsing algorithm.

Contributions. We show how to use standard programming language and compiler techniques to implement parsers for dependent grammars:

- We define the semantics of Gul, a minimal user-level language of dependent grammars. Gul supports binding semantic values and using them in parse constraints, as well as standard semantic actions. Gul bindings are lexically scoped.
- We define the semantics of Gil, a point-free intermediate language of dependent grammars. Gil grammars parse inputs while passing semantic values from left to right (like an L-attributed grammar with guarded reductions), and, in our experience, it can be supported by most existing parsing engines with little difficulty.
- We define a novel source-to-source transformation for splitting a Gul grammar into (1) a Gil grammar and (2) a coroutine for managing binding and executing semantic actions.
- We have validated our choice of features in Gul by using it to implement grammars taken from a wide variety of domains.
- We have validated our technique by implementing Gil with a variety of different parsing backends, either through extension or directly on top of native features. These backends include a scannerless Earley parser, a GLR parser, arrow-style parser combinators, and PEG parser combinators.
- Finally, we have proven that our translation from Gul to Gil is semantics-preserving. The paper includes the statement of our central theorem, and a number of significant supporting lemmas, along with brief summaries of their proofs.

An extended version of the material in this paper can be found in a companion technical report [9].

2 Gul, a User-Level Language

Gul is the user-level dependent grammar language that we will use throughout the paper. Gul is a minimal language that omits many features of our parser generator, Yakker; however, Yakker itself implements most of these features by translation to Gul. Most of the features of Gul will be familiar to anyone who has used a lexer or parser generator. The more unusual aspects are these:

- We support all context free grammars, even ambiguous grammars. We do not require grammars to avoid left recursion, or be in a restricted class such as the LALR(1) or LL(k) grammars.
- We include parsing constraints, @when(e), which act to prune possible parses.
- We support *foreign parsers* with the form @box(e). For example, e could be a library function for parsing one of the hundreds of existing time and date formats.

Gul Syntax. We define Gul's syntax as follows:

$$G = (A_1(x_1) = R_1), \ldots$$
$$R = \epsilon \mid c \mid (R \mid R) \mid ({*}^{x=e} R) \mid (x{=}R\ R) \mid \{e\} \mid A(e) \mid \text{@when}(e) \mid \text{@box}(e)$$

A Gul *grammar* is a sequence of definitions for *nonterminals* in terms of *right sides*. We use G, A, and R to range over Gul grammars, nonterminals, and right sides, respectively. Gul right sides are based on regular expressions, including the empty string ϵ, *terminals* c, alternation, and Kleene closure (written as a prefix '*'). The Kleene closure performs a fold over a portion of the input. The expression e provides an initial value, and right-side R plays the role of a combining function: x is bound in R's scope to the previous accumulating value and R's result provides the new value. The expression e is taken from some general-purpose programming language, which we call the *target* language. The right side $(x{=}R_1\ R_2)$ is the concatenation of R_1 and R_2, where x is bound to the semantic value of R_1 in the scope R_2. *Semantic actions* are written $\{e\}$. Gul nonterminals are defined with formal parameters ranging over semantic values, and are applied to target-language expressions. Parsing constraints are written @when(e), and foreign parsers are written @box(e).

Our techniques are not specific to any particular target language, but for the sake of concreteness we will start by assuming some variant of the untyped, call-by-value lambda calculus.

Notational Conveniences. In our examples, we will write concrete terminals in quotes, for example, '**b**' for the ASCII character lowercase b. We assume that the target language has a distinguished unit value, written (), as well as booleans and some notion of sets (used in the semantics of @box(e)). If the parameter of a nonterminal A is not used in its right side, we omit it, and similarly we write $(R_1\ R_2)$ for a concatenation which does not require binding. A Kleene-closure which accumulates the unit value can be written $({*}R)$. We may omit the parentheses in $({*}R)$, $({*}^{x=e}R)$, $(R_1\ R_2)$, $(R_1 \mid R_2)$, and $(x{=}R_1\ R_2)$ when this does not cause confusion. We write @pos for a @box that evaluates to the current input position, without consuming any input.

Gul Semantics. We now discuss the unusual aspects of Gul's semantics (we give the complete semantics in the technical report [9]). The semantics is defined by rules assuming a fixed grammar, G, and a fixed input, D, and they make use of the target language semantics via a partial evaluation function, eval(E, e), where E is an environment mapping variables to values.

The rules define judgments of the form $\langle E, i\rangle \stackrel{R}{\Longrightarrow} \langle v, i'\rangle$, meaning that right side R evaluates to semantic value v in environment E, starting at input position i and finishing at position i'. Evaluation can be nondeterministic: we can have $\langle E, i\rangle \stackrel{R}{\Longrightarrow} \langle v_1, i_1\rangle$ and $\langle E, i\rangle \stackrel{R}{\Longrightarrow} \langle v_2, i_2\rangle$ where $v_1 \neq v_2$, or $i_1 \neq i_2$, or both.

These three rules show that we use a standard call-by-value semantics:

$$\frac{\text{eval}(E, e) = v}{\langle E, i\rangle \stackrel{\{e\}}{\Longrightarrow} \langle v, i\rangle} \qquad \frac{\langle E, i\rangle \stackrel{R_1}{\Longrightarrow} \langle v_1, i_1\rangle \quad \langle E[x = v_1], i_1\rangle \stackrel{R_2}{\Longrightarrow} \langle v_2, i_2\rangle}{\langle E, i\rangle \stackrel{(x=R_1\ R_2)}{\Longrightarrow} \langle v_2, i_2\rangle} \qquad \frac{\text{eval}(E, e) = v, \quad (A(x) = R) \in G \quad \langle [x = v], i\rangle \stackrel{R}{\Longrightarrow} \langle v_1, i_1\rangle}{\langle E, i\rangle \stackrel{A(e)}{\Longrightarrow} \langle v_1, i_1\rangle}$$

A semantic action $\{e\}$ evaluates to the value of e without consuming input; a concatenation $(x{=}R_1\ R_2)$ evaluates R_1, binds its value to x, then evaluates R_2; and $A(e)$ evaluates e, binds it to the formal parameter of A, then parses according to the right side of A.

The semantics of parsing constraints and foreign parsers are given as follows:

$$\frac{\text{eval}(E, e) = \text{true}}{\langle E, i\rangle \xrightarrow{\text{@when}(e)} \langle (), i\rangle} \qquad \frac{\langle v, j\rangle \in \text{eval}(E, e(D)(i))}{\langle E, i\rangle \xrightarrow{\text{@box}(e)} \langle v, j\rangle}$$

The rule for @when(e) states that no progress can be made unless the constraint e is satisfied (there is no rule for the false case). To evaluate @box(e), we evaluate e applied to the complete input D and the current input position i. The foreign parser can be nondeterministic—it may return more than one result $\langle v, j\rangle$—but we require $j \geq i$. Note that the expression e can include values bound within the grammar (e.g., by (x=R_1 R_2)). Furthermore, a foreign parser is free to examine the complete input, and not just the portion between i and j. Note that foreign parsers subsume semantic actions, parsing constraints, terminals, and the empty string. Similarly, Kleene closure could be encoded using an additional nonterminal. Howeve, we have chosen to include those forms natively for reasons discussed at the end of Section 3.

We say that *a grammar G accepts input D with value v* if $\langle \cdot, 0\rangle \xrightarrow{A_1} \langle v, |D|\rangle$, where A_1 is the implicit start symbol of G. While we restrict our definition to parses which begin with an empty environment, in practice, we expect that grammars will be written with respect to some distinguished environment E_{init}, which may contain bindings for library functions, foreign parsers, etc. We can simulate such an environment simply by substituting the contents of E_{init} into our grammar before parsing.

We give an example Gul grammar in Section 4.2.

3 The Intermediate Language Gil

Gil is a lower-level language that corresponds closely to context-free grammars extended to support semantic values.

Gil Syntax. We define Gil's syntax as follows:

$$g = (A_1 = r_1), \ldots$$
$$r = \epsilon \mid c \mid (r \mid r) \mid (^*r) \mid (r\ r) \mid \{f\} \mid A(f_{\text{arg}}, f_{\text{ret}}) \mid \text{@when}(f_{\text{pred}}, f_{\text{next}}) \mid \text{@box}(f_{\text{box}}, f_{\text{ret}})$$

Gil, like Gul, is based on regular expressions over terminals and nonterminals. To distinguish between Gul and Gil we use g, r, and f to range over Gil grammars, right sides, and target language expressions, instead of Gul's G, R, and e. Gil lacks the binding forms of Gul: nonterminals are defined without a formal parameter, and there is no binding concatenation. Note that in Gil, nonterminals, constraints and foreign parsers take two arguments, whose purpose we will explain in a moment.

Gil Semantics. We give the full semantics of Gil in the technical report [9], and note a few key points here in the main text. Gil right sides are semantic-value *transformers*—they relate input values to output values—and thus, each right side takes an *implicit* value parameter. Semantic actions are the base value transformers, and our rule for concatenation shows that Gil threads values from left to right across parses:

$$\frac{f(v) = v_1}{\langle v, i\rangle \xrightarrow{\{f\}} \langle v_1, i\rangle} \qquad \frac{\langle v, i\rangle \xrightarrow{r_1} \langle v_1, i_1\rangle,\ \langle v_1, i_1\rangle \xrightarrow{r_2} \langle v_2, i_2\rangle}{\langle v, i\rangle \xrightarrow{(r_1 r_2)} \langle v_2, i_2\rangle}$$

Here are the rules for parsing constraints, nonterminals, and foreign parsers:

$$\frac{\begin{array}{l} f_{\text{pred}}(v) = \text{true} \\ (v' = f_{\text{next}}(v)) \end{array}}{\langle v, i\rangle \xrightarrow{@\text{when}(f_{\text{pred}}, f_{\text{next}})} \langle v', i\rangle} \quad \frac{\begin{array}{l} f_{\text{arg}}(v) = v_1, (A = r) \in g \\ \langle v_1, i\rangle \xrightarrow{r} \langle v_2, i_2\rangle \\ f_{\text{ret}}(v)(v_2) = v_3 \end{array}}{\langle v, i\rangle \xrightarrow{A(f_{\text{arg}}, f_{\text{ret}})} \langle v_3, i_2\rangle} \quad \frac{\begin{array}{l} \langle v_1, i_1\rangle \in f_{\text{box}}(v)(D)(i) \\ f_{\text{ret}}(v)(v_1) = v_2 \end{array}}{\langle v, i\rangle \xrightarrow{@\text{box}(f_{\text{box}}, f_{\text{ret}})} \langle v_2, i_1\rangle}$$

The first argument of a parsing constraint is used to compute a boolean determining whether parsing will continue, while the second is for calculating the transformed value. Nonterminals and boxes use their first argument to calculate the argument of the nonterminal or box, and the second to merge the result value with the original value. For example, if we define

$$\text{zero} = \textbf{`0'}\ \{\lambda v.2 \times v\}, \qquad \text{one} = \textbf{`1'}\ \{\lambda v.(2 \times v) + 1\},$$

then we can calculate the binary value of a sequence of 1s and 0s with

$$\text{bits} = \{\lambda v.0\}\ {*}(\text{zero}(\lambda v.v, \lambda v.\lambda v_2.v_2) \mid \text{one}(\lambda v.v, \lambda v.\lambda v_2.v_2)).$$

Here we use the action $\{\lambda v.0\}$ to initialize the value to 0. The function $\lambda v.v$ used in the argument positions for zero and one simply propagates the current value to those nonterminals. The function $\lambda v.\lambda v_2.v_2$ is used on the return, and it sets the new current value to the value v_2 returned from the nonterminal.

Finally, we can calculate a sum with this right side:

$$\text{bits}(\lambda v.(), \lambda v.\lambda v_1.v_1)\ \text{`+'}\ \text{bits}(\lambda v_1.(), \lambda v_1.\lambda v_2.v_1 + v_2).$$

Here the value returned from the first parse of bits is bound to v_1, and the value from the second parse of bits is bound to v_2. The function $\lambda v_1.\lambda v_2.v_1 + v_2$ performs the addition. Notice that there are two occurrences of (λv_1), one for each parse of bits; the semantics of nonterminals ensures that all occurrences of v_1 end up bound to the same value.

From these examples, we can see that the second argument of a nonterminal acts something like a continuation. Unlike in continuation-passing style, however, the continuation is *not* passed to the right side of the nonterminal; it is invoked by the caller, and not the callee. This is necessary to achieve maximal sharing to efficiently parse ambiguous grammars, which may require multiple parses of a single nonterminal at the same input position and with the same input parameter, but with different continuations.

In Gil, foreign parsers could subsume the empty string, terminals, and parsing constraints, and Kleene closure could be encoded using an additional nonterminal. We have retained these features because they are either supported natively by existing context-free parsing engines or could be more efficiently implemented on top of existing features than the more general @box.

4 The Coroutine Transformation

In this section, we show how to compile a Gul rule with bindings, parsing constraints, and other semantic actions into a Gil rule in which all of the semantic elements of the Gul rule have been gathered together into one Gil action (value transformer). This single Gil action is used as a sort of coroutine by the parsing engine as it processes the input according to the rest of the Gil rule.

4.1 Assumptions on the Target Language

The coroutine is a target language program that we build from the actions in the original Gul rule. We treat these actions opaquely, in a cut-and-paste fashion; consequently, we limit our assumptions about the target language and make our techniques more widely applicable. Nevertheless, to build the coroutine, we will have to assume that some language features are available. Essentially, we require the target language to support some features of an untyped call-by-value lambda calculus, as indicated by the following grammar of expressions:

$$\begin{aligned} e &= x \mid (e\ e) \mid (\lambda x.e) \mid (\text{fun}\, f\ x.e) \mid () \mid \ell \mid \underline{\lambda}\ C \mid \ldots \\ C &= \ell.e \mid (C \mid C) \end{aligned}$$

We are assuming that we can use target language variables and function application, that we have first-class and recursive functions, and we have a distinguished unit value (). We assume that we can use a countable set of *labels*, ranged over by ℓ; for concrete labels, we use underlined integers, like $\underline{3}$. We also make use of a match-function construct: $\underline{\lambda}(\ell_1.e_1 \mid \cdots \mid \ell_n.e_n)$. Here, we expect that a match-function is applied to a label ℓ_i, and the result of the application is the corresponding case e_i.[1] Finally, we permit let expressions which can be desugared in the standard way.

Note that we have not said that the target language *is* an untyped lambda calculus—it is sufficient for these features to be embeddable in the target language. In Section 5, we discuss the exact properties that we require of the target language. When the target language is statically typed, there are additional considerations, which we discuss in Section 6.

4.2 Coroutines by Example

To illustrate Gul-to-Gil compilation, we use an example adapted from the grammar for the IMAP mail protocol:

$$\text{literal} = \text{`\{'}\ x{=}\text{number}\quad \text{`\}'}\ p_1{=}\text{@pos}\quad {*}\text{CHAR8}\ p_2{=}\text{@pos}\quad \text{@when}(p_2 - p_1 {=} x)$$

An IMAP literal is a number surrounded by braces, followed by a sequence of characters (CHAR8s). We assume that number is a nonterminal that matches a

[1] As a corollary of our correctness proof, we know that we cannot have match failures in our construction.

sequence of ASCII digits and returns the equivalent semantic integer as its result. Recall that @pos is an abbreviation for a foreign parser that matches the empty string and returns the input position, so that p_1=@pos binds p_1 to the position in the input just after the right brace, and p_2=@pos binds p_2 to a position after some number of CHAR8s. The parse constraint @when($p_2 - p_1 = x$) matches the empty string if the predicate $(p_2 - p_1 = x)$ returns true, and otherwise fails to match anything.[2]

We transform this Gul rule into the following Gil rule:

$$\text{literal} = \{f_{\text{init}}\}\ \text{`\{'}\ \text{number}(f_1, f_2)\ \text{`\}'}\ \{f_3\}\ {}^*\text{CHAR8}\ \{f_4\}\ \text{@when}(f_5, f_6)$$

(We will define f_{init} and $f_{1\text{–}6}$ shortly.)

Recall that every Gil rule is a value transformer, and the initial value of a rule is its (implicit) parameter. Here, literal has no parameter, so we will use the unit value () for its initial value. According to the Gil semantics and the right side of the rule, we can begin parsing a literal by passing the initial value to f_{init}, which is itself a value transformer that we define as follows:

$$\begin{aligned} f_{\text{init}} = \lambda -.&\underline{\lambda}\, \underline{1}.() \\ &\mid \underline{2}.\lambda x.\underline{\lambda}\, \underline{3}.\text{let } p_1 = \text{pos}(); \\ &\qquad\qquad \underline{\lambda}\, \underline{4}.\text{let } p_2 = \text{pos}(); \\ &\qquad\qquad\quad \underline{\lambda}\, \underline{5}.(p_2 - p_1 = x) \\ &\qquad\qquad\quad \mid \underline{6}.() \end{aligned}$$

As we will see, f_{init} is the coroutine that carries out all of the semantic actions of the original Gul rule.

The Gil parsing engine starts parsing the rule by applying f_{init} to the current value, and expects to get a new value in return. f_{init} takes the current value and ignores it ($\lambda -$), since it is unit. f_{init} returns a new value (beginning with $\underline{\lambda}\,\underline{1}$) that incorporates all of the semantic actions of the original Gul rule. The parser will pass this value through a series of the other transformers $f_{1\text{–}5}$ of the rule to execute the semantic actions as required.

It is helpful to annotate f_{init} to highlight the values that will be passed to each transformer by the parser:

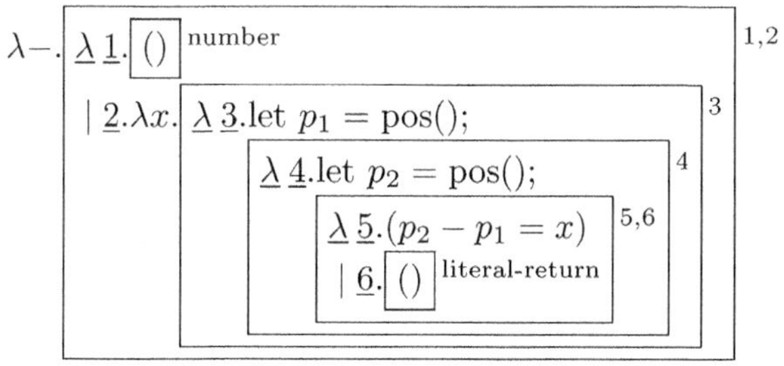

[2] IMAP literals can be implemented more efficiently in Gul, but this simple version serves better for our exposition. Also, this example can be generalized to support repetition of arbitrary-length nonterminals by including a counter variable on the Kleene-closure and comparing it to x in the constraint.

Here, we have boxed each expression that will compute a return value for a transformer. The label of a box indicates which transformer or transformers will receive the value. For example, f_{init} returns a value that will be passed to f_1 and f_2, so we box the return value and label it with $1, 2$.

Parsing continues by reading a left brace character, reaching number(f_1, f_2) in the right side. We apply f_1 to the current value (the 1,2-box) to calculate the parameter to number. We define f_1 simply as $\lambda v.v(\underline{1})$, so we end up applying the value to $\underline{1}$, hence the $(\underline{\lambda}\ \underline{1})$ case of the 1,2-box is evaluated. This returns $()$, since number takes no parameters; we have boxed this and labeled it to indicate that it will be the initial value passed to number.

The parsing engine uses f_2 to handle the binding of x to the result of number. We define $f_2 = \lambda v.v(\underline{2})$, so we end up applying the 1,2-box to $\underline{2}$, and hence the $(\mid \underline{2})$ case is evaluated. The parsing engine applies this to the result of number. The number is bound to x and the 3-box becomes the new current value.

Next, the parsing engine applies f_3 to the current value. We define $f_3 = \lambda v.v(\underline{3})$, so the current input position is bound to p_1, and the 4-box becomes the new value.

$f_{4\text{–}6}$ are defined in the same way as $f_{1\text{–}3}$, so the parsing engine ends up using the 4-box to bind p_2, and the 5,6-box to calculate the predicate $(p_2 - p_1 = x)$. If this evaluates to true, the engine uses the 5,6 box to calculate the final value, $()$, of the successful parse; otherwise, this run of the parse fails.

4.3 Coroutines Formalized

We now formalize the translation of Gul into Gil. We begin with a property that conservatively approximates when nonterminals and right sides make use of Gul's context-sensitive features. We term this property *relevance.*

Definition 1 (Relevance). *The relevance of the nonterminals and right sides of a grammar are defined as the least relations satisfying the following properties:*

- *A right side is* relevant *if it includes a target-language expression or a* relevant *nonterminal.*
- *A nonterminal is* relevant *if its right-side is* relevant.

Notice that bindings do not impact relevance, because what matters for parsing is whether the binding is used.

Irrelevant and relevant right-sides are handled differently by our translation. Therefore, to reduce the number of cases that need be considered during the translation, we specify a normal form for grammars that places syntax-directed constraints on the relevance of subterms. Normalized grammars use an extended syntax that includes the forms $(R_1\ R_2)$, $(^*R)$ and A, which are only abbreviations in Gul.

Definition 2 (Normalization). *A right side R is* normalized *if every subterm R' of R satisfies the following properties:*

N1 *If R' is $(x{=}R_1\ R_2)$ then both R_1 and R_2 are relevant.*
N2 *If R' is $(R_1\ R_2)$ then at least R_1 is not relevant.*

N3 *If R' is $(R_1 \mid R_2)$ then R_1 and R_2 share the same relevance.*
N4 *If R' is $({*}R_1)$ then R_1 is not relevant.*
N5 *If R' is $({*}^{x=e}R_1)$ then R_1 is relevant.*
N6 *If R' is A then the right-side defining A in G is not relevant.*
N7 *If R' is $A(e)$ then the right-side defining A in G is relevant.*

A grammar G is normalized *if every rule satisfies the following properties:*

N8 *If $(A(x) = R) \in G$ then R is relevant.*
N9 *If $(A = R) \in G$ then R is not relevant.*

Any right side R can be transformed into a normalized right side accepting the same language, and similarly for any grammar. We illustrate such transformations in [9].

Once a grammar has been normalized, we can translate its rules into Gil as follows. If R is not relevant, then R only uses syntax common to both Gul and Gil—that is, R is a Gil right side. In that case, the Gul rule $A = R$ is translated to the Gil rule $A = R$. If R is relevant, then a Gul rule $A(x) = R$ is turned into a Gil rule by a sequence of transformations, as indicated in the following definition. Below, we describe each of the transformations in turn.

Definition 3 (Gul-to-Gil Transformation). *We say that a normalized Gul grammar G transforms to a Gil grammar g, written $G \Rightarrow g$, iff*

- *If $(A = R) \in G$ then $(A = R) \in g$.*
- *If $(A(x) = R) \in G$ then $(A = \{\lambda x.\underline{\lambda}(\mathcal{C}[\![\mathcal{E}[\![R_\ell]\!]]\!][\cdot])\}\ \mathcal{D}[\![R_\ell]\!]) \in g$, where $R_\ell = \mathcal{L}[\![R]\!]$.*

Labeling $\mathcal{L}[\![\cdot]\!]$. Our first step is to add *labels* to Gul right sides. These labels serve to synchronize the construction of coroutines with the insertion of dispatch functions. The insertion of labels considerably simplifies the specification of those two phases, which otherwise could not be specified independently.

We only need to add labels to relevant subterms of a right side. The labeling transformation is given in Figure 1. We use underlined integers for labels, and use ℓ to range over integers used as labels. Each label identifies a control-flow point in the right side: in ${}^{\ell}R$, ℓ is the control-flow point just before evaluating R, and in R^{ℓ}, ℓ is the control-flow point just after evaluating R. In the case for sequences, we do not label subterm R_1, because we are guaranteed, by normalization, that it is irrelevant.

Erasing $\mathcal{E}[\![\cdot]\!]$. The coroutine for a Gul right side is constructed exclusively from relevant subterms of the right side. We can simplify the definition of coroutine production if we first erase all subterms that are not relevant. A suitable transformation is given in Figure 2. It has the important property that the resulting right side exactly preserves the control-flow of the labels of the original right side. The interesting case is for sequences, which, by normalization, are the only place irrelevant terms may appear within relevant terms. Notice that the result of erasing looks like a labeled, nondeterministic program.

$\boxed{\mathcal{L}[\![R]\!] = R'}$ (R is normalized)

If R is not relevant, then $\mathcal{L}[\![R]\!] = R$.

Otherwise, $\mathcal{L}[\![R]\!]$ is defined by the following cases. In each case, ℓ and ℓ' denote fresh labels.

$$\mathcal{L}[\![\{e\}]\!] = {}^{\ell}\{e\}$$

$$\mathcal{L}[\![A(e)]\!] = {}^{\ell}A(e)^{\ell'}$$

$$\mathcal{L}[\![@\mathrm{box}(e)]\!] = {}^{\ell}@\mathrm{box}(e)^{\ell'}$$

$$\mathcal{L}[\![@\mathrm{when}(e)]\!] = {}^{\ell}@\mathrm{when}(e)^{\ell'}$$

$$\mathcal{L}[\![(R_1 \mid R_2)]\!] = (\mathcal{L}[\![R_1]\!] \mid \mathcal{L}[\![R_2]\!])$$

$$\mathcal{L}[\![(R_1\ R_2)]\!] = (R_1\ \mathcal{L}[\![R_2]\!])$$

$$\mathcal{L}[\![(x{=}R_1\ R_2)]\!] = {}^{\ell}(x{=}\mathcal{L}[\![R_1]\!]\ \mathcal{L}[\![R_2]\!])$$

$$\mathcal{L}[\![(*^{x=e} R)]\!] = {}^{\ell}(*^{x=e} \mathcal{L}[\![R]\!])^{\ell'}$$

Fig. 1. Labeling right sides

$\boxed{\mathcal{E}[\![R]\!] = R'}$ (R is relevant and normalized)

$$\mathcal{E}[\![{}^{\ell}\{e\}]\!] = {}^{\ell}\{e\}$$

$$\mathcal{E}[\![{}^{\ell}A(e)^{\ell'}]\!] = {}^{\ell}A(e)^{\ell'}$$

$$\mathcal{E}[\![{}^{\ell}@\mathrm{box}(e)^{\ell'}]\!] = {}^{\ell}@\mathrm{box}(e)^{\ell'}$$

$$\mathcal{E}[\![(R_1 \mid R_2)]\!] = (\mathcal{E}[\![R_1]\!] \mid \mathcal{E}[\![R_2]\!])$$

$$\mathcal{E}[\![(R_1\ R_2)]\!] = \mathcal{E}[\![R_2]\!]$$

$$\mathcal{E}[\![{}^{\ell}(x{=}R_1\ R_2)]\!] = {}^{\ell}(x{=}\mathcal{E}[\![R_1]\!]\ \mathcal{E}[\![R_2]\!])$$

$$\mathcal{E}[\![{}^{\ell}(*^{x=e} R)^{\ell'}]\!] = {}^{\ell}(*^{x=e} \mathcal{E}[\![R]\!])^{\ell'}$$

Fig. 2. Erasing irrelevant subterms

Coroutine Production $\mathcal{C}[\![\cdot]\!]$. Given a labeled Gul right side R, we construct the match-cases of its coroutine using the function $\mathcal{C}[\![\cdot]\!]$, defined in Figure 3. The function makes use of *contexts* defined by the grammar

$$K = [\cdot] \mid x\ ([\cdot]),$$

and we write $K[e]$ to "fill the hole" of K, resulting in a target expression. Our contexts are much simpler than typical contexts used in programming languages: they have only two forms, and they cannot bind variables. $\mathcal{C}[\![\cdot]\!]$ is written in the style of a continuation-passing transform, and we use contexts K as the continuation argument of the transform. By using contexts, rather than target language expressions, as arguments to the transform, we obtain a one-pass algorithm whose result does not have administrative redexes [3].

The first case of Figure 3 handles semantic actions. Unlike in Gul, the results of semantic actions are not passed to the parsing engine, but are instead passed directly to the context K. This directness has some helpful implications for typed target languages, which we discuss in Section 6. The case for constraints splits its arguments into two match-cases, one for each label. The first evaluates the predicate and the second (invoked when the predicate is true) evaluates the input continuation. In Gul, constraints always have unit as their semantic value, so we pass the continuation the unit value. The case for nonterminals is quite similar to that of constraints, but reifies the continuation as a function expecting the return value of the nonterminal. The case for box does the same.

$\boxed{\mathcal{C}[\![R]\!]K = C}$

$\mathcal{C}[\![^{\ell}\{e\}]\!]K = \ell.K[e].$

$\mathcal{C}[\![^{\ell}@\text{when}(e)^{\ell'}]\!]K = (\ell.e \mid \ell'.K[()]).$

$\mathcal{C}[\![^{\ell}A(e)^{\ell'}]\!]K = (\ell.e \mid \ell'.\lambda x.K[x])$
where x is a fresh variable.

$\mathcal{C}[\![^{\ell}@\text{box}(e)^{\ell'}]\!]K = (\ell.e \mid \ell'.\lambda x.K[x])$
where x is a fresh variable.

$\mathcal{C}[\![(R_1 \mid R_2)]\!]K = (\mathcal{C}[\![R_1]\!]K \mid \mathcal{C}[\![R_2]\!]K).$

$\mathcal{C}[\![^{\ell}(x{=}R_1\ R_2)]\!]K =$
$\quad \ell.\text{let } g\ x = \underline{\lambda}(\mathcal{C}[\![R_2]\!]K);$
$\quad\quad \underline{\lambda}(\mathcal{C}[\![R_1]\!](g[\cdot]))$

$\mathcal{C}[\![^{\ell}(*^{x=e}R)^{\ell'}]\!]K =$
$\quad \ell.\text{let rec } g\ x = \underline{\lambda}(\ell'.K[x] \mid \mathcal{C}[\![R]\!](g[\cdot]));$
$\quad\quad g(e)$

Fig. 3. Coroutine production. In the last two cases, g denotes a fresh variable.

$\boxed{\mathcal{D}[\![R]\!] = r}$ (R is normalized)

If R is not relevant, then $\mathcal{D}[\![R]\!] = R$.

Otherwise, $\mathcal{D}[\![R]\!]$ is defined as follows, where $\text{d}(\ell) = \lambda v.v(\ell)$:

$\mathcal{D}[\![^{\ell}\{e\}]\!] = \{\text{d}(\ell)\}$

$\mathcal{D}[\![^{\ell}@\text{when}(e)^{\ell'}]\!] = @\text{when}(\text{d}(\ell), \text{d}(\ell'))$

$\mathcal{D}[\![^{\ell}@\text{box}(e)^{\ell'}]\!] = @\text{box}(\text{d}(\ell), \text{d}(\ell'))$

$\mathcal{D}[\![^{\ell}A(e)^{\ell'}]\!] = A(\text{d}(\ell), \text{d}(\ell'))$

$\mathcal{D}[\![(R_1 \mid R_2)]\!] = (\mathcal{D}[\![R_1]\!] \mid \mathcal{D}[\![R_2]\!])$

$\mathcal{D}[\![(R_1\ R_2)]\!] = (R_1\ \mathcal{D}[\![R_2]\!])$

$\mathcal{D}[\![^{\ell}(x{=}R_1\ R_2)]\!] = \{\text{d}(\ell)\}\ \mathcal{D}[\![R_1]\!]\ \mathcal{D}[\![R_2]\!]$

$\mathcal{D}[\![^{\ell}(*^{x=e}R)^{\ell'}]\!] = \{\text{d}(\ell)\}\ {*}(\mathcal{D}[\![R]\!])\ \{\text{d}(\ell')\}$

Fig. 4. The dispatching transformation

In the case of choice, we simply combine the match-cases of each branch into a single set of match cases. In the case for binding, we reify the continuation for R_1 as a (bound) function before transforming R_1. This detail prevents the inadvertent capture of free variables in R_2 by bindings in R_1. Since we are treating the semantic actions in Gul grammars opaquely (Section 4.1), we do not have the luxury of alpha-varying right-sides. We do, however, assume the ability to generate variables which are fresh with respect to target-language expressions.

Finally, the case for fold performs a reification just as in the binding case. The coroutine uses a recursive function, and combines the case for exiting the fold with the cases of the fold body. We provide an initial value to x by applying the function to expression e, and bind x to the body's most recent semantic value in each iteration of the function.

Dispatching $\mathcal{D}[\![\cdot]\!]$. We transform the labeled Gul right side to a Gil right side by replacing each label occurrence ℓ with a *dispatch* function $(\lambda v.v(\ell))$, which "informs" the coroutine of the current position in the control-flow graph. The transformation is given in Figure 4. As with labeling, we ignore R_1 in the case for sequences.

5 Correctness

The goal of our coroutine transformation is to simplify both the task of implementing a dependent parsing system and the task of proving said system correct. This section discusses correctness: specifically, that the result of our transformation parses the same language and results in the same value as the original Gul grammar, under appropriate conditions. We provide a summary of our correctness results here, and leave an extended discussion to our companion technical report [9].

An essential goal of our construction has been to avoid dealing with the details of the target language, as we discussed earlier. Our metatheory retains this focus, by stating and proving our theorem with respect to an *abstract* target language. Instead of a concrete language, we have derived a set of properties that we require of the evaluation function of the language in order to prove our soundness and completeness result. These properties are given in [9], and are unexceptional.

In the theorem and lemmas that follow, we use some well-formedness conditions for grammars, expressions, contexts and right-sides. These conditions essentially ensure that variables and nonterminal names are properly bound. Only well-formedness of contexts requires, in addition, *totality* from the context: if its hole is filled with a closed value, it must evaluate to a value. The formal definitions of well-formedness can be found in [9].

It is worth noting that we require call-by-value evaluation for the function constructs used by coroutines. This constraint is needed for soundness because we have defined Gul with a call-by-value semantics; a call-by-name semantics for coroutines would result in some Gil parses succeeding where Gul parses fail. We believe it would be straightforward to adapt Gul, Gil, and our transformation to a call-by-name semantics.

Theorem 1, below, states the main result of this section.

Theorem 1. *If G is normalized, $WF(G)$, and $G \Rightarrow g$, then*

1. *If $(A = R) \in G$ and $(A = r) \in g$, then for all inputs,*
   (a) *if $\langle \cdot, 0\rangle \stackrel{R}{\Longrightarrow} \langle v, i\rangle$ then $\langle (), 0\rangle \stackrel{r}{\rightarrow} \langle (), i\rangle$, and*
   (b) *if $\langle (), 0\rangle \stackrel{r}{\rightarrow} \langle (), i\rangle$ then $\langle \cdot, 0\rangle \stackrel{R}{\Longrightarrow} \langle (), i\rangle$.*
2. *If $(A(x) = R) \in G$ and $(A = r) \in g$, and v closed, then for all inputs,*
   (a) *if $\langle [x{=}v], 0\rangle \stackrel{R}{\Longrightarrow} \langle v', i\rangle$ then $\langle v, 0\rangle \stackrel{r}{\rightarrow} \langle v', i\rangle$, and*
   (b) *if $\langle v, 0\rangle \stackrel{r}{\rightarrow} \langle v', i\rangle$ then $\langle [x{=}v], 0\rangle \stackrel{R}{\Longrightarrow} \langle v', i\rangle$.*

In order to prove Theorem 1, we will state and prove stronger results for both relevant and irrelevant terms. We need the stronger statements because the theorem describes properties of whole rules, while we need to know properties of individual right-sides. Yet, this change is not as easy as it might sound. The coroutine transformation is not local to right sides, but global to an entire rule. Therefore, we must relate the coroutine that would be generated for a particular right-side in *isolation* to the coroutine of the rule of which the right side is part.

A first attempt might be to relate the coroutines with equivalence. However, equivalence alone is too strict for relating our local and global coroutines because the case for alternatives and fold both locally require a *smaller* coroutine—one with fewer match cases—than that provided by the surrounding context. Therefore, we extend equivalence to an ordering relation on expressions, similar to subtyping. We call this relation *sufficiency*, written $E \vdash e \Rightarrow e'$, and read "$e$ is sufficient for e'."

Informally, an expression e is sufficient for an expression e' if e can be used in place of e'. In the study of subtyping, this is often called the *principal of safe substitution* [16]. We capture this notion formally in the following lemma, which we use throughout our proof of Lemma 3, below.

Lemma 1. *Let* $e = \underline{\lambda}(\ell_1.e_1 \mid \ldots \mid \ell_n.e_n)$. *If* $WF(E,e)$ *and* $E \vdash e' \Rightarrow e$ *then* $E \vdash e'\ \ell_i \equiv e\ \ell_i$, *for* $i = 1$ *to* n.

We now state the two essential lemmas used in proving the soundness and completeness of our transformation of Gul grammars. Note that both of these lemmas assume an implicit Gul grammar G, which is normalized and well-formed, and a corresponding, implicit, Gil grammar g, for which $G \Rightarrow g$ holds. The first lemma addresses irrelevant right sides, on which the translation has little effect.

Lemma 2 (Translation correctness for irrelevant terms). *If R is irrelevant and normalized, then*

a) If $\langle E, i\rangle \overset{R}{\Longrightarrow} \langle v', i'\rangle$ *then* $\forall v,\ \langle v, i\rangle \overset{R}{\longrightarrow} \langle v, i'\rangle$.
b) If $\langle v, i\rangle \overset{R}{\longrightarrow} \langle v', i'\rangle$ *then* $v = v'$ *and* $\forall E,\ \langle E, i\rangle \overset{R}{\Longrightarrow} \langle (), i'\rangle$.

The second lemma addresses relevant right sides. Notice how we relate the current Gil value v_1 with the right-side's coroutine via the sufficiency relation. Notice further, though, that our result involves *equivalence*. This apparent strengthening is due to Lemma 1 above.

Most of the proof of this lemma involves reasoning about the evaluation behavior of the generated coroutines.

Lemma 3 (Translation correctness for relevant terms). *If R is relevant and normalized,* $WF(E,\ R)$, $WF(E,\ K)$, v_1 *is closed,* $R_\ell = \mathcal{L}[\![R]\!]$, *and* $E \vdash v_1 \Rightarrow \underline{\lambda}(\mathcal{C}[\![\mathcal{E}[\![R_\ell]\!]]\!]K)$ *then*

a) If $\langle E, i\rangle \overset{R}{\Longrightarrow} \langle v, i'\rangle$ *then* $\exists v_2.\ \langle v_1, i\rangle \xrightarrow{\mathcal{D}[\![R_\ell]\!]} \langle v_2, i'\rangle$ *and* $E \vdash K[v] \equiv v_2$.
b) If $\langle v_1, i\rangle \xrightarrow{\mathcal{D}[\![R_\ell]\!]} \langle v_2, i'\rangle$ *then* $\exists v.\ \langle E, i\rangle \overset{R}{\Longrightarrow} \langle v, i'\rangle$ *and* $E \vdash K[v] \equiv v_2$.

6 Typed Target Languages

Up until now we have assumed that our target language is untyped. However, we have implemented our parser generator, Yakker, in a statically typed language (OCaml), and this requires a few modifications to our coroutine transformation.

The principal difficulty is that many parsing engines need to manipulate collections of semantic values, for example, on a semantic-value stack. ML's homogeneous data structures therefore require us to give our semantic values (coroutines) a uniform type. Since our coroutines return a number of types (booleans for parsing constraints, foreign parsers, etc.), we must wrap them in a union datatype.

This sort of type casting is standard in ML parsers. The coroutine transformation significantly simplifies matters, however, because the types of Gul-bound variables do not appear in the coroutine union type: all bindings are implemented by closures, which hide the types of free variables. This is a key reason that we prefer coroutines over our original implementation of dependent parsing that used explicit environments.

We use a separate union type for call arguments and return values, which we call the *value* type. In Yakker, we currently require user annotations to specify argument and return types, and we construct the value type and insert the necessary injections and projections automatically. (The type annotations are not strictly necessary, e.g., the dypgen parser generator is able to eliminate them by type inference.) The coroutine type is then given as follows:

```
type value
type coroutine =
  | Bool of boolean
  | Value of value
  | Return of coroutine → coroutine
  | Box of int → input → (coroutine ∗ int) list
  | Continue of int → coroutine
```

Next, we must add the necessary injections and projections to and from the coroutine type. We add injections in the translation from Gul to the coroutine, and we add projections in the translation from Gul to Gil. The addition of injections is largely straightforward, and we only note that every nonterminal must end with a Value injection, which can be accomplished by setting the context used to construct the initial coroutine to Value[·].

Projections are similarly straightforward. First, change dispatch functions to project from the Continue branch and then compose every dispatch with a projection appropriate to the location of the dispatch. So, for example, a dispatch located in a @box would be followed by a projection from the Box branch. Second, the initial coroutine must begin by projecting its argument from the Value branch, as must all f_{ret} functions. For example, here is the typed rule for nonterminals:

$$\mathcal{C}[\![{}^{\ell}A(e)^{\ell'}]\!]K = \big(\ell.\text{Value}(e) \mid \ell'.\lambda\text{Value}(x).K[x]\big) \text{ where } x \text{ is fresh.}$$

Notice that the first match-case performs an injection, whereas the second case uses pattern matching to perform a projection.

7 Evaluation

We have investigated several practical aspects of our method.

Implementing Gil. To evaluate the difficulty of extending a context-free parsing algorithm to support the additional features of Gil, we implemented Gil on four different back ends:

Scannerless Earley. Our main implementation is a transducer-based, scannerless Earley parsing engine. Earley parsing is a general context-free parsing method that relies on nondeterministic, breadth-first exploration of possible parses. The standard Earley algorithm implements parse recognition without semantic values; we had to add semantic values to the algorithm, but this was a straightforward modification. The overall structure of the algorithm remained unchanged.

PEG. We have a Parsing Expression Grammar [5] interpretation of Gil. It supports all the features of Gil, but interprets choice as deterministic and prioritized (first match). The coroutine translation is fully compatible with the PEG back end, despite the different choice semantics, and required no modifications to be retargeted.

GLR. dypgen [13] is a GLR parser generator written in OCaml. dypgen has native support for "flowing" a value through a parse and supports most of the features of Gil[3], so no modifications to dypgen were necessary to support coroutines. However, implementing the semantics of Gil on dypgen did require a fairly deep and precise understanding of dypgen's semantics.

Memoizing Parser Combinators. Our final back end is a set of parser combinators based on Johnson's memoizing, top-down parser combinators for all context-free grammars [11]. Our combinators are fairly faithful to Johnson's originals, fixing one significant performance problem and adjusting for the differences between Scheme and OCaml. The added support for Gil's context-sensitive features had a trivial impact on the difficulty of implementing the combinators. As with the other back ends, the use of coroutines with parser combinators required no modifications to the coroutine generator.

Although every parsing algorithm is different, our experience with these four back ends convinces us that extending existing context-free parsing algorithms to support the additional features of Gil is usually straightforward, and certainly simpler than extending them with environments, as in our earlier work.

We found that to support Gil, the parsing engine needs three essential elements: (1) it must thread semantic values along with parses; (2) it must include a mechanism for abandoning a parse; and (3) it must support nonterminals parameterized by semantic values. Note that (1) is usually already a feature of any practical parsing tool. For (2), note that we are starting from parsing engines which can already parse all context-free languages, including ambiguous languages; such parsers necessarily include machinery for attempting multiple parses and abandoning failed parses. Parameters for nonterminals (3) are very

[3] Note that dypgen also has support for Gul-style dependency, implemented, in part, with explicit environment manipulations. Nevertheless, our ability to target dypgen based only on the Gil-relevant features demonstrates the applicability of our coroutine translation to a GLR engine.

naturally supported by top-down parsers. In bottom-up parsers they are less common, but we did not find them difficult to implement with dypgen's existing features, for example.

Implementing the coroutine transformation. We use the coroutine transformation in the front end of our Yakker parser generator. While our experience is subjective, we found the translation from paper to software to be straightforward. The core of our actual implementation is nearly identical to the pipeline presented in this paper. The major difference is that our front end supports many features that we have not mentioned, and, consequently, we implemented the coroutine transformation without normalization and erasing, at the cost of additional cases to consider in the other stages of the transformation. Based on our experience, we feel that the formal presentation in this paper contains sufficient information for a practical implementation.

Use cases. Finally, we have written a variety of examples in Yakker's Gul-style language. These examples demonstrate the practical utility of the features supported by Gul, lending weight to the argument for dependent parsing. In addition, our ability to generate working parsers from our grammars demonstrates that our technique works in practice, not just in theory. The examples are described in [9], and include languages like OCaml, JavaScript, Python, and Aurochs PEGs, and data formats including IMAP messages, IETF RFC grammars, Mail.app mailboxes, and the many formats expressible in the PADS languages.

8 Related Work

In earlier work, we presented a formalism that incorporated support for dependent parsing, scannerless parsing, full context-free grammars and foreign parsers [10]. That work focused on the correctness of the translation from grammars to transducers and their execution using an Earley-style algorithm. This work represents a significant advance beyond our previous work. It proposes a fundamentally different, and more general, approach to the handling of dependency, both in theory and in practice. Our separation of binding concerns into a coroutine means that correctness proofs of other techniques can be free of all the binding and environment concerns which played such a prominent role in our previous work. The same benefits carry over to the implementation, as we discussed in Section 7. In addition, our user-level language Gul differs from the grammar language of our previous work in a number of useful ways. It adds lexical scoping of variables, return values for nonterminals, binding to nested right-sides, and a functional interpretation of binding. Also, boxes now have access to the entire input. Moreover, our theory makes explicit the requirements we place on the target language, rather than supposing an untyped lambda calculus.

There are many alternative grammar formalisms for supporting some degree of context sensitivity. We have compared many of the closely related formalisms with our dependent grammars in earlier work [10]. However, we add here a brief comparison with definite clause grammars (DCGs) [15], a popular formalism for specifying grammars as logic programs. While the power of a particular formulation of DCGs depends on that of the underlying logic language, there are certainly examples with as much power as Gul. Moreover, the support for unification in logic languages provides a more flexible interpretation of variable bindings. However, DCGs rely critically on the features and semantics of the logic language in which they are embedded. In contrast, we are striving to provide an approach to implementing dependent parsing that is compatible with many different parsing algorithms, and applicable across many different programming languages.

Of the existing approaches to handling dependent parsing, the most straightforward is to compile grammars into recursive-descent parsers where binding and expressions in the grammar are copied directly into the target language of the parser. This approach is taken, for example, by the compiler of the PADS data description language [4]. In the case of embedded grammar languages, like monadic parser combinators, the binding support of the target language is even used directly [8,12].

However, this higher-order approach results in much of the grammar being trapped under lambdas, thereby prohibiting useful analyses and transformations which can be critical for performance or even termination (for example, the recent left-corner transform for typed grammars [1]) [12,19]. Paterson proposed the *arrow notation* as an alternative approach that allows such analyses and transformations for arrow combinators [14]. In essence, the translation of the arrow notation to (point-free) arrow combinators "pushes down" binders to the computations that use them, while "lifting" the other elements (in our case, grammar constructs) out from beneath the binders. All bound variables are collected in a tuple which is threaded through the computation.

Our coroutine transformation can be viewed as an alternative translation to point-free style that is better suited to our goal of supporting a wide variety of target languages and reusing existing parsing engines. In particular, we want to support table-based parsers (such as LR, GLR, and Earley parsers) and ML-style typed languages. These parsers require a uniform type for semantic values. Therefore, if we used environment tuples as semantic values, we would have to wrap them in a union type, e.g., to place them on a semantic value stack. Specifying such a union type would require either that the parser generator discover the types of all bound variables or that the user write them down, both of which we want to avoid; the former, so as not to further constrain the choice of target language, and the latter, so as not to burden the user. In our method, the bound values are stored in closures and hence their type is hidden from the type of our semantic values (the coroutines).

Coroutines and parsing have a long history together. For example, Conway originally introduced coroutines as a way to structure a one-pass compiler, including lexer and parser [2], and Warren used them in evaluating the attributes of an attribute grammar [20]. Our work differs from most uses of coroutines in an essential technical detail. In the standard approach, there is dynamically only one instance of any given coroutine, and, at each invocation, it resumes from the last point at which it yielded. Furthermore, the coroutine itself is responsible for maintaining its state (including its last code location). In contrast, our coroutines are pure (assuming pure embedded actions), which has two major implications: the parsing engine is responsible for maintaining the current version of any coroutine, and it is free to duplicate a coroutine as necessary for exploring different parsing branches.

Technically, our coroutines are closer to trampolined computations than to classic coroutines. Our method of implementing our coroutines is very close to the trampolined style of Ganz, et al., in which a computation is written such that its control flow can be managed externally by a so-called *trampoline* [6]. Our approach is different in two ways. First, because of our concern for sharing nonterminal parses, we needed to extend their method with a novel treatment of call and return. Second, our trampoline—the parsing engine—has a closer relationship with the coroutine. Instead of simply "bouncing" the coroutine at each step, it guides the control flow with the integer argument to the coroutine's closure. Moreover, our coroutines communicate information back to the parsing engine, whether for foreign parsers or for parsing constraints.

References

1. Baars, A., Swierstra, S.D., Viera, M.: Typed transformations of typed grammars: The left corner transform. In: Proceedings of the Ninth Workshop on Language Descriptions, Tools, and Applications, LDTA 2009, pp. 8–33 (March 2009)
2. Conway, M.E.: Design of a separable transition-diagram compiler. Commun. ACM 6(7), 396–408 (1963)
3. Danvy, O., Filinski, A.: Representing Control: A study of the CPS transformation. Mathematical Structures in Computer Science 2(4), 361–391 (1992)
4. Fisher, K., Gruber, R.: PADS: A domain specific language for processing ad hoc data. In: PLDI 2005: Programming Language Design and Implementation, pp. 295–304. ACM Press, New York (2005)
5. Ford, B.: Parsing expression grammars: a recognition-based syntactic foundation. In: POPL 2004: ACM Symposium on Principles of Programming Languages, pp. 111–122. ACM Press, New York (2004)
6. Ganz, S.E., Friedman, D.P., Wand, M.: Trampolined style. In: ICFP 1999: Proceedings of the Fourth ACM SIGPLAN International Conference on Functional Programming, pp. 18–27. ACM, New York (1999)
7. HTML5 (including next generation additions still in development) Draft Standard October 6 (2010), `http://www.whatwg.org/specs/web-apps/current-work/`
8. Hutton, G., Meijer, E.: Monadic parsing in Haskell. Journal of Functional Programming 8(4), 437–444 (1998)
9. Jim, T., Mandelbaum, Y.: A new method for dependent parsing. Technical Report TD:100334, AT&T Labs—Research (2011)
10. Jim, T., Mandelbaum, Y., Walker, D.: Semantics and algorithms for data-dependent grammars. In: POPL 2010: Proceedings of the 37th Annual ACM SIGPLAN-SIGACT Symposium on Principles of Programming Languages, pp. 417–430. ACM, New York (2010)

11. Johnson, M.: Memoization in top-down parsing. Computational Linguistics 21(3), 405–417 (1995)
12. Leijen, D., Meijer, E.: Parsec: Direct style monadic parser combinators for the real world. Technical Report UU-CS-2001-27, Department of Computer Science, Universiteit Utrecht (2001)
13. Onzon, E.: Dypgen: self-extensible parsers and lexers for OCaml, `http://dypgen.free.fr/`
14. Paterson, R.: A new notation for arrows. In: ICFP 2001: Proceedings of the Sixth ACM SIGPLAN International Conference on Functional Programming, pp. 229–240. ACM, New York (2001)
15. Pereira, F.C.N., Warren, D.H.D.: Definite clause grammars for language analysis. Artificial Intelligence 13, 231–278 (1980)
16. Pierce, B.C.: Types and Programming Languages. MIT Press, Cambridge (2002)
17. Scott, E.: SPPF-style parsing from Earley recognisers. In: Proceedings of the Seventh Workshop on Language Descriptions, Tools, and Applications (LDTA 2007). Electronic Notes in Theoretical Computer Science, vol. 203, pp. 53–67. Elsevier, Amsterdam (2008)
18. Scott, E., Johnstone, A.: Right nulled GLR parsers. ACM Transactions on Programming Languages and Systems 28(4), 577–618 (2006)
19. Swierstra, S.D., Azero Alcocer, P.R.: Fast, error correcting parser combinatiors: A short tutorial. In: Bartosek, M., Tel, G., Pavelka, J. (eds.) SOFSEM 1999. LNCS, vol. 1725, pp. 112–131. Springer, Heidelberg (1999)
20. Warren, S.K.: The coroutine model of attribute grammar evaluation. PhD thesis, Rice University, Houston, TX, USA (1976)

Static Analysis of Run-Time Errors in Embedded Critical Parallel C Programs*

Antoine Miné

CNRS & École Normale Supérieure
45, rue d'Ulm
75005 Paris, France
mine@di.ens.fr

Abstract. We present a static analysis by Abstract Interpretation to check for run-time errors in *parallel* C programs. Following our work on Astrée, we focus on embedded critical programs without recursion nor dynamic memory allocation, but extend the analysis to a static set of threads. Our method iterates a slightly modified non-parallel analysis over each thread in turn, until thread interferences stabilize. We prove the soundness of the method with respect to a sequential consistent semantics and a reasonable weakly consistent memory semantics. We then show how to take into account mutual exclusion and thread priorities through partitioning over the scheduler state. We present preliminary experimental results analyzing a real program with our prototype, Thésée, and demonstrate the scalability of our approach.

Keywords: Parallel programs, static analysis, Abstract Interpretation, run-time errors.

1 Introduction

Ensuring the safety of critical embedded software is important as a single "bug" can have catastrophic consequences. Previous work on the Astrée analyzer [5] demonstrated that static analysis by Abstract Interpretation could help, when specializing an analyzer to a class of programs (synchronous control/command avionics C software) and properties (run-time errors). In this paper, we describe ongoing work to achieve similar results for *parallel* embedded programs. We wish to match the current trend in critical embedded systems to switch from large numbers of single-program processors communicating through a common bus to single-processor multi-threaded applications communicating through a shared memory (for instance, in the context of Integrated Modular Avionics). We focus on detecting the same kinds of run-time errors as Astrée does (arithmetic and memory errors) and take data-races into account (as they may cause such errors), but we ignore other concurrency errors (such as dead-locks, live-locks, or priority inversions), which are orthogonal.

* This work is supported by the INRIA project "Abstraction" common to CNRS and ENS in France.

G. Barthe (Ed.): ESOP 2011, LNCS 6602, pp. 398–418, 2011.
© Springer-Verlag Berlin Heidelberg 2011

Our method is based on Abstract Interpretation [7], a general theory of the approximation of semantics, which allows designing static analyzers that are sound by construction, i.e., consider a superset of all program behaviors and thus cannot miss any bug, but can cause spurious alarms due to over-approximations. At its core, our method performs an analysis of each thread considering an abstraction of the effects of the other threads (called interferences). Each analysis generates a new set of interferences, and threads are re-analyzed until a fixpoint is reached. Thus, few modifications are required for a non-parallel analyzer to analyze parallel programs. Moreover, we show that few thread re-analyses are required in practice, resulting in a scalable analysis.

As we target embedded software, we can safely assume that there is no recursion nor dynamic allocation of memory, threads, or locks, which makes the analysis easier. In return, we handle two subtle points. Firstly, we consider a weakly consistent memory model: memory accesses not protected by mutual exclusion may cause behaviors that are not the result of any thread interleaving to appear, as they expose to concurrent threads compiler optimizations that are transparent on non-parallel programs. We handle this by proving that our semantics is invariant by some classes of program transformations. Secondly, we take into account the effect of a real-time scheduler that schedules the threads on a single processor according to strict, fixed priorities: only the unblocked thread of highest priority may run. This ensures some mutual exclusion properties that our target program exploits, and so should our analysis. This is achieved by partitioning with respect to an abstraction of the global scheduling state.

Our paper is organized as follows: Sec. 2 presents a classic non-parallel semantics, Sec. 3 considers threads in a shared memory, and Sec. 4 adds support for locks and priorities; Sec. 5 presents our prototype and experimental results, Sec. 6 discusses related work, and Sec. 7 concludes and envisions future work. We alternate between two kinds of semantics: semantics based on control paths, that can model precisely thread interleavings, and semantics by structural induction on the syntax, that give rise to effective abstract interpreters. Figure 1 summarizes the semantics introduced in the paper, using $\subseteq$ to denote the "is less abstract than" relation. Our analysis has already been mentioned, briefly and informally, in [4, § VI]. We offer here a formal, rigorous treatment.

2 Non-parallel Programs

This section recalls a classic static analysis by Abstract Interpretation of the run-time errors of *non-parallel* programs, as performed for instance by Astrée [5]. The formalization introduced here will be extended later to parallel programs, and it will be apparent that an analyzer for parallel programs can be constructed by extending an analyzer for non-parallel programs with few changes.

2.1 Syntax

For the sake of exposition, we reason on a vastly simplified programming language. However, the results extend naturally to a realistic language, such as the

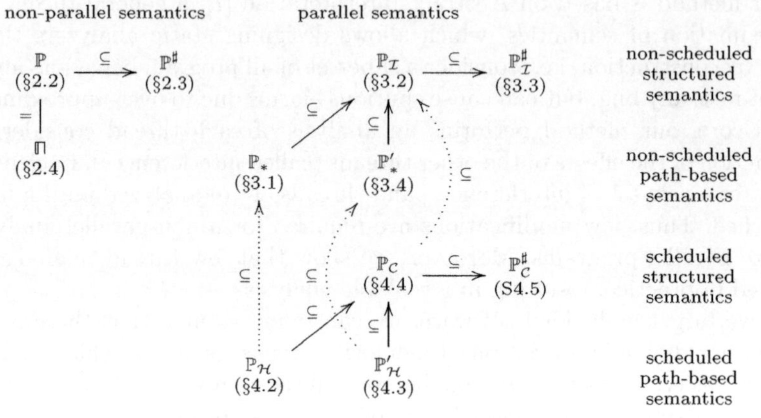

Fig. 1. Semantics defined in this paper

subset of C excluding recursion and dynamic memory allocation. We assume a fixed, finite set $\mathcal{V}$ of variables and $\mathcal{F}$ of function names. A program has an entry-point $entry \in \mathcal{F}$ and associates to each function name $f \in \mathcal{F}$ a structured statement $body(f) \in stat$ in the following grammar:

$$
\begin{array}{lll}
stat ::= X \leftarrow expr & \textit{(assignment, } X \in \mathcal{V}\textit{)} & \\
\quad\mid \ \textbf{if } expr \textbf{ then } stat & \textit{(conditional)} & \\
\quad\mid \ \textbf{while } expr \textbf{ do } stat & \textit{(loop)} & \\
\quad\mid \ stat;\ stat & \textit{(sequence)} & (1)\\
\quad\mid \ f() & \textit{(function call, } f \in \mathcal{F}\textit{)} &
\end{array}
$$

$$
\begin{array}{l}
expr ::= X \mid [c_1, c_2] \mid expr \diamond_\ell expr \\
\text{where } X \in \mathcal{V},\ c_1, c_2 \in \mathbb{R} \cup \{\pm\infty\},\ \diamond \in \{+, -, \times, /\},\ \ell \in \mathcal{L}
\end{array}
$$

For the sake of simplicity, we do not handle local variables (all variables are visible at all program points) nor function arguments and returns. Due to the absence of recursion, these could be easily simulated by using a finite set of global variables. Our toy language is limited to a single data-type (real numbers in $\mathbb{R}$) and numeric expressions. Constants are actually constant intervals $[c_1, c_2]$, which return a fresh value between c_1 and c_2 when evaluated. This allows modeling non-deterministic expressions and inputs from the environment. Each operator $\diamond_\ell$ is tagged with a syntactic location ℓ and we denote by $\mathcal{L}$ the finite set of all syntactic locations. The output of an analyzer will be the set of locations ℓ with errors (or rather, a superset of them, due to approximations).

2.2 Concrete Structured Semantics $\mathbb{P}$

We present a concrete semantics, that is, the most precise mathematical expression of program semantics we consider. As it is undecidable, it will be abstracted in the next section to obtain a sound static analysis.

A program environment $\rho \in \mathcal{E}$ maps each variable to a value, i.e., $\mathcal{E} \stackrel{\text{def}}{=} \mathcal{V} \to \mathbb{R}$. The semantics $\mathbb{E}[\![\, e \,]\!]$ of an expression $e \in expr$ maps an environment to a set of values in $\mathcal{P}(\mathbb{R})$ (sets accounting for non-determinism) and a set of run-time error locations in $\mathcal{P}(\mathcal{L})$ (in our simple case, only for divisions by zero). It is defined by structural induction as follows:

$$
\begin{array}{l}
\forall e \in \mathit{expr},\ \mathbb{E}[\![\, e \,]\!] : \mathcal{E} \to (\mathcal{P}(\mathbb{R}) \times \mathcal{P}(\mathcal{L})) \\
\mathbb{E}[\![\, X \,]\!]\rho \stackrel{\text{def}}{=} (\{\, \rho(X) \,\}, \emptyset) \\
\mathbb{E}[\![\, [c_1, c_2] \,]\!]\rho \stackrel{\text{def}}{=} (\{\, c \in \mathbb{R} \mid c_1 \leq c \leq c_2 \,\}, \emptyset) \\
\mathbb{E}[\![\, e_1 \diamond_\ell e_2 \,]\!]\rho \stackrel{\text{def}}{=} \\
\qquad \text{let } (V_1, \Omega_1) = \mathbb{E}[\![\, e_1 \,]\!]\rho \text{ in} \\
\qquad \text{let } (V_2, \Omega_2) = \mathbb{E}[\![\, e_2 \,]\!]\rho \text{ in} \\
\qquad (\{\, x_1 \diamond x_2 \mid x_1 \in V_1,\ x_2 \in V_2,\ \diamond \neq / \vee x_2 \neq 0 \,\}, \\
\qquad \ \Omega_1 \cup \Omega_2 \cup \{\, \ell \mid \diamond = / \wedge 0 \in V_2 \,\}) \\
\text{where } \diamond \in \{\, +, -, \times, / \,\}
\end{array}
\tag{2}
$$

We now consider the complete lattice $\mathcal{D} \stackrel{\text{def}}{=} \mathcal{P}(\mathcal{E}) \times \mathcal{P}(\mathcal{L})$ with partial order $\sqsubseteq$ defined as the pairwise set inclusion $(A, B) \sqsubseteq (A', B') \stackrel{\text{def}}{\iff} A \subseteq A' \wedge B \subseteq B'$. We denote by $\sqcup$ the associated join, i.e., pairwise set union. The *structured* semantics $\mathbb{S}[\![\, s \,]\!]$ of a statement s is a morphism in $\mathcal{D}$ that, given a set of environments R and errors Ω before a statement s, returns the reachable environments after s as well as Ω enriched with the errors encountered during the execution of s:

$$
\begin{array}{l}
\forall s \in \mathit{stat},\ \mathbb{S}[\![\, s \,]\!] : \mathcal{D} \to \mathcal{D} \\
\mathbb{S}[\![\, X \leftarrow e \,]\!](R, \Omega) \stackrel{\text{def}}{=} \\
\qquad (\emptyset, \Omega) \sqcup \bigsqcup_{\rho \in R} \text{let } (V, \Omega') = \mathbb{E}[\![\, e \,]\!]\rho \text{ in } (\{\, \rho[X \mapsto v] \mid v \in V \,\}, \Omega') \\
\mathbb{S}[\![\, s_1;\ s_2 \,]\!](R, \Omega) \stackrel{\text{def}}{=} (\mathbb{S}[\![\, s_2 \,]\!] \circ \mathbb{S}[\![\, s_1 \,]\!])(R, \Omega) \\
\mathbb{S}[\![\, \textbf{if } e \textbf{ then } s \,]\!](R, \Omega) \stackrel{\text{def}}{=} (\mathbb{S}[\![\, s \,]\!] \circ \mathbb{S}[\![\, e \neq 0? \,]\!])(R, \Omega) \sqcup \mathbb{S}[\![\, e = 0? \,]\!](R, \Omega) \\
\mathbb{S}[\![\, \textbf{while } e \textbf{ do } s \,]\!](R, \Omega) \stackrel{\text{def}}{=} \\
\qquad \mathbb{S}[\![\, e = 0? \,]\!](\text{lfp}\, \lambda X.\, (R, \Omega) \sqcup (\mathbb{S}[\![\, s \,]\!] \circ \mathbb{S}[\![\, e \neq 0? \,]\!])X) \\
\mathbb{S}[\![\, f() \,]\!](R, \Omega) \stackrel{\text{def}}{=} \mathbb{S}[\![\, \mathit{body}(f) \,]\!](R, \Omega) \\
\mathbb{S}[\![\, e \bowtie 0? \,]\!](R, \Omega) \stackrel{\text{def}}{=} \\
\qquad (\emptyset, \Omega) \sqcup \bigsqcup_{\rho \in R} \text{let } (V, \Omega') = \mathbb{E}[\![\, e \,]\!]\rho \text{ in } (\{\, \rho \mid \exists v \in V,\ v \bowtie 0 \,\}, \Omega') \\
\text{with } \bowtie \in \{\, =, \neq \,\}
\end{array}
\tag{3}
$$

where $\rho[X \mapsto x]$ is the environment that maps X to x, and elements $Y \neq X$ to $\rho(Y)$. Loops and conditionals use the synthetic "guard" statements $e = 0?$ and $e \neq 0?$ that filter their argument and keep only those environments that may evaluate, respectively, to null (i.e., false) or non-null (i.e., true) values. Guards and assignments are collectively called *atomic statements*. The semantics of loops uses a least fixpoint operator lfp to compute a loop invariant. We have the following property:

Theorem 1. *$\forall s$, $\mathbb{S}[\![\, s \,]\!]$ is well defined and a strict, complete $\sqcup-$morphism.*

We can now define the concrete structured semantics of the program as follows:

$$
\mathbb{P} \stackrel{\text{def}}{=} \Omega, \text{ where } (-, \Omega) = \mathbb{S}[\![\, \mathit{entry}() \,]\!](\mathcal{E}_0, \emptyset) \tag{4}
$$

where $\mathcal{E}_0 \subseteq \mathcal{E}$ is a set of initial environments (e.g., $\mathcal{E}_0 \stackrel{\text{def}}{=} \{\, \rho_0 \,\}$ where $\forall X \in \mathcal{V}$, $\rho_0(X) = 0$). Thus, we observe the set of run-time errors that can appear in executions starting at the beginning of *entry* in an initial environment. Note that, as $\forall s$, $\mathbb{S}[\![s]\!](\emptyset, \Omega) = (\emptyset, \Omega)$, we also observe errors occurring in executions that loop forever or halt before the end of *entry*.

2.3 Abstract Structured Semantics $\mathbb{P}^\sharp$

The semantics $\mathbb{P}$ is not computable as it involves least fixpoints in an infinite-height domain $\mathcal{D}$. An effective analysis will instead compute an abstract semantics over-approximating the concrete one. This semantics is parametrized by an abstract domain of environments, i.e., a set $\mathcal{E}^\sharp$ of computer-representable abstract elements, with a partial order $\subseteq^\sharp$. Each abstract element represents a set of concrete environments through a monotonic concretization function $\gamma_\mathcal{E} : \mathcal{E}^\sharp \to \mathcal{P}(\mathcal{E})$. In particular, there is an element $\mathcal{E}_0^\sharp \in \mathcal{E}^\sharp$ representing initial environments: $\gamma_\mathcal{E}(\mathcal{E}_0^\sharp) \supseteq \mathcal{E}_0$. We also require a sound and effective abstract version of every concrete operator:

$$\begin{array}{l} \cup_\mathcal{E}^\sharp : (\mathcal{E}^\sharp \times \mathcal{E}^\sharp) \to \mathcal{E}^\sharp \\ \text{with } \forall A^\sharp, B^\sharp \in \mathcal{E}^\sharp,\ \gamma_\mathcal{E}(A^\sharp \cup_\mathcal{E}^\sharp B^\sharp) \supseteq \gamma_\mathcal{E}(A^\sharp) \cup \gamma_\mathcal{E}(B^\sharp) \end{array}$$

and, for atomic statements s, i.e., $s \in \{\, X \leftarrow e,\ e = 0?,\ e \neq 0?\,\}$:

$$\begin{array}{l} \mathbb{S}[\![s]\!]^\sharp : (\mathcal{E}^\sharp \times \mathcal{P}(\mathcal{L})) \to (\mathcal{E}^\sharp \times \mathcal{P}(\mathcal{L})) \\ \text{with } \forall (R^\sharp, \Omega),\ (\mathbb{S}[\![s]\!] \circ \gamma)(R^\sharp, \Omega) \sqsubseteq (\gamma \circ \mathbb{S}[\![s]\!]^\sharp)(R^\sharp, \Omega) \\ \text{where } \gamma(R^\sharp, \Omega) \stackrel{\text{def}}{=} (\gamma_\mathcal{E}(R^\sharp), \Omega) \end{array}$$

i.e., the soundness condition requires an abstract operator to output supersets of the environments and error locations returned by the concrete one. Finally, when $\mathcal{E}^\sharp$ has infinite strictly increasing chains, we require a widening operator $\triangledown_\mathcal{E}$ to ensure the convergence of abstract fixpoint computations in finite time:

$$\begin{array}{l} \triangledown_\mathcal{E} : (\mathcal{E}^\sharp \times \mathcal{E}^\sharp) \to \mathcal{E}^\sharp \\ \text{with } \forall A^\sharp, B^\sharp \in \mathcal{E}^\sharp,\ \gamma_\mathcal{E}(A^\sharp \triangledown_\mathcal{E} B^\sharp) \supseteq \gamma_\mathcal{E}(A^\sharp) \cup \gamma_\mathcal{E}(B^\sharp) \\ \text{and } \forall (Y_i^\sharp)_{i \in \mathbb{N}}, \text{ the sequence } X_0^\sharp \stackrel{\text{def}}{=} Y_0^\sharp,\ X_{i+1}^\sharp \stackrel{\text{def}}{=} X_i^\sharp \triangledown_\mathcal{E} Y_{i+1}^\sharp \\ \qquad\qquad \text{reaches a fixpoint } X_k^\sharp = X_{k+1}^\sharp \text{ for some } k \in \mathbb{N}. \end{array}$$

There exist many such abstract domains, for instance the interval domain [7], where an element of $\mathcal{E}^\sharp$ associates an interval to each variable, or the octagon domain [17], where an element of $\mathcal{E}^\sharp$ is a conjunction of constraints of the form $\pm X \pm Y \leq c$ with $X, Y \in \mathcal{V}$, $c \in \mathbb{R}$.

Given an abstract domain, we can provide an abstract semantics for non-atomic statements by induction, similarly to the concrete semantics (3), except that loops use the widening operator $\triangledown_\mathcal{E}$:

$$\begin{array}{l} \mathbb{S}[\![s_1;\ s_2]\!]^\sharp(R^\sharp, \Omega) \stackrel{\text{def}}{=} (\mathbb{S}[\![s_2]\!]^\sharp \circ \mathbb{S}[\![s_1]\!]^\sharp)(R^\sharp, \Omega) \\ \mathbb{S}[\![\textbf{if } e \textbf{ then } s]\!]^\sharp(R^\sharp, \Omega) \stackrel{\text{def}}{=} \\ \qquad (\mathbb{S}[\![s]\!]^\sharp \circ \mathbb{S}[\![e \neq 0?]\!]^\sharp)(R^\sharp, \Omega)\ \cup^\sharp\ \mathbb{S}[\![e = 0?]\!]^\sharp(R^\sharp, \Omega) \\ \mathbb{S}[\![\textbf{while } e \textbf{ do } s]\!]^\sharp(R^\sharp, \Omega) \stackrel{\text{def}}{=} \\ \qquad \mathbb{S}[\![e = 0?]\!]^\sharp(\text{lfp}\, \lambda X.\, X \triangledown ((R^\sharp, \Omega)\ \cup^\sharp\ (\mathbb{S}[\![s]\!]^\sharp \circ \mathbb{S}[\![e \neq 0?]\!]^\sharp) X)) \\ \mathbb{S}[\![f()]\!]^\sharp(R^\sharp, \Omega) \stackrel{\text{def}}{=} \mathbb{S}[\![\mathit{body}(f)]\!]^\sharp(R^\sharp, \Omega) \end{array} \tag{5}$$

where $(R_1^\sharp, \Omega_1) \cup^\sharp (R_2^\sharp, \Omega_2) \stackrel{\text{def}}{=} (R_1^\sharp \cup_\mathcal{E}^\sharp R_2^\sharp,\ \Omega_1 \cup \Omega_2)$ and $(R_1^\sharp, \Omega_1) \triangledown (R_2^\sharp, \Omega_2) \stackrel{\text{def}}{=} (R_1^\sharp \triangledown_\mathcal{E} R_2^\sharp,\ \Omega_1 \cup \Omega_2)$. The program semantics is, similarly to (4):

$$\mathbb{P}^\sharp \stackrel{\text{def}}{=} \Omega, \text{ where } (-, \Omega) = \mathbb{S}[\![\, entry() \,]\!]^\sharp(\mathcal{E}_0^\sharp, \emptyset) \ . \tag{6}$$

The following theorem states the soundness of the abstract semantics:

Theorem 2. $\mathbb{P} \subseteq \mathbb{P}^\sharp$.

As our programs have no recursive procedures, the recursion in $\mathbb{S}[\![\cdot]\!]^\sharp$ is bounded and we obtain an effective and sound static analysis. It is flow-sensitive and fully context-sensitive (behaving as if all function calls were inlined). It is relational whenever $\mathcal{E}^\sharp$ is (e.g., with octagons [17]). Moreover, the number of abstract elements to keep in memory does not depend on the program size but on the maximum nesting of conditionals and loops: the analyzer is thus very memory friendly, which is critical to analyze large programs, as in Astrée [5].

2.4 Concrete Path-Based Semantics Π

We now propose an alternative concrete semantics based on control paths, which will come handy when considering parallel programs interleaving several threads. For non-parallel programs, its output is equal to that of the structured one.

A control path p is a finite sequence of atomic statements (i.e., $X \leftarrow e$, $e = 0?$, $e \neq 0?$). We denote by Π the set of all control paths. The set of paths $\pi(s) \subseteq \Pi$ of a statement s is defined as follows:

$$\begin{array}{l}
\pi(X \leftarrow e) \stackrel{\text{def}}{=} \{\, X \leftarrow e \,\} \\
\pi(s_1;\ s_2) \stackrel{\text{def}}{=} \pi(s_1); \pi(s_2) \\
\pi(\textbf{if } e \textbf{ then } s) \stackrel{\text{def}}{=} (\{\, e \neq 0? \,\}; \pi(s)) \cup \{\, e = 0? \,\} \\
\pi(\textbf{while } e \textbf{ do } s) \stackrel{\text{def}}{=} (\text{lfp}\, \lambda X. \{\, \epsilon \,\} \cup (X; \{\, e \neq 0? \,\}; \pi(s))); \{\, e = 0? \,\} \\
\pi(f()) \stackrel{\text{def}}{=} \pi(body(f))
\end{array} \tag{7}$$

where ϵ denotes then empty path, and ; denotes path concatenation (by analogy with statement sequencing s_1; s_2) and is naturally extended to sets of paths. When s contains a loop, $\pi(s)$ is infinite, although many paths may be infeasible, i.e., have no corresponding execution (e.g., if all loops have a static bound).

Using the definitions from the structured semantics (3), we can define the semantics $\Pi[\![\, P \,]\!]$ of a set of paths $P \subseteq \Pi$ as:

$$\Pi[\![\, P \,]\!](R, \Omega) \stackrel{\text{def}}{=} \bigsqcup \{\, \mathbb{S}[\![\, s_1; \ldots; s_n \,]\!](R, \Omega) \mid s_1; \ldots; s_n \in P \,\} \tag{8}$$

which is similar to the standard *meet over all paths* solution[1] of data-flow problems [18, § 2], but for concrete executions in the infinite-height lattice $\mathcal{D}$. The meet over all paths and maximum fixpoint solutions of data-flow problems are equal for distributive frameworks; similarly, our structured and path-based concrete semantics (based on complete $\sqcup-$morphisms) are equal:

Theorem 3. $\forall s \in stat$, $\Pi[\![\, \pi(s) \,]\!] = \mathbb{S}[\![\, s \,]\!]$.

[1] The lattices used in data-flow analysis and abstract interpretation are dual: the former uses a meet to join paths while we employ a join.

3 Parallel Programs in Shared Memory

In this section, we consider several threads that communicate through a shared memory, without any synchronization primitive. We also discuss memory consistency models and their effect on the semantics and static analysis.

A program has now a fixed, finite set $\mathcal{T}$ of threads. Each thread $t \in \mathcal{T}$ has an entry-point function $entry_t \in \mathcal{F}$. All the variables in $\mathcal{V}$ are shared and can be accessed by all threads.[2]

3.1 Concrete Interleaving Semantics $\mathbb{P}_*$

The simplest and most natural model of parallel program execution considers all possible interleavings of control paths from all threads. These correspond to *sequentially consistent executions*, as coined by Lamport [15]. A parallel control path p is a finite sequence of pairs (s, t), where s is an atomic statement and $t \in \mathcal{T}$. The semantics $\Pi_*[\![P]\!]$ of a set of parallel control paths P is:

$$\Pi_*[\![P]\!](R, \Omega) \stackrel{\text{def}}{=} \bigsqcup \{ \mathbb{S}[\![s_1; \ldots; s_n]\!](R, \Omega) \mid (s_1, -); \ldots; (s_n, -) \in P \} \quad (9)$$

We denote by π_* the set of all parallel control paths in the program:

$$\pi_* \stackrel{\text{def}}{=} \{ p \mid \forall t \in \mathcal{T},\ \text{proj}_t(p) \in \pi(body(entry_t)) \} \quad (10)$$

where $\text{proj}_t(p)$ projects p on a thread t by extracting the maximal path $s_1; \ldots; s_n$ such that $(s_1, t); \ldots; (s_n, t)$ is a sub-path of p. The semantics $\mathbb{P}_*$ of the parallel program is then:

$$\mathbb{P}_* \stackrel{\text{def}}{=} \Omega, \text{ where } (-, \Omega) = \Pi_*[\![\pi_*]\!](\mathcal{E}_0, \emptyset) \ . \quad (11)$$

3.2 Concrete Interference Semantics $\mathbb{P}_{\mathcal{I}}$

Because it reasons on infinite sets of paths, the interleaving concrete semantics is not easily amenable to flow-sensitive abstractions. We propose here a more abstract semantics that can be expressed by induction on the syntax and will lead to an effective static analysis after further abstraction.

We start by enriching the non-parallel semantics of Sec. 2.2 with a notion of interference. We call *interference* a triple $(t, X, v) \in \mathcal{I}$, where $\mathcal{I} \stackrel{\text{def}}{=} \mathcal{T} \times \mathcal{V} \times \mathbb{R}$, indicating that the thread t can set the variable X to the value v. The semantics of expressions is updated to take as extra arguments the current thread t and an interference set $I \subseteq \mathcal{I}$. When fetching a variable $X \in \mathcal{V}$, each interference on X from other threads is applied:

$$\mathbb{E}_{\mathcal{I}}[\![X]\!](t, \rho, I) \stackrel{\text{def}}{=} (\{ \rho(X) \} \cup \{ v \mid (t', X, v) \in I,\ t \neq t' \}, \emptyset) \quad (12)$$

while other functions are not changed with respect to (2), apart from propagating t and I recursively. As the interference is chosen non-deterministically, distinct occurrences of X in an expression may evaluate to different values. The

[2] As the set of threads is finite, thread-local variables, such as function locals and parameters, could be handled by duplicating the functions and renaming the variables.

$\mathcal{E}_0$: `flag1` = `flag2` = 0	

`flag1 ← 1;`
`if (flag2 = 0)`
critical section
	`flag2 ← 1;`
	`if (flag1 = 0)`
	critical section

(a) Mutual Exclusion Algorithm.

$\mathcal{E}_0$: `x` = `y` = 0	
`x ← x + 1;` `y ← x;`	`x ← x + 1;`

(b) Parallel Incrementation.

Fig. 2. Incompleteness examples for the interference semantics

semantics of statements is also enriched with interferences and is now a complete $\sqcup$−morphism in the complete lattice $\mathcal{D}_\mathcal{I} \stackrel{\text{def}}{=} \mathcal{P}(\mathcal{E})\times\mathcal{P}(\mathcal{L})\times\mathcal{P}(\mathcal{I})$. The semantics of an assignment in a thread t both uses and enriches the interference set:

$$\begin{aligned}&\mathbb{S}_\mathcal{I}[\![X \leftarrow e,\, t]\!](R,\Omega,I) \stackrel{\text{def}}{=}\\ &\quad(\emptyset,\Omega,I) \sqcup \textstyle\bigsqcup_{\rho\in R} (\{\,\rho[X\mapsto v] \mid v\in V\,\},\, \Omega',\, \{\,(t,X,v)\mid v\in V\,\})\\ &\qquad\qquad\text{where } (V,\Omega') = \mathbb{E}_\mathcal{I}[\![e]\!](t,\rho,I)\ .\end{aligned} \tag{13}$$

The other functions (not presented here) are easily derived: guards $e \bowtie 0?$ pass I to $\mathbb{E}_\mathcal{I}[\![e]\!]$ and return I unchanged, while non-atomic statements are similar to (3), replacing $\mathbb{S}[\![\cdot]\!]$ with $\mathbb{S}_\mathcal{I}[\![\cdot]\!]$. Moreover, using $\mathbb{S}_\mathcal{I}[\![\cdot]\!]$ in (8) defines a path-based semantics with interference $\Pi_\mathcal{I}[\![P,\, t]\!]$. Theorem 3 naturally becomes:

Theorem 4. $\forall t \in \mathcal{T},\ s \in \mathit{stat},\ \Pi_\mathcal{I}[\![\pi(s),\, t]\!] = \mathbb{S}_\mathcal{I}[\![s,\, t]\!]$.

The semantics $\mathbb{S}_\mathcal{I}[\![s,t]\!]$ still considers a statement s from a single thread t. To take into account multiple threads, we iterate the analysis of all threads until errors and interferences are stable:

$$\begin{aligned}&\mathbb{P}_\mathcal{I} \stackrel{\text{def}}{=} \Omega,\ \text{where } (\Omega,-) \stackrel{\text{def}}{=}\\ &\quad\text{lfp}\,\lambda(\Omega,I).\ \textstyle\bigsqcup_{t\in\mathcal{T}} \text{ let } (-,\Omega',I') = \mathbb{S}_\mathcal{I}[\![\mathit{entry}_t(),\, t]\!](\mathcal{E}_0,\Omega,I) \text{ in } (\Omega',I')\ .\end{aligned} \tag{14}$$

The interference semantics is sound with respect to the interleaving one (11):

Theorem 5. $\mathbb{P}_* \subseteq \mathbb{P}_\mathcal{I}$.

However, it is generally not complete. Consider, for instance the program fragment in Fig. 2(a) inspired from Dekker's mutual exclusion algorithm. According to the interleaving semantics, both threads can never be in their critical section simultaneously. The interference semantics, however, allows thread 1 to read `flag2` as either 0 (from $\mathcal{E}_0$) or 1 (from interferences) at any program point, and likewise for thread 2 and `flag1`, and so, there is no mutual exclusion. In Fig. 2(b), two threads increment the same zero-initialized variable `x`. According to the interleaving semantics, either the value 1 or 2 is stored into `y`. However, in the interference semantics, the fixpoint builds a growing set of interferences, up to $\{\,(t,\mathtt{x},i)\mid t\in\mathcal{T},\ i\in\mathbb{N}\,\}$, as each thread increments the possible values written by the other thread, resulting in any positive value being written into `y`.

3.3 Abstract Interference Semantics $\mathbb{P}^\sharp_\mathcal{I}$

The concrete interference semantics is defined by structural induction. It can thus be easily abstracted. We assume, as in Sec. 2.3, the existence of an abstract domain $\mathcal{E}^\sharp$ abstracting sets of environments, with a concretization $\gamma_\mathcal{E}$ and an element $\mathcal{E}_0^\sharp$ abstracting $\mathcal{E}_0$. Additionally, we assume the existence of an abstract domain $\mathcal{N}^\sharp$ that abstracts sets of reals. It is equipped with a concretization $\gamma_\mathcal{N} : \mathcal{N}^\sharp \to \mathcal{P}(\mathbb{R})$, a least element $\bot_\mathcal{N}^\sharp$ such that $\gamma_\mathcal{N}(\bot_\mathcal{N}^\sharp) = \emptyset$, an abstract join $\cup_\mathcal{N}^\sharp$ and, if it has strictly increasing infinite chains, a widening $\triangledown_\mathcal{N}$. Interferences are then abstracted using the domain $\mathcal{I}^\sharp \stackrel{\text{def}}{=} (\mathcal{T} \times \mathcal{V}) \to \mathcal{N}^\sharp$, with concretization $\gamma_\mathcal{I}(I^\sharp) \stackrel{\text{def}}{=} \{\, (t, X, v) \,|\, v \in \gamma_\mathcal{N}(I^\sharp(t, X)) \,\}$, and $\cup_\mathcal{I}^\sharp$ and $\triangledown_\mathcal{I}$ defined point-wise. Abstract semantic functions now have the form: $\mathbb{S}_\mathcal{I}[\![\cdot]\!]^\sharp : \mathcal{D}_\mathcal{I}^\sharp \to \mathcal{D}_\mathcal{I}^\sharp$ with $\mathcal{D}_\mathcal{I}^\sharp \stackrel{\text{def}}{=} \mathcal{E}^\sharp \times \mathcal{P}(\mathcal{L}) \times \mathcal{I}^\sharp$, and the soundness condition becomes:

$$(\mathbb{S}_\mathcal{I}[\![s, t]\!] \circ \gamma)(R^\sharp, \Omega, I^\sharp) \sqsubseteq (\gamma \circ \mathbb{S}_\mathcal{I}[\![s, t]\!]^\sharp)(R^\sharp, \Omega, I^\sharp)$$

where $\gamma(R^\sharp, \Omega, I^\sharp) \stackrel{\text{def}}{=} (\gamma_\mathcal{E}(R^\sharp), \Omega, \gamma_\mathcal{I}(I^\sharp))$, i.e., the abstract function over-approximates environment, error, and interference sets.

Classic abstract domains can be easily converted to the interference semantics. Consider, for instance, the case of an assignment $(R^{\sharp\prime}, \Omega', I^{\sharp\prime}) = \mathbb{S}_\mathcal{I}[\![X \leftarrow e, t]\!]^\sharp(R^\sharp, \Omega, I^\sharp)$, when $\mathcal{N}^\sharp$ is the interval domain [7] and $\mathcal{E}^\sharp$ is an arbitrary domain. For each variable Y occurring in e, we compute its abstract interference: $Y^\sharp \stackrel{\text{def}}{=} \bigcup_\mathcal{N}^\sharp \{\, I^\sharp(t', Y) \,|\, t \neq t' \,\}$. If $Y^\sharp \neq \bot_\mathcal{N}^\sharp$, then Y is substituted in e with the interval constant $Y^\sharp \cup_\mathcal{N}^\sharp \mathit{itv}_Y(R^\sharp)$ (where $\mathit{itv}_Y(R^\sharp)$ extracts the bounds of Y in the abstract environment $R^\sharp$) to get an expression e'. The result abstract environment and error set can now be computed using the native operators on $\mathcal{E}^\sharp$ as $(R^{\sharp\prime}, \Omega') = \mathbb{S}[\![X \leftarrow e']\!]^\sharp(R^\sharp, \Omega)$. Finally, $I^{\sharp\prime} = I^\sharp[(t, X) \mapsto \mathit{itv}_X(R^{\sharp\prime}) \cup_\mathcal{N}^\sharp I^\sharp(t, X)]$. Note that $\mathcal{I}^\sharp$ is not isomorphic to the interval domain [7]: the former abstracts $\mathcal{V} \to \mathcal{P}(\mathbb{R})$ and the later $\mathcal{P}(\mathcal{V} \to \mathbb{R})$. Sound abstractions for atomic statements then lift by induction on the syntax to sound abstractions for all statements, as in (5). Finally, an abstraction of the interference fixpoint (14) can be computed by iteration on abstract interferences, using a widening to ensure termination:

$$\begin{array}{l} \mathbb{P}_\mathcal{I}^\sharp \stackrel{\text{def}}{=} \Omega, \text{ where } (\Omega, -) \stackrel{\text{def}}{=} \\ \quad \text{lfp}\, \lambda(\Omega, I^\sharp). \forall t \in \mathcal{T}, \text{ let } (-, \Omega'_t, I_t^{\sharp\prime}) = \mathbb{S}_\mathcal{I}[\![\mathit{entry}_t(), t]\!]^\sharp(\mathcal{E}_0^\sharp, \Omega, I^\sharp) \text{ in} \\ \quad\quad (\bigcup_{t \in \mathcal{T}} \Omega'_t,\; I^\sharp \triangledown_\mathcal{I} \bigcup_\mathcal{I}^\sharp \{\, I_t^{\sharp\prime} \,|\, t \in \mathcal{T} \,\}) \ . \end{array} \tag{15}$$

The following theorem states the soundness of the analysis:

Theorem 6. $\mathbb{P}_\mathcal{I} \subseteq \mathbb{P}_\mathcal{I}^\sharp$.

The obtained analysis remains flow-sensitive and can be relational (provided that $\mathcal{E}^\sharp$ is relational) within each thread, but abstracts interferences in a flow-insensitive and non-relational way. It is expressed as an outer iteration that completely re-analyzes each thread until the abstract interferences stabilize, and so, can be implemented easily on top of existing non-parallel analyzers. Compared to a non-parallel program analysis, the cost is multiplied by the number of outer iterations required to stabilize interferences. This number remained very low in our experiments (Sec. 5). More importantly, the overall cost is not related to the (combinatorial) number of interleavings, but rather to the amount of abstract interferences $I^\sharp$, i.e., of actual communications between the threads. The speed of convergence can be controlled by adapting the widening $\triangledown_{\mathcal{N}}$.

3.4 Weakly Consistent Memory Semantics $\mathbb{P}'_*$

The interleaving concrete semantics $\mathbb{P}_*$ of Sec. 3.1, while simple, is not realistic. A first issue is that, as noted by Reynolds in [21], such a semantics requires choosing a level of granularity, i.e., some basic set of operations that are assumed to be atomic. In our case, we assumed assignments and guards to be atomic. In contrast, an actual system may schedule a thread within an assignment and cause `x` to be 1 at the end of the program in Fig. 2(b) instead of the expected value, 2. A second issue, noted by Lamport in [14], is that the latency of loads and stores in a shared memory may break the sequential consistency in true multiprocessor systems: threads running on different processors may not agree on the value of a shared variable. E.g., in Fig. 2(a), each thread may acknowledge the change of value of a flag after it has tested the other one, causing both critical sections to be entered simultaneously. Moreover, Lamport noted in [15] that reordering of independent loads and stores in one thread by the processor can also break sequential consistency (for instance performing the load from `flag2` after the store to `flag1` instead of before in the left thread of Fig. 2(a)). More recently, it has been observed [16] that optimizations in modern compilers have the same ill-effect even on mono-processor systems: program transformations that are perfectly safe on a thread considered in isolation (for instance, reordering the assignment `flag1` $\leftarrow$ 1 and the test `flag2 = 0`) can cause non sequentially consistent behaviors to appear. In this section, we show that the interference semantics correctly handles these issues, by proving that it is invariant under a "reasonable" class of program transformations.

Acceptable program transformations of a thread are defined with respect to the path-based semantics $\mathbb{\Pi}$ of Sec. 2.4. A transformation of a thread t is acceptable if it gives rise to a set $\pi'(t) \subseteq \Pi$ of control paths such that every path $p' \in \pi'(t)$ can be obtained from a path $p \in \pi(body(entry_t))$ by a sequence of elementary transformations from Def. 1 below, $q \rightsquigarrow q'$ indicating that the statement sequence q in a path can be replaced with q'. These transformations can only reduce the amount of errors and interferences, so that an analysis of the original program is sound with respect to the transformed one. In Def. 1, we say that $X \in \mathcal{V}$ is fresh if it does not occur in any thread; $X \in \mathcal{V}$ is local if it occurs in the current thread only; $s[e'/e]$ is the statement s where some but not necessarily all occurrences of expression e may be changed into e'; var(e) is the set of variables appearing in e; lval(s) is the set of variables modified by s; nonblock(e) hods if evaluating e cannot block the program: $\forall \rho$, $\mathbb{E}[\![\, e \,]\!]\rho = (V, -)$ with $V \neq \emptyset$; e is deterministic if, moreover, $|V| = 1$; noerror(e) holds if evaluating e is always error-free: $\forall \rho$, $\mathbb{E}[\![\, e \,]\!]\rho = (-, \emptyset)$.

Definition 1 (Elementary path transformations)

1. *Redundant store elimination:* $X \leftarrow e_1; X \leftarrow e_2 \rightsquigarrow X \leftarrow e_2$ *when* $X \notin$ var(e_2) *and* nonblock(e_1).
2. *Identity store elimination* $X \leftarrow X \rightsquigarrow \epsilon$.

3. *Reordering of assignments:* $X_1 \leftarrow e_1; X_2 \leftarrow e_2 \rightsquigarrow X_2 \leftarrow e_2; X_1 \leftarrow e_1$ *when* $X_1 \notin \mathrm{var}(e_2)$, $X_2 \notin \mathrm{var}(e_1)$, *and* $\mathrm{nonblock}(e_1)$.
4. *Reordering of guards:* $e_1 \bowtie 0?; e_2 \bowtie 0? \rightsquigarrow e_2 \bowtie 0?; e_1 \bowtie 0?$ *when* $\mathrm{noerror}(e_2)$.
5. *Reorder guard before assignment:* $X_1 \leftarrow e_1; e_2 \bowtie 0? \rightsquigarrow e_2 \bowtie 0?; X_1 \leftarrow e_1$ *when* $X_1 \notin \mathrm{var}(e_2)$ *and either* $\mathrm{nonblock}(e_1)$ *or* $\mathrm{noerror}(e_2)$.
6. *Reorder assignment before guard:* $e_1 \bowtie 0?; X_2 \leftarrow e_2 \rightsquigarrow X_2 \leftarrow e_2; e_1 \bowtie 0?$ *when* $X_2 \notin \mathrm{var}(e_1)$, X_2 *is local, and* $\mathrm{noerror}(e_2)$.
7. *Assignment propagation:* $X \leftarrow e; s \rightsquigarrow X \leftarrow e; s[e/X]$ *when* $X \notin \mathrm{var}(e)$, $\mathrm{var}(e)$ *are local, and e is deterministic.*
8. *Sub-expression elimination:* $s_1; \ldots; s_n \rightsquigarrow X \leftarrow e; s_1[X/e]; \ldots; s_n[X/e]$ *when X is fresh,* $\forall i$, $\mathrm{var}(e) \cap \mathrm{lval}(s_i) = \emptyset$, *and* $\mathrm{noerror}(e)$.
9. *Expression simplification:* $s \rightsquigarrow s[e'/e]$ *when* $\forall \rho, I$, $\mathbb{E}_{\mathcal{I}}[\![e]\!](t, \rho, I) \sqsupseteq \mathbb{E}_{\mathcal{I}}[\![e']\!](t, \rho, I)$.

Store latency can be simulated using rules 8 and 3. Breaking a statement into several ones (i.e., reducing the granularity of atomicity) is possible with rules 7 and 8. Global optimizations, such as constant propagation and folding, can be achieved using rules 7 and 9, while rules 1–6 allow peephole optimizations. Additionally, thread transformations that respect the set of control paths (such as loop unrolling or function inlining) are acceptable.

Given the set of transformed paths $\pi'(t)$, the interleaved executions π'_* and the semantics $\mathbb{P}'_*$ can be defined as in (10), (11):

$$\begin{aligned} \pi'_* &\stackrel{\text{def}}{=} \{\, p \mid \forall t \in \mathcal{T},\ \mathrm{proj}_t(p) \in \pi'(t) \,\} \\ \mathbb{P}'_* &\stackrel{\text{def}}{=} \Omega, \text{ where } (-, \Omega) = \Pi_*[\![\pi'_*]\!](\mathcal{E}_0, \emptyset) \ . \end{aligned} \tag{16}$$

The following theorem extends Thm. 5 to transformed programs:

Theorem 7. $\mathbb{P}'_* \subseteq \mathbb{P}_{\mathcal{I}}$.

However, it is not complete. The two semantics coincide, for instance, in the program of Fig. 2(a). However, in the case of Fig. 2(b), the interference semantics assumes that `y` can take any positive value, while the interleaving semantics after program transformation still only allows the values 1 and 2. Note also that Thm. 7 holds for our "reasonable" collection of program transformations, but may not hold when considering "unreasonable" ones. For instance, `flag1` $\leftarrow$ `1` should not be replaced (e.g., by a misguided prefetching optimizer) with `flag1` $\leftarrow$ `42; flag1` $\leftarrow$ `1` in Fig. 2(a), as this would cause the value 42 to be possibly seen by the other thread. Our interference semantics disallows such "out-of-thin-air" values to be introduced. This is consistent with other semantics, such as the Java one [16,22]. Another example of invalid transformation is the reordering of assignments $X_1 \leftarrow e_1; X_2 \leftarrow e_2 \rightsquigarrow X_2 \leftarrow e_2; X_1 \leftarrow e_1$ when e_1 may block the program (e.g., due to a division by 0) as the transformed program could expose errors in e_2 that cannot occur in the original program. Nevertheless, Def. 1 is not exhaustive and could be extended with some other "reasonable" transformations.

4 Parallel Programs with a Scheduler

The language and semantics of the preceding section are now extended to handle explicit synchronization primitives and a real-time scheduler.

4.1 Priorities and Synchronization Primitives

We denote by $\mathcal{M}$ a finite, fixed set of non-recursive mutual exclusion locks, so-called *mutexes*. The language (1) of Sec. 2.1 is enriched with primitives to control mutexes and scheduling as follows:

$$\begin{array}{rll} stat ::= & \mathbf{lock}(m) & (\textit{mutex locking},\ m \in \mathcal{M}) \\ \mid & \mathbf{unlock}(m) & (\textit{mutex unlocking},\ m \in \mathcal{M}) \\ \mid & X \leftarrow \mathbf{islocked}(m) & (\textit{mutex testing},\ X \in \mathcal{V},\ m \in \mathcal{M}) \\ \mid & \mathbf{yield} & (\textit{thread pause}) \end{array} \tag{17}$$

These new statements are considered to be atomic and the set of paths of a program (7) is extended by stating $\pi(s) \stackrel{\text{def}}{=} \{ s \}$ for them. We also assume that threads have fixed and distinct priorities. Thus, we denote threads in $\mathcal{T}$ simply by numbers from 1 to $|\mathcal{T}|$, being understood that thread t has a strictly higher priority than thread t' when $t > t'$.

Our scheduling model is that of real-time processes, found in embedded systems (e.g, the ARINC 653 specification [2]) and as an extension to POSIX threads. Moreover, we consider that a single thread can execute at a given time (e.g., when all threads share a single processor). In this model, the unblocked thread with the highest priority always runs. All threads start unblocked but may block voluntarily by locking a mutex that is already locked or by yielding, which allows lower priority threads to run. Yielding denotes blocking for a non-deterministic amount of time, which is useful to model timers (as we abstract away actual time) or waiting for some external resource. A lower priority thread can be preempted when unlocking a mutex if a higher priority thread is waiting for this mutex. It can also be preempted at any point by a yielding higher priority thread that wakes up non-deterministically. Thus, we cannot assume that a blocked thread is necessarily waiting at a synchronization statement.

This scheduling model is precise enough to take into account fine mutual exclusion properties that would not hold if we considered arbitrary preemption or true parallel executions on concurrent processors (as found, e.g, in desktops). For instance, in Fig. 3, the high priority thread avoids a call to **lock** / **unlock** by testing with **islocked** whether the low priority thread acquired the lock and, if not, executes its critical section (modifying Y and Z) confident that the low priority thread cannot execute and enter its critical section before the high priority thread explicitly **yield**s. Such reasoning is required to analyze precisely our target application (Sec. 5), and requires the real-time scheduler and single-processor hypotheses assumed in this section.

low priority	high priority
$\mathbf{lock}(m)$;	$X \leftarrow \mathbf{islocked}(m)$;
$Y \leftarrow 1$;	**if** $X = 0$ **then**
$Z \leftarrow 1$;	$Z \leftarrow 2$;
$T \leftarrow Y - Z$;	$Y \leftarrow 2$;
$\mathbf{unlock}(m)$;	**yield**;

Fig. 3. Using priorities to ensure mutual exclusion

4.2 Concrete Scheduled Interleaving Semantics $\mathbb{P}_{\mathcal{H}}$

We now refine the semantics of Sec. 3 to take scheduling into account, starting with the concrete interleaving semantics $\mathbb{P}_*$ of Sec. 3.1. Interleavings that do not respect mutual exclusion or priorities are excluded, and thus, we observe fewer behaviors. This is materialized by the dotted $\subseteq$ arrows between concrete semantics in Fig. 1 (no such property holds for abstract semantics as they are generally non-monotonic due to the use of widenings).

We define a domain of scheduler states $\mathcal{H}$ that associates to each thread whether it is ready, yielding, or waiting for some mutex, as well as the set of mutexes it holds: $\mathcal{H} \stackrel{\text{def}}{=} (\mathcal{T} \to \{\, ready, yield, wait(m) \mid m \in \mathcal{M} \,\}) \times (\mathcal{T} \to \mathcal{P}(\mathcal{M}))$. The domain of statements becomes: $\mathcal{D}_{\mathcal{H}} \stackrel{\text{def}}{=} \mathcal{P}(\mathcal{H} \times \mathcal{E}) \times \mathcal{P}(\mathcal{L})$. The semantics of atomic statements is decomposed into three steps. Firstly, the function $\text{enabled}_t : \mathcal{D}_{\mathcal{H}} \to \mathcal{D}_{\mathcal{H}}$ that keeps only the states where a given thread t can run:

$$\text{enabled}_t(R, \Omega) \stackrel{\text{def}}{=} (\{\, ((b,l),\rho) \in R \mid b(t) = ready \wedge \forall t' > t,\, b(t') \neq ready \,\}, \Omega) \ .$$

Secondly, the semantic function $\mathbb{S}'_{\mathcal{H}}[\![\, s, t \,]\!]$ for atomic statements s in thread t:

$$\begin{array}{l}
\mathbb{S}'_{\mathcal{H}}[\![\, \mathbf{yield}, t \,]\!](R,\Omega) \stackrel{\text{def}}{=} (\{\, ((b[t \mapsto yield], l), \rho) \mid ((b,l),\rho) \in R \,\}, \Omega) \\
\mathbb{S}'_{\mathcal{H}}[\![\, \mathbf{lock}(m), t \,]\!](R,\Omega) \stackrel{\text{def}}{=} (\{\, ((b[t \mapsto wait(m)], l), \rho) \mid ((b,l),\rho) \in R \,\}, \Omega) \\
\mathbb{S}'_{\mathcal{H}}[\![\, \mathbf{unlock}(m), t \,]\!](R,\Omega) \stackrel{\text{def}}{=} (\{\, ((b, l[t \mapsto l(t) \setminus \{\, m \,\}]), \rho) \mid ((b,l),\rho) \in R \,\}, \Omega) \\
\mathbb{S}'_{\mathcal{H}}[\![\, X \leftarrow \mathbf{islocked}(m), t \,]\!](R,\Omega) \stackrel{\text{def}}{=} \\
\qquad (\{\, ((b,l), \rho[X \mapsto 0]) \mid ((b,l),\rho) \in R,\, \forall t' \in \mathcal{T},\, m \notin l(t') \,\} \cup \\
\qquad\ \ \{\, ((b,l), \rho[X \mapsto 1]) \mid ((b,l),\rho) \in R,\, \exists t' \in \mathcal{T},\, m \in l(t') \,\}, \Omega) \\
\mathbb{S}'_{\mathcal{H}}[\![\, s, t \,]\!](R,\Omega) \stackrel{\text{def}}{=} \\
\qquad (\{\, ((b,l), \rho') \mid ((b,l),\rho) \in R,\, (R', -) = \mathbb{S}[\![\, s \,]\!](\{\, \rho \,\}, \Omega),\, \rho' \in R' \,\}, \Omega') \\
\qquad \text{where } (-, \Omega') = \mathbb{S}[\![\, s \,]\!](R, \Omega), \text{ for all other statements } s, \text{ using (3).}
\end{array}$$

Thirdly, a scheduler step that wakes up yielding threads non-deterministically and gives each available mutex to the highest priority thread waiting for it:

$$\begin{array}{l}
\text{sched}(R,\Omega) \stackrel{\text{def}}{=} (\{\, ((b',l'),\rho) \mid ((b,l),\rho) \in R \,\}, \Omega), \text{ where} \\
\quad \forall t, \text{ if } b(t) = wait(m) \wedge \forall t' \neq t,\, m \notin l(t') \wedge \forall t' > t,\, b(t') \neq wait(m) \\
\qquad \text{then } b'(t) = ready \text{ and } l'(t) = l(t) \cup \{\, m \,\} \\
\qquad \text{else } l'(t) = l(t) \text{ and } b'(t) = b(t) \vee (b'(t) = ready \wedge b(t) = yield) \ .
\end{array}$$

The semantics of an atomic statement s in a thread t combines all three steps:

$$\mathbb{S}_{\mathcal{H}}[\![\, s, t \,]\!] \stackrel{\text{def}}{=} \text{sched} \circ \mathbb{S}'_{\mathcal{H}}[\![\, s, t \,]\!] \circ \text{enabled}_t \ . \qquad (18)$$

The semantics $\Pi_{\mathcal{H}}[\![P]\!]$ of a set P of interleaved paths and the semantics $\mathbb{P}_{\mathcal{H}}$ of the program are then defined, similarly to Sec. 3.1, (9)–(11), as:

$$\begin{aligned} &\Pi_{\mathcal{H}}[\![P]\!](R,\Omega) \stackrel{\text{def}}{=} \\ &\quad \bigsqcup \{ (\mathbb{S}_{\mathcal{H}}[\![s_n, t_n]\!] \circ \cdots \circ \mathbb{S}_{\mathcal{H}}[\![s_1, t_1]\!])(R,\Omega) \mid (s_1,t_1);\ldots;(s_n,t_n) \in P \} \\ &\mathbb{P}_{\mathcal{H}} \stackrel{\text{def}}{=} \Omega, \text{ where } (-,\Omega) = \Pi_{\mathcal{H}}[\![\pi_*]\!](\{h_0\} \times \mathcal{E}_0, \emptyset) \end{aligned} \tag{19}$$

where $h_0 \stackrel{\text{def}}{=} (\lambda t.\, \mathit{ready}, \lambda t.\, \emptyset)$ denotes the initial scheduler state. As in Sec. 3.1, many control paths in π_* are unfeasible, i.e., return an empty set of environments, some of which are now ruled-out by the enabled_t function. Nevertheless, errors from a feasible prefix of an unfeasible path are still taken into account. This includes, in particular, any error that occurs before a deadlock.

4.3 Scheduled Weakly Consistent Memory Semantics $\mathbb{P}'_{\mathcal{H}}$

In addition to restricting the interleaving of threads, synchronization primitives also have an effect when considering weakly consistent memory semantics: they enforce some form of sequential consistency at a coarse granularity level. More precisely, the compiler and processor handle synchronization statements specially, introducing the necessary flushes into memory and register reloads, and refraining from optimizing across them.

We thus adapt the semantics $\mathbb{P}'_*$ of Sec. 3.4 as follows. We consider a transformed thread as a set of paths $\pi'(t)$ obtained from $\pi(\mathit{body}(\mathit{entry}_t))$ using elementary path transformations from Def. 1, but no transformation should cross any synchronization primitive **lock**(m), **unlock**(m), **yield** or $X \leftarrow$ **islocked**(m). Let π'_* be defined as before as the interleaving of paths from all $\pi'(t)$. The scheduled weakly consistent memory semantics is, based on (19):

$$\mathbb{P}'_{\mathcal{H}} \stackrel{\text{def}}{=} \Omega, \text{ where } (-,\Omega) = \Pi_{\mathcal{H}}[\![\pi'_*]\!](\{h_0\} \times \mathcal{E}_0, \emptyset) \ . \tag{20}$$

4.4 Concrete Scheduled Interference Semantics $\mathbb{P}_{\mathcal{C}}$

We now provide a structured version of the scheduled interleaving semantics $\mathbb{P}_{\mathcal{H}}$. Similarly to Sec. 3.2, it is based on a notion of interferences, and it is not complete. To avoid considering interferences between parts of threads that are in mutual exclusion, interferences are partitioned with respect to a thread-local view of scheduler configurations. The finite set of configurations $\mathcal{C}$ is defined as:

$$\mathcal{C} \stackrel{\text{def}}{=} \mathcal{P}(\mathcal{M}) \times \mathcal{P}(\mathcal{M}) \times \{ \mathit{weak}, \mathit{sync}(m) \mid m \in \mathcal{M} \}$$

where the first subset of $\mathcal{M}$ denotes the mutexes locked by the thread while the second one denotes the mutexes held by no thread at all (as tested with **islocked**). The last component in $\mathcal{C}$ allows distinguishing between two kinds of interferences, which are depicted in Fig. 4: weakly consistent interferences (*weak* component in $\mathcal{C}$) corresponding to read / write pairs not protected by mutual exclusion (Fig. 4.(a)), and well synchronized interferences ($\mathit{sync}(m)$ component in $\mathcal{C}$) where both the read and the write are protected by the same mutex m

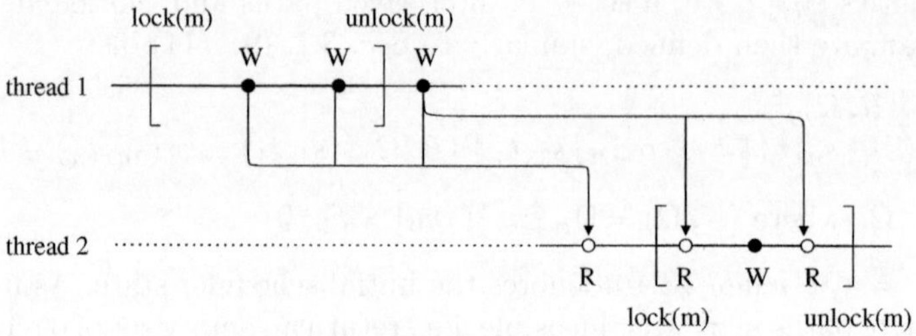

(a) Weakly consistent interferences.

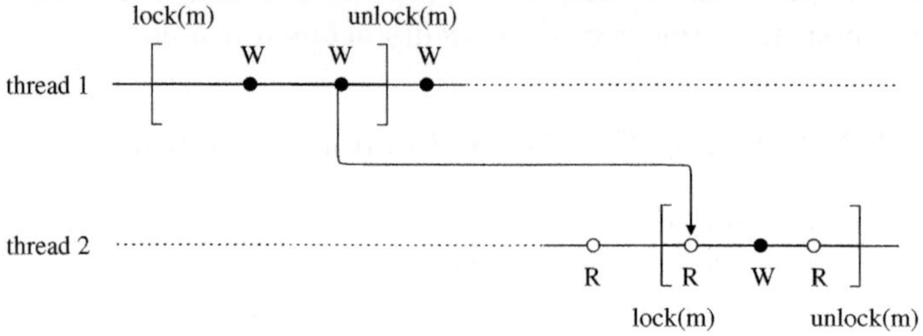

(b) Well synchronized interferences.

Fig. 4. Weakly consistent versus well synchronized scheduled interferences

(Fig. 4.(b)). Weakly consistent interferences behave as in Sec. 3.2. For well synchronized accesses, only the last write before unlocking a mutex affects a read, and only until the variable read is overwritten while the mutex is held. The partitioned domain of interferences is then: $\mathcal{I} \stackrel{\text{def}}{=} \mathcal{T} \times \mathcal{C} \times \mathcal{V} \times \mathbb{R}$.

The semantics of a variable X read from an environment $\rho \in \mathcal{E}$ by a thread t is similar to (12), but we only apply the weakly consistent interferences from $I \subseteq \mathcal{I}$ that are not in mutual exclusion with a current configuration $c \in \mathcal{C}$:

$$\begin{array}{l} \mathbb{E}_{\mathcal{C}}[\![\, X \,]\!](t, c, \rho, I) \stackrel{\text{def}}{=} \\ \quad (\{\, \rho(X) \,\} \cup \{\, v \mid (t', c', X, v) \in I,\ t \neq t \wedge excl(c, c') \,\},\ \emptyset) \\ \text{where } excl((l, u, s), (l', u', s')) \stackrel{\text{def}}{\iff} l \cap l' = u \cap l' = u' \cap l = \emptyset \wedge s = s' \ . \end{array} \tag{21}$$

Other constructions are handled as in (2), where t, c, I are passed unused and unchanged. To handle precisely the **islocked** primitive in code similar to Fig. 3, it is necessary to represent some relationship between environments and scheduler states. Hence, environments are also partitioned with respect to $\mathcal{C}$, although the third component of configurations is not used and always set to *weak*. The semantic domain of statements is now $\mathcal{D}_{\mathcal{C}} \stackrel{\text{def}}{=} \mathcal{P}(\mathcal{C} \times \mathcal{E}) \times \mathcal{P}(\mathcal{L}) \times \mathcal{P}(\mathcal{I})$, partially ordered by point-wise set inclusion. The semantics of assignments is similar to that of (13), applied point-wise to each configuration:

$$\begin{array}{l} \mathbb{S}_{\mathcal{C}}[\![\, X \leftarrow e, t \,]\!](R, \Omega, I) \stackrel{\text{def}}{=} (\emptyset, \Omega, I) \sqcup \\ \quad \bigsqcup_{(c,\rho) \in R} (\{\, (c, \rho[X \mapsto v]) \mid v \in V \,\},\ \Omega',\ \{\, (t, c, X, v) \mid v \in V \,\}) \\ \qquad \text{where } (V, \Omega') = \mathbb{E}_{\mathcal{C}}[\![\, e \,]\!](t, c, \rho, I) \ . \end{array}$$

The semantics of synchronization primitives is as follows:

$$\begin{array}{l}
\mathbb{S}_C[\![\, \mathbf{lock}(m),\ t \,]\!](R, \Omega, I) \stackrel{\text{def}}{=} \\
\quad (\{\, ((l \cup \{\, m \,\}, \emptyset, s), \rho') \mid ((l, -, s), \rho) \in R,\ \rho' \in in(t, l, m, \rho, I) \,\}, \\
\quad \Omega,\ I \cup \bigcup \{\, out(t, l, m', \rho) \mid ((l, u, -), \rho) \in R,\ m' \in u \,\}) \\
\mathbb{S}_C[\![\, \mathbf{unlock}(m),\ t \,]\!](R, \Omega, I) \stackrel{\text{def}}{=} \\
\quad (\{\, ((l \setminus \{\, m \,\}, u, s), \rho) \mid ((l, u, s), \rho) \in R \,\}, \\
\quad \Omega,\ I \cup \bigcup \{\, out(t, l \setminus \{\, m \,\}, m, \rho) \mid ((l, -, -), \rho) \in R \,\}) \\
\mathbb{S}_C[\![\, \mathbf{yield},\ t \,]\!](R, \Omega, I) \stackrel{\text{def}}{=} \\
\quad (\{\, ((l, \emptyset, s), \rho) \mid ((l, -, s), \rho) \in R \,\}, \\
\quad \Omega,\ I \cup \bigcup \{\, out(t, l, m', \rho) \mid ((l, u, -), \rho) \in R,\ m' \in u \,\})
\end{array} \tag{22}$$

$$\begin{array}{l}
\mathbb{S}_C[\![\, X \leftarrow \mathbf{islocked}(m),\ t \,]\!](R, \Omega, I) \stackrel{\text{def}}{=} \\
\quad (\{\, ((l, u \cup m_t^*, s), \rho'[X \mapsto 0]) \mid ((l, u, s), \rho) \in R,\ \rho' \in in(t, l, m, \rho, I) \,\} \cup \\
\quad \{\, ((l, u \setminus \{\, m \,\}, s), \rho[X \mapsto 1]) \mid ((l, u, s), \rho) \in R \,\}, \\
\quad \Omega,\ I \cup \{\, (t, c, X, v) \mid v \in \{\, 0, 1 \,\},\ (c, -) \in R \,\}) \\
\text{where } m_t^* \stackrel{\text{def}}{=} \{\, m \,\} \text{ if no thread } t' > t \text{ can lock } m, \text{ and } \emptyset \text{ otherwise} \\
in(t, l, m, \rho, I) \stackrel{\text{def}}{=} \\
\quad \{\, \rho' \mid \forall X \in \mathcal{V},\ \rho'(X) = \rho(X) \vee (t', (l', \emptyset, sync(m)), X, \rho'(X)) \in I, \\
\quad\ \ t \neq t',\ l \cap l' = \emptyset \,\} \\
out(t, l, m, \rho) \stackrel{\text{def}}{=} \{\, (t, (l, \emptyset, sync(m)), X, \rho(X)) \mid X \in \mathcal{V} \,\}\ .
\end{array}$$

The functions $in(t, l, m, \rho, I)$ and $out(t, l, m, \rho)$ respectively model entering and exiting a critical section protected by a mutex m in a thread t that also holds the mutexes in l: *out* collects a set of well synchronized interferences from an environment, while *in* applies them to an environment. Obviously, **lock**(m) uses *in* on m, while **unlock** uses *out*. Additionally, $X \leftarrow$ **islocked**(m) creates two partitions: one where $X = 1$, and one where $X = 0$ and m is assumed to be unlocked, which is remembered in u. However, the assumption that m is unlocked only stands if the thread cannot be preempted at any point by a higher priority thread locking m, hence the side-condition on m_t^* — in practice, this condition is checked by remembering in the semantics which **lock**s are issued by each thread; we do not present this for lack of space. Moreover, it stands only until the thread calls a blocking primitive (i.e., **lock** or **yield**), which gives the opportunity to a lower priority thread to lock m. Thus, blocking primitives use *out* to exit critical sections protected by all $m \in u$. Note that by replacing $X \leftarrow$ **islocked**(m) with $X \leftarrow [0, 1]$, we would obtain a less precise semantics, but which is also sound for true parallel or non real-time systems. We do not show the semantics of guards and non-atomic statements; they can be derived from (3) easily. The semantics $\mathbb{P}_C$ of a program has the same fixpoint form as (14):

$$\begin{array}{l}
\mathbb{P}_C \stackrel{\text{def}}{=} \Omega, \text{ where } (\Omega, -) \stackrel{\text{def}}{=} \operatorname{lfp} \lambda(\Omega, I). \\
\quad \bigsqcup_{t \in \mathcal{T}} \text{let } (-, \Omega', I') = \mathbb{S}_C[\![\, entry_t(),\ t \,]\!](\{c_0\} \times \mathcal{E}_0, \Omega, I) \text{ in } (\Omega', I')
\end{array} \tag{23}$$

where the initial configuration is $c_0 \stackrel{\text{def}}{=} (\emptyset, \emptyset, weak) \in \mathcal{C}$.

The semantics is sound with respect to that of Secs. 4.2–4.3:

Theorem 8. *$\mathbb{P}_{\mathcal{H}} \subseteq \mathbb{P}_C$ and $\mathbb{P}'_{\mathcal{H}} \subseteq \mathbb{P}_C$.*

As in Sec. 3.4, this semantics is not complete. An additional loss of precision comes from the handling of well synchronized accesses. A main limitation is that such accesses are handled in a non-relational way, hence $\mathbb{P}_{\mathcal{C}}$ cannot represent relations enforced at the boundaries of critical sections but broken within, while $\mathbb{P}_{\mathcal{H}}$ can. For instance, in Fig. 3, we cannot prove that $Y = Z$ holds outside critical sections, but only that $Y, Z \in [1, 2]$. This shows in particular that even programs without data-races have behaviors in $\mathbb{P}_{\mathcal{C}}$ outside the sequentially consistent ones. Yet, we can prove that $T = 0$, i.e., the assignment to T is free from interference. Our implementation is actually a little smarter than (22) and uses a modified *out* that does not consider interferences for variables not modified while m is held. Finally, our implementation can also report data-races by simply inspecting the set of interferences during each assignment.

4.5 Abstract Scheduled Interference Semantics $\mathbb{P}^{\sharp}_{\mathcal{C}}$

The interference semantics with scheduler $\mathbb{P}_{\mathcal{C}}$ can be abstracted similarly to $\mathbb{P}_{\mathcal{I}}$. As in Sec. 3.3, we assume the existence of two abstract domains $\mathcal{E}^{\sharp}$ and $\mathcal{N}^{\sharp}$ abstracting respectively $\mathcal{P}(\mathcal{E})$ and $\mathcal{P}(\mathbb{R})$. We lift these domains by partitioning under $\mathcal{C}$: $\mathcal{D}^{\sharp}_{\mathcal{C}} \stackrel{\text{def}}{=} (\mathcal{C} \to \mathcal{E}^{\sharp}) \times \mathcal{P}(\mathcal{L}) \times \mathcal{I}^{\sharp}$, where abstract interferences are in $\mathcal{I}^{\sharp} \stackrel{\text{def}}{=} (\mathcal{T} \times \mathcal{C} \times \mathcal{V}) \to \mathcal{N}^{\sharp}$. The concretization is: $\gamma(R^{\sharp}, \Omega, I^{\sharp}) \stackrel{\text{def}}{=} (\{\, (c, \rho) \mid \rho \in \gamma_{\mathcal{E}}(R^{\sharp}(c)) \,\}, \Omega, \{\, (t, c, X, v) \mid v \in \gamma_{\mathcal{N}}(I^{\sharp}(t, c, X)) \,\})$. Sound abstract transfer functions can be derived easily from those in $\mathcal{E}^{\sharp}$ and $\mathcal{N}^{\sharp}$. For instance, the assignment is similar to that of Sec. 3.3, except that it is applied point-wise to each $R^{\sharp}(c)$ and it only considers the abstract interferences from the configurations not in mutual exclusion with c. Synchronisation primitives are implemented mostly by joining partitions (using $\cup^{\sharp}_{\mathcal{E}}$) and copying non-relational information between $\mathcal{E}^{\sharp}$ and $\mathcal{N}^{\sharp}$ (for *in* and *out*). Transfer functions for non-atomic statements are derived as in (5). Finally, the abstract analysis $\mathbb{P}^{\sharp}_{\mathcal{C}}$ computes a fixpoint over the interferences identical to (15). The resulting analysis is sound:

Theorem 9. $\mathbb{P}_{\mathcal{C}} \subseteq \mathbb{P}^{\sharp}_{\mathcal{C}}$.

Due to partitioning, $\mathbb{P}^{\sharp}_{\mathcal{C}}$ is less efficient than $\mathbb{P}^{\sharp}_{\mathcal{I}}$. However, partitioned environments are mostly empty: Sec. 5 shows that, in practice, at most program points, $R^{\sharp}(c) = \bot^{\sharp}_{\mathcal{E}}$ except for a few of configurations. Partitioned interferences are less sparse because, being flow-insensitive, they accumulate information for configurations reachable from any program point. However, this is not problematic: as interferences are non-relational, a large number of partitions can be manipulated efficiently. Thanks to partitioning, the precision of $\mathbb{P}^{\sharp}_{\mathcal{C}}$ is much better than $\mathbb{P}^{\sharp}_{\mathcal{I}}$ in the presence of locks and priorities. For instance, $\mathbb{P}^{\sharp}_{\mathcal{C}}$ can discover that $T = 0$ in Fig. 3, while the analysis of Sec. 3.3 would only discover that $T \in [-1, 1]$ due to spurious interferences from the high priority thread.

5 Experimental Results

The abstract analysis of Sec. 4.5 has been implemented in Thésée, our prototype analyzer. It analyzes C without recursion nor dynamic memory allocation.

It is sound, and checks for integer and float arithmetic overflows, divisions by zero, invalid array and pointer accesses, and assertion failures. It also reports data-races, but ignores other parallel-related hazards. In particular, it does not check for dead-locks nor unbounded priority inversions. In fact, they cannot occur in our target application as all locks have a timeout. Thésée is based on Astrée [5], a static analyzer for synchronous embedded C software, which was successfully applied to prove the absence of run-time errors in large critical control/command software from Airbus [10]. Thésée benefited directly from Astrée's numerous abstract domains and iteration strategies targeting embedded C code. The adaptation to the analysis of parallel programs, including the addition of the interference fixpoint iterator and the scheduler partitioning domain, required adding approximately 6 KLines of code to the 100 KLines analyzer, and did not require any structural change.

Our target parallel application is another large program from Airbus consisting of 1.6 MLines of C code and 15 threads. It runs under an ARINC 653 real-time OS [2]. The code is quite complex as it mixes string formatting, list sorting, network protocols (e.g., TFTP), and automatically generated synchronous logic. The program was completed with a 2 500 line hand-written model of the ARINC 653 OS implementing the various API calls, in C enriched with analyzer-specific intrinsics (mutex lock, unlock, etc.).

The analysis currently takes 14h on our 2.66 GHz 64-bit intel server using one core. An important result is that only four iterations are required to stabilize abstract interferences. Moreover, there are a maximum of 52 partitions for abstract interferences and 4 partitions for abstract environments, so that the analysis fits in 32 GB of memory. The analysis generates around 7600 alarms. This high number is understandable: Thésée is naturally tuned for avionic control/command software as it inherits abstract domains $\mathcal{E}^\sharp$, $\mathcal{N}^\sharp$ from Astrée, but the analyzed program is not limited to control/command processing. We started adapting these domains and can already report some improvements compared to earlier experimental results (50h and 12000 alarms [4, § VI]), using the same iterator and scheduler partitioning. However, independently from the choice of abstract domains $\mathcal{E}^\sharp$, $\mathcal{N}^\sharp$, a better treatment of well synchronized interferences will surely be required to achieve zero false alarms. Following the design-by-refinement of Astrée [5], we have focused on the analysis of a single (albeit large and complex) real-life software and started refining the analyzer to lower the number of alarms.

6 Related Work

There are far too many works on the semantics and analysis of parallel programs to provide a fair survey and comparison here. Instead, we focus on a few works that, we hope, provide a fruitful comparison with ours.

The idea of attaching to each thread location a local invariant and to handle proofs of parallel programs as that of sequential programs with interferences dates back to the Hoare-style proof method of Owicki and Gries [19] and Lamport

[13] and has been well studied since (see [9] for a modern account and a partial survey). It has been studied from an Abstract Interpretation point of view in [8] and applied to static analysis. Two examples are the analysis of C with POSIX threads by Carré and Hymans [6] and that of Java with its weak memory model by Ferrara [11]. Unlike those, we do not handle thread creation, but we do take into account scheduler properties. Fully flow-insensitive analyses, e.g. Steensgaard's popular points-to analysis [23], naturally handle parallel programs. Unfortunately, the level of accuracy required to prove safety properties demands the use of (at least partially) flow-sensitive and relational methods, which we do.

Model-checking also has a long history of verifying parallel systems, including recently weak memory models [3]. Partial order reduction methods [12] are used to limit the number of interleavings to consider, with no impact on completeness. In contrast, we abstract the problem sufficiently so that no interleaving need to be considered at all, at the cost of completeness. Unlike context-bounded approaches [20], our method considers all executions until completion.

Weakly consistent memory models have been studied mostly for hardware [1]. Pugh pioneered its use in programming language semantics, culminating with the Java memory model [16]. It is described in terms of implicit conditions on interleaved execution traces and is quite complex. We chose instead a generative approach based on control path transformations matching closely optimization models, similarly to the work of Saraswat et al. [22]. Our focus is on models that are realistic and can be abstracted into interference semantics suitable for efficient static analysis.

7 Conclusion

We presented a static analysis to detect all run-time errors in embedded C software with several threads communicating through a shared memory with weak consistency and scheduled according to strict priorities. Our method is based on a notion of interferences and partitioning with respect to a scheduler state. It can be implemented on top of analyzers for sequential programs, leveraging a growing library of abstract domains. Promising early experimental results on real code demonstrate the scalability of the approach.

A broad avenue for future work is to bridge the gap between the interleaving semantics and its incomplete abstraction in terms of interferences. Abstracting well synchronized accesses in a non-relational way is a severe limitation that we wish to suppress. We also wish to add support for other synchronization primitives, such as condition variables and atomic variables, and exploit more properties of real-time schedulers. A more precise analysis may require the use of history-sensitive abstractions, an avenue we wish to explore. Moreover, more precise or more general interference semantics could be designed by adjusting the notion of weak memory consistency. Finally, we wish, in future work, to analyze errors specifically related to parallelism, such as dead-locks, live-locks, and priority inversions, including quantitative time-related properties (e.g., bounded priority inversions).

References

1. Adve, S.V., Gharachorloo, K.: Shared memory consistency models: A tutorial. IEEE Comp. 29(12), 66–76 (1996)
2. Aeronautical Radio, Inc. (ARINC). ARINC 653, http://www.arinc.com/
3. Atig, M.F., Bouajjani, A., Burckhardt, S., Musuvathi, M.: On the verification problem for weak memory models. In: 37th ACM SIGACT/SIGPLAN Symp. on Principles of Prog. Lang., pp. 7–18. ACM, New York (2010)
4. Bertrane, J., Cousot, P., Cousot, R., Feret, J., Mauborgne, L., Miné, A., Rival, X.: Static analysis and verification of aerospace software by abstract interpretation. In: AIAA Infotech@Aerospace, vol. AIAA-2010-3385, pp. 1–38. AIAA (American Institute of Aeronautics and Astronautics) (April 2010)
5. Blanchet, B., Cousot, P., Cousot, R., Feret, J., Mauborgne, L., Miné, A., Monniaux, D., Rival, X.: A static analyzer for large safety-critical software. In: ACM SIGPLAN Conf. on Prog. Lang. Design and Implementation, pp. 196–207. ACM, New York (2003)
6. Carré, J.-L., Hymans, C.: From single-thread to multithreaded: An efficient static analysis algorithm. Technical Report arXiv:0910.5833v1, EADS (October 2009)
7. Cousot, P., Cousot, R.: Abstract interpretation: A unified lattice model for static analysis of programs by construction or approximation of fixpoints. In: 4th ACM Symp. on Principles of Prog. Lang., pp. 238–252. ACM, New York (1977)
8. Cousot, P., Cousot, R.: Invariance proof methods and analysis techniques for parallel programs. In: Automatic Prog. Construction Techniques, ch. 12, pp. 243–271. Macmillan, New York (1984)
9. de Roever, W.-P., de Boer, F., Hanneman, U., Hooman, J., Lakhnech, Y., Poel, M., Zwiers, J.: Concurrency Verification: Introduction to Compositional and Noncompositional Methods. Cambridge University Press, Cambridge (2001)
10. Delmas, D., Souyris, J.: Astrée: from research to industry. In: Riis Nielson, H., Filé, G. (eds.) SAS 2007. LNCS, vol. 4634, pp. 437–451. Springer, Heidelberg (2007)
11. Ferrara, P.: Static analysis via abstract interpretation of the happens-before memory model. In: Beckert, B., Hähnle, R. (eds.) TAP 2008. LNCS, vol. 4966, pp. 116–133. Springer, Heidelberg (2008)
12. Godefroid, P.: Partial-Order Methods for the Verification of Concurrent Systems – An Approach to the State-Explosion Problem. PhD thesis, University of Liege, Computer Science Department (1994)
13. Lamport, L.: Proving the correctness of multiprocess programs. IEEE Trans. on Software Engineering 3(2), 125–143 (1977)
14. Lamport, L.: Time, clocks, and the ordering of events in a distributed system. ACM Comm. 21(7), 558–565 (1978)
15. Lamport, L.: How to make a multiprocessor computer that correctly executes multiprocess programs. IEEE Trans. on Computers 28, 690–691 (1979)
16. Manson, J., Pugh, B., Adve, S.V.: The Java memory model. In: 32nd ACM SIGPLAN/SIGACT Symp. on Principles of Prog. Lang., pp. 378–391. ACM, New York (2005)
17. Miné, A.: The octagon abstract domain. Higher-Order and Symbolic Computation 19(1), 31–100 (2006)
18. Nielson, F., Nielson, H.R., Hankin, C.: Principles of Program Analysis. Springer, Heidelberg (1999)
19. Owicki, S., Gries, D.: An axiomatic proof technique for parallel programs I. Acta Informatica 6(4), 319–340 (1976)

20. Qadeer, S., Rehof, J.: Context-bounded model checking of concurrent software. In: Halbwachs, N., Zuck, L.D. (eds.) TACAS 2005. LNCS, vol. 3440, pp. 93–107. Springer, Heidelberg (2005)
21. Reynolds, J.C.: Toward a grainless semantics for shared-variable concurrency. In: Lodaya, K., Mahajan, M. (eds.) FSTTCS 2004. LNCS, vol. 3328, pp. 35–48. Springer, Heidelberg (2004)
22. Saraswat, V.A., Jagadeesan, R., Michael, M.M., von Praun, C.: A theory of memory models. In: 12th ACM SIGPLAN Symp. on Principles and Practice of Parallel Prog., pp. 161–172. ACM, New York (2007)
23. Steensgaard, B.: Points-to analysis in almost linear time. In: 23rd ACM SIGPLAN/SIGACT Symp. on Principles of Prog. Lang., pp. 32–41. ACM, New York (1996)

Algorithmic Nominal Game Semantics

Andrzej S. Murawski[1,⋆] and Nikos Tzevelekos[2,⋆⋆]

[1] Department of Computer Science, University of Leicester
University Road, Leicester LE1 7RH, UK
[2] Oxford University Computing Laboratory
Wolfson Building, Parks Road, Oxford OX1 3QD, UK

Abstract. We employ automata over infinite alphabets to capture the semantics of a finitary fragment of ML with ground-type references. Our approach is founded on game semantics, which allows us to translate programs into automata in such a way that contextual equivalence is characterized by a finitary notion of bisimilarity. As a corollary, we derive a decidability result for a class of first-order programs, including open ones that contain unspecified first-order procedures.

1 Introduction

Recent years have seen a surge of interest in automata-theoretic models over infinite alphabets. It stemmed from the realization that finite automata, while immensely successful, do not lend satisfactory representations of a variety of interesting phenomena. In program verification, for instance, one might want to consider the interaction of unboundedly many agents, each of which issues requests that have to be traceable. In database theory, in turn, integrity constraints are often expressed in terms of data *values* possibly drawn from an infinite set (as opposed to data labels, which come from a finite one). Since giving automata too much power in manipulating values from an infinite domain quickly results in undecidability, decidable models over infinite alphabets have to be restricted so that the values can only be tested for equality. A number of such formalisms have been proposed in recent years: register automata [7], pebble automata [14] and data automata [3], to name a few.

The general goal of our paper is to draw techniques from these developments, adapt them to use in programming language semantics so that, ultimately, they can be applied to program verification: in our case, to automated equivalence checking.

Our results will concern Reduced ML [16], which is a subset of ML with ground-type references only (neither higher-order functions nor reference names can be stored in memory). This is a simple fundamental language that combines functional and imperative programming in a minimal fashion and in the style of ML. Despite its simplicity, it gives rise to a subtle theory of contextual program

⋆ Supported by an EPSRC Advanced Research Fellowship (EP/C539753/1).
⋆⋆ Supported by EPSRC (EP/F067607/1).

G. Barthe (Ed.): ESOP 2011, LNCS 6602, pp. 419–438, 2011.
© Springer-Verlag Berlin Heidelberg 2011

equivalence, which comprises elements of secrecy, freshness, locality and object identity. Here are several sample (in)equivalences that can be (dis)proved in an automated fashion using our results.

– Dynamically generated reference names are private[1].

$$\vdash \mathsf{let}\, n = \mathsf{ref}(0)\;\mathsf{in}\;\lambda x^{\mathsf{int\,ref}}.(x =_{\mathsf{int\,ref}} n) \quad\cong\quad \lambda x^{\mathsf{int\,ref}}.\mathit{false} : \mathsf{int\,ref} \to \mathsf{bool}$$

– Intermediate states of computation are invisible.

$$x : \mathsf{int\,ref} \vdash x := 0; x := 1 \quad\cong\quad x := 1 : \mathsf{unit}$$

– Local declarations and function abstraction do not commute in general.

$$\vdash \lambda x^{\mathsf{unit}}.\mathsf{let}\, n = \mathsf{ref}(0)\;\mathsf{in}\; n \quad\not\cong\quad \mathsf{let}\, n = \mathsf{ref}(0)\;\mathsf{in}\;(\lambda x^{\mathsf{unit}}.n) : \mathsf{unit} \to \mathsf{int\,ref}$$

– But they do sometimes, at the cost of explicit initialization.

$$\begin{aligned} f : \mathsf{int\,ref} \to \mathsf{int} \vdash\ & \lambda x^{\mathsf{unit}}.\mathsf{let}\, n = \mathsf{ref}(0)\;\mathsf{in}\; f(n) \\ \cong\ & \mathsf{let}\, n = \mathsf{ref}(0)\;\mathsf{in}\;\lambda x^{\mathsf{unit}}.n := 0; f(n) : \mathsf{unit} \to \mathsf{int} \end{aligned}$$

– In a similar fashion local variables can be globalized.

$$\begin{aligned} &\mathit{guard} : \mathsf{unit} \to \mathsf{int},\ \mathit{body} : \mathsf{int\,ref} \to \mathsf{unit} \vdash \\ &\qquad \mathsf{while}\; \mathit{guard}()\; \mathsf{do}\; (\mathsf{let}\, n = \mathsf{ref}(0)\;\mathsf{in}\; \mathit{body}(n)) \\ &\qquad \cong\ \mathsf{let}\, n = \mathsf{ref}(0)\;\mathsf{in}\;(\mathsf{while}\; \mathit{guard}()\; \mathsf{do}\; (n := 0; \mathit{body}(n))) : \mathsf{unit} \end{aligned}$$

– Not all differences between names can be picked up by the environment, as reference names are not storable.

$$\begin{aligned} f : \mathsf{int\,ref} \to \mathsf{unit} \vdash\ & \mathsf{let}\, n_1 = \mathsf{ref}(0)\;\mathsf{in}\;\mathsf{let}\, n_2 = \mathsf{ref}\;(0)\;\mathsf{in}\; f(n_1); (n_2 := !n_1); n_2 \\ \cong\ & \mathsf{let}\, n = \mathsf{ref}\;0\;\mathsf{in}\; f(n); n : \mathsf{int\,ref} \end{aligned}$$

In order to derive decidability results for program equivalence, we shall consider a finitary fragment of Reduced ML: with finite datatypes, no recursion and restricted higher-order types. To be exact, our approach will be applicable to terms $\Gamma \vdash M : \theta$, where θ as well as the type of each identifier in Γ is of the form β or $\beta \to \beta$, and β stands for any base type (unit, int or int ref), like in all of the examples given above.

To enable a systematic and computer-aided verification of equivalence between such terms, we translate them into a special class of automata over infinite alphabets in such a way that languages accepted by the automata will be faithful representations of their fully abstract game semantics [12].

Game semantics views interaction as an exchange of moves (play) between two players representing the environment (Opponent) and the program (Proponent) respectively. In our particular game model the moves will contain (reference) names drawn from a countable set of locations. Each move will also be equipped with a carefully selected fragment of the current heap, represented as a set of

[1] $x =_{\mathsf{int\,ref}} r$ denotes reference equality test.

(*name*,*value*) pairs. The involvement of an infinite set of names makes it very natural to view such plays as words over an infinite alphabet.

The automata we employ are deterministic variants of fresh-register automata [17], which themselves build upon register automata [7]: each automaton will be equipped with a finite set of registers in which names can be stored for future reference. The automata are designed in such a way that, in the spirit of register automata, they can classify each name coming from the environment as known (currently stored in one of the registers) or as *locally* fresh – not present in current memory. On the other hand, the names that a program can send to its environment will be either those already in its memory, or *globally* fresh ones, i.e. names that have not been encountered thus far, but can be obtained on demand by invoking a fresh-name generator, in the style of fresh-register automata. We therefore see that local freshness is inherently a property of Opponent, while global freshness is specific to Proponent.

Our decision procedure comprises three stages.

- First we construct automata that represent term behaviour (in the sense of game semantics) under the liberal assumption that the environment is capable of distinguishing all names created by the program and modifying the corresponding values at any time.
- Subsequently we refine the automata so that they capture exactly the interactions with contexts of Reduced ML.
- Finally, we introduce a finite notion of bisimilarity on the automata to ascertain that they represent equivalent interactions. Because the underlying game model is fully abstract, this relates contextual equivalence to decidable bisimilarity.

On the whole, our work combines automata-theoretic and semantic insights to develop a new verification routine.

Related Work. We make a notable step towards a full classification of decidable fragments of Reduced ML. Our results apply to reference types, while all earlier work [6,10,13] on that topic was based on the game model of RML [1], a variant of Reduced ML with "bad variables" (terms of type int ref with designated methods for reading and writing). Consequently, when reference types were present in a typing judgment the induced notion of equivalence was strictly stronger than in Reduced ML proper. For example, $x := !x$ and () could be distinguished by a bad variable that crashes on dereferencing. Another drawback of RML was that reference equality could not be studied, as it did not make sense. RML had a definite advantage though, as the associated game model was based on a finite set of moves. Equivalence in Reduced ML turns out much more subtle and the corresponding fully abstract game model [12] is unsuited to finite-alphabet representations. It so happens that the presence of bad variables does not change the induced observational equivalence in the call-by-name case of Idealized Algol [8], where a complete map of decidable fragments already exists [11] and increases in complexity (of deciding equivalence) are tightly linked to type-theoretic order.

$$\theta ::= \mathsf{unit} \mid \mathsf{int} \mid \mathsf{int\,ref} \mid \theta \to \theta$$

$$\frac{}{\Gamma \vdash () : \mathsf{unit}} \qquad \frac{i \in \{0, \cdots, max\}}{\Gamma \vdash i : \mathsf{int}} \qquad \frac{\Gamma \vdash M : \theta}{\pi(\Gamma) \vdash M : \theta}\ \pi \in Perm(\Gamma)$$

$$\frac{\Gamma \vdash M : \mathsf{int} \quad \Gamma \vdash M_0 : \theta \quad \cdots \quad \Gamma \vdash M_{max} : \theta}{\Gamma \vdash \mathsf{case}(M)[M_0, \cdots, M_{max}] : \theta} \qquad \frac{\Gamma \vdash M : \mathsf{int} \quad \Gamma \vdash N : \mathsf{unit}}{\Gamma \vdash \mathsf{while}\, M\, \mathsf{do}\, N : \mathsf{unit}}$$

$$\frac{\Gamma \vdash M : \mathsf{int\,ref}}{\Gamma \vdash !M : \mathsf{int}} \qquad \frac{\Gamma \vdash M : \mathsf{int\,ref} \quad \Gamma \vdash N : \mathsf{int}}{\Gamma \vdash M := N : \mathsf{unit}} \qquad \frac{\Gamma \vdash M : \mathsf{int}}{\Gamma \vdash \mathsf{ref}\, M : \mathsf{int\,ref}}$$

$$\frac{}{\Gamma, x : \theta \vdash x : \theta} \qquad \frac{\Gamma \vdash M : \theta \to \theta' \quad \Gamma \vdash N : \theta}{\Gamma \vdash MN : \theta'} \qquad \frac{\Gamma, x : \theta \vdash M : \theta'}{\Gamma \vdash \lambda x^{\theta}.M : \theta \to \theta'}$$

Fig. 1. Syntax of $\mathsf{RedML_{fin}}$

Contextual equivalence in ML-like languages, also those richer than Reduced ML, has also been studied extensively using relational techniques [15,2,4], albeit without decidability results.

2 Finitary Reduced ML

Finitary Reduced ML ($\mathsf{RedML_{fin}}$) is the (call-by-value) λ-calculus over the ground types unit, int, int ref augmented with (*finitely* many) integer constants $0, \cdots, max$, branching, looping and reference manipulation. Its typing rules are given in Figure 1. Note that we have not included reference equality testing, as it is expressible [15] (assuming $max > 0$). For instance, one can define $\mathsf{eq_{int\,ref}} : \mathsf{int\,ref} \to \mathsf{int\,ref} \to \mathsf{int}$ to be

$$\begin{aligned}\lambda x^{\mathsf{int\,ref}}.\lambda y^{\mathsf{int\,ref}}.\ & \mathsf{let}\, v_x = \mathsf{ref}\, !x\, \mathsf{in} \\ & \mathsf{let}\, v_y = \mathsf{ref}\, !y\, \mathsf{in} \\ & \mathsf{let}\, b = \mathsf{ref}\, 0\, \mathsf{in} \\ & \quad (x := 0; y := 1; (\mathsf{if}\, !x = 1\, \mathsf{then}\, b := 1\, \mathsf{else}\, ()); x := !v_x; y := !v_y; !b).\end{aligned}$$

In the above and in what follows, we write

- $\mathsf{let}\, x = M\, \mathsf{in}\, N$ for the term $(\lambda x^{\theta}.N)M$;
- $M; N$ for the term $(\lambda x^{\theta}.N)M$, if x is not free in N;
- $\mathsf{if}\, M\, \mathsf{then}\, M_1\, \mathsf{else}\, M_0$ for $\mathsf{case}(M)[M_0, M_1, \cdots, M_1]$;
- and $M =_{\mathsf{int\,ref}} N$ for $\mathsf{eq_{int\,ref}}\, M\, N$.

We refer the reader to [16] for a detailed exposition of the operational semantics.

Definition 1. *Two terms-in-context $\Gamma \vdash M : \theta$ and $\Gamma \vdash N : \theta$ are contextually* equivalent *if, and only if, for any* $\mathsf{RedML_{fin}}$*-context $C[-]$ such that $\vdash C[M], C[N] : \mathsf{unit}$, $C[M]$ evaluates to $()$ iff $C[N]$ does. Then we write $\Gamma \vdash M \cong N : \theta$.*

In this paper we show that contextual equivalence is decidable for a fragment of $\mathsf{RedML_{fin}}$, called $\mathsf{RedML}_{\mathsf{fin}}^{\beta\to\beta}$, to be defined next.

Definition 2. *Suppose* $\Gamma = [x_1 : \theta_1, \cdots, x_m : \theta_m]$. *The term-in-context* $\Gamma \vdash M : \theta$ *belongs to* $\mathsf{RedML}_{\mathsf{fin}}^{\beta\to\beta}$ *provided each of* $\theta_1, \cdots, \theta_m, \theta$ *is generated by the grammar*

$$\theta ::= \quad \beta \mid \beta \to \beta$$

in which β *stands for any base type (*unit, int *or* $\mathsf{int\,ref}$*).*

In Section 4 we shall define a class of automata over infinite alphabets to which terms of $\mathsf{RedML}_{\mathsf{fin}}^{\beta\to\beta}$ will be translated in Sections 5 and 6. In order to make the translation more concise, we are going to focus on translating terms in canonical form only. The canonical shapes are defined as follows.

$$\begin{array}{l}\mathbb{C} ::= () \mid i \mid x^{\mathsf{int\,ref}} \mid \mathsf{case}(x^{\mathsf{int}})[\mathbb{C}, \cdots, \mathbb{C}] \mid (\mathsf{while}\,(!x^{\mathsf{int\,ref}})\,\mathsf{do}\,\mathbb{C}); \mathbb{C} \mid \\ \quad (x^{\mathsf{int\,ref}} := i); \mathbb{C} \mid \mathsf{let}\, y^{\mathsf{int}} = !x^{\mathsf{int\,ref}} \,\mathsf{in}\, \mathbb{C} \mid \mathsf{let}\, x^{\mathsf{int\,ref}} = \mathsf{ref}\,(0)\,\mathsf{in}\,\mathbb{C} \mid \\ \quad \lambda x^{\beta}.\mathbb{C} \mid \mathsf{let}\, y^{\beta} = z()\,\mathsf{in}\,\mathbb{C} \mid \mathsf{let}\, y^{\beta} = z\,i\,\mathsf{in}\,\mathbb{C} \mid \mathsf{let}\, y^{\beta} = z\,x^{\mathsf{int\,ref}}\,\mathsf{in}\,\mathbb{C}\end{array}$$

Lemma 3. *Let* $\Gamma \vdash M : \theta$ *be an* $\mathsf{RedML}_{\mathsf{fin}}^{\beta\to\beta}$*-term. There exists a* $\mathsf{RedML}_{\mathsf{fin}}^{\beta\to\beta}$*-term* $\Gamma \vdash \mathbb{C}_M : \theta$ *in canonical form, effectively constructible from* M*, such that* $\Gamma \vdash M \cong \mathbb{C}_M$*.*

Proof. $\mathbb{C}_M$ can be obtained via a series of η-expansions, β-reductions and commuting conversions involving let and case. □

3 Game Semantics

In this section we briefly recapitulate the game semantics of Reduced ML [12], insofar as it concerns modelling $\mathsf{RedML}_{\mathsf{fin}}^{\beta\to\beta}$. We present it in a more concrete way, specialized to the types of $\mathsf{RedML}_{\mathsf{fin}}^{\beta\to\beta}$, along with examples that motivate the respective technical conditions.

Game semantics views computation as a dialogue between the environment (Opponent, O) and the program (Proponent, P). The game model we are going to sketch falls into the realm of *nominal game semantics*: moves may involve *names* drawn from an infinite set $\mathbb{A}$. Consequently, we can apply name-permutations to moves, plays and strategies. Put otherwise, they form *nominal sets* [5]. We begin with some auxiliary definitions before specifying what it means to play our games.

Definition 4. – *For every type* θ *let us define the associated set of labels* $\mathcal{L}_\theta$ *as follows:* $\mathcal{L}_{\mathsf{unit}} = \{\star\}$, $\mathcal{L}_{\mathsf{int}} = \{0, \cdots, max\}$, $\mathcal{L}_{\mathsf{int\,ref}} = \mathbb{A}$, $\mathcal{L}_{\beta\to\beta'} = \{\star\}$. *We shall write* $\mathcal{L}$ *for the set of all labels.*

– *Given a* $\mathsf{RedML}_{\mathsf{fin}}^{\beta\to\beta}$ *typing judgment* $\Gamma \vdash M : \theta$ *we write* $\mathcal{T}_{\Gamma\vdash\theta}$ *for the set of associated* tags, *defined to be*

$$\{\mathsf{c}_x, \mathsf{r}_x \mid (x : \theta_x) \in \Gamma,\ \theta_x \not\equiv \beta\} \cup \{\mathsf{r}_\downarrow\} \cup \{\mathsf{c}, \mathsf{r} \mid \theta \not\equiv \beta\}$$

Thus, for each function-type identifier x in Γ, we have introduced tags c_x and r_x. They can be viewed as calls and returns related to that identifier. Similarly, $\mathsf{r}_\downarrow$ can be taken to correspond to the fact that M was successfully evaluated, and, if θ is a function type, c and r refer respectively to calling the corresponding value and obtaining a result.

Given $\Gamma \vdash M : \theta$, $\ell \in \mathcal{L}$ and $t \in \mathcal{T}_{\Gamma\vdash\theta}$, we shall say that the pair (ℓ, t) is *consistent* if the following conditions are satisfied.

- If $t = \mathsf{r}_\downarrow$ then $\ell \in \mathcal{L}_\theta$.
- If $t = \mathsf{c}_x$ then $\theta_x \equiv \beta \to \beta'$ and $\ell \in \mathcal{L}_\beta$.
- If $t = \mathsf{r}_x$ then $\theta_x \equiv \beta \to \beta'$ and $\ell \in \mathcal{L}_{\beta'}$.
- If $t = \mathsf{c}$ then $\theta \equiv \beta \to \beta'$ and $\ell \in \mathcal{L}_\beta$.
- If $t = \mathsf{r}$ then $\theta \equiv \beta \to \beta'$ and $\ell \in \mathcal{L}_{\beta'}$.

Suppose $\Gamma = [x_1 : \theta_1, \cdots, x_m : \theta_m]$. The set of *initial moves* I_Γ is defined to be $\{(\ell_1, \cdots, \ell_m) \mid \ell_i \in \mathcal{L}_{\theta_i}, 1 \le i \le m\}$.

Definition 5. *A* play[2] *over $\Gamma \vdash \theta$ is a (possibly empty) sequence of the form $\iota(\ell_1, t_1) \cdots (\ell_k, t_k)$ such that $\iota \in I_\Gamma$, all pairs (ℓ_i, t_i) are consistent and $t_1 \cdots t_k$ is a prefix of a word matching $X\mathsf{r}_\downarrow(\mathsf{c}X\mathsf{r})^*$, where $X = (\sum_{\substack{(x:\theta_x)\in\Gamma \\ \theta_x \not\equiv \beta}} (\mathsf{c}_x\, \mathsf{r}_x))^*$. We assume that $X\mathsf{r}_\downarrow(\mathsf{c}X\mathsf{r})^*$ degenerates to $X\mathsf{r}_\downarrow$ if c, r are not available (i.e. θ is a base type). A play is* complete *whenever $t_1 \cdots t_k$ matches a word from $X\mathsf{r}_\downarrow(\mathsf{c}X\mathsf{r})^*$.*

The shape of plays can be thought of as a record of computation. First, calls are being made to the free identifiers of function type (expression X), then a value is reached ($\mathsf{r}_\downarrow$) and, if the type of the value is a function type, we have a series of calls and returns with external calls in-between ($(\mathsf{c}X\mathsf{r})^*$).

We shall refer to ι and (ℓ_i, t_i) as *moves*. Moves are assigned ownership as follows: ι and those with tags r_x, c belong to O (environment) and the rest (tags $\mathsf{c}_x, \mathsf{r}_\downarrow, \mathsf{r}$) belong to P (program). We shall write o and p to range over O- and P-moves respectively. We shall say that $\ell \in \mathbb{A}$ is an O-name (resp. P-name) in a given play s, provided the first occurrence of ℓ was in an O-move (resp. P-move). The set of O- and P-names in s will be denoted by $O(s)$ and $P(s)$ respectively.

The fully abstract game model of Reduced ML [12] is based on a more complicated notion of plays, in which each move can contain a store. Since we are considering a language with ground-type references only, i.e. references names themselves cannot be stored, programs will not be able, in general, to remember all names obtained from the environment. Accordingly, we shall not insist that the stores contain values for all names introduced by O, but only those that are potentially available to the program. Intuitively, these are environment names that the program has managed to bind. The notion of P-view helps to capture this concept.

[2] Readers familiar with game semantics will notice that we omit justification pointers in plays. This is because they are uniquely recoverable with the help of tags.

Definition 6. *Given a play s, we define its P-view $\ulcorner s \urcorner$ as follows.*

$$\begin{aligned} \ulcorner \iota \urcorner &= \iota \\ \ulcorner s\,(\ell_{\mathsf{r}}, \mathsf{r}_x) \urcorner &= \ulcorner s \urcorner (\ell_{\mathsf{r}}, \mathsf{r}_x) \\ \ulcorner s\,(\ell_{\mathsf{c}}, \mathsf{c}) \urcorner &= \ulcorner s' \urcorner (\ell_{\mathsf{r}_\downarrow}, \mathsf{r}_\downarrow)\,(\ell_{\mathsf{c}}, \mathsf{c}) \qquad s = s'(\ell_{\mathsf{r}_\downarrow}, \mathsf{r}_\downarrow)s'' \\ \ulcorner s p \urcorner &= \ulcorner s \urcorner p \end{aligned}$$

It can be checked that the P-view of a play is also a play. Given a play s, the set $\mathsf{Av}_{\mathsf{P}}(s)$ of P-available names is defined as $P(s) \cup O(\ulcorner s \urcorner)$. We can now define a new notion of play, in which players can play moves equipped with stores (moves-with-store, for short).

Definition 7. *A* play-with-store *over $\Gamma \vdash \theta$ is a sequence $m_1^{\Sigma_1} \cdots m_k^{\Sigma_k}$ of moves-with-store satisfying the conditions below.*

- *$m_1 \cdots m_k$ is a play over $\Gamma \vdash \theta$.*
- *For any P-move $m_{2i} = (\ell_{2i}, t_{2i})$, if $\ell_{2i} \in O(m_1 \cdots m_{2i})$ then $\ell_{2i} \in \ulcorner m_1 \cdots m_{2i-1} \urcorner$.*
- *For any $1 \leq i \leq k$, Σ_i is a partial function from $\mathbb{A}$ to $\{0, \cdots, max\}$ such that $\mathsf{dom}(\Sigma_i) = \mathsf{Av}_{\mathsf{P}}(m_1 \cdots m_i)$.*

Using the richer notion of play we define strategies.

Definition 8. *A* strategy *σ is a non-empty, even-prefix closed set of plays-with-store closed under name-permutation. Given a play s, let us write $[s]$ for its equivalence class with respect to name-permutation. A* deterministic *strategy is also required to satisfy the following condition: whenever $s_1 o_1^{\Sigma_1} p_1^{\Sigma_1'}, s_2 o_2^{\Sigma_2} p_2^{\Sigma_2'} \in \sigma$, $[s_1 o_1^{\Sigma_1}] = [s_2 o_2^{\Sigma_2}]$, then $[s_1 o_1^{\Sigma_1} p_1^{\Sigma_1'}] = [s_2 o_2^{\Sigma_2} p_2^{\Sigma_2'}]$.*

We have shown how to assign deterministic strategies to programs of Reduced ML in [12]. Let us write $[\![\Gamma \vdash M : \theta]\!]_0$ for the deterministic strategy corresponding to the $\mathsf{RedML}_{\mathsf{fin}}^{\beta\to\beta}$-term $\Gamma \vdash M : \theta$.

Example 9.
- $[\![\, \vdash \lambda x^{\mathsf{unit}}.\mathsf{let}\, n = \mathsf{ref}(0)\,\mathsf{in}\, n : \mathsf{unit} \to \mathsf{int\,ref}]\!]_0$ consists of plays of the following shape

$$\begin{matrix} \iota^{\emptyset} & (\star, \mathsf{r}_\downarrow)^{\emptyset} & (\star, \mathsf{c})^{\Sigma_0'} & (n_1, \mathsf{r})^{\Sigma_1} & (\star, \mathsf{c})^{\Sigma_1'} & (n_2, \mathsf{r})^{\Sigma_2} & \cdots (\star, \mathsf{c})^{\Sigma_{i-1}'} & (n_i, \mathsf{r})^{\Sigma_i} & (\star, \mathsf{c})^{\Sigma_i'} \cdots \\ O & P & O & P & O & P & O & P & O \end{matrix}$$

  where $\Sigma_0' = \emptyset$ and, for all $i > 0$, $\Sigma_i = \Sigma_{i-1}' \cup \{(n_i, 0)\}$, $\mathsf{dom}(\Sigma_i') = \mathsf{dom}(\Sigma_i)$. Moreover, for any $i \neq j$ we have $n_i \neq n_j$. Note that Σ_i' can be different from Σ_i, i.e. the environment is free to change the values stored at all of the locations that have been revealed to it. Here the stores keep on growing as the names are being generated by the program.
- $[\![\, \vdash \lambda x^{\mathsf{int\,ref}}.\mathsf{case}(!x)[1, 0, 0, \cdots, 0] : \mathsf{int\,ref} \to \mathsf{int}]\!]_0$ generates, among others, the play

$$\iota^{\emptyset}\ (\star, \mathsf{r}_\downarrow)^{\emptyset}\ (n, \mathsf{c})^{(n,2)}\ (0, \mathsf{r})^{(n,2)}\ (n', \mathsf{c})^{(n',0)}\ (1, \mathsf{r})^{(n',0)}\ (n, \mathsf{c})^{(n,0)}\ (1, \mathsf{r})^{(n,0)}.$$

  Note that in the play above the store does not grow as the names are being played by the environment and they disappear from P-view after each call.

By comparing strategies corresponding to terms we cannot yet prove all equivalences. This is because strategies do not take into account the fact that the environment (O) must also be subjected to restrictions concerning recognizability and visibility of names.

Example 10. The following equivalences hold. Yet, strategies corresponding to the terms on the left contain plays-with-store, given below, that seem to contradict this.

1. $f : \mathsf{int\,ref} \to \mathsf{unit} \vdash \mathsf{let}\, n = \mathsf{ref}(0)\,\mathsf{in}\, fn;\, (\lambda x^{\mathsf{int\,ref}}.\mathsf{eq}_{\mathsf{int\,ref}}\, x\, n)$
$\cong\ \mathsf{let}\, n = \mathsf{ref}(0)\,\mathsf{in}\, fn;\, (\lambda x^{\mathsf{int\,ref}}.0) : \mathsf{int\,ref} \to \mathsf{int}$

$$\begin{matrix} \star^{\emptyset} & (n, \mathsf{c}_f)^{(n,0)} & (\star, \mathsf{r}_f)^{(n,2)} & (\star, \mathsf{r}_{\downarrow})^{(n,2)} & (n, \mathsf{c})^{(n,2)} & (1, \mathsf{r})^{(n,2)} \\ O & P & O & P & O & P \end{matrix}$$

2. $f : \mathsf{int\,ref} \to \mathsf{unit} \vdash \mathsf{let}\, n = \mathsf{ref}(0)\,\mathsf{in}\, fn; n := 0;\, (\lambda x^{\mathsf{unit}}.\mathsf{case}(!n)[1, 0, 0, \cdots]) \cong$
$\mathsf{let}\, n = \mathsf{ref}(0)\,\mathsf{in}\, fn;\, (\lambda x^{\mathsf{unit}}.1) : \mathsf{unit} \to \mathsf{int}$

$$\star\ (n, \mathsf{c}_f)^{(n,0)}\ (\star, \mathsf{r}_f)^{(n,k)}\ (\star, \mathsf{r}_{\downarrow})^{(n,0)}\ (\star, \mathsf{c})^{(n,1)}\ (0, \mathsf{r})^{(n,1)}$$

In 1. O played a P-name that could not possibly be remembered by a context with ground-type references. In 2. O changes the value stored at such a location. This mismatch motivates further restrictions on the shape of strategies that are dual to those already imposed on P.

Definition 11. *Given a play s, we define its O-view ($\llcorner s \lrcorner$) as follows.*

$$\begin{aligned} \llcorner \epsilon \lrcorner &= \epsilon \\ \llcorner \iota\, s\, (\ell_{\mathsf{c}_x}, \mathsf{c}_x) \lrcorner &= \iota\, (\ell_{\mathsf{c}_x}, \mathsf{c}_x) \\ \llcorner \iota\, s\, (\ell_{\mathsf{r}_{\downarrow}}, \mathsf{r}_{\downarrow}) \lrcorner &= \iota\, (\ell_{\mathsf{r}_{\downarrow}}, \mathsf{r}_{\downarrow}) \\ \llcorner s\, (\ell_{\mathsf{r}}, \mathsf{r}) \lrcorner &= \llcorner s' \lrcorner\, (\ell_{\mathsf{c}}, \mathsf{c})\, (\ell_{\mathsf{r}}, \mathsf{r}) \qquad s = s'\, (\ell_{\mathsf{c}}, \mathsf{c}) s'' \text{ and } \mathsf{c} \notin s'' \\ \llcorner s\, o \lrcorner &= \llcorner s \lrcorner\, o \end{aligned}$$

The side condition in the last but one case stipulates that $(\ell_{\mathsf{c}}, \mathsf{c})$ be the last move in s with tag c (i.e. c matches r).

Returning to our examples, we can now see that in the fifth move O was playing/modifying a location from outside the current O-view.

Definition 12.
- *A* play-with-store $m_1^{\Sigma_1} \cdots m_k^{\Sigma_k}$ *is* relevant *if, for all O-moves $(\ell_{2i+1}, t_{2i+1})^{\Sigma_{2i+1}}$ $(1 < 2i + 1 \leq k)$ the following conditions hold.*
  - *If $\ell_{2i+1} \in P(m_1 \cdots m_{2i+1})$ then $\ell_{2i+1} \in \llcorner m_1 \cdots m_{2i} \lrcorner$.*
  - *For any $n \in P(m_1 \cdots m_{2i})$, if $n \notin \llcorner m_1 \cdots m_{2i} \lrcorner$ then $\Sigma_{2i+1}(n) = \Sigma_{2i}(n)$.*
- *A* protoplay *is a sequence of moves-with-stores $m_1^{\Sigma_1} \cdots m_k^{\Sigma_k}$ such that $m_1 \cdots m_k$ is a play and, for any $1 \leq i \leq k$,*
  - *$n \in \mathsf{dom}(\Sigma_i) \cap P(m_1 \cdots m_i)$ iff $n \in \llcorner m_1 \cdots m_i \lrcorner$;*
  - *$n \in \mathsf{dom}(\Sigma_i) \cap O(m_1 \cdots m_i)$ iff $n \in \ulcorner m_1 \cdots m_i \urcorner$.*

Let us write $[\![\Gamma \vdash M : \theta]\!]_1$ for the set of protoplays obtained by restricting $[\![\Gamma \vdash M : \theta]\!]_0$ to relevant plays and subsequently constraining stores to contain only P-names occurring in the suitable O-view. Protoplays are still not sufficient to prove all equivalences, because they do not convey the idea that the environment might not be able to recognize all different P-names.

Example 13. The following terms are equivalent, yet they induce different protoplays.

$$\begin{array}{rl} f : \mathsf{int\,ref} \to \mathsf{unit} \vdash & \mathsf{let}\, n_1 = \mathsf{ref}(0)\, \mathsf{in}\, \mathsf{let}\, n_2 = \mathsf{ref}\,(0)\, \mathsf{in}\, f(n_1); (n_2 := !n_1); n_2 \\ \cong & \mathsf{let}\, n = \mathsf{ref}\,(0)\, \mathsf{in}\, f(n); n : \mathsf{int\,ref} \end{array}$$

$$\star^{\emptyset}\,(n_1,\mathsf{c}_f)^{(n_1,0)}\,(\star,\mathsf{r}_f)^{(n_1,k)}\,(n_2,\mathsf{r}_\downarrow)^{(n_2,k)} \qquad \star^{\emptyset}\,(n,\mathsf{c}_f)^{(n,0)}\,(\star,\mathsf{r}_f)^{(n,k)}\,(n,\mathsf{r}_\downarrow)^{(n,k)}$$

In an interaction the environment will only be able to detect a difference between two P-names if they occur in the same O-view. Consequently, if P repeats a name introduced by himself, but none of the previous occurrences are present in the O-view, the name should present itself to the environment as if it were fresh. This motivates the last definitions.

Definition 14. *Given a protoplay s, let us subject it to the following refreshment routine: as long as $s = s_1(\ell,t)^{\Sigma}s_2$, where (ℓ,t) is a P-move, $\ell \in P(s)$, ℓ occurs in s_1, but its only occurrence in $\llcorner s_1(\ell,t) \lrcorner$ is in the final move, apply the following to s*

- *if $t = \mathsf{r}_\downarrow$ then replace ℓ with a fresh name.*
- *if $t = \mathsf{c}_x$ then replace ℓ with a fresh name and, provided ℓ occurs there, also in the following O-move;*
- *if $t = \mathsf{r}$ then replace ℓ with a fresh name and, provided ℓ occurs there, in all the following moves with tags c and r.*

Definition 15. *Let $[\![\Gamma \vdash M : \theta]\!]_2$ consist of protoplays from $[\![\Gamma \vdash M : \theta]\!]_1$ refreshed according to Definition 14.*

A play-with-store or a protoplay will be called complete, if the underlying play is complete. Given a set S of plays-with-store or protoplays, let us write $\mathsf{comp}(S)$ for the subset of S consisting of complete elements only.

Theorem 16 (Lemma 17 [12]). *For any $\mathsf{RedML}_{\mathrm{fin}}^{\beta\to\beta}$-terms $\Gamma \vdash M_1, M_2 : \theta$, $\Gamma \vdash M_1 \cong M_2 : \theta$ if, and only if, $\mathsf{comp}([\![\Gamma \vdash M_1 : \theta]\!]_2) = \mathsf{comp}([\![\Gamma \vdash M_2 : \theta]\!]_2)$.*

In Section 5, for a given term $\Gamma \vdash M : \theta$ of $\mathsf{RedML}_{\mathrm{fin}}^{\beta\to\beta}$ in canonical form, we shall construct a family of automata representing $[\![\Gamma \vdash M : \theta]\!]_0$. It will be refined in Section 6 to represent $[\![\Gamma \vdash M : \theta]\!]_2$. Section 7 will be devoted to crafting a bisimulation relation that will enable us to implement the equivalence test from Theorem 16.

4 Automata

As Example 9 demonstrates, the stores present in plays can grow indefinitely and, even though we shall work with infinite alphabets, we cannot afford to represent them literally, as this would amount to being able to memorize an unbounded supply of names. Instead we shall skip store information in O-moves on the understanding that, whenever this is done, the omitted value could be arbitrary. Similarly, if store values are omitted for P-moves, it will be the case that P does not change them, i.e. they remain the same as in the previous O-move. According to this convention the first play from Example 9 can be faithfully represented by $\iota^{\emptyset}\,(\star, \mathsf{r}_{\downarrow})^{\emptyset}\,(\star, c)^{\emptyset}\,(n_1, r)^{(n_1,0)}\,(\star, c)^{\emptyset}\,(n_2, r)^{(n_2,0)}\,\cdots$.

Next we introduce the kind of automata that will be used as acceptors of (representatives of) plays. In a single transition step they will be able to read a (representation of a) single move-with-store $(\ell, t)^{\Sigma}$ (subject to the condition that Σ is a subset of the actual store). On the technical level, the automata are a variant of fresh-register automata [17], adapted to process plays-with-stores. Their sets of states will be partitioned into O- and P-states, which correspond to the stages of play when O and P respectively are about to make a move. The machines will be equipped with a finite number of registers for storing names. At O-states they will be able to recognize whether the currently read name is present in one of the registers. At P states they will be able to process a currently stored name or a fresh one (one that has not been processed so far).

To enable a finite specification of the automata and to describe their semantics we introduce the following definitions. Recall that $\mathbb{A}$ is the set of names. Let $\mathbb{C} = \{\star, 0, \cdots, max\}$ be the set of *constants*. Let us also fix a finite set $\mathbb{T}$ of *tags* and a positive integer n.

Definition 17. – $\mathbb{L} = \mathbb{C} \cup \{\, \mathsf{fr}(i), \mathsf{kn}(i) \mid 1 \le i \le n \,\}$ *is the set of* symbolic labels. *We use ℓ to range over its elements.*
- Reg *is the set of all* $\rho : \{1, \cdots, n\} \to \mathbb{A} \cup \{\sharp\}$ *such that* $\rho(i) = \rho(j) \in \mathbb{A}$ *implies* $i = j$. *Its elements will be called* register assignments *and, from now on, we shall use ρ to range over them.*
- $\mathsf{Sto}^{\mathsf{s}} = \{1, \ldots, n\} \to \{\sharp, 0, \ldots, max\}$ *is the set of* symbolic stores, *which will be ranged over by S.*
- Sto *is the set of partial functions* $\Sigma : \mathbb{A} \rightharpoonup \{0, \ldots, max\}$ *such that* $\mathsf{dom}(\Sigma)$ *contains at most n elements. Its elements will be referred to as* stores *and ranged over by Σ.*
- $\mathsf{LT} = \mathbb{L} \times \mathbb{T} \times \mathsf{Sto}^{\mathsf{s}}$ *is the set of* transition labels, *ranged over by* $(\ell, t)^S$.

We shall abuse notation somewhat and write $\mathsf{dom}(\rho)$ for the set $\rho^{-1}(\mathbb{A})$, and similarly for $\mathsf{dom}(S)$. Given a pair $(\rho, S) \in \mathsf{Reg} \times \mathsf{Sto}^{\mathsf{s}}$ such that $\mathsf{dom}(\rho) = \mathsf{dom}(S)$, we can derive the store $\mathsf{Sto}(\rho, S) = \{\, (\rho(i), S(i)) \mid i \in \mathsf{dom}(\rho) \,\}$.

We can now define (n_{r}, n)-automata, which will be used for representing game semantics. An (n_{r}, n)-automaton is equipped with n registers, the first n_{r} of which will be read-only.

Definition 18. *An* (n_{r}, n)**-automaton** *of type θ is given as a quintuple* $\mathcal{A} = \langle Q, q_0, \rho_0, \delta, F \rangle$ *where:*

– Q *is a finite set of states, partitioned into* Q_O *(O-states) and* Q_P *(P-states);*
– $q_0 \in Q_P$ *is the initial state;*
– $\rho_0 \in \mathsf{Reg}$ *is the initial register assignment such that* $\mathsf{dom}(\rho_0) = \{1, \cdots, n_\mathsf{r}\}$*;*
– $\delta \subseteq (Q_O \times \mathsf{LT} \times Q_P) \cup (Q_P \times \mathsf{LT} \times Q_O) \cup (Q_O \times \mathcal{P}(\{n_\mathsf{r}+1, \ldots, n\}) \times Q_O) \cup (Q_P \times \mathcal{P}(\{n_\mathsf{r}+1, \ldots, n\}) \times Q_P)$ *is the transition relation;*
– $F \subseteq Q_O$ *is the set of final states.*

Additionally, the following properties must hold.

– *if* $(q, (\ell, t)^S, q') \in \delta$ *and* $\ell = \mathsf{fr}(i)$ *then* $i > n_\mathsf{r}$ *and* $i \in \mathsf{dom}(S)$*.*
– *if* θ *is a base type then there is a unique final state* q_F*, and* $\delta \upharpoonright \{q_F\} = \emptyset$ *(no outgoing transition).*

Our automata operate on words over the infinite alphabet $(\mathbb{C} \cup \mathbb{A}) \times \mathbb{T} \times \mathsf{Sto}$. We shall write $(\ell, t)^\Sigma$ to refer to its elements. We first explain the meaning of the transition function informally. Suppose $\mathcal{A}$ is at state q_1 and ρ is the current register assignment.

– If $(q_1, (\ell', t)^S, q_2) \in \delta$, $\mathcal{A}$ can move to state q_2 on the input symbol $(\ell, t)^\Sigma$ if one of the following conditions is satisfied.
  • $\ell \in \mathbb{C}$, $\ell' = \ell$, $\mathsf{dom}(S) \subseteq \mathsf{dom}(\rho)$ and $\Sigma = \mathsf{Sto}(\rho, S)$.
  • $\ell \in \mathbb{A}$, $\ell' = \mathsf{kn}(i)$, $\rho(i) = \ell$, $\mathsf{dom}(S) \subseteq \mathsf{dom}(\rho)$ and $\Sigma = \mathsf{Sto}(\rho, S)$.
  • $\ell \in \mathbb{A}$, $\ell' = \mathsf{fr}(i)$, $\mathsf{dom}(S) \subseteq \mathsf{dom}(\rho) \cup \{i\}$, $\Sigma = \mathsf{Sto}(\rho[i \mapsto \ell], S)$ and
    * either $q_1 \in Q_O$ and ℓ does not belong to $\rho(\{1, \cdots, n\})$ (*locally fresh*),
    * or $q_1 \in Q_P$ and ℓ has not appeared in the current run of $\mathcal{A}$ (*globally fresh*).

  In this case the automaton also sets $\rho(i)$ to ℓ.
– If $(q_1, N, q_2) \in \delta$, where N is a subset of writable register indices, $\mathcal{A}$ can clear all registers in N (i.e. set $\rho(i) = \sharp$ for all $i \in N$) and move to q_2 without reading any input symbol (ϵ-transition).

The above is formalized next. A *configuration* of $\mathcal{A}$ is a triple $(q, \rho, H) \in \hat{Q}$, where $\hat{Q} = Q \times \mathsf{Reg} \times \mathcal{P}_{\mathsf{fn}}(\mathbb{A})$ and $\mathcal{P}_{\mathsf{fn}}(\mathbb{A})$ is the set of finite subsets of $\mathbb{A}$.

Definition 19. *Let* $\mathcal{A} = \langle Q, q_0, \rho_0, \delta, F \rangle$ *be an* (n_r, n)*-automaton. The configuration graph* $(\hat{Q}, \longrightarrow_\delta)$ *of* $\mathcal{A}$ *is defined as follows (transitions are labelled by* ϵ *or elements of* $(\mathbb{C} \cup \mathbb{A}) \times \mathbb{T} \times \mathsf{Sto}$*). For all* $(q, \rho, H) \in \hat{Q}$ *and* $(q, (\ell, t)^S, q') \in \delta$*:*

– *if* $\ell \in \mathbb{C}$ *and* $\mathsf{dom}(S) \subseteq \mathsf{dom}(\rho)$ *then* $(q, \rho, H) \xrightarrow{(\ell,t)^\Sigma}_\delta (q', \rho, H)$ *where* $\Sigma = \mathsf{Sto}(\rho, S)$*,*
– *if* $\ell \notin \mathbb{C}$ *and* $\mathsf{dom}(S) \subseteq \mathsf{dom}(\rho')$ *then* $(q, \rho, H) \xrightarrow{(\ell,t)^\Sigma}_\delta (q', \rho', H')$ *where* $\Sigma = \mathsf{Sto}(\rho', S)$*,* $H' = H \cup \{\ell\}$*, and*
  • *if* $\ell = \mathsf{kn}(i)$ *then* $\ell = \rho(i)$ *and* $\rho' = \rho$*,*
  • *if* $\ell = \mathsf{fr}(i)$ *and* $q \in Q_O$ *then* $\ell \notin \rho(\{1, \cdots, n\})$ *and* $\rho' = \rho[i \mapsto \ell]$*,*
  • *if* $\ell = \mathsf{fr}(i)$ *and* $q \in Q_P$ *then* $\ell \notin \rho(\{1, \cdots, n_\mathsf{r}\}) \cup H$ *and* $\rho' = \rho[i \mapsto \ell]$*.*

Moreover, for all $(q, \rho, H) \in \hat{Q}$ *and* $(q, N, q') \in \delta$ *we have* $(q, \rho, H) \xrightarrow{\epsilon}_\delta (q', \rho', H)$*, where* $\rho' = \rho[N \mapsto \sharp]$*. The set of strings* accepted *by* $\mathcal{A}$ *is defined to be*

$$\mathcal{L}(\mathcal{A}) = \{\, \vec{\ell} \in ((\mathbb{C} \cup \mathbb{A}) \times \mathbb{T} \times \mathsf{Sto})^* \ \mid\ (q_0, \rho_0, \emptyset) \xrightarrow{\vec{\ell}}\!\!\!\twoheadrightarrow_\delta (q, \rho, H), \quad q \in F \,\}.$$

Definition 20. *We say that* $\mathcal{A}$ *is* deterministic *if, for any reachable configuration* $\hat{q}$ *and any* $\hat{q} \xrightarrow{\ell_1}_\delta \hat{q}_1, \hat{q} \xrightarrow{\ell_2}_\delta \hat{q}_2$*, if* $\ell_1 = \ell_2$ *then* $\hat{q}_1 = \hat{q}_2$*.*

Here is a structural constraint that guarantees determinacy.

Definition 21. $\mathcal{A}$ *is* strongly deterministic *if:*

- *for each* $q \in Q_P$ *there exists* at most *one transition out of* q*:* $|\delta \upharpoonright \{q\}| \leq 1$*;*
- *for each* $q \in Q_O$ *and* $(q, (\ell_1, t)^{S_1}, q_1), (q, (\ell_2, t)^{S_2}, q_2) \in \delta$*:*
  - *if* $\ell_1 = \mathsf{fr}(i_1)$ *and* $\ell_2 = \mathsf{fr}(i_2)$ *then* $i_1 = i_2$*,*
  - *if* $\ell_1 = \ell_2$ *and* $S_1 = S_2$ *then* $q_1 = q_2$*,*
  - $\mathsf{dom}(S_1) \setminus \{ i \mid \ell_1 = \mathsf{fr}(i) \} = \mathsf{dom}(S_2) \setminus \{ i \mid \ell_2 = \mathsf{fr}(i) \}$.
- *for any* $q_1 \in Q_O$*, if there exists* $q_2 \in Q_O$ *such that* $(q_1, N, q_2) \in \delta$*, then this is the only outgoing transition from* q_1*:* $|\delta \upharpoonright \{q_1\}| = 1$*.*

Definition 22. *Let* $\mathcal{A} = \langle Q, q_0, \rho_0, \delta, q_F \rangle$ *be a strongly deterministic automaton of base type. We define the set of* quasi-final *states* E *to be the set of states that reach* q_F *in one step. Then* E *is canonically partitioned as* $E = \biguplus_{(\ell,t)^S} E_{(\ell,t)^S}$ *where* $E_{(\ell,t)^S} = \{ q \in Q \mid (q, (\ell, t)^S, q_F) \in \delta \}$ *and* $\mathcal{A}$ *is uniquely determined by the structure* $\mathcal{A}^- = \langle Q, q_0, \rho_0, \delta, E \rangle$*.*

The following remark sheds some light on the formal nominal setting underlying our constructions. It can be safely skipped by readers not familiar with nominal sets [5].

Remark 23. Note that the initial register assignments of our automata contain names. One can view the automata as elements of nominal sets where name-permutation works as follows: for any name-permutation π, $\pi \cdot \langle Q, q_0, \rho_0, \delta, F \rangle = \langle Q, q_0, \pi \cdot \rho_0, \delta, F \rangle$, where $\pi \cdot \rho = \pi \circ \rho$. Note that then $\mathcal{L}(\pi \cdot \mathcal{A}) = \pi \cdot \mathcal{L}(\mathcal{A})$.

Moreover, the indexed families of automata to be used in the next definition are of nominal nature. Let X be a nominal set. By an X-indexed family of automata of type θ we mean a set $\{ \mathcal{A}_x \mid x \in X \}$ such that each $\mathcal{A}_x$ is an (n_{r}^x, n^x)-automaton of type θ and, moreover, for any name-permutation π, $\mathcal{A}_{\pi \cdot x} = \pi \cdot \mathcal{A}_x$.

5 From Terms to Plays-with-Stores

Let $\Gamma = [x_1 : \theta_1, \cdots, x_m : \theta_m]$ and $\Gamma \vdash \mathbb{C} : \theta$ be a $\mathsf{RedML}_{\mathrm{fin}}^{\beta \to \beta}$-term in canonical form. Let us write $I_{\Gamma \vdash \theta}^{+}$ for the set of plays-with-store of length 1 over $\Gamma \vdash \theta$. Recall that each of them will have the form ι^{Σ_0}, where $\iota \in I_\Gamma$, i.e. $\iota = (\ell_1, \cdots, \ell_m)$, where $\ell_i \in \mathcal{L}_{\theta_i}$. Let $\mathcal{L}_\iota = \{ \ell_i \,|\, \theta_i \equiv \mathsf{int\,ref} \}$ and $n_\iota = |\mathcal{L}_\iota|$. Then $\mathsf{dom}(\Sigma_0) = \mathcal{L}_\iota$. Let $\mathsf{idx} : \{1, \cdots, n_\iota\} \to \{1, \cdots, m\}$ be defined by $\mathsf{idx}(i) = j$ if $\ell_j \in \mathcal{L}_\iota$, there are $i-1$ different names in ι to the left of ℓ_j ($|\{\ell_1, \cdots, \ell_{j-1}\} \cap \mathcal{L}_\iota| = i-1$) and ℓ_j is not among them ($\ell_j \notin \{\ell_1, \cdots, \ell_{j-1}\}$).

We now instantiate the automata defined in the previous section by using the finite set of tags $\mathbb{T} = \mathcal{T}_{\Gamma \vdash \theta}$. A canonical form of $\mathsf{RedML}_{\mathrm{fin}}^{\beta \to \beta}$ will be translated into a family of automata indexed by $I_{\Gamma \vdash \theta}^{+}$. For each $\iota^{\Sigma_0} \in I_{\Gamma \vdash \theta}^{+}$, the corresponding automaton will accept exactly the words w such that $\iota^{\Sigma_0} w$ is a complete play induced by the canonical form. The family will be infinite, but *finite* when considered up to name-permutability.

Definition 24. *For any* $\mathsf{RedML}_{\mathsf{fin}}^{\beta\to\beta}$*-term* $\Gamma \vdash \mathbb{C} : \theta$ *in canonical form we define an* $I^+_{\Gamma\vdash\theta}$*-indexed family of automata* $\llparenthesis\, \mathbb{C} \,\rrparenthesis = \{\, \llparenthesis\, \mathbb{C} \,\rrparenthesis_{\iota^{\Sigma_0}} \mid \iota^{\Sigma_0} \in I^+_{\Gamma\vdash\theta} \,\}$ *by induction on the shape of* $\mathbb{C}$*. In all cases* $\llparenthesis\, \mathbb{C} \,\rrparenthesis_{\iota^{\Sigma_0}}$ *will have* $n_{\mathsf{r}}^{\iota^{\Sigma_0}} = n_\iota$ *read-only registers and the initial assignment will be* $\rho_0^{\iota^{\Sigma_0}}(i) = \ell_{\mathsf{idx}(i)}$*. The precise number of registers can be calculated easily by reference to the constituent automata. Let us write* S_0 *for the function* $S_0 : \{1, \cdots, n\} \to \{\sharp, 0, \cdots, max\}$ *defined by* $S_0(i) = \Sigma_0(\ell_{\mathsf{idx}(i)})$ $(1 \le i \le n_\iota)$ *and* $S_0(i) = \sharp$ $(i > n_\iota)$*. The base and inductive cases are as follows.*[3]

- $\llparenthesis\, () \,\rrparenthesis_{\iota^{\Sigma_0}} = \quad q_0 \xrightarrow{(\star,\mathsf{r}_\downarrow)^{S_0}} q_F$
- $\llparenthesis\, j \,\rrparenthesis_{\iota^{\Sigma_0}} = \quad q_0 \xrightarrow{(j,\mathsf{r}_\downarrow)^{S_0}} q_F$
- $\llparenthesis\, x^{\mathsf{int\,ref}} \,\rrparenthesis_{\iota^{\Sigma_0}} = \quad q_0 \xrightarrow{(\mathsf{kn}(j),\mathsf{r}_\downarrow)^{S_0}} q_F$ *, where* $x \equiv x_k$ *and* $\ell_{\mathsf{idx}(j)} = \ell_k$
- $\llparenthesis\, \mathsf{case}(x)[\mathbb{C}_0, \cdots, \mathbb{C}_{max}] \,\rrparenthesis_{\iota^{\Sigma_0}} = \llparenthesis\, \mathbb{C}_j \,\rrparenthesis_{\iota^{\Sigma_0}}$*, where* $x \equiv x_k$ *and* $\ell_k = j$
- $\llparenthesis\, (x := i); \mathbb{C} \,\rrparenthesis_{\iota^{\Sigma_0}} = \llparenthesis\, \mathbb{C} \,\rrparenthesis_{\iota^{\Sigma_0'}}$*, where* $x \equiv x_k$ *and* $\Sigma_0' = \Sigma_0[\ell_k \mapsto i]$
- $\llparenthesis\, \mathsf{let}\, y = !x\, \mathsf{in}\, \mathbb{C} \,\rrparenthesis_{\iota^{\Sigma_0}} = \llparenthesis\, \mathbb{C} \,\rrparenthesis_{(\iota\, \Sigma_0(\ell_k))^{\Sigma_0}}$*, where* $x \equiv x_k$
- $\llparenthesis\, \mathsf{let}\, y^{\mathsf{unit}} = z()\, \mathsf{in}\, \mathbb{C} \,\rrparenthesis_{\iota^{\Sigma_0}}$ *is given by* $q_0 \xrightarrow{(\star,\mathsf{c}_z)^{S_0}} q_1 \xrightarrow{(\star,\mathsf{r}_z)^{S}} \llparenthesis\, \mathbb{C} \,\rrparenthesis_{(\iota\, \star)^{\Sigma_S}}$ *, where* S *ranges over all symbolic stores with domain* $\{1, \ldots, n_\iota\}$ *and* $\Sigma_S(\ell_{\mathsf{idx}(i)}) = S(i)$*.*
- $\llparenthesis\, \mathsf{let}\, y^{\mathsf{int}} = z()\, \mathsf{in}\, \mathbb{C} \,\rrparenthesis_{\iota^{\Sigma_0}} = \quad q_0 \xrightarrow{(\star,\mathsf{c}_z)^{S_0}} q_1 \xrightarrow{(j,\mathsf{r}_z)^{S}} \llparenthesis\, \mathbb{C} \,\rrparenthesis_{(\iota\, j)^{\Sigma_S}}$ *with* S *as above and* $0 \le j \le max$*.*
- $\llparenthesis\, \mathsf{let}\, y^{\mathsf{int\,ref}} = z()\, \mathsf{in}\, \mathbb{C} \,\rrparenthesis_{\iota^{\Sigma_0}} = \quad q_0 \xrightarrow{(\star,\mathsf{c}_z)^{S_0}} q_1$, $\quad q_1 \xrightarrow{(\mathsf{kn}(j),\mathsf{r}_z)^{S}} \llparenthesis\, \mathbb{C} \,\rrparenthesis_{(\iota\, \rho_0(j))^{\Sigma_S}}$, $\quad q_1 \xrightarrow{(\mathsf{fr}(n_\iota+1),\mathsf{r}_z)^{S'}} \llparenthesis\, \mathbb{C} \,\rrparenthesis_{(\iota\, a)^{\Sigma_{S'}}}$

  where $1 \le j \le n_\iota$*,* S *is as above,* a *is a name that does not occur in* ι*,*[4] S' *ranges over symbolic stores with domain* $\{1, \cdots, n_\iota + 1\}$*,* $\Sigma_{S'}(\ell_{\mathsf{idx}(i)}) = S'(i)$ $(1 \le i \le n_\iota)$ *and* $\Sigma_{S'}(a) = S'(n_\iota + 1)$
- $\llparenthesis\, \mathsf{let}\, y^\beta = z\, i\, \mathsf{in}\, \mathbb{C} \,\rrparenthesis_{\iota^{\Sigma_0}}$ *and* $\llparenthesis\, \mathsf{let}\, y^\beta = z\, x^{\mathsf{int\,ref}}\, \mathsf{in}\, \mathbb{C} \,\rrparenthesis_{\iota^{\Sigma_0}}$ *are defined similarly to the above.*

  $\{n_\iota+1, \ldots, n\}$
- $\llparenthesis\, \lambda x^{\mathsf{unit}}.\mathbb{C} \,\rrparenthesis_{\iota^{\Sigma_0}} = \quad q_0 \xrightarrow{(\star,\mathsf{r}_\downarrow)^{S_0}} q_1 \xrightarrow{(\star,\mathsf{c})^{S}} (\llparenthesis\, \mathbb{C} \,\rrparenthesis_{(\iota\, \star)^{\Sigma_S}}[\mathsf{r}/\mathsf{r}_\downarrow])$ *, where the loopback connects the final state of* $\llparenthesis\, \mathbb{C} \,\rrparenthesis_{(\iota\, \star)^{\Sigma_S}}[\mathsf{r}/\mathsf{r}_\downarrow]$ *to* q_1*. Note that* S *ranges over all symbolic stores with domain* $\{1, \ldots, n_\iota\}$ *and* $\Sigma_S(\ell_{\mathsf{idx}(i)}) = S(i)$ $(1 \le i \le n_\iota)$*. The other cases of* λ*-abstraction are dealt with in a similar way.*
- *Case of* $\mathsf{let}\, x^{\mathsf{int\,ref}} = \mathsf{ref}\,(0)\, \mathsf{in}\, \mathbb{C}$*. Let* a *be a name not in* ι*, let* $\Sigma_0' = \Sigma_0[a \mapsto 0]$ *and consider the* $(n_\iota + 1, n)$*-automaton* $\llparenthesis\, \mathbb{C} \,\rrparenthesis_{(\iota\, a)^{\Sigma_0'}}$*. For each* $0 \le j \le max$ *define an* (n_ι, n)*-automaton* $\llparenthesis\, \mathbb{C} \,\rrparenthesis^{(j)}_{\iota^{\Sigma_0}}$ *to be a copy of* $\llparenthesis\, \mathbb{C} \,\rrparenthesis_{(\iota\, a)^{\Sigma_0'}}$ *in which*

---

[3] Note that we ignore initial register assignments of automata that do not appear in starting positions in the diagrams.

[4] Any such choice of a yields the same automaton $\llparenthesis\, \mathbb{C} \,\rrparenthesis_{(\iota\, a)^{\Sigma_{S'}}}$ after its initial register assignment is removed.

- *all transitions with label* $\mathsf{kn}(n_\iota + 1)$ *are removed,*
- *all transitions with symbolic store* S *such that* $S(n_\iota + 1) \neq j$ *are removed,*
- *and* $n_\iota + 1$ *is removed from all symbolic stores in remaining transitions.*

We define $\llparenthesis\, \mathsf{let}\, x^{\mathsf{int\,ref}} = \mathsf{ref}\,(0)\, \mathsf{in}\, \mathbb{C} \,\rrparenthesis$ *as an* (n_ι, n)*-automaton obtained by interconnecting* $\llparenthesis \mathbb{C} \rrparenthesis^{(0)}_{\iota\Sigma_0}, \cdots, \llparenthesis \mathbb{C} \rrparenthesis^{(max)}_{\iota\Sigma_0}$ *and* $\llparenthesis \mathbb{C} \rrparenthesis_{(\iota\, a)\Sigma_0'}$.

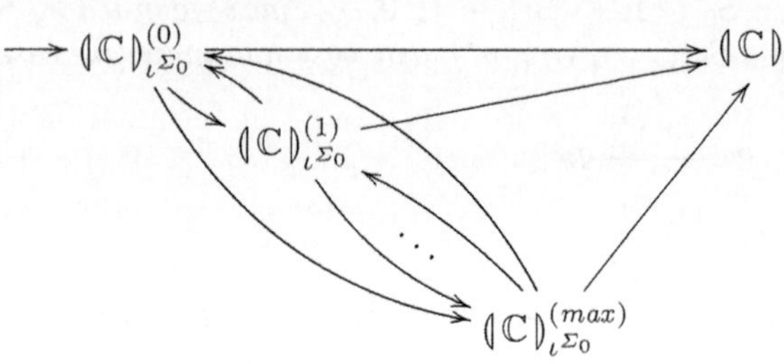

The transitions between the copies (arrows in the figure) are as follows. For each $q_1 \xrightarrow{(\ell,t)^S} q_2$ *in* $\llparenthesis \mathbb{C} \rrparenthesis_{\iota\Sigma_0'}$*, where* q_1 *is a P-state:*

- *if* $\ell \neq \mathsf{kn}(n_\iota + 1)$ *then, for each* $j \neq S(n_\iota + 1)$*, we add a transition from the state* q_1 *of* $\llparenthesis \mathbb{C} \rrparenthesis^{(j)}_{\iota\Sigma_0}$ *to state* q_2 *of* $\llparenthesis \mathbb{C} \rrparenthesis^{(S(n_\iota+1))}_{\iota\Sigma_0}$*, with label* $(\ell, t)^{S \restriction (\mathsf{dom}(S) \setminus \{n_\iota + 1\})}$*;*
- *if* $\ell = \mathsf{kn}(n_\iota + 1)$ *then, for each* $0 \leq j \leq max$*, we add a transition from the state* q_1 *of* $\llparenthesis \mathbb{C} \rrparenthesis^{(j)}_{\iota\Sigma_0}$ *to state* q_2 *of* $\llparenthesis \mathbb{C} \rrparenthesis_{\iota\Sigma_0'}$*, with label* $(\mathsf{fr}(n_\mathsf{r} + 1), t)^S$.

– *For* $(\mathsf{while}\,(!x)\,\mathsf{do}\,\mathbb{C}); \mathbb{C}'$*, let* $\Sigma_0, \ldots, \Sigma_h$ *be all the stores with the same domain as* Σ_0*. Assume* $x \equiv x_k$*. Recall the presentation of an automaton given in Definition 22. We define* $\llparenthesis (\mathsf{while}\,(!x)\,\mathsf{do}\,\mathbb{C}); \mathbb{C}' \rrparenthesis_{\iota\Sigma_0}$ *to be* $\llparenthesis \mathbb{C}' \rrparenthesis_{\iota\Sigma_0}$ *if* $\Sigma_0(\ell_k) = 0$*. Otherwise it is defined to be a combination of* $\llparenthesis \mathbb{C} \rrparenthesis^-_{\iota\Sigma_0}, \cdots, \llparenthesis \mathbb{C} \rrparenthesis^-_{\iota\Sigma_h}$ *and* $\llparenthesis \mathbb{C}' \rrparenthesis_{\iota\Sigma_0}, \cdots, \llparenthesis \mathbb{C}' \rrparenthesis_{\iota\Sigma_h}$ *connected together as explained below.*

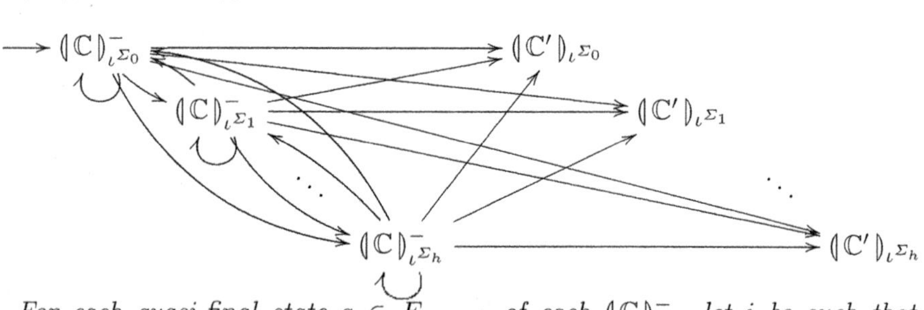

For each quasi-final state $q \in E_{(\star, \mathsf{r}_\downarrow)^S}$ *of each* $\llparenthesis \mathbb{C} \rrparenthesis^-_{\iota\Sigma_i}$ *let* i *be such that* $\ell_{\mathsf{idx}(i)} = \ell_k$*. Add transitions labelled* $\{n_\iota + 1, \ldots, n\}$ *in the following cases.*

- *If* $S(i) = 0$*, add one from* q *to the initial state of* $\llparenthesis \mathbb{C}' \rrparenthesis_{\iota\Sigma_S}$*,*
- *if* $S(i) \neq 0$ *add one from* q *to the initial state of* $\llparenthesis \mathbb{C} \rrparenthesis^-_{\iota\Sigma_S}$.

We shall now formalize in what sense the automata defined above can be taken to represent strategies.

Definition 25. *Let* $s = m_1^{\Sigma_1} \cdots m_k^{\Sigma_k}$ *be a play over* $\Gamma \vdash \theta$ *and* $t = m_1^{\Theta_1} \cdots m_k^{\Theta_k}$ *be a sequence of moves-with-store. We say that* s *is an* extension *of* t *if the following conditions are satisfied.*

– *$\Theta_i \subseteq \Sigma_i$ $(1 \leq i \leq k)$*
– *For any $1 \leq i \leq \lfloor k/2 \rfloor$, if $a \in \mathsf{dom}(\Sigma_{2i}) \setminus \mathsf{dom}(\Theta_{2i})$ then $\Sigma_{2i-1}(a)$ is defined and $\Sigma_{2i}(a) = \Sigma_{2i-1}(a)$.*

Note that, because s is a play, the clause about $\Sigma_{2i-1}(a)$ being defined amounts to stipulating that $\Theta_{2i}(a)$ be defined if the first occurrence of a in $m_1 \cdots m_k$ is in m_{2i}. Observe that this is always the case for words accepted by automata from Definition 24, as the store values are always printed out for fresh labels. Let us write $\mathsf{ext}(t)$ for the set of all extensions of t.

Lemma 26. *For any $\iota^{\Sigma_0} \in I^{+}_{\Gamma \vdash \theta}$, the automaton $(\!|\mathbb{C}|\!)_{\iota^{\Sigma_0}}$ is strongly deterministic and $\bigcup_{t \in \mathcal{L}((\!|\mathbb{C}|\!)_{\iota^{\Sigma_0}})} \mathsf{ext}(\iota^{\Sigma_0} t) = \{\, \iota^{\Sigma_0} t \mid \iota^{\Sigma_0} t \in \mathsf{comp}([\![\Gamma \vdash \mathbb{C} : \theta]\!]_0)\,\}$.*

Proof. Strong determinacy follows from the shape of the automata. For the latter part, the non-trivial cases are:

$\mathsf{let}\, x = \mathsf{ref}\,(0)\,\mathsf{in}\, \mathbb{C}$: The role of $(\!|\mathbb{C}|\!)^{(j)}_{\iota^{\Sigma_0}}$ $(0 \leq j \leq max)$ is to mimic the strategy corresponding to $\mathsf{let}\, x = \mathsf{ref}\,(0)\,\mathsf{in}\, \mathbb{C}$ before the name a (corresponding to the reference name x) is revealed. Accordingly, O is not allowed to play the name for the first time (as in the definition of composition [12]) or change store-values associated with a. P can still change them, though, and the current value at a is represented by the superscript (j). If P reveals the name for the first time, a fresh name is generated, written to register $n_\iota + 1$, and computation proceeds to $(\!|\mathbb{C}|\!)_{\iota^{\Sigma'_0}}$.

$\lambda x^{\beta}.\mathbb{C}$: Correctness follows from the fact that the strategy corresponding to $\lambda x^{\beta}.\mathbb{C}$ is single-threaded, i.e., following $(\star, \mathsf{r}_\downarrow)$, it is an interleaving of independent copies of strategies for $\mathbb{C}$.

$(\mathsf{while}\,(!x)\,\mathsf{do}\,\mathbb{C}); \mathbb{C}'$: Observe that the strategy for $(\mathsf{while}\,(!x)\,\mathsf{do}\,\mathbb{C})$ can be viewed as a subset of the single-threaded strategy for $\lambda y^{\mathsf{unit}}.\mathsf{if}\,!x\,\mathsf{then}\,\mathbb{C}\,\mathsf{else}\,()$, where the final values of free variables are communicated to the next thread and on reaching 0 by x control is transferred to the strategy for $\mathbb{C}'$. This is precisely what the construction achieves. □

6 Automata for Protoplays

In this section we shall transform the automata representing $[\![\Gamma \vdash \mathbb{C}]\!]_0$ to represent $[\![\Gamma \vdash \mathbb{C}]\!]_2$. To that end, we need to focus on protoplays that have been refreshed according to Definition 14. Such protoplays adhere to a specific pattern with respect to P-names: any P-name that appears in the O-view for the first time has not appeared earlier. This implies that in each such protoplay $s = s_1(\ell, t)^{\Sigma}$ with $\ell \in P(s)$:

– if $t = \mathsf{c}_x$ or $t = \mathsf{r}_\downarrow$ then ℓ is fresh for s_1,
– if $t = \mathsf{r}$ then either ℓ is fresh for s_1 or it has been introduced by some move with tag r.

The moral is that P-names introduced with tag c_x or $\mathsf{r}_\downarrow$ are played only once. In the former case, O may play them in his next move, but then they will not reappear in the protoplay. In the latter case, no moves can be made after the P-name ($\theta \equiv \mathsf{int\,ref}$). Hence, we can safely replace P-names introduced with tags c_x and $\mathsf{r}_\downarrow$ by dummy labels ($\circledast$) and still have a faithful representation, provided their values are remembered. We shall accommodate them in special labels so that the representation is still a protoplay, albeit in the following extended syntax.

Remark 27. Using $\circledast$ will also let us see that for terms $\Gamma \vdash \mathbb{C} : \beta$ one does not need globally fresh transitions. Hence the corresponding automata will then be variants of register automata [7] rather than fresh-register automata [17].

Definition 28. – *For every base type β we define the set of extended labels $\mathcal{L}^+_\beta = \mathcal{L}_\beta \cup \{\, \ell\langle i\rangle \mid \ell \in \mathcal{L}_\beta \cup \{\circledast\},\ 0 \le i \le max \,\}$.*

– *We define the set of transition labels $\mathbb{L}^+ = \mathbb{L} \cup \{\, \ell\langle i\rangle \mid \ell \in \mathbb{L} \cup \{\circledast\},\ 0 \le i \le max \,\}$.*

We proceed to define a translation from an automaton $\mathcal{A}$ in the original syntax to an automaton $\mathcal{A}^+$ in the extended one, following the intuitions described above. As a first step, we are going to enrich $\mathcal{A}$ with information about ownership of the names that are currently stored in the registers. This is concretely achieved as follows.

Definition 29. *For each automaton $\mathcal{A} = \langle Q, q_0, \rho_0, \delta, F\rangle$ construct the automaton $\mathcal{A}^+ = \langle Q', q'_0, \rho'_0, \delta', F'\rangle$ by setting*

$$Q' = \{\, (q, N_O, N_P) \in Q \times \mathcal{P}(\{1,\dots,n\})^2 \mid N_O \cap N_P = \emptyset,\ \{1,\dots,n_{\mathsf{r}}\} \subseteq N_O \,\},$$

$q'_0 = (q_0, \{1,\dots,n_{\mathsf{r}}\}, \emptyset)$, $\rho'_0 = \rho_0$, $F' = Q' \upharpoonright F$, and defining δ' as follows.

– *If $q \xrightarrow{(\ell,t)^S} q'$ in $\mathcal{A}$ then $(q, N_O, N_P) \xrightarrow{(\ell,t)^S} (q', N_O, N_P)$, provided $\mathsf{dom}(S) = N_O \cup N_P$ and $\ell \in \mathbb{C} \cup \{\mathsf{kn}(i) \mid i \in N_O \cup N_P\}$.*

– *If $q_O \xrightarrow{(\mathsf{fr}(i),t)^S} q_P$ in $\mathcal{A}$ then $(q_O, N_O, N_P) \xrightarrow{(\mathsf{fr}(i),t)^S} (q_P, N_O \cup \{i\}, N_P \setminus \{i\})$, provided $\mathsf{dom}(S) = N_O \cup N_P$. If the transition is from q_P to q_O, the dual holds.*

– *If $q \xrightarrow{N} q'$ in $\mathcal{A}$ then $(q, N_O, N_P) \xrightarrow{N} (q', N_O \setminus N, N_P \setminus N)$.*

For each $q \in Q'$ we shall write $O(q)$ and $P(q)$ for its second and third components respectively. We say $\mathcal{A}^+$ is *non-overwriting* if, for any $q \xrightarrow{(\mathsf{fr}(i),t)^S} q'$, we have that $i \notin O(q) \cup P(q)$. Observe that the constructions presented in Definition 24 always yield non-overwriting automata. We can show that the new automaton reaches state q only if its non-empty registers are those in $N_O(q) \cup N_P(q)$ and, moreover, each register in $N_O(q)$ (resp. $N_P(q)$) is filled with an O-name (a P-name). Note also that $\mathcal{A}^+$ is strongly deterministic, if $\mathcal{A}$ was.

For the next step, recall that we are using a finite set of tags $\mathbb{T} = \mathcal{T}_{\Gamma \vdash \theta}$, for some Γ, θ. The new automaton will feature states augmented with an extra component N to record those P-names that were originally introduced by c_x-moves but have been replaced by $\circledast$. For O-states we need an extra component

S which records the symbolic store prior to hiding, and also an index $i \in N \cup \{\text{-}\}$ reporting whether the preceding move was a name replaced now by $\circledast$ (by convention, if the preceding move was not such then the index is set to '-').

Definition 30. *Let $\mathcal{A}^+ = \langle Q, q_0, \rho_0, \delta, F \rangle$ be non-overwriting. We define an automaton $\overline{\mathcal{A}^+} = \langle Q', q_0', \rho_0', \delta', F' \rangle$ with labels from $\mathbb{L}^+$ by setting*

$$\begin{aligned} Q' = \{\, (q, N) \mid q \in Q_P,\ N \subseteq P(q) \,\} \ \cup \\ \{\, (q, N, S, i) \mid q \in Q_O,\ N \subseteq P(q),\ S \in \mathsf{Sto}^{\mathsf{s}},\ i \in N \cup \{\text{-}\} \,\} \end{aligned}$$

$q_0' = (q_0, \emptyset)$, $\rho_0' = \rho_0$, $F' = Q' \restriction F$ and by defining δ' as follows.

$$\frac{q_P \xrightarrow{(\ell,\mathsf{c}_x)^S} q \quad \ell \in \mathbb{C} \cup \{\mathsf{kn}(j) \mid j \in O(q)\}}{(q_P, N) \xrightarrow{(\ell,\mathsf{c}_x)^{S \restriction O(q)}} (q, N, S, \text{-})} \qquad \frac{q_O \xrightarrow{(\ell,\mathsf{r}_x)^S} q \quad \ell \notin \{\mathsf{kn}(j) \mid j \in P(q)\}}{(q_O, N, S', i) \xrightarrow{(\ell\langle S(i)\rangle,\mathsf{r}_x)^{S \restriction O(q)}} (q, N)}\ {\scriptstyle \begin{array}{l} S\restriction(N\setminus\{i\}) = S'\restriction(N\setminus\{i\}) \\ i \in N \end{array}}$$

$$\frac{q_P \xrightarrow{(\mathsf{kn}(j),\mathsf{c}_x)^S} q \quad j \in P(q)}{(q_P, N) \xrightarrow{(\circledast\langle S(j)\rangle,\mathsf{c}_x)^{S \restriction O(q)}} (q, N, S, j)} \qquad \frac{q_O \xrightarrow{(\mathsf{kn}(j),\mathsf{r}_x)^S} q \quad j \in P(q)}{(q_O, N, S', j) \xrightarrow{(\circledast\langle S(j)\rangle,\mathsf{r}_x)^{S \restriction O(q)}} (q, N)}\ {\scriptstyle S\restriction(N\setminus\{j\}) = S'\restriction(N\setminus\{j\})}$$

$$\frac{q_P \xrightarrow{(\mathsf{fr}(j),\mathsf{c}_x)^S} q}{(q_P, N) \xrightarrow{(\circledast\langle S(j)\rangle,\mathsf{c}_x)^{S \restriction O(q)}} (q, N \cup \{j\}, S, j)} \qquad \frac{q_O \xrightarrow{(\ell,\mathsf{r}_x)^S} q \quad \ell \notin \{\mathsf{kn}(j) \mid j \in P(q)\}}{(q_O, N, S', \text{-}) \xrightarrow{(\ell,\mathsf{r}_x)^{S \restriction O(q)}} (q, N)}\ {\scriptstyle S\restriction N = S'\restriction N}$$

$$\frac{q_P \xrightarrow{(\ell,\mathsf{r})^S} q \quad \ell \notin \{\mathsf{kn}(j) \mid j \in N\}}{(q_P, N) \xrightarrow{(\ell,\mathsf{r})^{S \restriction O(q) \cup (P(q)\setminus N)}} (q, N, S, \text{-})} \qquad \frac{q_O \xrightarrow{(\ell,\mathsf{c})^S} q \quad \ell \notin \{\mathsf{kn}(j) \mid j \in N\}}{(q_O, N, S', \text{-}) \xrightarrow{(\ell,\mathsf{c})^{S \restriction O(q) \cup (P(q)\setminus N)}} (q, N)}\ {\scriptstyle S\restriction N = S'\restriction N}$$

$$\frac{q_P \xrightarrow{(\mathsf{kn}(j),\mathsf{r})^S} q \quad j \in N}{(q_P, N) \xrightarrow{(\mathsf{fr}(j),\mathsf{r})^{S \restriction O(q) \cup \{j\} \cup (P(q)\setminus N)}} (q, N \setminus \{j\}, S, \text{-})} \qquad \frac{q \xrightarrow{N'} q'}{(q, N, \dots) \xrightarrow{N'} (q', N \setminus N', \dots)}$$

$$\frac{q_P \xrightarrow{(\mathsf{kn}(j)/\mathsf{fr}(j),\mathsf{r}_\downarrow)^S} q}{(q_P, N) \xrightarrow{(\circledast\langle S(j)\rangle,\mathsf{r}_\downarrow)^{S \restriction (O(q)\setminus\{j\})}} (q, N, S, j)} \qquad \frac{q_P \xrightarrow{(\ell,\mathsf{r}_\downarrow)^S} q \quad \ell \in \mathbb{C}}{(q_P, N) \xrightarrow{(\ell,\mathsf{r}_\downarrow)^{S \restriction O(q)}} (q, N, S, \text{-})}$$

Let us write $[\![\Gamma \vdash \mathbb{C} : \theta]\!]_2^{\iota^{\Sigma_0}}$ for all the protoplays from $[\![\Gamma \vdash \mathbb{C} : \theta]\!]_2$ that begin with ι^{Σ_0}.

Lemma 31. *For any $\iota^{\Sigma_0} \in I^+_{\Gamma\vdash\theta}$, the automaton $\overline{(\!|\mathbb{C}|\!)^+_{\iota^{\Sigma_0}}}$ is non-blocking, strongly deterministic, non-overwriting and*[5] $\bigcup_{t \in \mathcal{L}(\overline{(\!|\mathbb{C}|\!)^+_{\iota^{\Sigma_0}}})} \mathsf{ext}(\iota^{\Sigma_0} t) = \mathsf{comp}([\![\Gamma \vdash \mathbb{C} : \theta]\!]_2^{\iota^{\Sigma_0}})$.

Proof. Note that the computation histories of the new automata have been obtained by restricting the automata obtained from Lemma 26 so that they trace out relevant plays only:

- O never uses P-names invisible to him thanks to rules[6] 4 (j in $\mathsf{kn}(j)$ has to match (q_O, N, S', j)) and 6 ($\ell \notin \{\mathsf{kn}(j) \mid j \in N\}$),

---

[5] Here $\mathsf{ext}(\cdots)$ will stand for the set of extensions with respect to *protoplays*.

[6] Counting from left to right, top to bottom.

– O will not change values referred to by P-names not available to him, because restrictions of the form $S \upharpoonright \cdots = S' \upharpoonright \cdots$ forbid that.

The labels generate protoplays, because of the $S \upharpoonright \cdots$ restrictions on symbolic stores. The refreshments of Definition 14 are performed via rules 9 and 11 (as well as introducing $\circledast$ in rules 3 and 5, if the P-names were introduced with c_x tags). Consequently, the lemma follows from Lemma 26. □

From now on we shall assume that from each non-initial state of $\overline{(\!|\mathbb{C}|\!)^{+}_{\iota\Sigma_0}}$ it is possible to reach a final state (if this is not the case, states violating this reachability requirement can be removed without affecting the above lemma). Note that because of strong determinacy, this implies that the automata will not have ϵ-cycles. This technical assumption will allow us to relate language equivalence to bisimulation in the next section.

7 Bisimulation

Here we define a notion of (weak) bisimilarity that will allow us to carry out the test from Theorem 16. Note that, given a term, our second translation to automata yields representatives for each complete protoplay in $[\![\cdots]\!]_2$. These representatives are by no means canonical, as can be seen below.

Example 32. The following terms are equivalent.

$$f : \mathsf{unit} \to \mathsf{int\,ref} \vdash\ f(); f() \quad \cong$$
$$\mathsf{let}\, z = \mathsf{ref}\,(2)\, \mathsf{in\,while}\,(!z)\, \mathsf{do}\,(f(); z := \mathsf{case}(!z)[0,0,1,\cdots]) : \mathsf{unit}$$

The corresponding automata for $[\![\cdots]\!]_0$ (and $[\![\cdots]\!]_2$, which coincides with $[\![\cdots]\!]_0$ in this case) accept respectively the words given below.

$$(\star,\mathsf{c}_f)^{\emptyset}(n_1,\mathsf{r}_f)^{(n_1,k_1)}(\star,\mathsf{c}_f)^{(n_1,k_1)}(n_2,\mathsf{r}_f)^{\{(n_1,k_1'),(n_2,k_2)\}}(\star,\mathsf{r}_{\downarrow})^{\{(n_1,k_1'),(n_2,k_2)\}}$$
$$(\star,\mathsf{c}_f)^{\emptyset}(n_1,\mathsf{r}_f)^{(n_1,k_1)}(\star,\mathsf{c}_f)(n_2,\mathsf{r}_f)^{(n_2,k_2)}(\star,\mathsf{r}_{\downarrow})^{\emptyset}$$

The notion of bisimulation to be introduced aims to identify different representatives of identical protoplays by checking that they represent consistent store histories. First we define it on configuration graphs of automata. Let us say that that stores Σ_1, Σ_2 are *compatible*, written $\Sigma_1 \asymp \Sigma_2$, if $\Sigma_1 \cup \Sigma_2$ is a valid store (i.e. for all $a \in \mathsf{dom}(\Sigma_1) \cap \mathsf{dom}(\Sigma_2)$, $\Sigma_1(a) = \Sigma_2(a)$).

Definition 33. *Let $\mathcal{A}_i = \langle Q_i, q_{0i}, \rho_{0i}, \delta_i, F_i\rangle$ be automata of type θ, for $i = 1,2$, and let us write F_i^{ϵ} for the set of states that can reach some final state by means of empty transitions. We call a relation $R \subseteq \hat{Q}_1 \times \mathsf{Sto}_{n_1+n_2} \times \hat{Q}_2$ a* simulation *on $\mathcal{A}_1$ and $\mathcal{A}_2$ if, for all $(\hat{q}_1, \Sigma, \hat{q}_2) \in R$,*

– *if $\pi_1(\hat{q}_1) \in F_1$ then $\pi_1(\hat{q}_2) \in F_2^{\epsilon}$, ($\pi_1$ the first-projection function);*
– *if $\hat{q}_1 \xrightarrow{(\ell,t)^{\Sigma_1}}_{\delta_1} \hat{q}_1'$ and $\pi_1(\hat{q}_1) \in Q_{1O}$ then either $\hat{q}_2 \xrightarrow{\epsilon}_{\delta_2} \hat{q}_2'$ and $(\hat{q}_1, \Sigma, \hat{q}_2') \in R$, or there is a finite $D \subseteq \mathbb{A}$ such that, for all $\Sigma_2 \asymp \Sigma_1$ with $\mathsf{dom}(\Sigma_2) = D$, there is some $\hat{q}_2 \xrightarrow{(\ell,t)^{\Sigma_2}}_{\delta_2} \hat{q}_2'$ with $(\hat{q}_1', \Sigma_1 \cup \Sigma_2, \hat{q}_2') \in R$;*

– *if* $\hat{q}_1 \xrightarrow{(\ell,t)^{\Sigma_1}}_{\delta_1} \hat{q}_1'$ *and* $\pi(\hat{q}_1) \in Q_{1P}$ *then either* $\hat{q}_2 \xrightarrow{\epsilon}_{\delta_2} \hat{q}_2'$ *and* $(\hat{q}_1, \Sigma, \hat{q}_2') \in R$*, or there is some* $\hat{q}_2 \xrightarrow{(\ell,t)^{\Sigma_2}}_{\delta_2} \hat{q}_2'$ *with* $(\hat{q}_1', \Sigma_1 \cup \Sigma_2, \hat{q}_2') \in R$ *and* $\Sigma_2 \asymp \Sigma_1 \cup (\Sigma \restriction (\mathsf{dom}(\Sigma) \setminus \mathsf{dom}(\Sigma_1)))$*;*
– *if* $\hat{q}_1 \xrightarrow{\epsilon}_{\delta_1} \hat{q}_1'$ *then* $(\hat{q}_1', \Sigma, \hat{q}_2) \in R$*.*

We call R *a* bisimulation *if both* R *and* R^{-1} *are simulations. We say that* $\mathcal{A}_1$ *and* $\mathcal{A}_2$ *are* bisimilar*, written* $\mathcal{A}_1 \sim \mathcal{A}_2$*, if there is a bisimulation* R *such that* $((q_{01}, \rho_{01}, \emptyset), \emptyset, (q_{02}, \rho_{02}, \emptyset)) \in R$*.*

Although bisimilarity is an infinite notion, we can capture it with a finite (and, hence, decidable) notion of *symbolic bisimilarity*, which relates states of the automata augmented with auxiliary finite structure, rather than configurations. This can be achieved by keeping a log of how the registers of the two automata are dynamically related, that is, which of their registers contain common names and which contain private ones. Transitions can then be simulated by referring to that log and updating it. For example, at the symbolic level, a transition of the form $q_1 \xrightarrow{(\mathsf{kn}(i),t)^{S_1}} q_1'$ of automaton $\mathcal{A}_1$ can be matched by $\mathcal{A}_2$ with $q_2 \xrightarrow{(\mathsf{kn}(j),t)^{S_2}} q_2'$ if we know that registers i and j are related, and symbolic stores S_1 and S_2 are equal at their related registers. If, however, our log tells us that i is private to $\mathcal{A}_1$, then $\mathcal{A}_2$ can only simulate it by $q_2 \xrightarrow{(\mathsf{fr}(j),t)^{S_2}} q_2'$ if q_1, q_2 are O-states.

Lemma 34. $\overline{(\!|\mathbb{C}_1|\!)^{+}_{\iota\Sigma_0}} \sim \overline{(\!|\mathbb{C}_2|\!)^{+}_{\iota\Sigma_0}}$ *iff* $\mathsf{comp}([\![\Gamma \vdash \mathbb{C}_1]\!]_2^{\iota\Sigma_0}) = \mathsf{comp}([\![\Gamma \vdash \mathbb{C}_2]\!]_2^{\iota\Sigma_0})$.

Proof. L2R: Take $s \in \mathsf{comp}([\![\Gamma \vdash \mathbb{C}_1]\!]_2^{\iota\Sigma_0})$. By Lemma 31 there exists $t_1 \in \mathcal{L}(\overline{(\!|\mathbb{C}_1|\!)^{+}_{\iota\Sigma_0}})$ such that $s \in \mathsf{ext}(\iota^{\Sigma_0}t_1)$. Because $\overline{(\!|\mathbb{C}_1|\!)^{+}_{\iota\Sigma_0}} \sim \overline{(\!|\mathbb{C}_2|\!)^{+}_{\iota\Sigma_0}}$ we can find $t_2 \in \mathcal{L}(\overline{(\!|\mathbb{C}_2|\!)^{+}_{\iota\Sigma_0}})$ such that $s \in \mathsf{ext}(\iota^{\Sigma_0}t_2)$ by using s to resolve choices of missing store values in the corresponding bisimulation game. Hence $s \in \mathsf{comp}([\![\Gamma \vdash \mathbb{C}_2]\!]_2^{\iota\Sigma_0})$. The other inclusion is symmetric.

R2L: Suppose $\overline{(\!|\mathbb{C}_1|\!)^{+}_{\iota\Sigma_0}} \not\sim \overline{(\!|\mathbb{C}_2|\!)^{+}_{\iota\Sigma_0}}$. Because the automata are deterministic, accept the same sets of extensions with respect to protoplays and final states can always be reached, there must exist $s \in \mathsf{comp}([\![\Gamma \vdash \mathbb{C}_1]\!]_2^{\iota\Sigma_0}) = \mathsf{comp}([\![\Gamma \vdash \mathbb{C}_2]\!]_2^{\iota\Sigma_0})$ and $j \in \{1,2\}$ such that $s \in \mathsf{ext}(\iota^{\Sigma_0}t_j)$, where $t_j \in \mathcal{L}(\overline{(\!|\mathbb{C}_j|\!)^{+}_{\iota\Sigma_0}})$, but $s \notin \mathsf{ext}(\iota^{\Sigma_0}t_{3-j})$ for any $t_{3-j} \in \mathcal{L}(\overline{(\!|\mathbb{C}_{3-j}|\!)^{+}_{\iota\Sigma_0}})$, which contradicts Lemma 31. □

Theorem 35. *Program equivalence for* $\mathsf{RedML}_{\mathrm{fin}}^{\beta\to\beta}$ *terms is decidable.*

Proof. Let k be the number of equivalence classes of initial moves I_Γ with regard to name-permutability and let $\iota_0, \cdots, \iota_k$ be their representatives. Then it suffices to verify $\overline{(\!|\mathbb{C}_1|\!)^{+}_{\iota\Sigma_0}} \sim \overline{(\!|\mathbb{C}_2|\!)^{+}_{\iota\Sigma_0}}$ for all $\iota = \iota_0, \cdots, \iota_k$ and all possible stores Σ_0 with domain $\mathcal{L}_\iota$. Altogether only finitely many bisimulation queries need to be made. □

8 Further Work

It would be desirable to understand what other models over infinite alphabets are suitable for representing $\mathsf{RedML}_{\mathrm{fin}}$-terms featuring more complicated types. For instance, it seems that a variant of pushdown automata would be needed to capture terms of type $\vdash (\mathsf{unit} \to \mathsf{unit}) \to \mathsf{unit}$. Another interesting avenue for future work concerns investigating relationships between automata over infinite alphabets and history-dependent automata [9].

References

1. Abramsky, S., McCusker, G.: Call-by-value games. In: Nielsen, M. (ed.) CSL 1997. LNCS, vol. 1414, pp. 1–17. Springer, Heidelberg (1998)
2. Ahmed, A., Dreyer, D., Rossberg, A.: State-dependent representation independence. In: Proc. of POPL, pp. 340–353. ACM, New York (2009)
3. Bojańczyk, M., Muscholl, A., Schwentick, T., Segoufin, L., David, C.: Two-variable logic on words with data. In: Proceedings of LICS, pp. 7–16 (2006)
4. Dreyer, D., Neis, G., Birkedal, L.: The impact of higher-order state and control effects on local relational reasoning. In: Proc. of ICFP, pp. 143–156. ACM, New York (2010)
5. Gabbay, M.J., Pitts, A.M.: A new approach to abstract syntax with variable binding. Formal Aspects of Computing 13, 341–363 (2002)
6. Ghica, D.R.: Regular-language semantics for a call-by-value programming language. In: Proc. of MFPS. ENTCS, vol. 45. Elsevier, Amsterdam (2001)
7. Kaminski, M., Francez, N.: Finite-memory automata. Theor. Comput. Sci. 134(2), 329–363 (1994)
8. McCusker, G.: On the semantics of Idealized Algol without the bad-variable constructor. In: Proc. of MFPS. ENTCS, vol. 83. Elsevier, Amsterdam (2003)
9. Montanari, U., Pistore, M.: An introduction to history dependent automata. In: ENTCS vol. 10 (1997)
10. Murawski, A.S.: Functions with local state: regularity and undecidability. Theor. Comput. Sci. 338(1/3), 315–349 (2005)
11. Murawski, A.S., Ong, C.-H.L., Walukiewicz, I.: Idealized Algol with ground recursion and DPDA equivalence. In: Caires, L., Italiano, G.F., Monteiro, L., Palamidessi, C., Yung, M. (eds.) ICALP 2005. LNCS, vol. 3580, pp. 917–929. Springer, Heidelberg (2005)
12. Murawski, A.S., Tzevelekos, N.: Full abstraction for Reduced ML. In: de Alfaro, L. (ed.) FOSSACS 2009. LNCS, vol. 5504, pp. 32–47. Springer, Heidelberg (2009)
13. Murawski, A.S., Tzevelekos, N.: Block structure vs scope extrusion: between innocence and omniscience. In: Ong, L. (ed.) FOSSACS 2010. LNCS, vol. 6014, pp. 33–47. Springer, Heidelberg (2010)
14. Neven, F., Schwentick, T., Vianu, V.: Finite state machines for strings over infinite alphabets. ACM Trans. Comput. Log. 5(3), 403–435 (2004)
15. Pitts, A.M., Stark, I.D.B.: Operational reasoning for functions with local state. In: Gordon, A.D., Pitts, A.M. (eds.) Higher-Order Operational Techniques in Semantics, pp. 227–273. Cambridge University Press, Cambridge (1998)
16. Stark, I.D.B.: Names and Higher-Order Functions. PhD thesis, University of Cambridge Computing Laboratory, Technical Report No. 363 (1995)
17. Tzevelekos, N.: Fresh-register automata. In: Proceedings of POPL. ACM, New York (2011)

The Relationship between Separation Logic and Implicit Dynamic Frames

Matthew J. Parkinson[1] and Alexander J. Summers[2]

[1] Microsoft Research Cambridge
mattpark@microsoft.com
[2] ETH Zurich
alexander.summers@inf.ethz.ch

Abstract. Separation logic is a concise method for specifying programs that manipulate dynamically allocated storage. Partially inspired by separation logic, Implicit Dynamic Frames has recently been proposed, aiming at first-order tool support. In this paper, we provide a total heap semantics for a standard separation logic, and prove it equivalent to the standard model. With small adaptations, we then show how to give a direct semantics to implicit dynamic frames and show this semantics correctly captures the existing definitions. This precisely connects the two logics. As a consequence of this connection, we show that a fragment of separation logic can be faithfully encoded in a first-order automatic verification tool (Chalice).

1 Introduction

Separation logic (SL) [5,11] is a popular approach to specifying the behaviour of programs, as it naturally deals with the issues of aliasing. Separation logic assertions extend classical logic with extra connectives and predicates to describe memory layout. This makes it difficult to reuse current tool support for verification. Implicit Dynamic Frames (IDF) [15] was developed to give the benefits of separation logic specifications while leveraging existing tool support for first-order logic.

Although IDF was partially inspired by separation logic, there are many differences between SL and IDF that make understanding their relationship difficult. SL does not allow expressions that refer to the heap, while IDF does. SL is defined on partial heaps, while IDF is defined using total heaps and permission masks. The semantics of IDF are only defined by its translation to first-order verification conditions, while SL has a direct Kripke semantics for its assertions. These differences make it challenging to understand the relationship between the two approaches.

In this paper, we develop an extended separation logic that both captures the original semantics of separation logic, and correctly captures the semantics of IDF. To achieve this we provide a separation logic based on total heaps and a permission mask. The permission mask specifies the locations in the heap which are safe to access. Our formulation allows expressions that access the

G. Barthe (Ed.): ESOP 2011, LNCS 6602, pp. 439–458, 2011.
© Springer-Verlag Berlin Heidelberg 2011

heap to be defined, however it complicates the definition of the separation logic "magic wand" connective. In order to faithfully capture the original semantics of separation logic, and thus use magic wand to give the weakest pre-condition of commands, we present a non-standard definition of magic wand that includes changes to the total heap.

We also show that this extended separation logic correctly captures the semantics of the IDF formulas, we focus on the form of IDF found in the concurrent verification tool Chalice [9]. As the semantics of IDF formulas are only defined indirectly via weakest pre-condition calculations for a language using them, we show that the verification conditions (VCs) generated by the existing Boogie2 [8] encoding and the VCs generated from the separation logic proof rules are logically equivalent. This shows that our model directly captures the semantics of IDF.

This strong correspondence enables us to encode a fragment of separation logic containing separating conjunction, points to assertions, equalities and conditionals on pure assertions (a typical fragment used in verification tools), into Chalice - a tool based on first-order theorem proving.

Outline. The paper is structured as follows. We begin by presenting the background definitions of both separation logic and implicit dynamic frames (§2); we then develop our extended separation logic (§3). We prove the correspondence between VCs in the two approaches (§4). Finally, we discuss related work (§5) and consider possible extensions and conclude (§6).

The contributions of this paper are as follows:

- We define a total heap semantics for separation logic, and prove it equivalent with the standard (partial heaps) semantics for the logic.
- We define a direct semantics for the implicit dynamic frames logic (the specification logic of the Chalice tool), which has so far only been given a semantics implicitly, via verification conditions.
- We show how to encode a standard fragment of separation logic into an implicit dynamic frames setting, preserving its semantics.
- We show that verification conditions as computed for separation logic coincide via our translation and semantics with the verification conditions computed by Chalice.

2 Background and Motivation

2.1 Standard Separation Logic

Separation logic [5,11] is a verification logic which was originally introduced to handle the verification of sequential programs in languages with manual memory management such as C. The key feature of the logic is the ability to describe the behaviour of commands in terms of disjoint heap fragments, greatly simplifying the work required when "framing on" extra properties in a modular setting. Since its inception, separation logic has evolved in a variety of ways. In particular, variants of separation logic are now used for the verification of object-oriented languages with garbage collection, such as Java and C♯ [12].

In order to handle concurrency, separation logic has been extended to consider its basic points-to assertions as *permissions* [10], determining which thread is allowed to read and write the corresponding state. To gain flexibility, *fractional permissions* [4,3] were introduced, allowing the permissions governed by points-to assertions to be split and combined. A fractional permission is a rational number $0 < \pi \leq 1$, where 1 denotes full and exclusive (read/write) permission, and any other permission denotes read-only permission. In this paper we focus on the following core fragment of separation logic with fractional permissions.

Definition 1 (Separation Logic Assertions (*SL*)). *We assume a set of* object identifiers[1], *ranged over by* ι. *We also assume a set of* field identifiers, *ranged over by* f. Values, *ranged over by* v *are either object identifiers, integers, or the special value* **null**.

The syntaxes of separation logic expressions (ranged over by e*) and assertions (ranged over by* a, b*) are defined as follows*[2]*. In this definition,* n *ranges over integer constants, and* $0 < \pi \leq 1$.

$$
\begin{aligned}
e &::= x \mid \textbf{null} \mid n \\
a &::= e = e \mid e.f \overset{\pi}{\mapsto} e \mid a * a \mid a \mathrel{-\!\!*} a \mid a \wedge a \mid a \vee a \mid a \rightarrow a
\end{aligned}
$$

We will refer to this separation logic simply as SL hereafter.

The key feature of separation logic is the facility to reason locally about separate heap portions. As such, the standard semantics for separation logic is formulated in terms of judgements parameterised by partial heaps (sometimes called *heap fragments*), which can be split and combined together as required. The critical new connectives are the *separating conjunction* $*$, and the *magic wand* $-\!\!*$. The separating conjunction $a * b$ expresses that a and b are true and depend on disjoint fragments of the heap. The magic wand $a -\!\!* b$ expresses that if any extra partial heap satisfying a is combined with the current partial heap, then the resulting heap is guaranteed to satisfy b.

Fractional permissions[3] are employed to manage shared memory concurrency in the usual way - a thread may only read from a heap location if it has a non-zero permission to the location, and it may only write to a location if it has the whole (full) permission to it. By careful permission accounting, it can then be guaranteed that a thread can never modify a heap location while another thread can read it. Note that permissions are handled (via points-to predicates $e.f \overset{\pi}{\mapsto} e'$) on a per-field basis: it is possible for an assertion to provide permission for only one field of an object. This fine granularity of permissions allows for greater

1 These could be considered to be addresses, but we choose to be parametric with the concrete implementation of the heap.

2 Note that variables x need not be program variables, but can also be specification-only variables (sometimes called *logical*, *ghost* or *specification variables*).

3 Chalice, described in the next subsection, actually uses a slight variation on fractional permissions to make automatic theorem proving easier.

flexibility in the resulting logic - it can be specified that different threads have access to different fields of an object at the same time, for example. Combination of partial heaps includes combination of their permissions, where they overlap.

Definition 2 (Partial Fractional Heaps)

- *A* partial fractional heap *h is a partial function from pairs* (ι, f) *of object-identifier and field-identifier to pairs* (v, π) *of value and* non-zero *permission* π. *Partial heap lookup is written* $h[\iota, f]$, *and is only defined when* $(\iota, f) \in dom(h)$.
- *Partial heap extension:* $h_1 \subseteq h_2$, *iff* $\forall(\iota, f) \in dom(h_1).\ h_2[\iota, f] = h_1[\iota, f]$.
- *Partial heap compatible:* $h_1 \perp h_2$ *iff* $\forall(\iota, f) \in dom(h_1) \cap dom(h_2). \downarrow_1(h_1[\iota, f]) = \downarrow_1(h_2[\iota, f]) \ \wedge\ \downarrow_2(h_1[\iota, f]) + \downarrow_2(h_2[\iota, f]) \leq 1$.
- *The combination of two partial heaps, written* $h_1 * h_2$, *is defined only when* $h_1 \perp h_2$ *holds, by the following equations:*

$$dom(h_1 * h_2) = dom(h_1) \cup dom(h_2)$$
$$\forall(\iota, f) \in dom(h_1 * h_2).$$
$$(h_1 * h_2)[\iota, f] = \begin{cases} (\downarrow_1(h_1[\iota, f]), \downarrow_2(h_1[\iota, f])) & \text{if } (\iota, f) \notin dom(h_2) \\ (\downarrow_1(h_2[\iota, f]), \downarrow_2(h_2[\iota, f])) & \text{if } (\iota, f) \notin dom(h_1) \\ (\downarrow_1(h_1[\iota, f]), (\downarrow_2(h_1[\iota, f]) + \downarrow_2(h_2[\iota, f]))) & \text{otherwise} \end{cases}$$

We use $\downarrow_n$ *to denote the nth component of a tuple.*

There are two main flavours of separation logic studied in the literature: *classical* separation logic, and *intuitionistic* separation logic. In this paper, we consider *intuitionistic* separation logic. In intuitionistic separation logic, truth of assertions is closed under heap extension, which is appropriate for a garbage-collected language such as Java/C♯, rather than a language with manual memory management, such as C. The standard intuitionistic separation logic semantics for our fragment *SL* is defined as follows.

Definition 3 (Standard Semantics for *SL*). *Environments* σ *are partial functions*[4] *from variable names to values. Separation logic expression semantics,* $[\![e]\!]_\sigma$ *are defined by* $[\![x]\!]_\sigma = \sigma(x)$, $[\![n]\!]_\sigma = n$ *and* $[\![\mathtt{null}]\!]_\sigma = \mathtt{null}$. *The semantics of assertions is then as follows:*

$$\begin{array}{lll}
h, \sigma \models_{SL} e_1.f \overset{\pi}{\mapsto} e_2 & \iff & \downarrow_2(h[[\![e_1]\!]_\sigma, f]) \geq \pi \ \wedge\ \downarrow_1(h[[\![e_1]\!]_\sigma, f]) = [\![e_2]\!]_\sigma \\
h, \sigma \models_{SL} e = e' & \iff & [\![e]\!]_\sigma = [\![e']\!]_\sigma \\
h, \sigma \models_{SL} a * b & \iff & \exists h_1, h_2.(\ h = h_1 * h_2 \ \wedge\ h_1, \sigma \models_{SL} a \ \wedge\ h_2, \sigma \models_{SL} b) \\
h, \sigma \models_{SL} a \mathrel{-\!\!*} b & \iff & \forall h'.(\ h' \perp h \ \wedge\ h', \sigma \models_{SL} a \ \Rightarrow\ h * h', \sigma \models_{SL} b) \\
h, \sigma \models_{SL} a \wedge b & \iff & h, \sigma \models_{SL} a \ \wedge\ h, \sigma \models_{SL} b \\
h, \sigma \models_{SL} a \vee b & \iff & h, \sigma \models_{SL} a \ \vee\ h, \sigma \models_{SL} b \\
h, \sigma \models_{SL} a \rightarrow b & \iff & \forall h'.(\ h \subseteq h' \ \wedge\ h', \sigma \models_{SL} a \ \Rightarrow\ h', \sigma \models_{SL} b)
\end{array}$$

[4] However, we assume that all applications of environments are well-defined; i.e., whenever we write $\sigma(x)$, that $x \in dom(\sigma)$. This assumption is justified so long as the program and specifications are type-checked appropriately.

The semantics for the separating conjunction and magic wand express the required splitting and combination of partial heaps. The semantics for logical implication $\rightarrow$ considers all possible extensions of the current heap, so that assertion truth is closed under heap extension [5].

Assume/Assert. Verification in Boogie2 and related technologies uses two commands commonly to encode verification: `assume` A and `assert` A. The first allows the verification to work forwards with the additional assumption of A, while the second requires A to hold otherwise it will be considered a fault. These can be given weakest precondition semantics of:

$$wp(\texttt{assert } A, B) = A \wedge B \qquad\qquad wp(\texttt{assume } A, B) = A \Rightarrow B$$

From a verification perspective, these primitives can be used to encode many advanced language features. For example, in a modular verification setting with a first-order assertion language, a method-call is encoded by a sequence `assert` *pre*; `havoc`(*Heap*); `assume` *post*, in which *pre* and *post* are the pre- and post-conditions of the method respectively, and `havoc(.)` is a Boogie command that causes the prover to forget all knowledge about a variable/expression.

With separation logic, there are two forms of conjunction and implication, the standard (additive) ones $\wedge$ and $\rightarrow$, and the separating (multiplicative) ones $*$ and $-\!\!*$. This naturally gives rise to a second form of assume and assert for the multiplicative connectives ($\texttt{assume}^*$ and $\texttt{assert}^*$), with the following weakest precondition semantics:

$$wp(\texttt{assert}^*\ A,\ B) = A * B \qquad\qquad wp(\texttt{assume}^*\ A,\ B) = A -\!\!* B$$

These commands can be understood as follows: $\texttt{assert}^*$ A removes a heap fragment satisfying A, and $\texttt{assume}^*$ A adds a heap fragment satisfying A. In a verification setting where assertions express permissions as well as functional properties, these can be used to correctly model the transfer of permissions when encoding various constructs. In a separation logic setting, a method call is encoded as $\texttt{assert}^*$ *pre*; $\texttt{assume}^*$ *post*.

In Chalice, which handles an assertion logic based on Implicit Dynamic Frames, functional verification is based on two new commands: `inhale` A and `exhale` A, which are also given an intuitive semantics of adding and removing access to state. One outcome of this paper is to make this intuitive connection between `inhale`/`exhale` and $\texttt{assume}^*$/$\texttt{assert}^*$ formal, by defining a concrete and common semantics which can correctly characterise both assertion languages.

2.2 Chalice and Implicit Dynamic Frames

The original concept of Dynamic Frames comes from the PhD thesis of Kassios [7,6]. The idea is to tackle the frame problem by allowing method specifications to declare the portion of the heap they may modify (a "frame" for the method call) via functions of the heap. The computed frames are therefore dynamic, in the sense that the actual values determined by these functions may change as the heap itself gets modified. Implicit Dynamic Frames [15,14] takes a different approach to computing frames - a first-order logic is extended with a new kind of assertion called an *accessibility predicate* (written e.g., as $acc(x.f)$) whose role is to represent a permission to a heap location $x.f$. In a method pre-condition, such an accessibility predicate indicates that the method requires permission to $x.f$ in order to be called - usually because this location might be read or written to in the method implementation. By imposing the restriction that heap dereference expressions (whether in assertions or in method bodies) are only allowed if a corresponding permission has already been acquired, this specification style allows a method frame to be calculated implicitly from its pre-condition.

Chalice [9] is a tool written for the automatic verification of concurrent programs. It handles a fairly simple imperative language, with classes (but no inheritance), and several interesting concurrency features (locks, channels, fork/join of threads). The tool proves partial correctness of method specifications, as well as absence of deadlock. The core of the methodology is based on the Implicit Dynamic Frames specification logic, using accessibility predicates to handle the permissions necessary to avoid data races between threads.

In this paper we ignore the deadlock-avoidance aspects of Chalice, and focus on the aspects which guarantee functional correctness. Verification in Chalice is defined via an encoding into Boogie2, in which two auxiliary Chalice commands `inhale` p and `exhale` p are used. These commands reflect the addition and removal of permissions from the state, as well as expressing assumptions and assertions about the heap. For example, method calls are represented by `exhale` *pre*; `inhale` *post*. The command `exhale` *pre* has the effect of giving up any permissions mentioned in accessibility predicates in *pre*, and generating `assert` statements for any logical properties such as heap equalities. Dually, `inhale` *post* has the effect of adding any permissions mentioned in *post* and *assuming* any logical properties.

Definition 4 (Our Chalice Subsyntax). *Expressions E and assertions p in our fragment of Chalice are given by the following syntax definitions:*

$$E ::= x \mid n \mid \mathit{null} \mid E.f$$
$$p ::= E = E \mid acc(E.f, \pi) \mid p * p$$

Note that Chalice actually uses the symbol for logical conjunction ($\wedge$ or &&) where we write $*$ above. However, in terms the semantics of the logic this is misleading - in general it is not the case that $p \wedge p$ (as written in Chalice) is equivalent to p. Chalice's conjunction treats permissions multiplicatively, that is $acc(x.f, 1) \wedge acc(x.f, 1)$ is actually equivalent to falsity. As we will show, Chalice conjunction is actually directly related to the separating conjunction of separation logic, hence our choice of notation here. Where we use the symbol $\wedge$ later in the paper, we mean the usual (additive) conjunction, just as in SL.

Chalice performs verification condition generation via an encoding into Boogie2, which makes use of two special variables $\mathcal{P}$ and $\mathcal{H}$. The former maps object identifier and field name pairs to permissions, in this instance a fractional permission, and is used for bookkeeping of permissions[5]. The latter maps object identifier and field name pairs to values, and is used to model the heap of the real program. These maps can be read from (e.g., $\mathcal{P}[o, f]$) and updated (e.g., $\mathcal{P}[o, f] := 1$) from within the Boogie2 code, which allows Chalice to maintain their state appropriately to reflect the modifications made by the source program. In particular, the `inhale` and `exhale` commands have semantics which include modifications to the $\mathcal{P}$ map, to reflect the addition or removal of permissions by the program.

The critical aspect of Chalice's approach to data races, is to guarantee that assertions about the heap are only allowed when at least some permission is held to each heap location mentioned. This means that assertions cannot be made when it might be possible for other threads to be changing these locations - all logical properties used in the verification are then made robust to possible interference. Syntactically, this is enforced by requiring that assertions used in verification contracts are *self-framing* [6] - which means that the assertion includes enough accessibility predicates to "frame" its heap expressions. For example, the assertion $x.f = 5$ is not self-framing, since it refers to the heap location $x.f$ without permission. On the other hand, $(acc(x.f, 1) * x.f = 5)$ is self-framing.

3 A Total Heaps Semantics for Separation Logic

In this section we present a semantics for separation logic, which is based on states consisting of a *total* heap and a separate permission mask. Intuitively, the idea is that the permission mask specifies which locations in the heap we currently have permission to - this subset of the heap approximately corresponds with the partial heap which would be used in the standard semantics. The advantage of such a semantics is that it is simpler to relate to other logics with similar semantics and to encodings into first-order logic, as we will show later.

To facilitate comparisons, we define our semantics for an *extended* separation logic syntax, including not only the constructs of Definition 1, but also accessibility predicates from Implicit Dynamic Frames, and an enriched expression syntax that depend on the heap.

Definition 5 (Extended Separation Logic). *We define the expressions E and assertions A of* extended separation logic *(SL^+), by the following grammar (in which n stands for any integer constant):*

$$\begin{aligned} e &::= x \mid \textit{\textbf{null}} \mid n \\ E &::= e \mid E.f \\ A &::= E = E \mid e.f \overset{\pi}{\mapsto} e \mid A * A \mid A \mathrel{-\!\!*} A \mid A \wedge A \mid A \vee A \mid A \rightarrow A \mid acc(E.f, \pi) \end{aligned}$$

Note that the syntax of separation logic assertions (ranged over by a; see Definition 1) is a strict subset of the SL^+ assertions A defined above. The syntax of separation logic expressions e is also a strict subset of SL^+ expressions E.

[5] Technically, one should think of $\mathcal{P}$ as a *ghost variable*, since it does not correspond to real data of the original program.

Our aim is to give a total heap semantics for this more-general assertion language, implicitly defining a suitable semantics for both the fragment corresponding to *SL* assertions, and that corresponding to the assertions of Implicit Dynamic Frames. This semantics depends on states which are specified by a combination of a total heap and a permission mask which separately tracks permissions to heap locations.

Definition 6 (Total Heaps and Permission Masks). *A* total heap H *is a total map from pairs of object-identifier* o *and field-identifier* f *to* values v. *Heap lookup is written* $H[o,f]$.

A permission mask Π *is a total map from pairs of object-identifier and field-identifier to permissions. Permission lookup is written* $\Pi[o,f]$.

We write $\Pi_1 \subseteq \Pi_2$ *for* permission extension, *i.e.,* $\forall (o,f).\ \Pi_1[o,f] \leq \Pi_2[o,f]$.

We write $\varnothing$ *for the* empty permission mask; *i.e., the mask which assigns* 0 *to all locations.*

Evaluation of extended separation logic expressions depends on a given environment and heap, and is defined by:

$$[\![x]\!]_{\sigma,H} = \sigma(x) \quad [\![n]\!]_{\sigma,H} = n \quad [\![E.f]\!]_{\sigma,H} = H[[\![E]\!]_{\sigma,H}, f] \quad [\![\texttt{null}]\!]_{\sigma,H} = \texttt{null}$$

The meaning of separation logic expressions is preserved (and is independent of the heap), as the following lemma shows:

Lemma 1. $\forall e, \sigma, H.\ [\![e]\!]_{\sigma,H} = [\![e]\!]_{\sigma}$

In order to define our semantics, we need to be able to combine permission masks:

Definition 7 (Combining Permission Masks). *Two permission masks* Π_1 *and* Π_2 *are* compatible, *written* $\Pi_1 \perp \Pi_2$, *if it holds that:*

$$\forall (o,f).\ \Pi_1[o,f] + \Pi_2[o,f] \leq 1$$

The combination *of two permission masks, written* $\Pi_1 * \Pi_2$ *is undefined if* Π_1 *and* Π_2 *are not compatible, and is otherwise defined pointwise to be the following permission mask:*

$$(\Pi_1 * \Pi_2)[o,f] = \Pi_1[o,f] + \Pi_2[o,f]$$

To define and prove results about our semantics, we need operations for replacing and removing portions of a heap, according to a specified permission. To this end, we introduce the following auxiliary definitions.

Definition 8 (Total Heap Operations). *Two heaps* H_1 *and* H_2 agree on permissions Π, *written* $H_1 \overset{\Pi}{\equiv} H_2$, *if the two heaps agree on all locations given non-zero permission by* Π, *i.e.,*

$$H_1 \overset{\Pi}{\equiv} H_2 \iff \forall o, f. \Pi[o,f] > 0 \ \Rightarrow\ H_2[o,f] = H_1[o,f]$$

The restriction of H to Π, *written* $H \restriction \Pi$ *is a* partial fractional heap, *defined by:*

$$dom(H \restriction \Pi) = \{(o, f) \mid \Pi[o, f] > 0\}$$
$$\forall (o, f) \in dom(H \restriction \Pi). \downarrow_1((H \restriction \Pi)[o, f]) = H[o, f]$$
$$\forall (o, f) \in dom(H \restriction \Pi). \downarrow_2((H \restriction \Pi)[o, f]) = \Pi[o, f]$$

The main difficulty in defining a semantics for *SL* using total heaps is getting the treatment of the magic wand connective correct. Since the standard semantics of this connective involves a quantification over all partial heaps which can be combined with the current one (i.e., all those which are compatible), it is not obvious how a corresponding definition can be made when starting from a total heap. The key idea is to model the "addition" of a new heap fragment which takes place in the standard semantics by acquiring some additional permissions, and then considering all possible heaps which have different values at the locations corresponding to these new permissions. In this way, the "newly acquired" region of our total heap can take on arbitrary new values. We model this by considering all heaps which agree with the current heap over the part to which any permission is held, and also satisfy the requirements of the "additional" heap.

Definition 9 (Total Heap Semantics for SL^+). *We define validity of SL^+-assertions with respect to a specified total heap H and permission mask Π recursively on the structure of the assertion:*

$$\begin{aligned}
H, \Pi, \sigma \models_{SL^+} e.f \overset{\pi}{\mapsto} e' &\iff \Pi[\llbracket e \rrbracket_{\sigma,H}, f] \geq \pi \ \wedge\ H[\llbracket e \rrbracket_{\sigma,H}, f] = \llbracket e' \rrbracket_{\sigma,H} \\
H, \Pi, \sigma \models_{SL^+} A * B &\iff \exists \Pi_1, \Pi_2. (\Pi = \Pi_1 * \Pi_2 \ \wedge\ H, \Pi_1, \sigma \models_{SL^+} A \ \wedge \\
&\qquad\qquad H, \Pi_2, \sigma \models_{SL^+} B) \\
H, \Pi, \sigma \models_{SL^+} A \mathrel{-\!\!*} B &\iff \forall \Pi', H'. (\Pi' \bot \Pi \ \wedge\ H' \overset{\Pi}{\equiv} H \ \wedge\ H', \Pi', \sigma \models_{SL^+} A \\
&\qquad\qquad \Rightarrow H', \Pi * \Pi', \sigma \models_{SL^+} B) \\
H, \Pi, \sigma \models_{SL^+} A \wedge B &\iff H, \Pi, \sigma \models_{SL^+} A \ \wedge\ H, \Pi, \sigma \models_{SL^+} B \\
H, \Pi, \sigma \models_{SL^+} A \vee B &\iff H, \Pi, \sigma \models_{SL^+} A \ \vee\ H, \Pi, \sigma \models_{SL^+} B \\
H, \Pi, \sigma \models_{SL^+} A \rightarrow B &\iff \forall \Pi', H'. (\Pi \subseteq \Pi' \ \wedge\ H' \overset{\Pi}{\equiv} H \ \wedge\ H', \Pi', \sigma \models_{SL^+} A \\
&\qquad\qquad \Rightarrow H', \Pi', \sigma \models_{SL^+} B) \\
H, \Pi, \sigma \models_{SL^+} acc(E.f, \pi) &\iff \Pi[\llbracket E \rrbracket_{\sigma,H}, f] \geq \pi \\
H, \Pi, \sigma \models_{SL^+} E = E' &\iff \llbracket E \rrbracket_{\sigma,H} = \llbracket E' \rrbracket_{\sigma,H}
\end{aligned}$$

Note the similarity between the definitions for magic wand $\mathrel{-\!\!*}$ and logical implication $\rightarrow$.[6] This is because both cases involve heap extension in the partial heap semantics; in our total heap semantics we model heap extension by enabling the assignment of new arbitrary values to the part of the heap we have not yet acquired permission to. We observe that validity of assertions in this semantics is closed under permission extension.

[6] Note the intuitionistic implication can be defined in terms of the pointwise classical implication ($\rightarrow_c$) in separation logic: $A \rightarrow B \iff \text{true} \mathrel{-\!\!*} (A \rightarrow_c B)$.

Proposition 1. *If $H, \Pi, \sigma \models_{SL^+} A$ and $\Pi \subseteq \Pi'$ then $H, \Pi', \sigma \models_{SL^+} A$.*

Proof. *By straightforward induction on the structure of the assertion A.*

Semantically, an assertion is *framed* by a permission mask if it only depends on the values of heap locations which the permission mask assigns permission to. An assertion is semantically *self-framing* if it is only true for permission masks large enough to frame it. These semantic notions of framing and self-framing are formalised as follows:

Definition 10 (Framing, Self-Framing and Pure Assertions). *A permission mask Π'* frames *an assertion A (Π' frames A) if and only if:*

$$\forall \Pi, H, \sigma, H'.\ (H, \Pi, \sigma \models_{SL^+} A \wedge H' \stackrel{\Pi'}{\equiv} H \Rightarrow H', \Pi, \sigma \models_{SL^+} A)$$

An assertion A is self-framing *if and only if it is only satisfied under permission masks which frame it, i.e.,*

$$\forall \Pi, H, \sigma, H'.\ (H, \Pi, \sigma \models_{SL^+} A \wedge H' \stackrel{\Pi}{\equiv} H \Rightarrow H', \Pi, \sigma \models_{SL^+} A)$$

An assertion A is pure[7] *if and only if it doesn't depend on permissions, i.e.,*

$$\forall \Pi, H, \sigma.\ (H, \Pi, \sigma \models_{SL^+} A \Rightarrow H, \varnothing, \sigma \models_{SL^+} A)$$

For example, the assertion $x.f = 5$ is only framed by permission masks which give permission to location (x, f). It is not self-framing, since with an environment σ such that $\sigma(x) = \iota$, a heap H such that $H[\iota, f] = 5$ and an empty permission mask Π, we have $H, \Pi, \sigma \models_{SL^+} x.f = 5$. However, the heap $H' = H[(\iota, f) \mapsto 4]$ satisfies $H' \stackrel{\Pi}{\equiv} H$, but we have $H', \Pi, \sigma \not\models_{SL^+} x.f = 5$. On the other hand, the assertions $acc(x.f, 1) * x.f = 5$ and $x.f \stackrel{1}{\mapsto} 5$ are both self-framing.

Intuitively, self-framing assertions are robust to arbitrary interference on the rest of the heap. For separation logic assertions, this property holds naturally, since it is impossible for an assertion to talk about the heap without including the appropriate "points-to" predicates, which force the corresponding permissions to be held.

Lemma 2. *All separation logic assertions a (Defn 1) are self-framing.*

Proof. *We prove, by straightforward induction on the structure of the assertion a, the equivalent statement:*

$$\forall a, H, \Pi.\ (H, \Pi, \sigma \models_{SL^+} a \Leftrightarrow \forall H'.\ (H' \stackrel{\Pi}{\equiv} H \Rightarrow H', \Pi, \sigma \models_{SL^+} a))$$

We now turn to relating our total heap semantics for separation logic, with the standard semantics. To do this, we need to relate partial heaps with pairs of total heap and permission mask. Given any total heap H and permission mask Π we can construct a corresponding partial heap $H \upharpoonright \Pi$. Conversely, any partial heap h can be represented as the restriction of a total heap H to the permission mask

[7] We may have considered *pure* assertions to depend on the heap as well. This however, does not have the right logical characterisation: A is pure iff $\forall B, A * B = A \wedge B$.

corresponding to all the permissions in h. This representation however, is not unique - there are many such total heaps H we could choose such that $h = H \upharpoonright \Pi$. However, the different choices of H can only differ over the locations given no permission in Π, and the previous lemma demonstrates that such differences do not affect the semantics of assertions. For our correspondence result, it is therefore without loss of generality to consider partial heaps constructed by $H \upharpoonright \Pi$. We can then show that our total heap semantics for SL is sound and complete with respect to the standard semantics:

Theorem 1 (Correctness of Total Heap Semantics). *For all SL-assertions a, environments σ, total heaps H, and permission mask Π:*

$$H, \Pi, \sigma \vDash_{SL^+} a \iff (H \upharpoonright \Pi), \sigma \vDash_{SL} a$$

Proof. *By induction on the structure of the assertion a, using Lemma 1.*

This result demonstrates that our total heap semantics correctly models the standard semantics of separation logic assertions. However, because our assertion language is more general than that of separation logic, not all properties of the separation logic connectives transfer across to the full generality of SL^+. For example, in separation logic, the assertions $a \mathrel{-\!\!*} (b \mathrel{-\!\!*} c)$ and $(a * b) \mathrel{-\!\!*} c$ are (always) equivalent. This is not quite the case in SL^+. In order to precisely characterise the laws which hold, we require a notion of semantic entailment.

Definition 11 (Semantic Entailment, Validity and Equivalence). *A SL^+ assertion A is* semantically valid *(written $\vDash_{SL^+} A$) if it holds in all situations; i.e.,*

$$\vDash_{SL^+} A \Leftrightarrow \forall H, \Pi, \sigma.\ H, \Pi, \sigma \vDash_{SL^+} A$$

Given SL^+ assertions A and B, we say that A semantically entails *B (and write $A \vDash_{SL^+} B$) if and only if B holds whenever A does; i.e.,*

$$A \vDash_{SL^+} B \Leftrightarrow \forall H, \Pi, \sigma.\ (H, \Pi, \sigma \vDash_{SL^+} A \Rightarrow H, \Pi, \sigma \vDash_{SL^+} B)$$

Given SL^+ assertions A and B, we say that A is equivalent to *B (and write $A \equiv_{SL^+} B$) if and only if $A \vDash_{SL^+} B$ and $B \vDash_{SL^+} A$.*

We can now show how various laws which hold for separation logic transfer (in some cases partially) to our more general setting of SL^+.

Proposition 2. *For all SL^+ assertions A_1, A_2, A_3:*

1. $\vDash_{SL^+} A_1 * (A_1 \mathrel{-\!\!*} A_2) \rightarrow A_2$ *and* $\vDash_{SL^+} A_1 \wedge (A_1 \rightarrow A_2) \rightarrow A_2$
2. $A_1 \mathrel{-\!\!*} (A_2 \mathrel{-\!\!*} A_3) \vDash_{SL^+} (A_1 * A_2) \mathrel{-\!\!*} A_3$ *and* $A_1 \rightarrow (A_2 \rightarrow A_3) \vDash_{SL^+} (A_1 \wedge A_2) \rightarrow A_3$
3. $\forall H, \Pi, \sigma,$ *if* $\forall \Pi'.\ (\Pi' \bot \Pi) \wedge H, \Pi', \sigma \vDash_{SL^+} A_1 \Rightarrow \Pi * \Pi'$ *frames* A_1*, then:* $H, \Pi, \sigma \vDash_{SL^+} (A_1 * A_2) \mathrel{-\!\!*} A_3 \Rightarrow H, \Pi, \sigma \vDash_{SL^+} A_1 \mathrel{-\!\!*} (A_2 \mathrel{-\!\!*} A_3)$
4. $\forall H, \Pi, \sigma,$ *if* $\forall \Pi'.\ (\Pi' \bot \Pi) \wedge H, \Pi * \Pi', \sigma \vDash_{SL^+} A_1 \Rightarrow \Pi * \Pi'$ *frames* A_1*, then:* $H, \Pi, \sigma \vDash_{SL^+} (A_1 \wedge A_2) \rightarrow A_3 \Rightarrow H, \Pi, \sigma \vDash_{SL^+} A_1 \rightarrow (A_2 \rightarrow A_3)$
5. *If* $A_1 \vDash_{SL^+} (A_2 \mathrel{-\!\!*} A_3)$ *then* $(A_1 * A_2) \vDash_{SL^+} A_3$
6. *If* A_1 *is self-framing and* $(A_1 * A_2) \vDash_{SL^+} A_3$ *then* $A_1 \vDash_{SL^+} (A_2 \mathrel{-\!\!*} A_3)$

To see that the usual separation logic laws do not all hold in general, consider for example the two assertions $P_1 \stackrel{def}{=} (x.f = 1 \mathrel{-\!\!*} (x.f = 2 \mathrel{-\!\!*} 1 = 2))$ and $P_2 \stackrel{def}{=} (x.f = 1 * x.f = 2) \mathrel{-\!\!*} 1 = 2$. The assertion P_2 is always true, essentially because no heap exists which satisfies $(x.f = 1 * x.f = 2)$, and so the implication in the semantics of the wand holds vacuously. However, the assertion P_1 is not always true - if we consider the case where we do not have permission to $x.f$ when checking the wand, we can pick two heaps which agree on our existing permissions and which assign $x.f$ the values 1 and 2 respectively. However, $1 = 2$ will of course be false in any configuration.

The usual separation logic laws do however hold for self-framing assertions (which by Lemma 2) includes all separation logic assertions).

Corollary 1. *For all self-framing SL^+ assertions A_1, A_2, A_3:*

1. $\models_{SL^+} A_1 * (A_1 \mathrel{-\!\!*} A_2) \rightarrow A_2$
2. $\models_{SL^+} A_1 \wedge (A_1 \rightarrow A_2) \rightarrow A_2$
3. $A_1 \mathrel{-\!\!*} (A_2 \mathrel{-\!\!*} A_3) \equiv_{SL^+} (A_1 * A_2) \mathrel{-\!\!*} A_3$
4. $A_1 \rightarrow (A_2 \rightarrow A_3) \equiv_{SL^+} (A_1 \wedge A_2) \rightarrow A_3$
5. $A_1 \models_{SL^+} (A_2 \mathrel{-\!\!*} A_3)$ *if and only if* $(A_1 * A_2) \models_{SL^+} A_3$

To complete this section, we observe that we are able to eliminate the "points-to" assertions from our syntax without loss of expressiveness. This is because of the following proposition:

Proposition 3. *For all e,f,e',π we have $e.f \overset{\pi}{\mapsto} e' \equiv_{SL^+} acc(e.f, \pi) * e.f = e'$.*

Proof. Directly from the semantics.

This result along with Theorem 1 shows that we can faithfully represent *SL* assertions in an implicit dynamic frames logic, in which permissions are tracked by accessibility predicates, and assertions about the heap are managed independently. Because our proofs are inductive on the structure of assertions, this representation result can also be applied to any fragments of *SL*. In particular, if we take the core fragment of *SL* typically supported by tools (in which assertions are built from separating conjunction and a restricted form of implication in which $A \rightarrow B$ is only allowed if A is permission-free), then we can faithfully encode this fragment into the logic of Chalice (Definition 4).

However, Chalice has its own semantics for this logic, which is implicitly defined via the weakest-precondition semantics for the language. Therefore, in order to provide a strong connection between standard separation logic and the Chalice methodology we must also show that our total heap semantics can be used to accurately reflect the semantics of Chalice. This is the focus of the next section.

4 Verification Conditions

In this section, we precisely connect the semantics of our assertion language with Chalice. Chalice does not provide a direct model for its assertion language.

It instead defines the semantics of assertions using the weakest pre-condition semantics of the commands `inhale` and `exhale`. We show that this semantics precisely corresponds with the semantics in SL^+.

4.1 Chalice

Chalice is defined by a translation into Boogie2 [8], which generates verification conditions on a many-sorted classical logic with first-order quantification. It has sorts for mathematical maps, which are used by Chalice to encode both the heap and the permission mask. We use ϕ to range over formulas in this logic, and $\sigma \vDash_{FO} \phi$ to mean ϕ holds in the standard semantics of first-order logic given the interpretation of free variables σ, and $\vDash_{FO} \phi$ means holds in all interpretations.

The definitions throughout this section generate expressions that have these two specific free variables: $\mathcal{H}$ for the current heap, and $\mathcal{P}$ for the current permission masks. Thus, $\mathcal{H}[x, f] = 5$ means in the current heap the variable x's field named f contains value 5. In the assertion logic, this corresponds to $x.f = 5$ where the heap access is implicit.

To enable us to relate the verification conditions in separation logic with those in Chalice, we need to be able to relate formulas in one approach with the other. We can provide a syntactic translation from the Chalice assertion logic into the first-order logic.

Definition 12. *We translate expressions that implicitly access the heap into expressions that explicitly access the heap as follows:*

$$\llbracket x \rrbracket = x \qquad \llbracket \mathbf{null} \rrbracket = \mathbf{null} \qquad \llbracket E.f \rrbracket = \mathcal{H}[\llbracket E \rrbracket, f]$$

and we translate formulas as follows:

$$\begin{aligned} \llbracket acc(E.f, \pi) \rrbracket &= \mathcal{P}[\llbracket E \rrbracket, f] \geq \pi \\ \llbracket p * q \rrbracket &= \exists \mathcal{P}_1, \mathcal{P}_2.\ \llbracket p \rrbracket[\mathcal{P}_1/\mathcal{P}] \wedge \llbracket q \rrbracket[\mathcal{P}_2/\mathcal{P}] \wedge (\mathcal{P}_1 * \mathcal{P}_2 = \mathcal{P}) \\ \llbracket E = E' \rrbracket &= \llbracket E \rrbracket = \llbracket E' \rrbracket \end{aligned}$$

where $[\mathcal{P}_1/\mathcal{P}]$ means the replacement of $\mathcal{P}$ with $\mathcal{P}_1$, and $\mathcal{P}_1 * \mathcal{P}_2 = \mathcal{P}$ is a ternary predicate, true if and only if $\forall i. \mathcal{P}_1(i) + \mathcal{P}_2(i) \leq 1 \wedge \mathcal{P}(i) = \mathcal{P}_1(i) + \mathcal{P}_2(i)$.

For example, the formula $acc(x.f, \pi) * x.f = 5$ will be translated to

$$\exists \mathcal{P}_1, \mathcal{P}_2.\ (\mathcal{P}_1[x.f] \geq \pi) \wedge (\mathcal{H}[x, f] = 5) \wedge \mathcal{P} = \mathcal{P}_1 * \mathcal{P}_2$$

which we can simplify to $(\mathcal{P}[x.f] \geq \pi) \wedge (\mathcal{H}[x, f] = 5)$, that is the current heap contains 5 at x, f and the current permission mask has at least π permission on that location.

By interpreting the heap variable with concrete heap, and the permission mask variable with a concrete permission mask, we can show that the translated formula is true iff the original SL^+ formula was true.

Lemma 3. $\sigma, \mathcal{H} \mapsto H, \mathcal{P} \mapsto \Pi \vDash_{FO} \llbracket p \rrbracket \iff H, \Pi, \sigma \vDash_{SL^+} p$
where $\sigma, \mathcal{H} \mapsto H, \mathcal{P} \mapsto \Pi$ is an interpretation that has all the mappings of σ and additionally maps the current heap, $\mathcal{H}$, and permission mask, $\mathcal{P}$, to the heap, H, and the permission mask, Π.

Chalice does not allow arbitrary formulas to be used as argument to `inhale` and `exhale`: it restricts the formulas to be self-framing. Chalice does not use the semantic check from earlier, but instead uses a syntactic formulation that checks self-framing from left-to-right. Note that this means that syntactic self-framing is not symmetric with respect to $*$. For instance, $acc(x.f,\pi) * x.f = 5$ is syntactically self-framing, but $x.f = 5 * acc(x.f,\pi)$ is not. Somewhat surprisingly this is required by the way the verification conditions are generated.

Definition 13. *We define the footprint*[8] *of a formula; an expression with the $\mathcal{H}$ variable free in it, that has the type of a set of locations and field name pairs.*

$$\mathsf{foot}(E = E') = \{\} \qquad \mathsf{foot}(acc(E.f,\pi)) = \{(\llbracket E \rrbracket, f)\}$$
$$\mathsf{foot}(A * B) = \mathsf{foot}(A) \cup \mathsf{foot}(B)$$

We define a boolean expression $\mathsf{syn\_framed}_\psi(E)$ to mean that all the fields mentioned in E are in the set ψ.

$$\mathsf{syn\_framed}_\psi(E.f) = \mathsf{syn\_framed}_\psi(E) \wedge \llbracket E \rrbracket.f \in \psi$$
$$\mathsf{syn\_framed}_\psi(x) = \mathsf{syn\_framed}_\psi(\mathtt{null}) = \mathsf{True}$$

We lift this to formulas as

$$\begin{aligned}
&\mathsf{syn_framed}_\psi(E = E') \iff \mathsf{syn_framed}_\psi(E) \wedge \mathsf{syn_framed}_\psi(E') \\
&\mathsf{syn_framed}_\psi(acc(E.f,\pi)) \iff \mathsf{syn_framed}_\psi(E.f) \\
&\mathsf{syn_framed}_\psi(A * B) \iff \mathsf{syn_framed}_\psi(A) \wedge \mathsf{syn_framed}_{\psi \cup \mathsf{foot}(A)}(B)
\end{aligned}$$

Note that when we check that B is framed in $A * B$, we can use the footprint of A; these syntactic checks do not treat $*$ as associative and commutative.

A formula, A, is syntactically self-framing, if it is framed by the empty set, $\mathsf{syn\_framed}_\varnothing(A)$.

We can now provide the definitions of the weakest pre-conditions of the commands for `inhale` and `exhale`. In Figure 1, we present the weakest pre-conditions of commands in Chalice from [9]. We write $wp_{\mathrm{ch}}(C,\phi)$ for the weakest pre-condition of the command C given the post-condition ϕ. Chalice models the inhaling and exhaling of permission by mutating the permission mask variable. To exhale an equality (or any formula not mentioning the permission mask) we simply assert it must be true. This does not need to modify the permission mask. To exhale $p * q$, first we exhale p and then q. When an access predicate is exhaled, first we check that the permission mask contains sufficient permission, and then we remove the permission from the mask.

To inhale an equality, it is simply the same as assuming it. To inhale a $p * q$, we first inhale p and then q. There are two cases for inhaling a permission: (1) we don't currently have any permission to that location; and (2) we do currently have permission to that location. The first case proceeds by adding the permission, and then havocing the contents of that location, that is, making sure any previous value of the variable has been forgotten. The second case simply adds the permission to the permission mask.

[8] $\mathsf{foot}(\_)$ corresponds to the *required access set* in [15].

$$wp_{\mathrm{ch}}(\texttt{exhale}(E = E'), \phi) = wp_{\mathrm{ch}}(\texttt{assert}\ \llbracket E = E' \rrbracket, \phi)$$

$$wp_{\mathrm{ch}}(\texttt{exhale}(p_1 * p_2), \phi) = wp_{\mathrm{ch}}(\texttt{exhale}(p_1); \texttt{exhale}(p_2), \phi)$$

$$wp_{\mathrm{ch}}(\texttt{exhale}(acc(E.f, \pi), \phi) \\ = wp_{\mathrm{ch}}(\texttt{assert}(\mathcal{P}[\llbracket E \rrbracket, f]) \geq \pi; \mathcal{P}[\llbracket E \rrbracket, f] := \mathcal{P}[\llbracket E \rrbracket, f] - \pi, \phi)$$

$$wp_{\mathrm{ch}}(\texttt{inhale}(E = E'), \phi) = wp_{\mathrm{ch}}(\texttt{assume}\ \llbracket E = E' \rrbracket, \phi)$$

$$wp_{\mathrm{ch}}(\texttt{inhale}(p_1 * p_2), \phi) = wp_{\mathrm{ch}}(\texttt{inhale}(p_1); \texttt{inhale}(p_2), \phi)$$

$$wp_{\mathrm{ch}}(\texttt{inhale}(acc(E.f, \pi), \phi) \\ = wp_{\mathrm{ch}}(\texttt{assume}(\mathcal{P}[\llbracket E \rrbracket, f] = 0); \mathcal{P}[\llbracket E \rrbracket, f] := \pi; \texttt{havoc}(\mathcal{H}[\llbracket E \rrbracket, f]), \phi) \\ \wedge wp_{\mathrm{ch}}(\texttt{assume}(0 < \mathcal{P}[\llbracket E \rrbracket, f] \leq 1 - \pi); \mathcal{P}[\llbracket E \rrbracket, f] \mathrel{+}= \pi;, \phi)$$

where

$$wp_{\mathrm{ch}}(\mathcal{P}[o, f] := x, \phi) = \phi[upd(\mathcal{P}, (o, f), x)/\mathcal{P}]$$
$$wp_{\mathrm{ch}}(\texttt{havoc}(\mathcal{H}[x, f]), \phi) = \phi[upd(\mathcal{H}, (x, f), z)/\mathcal{H}] \qquad \text{fresh z}$$
$$wp_{\mathrm{ch}}(\texttt{assume}\ E, \phi) = E \rightarrow \phi$$
$$wp_{\mathrm{ch}}(\texttt{assert}\ E, \phi) = E \wedge \phi$$
$$wp_{\mathrm{ch}}(C_1; C_2, \phi) = wp_{\mathrm{ch}}(C_1, wp_{\mathrm{ch}}(C_2, \phi))$$

where $upd(a, b, c)[b] = c$ and $upd(a, b, c)[d] = a[d]$ provided $d \neq b$.

Fig. 1. Abridged weakest pre-condition semantics for Chalice [9]

4.2 Relationship

In the rest of this section, we show that the verification conditions (VCs) generated by Chalice are equivalent to those generated by SL^+. We focus on the `inhale` and `exhale` commands as these represent the semantics of the Chalice assertion language. By showing the equivalence, we show that our model of SL^+ is also a model for Chalice.

We write $wp_{\mathrm{sl}}(C, A)$, to be the weakest pre-condition in SL^+ of the formula A with respect to the command C. We treat `inhale` and `exhale` as the multiplicative versions of `assume` and `assert` (see §2.1), and thus have the following weakest pre-conditions:

$$wp_{\mathrm{sl}}(\texttt{exhale}(A), B) = A * B \qquad wp_{\mathrm{sl}}(\texttt{inhale}(A), B) = A \mathrel{-\!\!*} B$$

Our core result is to show that both `inhale` and `exhale` have equivalent VCs in the two approaches.

Definition 14 ($equiv(C)$)**.** *We define the VCs of a command as equivalent in both systems, $equiv(C)$, iff for every self-framing SL^+ assertions, A, we have*

$$\vDash_{FO} \llbracket wp_{\mathrm{sl}}(C, A) \rrbracket \iff wp_{\mathrm{ch}}(C, \llbracket A \rrbracket)$$

Our notion of equivalence of VCs only requires commands to have equivalent weakest pre-conditions for self-framing post-conditions, thus we need to show that each command preserves self-framing. If commands did not preserve self-framing, then sequencing could not be proved by induction on the subcommands.

Lemma 4. *Each command preserves semantic self-framing: If A and p are self-framing, then so are $wp_{\text{sl}}(\texttt{inhale}\ p, A)$ and $wp_{\text{sl}}(\texttt{exhale}\ p, A)$.*

The key to showing our semantics for SL^+ correctly embodies Chalice is to show that the VCs generated for the `inhale` and `exhale` commands are equivalent. The `exhale` is straightforward.

Lemma 5. $\forall p.\ equiv(\texttt{exhale}\ p)$

Proof. *By induction on p.*

The proof of `inhale` is more involved. This depends on the inhaled formula being syntactically self-framing. We must first prove a collection of lemmas to enable the proof to proceed by induction. (1) We need to connect the weakest pre-condition of an inhale with the footprint of a formula: that is, know that inhaling a formula adds its footprint to the permission mask. (2) The Chalice's VCs break `inhale` $p * q$ into two `inhale`s. This logically corresponds to currying/uncurrying a wand formula in SL^+, but this is only true if the first formula is framed in the current world, so we need an analog of this for the VC world. Finally, (3) we need to know that introducing additional havocs to locations outside the current permission mask does not affect the weakest pre-condition assuming that the post-condition is framed by the current permission mask.

Lemma 6

1. $wp_{\text{ch}}(\textit{assume}(\psi < \mathcal{P}); \texttt{inhale}\ p, A)$ *is equivalent to* $wp_{\text{ch}}(\textit{assume}(\psi < \mathcal{P}); \texttt{inhale}\ p\ ; \textit{assume}(\psi \cup \textit{foot}(p) < \mathcal{P}), A)$;
2. *If* $\textit{syn\_framed}_{\psi}(p_1)$, *then* $wp_{\text{ch}}(\textit{assume}(\psi < \mathcal{P}), \llbracket p_1 \mathrel{-\!\!*} (p_2 \mathrel{-\!\!*} A)\rrbracket)$ *is equivalent to* $wp_{\text{ch}}(\textit{assume}(\psi < \mathcal{P}), \llbracket (p_1 * p_2) \mathrel{-\!\!*} A\rrbracket)$; *and*
3. *If* $\textit{syn\_framed}_{\psi}(A)$, *then* $wp_{\text{ch}}(\textit{assume}(\psi < \mathcal{P}); \textit{havoc}(\mathcal{H}[\overline{\mathcal{P}}]), \llbracket A\rrbracket)$ *is equivalent to* $wp_{\text{ch}}(\textit{assume}(\psi < \mathcal{P}), \llbracket A\rrbracket)$.

where $\psi < \mathcal{P}$ *means* $\forall i \in \psi.\mathcal{P}[i] \neq 0$, *and* $\textit{havoc}(\mathcal{H}[\overline{\mathcal{P}}])$ *means* **havoc** *every field in the heap with no permission in* $\mathcal{P}$.

Proof. 1. By induction on p.
2. Direct consequence of Proposition 2.3 and 2.2.
3. From definition of framing.

We want to show that if p is syntactically self-framing, then `inhale` p is equivalent in both approaches. However, we need to prove a stronger fact that accounts for the permissions we may have inhaled so far. In particular, as `inhale` $p_1 * p_2$ is implemented by first inhaling p_1 and then p_2, when we consider inhaling p_2 it may not be self-framing. However, the context will have inhaled sufficient permissions that it is framed in that context. We prove that the VCs are equivalent in a context in which the inhale is framed.

Lemma 7. *If* $\textit{syn\_framed}_{\psi}(p)$ *and* $\textit{syn\_framed}_{\psi \cup \textit{foot}(p)}(A)$, *then*

$$wp_{\text{ch}}(\textit{assume}(\psi < \mathcal{P});\ \texttt{inhale}\ p, \llbracket A\rrbracket) \iff wp_{\text{ch}}(\textit{assume}(\psi < \mathcal{P}), \llbracket wp_{\text{sl}}(\texttt{inhale}\ p, A)\rrbracket)$$

Proof. By induction on p. The $*$ case uses Lemma 6.1 to rearrange the program so that the inductive hypothesis can be used on q_2, and Lemma 6.2. is used to rearrange separation logic assertion:

$$\begin{aligned}
& wp_{\text{ch}}(\texttt{assume}(\psi < \mathcal{P});\ \texttt{inhale}\ q_1 * q_2, \llbracket Q \rrbracket) \\
\Leftrightarrow\ & wp_{\text{ch}}(\texttt{assume}(\psi < \mathcal{P}); \texttt{inhale}\ q_1; \texttt{assume}(\psi \cup \mathsf{foot}(q_1) < \mathcal{P}); \texttt{inhale}\ q_2, \llbracket Q \rrbracket) \\
\Leftrightarrow\ & wp_{\text{ch}}(\texttt{assume}(\psi < \mathcal{P}); \texttt{inhale}\ q_1; \texttt{assume}(\psi \cup \mathsf{foot}(q_1) < \mathcal{P}); \llbracket q_2 \mathrel{-\!\!*} Q \rrbracket) \\
\Leftrightarrow\ & wp_{\text{ch}}(\texttt{assume}(\psi < \mathcal{P}); \texttt{inhale}\ q_1, \llbracket q_2 \mathrel{-\!\!*} Q \rrbracket) \\
\Leftrightarrow\ & wp_{\text{ch}}(\texttt{assume}(\psi < \mathcal{P}), \llbracket q_1 \mathrel{-\!\!*} (q_2 \mathrel{-\!\!*} Q) \rrbracket) \\
\Leftrightarrow\ & wp_{\text{ch}}(\texttt{assume}(\psi < \mathcal{P}), \llbracket (q_1 * q_2) \mathrel{-\!\!*} Q \rrbracket) \\
\Leftrightarrow\ & wp_{\text{ch}}(\texttt{assume}(\psi < \mathcal{P}), \llbracket wp_{\text{sl}}(\texttt{inhale}\ q_1 * q_2, Q) \rrbracket)
\end{aligned}$$

The *acc* case uses Lemma 6.3 to show that their is no difference between havocing just the inhaled location, and havoc all locations that you do not have permissions to. Assume that $\mathcal{P}[\llbracket E \rrbracket.f] = 0$,

$$\begin{aligned}
& wp_{\text{ch}}(\texttt{assume}(\psi < \mathcal{P}); \texttt{inhale}\ acc(E.f, \pi), \llbracket Q \rrbracket) \\
\Leftrightarrow\ & wp_{\text{ch}}(\texttt{assume}(\psi < \mathcal{P}); \texttt{inhale}\ acc(E.f, \pi); \texttt{havoc}(\mathcal{H}[\overline{\mathcal{P}}]), \llbracket Q \rrbracket) \\
\Leftrightarrow\ & wp_{\text{ch}}(\texttt{assume}(\psi < \mathcal{P}); \mathcal{P}[\llbracket E \rrbracket.f] := \pi; \texttt{havoc}(\mathcal{H}[\llbracket E \rrbracket.f]); \texttt{havoc}(\mathcal{H}[\overline{\mathcal{P}}]), \llbracket Q \rrbracket) \\
\Leftrightarrow\ & wp_{\text{ch}}(\texttt{assume}(\psi < \mathcal{P}); \texttt{havoc}(\mathcal{H}[\overline{\mathcal{P}}]); \mathcal{P}[\llbracket E \rrbracket.f] := \pi, \llbracket Q \rrbracket) \\
\Leftrightarrow\ & wp_{\text{ch}}(\texttt{assume}(\psi < \mathcal{P}), \llbracket acc(E.f, \pi) \mathrel{-\!\!*} Q \rrbracket) \\
\Leftrightarrow\ & wp_{\text{ch}}(\texttt{assume}(\psi < \mathcal{P}), \llbracket wp_{\text{sl}}(\texttt{inhale}\ acc(E.f, \pi), Q) \rrbracket)
\end{aligned}$$

Case where $\mathcal{P}[\llbracket E \rrbracket.f] \neq 0$ follows similiarly.

Corollary 2. *If p is syntactically self-framing, then equiv(`inhale` p).*

Proof. As we only consider self-framing post-conditions follows trivially from previous lemma.

Remark 1. Without the syntactic self-framing requirement on inhales, it would be unsound to break `inhale` $A * B$ into `inhale` A; `inhale` B. In particular, in the Chalice semantics, the behaviour of `inhale`$(A * B)$ and `inhale`$(B * A)$ are different. For instance, consider `inhale`$(x.f = 3 * acc(x.f))$ and `inhale`$(acc(x.f) * x.f = 3)$.

$$\begin{aligned}
wp_{\text{ch}}(\texttt{inhale}(x.f = 3 * acc(x.f)), \llbracket x.f = 3 \rrbracket) &\iff x.f \neq 3 \\
wp_{\text{ch}}(\texttt{inhale}(acc(x.f) * x.f = 3), \llbracket x.f = 3 \rrbracket) &\iff \mathsf{true}
\end{aligned}$$

The translation given by Smans *et al.* [15] does not suffer this problem as it does the analogue of `inhale` in a single step. However, it checks self-framing in a similar way, and thus would also rule out the first `inhale`.

In this section, we have shown that the encoding of `inhale` and `exhale` into Boogie2 is equivalent to the separation logic weakest pre-condition semantics. As a consequence, we have shown two things: (1) our model accurately reflects the semantics of Chalice's assertion language, and (2) a fragment of separation logic can be directly encoded into Chalice precisely preserving its semantics.

5 Related Work

In this paper, we have provided a version of separation logic [5,11], which allows arbitrary expressions over the heap. We have modified the standard presentation of an object-oriented heap for separation logic [12] to separate the notion of access from value. Most previous separation logics have combined these two concepts. One notable exception is the separation logic for reasoning about Cminor [1]. This logic also separates the ability to access memory, the mask, from the actual contents of the heap. The choice in this work was to enable a reuse of a existing operational semantics for Cminor, rather than producing a new operational semantics involving partial states. In the Cminor separation logic, they do not consider the definition of magic wand, or weakest pre-condition semantics, which is crucial for the connection with Chalice [9].

Smans' original presentation of IDF was implemented in a tool, VeriCool [15,14]. The results in this paper, should also apply to the verification conditions generated by VeriCool. In recent work, Smans *et al.* [16] describe an IDF approach as a separation logic. However, they do not present a model of the assertions, just the VCs of their analog of inhale and exhale. Hence, it does not provide the strong connection between the VCs and the model of separation logic that we have provided.

There have been many other approaches based on dynamic frames [6,7] to enable automated verification with standard verification tool chains, for instance, Dafny [13] and Region Logic [2]. Like Chalice, both also encoded into Boogie2. The connection between these logics and separation logic is less clear. They explicitly talk about the footprint of an assertion, rather than implicitly. However, our new separation logic might facilitate greater comparison.

6 Extensions and Applications

In this section we highlight the potential impact of our connection between separation logic and the implicit dynamic frames of Chalice, by explaining several ways in which ideas from one world can be transferred to the other.

Supporting Extra Connectives. Our extended separation logic supports many more connectives than have previously existed in implicit dynamic frames logics. For example, the support for a "magic wand" in the logic (or indeed an unrestricted logical implication) is a novel contribution, which paves the way for investigating how to extend Chalice to support this much-richer assertion language. While a formal semantics for the magic wand does not immediately tell us how to implement inhaling and exhaling such assertions correctly, it provides us with a means of formally evaluating such a proposal. Furthermore, our direct semantics for the assertion logic of Chalice provides a means of judging whether a particular implementation is faithful to the intended logical semantics.

Evaluating the Chalice Implementation. Various design decisions in the Chalice methodology can be evaluated using our formal semantics. For example,

Chalice deals with potential interference from other threads by "havocing" heap locations whenever permission to the location is newly granted. An alternative design would be to "havoc" such locations whenever all permission to them was *given up* in an exhale, instead. This would provide different weakest pre-conditions for Chalice commands, and it would be interesting to investigate what differences this design decision makes from a theoretical perspective. Our results provide the necessary basis for such investigations.

Separation logics typically feature recursive (abstract) predicates in their assertion language. The Chalice tool also includes an experimental implementation of recursive predicates (without arguments), along with the use of "functions" in specifications to describe properties of the state in a way which could support information hiding. In the course of investigating how to extend our results to handle predicates in the assertion logics, we discovered that the current approach to handling predicates/functions in Chalice is actually unsound in the presence of functions and the decision to havoc on inhales rather than exhales. We, and the Chalice authors, are now working on a redesign of Chalice predicates based on our findings. As above, the formal semantics and connections we have provided give us excellent tools for evaluating such a redesign.

Implementing Separation Logic. One exciting outcome of the results we have presented is that a certain fragment of separation logic specifications can be directly represented in implicit dynamic frames and automatically verified using the Chalice tool. This is a consequence of three results:

1. We have shown that our total heap semantics for separation logic coincides with its prior partial heaps semantics.
2. We have shown that we can replace all "points-to" predicates with logical primitives from implicit dynamic frames, preserving semantics.
3. We have shown that the Chalice weakest-pre-condition calculation agrees with the weakest pre-conditions used in separation logic verification.

The critical aspect which is missing is the treatment of predicates - once we can extend our correspondence results to handle recursively-defined predicates in the logics (which are used in virtually all separation logic verification examples), then it will be possible to exploit our work to use Chalice to implement separation logic verification. This will open up many interesting practical areas of work, in comparing the performance and encodings of verification problems between Chalice and separation logic based tools.

Old Expressions. We have also observed that the use of a total heap semantics seems to make it easy to support certain extra specification features in a separation logic assertion language. In particular, the use of "old" expressions in method contracts (allowing post-conditions to explicitly mention values of variables and heap locations in the pre-state of the method call) is awkward to support in a partial heaps semantics, since it expresses relationships between partial heap fragments which may not have obviously-related domains. As a consequence, separation logic based tools typically do not support this feature.

However, with our total heap semantics it seems rather easy to evaluate old expressions by simply replacing our total heap with a copy of the pre-heap. While the details remain to be worked out, this seems to suggest that both separation logic and implicit dynamic frames can be made more expressive using the connections proved in our work.

Acknowledgements

We thank Mike Dodds, David Naumann, Ioannis Kassios, Peter Müller and Sophia Drossopoulou for feedback on drafts of this paper.

References

1. Appel, A.W., Blazy, S.: Separation logic for small-step Cminor. In: Schneider, K., Brandt, J. (eds.) TPHOLs 2007. LNCS, vol. 4732, pp. 5–21. Springer, Heidelberg (2007)
2. Banerjee, A., Naumann, D., Rosenberg, S.: Regional logic for local reasoning about global invariants. In: Ryan, M. (ed.) ECOOP 2008. LNCS, vol. 5142, pp. 387–411. Springer, Heidelberg (2008)
3. Bornat, R., Calcagno, C., O'Hearn, P., Parkinson, M.: Permission accounting in separation logic. In: POPL, pp. 259–270 (2005)
4. Boyland, J.: Checking interference with fractional permissions. In: Cousot, R. (ed.) SAS 2003. LNCS, vol. 2694, Springer, Heidelberg (2003)
5. Ishtiaq, S.S., O'Hearn, P.W.: BI as an assertion language for mutable data structures. In: POPL, pp. 14–26. ACM Press, New York (2001)
6. Kassios, I.T.: Dynamic frames: Support for framing, dependencies and sharing without restrictions. In: Misra, J., Nipkow, T., Karakostas, G. (eds.) FM 2006. LNCS, vol. 4085, pp. 268–283. Springer, Heidelberg (2006)
7. Kassios, I.T.: A Theory of Object Oriented Refinement. PhD thesis (2006)
8. Leino, K.R.M.: This is Boogie 2, `http://research.microsoft.com/en-us/um/people/leino/papers.html`
9. Leino, K.R.M., Müller, P.: A basis for verifying multi-threaded programs. In: Castagna, G. (ed.) ESOP 2009. LNCS, vol. 5502, pp. 378–393. Springer, Heidelberg (2009)
10. O'Hearn, P.W.: Resources, concurrency and local reasoning. In: TCS (2007)
11. O'Hearn, P.W., Reynolds, J.C., Yang, H.: Local reasoning about programs that alter data structures. In: Fribourg, L. (ed.) CSL 2001 and EACSL 2001. LNCS, vol. 2142, pp. 1–19. Springer, Heidelberg (2001)
12. Parkinson, M.: Local Reasoning for Java. PhD thesis, University of Cambridge (November 2005)
13. Rustan, K., Leino, M.: Dafny: An automatic program verifier for functional correctness. In: Clarke, E.M., Voronkov, A. (eds.) LPAR-16 2010. LNCS, vol. 6355, pp. 348–370. Springer, Heidelberg (2010)
14. Smans, J.: Specification and Automatic Verification of Frame Properties for Java-like Programs (Specificatie en automatische verificatie van frame eigenschappen voor Java-achtige programma's). PhD thesis, FWO-Vlaanderen (May 2009)
15. Smans, J., Jacobs, B., Piessens, F.: Implicit dynamic frames: Combining dynamic frames and separation logic. In: Drossopoulou, S. (ed.) ECOOP 2009. LNCS, vol. 5653, pp. 148–172. Springer, Heidelberg (2009)
16. Smans, J., Jacobs, B., Piessens, F.: Heap-dependent expressions in separation logic. In: Hatcliff, J., Zucca, E. (eds.) FMOODS 2010. LNCS, vol. 6117, pp. 170–185. Springer, Heidelberg (2010)

Precise Interprocedural Analysis in the Presence of Pointers to the Stack

Pascal Sotin and Bertrand Jeannet

INRIA
{Pascal.Sotin,Bertrand.Jeannet}@inria.fr

Abstract. In a language with procedures calls and pointers as parameters, an instruction can modify memory locations anywhere in the call-stack. The presence of such side effects breaks most generic interprocedural analysis methods, which assume that only the top of the stack may be modified. We present a method that addresses this issue, based on the definition of an equivalent local semantics in which writing through pointers has a local effect on the stack. Our second contribution in this context is an adequate representation of summary functions that models the effect of a procedure, not only on the values of its scalar and pointer variables, but also on the values contained in pointed memory locations. Our implementation in the interprocedural analyser PInterproc results in a verification tool that infers relational properties on the value of Boolean, numerical and pointer variables.

1 Introduction

Relational interprocedural analysis is a well-understood static analysis technique [7,26,20]. It consists in associating at each program point a *relation* between the input state and the current state of the current procedure, so that at the exit point of a procedure P one obtains its input/output *summary function* capturing the effect of a call to P. Interprocedural analysis is also a form of modular analysis that enables the analysis of recursive programs.

Applying it requires the ability to identify precisely the input context of a procedure in the program, that is, the relevant part of the call-context that influences the execution of the callee procedure, as well as the output context, that is, the part of the state-space that may be altered by the procedure. This might be more or less simple:

- it is simple for procedures taking integer parameters and returning integer results; summary functions are relations $R \subseteq \mathbb{Z}^n$
- if a procedure accesses and modifies global variables, these may be treated as implicit input/output parameters that are added to the explicit ones; this applies to procedures manipulating dynamically allocated objects, if the memory heap is viewed as a special global variable [25,17].

This paper addresses the case where procedures might take pointer parameters referring to stack variables, as in Fig. 2. This occurs in C/C++ programs, and in a weaker way in Pascal and Ada languages through reference parameter passing.

G. Barthe (Ed.): ESOP 2011, LNCS 6602, pp. 459–479, 2011.
© Springer-Verlag Berlin Heidelberg 2011

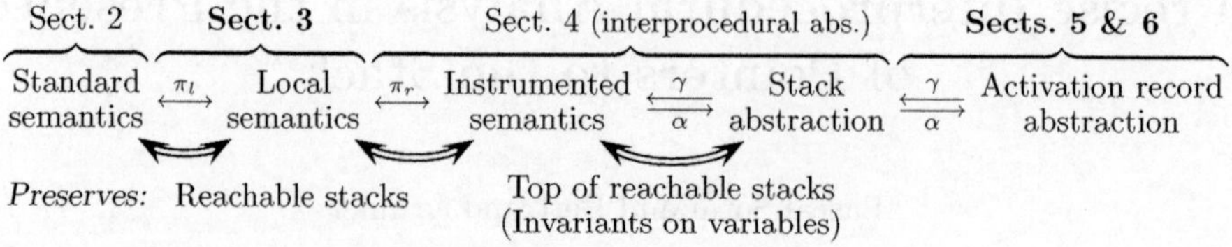

Fig. 1. Methodology followed in the paper

Pointers to the execution stack raise two difficulties in this context:

(*i*) the effect of an instruction `*p=*p+1` might modify a location anywhere in the stack, instead of being located in the top activation record;
(*ii*) aliasing of different pointer expressions referring to the same location.

Point (*i*) makes difficult to isolate precisely the effective input context of a procedure, keeping in mind that filtering out the irrelevant parts of the call-context is important for modularity and thus efficiency. This has been addressed in [2] for the simpler case of references, and in [31] in for general pointers, but in a less general way that us. Point (*ii*) is a widely studied problem in compiler optimisation and program verification. Points-to or alias analysis have been widely studied [13]. However, most work target compiler optimisation and the precision achieved is insufficient for program verification. Array and shape analyses [11,25,17], which may be seen as sophisticated alias analyses, target automatic program parallelization or program verification, but focus mainly on arrays or heap objects, and much less on pointers to the stack in an interprocedural context. We also observe that many established static analyzers avoid this specific problem: Astrée [8] inlines on the fly procedure calls and does not perform an interprocedural analysis. This is also the case for Fluctuat [9]. Caduceus [10], before being embedded in Frama-C, explicitly discarded pointers on the stack. On the other hand, PolySpace Verifier [24] has necessarily a specific treatment for them, but the technique is unknown (unpublished).

Our goal is thus to enhance existing interprocedural analysis that infers invariants on the values of scalar variables with the treatment of pointers to the execution stack. Typically, we want to infer an enough precise summary function for the `swap` procedure, in order to infer the postcondition below:

$$\{0 \leq x \leq 2y \leq 10\} \texttt{ swap(\&x,\&y) } \{0 \leq y \leq 2x \leq 10\}$$

Our approach is based on abstract interpretation [6]. We focus on pointers to the stack and we do not consider global variables, structured types and dynamic allocation; the combination with these features is discussed in the conclusion.

Our approach is original in several ways:

- our approach derives an effective analysis by decomposing it in the well-identified steps depicted on Fig. 1, and delays approximations on pointers and scalar variables to the last step, instead of mixing interprocedural and data abstractions;
- as a result, we perform in parallel an alias and a scalar analysis;

- we infer summary functions and invariance properties that are fully relational between alias properties (on pointers) and scalar properties (on Booleans and integers), and we define a symbolic representation for such properties;
- in the special case of Boolean programs, we prove our analysis to be exact.

Outline and contributions. Fig. 1 depicts graphically the methodology followed in the paper and emphasises (in bold font) our theoretical contributions. Sect. 2 describes the analysed language. Sect. 3 propose an alternative *local* semantics, in which the input context of a procedure is made explicit and the effect of a procedure is local (within the top of the activation stack). We prove this semantics to be equivalent to the standard one. Sect. 4 reminds how relational interprocedural analysis can be expressed as a stack abstraction [19], which allows us to formalize correctness proofs (available in [28]). It reduces the analysis on stacks to an analysis on activation records. Sect. 5 investigates the problem of representing efficiently sets and relations on activation records. Sect. 6 describes the abstraction of activation records with the BddApron library and shows an experiment with the PInterproc analyzer that we implemented. It discusses alternative abstract domains that lead to more classical analyses. Sect. 7 discusses related work and we draw some perspectives in Sect. 8.

2 The Language and Its Standard Semantics

We extend with pointers (Tab. 1) the language analysed by Interproc [16], which features procedures with call-by-value parameter passing, local variables, numerical and boolean expressions, assignments, conditionals and loops, see Figs. 2, 7 and 9. Our language excludes structured types and dynamically allocated objects.

We consider types of the form $\tau_0{*}^k = \tau_0 \overbrace{*\cdots*}^{k}$ and left values are of the form $*^k$ id, which can be found either on the left side of an assignment, or anywhere in expressions (like `**x + *y - 2`). We also have the nil pointer constant and the expression &id. Procedure calls have the form $\mathbf{y} = P(\mathbf{x})$, where $\mathbf{x}$ and $\mathbf{y}$ are the vectors of effective input and output parameters. Procedure definitions have the form

$$\begin{array}{l}\textbf{proc } P(fp_1 : t_1, \ldots, fp_m : t_m) : (fr_1 : t'_1, \ldots, fr_n : t'_n)\\ \textbf{var } z_1 : t''_1, \ldots, z_p : t''_p;\\ \textbf{begin} \ldots \textbf{end}\end{array}$$

where **fp** and **fr** are (vectors of) formal input and output parameters, **z** are the local variables, and **t**, **t'**, **t"** their associated type. We write $\mathbf{fp}^{(i)}$ for the ith component of the vector. The code of the full program is modelled with a Control Flow Graph (CFG), Fig. 2, in which an edge is either

- an intraprocedural edge $c \xrightarrow{\texttt{instr}} c'$ (test or assignment),
- a call edge $c \xrightarrow{\texttt{call y=}P\texttt{(x)}} s$ linking a *call point* c (in the caller) to the *start point* s of the callee,

Table 1. Language extension

(a) Types.

$\tau ::= \tau_0$	
$\mid \tau*$	
$\tau_0 ::=$ `bool`	
$\mid$ `int`	

(b) Expressions.

$\mathit{left} ::=$	id	variable
$\mid$	$*\mathit{left}$	dereferencing
$\mathit{expr} ::=$	left	read memory
$\mid$	&id	address taking
$\mid$	`nil`	nil pointer
$\mid$	...	

Table 2. Semantic domains

$$\overbrace{\langle n, F\rangle}^{\Gamma} \in \mathit{Stack} = \mathbb{N} \times (\mathbb{N} \to \mathit{Act})$$

$$\mathit{Act} = \mathit{Var} \to \overbrace{\mathit{Addr} \cup \mathit{Scalar}}^{\mathit{Val}}$$

$$\mathit{Addr} = (\mathbb{N} \times \mathit{Var}) \cup \{\mathit{nil}, \bot\}$$

$$\mathit{Scalar} = \mathbb{B} \cup \mathbb{Z}$$

```
proc swap(p:int*,q:int*) returns ()
var tmp:int;
begin            // (s)
    tmp = *p;
    *p = *q;
    *q = tmp;    // (e)
end
var a:int,b:int,
    x:int*,y:int*;
begin
  x=&a; y=&b; // (c1)
  swap(x,y);  // (r1)=(c2)
  swap(y,x);  // (r2)
end
```

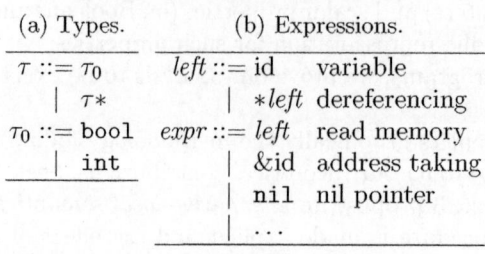

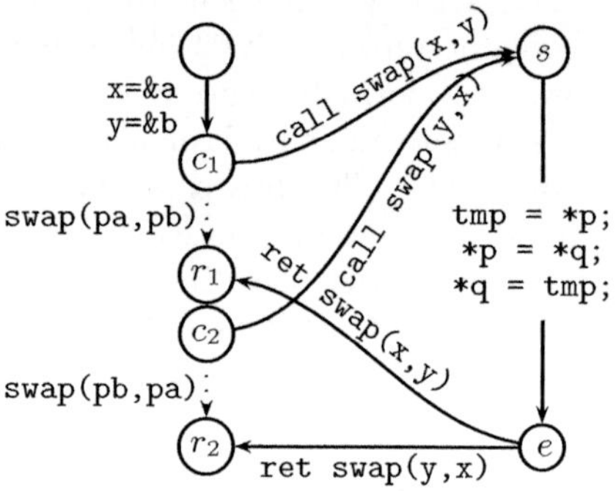

Fig. 2. Program example and Control Flow Graph (CFG)

– or a return edge $e \xrightarrow{\texttt{call y=}P(\texttt{x})} r$ linking the *exit point* e of the callee procedure to a *return point* r of the caller.

The return point associated to a call point c will be denoted by $\mathrm{ret}(c)$.

Semantics. The semantic domains are given on Tab. 2. A program state is a stack of activation records. A stack $\Gamma = \langle n, F\rangle$ is defined by its size n and a function $F : [1..n] \to \mathit{Act}$ that returns the activation record at the given index. An activation record contains the current control point encoded in a pc variable and the values of the local variables. A pointer value is either the null value *nil*, the special value $\bot$ denoting a pending pointer, or a normal address (n, id), referring to the variable id located at the index n. A pending pointer value $\bot$ typically occurs when a callee procedure returns a pointer to one of its local variables. We adopt the following alternative view of the stack:

$$\mathit{Stack} = \mathbb{N} \times \big(\mathbb{N} \to \overbrace{(\mathit{Var} \to \mathit{Val})}^{\mathit{Act}}\big) \simeq \mathbb{N} \times \big((\mathbb{N} \times \mathit{Var}) \to \mathit{Val}\big)$$

Tab. 3 defines the semantics of expressions. The semantics of a nil or a pending pointer dereference is undefined.

The semantics of the language is given as a transition system $(\mathit{Stack}, I, \leadsto)$, where $\leadsto$ is a transition relation on stacks and I is the set of initial stacks of height one. Tab. 4 defines $\leadsto$ for the interprocedural edges of the CFG. The call

Table 3. Standard semantics: expressions

$[\![left]\!]^{\mathcal{A}} : Stack \to \mathbb{N} \times Var$	Address of a left value
$[\![expr]\!]^{\mathcal{V}} : Stack \to (\mathbb{N} \times Var) \cup \{nil, \bot\} \cup Scalar$	Value of an expression
$[\![\mathrm{id}]\!]^{\mathcal{A}} = \langle n, \mathrm{id} \rangle$	$[\![left]\!]^{\mathcal{V}} = F([\![left]\!]^{\mathcal{A}})$
$[\![{*left}]\!]^{\mathcal{A}} = [\![left]\!]^{\mathcal{V}}$	$[\![\&\mathrm{id}]\!]^{\mathcal{V}} = [\![\mathrm{id}]\!]^{\mathcal{A}}$
when $[\![left]\!]^{\mathcal{V}} \notin \{nil, \bot\}$	$[\![\mathtt{nil}]\!]^{\mathcal{V}} = nil$
	(The argument $\Gamma = \langle n, F \rangle$ is implicit)

Table 4. Standard semantics: transitions

$$\frac{\begin{array}{ll} & F(n,\mathtt{pc}) = c \quad F'(n{+}1,\mathtt{pc}) = c' \\ \forall i, & F'(n{+}1,\mathbf{fp}^{(i)}) = F(n,\mathbf{x}^{(i)}) \\ \forall z \in Var_{\mathcal{T}*} \backslash \mathbf{fp}, & F'(n{+}1,z) = nil \\ \forall z \in Var_{\mathcal{T}_0} \backslash \mathbf{fp}, & F'(n{+}1,z) \in Scalar \\ \forall z \in Var, \forall k \leq n, & F'(k,z) = F(k,z) \end{array}}{\langle n, F \rangle \rightsquigarrow \langle n{+}1, F' \rangle} \qquad (\text{Call } c \xrightarrow{\mathtt{call\ y{:=}}P\mathtt{(x)}} c')$$

$$\frac{\begin{array}{c} F(n{+}1,\mathtt{pc}) = c \\ F' = F\left[\begin{array}{l} \langle n,\mathtt{pc} \rangle \mapsto c' \\ \langle n, \mathbf{y}^{(i)} \rangle \mapsto F(n{+}1,\mathbf{fr}^{(i)}) \end{array}\right] \\ F'' = F'[\ a \mapsto \bot \ \mathit{if}\ F'(a) = \langle n{+}1, \mathrm{id} \rangle\ ] \end{array}}{\langle n{+}1, F \rangle \rightsquigarrow \langle n, F'' \rangle} \qquad (\text{Ret } c \xrightarrow{\mathtt{ret\ y{:=}}P\mathtt{(x)}} c')$$

copies the effective parameters in the formal parameters. It also initializes the local variables of pointer type to *nil*. The return copies the formal results in the effective results, then it forgets the last activation record. Pointers to addresses of this activation record are turned to pending values. Intraprocedural edges generate simpler transitions, like choosing the next control point for tests, and updating the stack for assignments. In this semantics, undefinedness (comparison with a pending value or invalid dereference) generates a sink state without successors.

Analysis goal. Our aim is to perform a reachable state analysis of such programs and more precisely to compute for each program point an invariant on the values of variables. Formally, the set of reachable stacks is $Reach(I, \rightsquigarrow) = \{\Gamma \mid \exists \Gamma_0 \in I, \Gamma_0 \rightsquigarrow^* \Gamma\}$, and our goal is to compute the set of top activation records of these stack.

We want to apply relational interprocedural analysis methods for this purpose. As discussed in the introduction, this requires to identify the input context of a procedure, which may include in our case the content of a pointed location anywhere in the stack, which may be later modified by the procedure during its execution. In contrast, general interprocedural analysis techniques [20] assume that side-effects performed by a procedure are limited to the current activation record.

3 An Equivalent Local Semantics

The aim of this section is to define a *local* semantics in which the effect of a procedure is limited to the top activation record. The idea of this semantics, inspired by [2], is that a procedure works on local copies (called *external locations*) of the locations that it can reach with its pointer parameters.

The first challenge is to take into account aliasing properties between pointer parameters and to define a correct input parameter passing mechanism. Consider

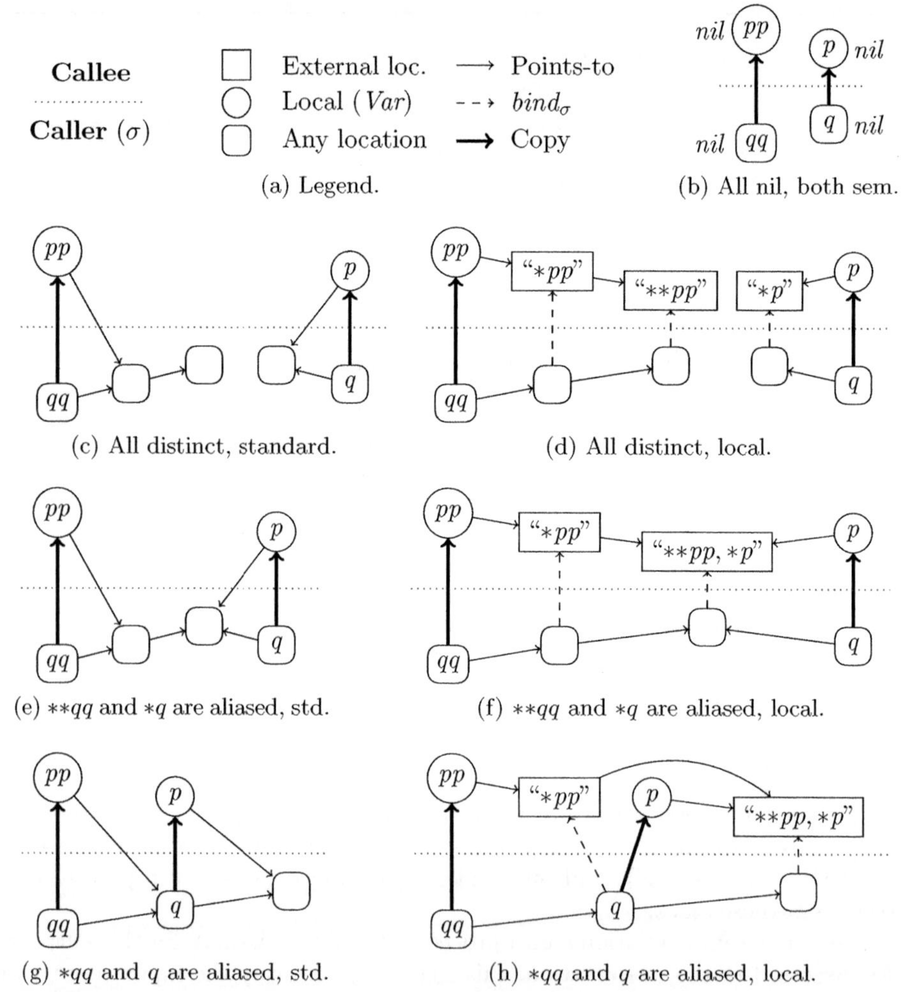

(a) Legend. (b) All nil, both sem.

(c) All distinct, standard. (d) All distinct, local.

(e) $**qq$ and $*q$ are aliased, std. (f) $**qq$ and $*q$ are aliased, local.

(g) $*qq$ and q are aliased, std. (h) $*qq$ and q are aliased, local.

Fig. 3. Procedure call in the standard and local semantics: call `f(qq,q)` to a procedure `f(int** pp, int* p)`

a call `f(qq,q)` to a procedure `f(int** pp, int* p)`. Fig. 3 considers different aliasing situation between qq and q in the caller, and the consequences on the set of external locations in the callee. We depict the situation on the left for the standard semantics, on the right for the local semantics. We will define a function *bind*, depicted with dashed arrows, that maps locations in the caller to external locations in the callee that are reachable from its input parameters. Figs. 3(g)(h) illustrates a non trivial situation: in the caller, qq points to q, but in the callee pp does not point to p.

The second point is then to define a correct return parameter passing mechanism. When the procedure f returns, the modifications on its external locations should be propagated back to the corresponding locations in the caller, which may be themselves local or external w.r.t. their own caller.

3.1 Local Semantics

Tab. 5 defines the semantic domains. Values can be stored as before in local variables, but also in external locations. These external locations are identified by the set of left values that refer to them at the beginning of the current procedure. Fig. 3 illustrates this naming scheme.

Table 5. Semantic domains

$$\begin{aligned} \Gamma \in \mathit{Stack} &= \mathit{Act}^\star \\ \sigma \in \mathit{Act} &= \mathit{Loc} \rightarrow \overbrace{\mathit{Loc} \cup \{\mathit{nil}, \bot\} \cup \mathit{Scalar}}^{\mathit{Val}} \\ l \in \mathit{Loc} &= \mathit{Var} \cup \mathit{External} \\ \mathit{External} &= \mathcal{P}(\mathit{Deref}) \\ \mathit{Deref} &= \{*^k \mathbf{fp}^{(i)}\} \end{aligned}$$

The evaluation of the expressions are the same as in Tab. 1b, except that left values are now all fetched in the top activation record σ. We have $[\![\mathit{left}]\!]^{\mathcal{V}}_\sigma = \sigma([\![\mathit{left}]\!]^{\mathcal{A}}_\sigma)$ and $[\![\mathrm{id}]\!]^{\mathcal{A}}_\sigma = \mathrm{id}$. The semantics of an interprocedural instruction is captured by a relation $R_{\mathrm{instr}}(\sigma, \sigma')$ between two top activation records.

Binding. The key point of the local semantics lies in the procedure calls and returns. The external locations (*ie.* local copies) have to be determined and valued at call time, then propagated back at return time.

The purpose of the function bind_σ is to map locations of the caller that can be reached by effective parameters to the external locations in the callee:

$$\begin{aligned} &\mathit{bind}_\sigma : \mathit{Loc}_{(\mathsf{Caller})} \rightarrow \mathit{External}_{(\mathsf{Callee})} \\ &\mathit{bind}_\sigma(l) = D \quad \text{if} \quad D = \left\{ *^k \, \mathbf{fp}^{(i)} \;\middle|\; [\![*^k \mathbf{x}^{(i)}]\!]^{\mathcal{V}}_\sigma = l \wedge k \geq 1 \right\} \neq \emptyset \end{aligned} \tag{1}$$

with $\sigma \in \mathit{Act}_{(\mathsf{Caller})}$ being the activation record at the call point. The function $\mathit{bind}_\sigma(l)$ binds a location l of the caller to the set of dereferences in the callee that can refer to it at call time. If this set is empty, $\mathit{bind}_\sigma(l)$ is undefined and l cannot be modified by the callee. The constraint $k \geq 1$ reflects the fact that modifications of the formal parameters do not alter the effective parameters (call-by-value). This function is injective and can be reversed into the function $\mathit{bind}_\sigma^{-1}$. Fig. 3 depicts bind_σ for different contexts σ.

Table 6. Local semantics: transitions

$$\widetilde{bind_\sigma}(v) = \begin{cases} bind_\sigma(v) & \text{if } v \in Loc \\ v & \text{otherwise} \end{cases} \qquad \widetilde{bind_\sigma^{-1}}(v) = \begin{cases} bind_\sigma^{-1}(v) & \text{if } v \in \mathcal{P}(Deref) \\ \bot & \text{if } v \in Var \\ v & \text{otherwise} \end{cases}$$

(Pass) (Pass^{-1})

$$\frac{R^+_{\mathbf{y}:=P(\mathbf{x})}(c)(\sigma,\sigma') \begin{cases} \sigma(\mathrm{pc}) = c \wedge \sigma'(\mathrm{pc}) = c' \\ \forall i, & \sigma'(\mathbf{fp}^{(i)}) = \widetilde{bind_\sigma}(\sigma(\mathbf{x}^{(i)})) \\ \forall e \in dom(bind_\sigma^{-1}), & \sigma'(e) = bind_\sigma \circ \sigma \circ bind_\sigma^{-1}(e) \\ \forall z \in Var_{\tau *} \backslash \mathbf{fp}, & \sigma'(z) = nil \\ \forall z \in Var_{\tau_0} \backslash \mathbf{fp}, & \sigma'(z) \in Scalar \end{cases}}{\Gamma.\sigma \rightarrow \Gamma.\sigma.\sigma'}$$

(CallL $c \xrightarrow{\texttt{call } \mathbf{y}=P(\mathbf{x})} c'$)

$$\frac{R^-_{\mathbf{y}:=P(\mathbf{x})}(c)(\sigma,\sigma',\sigma'') \begin{cases} \sigma(\mathrm{pc}) = c \wedge \sigma'(\mathrm{pc}) = c' \wedge \sigma''(\mathrm{pc}) = \mathrm{ret}(c) \\ \sigma''_{\mathrm{side}} = \sigma \left[l \mapsto \widetilde{bind_\sigma^{-1}} \circ \sigma' \circ bind_\sigma(l) \;\middle|\; l \in dom(bind_\sigma) \right] \\ \sigma'' = \sigma''_{\mathrm{side}} \left[\mathbf{y}^{(i)} \mapsto \widetilde{bind_\sigma^{-1}}(\sigma'(\mathbf{fr}^{(i)})) \right] \end{cases}}{\Gamma.\sigma.\sigma' \rightarrow \Gamma.\sigma''}$$

(RetL $c' \xrightarrow{\texttt{ret } \mathbf{y}=P(\mathbf{x})} \mathrm{ret}(c)$)

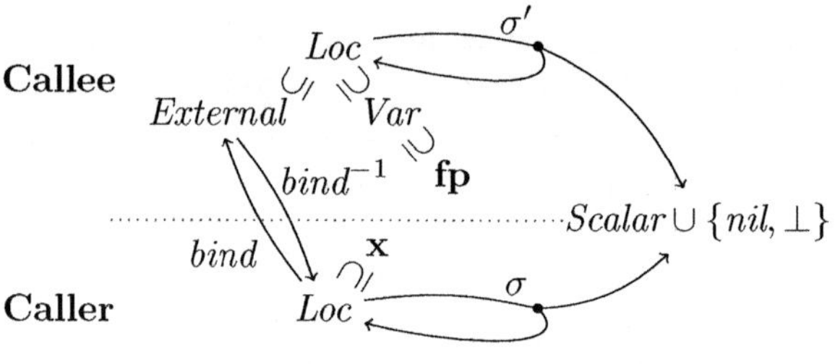

Fig. 4. Binding

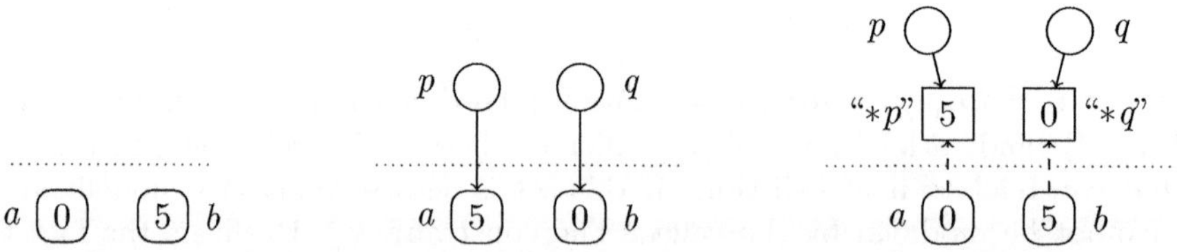

(a) Before call. (b) Before return, standard. (c) Before return, local.

Fig. 5. Standard and local stack before returning from `swap(&a,&b)`

Procedure calls and returns. Tab. 6 formalizes the transitions, and Fig. 4 illustrates the relationships between the involved sets and functions.

During a procedure call, a new activation record σ' is pushed on the stack, and initialized with the adequate values in the caller (parameters, external locations). The return operation first propagates the side effects by copying back the externals, then copies the return values and pops the activation record. The copies between caller and callee rely on the functions $\widetilde{bind_\sigma}$ and $\widetilde{bind_\sigma^{-1}}$ which take care of address conversion.

3.2 Preservation of Properties by the Local Semantics

Proving that the standard and local semantics are equivalent w.r.t. reachability properties raises a technical difficulty: side-effects due to pointers to the stacks are propagated immediately in the standard semantics, whereas this propagation is delayed until procedure return in the local semantics, as illustrated on Fig.5.

To deal with this, we define a function that "projects" a local stack into a standard stack and takes care of the above-mentioned propagation. We first define a function $address : \mathbb{N} \times Loc \to \mathbb{N} \times Var$ that returns the original variable in the stack referred to by a location at the ith activation record in a local stack $\sigma_1 \dots \sigma_n$:

$$address(i,l) = \begin{cases} address(i-1, bind^{-1}_{\sigma_{i-1}}(l)) & \text{if } l \in External \\ \langle i, l \rangle & \text{if } l \in Var \end{cases}$$

This function is then generalized to values:

$$\widetilde{address}(i,v) = \begin{cases} address(i,v) & \text{when } v \in Loc \\ v & \text{when } v \in \{nil, \bot\} \cup Scalar \end{cases}$$

We last define a function that assigns values to variables in a standard stack, possibly by searching the external location representing it at the highest index in the local stack:

$$value(i,z) = \begin{cases} value(i+1, bind_{\sigma_i}(z)) & \text{if } z \in dom(bind_{\sigma_i}) \wedge i \neq n \\ \widetilde{address}(i, \sigma_i(z)) & \text{otherwise} \end{cases}$$

Definition 1. *The projection function* $\pi_l : Stack_{ins} \to Stack_{std}$ *is defined by*
$$\pi_l(\sigma_1 \dots \sigma_n) = \langle n, F \rangle \text{ where } F(i,z) = value(i,z)$$

π_l is not injective because a local stack keeps track of past values of variables when these are copied in external locations. For instance, if one considers the local stack on Fig. 5c, modifying the value of location a does not modify its image by π.

Thm. 1 states that both transition systems behave the same way (proof in appendix). We can thus compute the exact reachability set in the standard semantics by computing it in the local semantics and projecting the result (Cor. 1).

Theorem 1. $\pi_l(i) = s \Rightarrow \begin{cases} \forall s', s \rightsquigarrow s' \Rightarrow \exists i', i \to i' \wedge \pi_l(i') = s' \\ \forall i', i \to i' \Rightarrow \exists s', s \rightsquigarrow s' \wedge \pi_l(i') = s' \end{cases}$

Corollary 1. $Reach(I, \rightsquigarrow) = \pi_l(Reach(I, \to))$

4 Interprocedural Abstraction

The previous section defined a local semantics in which side-effects involve only the top of the stack, so as to enable the application of relational interprocedural analysis techniques, which manipulate *relations* between activation records (but not relations between stacks). In this section, we formalize a relational interprocedural analysis based on the local semantics.

As explained in the introduction, relational interprocedural analysis associates at each program point a *relation* between the input state and the current state of the current procedure, so that the exit point of a procedure contains its input/output *summary*. Fig. 6 illustrates the use of the summary X_e which captures the effect of a call to P_j to obtain the relation X_r at the return point.

We follow the formalization of [19], that reformulates classical presentations [7,26,20] by deriving relational interprocedural analysis as an abstract interpretation of the concrete (local effects) semantics. The advantage of this formalization is twofold:

- it allows to derive automatically abstract transfer functions and to prove their correctness; this is not obvious when the input and output parameter passing mechanisms are as complex as in Tab. 6; for instance [20] does not investigate this issue.
- it separates the abstraction made by the interprocedural analysis method from the abstraction performed on activation records, as depicted on Fig. 1.

Relational instrumentation. Establishing a relation between the input and the current state at any point of a procedure requires to memorize the input state. We thus consider an semantics on instrumented pairs $(\sigma^0, \sigma) \in Act^2$ where σ_0 is the input state. Alternatively (as in [19]), it can be seen as introducing copies $\mathbf{fp}_0$ and $\mathbf{l}_0$ of the formal parameters and external locations in σ.

Formally, this *relational instrumentation* is defined from any local transition system $(Act^*, I, \rightarrow)$ by a transition system $((Act \times Act)^*, I', \hookrightarrow)$ where $I' = \{(\sigma, \sigma) \mid \sigma \in I\}$ and $\hookrightarrow$ is defined by the rules of Tab. 7. It is clear that there is a one-to-one correspondence between the executions of the transition

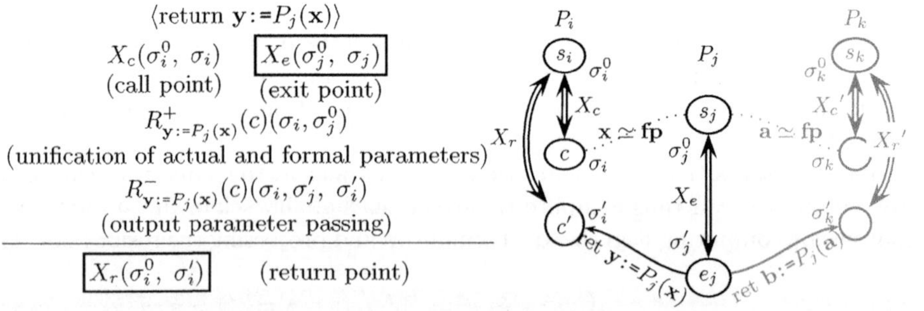

Fig. 6. Procedure return in relational interprocedural analysis. The relation X_r at return point is obtained by a (special) composition of relations X_c and X_e.

Table 7. Relational instrumentation for interprocedural analysis

$$\frac{\Gamma.\sigma \to \Gamma.\sigma'}{\Upsilon.\langle\sigma^0,\sigma\rangle \hookrightarrow \Upsilon.\langle\sigma^0,\sigma'\rangle} \text{ (IntraI)}$$

$$\frac{\Gamma.\sigma \to \Gamma.\sigma.\sigma'}{\Upsilon.\langle\sigma^0,\sigma\rangle \hookrightarrow \Upsilon.\langle\sigma^0,\sigma\rangle.\langle\sigma',\sigma'\rangle} \text{ (CallI)} \qquad \frac{\Gamma.\sigma.\sigma' \to \Gamma.\sigma''}{\Upsilon.\langle\sigma^0,\sigma\rangle.\langle\sigma^{0'},\sigma'\rangle \hookrightarrow \Upsilon.\langle\sigma^0,\sigma''\rangle} \text{ (RetI)}$$

Table 8. Abstract postcondition defining a forward semantics on activation records

$post^\sharp(\tau) : \mathcal{P}(Act^2) \to \mathcal{P}(Act^2)$ defined by $Y^\sharp = post^\sharp(\tau)(X^\sharp)$ with

$$\tau = c \xrightarrow{\texttt{instr}} c' \qquad Y^\sharp = \left\{ \langle\sigma^0,\sigma'\rangle \,\middle|\, \begin{array}{c} \langle\sigma^0,\sigma\rangle \in X^\sharp \\ R_{\texttt{instr}}(c,c')(\sigma,\sigma') \end{array} \right\} \tag{2}$$

$$\tau = c \xrightarrow{\texttt{call y=}P_j\texttt{(x)}} s_j \qquad Y^\sharp = \left\{ \langle\sigma_j,\sigma_j\rangle \,\middle|\, \begin{array}{c} \langle\sigma^0,\sigma\rangle \in X^\sharp \\ R^+_{\mathbf{y}=P(\mathbf{x})}(c)(\sigma,\sigma_j) \end{array} \right\} \tag{3}$$

$$\tau = e_j \xrightarrow{\texttt{ret y=}P_j\texttt{(x)}} \mathrm{ret}(c) \quad Y^\sharp = \left\{ \langle\sigma^0,\sigma'\rangle \,\middle|\, \begin{array}{c} \langle\sigma^0,\sigma\rangle \in X^\sharp \wedge \langle\sigma_j^0,\sigma_j\rangle \in X^\sharp \\ R^+_{\mathbf{y}=P(\mathbf{x})}(c)(\sigma,\sigma_j^0) \\ R^-_{\mathbf{y}=P(\mathbf{x})}(c)(\sigma,\sigma_j,\sigma') \end{array} \right\} \tag{4}$$

systems $\to$ and $\hookrightarrow$. The second important point is that all stacks reachable by $\hookrightarrow$ are coherent stacks (see Definition 2).

Definition 2 (Coherent stack). *Given a local semantics* $(Act^*, I, \to)$*, an instrumented stack* $\Upsilon = \langle\sigma_1^0,\sigma_1\rangle \ldots \langle\sigma_n^0,\sigma_n\rangle$ *in* $(Act^2)^\star$ *is* coherent *if* $\forall i < n :$ $R^+(\sigma_i, \sigma_{i+1}^0)$*, where* $R^+(\sigma,\sigma') = \exists\Gamma : \Gamma.\sigma \to \Gamma.\sigma.\sigma'$.

Reachable stacks are coherent because initial stacks are so, and this property is preserved by all transitions in Tab. 7. If $R^+(\sigma,\sigma')$, we say that σ is a *valid call-context* for σ'. We write $\mathcal{C}((Act^2)^\star)$ for the set of coherent stacks.

Stack abstraction and induced forward semantics. The stack abstraction consists in collapsing sets of stacks into sets of activation records, and conversely in using the coherence property to rebuild stacks. We define the Galois connection $\mathcal{P}(\mathcal{C}((Act^2)^\star)) \underset{\alpha}{\overset{\gamma}{\leftrightarrows}} \mathcal{P}(Act^2)$ with:

$$\alpha(X) = \{v_i \mid v_1 \cdots v_n \in X \wedge 1 \le i \le n\} \tag{5}$$

$$\gamma(X^\sharp) = \left\{ v_1 \cdots v_n \,\middle|\, \begin{array}{c} \forall 1 \le i \le n, v_i \in X^\sharp \\ v_1 \cdots v_n \text{ is coherent} \end{array} \right\} \tag{6}$$

Let $post(c \xrightarrow{\texttt{instr}} c') : \mathcal{P}(\mathcal{C}((Act^2)^\star)) \to \mathcal{P}(\mathcal{C}((Act^2)^\star))$ be the concrete postcondition operator associated to a CFG edge, which can be deduced from Tabs. 6

and 7. The induced abstract postcondition is defined in Tab. 8. Notice that Eqn. (4) reformulates the rule of Fig. 6; the condition $R^+_{\mathtt{y}=P(\mathtt{x})}(c)(\sigma,\sigma_j^0)$ tells that σ is valid context for σ_j^0.

Proposition 1 (*post*$^\sharp$ is a correct approximation of *post*)
For any τ, $post^\sharp(\tau)\circ\alpha \sqsupseteq \alpha\circ post(\tau)$.
If τ is not a return transition, then $post^\sharp(\tau)\circ\alpha = \alpha\circ post(\tau)$.

Not surprisingly, the transfer function is less precise for return transitions. However, generalizing a result of [19] we get the following optimality result that reformulates in our setting the Interprocedural Coincidence Theorem of [20].

Theorem 2. $lfp(\lambda X^\sharp \,.\, \alpha(I')\sqcup post^\sharp(X^\sharp)) = \alpha(Reach(I,\hookrightarrow)) = hd(Reach(I,\hookrightarrow))$

This means that as far as we are interested in invariants at each control point, which concern only top activation records of reachable stacks, the stack abstraction is exact.

5 Representing Sets and Relations of Activation Records

Let us remind the steps we followed, depicted in Fig. 1: we defined in Sect. 3 a local semantics, to which we apply the stack abstraction defined in Sect. 4, so as to obtain a reachability analysis on sets of activation records. In this section, we discuss the encoding of activation records by functions of signature $Id \rightarrow \mathbb{B}\cup\mathbb{E}\cup\mathbb{Z}$, and their symbolic manipulation with logical formula ($\mathbb{E}$ denotes enumerated values). This is a first step toward an abstraction leading to an effective implementation.

External locations and pointers. The set of external locations appears both in the domain and the codomain of activation records σ, see Tab. 5. Two facts are important:

(1) the set of *potential* external locations $External = \mathcal{P}(\{*^k fp^{(i)}\})$ is finite;
(2) the set of *active* external locations depends through the function $bind_\sigma$ on the call-context σ, see Fig. 3, and it is much smaller.

(1) implies that the domain of σ is finite and that the value of pointers belongs to a finite set. (2) comes from two properties: for a given call-context σ,
- typing forbids some subsets: all elements of $bind_\sigma(l) \in External = \mathcal{P}(Deref)$ represent aliased dereferences and thus have the same type;
- for two locations $l_1 \neq l_2$, $bind_\sigma(l_1)$ and $bind_\sigma(l_2)$ are disjoints.

We thus pick a representative for each set with a function $repr : \mathcal{P}(Deref) \rightarrow Deref$ defined by $repr(D) = \min_\preceq D$ with $*^{k_1}fp^{(i_1)} \preceq *^{k_2}fp^{(i_2)} \Leftrightarrow i_1 \leq i_2$. The order $\preceq$ is a total order on D because of the above-mentioned typing property.

As a result, an activation record can be represented with a function of signature $Id \rightarrow \mathbb{B}\cup\mathbb{E}\cup\mathbb{Z}$ with $Id = Var \cup External$ and $\mathbb{E} = \{nil\}\cup Var \cup External$.

Concerning the number of external locations, in a procedure of signature $(fp^{(1)} : \tau_0 *^{k_1}, \ldots, fp^{(n)} : \tau_0 *^{k_n})$ in which all scalars pointed by formal parameters

```
proc swapi(p:int**,q:int**)
begin
  **p = **p + 1;
  **q = **q + 1;
  (*p,*q) = (*q,*p);
end
```

$$\mathsf{p}=\mathsf{p}_0=\&\text{“}{*}\mathsf{p}\text{”} \wedge \text{“}{*}\mathsf{p}\text{”}_0=\&\text{“}{*}{*}\mathsf{p}\text{”} \wedge \text{“}{*}{*}\mathsf{p}\text{”}_0=10\wedge$$
$$\mathsf{q}=\mathsf{q}_0=\&\text{“}{*}\mathsf{q}\text{”} \wedge \text{“}{*}\mathsf{q}\text{”}_0=\&\text{“}{*}{*}\mathsf{q}\text{”} \wedge \text{“}{*}{*}\mathsf{q}\text{”}_0=20\wedge$$
$$\text{“}{*}\mathsf{p}\text{”}=\&\text{“}{*}{*}\mathsf{q}\text{”} \wedge \text{“}{*}\mathsf{q}\text{”}=\&\text{“}{*}{*}\mathsf{p}\text{”}\wedge$$
$$\text{“}{*}{*}\mathsf{p}\text{”}=\text{“}{*}{*}\mathsf{p}\text{”}_0+1 \wedge \text{“}{*}{*}\mathsf{q}\text{”}=\text{“}{*}{*}\mathsf{q}\text{”}_0+1$$

(a) At exit point: logical representation

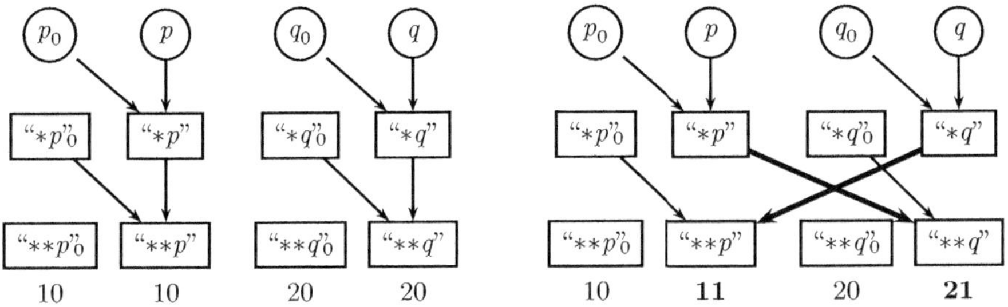

(b) At start point (c) At exit point

Fig. 7. Duplication of locations and examples of a summary function

have the same type τ_0, we have thus $\sum_{1\leq i\leq n} k_i$ external locations, which are all active if there is no aliasing at all. If there are several scalar types involved, we sum up the sums associated to each scalar type.

Representing sets. Our logical formula will use the following atoms:

$p=\&\mathtt{x}$	p points to variable x	$l_1=l_2$	l_1 and l_2 have same value
$p=\&l$	p points to location l	$l=7$	location l contains scalar 7

For example, we can describe the set of activation records

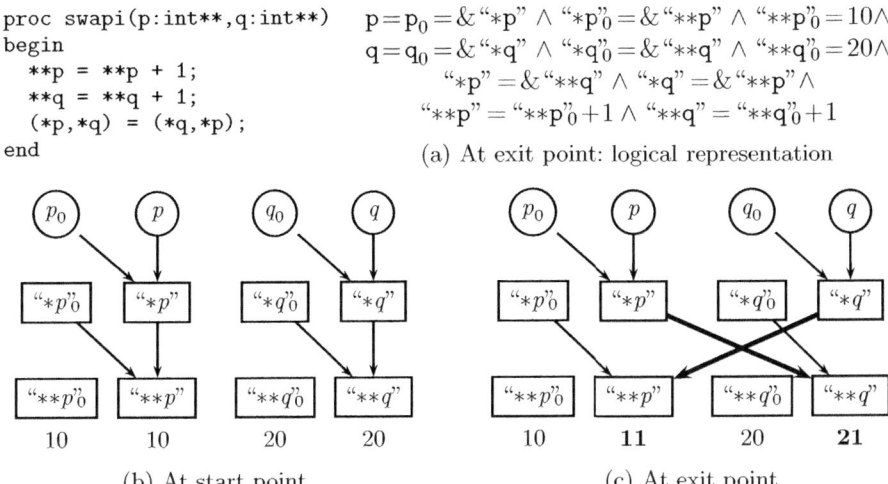

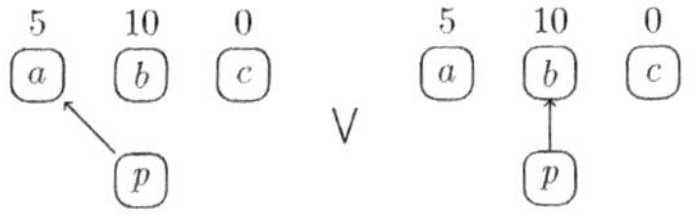

with $X = (\mathsf{p}=\&\mathsf{a} \vee \mathsf{p}=\&\mathsf{b})\wedge$
$\mathsf{a}=5 \wedge \mathsf{b}=10 \wedge \mathsf{c}=0$

Instrumented activation records. We actually represent pairs $\langle\sigma^0,\sigma\rangle$ of activation records in Tab. 8 with single activation records containing copies $\mathbf{fp}_0$ and $\mathbf{l}_0$ of formal parameters and external locations. Fig. 7 illustrates this point. Fig. 7b depicts the activation record at the start point of the procedure, and Fig. 7c shows the modified values (in bold lines) at the exit point. Fig. 7a represent it as a logical formula. We remind that keeping the values of locations $\mathbf{fp}_0$ and $\mathbf{l}_0$ will allow to select valid calling context for procedure return, see Fig. 6.

Representing relations. In Tab. 8, postconditions associated to call and return are based on the relation $R^+(\sigma,\sigma')$ defined in Tab. 6 that relates a call-context to the initial activation record in the callee. We illustrate the transcription of this relation with a quantifier-free logical formula. Consider the function

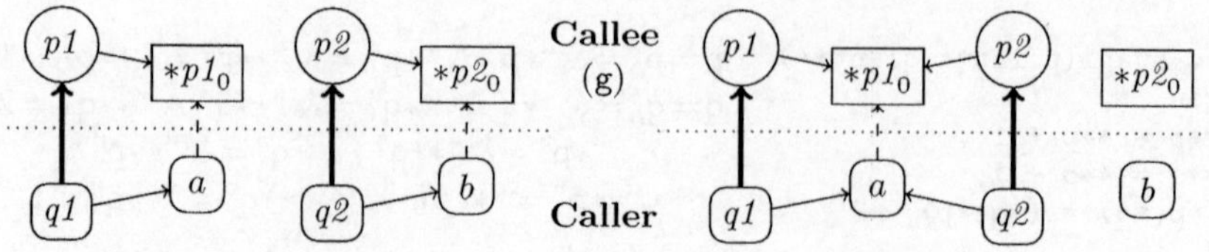

Fig. 8. Distinct aliasing, distinct bindings

`g(int* p1, int* p2)` and a call instruction `g(q1,q2)` in the context depicted on Fig. 8 where `q1` and `q2` can point to `a` and/or `b`, see Fig. 8. We have

$$
\begin{aligned}
R^{+}_{\mathtt{g(q1,q2)}} = & (\mathtt{q1}=nil && \Leftrightarrow \mathtt{p1}=nil) \\
\wedge & (\mathtt{q1}=\bot && \Leftrightarrow \mathtt{p1}=\bot) \\
\wedge & (\mathtt{q1}=\&\mathtt{a} && \Leftrightarrow (\mathtt{p1}=\&\text{``}{*}\mathtt{p1}\text{''} \wedge \text{``}{*}\mathtt{p1}\text{''}=\mathtt{a})) \\
\wedge & (\mathtt{q1}=\&\mathtt{b} && \Leftrightarrow (\mathtt{p1}=\&\text{``}{*}\mathtt{p1}\text{''} \wedge \text{``}{*}\mathtt{p1}\text{''}=\mathtt{b})) \\
\wedge & (\mathtt{q2}=nil && \Leftrightarrow \mathtt{p2}=nil) \\
\wedge & (\mathtt{q2}=\bot && \Leftrightarrow \mathtt{p2}=\bot) \\
\wedge & ((\mathtt{q2}\neq\mathtt{q1}\wedge\mathtt{q2}=\&\mathtt{a}) && \Leftrightarrow (\mathtt{p2}=\&\text{``}{*}\mathtt{p2}\text{''} \wedge \text{``}{*}\mathtt{p2}\text{''}=\mathtt{a})) \\
\wedge & ((\mathtt{q2}\neq\mathtt{q1}\wedge\mathtt{q2}=\&\mathtt{b}) && \Leftrightarrow (\mathtt{p2}=\&\text{``}{*}\mathtt{p2}\text{''} \wedge \text{``}{*}\mathtt{p2}\text{''}=\mathtt{b})) \\
\wedge & (\mathtt{q2}=\mathtt{q1} && \Leftrightarrow \mathtt{p2}=\mathtt{p1})
\end{aligned}
$$

When `q1` and `q2` are aliased ($\mathtt{q2} = \mathtt{q1}$), the value of "*p2" is unconstrained. The external location used is still named *p1, meaning that $repr(\{{*}\mathtt{p1}, {*}\mathtt{p2}\}) = {*}\mathtt{p1}$. Generally speaking we have to enumerate the possible values of the actual parameter $q1, q2$, and in each case assigning the correct value for the formal parameters, according to Tab. 6.

Once sets of and relations on activation records are represented with such logical formula, it is possible to compute the application of the relation to a set or to perform relation composition.

6 Abstracting Sets of Activation Records

The forward semantics of Tab. 8 manipulates activation records, the structure of which has been investigated in the previous section. We begin by an important result:

> *For recursive Boolean programs with pointers on the stacks, we obtain an exact analysis w.r.t. invariance properties that can be implemented.*

This is a consequence of Theorems 1 and 2, and the observation that the state-space induced by activation records is finite in this case. However in the presence of numerical variables it is not any more the case, and we need to perform an abstraction. We start by describing the one we implemented in our tool, and we then discuss alternatives which also abstract pointers and lead to more classical analyses.

Logico-numerical abstraction with BddApron. BddApron [14] is a static analysis library that provides an abstract domain based on the following Galois connection:

$$\mathcal{P}(Id \to \mathbb{B} \cup \mathbb{E} \cup \mathbb{Z}) \underset{\alpha_{\mathcal{N}}}{\overset{\gamma_{\mathcal{N}}}{\leftrightarrows}} A = (\mathbb{B}^n \to \mathcal{N})$$

where *Id* is a finite set of identifiers, $\mathbb{E}$ is a set of user-defined enumerated types, and $\mathcal{N}$ is any abstract domain for numerical variables provided by the APRON library [18], for instance intervals or convex polyhedra. This abstraction treats finite-state expressions exactly and approximates the operations involving numerical tests and assignments. Abstract values are efficiently represented using MTBDDs with numerical abstract values in terminal nodes; we use for this the CUDD library [27].

As discussed in the previous section, an activation record can be encoded with a function $Id \rightarrow \mathbb{B} \cup \mathbb{E} \cup \mathbb{Z}$, thus sets of activations records can be effectively abstracted with this library. We implemented a version of the Interproc analyzer [16] based on it, that analyses the class of program defined in Sect. 2.

We obtain a tool called PInterproc that infers at each program point invariants that are fully relational between aliasing/pointer properties and invariance/scalar properties. PInterproc can be tried on-line[1] on a number of examples, or on any program provided by the user.

Compared to the original version of Interproc, PInterproc has to preprocess expressions and assignments before feeding them to BddApron. Expressions like `*p+*q>=0` are typically expressed as conditional expressions

```
(if p=&a then a else b) + (if q=&a then a else b) >= 0
```

which are supported by the library and normalized by pushing operations `+`,`>=` under the tests. Assignments like `*p:=e` are decomposed in

```
if p=&a then a:=e else b:=e
```

The relation R^+ discussed in Sect. 5 is encoded exactly as a Boolean expression with equality constraints on numerical locations, whereas relation $R^-(\sigma, \sigma', \sigma'')$ defined in Tab. 6 and used in Eqn. (4) is actually encoded as a parallel assignment defining σ''.

Example of analysis. We consider the procedure of Fig. 9 that transfers the content of a pointed integer into another one, in a way similar to bank account transfer. The source is set to 0 and its value is credited to the destination. If the source or destination are *nil*, then no movement is performed. We show that the summaries generated by our analysis are alias-sensitive, and more generally context sensitive. The summary generated for procedure `transfer` (at `(4)`) is dependent from the possible aliasing contexts. We show (partial) invariant at point `(4)` and its call-context dependencies:

$$
\texttt{(4)}\ \left|\begin{array}{ll}
\left(\begin{array}{l} \texttt{src}=\&\text{``}{*}\texttt{src}\text{''} \wedge \texttt{dest}=\&\text{``}{*}\texttt{dest}\text{''} \\ \wedge 0 \le \text{``}{*}\texttt{src}\text{''}_0 \le 10 \wedge \text{``}{*}\texttt{dest}\text{''}_0 = 3 \\ \wedge \text{``}{*}\texttt{src}\text{''} = 0 \wedge \text{``}{*}\texttt{dest}\text{''} = \text{``}{*}\texttt{dest}\text{''}_0 + \text{``}{*}\texttt{src}\text{''}_0 \end{array}\right) & \text{from } \texttt{(1)} \\
\vee \left(\begin{array}{l} \texttt{src}=\&\text{``}{*}\texttt{src}\text{''} \wedge \texttt{dest}=\mathit{nil} \\ \wedge 11 \le \text{``}{*}\texttt{src}\text{''}_0 \le 13 \wedge \text{``}{*}\texttt{src}\text{''} = \text{``}{*}\texttt{src}\text{''}_0 \end{array}\right) & \text{from } \texttt{(2)} \\
\vee \left(\begin{array}{l} \texttt{src}=\&\text{``}{*}\texttt{src}\text{''} \wedge \texttt{dest}=\&\text{``}{*}\texttt{src}\text{''} \\ \wedge 11 \le \text{``}{*}\texttt{src}\text{''}_0 \le 13 \wedge \text{``}{*}\texttt{src}\text{''} = 0 \end{array}\right) & \text{from } \texttt{(3)}
\end{array}\right.
$$

[1] `http://pop-art.inrialpes.fr/interproc/pinterprocweb.cgi`

```
var a:int,b:int;
begin
  a = 0;
  while(a <= 10) do
    b = 3;
    transfer(&a,&b); // (1)
  done;
  transfer(&a,nil);   // (2)
  transfer(&a,&a);    // (3)
end
```

```
proc transfer (src:int*,dest:int*)
begin
  if (not (src == nil)) and
     (not (dest == nil)) then
    *dest = *dest + *src;
    *src = 0;
  endif;    // (4)
end
```

Fig. 9. Bank account transfer program

The aliasing context at call point (3) exhibits what can be a bad behaviour of the procedure (money or debt disappeared), when both parameters points to the same integer. Other experiments can be found at the webpage of PInterproc.

Complexity. Due to space constraints, we produce only a rough complexity analysis. Assuming $l = l_p + l_b + l_n$ external locations, resp. decomposed resp. into locations of pointer, Boolean, and numerical type (see Sect. 5 for an evaluation of l) and $v = v_p + v_b + v_n$ local variables decomposed in the same way, an abstract value can be represented by a MTBDD

- with at most $2(l_p + v_p)\log_2(l + v) + 2(l_b + v_b)$ Boolean variables,
- and with numerical abstract values on at most $2(l_n + v_n)$ dimensions.

The factor 2 is due to the copies of formal parameters and external locations. The discussion in Sect. 5 about the number of possible locations and the effective size of enumerated types encoding pointer values is very important in practice for efficiently encoding activation records and for controlling the number of disjunctions to handle in expressions and assignments. In particular the term $\log_2(l + v)$ totally ignores the type information that restricts the possible values of pointers, whereas our implementation performs such optimizations.

Alternative abstractions. An important idea of this work is to derive an effective analysis by decomposing it in the well-identified steps depicted on Fig. 1, and to delay as much as possible approximations on pointers and variables. We show here that our methodology allows to express more classical, previously published analyses. We assume that an activation record is encoded with a function $Id \to \mathbb{B} \cup \mathbb{E} \cup \mathbb{Z}$ and we decompose $Id = Id_p \cup Id_s$ into identifiers of resp. pointer and scalar types.

- We can obtain a pure alias analysis if we forget the values of scalars, using the abstraction

$$\mathcal{P}(Id \to \mathbb{B} \cup \mathbb{E} \cup \mathbb{Z}) \underset{\alpha}{\overset{\gamma}{\longleftrightarrow}} A = \mathcal{P}(Id_p \to \mathbb{E}) \simeq \mathcal{P}(\mathbb{B}^n)$$

  This defines a flow-sensitive, context-sensitive, and fully relational interprocedural alias analysis, in which procedure summaries establishes a relation between aliasing properties at start and exit points.

- If we perform a further non-relational abstraction:

$$\mathcal{P}(Id_p \to \mathbb{E}) \xleftrightarrow[\alpha]{\gamma} (Id_p \to \mathcal{P}(\mathbb{E}))$$

we obtain a flow-sensitive, context-insensitive interprocedural points-to analysis. Procedure summaries are of the form $P_{in} \wedge P_{out}$ and does not really relate input to output alias properties.
- We can also obtain the reduced product of an alias and a scalar analysis as follows:

$$\mathcal{P}(Id \to \mathbb{B} \cup \mathbb{E} \cup \mathbb{Z}) \xleftrightarrow[\alpha]{\gamma} \mathcal{P}(Id_p \to \mathbb{E}) \times \mathcal{P}(Id_s \to \mathbb{B} \cup \mathbb{Z})$$

The two analyses interacts during the fixpoint computation; typically the logico-numerical abstract domain will query the alias property when computing the effect of an assignment `*p=*p+1`, to know to which location p may point to.

7 Related Work

In 2001, Hind made a survey [13] of twenty years of pointer analysis. It is legitimate to ask what is the contribution of our paper in such a well-studied field. First we emphasize that most pointer analyses try to determine the possible aliasing in a program, regardless of the boolean and numerical values manipulated. One of our contribution is to allow the functional analysis of programs with pointers, in which the aliasing information both benefits from and benefits to the logico-numerical information.

Alias analysis for compilation. Pointer analyses that are directed to program optimisation are not suitable for a precise data-flow analysis (DFA). Andersen [1] and Steensgaard [29] founded two families of algorithms for *flow-insensitive* points-to analysis. Their methods lead to fast analysis (million lines of code), with a precision sufficient for optimisation but unfortunately insufficient for program functional analysis. In [13], Hind reported the point of view of Manuel Fähndrich, who states that "For error detection and program understanding, [...] there seems to be a lower bound on precision, below which, pointer information is pretty useless". However, we share with those analyses the concern of a precision adapted to the "client analysis" needs (eg. [5] and [12]). In our approach, the pointer analysis is merged with the logico-numerical analysis, which enhances the precision of both analyses.

The abstract domain library BddApron we use relies on BDDs to encode the value of pointers. BDDs have already been used in alias analysis, together with Datalog, for a context-sensitive, flow-insensitive points-to analysis for Java [30], but they are necessarily more efficient than analysis in pure Datalog [3]. We actually use BDDs in combination with numerical values, so the observation of [3] does not apply as is to our case.

Alias analysis for verification. Precise, but expensive, pointer analyses have also been proposed. For example, Landi and Ryder [21] tackles the may-alias problem and they merge into an algorithm the semantic work we did in Section 3 and an abstraction (less precise than the one we present in Section 4 and 6) This fusion of two distinct aspects of the analysis prevent the reuse of the algorithm with different abstraction schemes. Wilson and Lam [31] presents a lot of similarities with our work. They tackle more general C programs and they use a notion of external locations. However, they only address may-analysis of pointers (thus ignoring properties on scalars), and their analysis is defined by algorithms and not by semantic domains. Compared to our work, the lack of such a formalisation makes difficult its generalization to a different context (eg, combining it with scalar analysis using BDDs and convex polyhedra, or with shape analysis using a shape domain) and forbids soundness proofs. (available in [28]). The work that actually inspired us for the local semantics is Bourdoncle's [2], in which the semantics adaptation (of reference parameters) is done independently of the abstraction step. As this work targets the Pascal language it does not handle pointers to the stack. Pointer parameters bring more difficulties for the analysis and for context determination than reference parameters.

Pointers on the execution stack are different from pointers within the heap. Interprocedural shape analyses like [25,17] address the specific problem of verifying the recursive data-structures in the heap. They are both based on a relational interprocedural analysis, but [25] uses a tabulated representation for summary functions whereas [17] exploits a more symbolic representation of relations between input/output memory heaps, in a spirit similar to Sect 5. Control-flow analysis (CFA) aims at discovering the partly implicit control flow of higher-order or object-oriented programs such as JAVA (see [22] for a survey). CFA often includes rather precise alias analysis, but of pointers to the heap only, as such programs do not have pointers to the execution stack.

Inferring invariants on variables of programs. The original Interproc analyser deals with a simple language with procedures and recursive calls. It cannot handle most C-like programs since they often rely on pointers, dynamic allocation and arrays. The work we present here is a step toward the C language. As mentioned in the introduction, several well-established C analysers like Astrée [8] and Fluctuat [9] that infer sophisticated properties on numerical variables target specific kinds of programs for which they can inline procedures, so they only need to handle intraprocedural use of pointers (eg. see [23] for Astrée).

8 Conclusion

We addressed the problem of interprocedural analysis in the presence of pointers to the stacks. By doing so, we make a step toward the analysis of C codes which often rely on pointers as parameters and side-effects.

Our approach follows the abstract interpretation scheme depicted on Fig. 1 and carefully separate semantic and algorithmic issues. The first contribution of the paper is an alternative *local* semantics for our language, in which the instructions act locally on the stack, even in the presence of pointers and side-effects. We prove it to be equivalent to the original semantics, which is not so straightforward. We are convinced that this approach can be easily generalized to more complex languages with dynamic allocation.

We then apply relational interprocedural analysis to this local semantics, which result in a forward semantics manipulating sets of activation records. Our second contribution concerns the symbolic representation of such activation records, that relate alias properties on pointers and properties on scalar variables and locations pointed to by pointers. We abstract these activation records with the relational abstract domains provided by the library BddApron, and we implemented the PInterproc analyzer as an extension of the Interproc for programs with pointers on local variables.

We prove as a side-effect that for Boolean programs, our analysis is exact w.r.t. invariance properties at each control point. We also show in Sect. 6 that by further abstractions our approach leads to known alias analysis techniques, that are less precise but more efficient.

The main question in our view is to which extend our approach can be generalized to more expressive programs. Concerning global variables, one can push them on the stack when instrumenting them (see [15]) and the main change is that the domain of pointer values is larger, as we get more locations in stacks. Adding structured types (*eg.* records) raises two difficulties: aliasing properties are more complex, and it becomes possible to build an unbounded linked list on the call stack, which induces an unbounded number of external locations in our local semantics. This calls for a mechanism to merge external locations, as done in shape analysis [4,25,17]. At last, in the presence of dynamically allocated objects, we are convinced that one can still exploit our local semantics, and the question is how to combine an existing shape abstract domain with our abstraction for scalar and pointer variables.

Acknowledgements. The authors thanks Pascal Fradet for its suggestions and the anonymous reviewers for their comments and pointers to related work.

References

1. Andersen, L.: Program Analysis and Specialization for the C Programming Language. Ph.D. thesis (1994), `http://ftp.diku.dk/pub/diku/semantics/papers/D-203.dvi.Z`
2. Bourdoncle, F.: Interprocedural Abstract Interpretation of Block Structured Languages with Nested Procedures, Aliasing and Recursivity. In: Deransart, P., Małuszyński, J. (eds.) PLILP 1990. LNCS, vol. 456, Springer, Heidelberg (1990)
3. Bravenboer, M., Smaragdakis, Y.: Strictly declarative specification of sophisticated points-to analyses. In: Object-Oriented Programming, Systems, Languages, and Applications, OOPSLA 2009 (2009)
4. Chase, D.R., Wegman, M., Zadeck, F.K.: Analysis of pointers and structures. In: Prog. Lang. Design and Implementation, PLDI 1990 (1990)
5. Chatterjee, R., Ryder, B.G., Landi, W.: Relevant context inference. In: Principles of Prog. Languages, POPL 1999 (1999)
6. Cousot, P., Cousot, R.: Abstract interpretation: a unified lattice model for static analysis of programs by construction or approximation of fixpoints. In: Principles of Prog. Languages, POPL 1977 (1977)

7. Cousot, P., Cousot, R.: Static determination of dynamic properties of recursive procedures. In: IFIP Conf. on Formal Description of Programming Concepts (1977)
8. Cousot, P., Cousot, R., Feret, J., Mauborgne, L., Miné, A., Rival, X.: Why does astrée scale up? Formal Methods in System Design 35(3) (2009)
9. Delmas, D., Goubault, E., Putot, S., Souyris, J., Tekkal, K., Védrine, F.: Towards an industrial use of fluctuat on safety-critical avionics softwar. In: Alpuente, M., Cook, B., Joubert, C. (eds.) FMICS 2009. LNCS, vol. 5825, pp. 53–69. Springer, Heidelberg (2009)
10. Filliâtre, J.C., Marché, C.: Multi-prover verification of C programs. In: Davies, J., Schulte, W., Barnett, M. (eds.) ICFEM 2004. LNCS, vol. 3308, pp. 15–29. Springer, Heidelberg (2004)
11. Halbwachs, N., Péron, M.: Discovering properties about arrays in simple programs. In: Prog. Lang. Design and Implementation, PLDI 2008. ACM, New York (2008)
12. Heintze, N., Tardieu, O.: Demand-driven pointer analysis. In: Prog. Lang. Design and Implementation, PLDI 2001 (2001)
13. Hind, M.: Pointer analysis: haven't we solved this problem yet? In: Prog. Analysis For Software Tools and Engineering, PASTE 2001 (2001)
14. Jeannet, B.: The BDDAPRON logico-numerical abstract domains library, `http://www.inrialpes.fr/pop-art/people/bjeannet/bjeannet-forge/bddapron/`
15. Jeannet, B.: Relational interprocedural verification of concurrent programs. In: Software Engineering and Formal Methods, SEFM 2009. IEEE, Los Alamitos (2009)
16. Jeannet, B., Argoud, M., Lalire, G.: The INTERPROC interprocedural analyzer, `http://pop-art.inrialpes.fr/interproc/interprocweb.cgi`
17. Jeannet, B., Loginov, A., Reps, T., Sagiv, M.: A relational approach to interprocedural shape analysis. ACM Trans. On Programming Languages and Systems (TOPLAS) 32(2) (2010)
18. Jeannet, B., Miné, A.: APRON: A library of numerical abstract domains for static analysis. In: Bouajjani, A., Maler, O. (eds.) CAV 2009. LNCS, vol. 5643, pp. 661–667. Springer, Heidelberg (2009), `http://apron.cri.ensmp.fr/library/`
19. Jeannet, B., Serwe, W.: Abstracting call-stacks for interprocedural verification of imperative programs. In: Rattray, C., Maharaj, S., Shankland, C. (eds.) AMAST 2004. LNCS, vol. 3116, pp. 258–273. Springer, Heidelberg (2004)
20. Knoop, J., Steffen, B.: The interprocedural coincidence theorem. In: Pfahler, P., Kastens, U. (eds.) CC 1992. LNCS, vol. 641, Springer, Heidelberg (1992)
21. Landi, W., Ryder, B.G.: A safe approximate algorithm for interprocedural pointer aliasing. In: PLDI (1992)
22. Midtgaard, J.: Control-flow analysis of functional programs. ACM Computing Surveys (2011); preliminary version available as BRICS technical report RS-07-18
23. Miné, A.: Field-sensitive value analysis of embedded C programs with union types and pointer arithmetics. In: Languages, Compilers and Tools for Embedded Systems, LCTES 2006 (2006)
24. Polyspace, `http://www.mathworks.com/products/polyspace/`
25. Rinetzky, N., Sagiv, M., Yahav, E.: Interprocedural shape analysis for cutpoint-free programs. In: Hankin, C., Siveroni, I. (eds.) SAS 2005. LNCS, vol. 3672, pp. 284–302. Springer, Heidelberg (2005)
26. Sharir, M., Pnueli, A.: Semantic foundations of program analysis. In: Muchnick, S., Jones, N. (eds.) Program Flow Analysis: Theory and Applications, ch. 7. Prentice-Hall, Englewood Cliffs (1981)
27. Somenzi, F.:CUDD: Colorado University Decision Diagram Package, `ftp://vlsi.colorado.edu/pub`

28. Sotin, P., Jeannet, B.: Precise interprocedural analysis in the presence of pointers to the stack (January 2011), http://hal.archives-ouvertes.fr/inria-00547888/fr/
29. Steensgaard, B.: Points-to Analysis in Almost Linear Time. In: Principles of Prog. Languages, POPL 1996 (1996)
30. Whaley, J., Lam, M.S.: Cloning-based context-sensitive pointer alias analysis using binary decision diagrams. In: Prog. Lang. Design and Implementation, PLDI 2004 (2004)
31. Wilson, R.P., Lam, M.S.: Efficient context-sensitive pointer analysis for c programs. In: Prog. Lang. Design and Implementation, PLDI 1995 (1995)

General Bindings and Alpha-Equivalence in Nominal Isabelle

Christian Urban and Cezary Kaliszyk

TU Munich, Germany

Abstract. Nominal Isabelle is a definitional extension of the Isabelle/HOL theorem prover. It provides a proving infrastructure for reasoning about programming language calculi involving named bound variables (as opposed to de-Bruijn indices). In this paper we present an extension of Nominal Isabelle for dealing with general bindings, that means term-constructors where multiple variables are bound at once. Such general bindings are ubiquitous in programming language research and only very poorly supported with single binders, such as lambda-abstractions. Our extension includes new definitions of α-equivalence and establishes automatically the reasoning infrastructure for α-equated terms. We also prove strong induction principles that have the usual variable convention already built in.

1 Introduction

So far, Nominal Isabelle provided a mechanism for constructing α-equated terms, for example lambda-terms, $t ::= x \mid t\ t \mid \lambda x.\ t$, where free and bound variables have names. For such α-equated terms, Nominal Isabelle derives automatically a reasoning infrastructure that has been used successfully in formalisations of an equivalence checking algorithm for LF [18], Typed Scheme [17], several calculi for concurrency [2] and a strong normalisation result for cut-elimination in classical logic [21]. It has also been used by Pollack for formalisations in the locally-nameless approach to binding [14].

However, Nominal Isabelle has fared less well in a formalisation of the algorithm W [19], where types and type-schemes are, respectively, of the form

$$T ::= x \mid T \rightarrow T \qquad S ::= \forall\,\{x_1,\ldots,x_n\}.\ T \tag{1}$$

and the $\forall$-quantification binds a finite (possibly empty) set of type-variables. While it is possible to implement this kind of more general binders by iterating single binders, this leads to a rather clumsy formalisation of W.

Binding multiple variables has interesting properties that cannot be captured easily by iterating single binders. For example in the case of type-schemes we do not want to make a distinction about the order of the bound variables. Therefore we would like to regard the first pair of type-schemes as α-equivalent, but assuming that x, y and z are distinct variables, the second pair should *not* be α-equivalent:

$$\forall\,\{x, y\}.\ x \rightarrow y \approx_\alpha \forall\,\{y, x\}.\ y \rightarrow x \qquad \forall\,\{x, y\}.\ x \rightarrow y \not\approx_\alpha \forall\,\{z\}.\ z \rightarrow z \tag{2}$$

G. Barthe (Ed.): ESOP 2011, LNCS 6602, pp. 480–500, 2011.
© Springer-Verlag Berlin Heidelberg 2011

Moreover, we like to regard type-schemes as α-equivalent, if they differ only on *vacuous* binders, such as

$$\forall\{x\}.\, x \rightarrow y \;\approx_\alpha\; \forall\{x, z\}.\, x \rightarrow y \tag{3}$$

where z does not occur freely in the type. In this paper we will give a general binding mechanism and associated notion of α-equivalence that can be used to faithfully represent this kind of binding in Nominal Isabelle.

However, the notion of α-equivalence that is preserved by vacuous binders is not always wanted. For example in terms like

$$\texttt{let}\ x = \mathit{3}\ \texttt{and}\ y = \mathit{2}\ \texttt{in}\ x - y\ \texttt{end} \tag{4}$$

we might not care in which order the assignments $x = \mathit{3}$ and $y = \mathit{2}$ are given, but it would be often unusual to regard (4) as α-equivalent with

$$\texttt{let}\ x = \mathit{3}\ \texttt{and}\ y = \mathit{2}\ \texttt{and}\ z = \mathit{foo}\ \texttt{in}\ x - y\ \texttt{end}$$

Therefore we will also provide a separate binding mechanism for cases in which the order of binders does not matter, but the "cardinality" of the binders has to agree.

However, we found that this is still not sufficient for dealing with language constructs frequently occurring in programming language research. For example in `let`s containing patterns like

$$\texttt{let}\ (x, y) = (\mathit{3}, \mathit{2})\ \texttt{in}\ x - y\ \texttt{end} \tag{5}$$

we want to bind all variables from the pattern inside the body of the `let`, but we also care about the order of these variables, since we do not want to regard (5) as α-equivalent with

$$\texttt{let}\ (y, x) = (\mathit{3}, \mathit{2})\ \texttt{in}\ x - y\ \texttt{end}$$

As a result, we provide three general binding mechanisms each of which binds multiple variables at once, and let the user chose which one is intended in a formalisation.

By providing these general binding mechanisms, however, we have to work around a problem that has been pointed out by Pottier [13] and Cheney [5]: in `let`-constructs of the form

$$\texttt{let}\ x_1 = t_1\ \texttt{and} \ldots\ \texttt{and}\ x_n = t_n\ \texttt{in}\ s\ \texttt{end}$$

we care about the information that there are as many bound variables x_i as there are t_i. We lose this information if we represent the `let`-constructor by something like

$$\texttt{let}\ (\lambda x_1 \ldots x_n \,.\, s)\ [t_1, \ldots, t_n]$$

where the notation $\lambda\_\,.\,\_$ indicates that the list of x_i becomes bound in s. In this representation the term $\texttt{let}\ (\lambda x \,.\, s)\ [t_1, t_2]$ is a perfectly legal instance, but the lengths of the two lists do not agree. To exclude such terms, additional predicates about well-formed terms are needed in order to ensure that the two lists are of equal length. This can result in very messy reasoning (see for example [2]). To avoid this, we will allow type specifications for `let`s as follows

$$\begin{array}{lcl} trm & ::= & \ldots \mid \texttt{let}\ as{::}assn\ \ s{::}trm\quad \textbf{bind}\ bn(as)\ \textbf{in}\ s \\ assn & ::= & \texttt{anil} \mid \texttt{acons}\ name\ trm\ assn \end{array}$$

where *assn* is an auxiliary type representing a list of assignments and *bn* an auxiliary function identifying the variables to be bound by the `let`. This function can be defined by recursion over *assn* as follows

$$bn(\texttt{anil}) = \varnothing \qquad bn(\texttt{acons}\ x\ t\ as) = \{x\} \cup bn(as)$$

The scope of the binding is indicated by labels given to the types, for example *s::trm*, and a binding clause, in this case **bind** *bn*(*as*) **in** *s*. This binding clause states that all the names the function *bn*(*as*) returns should be bound in *s*. This style of specifying terms and bindings is heavily inspired by the syntax of the Ott-tool [16].

However, we will not be able to cope with all specifications that are allowed by Ott. One reason is that Ott lets the user specify "empty" types like $t ::= t\ t \mid \lambda x.\ t$ where no clause for variables is given. Arguably, such specifications make some sense in the context of Coq's type theory (which Ott supports), but not at all in a HOL-based environment where every datatype must have a non-empty set-theoretic model.

Another reason is that we establish the reasoning infrastructure for α-*equated* terms. In contrast, Ott produces a reasoning infrastructure in Isabelle/HOL for *non*-α-equated, or "raw", terms. While our α-equated terms and the raw terms produced by Ott use names for bound variables, there is a key difference: working with α-equated terms means, for example, that the two type-schemes

$$\forall \{x\}.\, x \rightarrow y \;= \forall \{x, z\}.\, x \rightarrow y$$

are not just α-equal, but actually *equal*! As a result, we can only support specifications that make sense on the level of α-equated terms (offending specifications, which for example bind a variable according to a variable bound somewhere else, are not excluded by Ott, but we have to).

Although in informal settings a reasoning infrastructure for α-equated terms is nearly always taken for granted, establishing it automatically in Isabelle/HOL is a rather non-trivial task. For every specification we will need to construct type(s) containing as elements the α-equated terms. To do so, we use the standard HOL-technique of defining a new type by identifying a non-empty subset of an existing type. The construction we perform in Isabelle/HOL can be illustrated by the following picture:

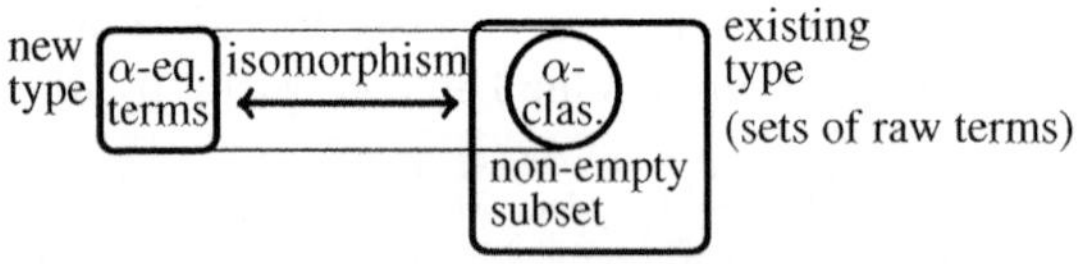

We take as the starting point a definition of raw terms (defined as a datatype in Isabelle/HOL); then identify the α-equivalence classes in the type of sets of raw terms according to our α-equivalence relation, and finally define the new type as these α-equivalence classes (non-emptiness is satisfied whenever the raw terms are definable as datatype in Isabelle/HOL and our relation for α-equivalence is an equivalence relation).

The problem with introducing a new type in Isabelle/HOL is that in order to be useful, a reasoning infrastructure needs to be "lifted" from the underlying subset to the new type. This is usually a tricky and arduous task. To ease it, we re-implemented in Isabelle/HOL [8] the quotient package described by Homeier [6] for the HOL4 system. This package allows us to lift definitions and theorems involving raw terms to definitions and theorems involving α-equated terms. For example if we define the free-variable function over raw lambda-terms

$$fv(x) = \{x\} \qquad fv(t_1\ t_2) = fv(t_1) \cup fv(t_2) \qquad fv(\lambda x.t) = fv(t) - \{x\}$$

then with the help of the quotient package we can obtain a function fv^α operating on quotients, or α-equivalence classes of lambda-terms. This lifted function is characterised by the equations

$$fv^\alpha(x) = \{x\} \qquad fv^\alpha(t_1\ t_2) = fv^\alpha(t_1) \cup fv^\alpha(t_2) \qquad fv^\alpha(\lambda x.t) = fv^\alpha(t) - \{x\}$$

(Note that this means also the term-constructors for variables, applications and lambda are lifted to the quotient level.) This construction, of course, only works if α-equivalence is indeed an equivalence relation, and the "raw" definitions and theorems are respectful w.r.t. α-equivalence. To sum up, every lifting of theorems to the quotient level needs proofs of some respectfulness properties (see [6]). In the paper we show that we are able to automate these proofs and as a result can automatically establish a reasoning infrastructure for α-equated terms.

Contributions: We provide three new definitions for when terms involving general binders are α-equivalent. These definitions are inspired by earlier work of Pitts [11]. By means of automatic proofs, we establish a reasoning infrastructure for α-equated terms, including properties about support, freshness and equality conditions for α-equated terms. We are also able to derive strong induction principles that have the variable convention already built in. The method behind our specification of general binders is taken from the Ott-tool, but we introduce crucial restrictions, and also extensions, so that our specifications make sense for reasoning about α-equated terms. The main improvement over Ott is that we introduce three binding modes (only one is present in Ott), provide formalised definitions for α-equivalence and for free variables of our terms, and also derive a reasoning infrastructure for our specifications from "first principles".

2 A Short Review of the Nominal Logic Work

At its core, Nominal Isabelle is an adaption of the nominal logic work by Pitts [12]. This adaptation for Isabelle/HOL is described in [7] (including proofs). We shall briefly review this work to aid the description of what follows.

Two central notions in the nominal logic work are sorted atoms and sort-respecting permutations of atoms. We will use the letters a, b, c, ... to stand for atoms and p, q, ... to stand for permutations. The purpose of atoms is to represent variables, be they bound or free. It is assumed that there is an infinite supply of atoms for each sort. In the interest of brevity, we shall restrict ourselves in what follows to only one sort of atoms.

Permutations are bijective functions from atoms to atoms that are the identity everywhere except on a finite number of atoms. There is a two-place permutation operation written $\_ \bullet \_ :: perm \Rightarrow \beta \Rightarrow \beta$ where the generic type β is the type of the object over which the permutation acts. In Nominal Isabelle, the identity permutation is written as 0, the composition of two permutations p and q as $p + q$, and the inverse permutation of p as $- p$. The permutation operation is defined over the type-hierarchy [7]; for example permutations acting on products, lists, sets, functions and booleans are given by:

$$p \bullet (x, y) \stackrel{def}{=} (p \bullet x, p \bullet y) \quad p \bullet [] \stackrel{def}{=} [] \quad p \bullet X \stackrel{def}{=} \{p \bullet x \mid x \in X\}$$
$$p \bullet b \stackrel{def}{=} b \quad p \bullet (x{::}xs) \stackrel{def}{=} (p \bullet x){::}(p \bullet xs) \quad p \bullet f \stackrel{def}{=} \lambda x.\, p \bullet (f\ (- p \bullet x))$$

Concrete permutations in Nominal Isabelle are built up from swappings, written as $(a\ b)$, which are permutations that behave as follows:

$$(a\ b) = \lambda c.\ \textit{if } a = c \textit{ then } b \textit{ else if } b = c \textit{ then } a \textit{ else } c$$

The most original aspect of the nominal logic work of Pitts is a general definition for the notion of the "set of free variables of an object x". This notion, written $\textit{supp}\ x$, is general in the sense that it applies not only to lambda-terms (α-equated or not), but also to lists, products, sets and even functions. The definition depends only on the permutation operation and on the notion of equality defined for the type of x, namely:

$$\textit{supp}\ x \stackrel{def}{=} \{a \mid \textit{infinite}\ \{b \mid (a\ b) \bullet x \neq x\}\} \qquad (6)$$

There is also the derived notion for when an atom a is *fresh* for an x, defined as $a \# x \stackrel{def}{=} a \notin \textit{supp}\ x$. We use for sets of atoms the abbreviation $as\ \#^*\ x$, defined as $\forall a{\in}as.\ a \# x$. A striking consequence of these definitions is that we can prove without knowing anything about the structure of x that swapping two fresh atoms, say a and b, leaves x unchanged, namely if $a \# x$ and $b \# x$ then $(a\ b) \bullet x = x$. While in the older version of Nominal Isabelle, we used extensively this property to rename single binders, it proved too unwieldy for dealing with multiple binders. For such binders the following generalisations turned out to be easier to use.

Property 1. *If* $\textit{supp}\ x\ \#^*\ p$ *then* $p \bullet x = x$.

Property 2. For a finite set as and a finitely supported x with $as\ \#^*\ x$ and also a finitely supported c, there exists a permutation p such that $p \bullet as\ \#^*\ c$ and $\textit{supp}\ x\ \#^*\ p$.

The idea behind the second property is that given a finite set as of binders (being bound, or fresh, in x is ensured by the assumption $as\ \#^*\ x$), then there exists a permutation p such that the renamed binders $p \bullet as$ avoid c (which can be arbitrarily chosen as long as it is finitely supported) and also p does not affect anything in the support of x (that is $\textit{supp}\ x\ \#^*\ p$). The last fact and Property 1 allow us to "rename" just the binders as in x, because $p \bullet x = x$.

Most properties given in this section are described in detail in [7] and all are formalised in Isabelle/HOL. In the next sections we will make extensive use of these properties in order to define α-equivalence in the presence of multiple binders.

3 General Bindings

In Nominal Isabelle, the user is expected to write down a specification of a term-calculus and then a reasoning infrastructure is automatically derived from this specification (remember that Nominal Isabelle is a definitional extension of Isabelle/HOL, which does not introduce any new axioms).

In order to keep our work with deriving the reasoning infrastructure manageable, we will wherever possible state definitions and perform proofs on the "user-level" of Isabelle/HOL, as opposed to write custom ML-code. To that end, we will consider first pairs (as, x) of type $(atom\ set) \times \beta$. These pairs are intended to represent the abstraction, or binding, of the set of atoms *as* in the body x.

The first question we have to answer is when two pairs (as, x) and (bs, y) are α-equivalent? (For the moment we are interested in the notion of α-equivalence that is *not* preserved by adding vacuous binders.) To answer this question, we identify four conditions: *(i)* given a free-atom function *fa* of type $\beta \Rightarrow atom\ set$, then x and y need to have the same set of free atoms; moreover there must be a permutation p such that *(ii)* p leaves the free atoms of x and y unchanged, but *(iii)* "moves" their bound names so that we obtain modulo a relation, say $\_\ R\ \_$, two equivalent terms. We also require that *(iv)* p makes the sets of abstracted atoms *as* and *bs* equal. The requirements *(i)* to *(iv)* can be stated formally as the conjunction of:

$$
\begin{array}{l}
(as, x) \approx_{set}^{R, fa, p} (bs, y) \stackrel{def}{=} \\
\quad \begin{array}{llll}
(i) & fa\ x - as = fa\ y - bs & (iii) & (p \bullet x)\ R\ y \\
(ii) & fa\ x - as \ \#^*\ p & (iv) & p \bullet as = bs
\end{array}
\end{array}
\tag{7}
$$

Note that this relation depends on the permutation p; α-equivalence between two pairs is then the relation where we existentially quantify over this p. Also note that the relation is dependent on a free-atom function *fa* and a relation R. The reason for this extra generality is that we will use $\approx_{set}$ for both "raw" terms and α-equated terms. In the latter case, R will be replaced by equality $=$ and we will prove that *fa* is equal to *supp*.

The definition in (7) does not make any distinction between the order of abstracted atoms. If we want this, then we can define α-equivalence for pairs of the form (as, x) with type $(atom\ list) \times \beta$ as follows

$$
\begin{array}{l}
(as, x) \approx_{list}^{R, fa, p} (bs, y) \stackrel{def}{=} \\
\quad \begin{array}{llll}
(i) & fa\ x - set\ as = fa\ y - set\ bs & (iii) & (p \bullet x)\ R\ y \\
(ii) & fa\ x - set\ as \ \#^*\ p & (iv) & p \bullet as = bs
\end{array}
\end{array}
\tag{8}
$$

where *set* is the function that coerces a list of atoms into a set of atoms. Now the last clause ensures that the order of the binders matters (since *as* and *bs* are lists of atoms).

If we do not want to make any difference between the order of binders *and* also allow vacuous binders, that means *restrict* names, then we keep sets of binders, but drop condition *(iv)* in (7):

$$
\begin{array}{l}
(as, x) \approx_{set+}^{R, fa, p} (bs, y) \stackrel{def}{=} \\
\quad \begin{array}{llll}
(i) & fa\ x - as = fa\ y - bs & (iii) & (p \bullet x)\ R\ y \\
(ii) & fa\ x - as \ \#^*\ p & &
\end{array}
\end{array}
\tag{9}
$$

It might be useful to consider first some examples how these definitions of α-equivalence pan out in practice. For this consider the case of abstracting a set of atoms over types (as in type-schemes). We set R to be the usual equality $=$ and for $fa(T)$ we define

$$fa(x) = \{x\} \qquad fa(T_1 \rightarrow T_2) = fa(T_1) \cup fa(T_2)$$

Now recall the examples shown in (2) and (3). It can be easily checked that $(\{x, y\}, x \rightarrow y)$ and $(\{y, x\}, y \rightarrow x)$ are α-equivalent according to $\approx_{set}$ and $\approx_{set+}$ by taking p to be the swapping $(x\ y)$. In case of $x \neq y$, then $([x, y], x \rightarrow y) \not\approx_{list} ([y, x], x \rightarrow y)$ since there is no permutation that makes the lists $[x, y]$ and $[y, x]$ equal, and also leaves the type $x \rightarrow y$ unchanged. Another example is $(\{x\}, x) \approx_{set+} (\{x, y\}, x)$ which holds by taking p to be the identity permutation. However, if $x \neq y$, then $(\{x\}, x) \not\approx_{set} (\{x, y\}, x)$ since there is no permutation that makes the sets $\{x\}$ and $\{x, y\}$ equal (similarly for $\approx_{list}$). It can also relatively easily be shown that all three notions of α-equivalence coincide, if we only abstract a single atom.

In the rest of this section we are going to introduce three abstraction types. For this we define

$$(as, x) \approx_{abs\_set} (bs, x) \stackrel{def}{=} \exists p.\ (as, x) \approx_{set}^{=,\ supp,\ p} (bs, x) \qquad (10)$$

(similarly for $\approx_{abs\_set+}$ and $\approx_{abs\_list}$). We can show that these relations are equivalence relations.

Lemma 1. *The relations $\approx_{abs\_set}$, $\approx_{abs\_list}$ and $\approx_{abs\_set+}$ are equivalence relations.*

Proof. Reflexivity is by taking p to be 0. For symmetry we have a permutation p and for the proof obligation take $-p$. In case of transitivity, we have two permutations p and q, and for the proof obligation use $q + p$. All conditions are then by simple calculations.

This lemma allows us to use our quotient package for introducing new types β *abs_set*, β *abs_set+* and β *abs_list* representing α-equivalence classes of pairs of type (*atom set*) $\times$ β (in the first two cases) and of type (*atom list*) $\times$ β (in the third case). The elements in these types will be, respectively, written as $[as]_{set}.x$, $[as]_{set+}.x$ and $[as]_{list}.x$, indicating that a set (or list) of atoms *as* is abstracted in x. We will call the types *abstraction types* and their elements *abstractions*. The important property we need to derive is the support of abstractions, namely:

Theorem 1 (Support of Abstractions). *Assuming x has finite support, then*

$$\begin{array}{lclcl} supp\ [as]_{set}.x & = & supp\ [as]_{set+}.x & = & supp\ x - as, \text{ and} \\ supp\ [bs]_{list}.x & = & supp\ x - set\ bs & & \end{array}$$

This theorem states that the bound names do not appear in the support. For brevity we omit the proof and again refer the reader to our formalisation in Isabelle/HOL.

The method of first considering abstractions of the form $[as]_{set}.x$ etc is motivated by the fact that we can conveniently establish at the Isabelle/HOL level properties about them. It would be laborious to write custom ML-code that derives automatically such properties for every term-constructor that binds some atoms. Also the generality of the definitions for α-equivalence will help us in the next sections.

4 Specifying General Bindings

Our choice of syntax for specifications is influenced by the existing datatype package of Isabelle/HOL and by the syntax of the Ott-tool [16]. For us a specification of a term-calculus is a collection of (possibly mutual recursive) type declarations, say $ty_1^\alpha, \ldots, ty_n^\alpha$, and an associated collection of binding functions, say $bn_1^\alpha, \ldots, bn_m^\alpha$. The syntax in Nominal Isabelle for such specifications is roughly as follows:

$$\begin{array}{ll}
\begin{array}{l}\text{type}\\ \text{declaration part}\end{array} & \left\{\begin{array}{l}\textbf{nominal_datatype}\ ty_1^\alpha = \ldots\\ \textbf{and}\ ty_2^\alpha = \ldots\\ \ldots\\ \textbf{and}\ ty_n^\alpha = \ldots\end{array}\right.\\
\begin{array}{l}\text{binding}\\ \text{function part}\end{array} & \left\{\begin{array}{l}\textbf{binder}\ bn_1^\alpha\ \textbf{and} \ldots \textbf{and}\ bn_m^\alpha\\ \textbf{where}\\ \ldots\end{array}\right.
\end{array} \tag{11}$$

Every type declaration $ty_{1..n}^\alpha$ consists of a collection of term-constructors, each of which comes with a list of labelled types that stand for the types of the arguments of the term-constructor. For example a term-constructor C^α might be specified with

$$C^\alpha\ \mathit{label}_1{::}ty'_1\ \ldots\ \mathit{label}_l{::}ty'_l\quad \mathit{binding\_clauses}$$

whereby some of the $ty'_{1..l}$ can be contained in the collection of $ty_{1..n}^\alpha$ declared in (11). In this case we will call the corresponding argument a *recursive argument* of C^α. The labels annotated on the types are optional. Their purpose is to be used in the (possibly empty) list of *binding clauses*, which indicate the binders and their scope in a term-constructor. They come in three *modes*:

bind *binders* **in** *bodies*   **bind (set)** *binders* **in** *bodies*   **bind (set+)** *binders* **in** *bodies*

The first mode is for binding lists of atoms (the order of binders matters); the second is for sets of binders (the order does not matter, but the cardinality does) and the last is for sets of binders (with vacuous binders preserving α-equivalence). As indicated, the labels in the "**in**-part" of a binding clause will be called *bodies*; the "**bind**-part" will be called *binders*. In contrast to Ott, we allow multiple labels in binders and bodies.

There are also some restrictions we need to impose on our binding clauses in comparison to the ones of Ott. The main idea behind these restrictions is that we obtain a sensible notion of α-equivalence where it is ensured that within a given scope an atom occurrence cannot be both bound and free at the same time. The first restriction is that a body can only occur in *one* binding clause of a term constructor (this ensures that the bound atoms of a body cannot be free at the same time by specifying an alternative binder for the same body).

For binders we distinguish between *shallow* and *deep* binders. Shallow binders are just labels. The restriction we need to impose on them is that in case of **bind (set)** and **bind (set+)** the labels must either refer to atom types or to sets of atom types; in case of **bind** the labels must refer to atom types or lists of atom types. Two examples for the use of shallow binders are the specification of lambda-terms, where a single name is bound, and type-schemes, where a finite set of names is bound:

nominal_datatype *lam* =
  Var name
  | *App lam lam*
  | *Lam x::name t::lam* **bind** *x* **in** *t*

nominal_datatype *ty* =
  TVar name
  | *TFun ty ty*
and *tsc* = *All xs::(name fset) T::ty* **bind (set+)** *xs* **in** *T*

In these specifications *name* refers to an atom type, and *fset* to the type of finite sets. Note that for *lam* it does not matter which binding mode we use. The reason is that we bind only a single *name*. However, having **bind (set)** or **bind** in the second case makes a difference to the semantics of the specification (which we will define in the next section).

A *deep* binder uses an auxiliary binding function that "picks" out the atoms in one argument of the term-constructor, which can be bound in other arguments and also in the same argument (we will call such binders *recursive*, see below). The binding functions are expected to return either a set of atoms (for **bind (set)** and **bind (set+)**) or a list of atoms (for **bind**). They can be defined by recursion over the corresponding type; the equations must be given in the binding function part of the scheme shown in (11). For example a term-calculus containing *Let*s with tuple patterns might be specified as:

nominal_datatype *trm* =
  Var name
  | *App trm trm*
  | *Lam x::name t::trm* **bind** *x* **in** *t*
  | *Let p::pat trm t::trm* **bind** $bn(p)$ **in** *t*
and *pat* = *PNil* | *PVar name* | *PTup pat pat*   (12)
binder *bn::pat* ⇒ *atom list*
where $bn(PNil) = []$
  | $bn(PVar\ x) = [atom\ x]$
  | $bn(PTup\ p_1\ p_2) = bn(p_1)\ @\ bn(p_2)$

In this specification the function *bn* determines which atoms of the pattern *p* are bound in the argument *t*. Note that in the second-last *bn*-clause the function *atom* coerces a name into the generic atom type of Nominal Isabelle [7]. This allows us to treat binders of different atom type uniformly.

As said above, for deep binders we allow binding clauses such as *Bar p::pat t::trm* **bind** $bn(p)$ **in** *p t* where the argument of the deep binder also occurs in the body. We call such binders *recursive*. To see the purpose of such recursive binders, compare "plain" *Let*s and *Let_rec*s in the following specification:

nominal_datatype *trm* = ...
  | *Let as::assn t::trm* **bind** $bn(as)$ **in** *t*
  | *Let_rec as::assn t::trm* **bind** $bn(as)$ **in** *as t*
and *assn* = *ANil* | *ACons name trm assn*   (13)
binder *bn::assn* ⇒ *atom list*
where $bn(ANil) = []$
  | $bn(ACons\ a\ t\ as) = [atom\ a]\ @\ bn(as)$

The difference is that with *Let* we only want to bind the atoms $bn(as)$ in the term *t*, but with *Let_rec* we also want to bind the atoms inside the assignment. This difference has consequences for the associated notions of free-atoms and α-equivalence.

To make sure that atoms bound by deep binders cannot be free at the same time, we cannot have more than one binding function for a deep binder. Consequently we exclude specifications such as

$$\begin{array}{ll} \mathit{Baz}_1\ p{::}\mathit{pat}\ t{::}\mathit{trm} & \textbf{bind}\ \mathit{bn}_1(p)\ \mathit{bn}_2(p)\ \textbf{in}\ t \\ \mathit{Baz}_2\ p{::}\mathit{pat}\ t_1{::}\mathit{trm}\ t_2{::}\mathit{trm} & \textbf{bind}\ \mathit{bn}_1(p)\ \textbf{in}\ t_1,\ \textbf{bind}\ \mathit{bn}_2(p)\ \textbf{in}\ t_2 \end{array}$$

Otherwise it is possible that bn_1 and bn_2 pick out different atoms to become bound, respectively be free, in p. (Since the Ott-tool does not derive a reasoning infrastructure for α-equated terms with deep binders, it can permit such specifications.)

We also need to restrict the form of the binding functions in order to ensure the *bn*-functions can be defined for α-equated terms. The main restriction is that we cannot return an atom in a binding function that is also bound in the corresponding term-constructor. That means in (12) that the term-constructors *PVar* and *PTup* may not have a binding clause (all arguments are used to define *bn*). In contrast, in case of (13) the term-constructor *ACons* may have a binding clause involving the argument *trm* (the only one that is *not* used in the definition of the binding function). This restriction is sufficient for lifting the binding function to α-equated terms.

In the version of Nominal Isabelle described here, we also adopted the restriction from the Ott-tool that binding functions can only return: the empty set or empty list (as in case *PNil*), a singleton set or singleton list containing an atom (case *PVar*), or unions of atom sets or appended atom lists (case *PTup*). This restriction will simplify some automatic definitions and proofs later on.

In order to simplify our definitions of free atoms and α-equivalence, we shall assume specifications of term-calculi are implicitly *completed*. By this we mean that for every argument of a term-constructor that is *not* already part of a binding clause given by the user, we add implicitly a special *empty* binding clause, written **bind** $\varnothing$ **in** *labels*. In case of the lambda-terms, the completion produces

$$\begin{array}{l} \textbf{nominal\_datatype}\ \mathit{lam} = \\ \quad \mathit{Var}\ x{::}\mathit{name}\quad \textbf{bind}\ \varnothing\ \textbf{in}\ x \\ \quad \mid \mathit{App}\ t_1{::}\mathit{lam}\ t_2{::}\mathit{lam}\quad \textbf{bind}\ \varnothing\ \textbf{in}\ t_1\ t_2 \\ \quad \mid \mathit{Lam}\ x{::}\mathit{name}\ t{::}\mathit{lam}\quad \textbf{bind}\ x\ \textbf{in}\ t \end{array}$$

The point of completion is that we can make definitions over the binding clauses and be sure to have captured all arguments of a term constructor.

5 Alpha-Equivalence and Free Atoms

Having dealt with all syntax matters, the problem now is how we can turn specifications into actual type definitions in Isabelle/HOL and then establish a reasoning infrastructure for them. As Pottier and Cheney pointed out [13,5], just re-arranging the arguments of term-constructors so that binders and their bodies are next to each other will result in inadequate representations in cases like $\mathit{Let}\ x_1 = t_1 \ldots x_n = t_n\ \mathit{in}\ s$. Therefore we will first extract "raw" datatype definitions from the specification and then define explicitly an α-equivalence relation over them. We subsequently construct the quotient of the datatypes according to our α-equivalence.

The "raw" datatype definition can be obtained by stripping off the binding clauses and the labels from the types. We also have to invent new names for the types ty^α and term-constructors C^α given by the user. In our implementation we just use the affix "*_raw*". But for the purpose of this paper, we use the superscript $\_^\alpha$ to indicate that a notion is given for α-equivalence classes and leave it out for the corresponding notion given on the "raw" level. So for example we have $ty^\alpha \mapsto ty$ and $C^\alpha \mapsto C$ where ty is the type used in the quotient construction for ty^α and C is the term-constructor on the "raw" type ty.

We subsequently define each of the user-specified binding functions $bn_{1..m}$ by recursion over the corresponding raw datatype. We can also easily define permutation operations by recursion so that for each term constructor C we have that

$$p \bullet (C\ z_1\ \ldots\ z_n) = C\ (p \bullet z_1)\ \ldots\ (p \bullet z_n) \tag{14}$$

The first non-trivial step we have to perform is the generation of free-atom functions from the specification. For the *raw* types $ty_{1..n}$ we define the free-atom functions $fa\_ty_{1..n}$ by recursion. We define these functions together with auxiliary free-atom functions for the binding functions. Given raw binding functions $bn_{1..m}$ we define $fa\_bn_{1..m}$. The reason for this setup is that in a deep binder not all atoms have to be bound, as we saw in the example with "plain" *Lets*. We need therefore a function that calculates those free atoms in a deep binder.

While the idea behind these free-atom functions is clear (they just collect all atoms that are not bound), because of our rather complicated binding mechanisms their definitions are somewhat involved. Given a term-constructor C of type ty and some associated binding clauses $bc_1 \ldots bc_k$, the result of $fa\_ty\ (C\ z_1\ \ldots\ z_n)$ will be the union $fa(bc_1) \cup \ldots \cup fa(bc_k)$ where we will define below what fa for a binding clause means. We only show the details for the mode **bind (set)** (the other modes are similar). Suppose the binding clause bc_i is of the form **bind (set)** $b_1 \ldots b_p$ **in** $d_1 \ldots d_q$ in which the body-labels $d_{1..q}$ refer to types $ty_{1..q}$, and the binders $b_{1..p}$ either refer to labels of atom types (in case of shallow binders) or to binding functions taking a single label as argument (in case of deep binders). Assuming D stands for the set of free atoms of the bodies, B for the set of binding atoms in the binders and B' for the set of free atoms in non-recursive deep binders, then the free atoms of the binding clause bc_i are

$$fa(bc_i) \stackrel{def}{=} (D - B) \cup B'. \tag{15}$$

The set D is formally defined as $D \stackrel{def}{=} fa\_ty_1\ d_1 \cup \ldots \cup fa\_ty_q\ d_q$ where in case d_i refers to one of the raw types $ty_{1..n}$ from the specification, the function fa_ty_i is the corresponding free-atom function we are defining by recursion; otherwise we set $fa\_ty_i\ d_i = supp\ d_i$.

In order to formally define the set B we use the following auxiliary bn-functions for atom types to which shallow binders may refer

$$bn_{atom}\ a \stackrel{def}{=} \{atom\ a\} \quad bn_{atom\_set}\ as \stackrel{def}{=} atoms\ as \quad bn_{atom\_list}\ as \stackrel{def}{=} atoms\ (set\ as)$$

Like the function *atom*, the function *atoms* coerces a set of atoms to a set of the generic atom type. The set B is then formally defined as

$$B \stackrel{def}{=} bn\_ty_1\ b_1 \cup ... \cup bn\_ty_p\ b_p$$

where we use the auxiliary binding functions for shallow binders. The set B' collects all free atoms in non-recursive deep binders. Let us assume these binders in bc_i are $bn_1\ l_1, \ldots, bn_r\ l_r$ with $l_{1..r} \subseteq b_{1..p}$ and none of the $l_{1..r}$ being among the bodies $d_{1..q}$. The set B' is defined as

$$B' \stackrel{def}{=} fa\_bn_1\ l_1 \cup ... \cup fa\_bn_r\ l_r$$

This completes the definition of the free-atom functions $fa\_ty_{1..n}$.

Note that for non-recursive deep binders, we have to add in (15) the set of atoms that are left unbound by the binding functions $bn_{1..m}$. We used for the definition of this set the functions $fa\_bn_{1..m}$, which are also defined by mutual recursion. Assume the user specified a bn-clause of the form $bn\ (C\ z_1\ \ldots\ z_s) = rhs$ where the $z_{1..s}$ are of types $ty_{1..s}$. For each of the arguments we calculate the free atoms as follows:

- $fa\_ty_i\ z_i$ provided z_i does not occur in rhs (that means nothing is bound in z_i by the binding function),
- $fa\_bn_i\ z_i$ provided z_i occurs in rhs with the recursive call $bn_i\ z_i$, and
- $\varnothing$ provided z_i occurs in rhs, but without a recursive call.

For defining $fa\_bn\ (C\ z_1\ \ldots\ z_n)$ we just union up all these sets.

To see how these definitions work in practice, let us reconsider the term-constructors *Let* and *Let_rec* shown in (13) together with the term-constructors for assignments *ANil* and *ACons*. Since there is a binding function defined for assignments, we have three free-atom functions, namely fa_{trm}, fa_{assn} and fa_{bn} as follows:

$$\begin{array}{ll}
fa_{trm}\ (Let\ as\ t) & = (fa_{trm}\ t - set\ (bn\ as)) \cup fa_{bn}\ as \\
fa_{trm}\ (Let_rec\ as\ t) & = (fa_{assn}\ as \cup fa_{trm}\ t) - set\ (bn\ as) \\
fa_{assn}\ (ANil) & = \varnothing \\
fa_{assn}\ (ACons\ a\ t\ as) & = (supp\ a) \cup (fa_{trm}\ t) \cup (fa_{assn}\ as) \\
fa_{bn}\ (ANil) & = \varnothing \\
fa_{bn}\ (ACons\ a\ t\ as) & = (fa_{trm}\ t) \cup (fa_{bn}\ as)
\end{array}$$

Recall that *ANil* and *ACons* have no binding clause in the specification. The corresponding free-atom function fa_{assn} therefore returns all free atoms of an assignment (in case of *ACons*, they are given in terms of *supp*, fa_{trm} and fa_{assn}). The binding only takes place in *Let* and *Let_rec*. In case of *Let*, the binding clause specifies that all atoms given by $set\ (bn\ as)$ have to be bound in t. Therefore we have to subtract $set\ (bn\ as)$ from $fa_{trm}\ t$. However, we also need to add all atoms that are free in as. This is in contrast with *Let_rec* where we have a recursive binder to bind all occurrences of the atoms in $set\ (bn\ as)$ also inside as. Therefore we have to subtract $set\ (bn\ as)$ from both $fa_{trm}\ t$ and $fa_{assn}\ as$.

An interesting point in this example is that a "naked" assignment (*ANil* or *ACons*) does not bind any atoms, even if the binding function is specified over assignments. Only in the context of a *Let* or *Let_rec*, where the binding clauses are given, will some atoms actually become bound. This is a phenomenon that has also been pointed out in [16]. For us this observation is crucial, because we would not be able to lift the *bn*-functions to α-equated terms if they act on atoms that are bound. In that case, these functions would *not* respect α-equivalence.

Next we define the α-equivalence relations for the raw types $ty_{1..n}$ from the specification. We write them as $\approx ty_{1..n}$. Like with the free-atom functions, we also need to define auxiliary α-equivalence relations $\approx bn_{1..m}$ for the binding functions $bn_{1..m}$, To simplify our definitions we will use the following abbreviations for *compound equivalence relations* and *compound free-atom functions* acting on tuples.

$$(x_1,\ldots,x_n)\ (R_1,\ldots,R_n)\ (x'_1,\ldots,x'_n) \stackrel{def}{=} x_1\ R_1\ x'_1 \wedge \ldots \wedge x_n\ R_n\ x'_n$$

$$(fa_1,\ldots,fa_n)\ (x_1,\ldots,x_n) \stackrel{def}{=} fa_1\ x_1 \cup \ldots \cup fa_n\ x_n$$

The α-equivalence relations are defined as inductive predicates having a single clause for each term-constructor. Assuming a term-constructor C is of type ty and has the binding clauses $bc_{1..k}$, then the α-equivalence clause has the form

$$\frac{prems(bc_1)\ \ldots\ prems(bc_k)}{C\ z_1\ \ldots\ z_n\ \approx ty\ C\ z'_1\ \ldots\ z'_n}$$

The task below is to specify what the premises of a binding clause are. As a special instance, we first treat the case where bc_i is the empty binding clause of the form

$$\textbf{bind (set)}\ \varnothing\ \textbf{in}\ d_1\ldots d_q.$$

In this binding clause no atom is bound and we only have to α-relate the bodies. For this we build first the tuples $D \stackrel{def}{=} (d_1,\ldots,d_q)$ and $D' \stackrel{def}{=} (d'_1,\ldots,d'_q)$ whereby the labels $d_{1..q}$ refer to arguments $z_{1..n}$ and respectively $d'_{1..q}$ to $z'_{1..n}$. In order to relate two such tuples we define the compound α-equivalence relation R as follows

$$R \stackrel{def}{=} (R_1,\ldots,R_q) \tag{16}$$

with R_i being $\approx ty_i$ if the corresponding labels d_i and d'_i refer to a recursive argument of C with type ty_i; otherwise we take R_i to be the equality $=$. This lets us define the premise for an empty binding clause succinctly as $prems(bc_i) \stackrel{def}{=} D\ R\ D'$, which can be unfolded to the series of premises $d_1\ R_1\ d'_1\ \ldots\ d_q\ R_q\ d'_q$. We will use the unfolded version in the examples below.

Now suppose the binding clause bc_i is of the general form

$$\textbf{bind (set)}\ b_1\ldots b_p\ \textbf{in}\ d_1\ldots d_q. \tag{17}$$

In this case we define a premise P using the relation $\approx_{set}$ given in Section 3 (similarly $\approx_{set+}$ and $\approx_{list}$ for the other binding modes). This premise defines α-equivalence of two abstractions involving multiple binders. As above, we first build the tuples D and D' for the bodies $d_{1..q}$, and the corresponding compound α-relation R (shown in (16)). For $\approx_{set}$ we also need a compound free-atom function for the bodies defined as

$$fa \stackrel{def}{=} (fa\_ty_1,\ldots,fa\_ty_q)$$

with the assumption that the $d_{1..q}$ refer to arguments of types $ty_{1..q}$. The last ingredient we need are the sets of atoms bound in the bodies. For this we take

$$B \stackrel{def}{=} bn\_ty_1\ b_1 \cup \ldots \cup bn\_ty_p\ b_p\ .$$

Similarly for B' using the labels $b'_{1..p}$. This lets us formally define the premise P for a non-empty binding clause as:

$$P \stackrel{def}{=} \exists p.\ (B, D) \approx_{set}^{R, fa, p} (B', D')\ .$$

This premise accounts for α-equivalence of the bodies of the binding clause. However, in case the binders have non-recursive deep binders, this premise is not enough: we also have to "propagate" α-equivalence inside the structure of these binders. An example is *Let* where we have to make sure the right-hand sides of assignments are α-equivalent. For this we use relations $\approx bn_{1..m}$ (which we will formally define shortly). Let us assume the non-recursive deep binders in bc_i are $bn_1\ l_1, \ldots, bn_r\ l_r$. The tuple L is then $(l_1,\ldots,l_r)$ (similarly L') and the compound equivalence relation R' is $(\approx bn_1,\ldots,\approx bn_r)$. All premises for bc_i are then given by

$$prems(bc_i) \stackrel{def}{=} P\ \wedge\ L\, R'\, L'$$

The auxiliary α-equivalence relations $\approx bn_{1..m}$ in R' are defined as follows: assuming a *bn*-clause is of the form $bn\ (C\ z_1\ \ldots\ z_s) = rhs$ where the $z_{1..s}$ are of types $ty_{1..s}$, then the corresponding α-equivalence clause for $\approx bn$ has the form

$$\frac{z_1\ R_1\ z'_1\ \ldots\ z_s\ R_s\ z'_s}{C\ z_1\ \ldots\ z_s \approx bn\ C\ z'_1\ \ldots\ z'_s}$$

In this clause the relations $R_{1..s}$ are given by

- $z_i \approx ty\ z'_i$ provided z_i does not occur in *rhs* and is a recursive argument of C,
- $z_i = z'_i$ provided z_i does not occur in *rhs* and is a non-recursive argument of C,
- $z_i \approx bn_i\ z'_i$ provided z_i occurs in *rhs* with the recursive call $bn_i\ x_i$ and
- *True* provided z_i occurs in *rhs* but without a recursive call.

This completes the definition of α-equivalence. As a sanity check, we can show that the premises of empty binding clauses are a special case of the clauses for non-empty ones (we just have to unfold the definition of $\approx_{set}$ and take *0* for the existentially quantified permutation).

Again let us take a look at a concrete example for these definitions. For (13) we have three relations $\approx_{trm}$, $\approx_{assn}$ and $\approx_{bn}$ with the following clauses:

$$\frac{\exists p.\ (bn\ as, t) \approx_{list}^{\approx trm, fa_{trm}, p} (bn\ as', t') \quad as \approx_{bn} as'}{Let\ as\ t \approx_{trm} Let\ as'\ t'}$$

$$\frac{\exists p.\ (bn\ as, (as, t)) \approx_{list}^{(\approx assn, \approx trm), (fa_{assn}, fa_{trm}), p} (bn\ as', (as, t'))}{Let\_rec\ as\ t \approx_{trm} Let\_rec\ as'\ t'}$$

$$\frac{}{ANil \approx_{assn} ANil} \qquad \frac{a = a' \quad t \approx_{trm} t' \quad as \approx_{assn} as'}{ACons\ a\ t\ as \approx_{assn} ACons\ a'\ t'\ as}$$

$$\frac{}{ANil \approx_{bn} ANil} \qquad \frac{t \approx_{trm} t' \quad as \approx_{bn} as'}{ACons\ a\ t\ as \approx_{bn} ACons\ a'\ t'\ as}$$

Note the difference between $\approx_{assn}$ and $\approx_{bn}$: the latter only "tracks" α-equivalence of the components in an assignment that are *not* bound. This is needed in the clause for *Let* (which has a non-recursive binder).

6 Establishing the Reasoning Infrastructure

Having made all necessary definitions for raw terms, we can start with establishing the reasoning infrastructure for the α-equated types $ty^{\alpha}_{1..n}$, that is the types the user originally specified. We sketch in this section the proofs we need for establishing this infrastructure. One main point of our work is that we have completely automated these proofs in Isabelle/HOL.

First we establish that the α-equivalence relations defined in the previous section are equivalence relations.

Lemma 2. *Given the raw types $ty_{1..n}$ and binding functions $bn_{1..m}$, the relations $\approx ty_{1..n}$ and $\approx bn_{1..m}$ are equivalence relations.*

Proof. The proof is by mutual induction over the definitions. The non-trivial cases involve premises built up by $\approx_{set}$, $\approx_{set+}$ and $\approx_{list}$. They can be dealt with as in Lemma 1.

We can feed this lemma into our quotient package and obtain new types $ty^{\alpha}_{1..n}$ representing α-equated terms of types $ty_{1..n}$. We also obtain definitions for the term-constructors $C^{\alpha}_{1..k}$ from the raw term-constructors $C_{1..k}$, and similar definitions for the free-atom functions $fa\_ty^{\alpha}_{1..n}$ and $fa\_bn^{\alpha}_{1..m}$ as well as the binding functions $bn^{\alpha}_{1..m}$. However, these definitions are not really useful to the user, since they are given in terms of the isomorphisms we obtained by creating new types in Isabelle/HOL (recall the picture shown in the Introduction).

The first useful property for the user is the fact that distinct term-constructors are not equal, that is

$$C^{\alpha}\, x_1 \,\ldots\, x_r \neq D^{\alpha}\, y_1 \,\ldots\, y_s \tag{18}$$

whenever $C^{\alpha} \neq D^{\alpha}$. In order to derive this fact, we use the definition of α-equivalence and establish that

$$C\, x_1 \,\ldots\, x_r \not\approx ty\; D\, y_1 \,\ldots\, y_s \tag{19}$$

holds for the corresponding raw term-constructors. In order to deduce (18) from (19), our quotient package needs to know that the raw term-constructors C and D are *respectful* w.r.t. the α-equivalence relations (see [6]). Assuming, for example, C is of type ty with argument types $ty_{1..r}$, respectfulness amounts to showing that

$$C\, x_1 \,\ldots\, x_r \approx ty\; C\, x'_1 \,\ldots\, x'_r$$

holds under the assumptions that we have $x_i \approx ty_i\; x'_i$ whenever x_i and x'_i are recursive arguments of C and $x_i = x'_i$ whenever they are non-recursive arguments. We can prove this implication by applying the corresponding rule in our α-equivalence definition and by establishing the following auxiliary implications

$$\begin{array}{ll} (i)\; x \approx ty_i\; x' \Rightarrow fa\_ty_i\, x = fa\_ty_i\, x' & (iii)\; x \approx ty_j\; x' \Rightarrow bn_j\, x = bn_j\, x' \\ (ii)\; x \approx ty_j\; x' \Rightarrow fa\_bn_j\, x = fa\_bn_j\, x' & (iv)\; x \approx ty_j\; x' \Rightarrow x \approx bn_j\; x' \end{array} \tag{20}$$

They can be established by induction on $\approx ty_{1..n}$. Whereas the first, second and last implication are true by how we stated our definitions, the third *only* holds because of our restriction imposed on the form of the binding functions—namely *not* returning any bound atoms. In Ott, in contrast, the user may define $bn_{1..m}$ so that they return bound atoms and in this case the third implication is *not* true. A result is that the lifing of the corresponding binding functions in Ott to α-equated terms is impossible.

Having established respectfulness for the raw term-constructors, the quotient package is able to automatically deduce (18) from (19). Having the facts (20) at our disposal, we can also lift properties that characterise when two raw terms of the form

$$C\, x_1 \,\ldots\, x_r \approx ty\; C\, x'_1 \,\ldots\, x'_r$$

are α-equivalent. This gives us conditions when the corresponding α-equated terms are *equal*, namely $C^\alpha\, x_1 \,\ldots\, x_r = C^\alpha\, x'_1 \,\ldots\, x'_r$. We call these conditions as *quasi-injectivity*. They correspond to the premises in our α-equivalence relations.

Next we can lift the permutation operations defined in (14). In order to make this lifting to go through, we have to show that the permutation operations are respectful. This amounts to showing that the α-equivalence relations are equivariant [7]. As a result we can add the equations

$$p \bullet (C^\alpha\, x_1 \,\ldots\, x_r) = C^\alpha\, (p \bullet x_1) \,\ldots\, (p \bullet x_r) \tag{21}$$

to our infrastructure. In a similar fashion we can lift the defining equations of the free-atom functions $fn\_ty^\alpha_{1..n}$ and $fa\_bn^\alpha_{1..m}$ as well as of the binding functions $bn^\alpha_{1..m}$ and the size functions $size\_ty^\alpha_{1..n}$. The latter are defined automatically for the raw types $ty_{1..n}$ by the datatype package of Isabelle/HOL.

Finally we can add to our infrastructure a cases lemma (explained in the next section) and a structural induction principle for the types $ty^\alpha_{1..n}$. The conclusion of the induction principle is of the form $P_1\, x_1 \wedge \ldots \wedge P_n\, x_n$ whereby the $P_{1..n}$ are predicates and the $x_{1..n}$ have types $ty^\alpha_{1..n}$. This induction principle has for each term constructor C^α a premise of the form

$$\forall x_1 \ldots x_r.\; P_i\, x_i \wedge \ldots \wedge P_j\, x_j \Rightarrow P\; (C^\alpha\, x_1 \,\ldots\, x_r) \tag{22}$$

in which the $x_{i..j} \subseteq x_{1..r}$ are the recursive arguments of $C^\alpha_\cdot$

By working now completely on the α-equated level, we can first show that the free-atom functions and binding functions are equivariant, namely

$$p \bullet (fa\_ty^\alpha_i\; x) = fa\_ty^\alpha_i\, (p \bullet x) \qquad p \bullet (bn^\alpha_j\; x) = bn^\alpha_j\, (p \bullet x)$$
$$p \bullet (fa\_bn^\alpha_j\; x) = fa\_bn^\alpha_j\, (p \bullet x)$$

These properties can be established using the induction principle for the types $ty^\alpha_{1..n}$. Having these equivariant properties established, we can show that the support of term-constructors C^α is included in the support of its arguments, that means

$$supp\; (C^\alpha\, x_1 \,\ldots\, x_r) \subseteq (supp\; x_1 \cup \ldots \cup supp\; x_r)$$

holds. This allows us to prove by induction that every x of type $ty^\alpha_{1..n}$ is finitely supported. Lastly, we can show that the support of elements in $ty^\alpha_{1..n}$ is the same as $fa\_ty^\alpha_{1..n}$. This fact is important in a nominal setting, but also provides evidence that our notions of free-atoms and α-equivalence are correct.

Theorem 2. *For $x_{1..n}$ with type $ty^{\alpha}_{1..n}$, we have $supp\ x_i = fa\_ty^{\alpha}_i\ x_i$.*

Proof. The proof is by induction. In each case we unfold the definition of *supp*, move the swapping inside the term-constructors and then use the quasi-injectivity lemmas in order to complete the proof. For the abstraction cases we use the facts derived in Theorem 1.

To sum up this section, we can establish automatically a reasoning infrastructure for the types $ty^{\alpha}_{1..n}$ by first lifting definitions from the raw level to the quotient level and then by establishing facts about these lifted definitions. All necessary proofs are generated automatically by custom ML-code.

7 Strong Induction Principles

In the previous section we derived induction principles for α-equated terms. We call such induction principles *weak*, because for a term-constructor $C^{\alpha}\ x_1 \ldots x_r$ the induction hypothesis requires us to establish the implications (22). The problem with these implications is that in general they are difficult to establish. The reason is that we cannot make any assumption about the bound atoms that might be in C^{α}.

In [20] we introduced a method for automatically strengthening weak induction principles for terms containing single binders. These stronger induction principles allow the user to make additional assumptions about bound atoms. To sketch how this strengthening extends to the case of multiple binders, we use as running example the term-constructors *Lam* and *Let* from example (12). Instead of establishing $P_{trm}\ t \wedge P_{pat}\ p$, the stronger induction principle for (12) establishes properties $P_{trm}\ c\ t \wedge P_{pat}\ c\ p$ where the additional parameter c controls which freshness assumptions the binders should satisfy. For the two term constructors this means that the user has to establish in inductions the implications

$$\forall a\, t\, c.\ \{atom\ a\} \#^*\ c \wedge (\forall d.\ P_{trm}\ d\ t) \Rightarrow P_{trm}\ c\ (Lam\ a\ t)$$
$$\forall p\, t\, c.\ (set\ (bn\ p))\ \#^*\ c \wedge (\forall d.\ P_{pat}\ d\ p) \wedge (\forall d.\ P_{trm}\ d\ t) \wedge \Rightarrow P_{trm}\ c\ (Let\ p\ t)$$

In [20] we showed how the weaker induction principles imply the stronger ones. This was done by some quite complicated, nevertheless automated, induction proof. In this paper we simplify this work by leveraging the automated proof methods from the function package of Isabelle/HOL. The reasoning principle these methods employ is well-founded induction. To use them in our setting, we have to discharge two proof obligations: one is that we have well-founded measures (for each type $ty^{\alpha}_{1..n}$) that decrease in every induction step and the other is that we have covered all cases. As measures we use the size functions $size\_ty^{\alpha}_{1..n}$, which we lifted in the previous section and which are all well-founded.

What is left to show is that we covered all cases. To do so, we use a *cases lemma* derived for each type. For the terms in (12) this lemma is of the form

$$\frac{\forall x.\ t = Var\ x \Rightarrow P_{trm} \qquad \forall a\, t'.\ t = Lam\ a\ t' \Rightarrow P_{trm} \qquad \forall t_1\, t_2.\ t = App\ t_1\ t_2 \Rightarrow P_{trm} \qquad \forall p\, t'.\ t = Let\ p\ t' \Rightarrow P_{trm}}{P_{trm}} \tag{23}$$

where we have a premise for each term-constructor. The idea behind such cases lemmas is that we can conclude with a property P_{trm}, provided we can show that this property holds if we substitute for t all possible term-constructors.

The only remaining difficulty is that in order to derive the stronger induction principles conveniently, the cases lemma in (23) is too weak. For this note that in order to apply this lemma, we have to establish P_{trm} for *all Lam-* and *all Let*-terms. What we need instead is a cases lemma where we only have to consider terms that have binders that are fresh w.r.t. a context c. This gives the implications

$$\forall a\, t'.\ t = Lam\ a\ t' \wedge \{atom\ a\} \#^*\ c \Rightarrow P_{trm}$$
$$\forall p\, t'.\ t = Let\ p\ t' \wedge (set\ (bn\ p)) \#^*\ c \Rightarrow P_{trm}$$

which however can be relatively easily be derived from the implications in (23) by a renaming using Properties 1 and 2. In the first case we know that $\{atom\ a\} \#^*\ Lam\ a\ t$. Property (2) provides us therefore with a permutation q, such that $\{atom\ (q \bullet a)\} \#^*\ c$ and $supp\ (Lam\ a\ t) \#^*\ q$ hold. By using Property 1, we can infer from the latter that $Lam\ (q \bullet a)\ (q \bullet t) = Lam\ a\ t$ and we are done with this case.

The *Let*-case involving a (non-recursive) deep binder is a bit more complicated. The reason is that the we cannot apply Property 2 to the whole term *Let p t*, because *p* might contain names that are bound (by *bn*) and so are free. To solve this problem we have to introduce a permutation function that only permutes names bound by *bn* and leaves the other names unchanged. We do this again by lifting. For a clause $bn\ (C\ x_1\ \ldots\ x_r) = rhs$, we define

$$p \bullet_{bn} (C\ x_1\ \ldots\ x_r) \stackrel{def}{=} C\ y_1\ \ldots\ y_r \text{ with } \begin{cases} y_i \stackrel{def}{=} x_i \text{ provided } x_i \text{ does not occur in } rhs \\ y_i \stackrel{def}{=} p \bullet_{bn'} x_i \text{ provided } bn'\, x_i \text{ is in } rhs \\ y_i \stackrel{def}{=} p \bullet x_i \text{ otherwise} \end{cases}$$

Now Properties 1 and 2 give us a permutation q such that $(set\ (bn\ (q \bullet_{bn} p)) \#^*\ c$ holds and such that $[q \bullet_{bn} p]_{list}.(q \bullet t)$ is equal to $[p]_{list}.\ t$. We can also show that $(q \bullet_{bn} p) \approx_{bn} p$. These facts establish that $Let\ (q \bullet_{bn} p)\ (p \bullet t) = Let\ p\ t$, as we need. This completes the non-trivial cases in (12) for strengthening the corresponding induction principle.

8 Related Work

To our knowledge the earliest usage of general binders in a theorem prover is described in [10] about a formalisation of the algorithm W. This formalisation implements binding in type-schemes using a de-Bruijn indices representation. Since type-schemes in W contain only a single place where variables are bound, different indices do not refer to different binders (as in the usual de-Bruijn representation), but to different bound variables. A similar idea has been recently explored for general binders in the locally nameless approach to binding [3]. There, de-Bruijn indices consist of two numbers, one referring to the place where a variable is bound, and the other to which variable is bound. The reasoning infrastructure for both representations of bindings comes for free in theorem provers like Isabelle/HOL or Coq, since the corresponding term-calculi can be implemented as "normal" datatypes. However, in both approaches it seems difficult to achieve our fine-grained control over the "semantics" of bindings (i.e. whether the order of binders should matter, or vacuous binders should be taken into account).

Another technique for representing binding is higher-order abstract syntax (HOAS). This technique supports very elegantly many aspects of *single* binding, and impressive work has been done that uses HOAS for mechanising the metatheory of SML [9]. We are, however, not aware how multiple binders of SML are represented in this work. Judging from the submitted Twelf-solution for the POPLmark challenge, HOAS cannot easily deal with binding constructs where the number of bound variables is not fixed. In the second part of this challenge, *Let*s involve patterns that bind multiple variables at once. In such situations, HOAS seems to have to resort to the iterated-single-binders-approach with all the unwanted consequences when reasoning about the resulting terms.

The most closely related work to the one presented here is the Ott-tool [16] and the Cαml language [13]. Ott is a nifty front-end for creating LaTeX documents from specifications of term-calculi involving general binders. For a subset of the specifications Ott can also generate theorem prover code using a raw representation of terms, and in Coq also a locally nameless representation. The developers of this tool have also put forward (on paper) a definition for α-equivalence of terms that can be specified in Ott. This definition is rather different from ours, not using any nominal techniques. To our knowledge there is no concrete mathematical result concerning this notion of α-equivalence. Also the definition for the notion of free variables is work in progress.

Although we were heavily inspired by the syntax of Ott, its definition of α-equivalence is unsuitable for our extension of Nominal Isabelle. First, it is far too complicated to be a basis for automated proofs implemented on the ML-level of Isabelle/HOL. Second, it covers cases of binders depending on other binders, which just do not make sense for our α-equated terms. Third, it allows empty types that have no meaning in a HOL-based theorem prover. We also had to generalise slightly Ott's binding clauses. In Ott you specify binding clauses with a single body; we allow more than one. We have to do this, because this makes a difference for our notion of α-equivalence in case of **bind (set)** and **bind (set+)**. Because of how we set up our definitions, we also had to impose some restrictions (like a single binding function for a deep binder) that are not present in Ott.

Pottier presents in [13] a language, called Cαml, for representing terms with general binders inside OCaml. This language is implemented as a front-end that can be translated to OCaml with the help of a library. He presents a type-system in which the scope of general binders can be specified using special markers, written *inner* and *outer*. It seems our and his specifications can be inter-translated as long as ours use the binding mode **bind** only. However, we have not proved this. Pottier gives a definition for α-equivalence, which also uses a permutation operation (like ours). Still, this definition is rather different from ours and he only proves that it defines an equivalence relation. A complete reasoning infrastructure is well beyond the purposes of his language. Similar work for Haskell with similar results was reported by Cheney [4].

In a slightly different domain (programming with dependent types), the paper [1] presents a calculus with a notion of α-equivalence related to our binding mode **bind (set+)**. The definition in [1] is similar to the one by Pottier, except that it has a more operational flavour and calculates a partial (renaming) map. In this way, the definition can deal with vacuous binders. However, to our best knowledge, no concrete mathematical result concerning this definition of α-equivalence has been proved.

9 Conclusion

We have presented an extension of Nominal Isabelle for dealing with general binders, that is term-constructors having multiple bound variables. For this extension we introduced new definitions of α-equivalence and automated all necessary proofs in Isabelle/HOL. To specify general binders we used the specifications from Ott, but extended them in some places and restricted them in others so that they make sense in the context of α-equated terms. We also introduced two binding modes (set and set+) that do not exist in Ott. We have tried out the extension with calculi such as Core-Haskell, type-schemes and approximately a dozen of other typical examples from programming language research [15].

We have left out a discussion about how functions can be defined over α-equated terms involving general binders. In earlier versions of Nominal Isabelle this turned out to be a thorny issue. We hope to do better this time by using the function package that has recently been implemented in Isabelle/HOL and also by restricting function definitions to equivariant functions (for them we can provide more automation).

Acknowledgements. We thank Peter Sewell for making the informal notes [15] available to us and also for patiently explaining some of the finer points of the Ott-tool.

References

1. Altenkirch, T., Danielsson, N.A., Löh, A., Oury, N.: PiSigma: Dependent Types Without the Sugar. In: Blume, M., Kobayashi, N., Vidal, G. (eds.) FLOPS 2010. LNCS, vol. 6009, pp. 40–55. Springer, Heidelberg (2010)
2. Bengtson, J., Parrow, J.: Psi-Calculi in Isabelle. In: Berghofer, S., Nipkow, T., Urban, C., Wenzel, M. (eds.) TPHOLs 2009. LNCS, vol. 5674, pp. 99–114. Springer, Heidelberg (2009)
3. Charguéraud, A.: The Locally Nameless Representation. To appear in J. of Automated Reasoning
4. Cheney, J.: Scrap your Nameplate (Functional Pearl). In: Proc. of the 10th ICFP Conference, pp. 180–191 (2005)
5. Cheney, J.: Toward a General Theory of Names: Binding and Scope. In: Proc. of the 3rd MERLIN Workshop, pp. 33–40 (2005)
6. Homeier, P.: A Design Structure for Higher Order Quotients. In: Hurd, J., Melham, T. (eds.) TPHOLs 2005. LNCS, vol. 3603, pp. 130–146. Springer, Heidelberg (2005)
7. Huffman, B., Urban, C.: Proof Pearl: A New Foundation for Nominal Isabelle. In: Kaufmann, M., Paulson, L.C. (eds.) ITP 2010. LNCS, vol. 6172, pp. 35–50. Springer, Heidelberg (2010)
8. Kaliszyk, C., Urban, C.: Quotients Revisited for Isabelle/HOL. To appear in the Proc. of the 26th ACM Symposium on Applied Computing (2011)
9. Lee, D.K., Crary, K., Harper, R.: Towards a Mechanized Metatheory of Standard ML. In: Proc. of the 34th POPL Symposium, pp. 173–184 (2007)
10. Naraschewski, W., Nipkow, T.: Type Inference Verified: Algorithm W in Isabelle/HOL. J. of Automated Reasoning 23, 299–318 (1999)

11. Pitts, A.: Notes on the Restriction Monad for Nominal Sets and Cpos. Unpublished notes for an invited talk given at CTCS (2004)
12. Pitts, A.M.: Nominal Logic, A First Order Theory of Names and Binding. Information and Computation 183, 165–193 (2003)
13. Pottier, F.: An Overview of Cαml. In: *ACM Workshop on ML*. ENTCS, vol. 148, pp. 27–52 (2006)
14. Sato, M., Pollack, R.: External and Internal Syntax of the Lambda-Calculus. J. of Symbolic Computation 45, 598–616 (2010)
15. Sewell, P.: A Binding Bestiary. Unpublished notes
16. Sewell, P., Nardelli, F.Z., Owens, S., Peskine, G., Ridge, T., Sarkar, S., Strniša, R.: OTT: Effective Tool Support for the Working Semanticist. J. of Functional Programming 20(1), 70–122 (2010)
17. Tobin-Hochstadt, S., Felleisen, M.: The Design and Implementation of Typed Scheme. In: Proc. of the 35rd POPL Symposium, pp. 395–406 (2008)
18. Urban, C., Cheney, J., Berghofer, S.: Mechanizing the Metatheory of LF. In: Proc. of the 23rd LICS Symposium, pp. 45–56 (2008)
19. Urban, C., Nipkow, T.: Nominal Verification of Algorithm W. In: Huet, G., Lévy, J.-J., Plotkin, G. (eds.) From Semantics to Computer Science. Essays in Honour of Gilles Kahn, pp. 363–382. Cambridge University Press, Cambridge (2009)
20. Urban, C., Tasson, C.: Nominal techniques in isabelle/HOL. In: Nieuwenhuis, R. (ed.) CADE 2005. LNCS (LNAI), vol. 3632, pp. 38–53. Springer, Heidelberg (2005)
21. Urban, C., Zhu, B.: Revisiting Cut-Elimination: One Difficult Proof is Really a Proof. In: Voronkov, A. (ed.) RTA 2008. LNCS, vol. 5117, pp. 409–424. Springer, Heidelberg (2008)

Author Index

Author Index

GPSR Compliance

The European Union's (EU) General Product Safety Regulation (GPSR) is a set of rules that requires consumer products to be safe and our obligations to ensure this.

If you have any concerns about our products, you can contact us on ProductSafety@springernature.com

In case Publisher is established outside the EU, the EU authorized representative is:

Springer Nature Customer Service Center GmbH
Europaplatz 3
69115 Heidelberg, Germany

Batch number: 09490872

Printed by Printforce, the Netherlands